D0936523

Studies in Human Sexuality

Studies in Human Sexuality
A Selected Guide

Second Edition

SUZANNE G. FRAYSER   **THOMAS J. WHITBY**

1995
Libraries Unlimited, Inc.
Englewood, Colorado

LIBRARIES UNLIMITED, INC.
P.O. Box 6633
Englewood, Colorado 80155-6633
1-800-237-6124

Library of Congress Cataloging-in-Publication Data

Frayser, Suzanne G.
    Studies in Human sexuality : a selected guide / Suzanne G.
Frayser, Thomas J. Whitby. -- 2nd ed.
    xx, 737 p. 17x25 cm.
    Includes bibliographical references and index.
    ISBN 1-56308-131-8
    1. Sex--Bibliography. 2. Reference books--Sex. 3. Best books.
I. Whitby, Thomas J.   II. Title.
Z7164.S42F73   1995
[HQ21]
016.3067--dc20   95-4259
                                                          CIP

Within that domain [biology and the life sciences], however, the most backward region of scientific exploration pertains to problems about love and sexuality.

Irving Singer, *The Nature of Love*, 1984

Likewise, just as arts of very contrasting kinds may be invested with beauty, so sex, which has its own kind of beauty, suffuses every sector of life, of individuals, and of societies, where earlier it had passed unnoticed. Now its image, once hidden or undeveloped, emerges from the unconscious like a photographic plate in developing fluid.

Philippe Ariès, *Western Sexuality*, 1985

It's a stampede, a demoniacal typhoon of sexuality—mankind trampling in sexual precincts.

Saul Bellow, *Vanity Fair*, May 1987

It is critical that we expand rather than narrow our notions of sexuality.

Erica Jong, *Playboy*, March 1993

Contents

Part III—BIBLIOGRAPHIES

Preface to the Second Edition

The purpose of this new, expanded edition of *Studies in Human Sexuality* remains the same as before: to provide scholars, professionals, students, and laypersons with a bibliographic guide, comprehensive in scope, to the best books in the English language on the subject of human sexuality. Within the biological, social and behavioral sciences, and the humanities, it covers such general areas as medicine, psychology, anthropology, sociology, religion, law, education, history, literature, and the arts. It also highlights the pressing issues of the day with abstracts on abortion, AIDS, child sexual abuse, incest, rape, sexual harassment, homosexuality, pornography, and prostitution.

Our method of compilation also remains the same. We have tried to select the best books available, some old, some new, in the diverse fields of human sexuality. We could not, however, select for abstracting every book available—we had to take only a limited number of books for each discipline and at the same time retain a balanced approach to the literature. We continue to express an impartial approach to our abstracting of books representing different, often conflicting, points of view.

We also want to present here the same bibliometric analysis that was featured in the first edition, showing the continued growth of the sexological literature. Not all of the books making up the present edition are confined to the current literature: a sizable portion of it antedates the 1980s, as shown in the table. The early years of the 1990s continue to reflect the enthusiasm for an in-depth exploration of sexual topics as investigative reporting as well as popular and scholarly work proceeds.

Growth of the Literature in the Field of Human Sexuality

Pre-nineteenth century	7
Nineteenth century	5
1900-1909	7
1910-1919	4
1920-1929	11
1930-1939	12
1940-1949	6
1950-1959	16
1960-1969	61
1970-1979	258
1980-1989	522
1990-1994	182
Total	1091
Adjusted total*	1099

*Includes individually counted volumes in multi-volume sets (e.g., Michel Foucault's three-volume *The History of Sexuality*).

Aside from the fact that we have increased the number of abstracts from 627 to 1,091, the substantive difference between the two editions may be gauged by the addition of abstracts for books that fill gaps in our earlier coverage. For example, studies by such pioneers in sexology as Albert Moll, August Forel, and Wilhelm

Stekel are now included, and topics overlooked before are now represented. *Misogyny*, *Vaginismus*, *Footbinding*, *Eunuchism*, and *Flagellation* are some of the new topics in this guide. Also, we have made certain areas of coverage more representative of what is being published. *Abortion*, for example, is now represented by abstracts of sixteen books as compared to only three in the first edition. *Prostitution*, always an area of abundant literature, has been geographically subdivided in the classification to accommodate many new abstracts. *Sex Crimes* is an altogether new category for this edition, as are *Burlesque*, *Sex Ratio*, and *Pedophilia*. *Satire* and *Puns* have been added to the humor category.

The classified table of contents has been buttressed by the inclusion of new headings, the revision of old headings, and the division and subdivision of existing headings where the quantity of abstracts warranted such action. *Homosexual* and *Prostitution* are good examples. We are pleased, however, by how well our classification, on which the table of contents is based, has accommodated these adjustments to its general structure over the past eight years.

This book is a bibliographic gold mine. Besides the forty-six monographic bibliographies abstracted in part III, there is a bibliographic thread running through and connecting nearly all the books abstracted. This represents a mother lode of material that investigators should find helpful in undertaking and pursuing research.

This book also provides an indication of trends in the monographic literature on human sexuality. The introduction of the first edition articulated many of those trends in terms of the major categories of the classification scheme. In terms of general issues, there are ongoing attempts to define the field of human sexuality and to develop a consistent vocabulary for it; several dictionaries, encyclopedias, and alphabetical guides to specific topics have appeared since publication of the first edition. Histories and interpretations of sexology offer overviews of its meaning, and major figures in the field are now synthesizing their past research into succinct forms. Critical evaluations of the constructs used to describe sexuality have increased as cultural analysis and the concepts of social construction/deconstruction have gained popularity with social scientists. Self-help books continue to flood the market, particularly those dealing with the link between sex and relationships, and educational texts are increasingly interdisciplinary in perspective.

Specialized monographs on specific topics continue to appear, and authors are increasingly drawn from a wider range of disciplines, including philosophy, religion, law, political science, psychiatry, and biology. Edited collections of papers summarizing the state of knowledge in specific disciplines and subjects have become important avenues for presenting interdisciplinary findings.

Normal psychosexual development during the periods of childhood and aging receive little, though continuing attention. Rather than stressing normalcy, topics such as sexual functioning, social patterns of sexual behavior, and cultural expressions of sexuality place more emphasis on disease (e.g., AIDS, other STDs), sexual problems (e.g., gender identity disorders, paraphilias), sexual coercion of various kinds (e.g., child sexual abuse, sexual harassment, rape), and deviance (e.g., prostitution, sex crimes). A focus on gender as a social construct rather than on sexual behavior per se guides the perspectives of many of the new monographs on cross-dressing, third genders, and gender roles. Of note is the increase in books on men's roles and feminist responses to cultural themes (e.g., beauty, body image) that seem to erode the promises of equality. Discussions of the politics of gender, sexual orientation, sexuality education, and reproductive rights are of major concern, and cross-cultural monographs and perspectives on sexuality are on the rise. Finally, studies critical of Judeo-Christian and Islamic values affecting sexual behavior and the institutions that propagate them, have come from reformers both within and without the religious community, essentially calling for a less rigid and more sympathetic understanding of human sexuality.

Favorable reviews of the first edition of *Studies in Human Sexuality*, as well as our continuing interest in the types of new books being published in the field, encouraged us to undertake this second edition. We hope that this compilation of informative abstracts of books in English will satisfy both readers and reviewers as much as the first edition did. In any case, we have learned a great deal from developing this guide and believe that this work will provide not only information about the specific books included, but also an illuminating perspective on the role of sexuality during the last three decades of the twentieth century.

Thomas J. Whitby
Suzanne G. Frayser

Preface to the First Edition

We have tried to do two things in this guide: to provide a selection of highly influential and informative sex books of our times and to prepare informative abstracts of those books in an unbiased manner. We hope we have succeeded. To our knowledge, this is the first endeavor to provide a balanced overview of the monographic literature in the broad field of sexology by presenting lengthy, informative abstracts in terms of a detailed conceptual scheme.

Our selection of titles derives largely from personal knowledge, the recommendations of professional colleagues, existing bibliographies, and the identification of references in books being read. The human sexuality classification, devised as an organizational framework for the guide, disclosed gaps in our coverage as we progressed and served to channel our efforts in selecting appropriate titles. Pure coincidence sometimes played a part, as when we discovered titles in bookstores and libraries while browsing.

Always in our search for prospective titles, we were looking for the basic writings of the pioneers in sexology (Sigmund Freud, Havelock Ellis, and others); the works of the leading figures currently working in the field; books perceived as having an important societal impact or which we believe reflect the major areas and issues of concern today; and books that are not only informative but also well written, well researched, and aesthetically appealing.

Originally we intended to include only books published after 1970 because we thought that more current studies would be of most use to professionals and others interested in the field. However, this cut-off date had the disadvantage of excluding some of the classic literature in the field, and we realized that the volume of literature in sexology before Kinsey was not overwhelming and that landmark works, which towered like mountain peaks over their surroundings, could be readily identified.

Employing a broad interdisciplinary approach, we have endeavored to incorporate popular, technical, and scholarly works from a variety of fields, including anthropology, biology, history, law, literature and the arts, medicine, politics, psychology, psychiatry, and sociology, as well as available, albeit sparse, reference materials. Perhaps this is too large a universe to embrace in a single undertaking; our temerity stems perhaps from our assumption that by limiting ourselves to the monographic literature, we stood a good chance of achieving our goal of abstracting a relatively fixed number of books from various fields. Happily we reached, and in fact exceeded, our numerical goal of 500 titles.

It would be comforting to be able to claim that we have covered the literature on human sexuality completely. But such an extravagant claim, in view of the information explosion in the field, could be easily discounted. Realizing that completeness is elusive, even asymptotic, we have striven instead for comprehensiveness, using certain selection practices to assure ourselves of both wide and balanced coverage of the subject's literature.

The table below presents an analysis of the 627 book entries in the main body and addendum of the guide in terms of publication date and original date of the material. This perspective indicates the explosive growth of information in the field of human sexuality, especially in the twentieth century.

Growth of Literature in the Field of Human Sexuality

Pre-Nineteenth century	6
Nineteenth century	4
1900-1909	2
1910-1919	2
1920-1929	9
1930-1939	8
1940-1949	5
1950-1959	11
1960-1969	46
1970-1979	219
1980-1987	323
Total	631*

*Includes individually counted volumes in multi-volume sets (e.g., Michel Foucault's three-volume *The History of Sexuality*).

Because it is based either on original publication dates or the approximate dates of the original works, rather than the publication dates for the editions and printings of the works actually abstracted, the table gives a true picture of the growth of the sexological literature. A number of the works abstracted antedate the twentieth century. These early works, precursors of later writings, range in date from the first century A.D. to the mid-nineteenth century. After several decades of statistically insignificant data for the twentieth century, noticeable growth occurred during the 1920s and 1930s, followed by an understandable decline in the 1940s. Following World War II, steady growth again took place, gained momentum in the 1960s, and seemed to explode dramatically in the 1970s and the early 1980s. While these figures are impressionistic only, a more complete bibliometric analysis of all titles published over the years would provide a more accurate picture of the growth of the sexological literature. Suffice it to say that the literature on human sexuality seems to be growing at an exponential rate and that there is no reason to think that it will either level off or decline in the near future.

Classification. The interrelationship of biological, social, and cultural aspects of human sexuality has been the theoretical principle forming the basis of our classification. Modified by certain practical considerations, this principle has guided the development of the system to its present configuration. Creating a detailed classification of human sexuality as a framework for our compilation was a good decision. As we progressed it provided a systematic base that exposed our strengths and weaknesses. It shows, for example, that we now have thirty-three bibliographies, twenty-six sex surveys, and twenty-three autobiographical and biographical works, but only six dictionaries and encyclopedias, with certain subjects (kissing, breast-feeding, jealousy) represented by but one book each. While other methods of organizing bibliographic materials are possible, we believe that our classification is designed to provide the user not only with an appreciation of the scope of the field but also with systematic access to the contents of the guide. Like ideas are associated in the scheme: all major concepts associated with human reproduction (e.g., menstruation, conception, pregnancy, birth control, etc.) are clustered under "Reproductive Cycle"; the main types of sexual abuse (e.g., incest, rape, child abuse) are kept together; and cross-cultural, ethnographic, and area studies are in one place.

Organization. The three parts into which the guide is divided reflect the theoretical and practical aspects of the classification. Part I, "General," contains the reference works as well as those general subjects—history, research, education—which cut across all specialized fields. Part II, "Topical Guide," most closely reveals the theoretical underpinnings of our scheme by logically organizing the biological, social, and cultural dimensions of human sexuality. Part III, "Bibliographies," closes out the classification by concentrating material that leads beyond the confines of the guide and into the more detailed type of material found in the periodical and report literature.

Abstracts. The abstracts we have written about the books in this guide are informative rather than indicative or evaluative. Anyone familiar with the major abstracting services (*Biological Abstracts, Chemical Abstracts*, and the like) can appreciate the type of abstract found in them—generally highly descriptive abstracts providing in succinct form the salient information in the item being abstracted, usually a journal article or a conference paper. The terse statements give the purpose of the work, significant data, and conclusions. We have used a similar approach for the abstracts in our guide. Instead of periodical articles and papers, however, we have focused on monographic works—reference books, studies, collections, surveys, bibliographies, and the like, all of which we view as studies. Our abstracts average about 300 words in length, some exceeding, others falling short, of that figure. The longest abstract in our guide—one for the 2,000-page *Final Report* of the Commission on Pornography and Obscenity—runs to about 600 words.

Obviously, it has been necessary to examine these works rather carefully. In most cases, the authors completely read each book included in this guide. We hope that the informative abstracts produced accurately reflect the contents of the books. A special effort has also been made by all the contributors to be unbiased in their descriptions of the contents of the books included. We consciously included works which reflect a variety of points of view—conservative and liberal, feminist and traditional, secular and religious, scholarly and popular—about sexuality. However much one might want to express his or her feelings about certain books, everyone submerged personal opinion in the belief that the reader will want to know the author's thinking and method rather than our opinions. We hope we have succeeded in rendering the authors' viewpoints faithfully and fairly. By adopting this approach we endeavor to provide a basis for users of this guide to decide for themselves what they choose to read.

Indexes. For direct content accessibility to the abstracts, three detailed alphabetical indexes have been prepared. The *author* index provides access to all those who may be considered under a broad definition of authorship: editors, compilers, illustrators, photographers, and translators as well as authors and co-authors proper. The *title* index includes main titles, distinctive subtitles, translated titles, and various kinds of other titles normally encountered in bibliographic work. The most complex of the direct-access indexes for this guide is the *subject* index. It contains not only terms and expressions as subjects but also personal names, corporate names, and titles when these are identified as subjects in books being abstracted. Cross-references (*see* and *see also*) have been used to interrelate synonymous, hierarchical, and collateral index terms.

Both the detailed classification in the front of the book, acting as a table of contents, and the alphabetical indexes at the back of the book provide access to the contents of the guide. The classification is intended to be used systematically while the alphabetical indexes are designed for quick, easy access to particular information. These methods complement each other, and the astute user will probably take advantage of both systems.

Finally, we want to say something about the genesis of our work. Four years ago, Suzanne G. Frayser and I met when she appeared as a guest in a science resources class I was teaching in the Graduate School of Librarianship and Information Management. She was scheduled to teach a course in human sexuality in the fall quarter at the University of Denver. Over coffee after we met, we discovered our mutual interest in sex, she from the anthropological point of view and I from the bibliographic standpoint. Discussing the availability of reference materials in the field of human sexuality, we concluded that what the field needed at this time was a guide to resources along the lines of those available in such traditional sciences as chemistry, physics, geology, etc., but with an interdisciplinary perspective and combining the theoretical with the practical. This suggested that a modest beginning could be made in that direction if we focused our attention on the available book literature on human sexuality. Deciding that the time was right to pursue this idea, we brought it as a suggestion to the attention of Bohdan Wynar, Editor-in-Chief of Libraries Unlimited, Inc. He gave us the green light. That was in fall 1983; now, four years later, our work, done without outside funding but with lots of help and encouragement from others, is a reality. We hope that our efforts will prove useful to you. In addition, we would appreciate your suggestions of titles that could fill in existing gaps in our coverage and enhance future editions of this work. We view our guide as an initial overview rather than a final pronouncement on the rich range of literature that the field of sexology has to offer.

The coding placed at the head of each entry is used to suggest the appropriate reading level or audience for the book abstracted. These codes (**PR**, **IL**, **PO**, **YA**, **CH**) stand for professional, intelligent layperson, popular, young adult, and children respectively.

Thomas J. Whitby

Acknowledgments

We want to thank the following who gave so freely of their time and talent in writing abstracts for us. Each abstract carries the initials of the abstractor or other source as indicated below.

JA   Judith Axelrad, M.L.S., Humanities Librarian, Denver Public Library, Denver, Colorado

JPC   Joseph P. Consoli, Ph.D., Humanities Bibliographer, Archibald Stevens Alexander Library, Rutgers University, New Brunswick, New Jersey

MC   Martha Cornog, M.A., M.S., Manager, Membership Services, American College of Physicians, Philadelphia, Pennsylvania

LF   Louise Forsleff, Ph.D., Professor, School of Community Health Services, Western Michigan University, Kalamazoo, Michigan

SDH   Susan D. Herring, M.A., Reference Librarian, University of Alabama in Huntsville, Huntsville, Alabama

MM   Margo Mead, M.L.S., M.A., Reference Librarian, University of Alabama in Huntsville, Huntsville, Alabama

EBS   Edward B. Sadowski, M.A., Adult Services Librarian, Edwin A. Bemis Public Library, Littleton, Colorado

DJS   David J. Severn, S.M., Medical Editor (deceased), Monett, Missouri

FGW Frank G. Whitby, Ph.D., Biochemistry, Rice University, Houston, Texas

Abstractors who contributed to the first edition but not to the present edition, include Anne Bolin (AB), Rose Cook (RC), Richard Lietz (RL), Dorothy M. Penny (DP), and Neil Woodward (NW). Their initials appear at the end of the abstracts they wrote.

Selected authors who, when asked, provided descriptive abstracts of their books.

We also wish to express our appreciation to the following:

Eugene R. August, Department of English, the University of Dayton, for permission to use several abstracts from *Men's Studies*, and Esther Stineman, who also consented to use of several abstracts from *Women's Studies*.

The library staff of Penrose Library, University of Denver, especially Kader Novibat of the interlibrary loan service, who succeeded in getting many scarce items that were not available locally, and Zarin Xavier of the circulation department, who graciously facilitated the location of library books..

The library staffs of the Edwin A. Bemis Public Library, Littleton, Colorado, and the Koelbel Public Library of the Arapahoe Library District, Arapahoe County, Colorado.

Those publishers who readily gave us permission to quote at length from their publications.

Bohdan S. Wynar, Editor-in-Chief, Libraries Unlimited, Inc., and his talented staff, especially Judy Gay Matthews, who in her editorial capacity, scrutinized and improved the abstracts in this compilation.

Finally, Suzanne Frayser gives her heartfelt thanks to her mother and father, Steve Banks, Carolyn and Les Hartshorn, Leslie Reingold, Barney Alexander, Karen Carlston, Judith Reynolds, Daniel Depperman, and Tom and Mary Whitby, for their loving support during the writing of this edition. Thomas Whitby would like to thank Mary Whitby and their children (Philip, Irene Holland, Michael, Daniel, Helen Stamenković, and Frank) who, with patience, understanding, and amusement, have supported the authors over the past decade, and their son-in-law Stanislav Stamenković and daughter-in-law, Dr. Carrie Byington, for their moral support.

Note Well

The coding placed at the head of each entry is used to suggest the appropriate reading level or audience for the book abstracted. These codes (**PR, IL, PO, YA, CH**) stand for professional, intelligent layperson, popular, young adult, and children, respectively.

We were fortunate to be able to add 31 abstracts of primarily 1994 books during the production process. Thus, instead of the 1,060 abstracts that were completed at the end of 1993 when the manuscript was initially finished, we now have a total of 1,091 abstracts. These additional abstracts are indicated by a number followed with a lowercase letter (e.g., 277a).

Part

I

GENERAL

1

Reference Works

ENCYCLOPEDIAS & DICTIONARIES

(For related material see also entries 628, 922)

PR,IL

1. Bullough, Vern L., and Bonnie Bullough, eds. **Human Sexuality: An Encyclopedia.** New York: Garland, 1994. 643 p. (Garland Reference Library of Social Science; vol. 685). Includes bibliographies and index. ISBN 0-8240-7972-8.

This is the first major general encyclopedia on human sexuality since the publication of the two-volume *Encyclopedia of Sexual Behavior*, edited by Albert Ellis and A. Abarbanel in 1961. Compiled for intelligent laypeople and professionals, *Human Sexuality* covers a broad range of general as well as narrow sexological topics. The 100 contributors, drawn from such diverse disciplines as anthropology, sociology, psychology, psychiatry, politics, education, arts and literature, research, and other fields, have written over 200 authoritative articles that reflect a range of distinct viewpoints. These contributors and their affiliations are listed in the front of the book.

Arranged alphabetically throughout, the encyclopedia's signed entries include both lengthy articles on such topics as Abortion; AIDS; Anthropology: Influence of Culture on Sex; Censorship and Sex; Gender; Law and Sex; Movies: Sexuality in Cinema; Pornography; Prostitution; and Science and Sexology; and many brief biographical sketches of major contributors to sexology. Most of the articles include a list of additional bibliographic references useful for further reading.

The editors point out that two recent works, the *Encyclopedia of Homosexuality* (1990), edited by Wayne F. Dynes, and *A Descriptive Dictionary and Atlas of Sexology* (1991), edited by Robert T. Francoeur, Timothy Perper, and Norman A. Scherzer, fully complement this work to a surprising degree with "brief definitions of many of the sexual phenomena on which we had originally planned articles" (p. ix).

The single appendix, contributed by Martha Cornog, also provides a useful guide to additional sources of information. An alphabetically arranged combined name and subject index completes this comprehensive encyclopedia. (TJW)

PR,IL,PO

2. Camphausen, Rufus C., comp. **The Encyclopedia of Erotic Wisdom; A Reference Guide to the Symbolism, Techniques, Rituals, Sacred Texts, Psychology, Anatomy, and History of Sexuality.** Rochester, Vt.: Inner Traditions International, 1991. 269 p. Includes bibliography and indexes. ISBN 0-89281-321-0.

According to the compiler's "Note to the Reader on Using the Encyclopedia," this work was designed and prepared to provide easy access "to a variety of lesser-known facts covering eros and sexuality." It thus includes information on substances, ancient deities and demons, exotic symbols, sexual techniques and exercises, mystery schools, phallic worship, and so forth. It excludes information about Freudian theory, AIDS, hygiene, fetishism, and homosexuality. Camphausen states that the "encyclopedia embraces inner and outer Tantrik and Taoist teachings," together with secrets of Western alchemists and cabalists, as well as up-to-date information concerning the brain, mind, and body, especially where they affect the erotic and sexual. In brief, this work provides information about varieties of sexual experience and introduces and clarifies concepts from other cultures.

3

The flavor of this reference work is expressed by a sampling of specific headings: Abraham; Absinthe; Algolagnia; Bacchantes; Bhakti Yoga; Castration; Chakra; Coitus a Tergo; Defloration; Erotomania; Ganesh; Gnosticism; G-spot; Hinduism; Infibulation; Jade Gate; Ka'bah; Lingam; Mahayana; Orgasm; Phallic Worship; Saturnalia; Trilinga; Venus; Yoni; and so forth. The articles, some quite lengthy, provide the user with knowledge not found in the typical encyclopedia. Entries dealing with the myriad aspects of female sexuality are notable for their sensitivity.

Alphabetically arranged and freely illustrated, the encyclopedia has numerous cross-references, and 27 thematic indexes providing direct access to the estimated 900 entries. (TJW)

IL

3. Carrera, Michael A. **The Language of Sex: An A to Z Guide.** New York: Facts on File, 1992. 180 p. Includes bibliography and index. ISBN 0-8160-2397-2.

Michael Carrera, a distinguished sex educator who currently directs the National Sexuality Training Center for the Children's Aid Society, has developed a reference work that presents sexuality in a "comprehensive, multidimensional fashion that goes beyond the mere description of sexual behavior." Based on the idea that "sexual ignorance is not bliss," the book provides nontechnical, easy-to-understand descriptions of terms and concepts related to human sexuality. Intended for laypeople rather than for specialists, it includes such basic information as descriptions of sexual and reproductive anatomy and physiology (e.g., x chromosome, follicle stimulating hormone, fallopian tubes, penis, labia majora); "normal" lifecycle events in the sexual and reproductive cycles (e.g., adolescence, pregnancy, climacteric); physical problems (e.g., cystitis, Candida albicans, cervical dysplasia); sexually transmitted diseases (e.g., AIDS, gonorrhea, condyloma acuminatum, chlamydia, trachomatis, crabs); medical interventions and medications (e.g., estrogen replacement therapy, hysterectomy, artificial insemination); behavioral and psychological difficulties (e.g., rape, incest); variations in sexual behavior (e.g., bondage and discipline, sadomasochism); and birth control (e.g., abortion, birth control pill, condom).

Resources for information on STDs, family planning, AIDS, gender, sexual abuse, and national sexuality organizations follow the alphabetized entries as does a bibliography of primarily trade books on abortion, AIDS, aging and sexuality, contraception, female sexuality, gender identity, sex roles, sexual orientation, infertility, major sex surveys, male sexuality, menopause, religion and sexuality, sexual abuse and sexual assault, sexual function and dysfunction, sexuality in illness and disability, sexually transmitted diseases, the life cycle and sexuality, and general books on sexuality. (SGF)

PR,IL

4. Dynes, Wayne R., Warren Johansson, and William A. Percy, eds. **Encyclopedia of Homosexuality.** With the assistance of Stephen Donaldson. New York: Garland, 1990. 2 v. (1484 p.). Includes bibliographies and index. ISBN 0-8240-6544-1.

In the preface the editors claim that "this encyclopedia is the first attempt to bring together, interrelate, summarize, and synthesize this outpouring of controversial and often contradictory writings and to supplant the pseudo-scholarship, negative or positive propaganda, and apologetics that are still appearing" (p. ix). This statement emerges from the recognition of the vast amount of writing that has appeared since 1969 and despite the longstanding suppression of any mention of homosexuality in public discourse and writing.

Intended not only for scholars but for "all likely users," the encyclopedia should prove of great practical value, including helping heterosexuals attempting to understand homosexuality. It covers the central subject of homosexuality, but also embraces female homosexuality (lesbianism), bisexuality, contributions of heterosexuals to the subject, nongenital passionate love of one male for another, and the effects of homophilia and homophobia on virtually every field of human endeavor.

With over 770 articles, the encyclopedia is interdisciplinary, transhistorical, and, within limits, cross-cultural. In addition to Europe and North America, it provides treatment of Africa, Asia, Latin America, the Pacific, and preliterate peoples.

The articles are thematic, topical, and biographical. Thus there are articles on both broad and narrow topics (sociology, labeling), particular times and places (Greece, Ancient, Chicago), and deceased individuals (Magnus Hirschfeld). Amply cross-referenced and with a detailed index at the end of volume two, the articles in this encyclopedia are readily accessed. Aiding the more systematically-minded user is the "Reader's Guide" at the beginning of volume one; it consists of some 45 main headings, such as Groups, History, Music, and Rulers, each divided by narrower subheadings. The articles, often lengthy, are alphabetically arranged. Articles, many of them contributed by the editors, are signed and accompanied by short bibliographies of books and articles. For anyone wishing to find a solid basis for the systematic study of homosexuality, this is the source. (TJW)

PR,IL

5. Ellis, Albert, and Albert Abarbanel. **The Encyclopedia of Sexual Behavior.** New York: Hawthorn Books, 1967. 1072 p. First edition, 1961. Includes bibliography and index.

The goal of the editors of this single-volume encyclopedia was to produce a work that "would be comprehensive, authoritative, inclusive of wide-ranging viewpoints, and truly international" (p. xvii). This was achieved through the contributions of 97 experts (psychotherapists, psychiatrists, physicians, sociologists, anthropologists, and religious leaders) whose credentials are listed in the front of the volume. Leo P. Chall's article, "Advances in Modern Sex Research," provides an overview and historical context for the 110 topical papers which follow. There are individual papers on aspects of the biology, psychology, sociology, anthropology, history, and geography of sex. Papers explore sex in Australia and New Zealand, Europe, Great Britain, India and Pakistan, Israel, Latin America, the Orient, Polynesia, Scandinavia, and the Soviet Union; sex life among Africans, American Indians, and the African and American Negro; and sex from the viewpoints of Catholicism, Islam, Judaism, and Protestantism. Particularly noteworthy are articles by major figures in the study of sexual behavior, including "Coitus" by Albert Ellis, "Hermaphroditism" by John Money, "Population and Sex" by Kingsley Davis, "Sex Research Institutes" by Wardell B. Pomeroy and Hedwig Leser, "Culture and Sex" by Clellan S. Ford, "The Psychology of Pornography" by Phillis C. Kronhausen and Eberhard W. Kronhausen, and "Anatomy of the Female Orgasm" by William H. Masters and Virginia E. Johnson. Two aids providing quick subject access to the volume's contents are a detailed index and an analytical guide that categorizes specific topics with page references under twenty-nine key conceptual themes (e.g., demography, ethics, law, love, marriage, and pornography). Bibliographic references for further reading accompany each article. Despite its vintage, this work is one of the few authoritative encyclopedias available in the field of sexual behavior and is particularly useful in articulating both the history and the state of sex research in the mid-1960s. (TJW)

PO

6. **Encyclopedia of Love & Sex: A Comprehensive Guide to the Physiology of Sex, the Art of Loving, and the Psychology of Love.** New York: Crescent Books, 1983. 256 p. Published originally in London by Cavendish in 1972. ISBN 0-517-10550-0.

This so-called encyclopedia attempts to "deal frankly, simply, and in vivid pictorial terms with some of the basic problems of sex and sexual relationships" (p. 2). It is divided into three sections, each of which is subarranged by topical chapters. Typical chapter headings in the thirty-three chapters of the first section, "The Physiology of Sex," are "Female Sex Organs," "Menstruation," "Male Sex Organs," "Conception and Misconception," "Contraception Now," and "Venereal Diseases." The second section, "The Art of Loving," discusses such topics as "Is Orgasm Always Necessary?" "What Is 'Normal' Sex?" "Oral Sex in Love-play," and "Does a Man Get Too Old for Sex?" Chapters in the last section, "The Psychology of Love," cover "What Making Love Means," "The Psychology of the Female," "Premature Ejaculation: Causes and Treatment," "Sexual Inhibitions," "Fantasies," and the like. Overall, the book covers biological, psychological, social, cultural, and historical perspectives on the sexual and reproductive elements of human sexuality. The text is well-written and attractively illustrated throughout with contemporary photographs, historical sculptures, drawings and pictures, and graphs and charts. However, the articles are for the most part signed by individuals whose affiliations are not included. There is no introduction to this collection of articles, and no one is acknowledged as responsible for its compilation and editing. It also lacks both bibliographic references and an index. It does not contain the documentation of a scholarly source such as *The Encyclopedia of Sexual Behavior.* (TJW)

PR,IL

7. Francoeur, Robert T., Editor-in-Chief, Timothy Perper and Norman A. Scherzer, Coeditors. In collaboration with George P. Sellmer and Martha Cornog. **A Descriptive Dictionary and Atlas of Sexology.** New York: Greenwood Press, 1991. 768 p. Includes bibliographic references. ISBN 0-313-25943-7.

Each discipline uses a different language to refer to aspects of sexuality. Biologists may be quite precise in their definitions of anatomy and physiology but less clear in their articulation of terms used in the social sciences. In addition, there are different languages of sex, e.g., polite, slang, technical, the usage of which depends on context. Therefore, " . . . definitions of sexual terms and phrases do not have a rock-hard basis in lexico-graphic truth, but receive meaning only in the flux and change of usage among many people of varied backgrounds and sexual moralities" (p. xv). These are among the many pitfalls of defining sexual terms.

The compilers of this dictionary have extensive background in sexology and are familiar with the ways in which the lack of clarity of terms can have an impact on research and education. Francoeur has authored or edited over twenty books on human sexuality and evolution, including college texts. Perper has studied courtship and flirtation for over a decade, and Scherzer has taught college courses in sexuality for over twenty years. With the assistance of Cornog and Sellmer, they are careful and precise in their objectives and criteria for developing this volume.

With the overall goal of providing a "common basis for communication by bringing together terms and definitions from all the disciplines" (p. ix), they chose to define terms on the basis of their domain of usage rather than supply limited prescriptive definitions. When appropriate, they supply background information to clarify the nature of the terms being defined. To choose terms to include, they referred to previous dictionaries of sexuality, including feminist and medical references, as well as the work of John Money, who has been responsible for the generation of major terms in the field, e.g., gender role and gender identity. Terms were cross-checked against glossaries and indexes in all available human sexuality college texts.

The more than 6,000 entries include the names of organizations, biographical information on important contributors to the field, court cases, novels, words from other cultures, historical information, theoretical concepts, and details of anatomy and physiology. Extensive cross-references aid the reader in locating and supplementing information. The appendixes also facilitate location of information: philias and paraphilias, phobias and anxieties, biographical sketches, and an atlas of human sexuality, including diagrams of anatomy and physiology and sexual development. The collaborators hope that this dictionary and atlas will enhance communication about human sexuality among the disciplines and contribute to the development of a consistent vocabulary among sexologists. (SGF)

IL,PO

7a. Gilbert, Harriett, ed. **Fetishes, Florentine Girdles, and Other Explorations into the Sexual Imagination.** New York: Harper Perennial, 1994. 290 p. Includes bibliographic references. ISBN 0-06-273313-3.

Described by the publisher as "a provocative . . . feminist's companion to the major religious, scientific, political and philosophical theories about sexuality as well as to the artists who have attempted to understand and represent the subject," this book is intended as "a tourist guide to the structures that contain, explain, and express our sexualities." Gilbert, a writer and broadcaster, has brought together an idiosyncratic collection of entries relating to the sexual imagination. Asserting that "[o]ur understanding of what sex means, the forms in which we express and discuss it, the fantasies that we weave around it are entirely artificial, manufactured," aspects of the sexual imagination are almost limitless.

Written by "an international team of [ninety-five] feminist authorities," the 350 alphabetically arranged entries are miniature essays rather than impartial descriptions of the topics. Most entries contain words in bold print that serve as cross-references to other relevant entries. In addition, there are many cross-references as well as selected bibliographic citations following each entry.

Topics covered are eclectic and were selected on the basis of "common sense . . . circumstance, chance, and whim." Many are based on the Western, literary tradition. Topics can be characterized according to major themes: names of novels (e.g., *The Arabian Nights*, *The Story of O*, *Orlando*); writers, poets, filmmakers, playwrights, artists, photographers (e.g., Maya Angelou, Ernest James Bellocq, Brian de Palma, Ernest Hemingway, Frida Kahlo, Sylvia Plath); sexual practices and concepts (e.g., androgyny, circumcision, erotica, rape); philosophies (e.g., Judaism, Hinduism); sexologists (e.g., Magnus Hirschfeld, Alfred Kinsey); psychologists (e.g., Karen Horney); and feminists (e.g., Andrea Dworkin, Emma Goldman). Many of the creative artists cited are from Europe, yet the topics discussed span different cultures, historical periods, genders, and points of view.

Interspersed throughout the text are thirty-five black-and-white illustrations. They range from drawings in Japanese comic books and Bellocq's photograph of a Storyville prostitute to Degas's "Waiting," Picasso's "Satyr and Sleeping Woman," and Hokusai's "A Couple Making Love." Overall, Gilbert hopes that the book is one "that entertains as much as it informs." (SGF)

IL,PO

8. Goldenson, Robert M., and Kenneth N. Anderson. **The Language of Sex from A to Z.** New York: World Almanac, 1986. 314 p. ISBN 0-88687-260-X.

Touted by the publisher as "the first book of its kind," this alphabetically arranged dictionary contains approximately 5,000 terms and expressions selected from the expanding field of sexology, defined by the authors as "the scientific study of sexuality and sexual behavior." Drawing terminology from many disparate disciplines, such as anatomy and physiology, anthropology, psychology, sociology, medicine, religion, and law, it reflects the origin, history, and substantive content of those fields. In addition to the technical sex vocabulary of each discipline, this comprehensive work includes the names of notable contributors (e.g., Sigmund Freud, Havelock Ellis, Magnus Hirschfeld, Alfred Kinsey, Marquis de Sade, and others) to sexology, colloquial expressions, homosexual slang, and titles of well-known reports (Hite Report, Kinsey Report), and all the "dirty" words. By providing clearly written definitions for the general reader as well as the scholar, this dictionary attempts to fill a longstanding gap in the literature of sexology. (TJW)

PO

9. Hegeler, Inge, and Sten Hegeler. **An ABZ of Love.** Drawings by Eiler Krag. Translated by David Hohnen. New York: New American Library, 1974. 342 p.

Published in Danish and English, Inge Hegeler and Sten Hegeler's dictionary became popular overnight. Written "for couples in their thirties or forties and thus also . . . for the young and those who have embarked upon, or who are about to embark upon, a relationship" (p. 5), the material is presented in lexical form to facilitate access to the ideas about erotic lovemaking that the authors deem significant. Consisting of some 400 entries, alphabetically arranged with numerous cross-references, the selections range from such technical terms as "anaphrodisiac," "erotographomania," and "titillatio clitoridis," to the familiar "coitus," "orgasm," and "penis." Popular expressions are included:

"peeping Tom," "penis envy," and "soixante-neuf." There are also entries for prominent sexologists (Freud, Kinsey), abstract concepts (gallantry, jealousy, responsibility), fields of knowledge (anthropology, psychology), diseases and disorders (venereal diseases, hysteria), sexual practices (incest, masturbation, rape), and particular headings favored by the authors ("facts, facing up to"; "parts, private"; and "words, naughty"). With comments about Danish sexual practices under many headings and such entries as "Mødrehjaelpen (mothers' aid centres)" and "Stork Fountain in Copenhagen," the reader is also treated to a Danish perspective on human sexuality. Sensibly written, often humorous, and pointedly illustrated, the Hegelers' book serves the double function of ready-reference and lovemaking guide. (TJW)

PR,IL
  10. Kahn, Ada P., and Linda Hughey Holt. **The A-Z of Women's Sexuality.** New York: Facts on File, 1990. 362 p. Includes bibliography and index. ISBN 0-8160-1996-7.

   This approximately 2,000 entry reference work, intended mainly for women and health professionals, provides both concise definitions and lengthier explanations of terminology in the field of female sexuality. The terms, expressions, abbreviations, and names of individuals and organizations included in this alphabetically arranged work are taken from various fields of knowledge, including biology, medicine, psychology, psychoanalysis, law, history, and sexology. Extensively cross-referenced, it embraces entries for allergies, drugs, diseases, phobias, tests, familiar allusions (Don Juan), classical allusions (Eros), and other pertinent concepts. Expanded entries appear for such complex subjects as childbirth, coitus, contraception, developmental stages, and the like. Biographical sketches appear for such major contributors to female sexuality as Sigmund Freud, Marie Bonaparte, Karen Horney, Alfred Adler, Alfred C. Kinsey, and Leopold von Sacher-Masoch. Entries for key organizations, such as Planned Parenthood Federation of America and the Association of Reproductive Health Professionals, also appear. Sprinkled throughout the text are sketches and diagrams illustrating such concepts as female genitalia, penis, pelvic examination, and ectopic pregnancy.

   The book's extensive bibliography, systematically arranged, is noteworthy. Carefully written and readily accessible, the information in this book should prove useful to laypersons and professionals. (TJW)

IL
  11. Love, Brenda. **The Encyclopedia of Unusual Sex Practices.** Introduction by Michael Perry. Fort Lee, N.J.: Barricade Books, 1992. 336 p. Includes bibliography, index, and glossary. ISBN 0-942637-64-X.

   Containing over 700 entries and more than 150 original illustrations, this volume by lecturer Brenda Love ("licensed pilot, skydiver and businesswoman") documents a wide range of sexual practices, devices, and concepts in an effort to "provide objective information about how human beings behave . . . to educate readers, and to do so without censorship." Twenty-two consultants, ranging from a free-lance writer, an officer in the National Leather Association, a "kinky" blacksmith, and an S/M player to professionals in psychology, human sexuality, medicine, and counseling, aided Love in generating and verifying the entries, the sources of which included "other authors and practitioners, individuals whose lectures (she had) attended, sometimes with demonstrations by people whom (she had) interviewed." Not intended as a user's manual or guide to experimentation, each entry usually begins with a description of the practice, its history, current use, and cautions about possible dangerous consequences of the practice. The author provides numerous cross-references, a glossary, appendix of names and addresses of suppliers, bibliography, and an index to access information.

   As sexologist Michael Perry notes in the introduction, this encyclopedia has gone beyond "the usual to the truly bizarre and beyond fantasy to the outskirts of reality itself. It carves a path through sexual history and cultures and practices, both local and foreign" (p. xi). Examples of entries range from descriptions of courtship, sexual anatomy, aphrodisiacs, phobias, marriage, grooming, and pornography to a wide variety of paraphilias, cock rings, pubic hair sculpturing, snuff films, stretching, genital/anal inserts, piercings, and the use of power tools in sex games. Love explains little-known practices such as scrotal infusion ("the process by which a solution is injected into the scrotal sack"), somnophilia ("those who are sexually stimulated by fondling or having sex with a sleeping partner"), and fellching ("either stuffing animals into the vagina or anus, or to a partner sucking semen out of one of these orifices"). Unlikely to be found in a dictionary, most of the practices in this encyclopedia illustrate the diversity of human sexuality. (SGF)

PO

12. McDonald, James. **A Dictionary of Obscenity, Taboo & Euphemism.** London: Sphere Books, 1989. 167 p. Includes bibliography. ISBN 0-7474-0166-7.

Intended for a general audience, this short dictionary of profanity, obscene words (many of which are taboo in English-speaking communities), and euphemisms contains about 350 entries, including numerous cross-references. Alphabetically arranged, the entries contain terse definitions and entertaining annotations.

Not a scholarly etymological dictionary, McDonald's work does provide essential information for the everyday user, identifying, for example, whether a particular term is colloquial or not. From a historical standpoint, McDonald discusses each expression fully, pointing out, when possible, the origin of the term, its evolution, and the development of synonyms. Highly selective, the dictionary deals with only the principal obscene, taboo, and euphemistic terms associated primarily with sex and excretion.

Typical entries are as follows:

CHERRY
(col.) *The hymen, hence figuratively virginity.*
This is primarily an American term, the details of the loss of one's cherry being a
favourite topic of conversation in the USA.
LINGAM
The penis.
This is a Sanskrit word meaning "the sign of the male." It is the masculine counterpart
of the feminine YONI.

Words such as these are used in English because they avoid the pejorative associations of native words, and the clinical formality of Latin ones.

This British dictionary has a decidedly international perspective, reflecting expressions originating in English-speaking countries. (TJW)

PR,IL

13. Richter, Alan. **Dictionary of Sexual Slang: Words, Phrases, and Idioms from AC/DC to Zig-zig.** New York: Wiley, 1993. 250 p. Includes bibliography. ISBN 0-471-54057-9.

After finishing a doctorate in philosophy at Birkbeck College, London University, British lexicographer Richter began his career in lexicography. His interest in sexual slang also began then, when he realized that "about every third word in the English language has, or has had, a sexual meaning or connotation, or so it seemed." In his opinion, no other language rivals the "variety, color, or sheer number of sexual terms" in the English language. The exclusive focus of this book is on the sexual meanings of words and phrases in English over the past 500 years, even though Richter acknowledges that the language of sexuality is broader, including formal and non-verbal communication. The emphasis is on slang—informal terms with elements of the "taboo"—rather than on technical or standard sexual language; it is the language regarded as the "outsider" in polite society.

Alphabetically listed by head word or main entry, all of the more than 4,000 words and phrases focus on sexual actions, sexual organs, and sexual roles rather than on aspects of reproduction (e.g., menstruation, pregnancy). They seldom include medical, legal, or anatomical sexual terms. Richter tried to select a comprehensive range of terms, cataloging "the wonderfully varied English language as it has evolved and been applied to sexuality." When available, he provides the etymology, nature of the term, time of use, and metaphors that apply to the entry. Subentries relate to the main listing, and "pithy or poetic coinages" of the words are added to many listings. "Dash one's doodle," "laborer of nature," and "over the shoulder boulder holder" are examples of some of the phrases that Richter defines.

As basic aspects of our lives, sexuality and language intersect in sexual slang. Richter notes two major themes that pervade this language. First, much of the sexual language is "blatantly male-centered" with a "heterosexual-dominant" bias. Second, it is rich in metaphors from nature (body, animality, nature, death, food/eating) and culture (aggression/war, religion, sport, music, names). Richter notes that the process of slang adding "color, humor, and grit" to our language continues today. (SGF)

PO
14. Rodgers, Bruce. **Gay Talk: A (Sometimes Outrageous) Dictionary of Gay Slang.** New York: Paragon Books, 1972. 265 p. Originally published by Straight Arrow Books and titled *The Queens' Vernacular*. Includes bibliography and index. ISBN 0-399-50392-7.

This work is an "admittedly random, passionately gathered and meticulously collated" dictionary of gay slang. For years the author sought out and interviewed hundreds of informants in bars, steam baths, dance halls, public toilets, and on the streets. Many of the 12,000 entries include quoted examples to clarify the meaning of the definitions. For many entries the author also provides pronunciation key, derivation (where known), and time spoken. This dictionary is not meant to be representative of typical, everyday gay speech, but is presented as an indication of slang as a language of social protest, variously used by members of the gay subculture. If the contents of this lexicon are regarded in the true sense of words as symbols, they provide clues about the content and meaning of the gay world. They are not only reflective of prejudice against this particular subculture but also expressive of gay experience within that social context. (SGF)

PR,IL,PO
15. Trimmer, Eric J., ed. **The Visual Dictionary of Sex.** New York: A&W Publishers, 1977. 321 p. Includes bibliography and index. ISBN 0-89479-006-4.

The full range of sexual topics is represented in words and pictures in this visually explicit reference book for the layperson. Although words are defined throughout, the presentation is more in line with a systematically organized encyclopedia. The verso of the title page identifies nine consultants and twenty-seven contributors from around the world, as well as a medical editor-in-chief, Dr. Eric J. Trimmer, but it is impossible to tell by whom the twenty-seven unsigned chapters into which the book is organized were written. Nevertheless, each breezily captioned chapter focuses on a basic vocabulary and knowledge of a single subject area. Chapter 1, "The Liberators," is a clear accounting of those men and women who have made important contributions to our knowledge of human sexuality, including Freud, Ellis, Krafft-Ebing, Sanger, Stopes, Reich, Kinsey, and Masters and Johnson. Chapter 27, "Clinic," treats gynecology, hygiene, the menstrual cycle, pregnancy tests, and so forth with authority. Stark photographs and lurid drawings, as well as frank but accurate discussions, characterize such chapters as "Sexploitation," "Prostitution," and "In the Sex Store." Replete with illustrations, many of them in color, this reference is a compendium of information that may be appreciated by layperson and professional alike. An extensive bibliography of books relating to each chapter and a detailed index further increase the utility of this unique reference source. (TJW)

TERMINOLOGY. NOMENCLATURE. THESAURI

PR

16. Adams, J. N. **The Latin Sexual Vocabulary.** Baltimore, Md.: Johns Hopkins University Press, 1982. 272 p. Includes bibliographic footnotes and indexes. ISBN 0-8018-2968-2.

Although complemented by modern scholarship, the primary sources of the Latin sexual vocabulary examined in this scholarly study are such Roman writers as Martial, Catullus, Cicero, Horace, Juvenal, Ovid, Petronius, and others. Used in comedy, epigrams, graffiti, satire, oratory, elegy, and other forms of writing, Latin sexual terms pervaded all walks of Roman life.

Adams devotes separate chapters to the word *mentula*, the Latin word for penis; the words for the female genitalia, such as *cunnus*; *culus*, the basic word for the anus; and the vocabulary relating to sexual acts. In each case, obscene metaphors, euphemisms, and the like are identified in passages from Latin writings, which are quoted but, unfortunately, not translated. Detailed examination of these terms follows, bringing out interrelationships and often showing the influence of the Greek.

Although there are many direct and obscene Latin terms for sexual parts of the body and for various sexual and excretory acts, Adams suggests that metaphors and euphemistic designations provide the bulk of the attested terms for these purposes. He also states that the uses of obscenity in Roman life were manifold, including obscene terms for warding off the evil eye or evil influences, aggression and humiliation, humor and outrageousness, and titillation. Festivals, weddings, and the like were often the occasions for obscene displays, as at the festival of Liber when phalluses were placed in carts and displayed at crossroads in the country.

Altogether Adams examines 800 Latin sexual terms, which are listed in a separate index. In an appendix he discusses Latin words relating to bodily excretory functions. (TJW)

PR

17. Brooks, JoAnn, and Helen C. Hofer. **Sexual Nomenclature: A Thesaurus.** Institute for Sex Research, Indiana University. Boston: G. K. Hall, 1976. 403 p. ISBN 0-8161-0044-6.

Produced by the Institute for Sex Research, Indiana University, on the basis of a grant from the National Institute of Mental Health in 1970, this thesaurus covers comprehensively the vocabulary of sexual behavior. Designed for the purpose of indexing the varied collections (books, journal articles, drawings, prints, paintings, photographs, films, objets d'art, novelty items) at the Institute so that they may be more readily accessible to researchers, it is an alphabetically arranged list of the terms and expressions encountered in the literature of sexual behavior. It shows by means of a typical thesaurus cross-referencing system the relationships between concepts, whether they be synonymous, collateral, or hierarchical. The vocabulary entries, traditionally called descriptors, embrace some 2,000 concepts as well as about 250 cross-references. A scope note defines each descriptor so that there will be uniformity in the application of the system by different indexers. A concordance follows the thesaurus section and provides alphabetical access to individual words in the multiword descriptors. When the *Thesaurus* was published the Institute's library contained some 36,000 items, 14,000 of which had already been indexed using this system, which resulted in the publication of the *Catalog of Periodical Literature in the Social and Behavioral Sciences Section, Library of the Institute for Sex Research . . . 1973-1975* (1976). It is the intention of the Institute to update the *Thesaurus* from time to time, and it is hoped that it "will represent the beginning of vocabulary standardization in this multidisciplinary field" (p. xii). (TJW)

PR,IL
18. Murray, Thomas E., and Thomas R. Murrell. **The Language of Sadomasochism: A Glossary and Linguistic Analysis.** New York: Greenwood Press, 1989. 197 p. Includes bibliographies and index. ISBN 0-313-26481-3.

Some 800 words and phrases comprise the central section of this study of the specialized vocabulary widely used by sadomasochists. The compilers base their investigation of this private language on such available communication channels as newspapers, magazines, bulletin boards, special clubs, organizations and associations, and personal conversations with sadomasochists. The vocabulary itself, its origins reaching far back into history, is mainly a twentieth century development stemming from the relaxation of sexual taboos in the 1960s.

Sadomasochism as a subculture in the United States "cuts across most, if not all, cultural and subcultural boundaries and it encompasses all those people who derive some measure of sexual satisfaction from depictions of and participation in activities in which the giving and receiving of pain can lead to sexual satisfaction either directly or as a prelude to sexual intercourse" (p. 4). For communication the practitioners have developed a highly structured language "to clearly inform other sadomasochists of a member's presence, preferences, and limits, while at the same time protecting the member from unwanted discovery by nonmembers of the subculture."

The early investigators of sadomasochism—Sigmund Freud, Richard von Krafft-Ebing, and Havelock Ellis endeavored to define sadomasochism. Indeed, Krafft-Ebing coined the individual words *sadism* and *masochism* on the basis of the novels of the Marquis de Sade and Leopold von Sacher-Masoch. Much of the understanding of the phenomenon derives not only from literature but also from medieval religious practices including flagellation as a relatively harmless method of chastisement. The authors state that sexual sadomasochism as practiced today "is an activity more suited to the theater, in which the players take on roles . . . for the specific purpose of giving and receiving pleasure mutually through the medium of the giving and receiving of pain" (p. 7).

Arranged alphabetically, each word is identified by part of speech followed by etymology (in parenthesis), definition or definitions, a citation illustrating the actual usage of the term or expression (given in quotes), and finally a reference to the source of the entry. It includes such readily recognized terms as *bondage, discipline, enema,* and *golden showers*, as well as some less palatable terms such as *breast torture* and *cum freak*. A typical entry is:

> **feminize**   v (OED 1652 'make feminine'; probably 20th century) Force a submissive male to dress in women's lingerie as a means of humiliating him. "I would like to be feminized and soundly spanked" (*Corporal* 10, no.3:38). *See also* forced feminization.

The work concludes with a linguistic analysis of the vocabulary, extensive bibliographic afternotes and references, and an index of synonyms. (TJW)

IL,PO
19. Paros, Lawrence. **The Erotic Tongue: A Sexual Lexicon.** Seattle, Wash.: Madrona, 1984. 241 p. ISBN 0-88089-001-0.

On July 3, 1978 a UPI bulletin announced that the Supreme Court "upheld, 5-4, a ban against airing seven 'filthy' words when children might be listening." Of course, when the story appeared in the newspapers the offending words were missing. Only by writing to certain papers were readers able to obtain a list of the words (which were "c**ks**ker, c**t, f**k, motherf**ker, p*ss, s**t, and t*t). Essentially these are the notorious four-letter words. The author of *The Erotic Tongue* has made five of these words the basis for his study of the derivation, meaning, and use of erotic words. His acknowledgments are to the authors and compilers of standard sources of information about these words, and he draws on classical works from the eighteenth and nineteenth centuries as well as on such well-known works as *The Oxford English Dictionary*, H. L.

Mencken's *The American Language*, John Ciardi's *A Browser's Dictionary*, and *Maledicta: The International Journal of Verbal Aggression*. In thirteen chapters bearing such provocative titles as "The Big F," "Spare Parts," "Different Strokes," "Act One," and "Let Me Count the Ways," the author wittily, hilariously, and bluntly delves into the etymology of basic words, exploring their origin, meaning, evolution, and usage in prose and poetry over the years. Examples can be serious, sad, scientific, or as terribly funny as this Mae West one-liner:

"Is that a gun in your pocket, or are you just glad to see me?"

or as suggestive as the wall hanging at Vassar College in the 1960s:

"When better men are made,
Vassar women will *make* them."

And so it goes. To quote that redoubtable wordsmith, Willard Espy, "The ancient Greeks had a word for it. Nowadays, though, we have enough to add up to this copious and entertaining lexicon." Alas, the book lacks an index to the 1,000 or so erotic words and expressions dealt with. (TJW)

PR,IL
20. Richter, Alan. **The Language of Sexuality.** Jefferson, N.C.: McFarland, 1987. 151 p. Includes bibliography, index, and glossary. ISBN 0-89950-245-8.

The goal of this small book is to demonstrate "how much of our ordinary language or terminology serves to provide metaphors for describing or understanding sexual activities, attitudes, organs, and so on" (p. 15). The first chapter explores the general connection between human language and sex; it provides the theoretical framework within which to interpret the specific terms discussed in the rest of the book. Richter points out how the grammar and content of the English language reveal the importance of sexuality in English-speaking cultures. He demonstrates his emphasis by identifying classes of words with sexual meaning; dividing the words by levels of acceptability and spheres of usage (scientific, slang, informal expression, euphemism, taboo); and parceling out the focus of the content.

Each of the remaining chapters attempts to illustrate the general points made in the first chapter. Each chapter is organized around a class of terms that relate to different aspects of sexuality: intercourse, female sex organs, male sex organs, and other aspects (actions, oral sex, people, states, aids, and objects). After this initial classification, sexual terms are grouped according to their association with such content categories as nature (e.g., flowers, animals) and culture (e.g., food, clothes, tools). Richter discusses the etymology of some words and briefly speculates on the reasons for the meaning of others. No one theory is used to explain the diversity of meanings and classifications. Rather, hypotheses are offered to explain individual components of the language of sexuality. The emphasis in the book is on a description of the language itself. A glossary provides a quick review of the extensive terminology discussed in the text and serves as an abbreviated dictionary. However, the book is not meant as a dictionary. Rather, it is intended to introduce and grapple with questions such as: Why do so many English words have sexual meanings and connotations? What is the role of the language of sexuality in human life? How can these terms be meaningfully classified and explained? (SGF)

IL
21. Sagarin, Edward. **The Anatomy of Dirty Words.** With an introduction by Professor Allen Walker Read. New York: Lyle Stuart, 1962. 220 p. Includes bibliography and indexes.

Applying the theoretical views of renowned linguists Edward Sapir and Benjamin Lee Whorf, Sagarin contends that language reflects culture that, in turn, is influenced by language itself. Language is a cultural or social product that appreciably determines how people view the world. Thus, assuming many kinds and levels of language, there are widely divergent ways of interpreting reality.

In this well-documented study of one aspect of language, such as obscenity, Sagarin examines the origin, development, and use of tabooed words and phrases in the English language. These constitute a shadow language, a type of vulgar expression that, until recently, went unrecognized in dictionaries. Constantly augmented by "forbidden words, verbal taboos, foul language banished by the elite from the tongue of propriety" (p. 34), the outlawed language consists, in the main, of words and phrases reflecting socially unpleasant biological functions, such as defecation, urination, and sexual activities.

Sagarin analyzes these stigmatized words representing the processes, products, and organs of excretion and sexuality. There are several vocabularies for these concepts: the official and accepted language, usually medical or juridical; less technical words and phrases; euphemisms; and "dirty" words. Related examples of each are "copulation," "to have sexual intercourse," "to make love," and "to screw," respectively. In everyday speech the most commonly used are the monosyllabic "dirty" words; these are the only words many people have for these concepts. They are clear, meaningful, accurately descriptive, and easy to use.

Sagarin believes that these "dirty" words arose in Western culture because of the aura of privacy, shame, and guilt surrounding the processes and products of excretion and sexuality. Society, looking for suitable ways to express the embarrassing concepts, latched on to various linguistic devices that seemed simple and direct: euphemisms, initialisms, foreignisms, and, of course, four-letter words.

A strange outcome was the appropriation of "dirty" words for common usage as slang in nonbiological connotations. Examples include "The boss is really pissed off," and "So-and-so got a shitty deal." One can only speculate that the availability of these "dirty" words readily lent itself to the expression of negative thoughts.

In conclusion, Sagarin states that the taboo on "dirty" words remained absolute until about 1930, when it began to relax. Today, anything is printable and the tabooed language has come out of the shadows. However, because of the inherently blunt and derogatory nature of these words, Sagarin sees the new openness toward the "dirty" words (which are now in dictionaries) as perpetuating the old antisexual and puritan attitudes toward sexuality and biological functions. In other words, language is the shaper of ideas, not merely the mirror of them. (TJW)

HANDBOOKS & MANUALS

(For related material see also entry 339)

IL,PO

22. Carrera, Michael. **Sex: The Facts, the Acts and Your Feelings.** New York: Crown, 1981. 448 p. Includes bibliography and index. ISBN 0-517-54498-9.

Much too often, "sex" is equated with genital activity and is separated from the thoughts, feelings, needs, and relationships of the total person. "This book is about an integrated, informed, creative expression of sexuality" (p. 9) and seeks to explore all dimensions of sexuality in an effort to present a basis for a "true" understanding of the topic. Carrera, chairperson of SIECUS (Sex Information and Education Council of the U.S.) and a professor of community health education at Hunter College, claims that his book is different from other sex books because it treats sexuality within the context of the whole person by considering both behavior and feelings. The basic dimensions that he explores are (1) facts (the foundation of understanding), (2) myths (irrational fears, misinformation), (3) age (a qualifier of sexual expression), (4) feelings (private convictions and concerns that condition behavior), (5) relationships (the rewards and problems of sharing sexual expression with others), (6) culture and religion (major social and religious forces that determine the approval of behavior), and (7) problems (what may go wrong, why, and what to do about it). The first and major portion of the book (380 pages) discusses facts and feelings about sexuality under twenty-one categories, including ages and stages, birth control, body image, disability, erotica, fetishism, sexual orientation, incest, rape, sex education, and STDs. A much less extensive section (50 pages) on acts and feelings deals with specific sexual acts and techniques (kissing, masturbation, oral sex, positions for intercourse, sex during pregnancy, touch, and caressing). The final sections provide an illustrated glossary/index to terms used throughout the text and helpful addresses for contacting organizations about specific issues. The clarity of the text is enhanced by its lack of jargon, 200 sensitive and informative line drawings, frequent question and answer sequences about topics often asked the author, and highlighting of major points using underlining and asterisks. The author's attention to the myths and cultural expectations that surround each topic are particularly useful in diffusing private doubts and insecurities about sexuality. He encourages us all to appreciate his point that the fulfillment of our sexual selves is a lifelong process, which can integrate the diverse facets of our humanity. (SGF)

PO

23. Diagram Group. **Sex: A User's Manual.** New York: G. P. Putnam's Sons, 1981. 192 p. Includes bibliography and index. ISBN 0-399-50517-2.

This up-to-date visual guide on just about every aspect of the human sexual experience is produced by the Diagram Group, a London-based team of researchers, writers, designers, and artists who create highly illustrated books for adults and children. In fifteen vividly illustrated chapters, human sexuality is covered in a clear, concise, correct, and easy-to-understand manner. The work is nontechnical but accurate, explicit but nonpornographic. The chapters, each exploring from three to ten subtopics, are entitled "Sex and Society," "Physiology of Sex," "Discovering Sexuality," "Attraction and Courtship," "The Sexual Process," "Sexual Intercourse," "Birth Control," "Infertility," "Average Sexual Experience," "Aging and Sex," "Sexual Problems," "Sexual Infections," "Homosexuality," "Unconventional Sex," and "Sex and Crime." Much of the information is of a statistical nature and is presented in charts and graphs; all of it is well documented from studies (Kinsey, Hite, Weinberg, etc.) that are listed in the bibliography. A great deal of practical information, advice, and suggestions (graphically presented, of course) are given on such topics as intercourse positions, birth control devices, impotence, and venereal diseases, among others. (TJW)

IL,PO

24. Diamond, Milton. **The World of Sexual Behavior: Sexwatching.** New York: Gallery Books, 1984. 256 p. Includes bibliography and index. ISBN 0-8317-9442-9.

The author, a professor of anatomy and reproductive biology at the John A. Burns School of Medicine, University of Hawaii, introduces the reader to the world of sexwatching, a multifaceted look at sex, where sex is dealt with as "a series of increasingly complex relationships, beginning with the individual, then expanding to the couple, the family, and society at large" (p. 23). Although related to reproduction, sex is not confined to the idea that having children is the purpose of most sexual activity.

The first chapter defines the domain of sexuality, from a basic definition, through an exploration of its history, to some important principles for sifting through data on sexuality. These principles include (1) emotional attitudes accompanying "facts" about sex; (2) data about trends gathered from individuals; (3) the importance of distinguishing between reality and expectations; and (4) the reliability of information on sexuality, which is only as strong as the methods and samples used to generate it. They also guide the presentation of data on a wide range of topical subjects in the subsequent chapters: sexual attraction, sexual aspects of the body, sexual stimulants and depressants, nonverbal communication, sexual development, sexual differences (homosexuality, bisexuality), deviations (transvestism, incest), the importance of love, the elements of a relationship, sexual response, sexually transmitted diseases, reproduction, contraception, and sexual/social issues (pornography, rape, prostitution). The final chapter suggests some possible, future trends in sexual behavior. This multidisciplinary work is filled with over 200 illustrations that complement its detailed descriptive text. (SGF)

IL
25. Haeberle, Erwin J. **The Sex Atlas.** New Popular Reference Edition. New York: Continuum, 1982. 538 p. Includes bibliography and index. ISBN 0-8264-0178-3.

Like the mythical Titan, Atlas, who had to support the heavens on his shoulders, Haeberle undertakes the heavy task of analyzing, evaluating, and summarizing the most widely accepted current knowledge about human sexuality. His aim is to provide the reader with a well-organized and systematic frame of reference from which to derive an overview and understanding of human sexuality. Drawing on the works of Kinsey, Ford and Beach, Kirkendall, Money, and Masters and Johnson, Haeberle presents a clearly written, easy-to-understand work. He starts "from scratch" and does not assume any prior knowledge of the subject, yet he does not "talk down" to the reader. Although he does not present any new findings or primary research of his own, Haeberle contributes a lucid, well-balanced introduction to three major facets of human sexuality: (1) biological, (2) psychological, and (3) sociocultural. The first part of the book focuses on the human body (sexual differentiation, the male and female bodies, reproduction, and physical problems) while the second part concentrates on human sexual behavior (development, types of sexual activity, and sexual maladjustment). The third part of the book relates to sex and society (social roles of males and females, conformity and deviance, marriage and the family, the sexually oppressed, and the sexual revolution). Helpful features of the book include the simplification of professional language, clear definition of terms, frequent cross-references, tasteful and informative drawings and photographs, historical background on a variety of topics, a glossary of sexual slang, further references and recommended reading at the end of each chapter, and an extensive bibliography and resource guide at the end of the book. (SGF)

PR
26. Wolman, Benjamin B., and John Money, eds. **Handbook of Human Sexuality.** Englewood Cliffs, N.J.: Prentice-Hall, 1980. 365 p. Includes bibliographic references and index. ISBN 0-13-378422-3.

The editors, both of whom are distinguished and prolific authors in the field of psychology, have organized the nineteen chapters of this handbook into three major sections, which correspond to "salient areas" of human sexuality: (1) its developmental phase, (2) sex and society, and (3) sexual disorders and their treatment. The first part presents information on developmental aspects of sexuality through different parts of the life cycle: prenatal (Mazur and Money), birth to two years (Higham), childhood (Martinson, Modaressi), early adolescence (Meyer-Bahlberg), adolescence (Shah and Zelnik), marriage (Williams), and aging (Silny). The second section spans both historical and contemporary perspectives in social, cultural, and legal issues related to sexuality: sexuality from an anthropological perspective (Fisher), sex and power (Wolman), sex and the law (Dolgin and Dolgin), sex discrimination (Heilman), and pornography (Athanasiou). The final section reviews a variety of sexual disorders and treatment approaches: disorders of gender identity and role (Money and Wiedeking), psychoanalytic (Meissner) and behavioral (Fensterheim and Kantor) approaches to sexual behavior, the treatment methods of Masters and Johnson (Waggoner) and of Helen S. Kaplan (Witkin and Kaplan), and a holistic approach to sex therapy (Witkin).

Although the authors are experts drawn from a variety of disciplines (law, sociology, anthropology, and biology), sixteen of the twenty-three contributors are from the fields of psychology and psychiatry. Each chapter provides an overview of theory and research on the topic and follows with a relatively extensive bibliography. Given the diversity of authors and subjects, a variety of perspectives is presented. No attempt is made to develop one consistent point of view for the book as a whole. (SGF)

SOURCEBOOKS. DIRECTORIES

(For related material see also entries 329, 358, 372, 1050)

PR
27. Bianco, Fernando, Loretta Haroian, and Gorm Wagner, eds. **International Who's Who in Sexology.** 1st ed. Compiled by The Institute for Advanced Study of Human Sexuality. San Francisco: Specific Press, 1986. 230 p. Includes index. ISBN 0-93084604-4.

A project of the Exodus Trust, a California nonprofit organization dedicated to the advancement of sexology through the National Sex Forum and the Institute for Advanced Study of Human Sexuality, *International Who's Who in Sexology* lists 1,440 individuals from fifty-two countries around the world. In addition to vital statistics and educational records, the entries contain important information relating to careers, activities, years in the sexological field, published works, research interests, memberships, and addresses. These compact entries are arranged alphabetically by country and within the United States and Canada by state and province. Several useful listings follow the main body of the directory: entry abbreviations, educational centers, organizations and associations, and newsletters and journals. A statement about the Exodus Trust completes this resource. (TJW)

PR,IL
28. Costa, Joseph J. **Abuse of Women: Legislation, Reporting, and Prevention.** Lexington, Mass.: Heath, 1983. 674 p. Includes bibliography and index. ISBN 0-669-05374-0.

Estimates of the prevalence of mate abuse in the United States range from 10 to 50 percent of all families. Until the 1970s, very little was written on the violence that occurs "behind closed doors." The author addresses the magnitude of the problem by compiling and organizing extensive information on sources and resources available to abused women. The first four chapters provide an informative, much-needed orientation to the spectrum of research and resources focused on mate abuse: (1) a summary of the literature on wife abuse, (2) answers to the often asked question of why abused wives stay with their husbands, (3) a review of legal help for battered women, and (4) an overview of state legislation on domestic violence. The last four chapters detail helpful resources for those involved in abuse: (1) government services for battered women, (2) programs for men who batter, (3) services for women, and (4) films and videotapes about spouse abuse. The appendixes and bibliography include an alphabetical listing of shelters, projects, and agencies as well as an extensive, 294-page bibliography of books and articles about mate abuse. This well-written, well-organized reference tool would be useful to health professionals, educators, librarians, researchers, and victims of abuse. It expresses an overall theme that "someone out there cares." (SGF)

PR
29. Norback, Judith, and Patricia Weitz, eds. **Sourcebook of Sex Therapy: Counseling and Family Planning.** New York: Van Nostrand Reinhold, 1983. 331 p. Includes index. ISBN 0-442-21204-6.

This reference work is intended for physicians, social workers, counselors, therapists, and ministers who work in the expanding areas of sex therapy and family planning. It covers a wide range of subjects, such as abortion, infertility, homosexuality, contraception, sexually transmitted diseases, and rape. Each section has brief explanatory material, with the majority of the text being lists of addresses and telephone numbers of individuals, institutions, and organizations that specialize in the topic being treated. These lists have been secured from national groups in their fields; for example, the American Association of Sex Educators, Counselors and Therapists provided the list of recognized sex educators. One chapter presents information about career choices in the specialties of sex therapy, family counseling, family planning, and nurse-midwifery. The section on contraception contains charts giving the effectiveness, advantages, possible side effects, and long-term factors of various forms of contraception. The medical and legal aspects of rape, laws concerning rape passed by individual states, and rape treatment and prevention resources are also included.

This sourcebook can be used as a reference work by all libraries and organizations that deal with the issues it covers and can furnish easy-to-use information for health care providers working in these emerging specialties. (**ARBA 1984**)

PR

30. Society for the Scientific Study of Sex. **Membership Handbook, 1992-1993.** Mount Vernon, Iowa: SSSS, 1993. 127 p.

In addition to listing approximately 1,200 members with addresses and telephone numbers, this handbook includes other pertinent organizational information. It lists members of the Board of Directors for 1992-1993; officers for the Eastern, Western, and Midcontinent regions; past presidents of SSSS (1958-1994); various society award recipients; society fellows; sponsoring members; committee chairs; those connected with the Foundation for the Scientific Study of Sex, a nonprofit entity of SSSS supporting scientific research related to sexuality; and the editors of the *Journal of Sex Research*, *The Society Newsletter*, and the *Annual Review of Sex Research*. The directory concludes with the text of the "Constitution" and the "Statement of Ethical Guidelines" of the SSSS. (TJW)

PR,IL,PO

31. Treboux, Dominique, with the assistance of Elizabeth I. Lopez. **T.A.P.P. Sources: A National Directory of Teenage Pregnancy Prevention Programs.** Metuchen, N.J.: Scarecrow Press, 1989. 557 p. ISBN 0-8108-2277-6.

The United States leads the developed countries in its rate of teenage pregnancies. Currently, over one in five sexually active teenage girls in the U.S. becomes pregnant. Such pregnancies often have negative effects on the quality of life of both the young mothers and their children. Pregnancy prevention programs are one way to address this growing problem. The Women's Action Alliance, a national nonprofit organization whose aims include facilitating equality for all women, began the Teenage Pregnancy Prevention Project in 1987. This directory is a product of that project. Its purpose is to "enable new and existing programs to easily access the work and wisdom of others in the field, to facilitate coordination of services, and to promote state-wide networking" (p. vi).

The state-by-state directory of over 500 teenage pregnancy prevention programs was compiled from responses to surveys distributed to teenage pregnancy prevention programs in a variety of clinical, community, and educational settings. Programs are further classified by city under the state heading. In addition to basic information such as address, telephone number, type of agency, scope, target population, fees, and parental notification policies, the description of each program includes goals, direct services, indirect services, special services, and funding sources.

The author, a developmental psychologist at Fordham University, addresses two issues in the introductory chapters. First, Treboux describes the major types of pregnancy prevention programs (those providing direct and/or indirect services) and the prevention strategies they use, e.g., more sex education, a holistic approach to teen sex, coordinated efforts. Second, she deals with the importance of incorporating an understanding of the role of sex role stereotyping on teenage sexual behavior into prevention strategies. Unfortunately, few programs have done this. For example, the stereotype that boys know everything about sex deters them from seeking accurate information. The stereotype that girls are not supposed to be interested in sex dissuades them from using contraception, even though it is available. Treboux suggests that sex education needs to be freed from such gender role distortion. Both males and females need to be well-informed about sex so that they can make responsible decisions. (SGF)

32. Webster, Linda, comp. and ed. **Sexual Assault and Child Sexual Abuse: A National Directory of Victim/Survivor Services and Prevention Programs.** Phoenix, Ariz.: Oryx Press, 1989. 353 p. Includes bibliography and indexes. ISBN 0-89774-445-4.

Sexual assault and child sexual abuse affect a relatively large portion of the American population. According to the introduction to this volume, by age 18, one-third of girls and one-sixth of boys will be sexually abused. This book is designed to "assist victims/survivors, their families and friends, to find the help they need."

Webster, an information specialist in the areas of education, library science, and health/social science, compiled over 3,000 entries on the basis of pre-existing national directories, database printouts, and responses of organizations to one of three mailings requesting information from 10,000 agencies. Webster's main goal is to provide a basic compilation of resources available, not to recommend them or judge their quality.

The directory includes a wide range of resources—from domestic violence shelters and victim assistance programs to counseling services, support groups, and prevention programs. Organized in five parts, the bulk of the book consists of 2,700 local agency profiles, arranged alphabetically by state and city. Each profile includes the name, address, telephone number, hours of operation, type of agency, contact names, geographical areas served, years in operation, and some description of services. Appendix A focuses on 268 state listings, organized by state and alphabetized by agency names. Appendix B follows with a national listing of over 100 agencies, grouped by subject and alphabetized by organization. An alphabetized listing of facilities mentioned in agency profiles is followed by an index of specialized services (art therapy, body work/massage, etc.) and clientele (blind, ethnic, adolescent offenders, etc.) mentioned in the profile. The fund of shared resources compiled in this directory enable service providers, victims, and other concerned individuals to network and support each other. Included in the introduction are a brief bibliography of books on such topics as self-defense and rape prevention, sexual harassment, adult survivors, and materials for parents and teachers. (SGF)

2

Theoretical Overviews. Philosophy

(For related material see also entries 73, 405, 961)

PR,IL
33. Bloch, Iwan. **The Sexual Life of Our Time in Its Relations to Modern Civilization.** Translated from the Sixth German Edition by M. Eden Paul. New York: Rebman Co., 1914. 790 p. First published September 1908. Includes bibliographic footnotes and indexes.

Written for lawyers and physicians, *The Sexual Life of Our Time* is meant to be a "complete encyclopedia of the sexual sciences" (p. xi). Iwan Bloch, a Berlin physician specializing in diseases of the skin and sexual system, was one of Europe's twentieth century pioneers of sexual science, whose aim was to reach "truth, not a theory." By considering the multifaceted aspects of sexuality, he seeks to provide more than a medical consideration of sexual life, which he thinks should be regarded "as a part of the general science of mankind." In the preface Bloch seeks to provide more than a medical consideration of sexual life, which he thinks should be regarded "as a part of the general science of mankind." In the preface he states the significance of this work: "Hitherto there has existed no single comprehensive treatise on the whole of the sexual life, in which a critical study has been made of the numerous and valuable researches and labors in all departments of sexual science" (p. x).

Modern "love" goes beyond marriage and children to reflect the individuality and being of civilized humans, who combine both physical and spiritual aspects of sex in their lives in "distance-love" (in contrast to "fusion-love," which serves reproductive purposes). Distance-love is a human process dependent on the brain—an evolutionary advance of conscious will over animal rutting. The origin of sexual life is in the psychic and physical difference between the sexes, which has become more pronounced as civilization has progressed; these differences do not express female inferiority but only a different adaptation to reproduction. Love is necessary for individual growth, including spiritual growth. In this sense, "the history of religion can be regarded as the history of a peculiar mode of manifestation of the human sexual impulse, especially in its influence on the imagination and its products" (p. 97). Free love is a desirable sexual union "based on intimate love, personal harmony, and spiritual affinity," into which both parties enter freely. The need for variety in sexual relationships and the influence of external stimuli on sex are important influences on sexual perversions, aberrations, and abnormalities. Homosexuality is unlikely to be altered, and most homosexuals are "thoroughly healthy, free from hereditary taint, physically and psychically normal." Sadism, masochism, and fetishism are biological conditions, but incest and other sexual perversions are generally connected with a social problem. Sexual problems such as venereal disease and prostitution require the education of the next generation to deal with them. In sum, Bloch concludes: "Truth is always a good thing, even truth regarding the sexual life ... let us imprint upon our sexual conscience three words—health, purity, responsibility" (pp. 755, 765). (SGF)

IL
34. Davis, Murray S. **Smut: Erotic Reality/Obscene Ideology.** Chicago: University of Chicago Press, 1983. 313 p. Includes bibliography and index. ISBN 0-226-13791-0.

Using a phenomenological approach derived from Alfred Schultz's phenomenology and Jean-Paul Sartre's existentialism to gain an understanding of human sexuality, Davis examines pornography and the writings of philosophers and theologians on sex. Believing that his study will provide a better understanding of sex than either Freud's sexual instinct or Kinsey's statistical studies of human sexual behavior, he postulates an erotic reality as opposed to an everyday reality. In shifting from one reality to another, one experiences an alteration of consciousness. One "who is sexually aroused experiences the world differently from someone who is not" (p. 12). Buttressing his thought with literary quotations, Davis examines the temporal, spatial, social, and physical variables that affect sexual arousal; he then analyzes phenomenologically the stages that constitute the slide into and out of erotic reality.

In part 2, "Smut Structure," Davis examines the ideological position of those who have transformed sex into something dirty. He dubs this group the Jehovanists (church fathers, various religious groups, social reformers, etc.) and proceeds "to work out the world view of those in our society who are opposed in principle to most aspects of sex" (p. 95). The reasons for their stances are a belief that sex is inherently dirty and a psychological fear that sexual activities will adversely affect the participants and ultimately society itself. While the Jehovanists barely tolerate "normal" sex within marriage, they regard nonmarital sex and sexual perversions (homosexuality, masturbation, incest, sadomasochism, fetishism, etc.) as anathema.

In part 3, "The War of the World Views," Davis first traces the historical development of the Jehovanist world view from Adam and Eve (who felt compelled to cover their genitals after eating the forbidden fruit) to the present, identifying the sources which fleshed out this belief system: Leviticus, St. Paul, St. Augustine, Aquinas, Luther, Calvin, and Kant. He continues with an examination of two different world views: the Gnostic and the Naturalistic. The Gnostic uses sex to spread havoc in the world by "shattering social roles, public organizations, and even natural laws." Its principal architect was the Marquis de Sade (1740-1814), and its adherents have included the likes of Baudelaire, Swinburne, Jean Genet, and Marcus Vassi, the pornographic magazine *Hustler*, and the musicians Mick Jagger and Alice Cooper. The Naturalistic world view, in contrast to the Jehovanistic and the Gnostic, does not view sex as dirty; rather it considers sex as a fact of everyday life. While its roots go back to antiquity, its modern developers have included Havelock Ellis, Sigmund Freud, Alfred Kinsey, and Masters and Johnson.

The author compares and contrasts these widely disparate world views, pointing out that we live in a transitional period between one sexual ideology (Jehovanism) and another (Naturalism). Finally, the author attempts to synthesize the truths inherent in these three systems: Jehovanism's notion of identity exchange during intercourse, Gnosticism's critical stance toward existing systems, and Naturalism's disarming attitude toward sex, which minimizes its threat. (TJW)

PR,IL

35. Ellis, Havelock. **Studies in the Psychology of Sex.** New York: Random House, 1936. 2v. Includes bibliographic references and indexes.

Because of the adverse moral climate in England, the first volume of Ellis's classic *Studies in the Psychology of Sex* appeared first in German in 1896. Although the English-language version was published in 1897, a lawsuit in 1898 prevented its sale and distribution. Between 1901 and 1910, an American publisher, F. A. Davis Company of Philadelphia, issued the *Studies* volume by volume. A final volume, *Sex and Society*, appeared in 1928. Several times revised and enlarged, the work has, in the present two-volume edition by Random House, "reached . . . its final shape" (p. xi). The content of this massive work may be best described by the simple expedient of giving the tables of contents of the two volumes. Volume I is composed of part 1: "The Evolution of Modesty," "The Phenomena of Sexual Periodicity," and "Auto-eroticism"; part 2: "Analysis of the Sexual Impulse," "Love and Pain," "The Sexual Impulse in Women"; part 3: "Sexual Selection in Man"; and part 4, "Sexual Inversion." Volume II is composed of part 1: "Erotic Symbolism," "The Mechanism of Detumescence," and "The Psychic State in Pregnancy"; part 2: "Eonism and Other Supplementary Studies"; and part 3: "Sex in Relation to Society." Ellis regarded sex as "the central problem of life" (p. xxix); accordingly the bulk of his work is concerned with the natural impulse of the individual.

The last part of volume II, however, "is concerned with that impulse as it is woven into the whole social texture" (p. xxii). While this monumental study is mainly about normal sexuality, it can be used "for a broad understanding of the complex social problem of sexual deviance" (Vol. I, p. viii). Each part of this work has its own author and subject indexes, and there are cumulative indexes at the end of the book. The work is fully documented throughout. (TJW)

PR,IL
36. Forel, August. **The Sexual Question: A Scientific, Psychological, Hygienic and Sociological Study.** English adaptation from the Second German Edition, Revised and Enlarged, by C. F. Marshall. Revised edition. New York: Physicians and Surgeons Book Co., 1924. 536 p. Copyright 1906. Includes bibliographic remarks and index.

August Forel, a psychiatrist and director of an insane asylum in Zurich, Switzerland, who earned M.D., Ph.D., and LL.D. degrees, was one of the European pioneers in the study of human sexuality in the early twentieth century. In *The Sexual Question* Forel focuses on two "fundamental" ideas: the "study of nature" and the "study of the psychology of marriage in health and in disease" (preface). His objective is to "study the sexual question under all of its aspects: scientific, ethnological, pathological and social, and to seek the best solution of the numerous problems connected with it" (p. 3). Based on his personal experience with both "normal" and "pathological" mentalities, Forel attempts to deal with the fundamental sexual question: How to adapt the basic object of all sexual functioning and love—reproduction of the species—to happiness and joy. The answer requires the elucidation of traditional prejudices and prudery about sex from a naturalistic, physiological, psychological, and social point of view.

The first seven chapters describe the natural history and psychology of sexual life, beginning with the reproduction and evolution of living beings followed by a discussion of the natural condition and mechanism of human coitus, pregnancy, and sexual characteristics. The sexual appetite or instinct in higher animals is based on a "durable sympathy between the sexes" but may oppose love at times and manifest itself differently in men and women. Love derives from a combination of sexual passion and "hereditary and instinctive sentiments of sympathy." Variations in sexual life and marriage are described (based on Westermarck's work), followed by a chapter on sexual evolution, a process where phylogeny determines ontogeny. Chapter 8, "Sexual Pathology," draws on Krafft-Ebing's work, from which Forel concludes that the brain is central in developing sexual pathologies such as sadism, masochism, and homosexuality. The balance of the book deals with the social role of the sexual life in such areas as prostitution, religion, medicine, morality, politics, art, and education. (SGF)

PR,IL
37. Freud, Sigmund. **Three Essays on the Theory of Sexuality.** Translated and newly edited by James Strachey. New York: Basic Books, 1962. 130 p. Includes bibliography and index.

The original edition of these three essays appeared in 1905. Subsequently, the German text was re-edited with additions and changes in 1910, 1915, and 1920. The present translation of the text from *The Standard Edition* of Freud's works contains the prefaces of those editions plus all changes made to the text from time to time as well as explanatory comments by the editor.

Freud's three classic essays deal with sexual variations, infantile sexuality, and mature sexuality. In the first essay, "The Sexual Aberrations," Freud derives his information from the writings of well-known investigators (Krafft-Ebing, Havelock Ellis, Magnus Hirschfeld, and others) as well as from his own clinical findings. Assuming a sexual instinct, manifested in the libido, he establishes (1) a "sexual object" from which emanates an attraction, and (2) a "sexual aim," an act that the instinct intends to carry out. He then proceeds to examine deviations in both of these. Deviations in regard to the sexual object include inversion (i.e., homosexuality), sex with children, and sex with animals (i.e., bestiality).

The normal sexual aim is copulation. Deviations from it embrace certain "perversions," which are conventionally considered shameful and disgusting. This shame and disgust stamps these activities (e.g., sexual use of the anus) as perversions. Other perversions include fetishism, where parts of the body, or even clothing, are substituted for the sexual object; voyeurism; and sadomasochism. Interestingly, elements of these perversions are "rarely absent from the sexual life of healthy people" (p. 26). It is difficult to distinguish between what is just normally physiological and what is pathological. The investigation of the behavior of psychoneurotics (those suffering from hysteria, obsessional neurosis, dementia praecox, and even paranoia) is accomplished by means of the psychoanalytic technique introduced in 1893 by Freud and Josef Breuer. Freud suggests that "a particularly strongly developed tendency to perversions is among the characteristics of psychoneurotic constitutions" (p. 37).

In the second essay, "Infantile Sexuality," Freud shows that, in contradiction to the popular belief that sexual feelings begin at puberty, the sexual instinct manifests itself in early childhood. The suppression of this notion may be attributed to infantile amnesia, which prevents one from recalling childhood memories of sexual experiences. Freud claims that psychoanalysis as well as direct observation of early childhood behavior demonstrate the existence of infantile sexuality. Infantile sexual activity includes thumb sucking, anal excitation, and masturbation as well as other components of the sexual instinct: scopophilia, exhibitionism, and cruelty.

In the third essay, "The Transformations of Puberty," Freud points out that the sexual instinct finds its primary sexual object in the opposite sex, and the sexual aim becomes focused in the genital zone. The "sexual aim in men consists in the discharge of the sexual products," accompanied by great pleasure. The function of the erotogenic zones in producing sexual excitation is explored; attention is directed to the role of the eye, the hand, and other zones in producing pleasure. Finally, the satisfaction derived from the pleasure brought about by the discharge of sexual substances temporarily extinguishes the tension of the libido. Freud (ahead of his time) hypothesizes about the chemical basis of sexual excitation. In outlining the differences between men and women, Freud observes that the "leading erotogenic zone in female children is located at the clitoris." At puberty clitoral sexuality is transferred to the vaginal orifice, which becomes the new leading erotogenic zone.

Freud concludes by showing that many examples of psychoneuroses arise out of failures in the normal development of the libido. (TJW)

PR

38. Gagnon, John H., and William Simon. **Sexual Conduct: The Social Sources of Human Sexuality.** Chicago: Aldine, 1973. 316 p. (Observations). Includes bibliographic footnotes and index. ISBN 0-202-30262-8.

Sociologists Gagnon and Simon present a sociological model of human sexuality that represents a major departure from some traditional approaches to the subject. Although sexual behavior may be grounded in biological capacities and processes, it is no more based on them than any other behavior is. The "myth of naturalness" has deluded professionals into placing too much emphasis on biological aspects of sexuality. Therefore, the authors question both Freud's view of sex as an innate drive that seeks satisfaction and his conceptualization of universal stages of psychosexual development. Sexual behavior is much too variable to be explained by universal drives. While Kinsey's work has the merit of focusing on behavior, it does not include such consideration of the social and cultural sources of meaning for the behavior. It is the intersection of meaning and behavior that produces sexual conduct.

The concept of "scripting" is central to an understanding of human sexuality because "all human sexual behavior is socially scripted behavior." A script (1) defines the situation, (2) names the actors, and (3) plots the behavior; without these elements, nothing labeled "sexual" is likely to happen. Consequently, a variety of sexual experiences (childhood and adolescence, postadolescent sexual development, sex education) and activities (homosexuality, lesbianism, prostitution, pornography) are interpreted as the result of a complex psychosocial process of development during which events become embedded in social scripts; sexual activities are learned and provide the channels through which biological occurrences are expressed. Viewed in this way, sexual development is a variable, sociocultural invention; the sociocultural gives sex its meaning and social myths invest it with power. Rather than relegating the study of sexuality to an isolated domain of sexology with special rules for its investigation, it is more fruitful to examine it by applying the same canons of research employed in the conventional disciplines, such as sociology and psychology. (SGF)

IL

39.   Gonzalez-Crussi, F. **On the Nature of Things Erotic.** San Diego: Harcourt Brace Jovanovich, 1988. 197 p. Includes bibliographic notes. ISBN 0-15-169966-6.

Astute observations on various expressions of eroticism characterize this collection of essays by Gonzalez-Crussi who, like the great essayists of the past, informs with style as well as content.

In the first essay, the author explores on mythological, romantic, biological, and philosophical grounds the origin of sex, the meaning of erotic attraction, and the nature of androgyny. Then he plumbs the core of jealousy in males, especially its extreme form, characterized by swift revenge, as recognized in the macho system of honor traditionally displayed in Spain, adding the hope of drugs and laughter as cures. An essay, "The Remedies of Love," discloses how our forebears valiantly but ineffectively struggled with the love passion, considering it a physical malady and attempting such remedies as denigration of the love object, medicines, strenuous exercise, ardent study, disgust engendered by satiety, bleeding, shock therapy, and so forth. In "The Divine Marquis" the author describes the paradox inherent in sadism/masochism by examining the life and writings of the Marquis de Sade.

Also reviewed are Greek and Roman attitudes toward women in terms of heterosexuality and homosexuality, the Christian perspective, the contradictory views of women as objects of contempt and reverential awe in medieval times, and the no less conflicting modern view of woman as independent, self-reliant, and competitive, yet having the stature of idol. An essay based on a fourteenth century Chinese text identifies the conditions, attributes, and techniques of seduction (as distinguished from courting) that remain appropriate in present-day conditions. The author deals with the power of erotic passion in an essay that focuses on certain views of Greco-Roman thinkers and Christian theologians in contrast to an Oriental and mystical perspective emphasizing sexual pleasure. Gonzalez-Crussi's last essay examines the value of concealment and secrecy in love, providing many lugubrious examples of deception on the part of lovers and pleasure seekers.

The thrust of this collection of elegant essays is to evoke in the reader a sense of the complex and contradictory nature of the erotic. (TJW)

PR,IL

40.   Guyon, René. **The Ethics of Sexual Acts.** Translated by J. C. Flugel and Ingeborg Flugel. With an introduction by Norman Haire. With a new introduction by Harry Benjamin. New York: Knopf, 1958. xxvii, 383 p. (Studies in Sexual Ethics, vol. 1). Originally published in 1934. Includes bibliographic footnotes and index. Translation of *La Légitimité des actes sexuels.*

Prominent French sexologist René Guyon (1876-19??) summarizes his views on sex in a monumental ten-volume set entitled *Studies in Sexual Science,* of which the present work is volume one. Here he concentrates on sexual ethics, beginning with introductory comments about the general pervasiveness and imperiousness of the sexual drive and the persistent resistance to sexual expression by religious and philosophic groups and prohibitionistic societies. He pays tribute to the contributions of Sigmund Freud, especially his method of psychoanalysis and the realities of childhood sexuality. He also points to the need to separate the functions of reproduction and sexual pleasure.

Following a chapter on the physiology of sex, Guyon delves into the morality of sexual acts, taking the position that the sexual organs should be viewed as any other part of the body, and pointing out that the "moral elements in sex are all creations of the human mind which have been superimposed upon the original physiological facts" (p. 113). These elements are conventions which either exalt or venerate the reproductive organs, as in phallic worship, or proscribe, dishonor, and conceal them. These latter negative conventions, characteristic of the Judeo-Christian religions, are sexual taboos brought on by special social and religious education. They are dogmatic expressions of sexual moralists and societies. Guyon questions whether it is legitimate and justifiable to impose sanctions on the exercise of the sexual organs that afford great pleasure. He demonstrates that one cannot justify the taboos on the grounds of either disgust or modesty, which the enemies of sex have attempted to do. Those responsible for the sexual taboos "insist upon a renunciation of the pleasures and enjoyments of life on earth," for they regard this world as a "vale of tears." For centuries humans have suffered "the devaluation of sexual pleasure, the procuring of which has, in defiance of all logic, been treated as a shameful and immoral act" (p. 132).

Guyon next delves into the origin of the sexual taboo and how it gained ascendancy in the Jewish theory of sex. He also discusses chastity as complementary to the sexual taboo and the development of neuroses due to sexual repression.

Guyon then reveals his own mechanistic theory of sexuality and its relation to morals. Following a severe critique of psychiatry, Freud, and psychoanalysis for their terminological deficiencies and for not going far enough in separating the normal from the abnormal, Guyon states that the true ego is inseparable from sex. "It is born in complete harmony with sexuality, a fact which finds expression in the infantile manifestations of sex" (p. 294). He believes that "sex and its activities should be removed from the sphere of morals, and should be judged from the points of view of physiology, psycho-physiology or hygiene only" (p. 380).

One of the final chapters concerns the so-called sexual aberrations (exhibitionism, incest, homosexuality), that from his point of view are perfectly rational and not perverse at all. The last chapter deals with individualized love, which Guyon defines as "only sexual desire concentrated on a single person" (p. 353). It flourishes only so long as the desire itself continues to exist; it changes (as in marriage) to affection based on habit that has little to do with sexual pleasure.

Guyon's second book in his overview of sexology is *Sexual Freedom*, published in 1939, which discusses the need for sexual freedom and justifies sex acts that stay within the society's ethical boundaries. It complements the first volume in establishing principles of sexual legitimacy and freedom, which are then applied to major sexual problems of civilization, addressed in volumes III through VII. (TJW)

PO

41. Haddon, Celia. **The Sensuous Lie.** New York: Stein and Day, 1983. 225 p. Includes bibliography and index. ISBN 0-8128-2883-6.

Early sex reformers tried to examine sex in a rational manner, taking it out of the realm of morals and religion into a more open arena of intellectual discussion and argument. However, a new orthodoxy has emerged. Based on the belief that sexual health is of major importance in maintaining a happy marriage, establishing personal well-being, and providing a sound basis for individual identity, this orientation has overemphasized the centrality of sexual activity for happiness. The goal of this book is to trace the evolution of today's sexual orthodoxy in order to understand how the assumptions and views of influential sexologists have led to the current trend.

First, Haddon traces the roots of what she regards to be three major myths: (1) sex is fun; (2) sex is natural; and (3) sex is healthy. Three well-known experts in the field of sexuality are responsible for developing these ideas. Havelock Ellis' historical research pointed out that sex should be pleasurable. Alfred Kinsey's surveys placed a range of sexual behavior in the realm of biological normalcy, while William Masters and Virginia Johnson's physiological studies of sexual response defined sexual expression as a matter of health. Second, Haddon shows how the language of science and health was perpetuated in marriage and sex manuals that established standards for the general public. Nevertheless, Haddon questions whether sex is fun, natural, or healthy. By comparing human sexuality with that of other primates, looking at sex within the context of marriage, and considering the consequences of chastity, she concludes that unrealistic expectations about sexual activity have fostered more unhappiness than satisfaction. She thinks that contemporary individuals need more instruction about how to love than how to have intercourse. (SGF)

IL

42. Koestenbaum, Peter. **Existential Sexuality: Choosing to Love.** Englewood Cliffs, N.J.: Prentice-Hall, 1974. 179 p. (Spectrum Books in Humanistic Psychology). Includes index. ISBN 0-13-294934-2.

In this work, Koestenbaum, a professor of philosophy, explains how the existential system can be applied to sexual and family relations. Based in part on field-of-consciousness theory, the existential method centers around the premise that people are free to make choices in life and love, and that happiness is maximized when their nature is understood and when the choices are made in harmony with this nature. A person must learn to evaluate his or her needs, desires, and limitations as well as those of others, and to face the terms and consequences of his or her choices (accept responsibility) within that framework.

The book is divided into two parts, "Love" and "Sex," and the existential view of these two aspects of the human experience is concretized with actual case histories of relationship problems and with self-tests that the reader can take to evaluate his or her own feelings and behavior. Chapters cover such topics as the nature of love, perversions, orgasm, abortion, and parenthood. The author shows how, through a decision for existential sex, a couple can achieve enhanced sexual fulfillment, or "authentic sex." A key to this achievement is "full embodiment" or "body authenticity," which is explained and then accompanied with psychological exercises to help develop this state. In addition, a separate chapter explores how the existential approach can be used in therapy.

An appendix, "The Master Table," outlines existential philosophy over the last 100-plus years, formulated with emphasis on the practical application of those philosophic insights. (EBS)

PO

43. Leonard, George. **The End of Sex: Erotic Love After the Sexual Revolution.** Los Angeles: J. P. Tarcher, 1983. 236 p. Includes bibliographic notes and index. ISBN 0-87477-178-1.

Sex—"an activity, a field of study, an entity that somehow seems to exist almost entirely separated from the rest of life" (p. 11). Sex is not only divorced from creation, it is used to sell commercial products. It has become trivial and impersonal, an abstract concept that does not exist in nature and is therefore "not real." Such is the author's view of "sex." Therefore, the end of "sex" means the end of separating sex from the rest of our lives, of trivializing and dehumanizing it, and of adhering to the dictates of an abstraction. As Leonard puts it, "We need to reconnect the bedroom with the rest of our lives, with society, and nature, and perhaps with the stars. . . . We need to appreciate the connection between the erotic and the creative. We need . . . to reawaken to the almost-endless, half-forgotten, life-transforming powers of full-bodies, fully committed erotic love" (p. 13). This book is about renewing erotic love, not a cookbook on how to make love. Each part explores an element of this process. Part I, "Love's Power," describes the physical and psychological transformation of a person during an act of love. Part II, "Love's Promise," presents three aspects of the author's personal erotic development. Part III, "Eros Betrayed," investigates the cultural contradictions that relate to erotic life in the culture. The last part, "Revisioning the Erotic," speculates about the erotic possibilities of the body, the person, and the society that extend beyond the end of sex after the sexual revolution. This well-written reinterpretation of intimacy tries to present a balance between feeling and behaving, love and intercourse, the person and his or her physical attributes, and change and stability. The body becomes a metaphor for changes in and the expression of personal relationships. (SGF)

PR,IL

44. Malinowski, Bronislaw. **Sex and Repression in Savage Society.** Cleveland, Ohio: World, 1966. 251 p. First published in 1927. Includes bibliographic notes and index.

On one level, Malinowski's book is a recognition of the valuable work of the psychoanalytic school in focusing attention on the origin of culture, the dynamics of family structure, and on human sexuality. The main thrust of this classic work, however, is an argument opposing the basic Freudian notion of the universality of the Oedipus complex, which Freud claimed arose out of a primeval crime when sons were killing their fathers, having sex with their mothers, and then developing the incest taboo to atone for their guilt. This accounts for the beginning of culture. According to Freud, male children have a built-in hatred for their fathers and a desire to replace their fathers in the affections of their mothers. This stems from the early foundation of the Oedipus complex. Malinowski rejects such concepts as "group mind" and "collective unconscious" as metaphysical conceptions arising out of armchair philosophizing about the origin of culture. In their place he substitutes the "family complex," a by-product of culture that depends on the placement of authority in the family. Hostility toward relatives relates to authority, not to a primeval crime.

Malinowski uses the example of matriliny in the society of the Trobriand Islanders to show that Freud's concept of the Oedipus complex is not universal. The evidence from a study of Trobriand family structure is that fear and tension exist between son and uncle, the mother's brother, and not between father and son. Indeed, the father's role is that of friendly companion and counselor to the children in the family, and there is no fear of mother/son incest. Instead, the incest taboo serves to keep brothers and sisters apart. In other words, the incest taboo is expressed differently in families governed by mother-right.

Malinowski shows "the influence of the family complex on the formation of myth, legend, and fairy tale, on certain types of savage and barbarous customs, forms of social organizations and achievements of material culture" (p. 20). Freudian interest in these anthropological problems, unfortunately, is affected by the "assumption that the Oedipus complex exists in all types of society" (p. 21).

Malinowski offers his own theory of the transition from nature to culture. He compares family units among our simian relatives with human family units. Regretting that anthropologists cannot study culture *in statu nascendi*, nor should they dream up singular "original events of cultural birth," he states that we can study correlations of the factors of cultural development and learn thereby. Such factors as implements and weapons, conceptual thought and language, and social and spiritual elements can be examined in their primitive form. He states that any "complexes" that humans might develop are "necessary by-products in the process of the gradual formation of culture" (p. 164).

Malinowski's book is an appeal for scientific truth and understanding, for collaboration among anthropologists, sociologists, psychoanalysts, and others. (TJW/SGF)

IL,PO

45. Masters, William H., Virginia E. Johnson, and Robert C. Kolodny. **Masters and Johnson on Sex and Human Loving.** Boston: Little, Brown, 1986. 598 p. Revised edition of *Human Sexuality*, 2nd ed., 1985. Includes bibliography and index. ISBN 0-316-54998-3.

Veteran sex researchers Masters and Johnson team up with their former coauthor and colleague, Kolodny, to produce a readable, multidisciplinary work on sex and human loving. The first few pages reveal the broad scope of the contents: "It is impossible to understand human sexuality without recognizing its multidimensional nature": private, public, historical, psychosocial, behavioral, clinical, and cultural. The authors broadly define sexuality as a dimension of personality rather than confining it to a capacity for erotic response alone.

After reviewing a variety of perspectives on sexuality, the authors present some basic information about sexual anatomy, physiology, and birth control; they then turn to a discussion of different developmental phases of sexuality and follow it with a consideration of gender roles. The rest of the book deals with a wide range of concerns: the relational context of sex (loving, intimacy, and communication); types of sexual relationships (heterosexual, bisexual, homosexual); varieties of sexual behavior, including solitary sexual behavior; sexual difficulties (coercive sex, sexual dysfunctions, sexual disorders, STDs); and routes to enhancing sexual satisfaction.

The text is laced with case histories, perspectives gleaned from the results of the authors' research experience, information that dispels myths surrounding sexual subjects, synopses of current research, elucidation of different perspectives on sexuality, practical information on what to do in a situation such as rape or incest, and guidelines for enhancing the quality of intimate relationships. Throughout, the authors reiterate their belief that sound knowledge of sexuality can enhance sexual satisfaction. They conclude their book with some optimistic speculations about the future of sexuality: greater importance given to sex education for children; no further increase in the sexual activity of adolescents; greater emphasis on long-term relationships; a more positive view toward aging and sexuality; and greater tolerance of homosexuality. (SGF)

PR,IL

46. May, Rollo. **Love and Will.** New York: Norton, 1969. 352 p. Includes index. ISBN 0-440-35027-1.

In the introduction to this psychoanalytic treatise, the author states that we are living in "an era of radical transition" in which the meaning of love has been lost, sexual technique has become a banal preoccupation, and the terms "will power" and "free will" have become meaningless. Modern society has become schizoid, in the sense of being out of touch and unable to feel.

The body of May's book is divided into three sections. In the first section, "Love," May compares modern society to the Victorian period. The Victorians desired love without sex, while contemporary individuals pursue sex without love. The emphasis has shifted to performance, often at the cost of feeling. The creative force of love, Eros, can only exist in company with passion. By separating love and sex, society is avoiding or repressing Eros. Many psychological problems are related to anger at or fear of the creative factor in sexual love. The Greeks viewed Eros as a daimon, defined as a natural creative or destructive force that has the power to overwhelm a person. The daimonic within the individual is the urge to affirm, perpetuate, or increase oneself, and the denial of the daimonic results in apathy or the death instinct.

In the second section, May discusses "Will" and the crisis facing both individuals and society since Freud destroyed the Victorian concept of "will power." Humans no longer feel in control of themselves, their world, or their future. May's answer to this is intentionality, "the structure which gives means to existence" (p. 223) or the capacity to have intentions or make decisions based on personal knowledge and perceptions of reality. Intentionality implies ability and identity and includes the potential for action.

The final section, "Love and Will," deals with the relationship between the two subjects. The two are seen as closely interrelated, with both being ways the individual deals with the world and elicits responses. However, if not kept in balance, each can block the other. Excessive will can preclude passionate love, and over-generalized love can result in passivity. Lasting love requires both erotic passion and fidelity. The uniting of love and will in the individual is a vital task pointing toward maturity and wholeness. The sex act itself contributes to deepening consciousness through tenderness, the affirmation of self, the enrichment and fulfillment of personality, the essential giving of the self, and the psychological union of consciousness at the climax. (SDH)

PR
47.   Rancour-Laferriere, Daniel. **Signs of the Flesh: An Essay on the Evolution of Hominid Sexuality.** Berlin: Mouton de Gruyter, 1985. 473 p. (Approaches to Semiotics; 71). Includes bibliography and index. ISBN 0-89925-121-8.

The interface between psychoanalysis, semiotics (the study of signs and how inter-preters analyze their meaning and function), and evolutionary biology as they apply to the evolution of human sexuality and how today's hominids engage in sexual relationships is the topic of this book. Rancour-Laferriere's aim is to emphasize that "somehow in the course of hominid evolution enormously complex systems of signs—semiotic complexes such as spoken language, gesture, religious rituals, courtship rituals, residence patterns, dreams, day-dreams, poetry, music, games, myths, kinship systems, avoidance rules, exchange systems, marriage rules, etc.—have managed to make the space between genes and behavior much larger than in any other creature on the planet. To discern just some of the specifically sexual structures lurking in this vast space is the purpose" (p. 62) of the book.

After defining some basic terms such as semiotics, evolutionary perspective, sociobi-ology, and psychoanalysis, and then explaining the link between these perspectives and some well-known aspects of human evolution, e.g., language, bipedalism, upright posture, absence of an ovulation signal, and diversity in human sexuality, the author turns to an examination of "signs of the flesh," the ways in which human evolution has produced anatomy, physiol-ogy, and relationships inscribed with meaning. Initial chapters deal with the importance of female orgasm. Rancour-Laferriere suggests that female orgasm developed to ensure copu-latory frequency in the absence of estrus; it became fully developed after upright posture and face-to-face intercourse began. Females had as much of a role in developing "the sexiest primate alive" as males did; female sexual choice in ancestral hominids is related to orgasmic consistency with a mate. Orgasm may have four functions: hedonic and domestic bliss functions for females and paternal confidence and potency functions for males. The author considers the environmental conditions that lead to the "ontogeny of her orgasms" and "Mr. Right"—the relationship of a girl with her mother and father. He discusses and translates the psychoanalytic notion of the Oedipus Complex (as interpreted by Freud, Klein, and others) into the semiotic hypothesis that "one's mate is an iconic sign of the way the opposite sex parent was experienced in the past." Such theory has relevance for spouse selection, incest avoidance, and maintenance of a long-term marriage. Later chapters address such topics as male altruism, virginity, the development of language, obscenities, sex differences, power asymmetry between the sexes, the breast, the penis, castration, homosexuality, and the couvade.

Rancour-Laferriere concludes that "the flesh is semiotizable." Because it can signify meaning, what it means depends on its interpreter and the context within which it occurs. What is adaptive in an evolutionary context channels the meaning that an individual attaches to sex. "[t]he signs of the flesh, and not only the flesh itself, are the product of natural selection. Sex will appear to be everything in precisely those situations where genes stand to benefit from the belief that sex is everything" (p. 388). (SGF)

PR
48.   Scruton, Roger. **Sexual Desire: A Moral Philosophy of the Erotic.** New York: Free Press, 1986. 428 p. Includes bibliographic notes and indexes. ISBN 0-02-92980-8.

Only rational beings experience sexual desire (as opposed to the procreative impulse). The distinctive phenomena of desire—sexual arousal, for example—are signs of an interpersonal intentionality. One consequence is that desire is essentially moralized, i.e., imbued with a sense of right and wrong, responsibility, innocence, and guilt. Another consequence is that desire is subject to the illusions contained within the concept of the person, and is therefore always built on shaky ground. Desire is distinguished from erotic love, and a theory of sexual perversion is offered. Finally, the book argues for a morality of temperance and fidelity, from Aristotelian premises about the nature of rational agency, and presents a sketch of a theory of sexual behavior. (Author)

[N.B. Roger Scruton is in the Department of Philosophy of Birkbeck College, University of London.]

PR

49. Soble, Alan, ed. **The Philosophy of Sex: Contemporary Readings.** Totowa, N.J.: Rowman and Littlefield, 1980. 412 p. Includes bibliographic notes. ISBN 0-8476-6292-6.

The essays in this collection were written between 1968 and 1978, chiefly by professors of philosophy at recognized American universities. The editor is a philosopher as well as the founder of The Society for the Philosophy of Sex and Love (1977).

In his lengthy introductory remarks, Soble states that philosophers of late have been asking such deceptively simple questions as "What *is* sex?" "What is sex *for*?" and "What is *good* sex?" In these collected essays the authors attempt to answer these questions from various philosophical standpoints—theoretical, methodological, and conceptual—by discussing, analyzing, and clarifying the conclusions of sex investigators in other disciplines.

The essays have been divided into two parts: part I, "The Analysis of Sexual Concepts," consisting of nine theoretical papers, and part II, "Sexuality and Society," focusing on causal connections among such issues as androgyny, pornography, censorship, and prostitution on the one hand, and politics, economics, and philosophy on the other.

Soble's personal perspective comes through in a set of theses he proposes: (1) human sexuality is not naturally heterosexual; (2) despite present-day permissiveness, there is continued opposition to the practice of masturbation; (3) the oppression of women and children is perpetuated through the nuclear family, which should be supplanted by the extended family; and (4) the family as presently maintained in Western society may be attributed to liberal capitalism. From a socialist perspective, Soble argues that sexism and the domination of women inherent in Western capitalist societies can be undermined by devoting more attention to the promotion of the androgynous/bisexual extended family. It is unclear how much support for his position may be found in the philosophically oriented essays in this collection. (TJW)

PR,IL

50. Socarides, Charles W. **Beyond Sexual Freedom.** New York: Quadrangle/New York Times, 1975. 181 p. Includes bibliography and index. ISBN 0-8129-0532-6.

In this book Socarides, a prominent psychoanalyst, presents his views on "current sexual practices, the nature of their powerful appeal, their motivational origins, and what they hold for all of us—beyond the promise of sexual freedom" (p. 3). He focuses his attention on such issues as pornography, homosexuality, group sex, communal living, and transsexual surgery. He believes that the high degree of sexual freedom attained in these areas has come upon us very rapidly, that insufficient attention has been given to their implications for society, and that a serious threat to the foundations of society, especially the family, has resulted.

Certain segments of society seem hell-bent on the destruction of the family. Socarides singles out for attention the radical elements in the women's liberation movement who look upon the family in our patriarchal society as the wellspring of everything that is wrong with society, particularly the domination of women by men. Such prominent figures as Germaine Greer and Margaret Mead, whose understanding of human nature, Socarides believes, is superficial, have lent credence to this view.

It behooves society at this juncture not to overlook the teachings of psychoanalysis in regard to sexuality. The author contends that many current sexual practices—homosexuality, group sex, etc.—are pursued without regard for the biological and psychological nature of humans. He says that our present era of sexual freedom when anything goes resembles "the stage of individual human life found in early childhood, . . . a period referred to as the phase of *polymorphous perverse sexuality*" (p. 20). Socarides also criticizes the research and writings of Kinsey, Masters and Johnson, and Alex Comfort, whose work, while contributing to the accelerating pace of sexual freedom, has not provided us with solutions to our sexual dilemmas.

In conclusion, Socarides laments our false sexual freedom that has turned everything we have traditionally regarded "as important in life upside down as if to say, 'If family doesn't work, let's try no-family.' 'If heterosexuality isn't satisfying, let's try homosexuality,' 'If tradition doesn't work, let's try anti-tradition,' 'If you don't like what sex you are, try the opposite'—in other words, let's unthinkingly turn the world on its head, for we can do anything we like; this is the voice of the beast of pride. The voice is still small, but it tries to rise to a roar. There is still time for the voice of reason to prevail" (p. 165).

In the final chapter, "Future Sex," Socarides speculates on the use of drugs and implanted electrodes to produce intense sexual gratification, asexual reproduction, prenatal inovulation, and the artificial womb. He believes that these developments presage a bleak future in which the inherent drives and emotions of humans will be ignored. (TJW)

IL

51. Sorokin, Pitirim A. **The American Sex Revolution.** Boston: Porter Sargent, 1956. 186 p.

Harvard Professor of Sociology (1930-1955) Sorokin presents in this small volume his personal assessment and condemnation of the American sexual revolution. This highly opinionated (and sparsely documented) work paints an apocalyptic view of Western society, and of America in particular: unless certain trends in the personal, social, and cultural lives of Americans, amounting to a preoccupation with sex, are reversed, a national calamity will ensue. In recent decades, the shrinking size of the family, desertions, and sharp increases in the divorce rate, attest to a general moral disintegration affecting not only the family but also the entire social fabric of organizations and institutions. Sociological data concerning premarital and extramarital sex, the number of illegitimate children, skyrocketing sales of contraceptives, etc., point to increasing sexual promiscuity, a kind of "sex anarchy" having momentous implications for the individual, the community, and the nation.

Sorokin has shown in his previous work (e.g., *Social and Cultural Dynamics*) that over the past five centuries there has been a change in the main values of the Western world, tantamount to the substitution of sensate (secular) for medieval (religious) ones. Even the former are deteriorating, and a kind of sexualization of society is occurring, especially in America and Western Europe, where every phase of culture—literature, painting and sculpture, music, theater, television and radio, the popular press, advertising, even science, religion, law, and politics—have been suffused with sex. It is this total bombardment of society by sex that bothers Sorokin: he believes it is responsible for many of our social ills, including crime.

In three chapters Sorokin discusses the "Effects of Sex Indulgence on the Individual and His Associates," the "Social and Cultural Effects of Sex Anarchy," and "Sex in the Creative Growth and the Decay of Societies." The fate of nations is the underlying current of thought in this book, and in "America at the Crossroads," Sorokin expresses concern about the lack of creativity in practically all fields of endeavor, claiming that we are lacking in will and drifting without a rudder, because of the depletion of our energies into sexual activity. He concludes that our hope lies in individuals taking constructive action: re-establishing a sane sex order and restoring the values associated with marriage and the family.

The material in this book was sparked by the author's article, "A Case Against Sexual Freedom" (1954), which readers urged him to expand into book form. The author realizes that his point of view is likely to be unpopular, for it advocates a highly restricted orientation to sexuality similar to that of the nineteenth century, a time of increasing liberalization of attitudes toward sexual behavior. (TJW)

PR,IL

52. Wilson, John. **Love, Sex, & Feminism: A Philosophical Essay.** New York: Praeger, 1980. 125 p. Includes bibliographic references. ISBN 0-03-056103-5.

Wilson, a lecturer and tutor at Oxford University, is an educator, philosopher, and author of several books in the fields of education and psychology. In this book he uses his philosophical skills to lay the foundation for a clear understanding of sexuality and its attendant concepts. He is concerned about understanding "sexuality" for three major reasons: (1) we are all involved in sexuality; (2) we are being bombarded by great quantities of practical, advisory, and pornographic literature; and (3) sexuality for us is "not a kind of optional exercise but something both inevitable and inevitably important" (p. v). The book is divided into two sections based on two sorts of questions that relate to sexuality. The concepts involving sexuality or eroticism itself are dealt with in part I, under such headings as "Sex, Perversion, and Morality," "Love," "Love-Objects and the Body," "Aggression," "Integrity," and "Obscenity and Censorship." Those concerned with sex in the sense of male and female sexuality—"Sexual Insults," "Sex Differences," "Equality, Wants, and Interests," "Power, Influence, and Justice," "Feminist Strategies," and "Abortion"—are examined in part II. A postscript looks at "Sex and Education." Topics are approached using the techniques of analytic philosophy, which directs attention to establishing the concepts and range of meaning that define what is being talked about. Wilson considers the meanings of such concepts as "love," "feminist," and "abortion." For example, he finds that the term "feminists" is a hopelessly vague description because, unlike the term "suffragists," it does not refer to a group with a particular platform. He also examines "abortion" in terms of whether an embryo is a person or not. This well-written, carefully reasoned philosophical essay provides a perspective on sexuality that may be helpful to professionals, such as psychologists, anthropologists, physicians, and others. (TJW)

3

Origins. Evolution

IL,PO

53. Cherfas, Jeremy, and John Gribbin. **The Redundant Male: Is Sex Irrelevant in the Modern World?** New York: Pantheon Books, 1984. 196 p. Includes bibliographic references and index. ISBN 0-394-74005-X.

At first glance, it seems that "men are at best parasites on women, and at worst totally redundant in the immediate evolutionary scheme" (p. 6). Using the Darwinian concept of natural selection, Cherfas and Gribbin, both writers and consultants for *New Scientist*, attempt to answer the question of why women bother to have sons. They divide their query into two different questions: (1) Why do human females reproduce sexually? and (2) Why are there two distinct genders? The initial chapters address basic elements of these questions. "What Is Sex?" focuses on genetic shuffling through meiosis as the main feature of sex. However, the female sacrifices half of her genetic material to engage in the process. "What Is Sex For?" is a more difficult question. The long-term benefits of sex, such as facilitation of quicker evolution and adaptation and avoidance of extinction, are easier to understand than its short-term advantages. Nevertheless, sex is a given. In "Why Two Sexes?" the question becomes why gender developed and whether it is also an immutable part of our existence. The basic distinction between male and female is that males produce small gametes and females, large ones. Given the need to recombine genetic material, females need to mate with males. Therefore, the male gamete has a role to play. The male investment in reproduction is cheap, based on the large number of gametes he can produce and the opportunities available to impregnate the female. That of the female is more costly, as she nurtures more reproductive material and has to parent offspring. These relative investments underlie the concept of gender. Despite possible alterations in the biological foundation of sex, gender may persist because of the ways in which sexual reproduction has shaped our way of life. The remaining chapters consider these effects. "Sex in the Wild" gives an overview of the effects of sexual reproduction on animal behavior in general. Mating systems in particular illustrate the common theme of female parental care and male competition for mates. "The Sexes in Balance" discusses why the sexes are kept in balance rather than opting for the sex that reproduces cheaply. The biological paradigm is transposed to social concerns in "Sex and Society" and "Of Sex and Apes." Only a biological framework makes sense of the differences between males and females. The concluding chapters reiterate the question of why sexual reproduction is necessary. The overall answer is that sex is advantageous when environmental changes favor differential genetic combinations. In "Sex 'N' Bugs" the authors offer the view that sex is a defense mechanism against pathogens. Therefore, males are not useless. As the authors put it, "we have the perfect answer to those women who see males for what they are, biological parasites on the parental care of females: if it weren't for men, you would all be riddled with disease" (p. 179). (SGF)

PR,IL

54. Daly, Martin, and Margo Wilson. **Sex, Evolution, and Behavior: Adaptations for Reproduction.** North Scituate, Mass.: Duxbury Press, 1978. 387 p. Includes bibliography, index, and glossary. ISBN 0-87872-156-8.

What is the rationale behind the duality of male/female? What differences between the sexes are basic? Why have some traits developed for males and females while others have not? One aim of this book is to make the case that "a comparative, evolutionary perspective can cast a good deal of light on human behavior and on the essential nature of woman and man" (p. 4). While Daly and Wilson's major explanatory level for sex differences is in terms of ultimate causation, they acknowledge that a full explanation must also include an understanding of proximate causation, ontogeny, and phylogeny. The authors draw primarily on a wealth of cross-species information from the biological sciences but also include data from the social and behavioral sciences to provide a synthetic framework with sociobiological outlines.

The authors assert that sexual reproduction is a product of evolution by natural selection, which has to be understood if the sexes are to be understood. According to the tenets of natural selection, organisms have strategies that function to maximize fitness, i.e., reproductive success. Sexual reproduction probably evolved because it introduces greater variability among sexually produced offspring. The differences between males and females can be viewed as a product of different reproductive strategies. Females invest more in each offspring than males and have a lower reproductive potential; thus, they are "reluctant" or selective in mating because mistakes are costly in terms of wasted mating and reproductive potential. Males have greater variance in their reproductive success and are "ardent" in competing for opportunities to inseminate females and gain access to the female's greater parental investment. Sexual differences in reproductive capacity, courtship, mortality, and mating systems follow from these basic strategies. While parental strategies may also contribute to reproductive success, they may do so at the expense of a mate. These reproductive strategies may be expressed in the proximate causes of sexual behavior in males and females. Physiological control mechanisms such as hormones may function to optimize the timing of female reproductive events and to activate competitive mating in males. Hormones organize the development of internal and external sexual organs and certain sex-typed aspects of the brain and behavior; developmental processes have a definite direction and can be interpreted functionally.

These general explanations for the origin of male and female differences can be applied to humans. Sexual differences in attitudes and choices are consistent with reproductive strategy theory. For example, males are more concerned with female fidelity than vice versa, and females are more selective of mates; males court females vigorously and are more likely to be promiscuous. Marriage patterns and incest avoidance can also be explained in these terms. The authors conclude that human sexual behavior can be partially understood in terms of evolutionary biology; the reproductive consequences of behavior aid in understanding the specializations of any species, including humans. (SGF)

IL
55.   Davis, Elizabeth Gould. **The First Sex.** New York: Putnam, 1971. 382 p. Includes bibliographic notes and index.

Two convergent themes run through this work. The first is that the earliest civilizations known to us are only remembered fragments of a much earlier and higher civilization. The second is that women have been the agents of civilization, playing the dominant role in preserving and renewing aspects of lost civilizations.

In this scholarly volume Davis marshals compelling evidence in support of both convictions and their convergence. Anthropological findings, philology, cartography, mythology, archaeology, sexual symbolism, origins of fetishes, profiles of medieval women and women of the Reformation and the eighteenth and nineteenth centuries by turn are skillfully presented as the case is built. The testimony of others, from the writings of Plato to television broadcasts by Buckminster Fuller, is woven into the argument.

The book ends on a note of prophecy—foreseeing that in the twenty-first century "not physical force, but spiritual force will lead the way. . . . And in this sphere woman will again predominate. She who was revered and worshipped by early man because of her power to see the unseen will once again be the pivot . . . about whom the next civilization will, as of old, revolve" (p. 339). (LF)

PR,IL,PO

56. Fisher, Helen E. **The Sex Contract: The Evolution of Human Behavior.** New York: Quill, 1983. 253 p. Includes bibliography and index. ISBN 0-688-01599-9.

According to Fisher, a physical anthropologist, many scientists have passed over the role of sex in human evolution. Nevertheless, she believes that sex is "the spark that . . . ignited all of human life" (p. 16). Drawing on data from her doctoral dissertation and other relevant materials from various disciplines, she reconstructs the development of human life from its prehominid and protohominid phases through its hominid stages to its emergence into truly human form.

The nature of sexual relationships was an integral part of this process. As self-sufficient protohominid females gradually became bipedal so that they could carry food to a central place in the savannah, their pelvic shape changed; the pelvic inlet was more constricted, and natural selection favored those females who gave birth to immature young. Since immature offspring required more nurturance and protection, mothers needed the cooperation of males to raise the young. Sexier females who copulated during periods other than estrus received more attention, protection, and food from males; these advantages led to the loss of estrus. Females who copulated with males soon after birth maintained temporary bonds with males, received food from them, enhanced their nutritional status, ovulated sooner, and thus bore offspring more frequently. The more offspring that females had, the more they needed the help of males. Therefore, selection favored males and females who could bond for a longer period of time. The sex contract began four million years ago when males and females established economic and sexual ties with each other; males provided meat and protection for the young in exchange for intercourse with females and the vegetables that they gathered. The bonding that males and females established with each other might be at the root of such emotions as jealousy and altruism; cognitive characteristics such as the capacity for complicated thought, the development of language, and the categorization of kin; and the generation of social rules. Therefore, bonding began as a part of the sex contract and continues as an essentially human attribute. This well-written book, geared to a general audience, shows how ancient behavior patterns may still be shaping our lives today. (SGF)

PR

57. Hrdy, Sarah Blaffer. **The Woman That Never Evolved.** Cambridge, Mass.: Harvard University Press, 1981. 256 p. Includes bibliographic notes and index. ISBN 0-674-95540-4.

The primary aim of this book is "to suggest a few plausible hypotheses about the evolution of woman that are more in line with current data" (p. 14). In the process, anthropologist Hrdy casts doubt upon some deeply held beliefs about the nature of females. How did woman actually evolve over the past seventy million years? Hrdy draws on extensive primate research, particularly recent studies on female primates in the wild, to support her view that female primates share a heritage of being competitive, socially involved, and sexually assertive. The woman that *never* evolved was less competitive, less egotistical, less interested in dominance, and more peaceful than man. The perception of woman's nature as innocent from lust or power, cooperative, and solitary is more a product of cultural construction than biological evidence.

Although attention has focused on the reproductive advantages of competition and sexual variety for men, little attention has been given to the reproductive advantages of such characteristics for females; they are viewed as aberrations or by-products of male evolution. Using a sociobiological perspective, Hrdy makes a case for reproductive advantages that would accrue to a sexually assertive, competitive female. Although large body size allowed males to dominate females, females have governed the breeding potential. A rare mammalian mating pattern like monogamy derives from constraints imposed on males by females who make male assistance essential because of the way they arrange themselves socially and geographically. Mating strategies depend on how well females tolerate each other, not on the tendencies of males. Every female is a "competitive, strategizing creature." Females may compete with each other or cooperate with other females to compete with other groups of females.

Despite claims to the contrary, there is variation in the reproductive success of females; there are differences in fertility and survival of offspring. The primate origins of female sexuality derive from behavior that improves the survival of offspring. Concealed ovulation, nonreproductive sexual activities, and orgasms are not unique to humans. Primate patterns of sexual activity are quite flexible and can lapse from cyclical patterns to situationally-dependent sex not governed by the menstrual cycle. Copulation functions for more than insemination; it can serve to attract a number of partners to a female, confuse paternity, and most important, forestall a male's interference in the survival of the female's offspring. Female genital stimulation can be reinforcing in itself and multiple orgasms would allow females to engage in multiple reproductive and nonreproductive encounters.

Hrdy's discussion of male/female inequality, mating patterns, and female primate sexuality leads her to conclude that human females are "radically different" from other primates. The prehominid primate's probable readiness to engage in a variety of reproductive and nonreproductive encounters has been restricted by rules and practices institutionalized to ensure paternity. Clitoridectomies, patrilocality, premarital chastity, the subordination of women, and the prevalence of male authority can be viewed in this light. An understanding of evolutionary history may aid in understanding contemporary sexual asymmetry among humans.

Readers can refer to Daly and Wilson's *Sex, Evolution, and Behavior* for an overview of sociobiological tenets. Symons's *The Evolution of Human Sexuality* is an example of the male-oriented interpretation of evolution that Hrdy attempts to balance. (SGF)

IL

58.   Jonas, Doris, and David Jonas. **Sex & Status.** New York: Stein and Day, 1980. 214 p. Originally published by Stein and Day in 1975. Includes bibliography and index. ISBN 0-8128-6069-1.

Sexual behavior as a function of status is the subject of this book by Jonas and Jonas, group and family therapy leaders and marriage counselors with professional backgrounds in anthropology and medicine. Status is defined as an aspect of group behavior that endows individuals with self-confidence and a feeling of success. It entitles them to form sexual bonds and reproduce, thus ensuring continuation of the species. Those who achieve status are the successful ones (the winners) in the struggle for dominance in life. The authors provide numerous examples of this from childhood, school life, and adulthood. They also make many interspecies comparisons. In all animal life social order arises out of the struggle for rank, or status. In nonhuman species the hierarchies that emerge are rigid and the life roles of individuals are fixed. With humans the situation is more complicated because of the influence of the brain which allows imagination, fantasy, and judgment to modify behavior. Besides a human being's special brain, another factor influencing his or her behavior is supersexuality (i.e., the capacity to perform sexually year around rather than at prescribed times). Yet another important biological factor modifying behavior is the hormonal outpouring which occurs in many situations: prior to mating, in violence of all kinds, in fighting, etc. Among animal species (except people), as a result of the struggle for existence, a natural balance is established between animal populations and their environments. The fit survive while the weaker members are allowed to perish. With humans, the opposite is often the case: they make every effort to preserve those who are physically and mentally deficient. Humanity even allows the deficient to reproduce in the belief that everyone is entitled to this right. Nevertheless, nature itself acts as a countervailing force in this matter: those who are ill-equipped to strive for status or those who have lost in the struggle for dominance, characterized as "losers" by the authors, do not have the same opportunities to procreate. Indeed, many of them suffer from sexual dysfunctions, if not permanently at least until more dominant roles are provided than in the social hierarchies. A great deal of sex therapy is concerned with treating the "losers" in the struggle for status. Treatment is difficult if it focuses on the specific problem, say, premature ejaculation, without taking into consideration the underlying causes. Attention to the patient's social status is likely to provide the key to the problem. A stronger case for the authors' position might have been made had supporting documentation beyond the bibliography at the end of the book been provided. The book represents a philosophical summing up of the authors' impressions about the nature of life, gleaned from their clinical experience and reading; it is not a research report or scientific study. (TJW/SGF)

IL

59. Margulis, Lynn, and Dorion Sagan. **Mystery Dance: On the Evolution of Human Sexuality.** New York: Summit Books, 1991. 224 p. Includes bibliographic notes and index.

Distinguished professor Margulis (Department of Botany at the University of Massachusetts at Amherst) and freelance writer Sagan team up to provide readers with an "evolutionary striptease," a mystery dance that "exposes the presumed sex lives and bodily appearances of our ancestors, human and prehuman." It is a speculative story of the evolution of human sexuality, drawn from philosophy, psychoanalysis, and scientific data. As the authors put it, "This book is set up as a kind of holographic theater, in which we show you evolution in reverse, from human to ape to reptile and beyond, exploring the evolution of men and women, sexual organs and sex roles, trusting commitments and erotic infidelities, love and lust." "Mystery dance" also refers to the human sex act itself, which expresses the human heritage and is the point where "reality hooks up with dream."

Each chapter focuses on a different aspect of human sexual evolution, linking it to similar traits in other animals or organisms and tying it to theoretical questions about its meaning. The first chapter considers such questions as: What is the significance of the size of the testes, the length of the penis, and the amount of sperm a man produces? Answers revolve around sperm competition and opportunities to reproduce. Implications relate to an understanding of jealousy, men's "greater promiscuity," and the origins of marriage and monogamy. The second chapter investigates cultural differences and biological similarities in male and female orgasms, exploring what role female orgasm may have played in evolution. While the penis conferred an advantage in sperm competition, "anatomically and physiologically the clitoris seems to be a diminutive version of the penis," without evolutionary significance. The third chapter seeks the origins and meaning of the "body electrick," aspects of female anatomy such as breasts and the hymen and her physiology such as the "loss of estrus" and menstruation. How do these relate to sexual selection, attraction, and reproduction? What does neotony have to do with the development of fetishes and attraction?

The farther reaches of the evolutionary striptease take the reader back to links with humans that have been given less attention than mammalian developments. The last three chapters draw attention to them: (1) the retention of the R-complex in the brain characteristics of reptiles, which may help us to understand sexual jealousy, same-gender violence, rape, dreams, and hierarchical obedience; (2) the meaning of phallic variety in the biological world, particularly its psychoanalytic interpretation; and (3) the sex lives of the protists and bacteria at the dawn of time, which suggest that sexually reproducing plants and animals, not sexual reproduction, was selected for in evolution. The question that concludes the book is why sex exists and persists. "Sex as the formation of individuals with genes from more than a single parent first appeared in promiscuous bacteria, but not until the evolution of protists did sex become necessary . . . for reproduction." Understanding the biological heritage of human sexuality continues, and "the dance never ends." (SGF)

PR
60. Margulis, Lynn, and Dorion Sagan. **Origins of Sex: Three Billion Years of Genetic Recombination.** New Haven, Conn.: Yale University Press, 1986. 258 p. (The Bio-origins Series). Includes bibliography, index, and glossary. ISBN 0-300-04619-7.

This book explores the origins of sex writ large—from its evolution in microorganisms to its expression in more complex forms of life. The analysis involves a detailed consideration of cell processes, particularly genetic recombination, over the past three billion years, because "sex, the pooling of genetic resources from two parents, is so intimately intertwined with cell processes that much of the origin and evolution of sex is the origin and evolution of life itself."

The main thesis, which "may come as a surprise to some," is that "ultimately males and females are different from each other not because sexual species are better equipped to handle the contingencies of a dynamically changing environment but because of a series of historical accidents that took place in and permitted the survival of ancestral protists . . . biparental sex itself did not immediately confer any great advantage upon those organisms in which it arose." Central to an understanding of this thesis is an exploration of sex and reproduction among bacteria and protists (a one-celled microorganism with a membrane-bounded nucleus), especially the dynamics of mitosis (cell division in which chromosomes are doubled, segregated, and dispersed to offspring cells), meiosis (a process of fertilization in which diploid cells are reduced to haploid ones), and DNA replication, repair, and mutation.

The initial chapters deal with some basic definitions: life (self-maintenance, growth, and reproduction), sex ("mixing of genetic sources"), reproduction ("copying resulting in the creation of additional live beings"), and evolution (selection pressures or mutations that lead to differential reproduction and changes in populations over time). Detailed explorations of the emergence of sexuality make up the core of the book: (1) how threats to DNA by ultraviolet light led to the emergence of sex; (2) recombination and bacterial mating; (3) the emergence of protists; (4) the origin of chromosomes; (5) chromosome deployment in mitosis; (6) cannibalism among microorganisms; and (7) mitosis, meiosis, and cell differentiation. The final chapters present the relevance of these ancient processes to the origin of eggs, sperm, and gender ("the entire complex of signals of mate recognition") and the implications of a common evolutionary legacy to all sexually reproducing organisms. The authors conclude that gender "is an epiphenomenon of meiotic sex and cell differentiation [and is] . . . determined in many different ways with different degrees of rigidity." Therefore, there can be many more than two genders. The problem in interpreting the origin and maintenance of sex has been their exploration primarily in vertebrates rather than investigating genetic recombination, meiotic sex, gender determination, and reproduction in a wider range of organisms. Consequently, the arguments become skewed by the bias of humans focusing on the origins of their own particular brand of sex as sexually reproducing vertebrates. Therefore, it may be difficult to conceptualize how the idea that "reproduction preceded all kinds of sex [and] is not an intrinsic part of the sexual process . . . [and that] meiotic sexuality was never selected for because it generated more variation than asexuality did." In sum, "sex should be thought of broadly." (SGF)

IL,PO
61. Morris, Desmond. **The Naked Ape: A Zoologist's Study of the Human Animal.** New York: McGraw-Hill, 1967. 252 p. Includes bibliography.

On publication Morris's *The Naked Ape* became a national bestseller. Its popularity stemmed from the fact that it addressed important questions about human's animal nature in terms of sex, the rearing of offspring, aggression, and the like. Morris, a zoologist, describes our species, *Homo sapiens*, as a naked ape, i.e., as one creature among 193 living species of primates, practically devoid of hair. Furthermore, with the largest and most imaginative brain, and possessing the largest penis relative to body size, man is unique among his peers.

In the introduction Morris criticizes early anthropologists, psychiatrists, and psychoanalysts in their attempts to understand human's basic nature. In hopes of finding basic truths about humans, the psychiatrists studied patients with serious psychological problems rather than normal people, while anthropologists dashed off to remote corners of the globe to study primitive peoples. Despite all of the exotic and interesting data anthropologists gathered, little of central importance to understanding our species was found. The reason is that these primitive peoples had been sidetracked into cultural blind alleys where their progress stopped. It would have been better, Morris believes, to have investigated "the common behavior patterns that are shared by all the ordinary, successful members of the major cultures" (p. 10). From Morris's standpoint, a more fruitful source of information about *Homo sapiens* is to be found in an examination of primate behavior, that of both the naked ape and the hairy ape.

Morris's chapter on the naked ape's sexual behavior in today's advanced societies is particularly instructive. He identifies three characteristic behavioral phases—pair formation, precopulative activity, and copulation—and provides both detailed descriptions of activities peculiar to each phase and explanations of bodily reactions during the activities. In drawing comparisons with other primates' sexual behavior, he concludes that the naked ape is the sexiest primate alive.

Of course, humans differ from the apes in many behavior patterns that are inherited from our simian ancestors. In order to survive and multiply our ancestors became in turn food gatherers and hunters. They also had to develop a better brain to compensate for their inadequate physique. This necessitated a much longer and more dependent childhood with the females staying at home minding the infants. Males cooperated in the hunt and used weapons. Out of these social developments came the patterns now dominant in human life.

The development of civilization has done little to alter the sexual system of the species, for it has happened too quickly for any fundamental biological advances to occur. Indeed, Morris believes that our "biological nature has moulded the social structure of civilization, rather than the other way around" (p. 84). Just beneath the veneer of society's gloss and glitter lies the naked ape. (TJW)

PR,IL

62. Sherfey, Mary Jane. **The Nature and Evolution of Female Sexuality.** New York: Random House, 1973. 188 p. Includes bibliography and glossary. ISBN 0-394-71806-2.

In her controversial presentation of the fundamental sexual nature of women, feminist psychiatrist Sherfey draws primarily on new ideas and information in biology and sex research to reassess the current psychiatric interpretation of female sexuality. Two major sets of findings contribute to her views.

First, she explicates the inductor theory of sexual differentiation. In essence, it posits that mammalian males are derived from an innate, genetically determined female morphology in all mammalian embryos; androgen is the hormonal substance that induces the transformation to male morphology. Such a shift was necessary to maintain the advantages of viviparity. Therefore, the long-held view of innate bisexuality of vertebrate embryos on which Freud based his theory of female psychosexual development is no longer valid. Freudian theory needs to be revised in light of these new findings.

Second, Sherfey was impressed by the initial findings of Masters and Johnson that clitoral and vaginal orgasms are physiologically the same and that women are capable of multiple orgasms. Using these major themes, Sherfey weaves an evolutionary picture of female sexuality that attempts to explain the inadequately understood issues of PMS, the shift from periodicity to the potential for continuous arousal, orgasm, and the human mating pattern. She proposes that "throughout primate evolution selective pressure has always tended in the direction of favoring the development of the longer duration of the intense orgasmic contractions in the females and the shorter, more intense contractions in the male. In general, the orgasm in the male is admirably designed to deposit the semen where it will do the most good, and in the female, to remove the largest amount of venous congestion in the most effective manner" (p. 80). Upright posture as well as greater buildup of the endometrium for implantation in the last two weeks of the menstrual cycle mean greater venous congestion in the female pelvis. This congestion may contribute to the discomfort of PMS and foster a greater desire for intercourse, that could release the congestion through orgasm. Nevertheless, the female "is sexually insatiable in the presence of the highest degrees of sexual satiation" (p. 112).

In the past, women probably eagerly pursued sexual activity. However, this behavior was not compatible with monogamous, sedentary cultures. When paternity and inheritance became as important as maternity, women's inordinate sexual desires had to be suppressed so that organized, civilized cultures could emerge. Sherfey thinks that this subjugation of female sexuality occurred fairly recently. Strong sexual desires in women persist because they are basic to a woman's nature. (SGF)

PR

63. Symons, Donald. **The Evolution of Human Sexuality.** New York: Oxford University Press, 1979. 358 p. Includes bibliography and index. ISBN 0-19-502535-0.

In this controversial application of the tenets of sociobiology to the evolution of human sexuality, anthropologist Symons attempts to demonstrate that "with respect to sexuality, there is a female human nature and a male human nature, and these natures are extraordinarily different"; they are a product of different adaptive responses to the exigencies of the long hunting and gathering phase of human evolutionary prehistory. Symons compiles a wealth of data from primatology, evolution, biology, psychology, sociocultural anthropology, and popular literature to account for the development of human sexuality and sex differences, not sex roles. He asserts that psychological differences in desire and disposition between men and woman may be innate rather than learned. He thinks that resistance to accepting this point of view stems from the long immersion of social and behavioral scientists in learning theory, with a concomitant lack of attention to biological processes; in addition, the application of principles of natural selection to humans implies a "mechanistic, utilitarian, unsentimental, tough-minded, and cynical" view of life, seemingly at odds with Western views of humanity.

The first chapter introduces evolutionary principles and the second deals with the difficult question of how to apply these tenets to humans. The remainder of the book tries to demonstrate that selection for reproductive success has resulted in consistent differences between males and females. Some of these differences are (1) the greater selective advantage of male orgasms, (2) the advantages for females of loss of estrus, (3) greater intrasexual competition among males, (4) the inclination of males to polygyny, (5) the universal occurrence of male jealousy, (6) the higher probability that males will be aroused by the sight of women and female genitals, (7) the importance of physical characteristics as determinants of female attractiveness, (8) a greater predisposition for men to desire a variety of sexual partners, and (9) the perception of copulation as a favor or service that women perform for men. Examination of hormonal evidence and homosexual experiences are used to test Symons's hypothesis that there are species-typical sex differences in sexual desire and disposition. Symons concludes that it was "the complexity of sexual opportunity and constraint in natural human environments that made adaptive a human psyche uniquely informed by sexuality." (SGF)

IL

64. Wilson, Glenn. **Love and Instinct: An Evolutionary Account of Human Sexuality.** New York: Quill, 1983. 252 p. Previously published in 1982 as *The Coolidge Effect.* Includes bibliography and index. ISBN 0-688-01899-8.

Wilson's major premise is that while much of human behavior is learned, a great deal of it is biologically based, indeed instinctive. Instinctive behavior has an evolutionary origin, the result of genetic changes, and readily accounts for many mental and emotional differences between men and women. In this book, psychiatrist Wilson applies sociobiological theory to human sexual and romantic behavior, a position that runs contrary to environmental explanations of behavior.

The existence of two sexes is responsible for sexual and romantic behavior leading to sexual intercourse and reproduction. Owing to the reshuffling of genes at conception, offspring are unique: those that are better able to adapt to the environment have a better chance for survival. Wilson considers sexual traits that are reproductively advantageous instinctive.

He also maintains that gender differences are partly determined by genetic factors operating through the hormones. He rejects the belief that the identical rearing of boys and girls would eliminate gender differences. In fact, the parental investment theory accounts for a great deal of male and female behavior. Men tend to be polygamous, highly competitive, and desirous of younger females as mates. Women prefer monogamy, are cautious, and less concerned about age of partners.

Wilson examines those genetically determined male and female sex differences (various physical differences, visual arousability, etc.) that are responsible for sexual attraction and arousal. He also believes that the incest taboo has a strong instinctual basis (it is not reproductively advantageous to copulate with parents, siblings, etc.) as well as a social one.

Wilson further states that sexual attractiveness probably determines initial choice of a mate, but that the pair-bond established survives for other reasons (duty, children, habit). Even regular copulation does not guarantee a stable marriage. According to Wilson, the instinct that underlies marriage "is that of sequestering a mate and protecting her from other males so that the husband can be sure of his paternity" (p. 135). Jealousy emerges as a basic emotion engendered by any attack on the matrimonial state. For different instinctual reasons men and women are jealous of each other. Love, however, is probably multifactorial; it is solidly established in childhood by imprinting, that sets up a mental model that we use to select a partner.

Wilson reviews the various theories of female orgasm. He discounts the belief that female orgasm performs "any very important evolutionary function"; otherwise "it would occur with a great deal more ease and with much greater reliability than it does" (p. 175). Clitoral orgasm is learned behavior, much like piano playing.

In the final chapters Wilson concerns himself with instinctual mechanisms in relation to sexual variations and with social influences on sexual behavior. (TJW)

4

Demographic Studies

PR,IL
65. Guttentag, Marcia, and Paul F. Secord. **Too Many Women? The Sex Ratio Question.** Beverly Hills, Calif.: Sage Publications, 1983. 277 p. Includes bibliographic notes and index. ISBN 0-8039-1918-2.

Guttentag and Secord, both social psychologists, trace a cause of many social phenomena to the relative balance of men versus women in a given social group. A high sex ratio of men versus women (more men than women) has tended throughout history and culture to be associated with men valuing, protecting, sheltering, and sometimes restricting women, together with substantial interest and investment by men in monogamy, marriage, family, and children. A low sex ratio by contrast (fewer men than women), has tended to be associated with promiscuity, higher divorce and separation rates, lesser valuing of women by men and more misogyny, and rise of feminist-type women's interest groups.

Guttentag and Secord describe in detail these correlations for classical Greece, medieval Europe, orthodox Jews, various groups in early America, modern white Americans, and modern black Americans. They describe two types of power: *structural power*, stemming from social, economic, and legal roles, which has been traditionally held by men across history and culture; and *dyadic power*, which is held by whichever sex is fewest and therefore has the greatest choice of potential mates. They show that the interaction between structural power constantly in the hands of men, and dyadic power shifting between men and women, has influenced past society and culture in relatively consistent ways.

However, scientific and technical changes in the last century have greatly reduced the salience of the major biological disparities between the sexes, which are the greater size and strength of men and the virtual unavoidability of childbearing for most women. This has resulted in women as well as men being able to achieve structural power. Thus the influence of dyadic power through sex ratios alone may have somewhat different effects in the future than in the past. (MC)

PR
66. Laslett, Peter. **Family Life and Illicit Love in Earlier Generations: Essays in Historical Sociology.** Cambridge: Cambridge University Press, 1977. 270 p. Includes bibliography and index. ISBN 0-521-21408-4.

The goal of this detailed, demographic, and scholarly study in historical sociology is to examine the general thesis that the distinguishing characteristics of the Western family over the past two to three hundred years have been the simultaneous presence of four interrelated traits: (1) a family or household composed primarily of parents and children; (2) a relatively late age of the mother during the period of childbearing; (3) often a theme of a companionate marriage with relatively few years separating the ages of the spouses, with the wife often being older than her husband; and (4) servants (people who do not belong to the immediate family) who are recognized and important members of many households. Laslett, Director of the Cambridge Group for the History of Population and Social Structure, focuses on how these characteristics compose the context for the socialization of young children and have an important impact on their personality formation, particularly in the pre-industrial era.

Laslett presents demographic evidence for establishing the credibility of his thesis, discussing each characteristic in turn as it applies to an individual's socialization in the life cycle as well as to phases of the family cycle. Among his findings are that parents and siblings have had a strong impact on the developing child in the Western family; that the physical removal of the father had a major impact on the nature of the family; that one-fifth to one-quarter of wives were older than their husbands; that most women gave birth to their children when they were in their late twenties or early thirties; and that servants were almost always members of the household.

This unique family pattern implied other social patterns which are documented in successive chapters: illegitimacy, children's parental deprivation, and the role of aged parents in the family. The chapter on "long-term trends in bastardy in England" discusses the patterns and implications of "illicit love," i.e., illegitimacy and pre-nuptial pregnancy. Rather than confirming the expectation that illegitimacy will be high when marriage is later or that illegitimacy figures reflect the prevalence of sexual intercourse outside of marriage, Laslett suggests that "something like a subsociety of the illegitimacy-prone may have existed over time" whose birth rates may explain illegitimacy ratios at specific phases of history, particularly the rise in the early seventeenth century and the dip in the 1810s. There is no necessary connection between sexual deprivation and children born out of wedlock. Laslett also shows that later marriage and motherhood as well as illegitimacy increased children's likelihood of being stepchildren or orphans. He concludes that parental deprivation in the seventeenth and eighteenth centuries' traditional societies was probably more common than it is now. In his chapter on the history of aging and the aged, Laslett disputes the idyllic idea of the elderly residing with their children more than they do today.

Laslett concludes his book by using European data on age at marriage and the birth of the first child to infer age at menarche in Europe since the Middle Ages; and by comparing trends in English and West European family life with the family and household structure of slaves on U.S. plantations, he suggests there is evidence of Western family types, even without legal, public sanction. (SGF)

5

Historical Works

HISTORY OF SEX

(For related material see also entries 123, 131, 344, 356, 365, 401, 403a, 459a, 466, 476, 498, 653, 750, 756, 768, 798, 803, 928, 931, 945a, 987, 989, 1003)

IL
67.   Barret-Ducrocq, Françoise. **Love in the Time of Victoria: Sexuality, Class and Gender in Nineteenth-Century London.** Translated by John Howe. London: Verso, 1991. 225 p. Includes bibliography. ISBN 0-86091-325-2.

Records of the Foundling Hospital, established in 1741 to provide shelter and care for London's abandoned children, are the basis for this study of the sexual behavior of parents of children born out of wedlock. Barret-Ducrocq's study also discusses the social milieu of lower-class working people—the domestics, laborers, skilled workers, etc.— who generally lived in crowded conditions in the poorer sections of London. Their story of sexual and moral behavior, previously glossed over by scholars of the Victorian era, has now been revealed through "the fortuitous discovery of a mine of private archive material" (p. 3).

Normally viewed as amoral by reformers and philanthropists, the applicants to the Foundling Hospital reveal in the now over 100-year-old blue files the details of their amorous encounters that produced so many illegitimate children. In 1801 the Foundling Hospital restricted admission to children under one year old. On the admission sheet the unwed mother had "to show that her good faith had been betrayed, that she had given way to carnal passion only after a promise of marriage or against her will, that she therefore had no other children, and that her conduct had always been irreproachable in every other respect" (p. 41). Furthermore, information on the sexual relations with her lover had to be disclosed. These verbatim, often poignant, statements about the amorous relations of the parents are the substance of this study. What do they reveal?

They reveal the many sides to the relationship between father and mother, such as how they met, intensity of sexual activity, length of courtship; promises of marriage; desertion by the father; impact of pregnancy; reactions of families, friends, fellow workers, and employers; emotional and practical support from individuals and organizations; etc.

Barret-Ducrocq believes that her study of the unique Foundling Hospital records has provided a needed correction to Victorian studies that portray nineteenth-century working men and women as social pariahs, mired in sin and debauchery. The testimonials examined expose the real conditions and attitudes of the lower classes, who demonstrated surprising moral strength in coping with the problem of illegitimacy. (TJW)

PR
68.   Birken, Lawrence. **Consuming Desire: Sexual Science and the Emergence of a Culture of Abundance, 1871-1914.** Ithaca, N.Y.: Cornell University Press, 1988. 167 p. Includes bibliography and index. ISBN 0-8014-2058-X.

According to historian Birken (Assistant Professor of History at N.Y.U.), sexuality and sexual science play important roles in Western culture, but their importance has not been adequately explained. The goals of this book are to try to understand when and why sexual science emerged and to explore its meaning for Western society. Using original sources in science emerged and to explore its meaning for Western society. Using original sources in evolutionary, economic, sexual, and analytic theory as well as the writings of sexologists published from 1871-1914, Birkin argues that sexology was "an ideology par excellence" that emerged from 1871-1914 within the context of broader changes in Western thought. It was no accident that sexual science developed when it did. The end of the nineteenth century and the beginning of the twentieth century brought with them major cultural and social transitions: (1) from a production-oriented to a consumer-oriented economy; (2) from a holist (i.e., the view that people are different from the start and are born into the society as different) to an individualistic (i.e., the view that people are similar from the start and become different only through social process) conception of the social order; and (3) from transcendent beliefs about the world, based on spiritual ideas, to a natural view of the world, stemming from Darwinian concepts of natural laws. The convergence of these transitions contributed to the development of sexology, an ideology that pushed individualistic and democratic principles to their limits by claiming, as Darwin did, that women and children have desires and that the distinction between normal and abnormal is a matter of degree, not kind. Consequently, previous definitions and rules of order—that spiritual or secular law determines what is right or wrong, legal or not legal—gave way to ideas of natural principles centered on the equality of all human beings and the importance of individual initiative and desires. The structure of thought in sexology symbolized these new principles and expressed the gradual loosening of control of people's lives by religion and the state.

Rather than contributing to a chronological narrative, each of the seven chapters in the book discusses one of the major themes in this phase of transition in Western intellectual history. The first chapter describes the dissolution of the past political economy as the new marginalist economics emerged after 1871. The second chapter discusses the ways in which the emergence of sexology paralleled economic developments, particularly tension between the values of production and consumption. Chapters 3 and 4 concentrate on ambiguities in evolutionary theory as they applied to ideas about sex, women, and children as well as about normalcy and abnormality. The fifth chapter is "explicitly historical," examining the interface between sexology, society, and the broader ideological context, a theme that is continued in chapter 6. The final chapter briefly articulates the ways that the themes discussed in the previous chapters mark the demise of hierarchy in favor of democratic principles. In sexology as in the economy, the emphasis was on needing what you want (consumer-oriented), not wanting what you need (production-oriented). Thus, desire became pivotal on many different levels. (SGF)

IL

69. Boucé, Paul-Gabriel, ed. **Sexuality in Eighteenth-Century Britain.** Totowa, N.J.: Manchester University Press, 1982. 262 p. Includes bibliographic notes and index. ISBN 0-7190-0865-4.

Using an interdisciplinary approach, editor Boucé has assembled twelve papers to explore various sociocultural aspects of sexuality in eighteen-century Britain. Providing a general background for later papers, Roy Porter explores Enlightenment attitudes of the élite in England, sandwiched between those of the common people, circumscribed by custom and superstition, and those of the courtly aristocracy, where sexual libertinism was rife. He avers that "the pursuit of pleasure leading to happiness, became seen in Enlightenment writers . . . as the behaviour dictated by Nature to man" (p. 4). Sexuality thereby pervaded the society, manifesting itself in such diverse fields as scientific writing, medicine, the belles-lettres, the stage, and male/female relationships.

Following Porter's general comments, editor Boucé writes about some commonly held but dated beliefs and myths concerning anatomy (penis size), physiology (menstruation, spermatogenesis), and pregnancy. Norah Smith takes up sexual mores and attitudes toward marriage and divorce in Scotland. Then Robert A. Erickson discusses in detail the style and language of a select number of books on midwifery. G. S. Rousseau examines Dr. Bienville's book *La Nymphomanie,* published in 1771, which is the first work on nymphomania and attributes the sexual disorder to the imagination. Peter Wagner's essay concerns criminal trial reports of sexual misconduct as a source of widely read erotic and pornographic literature. In "The Veil of Chastity," Ruth Perry examines the feminist views of Mary Astell, who provided reasons for women to opt for a celibate life.

Turning to the literary component of eighteenth-century sexuality, Boucé provides a paper by John V. Price that examines patterns of sexual behavior found in the eighteenth-century novels *Moll Flanders, Joseph Andrews, Clarissa,* and *Peregrine Pickle,* pointing out the serendipitous nature of sexual encounters. In "The Mythology of Love," Douglas Brooks-Davies points out the Venerean iconography in the writings of Pope, Fielding, Cleland, and Sterne. Arthur H. Cash focuses his attention on the bizarre birth of Tristrum Shandy in Samuel Richardson's novel by that name, elaborating on the shortcomings of the birthing devices of the day. Robert Adams Day writes about sex and scatology in the writings of Tobias Smollett. Finally, Pat Rogers directs the reader's attention to the titillating sexual ambiguities of the "breeches parts" in Restoration and eighteenth-century stage presentations. (TJW)

IL

70. Bullough, Vern L. **Sexual Variance in Society and History.** New York: Wiley, 1976. 715 p. Includes bibliographic notes and index. ISBN 0-471-12080-4.

Essentially a history of sex in the Western world, *Sexual Variance in Society and History* focuses on "attitudes toward sex and their relationship to certain forms of stigmatized sexual behavior, primarily homosexuality," but including the related activities of masturbation, transvestism, transsexualism, and bestiality. For perspective, sexual customs and attitudes in non-Western cultures—the Islamic world, India, and China—are also examined. Emphasized in this overview of attitudes are the influence of religions, the supportive role of legal codes, and the philosophical and scientific justifications of sexual behavior sanctioned by religion and the law. Owing to its hostility toward sexual expression in general, the author has labeled Western culture "sex-negative," contrasting it to the "sex-positive" cultures in other parts of the world. Bullough hopes that his book will help explain the reasons for the current assault (e.g., the liberation of women we are witnessing) on traditional Western values and attitudes toward sex. He also hopes that his overview of past and present investigations of Western sexuality will open up new horizons for the serious student of sex.

In part 1, "Background," there are separate chapters on the biological basis of human sexuality; sex customs of "primitive" societies; the sexual attitudes of early civilizations in the Middle East, including the Sumerian, Assyrian, Egyptian, and Persian; and last, the contributions made by the founders of Judaism, a religion of laws that regulated sexual activity.

Part 2, the "European Inheritance," expounds on the contributions of the Greeks and Romans to our sexual heritage, followed by an analysis of Christian hostility to sex and the reasons for designating Christianity a sex-negative religion.

In part 3, "Attitudes Toward Sex in the Non-Western World," Bullough claims that Islam is a sex-positive religion, and examines the salient features of Islam as they pertain to women and sex; he also explores Hinduism and Buddhism, including Tantrism, on the Indian subcontinent; and finally, he surveys the sex beliefs and practices of ancient China.

Part 4, "The Christian World," delves first into the importance of the split in the Church between the Eastern Orthodox Christians, based in Byzantium, and Roman Catholicism, centered in Rome, as it affected marriage, divorce, and sexual behavior and practices. Bullough traces the evolution of Christian thought on matters of sex in chapters on the early Middle Ages and the later Middle Ages in the West, culminating in a chapter on the impact of the thinking of Protestant reformers on such matters as marriage, celibacy, homosexuality, and the like.

Part 5, "New Horizons and the New World," shows that in the West from the sixteenth century to the nineteenth century the influence of religion waxed and waned. It vacillated from a series of restrictive movements, such as Puritanism, to the secular views of writers and philosophers who assumed a tolerant, even lax attitude toward sexual activity. To America the settlers brought the Puritan outlook, which condemned sex in America, England, and on the Continent, followed by a review of English law and law enforcement as they impinged on such phenomena as contraception, homosexuality, lesbianism, and sodomy, and a discussion of stigmatized sexual behaviors (i.e., homosexuality and lesbianism) in nineteenth-century America.

In the final part of the book, "The Twentieth Century: Problems and Prospects," Bullough notes the growing reaction to traditional sexual attitudes late in the nineteenth century and on into the twentieth century, manifest in studies and theorizing about sex, especially homosexuality; the emancipation of women; and advances in contraception and the birth control movement. Bullough says that at midcentury attitudinal change was approaching flood stage. In his last chapter, Bullough reviews positive changes in the sexual attitudes that have occurred, and hopes that his study of sexual variance will help the reader gain a new understanding of his or her sexual past and a fuller appreciation for others' varied sexual beliefs and behaviors. (TJW)

PR,IL
71. D'Emilio, John, and Estelle B. Freedman. **Intimate Matters: A History of Sexuality in America.** New York: Harper & Row, 1988. 428 p. Includes bibliography and index. ISBN 0-06-015855-7.

Organized according to a chronological framework, this historical account of American sexuality over the last 350 years traces the individual and social factors that have shaped a shift from the reproductive sexuality of the colonial period to the rise and fall of sexual liberalism in contemporary society. D'Emilio and Freedman, both of whom are historians, suggest that the themes of family-centered reproductive sexuality and nonreproductive, pleasure-focused, personally satisfying sexuality are more relevant to an understanding of the events that gave rise to sexual behavior and ideology in a particular era than the more familiar dichotomy of repression and freedom.

Each part of the book describes a segment of change: I—The Reproductive Matrix, 1600-1800; II—Divided Passions, 1780-1900; III—Toward a New Sexual Order, 1880-1930; IV—The Rise and Fall of Sexual Liberalism, 1920 to the present. Underlying each discussion is an emphasis on sexual meanings, sexual regulation, and sexual politics, all of which have changed over time. The meticulous documentation of the themes of each time period underscores the complexity of the American sexual landscape. D'Emilio and Freedman are careful to point out differences in the sexual milieu according to region (North/South, East/West), ethnic group (blacks, Native Americans, Mexicans, European immigrants, whites), gender (male/female, heterosexual/gay, lesbian), and socioeconomic status.

The meaning of sexuality was defined and applied differently to different groups. The dominant white, middle-class ideology was used to reinforce the prevailing gender, class, and ethnic distinctions. As the family, economy, and politics changed, so too did definitions of appropriate sexual behavior. The basis of sexual regulation has also changed from reliance on the family, church, and state to sanction behavior to trust in the medical profession, political groups, and the media. Like sexual meanings and sexual regulation, sexual politics is dynamic. It expresses particularly notable trends when an older order is being challenged by a new one or when gender inequality prompts women to resist the authority of men.

The picture that emerges is one of complex, shifting motifs that are layered upon each other over time, not the replacement of one simple set of themes by others. The changing nature of the family, politics, and the economy has shaped the changes. (SGF)

PR,IL
72. Flandrin, Jean-Louis. **Sex in the Western World: The Development of Attitudes and Behaviour.** Translated from the French by Sue Collins. Switzerland: Harwood Academic Publishers, 1991. 368 p. Translation of *Le Sexe et l'Occident.* Includes bibliographic notes and index. ISBN 3-7186-5201-3.

Originally published in 1981, this book is a collection of Flandrin's own studies, essays, and reviews on the development of sexual attitudes and behavior in Europe, mainly France, since the Middle Ages. Chapter 1, "Why Study the History of Sexuality?" presents Flandrin's views on abiding questions in the areas of love, religion, marriage, children, and sexuality. In it he also discusses historical methodology using statistics as applied in these areas.

Flandrin divides his book into four parts. Part one, "Love," contains four chapters on different aspects of love in the sixteenth, seventeenth, and eighteenth centuries. Chapter 2, for example, presents the results of a content analysis of book titles of sixteenth century books as compared with titles from 1961 in order to show the legally and socially accepted influence of ideas.

Part two, "Sexual Morality and Marital Relations," consists of chapters on (1) the Christian doctrine of marriage, (2) contraception, marriage, and sexual relations, and (3) the behavior of man and wife in the marriage bed.

Flandrin begins part three, "The Child and Procreation," with a review of Philippe Aries's book *Centuries of Childhood*, a seminal work for sociologists and historians, dealing with the history of childhood. Chapter 10, the largest in the book, examines "Attitudes Towards Young Children and Sexual Behaviour." Using a demographic approach, Flandrin explains such questions as the conditions favorable to infanticide in the seventeenth and eighteenth centuries; overpopulation in Christian societies; contraception and infanticide; the intentional killing of children through abortion, smothering, and abandonment; infant mortality; breast-feeding; wet nursing; and the theological concerns over these issues. Chapters 11 and 12 discuss adages and sayings dealing with children and the family and with proverbs concerning young women.

The last part of the book, "The Sex Lives of Single People," republishes two of Flandrin's essays: "Late Marriages and Sex Lives" (1972) and "Repression and Change in the Sex Lives of Young People" (1977). The last chapter is an in-depth review of Peter Laslett's book, *Family Life and Illicit Love in England*, a demographic study of illegitimacy.

Finally, Flandrin states: "The various chapters of this book will, I hope, be able to contribute by modifying our visions of love, of marriage and marital relations, of the parent-child relationship and of the sex lives of single people in a culture forgetful of history" (p. 3). (TJW)

PR,IL

73. Foucault, Michel. **The History of Sexuality.** Translated from the French by Robert Hurley. New York: Pantheon Books, 1978- . 4 v. Translation of *Histoire de la Sexualité*. Vol. 1, *An Introduction*, 1978, 168 p. Vol. 2, *The Use of Pleasure*, 1985, 293 p. Vol. 3, *The Care of the Self*, 1986, 275 p. Includes bibliographies and indexes. ISBN 0-394-41775-5 (v. 1); 0-394-54349-1 (v. 2); 0-394-54814-0 (v. 3).

In volume 1, Foucault, well known for his previous works, *Madness and Civilization* (1965) and *Discipline and Punishment: The Birth of the Prison* (1977), focuses his analytic powers on the history of sexuality since the end of the sixteenth century. He not only tries to present an overview of historically significant points and theoretical problems, but also aims to explore the nature of discourse on sex. In part 1, "We Other Victorians," he discusses a central issue: how to account for the way and degree to which sex is spoken about. In part 2, Foucault turns his attention to the repressive hypothesis according to which sexual behavior for economic reasons was gradually curtailed so that by the nineteenth century the bourgeois, capitalist, and industrial society of the West could be characterized as prudish, hypocritical, and inimical toward sex, casting a pall of silence, secrecy, and scorn over it. In contrast, he hypothesizes that this society "put into operation an entire machinery for producing true discourses concerning it. Not only did it speak of sex and compel everyone to do so; it also set out to formulate the uniform truth of sex. As if it suspected sex of harboring a fundamental secret. As if it needed this production of truth. As if it was essential that sex be inscribed not only in an economy of pleasure but in an ordered system of knowledge" (p. 69). In part 3, Foucault discusses a *scientia sexualis*, that was created to pursue the truth about sex through the mechanism of the confessional and other techniques of truth telling and the proliferation of discourse in fields of knowledge: medicine, psychiatry, sociology, and so forth. The result has been a deployment of sexuality into every aspect of our lives. Foucault discusses this deployment in detail in part 4. Examples of it are four key figures: the hysterical woman whose sexuality was analyzed and whose intrinsic pathology was integrated into medical practice; the masturbating child whose behavior became the focus of proscriptive attention from parents, educators, doctors, and psychologists; the Malthusian couple whose procreative behavior had to be socialized through economic, political, and medical measures; and finally, the perverse adult whose behavior became psychiatrized through normalization or pathologization. These cogent illustrations of power relations at the local level, the development of discourses and special languages centering on sex, and the diffusion of sexual knowledge everywhere are used to support Foucault's hypothesis about a widening of interest in sexuality as opposed to a repression of sexuality in the nineteenth century.

The second volume of Foucault's history of sexuality, *The Use of Pleasure*, focuses on "the manner in which sexual activity was problematized by philosophers and doctors in classical Greek culture of the fourth century B.C." (p. 12). Foucault believes that the Greeks based their pursuit of pleasure on stern principles that emerged from the efforts of philosophers and physicians to examine "sexual behavior as an ethical problem."

In volume 3, *The Care of the Self*, Foucault moves on to the first two centuries of our own era to examine the writings of philosophers (Plutarch, Epictetus, Marcus Aurelius, Seneca) and physicians (Galen, Athenaeus, Soranus, Rufus of Ephesus) dealing with various questions of sexuality: sexual activity and its attendant pleasure, care of the body in the interest of sexual activity, sexual relations between spouses, and the love of boys. Into all these questions crept notions of austerity and caution, that separated the thinking of this period from classical Greek thought and at the same time presaged "the lineaments of a future ethics, the ethics that one will find in Christianity, when the sexual act itself will be considered an evil" (p. 235). (TJW)

PR,IL

74. Gallagher, Catherine, and Thomas Laqueur, eds. **The Making of the Modern Body: Sexuality and Society in the Nineteenth Century.** Berkeley, Calif.: University of California Press, 1987. 242 p. Includes bibliographic notes and index. ISBN 0-520-05960-3.

The editors of this collection of eight essays state that, despite the Victorian reputation for sexual repression, nineteenth-century European society promoted discourse on the body and sexuality. In the main, these essays deal primarily with sex differences and bring to light diverse views from different perspectives: social, historical, anatomical, medical, political, cultural, and literary.

In the first essay, "Orgasm, Generation, and the Politics of Reproductive Biology," editor Laqueur states that a hierarchical model of sex differences, that presented the female body as "an inferior and inverted version of the male body," was replaced by a model of complementary difference in which the woman's "reproductive biology stressed the opposition of male and female bodies, the woman's automatic reproductive cycle, and her lack of sexual feeling" (p. viii). In "Skeletons in the Closet," Londa Schiebinger traces the efforts of anatomists to draw the female skeleton to show anatomical differences between the male and female. She further attributes European societies' belief in the natural inferiority of women to inherent sex differences in men and women as demonstrated by the anatomists. In the essay on the works of Thomas Malthus and Henry Mayhew, editor Gallagher shows how the healthy and vigorous body has a potentially harmful effect on the social body. For example, Malthus in his *Essay on Population* demonstrates that the body is at once a source of value and a source of misery in the sense that it reproduces itself while simultaneously causing a population problem.

In the essay "*Cage aux folles*," D. A. Miller analyzes Wilkie Collins's nineteenth-century sensation novel *The Woman in White* by showing the construction of femininity as "the imposition of male power on women." Mary Poovey's essay concerns the medical treatment of Victorian women. She takes the instance in 1847 when Dr. James Simpson began using chloroform as an anesthetic for women in childbirth. The ensuing debate brought out the concern about how women's bodies were perceived by the male medical profession. Laura Engelstein in "Morality and the Wooden Spoon" describes the range of medical attitudes toward the spread of syphilis in Russia during the nineteenth century. Believing that syphilis in rural areas was a nonvenereal disease fostered by close human contact and unsanitary habits, Russian doctors promoted political, cultural, and environmental solutions to the problem. They further believed that the sexual life of the peasant was minimal, restricted wholly to procreation. In contrast to the absence of state control of prostitution in Russia, the system of state regulation of prostitution in France is the subject of Alain Corbin's essay "Commercial Sexuality in Nineteenth-Century France." Corbin argues that the prostitute became an archetype of the sexualized female body, inspiring fear and the need for control. Her body was viewed as a sewer for social excesses, including disease, especially syphilis. Also focusing on nineteenth-century Parisian prostitution is Christine Buci-Glucksmann's essay "Catastrophic Utopia: The Feminine as Allegory of the Modern." Her paper is an analysis of Walter Benjamin's writings on Baudelaire's reflections about prostitution.

The editors suggest that twentieth-century writers, focused as they are on female sexuality and orgasm, should pay more attention to how the female body was viewed by society in the nineteenth century, giving recognition to the fact that as women became more sexually embodied, they were conceptualized as people without strong sexual feelings. (TJW)

IL

75. Gay, Peter. **The Bourgeois Experience: Victoria to Freud.** New York: Oxford University Press, 1984- . 3 v. Vol. 1, *Education of the Senses*, 1984, 534 p. Vol. 2, *The Tender Passion*, 1986, 490 p. Vol. 3, forthcoming. Includes bibliographic essays and indexes. ISBN 0-19-503352-3(v.1); 0-19-503741-3(v.2).

Education of the Senses focuses on sexual enlightenment of the bourgeois in the West (United States, England, France, Germany) from about 1820 to World War I or, metaphorically speaking, from Victoria to Freud. Gay analyzes nineteenth-century bourgeois culture from a psychoanalytic perspective, using it to penetrate the surface of accepted views and myths about Victorian society. His source documents are diaries, personal correspondence, sex surveys, medical texts, manuals of domestic economy, works of art, and other primary materials researched in archives and libraries. Information derived from these sources often contrasts with ideas provided in published works, giving the reader an understanding of the period quite different from the stereotypical views commonly held: that middle class society was hypocritical, its women unresponsive sexually, and its men inveterate womanizers, living a double standard. Gay examines a broad spectrum of nineteenth-century cultural features in the realm of sexuality: the feminist movement and male fear of women; sexism in the struggle for higher education for women; pain-coping methods in pregnancy and childbirth; expanding contraceptive techniques; the ignorance of sexual knowledge on the part of newlyweds; the environment of silence on sexual issues; the feeble attempts at sex education; the frantic opposition to masturbation from physicians, divines, and educators; sexual expression in painting and sculpture; and so forth. All of these separate strands are analyzed, interpreted, and woven into a grand cultural pattern that provides the reader with an understanding of how the nineteenth-century bourgeoisie were sensually and sexually informed. Two documents relied upon heavily by Gay are Mabel Loomis Todd's diary and the Mosher Survey. The former, by a prominent Amherst lady and lover of Austin Dickinson (the brother of Emily Dickinson), is a startlingly frank record of sexual activities; the latter is a survey of the sexual behavior of some forty-five Victorian women that would incline one to doubt the popular notion that such women were sexually anesthetized. Gay concludes that "the bourgeois experience was far richer than its expression, rich as that was; and it included a substantial measure of sensuality for both sexes, and of candor—in sheltered surroundings. It would be a gross misreading of this experience to think that nineteenth-century bourgeois did not know, or did not practice, or did not enjoy, what they did not discuss" (p. 458). A detailed forty-five page bibliographic essay treating sources chapter by chapter concludes this first volume.

Gay continues his exploration of nineteenth-century bourgeois culture in *The Tender Passion*, this time focusing on middle class attitudes and views of love and demonstrating that love as well as sex was a serious concern of the Victorians. Reflecting a Freudian view, he writes that "true love is the conjunction of concupiscence with affection." The compelling bourgeois romances of the German pair, Otto Beneke and Marietta Banks, and that of Walter Bagehot and Eliza Wilson, exemplify this conjunction of sex and love.

Gay identifies clues to nineteenth-century love through a searching examination of its manifestation, indeed sublimation, in such diverse fields as literature, music, art, nature study, and religion. Endowment of objects (music, the clouds, food, etc.) with sexual qualities they do not really possess was typical of the bourgeois approach to love. *The Tender Passion* complements *Education of the Senses* by providing a balanced picture of nineteenth-century emotional life. (TJW)

IL

76. Haller, John S., and Robin M. Haller. **The Physician and Sexuality in Victorian America.** Urbana, Ill.: University of Illinois Press, 1974. 331 p. Includes bibliography and index. ISBN 0-252-00207-5.

Haller and Haller define sexuality very broadly to encompass the totality of social relations between the sexes. Their concern is with the tensions that arose in these relations as Victorian America made the transition from a rural, preindustrial to an urbanized, industrial society—a transition creating dramatically new social patterns and necessitating the invention of new values and behaviors. In particular, the transformation of the family from a sphere of production to a sphere of privatized consumption threatened disruption of the traditional sexual division of labor. Haller and Haller see the manifestation of these tensions in Victorian society's preoccupation with sexuality; in the endless diagnoses of, treatises on, and claimed cures for the ills of masturbation, prostitution, pregnancy, menopause, women's "nervous disorders," and so on. They advance three particularly important theses concerning this period. First, they argue, it was at this time that physicians increasingly usurped the role formerly played by ministers as society's confessors and moral guardians. Second, they note that in this role physicians exercised a very conservative influence, particularly with regard to women's efforts to escape constricting sex roles. And third, they put forward a radical reinterpretation of the supposed "prudery" of Victorian women, viewing it as a form of sexual rebellion and as the only line of defense available under prevailing conditions. (**Women's Studies**, 1979)

IL

77. Hunt, Morton M. **The Natural History of Love.** New York: Knopf, 1959. 416 p. Includes bibliography and index.

Hunt's history of love through the ages takes the reader on a discursive investigation of the meaning of love and related concepts in Western society and then tries to answer the question, "What are these things that have been called love?" Using a variety of sources to answer that intriguing question—private correspondence; biographies; diaries; historians' anecdotes; rules of etiquette; the laws concerning adultery, divorce, and dowry; and manuals of courtship—Hunt presents changes in the concept of love throughout Western history. He covers ancient Greece, where love expressed itself primarily in prostitution and pederasty; Rome, the land of pagan love and adultery; and the "Dark Ages of Love," when Christian asceticism, expressed in the ideas of the Church fathers, influenced Roman morals. He graces the origin, development, and spread of courtly love in Western Europe from the time of the troubadours to the Courts of Love; he then reveals the excesses of Platonic love in European courts during the Renaissance as well as the witch hunts in northern Germany, and shows how these two extreme manifestations became fused by the seventeenth century into a saner view of love and marriage. Hunt shows how the Reformation, initiated by Martin Luther and strengthened by the brand of Puritanism espoused by John Calvin, while resulting in the blunting of love by doctrinal restraints and severe punishment for sinful sex, nevertheless accepted certain romantic ideals and the normality of sex within marriage. In the final chapters, Hunt discourses on (1) the rational love of the Enlightenment with its scorn of romantic love and penchant for assiduously cultivated manners, lechery, and cruelty; (2) nineteenth-century preoccupation with industrial middle-class romantic, or Victorian, love that nonetheless allowed women to begin their struggle for equal rights; and (3) love in the twentieth century (called the Age of Love) to blend romantic love and sex in marriage. Throughout this book, Hunt pays close attention to the status and condition of women in each historic period; the reader acquires a holistic view of love, sex, and marriage in a historical context. (TJW)

PR

78. Jacquart, Danielle, and Claude Thomasset. **Sexuality and Medicine in the Middle Ages.** Translated by Matthew Adamson. Princeton, N.J.: Princeton University Press, 1988. 242 p. Translation of: *Sexualité et savoir médical au Moyen Age.* Includes bibliographic notes and index. ISBN 0-691-05550-5.

Jacquart, a medical historian, and Thomasset, a philologist, present a scholarly and comprehensive study of sexuality as it was known to the medieval scientist. Beginning with male and female anatomy, the etymology of sexual terms is analyzed with comparisons between ancient Arabic texts and their Greek and Latin translations and interpretations. Understanding of anatomy was hindered not only by the lack of observation through autopsy but also by adherence to physiological principles that remained virtually unquestioned until the sixteenth century. These principles were influenced by Galen's presentation of the four Hippocratic humours. A physiological discussion of male and female sperm, menses, and coitus includes theories on purification and the mechanistic functions of the body.

The book moves beyond the purely physiological and investigates the art and pleasures of lovemaking as revealed in such medical writings as *De Amore* of Andreas Capellanus and the *Roman de la Rose.* Using the penitential literature and the literature of courtly love, as well as the writings attributed to the midwife Trotula of Salerno and other erotic texts, the authors show the dichotomy of sexual pleasure and sex for procreation. The book does not delve into reproduction, but does discuss methods of birth control, female fertility, and sexual dysfunction. Jacquart and Thomasset address the subjects of physiognomy, masturbation, and homosexuality in a chapter on the innocent and the guilty. The concluding chapter on the pathology of sexually transmitted diseases offers a treatise on leprosy and venereal diseases. This translation has been augmented by black-and-white illustrations and updated bibliographic information. (MM)

PR,IL

79. Maccubbin, Robert Purks, ed. **'Tis Nature's Fault: Unauthorized Sexuality During the Enlightenment.** Cambridge: Cambridge University Press, 1987. 260 p. Includes bibliographic notes. ISBN 0-521-34768-8.

In *'Tis Nature's Fault* editor Maccubbin collects eighteen essays about diverse and unauthorized aspects of sexuality in the Europe of the Enlightenment. He intends that the essays will be "an important first step toward integrating sexuality into our general understanding of eighteenth century culture."

First, Roy Porter writes about *Aristotle's Masterpiece*, a sexual advice book in English for married couples that appeared in 1690. A pseudo-Aristotelian work, it remained popular through the nineteenth century, promoting all aspects of reproduction, especially coitus, pregnancy, and childbirth. Jean Marie Goulemot examines the popular *Traité des superstitions* of Abbé Thiers for superstitions and magical sexual practices relating to infertility and impotence. And in his essay "Married But Not Churched," John R. Gillis looks closely at individual marriage practices among the lower classes in England when industrial organization was undergoing rapid change. Théodore Tarczylo in "Moral Values in *La Suite de l'Entretien*" examines several views on masturbation and chastity as expressed by the encyclopedist Denis Diderot and others. Vern Bullough writes about how prostitution was portrayed in literature and about efforts to reform the rampant prostitution of the time. James G. Turner discusses the term Libertinism as variously used in literature during the Enlightenment. In "Between the Licit and the Illicit," Jean-Pierre Guicciardi reveals how the public image of the sexual excesses of French monarch Louis XV led to the downfall of the *ancien regime.* In his essay, David Coward describes the obsessive sexuality of the writer Restif de la Bretonne, his shoe fetish and his penchant for incest.

Maccubbin inserts five essays concerning homosexuality, beginning with Randolph Trumbach's historiography, "Sodomitical Subcultures, Sodomitical Roles, and the Gender Revolution of the Eighteenth Century," followed by Michel Delon's "The Priest, the Philosopher, and Homosexuality in Enlightenment France," G. S. Rousseau's "The Pursuit of Homosexuality in the Eighteenth Century," Arend H. Huussen, Jr.'s "Sodomy in the Dutch Republic During the Eighteenth Century," and Michel Rey's "Parisian Homosexuals Create a Lifestyle, 1700-1750."

Included in the final group of essays are "The Censor Censured" by Peter Sabor, which discusses the expurgation of John Cleland's *Memoirs of a Woman of Pleasure"*; Paul-Gabriel Bouce's "Chthonic and Pelagic Metaphorization in Eighteenth-Century English Erotica"; Robert J. Ellrich's "Modes of Discourse and the Language of Sexual Reference in Eighteenth-Century French Fiction"; Robert L. Dawson's "The *Melange de poesies diverses* (1781) and the "Diffusion of Manuscript Pornography in Eighteenth-Century France"; and Armando Marchi's "Obscene Literature in Eighteenth-Century Italy: An Historical and Bibliographical Note." (TJW)

IL,PO

80. Money, John. **The Destroying Angel: Sex, Fitness & Food in the Legacy of Degeneracy Theory, Graham Crackers, Kellogg's Corn Flakes & American Health History.** Buffalo, N.Y.: Prometheus Books, 1985. 213 p. Includes bibliography and index. ISBN 0-87975-277-7.

Fully believing that history will repeat itself if its lessons are ignored, Money, Director of the Johns Hopkins Medical School's psychohormonal unit, in this metaphorically apt title, first reviews those antisexuality notions of the eighteenth and nineteenth centuries prevalent among the clergy and medical professionals and later transmitted to the United States, where they became shrill outbursts aimed at certain forms of sexual behavior.

Among those singled out for scrutiny are the efforts of such stalwarts as Simon André Tissot, the Swiss physician, who propounded a theory of degeneracy based on the rumored debilitating effects of masturbation; Sylvester Graham (1794-1851), the inventor of graham crackers, who, imbued with the tenets of degeneracy theory, promoted clean living through pure thoughts, good food, invigorating exercise, and sexual restraint; and John Harvey Kellogg (1856-1943) of cornflakes and Battle Creek Sanitarium fame, who came down hard on masturbation (the secret vice) as a cause of disease. All of these worthies wrote treatises about the dangers of vice and the salubrious effects of clean living.

Similarly, Money examines other personalities and events around the turn of the century: (1) the career of Anthony Comstock and the harmful effects of his brand of antisexualism; (2) the women's emancipation struggle; (3) the conflict within the American Medical Association over a paper by gynecologist Denslow Lewis describing explicitly but accurately the sexual act; (4) the psychoanalytic movement in medicine; and (5) Victorian sexual doctrine as reflected in attitudes toward pornographic materials.

The sexual doctrines of the past survive today in our views of childhood sexuality. Money says that "no child may grow up without becoming acquainted with the taboo of talking about sex," and awareness that "sexual evasiveness is classified as clean and pure" (p. 132). Inculcating such ideas (the destroying angel) will affect a child's sex life in adulthood.

At this point, Money introduces his idea of "sexual rehearsal play" on the part of children. Such expressed sexuality plus parental influences establishes one's "love-maps." He goes on to illustrate the significance of "lovemaps" by discussing their manifestation in psychosexual disorders, specifically the paraphilias. He describes and categorizes some thirty paraphilias, including such well-recognized ones as masochism and pedophilia, and those less well known: biastophilia (violent assault) and erotophono-philia (lust murder). Stored as erotic fantasies in lovemaps, the paraphilias may not be expressed until puberty, are stable throughout life, are commoner among males, and vary from the playful and harmless to the dangerous and destructive.

In the remainder of his book Money interrelates paraphilias, degeneracy theory, sexual contagion theory, and pornography. Finally, he describes the shortcomings of sexology as a discipline and laments the lack of funding for sex research, attributing the backwardness of the field to lingering and persistent antisexualism. (TJW)

PR,IL
81. Murstein, Bernard I. **Love, Sex, and Marriage Through the Ages.** Foreword by William M. Kephart. New York: Springer, 1974. 639 p. Includes bibliography and index. ISBN 0-8261-1460-1.

Intended for intelligent laypersons, students, and professionals, this comprehensive history of love, sex, and marriage is written from a general perspective, using "a representative sample of work from all possible sources" drawn from many fields, including literary, biographical, and scriptural works as well as historical, sociological, psychological, and anthropological writings. In his introduction, Murstein states the two purposes of this book: (1) to detect "the historical roots and antecedents of our present modes in love, sex, and marriage" and (2) "to provide a sourcebook of information." No overriding philosophy of history is apparent in this lengthy, descriptive work; instead Murstein prefers "to let the data speak for themselves." For each of the societies included, he describes its marriage customs and regulations, focusing on the group's conceptualization of marriage as well as on the expectations and problems of women and men in their marital roles. Murstein organizes the book into twenty-five chapters, each dealing with a specific topic or period, starting in chapter 2 with a review of theories on the origin of marriage, its classification, and peculiar features. In successive chapters he then examines Hebrew, Greek, Roman, and early Christian marriage, followed by chapters on marriage in the Middle Ages, the Renaissance, the Reformation, the Enlightenment, and the Victorian Age. Following a chapter on Sigmund Freud and Havelock Ellis, he takes up marriage in America from the Colonial period until today. He also deals with marriage, past and present, in certain select countries and regions, among them the Soviet Union, China, Japan, and black Africa. He concludes with chapters on the future of marriage, current marriage innovations, and an overview of the subject with some predictions. Extensive quotations drawn from the roughly 1,000-item bibliography form a notable feature of this sourcebook. (TJW)

IL
82. Pearsall, Ronald. **The Worm in the Bud: The World of Victorian Sexuality.** Toronto: Macmillan, 1969. 560 p. Includes bibliographic notes and index.

In *The Worm in the Bud*, Pearsall, a British historian specializing in the nineteenth century, provides an in-depth survey of Victorian sexuality. The book is divided into two parts. Part 1, "The Imperious Desire," begins with the accession of the eighteen-year-old Victoria to the throne of England in 1837, and a description of morality among the social classes of the time. In addition to the aristocracy, that eschewed conventional morality, there were the middle classes mistakenly attempting to model their behavior on the upper classes, and the working classes taking their cues from the middle classes. The center of

Victorian morality seems to have been the middle classes, that, with guidance from the medical profession and the clergy, thought of themselves as the upholders of sexual norms. It was a situation characterized by a double standard of sexual morality benefiting only the males in society, and a hypocritical attitude in public and private behavior. In chapters on the leisure classes, women in society, love and marriage, and the facts of life (childbirth, venereal diseases, birth control), Pearsall reveals the visible side of Victorian society.

Part 2, "The Victorian Buried Life," gives a view of the underside of society. Pearsall examines the rampant prostitution (including child prostitution), perversions (chiefly rape, child abuse, ritual flagellation in public schools, fetishisms, and the cult of the little girl), pornography (focusing on its production and distribution), the sexual humor of the times, and the language of sex. He also looks at the psychology of Victorian sex, exploring the prevailing attitudes, opinions, and theories of such notables as Dr. William Acton, a physician who railed against masturbation; Sigmund Freud, the founder of psychoanalysis; and John Ruskin, the great writer whose dreams, replete with sexual symbolism, were discussed. In the last chapter, Pearsall looks at those forces that were at odds with the prevailing sexual mores of society, especially homosexuality and lesbianism. English society throughout the nineteenth century was a scene of constantly changing attitudes and beliefs. Pearsall states that "one makes rash generalizations about Victorians and sex at one's peril."

Thoroughly documented, the book's endpapers present a "Sin Map of London in Victorian Times," showing the locations of brothels, flagellation establishments, introducing houses, sites of *tableaux vivants*, and pornographic publishers. (TJW)

PR,IL
83. Pomeroy, Sarah B. **Goddesses, Whores, Wives, and Slaves: Women in Classical Antiquity.** New York: Schocken Books, 1975. 265 p. Includes bibliography and index. ISBN 0-8052-3562-0.

To set down the largely unwritten history of women from the Bronze Age to the death of Constantine in A.D. 337 is the avowed purpose of this book by Pomeroy, Hunter College professor of classics. Her sources are archaeological and literary. Recognizing the difficulty in writing about all women in the ancient world and acknowledging the numerous gaps in the historical record, Pomeroy nevertheless emphasizes such social and cultural phenomena as male/female relationships, marriage, adultery, sexual behavior, and the like. She begins by examining the creation myths as told by Hesiod, the misogynistic Greek poet living in Boeotia around 700 B.C. Hesiod describes the creation of the first women, Pandora, to whom he attributes the woes of mankind; the birth of Aphrodite resulting from the union of the castrated genitals of Uranus and the sea; and the principal gods and goddesses of mythology. Pomeroy also brings out the vulnerability of women as revealed in sexual encounters (rapes) of mortals by the gods.

Following a brief examination of life in Sparta—woman as childbearer, men as warriors—during the Archaic period (800-500 B.C.), Pomeroy, using information from tombstone carvings, vase paintings, and various writings, reconstructs Athenian private life during the Classical period. She focuses on the seclusion of women within residential areas, the daily life of families, relationships within marriage, and Athenian sexuality, including penalties for adultery and, in contrast to restrictions on married women, the considerable freedom and influence enjoyed by prostitutes.

Pomeroy devotes a chapter to the images of women in the literature of Classical Athens: the plays of Sophocles, Euripedes, and Aristophanes, as well as the utopian writings of Plato. She points to the forceful heroines of comedy and tragedy, such as Medea, Phaedra, Lysistrata, and others, stating that their sex roles often seem to conflict with those of real Athenian women.

When the Macedonians swept down from the north in the fourth century B.C., their rulers (Philip II, Alexander) brought an end to the Greek city-states. This upheaval profoundly affected women's lives for the good: Macedonian princesses, upper-class women, and even courtesans, concubines, and prostitutes became increasingly independent, educated, and powerful. In the 300 year Hellenistic period, the nude female in sculpture and vase painting appears for the first time, which established the classic proportions of the female nude.

Pomeroy next turns to the status of women in the late Republic and early Empire periods. Following a discussion of marriage, divorce, remarriage, and adultery, she focuses on a woman's relationship to first her father and then her husband. She shows that upper-class Roman women had much greater freedom than Athenian women but still remained subordinate to their husbands. She then describes women of the Roman lower classes—slaves and freed men and women who married and had families, the former providing sexual services to their masters as well as being a main supply for the brothels.

The final chapter is devoted to the role of women in the religion of the Romans, focusing attention on the various cults, the 1,000-year history of the Vestal virgins, the cult of Mithras, and finally the amazing success of the cult of the Egyptian god Isis.

Pomeroy's purpose has been to discover "the realities of women's existence in the ancient world rather than concentrate on the images that men had of women." She states, moreover, that "we cannot tell how much to attribute to the living women of the period and how much is due to men's imagination" (p. 230). (TJW)

IL

84.   Riencourt, Amaury de. **Sex and Power in History.** New York: McKay, 1974. 469 p. ISBN 0-679-50490-7.

Advancing the thesis that modern civilization is doomed unless society makes the effort to understand the profound causes behind "contemporary woman's liberation drive toward a *decrease* in sexual differentiation, to the extent that it is leading toward androgyny and unisexual values" (p. x), de Riencourt takes us back to prehistoric times when man worshipped "womanhood (Mother Earth) . . . as the intermediary between man and nature's mysteries." He recreates the patriarchal revolution of some 3,500 years ago, when man, as a result of discovering the connection between sex and procreation, replaced Gaea, the mother Goddess, with a male god.

De Riencourt states that this book is "an all-inclusive interpretation of history from end to end, as seen through the interplay of the primary biosocial forces that have shaped it—the *yin* and *yang*, the female and male principles that are the warp and woof of an intricate tapestry" (p. vii). He adds that "for the first time . . . a study of human evolution focuses primarily on the female of the species and presents a comprehensive view of the influence, social position, economic status, and cultural influence of women throughout the ages."

He then traces the male/female power relationship through the "first female revolt" in the Greco-Roman period to the birth of Christianity, with its synthesis of feminine and masculine trends as well as Hebrew faith and Greek philosophy. He proceeds with a description of the leading types of womanhood: the barbarian woman, the medieval lady, the virago, the witch, the reformed woman, and the cultured woman; and brings the reader to a time when the male/female synthesis broke down with the Reformation, that expelled the female component of Christianity (the Virgin) and reverted to Old Testament patriarchalism, and the Renaissance, that broke the medieval symbolic thought and reverted to the rational thought of the Greeks and Romans. Male/female power relations were again disturbed as a result of the scientific and industrial revolutions: breakdown of the extended family as a unit and the increasing separation of the sexes resulting from urbanization and industrialization. Large segments of middle class women were idled and lowered to the rank of mere status symbols. This has brought about the present women's revolt, aggravated by the biological revolution now occurring. It is axiomatic, De Riencourt believes, that progress in evolution is stimulated by the *increase* in sexual differentiation. But the opposite is occurring: sexual differentiation is being decreased through the goals of the present-day feminist movement. As one reviewer of this book stated: "De Riencourt is ultimately committed to the necessity of sexual differentiation and urges a rebirth of cultural identification with the 'eternal feminine' as the path to salvation." (TJW)

PR,IL

85. Rousseau, George Sebastian, and Roy Porter, eds. **Sexual Underworlds of the Enlightenment.** Chapel Hill: University of North Carolina Press, 1988. 280 p. Includes bibliographic notes and index. ISBN 0-8078-1782-1.

P. G. Boucé's *Sexuality in Eighteenth-Century Britain* (1982) was a pioneer effort in dealing with the Enlightenment. However, significant gaps in information about this period remain. Research has focused on major figures and texts, primarily within a "respectable" domain. Little is known about either the beliefs and attitudes of all classes or the responses of individuals to the dominant literature of the day. The goal of this book is "frank debate about topics too infrequently discussed." It attempts to fill in gaps of information by focusing on the sexual underworld ("domains that lie in the margins of respectability"), e.g., male and female prostitution, lesbianism, transvestism, pornography, sodomy, homosexuality, and fantasy. This emphasis allows scholars to begin to grasp the entire range of sexual experience during the Enlightenment, not merely its most obvious facets.

In the introduction, editors Rousseau and Porter provide an overview of the ten chapters that make up the book. They trace interpretations of sexuality from Linnaeus's taxonomy of all living creatures as sexual entities to the "ethereal sensibilities" of the second half of the eighteenth century. The five chapters in section one, "Sex and Discourse," establish the importance of linking beliefs and behavior. Théodore Tarczylo points out that a unidimensional history of sexuality during the eighteenth century is misleading. Peter Wagner examines erotic and pornographic writings to discover the nature of sexual mentality that behavior possibly imitated. Randolph Trumbach explores a similar theme in an essay on prostitution and gender in the novel *Fanny Hill.* Paul-Gabriel Boucé's chapter considers the nature of the female imagination by looking at gynecological works and books about childbirth. Editor Rousseau discusses the issue of homosexual desire as expressed in the culture.

Section two, "Sex and Society," concentrates on behaviors indicative of sexual beliefs. Terry Castle discusses masquerade travesty as an indication of challenges to the traditional mores. Antony E. Simpson considers the effect of the age of female consent on prosecutions of rape. Editor Porter examines the possibility of female oppression at the hands of male midwives. Section three, "Sex at the Margins," considers socially defined fringe areas. Lynne Friedli discusses gender boundaries in relation to "passing women," and Gloria Flaherty looks at shamanism as it relates to sex. (SGF)

PR

86. Salisbury, Joyce, ed. **Sex in the Middle Ages: A Book of Essays.** New York: Garland, 1991. 258 p. (Garland Medieval Casebooks; vol. 3). Includes bibliographic notes and index. ISBN 0-8240-5766-X.

In the introduction to this collection of essays, Salisbury acknowledges that the definitive study of medieval sexuality has yet to be written, and that these thirteen essays, contributed by researchers from various fields of study, should lead to a better understanding of "the puzzle of medieval sexuality." In order to shed light on particular facets of medieval sexuality, Salisbury has organized the collection thematically into four parts: courtship, disclosure, diversity, and public implications.

The first essay in the courtship category is Jenny Jochens's "Before the Male Gaze," that reminds us that while physical beauty is at the core of sexual behavior, in Old Norse texts (family sagas) of Icelandic society, it was clothing, hair, and men's bodies that were the primary sources of attraction. Richard Kieckhafer in his essay, "Erotic Magic in Medieval Europe," explains the use of natural magic, demonic magic, and all sorts of magic amulets, philtres, and the like to induce people to have sex, to enhance sexual experience, to serve gynecological purposes, or to cure such ills as impotency. Esther Lastique and Helen Rodnite Lemay's essay, "A Medieval Physician's Guide to Virginity," is about a fifteenth-century book on the diseases of women (*De passionibus mulierum*), that deals in part with a medical situation arising out of the defloration or violation of a virgin.

Under the second theme, "Disclosure," are also three essays. Christopher Klein-henz in "Texts, Naked and Thinly Veiled" analyzes the erotic elements in medieval Italian poetry and prose. Margaret Schleissner in "A Fifteenth-Century Physician's Attitude Toward Sexuality" examines a translation of Dr. Johann Hartlieb's thirteenth-century *Secreta mulierum*, which is a male-to-male discourse about female nature and human reproduction. The third essay, "Sex and Confession in the Thirteenth Century," by Pierre J. Payer, explores how sex was a dominant theme of disclosure in confessional manuals.

The third theme of this collection is "Diversity." In "A Smorgasbord of Sexual Practices," Cathy Jorgensen Itnyre discusses the variety of sexual acts and myths in medieval Icelandic sagas, pointing out that despite their Christian beliefs the medieval Icelanders had a secular outlook about sex. Norman Roth in his essay about boy love in Hebrew and Arabic verse demonstrates in his analysis of "Fawn of My Delights" the existence of love among pre-pubescent boys in Hebrew and Arabic society. Editor Salisbury in her essay "Bestiality in the Middle Ages," reveals the "changing attitudes toward bestiality that led from classical mythology's praise of the practice to thirteenth-century scholastics who considered it the worst of the sexual sins" (p. xiv). Andreas Heusler's essay on the Icelandic saga "The Story of the Völsi," tells the story of household worship of a horse penis and the subsequent conversion of the household to Christianity.

The fourth thematic category, "Public Implications," consists of three papers. In "Saints and Sex, ca. 500-1100," Jane Tibbetts Schulenburg examines the *vitae* of saints in the Latin West from the sixth through the eleventh centuries, revealing such aspects of their lives as immaculate conception, ascetic lifestyles, temptations, celibacy, chastity, abstinence, and the like. J. D. Rolleston in his short essay *Penis Captivus*, provides quotations from medieval literature about the phenomenon of capture of the penis by the vagina during intercourse, and C. Grant Loomis does a similar analysis in "Three Cases of Vaginism." The final essay in this category is James A. Brundage's "The Politics of Sodomy." In it he reveals "the political use of sodomy as an instrument of royal as well as ecclesiastical power." (TJW)

PR,IL

87.   Seidman, Steven. **Romantic Longings: Love in America, 1830-1980.** New York: Routledge, 1991. 247 p. Includes bibliographic notes and index. ISBN 0-415-90404-8.

Seidman is Associate Professor of Sociology at SUNY, Albany. *Romantic Longings* is a study of intimacy in the United States from 1830 to 1980. It is based on various discourses as found in advice literature, popular medical texts, personal documents (diaries, letters, autobiographies) as well as in novels, sex surveys, and research materials. Seidman explores this intimate culture relating to sex and love in three distinct periods: the Victorian era (1830-1890), modern times (1890-1960), and the contemporary period (1960-1980). He documents a series of changes in the meaning of romantic love and analyzes "the changing conceptions and norms which define sex in relation to love in American culture" (p. 2).

Seidman focuses his attention on the "nonimmigrant, white middle class that resides chiefly in the Northeast" because "its size, social position and social impact justify its study" (p. 4). He also examines gender issues as they impact middle-class love, which is predominantly heterosexual although same-sex love is also significant.

In the earliest, Victorian, period a distinctive culture of intimacy came into being. "Love was considered an ideal basis and the essential state of marriage"; "sex was thought of as an equally vital part of marriage" (p. 7). But the Victorians desexualized love and desensualized sex. In the post-Victorian period, love "changed from having an essentially spiritual meaning to being conceived in a way that made it inseparable from the erotic longings and pleasures of sex" (p. 4). Seidman shows that a progressive "sexualization of love" as well as the legitimation of the erotic aspects of sex, occurred in this period. In the twentieth century an intimate culture of sex, valued for its sensually pleasurable and expressive qualities, arose. Sex for carnal pleasure became legitimized, although it was framed in a context of love. In the post-World War II period eroticism acquired value apart from love. Sex for the sake of sex became accepted. "By the 1960s the pleasurable and expressive qualities of sex were appealed to as a sufficient justification of sex" (p. 8).

Seidman does not accept the prevalent criticism that attributes "AIDS, herpes, escalating rates of divorce, illegitimacy and teen pregnancies, loneliness, violence against women, and the impoverishment and abandonment of our children" to expanded sexual freedom. He believes that these phenomena "are acceptable costs for expanded choice and an intimate culture that values erotic pleasure and variety" (p. 9). He spells out the opposition to the intimate culture of the day: it is a reform movement emanating primarily from feminist groups but also from others who resist pornography, crusade for teenage chastity, and try to medicalize casual sex as addiction. Seidman devotes a chapter to the intimate homosexual culture of both gays and lesbians, whose attitudes and behavior have paralleled those of heterosexuals over the same periods of time. (TJW)

IL,PO

88. Tannahill, Reay. **Sex in History.** New York: Stein and Day, 1980. 480 p. Includes bibliography and index. ISBN 0-8128-2580-2.

Sex in the sweep of history from prehistoric times to the present is the subject of this popular book by Tannahill, also the author of *Food in History.* Separate chapters are devoted to sex in the first civilizations (Sumerian, Egyptian, Assyrian, Hebrew), Greece, Rome, medieval Europe, China, India, the Near East, Latin America, and modern Europe and America. A selective perspective pervades the solid scholarship manifest throughout the text. Answers to a variety of abiding and important questions are presented in a dispassionate and objective fashion. Examples abound: When in the early period of recorded history did the sex roles of man and woman become distinguished? At what point in history did woman become subordinate to man the master? Did religion have a role in perpetuating man's view of himself as superior in all ways to woman in the early civilizations of the Near East? How enlightened were the views of the Church Fathers—St. Paul, Tertullian, St. Jerome, St. Augustine—on women, marriage, and sex? What Chinese philosophy relied heavily on manuals for the sex instruction of men and women? What were the effects of Victorian ideals on prostitution, the spread of venereal disease, and the rising taste for masochism? What factors in recent years have tended to undermine the ideal of the Victorian family structure? Thoughtful answers to these and many other intriguing questions are provided in this well-documented book. Tannahill has brought the story of humankind's sexual relationships through the ages. (TJW)

IL

89. Taylor, Gordon Rattray. **Sex in History.** London: Thames and Hudson, 1953. 336 p. (The Past in the Present). Includes bibliography and index.

Taylor, a successful science program writer for the BBC, disenchanted with the way historians have dealt with sex in history, has undertaken a study of changes in sexual attitudes in Western culture. Believing that history reveals the state of "warfare between the forces of the id and the taboos and inhibitions which man has erected to control them" (p. 9), he states that the "purpose of this book is to survey these various attempts to control the irrational as they have been developed in western Europe and particularly in England during the Christian era" (p. 13). He proposes to examine actual sexual behavior during particular periods and to compare it with the official codes of the time. A good example is the contrast between medieval sexual behavior, characterized by frank sexuality and license, and the efforts of the Roman Church to control that behavior with a strict moral code.

Using Freudian analysis, Taylor suggests that underlying sexual attitudes are two views of the world, supposedly engendered during childhood: one patrist (authoritarian, conservative, restrictive), the other matrist (democratic, progressive, permissive). Taylor uses this patrist/matrist duality to characterize sexual and other attitudes throughout history. He describes the matrist outburst in southern France at the time of the Trouba-dours (twelfth century) and the patrist reaction from the Church in its repression of the underlying Cathar movement. Another example at the close of the Middle Ages was the matter of witchcraft in northern Germany that was severely dealt with by the Inquisition, with direction from Rome. During ensuing periods of history (the Renaissance, the Reformation, etc.), sexual attitudes vacillated between the restrictive and the permissive.

In the final part, Taylor turns his attention to the origins of Christian sexual morality. Prior to the advent of Christianity many of the religions of the Near East worshipped female deities: temple prostitution was accepted behavior and sex was considered a sacrament. Judaism, Mithraism, and Christianity gradually replaced these mystery religions, substituting male gods for goddesses and establishing strict codes of conduct. In time, the Christian fathers (Augustine, Jerome, and others) made sex a sin, denigrated the status of women, and viewed intercourse as a necessary evil. This became the Church's prevailing attitude toward sex. History has shown the persistent struggle between the Church's patrist approach to sex and matrist tendencies in society. (TJW)

AUTOBIOGRAPHIES

(For related material see also entry 141)

PO
90.   Adler, Polly. **A House Is Not a Home.** New York: Rinehart, 1953. 374 p.
      After twenty-five years in the business of prostitution (1920-1945), Polly Adler closed the doors of "New York's most famous bordello." A product of the Roaring Twenties, Miss Adler gives an autobiographical account of how she left her home in Poland and, at the age of fourteen, came alone to America and rose meteorically to the top of her chosen field. After completing grade school in Holyoke, Massachusetts, and working in factories at low wages, she became acquainted with a Riverside Drive crowd. Before long she began her career as a madam; by 1924 she had become a New York celebrity. In *A House Is Not a Home*, Adler paints a vibrant picture of New York's social life in the 1920s, with its night clubs, theaters, restaurants, speakeasies, and brothels. Despite prohibition (1919-1933), liquor was plentiful and the gangsters prominent. It was the era of the "lost generation" and of "flaming youth," and in the clubs the socially elite rubbed elbows with the underworld. In this milieu, Adler's business prospered. In giving an insider's view of the profession, Adler focuses on her relations with the authorities, the customers, and her stable of girls. Commenting that "no woman is born a whore and any woman may become one," Adler explains how she recruited her girls, describes their daily routines, personal quirks, problems with customers, and their hopes for the future. She points out that "they knew it was a short-lived career and that, like baseball players, they had to be young to stay in the game. Therefore, the smart ones either saved their money against the day they would have to retire, or learned a trade, or worked out ways and means of snagging a rich husband" (p. 108). Following the crash of 1929, Adler for a time kept a low profile during the Seabury investigation into judicial bribe taking, police corruption, and vice. Financially pressed, she involuntarily teamed up with Dutch Schultz, the notorious New York racketeer, who used her establishment as a sanctuary for his gang. Following the repeal of the 18th Amendment, and after Schultz's death in 1935, Adler again did well. A raid on her house in 1935 brought her a conviction for running a disorderly house and she spent thirty days in jail. For another decade she continued her operations unabated, but ill health and several reverses persuaded her that the moment had come to end her colorful career. Encouraged by her lawyer, she returned to school, studied creative writing, and wrote the Polly Adler story. (TJW)

PO

91. Armstrong, Louise. **Kiss Daddy Goodnight: A Speak-Out on Incest.** New York: Pocket Books, 1979. 296 p. Includes bibliography and index. ISBN 0-671-49938-6.

The betrayal and horror that writer Louise Armstrong felt about an incestuous incident with her father persisted ten years after her father's death. The lingering feeling of violation of trust motivated her to investigate incest, not only in the professional literature but also from the experiences of the women themselves. She sought information through advertisements ("I am a woman writer, doing a first-person documentary book on incest. I would like to hear from others who had an actual or near-actual incest experience.") in newspapers, magazines, and the feminist press; she also received referrals from friends, acquaintances, and professionals. Overall, she spoke with 183 women of different social, ethnic, and economic backgrounds and chose to write about a few who seemed to represent "the variety of the impact effects of sexual abuse where some inner balance is present in the person." These women are survivors, not "losers," and could have been the girl next door. The goal of the book is to provide a "human document," a "bridge to understanding" that portrays the meaning and reality behind the label "victim of sexual molestation." Therefore, Armstrong purposely leaves out commentaries from "experts" and the professional literature.

The bulk of the book consists of women's highly personal descriptions of father-daughter incest. These intimate narratives are accounts of a wide range of types of incestuous contexts, a diversity of feelings, and a spectrum of coping tactics, all of which provide information to counter the myths that young girls either fantasize about or enjoy incest. Armstrong sees several common themes that pervade these diverse experiences: betrayal of trust, a sense of loss of both parents, and the man's perception of himself as an older child rather than as a parent in the family. She hopes that breaking silence about the violation of the taboo and refusing to sanction such behavior will cut down on its incidence as well as expose the denial and hysteria that surrounds it. (SGF)

PO

92. Barrows, Sydney Biddle, with William Novak. **Mayflower Madam: The Secret Life of Sydney Biddle Barrows.** New York: Arbor House, 1986. 291 p. ISBN 0-87795-722-3.

Cachet, an escort service operating in Manhattan for five and one-half years, was busted on October 11, 1984. Its owner and manager was Sydney Biddle Barrows, a descendant of Elder William Brewster, whose name appeared on the passenger list of the *Mayflower.* Miss Barrows (a.k.a. Sheila Devin) was charged with promoting prostitution—a felony; after a hard-fought court battle she pled guilty to the lesser charge of promoting prostitution in the third degree—a misdemeanor. Given an "unconditional discharge" by the judge, she paid a fine of $5,000.

This aptly titled book discloses in Barrows's own words how she got started in the escort business. It emphasizes her desire to run a high class enterprise that would be profitable both for her and the girls working for her. It discusses various aspects of the business: recruitment and training of call girls, advertising, security measures, client records, call girl/client relationships, earnings, hours of work, problems with landlords, and so forth.

Unlike brothels, where sex is *de rigueur*, escort service sex between a call girl and client is not necessarily a part of the evening's agenda, which may be purely social. It would be naive, however, to believe that sex did not occur on a regular basis. Indeed the girls were prepared and equipped for any eventuality.

Barrows dispels the ethical question concerning her service with this statement: "And I had no 'moral' problems, because escort services filled a human and age-old need" (p. 41). She adds to this later by saying: "For although we were ostensibly selling sex, what the girls were really providing was companionship and intimacy" (p. 134). Since the service catered to celebrities, diplomats, executives, professionals, and the like, she could claim that "our girls were among the highest-paid professional women in the country" (p. 130). Some call girls made as much as $1,000 a week in 1984. "A call girl," she notes, "is simply a woman who hates poverty more than she hates sin" (p. 130). After her trial, Barrows failed to reopen her escort service. (TJW)

IL,PO

93. Bengis, Ingrid. **Combat in the Erogenous Zone.** New York: Knopf, 1972. 260 p. ISBN 0-394-47550-X.

In converting that hoary expression "battle of the sexes" into "combat in the erogenous zone," Bengis, writing with surprising maturity, focuses on the struggle to emancipate herself from sexual roles assigned to her by society. Only in her twenties at the time this book was written, Bengis has managed to accumulate a rich store of experience in the sexual arena, which she analyzes in the three long essays that comprise this book: "Man-Hating," "Lesbianism," and "Love."

While admitting that she has not brought forth any "conclusions about the possibilities for love and hate among men and women," she does subject these emotions to a thorough examination, revealing in the process a host of consequences attendant upon their exercise. She says that the "conflict between love and lust, need and fear is a perpetual one, and perhaps the only reality that remains firm is the reality of conflict itself." In this context, she states that she is "in search of authenticity, in search of sex and love which reflect that authenticity" (p. xvii).

Defining man-hating as a defense against fear and pain, she explores in her first essay the many factors and situations that engender hate in her contact and relations with men (strangers and friends) and institutions. In her second essay she dissects her feelings and her relations with women in an effort to find out whether she is lesbian or not.

In the third and culminating essay, Bengis reflects on the fact that her expectations, beliefs, and behavior were shaped between the ages of sixteen and twenty-five (admittedly not a long period). Bengis says that she was taught that "women love, men screw; save yourself for marriage; taught: don't squander your inner resources on someone who will only squash them; taught: men have affairs, women don't; taught: men respect a woman who can say no; men want to marry virgins; taught: if you did what Anna Karenina did, you'll wind up where she wound up, dead on the railroad tracks. The moral of the story was: don't let your passions . . . run away with you. It can only lead to a bad ending" (pp. 197-198).

Bengis admits that these standards did her little good because they had changed by the time she was old enough to apply them. So she embraced the new norms of the 1960s and, fashioning her own outlook, experienced the emotional conflicts inherent in change. This situation is reflected in one of her last statements: "Permanence in love, of course, is just about impossible to achieve. But that doesn't make it any less desirable" (p. 253). (TJW)

IL,PO

93a. Berendzen, Richard, and Laura Palmer. **Come Here: A Man Overcomes the Tragic Aftermath of Childhood Sexual Abuse.** New York: Villard Books, 1993. 301 p. Includes bibliography. ISBN 0-679-41777-X.

Physically and sexually abused beginning when he was eight years old, Berendzen tells, in this poignantly titled confession, how he reluctantly responded to his mother's brusque command from her bedroom of their home in East Dallas, Texas, to "Come here." Lasting for several years, his ordeal abruptly ended when his mother was committed to an institution. Berendzen's reaction to the abuse was to bury it deep in his memory. It became his great secret, not revealed until much later in life. He also responded by excelling in school and going on to study physics at Southern Methodist University, the Massachusetts Institute of Technology, and Harvard University. He became an astronomer of note, taught at Boston University, and eventually, in 1980, became President of American University in Washington, D.C., where he strove to bolster the flagging quality of higher education at a school noted primarily for its social life.

Following the death of his father in 1987, Berendzen made phone calls to randomly selected child care providers, broaching the question of incestuous relations between parents and children. The situation erupted into a scandal in April 1990 when his calls, taped by the police, brought about his downfall. He resigned from his prestigious position, explaining that he had never engaged in any improper activities with children, and that he was only seeking information about child sexual abuse.

With support from his wife and daughters, Berendzen sought help from a sexual disorder clinic at Johns Hopkins Hospital in East Baltimore, Maryland. With difficulty he responded to the request, "Tell me about your first sexual experience." His great secret revealed, Berendzen was informed he had Post Traumatic Stress Disorder (PTSD) and needed treatment. Following a battery of tests and group therapy sessions, he left the clinic in May 1990, suffering from depression. To his family he revealed the reasons for his bizarre behavior and hoped for and received forgiveness and understanding. In due course he recovered, went public with his long-standing problem, and rejoined the faculty at American University, where he resumed teaching physics and astronomy. Today, in addition to his teaching, Berendzen devotes time to educating the public about child sexual abuse. (TJW)

PO

94. Brady, Katherine. **Father's Days: A True Story of Incest.** New York: Seaview Books, 1979. 216 p. ISBN 0-87223-539-4.

Katherine Brady grew up in a small midwestern town with her mother, father, sister, and brother. She seemed to be living the life of a popular young women; she was pretty, intelligent, and sought after by boys. She eventually married her high school beau, established a lovely home, began to develop a career, and was the mother of two children. However, those facts did not erase the anger, isolation, and guilt she felt as a consequence of a ten-year incestuous relationship with her father—an interaction that began when she was ten years old and shaped her entire life. Thirty-five at the time this book was written, the author, writing under a pseudonym, recounts the experiences of her childhood in order to help free herself of the emotional prison within which her secret engulfed her and to aid other incest victims with the knowledge that "you are not alone and you are not to blame." The highly personal account of father-daughter incest counters many myths about the nature of sexual interaction between parent and child and traces its impact on the victim's self-concept, her marriage, her children, her subsequent relationship with her mother and father, and her parents' relationship with each other. (SGF)

PO

95. Fleming, Karl, and Anne Taylor Fleming. **The First Time.** New York: Simon and Schuster, 1975. 319 p. ISBN 0-671-22070-5.

The main idea behind this series of vignettes was to "let people talk on their own terms and in their own terms and in their own language about how sex came into their lives." Fleming and Fleming, both writers by profession, derived their information from personal interviews with well-known personalities. Interviews were conducted separately by each of the authors and ranged in length from less than an hour to over ten; all were taped, edited, and presented as monologues, "totally faithful to the letter and spirit of their remarks." Although Fleming and Fleming wanted a cross-section of people in different professions, most are in the arts. They categorize the people who agreed to be part of the book as (1) uninhibited and casual in their discussions of sex; (2) in the process of finding themselves after being unhappy sexually; and (3) perceiving sex as a major American problem because they had terrible early sexual experiences.

The twenty-eight participants (fifteen males and thirteen females) span several generations: they include Alice Roosevelt Longworth, Mae West, Dr. Benjamin Spock, Rudy Vallee, Joseph Cotton, Joan Rivers, Erica Jong, Debbie Reynolds, Dyan Cannon, Victoria Principal, among others. The essays are more than a retelling of "the first time"; they involve an attempt by these notables to "sum themselves up sexually." Dyan Cannon confesses that "I was frigid until three years ago," Bob Guccione says that he thinks "women are much more sexually liberated than men," Joan Rivers comments "Everything came late to me. I didn't kiss a boy until the summer between high school and college." Fleming and Fleming did not set out to prove a point or to reach any conclusions; they leave this up to the reader. (SGF)

IL

96.   Harris, Frank. **My Life and Loves.** Edited and with an introduction by John F. Gallagher. New York: Grove Press, 1963. 1070 p. Originally copyrighted in 1925 by Frank Harris. Includes index.

Frank Harris (1856-1931), eminent journalist, biographer of Oscar Wilde and Bernard Shaw, author of short stories, plays, and novels, interpreter of Shakespeare, wrote *My Life and Loves* as an innovative kind of autobiography, one that was to reveal fully and honestly his sex life from earliest recollections as a child in Ireland through manhood. He succeeded to the extent that his book shocked contemporary society and was declared obscene by Justice Levy of the Supreme Court of New York. It did not become widely available in the United States until 1963 when Grove Press issued it in paperback. Surprisingly, careful examination of the book discloses only scattered sections devoted to Harris's *amours*; most of it focuses on a time when he was editor of several London periodicals and interacting with an astonishingly large number of great and near-great figures of the day, including Oscar Wilde, Sir Richard Burton, Lord Randolph Churchill, George Bernard Shaw, H. G. Wells, Guy de Maupassant, and others. Descriptions of his love affairs in the United States, on the Continent, and in England portray him as a highly sexed person who pursued attractive women. Using frank, blunt, and detailed language, he tells of his sexual experiences (all heterosexual) in Lawrence, Kansas, where he was a university student, in Athens where he was a tourist, in Paris, Nice, and San Remo, and in London, where his affairs included one long-standing relationship. Nothing is left to the imagination. His straightforward openness may explain why his autobiography was poorly received: nothing quite so frankly libidinous had ever been written by a person of recognized standing, and it offended the moralistically minded in England and America. It did, however, receive praise from Shaw in England and Mencken in the United States. It deserves to be read by students and scholars, not just for descriptions of Harris's sexual experiences, but as much for the vivid picture it paints of the literary, political, and social life of Victorian England in the closing decades of the nineteenth and the early years of the twentieth centuries. (TJW)

PO

97.   Hollander, Xaviera, with Robin Moore and Yvonne Dunleavy. **The Happy Hooker.** New York: Dell, 1972. 311 p.

With startling frankness, the "happy hooker" tells the story of her life with numerous lovers, male and female, in Holland, South Africa, and America. Her hypersexual and bisexual behavior leads her into prostitution and eventually into the management aspects (as a madam) of the oldest profession in the world. Starting with chapter 10, "The Oldest Profession Updated; Or: Behind Open Doors," the reader is introduced to the intricacies of brothel management: location, clientele, services, fees, staff (essentially prostitutes), recruitment, public relations, problems (primarily with the police), and payoffs. Hollander, who was twenty-eight when this book was written, does not employ pimps or direct a street operation, but claims instead to run a high-class establishment, catering mainly, but not exclusively, to bankers, stockbrokers, lawyers, insurance men, traveling salesmen, and other types from the financial world. Her clientele range in age from sixteen to seventy, are often married, lonely, and unhappy, and are seeking sexual experiences beyond their normal diet. Prostitution is, of course, illegal, so raids are not infrequent and payoffs to police and politicians are necessary. Through all of this Hollander, who is constantly in danger of being deported, maintains a happy stance, claiming that she likes her work and believes that it is serving a legitimate purpose: instructing the young, rejuvenating the old, and giving pleasure to the rest.

Despite the persistent efforts of governments and communities to terminate the activity, Hollander believes prostitution will survive because men want it to. Other books by this enterprising sexpert include *Xaviera on the Best Part of a Man* (1975) and *Xaviera's Supersex* (1976). (TJW)

[N.B. According to George H. Gordon, Xaviera Hollander "is a pseudonym for various slick magazine writers" (*Erotic Communications*, 1980, p. 7).]

PO

98. Lewin, Lauri. **Naked Is the Best Disguise: My Life as a Stripper.** New York: Morrow, 1984. 200 p. ISBN 0-688-02929-9.

In 1976 Lauri Lewin entered Boston's "Combat Zone" determined to become a stripper. Only sixteen years old and a high school student, she was vulnerable: in three weeks she was fired without payment for the sordid services she had performed at the Twilight Lounge. She returned to school, graduated, and entered college, supporting herself by working at odd jobs: waitress, office work, etc. At eighteen, less naive and more determined, she re-entered the Combat Zone and sought employment at the Nudie-Tease Nightclub as a stripper. Calling herself Lolita, Lewin stripteased in the afternoons and attended classes at the university in the mornings. Her personal interests revolved around relationships and school; she stripped for money to support herself and a growing cocaine habit. As she explains it, stripping is done to entice men into a place so that the strippers can persuade them to spend money. "The lure of female nakedness tricked men into spending large sums of money. The customers fantasized about women they did not know. Dancers approached customers with feigned interest. We drank water while pretending to drink vodka" (p. 143). In addition to stripteasing, there was also a floor show in a small room at the back of the club, called the Bare Beaver Bar, where the strippers enticingly exposed their genitals to the rapt gazes of the gawking customers. Perhaps as important as the details of stripteasing disclosed in this book are the personal relationships with customers and colleagues that Lauri Lewin explores during her five-year sojourn in the Combat Zone. Overall, Lewin has given the reader a personal, social, and cultural portrait of the stripper. Her own emotional confrontation with this life eventually led her to abandon the world of exotic dancers. She graduated summa cum laude from the University of Massachusetts and began a career as a counselor in a reproductive health center. (TJW)

PO

99. Lovelace, Linda, with Mike McGrady. **Ordeal.** New York: Bell, 1983. 253 p. Originally published in 1980 by The Citadel Press. ISBN 0-517-427915.

Published as a contradiction to such works as *Inside Linda Lovelace*, this autobiography, if accurate, tells the sad story of the gradual degradation of a young woman who overnight became a porno star. Threatened and held captive by her manager husband, she was subjected to every imaginable sexual aberration, including group rape, sadomasochistic rituals, and unnatural acts with animals. She is well known for the oral technique she developed, perfected, and brought to public attention in the popular pornographic film *Deep Throat*, in which she starred. Fame brought her to the attention of Hugh Hefner, who accommodated Lovelace and her husband in his Los Angeles headquarters, Playboy Mansion West; and of Sammy Davis, Jr., who befriended her for awhile. Eventually she was able to disentangle herself from the clutches of her husband, abandon the world of pornography, get married, become a mother, and try to live a normal family life, which is all she ever longed to do. Interestingly, she never profited monetarily from her career; she was exploited by those around her, especially her husband.

In her later book, *Out of Bondage* (1986), she explores in greater depth her life as a porno star, what she has endured socially since abandoning the life, and her subsequent marriage. For a feminist perspective on her life, read "The Real Linda Lovelace," an essay by Gloria Steinem in the book *Outrageous Acts and Everyday Rebellions*. (TJW)

PO

100. Morris, Jan. **Conundrum.** New York: New American Library, 1975. 194 p. Reprint of 1974 edition published by Harcourt Brace Jovanovich.

James Morris lived for forty-six years as a male. His physical appearance was that of a male and other people defined him as a male. Furthermore, he lived the role of a male: he climbed Mount Everest, served in the British army, married, had five children, and distinguished himself in his profession as an author. But then James Morris underwent an operation to change his sex organs and physical appearance from male to female. The body of James Morris was transformed to coincide with the identity that he had always felt—that of a female. At forty-six, James Morris became Jan Morris, the author of this book. In this absorbing story, Jan presents an autobiographical account of the thoughts and feelings that led up to her sex-change operation. It documents the intricate and delicate problem ("conundrum") with which a transsexual is faced: how is it possible to reconcile gender identity (one's private sense of oneself as a male or female) with gender role (the behavior one expresses that socially identifies one's gender) and physical sex (sexual anatomy and physiology, genetic sex)? Morris succinctly expresses the dilemma: "I was three or perhaps four years old when I realized that I had been born into the wrong body and should really be a girl. I remember the moment well, and it is the earliest memory of my life." Jan's description of her transsexualism not only demonstrates the difference between transsexualism and homosexuality and transvestism but also serves as a reminder of the diverse components of human sexuality that many of us take for granted. The book becomes a testimony to the scope of sexuality. (SGF)

PO

101. **My Secret Life.** Abridged but unexpurgated. Introduction by G. Legman. New York: Grove Press, 1982. 697 p. Published in 1966 by Grove Press. ISBN 0-394-17397-X.

My Secret Life is a prolonged tale of unremitting sexual activity by an unknown Victorian gentleman of independent means. Based on a diary begun in his mid-twenties, the book traces the author's sexual career over a period of many years from early childhood to late maturity. Enamored of women's bodies at a tender age, he pursued them relentlessly for sexual pleasure rather than for their companionship and ideas; indeed, his conversations with them dealt with only one topic: sex. His conquests encompassed servant girls, prostitutes (gay ladies), dissatisfied middle class married women, teenage virgins, and others. Although basically heterosexual, he sometimes had sex with young men for the experience and variety. He claims to have had sex with over 1,200 women of all races and stations in England and all the countries of Europe including Russia. While not all of these experiences are told, hundreds are described in great detail: how the encounters came about, where, with whom, what occurred, descriptions of female genitalia, the ecstatic reactions of partners, and so forth. Unrelieved by any references to religion, politics, art, or letters, the book focuses totally on sex. About midway through the author interjects a state-of-the-art discourse on sexual intercourse. Still later, he philosophizes about sexuality: in his single-minded view all sexual practices are permissible if done for mutual delight: only the simple act of coition, as animals do it, is beastly. Through imagination sexual intercourse can be elevated to a divine level of experience. In the words of Steven Marcus, author of *The Other Victorians*, this book depicts "the secret life of sexuality" of Victorian England, the underbelly of daily life not depicted by the great Victorian novelists. It is important not only as a segment of social history but also as one of the longest erotic autobiographies ever written. It is unequaled in the variety of sexual experience that it portrays as well as in the frankness of language used to describe these experiences. Scholars have failed to identify the author of this underground classic. However, in his lengthy introduction, Gershon Legman hypothesizes that the author is H. Spencer Ashbee, bibliographer and collector of erotica. Originally privately printed in Amsterdam in eleven volumes (the last volume appeared in 1894), the first public printing of this anonymous autobiography did not take place until 1966, when Grove Press published it in two volumes, complete and unexpurgated. (TJW)

PO

102. Pearl, Cora. **Grand Horizontal: The Erotic Memoirs of a Passionate Lady.** Edited by William Blatchford. New York: Stein and Day, 1983. 186 p. Originally published in 1890. ISBN 0-8128-2917-4.

This work was originally printed under the title *The Memoirs of Cora Pearl.* Another work, entitled *Mémoires de Cora Pearl,* had been published in 1886, but it proved to be exceedingly dull. In it prominent names were given pseudonyms, which were soon deciphered. The present work, however, with a fresh title apparently supplied by the editor, is anything but dull. As its editor comments in his introduction, "It is certainly rather more the kind of book one might expect (or, perhaps, hope) of her, showing a great deal of spirit and a fine disregard for the feelings of any of her lovers who might read it. It is also sufficiently frank to have made conventional publication impossible, containing some of the most explicit sexual passages written by any female author until our own time" (p. 10). The volume contains the reminiscences of Cora Pearl, born Emma Crouch in Plymouth, England, in 1837, daughter of the man whose song "Kathleen Mavourneen" is recognized worldwide. After a convent education in Boulogne, France, where, in addition to learning French, she was introduced to the pleasures of the flesh by her fellow students, she returned to England. There she took to the streets and shortly began her long career as a prostitute. She visited Paris in 1858 and quickly learned the business end of the oldest profession. As a celebrated Parisian courtesan, she maintained liaisons with lovers from every stratum of French society, including Prince Napoleon, Prince Achille de Murat, Prince William of Orange, and the Duc de Morny. During the Siege of Paris (1870-71), she remained in Paris, abandoning her business and giving herself up to helping those in need. Following the war, Cora Pearl, having lost her wealthy protectors, failed to recover her position in society. She lived fairly comfortably in Paris to the end of her days, dying of cancer in 1886. She was so famous in her day as a high-class courtesan that she was awarded an entry in Sir Leslie Stephen's well-known *Dictionary of National Biography.* (TJW)

IL,PO

103. Rhodes, Richard. **Making Love: An Erotic Odyssey.** New York: Simon & Schuster, 1992. 175 p. Includes bibliography. ISBN 0-671-78227-4.

In a revelatory mood, Richard Rhodes sets down the truth about his love life, obscuring only the identities of his lovers, which he reckons at eleven. He provides personal background: married twice, father, 51 years old, and Pulitzer Prize-winning author of *The Making of the Atomic Bomb.* Although he refers to his abused childhood, he pays most attention to early sex experiences at a boys' home: the exploration of masturbation, the pleasures of viewing so-called "dirty pictures," and hearing about bestiality from his chums. He ends his adolescent days by having his "first sex" at eighteen with a dance-hall girl and part-time prostitute.

An avid reader, Rhodes learns about sex techniques from T. H. Van de Velde's classic sex manual, *Ideal Marriage,* that he says misled him for years about the importance of simultaneous orgasm. He introduces the reader to a succession of sex partners, whom he identifies by initials only, two of whom were probably his former wives. He remarks, "Each of my partners made love differently. I made love differently with each of my partners" (p. 69). With them he explores the entire range of heterosexual lovemaking, leaving no detail undescribed.

Along the way Rhodes writes about pornography, which he says is "despised in part because it reveals sex's raw Dionysian bounty" (p. 98); "the crime pornography supposedly commits isn't the doing; it's the showing" (p. 99). He talks about porn stars (the prowess of Marilyn Chambers, the dimensions of John Holmes), his obsession with female orgasm, and his elaborate preparations for watching adult videos while masturbating. He also devotes a chapter to the penis, its dimensions and strange behavior.

He moves on to his role as editor for the best-selling book *ESO* [Extended Sexual Orgasm] by Alan Brauer and Donna Brauer (Warner, 1983). What he learns about extended sexual orgasm he applies to his relationship with G__, his last sex partner. Throughout the book Rhodes manages to establish links between childhood abuse from his stepmother and his sexual behavior. Preoccupation with keeping G__ at a multiple orgasmic level in his lovemaking leads to a rift between the two. Eventually reconciled to a more modest level of orgasmic intensity, Rhodes recognizes the childhood origin of his fixation, and, a wiser man, continues his sexual relationship with G__. (TJW)

BIOGRAPHIES

(For related material see also entries 175, 486, 825)

IL,PO

104. Barry, Joseph. **French Lovers: From Heloise and Abelard to Beauvoir and Sartre.** New York: Arbor House, 1987. 352 p. Includes bibliographic notes. Translation of: *À la française.* ISBN 0-87795-844-0.

Barry hazards a definition of French sexuality by suggesting that "it is sensuality sharpened by intellectuality." Believing that France has contributed "more in the ways and means, the lore and language, of love" than any other country, he has chronicled in this collection of ten biographical sketches the love lives of renowned French couples through nine centuries of French history. Because "all loves are remarkably contemporary," he believes that these accounts are relevant to our own time. He states philosophically, "I have come to believe that a prime indicator of a civilization is the one-to-one relationship of its people—man to man, woman to woman, woman to man; in short, its couples" (p. xi).

The sketches begin with "The Couple and the Cross: Abelard and Heloise," the twelfth-century tragic tale of forbidden love between a great philosopher-teacher and his apt sixteen-year-old pupil, eventuating in the religious life for both and their remarkable correspondence. The second essay, "The Lady and the Knight: Courtly Love," gives an account of courtly love as perceived by Chrétien de Troyes in the story of Lancelot and Queen Guinevere, and by Andreas Capellanus whose *De Arte Honesti Amandi* (*The Art of Courtly Love*) detailed the principles and proceedings of the French courts of love in the twelfth century.

Additional essays include "Renaissance Turning Points: Henry II and Diane de Poitiers; Monsieur and Madame de Montaigne"; "Jealousy: Molière and Armande"; "The Poet and the Scientist: Voltaire and the Marquise du Châtelet"; "Pain and Pleasure: The Marquis and the Marquise de Sade"; "Romantic Love and the Daily Life: Marie d'Agoult and Franz Liszt"; "One Plus One Equals the Twentieth Century: Gertrude Stein and Alice B. Toklas"; "The Reinvention of Romantic Love: Jean Cocteau and Jean Marais"; and "The Sexism of a 'Liberated' Couple: Jean-Paul Sartre and Simone de Beauvoir."

These stories, Barry states, demonstrate how two people can create a world within a world; he concludes that "one by one, then two by two, we can rise above our pasts—infancy, childhood, conditioning—to form pairs of equals. We have no blueprints. But there are examples, and France provides us with some of the finest" (p. xv). (TJW)

IL

105. Bloch, Iwan. **Marquis de Sade: His Life and Works.** Translated by James Bruce. New York: Castle Books, 1948. 128 p. Translation of: *Marquis de Sade: Der Mann und Seine Zeit.*

Bloch does three things in his biography of the notorious Marquis de Sade: (1) he describes social conditions in France in the eighteenth century; (2) he provides an introduction to the life and works of the Marquis; and (3) he examines the philosophy of sadism as implied in Sade's novels. In one of his novels, Sade called the eighteenth century "the age of complete corruption," a century devoted to the "systematizing of sexual pleasure and pursuits." The Marquis, a keen observer, captured the spirit of debauchery pervading all levels of French society: royalty, nobility, clergy, all the way down the social ladder to the peasants. Furthermore, art, literature, fashion, and social life were eroticized. Woman was worshipped and became influential. At the same time, life were eroticized. Woman was worshipped and became influential. At the same time, "the family broke up, love took on immoral forms, and was accompanied by a contempt for the feminine sex" (p. 23). Prostitution was rampant in the cities, especially Paris, where famous bordellos serving royalty and the nobility flourished. Even Louis XV had his private brothel, Deer Park. Popular sexual practices of the day included onanism, tribadism, pederasty, and flagellation.

A brief sketch of the life of the Marquis de Sade, called by some the philosopher of vice and the professor of crime, follows: He was born in 1740, spent twenty-seven years in jail for various sex offenses and crimes, wrote his books while incarcerated, and died in 1814. Bloch then examines in detail the famous novels depicting the debauchery of the day. The works analyzed include *Justine or the Misfortunes of Virtue*; *Juliette, Her Sister, or the Fortunes of Vice*; *Philosophy in the Boudoir*; and other lesser works. Bloch states that in addition to the complete preoccupation with the sexual functions and pursuits of humans, one also finds in these novels the blending of sex, crime, and destructive behavior of all kinds. The materialistic, atheistic, and antifeminist philosophy of these novels, promoting as they do the infliction of pain on others for sexual pleasure, has been called sadism. While believing that the works of Sade are "repugnant and repulsive and repellent to any person save the most degenerate libertine," Bloch contends that they "are extremely important and instructive for the history and culture of the human race" (p. 108).

Giving more attention to the private life of the Marquis, especially his relationships with family members and details about his several incarcerations, is Donald Thomas's *The Marquis de Sade* (Boston: New York Graphics Society, 1976). Thomas provides insight into Sade's philosophy as embodied in his writings. For example, he reveals how *The 120 Days of Sodom* came to be written, and the fate of this unusual work. A selected bibliography paves the way to further study of the renowned Marquis. (TJW)

IL

106.   Broun, Heywood, and Margaret Leech. **Anthony Comstock: Roundsman of the Lord.** New York: Literary Guild of America, 1927. 285 p. Includes bibliography and index.

Based primarily on newspaper accounts of the period, the annual reports of the Society for the Suppression of Vice (1874-1916), and the writings of Comstock himself, including his diary, this penetrating biography by Broun and Leech presents the colorful life of Anthony Comstock, the great crusader against obscene literature and the arts, gambling, and quackery in the United States in the latter half of the nineteenth century and the early years of the twentieth century. Aptly dubbed "roundsman of the Lord" by the authors, Comstock was born on March 7, 1844 in New Canaan, Connecticut of Puritan stock. Strongly influenced by Bible stories told by his mother, he grew to manhood in an aura of austerity and religiosity. He served in the Union Army from 1863 to 1865, all the while keeping a diary of his observations and activities. Following the Civil War, he went to work in a drygoods house and settled in Brooklyn. In January 1871 he married Margaret Hamilton, a woman ten years older than he. After their one child died within the year, they adopted a little girl whose mother had recently died.

Thoroughly self-righteous, Comstock in 1871 purged his neighborhood of saloons for violating the Sunday closing laws. Earlier his sympathy for the anti-obscenity stance of the Young Men's Christian Association led him to write to its officers decrying the evils of the day. Affiliating himself with the YMCA, there followed in 1872 the formation of a Committee for the Suppression of Vice with Comstock as its man in the field, setting out to destroy the "hydra-headed monster" of obscenity. Using the recently passed New York obscenity law of 1868, Comstock brought about the arrest of bookdealers and publishers for selling obscene books, pamphlets, postcards, and the like. Many of these people were jailed, driven out of business, and, in some cases, hounded to death. In his diary, Comstock repeatedly reveals his motives for conducting these campaigns against the producers and disseminators of "dirty" materials: invariably he says that he is doing it all "for Jesus" in order to protect the children and young people of this country.

Believing that existing federal legislation in the United States was not as effective as it might be, Comstock persuaded the United States Congress to pass his 1873 bill to strengthen existing legislation by prohibiting the mailing of obscene matter within the United States and its territories. At the age of 29, Comstock was appointed Special Agent of the Postmaster-General with broad powers to launch a vigorous campaign against the smut peddlars and purveyors of contraceptive remedies and devices. The Committee, with strong YMCA backing, became the Society for the Suppression of Vice. His campaign broadened to encompass advertisers, abortionists, birth control advocates, and quacks and vendors of patent medicines. Comstock's baneful influence lasted until 1915.

Although in later years his campaigns faltered as opposition forces came to oppose him on the grounds that his activities were violations of free speech and were unconstitutional, he nevertheless could boast by 1882 that many of his goals had been achieved and the country was practically rid of pornographic literature and art. He then turned his attention to gambling and was successful in closing down the Louisiana lottery. But when he took on classical art and literature and the suggestive belly dancing at the Columbian Exposition in Chicago in 1893, he was less successful. In 1905 George Bernard Shaw, in reaction to Comstock's efforts to have the play *Mrs. Warren's Profession* banned in New York, called the efforts of the crusader "comstockery." One of Comstock's last acts was to attend the International Purity Congress meeting in San Francisco in 1915 as President Wilson's representative. Apparently the trip was too strenuous for Comstock, and he died in September 1915.

The authors' assessment of Comstock as a man is that he was profoundly sincere, terribly honest, frightfully energetic, but arrogant, self-righteous, and puritanically high-minded. (TJW)

PO

107. Cahill, Marie. **Madonna.** New York: Gallery Books, 1991. 96 p. Includes discography and index. ISBN 0-8317-5705-1.

In words and pictures Cahill traces the career of Madonna Louise Veronica Ciccone, who was born on August 16, 1958 in Bay City, Michigan. Intelligent, talented, and determined, Madonna achieved early success as a dancer in New York City, where she was noted for her flamboyant style of dress. Here she also discovered her musical talents—writing music and singing. She exploded onto the entertainment scene in 1983 with her first rock music album, *Madonna*, featuring eight songs; it eventually sold three million copies. Other successful albums followed: *Like a Virgin* (1984), *True Blue* (1986), *Like a Prayer* (1989), and *I'm Breathless* (1990). Individual songs from these albums, such as "Like a Virgin," reached #1 on the charts, while "Material Girl," where Madonna cannily styled herself after Marilyn Monroe, peaked at #2. In all these offerings Madonna projects an image of raw sex appeal; she even calls herself "Boy Toy."

Madonna also made three tours: The Virgin Tour (1985), Who's That Girl (1987), begun as an AIDS fund-raiser, and Blonde Ambition (1990). All these forays featured exciting and often erotic dances. The Blonde Ambition tour, in particular, has been an especially provocative rock concert. Its sexy costumes, suggestive dancing, and raw banter, obviously intended to shock, brought negative reactions from Catholics in Italy where her efforts were condemned as indecent, obscene, and blasphemous. Blasphemous because Madonna mixed Christian symbols with sexually suggestive dancing.

Cahill also looks at Madonna's efforts in Hollywood where she has made five movies since 1985, the most successful being *Desperately Seeking Susan* (1985) and *Dick Tracy* (1990).

Claiming to be a serious artist projecting sexuality and power through music and dance, Madonna has captured the attention of youth worldwide, for whom she has become a role model for outlandish dress and behavior. The big question remains, Will Madonna continue to sustain her meteoric career through the nineties? Cahill thinks so. (TJW)

IL

108.   Cleugh, James. **The First Masochist: A Biography of Leopold von Sacher-Masoch.** New York: Stein and Day, 1967. 220 p. Includes bibliography and index.

It was Richard von Krafft-Ebing who coined the term "masochism" after reading accounts of Leopold von Sacher-Masoch's peculiar obsession of courting sexual abuse and pain. The latter was born in 1836 at Lemberg, capital of the province of Galicia in the northeast corner of the Austro-Hungarian Empire. As biographer Cleugh points out in *The First Masochist*—a balanced biography treating both the life and works of Sacher-Masoch—he was possessed of a lively imagination and a strong creative drive. He grew up to be a recognized writer, publishing original historical and literary works steadily from 1857 until his death. His most famous novels, *Don Juan von Kolomea* and *Venus im Pelz (Venus in Furs)* came out in 1864 and 1870 respectively; they embody his theory of sex and reflect his personal neuroses. Indeed, most of his novels express in one way or another features of Sacher-Masoch's life and thought. A quote from *Venus im Pelz* well expresses his philosophy of sex:

> I held sensuality to be sacred. In fact nothing else appeared sacred to me. There was something divine, I believed, about a beautiful woman, since the most important preoccupation of nature, the propagation of the species, is primarily her affair. I regarded the female as the personification of nature, the goddess Isis, and the male as her priest and slave. I recognized in her the same cruelty as that of nature, which rejects all that serves it as soon as the service provided is no longer needed. As for the man, ill-treatment and even death at the hands of a woman are experienced by him as voluptuous bliss. (p. 69)

For the practical realization of his "masochistic" schemes, Sacher-Masoch urged his women to sign agreements stipulating their relationship. The following excerpt from one, signed by Sacher-Masoch and Wanda von Dunayev, brings out their respective roles—his submissive—hers dominate—in the relationship:

> Your mind belongs to me in just the same way as your body and however much you may suffer you must nevertheless subordinate your sentiments and sensations entirely to my orders. I am to be allowed to inflict any torture upon you and even if I mutilate you, you must still endure it without complaint. You must work for me like a slave and even if I become very rich and let you want for everything and trample upon you, you would have to embrace without a murmur the foot which crushed you. (p. 100)

Sacher-Masoch had several relationships of this sort over the years. He was never wholly satisfied with them, for he never really found a woman who satisfied his criteria for such a dominant role. On his death, Sacher-Masoch, at one time seriously considered the successor to Goethe in the field of German letters, left behind "the modern theory of equality between the sexes in every activity, both mental and bodily, open to the human race." (p 128) (TJW)

IL

109.   Garde, Noel I. **Jonathan to Gide: The Homosexual in History.** New York: Vantage Press, 1964. 751 p. Includes bibliography and index.

This specialized biographical directory focuses on homosexuals in history from the Israelite crown prince Jonathan (c.1046-1013 B.C.), beloved of David, to the American poet Hart Crane. It contains short biographical sketches of some 300 notable men who are identified in the literature as being homosexual or of homoerotic temperament. The allegations of homosexuality are based on statements in various encyclopedias, works of literature, biographies, and studies, all listed in the bibliography. Arranged chronologically, the compilation constitutes a history of 3000 years of political and cultural history. The back of the book includes an alphabetical index as well as listings of the subjects broken down by professions or occupations and by nationalities. (TJW)

PR,IL
110. Gay, Peter. **Freud: A Life for Our Time.** New York: Norton, 1988. 810 p. Includes bibliographic notes and index. ISBN 0-393-02517-9.

This book is more than a biography of Freud; it is a voyage into the context of European social, cultural, and intellectual history of which Freud was a part, from his birth in Freiberg in 1856 to his death in London in 1939. Distinguished cultural historian Gay (Sterling Professor of History at Yale University) draws on Freud's voluminous correspondence with colleagues, friends, and family; his copious body of professional writings; and Ernest Jones's three volume biography, to document the life and influence of Freud, the founder of psychoanalysis and a revolutionary thinker who changed the pattern of Western thought. As a graduate of the Western New England Institute for Psychoanalysis, Gay brings the skills of a psychoanalyst to his assessment of Freud's life and work; throughout the text Gay analyzes and critiques Freud's writings in terms of their significance to the psychoanalytic movement and uses Freud's own discoveries as well as his methods to explore his life history.

The biography is divided into three parts: (1) "Foundations: 1856-1905"; (2) "Elaborations: 1902-1915"; and (3) "Revisions: 1915-1939." Gay notes that "most of Freud's writings bear the traces of his life" (p. 267), because Freud examined his own life to understand those of others. Freud was the first and "declared family favorite" of the seven children of Jacob Freud, a wool merchant, and Amalia Freud, Jacob's third wife who was twenty years his junior. He was "ambitious," "outwardly self-assured," "brilliant in school," and "a voracious reader." Part one discusses the formation of Freud's own family with Martha Bernays, whom he married in 1886 and was the mother of their six children; the beginning of his medical career, about which he had reservations from the beginning; the significance of Charcot, who "propelled him away from the microscope" toward psychology; his friendship with Wilhelm Fliess ("the midwife of psychoanalysis"), whom Freud labeled the "Other," "the alter" in his life; the publication in 1895 of *Studies in Hysteria*, which included the case of Anna O, the "founding case" of psychoanalysis; the development of Freud's analytic techniques (close observation, appropriate interpretation, free association, working through) by 1892; the articulation of some of the basic principles of psychoanalysis (e.g., the Oedipus Complex, repression, the struggle between desire and defense) in *The Interpretation of Dreams* (1900); the publication of *The Psychopathology of Everyday Life* (1901), that demonstrated the workings of the unconscious; and the publication of *Three Essays on the Theory of Sexuality* (1905), a seminal work that presented Freud's view that neuroses stem from unresolved sexual conflicts in childhood. The first fifty years of Freud's life were the basis for psychoanalysis, a "psychology for psychologists," that marked a departure from physiological explanations for mental life; Freud saw its goals as providing therapy and generating theory, detailing a "map of the mind."

Part two traces the impact of Freud's theories and the refinements he made in them. Of major importance during this period was the founding of the Wednesday Psychoanalytic Society (1902), that was the basis for the Vienna Psychoanalytic Society, founded in 1908, that became a model for subsequent psychoanalytic societies. Among the participants of the latter were Sando Ferenczi, Hanns Sachs, Max Eitingon, Carl G. Jung, Karl Abraham, Ludwig Binswanger, A. A. Brill, Ernest Jones, and Edoardo Weiss. Gay discusses the politics that impinged on the "embattled founder," particularly the breaks with Jung and Adler. Freud's analyses of the case histories of Dora, Little Hans, Rat Man, and Wolf Man condensed the basis for his analytic techniques, focusing on how to make the unconscious conscious. During this period, Freud applied the principles of psychoanalysis to culture in *Totem and Taboo* (1913).

Part three analyzes the last part of Freud's life when he introduced the idea of the superego in *The Ego and the Id* (1923); considered how to deal with the "dark continent" of women; became a mentor for his daughter Anna's psychoanalytic career; moved on to an analysis of religion and culture in *The Future of an Illusion* (1927) and *Civilization and Its Discontents* (1930); deepened his friendship with Lou Andreas-Salomé and Princess Maria Bonaparte; and became an exile in London during the Nazi occupation of Austria, receiving help from Ernest Jones, whom he regarded as a member of his family. In his last years, Freud wrote *Outline of Psychoanalysis*, his "testament to the profession he founded" (p. 634). At Freud's request, his personal physician Dr. Max Schur hastened his death by successive injections of morphine, as he agreed to do if the "torture" of Freud's cancer became unbearable. Gay concludes, "The old stoic had kept control of his life to the end" (p. 651). (SGF)

IL
111.   Grier, Barbara, and Coletta Reid, eds. **Lesbian Lives: Biographies of Women from the Ladder.** Baltimore, Md.: Diana Press, 1976. 433 p. Includes bibliographies and index. ISBN 0-88447-012-1.

Important for understanding the development of lesbian thought and consciousness, these selections were taken from *The Ladder*, that from 1956 to 1972 was the only journal providing a forum for lesbian thought and life. Among the biographical subjects in this volume are Amelia Earhart, Colette, Octave Thanet, Willa Cather, Mary Casal, Radclyffe Hall, H. D., Charlotte Cushman, Dame Ethel Smyth, Rosa Bonheur, Madame de Staël, Juliette Recamier, Dorothy Thompson, Margaret Fuller, Edith Hamilton, and Carey Thomas. Grier and Reid have divided the biographical materials (sketches, book reviews, and bibliographies on the "variant" women) into sections: "Famous Couples," "Adventurers," "Novelists," "Queens and Their Consorts," "Poets," "Artists," "Writers," and "Pathbreakers." Although not comprehensive, this is the best source for consistently well-written, well-researched articles on lesbian women. Lesbianism is stressed as a positive element of the women's lives. In addition to portraits of specific women, Grier and Reid have included articles on groups—"Poetry of Lesbiana: Lesbian Poets"; "Guiding Lights: Ladies Bountiful"; "Women Composers"; and "And the Ladies Gathered: Martha McWhirter's Female Communal Society." The introduction by Grier is an important commentary on lesbian culture and the role of *The Ladder* in the dissemination of lesbiana in the United States. The picture and bibliography that complement almost every article are further indicators of the usefulness of this volume. (**Women's Studies**, 1979)

IL
112.   Grosskurth, Phyllis. **Havelock Ellis: A Biography.** London: Allen Lane, 1980. 492 p. Includes bibliography. ISBN 0-7139-1071-2.

Both the life and works of Havelock Ellis are treated in this definitive biography by Grosskurth, Professor of English at the University of Toronto. Ellis was born in South London in 1859. His father, a sea captain, twice took him on voyages around the world. In his teens, he spent four years living an isolated existence in Australia, where he taught school. His interest in the study of sexuality began at this early juncture in his life. Returning to London, he studied medicine, eventually obtaining a degree in 1889.

Ellis's deep attachment to women—his mother and sisters, his three great loves (Olive Schreiner, Edith Lees, and Françoise Lafitte)—and many infatuations and friendships, including a long relationship with Margaret Sanger, are delightfully explored throughout the book, primarily on the basis of the vast correspondence he conducted with many of these ladies. His friendships with men, notably Arthur Symons, Edward Carpenter, and Hugh de Sélincourt, are fully described also. His correspondence with others (Ernest Jones, Edward Westermarck, Bronislaw Malinowski) on a great variety of questions and issues is extensive.

In the introduction, Grosskurth says that she has tried to "depict Ellis *in process*," to show him "in his approach to his work, his reaction to the world around him, how and why he loved certain people and why they loved him, and, most difficult of all, how he viewed himself" (p. xvi). Thus the reader gets a stunningly intimate view of Ellis's personal life, including his strange relationships with the women he loved (e.g., his wife of twenty-five years, Edith, was a professed lesbian) and glimpses of unusual sexual behavior (e.g., his penchant for urolagnia with his lady friends).

Ellis died in 1939, leaving an enormous body of written work, most of which is discussed by Grosskurth, especially his great work, *Studies in the Psychology of Sex*. She both reviews the bibliographic history of this work and analyzes the contents of each of its seven volumes. She also examines many of his other important works, including *Man and Woman* (1894), *The Dance of Life* (1923), and *My Life: Autobiography of Havelock Ellis* (1939).

Ellis's resolution as a youth "to make his life's work the exposure, the exploration, and the understanding of sex in all its manifestations" (p. xv) was, as is made evident by this biography, never broken. Along with Sigmund Freud, Richard von Krafft-Ebing, and Magnus Hirschfeld, he became one of the half dozen or so seminal figures in the development of sexology in the early years of the twentieth century. (TJW)

IL

113. Hall, Ruth. **Passionate Crusader: The Life of Marie Stopes.** New York: Harcourt Brace Jovanovich, 1977. 351 p. Includes bibliography and index. ISBN 0-15-171288-3.

Although deemed by some as egomaniacal and self-centered, no one denies that Stopes's life (1880-1958) was extraordinary by any standard. Her most memorable accomplishment was the founding of Great Britain's first birth control clinic. Stopes's visibility as a flamboyant spokeswoman for birth control and for a clearer public understanding of sexuality during the 1920s and 1930s overshadows her contributions as a noted paleobotanist. On a lesser scale, she dabbled in the arts. Hall, a journalist, has sifted through the huge corpus of documentation on this contradictory personality, to produce a biography that explores the contributions of Stopes as social pioneer but takes note of her many eccentricities as a private woman. Like many early birth control advocates, Stopes was elitist in her approach to the question, believing that the lower classes were unfit to breed more of their own. Her central belief was that the human race could be greatly improved by the eugenic application of birth control. Ironically, this stern approach was considered very liberal in Marie Stopes's day. Along with her outrageous pronouncements she had many good ideas that have had great impact in Britain—for example, that the state accept the responsibility to provide free birth control services, which has been the case in Britain since 1975. (**Women's Studies**, 1979)

IL,PO

114. Hayman, Ronald. **De Sade: A Critical Biography.** New York: Crowell, 1978. 253 p. Includes bibliography, index, and chronology. ISBN 0-690-01416-3.

In this biography of the Marquis de Sade, Hayman, English theatre director and literary critic, attempts to fathom the behavior of the notorious eighteen century libertine. The work begins with a detailed chronological table interrelating events in the Marquis's life with political and cultural occurrences. We discover that Donatien-Alphonse-François de Sade was born in Paris on June 2, 1740 at the Hôtel de Condé. Chapter 1 covers Sade's boyhood and youth until his marriage to Renée-Pélagie de Montreuil on May 17, 1763. During this period he receives a sound education; serves in the military, attaining the rank of captain; and has sexual relations with the Marquis de Lauris's twenty-two-year-old daughter from whom he contracts a venereal disease.

Chapters 2 and 3 first deal with Sade's mad adventure with a twenty-year-old working-class girl, Jeanne Testard, who later testifies that Sade blasphemed the Christian religion and coerced her into flagellating him. Hayman attributes these actions to Sade's atheistic hatred of religion and the psychological impact of strict Jesuit schooling and rigorous cavalry training. Then follow numerous affairs with actresses, dancers, and prostitutes in which flagellation and anal intercourse are dominant tendencies. These extramarital affairs are kept secret from his wife by his mother-in-law Madame de

Montreuil. He also fathers a son by his wife. Then comes the Rose Keller affair on Easter Sunday, April 3, 1768. For this sadistic adventure Sade is arrested and imprisoned for several months. He fathers a second son in June 1769 and a daughter in April 1771. He also has an affair with his sister-in-law Anne-Prospère, followed by a sadistic orgy with young prostitutes in Marseilles in June 1772. Arrested for sodomy and poisoning, the Parlement at Aix sentences him to death. He escapes to Italy with Anne-Prospère, but is again arrested on December 5, 1772 and imprisoned at Miolans in Sardinia. He escapes into hiding in April 1773. After several hectic years, marked by scandals, he is finally arrested in 1777 under a *lettre de cachet* and begins his long incarceration, first at Vincennes fortress and then in the Bastille.

Receiving regular visits from his wife from 1781 on, he begins to write, completing *Dialogue entre un prêtre et un moribund* in 1782; he also starts work on *Les 120 journées de Sodome*. In 1784 the authorities transfer Sade to the Bastille, where he is to remain until released on April 2, 1790. He transcribes the *120 journées* onto a forty-foot roll of thin paper about five inches wide. Not published until 1904, this erotically sadistic novel, left behind when he was freed from the Bastille, is Sade's most famous work. In it he describes 450 episodes in the most diverse sexual activity imaginable, including deflowering, sodomy, flagellation, coprophilia, torture, mutilation, and murder. Some of it is nonsexual and "pushes sadism beyond the limits of reason." During his incarceration in the Bastille, Sade completes several other noteworthy works, including the novel *Aline et Valcour*.

From 1790 to 1801, Sade enjoys freedom, begins a relationship with Marie-Constance Renelle, participates in the revolution, writes plays, and produces several significant works: *La Philosophie dans le boudoir, Justine* (1791) and *Juliette* (1797). Ostensibly imprisoned in 1801 for producing obscene writings, Sade denounces *Justine* "as infamous, disgusting, full of filth," and claims he was only its copyist. Until his death on December 2, 1814, Sade occupies a number of prisons and asylums: Sainte-Pélagie, Bicêtre, and Charenton.

Hayman explains why Sade's writings are considered dangerous: "No one has ever argued more uncompromisingly than Sade that we should give free rein to our destructive impulses, overcoming all inclination to altruism and remorse" (p. 226). He took "a totally negative view of human existence." In one of his letters to his wife he states: "I am a libertine, but I am neither a criminal nor a murderer" (p. 116). (TJW)

PR,IL

115. Jones, Ernest. **The Life and Work of Sigmund Freud.** Edited and abridged by Lionel Trilling and Steven Marcus. With an introduction by Lionel Trilling. New York: Basic Books, 1961. 541 p. Includes index.

This is the abridged version of Jones's monumental three-volume biography of Sigmund Freud, published between 1953 and 1957. In the preface Jones states the purpose of his book: "Its aims are simply to record the main facts of Freud's life" and "to try to relate his personality and the experiences of his life to the development of his ideas." Jones divides his biography into three books: "The Formative Years and the Great Discoveries, 1856-1900"; "Years of Maturity, 1901-1919"; and "The Last Phase, 1919-1939."

Sigmund Freud was born in 1856 in Freiberg, in Moravia (now Pribor, Czechoslovakia) and died in 1939 in London. In book I, Jones describes the family's move first to Leipzig, when Freud was three years old, and then a year later to Vienna, where he was to remain throughout most of his life. Jones describes Freud as an avid reader with a good memory, averse to music, and irreligious. Graduated from the Gymnasium *summa cum laude,* he was familiar with the classics and had a sound knowledge of several languages. His first erotic experience was an innocent affair with the daughter of a family friend when he was sixteen.

In a series of chapters, Jones examines Freud's choice of profession, his medical career, and his experimentation with and use of cocaine. He relates in detail Freud's betrothal and eventual marriage to Martha Bernays in 1886. He also describes Freud's friendships; personality traits; and ideas about women, the French and the English, and military service; thus providing an excellent portrait of Freud as a man.

Freud greatly admired the French physician, Charcot, under whom he studied at the Salpetriere in Paris, and who introduced him to the problem of hysteria. By 1893 Freud, a recognized authority on the subject of children's paralysis, switched from the use of hypnosis in the treatment of hysteria to the "free association" method in order to penetrate the realm of the unconscious. This marks the beginning of psychoanalysis, a term he first employed in 1896. He began to notice frequent allusions to sexual experiences in patients' memories. With Josef Breuer he collaborated to produce *Studies in Hysteria* (1895).

Freud's self-analysis began in 1897; from it emerged a greater understanding of childhood sexuality and an appreciation of dreams. He discovered what he took to be a general human characteristic: a boy's love for his mother and jealousy of his father. *The Interpretation of Dreams* was published in 1900.

In book II, Jones describes Freud's achievements, disappointments, and influence in the first two decades of the twentieth century. These include the emergence of the Vienna Psycho-Analytical Society; the publication of several important books: *The Psychopathology of Everyday Life* (1904), *Three Essays on the Theory of Sexuality* (1905), and *Totem and Taboo* (1913); collaboration with the Swiss psychiatrist C. G. Jung; a lectureship at Clark University in America; the spread of the psychoanalytic movement internationally; the defection of such important followers as Alfred Adler, Wilhelm Stekel, and Jung; and the formation of an inner group of analysts (Rank, Abraham, Eitingon, Jones, Ferenczi, Sachs, Freud) known as "the Committee." Jones concludes book II by describing the impact of the war years on Freud's work, which had diminished considerably.

Book III begins by showing Freud's interest in masochism, the pleasure principle, and the death instinct. Out of this emerged several books, including *Beyond the Pleasure Principle* (1920) and *The Ego and the Id* (1923). In 1923, Freud, then sixty-seven, had the first of thirty-three cancer operations on his mouth and jaw. In 1925, his *Autobiography*, highlighting his scientific career and ideas, was published. Freud's views on the future of psychoanalysis focused on lay analysis, child analysis, and an educational program for practitioners. This led to a dispute with the Americans over the education of psychoanalysts within the medical profession.

Civilization and Its Discontents was written in 1929; in it Freud writes about humanity's relation to the universe, the purpose of life, the pleasure-pain principle, and human happiness and guilt. Freud's last major work, *Moses and Monotheism*, was written in London, where he lived a short while before his death. In 1938 the spread of Nazism into Austria compelled him to abandon his home in Vienna.

Sigmund Freud opened up a whole new field of psychological study. By his profound insights into such submerged areas of the human psyche as sexuality, he also became one of the founding fathers of sexology. (TJW)

PR,IL

116. Kennedy, David M. **Birth Control in America: The Career of Margaret Sanger.** New Haven, Conn.: Yale University Press, 1970. 320 p. (Yale Publications in American Studies, 18). Includes bibliography and index.

This study is more fully a history of the birth control movement than a comprehensive biography of Margaret Sanger. Kennedy, Assistant Professor of History at Stanford University, emphasizes the intellectual, familial, and social influences that brought Sanger to a position of leadership in birth control from 1914 to 1942 (e.g., her Catholic girlhood and her awakening to the ideas of Havelock Ellis and Freud on sexuality). Although Sanger began as a radical, Kennedy points out the conservative support that her birth control reform movement attracted: eugenicists, in their campaigns to control immigrant population increase; Protestant churches, in their endorsements of family stability; and the federal government, in the self-serving interests of social control during the Great Depression and wartime. Kennedy sees Margaret Sanger as an emotional leader rather than an intelligent strategist, as one who never really understood the sexual ignorance of the masses. Although he credits her with dynamism, he depicts her as absorbed with her own heroism. The bibliographic essay, together with the selected bibliography, will well serve the researcher on Sanger and the birth control movement.

For a more complete account of the personal life of Sanger, see Madeline Gray's *Margaret Sanger: A Biography of the Champion of Birth Control* (New York: Marek, 1979). (**Women's Studies**, 1979)

IL

117. Lély, Gilbert. **The Marquis de Sade: A Biography.** New York: Grove Press, 1970. 464 p. Translation of: *La Vie du Marquis de Sade*. Originally published in two volumes in 1952 and 1957. Includes index.

Lély's biography of the infamous Marquis de Sade, based largely on primary source material (letters, legal documents, Sade's writings) is considered a definitive work. Following a background description of the Sade family (linked by marriage to the royal house of Bourbon) from the twelfth century to the birth of Donatien Alphonse François, Marquis de Sade, on June 2, 1740 in Paris, Lély presents the life of the Marquis in a strictly chronological fashion. Despite the unrelatedness sometimes of adjacent dated entries, Lély describes realistically and completely the Marquis's life until his death on December 2, 1814 in Charenton Asylum.

Lély describes the early period of the Marquis's life, from birth to his marriage in 1763, in terms of early childhood experiences, education, military service, and marriage to Lady Renée de Montreuil. Sade's libertinage began shortly after his marriage, resulting in his conviction and incarceration in various prisons for sexual excesses (adultery, incest, flagellation, sodomy, poisonings, and inflicted pain) and sundry liaisons with prostitutes stemming from the alleged "frigid and prim" behavior of the Marquise. He also had a torrid affair with his sister-in-law, Lady Anne.

Following an arrest by *lettre de cachet* in February 1777, Sade spent sixteen months in Vincennes Prison. Freed for thirty-nine days in 1778, he was rearrested and sent back to Vincennes for five and a half years. Suddenly transferred to the Bastille in 1784, Sade spent another five and a half years in prison.

Around 1780, as a prisoner, Sade began his enormous literary task. He considered this effort his salvation and purpose in life. In 1788 he drew up a catalog of his finished works, which included two volumes of plays; a philosophical novel, *Aline and Valcour*; the novel *Justine, or the Misfortunes of Virtue*; and four volumes of stories. He produced a great volume of correspondence, much of it with his devoted wife. In 1785 he began writing *The 120 Days of Sodom*, which he inscribed on thirty-nine feet of a roll of thin paper. When freed in 1789, Sade had to quickly hide the manuscript, which he never saw again. Rediscovered in the very cell that Sade occupied, it was preserved for many years and finally published by Iwan Bloch in 1904, a Berlin psychiatrist, under the pseudonym of Eugène Dühren.

From 1789 to 1792, Sade worked under the revolutionary regime: first as a prisoner in the Charenton Asylum for nine months, then freed by a Decree of the Assembly concerning prisoners detained by *lettre de cachet*, as an "active citizen" of the Place Vendome section, where as a Commissioner he prepared recommendations for the management of hospitals in Paris. He also saw to the production of his plays and the publishing of his writings. On Lady de Sade's formal separation from her husband, citizen Sade formed an alliance with a young actress under thirty, Marie Quesnet, that lasted until Sade's death twenty-four years later.

On March 6, 1801, Sade was seized and imprisoned in St. Pélagie prison for his writings, especially the novels *Justine* and *Juliette*. Then, following a short stay in Bicêtre Prison, he was once again transferred to Charenton, his last incarceration. Altogether Sade spent twenty-eight years as a prisoner. His last years were not uncomfortable: a sympathetic warden, freedom to perform his plays, plenty of books and writing materials to keep him occupied, and regular visits from Marie Quesnet made life bearable. The poet Guillaume Apollinaire stated that despite Sade's long imprisonment, the libertine remained "the freest soul that ever existed." (TJW)

PR,IL
118. Pomeroy, Wardell B. **Dr. Kinsey and the Institute for Sex Research.** New York: Harper & Row, 1972. 479 p. Includes index.

Pomeroy, Kinsey's closest associate for more than thirteen years, pays tribute to "the greatest figure in sex research since Freud" by reconstructing his life and work for a public that knows very little about Kinsey as a human being. Using his own recollections, a series of taped interviews with important people in Kinsey's life, and information from 45,000 letters in the files of the Institute for Sex Research, he traces Kinsey's life from his early years as a shy, lonely youngster in Hoboken, New Jersey, to his fame as a sex researcher in Bloomington, Indiana. In the process, he also reveals the climate of the times and the problems in conducting sex research.

Kinsey's career began as a biology professor at Indiana University, where he pursued his research on gall wasps. His interests began to shift in 1938 when he was named coordinator for a bold new course on marriage. Since there was scant literature on the subject, Kinsey decided to do his own research on sexual behavior by taking histories of his students. The search for histories began to absorb him completely, "and as he came to realize that he was working in a research field virtually unexplored, the scientist, the collector and the teacher came together in Kinsey the researcher in human sexual behavior" (pp. 61-62). Perfectionistic, controlling, persistent, thorough, versatile, private, and warm are all adjectives that apply to this remarkable man. "Collector" is the label that Pomeroy thinks best describes the complex dimensions of Kinsey's personality. And, through and through, he was the consummate scientist, who left no detail of his subject unexamined, including erotica, films, and photographs of sexual interaction, physiology, characteristics of other species, and the behavior of such diverse groups as prisoners, prostitutes, homosexuals, and dignitaries.

The research that preceded the "Kinsey Reports" was characterized by dogged persistence in obtaining lengthy, personal interviews; long hours of travel and daily work; immersion in the cultural context of the people interviewed; a fierce determination to protect peoples' privacy; an aversion to making value judgments about his respondents; and an honesty and enthusiasm that disarmed many of the staunchest skeptics.

However, the publication of *Sexual Behavior in the Human Male* (1948) and *Sexual Behavior in the Human Female* (1953) brought a barrage of unexpected publicity to this dedicated scientist. The public controversy over his findings, particularly in the *Female* volume, and an onslaught of criticism took their toll on the future of the Institute and on Kinsey's health. However, Kinsey's commitment to his work was total; his work was his world. As he said, "if I can't work, I'd rather die." When Kinsey died of an embolism in 1956 at the age of sixty-two, many of his dreams were unfulfilled; he had hoped to collect a total of 100,000 interviews and publish many more volumes on the research that he felt he had only begun to analyze. Nevertheless, he was "one of the most widely known scientists of this century" (p. 3). Pomeroy sums up Kinsey's lifework in eight major contributions: (1) the fact of the research itself; (2) the establishment of baselines; (3) individual variations; (4) the 0-6 scale for measuring homosexuality; (5) the concept of total outlet; (6) the difference in sexual behavior according to social levels; (7) the effects of aging on sexuality; and (8) the Institute for Sex Research. The library and archives at the Institute remain a monument to his devotion. Other details of the life of this pioneer in sex research may be found in another biography by a staff member at the Institute, Cornelia Christenson's *Kinsey, a Biography* (1971). (SGF)

PR,IL
119. Sharaf, Myron. **Fury on Earth: A Biography of Wilhelm Reich.** New York: St. Martin's Press/Marek, 1983. 550 p. Includes bibliography and index. ISBN 0-312-31370-5.

In *Let Us Now Praise Famous Men*, James Agee states, "Every fury on earth has been absorbed in time. . . . Official acceptance is the one surest sign of fatal misunderstanding." Sharaf, a psychoanalyst and a former student, patient, and colleague of Reich, aptly underscores the degree to which Reich's life could be misinterpreted. Variously characterized as ludicrous, pathetic, paranoid, bizarre, or sinister, Reich developed many novel, brilliant ideas that were often distorted by others and used to make him an object of attack. Sharaf highlights the influence of Reich's social context and personal life on the development of his career in an effort to understand the life of this extraordinary individual. He argues that Reich struggled to maintain contact with the core of his being; his "soaring intellect" and "emotional depth" could interact with his neuroses in either a creative or destructive way.

The suicide of Reich's mother when he was fourteen (soon after his father pressured him to confess his knowledge of her affair with a tutor) and his father's death from tuberculosis three years later produced unresolved tensions that Sharaf thinks shaped Reich's "sense of mission." The focus of psychoanalysis on examining psychological forces that lay beneath the surface of social life was particularly appealing to Reich. He soon became Freud's protégé in Vienna. However, while Reich received praise for his characterological work, his view of orgastic potency as the goal of psychoanalytic treatment met with disapproval. By 1934, Reich's attempts to unite a program of sexual reform with a Marxist political program further separated him from his psychoanalytic colleagues. Freud's eventual rejection of him was particularly disappointing. Nevertheless, in several phases of his life, Reich repeated a similar pattern: passionate commitment to an idea that was at odds with general consensus; rejection of advice from friends; polarization of colleagues, departure from personal and professional relations, and the establishment of new ones; and change in social and scientific perspective. Reich left five countries, married three times, had many affairs, and was embroiled in political and professional controversies. He delved into research in the social, behavioral, and natural sciences, exploring various dimensions of energy. His shift from Europe to America was marked by less emphasis on psychoanalysis and more dedication to understanding orgone energy—an energy outside of the body and outside of matter itself (in contrast to libido, that was contained in the body). Research on bions (vesicles that represent transitionary stages between living and nonliving substances), emphasis on physiology in therapeutic work (freeing energy from muscular armor), and interest in mother/infant interaction bridged the gap. His primary interest for the last seventeen years of his life as well as his major contribution was the concept of orgastic potency (the full expression of genitality), which became part of his understanding of orgone energy. His synthetic approach linked findings from behavioral and natural science to draw attention to the interaction between body and behavior as well as between cognition and sensation. He designed an accumulator ("orgone box") to demonstrate the presence of orgone energy. In his study of health and illness, he drew attention to the defenses of the disease host rather than to the disease agent and suggested that a dysfunction in an organism's biological energy could cause a degenerative disease such as cancer or schizophrenia.

However, the fruition of his life's work began to draw to a close in 1951 when the FDA accused him of promoting concepts of orgone energy to dupe the public into believing that his accumulator was a cure for cancer. A trial upheld the FDA's contention and the court ordered that Reich's writings on orgone energy were to be burned and his accumulators destroyed. After Reich's defiance of the court order, he was sent to prison. He died there of "heartbreak" in 1957 at the age of sixty.

Twenty-five years after his death, the rich legacy of Reich's ideas is only beginning to be explored. Sharaf suggests that "we tried to run from what he studied," perhaps because it dealt with issues that did not fit into the scientific or social paradigm of the time. (SGF)

PO

120.   Steinem, Gloria. **Marilyn.** Photographs by George Barris. New York: Henry Holt, 1986. 182 p. ISBN 0-8050-0060-7.

Why has Marilyn Monroe remained an icon of continuing power, and how do we understand her as an individual? Feminist Steinem and photographer Barris combine their talents to address these questions and to "set the record straight," as Marilyn wanted to do. Drawing on interviews that Barris conducted with Marilyn shortly before she died; text from Marilyn's unfinished autobiography, *My Story*; and materials from some of the more than forty books written about Marilyn, Steinem interprets the lives of Norma Jeane Baker, the vulnerable daughter of Gladys Baker Mortenson, and Marilyn Monroe, the sex goddess. The juxtaposition of role and person is a consistent theme in each chapter.

Norma Jeane was born on June 1, 1926 to a twenty-four-year-old divorcee, separated from her second husband and abandoned by her lover, Norma Jeane's father. She never met her father and rarely lived with her mother, who was often hospitalized for mental problems. She spent most of her childhood in foster homes and was sexually abused by a boarder when she was only eight years old. She lacked continuity, emotional security, and a person who loved her unconditionally for herself. Perhaps these deficits fed into her need for attention, approval, and love later on. As Steinem notes, "As you read and think about Marilyn, remember Norma Jeane" (p. 61).

Marilyn's career reflected Norma Jeane's needs. She refused to be a kept woman but gave sex as a "friendly reward" to men who helped or understood her. Linked to some of the world's most powerful men—Howard Hughes, Hugh Hefner, Robert Kennedy, John F. Kennedy, Frank Sinatra—and married three times, including a nine month marriage to baseball hero Joe DiMaggio and a marriage of several years to renowned playwright Arthur Miller, Marilyn maintained a romantic, idealistic attitude toward men. She only wanted to marry for love and to have children within marriage. She seemed to seek her identity through men, but men did not compensate for her lack of personal identity or control over her life. Although she craved the attention that her attractive body and mannerisms as Marilyn produced, her body became her prison. She experienced twenty or more surgical invasions, including twelve or thirteen abortions, before she died in 1962 at age thirty-six. She drank heavily, took drugs, and had difficulty sleeping. Although many of her eleven starring roles played up a dumb blonde image, she wanted to be more than a "celluloid aphrodisiac."

Why did Marilyn capture so much of the public's attention so long after her death? The sexy woman-child who rarely asked for anything for herself; who tried to please; who was so needy and innocent, triggered protectiveness and adoration from her primarily male admirers. Groucho Marx described her at twenty-three as "Mae West, Theda Bara, and Bo Peep—all rolled into one." Although the public praised her body, it gave less attention to her needy spirit. When she died, she remained the "unthreatening half-person that sex goddesses are supposed to be." Barris's photographs, taken in the last months of Marilyn's life, supplement the text to reveal Norma Jeane's spirit and Marilyn's persona. As Steinem concludes, when Marilyn Monroe died, "It was the lost possibilities of Marilyn Monroe that capture our imaginations. It was the lost Norma Jeane, looking out of Marilyn's eyes, who captured our hearts" (p. 180). (SGF)

PO

121.   Wallace, Irving, Amy Wallace, David Wallechinsky, and Sylvia Wallace. **The Intimate Sex Lives of Famous People.** New York: Delacorte Press, 1981. 618 p. Includes index.

The compilers, already well known for *The People's Almanac* and *The Book of Lists*, undertook this compilation because, to the best of their knowledge, "no one ... has yet written a comprehensive volume that reveals the sexual behavior of well-known and distinguished men and women in world history." How did they gather such seemingly private information?

They state that twenty persons in the United States and additional researchers in England, France, Italy, and Spain read over 1,500 biographies as well as autobiographies, memoirs, correspondence, dairies, journals, medical reports, and numerous other sources of information. The 207 personalities from the distant and recent past covered in this work include actors and actresses (Charlie Chaplin, Joan Crawford), artists (Picasso), authors and playwrights (Colette, Joyce, Wilde), poets (Swinburne), singers (Caruso, Callas), composers, musicians, and conductors (Chopin, Stokowski), rulers and royalty (Cleopatra, Henry VIII), political leaders (Jefferson), military persons (MacArthur), capitalists (Ford), religious figures (Father Divine, Brigham Young), psychologists, scientists, and philosophers (Freud, Marie Curie, Marx), courtesans and prostitutes (Cora Pearl), sex symbols (Clara Bow, Lord Byron), and a miscellaneous group including Josephine Baker, Milton Berle, and Babe Ruth. The technique used by the authors is to present briefly the biographee's claim to fame, describe the person, and then concentrate on his or her love and/or sex life, adding memorable thoughts made by the person on love, marriage, sex, men, women, etc. Fully illustrated with portraits (Marilyn Monroe's calendar shot is typical), the well-written sketches, although possibly humbling to ordinary mortals, are fun to read. (TJW)

PR,IL

122. Wolff, Charlotte. **Magnus Hirschfeld: A Portrait of a Pioneer in Sexology.** London: Quartet Books, 1986. 494 p. Includes bibliographies and index. ISBN 0-7043-2569-1.

Biographer Wolff, widely known for her books on bisexuality and lesbianism, has researched and written the major biography on one of the most distinguished and influential sexologists of the late nineteenth and early twentieth centuries. Using archival materials, interviews with those who knew him, original records and publications, as well as considerable secondary source materials, Wolff has woven a sharp picture of Magnus Hirschfeld from his childhood and student days until his mature years and death in Nice in 1935.

Son of a well-known physician, Hirschfeld was born on May 14, 1868 in Pomerania in the resort town of Kolberg on the shores of the Baltic Sea. After a happy childhood, he followed in his father's footsteps and chose to become a doctor rather than pursue philology or writing, his other great interests. In 1896 he settled in Charlottenburg, Berlin, advertising himself as a specialist in hydrotherapy, while his true interests focused on the varieties of love, especially homosexuality. Keeping his own homosexuality pretty much hidden, he wrote pseudonymously a thirty-four-page pamphlet, *Sappho and Socrates*, attempting to explain the love of men and women for members of their own sex. This work marks the beginning of his career as an advocate in the struggle to have Paragraph 175 of the Reichstrafgeseltzbuch abolished in Germany. One of the principal reasons for establishing the Wissenschaftlich-humanitäres Komitee (Scientific-Humanitarian Committee) on May 15, 1897 was to create an instrument to fight the mistreatment of homosexuals under the law.

In 1899 under the Committee's auspices, Hirschfeld started the *Jahrbuch für sexuelle Zwischenstufen* (*Yearbook for Sexual Intermediaries*) to communicate new knowledge about unorthodox sexuality, i.e., transvestism, androgyny, hermaphroditism, homosexuality. In 1908 he also started the first journal devoted to sexology, *Die Zeitschrift für Sexualwissenschaft* (*Journal of Sexual Science*), that carried contributions from the foremost sexologists of the day.

One of the fruits of these endeavors was Hirschfeld's study *Die Transvestiten*, published in 1910, in which he coined the word "transvestites." Another was the great work produced by Hirschfeld in 1914: *Die Homosexualität des Mannes und des Weibes* (*Homosexuality of Men and Women*). Based on information from 10,000 homosexuals, it is probably the most comprehensive study of homosexuals ever undertaken. He believed that homosexuality was a natural condition modified by circumstances.

Hirschfeld's greatest achievement was the founding of the Institut für Sexualwissenschaft (Institute for Sex Research) in 1919 in Berlin. It became internationally renowned not only for its research but also as a treatment and therapeutic center for people with sexual problems. Its library, exhibits, archives, and educational programs were outstanding. Unfortunately, after fourteen years of success and acclaim, this first-ever sex institute was destroyed in 1933 by the Nazis.

In 1921 Hirschfeld held the first International Congress for Sexual Reform in Berlin; this evolved, in 1928, into the World League for Sexual Reform at the second International Congress for Sexual Reform held in Copenhagen. Subsequently, these congresses were held in London (1929), Vienna (1930), and Brunn, Switzerland (1932).

Wolff describes other activities and aspects of Hirschfeld's productive life: involvement in the women's movement; promotion of national and international meetings; world travel; campaigns against alcoholism, drugs, and smoking; speechmaking in the interest of sexual enlightenment; etc.

Magnus Hirschfeld, whom some consider the founder of sexology, died in self-exile in France on his birthday in 1935. (TJW)

6

Readers. Collections.
Conference Proceedings

(For related material see also entries 456, 643, 682)

PR,IL

123. Ariès, Philippe, and André Béjin, eds. **Western Sexuality: Practice and Precept in Past and Present Times.** Translated by Anthony Forster. Oxford: Basil Blackwell, 1985. 220 p. (Family, Sexuality and Social Relations in Past Times). Translation of: *Sexualités Occidentales.* Includes bibliographic footnotes and index. ISBN 0-631-13476-X.

Organized by the late Philippe Ariès at L'Ecole des haute études en sciences sociales in 1979-80, this seminar examined different aspects of Western sexuality. The unifying theme of the seminar appears to be the historical background to the major issues in such areas of modern sexology as homosexuality, marriage, prostitution, Christian ethics, autoerotism, and the field of sexology itself. Participants included some of the foremost thinkers on sex and sexuality in the Western world.

Among the key papers presented at the seminar are Robin Fox's thoughts on basic patterns in the relations between the sexes from an evolutionary and sociobiological perspective; Michel Foucault's analysis of Cassian's writings on chastity and fornication in the context of monasticism; Philippe Ariès's explanation of St. Paul's categorization of the sins of the flesh; Michael Pollak, Paul Veyne, and Philippe Ariès's views on the history and nature of male homosexuality; Jacques Rossiaud's description of prostitution and prostitutes in French towns of the fifteenth century; Jean-Louis Flandrin and others' views on love and sex in married life; André Béjin's consideration of nine criteria in regard to extramarital unions; and Béjin's reports on (1) the decline of the psychoanalyst and the rise of the sexologist in the treatment of orgasmic dysfunctions and (2) the influence of sexologists in modern society and the heady concept of sexual democracy. All the papers in this important collection provide information affecting contemporary attitudes and thinking about sex and sexuality in modern society. (TJW)

PR

124. Beach, Frank A., ed. **Human Sexuality in Four Perspectives.** Baltimore, Md.: Johns Hopkins University Press, 1977. 330 p. Includes bibliographic references and indexes. ISBN 0-8018-1845-1.

The aim of this edited volume is to "achieve a synthesis which . . . will reveal general trends or principles that will help us to understand human sexuality, as we know it from personal experience, and as a subject of broad scientific and social significance" (p. 1). Each of the eleven chapters is written by a distinguished specialist on the subject addressed. Two approaches underlie the presentation of information. A cross-sectional, historical view concentrates on "currently observable sexual phenomena." A transtemporal view focuses on questions about how behavior patterns developed to their current form. These approaches complement each other to produce the four perspectives for which the volume is named. The developmental perspective explores the origins of sex differences as well as continuities and discontinuities in sexual development. Milton Diamond's "Human Sexual Development," John Money's "Human Hermaphroditism," and Jerome Kagan's "Psychology of Sex Differences" all address this theme. The sociological perspective examines sexual variations and gender differences within the broad context of social organization. William Davenport's "Sex in Cross-Cultural Perspective," Martin Hoffman's "Homosexuality," and Robert Stoller's "Sexual Deviations" relate to this viewpoint. The physiological perspective concentrates on the contribution that different organic systems (endocrine, nervous, muscular) contribute to patterns of sexual feelings and behavior. Richard Whalen's "Brain Mechanisms Controlling Sexual Behavior," Frank Beach's "Hormonal Control of Sex-Related Behavior," and Frederick Melges and David Hamburg's "Psychological Effects of Hormonal Changes in Women" develop this orientation. Finally, the evolutionary perspective considers the genetic and social processes that resulted in the socialization of sex and the sexualization of society. Frank Beach's chapter, "Cross-Species Comparisons and the Human Heritage" concludes the book on this global theme. Four indexes (subject, author, peoples and cultures, animal species) highlight the interdisciplinary flavor of the volume. (SGF)

IL

125. Calverton, V. F., and Samuel D. Schmalhausen, eds. **Sex in Civilization.** Introduction by Havelock Ellis. Garden City, N.Y.: Garden City, 1929. 709 p. Includes bibliography and index.

The editors of this huge collection of papers on sex in civilization, produced in the late twenties, point out that there has been a growing revolt against civilization ever since the industrial revolution. Part of this revolt has been the contributions to an understanding of the psychology of the individual from Freud, Adler, Jung, Stekel, and others of the psychoanalytic school. However, their contributions to a social understanding of sexual phenomena were negligible. This volume, summarizing the state of knowledge in human sexuality, will not only aid in understanding the individual personality but also "link up the individual to society" by means of addressing the social problems encompassed in this volume. According to Calverton and Schmalhausen, a hypocritical problem—pretense—pervades society in connection with human sexuality. For example, "the failure of the church to treat sex and natural impulse with dignity and candor is the largest single fact in that disintegration of personal codes which confronts us in these hectic times" (p. 11).

The thirty papers in this collection, grouped around six ideas, address pressing sexual problems in modern civilization. Every angle of the present revolt is addressed by knowledgeable people with varied viewpoints. In the introduction, Havelock Ellis expresses enthusiasm for the development of a science of sex, continued psychoanalytic investigations, sex education, the contribution of technology in controlling reproduction through contraception, and further studies of uncivilized peoples. He states that "these social movements and these currents of thought . . . mark Sex in Civilization in our time" (p. 23).

Section 1, Sex Through the Ages, contains papers by Robert Briffault ("Sex in Religion"), Alexander Goldenweiser ("Sex and Primitive Society"), Beatrice Forbes-Robertson Hale ("Women in Transition"), William McDougall ("Should All Taboos Be Abolished?"), Mary Ware Dennett ("Sex Enlightenment for Civilized Youth"), and Charlotte Perkins Gilman ("Sex and Race Progress").

Section 2, The Role of Sex in Behavior, includes papers by Joseph Jastrow ("The Implications of Sex"), A. A. Roback ("Sex in Dynamic Psychology"), Waldo Frank ("Sex Censorship and Democracy"), Judge Ben B. Lindsey ("Wisdom for Parents"), Huntington Cairns ("Sex and the Law"), Arthur Garfield Hays ("The Sexual Factor in Divorce"), and J. William Lloyd ("Sex, Jealousy and Civilization").

In section 3, Sex and Psycho-Sociology, are papers by V. F. Calverton ("Sex and Social Struggle"), Harry Elmer Barnes ("Sex in Education"), and Samuel D. Schmalhausen ("The Sexual Revolution").

Section 4, Sex and Psychoanalysis, has papers by Fritz Wittels ("Narcissism"), Smith Ely Jelliffe ("The Theory of the Libido"), Bernard Glueck ("The Psychoanalytic Approach"), E. Boyd Barrett ("The Psychoanalysis of Asceticism"), and Abraham Myerson ("Freud's Theory of Sex: A Criticism").

Section 5, The Clinical Aspects of Sex, presents papers by Margaret Sanger ("The Civilizing Force of Birth Control"), Phyllis Blanchard ("Sex in the Adolescent Girl"), G. V. Hamilton and Kenneth Macgowan ("Physical Disabilities in Wives"), J. Blake Eggen ("Sex and Insanity"), Ira S. Wile ("Sex and Normal Human Nature"), C. Elizabeth Goldsmith ("Sex Consciousness in the Child"), and William J. Fielding ("The Art of Love").

Finally, in section 6, Sex in Poetry and Fiction, are papers by Arthur Davison Ficke ("Note on the Poetry of Sex") and Robert Morss Lovett ("Sex and the Novel").

All of these contributions provide a comprehensive perspective on the state of sex knowledge in the first quarter of the twentieth century. Biographical sketches of the contributors are included at the end of the volume. (TJW)

PR,IL
126. Chasseguet-Smirgel, Janine. **Female Sexuality: New Psychoanalytic Views.** Foreword by Frederick Wyatt. Ann Arbor, Mich.: University of Michigan Press, 1970. 220 p. First published in 1964. Translation of: *Recherches psychoanalytiques nouvelles sur la sexualité feminine.* Includes bibliographic notes. ISBN 0-472-21900-6.

Originally published in 1964 and compiled by Chasseguet-Smirgel, this book brings together well-known psychoanalysts to investigate the question of female sexuality. Critical of Freud's views on the topic, these authors, according to Chasseguet-Smirgel, "have attempted as far as possible to free their theoretical ideas and their clinical interpretations from the unconscious fantasies which distort scientific objectivity."

Christian David examines masculine myths about femininity, such as "the image of woman as a deficient man" (p. 49). Béla Grunberger provides an outline for a study of narcissism in female sexuality. Catherine Luquet-Parat in "The Change of Object" deals with the Freudian "triple change": change of love object (mother to father), change of erogenous zone (clitoris to vagina), and the change from activity to one of passivity toward the love object (sadism to masochism).

Chasseguet-Smirgel in her paper deals with feminine guilt and the Oedipus complex. She discusses various cases in which "the mother was sadistic and castrating, the father was good and vulnerable" (p. 132). In the Oedipal situation women are conflicted because they need to choose "between mother and husband as the object of dependent attachment" (p. 134). Maria Torok discusses the significance of penis envy in women, hypothesizing female dependence and passivity that "imposes on women the envy of an emblem which serves to conceal her desires" (p. 170). Finally, Joyce McDougall examines homosexuality in women, concluding from her clinical studies that "faced with manifold psychic dangers the young woman thus turns to a homosexual love as a bulwark against them" and that "the price she must pay for her homosexual identity is the renunciation of all feminine sexual desire as well as of the children she unconsciously longs for" (p. 211).

In the foreword Frederick Wyatt presents an overview of the tasks of psychoanalysis in the future, especially in light of "the overwhelming importance of the mother for the personality and later sexual adjustment of the little girl."

Chasseguet-Smirgel is a professor at the Charles-de-Gaulle University in Lille, France. She held the Freud Memorial Chair at University College, London in 1982-83; was president of the Paris Psychoanalytic Society; and in 1988 winner of the Alexander von Humboldt Award for a project on the Nazi way of thinking. (TJW)

PR,IL
127. Cook, Mark, and Glenn Wilson, eds. **Love and Attraction: An International Conference.** Oxford: Pergamon Press, 1979. 554 p. Includes bibliographic references and index. ISBN 0-08-022234-X.

Impressed by the great variety of work being conducted in different countries, Cook and Wilson convened the International Conference on Love and Attraction, held at Swansea, Wales, in the summer of 1977. The published proceedings present some eighty papers on different aspects of human sexuality. These studies are contributions from an international group of psychologists, sociologists, anthropologists, biologists, psychiatrists, and other specialists from the United Kingdom, the United States, Canada, West Germany, Ghana, Sweden, Norway, the Netherlands, and Australia. Organized into twelve sections, each consisting of from four to eleven papers, the volume covers the following topics: physical attractiveness; nonverbal intimacy, attraction and friendship; mate selection; marital relations; romantic love; exchange theory applications to love and attraction; the social psychology of human sexuality; sexual behavior and society; sex therapy; erotica and arousal; infant and child sexuality; and pedophilia. Emphasizing attraction as it relates to love/sex, the research papers and theoretical speculations, together and individually, provide both the professional and the interested layperson with diverse perspectives about human sexual behavior. (TJW)

PR,IL
128. Freud, Sigmund. **Sexuality and the Psychology of Love.** With an introduction by the editor, Philip Rieff. New York: Collier Books, 1963. 223 p.
       Rieff, professor of sociology at the University of Pennsylvania, presents in this collection eighteen papers on sexuality by Sigmund Freud. Written between 1905 and 1938, they add to and expand Freud's ideas presented in *Three Essays on the Theory of Sexuality*. Indeed, the first paper, "My Views on the Part Played by Sexuality in the Aetiology of the Neuroses" (1905) was written shortly after *Three Essays* and relates closely to it.
       The 1908 polemical essay, " 'Civilized' Sexual Morality and Modern Nervousness" asserts the popular "frustration" theory of culture and neurosis. This theory is carried forward by the next paper, "Types of Neurotic Nosogenesis" (1912), where it may be termed "repression." These papers are followed by three contributions to the psychology of love, again stressing the tension between culture and natural man: "A Special Type of Object Choice Made by Men" (1010); "The Most Prevalent Form of Degradation in Erotic Life" (1912); and "The Taboo of Virginity" (1918). "The Predisposition to Obsessional Neurosis" (1913) is representative of Freud's writing on the phases through which the sexual instinct passes on its way to genitality.
       Freud deals with homosexuality in "A Case of Paranoia Running Counter to the Psychoanalytical Theory of the Disease" (1915) and in "The Psychogenesis of a Case of Homosexuality in a Woman" (1920), which shed some light on sexuality in women and directed attention to the universal bisexuality of human beings. Further discussion of homosexuality is found in "Certain Neurotic Mechanisms in Jealousy, Paranoia, and Homosexuality" (1922).
       In the classic essay, "A Child Is Being Beaten" (1919), Freud notes that infantile sexuality, under repression, "acts as the chief motive force in the formation of symptoms." "The Infantile Genital Organization of the Libido" (1923) supplements Freud's theory of sexuality.
       Two papers, "The Passing of the Oedipus-Complex" (1924) and "Some Psychological Consequences of the Anatomical Distinction Between the Sexes" (1925), contain brief explanations of comparative sexual development. Insights into the "mystery" of women may be found in the essay "Female Sexuality" (1931). Problems in the psychopathology of love and sexuality are discussed in the final essays: "Medusa's Head" (1922), that concerns castration; "Fetishism" (1927); and "Splitting of the Ego in the Defensive Process" (1938). (TJW)

PR
129. Geer, James H., and William T. O'Donohue, eds. **Theories of Human Sexuality.** New York: Plenum Press, 1987. 428 p. (Perspectives in Sexuality: Behavior, Research, and Therapy). Includes bibliographies and index. ISBN 0-306-42459-2.
       The editors of this collection of papers include fourteen selected approaches to the study of human sexuality for this volume in the Perspectives in Sexuality series. The diversity of these contributions stems from the fact that human sexuality is a multidisciplinary field deriving sustenance from anthropology, biology, history, psychology, religion, sociology, and other fields. The authors of these papers include leading contributors and proponents of these theoretical approaches.

Geer and O'Donohue's introduction claims that the collection "provides the broadest overview of sexuality presently available to the student of human sexuality." They point out that despite the great diversity in points of view taken by the authors, there emerges a high degree of compatibility that "allows interdisciplinary questions to be framed and studied." They further note that human sexuality has an ethical dimension that investigators must keep in mind.

Following the introduction, Geoffrey Parrinder "examines the relationships between religious faith and experience, and human sexuality." He raises the interesting question of the sexual nature of God, and describes the nature of theological inquiry into sex. Then Vern Bullough in "A Historical Approach" presents "a history of attitudes and beliefs about sex, rather than a history of sexual behavior *per se.*" Catherine A. MacKinnon follows with "A Feminist/Political Approach," arguing that "what men want sexually is women violated, women degraded, women tortured and killed." Donald Symons "examines the kinds of questions an evolutionary perspective on human behavior can address." Alphonso Lingis looks at the views of Sartre, Merleau-Ponty, and others in regard to a phenomenological approach to human sexuality. Lisa A. Serbin and Carol H. Sprafkin describe a developmental approach to sexuality from infancy through adolescence. William H. Davenport reviews work by anthropologists concerning sexuality, focusing on descriptive and comparative kinds of studies. The sociological approach is examined by John DeLamater who maintains that patterns of sexual behavior exist within every society. Soviet scholar Igor Kon reviews the literature from a wide range of human sciences in disclosing the sociocultural approach to the study of human sexuality. Nathaniel McConaghy reviews different learning approaches (conditioning theory, behaviorism, psychoanalysis, etc.) as they apply to specific areas of sexuality. Susan R. Walen and David Roth in "A Cognitive Approach" review the "major extant models of cognitive functioning and argue for the importance of cognitive processes in influencing sexual arousal and behavior." Professors William Simon and John H. Gagnon in their paper "A Sexual Scripts Approach" maintain that much of human sexual behavior can be understood from the perspectives of cultural scenarios, interpersonal scripts, and intrapsychic scripts. Ethel Spector Person examines Freud's theories of sex and their implications for a theory of personality and neurosis and reviews neo-Freudian critiques and revisions of Freud's original proposals. Finally, John Bancroft in "A Physiological Approach" looks at the role of hormones in human sexual behavior.

Absent from this compilation are approaches that do not derive from any theory of sexuality, e.g., that of Kinsey, described here as an actuarial approach; and that of Masters and Johnson, viewed here as dealing with a very limited aspect of human sexuality, a practical set of therapeutic procedures for the treatment of sexual problems. (TJW)

PR

130. International Congress of Medical Sexology, 3rd, Rome, 1978. **Medical Sexology.** Edited by Romano Forleo and Willy Pasini. Littleton, Mass.: PSG Publishing Co., 1980. 644 p. Includes bibliographies. ISBN 0-88416-255-9.

The third International Congress of Medical Sexology had over 300 presentations; 103 of them are presented in this volume. Editors Forleo and Pasini state that the second congress held in Montreal in 1976 established sexology as an interdisciplinary science while this third congress "resulted in a better synthesis between different cultures, philosophies, and disciplines," and "a movement full of interrogation rather than positive statements was noticed."

The 103 essentially empirical presentations include the research of such well-known figures as John Money, Richard Green, Erwin J. Haeberle, Wardell Pomeroy, Shere Hite, Glenn D. Wilson, Mary C. Calderone, Heino F. L. Meyer-Bahlburg, Joseph Shepher, Benjamin Graber, Georgia Kline-Graber, and others. The presentations are organized into thirteen subject areas: "Ethics and Sexuality" (seven papers); "Philosophic Views on Sex" (nine papers); "Sociology and Anthropology of Sexual Behavior" (ten papers); "Endocrinology and Sex Research" (seven papers); "Clinical Sexology" (eleven papers); "Homosexuality and Sexual Identity" (seven papers); "Sexuality and

Reproductive Life Events" (nine papers); "Sexuality and Aging" (three papers); "Sexuality and Disability" (four papers); "Sexuality and the Law" (five papers); "Sex Education" (eleven papers); the psychologic approach to "Sex Therapy" (fifteen papers); and the somatic approach to "Sex Therapy" (five papers).

The names of all contributors with their affiliations are listed in the front of the volume; unfortunately there is no index to this significant contribution to the field of sexology. It is also somewhat puzzling as to why this conference was titled Medical Sexology inasmuch as the approach seems to be highly interdisciplinary with discussions of sexual behavior, morality, law, and education. (TJW)

PR,IL
131. Jeffreys, Sheila, ed. **The Sexuality Debates.** New York: Routledge & Kegan Paul, 1987. 632 p. (Women's Source Library). Includes index. ISBN 0-7102-0936-3.

Drawing on pamphlets and papers from the Fawcett Library, the principal women's archive in Great Britain, Jeffreys has selected writings that impart some of the flavor of attitudes toward sexuality from the 1870s to the 1920s. Part one includes source material from nineteenth century male doctors whose opinions are presented as indicators of more widespread male beliefs about female sexuality. For example, clitoridectomies were thought to "cure" masturbation and prevent epilepsy. Part two focuses on writings associated with feminist campaigns around sexuality: attempts to repeal the Contagious Diseases Acts of the 1860s, that permitted police to subject women to examinations if they were suspected of prostitution; efforts to develop organizations promoting "social purity," struggles to obtain voting privileges for women, partly so that they could more effectively combat domestic violence and the sexual abuse of women and children. The last section deals with issues of feminism, sexuality, and the impact of sexual reform. The sex reform movement in Great Britain in the 1890s fanned the ire of feminists. Notions that men are innately aggressive and sadistic and that women are passive and masochistic or that infrequent sexual intercourse (heterosexual) would lead to illness did little to free women from what they regarded as male concepts of sexuality.

These documents show that there was considerable resistance to male interpretations of sexuality, even during times of Victorian "prudery." Jeffreys comments that the "period covered by the papers in this collection was a hugely important watershed period in the history of sexuality." She points out that the path to sexual freedom has not been a smooth one. At the turn of the century feminists analyzed the contribution of sex and role to women's oppression and tried to change male sexual behavior. She also notes that the new science of sexology and the sex reform movement were "hostile to feminism, women's independence, and self-determination." (SGF)

PR
132. Karasu, Toksoz B., and Charles W. Socarides, eds. **On Sexuality: Psychoanalytic Observations.** New York: International Universities Press, 1979. 412 p. Includes bibliography and indexes. ISBN 0-8236-3857-X.

Intended for psychoanalysts, psychiatrists, and other behavioral scientists, this collection of seventeen state-of-the-art papers presents developments in human sexuality from the psychoanalytic point of view. In the main, the authors are psychiatrists and psychoanalysts specializing in such diverse areas as infantile sexuality, adolescence, sexual perversions, education, sex therapy, and history. The editors believe that "sexual behavior is primarily a motivated field, and motivational analysis supplied by psychoanalysis is the only method by which science can reach the whole individual on the behavior level" (p. vii).

Recognizing the stages in the development of sexuality as the cornerstone of psychoanalytic theory, the editors give the lead paper to Eleanor Galenson and Herman Roiphe, who report on sex differences in infants during the second year of life. Then Aaron Esman writes about the impact of sexuality on adolescents; Irwin Marcus expresses his analysis-derived views on masturbation; Nathaniel Ross expands on the significance of infantile sexuality and intimacy in humans and animals; Edith Buxbaum deals with psychobiological events following birth in both mother and child; and John M. Ross explains the relatively neglected area of paternity.

Arno Karlen, who believes that the West remains uncomfortable about sexual activity, provides a panoramic view of sexual attitudes in history. Stuart A. Waltzman and Toksoz B. Karasu spell out the vicissitudes of sexuality in old age; three papers from the pens of Charles W. Socarides writing on theory, Vamik D. Volkan examining transsexualism, and Milton E. Jacovy exploring transvestitism convey an understanding of sexual perversions. Robert Dickes writes about the impact of the "New Sexuality" on psychiatric education; and Jules Glenn, Harvey B. Bezahler, and Sylvia Glenn describe a psychoanalytically-based education program for children. In her paper, Virginia L. Clower defends Freudian psychology of women. William A. Frosch, George L. Ginsberg, and Theodore Shapiro discuss impotence in light of the "New Sexuality." Edward M. Levine examines the consequences of accepting perversions as simply alternative life-styles. Finally, Toksoz B. Karasu, Maj-Britt Rosenbaum, and Inez Jerrett provide an overview of sex therapies in the United States.

The editors voice the hope that their examination of psychoanalytic perspectives "will lead to maturation, improvement, and healthy change, both for the individual and for society" (p. xi). (TJW)

IL

133.   Kaufman, Michael, ed. **Beyond Patriarchy: Essays by Men on Pleasure, Power, and Change.** Toronto: Oxford University Press, 1987. 322 p. Includes bibliographic notes. ISBN 0-19-540534-X.

Claiming motivation from the feminist movement, the authors of the papers in this collection, academics from Australia, Canada, England, and the United States, examine the institution of patriarchy, focusing on the structures of men's power and domination over women both at the individual level and at the social, political, economic, and ideological levels. Because the social structures of oppression and power are individually internalized, the authors admit to being influenced by patriarchal ideology and regimens, including "the nuclear family, the organization of working life, our conceptions of science, the prohibitions on homosexuality, sports, advertising, films, and political structures."

Part one, "Masculinity, Sexuality and Society," presents eight papers, including a lead paper by the Kaufman on "the individual construction of masculinity, that is, the manner in which patriarchy is developed and expressed within individual men and, more generally, within social structures." Then anthropologists Richard Lee and Richard Daly point out that patriarchy emerged as a coherent and dominant system only with the rise of state societies. Carmen Schifellite challenges the conclusions of sociobiologists that exaggerate the importance of physical differences in the sexes, and Tony Rotundo examines the continuing evolution of the institution of fatherhood in the United States. Gad Horowitz and Michael Kaufman apply psychoanalytic theory to the theory of male sexuality and its expression in male dominated societies. Gary Kinsman looks at homosexuality as a rather recent creation and raises the question of same-sex love as a universal possibility. Seymour Kleinberg describes the new masculinity of gay men and the constraints to gay male identity resulting from the AIDS epidemic. Finally, a review of the 1970's men's literature by Tim Carrigan, Bob Connell, and John Lee attempts to set a standard for the critical examination of such literature.

Part two, "Men, Work, and Cultural Life," presents seven papers on particular fields in which patriarchy prevails. Brian Easlea, a physicist, presents a history of the evolution of modern sciences with emphasis on the patriarchal assumptions and images intrinsic to nuclear physics. Based on personal experience as a shop steward at a Westinghouse plant, Stan Gray presents "a provocative exploration of the connection between the class oppression of male workers and their own oppressive behavior towards women." Michael Kimmel explains the "cult of masculinity in politics and society in the United States, from the contras to the cowboys." Bruce Kidd, a former Olympian, demonstrates the links between sports and patriarchy. Film critic Robin Wood explores the homosexual subtext in Hollywood films. In an original look at advertising, one of the most manipulative structures in our society, Andrew Wernick shows the flexibility of the dominant conceptions and portrayals of masculinity. Finally, Peter Fitting examines the images of men and women presented in the feminist utopian literature since the 1960s, thus providing a glimpse of a world freed of exploitation and oppression. (TJW)

IL

134. Kirkendall, Lester A., and Robert N. Whitehurst, eds. **The New Sexual Revolution.** With a preface by Paul Kurtz. Buffalo, N.Y.: Prometheus Books, 1972. 236 p. Includes bibliography.

All of the contributors to this collection of papers responded positively to the requests from Paul Kurtz, editor of *The Humanist*, and the editors of the present volume, to present their thoughts on the humanistic revolution reshaping America's sexual attitudes and behavior. Rejecting traditional Judeo-Christian sexual beliefs as based on myth and illusion, the contributors explore various areas of sexuality in search of a secular system to replace authoritarian standards "with roles intelligently developed from within human experience in terms of actual human needs and desires" (p. x). They accept the propositions that human happiness is the goal of man, that sexual enjoyment is a significant part of human happiness, and that sex should be approached not with fear or guilt but with openness and receptiveness. Although demanding reforms in existing laws affecting such issues as abortion, prostitution, homosexuality, and the like, the humanists insist on sexual responsibility grounded in rationally achieved conclusions.

Background papers to this interdisciplinary collection are provided by Robert W. Whitehurst, who examines the historical basis of American sexophobia; Herb Seal, who looks at cross-cultural sexual practices in the world to show the wide choice of alternatives of sexual behavior; and Wesley J. Adams, who discusses evolving sexual ethics within a democratic society as affected by the Kinsey findings and more recent investigations. Albert Ellis presents his ideas in "A Rational Sexual Morality" by advancing various propositions and rules of sexual conduct as components of an ethical code.

As contributions to understanding human sexuality, Leon Salzman writes about the proliferation of sex research since the Kinsey Reports; Walter R. Stokes examines current thinking in regard to autoerotic behavior; and Donald Cantor gives a status report on the homosexual revolution. Cultural problems are explored by Charles Winick in his paper on the decline in libido, the depolarization of sex, the widespread voyeurism throughout society, and the impact of genetic engineering; and by Edward Sagarin, who examines the issues of obscenity and pornography.

Luther G. Baker, Jr. probes the problem of single women in society, and Rustum Roy and Della Roy raise the question "Is Monogamy Outdated?" Sex education receives astute treatment from Lester A. Kirkendall in his paper and from Winfield W. Salisbury and Frances F. Salisbury in their paper, "Youth and the Search for Intimacy."

Finally, a section on population growth contains a paper by Edward Pohlman on contraception, one on the compatibility of population control and personal freedom by Alice Taylor Day, and one on sterilization by Garrett Hardin. Kirkendall concludes this volume by raising a host of questions concerning sex that need to be answered, and by emphasizing the desirability of the humanistic approach as exemplified by the papers presented in this collection. (TJW)

PR,IL

135. Kirkpatrick, Martha, ed. **Women's Sexual Experience: Explorations of the Dark Continent.** New York: Plenum Press, 1982. 328 p. (Women in Context: Development and Stresses). Includes bibliographic references and index. ISBN 0-306-40793-0.

Like its companion volume, *Women's Sexual Development*, this collection is a "potpourri of ideas, not campaign literature to promote a particular point of view." Its intent, according to Kirkpatrick, is "to evoke questions, delay convictions, invite controversy, and plead for opening minds." The collection is divided into two parts: part I contains five papers on the general condition of women's sexuality, while the ten papers in part II examine its special circumstances.

In the tone-setting first paper, Helen S. Kaplan and Erica Sucher describe the normal sexual development and responses of women based on current knowledge; this is followed by one paper on the sexual experience of Afro-American women and another on the sexual consequences of acculturation of American Indian women. A paper by Lillian B. Rubin on the sex and sexuality of women at mid-life, and another by B. Genevay in praise of older women, suggest that sex improves with age.

The first two contributions in part II deal with aspects of incest. In her paper on incest as the cradle of sexual politics, Louise Armstrong, the author of the popular book *Kiss Daddy Goodnight*, wonders about the "powerful need on the part of so many men to preserve the permission to exploit their children sexually." Roland Summit, in his paper on the reluctant discovery of incest, examines such aspects of incest as recognition, frequency, and treatment.

A series of four papers deals with the effects of teenage motherhood, the maturity of adolescent mothers, the impact of pregnancy on female sexuality, and factors affecting voluntary childlessness. Another series of papers on different aspects of female sexual experience follows. Lloyd M. Levin writes about the swinging lifestyle of some women; Jennifer James views the prostitute as a victim of various legal and social forces; and Edward M. Brecher writes about women as victims in society's efforts to cope with the problem of venereal disease.

Most of the papers in this collection are followed by stimulating comments from experts who may agree or disagree with the ideas presented in the main papers. (TJW)

IL,PO

136. McDermott, John Francis, ed. **The Sex Problem in Modern Society: An Anthology.** New York: Modern Library, 1931. 404 p. Includes bibliographic footnotes.

Intended for the lay reader, this selection of twenty-six papers clustered around eight broad headings presents diverse, often conflicting viewpoints on each of these facets of sex as they were perceived at the time. The distinguished authors express the state of thinking about sexuality during the first part of the twentieth century.

Essays by Bertrand Russell, Edward Sapir, and George Jean Nathan provide three perspectives on the ethics of sex; and Jacques Fischer, Samuel D. Schmalhausen, and Alfred Adler look at the psychology of sex from different sides. Havelock Ellis, Grace Potter, and Dora Russell provide three papers on the interrelationship of love and sex. Robert H. Lowie, Will Durant, Ben B. Lindsey and Wainright Evans, and V. F. Calverton present in their essays four views on different aspects of marriage. In their papers, Edward M. East, Franz Boaz, and Andre Siegfried deal with heredity, race, and eugenics. The problem of birth control receives attention from Margorie Wells, Margaret Sanger, Charles F. Potter, and Henry K. Norton. Joseph Collins, Phyllis Blanchard, and C. G. Jung focus their articles on the love and sex problems of adolescents. Finally, V. F. Calverton, Robert Herrick, Morris L. Ernst, and William Seagle deal with the treatment of sex in literature.

McDermott thinks that these papers help summarize the new twentieth-century openness about sex that contrasts with the attitudes and beliefs prevalent in the nineteenth century. (TJW)

PR

137. Money, John. **Venuses Penuses: Sexology, Sexosophy, and Exigency Theory.** Buffalo, N.Y.: Prometheus Books, 1986. 659 p. Includes bibliography. ISBN 0-87975-327-7.

This is a collection of forty-eight papers written by Money between 1948, when he published his first paper, and 1985. Divided into five parts, it reflects the evolution of his thinking and research on a diversity of topics centered around his human clinical and longitudinal research done at Johns Hopkins University's Psychohormonal Research

Unit, which he directs. Also included are papers he has written on aspects of sexology, sexosophy, and the exigency theory.

The material is grouped under five headings: "Research Theory and Design" (ten papers), "Gender Identity/Role Differentiation" (nine papers), "Homosexual/Bisexual/Heterosexual Gender Status" (eight papers), "Transsexualism and Paraphilia" (seven papers), and "Sexology and Sexosophy: Principles and Polemics" (fourteen papers).

An extensive bibliography of Money's work, including books; scientific papers; reviews; encyclopedia and textbook chapters; brief communications, abstracts, teaching notes; editorials and letters to the editor; book reviews; republications and translations; and films and tapes makes up a large section at the back of the book.

As a prologue, Money includes a professional biography outlining his educational career, research interests, achievements, and philosophical orientation. (TJW)

PR,IL

138. Peiss, Kathy, and Christina Simmons, eds. **Passion and Power: Sexuality in History.** Philadelphia: Temple University Press, 1989. 319 p. (Critical Perspectives on the Past). Includes bibliographic notes. ISBN 0-87722-596-6.

The contributors to this collection, especially editors Peiss and Simmons, along with Robert A. Padgug, conceive of sexuality as a separate entity with its own history but embedded in political, social, economic, and cultural conditions. In part I, "Sexuality and Historical Meaning," Peiss and Simmons state that as a result of the gay liberation movement and the feminist movement in the 1960s and 1970s, "older essentialist categories of sexual behavior and identity have been exploded" (p. 4), and are being replaced by newer sexual meanings and understanding. Padgug's essay, reprinted from a 1979 issue of *Radical History Review*, provides a Marxist approach to human sexuality. He states that biological sex is but a limiting precondition of human sexuality. A definition of sexuality must take into account its connection with such cultural entities as politics and the economy.

In part II, "The Emergence of Modern Sexuality, 1790-1930," the first paper, by Marybeth Hamilton Arnold, concerns sexual assault cases in New York City, giving the perspectives of both the victims and the male rapists and showing that the concerns of women were not their helplessness and virtue but rather their future ability to carry on in a competitive world. Editor Peiss's paper is about working-class sexuality, especially the way the so-called "charity girls," a class of urban white women in New York City, traded sexual favors for a good time. Jeffrey Weeks examines the various meanings that have historically been given to homosexuality and the recent emergence of the homosexual identity. Then George Chauncey, Jr. shows how homosexuality came to be distinguished from sexual inversion by the medical profession. The next paper describes the Heterodoxy Club of Greenwich Village, New York, that during its thirty-year history, beginning in 1912, was a forum for independent women who promoted feminist political and social issues, including challenges to sexual and gender roles. Photographs of some twenty-five heterodites accompany this essay. Jessie M. Rodrique's paper concerns the black community and the birth control movement in America.

Part III, "Sexual Conflicts and Cultural Authority, 1930-1960," consists of editor Simmons's paper on the contrast between Victorian morality and the new sexual morality as epitomized by the flapper; Elizabeth Fee's paper on the cultural aspects of venereal disease in Baltimore, Maryland; Estelle B. Freedman's paper on the transformation of "the psychopath into a violent, male, sexual criminal," that occurred during the 1930s, "when American criminologists became increasingly interested in sexual abnormality and male sexual crime"; and finally two essays on homosexuality: John D'Emilio's paper on the targeting of homosexuals and lesbians in the 1950s that, ironically, resulted in the forging of the gay liberation movement of the 1960s; and Elizabeth Lapovsky Kennedy and Madeline Davis's paper, documenting the political and social evolution of a working-class lesbian community, that focuses on an explanation of butch-fem roles from 1930 to 1965.

In part IV, "Private Passions and Public Debates, 1960 to the Present," Ann Barr Snitow addresses pornography for women as offered by mass market romances, such as the Harlequin romance novels; and Daphne Read writes about the construction of the anti-pornography views of radical feminists and the deconstruction of those views by a critical analysis of the film *Not a Love Story*. Finally, Robert A. Padgug writes about the impact of AIDS on the gay community and the restructuring of gay sexuality.

In the words of editor Peiss, "The essays in this volume, taken together, explore the way that sexuality has increasingly become a core element of modern social identity, constitutive of being, consciousness, and action" (p. 4). (TJW)

PR,IL

139. Sadock, Benjamin J., Harold I. Kaplan, and Alfred M. Freedman, eds. **The Sexual Experience.** Baltimore, Md.: Williams & Wilkins, 1976. 666 p. Includes bibliographies and index. ISBN 0-683-03374-3.

Intended for professionals as well as intelligent laypersons and students, this comprehensive, in-depth survey of sexuality consists of fifty papers, most of which were selected from *Comprehensive Textbook of Psychiatry-II*, covering "sex and sexual behavior from the historical, developmental, biological, functional, and social points of view" (p. v). The editors (three psychiatrists) believe that there is a "need for a book of this type, one that would provide a thorough overview of the field and one that sex trainees from various walks of life—medicine, clergy, nursing, social work, and psychology, among others—would find useful" (p. vi). Organized into twenty-four chapters, the text attempts to present "all the facts relating to normal and abnormal sexuality" and to review "various hypotheses and speculations relevant to the goal of sexual enrichment." Following an introductory chapter explaining concerns about sexuality, chapter 2 reviews the history of sex and sex research; chapter 3 explores the anatomy and physiological mechanisms of sexuality; chapter 4 covers the stages of sexual development; chapter 5 discusses sexual identity and sex role behavior; chapter 6 examines the techniques of coitus; and chapters 7 through 11 describe sexual behavior in relation to marriage and divorce, embracing premarital and extramarital intercourse. Transitional chapter 12 covers cross-cultural studies and animal studies of sex as well as the sociocultural roles of male and female, and chapter 13 covers many aspects of sex and medicine (surgery, illness, venereal diseases, drugs, contraception, and abortion). Chapter 14 explores sexual behavior and mental illness; chapter 15 examines different aspects of sexual variations and disorders (homosexuality, frigidity, dyspareunia, vaginismus, impotence, incest, etc.); chapter 16 covers various methods and aspects of treating sexual disorders; chapter 17 turns to a discussion of sex education; and chapters 18 through 23 embrace the relationships between cultural institutions (the arts, the law, marriage and divorce, pornography and prostitution, religion) and the sexual experience. Finally, a last chapter extensively reviews the women's movement and its profound effect upon men and women as well as society as a whole. (TJW)

IL,PO

140. Steinberg, David, ed. **The Erotic Impulse: Honoring the Sensual Self.** New York: Jeremy P. Tarcher, 1992. 312 p. ISBN 0-87477-697-X.

Some fifty contributions from as many contributors comprise this collection of papers and poems on various aspects of the erotic impulse. Such names as Summer Brenner, Jack Morin, Rollo May, and others make up part one, "The Nature of the Erotic Impulse." It provides an overview and introduction to the subsequent sections, that explore more specific aspects of erotic expression. Poems by Allen Ginsberg and James Broughton close out this part.

Part two, "Erotic Initiation and Passage," allows such well-known writers as Lonnie Barbach, Henry Miller, Gore Vidal, and others to disclose their introductions to the world of sex. The two poems ending this section are by James Joyce and e. e. cummings.

In part three, "The Erotic Imagination," Camille Paglia, Richard Goldstein, and others give their views on the erotic eye, pornography, erotic art, and other topics. Short statements on the sexual components in erotica are given by such well-known writers, photographers, poets, and artists as Lucien Clergue, Tee Corinne, Henry Miller, Anne Rice, and Marco Vassi.

Part four, "Erotic Differences Between Men and Women," offers papers by Anaïs Nin, Susie Bright, Nancy Friday, and others, and poems by Robert Bly and Carolyn Kleefeld revealing varied aspects of sex differences.

In part five, "The Suppression and Denial of Eros," authors Robert T. Francoeur, Marty Klein, Carol Cassell, Carole S. Vance, and others delve into such topics as religious suppression of sex, erotophobia, "good" girls, sexual politics, dirty talk, etc. It concludes with the poem "Us" by Anne Sexton.

Part six, "Erotic Frontiers," features writers Betty Dodson, Carol A. Queen, and others who describe the delights of masturbation, sadomasochism, and homosexuality.

In part seven, "Erotic Transcendence and Self-discovery," Kevin Regan, Margo Anand, Robert Bly, and others explore conjugal love, tantrism, lovemaking, and praise eros in poetry.

In the epilogue, editor Steinberg calls upon the readers of this book to recognize the world of eros, to use these writings "to help unravel the erotic tangle we find around us" (p. 302). (TJW)

PO

141. Steinem, Gloria. **Outrageous Acts and Everyday Rebellions.** New York: Holt, Rinehart and Winston, 1983. 370 p. Includes index. ISBN 0-03-063236-6.

Steinem, one of America's leading feminists, cofounder of *Ms.* magazine, and an active journalist, has put together this collection of her best writings. Most of the articles have appeared in the popular press and all of them relate to the basic theme of addressing women's concerns in the modern world and elucidating the real meaning of a feminist perspective that balances the full equality and humanity of both men and women. Those that relate most closely to aspects of human sexuality include "I Was a Playboy Bunny" (1983); "In Praise of Women's Bodies" (1981); "Transsexualism" (1977); "Erotica vs. Pornography" (1977-78); "Marilyn Monroe: The Woman Who Died Too Soon" (1972); "The Real Linda Lovelace" (1980); "The International Crime of Genital Mutilation" (1979); and "If Men Could Menstruate" (1978). One essay, "Ruth's Song (Because She Could Not Sing It)" depicts Steinem's life with her mother. The introductory and final chapters give fascinating details about her role as an organizer in the feminist movement and her efforts on behalf of the ERA. (TJW)

PR,IL

142. Stimpson, Catherine R., and Ethel Spector Person, eds. **Women: Sex and Sexuality.** Chicago: University of Chicago Press, 1980. 345 p. Includes bibliographic footnotes and index. ISBN 0-226-77477-5.

The twenty-two essays and review articles in this collection originally appeared in the summer and autumn 1980 issues of *Signs: Journal of Women in Culture and Society.* The editors of this summing-up of the thought and research on female sexuality at the end of the 1970s believe that human sexuality is embedded with meaning and involves the exploration of social and symbolic constructions of what seems natural; it "follows certain development patterns . . . responds to the mediation of culture" (p. 1). Therefore, the study of female sexuality is an interdisciplinary field and "no single perspective, no single discipline, can do intellectual justice to it" (p. 2). The articles begin with Elizabeth Janeway's tone-setting paper on the loss of sexual paradigms (in the sense Thomas Kuhn used that term) in modern society; Alix Kates Shulman's review of feminist accomplishments in the women's liberation movement from 1967 to 1980; and Ethel Spector Person's examination of psychoanalytic paradigms (Freud's libido theory and the appetitional theory of sexual motivation) and their import for a theory of female sexuality. More specific themes are taken up in later papers: lesbianism, reproductive freedom, menstruation and reproduction, pornography, and prostitution. Several papers review biological aspects of female sexuality, such as Susan W.

Baker's "Biological Influences on Human Sex and Gender" and Madeleine Goodman's "Toward a Biology of Menopause." Genres of literature dealing with female sexuality are reviewed by Ann Barr Snitow (sex novels by women, 1969-1979) and Ellen Ross (couples advice books in the late 1970s). Critical reviews of four books (*Homosexuality in Perspective*, by William H. Masters and Virginia E. Johnson; *The Hosken Report: Genital and Sexual Mutilation of Females*, by Fran P. Hosken; *Sexual Excitement*, by Robert J. Stoller; and *The History of Sexuality*. Vol. 1, *An Introduction*, by Michel Foucault) are provided. Finally, in an archives section two curious documents are included. One is a "set of letters from a young working-class woman to a psychiatrist" that describes her struggle with masochistic and lesbian tendencies. The other is the revelation by a Polish priest of the confessed sexual problems of women and how he advised them in line with the Church's doctrines. These latter papers represent responses by powerful institutions to female sexuality. (TJW)

7

Surveys & Statistical Works

(For related material see also entries 392a, 458, 500a)

PR,IL,PO

143. Blumstein, Philip, and Pepper Schwartz. **American Couples: Money, Work, Sex.** New York: Morrow, 1983. 656 p. Includes index. ISBN 0-688-03772.

Blumstein and Schwartz, both of whom have doctorates in sociology and teach at the University of Washington, depart from the usual emphasis on married couples to explore the nature of different types of American couples from several vantage points, including statistics and in-depth interviews. By encompassing cohabitors, marrieds, and homosexuals in their study they tap into a "naturally occurring experiment." The contrast between marrieds and cohabitors allows them to analyze the effect of marriage on heterosexual couples; the comparison of homosexuals with heterosexuals helps them examine how a couple operates when they don't have to deal with male/female differences; a gay/lesbian contrast allows an exploration of differences in the male/female contribution to relationships. Blumstein and Schwartz try to go beyond description and determine why people make the choices they do. Given their interest in the dynamics of decision making between partners, they chose to focus on three critical issues faced by all couples: work, money, and sex. They facilitate an understanding of their results in each topic area by setting off the major findings in italics and summarizing the results for each subgroup in bar graphs. The first two chapters provide a clear context for the rest of the book: one succinctly describes how the research was done and the second provides a fascinating historical perspective on the American couple. The first three sections focus on the issues of money, work, and sex. The epilogue discusses the importance of these issues from another perspective: who broke up and why. The next major portion of the book ("Couples' Lives") presents qualitative descriptions of five couples from each of the four types in the book.

The data for the book are based on a careful research design that taps quantitative and qualitative aspects of relationships. Blumstein and Schwartz tried to draw a large sample that avoided systematic bias. The 22,000 copies of the thirty-eight-page questionnaire on all aspects of a couple's life were distributed to a broad geographical range of respondents. They received 12,000 usable questionnaires returned by both partners in a relationship in which they lived together at least four days a week, had sex at some time in their relationship, and regarded themselves as a couple. Three hundred in-depth interviews at the couples' homes supplemented the questionnaire data. This well-written, thoughtful volume sets out a number of provocative questions, sifts through the data in a humanistic way, and provides sound information for reflection about the major issues that face all couples today. (SGF)

IL,PO

144. Brecher, Edward M. **Love, Sex, and Aging: A Consumers Union Report.** Boston: Little, Brown, 1984. 441 p. Includes index. ISBN 0-316-10718-2.

Misconceptions about love and sex after fifty abound. Many people share the view that older individuals lead frustrated or nonexistent sex lives. This belief is the product of a negative perception of aging that associates the process with social isolation, chronic illness, and general unhappiness. This book tries to correct many of these myths by using survey data as a basis for describing what the later years are really like. As one respondent put it, "Let us silver-haired sirens out of the closet! We have a lot to 'show and tell' the world" (p. 21). Out of 9,800 questionnaires sent to the readers of *Consumer Reports* and their friends and relatives, 4,246 were returned in usable form. The respondents exceed the size of Kinsey's sample of people between fifty and eighty and make up one of the largest geriatric samples for a sexuality study of the "mature years." The final questionnaire included sixty-four "objective" questions about background, health, opinions about a variety of contemporary sexual practices, friendship, love, and sexuality; fourteen of these issues were highlighted for further comments at the end of the questionnaire. Four essay questions concluded the questionnaire. Questions primarily dealt with preferences, opinions, and desires about love and sex, both past and present. The findings demonstrate that people over fifty are a diverse group who are involved in a variety of lifestyles, are often very happy, are sexually active, and are participants in the "sexual revolution."

Part 1 focuses on general aspects of the lives of married and unmarried people over fifty—sexual and nonsexual factors that contribute to life enjoyment. Topics include marital fidelity, satisfaction with sexual practices and frequency, loneliness, living arrangements, masturbation, and homosexual relationships, to name a few. Part 2 deals with the ways in which human sexuality changes in the later years: how attitudes and activities have departed from Victorian sexual options, how health relates to sexual activity, how menopause and postmenopausal hormone therapy affect behavior, and how respondents compensate for sexual changes as they age. This informative, well-written book aims to clarify readers' thoughts and feelings about love and sex in an effort to accurately describe options open to people in their later years. (SGF)

IL
145.   Coles, Robert, and Geoffrey Stokes. **Sex and the American Teenager.** New York: Harper & Row, 1985. 238 p. Includes index. ISBN 0-06-096002-7.

Distinguished psychiatrist and author, Coles teams up with journalist Stokes to provide a clearly written, sympathetic profile of a generation that could be called "the children of the children of Woodstock." They focus on two main questions about teenage sex: What do kids do? and How do they feel about it? The findings described in the book are based on 50,000 pages of transcribed interviews, academic and clinical experience, and the results of a *Rolling Stone* survey (containing 358 variables) of 1,067 teenagers who are members of varied types of households that are statistically representative of the U.S. population. Stokes claims that it is "the most accurate picture yet developed of sex and teenage Americans."

The book is divided into four parts. In part I, Coles presents a psychological perspective on the social and individual context of teenage sexuality. The "burst of self-consciousness" is one of the major psychological themes of adolescence. It is linked to the experience of attaining maturity and responding to its requirements. Sexual life is tied to a teenager's symbolic journey through physical change. In part II, Stokes presents the findings of the survey—"the social profile." Each of its fourteen sections is devoted to a specific topic that reveals important information for teachers, parents, shapers of public policy, and most of all, teenagers. Topics discussed in this part include sources of sexual information, the expression of intimacy, masturbation, virginity, relationships with parents, rape, sexual stimulants, birth control, abortion, and homosexuality. The dovetailing of statistics on sexual behavior with quoted comments from teenagers about feelings and beliefs provides insight into the ways that teenagers experience sex. Part III presents excerpts from interviews that intensify the personalization of the statistics. In part IV, Coles concludes by reiterating the theme established in the beginning—the importance of acknowledging the struggle involved in trying to gain some emotional control over sexual urges and the moral complexity of attempting to do so. (SGF)

PR
146.   Dickinson, Robert Latou, and Lura Beam. **A Thousand Marriages: A Medical Study of Sex Adjustment.** Foreword by Havelock Ellis. Westport, Conn.: Greenwood Press, 1970. 482 p. (Medical Aspects of Human Fertility Series). Originally published in 1931 by Williams & Wilkins. Includes index.

In the foreword, Havelock Ellis points out a number of contributions that this volume makes. First, it focuses on the sexual activities and relationships of a large number of "fairly normal people" rather than on "abnormals," as many earlier studies have. Second, Dickinson's work includes information derived from personal interviews with his patients about their intimate relationships as well as medical findings from gynecological examinations; he views their problems in the context of their lives as a whole rather than concentrating on malfunctions of the sex organs. Third, Dickinson talked with his patients over a period of years so that longitudinal portraits are obtained. Overall, the book offers analyses of sex lives during an epoch beginning in the late 1880s and ceasing after World War I.

The contents of the volume are based on 1,098 married patients' medical histories, which distinguished gynecologist Dickinson recorded during his forty-eight years of practice; records include entries from childhood to old age and cover an average of seven years of a couple's marital life. Information about general health, fertility, pelvic disorders, labor, anatomic variations in external and internal genitalia, intercourse, contraception, symptoms, and diagnoses are detailed. Separated or divorced women, widows, and wives living with husbands are classified according to their sexual adjustment. Almost half of the 768 women considered "settled" in their marriages expressed some degree of dissatisfaction; 175 cases of dyspareunia and 100 of frigidity were diagnosed. The point of the analysis is to diagnose the basis of sexual disorders, not to offer a therapeutic format. Statistical tables present many of the findings while case histories illustrate the problems. Among the conclusions are that a woman has a lifelong capacity for sexual desire; complete unity in marriage depends on sexual unity; abstinence in marriage is not practical; sexual problems are often the result of emotional difficulties, inadequate information, and poor technique, not the product of organic problems; and sexual habit can be indexed by anatomical factors.

A few other works published around the same time also deal with the sexual relationships of normal people. Katherine B. Davis's *Factors in the Sex Life of Twenty-Two Hundred Women* (1929) is a sociological study, while G. V. Hamilton's *A Research in Marriage* (1929) used questionnaires to study the sex lives of 100 married men and 100 married women. Also of interest are Clelia Mosher's records, published as *The Mosher Survey*, that also describe the thoughts and feelings of married women about their sexuality at the turn of the century. (SGF)

PR

147.   Gebhard, Paul H., and Alan B. Johnson. **The Kinsey Data: Marginal Tabulations of the 1938-1963 Interviews Conducted by the Institute for Sex Research.** Philadelphia: Saunders, 1979. 642 p. Includes index. ISBN 0-7216-4059-1.

This volume complements Kinsey's *Sexual Behavior in the Human Male* (1948) and *Sexual Behavior in the Human Female* (1953). Its 580 tables comprise data taken from over 18,200 case studies compiled between 1938 and 1963. Much of this information has not been previously published. Seven introductory chapters provide new background information on interviewing and sampling procedures used by the Institute for Sex Research, plus full commentary on how to interpret the tables.

As with the original Kinsey studies, the sample includes college and noncollege whites of both sexes. College blacks, but very few noncollege blacks, are included. There are also over 130 tables devoted to a homosexual sample. The data, presented mostly in percentages, cover basic social and physical information about the respondents, their attitudes toward particular sexual behavior, and types of sexual behavior regularly practiced or experienced. (**ARBA 1981**)

IL

148.   Grosskopf, Dianne. **Sex and the Married Woman.** New York: Simon & Schuster, 1983. 216 p. Includes index. ISBN 0-671-47283-6.

Married women's responses to a detailed survey of their sexual behavior, combined with personal observations and an analysis of their remarks by Grosskopf, are the subject of this book. Conducted by the Institute for Advanced Study of Human Sexuality in San

Francisco and commissioned by *Playgirl* magazine, the survey questioned 1,453 women on a wide range of topics: the importance of sex and sexual satisfaction; masturbation; orgasm; sex aids; sexual fantasies, practices, and preferences; sex as a service; pregnancy, childrearing, and contraception; and extramarital affairs. The 1,207 valid respondents, who were guaranteed anonymity, came from four areas: Ohio, North Carolina, Washington, D.C., and California. They were legally married and had their own families. Their average age was 35.3 but the range was from 17 to 70. Ethnically, 91 percent were white, 6 percent black, 1 percent Asian, 0.5 percent Hispanic, and 1.5 percent other. On the average they had been married for 14.2 years. Seventeen percent were Catholic, 67 percent Protestant, 3.8 percent Jewish, 2.6 percent other, and 9.6 percent of no religion. The number of questions asked ranged from five on masturbation to twenty-eight on extramarital sex. Some interesting general responses include the following: 48 percent were satisfied with their sex lives, 52 percent were "somewhat" or "not very" satisfied; 61 percent enjoyed masturbating, 39 percent did not; and 17 percent felt that moral or religious beliefs inhibited sexual activity, 83 percent felt that they did not. Grosskopf claims that this survey is an attempt to survey "married women representative of middle-class America." (TJW)

IL
149. Hass, Aaron. **Teenage Sexuality: A Survey of Teenage Sexual Behavior.** New York: Macmillan, 1979. 203 p. Includes bibliographic notes. ISBN 0-02-548930-5.

Hass, a clinical practitioner in the area of human sexuality, presents the findings of his research on teenage sexuality with the hope of reassuring adolescents of the normality of their behavior and feelings as well as giving parents an accurate idea of how their children may be dealing with their sexuality. The research is based on the results of a lengthy questionnaire about sexual attitudes and behavior that was completed by 625 teenagers (307 boys, 318 girls) between the ages of fifteen and eighteen. Ninety percent of the respondents were from the southern California area. Although the questionnaire allowed for some open-ended responses, Hass obtained a deeper understanding of his results by conducting personal interviews with 10 percent of the volunteers.

The findings of the questionnaires are presented in thirteen chapters, each of which addresses a relevant issue: romance and sex, dating, petting, oral sex, sexual intercourse, masturbation, orgasm, fantasy, the double standard, homosexuality, performance anxiety, pornography, and parents. Within each of the chapters, the results of responses to each question are discussed, noting differences between boys and girls as well as between age levels. Each conclusion is documented with comments by teenagers that capture the flavor of their opinions about the issue. Hass regards the detailed thoughts and feelings of teenagers about different areas of sexuality as a particularly important contribution of his book. Although there are considerable sexual differences in the attitudes and behavior of boys and girls, there is also a lot of overlap. Many of his results are consistent with those of Sorensen's 1973 study *Adolescent Sexuality in Contemporary America.* Overall, Hass concludes that teenagers do not hold values that are "casual" or indiscriminate; their sexual expression is "a vehicle" for communicating caring and intimacy. (SGF)

IL,PO
150. Hite, Shere. **The Hite Report: A Nationwide Study of Female Sexuality.** New York: Macmillan, 1976. 638 p. Includes bibliographic references. ISBN 0-671-06963-2.

Does having good sex have anything to do with having orgasms? Do you enjoy masturbation? What do you like and dislike about intercourse? What are your deepest longings for a relationship with another person? These are just a few of the fifty-eight questions that 3,019 women answered in response to four different versions of over 100,000 questionnaires distributed to women all over the country from 1972 to 1975. Respondents were readers of *Oui, Mademoiselle, Brides, Ms.,* and church newsletters as well as participants in women's movement groups; they included women from a variety of geographical, religious, educational, occupational, marital, and age groups. The goal of the questionnaires was to "ask women how they feel, what they like and what they think of sex." The book is meant to stimulate public discussion and a re-evaluation of sexuality by presenting verbatim samples of what women said about orgasm and the cultural definition of sex. Hite intentionally chose open-ended questions and a nonstatistical method of presentation of results to avoid setting up a standard for how women "should feel." She presents her new theory of female sexuality in the introductions and conclusions of the chapters (on masturbation, orgasm, intercourse, clitoral stimulation, lesbianism, sexual slavery, the sexual revolution, older women, and a new female sexuality). She asserts that past cultural definitions of sex were mechanical, limited to a reproductive model of foreplay, penetration, and intercourse with male orgasm as the climax and end of the encounter, and primarily under male control. Hite encourages women to redefine their sexuality in such a way that they allow themselves to accept a wide variety of options for physical intimacy. The extensive descriptions of sexual experiences presented in women's own words make up the bulk of the book and provide a verbal support network for exploring the dynamics of these new options. (SGF)

IL,PO
151. Hite, Shere. **The Hite Report on Male Sexuality.** New York: Knopf, 1981. 1129 p. ISBN 0-394-41392-X.

In this companion volume to *The Hite Report*, Hite attempts to demonstrate how American men behave, think, and feel about their sexuality and personal relationships and thus provide a forum within which men can express their views. Given the centrality of male sexuality to definitions of masculinity and the pivotal part masculinity plays in the world view of American culture, "what we are looking at in this book is far more than male sexuality—it is a way of life . . . a culture in microcosm." Consequently, the range of materials included is much broader than the topics described in the report on female sexuality (mainly orgasm and aspects of sexual enjoyment). The bulk of the book consists of quotations from replies to questionnaires, organized around a series of basic questions focused on understanding male sexuality, how men feel about sex, and what sex means to them. Chapters 1 ("Being Male") and 2 ("Relationships with Women") provide the context for subsequent chapters ("Intercourse and the Definition of Sex"; "Other Forms of Male Sexuality": "Men's View of Women and Sex"; "Rape, Paying Women for Sex, and Pornography"; "Sex and Love Between Men"; "The Sexuality of Older Men"; and "Thirty Men Speak About Their Lives"). Using a methodology similar to the 1976 study, Hite distributed 119,000 questionnaires to men of all ages, backgrounds, and viewpoints. From 1974 to 1978 she sent questionnaires to church groups, men's groups, sports groups, professional associations, readers of *Sexology* magazine, the paperback *Sexual Honesty, by Women for Women*, and *The Hite Report*, and to men who requested them in response to television, magazine, radio, and newspaper reports. The data consist of long, essay-type replies to the 168 open-ended questions on the 7,239 questionnaires that a "very wide and highly representative cross-section of men in America" completed. Replies were charted, categorized, and statistically computed. This book is the result of over five years of intensive research and Hite hopes that it will provide a basis for a new cultural interpretation of male sexuality by redefining the dimensions of sex and male sexuality. (SGF)

IL,PO
152. Hunt, Morton. **Sexual Behavior in the 1970s.** New York: Dell, 1975. 395 p. Originally published in 1974 by Playboy Press. Includes bibliography and index.

To what extent were Americans involved in a sexual revolution in the early 1970s, at the end of a generation of rapid and seemingly wide social change? What influence has "sexual liberation" had on American life? This study, commissioned by the Playboy Foundation (which often sponsors research on sexual behavior and promotes sex education) seeks to provide a sound basis for answering these questions by documenting the range of sexual attitudes and practices of Americans on a national scale. Although not so detailed and ambitious as the Kinsey surveys of 1948 and 1953, it explores all of the major areas studied by Kinsey in addition to a few (e.g., sadomasochism, group sex, anal intercourse) that he did not investigate. Hunt consistently compares this survey's results with those of Kinsey to indicate the direction and scope of changes that have occurred in the two decades that followed the early 1950s. Research Guild, Inc., an independent market survey and behavior research organization, not only designed and administered the questionnaire but also processed and analyzed the statistical data collected. They administered the basic questionnaire of 1,000-12,000 items (about individual background, sex education, attitudes toward sex education, and a complete sex history) to a random sample of adults in twenty-four American cities in 1972. The 2,026 people who completed the questionnaires "closely" parallel the American population of adults over eighteen.

Hunt, his wife, and other individuals who worked on the original survey, conducted 200 in-depth, tape-recorded interviews with a small sample of 200 adults (100 males and 100 females) to find out the meaning behind the trends that the survey revealed. These interviews form the basis for the quoted material in the book. Hunt does not try to seek the causes of the sexual revolution but discusses the meaning that the changes he presents have for people's individual lives. He examines attitudes in conjunction with behavior to reach his conclusions. The six chapters of the book (on sexual liberation, masturbation, marital sex, postmarital and extramarital sex, and deviant sexual behavior) provide a well-written, thoughtful analysis of the meaning of sexual liberation to the American public. Of particular interest are comparisons with Kinsey's results, the relevance of the age factor to sexual attitudes and behavior, and the definition of sexual freedom that people in the United States hold. (SGF)

PR,IL,PO

153. Janus, Samuel S., and Cynthia L. Janus. **The Janus Report on Sexual Behavior.** New York: Wiley, 1993. 430 p. Includes bibliographic notes and index. ISBN 0-471-52540-5.

Named for its authors, researcher and author (*The Death of Innocence* and *A Sexual Profile of Men in Power*) Samuel S. Janus, Ph.D., and Cynthia L. Janus, M.D., *The Janus Report* is their report of the findings of a nationwide survey of American sexuality. The purposes of the study were "to bring into clear focus sexual behavior *as lived by* Americans in the 1980s and early 1990s, and to examine how Americans engage in sex, what they believe about their sexuality, and the most relevant related social issues."

The research was conducted over nine years in two phases: (1) a pilot phase between 1983 and 1986 during which research tools were developed and (2) the large-scale, cross-sectional survey conducted between 1988 and 1992. The national survey was designed to represent every region of the contiguous forty-eight United States, and Janus and Janus think that "our demographics are sufficiently representative of the characteristics of the national population of the United States that our findings are likely generalizable for the country as a whole." Findings are based on 2,765 satisfactorily completed questionnaires, supplemented by 125 in-depth interviews.

Data reflect information derived from individuals that represent all stages of the adult life cycle, from eighteen to over sixty-five. Of particular interest was information on singles' lifestyles, sex within marriage, sex among the "postmature" groups, and the relationship between sexuality and family roles and divorce, which are discussed in the early chapters of the book. Later chapters evaluate the influence of income, religion, education, politics, and geographic region on sexual behavior.

After chronicling changes in sex research and the social context of sexual behavior in the U.S. since the early twentieth century, Janus and Janus state that "this background of social and sexual change has led us to seek valid, up-to-date information on sexual behavior in the U.S. This book is the result of that search." They present their findings in twelve chapters, each preceded by highlights of significant findings and questionnaire subjects tabulated in the chapters. Over 280 tables summarize findings discussed in more detail in each of the chapters. Each chapter has several excerpts from in-depth interviews, "in their own words."

Many of their findings reflect changes in sexual beliefs and behavior. For example, financial responsibility for the family is no longer a male prerogative and "the role of breadwinner is no longer an extension of a man's masculinity"; there is a trend toward partnership between spouses. The gender gap in sexual behavior is closing; both men and women are freer to explore their sexuality, whether married or not. There is less contrast between what singles and married people want out of a relationship. Men and women have active, vigorous sex lives in middle age and beyond. Masturbation is rather well accepted as "a common and even routine part of adult sexuality." And, contrary to conventional wisdom, males do not reach their sexual peak in their late teens; the frequency of men's sexual activity between ages twenty-seven and sixty-four is higher than those aged eighteen to twenty-six.

Janus and Janus conclude that individuals seem to prefer more selective sexual interaction rather than sexual experimentation with many partners. However, respondents express "unrest and indecision" about sexuality, even as they are actively involved with it in a more egalitarian and less shame-based way. (SGF)

PR,IL,PO
154. Kahn, Sandra S., and Jean Davis. **The Kahn Report on Sexual Preferences.** New York: St. Martin's Press, 1981. 278 p. Includes bibliographic notes and index. ISBN 0-312-71351-7.

Intrigued by the meager amount of research that had been conducted on female sexual preferences, Kahn, a full-time private therapist who works primarily with women, conducted a two-year study to determine the preferences of males and females for various sexual activities. Rather than drawing volunteers from a college/young adult population, she chose 200 heterosexual volunteers in the twenty-seven to forty-nine-year-old age group on the premise that these individuals have had enough time and experience to establish and know their sexual preferences. Subjects were chosen from lists of volunteers at Kahn's speaking engagements (women's and men's groups, professional groups, community organizations); those who were overeager, uncooperative, or biased by strict religious convictions were excluded. Subjects were white collar, middle-class whites from a Judeo-Christian background residing in the Chicago metropolitan area. The experiment consisted of two parts: (1) showing the subjects fifty-seven "pornographic" pictures on nineteen sexual themes that they were asked to rank in order of their preference and (2) assessing the same pictures in terms of what the subject thought his or her own sex and the opposite sex would prefer. The book provides background for and discussion of the rankings. The first chapter provides an orientation to the roots of gender-appropriate behavior in childhood and youth. Chapter 2 discusses methodology, and chapter 3 provides a self-testing guide for the reader to appraise his or her own preferences (using words rather than pictures). In chapter 4, the comparison of results (actual ranking of male/female preferences of sexual activities, male/female perceptions of the actual male/female rankings) shows the extent to which sexual preferences are in line with the preferences of the opposite sex and overall social/cultural expectations. The rest of the book discusses the significance of male/female preferences, their relevance to men and women in their adult lives, and their importance for the sex education of children. (SGF)

PR,IL
155. Kinsey, Alfred C., Wardell B. Pomeroy, and Clyde E. Martin. **Sexual Behavior in the Human Male.** Philadelphia: Saunders, 1948. 804 p. Includes bibliography and index.

A milestone in the study of sexuality, this book and its companion volume, *Sexual Behavior in the Human Female,* made at least three major contributions that set them apart from previous research on the subject: (1) utilization of large-scale survey techniques to "objectively" study sexual behavior; (2) data collection by personal interviews rather than questionnaires; and (3) accumulation of facts about sexual behavior in a manner that attempts to avoid social, moral, or theoretical interpretations of them. Kinsey modestly begins this volume by describing it as a "progress report from a case history study on human sexual behavior" and as a "fact-finding survey in which an attempt is being made to discover what people do sexually, and what factors account for differences in sexual behavior among individuals and among various segments of the population." As a zoologist who believed strongly in the canons of science, Kinsey began to study human sexuality ("one of the least explored segments of biology, psychology and sociology") with the methodological rigor that he employed in his research on four million gall wasps. His recurrent goal is "objectivity" and reporting "facts" about what people do, and his methodology represents a painstaking attempt to fulfill his objectives. The first part of the book ("History and Method") is a chronicle of a pioneering research team (Kinsey, Pomeroy, and Martin) that designed a method that could be applied to research on sexuality as well as to other human problems. They carefully describe why and how they obtained their final sample of 5,300 males and point out its advantages and weaknesses. They present their rationale for data collection through case histories rather than questionnaires and review the precise interview techniques they used to obtain information on a range of 300-531 well-defined items on private, emotionally laden aspects of sexual behavior. In addition, they discuss potential problems of reliability, validity, and statistical analysis and present the techniques they used to counter them.

The bulk of the book (parts II and III) is a report on the sexual behavior of the American male "as we find him." The authors do not describe or categorize behavior as normal/abnormal, moral/immoral, or bad/good, but present findings on a range of behavior according to twelve "biological and socio-cultural factors": sex, cultural group, marital status, age, age at onset of adolescence, educational level, parent's occupational class, subject's occupational class, rural/urban background, religious group, degree of adherence to religion, and geographical origin. Part II deals with how each of these factors affects sexual outlet. Part III discusses the sources of sexual outlet (masturbation, nocturnal emissions, heterosexual petting, premarital intercourse, marital intercourse, extramarital intercourse, intercourse with prostitutes, homosexual outlet, and animal contacts). Each chapter not only presents the incidences and frequencies for each topic but also includes operational definitions of terms, references to previous research, and a discussion of the social significance of the findings. An almost overwhelming number of statistics, charts, and tables supplement the text and attest to the conscientious attention to detail that permeates this first volume of the classic Kinsey Reports. (SGF)

PR
156.   Kinsey, Alfred C., Wardell B. Pomeroy, Clyde E. Martin, and Paul H. Gebhard. **Sexual Behavior in the Human Female.** By the staff of the Institute for Sex Research, Indiana University. Philadelphia: Saunders, 1953. 842 p. Includes bibliography and index.

This classic volume on the sexual behavior of the human female complements the volume on the male as a "fact-finding survey in which an attempt has been made to discover what people do sexually, what factors may account for their patterns of sexual behavior . . . and what social significance there might be in each type of behavior." Like the first "progress report," this study uses innovative techniques to obtain case histories from a large sample of personally interviewed respondents (5,940 white females living in the United States) as the basis for most of the statistical data. The authors use recorded data (diaries, sex calendars, drawings, scrapbooks, etc.), observed data (observations of mammals, clinical reports, and community studies), and information from previously published studies (from anthropology, law, etc.) to broaden the scope of this volume beyond that of the report on the male. Much of the discussion of the social significance of each type of sexual activity was drawn from these sources.

Part I reviews the historical background as well as the meticulous methodology employed in the study, detailing its definitions, procedures, and limitations. Continuing to believe that "there is an honesty in science which refuses to accept the idea that there are aspects of the material universe that are better not investigated . . . and an honesty in science which leads to a certain acceptance of the reality," Kinsey and his research associates present findings on the sexual activity of American females which were destined to explode cherished myths about American womanhood. The topics covered parallel those investigated for the male: preadolescent sexual development, masturbation, nocturnal sex dreams, premarital petting, premarital coitus, marital coitus, extramarital coitus, homosexual responses, and animal contacts. They also analyzed the relationship between each of these types of sexual outlets with twelve biologic and sociocultural variables (sex, cultural group, marital status, age, age at onset of adolescence, educational level, subject's occupational class, parent's occupational class, rural/urban background, religious group, degree of adherence to religion, and geographical origin). They follow each chapter with a summary of the data described and compare it with findings on the male. Part II continues the theme of comparing the sexual behavior of males and females. The last five chapters present a careful synthesis of current data on the anatomy of sexual response and orgasm, the physiology of sexual response and orgasm, psychological factors in sexual response (including data on differential responses to forms of erotic stimulation), neural mechanisms of sexual response, and hormonal factors in sexual response.

This publication represents fifteen years of research that continued despite some concerted attempts by opponents to stop the efforts of the authors at the Institute for Sex Research. Although Kinsey envisioned a twenty-year study and at least 100,000 case histories, the data derived from more than 16,000 interviews of males and females presented in the two volumes of the Kinsey Reports were sufficient to establish sexuality as a legitimate domain for scientific study. The Kinsey Reports are not only important for their methodology and place in the history of sex research; they are also relevant as a valuable source of information about sexuality and a standard by which to measure subsequent efforts. (SGF)

PR,IL
157. Klassen, Albert D., Colin J. Williams, and Eugene E. Levitt. **Sex and Morality in the U.S.: An Empirical Enquiry Under the Auspices of the Kinsey Institute.** Edited and with an Introduction by Hubert J. O'Gorman. Middletown, Conn.: Wesleyan University Press, 1989. 462 p. Includes bibliography and index. ISBN 0-8195-5224-0.

This work reports the findings of a 1970 national survey on sex, conducted under the auspices of the Institute for Sex Research at Indiana University. The goal of the survey was to identify the moral rules that people apply to sexual behavior and thus "extend and expand the type of research represented by the pioneering work of Dr. Kinsey and his associates," that focused on sexual behavior and eschewed research on morality. Like the Kinsey research, many individuals provided personal information about their sexuality; unlike Kinsey's sample, the authors claim that participants were part of a national representative sample. Responses from extensive interviews with 3,018 people were categorized by age, gender, race, marital status, education, socioeconomic status, geographic region, community size, religious affiliation, liberalism and conservatism. But, between 1970 and 1989, cost overruns, loss of funding, bureaucratic bungling and interpersonal conflict sidetracked reporting and publishing the findings of the research. Ultimately, sociologist O'Gorman of Wesleyan University took on the editing task, at the request of the Kinsey Institute.

Overall, the book is "the first . . . and remains the only national survey centered wholly on the sexual experiences and the sexual norms of a representative sample of the adult American population . . . these data are demonstrably relevant for an understanding of how Americans then (1970) and now define and respond to sexual situations." Since the survey began as a research project on attitudes toward homosexuality, four of the twelve chapters of the present volume discuss the stereotypes, attitudes and reactions to homosexuality as well as the structures and dynamics of anti-homosexual attitudes. The study's content became broader to include reports of sexual experience and moral judgments about such other sexual activities as premarital and extramarital sex, masturbation, and prostitution. Most of the book deals with the context of sexual norms: the sexual revolution, an overview of sexual norms in the U.S., influences on sexual morality, changes in sexual morality, accounting for sexual morality, reactions to norm violators, and sexual morality and contemporary society.

The text, replete with tables and figures, provides a national baseline dataset and defines the sexual norms during a specific period of American social history, before AIDS. The findings show that the sexual norms of Americans are more conservative than permissive; there was not a major shift away from traditional morality, despite media attention to sexual permissiveness. Older people are more conservative in their sexual norms than younger people, men, and singles. And, although almost half of the respondents thought they were more tolerant about non-marital sex than their parents, almost two-thirds agreed with their parents' beliefs about homosexuality.

Appendixes contain detailed information about the history and design of the study, training of field supervisors, pretesting of the interview questionnaire, the sample, tables of correlations and response distributions. (LF/SGF)

IL,PO

158. McGill, Michael E. **The McGill Report on Male Intimacy.** New York: Holt, Rinehart and Winston, 1985. 300 p. Includes index.

McGill's interest in explaining male intimate behavior is an outgrowth of his specialization in organizational behavior. Why men love as they do and what that means to them and those they love seem key to understanding the behavior of men in general. The major questions that McGill attempts to answer are whether differences exist in the intimate behavior of men and women, and if so, why. His conclusions are based on the responses of 1,383 (737 men and 646 women) individuals, aged eighteen to seventy-three, to his intimacy questionnaire, that measures six dimensions of intimate interactions with spouse or intimate other, parents, children, and friends.

Intimacy is "the state of being close" and is associated with time together, depth and breadth of interpersonal exchanges, exclusivity, and value attached to the relationship. Disclosure patterns about public, private, and personal information indicate who and how men love. Elements of a variety of relationships make up male intimacy. Men usually take on three roles with their wives: Reluctant Revealers, Cautious Confirmers, and Emotional Evaders; most men withhold something of themselves from their wives. In contrast, men may reveal personal information to another woman who may be a friend and/or sexual partner. Although relatives and friends are said to be important, the average man is rarely intimate with them. Male friendships are shallow and not characterized by much sharing.

Given the fragmentation of men's intimate relationships, how do men express love? They are most likely to use emotional surrogates to convey their love (e.g., sex, presents, listening). Intellectualization of emotions and taboos against touching can mask a man's loving intent. Although men may not behave in loving ways, it does not mean that men do not love. However, trust and disclosure may signal a loss of control over oneself and others.

McGill demonstrates the very real differences in the ways that men and women express intimacy. He concludes that men can become truly intimate if they are convinced that they gain more power and control from being close to others than from evading intimacy. (SGF)

IL

159. Mendola, Mary. **The Mendola Report: A New Look at Gay Couples.** New York: Crown, 1980. 269 p. Includes index. ISBN 0-517-541394.

Based on a nationwide survey of gay couples living together, this book aims to provide an "open and positive forum where lesbian and homosexual couples" can "explore the marital lifestyles of their peers." Fifteen hundred "Speak Out" questionnaires were sent to individuals and nonpolitical organizations for distribution throughout the United States. Bars and political organizations that might unduly represent a specific lifestyle were excluded, while many towns and cities in addition to San Francisco and New York were included to assure regional representation. The questionnaire was composed of thirty-five multiple choice and four essay questions on various aspects of committed relationships between gays. Approximately 27 percent of the questionnaires were returned (in comparison to the usual 5-10 percent return rate for this type of survey). Respondents were better educated and higher in socioeconomic status than the general population; most were over thirty (73 percent), professionals or managers (66 percent), in a permanently committed relationship (67 percent) for more than two years (65 percent). In addition, Mendola personally conducted an unspecified number of unpaid interviews of couples. The results of the survey provide a framework for presenting and discussing the interviews that make up the bulk of the text; their combined importance lies in their expression of the emotional and sexual dimensions of gay relationships as homosexuals and lesbians view them. Defining herself as a human being, woman, and lesbian, Mendola encourages a view of gays as whole people, not as individuals narrowly defined in terms of their sexual behavior. Therefore, chapters concentrate on a wide range of relationship issues: everyday living, gay parenthood, financial partnerships, family relations, divorce, and death; they also address problems of societal pressure and community relations. The overall theme of the book is that there is no essential difference between gay couples and heterosexual couples. (SGF)

IL,PO

159a. Michael, Robert T., John H. Gagnon, Edward O. Laumann, and Gina Kolata. **Sex in America: A Definitive Survey.** Boston: Little, Brown, 1994. 300 p. Includes index. ISBN 0-316-07524-8.

New York Times science reporter Kolata worked with researchers Michael (Dean of the Graduate School of Public Policy Studies at the University of Chicago), Gagnon (Professor of Sociology at the State University of New York at Stony Brook), and Laumann (Professor of Sociology at the University of Chicago) to provide a readable account of a scientific survey of Americans' sexual practices and beliefs. The book "offers the facts about Americans' sexual practices, putting them in a context that helps explain not only what we do but why" (p. 1).

The authors claim that this study departs from previous sex surveys ("the vast majority [of which] are unreliable; many are worse than useless" [p. 15]) in its methodologically sound approach to sexuality. One chapter discusses the limitations of such well-known studies as the Kinsey reports, Masters and Johnson's research, the Hite report, and the Janus report, and highlights the method of the national Health and Social Life Survey, the data from which form the basis for this book. With the goal of obtaining a representative sample of people in the United States, aged 18 to 59 and who speak English, the researchers went through a series of random selections—of geographic areas of the country; of cities, towns, and rural areas; of neighborhoods; of households—to arrive at the sample of individuals to interview. The one-and-one-half-hour confidential interviews of 3,432 respondents were carried out by 220 trained interviewers (mainly white women in their thirties and forties, managed by the National Opinion Research Center), over a seven-month period. They queried people first about their background (e.g., ethnicity, age, education, marital status, religion), then about marriage and children, and finally about sex. The study does not distinguish between heterosexuals and homosexuals, but includes respondents with social characteristics similar to those of the population of the United States.

The findings of the research challenge some widely held beliefs: that we can fall in love with anyone; that anything is possible for those who love; that marriage is "deadly" to sex; that everyone's having sex; that AIDS will eventually spread throughout the heterosexual population; that most married people are unfaithful; and that Americans are very sexual, engaging in a wide variety of sexual practices with a wide variety of partners. Rather, the authors claim "that sexual behavior is shaped by our social surroundings. . . . We do not have all the latitude we may imagine when we look for a partner, nor do we have all the choices in the world when we decide what to do in bed" (p. 16). Each chapter details what the data reveal about a specific topic, e.g., who our sex partners are, finding a partner, how many sex partners we have, how often we have sex, masturbation and erotica, practices and preferences, forced sex. The final chapter, "Sex and Society," integrates the findings of the study to reach the conclusion that people's sexual behavior does not depart a significant degree from their beliefs. "America is not the golden land of eroticism where everybody who is young and beautiful has a hot sex life. Nor is it a land where vast hordes of miserable people, kicked out of the sexual banquet, lick their wounds in silence and resentment. Instead, . . . it is a nation of people who are for the most part content, or at least not highly dissatisfied, with the sexual lots they have drawn" (p. 246).

Professionals and scholars may refer to the scientific study on which this popular version is based by consulting *The Social Organization of Sexuality: Sexual Practices in the United States* by Edward O. Laumann, John H. Gagnon, Robert T. Michael, and Stuart Michaels (University of Chicago Press, 1994). (SGF)

PR
160.   Mosher, Clelia Duel. **The Mosher Survey: Sexual Attitudes of 45 Victorian Women.** Edited by James MaHood and Kristine Wenburg. Introduction by Carl N. Degler. New York: Arno Press, 1980. 469 p. ISBN 0-405-13090-2.

While conducting research at the Stanford University Archives in 1973, historian Carl N. Degler discovered the unpublished research papers (*Hygiene and Physiology of Women*) of Clelia Duel Mosher (1863-1940). Volume X contained 650 pages of handwritten questionnaires, that Mosher administered to women from 1892 to 1920. Editors MaHood and Wenburg have clarified (*not* abridged or interpreted) the contents of these forms so that they are now readable and accessible as the Mosher Survey. Although the survey contains the responses of only forty-five women, it is important as a primary historical document containing direct statements about sex and marriage from women who were brought up during the Victorian era. It is probably the first American sex survey and certainly the first sex survey on women conducted by a woman sex researcher. Mosher began the survey as part of her preparation for a talk at the Mothers' Club at the University of Wisconsin; she continued to collect information to use in teaching and advising students at Stanford University. She gave no indication of why she chose to interview the respondents she did. Most (thirty-four of forty-five) of the respondents attended college or normal school, many (thirty of forty-five) worked as teachers before marriage, were in their thirties when they were interviewed, were white, married, and lived in the North or West. Mosher asked about frequency of intercourse, attitudes toward sex, ideal sex practices, number of conceptions, experience with and means of contraception, sleeping arrangements, and the condition of the bowels. She found that most women were poorly informed about sex before marriage, enjoyed sex, had experienced orgasm, and practiced effective birth control techniques beyond withdrawal and abstinence. Although Mosher provided no conclusions based on her data, she left a document that indicates the changes in sexual attitudes that were occurring at the turn of the century. (SGF)

IL,PO
161.   Pietropinto, Anthony, and Jacqueline Simenauer. **Beyond the Male Myth: What Women Want to Know About Men's Sexuality: A Nationwide Survey.** New York: Times Books, 1977. 430 p. ISBN 0-8129-0726-4.

In comparison with the amount of research conducted on women, studies devoted to men are scarce. Pietropinto, a psychiatrist and Simenauer, a journalist who has served as a psychiatric editor, assert that "much of the extant male lore, though promulgated widely as psychological fact, belongs more properly to the realm of modern mythology" (p. 19). Consequently, they designed a survey to go beyond the "male myth" by exploring the complexity of thoughts and feelings that "real-life" men in their "natural habitats" have about sexuality. On the basis of queries that women frequently have about men, Pietropinto and Simenauer developed a questionnaire that was distributed by a research service organization to over 4,000 men located in eighteen states and in Washington, D.C. Field agents approached men primarily in shopping centers, office building complexes, college campuses, tennis clubs, airports, and bus depots, and asked them to take twenty minutes to complete the questionnaire. Half of those approached agreed to participate. The agents attempted to select men from different age groups, from diverse levels of affluence, and from various ethnic backgrounds. The questionnaire consisted of two parts: (1) a forty-item, multiple choice section covering such topics as demographic characteristics, attitudes about sex and contemporary women, communication with women, fantasy, attitudes toward love, marriage, fidelity, and cheating, and (2) four essay questions to be answered in handwriting. The responses to the questionnaire constitute the data on which Pietropinto and Simenauer base their findings. They use the essays to present the "voices" of their subjects throughout the book. The focus of the book is an assessment of thoughts and feelings about behavior, not quantification of frequencies of sexual behavior. Topics discussed in each chapter correspond to major subjects investigated in the questionnaire: what turns men on and off, expectations about a sexual and/or marital partner, opinions about love, views about different kinds of relationships (marriage, other women, dream girls), and suggestions about how to communicate and deal with problems. They then compare and contrast their findings with those of Shere Hite, Alfred Kinsey, and Morton Hunt. They hope that their conclusions will benefit women by dispelling misconceptions about men and will aid men by giving them a forum to share and compare their experiences and thoughts with each other. (SGF)

IL,PO
162. Playboy Enterprises. **The Playboy Report on American Men.** Chicago: Playboy Enterprises, 1979. 59 p.
     This survey explores the values, attitudes, and goals of American males between the ages of eighteen and forty-nine. Between December 6, 1976 and January 12, 1977, 1,990 men were interviewed extensively on 400 "items." The survey was conducted for Playboy Enterprises by Louis Harris and Associates; analysis and interpretation of key data were made by William Simon and Patricia Y. Miller. Harris calls the sampling "representative." The survey discloses a rich diversity of male opinion, fairly evenly divided among four groups—traditionalists, conventionals, contemporaries, and innovators. Areas touched upon in the survey include basic values; family; love and sex; marriage and children; the outer man's appearance; religion and psychotherapy; attitudes toward drugs, money, and possessions; work; politics; and leisure. The survey found that most men are hardly playboys in their values and attitudes. Nearly 85 percent rated family life as very important for a satisfied life, while only 49 percent rated sex as similarly important. Married men had the highest levels of satisfaction with their sex lives, and three out of four men considered sexual fidelity very important for a successful marriage. Although 82 percent of the men believed in a Supreme Being, only 41 percent said religion was personally significant for them. Although work is important to men, most rated it below health, love, peace of mind, and family life as very important for a happy, satisfied life. In these and other areas too often subjected to impressionistic speculation, the Playboy survey offers hard information about American men's attitudes and values. (**Men's Studies**, 1985)

IL
163. Shanor, Karen. **The Shanor Study: The Sexual Sensitivity of the American Male.** New York: Dial Press, 1978. 274 p. Includes bibliography. ISBN 0-8037-7810-4.
     "The American male is a more complete person than contemporary views of him allow," Shanor concludes from her study utilizing 4,062 questionnaire responses and seventy interviews. She devotes separate chapters to orgasm (some men fake it on occasion), masturbation (it is performed more frequently since the time of Kinsey's study), and sexual fantasies. She then offers profiles of men in their forties (the mid-life transition is often a mid-life crisis), thirties (these men are often trapped between old and new cultural values), and twenties (freer in their sexual attitudes, these males pursue traditional careers but not "seriously"). For men fifty and older, sex can be a waning activity or a continuing source of enjoyment. In their teens males are troubled about their

sexual identity and performance, but usually they are actively pursuing information and experience. Later chapters touch upon sexual activity of black men and homosexuals, impotence, sadomasochistic fantasies, and characteristic behavior during sex. The final chapter provides an overview, an attempt to fix a representative portrait of current male sexuality in transition. Numerous quotes from Shanor's respondents are incorporated in the text. The appendix provides the questionnaire and statistical information. Shanor is president of Shanor Associates and a practicing psychotherapist. (**Men's Studies**, 1985)

IL

164.   Simenauer, Jacqueline, and David Carroll. **Singles: The New Americans.** New York: Simon & Schuster, 1982. 399 p. ISBN 0-671-25052-3.

In the early 1980s one of every three adults in the U.S. between the ages of twenty and fifty-five was single. Simenauer and Carroll, both professional writers, decided to write this book in an effort to establish a self-portrait of the sociological, psychological, and sexual aspects of this segment of the American population. A national survey of singles is the core of this book and most of the text is confined to describing its results. Simenauer and Carroll consulted with psychiatrists, psychologists, and sociologists to devise a final version of their fifty-five-question, multiple-choice questionnaire that 250 field representatives of a survey company administered to a national sample of 3,000 singles. They distributed questionnaires to such locations as colleges, singles apartment complexes, restaurants, health clubs, and places of work. The respondents came from 36 of the most populous states in the United States, from 57 major cities and from 275 metropolitan areas. Simenauer and Carroll claim that their sample is representative of singles in the nation as a whole although no statistics are presented to corroborate their contention. The chapters follow singles through different phases of their relationships: meeting, dating, being sexually intimate, living together or alone, and getting divorced. Each chapter has a similar format: presentation of the pertinent questions from the questionnaire, the results, and a brief discussion of the findings, often in the form of excerpts from essays written by singles. Major findings, secondary "bonus" findings, and profiles of singles who held specific attitudes are highlighted. Findings focus on such topics as attitudes toward singles bars, single parents, and sex on the first date. They reveal the conflict and myths that often surround such topics. Primarily descriptive rather than theoretical, this book is a "compendium of data covering practically every aspect of single life." (SGF)

PR,IL

165.   Sorensen, Robert C. **Adolescent Sexuality in Contemporary America: Personal Values and Sexual Behavior Ages Thirteen to Nineteen.** Introduction by Paul Moore, Jr. New York: World Publishing/Times Mirror, 1973. 549 p. Alternative title: *The Sorensen Report.* ISBN 0-529-04820-5.

Sorensen's definition of adolescent sexuality as a time "when adolescents adopt certain beliefs and forms of behavior in response to their sexual desires" (p. 3) highlights what he thinks are the most important ingredients for study: beliefs *and* behavior. Behavior alone does not truly reflect the complex dimensions of adolescent sexuality. Therefore, he chooses to investigate adolescent attitudes and then determine the degree to which attitude and behavior are related to each other. He considers his investigation the "first nationwide study of its kind in the United States" (p. 9).

An overarching goal of this research was to understand sexuality from the adolescent's point of view. Therefore, two data collection techniques were used to obtain honest replies directly from thirteen to nineteen year olds: (1) 200 personal, open-ended interviews designed to familiarize researchers with the language and emotions that teenagers attach to sexuality; and (2) 411 self-administered questionnaires, distributed to a national probability sample that conformed to the entire adolescent population in 1970.

The findings are presented in three major sections: "Personal Values and Sexual Attitudes"; "Sexual Behavior"; and "Adolescent Sexual Behavior and Social Change." A strong value system pervades adolescents' sexual attitudes and behavior. Sexual behavior is regarded as a "natural" activity, not an "immoral" one. Mutuality, personal intimacy and sharing, tolerance for the choices of others, a situational ethic, multiaffectional love, and the pleasurable intensity of feeling and meaning for the moment are some of the characteristics of adolescent sexuality. Although many of these young people want sex without marriage and do not require fidelity in a relationship, they are not promiscuous; they focus on the meaning of the relationship, which often takes the form of serial monogamy or sexual adventurism. Although most adolescents communicate very little with their parents about sex, they plan to do so with their own children. Most intend to marry and have children. However, they may be very careful about their selection of a mate; they are likely to live together before marriage and take into account some of the nonsexual characteristics of married life. The overall portrait of adolescents that emerges from this rich set of findings is of young people who value love and affectionate relationships and who are struggling to deal with men and women as whole people, not just as sexual beings. (SGF)

PO

166. Spada, James. **The Spada Report: The Newest Survey of Gay Male Sexuality.** New York: New American Library, 1979. 339 p.

Written by a freelance journalist who regularly contributes to such magazines as *The Advocate* and *In Touch*, *The Spada Report* presents the results of Spada's survey of the attitudes, activities, and lifestyles of 1,038 gay men; these findings are offered "in the hope of breaking down the barriers which separate so many of us" (p. 9). Ten thousand copies of a fifty-five-item, open-ended questionnaire were distributed primarily through reproduction of the questions in such national magazines as *The Advocate*, *Playguy*, and *Man's Way* between November 1976 and July 1978. Questionnaires were also given out at meetings, symposia, bookstores, gay bars and theaters, and by request through the mail. Most respondents were Caucasian, well educated (some college at a minimum), from the Northeast (26 percent) and Southwest (35 percent), and Protestant; their ages ranged from sixteen to seventy-seven, but most were between nineteen and forty-nine. Although Spada presents frequency distributions of answers to the questions in the appendix, the text itself is made up of diverse, verbatim responses to the six topical foci of the questionnaire: coming out, gay male sexuality, relationships, women, problems, and being gay. Rather than providing contextual or descriptive material about gays, Spada preferred "to allow the respondents to speak their minds with a minimum of intrusion of my own comments" (p. 319). (SGF)

IL

167. Starr, Bernard D., and Marcella Bakur Weiner. **The Starr-Weiner Report on Sex & Sexuality in the Mature Years.** New York: Stein and Day, 1981. 302 p. Includes bibliography and index. ISBN 0-8128-2750-3.

Sex is a part of life and can continue in some form forever. This is a major conclusion that transcends the topical headings of this report on sex and sexuality in the "mature years" after sixty. Far from being in a state of decline and decay, respondents to the survey on which the report is based have a strong, continuing interest in sex, are sexually active, show little embarrassment or anxiety about it, and are fairly satisfied with their current sex lives. In addition, they engage in a variety of sexual practices (including oral sex and masturbation) and feel that sex is as good as it was when they were younger.

The survey is based on data from 800 responses to a fifty-item, open-ended questionnaire distributed to audiences of elderly who attended programs presented by Starr and Weiner on "Love, Intimacy and Sex in the Later Years." Starr, a professor in the School of Education at Brooklyn College of CUNY and a research associate of CASE Center for Gerontological Studies at the Graduate Center of CUNY, and Weiner, Adjunct Professor of Psychology/Gerontology at CUNY, a consultant in gerontology, a practicing psychotherapist, and a delegate to the White House Conference on Aging, attribute their high (14 percent) response rate to their "personal" approach in giving out questionnaires. They arranged talks through local councils on aging, civic agencies, university professors with contacts in the community, professional colleagues, or older people who arranged programs for community centers. Audiences ranged in size from 25 to 300 people. Respondents share the following characteristics: (1) an age range from sixty to ninety-one; (2) 35 percent males, 65 percent females; (3) primarily from the Northeast (47 percent) and the West/Northwest (27 percent); (4) white; (5) living in the community, in their own homes, in senior residences, or with a relative; (6) higher educational level than most older adults; and (7) married (48 percent) or widowed (37 percent). The open-ended questionnaire that respondents had to fill in included a broad range of questions designed to emphasize the special concerns and problems of older adults. Subject headings of the chapters indicate the major content of the responses: interest in sex, masturbation, female orgasm and love experience, likes and dislikes, sex experiences and the ideal lover, intimate communication, older women alone, looking backward/looking forward. Initial chapters discuss the survey and the myths about sex and aging. The final chapters provide a practical guide for older people who want to improve their sexuality, and projections, based on the survey, of what kind of life the baby-boom generation can expect when it turns sixty in 2010. Throughout the book, Starr and Weiner provide useful background material on each topic they discuss and put sex and aging in the more embracing context of sexual concerns that all people share. (SGF)

PO
168. Tavris, Carol, and Susan Sadd. **The Redbook Report on Female Sexuality: 100,000 Married Women Disclose the Good News About Sex.** New York: Delacorte Press, 1975. 186 p. Includes bibliography and index. ISBN 0-440-07560-2.

In 1974 *Redbook* published a questionnaire entitled "How Do You Really Feel About Sex?" An unprecedented 100,000 replies to the survey were received from women who are generally younger, better educated, more affluent, and relatively more liberal than the average American. In addition, hundreds of letters accompanied the seventy-five-question, close-ended questionnaires on range of sexual experience and preference. The book is based on a random sample of 2,278 replies from married and remarried women as well as on unsolicited letters; a larger random sample of 18,000 was used for larger, comparative analyses. The responses "celebrate love, marriage and undisguised lust." Tavris and Sadd stress the importance of the survey as a picture of a large group of American women "who usually have neither the opportunity nor inclination to participate in sex surveys" and as a significant focus for eliciting dialogue about sexual issues. According to Tavris and Sadd, the book demonstrates some of the "good news" about men, women, and sex in relation to premarital sex, marital sex, and extramarital sex. For example, the stronger a woman's religious beliefs, the more likely she is to be satisfied sexually. Also, premarital sex has little effect on marriage, and promiscuity is not increasing among young women. Tavris and Sadd, both of whom hold doctorates in social psychology, are careful to note the pros and cons of sex surveys in the first chapter. They compare their results with those of other major sex surveys (the Kinsey Reports, the Hite report, etc.) and incorporate the findings of other relevant research into their discussions throughout the book. Written in a supportive, interesting, and careful manner, the book aims for the goals of Robert Levine, to whom it is dedicated: search for truths but help people to be comfortable and choose what is right for themselves. (SGF)

PO
169. Wolfe, Linda. **The Cosmo Report.** New York: Arbor House, 1981. 416 p. Includes index. ISBN 0-87795-315-5.

The idea for a sex survey of the *Cosmopolitan* readership was the product of brainstorming during a regular meeting of the *Cosmopolitan* staff, all of whom contributed questions for the questionnaire. The book is based on a synthesis of information derived from over 106,000 questionnaires returned to the magazine and 2,500 unsolicited letters received from women who wrote in response to the January 1980 *Cosmo* article, "The Sexual Profile of That Cosmo Girl." The respondents are generally women between the ages of eighteen and thirty-four who earn their livings as managers, administrators, office workers, technicians, and professionals in cities and the suburbs, and who are sexually experienced and experimental (the majority have had two to ten sex partners). The seventy-eight close-ended questions that they answered deal with their personal background (nine), sexual experience (forty-nine), and sexual manners and morals (twenty). Wolfe, a behavioral and social science writer, studied the statistical results handled by Simmons Market Research Bureau, analyzed the letters, and wrote the final report. Although the overall goal of the book is to assess the extent and effect of the "sexual revolution" among women, it can also be used as a "measuring rod" by which women can assess their own behavior in relation to contemporary patterns as well as a handbook of useful information about sex. Wolfe tries to offer "direction as well as report" about several dimensions of sexuality—psychological, social, and technical. Heavily interspersed with quotes from the respondents, the book spans many aspects of sexuality in five sections: (1) "Sexuality with Partners" (the first time; turn-ons; the whens, wheres, and how oftens of sex; sexual practices; orgasm with a partner), (2) "Private Sexuality" (masturbation, sexual fantasies, and dreams), (3) "The Human Arithmetic of Sex" (lovers, multiple partners, infidelity), (4) "Sexual Abuse" (incest, rape, and sexual molestation), and (5) "The Sexual Revolution" (evaluation). (SGF)

8

Research

BACKGROUND

PR

170.   Aberle, Sophie D., and George W. Corner. **Twenty-five Years of Sex Research: History of the National Research Council Committee for Research in Problems of Sex, 1922-1947.** Philadelphia: Saunders, 1953. 248 p. Includes bibliography and indexes.

Against a background of resistance to the investigation, or even discussion, of sex in American society, the Committee for Research in Problems of Sex of the National Research Council was established in 1921. Philanthropists, physicians, and scientists had urged the formation of such a group to study human sexual behavior. Recognizing diverse concerns in the area of human sexuality, such as women's call for a single standard of sexual morality, new knowledge of sexual aberrations and anomalies, concerns about prostitution, homosexuality, and the spread of venereal diseases, and Freudian revelations about the nature of sexuality, these eminent people pressed for a liberalization of scientific thought about sex as a natural phenomenon, and called for the investigation of the biological basis of sexual behavior. The Committee stated its purpose as follows: "To conduct, stimulate, foster, systematize, and coordinate research on sex problems to the end that conclusions now held may be evaluated and our scientific knowledge in this field increased as rapidly as possible" (p. 15). Although the Committee's work arose from concern about social problems, it aimed at the scientific study of sex as a biological phenomenon.

The range of the Committee's activities in the years 1922 to 1947 was very broad, covering anatomical and physiological, anthropological, psychological, and sociological aspects of sex. Chapter 3, "Contributions to Knowledge of Sex Biology," reviews work done on ovarian and testicular hormones, the pituitary hormones, and some general aspects of sex biology. Chapter 4, "Contributions to Knowledge of Neural and Psychological Aspects of Sex Behavior," reviews the Committee-supported work of such investigators as Alfred C. Kinsey and Lewis M. Terman of Stanford University, and others.

The Committee-subsidized research is given in appendix 7, "List of Grants," that provides information about grantee, institution, title of research, amount of grant, and year of work; and in appendix 8, "Published Reports of Investigations," which is a 106-page bibliography arranged by investigator.

In conclusion, Aberle and Corner point out that "the Committee has resolutely given preference to basic research instead of attempting the direct solution of practical problems" (p. 91). They further state, "By its mere existence, and by the prestige of its place in the National Research Council and its support by the Rockefeller Foundation, the Committee has been a very great influence in breaking down the taboos against scientific study of sex in the United States" (p. 89). (TJW)

IL,PO

171.   Brecher, Edward M. **The Sex Researchers.** With a foreword by William H. Masters and Virginia E. Johnson. Boston: Little, Brown, 1969. 354 p. Includes bibliography and index.

Brecher's curiosity about sex research was stimulated when he was ten years old and questioned the truth of his twelve-year-old friend's pronouncement that premarital sex would result in syphilis. He attests to his continuing interest in the subject by presenting this historical overview of what has been learned from the scientific study of sex. Focusing on the contributions of twenty-five sex researchers in the United States, Great Britain, and Europe from Victorian times to the present, Brecher attempts to provide a historical context within which nonspecialists can understand and evaluate the findings of research on human heterosexuality. Written in a nontechnical, free-flowing narrative style, the book combines biography with discussion of the research methods and findings of such early figures as Havelock Ellis, Krafft-Ebing, Freud, Van de Velde, and Blackwell, through Dickinson, Kinsey, Pomeroy, and Gebhard, to contemporary researchers like Schaefer, Sherfey, Money, Harlow, and Masters and Johnson. It balances theoretical interests with practical issues. As Masters and Johnson comment in the foreword and Brecher readily admits, the book is highly opinionated and selective in what it includes. It is meant to be neither a comprehensive history nor a textbook or reference work. Rather, it pursues a theme of showing the "gradual convalescence of our culture from a debilitating sexual disease," i.e., Victorianism. (SGF)

PR,IL
172. Bullough, Vern L., ed. **The Frontiers of Sex Research.** Buffalo, N.Y.: Prometheus Books, 1979. 190 p. Includes bibliographies. ISBN 0-87975-113-4.

Ongoing research in the field of human sexuality is reviewed in this collection of eighteen papers by sexologists, sociologists, psychologists, and others. Bullough, professor of history and founder of the Center for Sex Research at California State University, Northridge, states that "the field of sexual studies is just beginning to emerge as a serious one" and that most of the major researchers in the field are still active today, building on the groundwork laid by Alfred Kinsey, Havelock Ellis, and Magnus Hirschfeld. Researchers identified at the research frontier include J. Robert Bragonier and Barbara J. Bragonier (sex physiology), William E. Hartman and Marilyn Fithian (sexual dysfunction), Milton Diamond (sexual identity and sex roles), Julius H. Winer (transsexual surgery), Richard W. Smith (homosexuality), Veronica D. Elias (sexual conduct), James Elias (adolescent sexuality), John Money (erotic imagery), Thomas Coleman (sex and the law), and Lester A. Kirkendall (sex research itself). A number of other investigators discuss historical aspects of the field (Vern L. Bullough), the sexual revolution (Helen Colton), sex counseling (Bonnie Bullough), and sex research as a personal experience (Virginia Prince). "A Guide to Further Reading" suggests where to find reports of both ongoing and earlier research in monographs, specialized journals, and bibliographies. (TJW)

PR,IL
172a. Bullough, Vern L. **Science in the Bedroom: A History of Sex Research.** New York: Basic Books, 1994. 376 p. Includes bibliographic notes and index. ISBN 0-456-03020-3.

Bullough, a distinguished historian and author of numerous books about sexuality (e.g., *Sexual Variance in Society and History*, 1976; *Women and Prostitution* [with co-author Bonnie Bullough], 1987; *Cross-Dressing, Sex, and Gender* [with co-author Bonnie Bullough], 1993), inquires, "How did modern sex research develop?" Concentrating on the last 150 years, he describes the historical, social, cultural, and psychological contexts from which sex research emerged and developed. He pays attention to the background of major and lesser-well-known personalities influential in shaping sex research (e.g., Karl Heinrich Ulrichs, Richard von Krafft-Ebing, Magnus Hirschfeld, Clelia Mosher, Michel Foucault, Sigmund Freud, Havelock Ellis, William Masters, Virginia Johnson, John Money).

The first chapter highlights ideas about sexuality from the Greeks in the fourth century B.C. to scientists in the nineteenth century, when modern sexology began. Up to this time, concepts of sexuality represented a "hodgepodge of ideas and contributors" (p. 9). Much of the interest during this period was related to human anatomy and physiology and queries about how conception took place. Many of these ideas persisted until the nineteenth century, when several factors converged to create a climate conducive to the development of modern sexology: more specialization in science; the efforts of people labeled deviant, defective, or criminal to explain the basis of their own behavior; and feminism. These three factors pervade the discussions that follow on such topics as homosexuality, gender research, the American experience, and the changing social attitudes and personalities that facilitated sexological research.

Personal and social interest in the nature of and origins of homosexuality sparked much research in the late nineteenth and early twentieth centuries. Magnus Hirschfeld, Havelock Ellis, and Sigmund Freud dominated sexology in the early part of the twentieth century. Hirschfeld and Ellis contributed a great deal of empirical data, and Freud provided a systematic, theoretical framework for research and therapy, in addition to his case studies. Americans noticed the wide range of variations in sexual practices and added realism to their inquiries. By the 1920s and 1930s, the public was more willing to learn about sex, and endocrinological researchers made significant progress in understanding sexual physiology. More scholars and scientists explored sexual topics, including anthropologists, biologists, and psychologists. Freudian ideas were well-established by the 1940s and smoothed the way for public interest in the scientific, survey research on the sexual behavior of the human male and female by Kinsey, "the most influential sex researcher in the twentieth century." The development of oral contraceptives and new studies of human sexual response by Masters and Johnson ushered in the establishment of sexology as a new discipline. The interdisciplinary nature of the field and a social climate conducive to exploring diverse lifestyles led to almost a geometrical progression of sex research from the 1960s on. Masculinity, femininity, and cross-gender behavior took center stage as areas of investigation. Currently, sexology is on its way to becoming a science.

From its beginning as an adjunct to medical research in the early years of the twentieth century to the current proliferation of research from many disciplines, "Sexology as a science has made important contributions to society" (p. 299). (SGF)

PR
173. Bullough, Vern L. **The Society for the Scientific Study of Sex: A Brief History.** Mt. Vernon, Iowa.: Foundation for the Scientific Study of Sexuality, 1989. 35 p. Includes bibliography. ISBN 0-9624373-0-1.

Authored by Vern Bullough, a past president of the Society for the Scientific Study of Sex (SSSS) and contributor through his publications to several areas of human sexuality, this pamphlet presents an insider's view of the Society's history. Before discussing the Society's history, Bullough provides a brief review of the beginnings of research in the field of sexology, focusing on key developments in Germany during the nineteenth and early twentieth centuries as well as major contributions from Richard von Krafft-Ebing, Magnus Hirschfeld, and others. He also pays attention to the first international congresses on sexology that were initiated by some of these same leaders, and comments on the leading American researchers (Kinsey, Masters and Johnson) whose work preceded the establishment of the SSSS.

Based on interviews with other past presidents of the SSSS, together with his own personal recollections, Bullough recounts the humble beginning of the Society, which grew out of the efforts of Albert Ellis, Hans Lehfeldt, and Henry Guze. He describes the writing of the constitution, the recruitment of charter members, the early meetings in New York City, and the Society's final incorporation in New York State in 1965. He relates the growth and activities of the SSSS in its early years and the spinning off of SIECUS (Sex Information and Education Council of the U.S.) in 1964 and the organization of AASECT (American Association of Sex Educators, Counselors, and Therapists) in 1967. He discusses the reigns of the early presidents of SSSS, the establishment of *The Journal of Sex Research*, the problem of making SSSS a truly national organization, and international endeavors carried out by John Money. He points out that under later presidents, the organization was put on a more secure financial footing, strengthened by appointing an executive director, and forming regional groups in the West, East, and the Midwest.

As to the future, Bullough sees research and public policy as the main thrusts of the Society. Moreover, he states that in the United States we do not have adequate sex programs; we have not dealt very effectively with sexually transmitted diseases; sexual problems within marriage remain a major concern; adult-child sexual relations remain relatively unexplored; gender disphoria issues and endocrinological studies have just begun; and so forth. But, he points out, research is expanding in all these areas, and the Society has positioned itself to take the leadership in the exploration of all the key issues facing researchers and reformers today.

The appendixes of this short monograph include listings for past presidents (with their terms of office), the past presidents of the SSSS regions, the charter members of the Society, society fellows, and society award recipients, as well as additional listings of directors, members-at-large, and donors of the Foundation for the Scientific Study of Sexuality, which sponsored this brief history. (TJW)

PR,IL

174. Irvine, Janice M. **Disorders of Desire: Sex and Gender in Modern American Sexology.** Philadelphia: Temple University Press, 1990. 345 p. (Health, Society, and Policy). Includes bibliographic notes and index. ISBN 0-87722-898-1.

Irvine, a sociologist in the Community Health Program at Tufts University and a sex educator since the early 1970s, examines scientific sex research and its application, emphasizing "the efforts of sexology to prevail—both as a viable profession and as a science that would wield 'cultural authority' over issues of sex and gender" (p. 2). What have been the social and political factors that have created an identity crisis within the field and have resulted in conflict over control of cultural definitions of sex and gender?

Beginning with Bloch's formal conception of sexual science in Europe and continuing through later sexology, Irvine asserts that there has been a consistent biomedical emphasis in the field. Krafft-Ebing, Freud, Ellis, and Hirschfeld as well as Kinsey and Masters and Johnson express this essentialist theme. In contrast to the scientific study of sex is the humanistic tradition in sexology, that began with the work of Reich in the 1920s and flowered in the 1960s with the development of humanistic psychology, particularly the human potential movement. The focus of humanistic sexology is on sexual enhancement and fulfillment, on sexual expression and emotion, rather than on intellectual analyses of sexuality. The Institute for Advanced Study of Human Sexuality, SARs (Sexual Attitude Reassessments), and the therapeutic style of Hartman and Fithian emphasize this theme. The inclusion of these two approaches to human sexuality under the label "sexology" has generated conflict within the field and hindered the growth of sexology as a profession. Clinical programs of sex therapy and research on gender illustrate these issues.

Irvine discusses biomedical and humanistic trends in the development of sexology in terms of classic research on elements of professionalization: systematic theory and cognitive base (major enterprises of sexology and their underlying ideologies); authority over knowledge (role of sexology in the historical construction of sexual disease and a biomedically negotiated sexuality); sanctions of the broader community (how sexology relates to shifts in political, cultural, economic, and demographic variables); development of regulatory ethical codes as well as a culture of associations and organizations (sexology's internal process of professional consolidation).

Irvine concludes that sexology's current challenge is to "secure an authoritative and profitable niche in the area of human sexuality at a moment of fear and uncertainty" (p. 280). The field has accomplished some success in credibility by fostering more openness and enthusiasm for sex and by establishing professional organizations. Also, a few sexologists have achieved public respectability while other professionals are less subject to harassment for being involved in sex research. Nevertheless, she thinks that sexology has generally failed to establish its cultural authority over sexual knowledge and values. It lacks a power base; remains a "fragmented, diffuse, and defensive field" (p. 283); presents sexual issues in a cultural context where discourse on sex is marked by stigma, shame, and moralism; and generally adheres to a biomedical model that may contribute to professional respectability but constrains the development of the profession to a narrow niche. Irvine thinks that the growth of the field depends upon confrontation with its biases and methods; an understanding of the social construction of sexual definitions, categories, and behavior; and an exploration of the impact of politics on sexual discourse. The inclusion of diverse voices and a broader vision of the field will contribute to sexology's cultural legitimacy. (SGF)

PR,IL

174a.   Lichtenberg, Kara Ellynn. **A Research Guide to Human Sexuality.** New York: Garland, 1994. 497 p. (Garland Reference Library of Social Science; Vol. 836). Includes bibliography and indexes. ISBN 0-8153-0867-1.

Intended as a research guide, not a series of bibliographies on various subjects, this is "the first attempt to compile a comprehensive dictionary and research guide for those seeking information and materials on human sexuality and related topics, be they researchers, educators, clinicians, students, or the general public" (p. xv). It contains 1,000 print and electronic resources published in English, primarily between 1982 and 1993, although it does include classic references before 1982. Lichtenberg organizes a wide range of diverse materials from different disciplines (e.g., anthropology, biology, sociology, literature, psychology, social science, religious studies, women's studies), professions (e.g., counseling, law, medicine, public affairs), types of sources (e.g., scholarly, professional, governmental, commercial, popular), and points of view (e.g., Feminists Fighting Porn, NARAL, the National Pro-Family Coalition), and presents them in a logical, user-friendly format.

Each of the thirty chapters focuses on a specific type of resource for sex research, arranged into seven categories, each of which makes up one of nine major parts of the guide: (1) research assistance (libraries, reference works), (2) terminology (thesauri, subject dictionaries), (3) background sources (literature reviews, textbooks, encyclopedias, handbooks), (4) accessing tools (library catalogs, library classification systems, subject bibliographies, electronic databases, indexes and abstracts, directories, periodicals), (5) source materials (books, dissertations/theses, government documents, conferences and meetings), (6) statistical and survey data (public opinion polls, statistics, sexual behavior surveys, records, lists, facts), (7) tools (curriculum, measurement tools, data sets), (8) media resources (educational audiovisuals, entertainment films/'videos, television), and (9) human resources (experts, organizations/institutions).

Lichtenberg provides a brief introduction to each chapter, pointing out the usefulness of the resource. She also includes a "How to Find" shaded box that highlights how to locate the general and specific aspects of the topics, allowing the reader to find new resources beyond those in the guide. An often lengthy descriptive annotation accompanies each source listed, providing information about its scope and content. A consistent format for each chapter, many cross-references, a title index, and a name index contribute to the reader's ease in using the guide. Appendixes of the Library of Congress's subject headings and schedules are included to facilitate library research. (SGF)

IL

175.   Robinson, Paul. **The Modernization of Sex: Havelock Ellis, Alfred Kinsey, William Masters and Virginia Johnson.** New York: Harper & Row, 1977. 200 p. Includes index. ISBN 0-06-090548-4.

In contrast to the Victorians, who regarded sexual experience as either a "drain in vital energies" or a "threat to moral character," the modernists thought of it as "a worthwhile, though precarious human activity." They were "sexual enthusiasts" who raised questions about the range of legitimate sexual behavior, the need for variety in erotic life, the restriction of sexual experience to marriage, and the sexual equality of women with men. Robinson attempts to demonstrate the significance of sexual modernism as a legitimate component of intellectual history by analyzing the major works of four influential sexual thinkers—Havelock Ellis, Alfred Kinsey, and William Masters and Virginia Johnson—who shaped the form of this new sexual ethos. Havelock Ellis overshadows Freud as a central figure in developing sexual modernism. The first six volumes of his massive work, *Studies in the Psychology of Sex*, were published between 1897 and 1910; they established an enthusiastic, tolerant, and emotionally complex tone toward the study of sexuality that affected subsequent sexual theorizing. Although not thought of as a major theorist, Alfred Kinsey contributed more to thinking on the subject than the empirical data contained in his *Sexual Behavior in the Human Male* (1948) and *Sexual Behavior in the Human Female* (1953). He not only fostered tolerance toward homosexuality and the sexual activities of the young; he also demystified sex. Unlike Freud, who saw sex as fraught with danger, or Ellis, who tended to romanticize it, Kinsey was anti-romantic about the subject. Masters and Johnson went one step further than Kinsey's interviewing to collect their information on sexual behavior; they observed and measured sexual activity in the laboratory. Despite their reputation as dedicated researchers, Robinson claims that they were more interested in therapy and case studies than pure scientific research. And, although they advanced women's sexual rights by demonstrating the similarities in male and female sexual response, they are essentially conservative in adhering to middle class ideals about sex. In essence, they typify the modern mentality about sex—the coexistence of romantic and anti-romantic themes. Overall, Robinson examines the assumptions, biases, inconsistencies, and modes of reasoning that characterized the formulation of a systematic, explicit body of thought on the subject of sex in the twentieth century. (SGF)

In a new, 1989 preface to his book, Robinson highlights the current reaction to the sexual enthusiasm implied in the work of Havelock Ellis, et al., by discussing recent contributions of historian Peter Gay and philosopher Michel Foucault. These deep thinkers have questioned modernist thought about Victorian sexual repression, providing telling information and speculation about the very opposite. Furthermore, the views of Jerry Falwell and others in conjunction with the AIDS epidemic have cast a pall over sexual enthusiasm, resulting in sexual abstinence that can only be described as a "classic example of sublimation on a massive scale." (TJW)

PR,IL

176.   Weinberg, Martin S., ed. **Sex Research: Studies from the Kinsey Institute.** New York: Oxford University Press, 1976. 320 p. Includes bibliography. ISBN 0-19-502032-4.

Weinberg, Professor of Sociology at Indiana University and Senior Research Sociologist at the Institute for Sex Research, surveys in this book the work at the Institute for Sex Research in order to present its history and an overview of its publications and ideas from Kinsey's time to the present. He hopes that his presentation of selections of works from the Institute will "inform the reader about the social factors that influence human sexuality" because "the whole purpose behind the Institute for Sex Research is to dispel the myths and lack of knowledge that have for too long surrounded this elusive subject." Excerpts from the writings of three of Kinsey's closest colleagues (Paul Gebhard, Cornelia Christenson, and Wardell Pomeroy) provide a history of the Institute, including background on Kinsey's life and work. The rest of the book makes the findings of some of the major reports of the Institute accessible to the public in condensed form. Selections from *Sexual Behavior in the Human Male* and *Sexual Behavior in the Human Female* are followed by those from other Institute publications, that cover a wide range of topics in human sexuality: pregnancy, birth, abortion, sex offenders, homosexuality, fetishism, sadomasochism, nudity, cross-cultural variations, and eroticism in art and literature. The book conveys the central theme of the Institute: like other forms of behavior, sex can be approached in a direct way and can be understood as an experience shaped by social factors. It acquaints the reader with other members of the Institute's staff and demonstrates how work on human sexuality has proceeded at the Institute since Kinsey's death in 1956. (SGF)

METHODOLOGY. ETHICS

PR
177.   Beere, Carole A. **Sex and Gender Issues: A Handbook of Tests and Measures.**
New York: Greenwood Press, 1990. 605 p. Includes bibliographies and indexes. ISBN
0-313-27462-2.

In this compilation intended for researchers, Beere, Associate Dean for Graduate
Study and Research at Central Michigan University, has assembled and described 197
scales found in articles and reports identified in a wide variety of journals and documents.
She has arranged these scales by name in eleven categories as follows: Heterosexual
Relations (17 scales), Sexuality (41 scales), Contraception and Abortion (18 scales),
Pregnancy and Childbirth (20 scales), Somatic Issues (16 scales), Homosexuality (10
scales), Rape and Sexual Coercion (25 scales), Family Violence (9 scales), Body Image
and Appearance (17 scales), Eating Disorders (20 scales), and Other Scales (5 scales).

The scale descriptions follow a consistent pattern, providing the following information: title of scale as provided by author; author(s); date of earliest use; brief statement
of variables that scale is intended to measure; type of instrument, e.g., multiple choice
measure; description of the scale; sample items for each scale; previous subject groups,
e.g., college students; statement of appropriateness for subject groups; method of administration (usually self-administered); scoring method; development of the scale; reliability; validity; notes and comments; availability of scale; articles and reports that used the
scale; and, bibliography. An introduction to each section puts the scales in perspective.

This volume and its companion volume *Gender Roles* (Beere, 1990) are revisions of
her earlier work, *Women and Women's Issues: A Handbook of Tests and Measures* (Beere,
1979) and supersede it. Both are meant to facilitate researchers' tasks by locating valid
measures appropriate for research. The compilation contains an Index of Scale Titles, Index
of Scale Authors, Index of Variables Measured by Scales, and Index of Scale Users. (TJW)

PR
178.   Byrne, Donn, and Kathryn Kelley, eds. **Alternative Approaches to the Study of
Sexual Behavior.** Hillsdale, N.J.: Lawrence Erlbaum Associates, 1986. 224 p. Includes
bibliographies and indexes. ISBN 0-89859-677-7.

This volume includes an introductory paper on the multidisciplinary study of
sexual behavior; five papers explaining alternative approaches to the study of human
sexuality; a review of research on coition as an emotion; and a final paper discussing the
integration of sex research.

The main point made by Donn Byrne in his paper is that "biosexual, sociosexual,
and psychosexual research can be combined within a single framework . . . together they
provide an integrative picture of human sexual functioning" (p. 7).

George G. Gallup, Jr. states that the purpose of his paper "is to examine some
distinctive features of human sexual behavior and anatomy from the standpoint of
adaptive considerations related to the evolutionary history of our species" (p. 13). He
emphasizes genetic influences on sexual behavior and notes differences in male and
female sexuality as "a reflection of our evolutionary heritage, not environmental or
cultural influences" (pp. 39-40).

The paper by Raymond C. Rosen and J. Gayle Beck "reviews the development of
laboratory research methods" in the study of male and female sexual arousal. It emphasizes "issues such as the multifaceted nature of sexual response, the correspondence
between objective and subjective measures of arousal, the choice of theoretical models
being used to guide laboratory research, gender and individual differences, and the social
context of sex research" (p. 44).

Edgar Gregersen examines human sexuality from a cross-cultural perspective,
pointing out that the "strategy of cross-cultural study has been to try to develop a sample
of cultures, each of which is relatively independent of other cultures" (p. 88). He reviews

the history of cross-cultural studies, describes variations in sex customs around the world, and examines sexual customs, beliefs, and practices in select culture areas, such as Black Africa, the Middle East, and others.

Kathleen McKinney describes and illustrates the sociological approach to human sexuality. Specifically, she looks at the kinds of issues studied by sociologists; the theoretical perspectives adopted (learning theory, functionalism, labeling theory, conflict theory, symbolic interactionism, and exchange theory); research strategies used (case studies, experiments, observational research, survey research); and ethical and methodological problems that must be faced using the sociological approach.

William A. Fisher in his paper on the psychological approach to human sexuality uses the Sexual Behavior Sequence, a model that "deals with the roles of arousal, affect, and cognition as determinants of sexual behavior" (p. 132), as the basis of discussion.

Dolf Zillmann's paper proposes that coition be considered an emotional phenomenon and relates his work to that of Cannon (1929) who "promoted the view that acute emotional states are responses to environmental threats and that these responses are designed to aid the organism in coping with the threats" (p. 173).

Finally, Kathryn Kelley discusses the theoretical benefits of integrative sexological research; points out the methodological improvements in such research; and compares the various methods in terms of a number of dimensions relating to theory, content differences, and mechanisms, presenting the contributors' approaches in the form of a table. (TJW)

PR
179. Davis, Clive M., William L. Yarber, and Sandra L. Davis, eds. **Sexuality-Related Measures: A Compendium.** Lake Mills, Iowa: Graphic Publishing, 1988. 270 p. ISBN 0-9620581-0-6.

In the preface, the editors pinpoint the logic that underlies the need for this compendium of sexuality-related measures. An understanding of different forms of sexual expression requires research, that in turn requires reliable and valid measurement tools that are available to and used by professionals in the field. Sex researchers are faced with difficulties in obtaining access to sexuality-related measures other than those most widely used. The goal of this volume is to address the problem of availability of measures for sex researchers by providing "descriptions and, in most cases, complete reproductions of many of the most promising measurement tools" (preface).

To obtain the 109 measures that make up this book, the editors searched the published and some unpublished literature and asked colleagues for suggestions. The more than 100 original developers of the measures provided descriptions of their measures according to the following format: (1) name of measure; (2) what it measures; (3) a description of the measure; (4) response mode and timing; (5) reliability; and (6) validity. Each of these descriptions became one of the chapters in the book, arranged according to subject area. The topics covered relate to the disciplines of medicine, psychology, sociology, and anthropology; they include measures about abortion, education, experience, female sexuality, functioning, homosexuality, love, rape, satisfaction, STDs, transsexualism, and vasectomy. Although the book does not incorporate "all of even the fairly well-known instruments or many measures of assessments in an applied setting," the editors hope that the availability of the measures they did include will "stimulate more and better research by making the task of measurement or assessment easier." By adding the mailing address of each of the authors at the end of each description, the editors also hope to enhance communication between researchers and practitioners who can then develop new measures or refine the ones available. (SGF)

PR
180. Harding, Sandra, and Jean F. O'Barr, eds. **Sex and Scientific Inquiry.** Chicago: University of Chicago, 1987. 317 p. Includes bibliographic notes and index. ISBN 0-226-31627-0.

Selecting from fifty essays published in *Signs: Journal of Women in Culture and Society*, editors Harding, Professor of Philosophy and Director of Women's Studies at the University of Delaware, and O'Barr, Director of Women's Studies at Duke University and editor of *Signs*, bring together articles that relate to five major themes: (1) the social structure of science; (2) misuses and abuses of science and technology; (3) bias in the sciences; (4) the sexual meanings of science; and (5) epistemology and metatheory. The fifteen articles organized around these themes were written by academic women in departments of philosophy, biology, family studies, history, mathematics, sociology, psychology, and the humanities.

In the first section, historians Londa Schiebinger and Margaret W. Rossiter examine the social structure of science while Sandra L. Chaff presents photographs that convey the image of women in medicine in the nineteenth century. In the second part, Judith A. McGaw, Sally G. Allen, and Joanna Hubbs, and Inez Smith Reid deal with the uses and misuses of science and technology, examining such questions as the role of women in the history of American technology and the links between science, politics, and race. The largest section, the third, contains articles that challenge the value neutrality of science by elucidating biases in the models, problem definition, theory and construct construction, research design, data collection, and interpretation of results. Helen H. Lambert offers a perspective on sex differences that suggests it is a mistake for feminists to base their claims for social justice purely on cultural influences, while Patricia Y. Miller and Martha R. Fowlkes review behavioral and social models of female sexuality that depart from the Freudian model. Helen Longino and Ruth Doell focus on evolutionary studies and endocrinological research on behavioral sex differences as examples of ways in which sexism and androcentrism become part of the research process. Stephanie A. Shields and Donna Haraway examine the assumptions of specific scientific theories; Shields looks at sex differences in intelligence, while Haraway investigates the basis for assuming that dominance is a natural, physical-chemically based behavior. In the section on sexual meanings in science, both Evelyn Fox Keller and Susan Bordo point out that the ways in which men understand gender relations reinforce the sexual meanings in science. In the last section on epistemology and metatheory of science, Hilary Rose and Sandra Harding grapple with questions about the assumptions and theories of natural science in relation to feminist critiques of them.

Together, the essays provide a feminist critique of science, particularly the ways in which the history of science and its concepts, theories, and methods frame the ways in which researchers and theorists conceptualize and interpret human sexuality, especially female sexuality. (SGF)

PR

181. Masters, William H., Virginia E. Johnson, and Robert C. Kolodny, eds. **Ethical Issues in Sex Therapy and Research.** Boston: Little, Brown, 1977. 227 p. Includes bibliographic references and index. ISBN 0-316-54983-5.

This is a very significant reference source in the field of human sexuality. Topics evolved out of a conference organized and sponsored by the Reproductive Biology Research Foundation (January 22-23, 1976). Discussions were convened around the following topics: the historical background of ethical considerations in sex research and sex therapy; theological perspectives on the ethics of scientific investigation and treatment of human sexuality; ethical issues and requirements for sex research with humans; confidentiality; issues and attitudes in research and treatment of variant forms of human sexual behavior; the ethics of sex therapy; and the training of sex therapists. William H. Masters summed up the conference in an expression of the need for the incorporation of acceptable ethical standards in both treatment and research. He called for the establishment of training centers and treatment programs with appropriate institutional connections, stating that human sexology has yet to come into its academically recognized and legitimized scientific place in the medical community. (**Women's Studies**, 1979)

PR

182. Pomeroy, Wardell B., Carol C. Flax, and Connie Christine Wheeler. **Taking a Sex History: Interviewing and Recording.** New York: Free Press, 1982. 329 p. Includes index. ISBN 0-02-925370-5.

Prepared by one of Alfred Kinsey's original collaborators, Wardell Pomeroy, and two prominent sex therapists and educators, this volume proposes "to describe and explain the interviewing and coding system used by Kinsey and his colleagues, to provide an aid to a later generation of scholars and practitioners" (p. 1). The personal, structured interview is the method used to elicit a sex history. The primary emphasis of the book is on interviewing techniques (what questions to ask, how to phrase them, the order of presentation, etc.) within the framework of describing the recording instrument. All responses are recorded on an 8 by 11-inch sheet of paper, divided into blocks that correspond to each area of background or behavior of interest to the interviewer; responses are coded into a brief list of symbols that have meaning according to where they are coded on the block.

The initial chapters cover some general aspects of the interviewing process, detail the symbols of the "position code," and how to use the recording model. A common concern of interviewees is whether they are normal; the interviewer needs to be able to correct misinformation, provide accurate information when requested, and abide by a general interviewer rule when collecting sex information—"never make judgments about what people do or do not do." Since eliciting accurate and complete information is the object of the interview, a private setting and an accepting attitude set a trusting tone for the discussion. Providing positive feedback, opening and closing information doors, establishing a pattern via pegs (significant life events), using checklists, flowing with the respondent, avoiding euphemisms, using special vocabularies if necessary, and controlling the interview all enhance the accuracy of the information.

Each of the remaining chapters deals with the special interviewing techniques, symbols, and background information relevant to each category of information elicited in the interview. Health, family background, sex education, dreams, first coitus, contraception, erotic arousal, animal contacts, and anatomy are some of the subjects covered. Initially a chapter gives a brief introduction to the subject and discusses the significance of the questions as part of a sex history; the rest of the chapter provides responses that could occur and discusses how to interpret them or probe further. Figures show the way the code should be entered on the sheet. Final chapters demonstrate how the general model for taking a sex history can be applied to special populations, such as homosexuals or prostitutes. Not only does the book provide ways to accurately and confidentially collect and record information about a personal, sensitive area of a person's life; it also illustrates the meticulous logic and method that became the basis for the Kinsey reports. (SGF)

Sex Education

(For related material see also entries 592, 1044-1048, 1052)

PR,IL
183. Breasted, Mary. **Oh! Sex Education!** New York: Praeger, 1970. 343 p. Includes index.

In 1969, when Breasted, a contributor to the *Village Voice*, began her research about the sex education controversy, battles over the subject were taking place in thirty states. On the right were the Anti Sex Education forces (the "Antis") such as the John Birch Society and the Christian Crusaders; at the other extreme were supporters of sex education such as college professors and SIECUS (Sex Information and Education Council of the U.S.).

Written in a lively, often pungent yet humorous journalistic style, the book first examines the sex education controversy in Anaheim, California, where one of the most advanced sex education programs in the country had been instituted in 1965. Anaheim's program became a symbol for people on both sides of the issue and could be viewed as a microcosm of the concerns relevant to the country as a whole: parental roles and authority over children; beliefs about children's sexuality; religion and morality; the relevance of teachers and intelligentsia in sex education; political interpretations of sexuality; and personal crusades. Breasted describes a rich roster of characters who personify these forces, such as a school superintendent and a former director of the Family Living and Sex Education (FLSE) program who became symbols of the professional elite and casualties of the anti-sex education forces; housewives who became self-appointed guardians of children's morality; and a newspaper editor whose writing helped to undermine the FLSE program. Although over 90 percent of the parents in the area said they favored sex education, the Antis's appeals of God, country, and family succeeded in eroding much of the administrative support and educational materials for the program.

The other major part of the book explores related issues with their associated personalities from other parts of the country. Gordon Drake, author of the pamphlet "Is the School House the Proper Place to Teach Raw Sex?" and part of the Christian Crusade, is contrasted with the well-educated daughter of photographer Edward Steichen, Mary Calderone, who was director of Planned Parenthood and one of the founders of SIECUS. On an organizational level, the participants at the National Convention on the Crisis in Education, who were dedicated Antis, are contrasted with people who attended a meeting of the National Council on Family Relations, humanists who subscribe to a "worship of normalcy" and an "accommodation to current culture."

Breasted concludes that the sex education controversy boils down to a matter of faith, centering on the question of whether knowledge of sexuality is a good thing. One set of believers thinks that "sexual enlightenment contributed to any number of socially commendable attitudes" while the other was sure that it "created terrible and irresistible temptations that put a strain on every ounce of civilization in a child's mind." (SGF)

PR
184. Brown, Lorna, ed. **Sex Education in the Eighties: The Challenge of Healthy Sexual Evolution.** New York: Plenum Press, 1981. 264 p. (Perspectives in Sexuality). Includes bibliographic references and index. ISBN 0-306-40762-0.

This volume in the Perspectives in Sexuality series is dedicated to Mary Steichen Calderone, a cofounder in 1964 of the Sex Information and Education Council of the United States (SIECUS). In his preface, series editor Richard Green describes Calderone as "the foremost advocate of sex education in the United States." Editor Brown states that this wide-ranging collection of papers "shows how many different fields now have a sex education component." The twenty-one contributors are drawn from education, psychology, psychiatry, sociology, and anthropology, which highlights the interdisciplinary orientation of the book.

As background to the field, Lester A. Kirkendall gives a historical account of sex education in the United States from the beginning of the present century; and Harriet F. Pilpel and Laurie R. Rockett delve into the "legal and constitutional principles governing the questions of access to and control of sex education in the schools."

Sex education in different environments is dealt with in several papers: Mary Lee Tatum writes about sex education in the public schools, and Michael A. Carrera and Eugene A. Baker expound in detail on the successful human sexuality program that served as a model for sex education in a residential facility for problem children. Warren R. Johnson covers sex education for special populations, including the mentally handicapped, the physically disabled, the chronically ill, and the elderly. Herant A. Katchadourian describes the experience in sex education at Stanford University, the first major research university to establish an accredited undergraduate sexuality course, and evaluates current courses in sex education at the college level. Sex education at different age levels is dealt with in two papers: Floyd M. Martinson investigates the problem of the sex education of children from early childhood through elementary school, and Sol Gordon looks at the educational aspects of teenage sexuality.

The state of sex education in special fields, including religion, is also examined: William H. Genne's paper deals with sex education in religious settings, and includes a discussion of *The Interfaith Statement of Sex Education*, which was adopted by Protestant, Catholic, and Jewish organizations; David R. Mace explores the relationship between marriage counseling and sex education, while Jane M. Johnson relates sex education and family planning; Harold I. Lief examines the past and prospects for the future on sex education in medicine; and Harvey L. Gochros does the same for the allied health professionals in nursing, social work, law, and the ministry.

Educating the educators is a serious problem. Deryck Calderwood takes up this challenging problem and presents the curriculum content of a course in human sexuality that would stress knowledge, attitude, and methodology. Gary F. Kelly then presents his views on the difficult role of parents as sex educators, and Robert N. Butler and Myrna I. Lewis stress the importance of educating professionals about sex and aging. Eli A. Rubinstein shows how educators may use television as a useful sex education tool.

Finally, Mary S. Calderone reminisces about sex education and the work of SIECUS. She identifies six concepts that have become the basis of our current understanding of human sexuality: identification of human sexuality as a health entity, common usage of the term "sexuality" as distinguished from sex, enlistment of professionals of all disciplines, the beginnings of the sexuality movement at the international level, awareness of the sexual needs of sexually disenfranchised groups, and acceptance of the sexuality of children and infants. (TJW)

PR

185. Bruess, Clint E., and Jerrold S. Greenberg. **Sex Education: Theory and Practice.** Belmont, Calif.: Wadsworth, 1981. 319 p. Includes bibliographies and index. ISBN 0-534-00899-2.

The purpose of this book is to provide a "comprehensive coverage of the many aspects of human sexuality and the teaching skills that are necessary to prepare a sex educator" (p. xv). Applicable in virtually any sex education program, the practical ideas presented here in exercise form are intended to help the reader learn to be a sex educator.

The text is divided into eight parts: part I is an introduction to sex education and discusses such topics as traditional and contemporary concepts of human sexuality, the complexity of sexuality and the life cycle, and selected issues (masturbation, homosexuality, orgasms, etc.); part II contains ideas on how to start and expand a program; part III covers the biological, psychological, and sociological aspects of sex education; part

IV is about sexual decision making involving moral considerations deriving from contemporary religious positions; part V gets down to the basics of conducting sex education from the preschool level through college and adult education levels and deals with such topics as curriculum, lesson plans, etc.; and part VI focuses on evaluation of the sex education program and the sex educators.

Several appendixes cover the "National Council of Churches Interfaith Statement on Sex Education"; Michael A. Carrera's journal article "Training the Sex Educator: Guidelines for Teacher Training Institutions"; a listing of sex education resources; a paper on venereal disease education materials; the "Code of Ethics of the American Association of Sex Educators, Counselors, and Therapists"; and a discussion of various teaching strategies. (TJW)

PR

186. Cassell, Carol, and Pamela M. Wilson, eds. **Sexuality Education: A Resource Book.** New York: Garland, 1989. 446 p. (Garland Reference Library of Social Science, vol. 416). Includes bibliographies and index. ISBN 0-8240-7899-3.

The purpose of this reference work is to "describe a variety of ways to plan and implement sexuality education and to provide in-depth information on the current resources available." The editors, author and researcher Cassell and sexuality education program consultant Wilson, emphasize some of the themes of the book by its title, *Sexuality Education,* a concept that embraces emotions, relationships, psychological development, and behavioral processes, not merely sexual functioning or "sex" per se, which is often the interpretation of the widely used expression "sex education." They organize the essays of the thirty-eight contributors into four major sections: (1) Sexuality Education in the Family (topics include parent education, parent/child relationships, gay children, abuse prevention), (2) Sexuality Education in the Schools (topics: curricula for elementary schools, junior high school, senior high school, college, private and public schools, and information on teacher training), (3) Sexuality Education Programs in the Community (topics: education in the contexts of youth organizations, health agencies, churches, and address the problems of AIDS and program evaluation), and (4) Model Programs (topics: examples of specific programs such as the Teenage Communication Theater, mother/daughter workshops, and others).

The professional fields of the contributors—secondary or college education, family or population planning, mental health, medicine, religion, civic organizations—provide an interdisciplinary framework for approaching this immense topic. Each of the short essays is designed to address one practical aspect of conducting sexuality education. Cassell and Morris offer a very brief introduction to the topic of sex education. The first essay of each section provides an overview of the segment of education being considered. The first three sections are followed by an annotated bibliography of resources, categorized according to audience level (professionals, parents, young children, teens, etc.) and type of material (curricula, audiovisual, etc.). The book concludes with a brief section of addresses and telephone numbers of audiovisual distributors.

Despite the variety of contributors, the book reiterates a number of themes. Learning about sexuality is a life-long process; formal education is only a part of that process. Sexuality education should embrace the various contexts, feelings, and values that individuals experience, not merely focus on problems. Approaches to sexuality education need to foster communication and comfort with the subject. Sexuality education supplements rather than replaces education by parents, who are primarily responsible for the sexuality education of their children.

The essays are quite general, written in jargon-free prose, and provide an overview of problems and approaches in the field. The book provides a basic introduction to the subject for educators, counselors, administrators, and policymakers. (SGF)

IL,PO
187. McCary, James Leslie. **Sexual Myths and Fallacies.** New York: Van Nostrand Reinhold, 1971. 206 p. Includes bibliography, index, and glossary.

Recent research findings in a variety of fields (psychology, medicine, biology, and sociology) have shown that "accurate sex information is directly related to a stable and fulfilling sex life." However, myths and fallacies about sexuality abound in all segments of the population, including the educational and scientific communities. Consequently, they are often perpetuated by parents to their children and by teachers to their students. In an effort to "dissipate some of the clouds of misinformation enveloping the subject of human sexuality," McCary, a distinguished sex educator, selects eighty-three myths and fallacies that represent some of the "more sophisticated questions" asked him by students, physicians, lecture audiences, and private correspondents. The myths cluster around several major themes into which the book is divided: sexual physiology and functioning; sexual drive; reproduction and birth control; homosexuality; sexual disorders and sexual abnormalities, real and imagined; sex offenses; and "other fallacies." Examples of myths addressed are: "Athletic performance is diminished by sexual intercourse the night before," "Sexual intercourse should be avoided during pregnancy," "Alcohol is a sex stimulant," "Nymphomaniacs and satyromaniacs abound in our society," and "Pornography stimulates people to commit criminal sex acts." McCary then refutes each myth with scientific evidence.

A brief annotated bibliography of classic works on sexuality (e.g., Kinsey, Masters and Johnson, Ford and Beach) and a dictionary of sex-related terminology facilitate finding further information and in elucidating terms in the text. In the process of dispelling myths, McCary presents an overview of important concepts in the field of human sexuality. (SGF)

PR
188. Morrison, Eleanor S., and Mila Underhill Price. **Values in Sexuality: A New Approach to Sex Education.** New York: Hart, 1974. 219 p. Includes bibliography and index. ISBN 0-8055-0179-7.

Human sexuality is not limited to the genitals but encompasses an individual's entire personality. Therefore, fundamental issues of sexuality include personal values, self-image, mode of interaction, and lifestyle. It follows that sex education is not an exclusively cognitive domain, but includes the equally important area of affective responses. This book's goal is to present a new style of education for mature sexuality—one that emphasizes the interaction of small groups of people to elucidate their awareness of feelings and values about sex. Each section of the book includes exercises and activities focused on a specific theme—physiology, psychosexual development, sex roles, values clarification, dimensions in relationships, nonmarital sex, marriage, and parenthood. Each activity is organized by subject, materials needed, time required, objectives, rationale, and procedures. For example, the section on physiology includes a brainstorming session on sexual vocabulary that is aimed at encouraging the use of explicit language referring to sex. Additional sections at the end of the book include advice on starting discussions, methods for summarizing activities, and a short list of books that can supplement the text by providing expanded content for the issues addressed.

The teaching design for this book originated in Morrison's course on human sexuality at Michigan State University. However, it has been employed in training programs, consciousness raising groups, and church and family groups. Geared to high school and college level students, this book provides exercises that structure interaction so that the individual is permitted to explore and discuss sexual issues without the pressure of accepting a particular point of view. Self-awareness and an ability to process materials to make intelligent choices are the overall aims of this issue-oriented compilation of thought-provoking activities. (SGF)

IL,PO

189. Reinisch, June M., with Ruth Beasley. **The Kinsey Institute New Report on Sex: What You Must Know to Be Sexually Literate.** Edited and compiled by Debra Kent. New York: St. Martin's Press, 1990. 540 p. Includes bibliographies and index. ISBN 0-312-05268-5.

"The latest, accurate answers to the questions Americans most often ask about sex and related issues" are presented in this work, written by Reinisch, the Director of the Kinsey Institute for Research on Sex, Gender, and Reproduction at Indiana University. This report does not repeat Alfred Kinsey's famous studies on sexuality, but is meant to supplement them with a new national survey of sexual literacy commissioned by the Kinsey Institute. According to this poll, conducted by the Roper Organization, the majority of Americans are not sexually literate. The sex knowledge test, which most Americans failed, is included in the book for readers to take. All information is presented in an easy-to-read, question-and-answer format and covers the whole gamut of sex and reproduction, including sexual dysfunction; puberty and sexual development; bisexuality and homosexuality; contraception and parenthood; sexually transmitted diseases and reproductive health; sex and aging; male and female anatomy.

Numerous illustrations supplement the text. An appendix provides advice on locating, selecting, and evaluating professional services for treatment of sex problems. (EBS)

IL,YA

190. Skeen, Dick. **Different Sexual Worlds: Contemporary Case Studies of Sexuality.** Lexington, Mass.: Lexington Books, 1991. 179 p. Includes bibliographic references. ISBN 0-669-27278-7.

Based on interviews with over 200 people whose lives represent a broad range of sexual lifestyles in American society, sociologist Skeen selected ten cases that he thinks illustrate the meaning of sex in people's lives and show the diversity of possible sexual lifestyles. One case describes a woman who explores different sexual options after the traumatic end of her marriage. Another describes a successful band leader, whose life revolves around sex, drugs, and rock-and-roll. Other stories include the life of a Catholic priest; an upper-middle-class girl who left her family and became involved in prostitution; a gay male living with AIDS; and a female incest survivor trying to have a satisfying sexual relationship. Skeen's goal is to "share with students the viewpoints of subjects who live in different sexual worlds" (p. 177).

The case studies are designed to complement standard college texts on human sexuality by showing how the knowledge presented in the texts applies to people's real lives. It is meant to encourage the development of an integrated perspective on human sexuality and an understanding of the student's own sexual development. Skeen organizes each case to facilitate discussion in small and large classes. Each case study begins with a chronological review of the person's life, presented from their own point of view. Skeen then analyzes the case, pointing out significant issues that the story raises and relating it to current literature on the subject. A bibliography of suggested readings follows the analysis. Each case study concludes with a series of topical discussion questions designed to encourage students to think about the relevance of the case and the issues it raises for their own lives. The table of contents provides not only a brief synopsis of the story of each case but also a list of topics to which the cases relate.

Among the themes tapped are love, romance, and sexual fulfillment; the balance between passion and security; the impact of early family experiences on later sexuality; growth and change throughout life; pain and trauma in the face of sexual ideals. Skeen concludes that "the variety and power of the meanings we construct in our sexual lives is amazing" (p. 179); it is important that we understand people's different sexual worlds and move beyond erotocentrism. (SGF)

IL
191.   Szasz, Thomas. **Sex by Prescription.** Garden City, N.Y.: Anchor Press/Doubleday, 1980. 198 p. Includes bibliographic notes and index. ISBN 0-385-15898-X.

Szasz, well-known psychiatrist and author of books on psychiatry (e.g., *The Myth of Mental Illness*), examines the subject of sex in two fields, medicine and education. In the areas of sex therapy and sex education, Szasz believes that the public is being hoodwinked by well-intentioned people who should know better. The sex therapists, for example, have mistaken certain behavioral patterns in the sexual arena to be medical problems and have converted them into diseases that they call sexual dysfunctions and sexual disorders, and have recommended treatment. An example is premature ejaculation, the correction of which may be simply a matter of learning. According to Szasz, "Instead of regarding sexual dysfunctions as diseases, we could more profitably regard them as the solutions of certain life tasks—that is, as the expressions of the individual's life-style." Sex educators, like sex therapists, have also exceeded their authority, delving into areas of sexual behavior in which they have no business. It is all right to teach anatomy, physiology, genetics, and reproduction, but sex educators venture into the moral and ethical arena when they purvey opinions about erotic practices, teenage pregnancy, and contraception. Much of so-called sex education flies in the face of established religious and cultural practices and is bound to upset people with profound religious convictions, such as Jews, Christians, and Muslims who have their own ideas about sexual behavior. The sex educators in our public schools fail to recognize this and proceed blindly with their own secular approach to the subject under the guise of scientific thinking. Szasz also explores other fascinating areas, such as sex surgery and sex education for doctors in medical schools, all of which he thinks are a waste of time. Many of the modern approaches to the treatment of sexual problems and the sex education of children are dangerous trends, dehumanizing society and converting its members into docile slaves reminiscent of the inhabitants of the future society depicted in that classic work of prognostication, Huxley's *Brave New World* (1932). Szasz's work is an antidote to the abundance of materials promoting sex therapy and sex education. (TJW)

PR,IL,PO
192.   Wattleton, Faye, with Elisabeth Keiffer. **How to Talk with Your Child About Sexuality.** New York: Doubleday, 1986. 203 p. Includes bibliography, index, and glossary. ISBN 0-385-18444-1.

Drawing on her organization's seventy years of tradition in the field of family planning, Planned Parenthood's President presents a guide for parents, designed to prepare and assist them in their role as children's first and most effective teachers of sexuality. Reiterating Planned Parenthood's position that information and education are the foundation of sound decision making, Wattleton proceeds to describe how parents can adequately present information about sexuality that children want and need to know. Sexuality is regarded as part of the normal development and makeup of every human being. Instruction about it should be part of a lifelong process of communication within the family context.

The first section of the book addresses some of the issues that parents confront in teaching sexuality: how to talk about it without being self-conscious or threatened, how to begin, what to do, how to recognize issues of self-esteem, and how to develop the knowledge that it is safe to be sexual. It is important that both parents assume a role in communicating about sex with children of both sexes. Listening; allowing privacy; trusting; answering questions simply, honestly, and clearly; and presenting a united front all aid the process of inculcating a child's sense of self-worth and values.

The second section addresses "the facts" that children at different ages want to know. There is a progression from the preschooler's interest in concrete information about physical aspects of sex to the teenager's concern with associated moral, social, and emotional values. Discussion centers on providing parents with physical and psychological information about the top seven issues with which children are concerned: menstruation, wet dreams, masturbation, intercourse and pregnancy, birth control, sexually transmitted diseases, and homosexuality.

The final section deals with how to provide help in special situations: a teenager involved in a sexual relationship, including how to deal with an unintended pregnancy; recognition, confrontation, and prevention of sexual abuse, including rape and incest; the dilemma of the single parent who is dating; and parental guidelines for the prevention of "sexual casualties" among latchkey children.

Appendixes supplement the information in the text by adding a glossary of sexual terms; facts about sexually transmitted diseases; methods of contraception; and a selected bibliography of books, pamphlets, and teaching resources for parents as well as for children of different ages. Readers could also consult Snyder and Gordon's *Parents as Sexuality Educators* for other educational materials. (SGF)

TEXTBOOKS

PR,IL
193. Allgeier, Elizabeth Rice, and Albert Richard Allgeier. **Sexual Interactions.** 3rd edition. Lexington, Mass.: Heath, 1991. 819 p. Includes bibliography, indexes, and glossary. ISBN 0-669-24320-5.

In their updated and revised third edition of *Sexual Interactions*, first published in 1984, psychologists Elizabeth Rice Allgeier (Professor of Psychology, Bowling Green State University) and Albert Richard Allgeier (in private practice) reiterate the two main objectives that pervade all three editions of this college text on human sexuality: (1) to provide an integrative approach to human sexuality that recognizes that each individual's sexual experience is the product of a complex interaction of influences that are expressed in the unique context of a person's life and (2) to emphasize that human sexuality is a topic "of serious intellectual inquiry" (p. xi). Drawing from history and literature as well as from contemporary findings on sexuality from anthropology, biology, health education, medicine, sociology, and psychology, Allgeier and Allgeier present a "research-based approach with practical applications" that will allow students to make informed decisions about sexual choices in their own lives.

The first of twenty chapters puts human sexuality in perspective by describing the range of beliefs and behavior about sexual issues in different societies and at different time periods. Chapter 2 focuses on research in sexuality—the pioneers of sex research and the problems that face sex researchers—while chapter 3 outlines four theoretical perspectives (i.e., evolutionary, psychoanalytic, social learning, and sociological) that frame explanations of human sexuality. Chapter 4 deals with conception, prenatal development, and sexual differentiation, and chapter 5 focuses on anatomy, hormones, and the nervous system. Chapter 6 discusses sexual arousal and communication. Sexual behavior is the subject of chapter 7, followed by a discussion of the most recent research on sexual dysfunctions and therapy in chapter 8. Aspects of reproduction are the foci of chapters 9 ("Pregnancy and Birth"), 10 ("Contraception"), and 11 ("Resolving Unwanted Pregnancy"). Chapters 12 and 13 examine gender and sexuality during childhood, adolescence, and adulthood, and chapter 14 considers such topics as eating disorders, body image, diseases, and disabilities, emphasizing ways to enhance sexual health. Chapter 15 deals with variations in sexual orientation. Chapters 16 ("Sex for Profit"), 17 ("Sexually Transmitted Diseases"), 18 ("Sexual Coercion"), and 19 ("Atypical Sexual Activity") deal with contemporary social and psychological issues linked to sexuality. The text concludes with the more positive theme of "Loving Sexual Interactions." Boxes highlighting interesting information as well as many illustrations and photographs complement the text. A summary of major points in the chapter as well as a review of key concepts follow each chapter.

Supplementary materials to enhance both the teacher's and student's use of the text include an instructor's guide with a test item file (also available in computerized form), a study guide, a computerized study guide, a set of colored transparencies, and a periodic newsletter for all adopters. (SGF)

PR,IL

194. Crooks, Robert, and Karla Baur. **Our Sexuality.** 4th edition. Redwood City, Calif.: Benjamin/Cummings, 1990. 850 p. Includes bibliography, index, and glossary. ISBN 0-8053-0190-9.

In this fourth edition of their 1980 college text, Crooks, a psychologist who specializes in clinical and physiological psychology and has a substantial background in sociology, and Baur, a clinical social worker who specializes in sex therapy, continue to pursue their major goal for this text: "To provide a comprehensive and academically sound introduction to the biological, psychosocial, behavioral, and cultural aspects of sexuality, in a way that is personally meaningful to students" (p. x).

Drawing on a scholarly review of the literature (this edition has 500 new citations) and their files of information from clients and college students, Crooks and Baur attempt to present an integrated interdisciplinary approach to human sexuality that is nonjudgmental, egalitarian, and balanced in gender perspectives. Learning aids include critical thinking questions integrated into the text; health capsules summarizing important measures (discussed in the text) for preventing sexual problems and diseases; a glossary and pronunciation guide; a bibliography; and annotated suggested readings at the end of each chapter.

The organization of the contents proceeds in a "logical progression." Part one focuses on the social and cultural legacy of sex in United States society. Although attitudes and roles are changing, the legacies of the belief that sex is primarily for reproduction and the differences in expectations for men and women persist. Crooks and Baur use a psychosocial approach throughout the text to show that human sexuality is governed more by psychological factors (motivations, emotions, attitudes) and social conditioning (learned social expectations and mores) than by biological factors such as hormones or instincts. The last chapter of the first part, "Gender Issues," addresses the specific ways in which gender development is a product of multiple factors. Part two deals with the biological bases of sexual behavior, e.g., female and male sexual anatomy and physiology as well as sexual arousal and response. Part three includes discussions of sexual behavior, including the importance of love, communication, patterns of sexual behavior, and homosexuality. Part four focuses on sexuality and the life cycle and deals with contraception, the process and choice of conceiving children, childhood, adolescence, adulthood, and aging. Part five concerns sexual problems, e.g., sexual difficulties, enhancing sexual satisfaction, chronic illness, disability and sexual adjustment, and sexually transmitted diseases. The text concludes with discussions of social issues, e.g., atypical sexual behavior, sexual victimization, and sex for sale. (SGF)

IL

195. Francoeur, Robert T. **Becoming a Sexual Person.** 2nd edition. New York: Macmillan, 1991. 677 p. Includes bibliography, index, and glossary. ISBN 0-02-339220-7.

In this second edition of his 1982 text *Becoming a Sexual Person* (one of SIECUS' top-rated texts at the time), Francoeur, Professor of Biological and Allied Health Sciences at Fairleigh Dickinson University, updates his interdisciplinary approach to human sexuality by enhancing the range of viewpoints with the help of seventy special consultants who worked with him to "simplify and balance the treatments of complex and controversial issues" (p. ix).

Each part of the text stresses one of the main components of the bio-psycho-sociocultural approach. Part one, "Our Cultural Heritage," deals with social and cultural aspects of sex: a historical chronicle of changes in American culture; sexual values and behaviors in the Muslim Near East, in the Hindu traditions of India, in China, and in Latino cultures; the influence of values and beliefs on individual perceptions of sexual decisions. Part two, "The Personal Context," examines the biological and psychological interface in sexuality: prenatal gender development; anatomy and physiology of the sexual responses and reproduction; issues of birth control, sexual health, STDs, AIDS, childhood and adolescent sexuality. Part three, "The Interpersonal Context," focuses on the link between social and psychological aspects of sexuality: sexual desire and love play; intimacy and love; gender and erotic orientations and conflicts; sexual expressions, problems, and therapies; lifestyles. Part four, "The Social Context," deals with explicit social forms of sexuality: the law; prostitution and pornography; sexual coercion.

Each chapter includes diagrams, illustrations, pictures, and a summary of key concepts and terms. Summary questions aid the student in reflecting on the contents of the chapter. Suggested readings guide the student to more detailed explorations of issues introduced in the chapters, as does the lengthy bibliography at the end of the book. A glossary of terms as well as resources and hot lines for such topics as abortion, AIDS, disabilities and sexuality, gender conflict, gender orientation, sexual abuse and incest, and STDs, aid in the practical use of the work. A computerized test bank, an instructor's manual, and a study guide for students complement the volume. In addition, a set of transparencies, some in color, are available for use with the text.

By blending ethical, personal, social, cultural, and biological concerns about sexuality, Francoeur hopes to present a balanced, thought-provoking, and responsible view of human sexuality. His presentation highlights the major issues in the field without sacrificing their complexity. Although he answers many questions about sexuality, his text serves to question and evaluate issues. (SGF)

IL
196. Gagnon, John H. **Human Sexualities.** Glenview, Ill.: Scott, Foresman, 1977. 432 p. Includes bibliography, index, and glossary. ISBN 0-673-15033-X.

Drawing on the theoretical model that he introduced with William Simon in *Sexual Conduct*, Gagnon offers a text that applies the perspective of social scripting to a range of basic topical issues in the field of human sexuality. Gagnon titles his book *Human Sexualities* because he believes that there is no one human sexuality but a variety of ways to become, be, and express sexuality. He asserts from the beginning that his book has a social learning and developmental perspective, which he presents in the first few chapters ("Sources of Sexuality," "Changing Purposes of Sexuality," "Evaluating Sex Research"). He believes that "sexuality can best be understood as a pattern of learned human conduct, a set of skills and feelings—and that part of that understanding can come from using the tools of psychology and sociology" (p. 2). A sexual script is a device for guiding and understanding action: it is like a blueprint that shapes and controls sexual expression but does not detail every fiber of its content.

Although he does not subscribe to a conventional view of human development as a sequence of stages in which the past has priority over the future, Gagnon finds it convenient to organize most of his materials around the life cycle process. He discusses the early learning of sexuality and puberty, including the formation of gender identities and roles, sexual arousal and response, and masturbation, and then proceeds to a consideration of the development of heterosexuality, homosexuality, bisexuality, and marital and nonmarital sexuality. Variations in sexual expression (prostitution, sexual offenses and offenders, and sexual minorities), a tour of the erotic environment, and a discussion of sex therapy and physical health as it relates to sexual activities round out the text. (SGF)

PR
197. Hogan, Rosemarie Mihelich. **Human Sexuality: A Nursing Perspective.** New York: Appleton-Century-Crofts, 1980. 747 p. Includes bibliographic references and index. ISBN 0-8385-3956-4.

Written by a nurse for nursing students and graduate nurses in different settings, this text uses a multidimensional perspective and a nursing process framework to present current, accurate information, necessary for the nursing care of individuals. Two major themes underlie the materials presented: (1) nurses need to ensure that their own beliefs do not penalize or interfere with the treatment of patients whose beliefs and behavior are different from their own, and (2) sexuality relates to the entire human being, not just to sexual behavior per se. Although Hogan does not intend to train nurses as sex therapists, she does want to prepare health professionals to deal with sexual behavior and integrate it into health care. Unfortunately, very few nursing programs prepare nurses to address sexual issues. This book's comprehensive coverage of the subject is an effort to fill this gap.

The first unit presents background information necessary for an understanding of the topic of sexuality and its relation to nursing. Historical, biological (the life cycle, sexual response, sex drive, arousal, and intercourse), psychological (alternate forms of sexual expression, theories of functioning), and sociocultural (religion, learning) aspects are discussed. The second unit addresses questions of how to assist the patient in maintaining or attaining sexual health. Included are such topics as assessing a sexual problem, taking a sex history, understanding the impact of illness and hospitalization on sexuality, the sexual dimensions of the relationship between nurse and patient, and methods for teaching and counseling patients about sexuality. The third unit traces the development of sexuality through different parts of the life cycle, pointing out problems that may complicate healthy development. The fourth unit considers the reproductive consequences of sexual expression and deals with such issues as contraception, abortion, pregnancy, and birth. The last unit focuses on the specific effects of health deviations and therapies on sexual functioning: STDs, cancer, mutilating surgery and therapy, drugs, and impaired neurological, hormonal, cardiovascular-pulmonary, and urogenital functioning, as well as mental illness and retardation.

Each unit not only considers the biological, social, cultural, and psychological dynamics of each issue but also the nursing implications of a problem. Most chapters conclude with a summary and briefly annotated suggestions for further reading. Hogan hopes that this volume will not only impart information about sexuality but also inculcate an awareness of how beliefs, attitudes, and values affect nursing practice. (SGF)

IL

198. Hyde, Janet Shibley. **Understanding Human Sexuality.** 5th edition. New York: McGraw-Hill, 1994. 769 p. Includes bibliography, index, and glossary. ISBN 0-07-031615-5.

Hyde, Professor of Psychology and Women's Studies at the University of Wisconsin-Madison, has taught human sexuality since 1974. Given her graduate training in psychology, with specialties in behavioral genetics and statistics, and her current college teaching and research interests in the psychology of women and gender roles, she feels well qualified to present an interdisciplinary, survey approach to human sexuality, discussing its biological, sociological, and psychological dimensions. Her main goal in this book is to provide a readable, scholarly, and comprehensive introduction to human sexuality without assuming a student has had prior college courses in biology, sociology, or psychology. Her writing style is designed to facilitate learning rather than to "intimidate" students, and the illustrations were prepared to convey a lot of information clearly and simply. Three objectives underlie the text: (1) to provide practical information about sexuality and its problems, particularly psychological ones; (2) to help students become more comfortable with thinking about and discussing sex so that they can be rational decision makers about sex; and (3) to aid students in intelligently and critically evaluating the methods used in sex research.

The twenty-three chapters cover a wide range of topics that tap scholarly as well as popular interest in the major facets of the field: (1) anatomical and physiological (sex hormones, sexual differentiation, menstruation, menopause, conception, pregnancy, childbirth, contraception, abortion, STDs); (2) psychological and/or behavioral (arousal, sexual response, attraction, love, intimacy, female sexuality, male sexuality, sexual dysfunctions, sex therapy, sexual orientation, sex and the life cycle [childhood, adolescence, adulthood], sexual variations); and (3) social (gender roles, ethics, religion, law, sex education, sexual coercion, prostitution, pornography). Hyde points out that individual chapters can stand on their own so that instructors can order them according to their own needs. In addition to revisions of the chapters on contraception and abortion and STDs, the major addition to this fifth edition is an expansion of the multicultural perspective.

Each chapter begins with a content outline and a quotation from an expert on the subject to follow. "Focus" sections within the chapters detail information related to specific aspects of the topic, e.g., Kinsey, sexuality and disability, the Protestant ethic; sex as work. A running glossary of terms and their pronunciation is highlighted in the margins. Chapters conclude with a summary; review questions; questions for thought, discussion, and debate; and suggestions for further reading. The appendix, "A Directory of Resources in Human Sexuality," lists the names, addresses, and functions of major organizations dealing with health issues, sex education, sex research, sex therapy, lifestyle issues, media, sexual victimization, feminism, gender issues, and journals. The teaching resource package that accompanies the text includes an instructor's manual, test questions (also available on computer disc), and sixty-five full-color transparencies. (SGF)

IL

199. Katchadourian, Herant A., and Donald T. Lunde. **Fundamentals of Human Sexuality.** 3rd ed. New York: Holt, Rinehart and Winston, 1980. 534 p. Includes bibliography, index, and glossary. ISBN 0-03-042941-2.

Katchadourian and Lunde, both psychiatrists at the Stanford School of Medicine, wrote the first edition of this book to fill a perceived void for an adequate college level text for their human sexuality course in the Human Biology Program at Stanford University. Recognizing that there is more to sex than biology, they view sexuality as the outcome of biological, social, and psychological factors. Their book aims to provide information to answer three fundamental questions: (1) Why do we behave sexually? (2) How do we behave sexually?, and (3) How should we behave sexually? These concerns are reflected in the three major sections into which the book is divided: (1) biology (anatomy, physiology, hormones, conception, pregnancy, birth, contraception, and sexual disorders), (2) behavior (development through the life cycle, autoeroticism, intercourse, homosexuality, other sexual behaviors, e.g., fetishism, pedophilia, incest, transsexuality, sexual malfunctions, and therapy), and (3) culture (the relation of sex to law, morality, and society, primarily in the United States).

Considerations of evolutionary, cross-species, historical, and cross-cultural aspects of sexuality lace the text. However, sections on the erotic in art, literature, and film were deleted from the third edition because readers of the text said that they rarely used these sections. "Boxes" in each chapter elaborate on particular subjects of interest (e.g., masturbation in cross-cultural perspective, male fantasies). Line drawings, photographs, reproductions of artworks, and tables enhance the text.

Readers interested in a distilled version of Katchadourian's approach to his subject can refer to his short book, *Human Sexuality: Sense and Nonsense* (1974), written for Stanford alumni to acquaint them "with the salient facts in the area of human sexuality," and to "provide guidance in the often frustrating search for 'the right book.' " (SGF)

IL

200. McCary, James Leslie. **McCary's Human Sexuality.** 3rd ed. New York: Van Nostrand, 1978. 500 p. Includes bibliography, index, and glossary. ISBN 0-442-25249-8.

Convinced that "mature and healthy sexual attitudes and behavior rest on a firm foundation of accurate information presented honestly and directly" (p. ix), sex educator McCary presents the readers of this edition of his 1967 book with "the most current research in human sexuality"; he hopes that it will personally benefit students by fostering an understanding of the causes and effects of a wide range of sexual behavior.

The book is divided into six major parts. The introduction (part 1) examines some of the obstacles to sex education and discusses the personal and social toll of sexual ignorance. A long list of common myths and fallacies attests to misinformation about sexuality and accentuates the need for accurate information. An understanding of sexual physiology and functions is the goal of part 2, that includes information on the endocrine system; male and female sexual systems; menstruation and the climacteric; and fertilization, prenatal development, and birth. Communicating that a meaningful sexual relationship involves emotional, intellectual, and physical components, McCary discusses a variety of dimensions of the "sexual act" in part 3: intimacy and love, techniques of sexual arousal, aphrodisiacs and anaphrodisiacs, positions for intercourse, orgasm, birth control, and sex in the later years. Current attitudes toward sex in Western society and a review of the incidences and frequency of various types of sexual activity make up part 4. Part 5 details physical and emotional aspects of sexual dysfunctions, variances, diseases, and disorders. The last part, "Sex and Society," deals with the relation of sexual behavior to norms in the context of such issues as abortion, prostitution, illegitimacy, and pornography.

Illustrations concentrate on depicting anatomical aspects of sexuality but also include a few humorous cartoons. Although McCary intends to show the interactions of physiological, sociological, and psychological dimensions of sexuality, he does not include much information about such topics as psychosexual development, sex and the media, sex and religion, and sex research. (SGF)

PR
201. Mims, Fern H., and Melinda Swenson. **Sexuality: A Nursing Perspective.** New York: McGraw-Hill, 1980. 365 p. Includes bibliographies and index. ISBN 0-07-042388-1.

In 1963, only one medical school required a course dealing with the systematic study of human sexuality. By the late 1970s there were still very few sexuality texts geared to health care providers, and even fewer for nurses. This gap in the literature prompted Mims and Swenson, both nurses, to write a text for professional nurses, teachers of nurses, and nursing students. The goal of this book is to present theory and research about human sexuality so that it can be applied to nursing practice. The main framework that underlies the presentation of materials is the Mims-Swenson Sexual Health Model, that is described in the first chapter. The model is designed to aid nurses in promoting the sexual health of their clients and patients by increasing their knowledge of sexuality; enabling them to confront their own feelings and attitudes about sexuality; and developing assessment, intervention, and communication skills in all areas of sexual health. With the help of this model, they hope that the reader can deepen his or her knowledge and experience at an appropriate level.

The organization of the chapters is in line with this aim. Part 1 introduces the sexual health model, gives historical background on the study of sexuality, and provides basic information about sexual responses and dysfunction. The succeeding chapters emphasize teaching and learning about typical and atypical psychosexual development, reproductive decision making, health disruptions, and advanced intervention and research. Each chapter includes a series of learning activities, references, and bibliography. Later chapters focus on a problem orientation by outlining the data, assessing them, and suggesting a plan for intervention. Of particular interest are such pragmatic chapters as how to take a sex history; how to incorporate teaching about sexual health with a physical examination; a legal analysis of traditional and nontraditional lifestyles and how they may affect attitudes toward sex; sexual concerns of postcoronary patients; people with diabetes, spinal cord injuries, surgical interventions, and terminal illnesses; and the effects of medication on sexual functioning. (SGF)

IL
202. Offir, Carole Wade. **Human Sexuality.** New York: Harcourt Brace Jovanovich, 1982. 567 p. Includes bibliography, index, and glossary. ISBN 0-15-540428-8.

The primary aim of this textbook is to provide an integrated introduction to the study of human sexuality for a reader without any previous background either on the topic or in the disciplines from which so much research on sexuality is obtained (psychology, sociology, biology, medicine, physical education, and health education). Offir synthesizes research and information from a variety of fields to produce an interesting, well-written, and informative text. As a social scientist and a professional social science writer, Offir is able to blend understandable prose with a scholarly approach without oversimplifying the complexity of the issues with which she deals. "Sex in Perspective" (part I) attunes the reader to the historical and methodological intricacies of the study of sexuality. "The Psychobiology of Sex" (part II) deals with anatomy, physiology, and gender development, while "Sexual Behavior and Relationships" (part III) tackles such topics as love, sexual activities, homosexuality, and sexual problems and solutions. Developmental aspects of sexuality are included in "Sexuality Across the Life Span" (part IV). "Sex as a Social and Medical Issue" (part V) focuses on such issues as commercial sex, sexual abuse, sexually transmitted diseases, reproduction, and birth control. Offir addresses contemporary issues and questions that students might have about sexuality by including highlighted "boxes" that deal with such issues as the politics of sex research, the sex-change controversy, sex education for teenagers, and how to examine one's breasts. The book is replete with photographs, illustrations, and cartoons that appropriately complement the clear text. Other learning aids include outlines that precede each chapter; clear charts, tables, and figures; chapter summaries; a glossary of terms; and an extensive bibliography at the end of the book. An instructor's manual accompanies the textbook and includes summaries of chapters, suggestions for lectures, ideas for classroom discussion, supplementary readings, and multiple-choice and essay test questions. (SGF)

PR
203. Woods, Nancy Fugate. **Human Sexuality in Health and Illness.** 3rd ed. St. Louis, Mo.: Mosby, 1984. 476 p. Includes bibliographic references and index. ISBN 0-8016-5628-1.

Like the human body, sexuality has the potential to be healthy or unhealthy because it is not a purely biological phenomenon. An understanding of human sexuality involves a consideration of its psychological and sociocultural dimensions. The interaction of these variables affects sexual identity, role, and functioning. This compact book, written by a nurse for students and health practitioners, provides an overview of areas in which the intervention of health personnel can aid clients in dealing with situations that could threaten their sexual integrity. The topics discussed are meant to tap problems or situations commonly encountered in health practice.

The first section describes the "normal" development of sexuality through the life cycle, from the prenatal period to old age, and outlines the components of patterns of human sexual response. This general discussion lays the groundwork for understanding the problems an individual encounters in adapting to life events that threaten sexual integrity (pregnancy, abortion, sexual assault) or interfere with sexuality and sexual functioning (hospitalization, illness, surgery, trauma, drugs)—subjects that are discussed in two other major sections. Each section describes psychological, social, and biological dimensions of an issue, potential problems in development or response to a situation, and ways that a health professional can assess, intervene, and evaluate the problem.

The question is no longer *whether* a health practitioner should deal with issues that affect a client's sexual health, but *how*. The last unit considers the different roles a health professional can play in educating and counseling patients—from being a helpful role model to presenting formal instruction and counseling. (SGF)

GUIDES AND SELF-HELP BOOKS

Classic Guides to Love and Sex

(For related material see also entries 441, 969)

IL
204. Capellanus, Andreas. **The Art of Courtly Love.** With introduction, translation, and notes by John Jay Parry. New York: Ungar, 1959. 218 p. Republication of the Columbia University Press edition of 1941. Translation of: *De arte honeste amandi.* Includes bibliography.

Written in Latin toward the end of the twelfth century by Andreas Capellanus (known in France as André le Chapelain), *The Art of Courtly Love* is a codification of the doctrine of courtly love in all its particulars. Used as a guide in the courts of love in France and England to settle problems of romantic love, it consists of three books. Introductory book 1 deals with the nature of love, defining it as "a certain inborn suffering derived from the sight of and excessive meditation upon the beauty of the opposite sex, which causes each one to wish above all things the embraces of the other and by common desire to carry out all of love's precepts in the other's embrace" (p. 2). It explores the nature of courtship in a series of eight dialogues between men and women (commoners, simple nobility, higher nobility) of the same or different stations in life. In some circumstances, the male clergy are permitted to seek love, but nuns are off limits to everyone. Frequently, surprising statements are made in the dialogues (in a way, arguments): for example, in speaking to a woman of the simple nobility, a man of the higher nobility says, "But I am greatly surprised that you wish to misapply the term 'love' to that marital affection which husband and wife are expected to feel for each other after marriage, since everybody knows that love can have no place between husband and wife" (p. 17).

Book 2, "How Love May Be Retained," discusses the increase, decrease, and end of love; unfaithful lovers; royal decisions in specific cases of love; and finally, the origin of the thirty-one rules of love in King Arthur's court in Britain. Examples of these concisely written, aphoristic rules are: "He who is not jealous cannot love" (Rule II); and "A new love puts to flight an old one" (Rule XVII).

Strangely, book 3, "The Rejection of Love," does nothing to augment what has been stated in the previous books; instead, proceeding from the premise that love and women are sinful pursuits, it flatly contradicts all the advice given to lovers earlier.

This document offers the most provocative statement on the nature of courtly love that has come down to us from the Middle Ages. Book 3 notwithstanding, Capellanus "depicts passionate love as an ennobling experience," in effect raising the status of women in men's eyes and exerting a positive and lasting influence on the relations between the sexes down through the ages.

IL,PO

205. Chang, Jolan. **The Tao of Love and Sex: The Ancient Chinese Way to Ecstasy.** Foreword and postscript by Joseph Needham. New York: Dutton, 1977. 136 p. Includes bibliography and index. ISBN 0-525-47453-6.

This is a practical book on sexual loving that is based on the ancient Chinese philosophy of Taoism. The Tao of Loving, as expounded by Chang, is an explanation of the advice given by various authorities in classical works on Taoism, that considered lovemaking as part of the natural order of life. Among the ancient sex experts is Su Nu, female advisor to the Emperor Huang Ti, who might have lived during the Han Dynasty (206 B.C.-A.D. 219). At any rate, the utterances of Su Nu and others on the subject of sex are surprisingly modern and similar to the thinking of such researchers as Masters and Johnson. Specific concepts in the Taoist approach to sexual loving include ejaculation control, the distinction between orgasm and ejaculation, unusual thrusting techniques during intercourse, basic love positions with variations, and erotic kissing. Pervasive in the Tao of Loving is a strong emphasis on female satisfaction, achieved only through a proper balance and harmony of the forces of Yin (female) and Yang (male), opposites in the cosmic scheme of things. Benefits accruing to the practice of the Tao of Loving include the conquest of impotence, longevity, and the viability of May-September relationships. Although this work is addressed primarily to men, it is claimed that women are the automatic beneficiaries of the system as presented. The book contains a foreword by Joseph Needham, the renowned China scholar, in which Chang is lauded for bringing to the attention of Western culture the Chinese notion of the unity of sacred and profane love. A postscript, also by Needham, is an address in the Chapel of Caius College, Cambridge, on Whit Sunday, 1976, on the nature of Christian love that seems in conformity with the Tao of Love and Sex. The bibliography lists both Chinese and English texts. An expansion of the Taoistic concepts of lovemaking is to be found in Chang's 1983 follow-up book, *The Tao of the Loving Couple*. (TJW)

IL,PO
206. Devi, Kamala. **The Eastern Way of Love: Tantric Sex and Erotic Mysticism.**
Illustrated by Peter Schaumann. New York: Simon & Schuster, c1977, 1985. 160 p.
Includes bibliography and glossary. ISBN 0-671-60432-5.

Offering her view of Tantric sex rituals and exercises for Western readers, Devi
draws on personal experience and impressive background knowledge of Eastern and
Western sex practices. Tantra, she explains, is an ancient Indian philosophy derived from
Buddhism and Hinduism whose adherents, the Tantrics, taught a method of attaining
sexual ecstasy in order not only to experience pleasure but also to be one with the
universe. The Tantrics affirmed life in their art, writings, and religious rituals glorifying
sex. The divine, they say, is realized by using the senses, the mind, and the spirit to reach
sexual and mystical heights.

The Eastern Way of Love describes the various yogic methods of breathing, exercise,
meditation, and chants, or mantras, used by the Tantrics to put them in a state for the
enjoyment of sex and the attainment of spiritual ecstasy. Devi's chapter on Tantra sex rituals
explains how Kundalini, the symbolically coiled serpent as the Muladhara chakra (a sex nerve
center located between the anus and the genitals), is awakened and stimulated to move up
the spinal cord until it unites with the god Shiva in the head. For this experience, Devi provides
a chapter on Kundalini Yoga exercises for increasing sexual pleasure; another on techniques
for meditation, including use of Sanskrit mantras, such as "Om mani palme hum" (the jewel
in the lotus); another on techniques (kissing, massage, oral sex, etc.) for keeping ecstatic
feelings at a high level; still another on sexual positions, called asanas, to help attain cosmic
consciousness; and another on the prolongation of ecstasy.

Devi also discusses in separate chapters group sex rituals, sex games, sexual
potency in the aging, and pelvic muscle exercises for women to help them improve their
sexual performance. Attractive black-and-white and color drawings enhance the text by
illustrating intimate sex play and the asanas, or sexual positions. (TJW)

PO
207. Kalyanamalla. **Ananga Ranga.** Translated and edited by Tridibnath Ray. New
York: Citadel Press, 1964. 249 p.

The *Ananga Ranga* (*Theatre of Ananga*) is a famous Sanskrit work written by the poet
Kalyanamalla, a Brahmin and a courtier, sometime in the fifteenth or sixteenth centuries at
the request of a Muslim prince. Translated into English with extensive comments by
Tridibnath Ray, it is a sex guide stressing the physical side of love. Girindrashekhar Bose of
Calcutta states in the foreword that it "is mainly a compilation from authoritative ancient
works, and appears to have been written for the benefit of laymen." In the introduction Ray
gives an in-depth review of ancient Indian erotic writings leading up to the *Ananga Ranga*,
including Vatsyayana's *Kama Sutra*. Kalyanamalla addresses himself primarily to a male
audience, noting that "all of you who read this book shall know how delicious an instrument
is woman," who is capable "of giving the divinist pleasures" (p. 39, Burton translation). The
ten chapters intersperse the translated Sanskrit text with the observations of the translator; in
this edition it is sometimes difficult for the reader to distinguish between the text and the
comments. Chapter 1 presents a classification of women into four distinct kinds based on
physical appearance and sexual behavior; chapter 2 identifies female erogenous zones and
discusses methods of producing orgasm; chapter 3 examines the physical dimensions of male
and female genitalia and their effect on coitus; chapter 4 deals with female temperament and
disposition in the different stages of life and with the anatomy of female genitalia; chapter 5
delves into the regional differences among the women of India in terms of attire and amorous
proclivities; chapters 6 and 7 focus on those substances that enhance sexual performance,
alleviate deficiencies, improve appearance, attract mates, and so forth; chapter 8 examines
the pros and cons of extramarital relations; chapter 9 covers foreplay with an emphasis on
kissing; and chapter 10 describes numerous sexual positions for intercourse. Because the
Ananga Ranga was one of the most popular erotic works in the India of the past, the present
edition aims to inform current sexologists, physicians, Sanskrit scholars, and sociologists

about the state of knowledge of the "ancient East" concerning sex and its relation to contemporary thinking on the topic. (TJW)

IL
208. Kokkoka. **The Koka Shastra: Being the Ratirahasya of Kokkoka and Other Medieval Indian Writings on Love.** Translated and with an Introduction by Alex Comfort. Preface by W. G. Archer. New York: Stein and Day, 1965. 171 p. Includes bibliography.

In his introduction translator Comfort traces the history, development, and thought of various Sanskrit textbooks on love and sex. Labeled erotologies, they complement the Hindu sexual imagery resplendent on temple walls and common in religious everyday wares and ornaments. In existence for over 1,000 years, they include Vatsyayana's great work, *The Kama Sutra*, written sometime before A.D. 400; the *Ratirahasya of Kokkoka*, popularly known as the *Koka Shastra* (Koka's Book), written in the eleventh or twelfth centuries; the *Ananga Ranga* of Kalyanamalla, a fifteenth or sixteenth century successor to the *Kama Sutra*.

While the *Kama Sutra* belongs to ancient Hindu literature, the *Koka Shastra* relates to a different, medieval society, incorporating ideas not dealt with earlier. Comfort also characterizes many later texts on love, e.g., the *Ananga Ranga*, as examples that stretch from medieval times to the present. These are mostly imitative of the earlier works, although some have increased enhancements to existing practices.

The *Koka Shastra* is divided into fifteen parts: "Of the Physical Types and Their Seasons," "Of the Lunar Calendar," "Of Physical Types by Their Genital Characters," "Of Women by Their Ages, Temperaments and Dispositions," "Of Women by Custom and Place," "Of Embraces," "Of Kisses," "Of Love-marks," "Of Coition and the Various Coital Postures," "Of Love-blows and Love-cries," "The Wooing of a Bride," "Concerning Wives," "Concerning Relations with Strange Women," "Concerning Love-spells," and "Concerning Recipes." In the preface, W. G. Archer comments that Kokkoka "is concerned with how to make the most of sex, how to enjoy it and how to keep a woman happy. Moreover, . . . he takes it for granted that almost by definition the partner in sex will be the wife."

Comfort seems to have chosen to translate the *Koka Shastra* for good reason: in medieval India, in contrast to ancient India, morality was different: it had become more conservative with the result that women had less freedom than before and were more carefully watched. The options for the gentleman about town were fewer—premarital and extramarital sex were sharply constrained—and in his amorous pursuits he had to proceed cautiously. Hence, a text on love more in tune with the times and more reliable than the *Kama Sutra* had to be made available. It is these differences that the *Koka Shastra* recognizes. While the advice on coition remains pretty much unchanged, the conditions for love and sex had changed. Comfort's introduction and translation and Archer's lengthy preface reflect this. (TJW)

IL,PO
209. Ovid. **The Art of Love.** Translated by Henry T. Riley. Edited by Walter S. Kearing. Illustrated by Remo Farruggio. New York: Stravon, 1966. 126 p.

Ovid (43 B.C.-A.D. 17) was a great poet of the Roman leisure class. Acclaimed for his talent at an early age, he devoted himself to writing love poems. His *Ars amatoria* (*The Art of Love*) was completed when he was in his early forties. However, he was to be exiled by the Emperor Augustus, who deemed the work immoral. *The Art of Love* has become a classic guide to lovemaking, influencing lovers and writers across the centuries.

The *Art of Love*, book 1, "On Finding Love," and book 2, "On Making Love Last," provide advice to men. Book 3, "On Winning and Holding Love," provides corresponding advice to women.

Ovid, assuming the mantle of the guardian of love, focuses his counsel first on how a young man might find and win a lasting love object. The style of his counsel is indicated by the following examples. Speaking of the love object, he avers, "She will not come to you gliding through the yielding air; the fair one that suits must be sought with your eyes" (p. 16). He recommends the theater for pursuing prospects: "There you will find what you may love, what you may trifle with, both what you may once touch, and what you may wish to keep" (p. 17). Once identified, "Be not tired of praising either her face or her hair; her taper fingers too, and her small foot" (p. 42). To hold her, "Bring soft caresses, and words that delight the ear, that she may ever be joyous at your approach" (p. 56). In a similar vein advice is given to women.

What emerges from reading this short classic is that lovemaking is a desirable pursuit that requires concentration and a special talent on the part of men and women. It is, in fact, a pleasure to be enjoyed and participated in equally by both sexes. (TJW)

II,PO
210. 'Umar ibn Muhammed (al Nafzāwī, 16th century). **The Perfumed Garden of the Shaykh Nefzawi.** Translated by Sir Richard F. Burton. New York: Castle Books, 1964. 128 p.

The best-known example of a classic Islamic sex manual is *The Perfumed Garden* by Sheikh Nefzawi, who wrote it at the request of the Vizir of Abd-el-Aziz, the ruler of Tunis. Translated by Sir Richard Burton, the renowned British explorer, and published in 1886, this sixteenth-century guide colorfully and poetically discusses what people of that time thought were the most satisfactory characteristics of lovers and methods of lovemaking. Its twenty-one chapters cover a wide range of topics: chapter 6, "Concerning Everything That Is Favourable to the Act of Coition," describes twenty-six positions for coitus; chapter 9, "Sundry Names Given to the Sexual Organs of Women," examines the salient features of thirty-eight different kinds of vulvas; and chapter 18, "Prescriptions for Increasing the Dimensions of Small Members and for Making Them Splendid," advises a man who wants his penis ready for coition to "rub it before copulation with tepid water, until it gets red and extended by the flood flowing into it, in consequence of the heat; he must then anoint it with a mixture of honey and ginger, rubbing it in sedulously" (p. 117). Other chapter topics include descriptions of favorable and con-temptuous characteristics of men and women, symptoms and treatment of sterility and impotence, abortion, homosexuality, and advice about pregnancy and foretelling the sex of the fetus. The book provides an interesting comparison and contrast to current views of sex and reproduction and remains a noteworthy, cross-cultural document of the wide variety of cultural constructions of human sexuality. (TJW)

IL,PO
211. Vatsyayana. **The Kama Sutra of Vatsyayana.** Translated by Sir Richard Burton and F. F. Arbuthnot. Edited with a preface by W. G. Archer. Introduction by K. M. Panikkar. New York: Putnam, 1984. 223 p. Published in 1963 by G. P. Putnam's Sons. Includes bibliography. ISBN 0-425-06556-1.

The *Kama Sutra* (*Aphorisms of Love*), popularly stereotyped as a Hindu sex classic, was published in 1993 in English translation from the Sanskrit by Sir Richard F. Burton, the noted explorer and translator of *The Arabian Nights*, and his colleague, F. F. Arbuthnot. They had founded the Kama Shastra Society for the purpose of publishing Eastern erotic literature. Vatsyayana wrote the *Kama Sutra* sometime between the first and fourth centuries A.D. "while leading the life of a religious student and wholly engaged in the contemplation of the Deity" (p. 220). Therefore, Vatsyayana was being strongly influenced by his Dharma, Artha, and Kama, the three pillars of the Hindu religion representing religious duty, worldly welfare, and life of the senses respectively. His aim was to produce a work expressing the Indian attitude toward sex as a central and natural component of Indian thought and life.

The *Kama Sutra* is divided into seven parts: "Introduction," "On Sexual Union," "About the Acquisition of a Wife," "About a Wife," "About Wives of Other People," "About Courtesans," "On the Means of Attracting Others to Oneself." For the most part, the *Kama Sutra* is a treatise on sex relationships between the leisured man about town and the various women in his life: his wife, others' wives, courtesans, servants, and so forth. Given the basic role that Kama (sensual gratification) was thought to play in everyone's lives, the book is addressed to both men and women who strive to transform their sexual behavior into an act of divine creation. Although part II might be considered a sex manual in the modern sense, it is probably inadequate as a contemporary guide to sexual fulfillment. (TJW)

Contemporary Sex Manuals

(For related material see also entry 442)

IL,PO

212. Anand, Margo. **The Act of Sexual Ecstasy: The Path of Sacred Sexuality for Western Lovers.** Illustrated by Leandra Hussey. Los Angeles: Tarcher, 1989. 450 p. Includes index.

This guide promises to provide the reader who follows its detailed instructions with experiences in "High Sex," or ecstasy, at a level far beyond that of ordinary intercourse. Following years of study, practice, relaxation, and meditation, Anand, a psychologist specializing in enhancing sexuality, has put together this systematic training course in the art of sexual ecstasy. By following her step-by-step program featured in this book, one "can discover erotic bliss not by separating sex from other higher purposes and treating it as recreation only, but by cultivating the art of sexual ecstasy to reach higher states of consciousness and in this way deepening our intimacy with our loved ones" (p. 4).

Based largely on the Tantric blending of spirituality with sexuality, Anand's approach incorporates other methods of self-development derived from present-day sexology and psychology, then making it more suitable for Western lovers. "The training consists of three ten-day seminars held over a year-long period in which participants meet as a group to learn various practices that can heal their sexuality and bring joy to their lives" (p. 7).

Following a chapter on "How to Use This Book," Anand offers twelve chapters on different aspects of achieving sexual ecstasy. Chapter 1, "High Sex and the Tantric Vision," offers a vision of sacred sexuality with an overview of the principles of High Sex. Chapter 2, "Awakening Your Inner Lover," emphasizes the importance of loving oneself before loving another. Chapter 3, "Opening to Trust," refers to attaining trust with a partner. Chapter 4, "Skills for Enhancing Intimacy," pertains to seduction and the five senses. Chapter 5, "Honoring the Body Ecstatic," deals with rediscovering the body through ritual, ceremony, touching, and assuming various body positions. Chapter 6, "Opening the Inner Flute," prepares one for whole-body orgasm by teaching one how to open the hidden channel of energy flow through seven energy centers. Chapter 7, "Self-Pleasuring Rituals," teaches one how to give pleasure to oneself and one's partner. Chapter 8, "Harmonizing Your Inner Man and Inner Woman," advocates enacting gender roles while enhancing masculine and feminine polarities through the giving and receiving of blissful surprises. Chapter 9, "Awakening the Ecstatic Response," teaches one how to relax in different positions in order to awaken the orgasmic reflex. Chapter 10, "Expanding Orgasm," shows how tensions may be reduced in the genital area and how orgasm is enhanced by vaginal, penile, and anal stimulation. In chapter 11, "From Orgasm to Ecstasy," the partners, using advanced techniques from Taoist and Tantric traditions, direct orgasmic feelings from the genital area upwards through energy centers, or chakras, to the brain. The last chapter, "Riding the Wave of Bliss," involves a seven-step process integrating all that has been learned in order to experience sexual ecstasy.

These twelve chapters, or stages, Anand assures us, are the avenues to "High Sex," that should promote "a lifestyle that brings you pleasure and joy in all dimensions" (p. 425). Appendixes on "Safe Sex" and "Musical Selections" (used to create atmosphere during sessions) close out this practical book. (TJW)

IL,PO
213. Ayres, Toni, Phyllis Lyon, Ted McIlvenna, et al. **SARguide for a Better Sex Life: A Self-Help Program for Personal Sexual Enrichment/Education Designed by The National Sex Forum.** San Francisco: National Sex Forum, 1977. Includes bibliographies. ISBN 0-913566-02-0.

SAR stands for Sexual Attitude Restructuring, a step-by-step instructional program designed for couples and individuals by the National Sex Forum of San Francisco. It is an integral part of a broader program called Personal Sexual Enrichment/Education that the Forum developed as a self-help program to encourage individuals and couples to learn about their sexuality and create a better sex life for themselves. The *SARguide* is a structured workbook covering four weeks of class discussion, film viewing, at home exercises, readings, and maintaining a journal. In week no. 1, for example, discussions focus on the anatomy and physiology of the sexual response cycle, sexual fantasies, and masturbation, enriched by four videocassettes/films and augmented by readings and home exercises. Each week of the program is similarly structured. Before starting the program, each student fills in a sixty-three question Situational Assessment and completes a Sexual Experience Survey. Along with the journal maintained during the four-week course, these are equivalent to a personal sex history. Brief biographies of the eight men and women who wrote this guide are given at the back of the book. (TJW)

IL,PO
214. Barbach, Lonnie Garfield. **For Each Other: Sharing Sexual Intimacy.** New York: New American Library, 1984. 316 p. Includes bibliographic notes and index. ISBN 0-451-12802-8.

Based on nine years of work with people in therapy, this book was "conceived as a guide to help negotiate the complex aspects of a relationship that can affect sexual satisfaction" (p. 14). Each section describes major factors that affect sexual fulfillment and includes exercises for breaking old patterns and creating new ones. Section I deals with major areas that underlie sexual problems: role scripts, the dynamics of relationships (power, interdependence, feelings of adequacy), and physiological and emotional components of sexual response. Section II explores methods for analyzing sexual problems (e.g., observation) and ways to initiate change (e.g., risk taking and communication). Section III discusses reasons for orgasmic dysfunction and suggests ways to become orgasmic, such as increasing body acceptance, receptivity to stimulation, and vaginal sensitivity. Section IV deals with the problems of women who experience painful sex, and section V turns to the causes and solutions for lack of sexual interest and discrepancies in desire; the latter suggests ways to enhance routine, boring sex. The fifty exercises included in the book are extensions of the major themes of the text: sexual exploration as a process that continues throughout life and is linked to social, cultural, and psychological facets of a person's total existence. Readers especially interested in female orgasmic dysfunction may want to refer to Barbach's earlier book, *For Yourself.* Those who want amplification of men's and women's thoughts and feelings about sexual experiences can refer to *The Intimate Male: Candid Discussions About Women, Sex, and Relationships* by Linda Levine and Lonnie Barbach and to *Shared Intimacies: Women's Sexual Experiences* (Garden City, N.Y.: Anchor Press, 1980) by the same authors. These works provide clearly written, articulate descriptions of experiences, acknowledgment of fears and expectations related to the topics discussed, and suggestions for improvement. (SGF)

IL,PO
215. Barbach, Lonnie Garfield. **For Yourself: The Fulfillment of Female Sexuality.** Garden City, N.Y.: Anchor Press/Doubleday, 1976. 218 p. Published by Doubleday in 1975. Includes bibliography and index. ISBN 0-385-11245-9.

As a sex therapist and psychologist with the Human Sexuality Program at the University of California Medical Center in San Francisco, Barbach became keenly aware of the problems that women have in understanding their sexual natures and in reaching orgasm. In addition, she realized that the couple treatment approach of Masters and Johnson was unavailable or too expensive for many women who want help in dealing with sexual problems. Consequently, she and Nancy Carlsen developed a new kind of treatment program to provide help for a broad spectrum of women. The distinctiveness of the program lay in therapists dealing only with women in a group situation and combining a number of therapeutic techniques. The experiences of their "pre-orgasmic groups" (composed primarily of five to seven middle class, Caucasian, heterosexual women, aged eighteen to fifty-eight) became the basis for this book. The specific purpose of the book is to counteract the common complaint of lack of orgasm by teaching women about their bodies and orgasm, primarily by self-stimulation. The organization of the book follows the general structure of the preorgasmic group therapy program: (1) information on psychological and physiological aspects of female sexuality with the goal of helping a woman to assess her own attitudes and feelings about sex and to learn about her body and its needs, and (2) specific individual and partner "homework" exercises designed to aid a woman in reaching her own sexual potential and in overcoming her sexual difficulties. The broader purpose of this guide to the fulfillment of female sexuality is to provide the reader with adequate information, permission, and support so that she can explore the dimensions of her sexual being. Later chapters (sexual expansion, sex and pregnancy, menopause and aging, your responsibility to your body, bringing up children sexually, personal liberation) deal with this broader goal. The follow-up statistics compiled at the University of California Medical Center indicate that 93 percent of the participants in the program consistently experience orgasm, primarily by self-stimulation, and that more than 50 percent could experience orgasm with partners within three months after treatment. Therapists interested in running preorgasmic groups can refer to Barbach's *Women Discover Orgasm: A Therapist's Guide to a New Treatment Approach* (1980). (SGF)

PO
216. Calderone, Mary S., and Eric W. Johnson. **The Family Book About Sexuality.** Revised edition. Drawings by Vivien Cohen. New York: Harper & Row, 1989. 288 p. Includes bibliography, index, and glossary. ISBN 0-06-016068-3.
       Written by a leading sexologist and a sex educator, this book, intended for both children and adults, is a guide to sexuality. The first chapter, "Understanding Ourselves as Sexual People," describes the sexualization process—growing up with a sense of a sexual self, whereby gender identity is acquired and gender role behavior is learned through interaction with one's social environment. Chapter 2 explains the development and functioning of human sexual response systems, including arousal, nudity, masturbation, dysfunctions, learning techniques, and achieving intimacy. Chapters 3 and 4 explain human reproduction and family planning. Chapter 5, "Living Our Sexual Lives," discusses sexual programming before and after birth, how sexualization is helped or hindered, normalcy, homosexuality, bisexuality, sexuality and aging, separation, divorce, and death. Marriage is the topic of chapter 6, while chapter 7 explains the role of the family in the development of sexuality. Chapter 8 touches on the special problems of "the different ones, the lonely ones": the disabled, abused and neglected children, singles, and the elderly. Chapter 9, "Sex and Sexual Problems," discusses sex and religion, "victimless" crimes, child molestation, incest, pornography, prostitution, rape, sex and drugs, and other sexual behaviors with and without legal implications. Chapter 10 talks about sexually transmitted diseases. Chapter 11 offers guidelines for sex education programs. The last chapter, "Making Sexual Decisions," is addressed to young people and defines sexual responsibility. A fifty-two-page glossary of terms, called "Concise A-to-Z Encyclopedia" by the authors, and an annotated bibliography are included. (EBS)

PO
217. Castleman, Michael. **Sexual Solutions: An Informative Guide.** New York: Simon & Schuster, 1983. 286 p. Includes bibliography and index. ISBN 0-671-44756-4.

As the title implies, this book is about sexual problems, especially those that affect men and render their lovemaking ineffectual. It is written for men in jargon-free language from a man's point of view. Castleman is founding director of the Men's Reproductive Health Clinic in San Francisco, a public health facility focusing on men's birth control and sexual concerns. With the goal of problem-free lovemaking in mind, Castleman explores a host of concerns by first demythologizing sex in regard to certain fears men harbor as to penis size, instant erection, simultaneous orgasm, and the like and then promoting the idea of sensuality in lovemaking through relaxation, deep breathing, touching, massage, and other whole-body techniques. However, the principal problems he deals with are involuntary ejaculation, nonerection, and nonejaculation, which are his nonpejorative terminological equivalents for premature ejaculation, impotence, and ejaculatory incompetence. Additional problems for men include selection of birth control methods, sexual infections, self-examination of testicles and breasts for cancer, and what to do if one's lover is raped. Respect for women and an emphasis on similarities rather than differences between males and females are themes that permeate this book. Castleman also takes a look at sex films, magazines, and books as phenomena that foster many of the male myths and have a negative impact on lovemaking. The appendixes include a guide to men's and women's sexual anatomy and a national directory of sex therapists. (TJW)

IL,PO
218. Cauthery, Philip, Andrew Stanway, and Penny Stanway. **Loving Sex: A Lifetime Guide.** New York: Stein and Day, 1984. 442 p. Includes index. ISBN 0-8128-2968-9.
Believing that there has been an overemphasis on physical sex in our "genitally obsessed society," the authors of this book, all physicians involved in counseling adolescents and/or parents on sexuality, offer to families a nonjudgmental, comprehensive, yet practical guide that looks "at love and sex from the cradle to the grave and, with the benefit of knowledge of both family and psychosexual medicine, weaving a picture of interlinking complexity that shows how a child grows up to become a sexual person" (p. 11). They hope to put sexuality into a broad context and influence parents to change the ways they think of love and sex. Based on their own and others' clinical experiences, they concentrate on what they perceive most families want to know. In explaining the sexual components of the life cycle, the authors have written thirty-five chapters, beginning with "Baby and Childhood Sexuality" and moving through "Early Adolescence" and "Mid- and Late Adolescence" to "Courtship," "Engagement," "Romance," "Marriage as a Way of Life," and "Marriage, Divorce and Society." There are chapters on "Sex Differences," "Intercourse," :Loving Behaviour," "Conception and Infertility," "Pregnancy and Childbirth," and "Teaching Children About Sex." For those concerned with sexual problems, there are chapters on "Masturbation," "Sexual Morals," "Homosexuality," and "Prostitution." Final chapters cover "Sex and Health," "Sex in Old Age," and "Love." Tastefully illustrated with well-chosen photographs and drawings, this well-written book can be read from cover to cover or can be dipped into profitably at any juncture. Although it is provided with an index, it does lack a listing of other books for further reading. (TJW)

PO
219. Comfort, Alex, ed. **The Joy of Sex: A Cordon Bleu Guide to Lovemaking.** New York: Crown, 1972. 255 p. Includes index.
This book tries to do for lovemaking what *The Joy of Cooking* did for the culinary arts: present a "sophisticated and unanxious account of available dishes" that include the practical details of preparing a staple diet as well as directions for indulging in occasional, gourmet fantasies. The aim of the book is to reassure adult readers that common sex needs are not odd or weird and that sex can be a pleasurable, joyful experience. Geared to the average, sexually active reader who wants to enjoy sex and be responsible about it, the book stresses several basic themes: (1) sexual elaboration can be a form of adult play that is a part of love; (2) since love and sex are intertwined, satisfactory lovemaking involves feedback between partners; (3) people need to express many aspects of themselves in lovemaking in addition

to sex play centered on intercourse; and (4) there are very few rules that apply to lovemaking as long as partners do not engage in antisocial, dangerous, or unenjoyable activities. By helping readers use their creative imagination, the authors hope to foster a varied, satisfactory, and spontaneous love life. The first two chapters contextualize sexual behavior as a part of love and as a type of joy in life. The next few chapters describe in detail some of the numerous components of sexual behavior, providing information about practical aspects of lovemaking (beds, deodorants, nakedness, etc.), basic sexual stimulation and positions, and sexual enhancement. The authors integrate physical and psychological aspects of sexuality in their descriptions and emphasize that the behavior described represents a choice for couples, depending on individual needs. The final chapter deals with problems (rape, age, prostitution) that may relate to sexual activity. Comfort edited this guide to lovemaking based on the work of one couple and supplemented it with advice from some experts and a few other couples. The numerous, sensitively drawn, educational illustrations of Charles Raymond and Christopher Foss as well as the erotic Indian, Chinese, and Japanese color plates enliven this classic guide to healthy lovemaking. More advanced readers may wish to pursue this information with the companion volume, *More Joy* (1974). (SGF)

PO
220.   Comfort, Alex, ed. **The New Joy of Sex.** New York: Crown, 1991. 256 p. Includes index. ISBN 0-517-58583-9.
        The first edition of this book, published in 1972, sold over 8 million copies and became one of the classic sex guides of the 1970s. Over two decades later, *The New Joy of Sex* is a "completely revised" guide to address contemporary concerns. Although the headings are similar to the 1972 edition, much of the content is new. Dealing with practical issues like AIDS; contraception; male sexual dysfunction; overemphasis on the mechanics of sex; the sexuality of people with disabilities; and bothersome sexual behaviors are some of the new topics included. New illustrations, a dozen erotic duotone photos, and eighty-five full-color drawings complement the text.
        "The aim of the book is pleasure, not psychiatry . . .," and a major theme is to encourage people to develop their ability to engage in sex as play, whether in a "duet" or for a "solo performance." The book does not contain a lot of information on the biology or psychology of sex, nor does it give much attention to positions for intercourse. Rather, it emphasizes how "valid sex behaviors" work. The "main dish" in this new version is "loving, unselfconscious" sex, that is long, frequent, satisfying, varied, and stimulating to the creative imagination. The only rules are: (1) refrain from what is not enjoyable and (2) discover your partner's needs. The highest quality sex is most likely to develop in a loving relationship, where a couple matches up their needs and preferences, letting go of fears and guilt engendered by misinformation or no information. Comfort hopes that this book will facilitate responsible, happy, anxiety-free sex in the lives of ordinary people. (SGF)

PO
221.   Crenshaw, Theresa Larsen. **Bedside Manners: Your Guide to Better Sex.** New York: McGraw-Hill, 1983. 300 p. Includes index. ISBN 0-07-013581-9.
        Crenshaw, author of this practical guide to improved sexual behavior for women and men, is a medical doctor prominently involved in sex education, counseling, and therapy. She is also founder and director of the Crenshaw Clinic in San Diego. Because she could not find a popular book to recommend to her patients that dealt comprehensively with sexual functioning and dysfunctioning from the psychological, biological, and medical standpoints, she decided to write her own. *Bedside Manners* is the result.
        Bedside manners are the principles that make up the etiquette of sex, but they are not limited to the bedroom. The first six chapters deal with sexual relationships, what causes them to go awry, and what partners can do for them by understanding "cultural rituals that are destructive to good sex," by developing appropriate sexual manners, and by improving interpersonal communication skills. Chapters 7, 8, and 10 deal with the

physiology of sex: sexual response cycles for women and men, and orgasm. In chapter 9, "The Totaled Woman," Crenshaw looks at the common problem of sexual aversion. A return to female orgasm occurs in chapter 11, which men are encouraged to read because it focuses on techniques to enhance orgasm. Chapter 12 examines the causes, diagnosis, and treatment of premature ejaculation and ejaculatory incompetence. Chapter 13 takes up medical aspects of sexuality: vaginismus, sexual infections, hysterectomy, clitoridectomy, and prostate surgery. Chapter 14 provides up-to-date information on advances in sex therapy: pheromones, copulins, the G Spot, penile prosthesis, electroejaculation, and so forth. The last chapter provides sexual self-evaluation questionnaires to help people identify their sex problems and deal with them. (TJW)

IL
222.   Ellis, Albert. **The Sensuous Person: Critique and Corrections.** Secaucus, N.J.: Lyle Stuart, 1972. 236 p. Includes bibliography.
The well-known sexologist Albert Ellis challenges the ideas issued in a spate of bestselling sex guides of the late sixties and seventies: *The Sensuous Woman*, by "J"; *The Sensuous Man*, by "M"; *The Sensuous Couple*, by Dr. Robert Chartham; *Everything You Always Wanted to Know About Sex But Were Afraid to Ask* and *Any Woman Can!* by Dr. David Reuben. Ellis begins the first chapter, "Will the *Real* Sensuous Person Please Stand Up?" by attempting to clear up the public's "exceptionally confused" view of the Sensuous Person, namely, that the subject is not a new phenomenon, that "how-to-be-a-sexpot-in-ten-easy-lesson books have been popular in the English-speaking world for well over a hundred years; and in the middle of the nineteenth century hell knows how many zillions of pamphlets and books on one 'sensuous' technique alone were distributed in the United States." The book continues in this informal, colloquial tone, stylistically emulating the subjects of his criticism, at the same time discrediting the thunder of their messages.
In the first chapter, that provides a historical review of how-to sexual literature, Ellis graciously prefaces his assaults by acknowledging that he likes this breed of writings for a whole list of reasons, and that on the whole they do more good than harm. Setting this initial, token kindness aside, he proceeds to mercilessly pick apart these works for their considerable misinformation. In demolishing the credibility of these well-intentioned tomes, he points to the fact that most of the authors lack credentials to dish out sex advice. The advice given collectively is often contradictory, shows ignorance of human psychology, and is oblivious of individual personality differences, expecting all readers to fit rigid, perfectionist molds and behavioral scripts. He lists the numerous errors by the authors in dispensing often nonsensical information about sexuality that is totally unsubstantiated by scientific fact. Chief among the culprits who have "surely abused the mistake-making privilege" is David Reuben, "who one would have thought would have done much better about verifying his facts and presenting them in unembellished form." Among Reuben's gaffes are the erroneous assumptions that "all women primarily enjoy intercourse; that they all become desperately frustrated and unhappy when it is not sufficiently prolonged to give them an orgasm; that men who come quickly are lousy slobs for allowing themselves to commit this heinous deed; that all of them could train themselves to last longer." The citations of Reuben's mistakes cover the entire gamut of sexuality, including masturbation, impotence, frigidity, venereal diseases, and prostitution. (EBS)

PO
223.   Morgenstern, Michael. **How to Make Love to a Woman.** New York: Clarkson N. Potter, Inc., 1982. 150 p. ISBN 0-517-54706-6.
In this popular self-help book on love and sex, the reader is exposed to an informed layperson's view of how men should satisfy women emotionally and sexually. Morgenstern perceives the intimate relations between the sexes as having deteriorated drastically since the 1960s, so much so that many men and women are confused about their sex roles and are seeking solutions. He intends to help solve the problem with this practical guide to lovemaking for men. For the modern, independent woman, the solution seems to reside principally in a return to the cherished values of romantic love: flowers,

candlelight, music, etc. For men it is a matter of looking at women differently—not as property or as objects deserving pedestal status, but rather as equals who desire to share experiences. These attitudes have implications for sexual loving, and Morgenstern goes on to discuss in chapters 3 and 4 the qualities in men that women like (e.g., self-assurance, appealing physical attributes, charming voice, positive attitude toward women); and the fears men and women have about sex (e.g., not being attractive enough, size of breasts, pregnancy). In chapters 5 and 6 he examines courting and romance and seduction and arousal. In chapter 7 he stresses the importance of talking to each other before, during, and after sex. In chapter 8 he shows how the ideas of romance, equality, and sharing have an impact upon the techniques of sex: foreplay and afterplay, positions, oral sex, masturbation, etc. In chapter 9, "The Big 'O'," he takes up orgasm, explaining how the different kinds—single, multiple, sequential, and peritoneal—are achieved. In the last chapters he examines various notions and sources for clues as to how to make love to women: variety and novelty in sex, sex toys, pornography, professional lovers (i.e., gigolos), sex therapy. In this book a recommended sex role for men is spelled out in detail: it emphasizes a return to romantic love coupled with fervid sexuality. In the same practical vein is Alexandra Penney's book for women, *How to Make Love to a Man* (New York: Clarkson N. Potter, Inc., 1981). (TJW)

PO
224.   Petersen, James R. **The Playboy Advisor on Love & Sex.** Illustrated by Patrick Nagle. New York: Putnam, 1983. 285 p. Includes index. ISBN 0-399-50742-6.

Frank and humorous responses to real-life questions about sex from readers of the Playboy Advisor column in *Playboy* magazine characterize the content of this book. Petersen, the column's editor since 1973, has divvied up his selection from ten years of questions and answers into three broad sections: "The Body: An Owner's Manual"; "The Pursuit of Pleasure"; and "Notes from the Sexual Frontier." In section I, five chapters examine sexual problems (premature ejaculation, penis size, wet dreams, breast size, female ejaculation, drugs and sex, birth control, venereal diseases) put forth by curious males and females. In section II, questions and answers explore old and new sexual techniques for enhancing sexual pleasure: oral sex, anal sex, masturbation, fantasy, and sex toys. Section III delves into the impact of the sexual revolution on relations between the sexes in terms of dating, living together, married life, ménage à trois, group sex, and homosexuality. Answers are drawn from the expertise of over 300 advisors in the field and the commonsense wisdom of a few friends. For the record, the Playboy Advisor column first appeared in the September 1960 issue of *Playboy*; it dealt with such topics as fashion, dating, sports cars, tipping, and food. Sixty-three readers responded with more questions. By the end of the decade, up to 1,000 letters were being received each month from readers starved for information bearing on their sex lives. Consequently, Petersen thinks that the column provides valuable insight into the history of American culture. After characterizing available feminist literature on sex as "based on rage, anger, and violence," Petersen, "a sportswriter for America's favorite sport," justifies the importance of his "consumer reports of the erotic" by saying that the readers of *Playboy* "are the true pioneers of the sexual revolution. They don't need credentials, or computers, or statistics; they are in it up to their ears. The one thing they have in common is courage. They like sex. They like being in love. They are trying to work things out—without the dogma of sexual politics. They refuse to settle for second best. They do not whine or complain. They question. They go for it" (p. 13). Petersen notes that the volume is neither scientific nor comprehensive, but that it is "compassionate." (TJW)

PO
225.   Westheimer, Ruth. **Dr. Ruth's Guide to Good Sex.** Introduction by Helen Singer Kaplan. New York: Warner Books, 1983. 334 p. Includes bibliography and index. ISBN 0-446-51260-5.

"Dr. Ruth" is best known as the informative, compassionate, down-to-earth, and entertaining moderator of WYNY's weekly call-in radio show, "Sexually Speaking." She views her program as a form of education through which she imparts knowledge and communication that can aid people in enhancing their sex lives. As she puts it, "A healthy attitude toward one's own individual sex life is a happy, sensible, and imaginative attitude, free from peer pressure and free from pain and despair. That is what I want to promote." Dr. Ruth's background includes a doctorate in education (Columbia University), certification as a sex therapist (The New York Hospital—Cornell Medical Center), and work as a psychotherapist specializing in the treatment of sexual dysfunctions. As her former teacher, Helen Singer Kaplan, describes her, she has "a wonderful talent for translating the new technical and scientific information about sex into practical advice" (p. xiv). Written in straightforward, often humorous, conversational style, the book draws heavily on the questions of Dr. Ruth's clients, callers, and correspondents to define and explain a broad range of topics chosen for discussion in each chapter. Dr. Ruth deals with general concerns about sexuality (the need for sexual literacy, talking about sex, feeling good about sex, the importance of touching, relationships, normality, self-esteem), issues of interest to specific groups (sex and the elderly, gay sex, sex and the disabled, teen-age concerns), aspects of sexual health (contraception and STDs), and the particulars of sexual activity (sexual appetite, orgasm, positions, timing). The final chapters provide guidance in developing a satisfactory sexual marriage and present a sex information quiz that sums up some of the major points in the book. In offering advice to individuals, Dr. Ruth provides general information that dispels myths that many people share. (SGF)

IL,PO
226. Yaffé, Maurice, and Elizabeth Fenwick. **Sexual Happiness for Men: A Practical Approach.** Consultant Editor, Raymond C. Rosen. Illustrated by Charles Raymond. New York: Holt, 1988. 159 p. Includes bibliography and index. ISBN 0-8050-0690-7.

This illustrated guide to sexual fulfillment places particular emphasis on identifying problems in relationships and sexual functioning and suggesting options for their resolution. Designed as a self-help manual, it channels current research and practice into a practical reference format.

The first section, "Your Sexual Profile," contains a series of questions to indicate the reader's attitudes and behavior in the areas of sexual knowledge, sex drive, psychological well-being, satisfaction, sensuality, communication, confidence, technique, broadmindedness, and orientation; together, these make up the sexual profile of the reader, adding a personal perspective to the materials that follow. The second section contains a series of flow charts designed to self-diagnose sexual problems and difficulties and to suggest ways of dealing with them. Problems addressed include such issues as lack of interest, negative feelings, masturbation anxiety, low self-esteem, erection and ejaculation problems, sex and aging, and gender orientation. Section three presents specific suggestions for developing, sustaining, and enhancing a good sex life by expanding one's sexual repertoire, overcoming inhibitions and fear of intimacy, dealing with orientation problems, etc. The final two sections focus on relationship issues for men with steady partners, and for those who are single, questions about compatibility, communication, sex-drive discrepancy, understanding the other gender's feelings, jealousy, infidelity, and conception problems are dealt with as partnership issues; questions about being single, finding a partner, difficulties in sustaining relationships, and difficulties in developing social skills are dealt with as issues with which singles deal. Appendixes outline further resources for reading about sexuality and locating therapists.

Yaffé, a clinical psychologist who specializes in sex therapy and the analysis of sexual behavior, and Fenwick, who specializes in writing about medicine and health, organize the materials into an accessible format with many charts, illustrations, numerous cross-references, and succinct statements of advice. A companion volume, *Sexual Happiness for Women: A Practical Approach*, adopts a similar style in addressing women's problems. (SGF)

IL,PO

227. Zilbergeld, Bernie, with the assistance of John Ullman. **Male Sexuality: A Guide to Sexual Fulfillment.** Toronto: Bantam Books, 1981. 411 p. Includes bibliographic notes and index. ISBN 0-553-20450-5.

According to clinical psychologist Zilbergeld, "men have been duped about sex" by accepting a male mythology that traps them into believing such ideas as "men should not have, or at least not express, certain feelings"; "it's performance that counts"; "the man must take charge of and orchestrate sex"; and "a man always wants and is always ready to have sex." By learning such rules and concepts, men are drawn into a sexual fantasy land that is "destructive and a very inadequate preparation for a satisfying and pleasurable sex life." Therefore, the origin of male dissatisfaction with sex is cultural rather than personal. This book provides ways for men to unlearn unsatisfactory sexual scripts and explore other, more appropriate ways of being sexual. It is addressed primarily to heterosexual males, but it can be used by gays and women to enhance their relationships; its tone consistently acknowledges the individuality of sexual preferences and style.

After detailing the fantasy model of sex, Zilbergeld introduces descriptions and exercises for men to use to combat it. The first steps are to assess their present sex life, establish goals that form the basis for change, and accept realistic guidelines for meeting personal conditions for good sex. Conditions fall into two categories: (1) those that can be dealt with entirely on one's own, without anyone else's knowledge or participation and (2) those that require a partner's participation. Discussions of male anatomy and physiology, relaxation, masturbation, virginity, and abstinence relate to the first category of conditions, but most of the book is concerned with the second. Although some of the discussions concentrate on dealing with specific problems (e.g., ejaculatory control, erection, lasting longer, aging, and medical conditions such as medication, coronaries, and surgery), many are concerned with the relational context within which sexual activity operates. For instance, one chapter, "About Women," attempts to inform men not only about women's sexual anatomy and physiology but also about what women say they want from sex: shared contact and communication, gentleness, sensuality, sensitivity, and playfulness. Such knowledge may aid men in giving up an emphasis on performance and goal-oriented sex. Guidelines and exercises on assertiveness, touching, and listening try to aid communication about sexual needs.

"Dealing with a Partner" confronts the often unspoken but troublesome areas of a sexual relationship: talking about sex, contraception, saying "no," dealing with a new sexual partner, handling disagreements, and dealing with boredom in a long-term relationship. Contrary to popular myths, men's sexuality is every bit as complex as women's, even though it has not been given as much attention. This practical, clearly-written book not only defines the sexual complexity of males but also provides practical, easy-to-understand ways of dealing with it. The chapter references at the end of the book supplement the text by providing further sources of information for men who are interested in a specific issue. (SGF)

IL,PO

228. Zilbergeld, Bernie. **The New Male Sexuality.** New York: Bantam Books, 1992. 580 p. Includes bibliographic notes and index. ISBN 0-553-08253-1.

Clinical psychologist Zilbergeld's first book on male sexuality, *Male Sexuality* (1978), became a classic guide for men to develop sexual fulfillment; the *Washington Post* called it the "most humane, sympathetic, commonsensical book on the subject." In the sixteen years since it was published, social and cultural changes have altered the sexual issues with which men have to deal; *The New Male Sexuality* addresses these new concerns. Like *Male Sexuality*, it is a practical self-help book, written in down-to-earth language. Although there is some overlap in content and viewpoint, *The New Male Sexuality* is not a second edition of *Male Sexuality* but rather a new book dealing with contemporary sexual issues. Zilbergeld comments on some of the themes that he develops: "Throughout the book I offer the elements of a new model of sex, one that emphasizes pleasure, closeness, and self- and partner-enhancement rather than performance and scoring" (p. 4).

Good sex does not just happen; it has to be learned. First, it requires accurate information about your own sexuality, your partner's, and about sex itself. New chapters that address these elements are on sexual arousal, the nature of sexual normality, sex among singles, how to keep sex good over the years, and how to initiate sex. Other chapters relevant to this theme deal with the nature of sex, the penis, touching, and specifying your own personal conditions for good sex. Second, good sex means being realistic about sex and not buying into a fantasy model that includes ideas like "it's two feet long, hard as steel, always ready, and will knock your socks off." Since ideas about masculinity are often a part of the fantasy model and affect a man's sexual expectations, Zilbergeld includes a chapter dealing with male socialization ("The Making of Anxious Performers") as well as a final chapter centering on how men can be good fathers ("What You Can Do for Your Son"). Third, because good sex is likely to flourish in the context of a good relationship, Zilbergeld includes chapters on asserting yourself, connecting with your partner, being a good listener, expressing yourself, and dealing with conflict. Effective verbal and nonverbal communication about sex can enhance sexual interaction and the relationship. How do you know you've had good sex? Zilbergeld draws on a definition suggested by San Francisco sex therapist Carol Ellison: "You're having good sex if you feel good about yourself, good about your partner, and good about what you're doing. If later, after you've had time for reflection, you still feel good about yourself, your partner, and what you did, you know you've had good sex" (p. 67).

However, men have problems in developing good sex; they may feel driven or compulsive; have thoughts or feelings that get in the way of effective sexual functioning; have difficulties about timing, frequency, fantasies, or routine with their partners; or may engage in illegal activities. Over one-quarter of the book discusses problems like ejaculatory control, erection problems, sexual desire and activity, and then presents specific self-help exercises or recommendations for counseling to deal with them.

Overall, Zilbergeld normalizes a lot of feelings and experiences, giving men permission to be who they are. Numerous excerpts from case studies and specific suggestions (e.g., scripts about what to say in difficult situations) tie the text to the real lives and issues of contemporary men. (SGF)

Materials for Children

IL,PO
229. Calderone, Mary S., and James W. Ramey. **Talking with Your Child About Sex: Questions and Answers for Children from Birth to Puberty.** New York: Random House, 1982. 133 p. Includes bibliography and index. ISBN 0-394-52124-2.

Several assumptions set the stage for the contents of this book. Just like eating, sexual pleasure is also a primary life function, that requires guidance and support from caretakers during childhood so that sexual behavior can be accepted and enjoyed at each stage of development. Since children are sexual beings from birth on and learn about their sexuality in the process of growing up, it is essential that caretakers assume responsibility for socialization in this vital area so that children are prepared for the physical, social, and emotional changes and pitfalls that accompany adolescence.

Keeping these assumptions in mind, distinguished sexologist Calderone (a cofounder and president of SIECUS and a former medical director of the Planned Parenthood Federation of America) and her co-author, Ramey, have produced a short, readable guide to sexual socialization of children from birth to puberty. Using a developmental framework, they briefly describe the sexual feelings and behavior that children are likely to experience and express at each stage (newborn and first eighteen months, eighteen months to three years, three and four, five and six, seven through nine, and ten through twelve). Of particular use are descriptions of possible responses that caretakers may have to the sexuality of their children and suggestions for appropriate ways to answer children's questions at each stage. Therefore, the book serves the dual function of educating caretakers about their own feelings (erotic and otherwise) toward children's sexuality as well as preparing them for answering children's questions about their own sexuality. (SGF)

IL,PO,CH

230. Comfort, Alex, and Jane Comfort. **The Facts of Love: Living, Loving and Growing Up.** New York: Crown, 1979. 128 p. Includes index. ISBN 0-517-53839-3.

Intended for parents as well as their children, this handsomely illustrated book about sex has received high commendation from Patricia J. Campbell (*Sex Education Books for Young Adults 1892-1979*), who says that the Comforts "communicate their sense of celebration about the pleasures of sexuality, but with an emphasis on responsible, caring behavior." Based on the premise that sex education needs to be given before it is needed for practical purposes, the book attempts to make things easier in general by providing a bridge to communication about sex. In the section of the book titled "What Is Sex For?," the Comforts point out that "sex in humans has three uses—reproduction, relation and recreation (in other words, babies, love and fun). And this is the origin of a lot of the crossed wires and worry that have made one of the best things in life into one of the most anxious for humans. You need to know which of these three you are after, and which your partner is after" (p. 57). Accordingly, the Comforts have many things to say, advice if you will, on various topics relevant to these aims, such as contraception, virginity, nakedness, parents, fantasies, sex roles, marriage, alcohol and other drugs, diseases, and pornography. All of this material may seem to be heavy stuff for young minds. Nevertheless, the Comforts' overall theme remains an important consideration: advice about sex must be given before the need arises if it is to serve the useful purposes of preventing harm and facilitating the development of responsible, moral choices. The text was written with eleven-year-olds in mind, but older children and young adults will probably find it helpful. Parents, too, should benefit from reading it and knowing what kind of advice is being offered in the literature to their children. (TJW)

CH

231. Fassler, David, and Kelly McQueen. **What's a Virus, Anyway? The Kids' Book About AIDS.** Burlington, Vt.: Waterfront Books, 1990. 67 p. ISBN 0-914525-15-8.

Children hear much about AIDS through the media, at school, and at home. This book was designed to help parents and teachers begin to talk about AIDS with young children, and it provides them with basic information appropriate to this age group (approximately grades 1-5, and younger). In developing this book, Fassler and McQueen had the help of children between the ages of five and twelve and included their actual drawings and questions.

First the concept of a virus and how they cause sickness are presented. AIDS is described as a special kind of virus that kills white blood cells. This makes the person much sicker because white blood cells are needed to keep healthy. Next are listed the ways AIDS can be transmitted: needle sharing, sex, and placental transfer; and the ways AIDS is *not* transmitted: casual contact, mosquito bites, etc. Only minimal information is included about the sexual transmission of the disease.

The text stresses that different kinds of people can get AIDS, and people with AIDS are like everyone else. Some will live for a few years or longer, some will die in a short time. There is no cure for AIDS yet, although scientists and physicians are working to find one. Finally, the reader is invited to share feelings and questions about AIDS with parents, teachers, and medical professionals. (MC)

IL

232. Gordon, Sol, and Judith Gordon. **Raising a Child Conservatively in a Sexually Permissive World.** Revised and updated edition. New York: Simon & Schuster, 1989. 241 p. Includes bibliography and index. ISBN 0-671-68182-6.

Gordon and Gordon urge parents to be the principal sex educators of their children, to support them in developing healthy attitudes, and not to be apologetic about wanting to get across their own values. They consider teenage sexual intercourse to be a physical and emotional health hazard, and they support strengthening family life through open and honest communication between spouses and among parents and children.

The initial part of the book lays out Gordon and Gordon's philosophy about sexual communication in conservative families, promoting self-esteem in children, and coming to terms with sexuality. Two additional chapters discuss becoming an "askable" parent, and sexuality education in schools. The remainder of the book covers what types of sexual information, issues, and questions need to be addressed by parents for different age groups of children: preschool, preteen, and adolescents. Special situations are also mentioned: the single parent, the disabled child. The conclusion focuses on the roles of the mother, father, and grandparents in sex education; educating about moral and responsible sexuality; and the price of sexual ignorance in the next generation. (MC)

IL,PO,CH
233. McBride, Will, and Helga Fleischhauer-Hardt. **Show Me! A Picture Book of Sex for Children and Parents.** English language adaptation by Hilary Davies. New York: St. Martin's Press, 1975. 176 p. German edition published in 1974 by Jugenddienst-Verlag, Wuppertal. Includes bibliography.

This book, highly controversial when published, is intended for children and parents alike. It is both a picture essay showing the sexual development and sexual behavior of boys and girls from infancy through puberty as well as an instructional work aimed at indoctrinating young children with a sound understanding of their sexuality. The oversized book is handsomely made, combining the photographic talents of McBride, who also captioned the pictures, and the expert knowledge of Fleischhauer-Hardt, psychiatrist, child therapist, and parental advisor, who wrote the text.

The book is designed so that the child can thumb through it looking at the pictures while the parent discusses each image with him or her. The graphic full-page pictures depict naked children, sometimes with their mother or father, examining their bodies or asking questions or exclaiming about their sexual behavior. A typical sequence of pictures shows the mother cuddling and breast-feeding her baby while the children exclaim, "My mother's got a new baby. I'm really jealous, but I know babies have to be cuddled a lot. Everybody knows THAT! Look at him open his mouth! The way he's screaming, you'd think he was STARVING. Now he's finally FULL. Boy, he sure has a great filling station." This procedure is followed throughout the picture portion of the book, that covers many other topics, including genital differences, defecation and urination, erections, sex games children play, reaction to parents' sexual activities, masturbation, ejaculation, oral stimulation, and eventually intercourse, pregnancy, and birth. Finally the children, after witnessing all this, exclaim, "If you ask me . . . when I grow up, I want to be like FATHER. And I WANT TO BE LIKE MOTHER."

A Freudian perspective pervades the liberal philosophy of sex education advanced by Fleischhauer-Hardt. The ill effects of the Oedipus complex, penis envy, and the castration complex can be counteracted, she believes, by frank explanations of relevant questions raised by children in the early stages of their sexual development. In other words, this book, by openly depicting the sexuality of children and honestly discussing the facts with them, can serve to prevent the development of sexually warped adults. The result of this educational process should be informed adults imbued with loving and caring personalities, and who are free of sexual hang-ups. An appendix provides information for sexually active adolescents who need to know about contraception, abortion, and venereal disease. (TJW)

PR,IL
234. National Guidelines Task Force. **Guidelines for Comprehensive Sexuality Education: Kindergarten-12th Grade.** New York: SIECUS, 1991. 52 p. Includes appendixes.

Although 90 percent of parents want their children to have comprehensive sex education, less than 10 percent of them receive it. Most existing sex education programs begin late in high school and focus more on family, gender, and developmental issues than on sexual ones. Even AIDS curricula focus primarily on abstinence rather than safe sex; most mention condoms but few discuss how to use them. Meanwhile, every year one million teenaged women become pregnant; one in seven teens contracts a STD; and one in five hundred college students are infected with HIV. To meet the challenge of helping children become "sexually healthy and happy adults," in 1990 SIECUS (Sex Information and Education Council of the U.S.) convened the National Guidelines Task Force, chaired by William L. Yarber, Professor of Health Education at Indiana University; Debra Haffner, Executive Director of SIECUS, served as project director. The task force of leading health, education, and sex professionals developed the concepts and subconcepts that represent the foundation for comprehensive sex education in grades K through 12.

The guidelines are not a textbook or curriculum. Rather, they are a framework to facilitate the development or improvement of programs; to evaluate existing programs; to use for in-service education or teacher preparation; and to begin curriculum development at local levels. They are based on four major goals for sex education: (1) to provide accurate information about human sexuality; (2) to aid young people in developing values, attitudes, and insights; (3) to enhance relationships and interpersonal skills; and (4) to encourage responsibility.

The guidelines organize information about human sexuality around six key concepts—human development, relationships, personal skills, sexual behavior, sexual health, and society and culture—each of which is further related to four developmental levels of students, i.e., middle childhood (ages 5-8), preadolescence (ages 9-12), early adolescence (ages 12-15), and adolescence (ages 15-18).

Cognizant of the sensitive subject matter of a comprehensive sex education program, the Task Force encourages users of the guidelines to offer sexuality education as part of a comprehensive health education program; to utilize specially trained teachers to teach sex education; to involve the community in the development and implementation of a program; to relate materials to the multicultural needs of communities; and to address cognitive, affective, and behavioral dimensions of learning. Although a beginning, these guidelines are significant as the first national set of guidelines for comprehensive sex education in the United States. (SGF)

PO,CH
235. Schoen, Mark. **Bellybuttons Are Navels.** Illustrations by M. J. Quay. Foreword by Mary Steichen Calderone, M.D. Buffalo, N.Y.: Prometheus Books, 1990. 44 p. Includes a note to parents. ISBN 0-87975-585-7.

This picture book is designed for use by parents and educators with preschool and K-3 age children to help them learn to name and identify body parts, including sexual body parts, in a positive, accurate way. The aim is to help provide children from a young age with the ability to discuss genital anatomy frankly and correctly so that they can understand information and instruction about sexuality, reproduction, health and hygiene, and sexual abuse. A secondary purpose is to help them integrate acceptance of their genitals into acceptance of the total body.

In the story, a small brother and sister are taking a bath together. They begin by pointing out and naming parts of the face—eyes, nose, ears, mouth—then move on to arms, fingers, nipples, bellybuttons/navels, vulva, penis, scrotum, testicles, clitoris, buttocks, anus, legs, feet, and toes. Incidentally, a twelve-minute video with the same name is also available from the publisher. (MC)

PO,CH
236. Sheffield, Margaret. **Where Do Babies Come From?** Illustrated by Sheila Bewley. New York: Knopf, 1978. 33 p. ISBN 0-394-48482-7.

This short book is an adaptation of the award-winning BBC program "Where Do Babies Come From?" that deals with children's curiosity about the beginning of life. Designed for children about seven years of age or younger, the book presents the basic elements of reproduction from conception to birth by combining a soft, warm, colorful painting of a reproductive element on one page with a simple text accompanying it on the facing page. Illustrations include a woman nursing, a fetus inside the mother's womb, anatomical differences between males and females, a loving couple who are embracing while conceiving a child, stages of fetal development, and birth. Adults can read this book with children to answer basic questions such as "Where do I come from?" and "How was I born?" The sensitive drawings and the text of this overview tap the essential facts of sexual reproduction without detailing the intricacies of anatomy and physiology for which children of this age may not be prepared. (SGF)

Materials for Youth

(For related material see also entries 298, 312, 319)

PO,YA
237.   Bell, Ruth, et al. **Changing Bodies, Changing Lives: A Book for Teens on Sex and Relationships.** Revised and updated. New York: Vintage Books, 1987. 254 p. Includes index. ISBN 0-394-75541-3.
        Inspired by *Our Bodies, Ourselves* and motivated by the belief that "teenagers—and all of us—have a right to honest and thorough information about sex," the ten authors of this book (some of whom worked on *Our Bodies, Ourselves*) directly confront issues relevant to teenagers in the hope that it will serve to open a dialogue with teens about sex and relationships. This book has two major goals: (1) to give teenagers more information about their bodies and sex so that they can make responsible decisions about their future as well as feel good about themselves and (2) to provide an opportunity for teenagers to know that their own experiences are shared with their peers. The "backbone" of the book is based on three years of interviews with several hundred teenagers from a variety of backgrounds across the United States. Lengthy quotes and poems by these teenagers emphasize the relevance of their experiences.
        The book is divided into three sections: changes, sexuality, and taking care of yourself. The holistic perspective of the book is emphasized by its consideration of the physical and emotional aspects of these subjects. Practical information about menstruation, sexual problems, rape, suicide, alcohol and drug use, and birth control helps to dispel myths and provide needed guidance in these areas. Concern for the well-being of teens is also expressed by many graphic diagrams of important procedures such as inserting a diaphragm, putting on a condom, and conducting a self-examination of the genitals. The volume is replete with pictures, diagrams, tables, and "boxes" that highlight essential information. Options for value-laden decisions are presented without assuming the types of experiences to which adolescents have been exposed. Ordinary language is used to describe the issues, and pronunciation guides accompany more technical words. Parents are assured that good sex education will not make young people "go wild" but will aid them in becoming more well-informed decision makers.
        In the preface to this revised and updated edition, the authors state that "in 1980, when the first edition of this book appeared, we didn't know about AIDS. Now, just a mere seven years later, the tragedy of thousands of people dying of this sexually transmitted disease has made body and sex education an essential part of safe living. Everyone who is sexually active—and that is almost 100 percent of our population—must learn about responsible sexuality and how to keep themselves and others from getting AIDS." (SGF/TJW)

PO
238.   Cassell, Carol. **Straight from the Heart: How to Talk to Your Teenagers About Love and Sex.** New York: Simon & Schuster, 1988. 254 p. Includes bibliographic references. ISBN 0-671-66198-1.

Parents today, some of whom advocated sexual liberation when they were younger, wonder how well their children can deal with sexuality in a social context that allows them broader choices. Noted author, lecturer, and sex educator Cassell wrote this book as "a practical guide for parents, married or single, on how to help a son or daughter become a sane and sensible sexual person, without the sexual hang-ups of the past, but with an appreciation of the responsibility involved in having sexual choices." Drawing on her experience as a parent of six children, as a professional in the field of human sexuality, and on current theory and research, Cassell presents a perspective on each topic; guidelines on how to discuss the topic with a teenager; and a summary of factual information. Written in a conversational, down-to-earth, and often humorous style, the book provides suggestions for understanding the pressures with which teens have to deal; teens' views about parents; ways parents can clarify their own feelings and values about sex; and ways to open lines of communication between adults and teens (practice sessions are included). Cassell's approach is that of a compassionate mediator between the generations—a guide to ethical, responsible decisions by teenagers and a facilitator of routes for communication.

Several themes run through the topical discussions: (1) how to discuss sex; (2) the adolescent experience; (3) love; (4) what sex is; (5) the nature of relationships; (6) homosexuality and homophobia; (7) contraception; (8) pregnancy; (9) STDs. First, sexual ignorance is no gift. Teenagers will learn about sex one way or another and would like an honest discussion with their parents. Second, parents need to help their children in making decisions about sexuality issues, given the range of choices. Third, responsibility to self and others is an important consideration in any decision a teenager makes. Finally, we have not given enough attention to relationship issues like love, broken hearts, and sexual orientation—all of which are extremely important to teenagers. Ignoring these issues only results in uninformed decisions and potentially harmful consequences—suicide, disease, or pregnancy. (SGF)

PO,YA

239.   Gale, Jay. **A Parent's Guide to Teenage Sexuality.** New York: Henry Holt, 1989. 242 p. Includes bibliography, index, and glossary. ISBN 0-8050-0937-X.

This work by Gale, a psychologist, distinguishes itself from most sexuality guides by not just providing the "what" of information on the subject, but also the "how," as in how to approach the teen and how to communicate with him/her in regard to this most sensitive of topics.

In fact, the first half dozen or so chapters act as a preamble to the "nitty gritty" facts of sexuality, providing a philosophical and practical framework of what sex education is (chapter 1, "Your Child Will Receive a Sex Education, Whether You Like It or Not"; chapter 4: "Methods of Sex Education"). Gale devotes the first two chapters to addressing such things as "The Myth of the Sex Lecture" and the accompanying fears and discomfort on the part of the parent. In other words, understanding oneself as a parent vis-a-vis the adolescent looms as an important requisite to being able to talk about sex. Chapter 5 provides sensitivity training for the parent ("The Rodney Dangerfield Factor: Everyone Needs Respect"), with a follow-up chapter, "A Quick Primer on Communicating with Your Teenager."

After this first section, entitled "Your Role in Your Child's Sex Education," the book moves to part II, "What Your Teenager Needs to Know." Again, Gale lays a psychological foundation: in chapter 7, "Your Teenager Needs More Than Facts," he talks about adolescent self-esteem and issues of feeling sexual versus responsibility and moral values.

The remaining chapters discuss puberty, sexual intimacy, conception and contraception, sexually transmitted diseases and AIDS, and homosexuality. In the third section, "Special Situations, Special Needs," attention is given to the sexually active teenager, pregnancy, dealing with sexual trauma, if you're a single parent, the homosexual teenager, and the handicapped teenager. The few illustrations that accompany the text are excellent.

An appendix, "Finding Help," offers avenues for counseling, referral services, and further information. (EBS)

PO,YA

240. Gordon, Sol. **Facts About Sex for Today's Youth.** Illustrated by Vivien Cohen. Revised ed. New York: John Day, 1973. 48 p. ISBN 0-381-99648-4.

This purposely brief book was written for the average adolescent who is interested in receiving some clearly presented, basic information on sex and reproduction but does not wish to wade through technical descriptions of sexual response or essays on morality. Gordon, a clinical psychologist, hopes that parents with teenagers will read the entire book so that it can facilitate communication about sexuality, particularly as it relates to values and family life.

Each chapter discusses some common concerns of adolescents—anatomy and physiology of the male and female reproductive systems and how they relate to sexual intercourse, love, premarital sex, birth control, pregnancy and birth, and sexual problems and differences. Translations of technical terms into plain language (e.g., sexual intercourse is "getting laid," "sleeping together," and "having sex") occur throughout, as do reassurances about the normality of events most likely to occur in adolescence (e.g., masturbation, spontaneous erections, menstruation, "crushes," problems in coping with budding sexuality). Individual sexual problems (impotence, lack of orgasm), social problems (rape and VD), and differences (homosexuality) are acknowledged and explained. The book concludes with ten questions high school students ask the author most frequently about sex, such as "Do you think it's right to have sexual intercourse at our ages . . . 15, 16, 17?" "Does 'jerking off' frequently cause any harmful effects later?" "Can a girl become pregnant when she has intercourse for the first time?" and "How can you tell if you have VD?"

Explicit drawings of the sex organs, pregnancy and birth, contraceptive devices, sanitary napkins and tampons, and sexually developed young people enhance the information in the text. A series of references, selected for special groups (adolescent boys and girls, young children, parents, educators, religious people) can supplement the short descriptions in the book.

This book has gone through several editions since its original publication in 1969 as *Facts About Sex for Exceptional Youth.* Patty Campbell states that "in its 1978 and 1985 [sic] versions, it remains the best guide for unwilling or unskilled readers, both in early adolescence and up into the late teens." (SGF)

PO

241. Hatcher, Robert A., Shannon M. Dammann, and Julie Convisser. **Doctor, Am I a Virgin Again? Cases and Counsel for a Healthy Sexuality.** Atlanta, Ga.: Contraceptive Technology, 1990. 232 p. Includes resource lists, glossaries, and index.

Ignorance and communication problems can be dangerous to the sexual health of teenagers and young adults. Fifty percent of all first acts of intercourse occur without contraception; 10 percent of teens between fifteen and nineteen experience unintentional pregnancies each year. One in four girls and one in seven boys say they have been sexually abused before they are eighteen; one in four college women say they have experienced rape or attempted rape. And, 10 percent of female college students attending clinics show evidence of current or previous infection with chlamydia. When a society neglects education of youth about sexuality, it deprives them of the basis for making sound and healthy decisions. Such education is crucial since sex is an integral part as well as one of the most important aspects of an individual's personal and social life.

The goal of this book is to aid young people in making positive decisions about their sexuality to protect their health; increase their enjoyment; and to be considerate of others. Hatcher, Professor of Obstetrics and Gynecology at Emory University; Dammann, a recent graduate of Emory who writes on behalf of her young peers; and Convisser, a recent graduate of Williams College who specializes in family communication, collaborated to produce a relevant, sensitive, accurate presentation of information and anecdotes about sexual issues. Topics range from menstruation, a pelvic exam, contraception, and sexually transmitted diseases to sexual etiquette and decision-making about sexuality. Most chapters begin with a glossary of relevant terms and proceed to discuss, in plain English, the importance of the chapter's topic. One hundred and fifty actual cases illustrate the points of the text and indicate the misconceptions and human errors that individuals make about sex. For example, one woman relates how she used grape jelly in her diaphragm; a man comments on his diligence in using condoms by washing and reusing them!

The authors provide straightforward information about biological aspects of sexuality and refer readers to further information about the topics. They also provide guidelines for thinking about social and psychological aspects of sex, e.g., sexual etiquette, whether to have an AIDS test, deciding on a method of contraception. More than an "organ recital," this book confronts the complex issues of individual decision-making about sexual issues. (SGF)

PO,YA
242. Johnson, Eric W. **Sex: Telling It Straight.** Philadelphia: Lippincott, 1979. 112 p. Includes index. ISBN 0-397-01323-X.

This slender volume is an easy-to-read sex guide for adolescents. By not trying to double as a guide for both parents and children, the book utilizes a simple sentence structure and vocabulary so that even the weakest and youngest readers will have a chance of learning about sexuality on their own. The readability of the book is further enhanced with line drawings and phonetic guides to pronunciation of technical terms. In a very conversational manner and succinct form, the book presents practical information and advice without moralizing or preaching. As Johnson, a prominent sex educator, states in the preface, "Sex isn't bad or good. It just is. But how we use it is bad or good—for ourselves, for others." Knowledge, then, is the key to free will and responsible decisions. The chapter titles are "Sex, a Big Part of Life"; "Words and Sex"; "A Man's Sex Parts and How They Work"; "A Woman's Sex Parts and How They Work"; "Sexual Intercourse"; "How a Baby Is Born and What It Looks Like"; "Differences Between Men and Women"; "Masturbation"; "Having Sex Without Making Babies: Birth Control"; "A Problem of Sex: Babies Who Are Not Wanted"; "Another Problem of Sex: Abortion"; "Another Problem of Sex: VD"; "Some Other Problems of Sex"; "Homosexuality: Being 'Gay' "; "The Place of Sex in Life"; and "What Is Love?" (EBS)

YA
243. Johnson, Ervin "Magic." **What You Can Do to Avoid AIDS.** New York: Times Books, 1992. 192 p. Includes index. ISBN 0-8129-2063-5.

"Magic" Johnson is a well-known and well-liked basketball player who went public as a crusade against AIDS after he was diagnosed as HIV positive in 1991. His book is written to educate young people, and is designed to be read by teens and their parents. In preparing the book, Johnson collaborated with a number of experts and AIDS-related organizations, including former Surgeon General C. Everett Koop, the Centers for Disease Control, the American Foundation for AIDS Research, and Planned Parenthood.

Johnson's overall message is: "If you can wait [to have sex], wait . . . if you can't, be safe—*every time.*" He begins by exhorting parents to talk to their children about sex and AIDS/HIV. The seven chapters of the book are: "What Are HIV and AIDS?" (what the virus is and how it is and is not transmitted); "How to Be Sexually Responsible" (understanding sexual feelings and talking to your partner); "How to Have Safer Sex" (sexual expression without intercourse, how to buy and use condoms)' "How to Protect Yourself from Other Sexually Transmitted Diseases"; "If You Do Drugs or Drink" (stop or get help, but if you do shoot drugs, how to reduce the chances of getting HIV); "If You or Someone You Know Has HIV" (get treatment, support your friend); "If You're a Runaway or Homeless."

Throughout, questions and answers and mini-biographies of people with AIDS are interspersed with the text. Finally, Johnson's book includes a state-by-state directory of resources as well as a listing of Canadian resources. (MC)

PO,YA

244. Kaplan, Helen Singer. **Making Sense of Sex: The New Facts About Sex and Love for Young People.** Drawings by David Passalacqua. New York: Simon & Schuster, 1979. 154 p. Includes index. ISBN 0-671-25131-7.

According to Kaplan, a noted sex therapist, educator, and mother of three children, "making sense of sex" involves at least two tasks: (1) the presentation of facts about sex in a useful, reasonable manner and (2) communication of a clear, positive attitude about sex—that it is not only okay but also that its enjoyment is a natural, beautiful human experience. Written primarily for adolescents, this book attempts to present useful information about love and sex that will enhance the sexual development of young adults who are living in a society that has emphasized genital sex to the neglect of its emotional context. The explicit, open tone of the book tries to counter negative attitudes and myths that Kaplan thinks promote sexual problems and hamper a person's ability to love and have satisfying sexual experiences. The overall emphasis is on the link between human sexuality and the development of caring and loving relationships with others. The first chapter directly addresses the question of what "normal" lovemaking is; it dispels some myths about "having sex" by discussing male/female differences in sexual response and pinpointing the sources of some temporary problems in lovemaking. The succeeding chapters provide up-to-date information on the following topics: the biology of sex (mating, male and female genitals, gender development), the three phases of male and female sexual response (desire, excitement, orgasm), sexual problems (dysfunctions, variations, gender disturbances), "normal" sex (masturbation, fantasy, etc.), reproductive physiology (ovulation, menstruation, sperm production, conception, pregnancy), birth control, and sexually transmitted diseases. The book concludes with a chapter on sexual development and one on love that tie together a major theme implicit in the rest of the text: the mechanics of sex are important but are a less significant aspect of a person's life than a caring, intimate relationship with another person. The drawings of David Passalacqua greatly enhance the text. Parents and teachers also can benefit from the lessons presented in this clearly written, empathetic book for young people. (SGF)

PO,YA

245. Lauersen, Niels H., and Eileen Stukane. **You're in Charge: A Teenage Girl's Guide to Sex and Her Body.** New York: Fawcett Columbine, 1993. 345 p. ISBN 0-449-90464-4.

The title's tenet is the basis for this guide—namely, that by being armed with knowledge ("we believe in the intelligence of today's youth"), the adolescent girl can be in control of her life and avoid the pitfalls of pregnancy, sexually transmitted diseases, alcohol, drugs, eating disorders, stress, and other physical and mental land mines of growing up female.

The authors—one of whom is a prominent physician—utilized informal interactions with teenage girls as well as questionnaires to shape the content of this practical survival manual. Lauersen and Stukane also used the input of a diverse group of professionals to help further define the relevant issues and their proper answers.

The result is a readable, well-illustrated, well-rounded handbook that touches all the bases. The standard, predictable explanations of sexuality, pregnancy, contraceptives, and teenage health problems are covered amid some intriguing chapter headings: "How to Be Happy with Your Body"; "What Boys Are Going Through"; "How You Eat Reveals How You Feel About Yourself." Topics such as how skin and diet are related and how to deal with stress are interspersed with interesting side tidbits such as "Moments in the History of Hair." (EBS)

PO,YA

246. Madaras, Lynda. **Lynda Madaras Talks to Teens About AIDS: An Essential Guide for Parents, Teachers, and Young People.** Drawings by Jackie Aher. New York: Newmarket Press, 1988. 106 p. Includes index. ISBN 1-55704-009-5.

A deceptively slender volume, this handbook for parents, teachers, and young people is mainly about safe sex. The preface excerpts a 1988 newspaper article that states "although the number of teenagers with AIDS is minuscule compared with the 62,740 cases reported annually, the number of teenagers being diagnosed with AIDS each year is about doubling and that the scale of the problem should not be underestimated."

The first of five chapters, "AIDS: The Rumors and the Real Facts," gives a basic explanation of what AIDS is and how it can and cannot be contracted. The remaining chapters elaborate further the various ways AIDS is transmitted and what practices can minimize risk.

In the third chapter, a strong case is made for abstinence, arming the teen with ammunition against peer pressure and for making a decision to refrain from intercourse. Provided is a section on "Outercourse: A Safe, Satisfying Way of Being Intimate," that includes petting, manual stimulation, and dry kissing. The chapter concludes with guidelines for "safer sex," that includes the do's and don't's of condom use. Madaras states, "condoms can be very sexy if you make using them a part of, rather than an interruption to, your love-making," and most men say "they're really turned on when women put the condom on for them." Teamwork can be a pleasurable fulfillment of mutual responsibility.

This work has a number of helpful diagrams and illustrations as well as an appendix of sources for further information, including listings of pamphlets, videos, and hotlines. (EBS)

PO,CH

247. Madaras, Lynda, and Area Madaras. **What's Happening to My Body? A Growing Up Guide for Mothers and Daughters.** New York: Newmarket Press, 1983. 191 p. Includes bibliography and index. ISBN 0-937858-21-8.

Puberty is often a confusing, complicated, emotional period for pubescent children and their parents. Children want and need to know what is happening to them during this phase of their lives. However, parents may not know what to say or how to talk with their children about these issues. A one-shot "talk" about the facts of life is not sufficient to deal with the complexity of the process. This book, designed to be read by girls in the nine to thirteen-year-old age range, was written to provide essential details about anatomical and physiological changes in the female body during puberty. Madaras, whose young daughter contributed to this book, hopes that mothers and daughters will read it together so that they can understand the changes that are occurring and become closer and more comfortable with each other while discussing the topics. After a general discussion of what puberty is, Madaras discusses specific changes that occur in females during puberty: size and shape changes; the appearance of body hair, perspiration, and pimples; larger breasts; changes in the appearance of the vulva; changes in the reproductive organs; and the process of the menstrual cycle. Each chapter includes informative drawings as well as quotes from pubescent girls who were members of Madaras's class on preteen and teenage sexuality. The author discusses practical matters, such as the pros and cons of pads, tampons, and sponges for use during menstruation and ways to alleviate menstrual cramps. She fosters sexual and reproductive health by encouraging girls to touch, look, and be aware of bodily changes and by informing them about the symptoms of toxic shock and PMS; how to examine the breasts for lumps; and how to conduct a self-examination of the vulva, vagina, and cervix. The final chapters give an overview of changes that occur in pubescent boys and outline some sexual issues that may arise during puberty and the teen years: "crushes," dating, petting, intercourse, STDs, birth control, rape, incest, and homosexual feelings. As Ralph I. Lopez says in his foreword, "For mothers this will serve as a reminder of their own youth and help with the turmoils of their daughters' world; for fathers it is a 'must read' if they are to try to understand their daughters." (SGF)

PO

248. McCoy, Kathy. **The Teenage Body Book Guide to Sexuality.** Illustrations by Bob Stover. New York: Pocket Books, 1983. 128 p. Includes index. ISBN 0-671-54681-3.

In 1978, McCoy, an editor for *Teen* magazine, and Charles Wibbelsman, a specialist in adolescent medicine, published *The Teenage Body Book*, that discusses sexuality as part of overall physical and mental health. In its companion volume, *The Teenage Survival Guide* (1981), McCoy dealt more deeply with social and emotional problems. Material in these early works was updated and published in 1983 as *The Teenage Body Book Guide to Sexuality* and *The Teenage Body Book Guide to Dating*. The former is the first in a series of books dealing with topics of concern to teenagers. McCoy comments that this succinct, easy-to-read book "is designed to help you [teenagers] to understand your sexual anatomy; your sexual feelings, actions and alternatives; and to make choices that are right for you." McCoy highlights adolescent concerns by introducing parts of the text with personal inquiries from teenagers who wrote to *Teen* magazine in search of answers to their problems.

The first half of the book confronts some of the myths and anxiety that teenagers have by providing information and guidelines about broad sexual issues: the normality of sexual thoughts and feelings; anatomy and physiology of the male and female reproductive systems; the psychology of sexuality, including a discussion of fantasies, self-images, sexual preferences, sexual attitudes, and sexual values; the process of making responsible sexual choices; and uncertainties about such areas as masturbation, petting, foreplay, sexual intercourse, and communication in a sexual context. The second half of the book focuses on the specifics of birth control (including an identification of each method, who should and should not use it, its advantages and disadvantages, how to obtain it, how to determine an appropriate method for a particular lifestyle), sexually transmitted diseases (what they are, their symptoms, the dangers, the treatment), pregnancy (assessing the risk of getting pregnant, symptoms of pregnancy, and choices available if pregnant), and where to get help for such problems as pregnancy and disease. The last chapter reiterates themes that run through the text—that sexuality is a normal part of life and that it entails responsible choices. Throughout the book, the importance of having accurate information, recognizing social values and personal attitudes, developing self-esteem, and having sensitivity in making sexual choices is emphasized. Diagrams complement the text by depicting such images as four types of hymens; a circumcised and an uncircumcized penis; and the insertion of a diaphragm. As the cover says, the book contains "straightforward, no-nonsense answers to the questions you have about sex," presented in a sympathetic style. (SGF)

PO,YA
249. Mintz, Thomas, and Lorelie Miller Mintz. **Threshold: Straightforward Answers to Teenagers' Questions About Sex.** Illustrated by Lorelie Miller Mintz. New York: Walker, 1978. 120 p. Includes index. ISBN 0-8027-6307-3.

In simple language directed toward young readers, *Threshold* answers some of the most frequently asked questions of adolescents about puberty and sex. Written by a psychiatrist and his wife, the book is intended to help allay anxieties of adolescent change and to provide answers to questions that teenagers would often find too embarrassing to ask. The book is organized into seven chapters in a question-and-answer format. The first two chapters ("Puberty in Girls" and "Puberty in Boys") explain the physical changes that accompany puberty, including menstruation and ejaculation. Chapter 3, "Sexual Development in Girls and Boys," explains masturbation, orgasm, and sexual intercourse. Pregnancy and birth are covered in the next two chapters. Chapter 6, "Caution and Precaution," covers birth control, abortion, and venereal diseases. The final chapter, "Feelings," addresses feelings about the opposite sex, one's family, and oneself, and includes guidance in regards to dating and love. (EBS)

PO,YA
250. Pomeroy, Wardell B. **Boys and Sex.** A revised ed. of the classic book on adolescent male sexuality. New York: Delacorte Press, 1981. 187 p. Includes index. ISBN 0-440-00756-9.

Written by a co-author of the Kinsey Reports, this book explains sex and adolescence to boys and their parents (and would also be good reading for girls who want to expand their knowledge). The approach is simple and straightforward, explaining the mental and physical aspects of sexual feelings and behavior from the standpoint of the adolescent male. Pomeroy does not condemn youthful sex activity, stating in his afterword, "It isn't what you do sexually that matters, as long as you're not hurting someone else." Chapters cover the anatomy and physiology of sex, sex play before adolescence, masturbation, homosexuality, dating, petting, intercourse, and the consequences of intercourse. A final chapter answers questions most frequently asked by boys. Pomeroy has also written a similar primer for girls, *Girls and Sex* (1969). (EBS)

PO,YA
251. Westheimer, Ruth, and Nathan Kravetz. **First Love: A Young People's Guide to Sexual Information.** New York: Warner Books, 1985. 212 p. Includes index. ISBN 0-446-34092-8.

Psychosexual therapist "Dr. Ruth" and education professor Kravetz collaborate to produce a readable, informative young people's guide to sex information for both parents and teenagers. Although the first chapter of the book contains some basic information on the development of male and female sexual anatomy and physiology, primary emphasis in the rest of the book is on the psychological and social concerns about sexuality that may confront teenagers at this point in their lives.

Chapter 2 deals with questions about the relationship between love and sex and makes a case for the conclusion that kissing and petting, not intercourse, are appropriate expressions of love and happiness for teenagers. Nevertheless, the final decision about sexual expression is up to each individual, and the best way to deal with this decision is to be well informed about the expectations, dangers, and pleasures associated with sexual involvement. Chapter 3 discusses some of these issues—the pros and cons of being a virgin, masturbation, and sexual positions. Chapter 4 concentrates on getting along with people—the components of building a relationship that are the key to having good sex. Chapters 5 and 6 focus on what girls and boys ought to know. Girls, for example, ought to know what to expect from a gynecological exam, how to explain the process of menstruation, and how to handle relationships with parents, boys, and older men. Teenage boys should know, for example, how to recognize "bad" information about sex, understand the "uninvited erection," penis size, and premature ejaculation, and cope with men who may approach them. Controversial topics such as rape, incest, sexual abuse, homosexuality, and contraception are dealt with in later chapters. Advice on parent/teenager communication and ways to ask for help is also included. The advice is given with the purpose of making "people's lives happier and to offer a better understanding of sex."

Readers should make sure that they do not use the first printing of this book, that was recalled by the publisher because of a major error on lines 5 and 6 on page 195: the sentence said that the safe times for nonreproductive intercourse were the week before and the week after ovulation. It should have said that these were the UNSAFE times. (SGF)

Part

II

TOPICAL GUIDE

Developmental Aspects

OVERVIEWS. SEX DIFFERENCES

(For related material see also entries 37, 1015, 1052)

IL,PO

251a. Campbell, Anne, ed. **The Opposite Sex: The Complete Illustrated Guide to Differences Between the Sexes.** Topsfield, Mass.: Salem House, 1989. 256 p. Includes bibliography and index. ISBN 0-88162-369-5.

Campbell's compilation is a celebration of sex differences through the life course. In this oversized volume, made up of contributions from colleagues, Campbell vividly depicts in words and pictures how babies, children, adolescents, and adults differ in their sexual behavior and sex roles. She shows that both society and nature play significant parts in this gradual unfolding of human life.

Campbell divides the book into two parts. The first part, "Children: Girls and Boys," covers fifteen signed papers on the following topics: "Before Birth," "Early Infancy," "Adopting a Sex Role," "The Freudian View," "Brothers and Sisters," "When Mother Goes to Work," "The Roots of Aggression," "Toys and Play," "Friendship," "Skills and Aptitudes," "At School," "When Parents Split Up" "Moral Development," "Getting into Trouble," and "Puberty." The second part, "Adulthood: Men and Women," also covers fifteen topics: "Evolution," "Sexuality," "Attitudes to Love," "Marriage," "Who Looks After the Children?" "Violence Between the Sexes," "Emotion and Adjustment," "In the Workplace," "Influence and Persuasion," "Ambition and Leadership," "Creativity," "Styles of Communication," "In the Media," "Sex Stereotypes," and "Role Versatility."

Campbell, Associate Professor of Psychology at Rutgers University, has assembled a team of professionals to deal with the sex difference topics in a helpful and expert manner in the hope that their presentations will guide adults in their search for understanding problems that may occur between the sexes. Each topic, generously illustrated in black-and-white and color pictures and instructive diagrams, points out the wonder and excitement of life. Psychology professors Carol Jacklin and Carol Tavris served as distinguished consultants for this well-designed book. (TJW)

PR

252. Eysenck, Hans Jurgen. **Sex and Personality.** Austin, Tex.: University of Texas Press, 1976. 255 p. Includes bibliography and index. ISBN 0-292-77529-6.

The research reported in this volume was undertaken by Eysenck to account for differences in human sexual behavior. He sought to make predictive connections between personality theory and aspects of sexual behavior. Using the personality dimensions N (neuroticism), E (extroversion), and P (psychoticism), and the L (lie scale) developed in his earlier work as variables in predictions, Eysenck sought to demonstrate that individuals with different personalities will differ predictably in their sexual attitudes and behaviors. He paid particular attention to gender, age, and genetic, biological, and psychiatric variables. Each study is discussed in detail. Lengthy questionnaires were used from which a subset of variables was chosen for analysis. Scales were constructed for eleven primary attitude factors (permissiveness, satisfaction, neurotic sex, impersonal sex, pornography, sexual shyness, prudishness, sexual disgust, sexual excitement, physical sex, and aggressive sex) and for two "super factors" (sexual satisfaction and sexual libido).

Acknowledging the possibility of error in using small, time- and place-limited samples, Eysenck concludes that results with divergent groups were similar enough to permit generalization with some confidence. Among the key findings reported in his summarization are that a meaningful correlation exists between social attitudes in general and sex attitudes, and attitudes about sex fall in clusters that have clear psychological meaning. Personality dimensions, as measured by N, E, P, and L inventories, were consistently and predictably linked with high or low scores on the attitude scales and the libido and satisfaction scales. Marked gender differences appear on items and scales. Libido is the factor that shows the greatest divergence. However, on a two-dimensional grid, the sexes show strikingly similar patterns of correlation of the attitude scales with the super scales.

Eysenck discusses the social relevance of these and other findings and their implications in sex education, in the issues that surround pornography, and in a consideration of permissiveness in a democratic society. (LF)

PR,IL
253. Fausto-Sterling, Anne. **Myths of Gender: Biological Theories About Women and Men.** New York: Basic Books, 1985. 258 p. Includes bibliographic notes, index, and glossary. ISBN 0-465-04790-4.

Myths of Gender is both a scientific and a political statement. It shakes the foundations of many widely held biological theories about men and women and of the scientific process that produced them. Two major themes run through this thoroughly documented book. First, the search for fundamental biological causes of behavior is based on a false understanding of biology. Nature/nurture debates are fruitless because they pose unanswerable questions. The link between biology and behavior is part of a complex, dynamic process; understanding it demands a precise examination of the interaction between a biological being and the social environment, in which each can affect the other. Unidimensional explanations not only confuse the issues but also blind us to the fact that behavior can have many different causes. In sum, "any biological theory about human behavior that ignores the complex of forces affecting behavior as well as the profound two-way interactions between mind and body is scientifically hopeless" (p. 220). Second, scientists "peer through the prism of everyday culture" and their personal lives when they design studies. Investigations of gender are particularly subject to the influence of hidden agendas because they touch researchers so personally. Therefore, it is "inherently impossible for any individual to do unbiased research" in the areas of race, gender, or sexuality. Consequently, it is important that scientists be aware of and spell out their beliefs.

Most of the content of Fausto-Sterling's book aims to "take a flashlight and shine it in unlit corners of other people's research" (p. 10). A biologist trained in studying developmental genetics, she examines a series of scientific investigations of gender from the point of view of a "scientist who is also a feminist." She concentrates on four major questions: (1) Do male and female brains differ physically? (2) What is meant by genetically caused behavior and what is known about the embryological development of gender differences? (3) To what extent do hormones cause behavior? (Do menstruation and menopause cause women to be unstable? Does testosterone account for males being more aggressive than females?) and (4) Does an evolutionary framework explain present-day differences between men and women? Drawing on extensive research related to each of these questions, Fausto-Sterling logically dissects the evidence to draw conclusions about the validity of the interpretations. She not only exposes many myths in the process but also concludes that the dangers in adhering to simplistic biological explanations are to deny the possibility of social change and to stifle creative research that confronts the web of biological and social interactions with the expectation of no easy answers. (SGF)

PR,IL
254. Gilligan, Carol. **In a Different Voice: Psychological Theory and Women's Development.** Cambridge, Mass.: Harvard University Press, 1982. 184 p. Includes bibliography and index. ISBN 0-674-44544-9.

According to Gilligan, Associate Professor of Education at Harvard University, there is a disjunction between women's experiences and the way that human development is represented in psychological theories, that results in the interpretation of women's development as inferior, inadequate, or puzzling. Gilligan suggests that the problem may not lie in women's development but in the types of theories used to assess their development. Critical theory-building research in psychology has excluded women from these studies, resulting in a distortion of developmental theory in favor of men's experiences. Gilligan's book "records different modes of thinking about relationships and the association of these modes with male and female voices in psychological and literary texts and in the data of my research" (p. 1). Her goal is to present a clearer representation of women's development, one that will supplement current developmental theories to fashion a more balanced and enriched picture of human development that includes the experience of both sexes. Although she claims that the "different voice" she describes "is characterized not by gender but by theme" (p. 2), this book concentrates on the modes of thought that characterize a woman's voice as a different voice. Drawing on three empirical studies based on interviews about conceptions of self and morality and about experiences of conflict and choice—a college student study, an abortion decision study, and a rights and responsibilities study—Gilligan highlights the differences in men's and women's views of the world and their role in it.

The first chapter, "Woman's Place in Man's Life Cycle," is the theoretical cornerstone of the later chapters. The main thesis is that the nature of a person's concept of the world depends upon the position of the observer and the experiences that shape his/her observations. This is true of scientists as well as the average person. The theories of Freud, Erikson, Kohlberg, and Piaget all emphasize the importance of separation and individuation as stages indicative of mature psychological functioning and adequate moral development; they follow periods of attachment that need to be relinquished in the path of maturity. In contrast, Chodorow suggests that such theories bypass the developmental differences between men and women, setting up men's experiences as standards to which women are supposed to conform. During the first three years of life, when Stoller hypothesizes that gender identity is irreversibly set, a child is cared for by women. Chodorow thinks that this social situation sets up different dynamics of gender identity formation for men and women. Girls have ongoing relationships with their mothers, linking attachment to identity formation; boys separate from their mothers, linking masculinity with differentiation from women. Femininity is defined through attachment, context, and care while masculinity is defined through separation, individuation, and rules of fairness. However, the cultural definition of maturity as separation and individuation is at odds with women's experience and affects psychologists' evaluations of women's moral development, that focuses on retaining relationships rather than following rules of fairness. The rest of the book explains the ramifications of the contrast between the care and justice perspectives in relationships, responses to moral dilemmas, crises and transitions, and ideas about women's rights. Gilligan concludes that recognition of the importance of both attachment and separation as complementary rather than sequential aspects of development is the real path to discovering maturity. (SGF)

PR
255. Goy, Robert W., and Bruce S. McEwen. **Sexual Differentiation of the Brain: Based on a Work Session of the Neurosciences Research Program.** Cambridge, Mass.: MIT Press, 1980. 223 p. Includes bibliography and index. ISBN 0-262-07077-4.

This volume synthesizes the proceedings of a Neurosciences Research Program Work Session held on May 22-24, 1977; it reflects the "collaborative interaction, reviewing, and updating" of the report by the twenty participants, who are drawn from a variety of fields, including medicine (psychiatry, neuroscience, endocrinology, internal medicine, anatomy), psychology, sociology, and biology. (The Neurosciences Research Program is an interdisciplinary, interuniversity research center at MIT, the goal of which is to investigate how the nervous system mediates behavior.)

Operating on the assumption that behavioral sex differences are the product of genetic, hormonal, and environmental factors, the task of the work session was to explore the relative contribution that each of these factors makes to sexually dimorphic behavior. The book is divided into five parts, each of which deals with one aspect of understanding the causes of variations in sexually dimorphic behavior. Part I is a general introduction to the concept of sexually dimorphic behavior (in which males and females exhibit measurable differences in their behavioral responses) and the organizational hypothesis (that there is an intrinsic tendency for neural processes and reproductive organs to develop according to a female pattern of body structure and development). These researchers find a wide variation in behavioral and morphological dimorphism and present no evidence that would contradict the hypothesis that both organizational and activational mechanisms of gonadal hormones are represented among all vertebrate phyla. Furthermore, some dimorphism may have neither a genetic nor a hormonal basis. Part II tests the implications of the organizational hypothesis by looking at sex differences in the behavior of rodents, birds, and primates. Topics include biological and environmental determinants of sexual differentiation in humans, sexual dimorphism in human parenting, and the endocrinological basis for homosexuality among males. Part III deals with genetic aspects of sex differences in behavior and sexual differentiation; it includes what little is known about the genetic basis of sexual behavior patterns. Part IV, "Cellular and Molecular Aspects of Sexual Differentiation," focuses on the cellular organization and morphological sex differences of the gonadal and reproductive tract of birds and mammals. The final section, "Cellular Bases of Sexual Dimorphisms of Brain Structure and Function," suggests that there is no single hormonal agent responsible for the sexual differentiation of the brain in birds and mammals. Overall, Goy and McEwen conclude that "from our discussions, the biological substrate seems as important in humans as in other animals" (p. 156). (SGF)

PR

256. Katchadourian, Herant A., ed. **Human Sexuality: A Comparative and Developmental Perspective.** Berkeley, Calif.: University of California Press, 1979. 358 p. Includes bibliographic references and index. ISBN 0-520-03654-9.

According to Katchadourian, an investigation of sexual development through the life span is essential for a thorough understanding of human sexuality. The main purpose of this book is to bring together specialists from a variety of fields to address the issue of sexual development, particularly as it relates to gender identity and roles.

Two general essays introduce the contents. In the first, Katchadourian points out the wide range of meanings attached to the terminology of sex and gender and argues that it is important to have consistent terms, not only for interdisciplinary communication but also for conceptual clarity. In the second essay, Katchadourian and Martin suggest that it is possible to characterize the essential components of sexuality in terms of the "direction of sexual striving" and the "magnitude of sexual behavior."

The balance of the book is organized into five parts, each providing a different disciplinary perspective on sexual development. Within each part, one specialist provides an overview of major findings and theoretical views while a second critiques or supplements the first; a third contributor comments on the first two papers and suggests directions for further research.

In part I, "Evolutionary Perspectives," Lancaster, Alexander, and Beach examine the primate evidence in an effort to understand species-wide characteristics of human sexuality. Green, Davidson, and Ehrhardt discuss the significance of biological factors in sexual differentiation and behavior in part II, "Biological Perspectives." Three developmental psychologists, Luria, Maccoby, and Sears, analyze psychosocial dimensions of gender identity, role, and orientation in part III, "Psychological Perspectives." In part IV, "Sociological Perspectives," Gagnon, Lipman-Blumen and Leavitt, and Rainwater make a case for the impact of learning and social context on sexual behavior and expressions of gender identity. In the final part, "Anthropological Perspectives," Shapiro, LeVine, and Whiting point out the relevance of different cultural milieus in understanding gender roles, gender identity, and sexual behavior. No concluding chapter integrates the perspectives presented. Katchadourian admits that "the range and diversity of the viewpoints represented . . . do not add up to an integrated and coherent view of the subject." (SGF)

IL
257. Kitzinger, Sheila. **Woman's Experience of Sex.** Photography by Nancy Durrell McKenna. New York: Putnam, 1983. 320 p. Includes bibliography and index. ISBN 0-399-12856-5.

Written by an internationally recognized writer and educator in psychosexuality, this sensitive, solidly documented book discusses female sexuality from a woman's perspective. Based on the direct experiences of hundreds of women who talked with Kitzinger, it rejects the irrelevance to which women's feelings and behavior are assigned by male authors and attempts to demonstrate the dimensions of women's sex lives, that Kitzinger comments are "marvelously more complex than most books about sex would have us believe." Because sex involves the whole person and is not just genitally focused, Kitzinger examines sexuality in a variety of contexts. In the early chapters she deals with the body (genital anatomy and physiology, the effect of hormones) and feelings (sexual rhythms, masturbation, orgasm, and sexual fantasies). She then looks at sexual lifestyles, including marriage, lesbianism, and celibacy, as well as sexual relationships, embracing, talking about sex, developing confidence in sex, touching, massage, and handicaps. Succeeding chapters present a series of topics showing how sexuality changes for a woman at different times in her life. One chapter focuses on children and sex (childhood sexuality, baby massage, and talking to children about sex), and another, on transitions (the girl growing up, choosing a contraceptive, pregnancy, childbirth, menopause, and aging). The final chapters concentrate on various problems: sexual dysfunctions, sex and power (harassment, assault, and pornography), and the grief accompanying the death of a loved one (spouse, baby). The profuse, often explicit illustrations and photographs complement the text of this practical guide to sexuality. Its consideration of the link between sexuality and a woman's identity, values, emotions, and relationships make this book a useful source not only for women but also for those who love them. (TJW)

IL
258. Laqueur, Thomas. **Making Sex: Body and Gender from the Greeks to Freud.** Cambridge, Mass.: Harvard University Press, 1990. 313 p. Includes bibliographic notes and index. ISBN 0-674-54349-1.

Western perceptions of sex and gender are not static. As Laqueur demonstrates, a dramatic shift in these perceptions occurred around the eighteenth century, changing our very ways of thinking about ourselves.

From Galen to the Enlightenment, the human body was seen to reflect variations on one (male) ideal. This "one-sex model" was not just a philosophical construct; it was a pervasive belief that permeated Western culture. Scientific study supported it as much as theology did, and anatomy was used to reinforce it. The male and female reproductive organs were seen as essentially identical in all but position. Conception was believed to require orgasm by both partners. The possibility of the female body changing to male—a transformation repeatedly documented in scientific writing—made sexual identity a fluid concept. Sexual differences were not clearly marked by the body, and culturally-defined gender roles were necessary to determine sexual identity.

But during the eighteenth century woman became defined as a separate being, almost a separate species, from man. In the nineteenth century this reinterpretation was supported by both biology and psychology. Male and female reproductive organs became differentiated, even being renamed. Perceived differences in temperament between the sexes were attributed to the influence of the uterus. The sexuality of women was redefined: when female orgasm was found to be unnecessary for conception, the woman's role in intercourse became that of the passive partner with little sexual desire. Sexual anatomy became the defining factor in gender.

This shift in the perception of sex and gender was caused by a complex of views from science, philosophy, and politics. Science demonstrated the physical differences between male and female—but anatomy did not change over the centuries. Only the interpretation of it was altered. Philosophical evolution from a world view based on religion and the Great Chain of Being to one based on nature and objective analysis greatly affected that interpretation. In turn, that outlook made it possible for patriarchal politics to use the growing body of knowledge concerning physiological sex differences (however inaccurate that might be) to create gender definitions supporting the hierarchy of power. (SDH)

PR
259. Maccoby, Eleanor Emmons, and Carol Nagy Jacklin. **The Psychology of Sex Differences.** Stanford, Calif.: Stanford University Press, 1974. 634 p. Includes bibliography and index. ISBN 0-8047-0859-2.

In this sequel and supplement to *The Development of Sex Differences* (1966), Maccoby, a professor, and Jacklin, a research associate, both in the Department of Psychology at Stanford University, focus not only on the development of sex differences through childhood and adolescence (as in the earlier volume) but also on sex differences in intellectual performance and social behavior among adults. They concentrate on psychological development during the course of the life cycle rather than on sexual behavior per se. The goal of the volume is to determine which beliefs about sex differences are substantiated by the evidence. To do this, they present a thorough review and assessment of the research literature on sex differences published between 1966 and 1973.

The first two sections of the book establish the nature of differences that require explanation. Part 1, "Intellect and Achievement," reviews research on perception, learning, and memory; intellectual abilities and cognitive styles; and achievement motivation and self-concept. Part 2, "Social Behavior," covers research on temperament, social approach-avoidance, and power relationships. The third section summarizes the findings of the first two sections and addresses the question of how to explain patterns of similarity and difference between the sexes.

Overall, the evidence does not support many popular beliefs about psychological differences between the sexes. Girls are *not* more socially suggestible, better at rote learning and repetitive tasks, lacking in achievement motivation or self-esteem, affected by heredity, or more auditory than boys. Boys are *not* more analytic, visual, or affected by environment than girls. The well-established differences between the sexes are rather few. Boys are more aggressive than girls; and, while boys excel in their mathematical and visual-spatial abilities, girls have greater verbal ability.

The next question is what accounts for the small set of psychological differences that do exist? While imitation and differential reward and punishment are aspects of the acquisition of sex-typed behavior, a cognitive process of self-socialization is also involved. Methodological problems as well as firmly entrenched sexual stereotypes may have resulted in greater attention being paid to the differences rather than similarities between the sexes. The null hypothesis emerges as a plausible explanation for many psychological characteristics of the sexes. Maccoby and Jacklin conclude that the sexes are psychologically alike in many ways and that societies have the option of minimizing sex differences if they so choose.

The book ends with a 235-page annotated bibliography of over 1,400 research studies published since 1965, or not included in *The Development of Sex Differences*. The lengthy annotations summarize each study in terms of subjects, measures, and reesults, and they provide a valuable reference tool for researchers. (SGF)

PR,IL
260. May, Robert. **Sex and Fantasy: Patterns of Male and Female Development.** New York: Norton, 1980. 226 p. Includes bibliographic notes and index. ISBN 0-393-01316-2.

In the first half of this book, May examines diverse lines of fantasy-laden evidence to account for sex differences in men and women. To support his belief that men and women are inherently different from each other, psychologically as well as physically, he recounts two archetypal Greek myths (that of Phaethon and Phoebus on the one hand and Demeter and Persephone on the other); describes research into the fantasy patterns of men and women; and interprets separately the contrasting lives of a particular man and woman. These myths, fantasies, and lives display similar patterns of thought and behavior; the author chooses the word *pride* to sum up the male pattern and the word *caring* to characterize the female pattern.

To counter the argument of those who accept the position that sex differences are caused primarily by environmental factors, May turns his attention to a review of the abundant empirical literature on sex differences, that demonstrates that there are genetic, hormonal, cross-species, and cross-cultural differences between the sexes. He argues that we must honor the body as well as the culture; he says that "socialization, after all, does not write on a blank page" (p. 95). He goes on to examine the literature on sex differences in early infancy and in the area of children's play.

May adds to the evidence for sex differences by a psychoanalytic explanation of sex differentiation at various stages of male and female development (infancy, childhood, adolescence, adulthood). Incidentally, May provides insights into Freud's methods and evolving thought processes. Furthermore, he believes that because of their different sexual anatomy, men and women think differently about sexuality.

May also examines the argument for androgyny—the blending of all the good traits of males and females into one. He discounts this dream of androgynous perfection as fanciful and unreal. (TJW)

PR
261. Money, John. **Love and Love Sickness: The Science of Sex, Gender Difference, and Pair-Bonding.** Baltimore, Md.: Johns Hopkins University Press, 1980. 256 p. Includes bibliography, indexes, and glossary. ISBN 0-8018-2317-X.

Discarding previous analytic concepts such as motivation, nature/nurture, and mind/body, Money replaces them with gender-identity/role (G-I/R) as a new basis for understanding the full range of sex differences. He defines G-I/R as "anything and everything that has to do with behavioral and psychologic differences between the sexes, no matter whether the differences are intrinsically or extraneously related to the genitalia" (p. 12). G-I/R includes differences that are not only "sex-irreducible" (definitive, unchangeable differences, e.g., that males impregnate and females menstruate, gestate, and lactate) but also "sex-derivative" (bodily characteristics that may or may not be related to procreation or eroticism), "sex-adjunctive" (social responses constrained by sex-irreducible characteristics), and "sex-arbitrary" (arbitrarily coded by the culture on the basis of genital sex). He suggests that a 2X2X2 template composed of phylographic (species-shared)/idiographic (individually unique); nativistic (inborn)/culturistic (due to influence of economy and environment); and imperative (a species necessity)/adventive (one among two or more alternatives) distinctions can be used to explain any sexually dimorphic behavior. His overall point is that sexually dimorphic behavior is likely to be the result of multiple determinants, that are a product of a developmental sequence composed of biological, social, and psychological factors.

Using this theoretical backdrop, Money proceeds to illustrate his point of view by providing an overview of attitudes toward and studies of sex, drawn from history, sociology, psychology, anthropology, the law, medicine, and endocrinology. He first describes the developmental sequence that leads to adult G-I/R. He then documents different philosophies of sex ("sexosophy"), including their rules (e.g., age-avoidance, intimacy-avoidance, allosex-avoidance, concepts (e.g., "dirt," Mediterranean, Nordic, and Amerafrican cultural legacies), and attitudes (e.g., toward sex rehearsal play, adolescence, and pair-bonding). Phases of sexual eroticism (proception, acception, and conception), factors relevant in the origin of erotic/sexual dysfunctions (paraphilias, gender transpositions, erotic apathy or excess), aphrodisiacs, and pornography are considered. Money then points out that sexologists, who study sex and eroticism in humans and other species, have attempted to confront cultural constraints on sexuality; Kinsey, Zelnick and Kantner, and Masters and Johnson are particularly notable in this regard. However, American society tends to maximize rather than minimize sex differences. Nevertheless, studies of aggression (expressed as fighting, assertion, and dominance), parenting, reasoning, and psychohormonal dynamics show the similarity and malleability of human sexuality. Unfortunately, Money thinks that American society is "lovesick"; many couples are mismatched. He suggests that the bases of sexual-erotic pair-bonding described in this book may aid people in knowing the parameters of "love" and avoid or at least understand "lovesickness," that "flourishes on mismatching and pits a couple against one another in the power struggle of a chronic adversary relationship" (p. xv). (SGF)

PR
262. Money, John, and Anke A. Ehrhardt. **Man & Woman, Boy & Girl: The Differentiation and Dimorphism of Gender Identity from Conception to Maturity.** Baltimore, Md.: Johns Hopkins University Press, 1972. 311 p. Includes bibliography, indexes, and glossary. ISBN 0-8018-1406-5.

Transcending an orientation of psychosexual development, Money and Ehrhardt formulate a theory of behavioral dimorphism and differentiation of the sexes that stresses the interaction of hereditary endowment and environmental influence. The proposal of a theory that includes a comprehensive coverage of "all the determinants of human sexual behavior" leads the authors to draw on and integrate experimental and clinical data and concepts from a variety of fields, including genetics; embryology; neuroendocrinology; neurosurgery; social, medical, and clinical psychology; and social anthropology. And, for the first time, Money synthesizes twenty years of longitudinal case studies and research on clinical syndromes relevant to psychosexual functioning and gender identity differentiation, drawn from his files at the Johns Hopkins Hospital and School of Medicine.

An introductory chapter presents a synopsis of the theory that highlights the components of gender identity differentiation that are described in more detail in the chapters that follow. Money and Ehrhardt argue that gender identity emerges from a sequence of components that begin with conception and continue to interact with each other throughout maturity. Of particular importance is the distinction between physical sex (morphology), gender role (a public, behavioral expression of sex), and gender identity (the private experience of gender role). Chromosomal sex (the pattern of sex chromosomes) determines the differentiation of the sex glands (gonads) into ovaries or testes, that, in turn, influence the production of gonadal hormones that affect the infant's morphology. In the *absence* of testosterone and a Mullerian inhibiting substance, the fetus develops as a morphological female, regardless of chromosomal sex. The morphology of the external genitals influences not only the sex assignment of the infant and social responses to it but also the body image of the child and the eventual development of juvenile gender identity. During this time, behavior that complements the role of the morphological opposite sex and identifies with that of the same sex helps the child to establish an appropriate gender role. The first few years are particularly crucial in this process. At puberty, the release of hormones promotes physical changes that accentuate the morphological differences between the sexes and spark pubertal eroticism. The interaction of pubertal changes with juvenile gender identity produces adult gender identity. The authors maintain that gender identity is so firmly established by puberty that it cannot be changed.

The complexity of the process of gender differentiation is strikingly illustrated by cases in which there is a modification in the sequence of gender differentiation; for example, a conceptus may have an extra chromosome or a chromosomal male fetus may be insensitive to androgen and develop as a morphological female. Money and Ehrhardt devote a lot of attention to describing and analyzing the anatomy, physiology, psychology, and behavior of hermaphrodites or intersexes, whose reproductive systems are incompletely developed as male or female. The reality of these exceptional cases highlights the relative contribution that biological, social, and psychological factors make in shaping gender. (SGF)

PR

263.   Parsons, Jacquelynne E., ed. **The Psychobiology of Sex Differences and Sex Roles.** New York: McGraw-Hill, 1980. 319 p. Includes bibliographies and indexes. ISBN 0-07-048540-2.

According to Parsons, a psychology professor at the University of Michigan, the debate about the origin and existence of sex differences centers on the relative role that biology plays in producing them. The aim of this book is to assess evidence pertinent to biological explanations of sexual dimorphism. Each chapter deals with several relevant issues: (1) a definition of what biological influence includes, (2) a means to determine which biological processes are influential, (3) identification of mechanisms by which biological processes could be influential, (4) determination of how biological processes interact with other behavioral and social forces, and (5) the degree of malleability of biological influences.

Parts 1 and 2 focus on the role of biological processes in gender role dimorphism. In part 1, "Psychosexual Neutrality," Parsons examines some of the types of evidence used to generate hypotheses about biological influences and concludes that gender role diversity and flexibility are the rule rather than the exception. Petersen reviews and evaluates the current state of knowledge about biopsychosocial characteristics that differentiate the sexes and proposes a model that highlights the interaction between biology and experience. Broverman, Klaiber, and Vogel examine the relation of gonadal hormones to cognitive functioning while Kaplan reviews Money's studies on human sex hormone abnormalities in relation to the concept of androgyny.

Part 2, "Sexuality," examines the biological foundations of human sexual behavior and dysfunction. Ledwitz-Rigby attempts to determine biochemical and neurophysiological influences on sexual behavior by using sexual potency, libido, and sexual orientation as examples. Meyer-Bahlburg reviews the current state of knowledge of the psycho-neuro-endocrinology of sexual orientation while Falbo offers a social psychological model of human sexuality.

The last two parts examine the link between biological processes and patterns of fluctuations in female behavior. Part 3, "Women's Reproductive System and Life Cycles," concentrates on such issues as a critical review of American birth practices (Hahn and Paige), a review and appraisal of the literature on maternal stress in the postpartum period (Magnus), and the psychological dimensions of changing roles and hormones at mid-life (Notman). Part 4, "Cyclicity and Menstruation," includes a discussion of the usefulness of a sociocultural approach in understanding menstrual cycle research (Ruble, Brooks-Gunn, Clarke), the importance of relating psychological correlates of physiological changes to social context (Sherif), and the extent to which the menstrual cycle (biological time) and the calendar week (social time) affect mood and sexual behavior (Rossi and Rossi).

Overall, each of the authors, most of whom are psychologists, contributes to a general view that biological, social, and psychological processes interact to shape sex role behavior. (SGF)

PR,IL

264.   Russett, Cynthia Eagle. **Sexual Science: The Victorian Construction of Womanhood.** Cambridge, Mass.: Harvard University Press, 1989. 245 p. Includes bibliographic notes and index. ISBN 0-674-80290-X.

Russett, Professor of History at Yale University, spells out in the introduction her key interests: the intellectual impact of Darwinism and the history of women. Charles Darwin and T. H. Huxley emphasized that motherhood is woman's role in life. In this study, Russett reviews the scientific literature of the nineteenth and early twentieth centuries on the differences between men and women. She points out that with the publication of *The Subjection of Women* (1869), John Stuart Mill challenged the patriarchal foundation of Victorian society by proposing the equality of the sexes. He believed that nurture shaped character more than nature did. With this Darwin and a host of others disagreed, for they believed that woman's nature was rooted in biology. This controversy helped to create the possibility of a science of male/female relationships based on the sex differences between them.

Before focusing her attention on scientific developments of the nineteenth century, such as the creation of new social sciences (anthropology, sociology, psychology) inspired by advances in the natural sciences, Russett, cognizant of the long history of women's inferiority, reviews the opinions of Aristotle, Galen, William Harvey, and others. With the new sciences came an appreciation of the value of the hierarchical ordering of human knowledge, an improved understanding of scientific method, and a better awareness of the relationship of the social sciences to the physical and biological sciences.

In her study Russett aims to examine the theories of sexual differences derived from the emerging sciences in the context of the times. In turn, she explores the contributions of phrenology, craniology, physical anthropology, ethnology, evolution, and psychology from the standpoint of sex differences. In each field, the principal investigators pronounced the preeminence of men over women in many subjects. It became clear to these Victorian scholars that intellectually, physically, and even sexually men were superior to women. However, women were given the edge in such conservative qualities as nurturance, patience, and memory.

In search of the scientific basis for these conclusions about women's inferior status, scientists accepted and applied the notion that ontogeny recapitulates phylogeny; the Darwinian sexual selection hypothesis of the theory of evolution; the law of energy conservation, i.e., the First Law of Thermodynamics; the law of the division of labor with its emphasis on specialization; and the greater variability of males, a notion of Darwin's. All of these added up to what Russett calls the Victorian construction of womanhood.

This construction, or paradigm, came under sharp attack in the early years of the twentieth century with critical discoveries in heredity, cellular structure, and the physiology of reproduction. It also eroded with the decline of recapitulation theory and neo-Lamarckianism; the development of better statistical methods; and the shift from biological determinism to environmentalism.

Russett attributes much of the dismal history of sexual science to patriarchal attitudes that the nineteenth century scientists grew up with and were unable to overcome. Moreover, she gives credit to those feminists and a few enlightened men (J. S. Mill, William James, and others) who refused, despite the factual knowledge on obvious sex differences, to accept views that they saw as personal opinions and beliefs consigning women, without due consideration for cultural and social factors, to an inferior position with respect to men. (TJW)

IL

265. Tavris, Carol. **The Mismeasure of Woman.** New York: Simon & Schuster, 1992. 398 p. Includes bibliography and index. ISBN 0-671-66274-0.

In this work, Tavris analyzes in compelling detail, the mode of Western civilization that takes the human male as a standard or model and explains the human female in terms of divergence from the male standard. She draws evidence from psychology and sociology, citing the successive revision of the *Diagnostic and Statistical Manual of Mental Disorders* (DSM), Kinsey's research, studies of family violence, the codependency-dependency literature, and classical works like Erik Erikson's *Eight Stages of Man*. She draws on evidence from medicine, citing the extensive PMS literature, the absence of women subjects in medical research, and the long tradition of bias and error in physiology textbooks. She draws evidence from the law, citing court cases and judgments. She draws on evidence from the popular press, citing the feminizing of love, what she calls "the fables of female sexuality," the self-help literature on self-esteem, self-confidence, depression, and weight control that patronizes women, and such classics as *Cinderella* and *Sleeping Beauty*.

Tavris describes the "no-win" situation of women created by what she presents as three errors in popular and scientific thought, which she sees as harmful to women's self-concepts, to relationships, and to the position of women in society: "Men are normal; women, being 'opposite,' are deficient.... Men are normal; women are opposite from men, but superior to them.... Men are normal, and women should be like them" (p. 20).

This work proposes a more holistic view of women and men, minorities and majorities, a move beyond "particularization, in which each gender, race, or ethnicity seeks only its own validation, celebrates only itself and rewrites its history and character in false phrases of its own superiority" (p. 330), to find fresh ways of looking at old dilemmas and to expand our life stories in nondualistic ways to foster health in relationships, families, work and the environment of our planet. (LF)

PR
266. Teitelbaum, Michael S., ed. **Sex Differences: Social and Biological Perspectives.** Edited and with an introduction by Michael S. Teitelbaum. Garden City, N.Y.: Anchor Press/Doubleday, 1976. 232 p. Includes bibliographies and index. ISBN 0-385-00826-0.

In his introduction, Teitelbaum asserts that "it is clear that sex is both a social and biological characteristic." The goal of this book is to "examine human sex differences from this social-biological perspective." A brief review of the intellectual history of the debate about the relative importance of biological and social factors in shaping human behavior illustrates the degree to which research on sex differences has been hampered by the subtle political biases of scientists. It is Teitelbaum's hope that each of the chapters in the book will spark an examination of scientific assumptions and methodologies in this field.

Each of the five contributors provides an overview and assessment of the research on a topic of particular relevance to evaluating the social and biological dimensions of human sexuality. Physical anthropologist Lancaster, a specialist in primate social behavior and human evolution, reviews the research on sex role behavior in higher primates. She finds that the roles of males and females vary according to species and that it is "impossible" to generalize about sex roles from another primate species to humans, although human adaptive patterns (e.g., the role of husband-father, the family, the division of labor) are foreshadowed by primate forebears. Rather, she suggests that it is more productive to look at each species in its own terms. Reproductive biologist Barfield surveys and evaluates the degree to which biological processes (e.g., embryonic development, physiological characteristics) affect behavioral differences between the sexes (e.g., aggression, moods, mental behavior) and concludes that there is a constant interaction between biological and social forces in shaping personality and behavior; most characteristics are found in both sexes.

Cultural anthropologist Brown reviews the research on the division of labor in subsistence, a universal trait that might be explained in terms of sex-linked psychology and physiology. However, she thinks that cultural and environmental factors have more explanatory power. Sociologist Stewart examines the literature on sex differences in personality, ability, and achievement in terms of sex role socialization by the family, media, peers, and school. Beneath what appear to be actual sex differences is a considerable degree of overlap in male and female behavior. Finally, science historian Fee completes the book with an in-depth look at the way that social forces in Great Britain and the United States from 1860 to 1920 influenced the focus and findings of research on sex role differences. She reiterates the theme that Teitelbaum introduced at the beginning: scientists are very much a product of their own culture and are not exempt from bias in research on sex differences. (SGF)

LIFE CYCLE STAGES

(For related material see also entries 144, 145, 167)

PR,IL
267. Brown, Judith K., Virginia Kerns, et al. **In Her Prime: A New View of Middle-Aged Women.** Foreword by Beatrice Blyth Whiting. South Hadley, Mass.: Bergin & Garvey, 1985. 217 p. Includes index and bibliographies. ISBN 0-89789-056-6.

This collection of essays focuses on the experiences of middle-aged women in a variety of societies. The working definition of middle-aged women is "women who have adult offspring and who are not yet frail or dependent" (p. 2). When examined in cross-cultural perspective, physiological indicators like age and menopause are less significant than social markers. This book is unique because it deals with middle-aged women in developmental, cross-cultural, and evolutionary perspectives. In her introductory essay, anthropologist Brown points out that the onset of middle age is generally positive for women in nonindustrial societies. Women are free from the cumbersome restrictions that confined them as young women; have a wider range of authority, especially over younger kin; and are eligible for extra-domestic statuses and roles.

Lancaster and King's essay, "An Evolutionary Perspective on Menopause," considers whether menopause evolved as an adaptive pattern that actively promotes a nonreproductive period or as a byproduct of other processes. The following eleven essays, written primarily by anthropologists, are divided into sections based on level of social complexity of the society considered: small-scale traditional, intermediate, complex, and industrial. Lee discusses the !Kung hunter-gatherers among whom aging enhances more than weakens a women's power. Solway notes that women's status among the Bakgalagadi herders of Botswana increases as women have more autonomy; middle-age is not marked as a special category or status. In "Big Women of Kaliai" Counts observes that these horticulturalists in Papua New Guinea recognize more responsibility of older women. However, menopause is not recognized as a special period and women do not have symptoms of depression, hot flashes, etc. associated with it. Parenthood does not end with fertility; nurturance continues.

In contrast to the small-scale traditional societies, intermediate societies, whose subsistence is based on cultivation, reserve special statuses for women. Lambek observes that social adulthood evolves among women of the Comoro Islands, between the coast of East Africa and Madagascar. Among the Garifuna, black Carib villagers of Belize, Kerns discusses how rules about sexuality and behavior relate to different phases of the reproductive cycle while Boddy notes how social status increases among women in the Northern Sudan when their fertility is no longer jurally or biologically active. Among the Maori, Sinclair notes the dramatic improvement of women's status with middle age.

Among women in complex non-Western societies, women's position is enhanced as they age, but there are also some drawbacks. In India, Vatuk describes the continuing concern with the power of women's sexuality, regardless of age. As a woman ages, her social status increases, regardless of the state of her biological fertility. Raybeck compares the difference between traditional Chinese women and Malaysian women. Despite differences in overt status, women in both contexts enhance their status as they age—the Chinese, by direct economic participation and the Malaysian, by indirect influence through their children.

In industrial societies, women exercise a number of options at middle age. Datan, Antonorski, and Maoz demonstrate this diversity among women in five Israeli subcultures, and Kaufert examines the difference between the assumptions of medical models of menopause and Canadian women's experience of it.

In a concluding essay, Gutmann suggests that there be greater interdisciplinary cooperation in the study of women in mid-life. Both clinical and cross-cultural data show similarities in women's increase in social power as they age. He offers the possibility that these changes may be developmental in nature, not just a matter of flexibility of social rules and cultural expectations. (SGF)

PO

268. Butler, Robert N., and Myrna I. Lewis. **Love and Sex After 40: A Guide for Men and Women for Their Mid and Later Years.** New York: Harper & Row, 1986. 202 p. Includes bibliography, index, and glossary. ISBN 0-06-015491-8.

The proportion of older people in the American population continues to climb. Consequently, there is increasing concern not only about the aging process but also about what happens to sexuality over time. Unfortunately, many myths and fears surround these areas. People in their forties are worried about continuing to "perform," remain attractive, and retain a partner while those in their sixties have to confront social negativism toward sex in later life. By presuming that sexual desire automatically begins to decline in the forties, ebb in the fifties, and bottom out after sixty, many older people presume that sex is over.

Butler and Lewis address these problems by revising and incorporating the materials in their earlier book, *Love and Sex After 60* (1976), to produce a guide for people over forty who are interested in sex but have fears and problems about sexual expression during the later years. Butler is a Pulitzer Prize winning author and Chairman of the Department of Geriatrics at Mount Sinai Medical Center, the first department of its kind in an American medical school. Lewis, Butler's wife, is a psychotherapist, social worker, and gerontologist who is on the faculty at the Mount Sinai School of Medicine. They draw on current research findings as well as their own clinical experience to address some common concerns about sexuality in the later years.

The first part of the book deals with physical issues: normal physical changes in sexuality with age, effects of common medical problems (e.g., heart problems, diabetes, arthritis, hypertension, stroke) on sex; sexually transmitted diseases; diagnosis and treatment of physically caused impotence in men; estrogen anxiety and menopausal symptoms in women; the sexual effects of sex organ surgery; the effects of medications and alcohol on sex; and tips on health care (exercise, diet, rest) that promote sexual fitness. The second part addresses psychological issues; communication about emotions and sex; problems with partners; dating, remarriage, and children; and where to go for help with problems. Overall, Butler and Lewis reiterate the theme that sexual desires, pleasure, and behavior are part of a lifelong experience of affection, warmth, and sensuality. They hope that this book helps people to grow and enhance their sexuality throughout the later part of their lives. (SGF)

PR

269. Constantine, Larry L., and Floyd M. Martinson, eds. **Children and Sex: New Findings, New Perspectives.** Boston: Little, Brown, 1981. 288 p. Includes bibliographic references and index. ISBN 0-316-15331-1.

This multidisciplinary collection of "some of the best and most challenging of unpublished and recently published works on childhood sexuality" tries to make a valuable contribution to human sexuality by "dealing with children as fully sexual beings for whom sexuality and sexual experiences are not necessarily any less significant than for adults" (p. ix). Human sexuality at different points in life is viewed as variations on a theme rather than qualitatively different experiences. The authors are social scientists, psychologists, and psychiatrists with extensive experience in research or treatment of children. The contents span research findings, literature reviews, and hypotheses about important issues of childhood sexuality. Constantine and Martinson have divided the papers into six areas: cultural content, sexual behavior and development, sexual latency, sex in the family, effects of childhood sexual experiences, and children and sexual liberation. Current research is still in the early stages because of the common view of childhood sexuality as either nonexistent or a taboo subject, and findings are often conflicting; however, there is some agreement in several areas. Research among traditional cultures and some alternative Western cultures indicates that children are intrinsically sexual beings and possess both the need and the ability to have and enjoy sexual experiences. Autoerotic activities, peer sex play, and attempted intercourse are found among children in most societies. Negative experiences are often due more to societal and parental reactions than to any native response. The psychological trauma reported in many research studies on childhood sexual experiences, particularly incest, appears to be due to the populations studied (primarily referrals from prisons, police files, psychiatrists, or social workers) rather than to the experiences. Studies of self-selected or nonclinical individuals reflect mixed conclusions, but a general overview indicates that such experiences need not be traumatic, if they occur (1) in a stable, supportive environment, (2) between peers, (3) without force or coercion, and (4) without being followed by emotional trauma. There is also evidence that sexual experiences with older persons may be initiated or willingly accepted by children. The goals of the child and the older participant are usually different, with the child seeking affection, closeness, and emotional support rather than sexual fulfillment. The existence of childhood sexuality is still not widely accepted, but movements toward personal and societal liberation may lead to future acceptance of children as sexual beings with the right to explore, learn about, and enjoy their sexuality. (SDH)

PR,IL
270. Gadpaille, Warren J. **The Cycles of Sex.** Edited by Lucy Freeman. New York: Scribner's, 1975. 496 p. Includes bibliographic notes and index. ISBN 0-684-14224-4.

Gadpaille, a psychiatrist and psychoanalyst, attempts to trace the enormous complexities of normal sexual development from the earliest biological influences during fetal life until the last stages of aging. The book grew out of his many years as consultant to the Jefferson County School District in Colorado, in its Family Living Program, where he recognized the need for a technically comprehensive but readable overview of normal developmental influences and issues. In this book he includes relevant research and clinical data from psychoanalysis, clinical psychology, sociology, cultural and evolutionary anthropology, embryology, physiology, and nonhuman animal research.

Two principles underlie Gadpaille's concept of normal sexual development. One is the constant and inevitable interplay of nature and nurture; the human infant is not seen as a sexual *tabula rasa*, totally shaped by its postnatal experiences. Each individual brings to the world innate pan-human and innate sex-specific traits, as well as unique genetic and constitutional tendencies that influence sexuality throughout life. These constitute the substrate upon which parental, social, and cultural influences act to shape individual sexuality at any given time. Postnatal learning, both conscious and out-of-awareness, probably exerts the strongest influence on sexual development, and can distort or disrupt innate biology, but it can never fully erase the biological givens.

The second principle is that sexuality is not normally static, and sexual development never ends. New and changing circumstances throughout life demand changing adaptations. Gadpaille describes a predictable progression of cycles in which everyone returns to the fundamental issues of sexual desire versus sexual control, and reworks and refines the earlier resolutions in accord with the changed realities of each new stage of life. (Author)

PR
271. Goldman, Ronald, and Juliette Goldman. **Children's Sexual Thinking: A Comparative Study of Children Aged 5 to 15 Years in Australia, North America, Britain and Sweden.** London: Routledge & Kegan Paul, 1982. 485 p. Includes bibliography and indexes. ISBN 0-7100-0883-X.

This book attempts to demonstrate that children, like adolescents and adults, are active sexual thinkers, not only during the alleged latency period but also throughout their development. The first chapters review the theoretical and practical background for the study and present its research design. Goldman and Goldman define sexual thinking as "thinking about that broad area of sex and sexuality which impinges upon the child's world from birth," not just sexual intercourse. Despite much speculation about childhood sexuality by such eminent figures as Freud, Piaget, and Kohlberg, little substantive research has been directed toward testing the validity and universality of their formulations. Evidence from other cultures suggests that there are different expectations about children's sexual behavior and that there are other cognitive frameworks within which children can organize their thoughts about sexuality. Practical social issues involving sexuality face Western culture: earlier physical maturity, delay of age at marriage, teenage pregnancies, birth control, venereal disease, pornography, rape, divorce, and child molestation. However, few children learn about these issues through sex education programs; most need enlightenment. Consequently, the authors designed their research to "measure the extent of children's sexual knowledge, their sexual understanding at various ages, and to identify what processes of thought they use in trying to explain the biological functions and phenomena of their own bodies as they grow and change." The criteria of Piaget, Freud, and Kohlberg were used to test their cognitive theories. Samples of children aged five to fifteen, drawn from regional clusters of schools and stratified by socioeconomic status, ability, birth order, sex distribution, intact nuclear family, and a younger sibling, were selected in four countries—Australia, Great Britain, North America, and Sweden. Although they do not claim that their samples are strictly national ones, they do think that they describe rather typical children within each context.

The chapters that follow summarize the findings of the content of the interviews, that probe dimensions of the following areas: (1) aging and the best time to be alive in the life cycle, (2) the identity and roles of parents as mothers and fathers and as men and women, (3) children's perceptions of sex differences in the newborn and during puberty as well as indications of their own sexual preferences, (4) the origin of babies and the role of mothers and fathers in having them (procreation, gestation, birth) as well as not having them (contraception, abortion), (5) sex education, (6) clothes and nakedness, and (7) sexual vocabulary. In each chapter, numerous tables summarize the statistical results and a narrative summary concludes it.

In their discussion of the results, the authors present their major findings, that include the following points: (1) evidence supports Piaget's cognitive developmental stages in sexual thinking as well as Kohlberg's three levels of moral thinking; (2) findings do not support the idea of the Oedipus complex as a normal phase of child development; latency appears to be a myth; (3) retardation of sexual thinking occurs in English-speaking samples; this result may arise from inadequate sex education both at home and at school. The authors emphasize the need for a well-developed, sequential program of sex education. (SGF)

PR
272. Kirkpatrick, Martha, ed. **Women's Sexual Development: Explorations of** *Inner Space.* New York: Plenum Press, 1980. 298 p. (Women in Context: Development and Stresses). Includes bibliographic references and index. ISBN 0-306-40375-7.

This edited volume of papers represents a "variety of points of view on contemporary issues, controversies, and questions about female sexual development." Kirkpatrick does not try to present papers that reflect a consistent point of view; rather, she hopes the papers will stir controversy and stimulate questions by reflecting the ambiguity and disagreement that surround the topic. Although they are not grouped by subject area in the book, the sixteen chapters can be clustered according to several themes.

Some chapters deal directly with issues of development in the life cycle (Baill and Money's consideration of physiological aspects of female sexual development from conception through puberty and during gestation, lactation, and menopause; Galenson and Roiphe's revision of Freud's conceptualization of early female sexual development; Elmhurst's presentation of Klein's view of early stages of female psychosexual development; Stoller's analysis of the development of femininity in males and females; Ekstein's outline of the life cycle of the father-daughter relationship; and Adams-Tucker and Adams's consideration of the role that a father can play in his daughter's life. A couple of chapters focus on dealing with specific behaviors: Clower's discussion of the role of masturbation in female sexual development and function, or in particular situations; Ponse's study of self within a lesbian community, that demonstrates that sexual activity and identity do not necessarily overlap.

Another cluster of papers deals with the kind of social and cultural influences that affect female sexuality. Lewis presents a sweeping history of female sexuality in the United States from the nineteenth to the twentieth centuries while Canfield briefly discusses the implications of the sexual revolution for female choice. Roberts emphasizes that learning about sexuality is a lifelong process that goes beyond sex education. Oaks focuses on sexual attitudes expressed in folksongs while Ash considers the implications of terms used to refer to the vagina.

Finally, a few papers propose ways to find help in dealing with sexual problems: Rila and Steinhart describe a sex information switchboard, Lawrence and Edwards outline self-help sexual analysis and tips for gynecological self-help, and Downer portrays the advantages of women's self-help clinics and groups for promoting healthy sexuality. (SGF)

PR

272a. Martinson, Floyd M. **The Sexual Life of Children.** Westport, Conn.: Bergin & Garvey, 1994. 153 p. Includes bibliography and index. ISBN 0-89789-376-X.

Martinson, Research Professor of Sociology at Gustavus Adolphus College, has been one of the few contemporary researchers to write about *normal childhood sexuality*, attempting to provide empirical knowledge in an area where "neither the folk culture nor the scientific literature has had much to say on the subject" (p. viii). With more social interest in the distinctive attributes of childhood and sexuality in general, Martinson's goal is "to bring the reader up to date on what we know about early sexual development and sexual experience in the life of prepubescent children" (p. viii) and to "contribute to a freer and better informed atmosphere of discussion in the future" (p. ix).

Drawing on an array of research from different disciplines (e.g., biology, medicine/psychiatry, psychology, anthropology, sociology, law, political science), as well as from his own research, Martinson devotes separate chapters to synthesizing findings relating to important aspects of children's sexuality: early development and experience; self-stimulation; sex play; same-sex sex play; dreams, fantasies, and myths; sexual encounters with older children, adolescents, and adults; sexuality education; and the law and social contexts.

Children are "active and sensual, even before they are born" (p. 1), needing the affirmation of touch as well as "close, warm, gentle, caring" (p. 16) treatment during infancy and childhood to foster healthy, age-appropriate development, including sexual development. Self-stimulation and sex play as well as sexual dreams, fantasies, and myths are normal parts of children's sexual experience, even in U.S. society, where great restrictions are placed on children's sexual activity. Sexual encounters of children with older children, adolescents, and adults can be exploitative, abusive, and destructive; consequently, children "need to be educated in such a way to prepare them for the sexual life they are entering and to protect them, insofar as it is possible, from experiences that are not in their best interest" (p. 97). Legal and judicial decisions about children's sexuality reveal social perceptions about children's sexual nature and the contexts within which it should be expressed. Comparison of children's sex lives in Sweden and the United States demonstrates the influence of social context on children's sexual development.

Throughout, Martinson highlights data on what is currently known about normal childhood sexual development as well as the role that parents, caretakers, educators, and others can play in fostering healthy, normal sexual development in children. References for each chapter as well as a concluding bibliography provide further resources for those who wish to learn more about the topic and its surrounding controversies. (SGF)

PR,IL

273. Moll, Albert. **The Sexual Life of the Child.** Translated from the German by Dr. Eden Paul. With an introduction by Edward L. Thorndike. New York: Macmillan, 1924. 339 p. Originally published in 1908. Translation of: *Das Sexualleben des Kindes.* Includes bibliographic footnotes and index.

In his introduction, distinguished educational psychologist Edward L. Thorndike establishes the credibility and respectability of Dr. Moll's investigation of the origin and development of sexual acts and feelings during childhood and youth; he points out that Dr. Moll approaches the subject with "dignity and frankness" without a "taint" of gratifying a "low curiosity" in the topic. He concludes by stating, "Of all the causes of sexual disorder, the reading of scientific books by reputable men is surely the least" (p. viii). What follows is a study that not only contributed to Moll's place as a pioneer of modern sexology but also addresses issues that continue to stir controversy—the supposed sexual innocence of children; the role of sexuality in child development; gender differences in sexual expression; the importance of sex education; the origins of homosexuality; the consequences of pedophilia; and the veracity of children's testimony in court cases involving sexual abuse. There's a strikingly modern flavor to this book published in 1908.

Moll was a physician who used not only data about his patients but also the reports of healthy men and women to corroborate his descriptions of the sexual life of children;

he thought that using pathological manifestations of the "sexual impulse" would distort his presentation. In his preface Moll points out that understanding the sexual life of the child will enrich the knowledge of adult sexuality and provide necessary information for young people during an age of "sexual enlightenment." Unfortunately, "this department of knowledge has been ignored" (p. 10) and "this province of research has received but little scientific attention" (p. 16).

The first few chapters carefully describe the normal manifestations of the sexual impulse during childhood and establish that "in the child the sexual processes are much more extensive than has commonly been believed" (p. 109). It is a mistake to confuse the onset of procreative ability with the beginning of sexual behavior and thoughts that begin much earlier than puberty. Moll describes the physical and psychological changes in sexual development by gender and stage of childhood, discussing such issues as masturbation (which Moll regards as a normal part of development), objects of attraction, love and jealousy, physical responses, the apparent restraint of "voluptuous sensations" in females, and the capacity for coitus. A discussion of the types, etiology, and diagnoses of sexual pathology (e.g., very early or very late development of sexual impulses, homosexuality) follows that of normal developments. Moll's data do not convince him that homosexuality is a congenital condition; rather, it may develop during a undifferentiated stage of development during which the child is particularly susceptible to environmental influences.

The last few chapters consider the importance of the sexual life of the child. Moll argues that sexual enlightenment of children is necessary to protect them from the dangers of seduction, social degradation, health risks, and pedophilia. Acknowledging that existence of sexual feelings in children is not necessarily harmful since "in the education of the child the complete exclusion of sexual stimuli is impossible" (p. 248), sex education prevents and minimizes danger to children; proper control rather than negating sex is more sensible than lying to children. Children are more influenced by good examples than by good words. Unfortunately, "the very persons to whom today we have to look to effect the sexual enlightenment of children, are themselves to a great extent also in need of enlightenment" (p. 303). (SGF)

IL
274. Money, John, and Patricia Tucker. **Sexual Signatures: On Being a Man or a Woman.** Boston: Little, Brown, 1975. 250 p. Includes bibliography and index. ISBN 0-316-57826-6.

What does it mean to be a man or a woman? This clearly written book attempts to answer the complex questions of "where you are as a man or woman and how you got there." It examines sex differences in light of new findings in gender research, especially data drawn from gender identity clinics. Central themes include the importance of gender schema (a mental construct that is society's definition of what it means to be male or female), gender identity (your sense of yourself as male or female), and gender role (everything that you do to express a sense of yourself as male or female). Chapters 1-6 carefully explain how the interaction of anatomy, physiology (especially the roles of genes, hormones, and the brain), perception, social history, personal biography, and culture contribute to the eventual definition of a person's gender. The last two chapters discuss the implications of Money and Tucker's findings for contemporary social issues (liberationists, sex and the elderly, the disjunction between recreational and procreational sex, etc.). By tracing sexual differentiation from the beginning of life through adulthood, Money and Tucker demonstrate the intricate, step-by-step process of gender development and reinforce their point that sex differences are relative, not absolute. The book's discussion of the multifaceted dimensions of sexual differentiation could contribute to courses related to human sexuality offered by many disciplines; it could also be helpful to sex educators, counselors, and parents who seek a succinct, thoughtful account of the complex facets of masculinity and femininity. (SGF)

IL

275. Olds, Sally Wendkos. **The Eternal Garden: Seasons of Our Sexuality.** New York: Times Books, 1985. 325 p. Includes bibliography and index. ISBN 0-8129-1159-8.

Persuaded that "sexual turning points" play an integral and significant role in human development and failing to find, in the literature of the social sciences, the supporting framework of theory and research that she sought, Olds undertook this study of interrelationships between sexual development and life events across the entire life span. In personal, in-depth interviews she drew out the many different voices who speak through this book of experiences in childhood, adolescence, the transition years to adulthood or in one of the subsequent decades of adult life. Chapter headings such as "The Sensual Seedling," "Blooming Again," and "Perennial Passions" sustain the Eternal Garden theme. Skilled and intuitive as an interviewer, Olds sifted through the powerful rhythms of sexuality looking for patterns and teasing out answers to basic questions about effects of birth control advances, implications of casual sexual activity for marriage, connections between the sexual revolution and lack of desire, homosexuality, monogamy, open marriages, effects of parenthood on sexuality, special problems of newly single adults, mid-life crises, and sexual attitudes and activities in old age. Olds describes universally perceived "turning points" and acknowledges that idiosyncratic transitions influenced by variety in social and sexual mores also occur. Her summation offers a belief that "there *are* some basic, universal, absolute criteria for sexual morality"; that beyond those basic tenets a wide range of sexual choices is open to men and women as they seek expression of the vital life force of sexuality that extends and is variously expressed from cradle to grave. (LF)

PR

276. Perry, Michael E., ed. **Childhood and Adolescent Sexology.** Amsterdam: Elsevier, 1990. 448 p. (Handbook of Sexology; vol. 7). Includes bibliographies and index.

Perry comments in his preface that this volume "pioneers new territory . . . and clearly establishes that mature sexuality has its precursors in the prepubertal years of infancy and childhood" (p. 5). Historian Stevi Jackson corroborates Perry's point in his essay "Demons and Innocents: Western Ideas on Children's Sexuality in Historical Perspective." "Speculation on the nature and development of childhood and adolescent sexuality is a modern phenomenon, dependent upon concepts of relatively recent invention" (p. 45). The twenty-three articles, written by distinguished sex researchers from various disciplines (e.g., history, anthropology, biology, sociology, psychology, medicine) and countries, summarize much of the current information about child and adolescent sexuality; they are organized into four major parts, each preceded by a brief introduction by Perry.

The first part, "Sexosophy: Historical, Cultural, Legal, Religious, and Educational Concepts," consists of seven articles that provide overviews of conceptual issues relevant to understanding aspects of child and adolescent sexuality: historical and current concepts of pediatric and ephebiatric sexology (John Money) as well as Western ideas about childhood sexuality (Stevi Jackson); the role of professionals in anti-vice campaigns (Gregory A. Sprague); a cross-cultural perspective on the development of bisexuality (Gilbert Herdt); and current perspectives on religious doctrines of sexual and erotic development in children (Robert T. Francoeur); the legal status of the erotic and sexual rights of children (Floyd M. Martinson); and sexuality education (Sari Locker).

The second part, "Sexology: Prenatal, Infantile and Juvenile," concentrates on research about prepubertal sexual development, from discussions of prenatal and early critical learning periods (John Money), early infantile sexual and erotic development (Eleanor Galenson), and early childhood and juvenile sexual development and problems (Thore Langfeldt) to broader summaries of empirical research on prepubertal sexuality (Ernest Borneman), and children's sexual thinking (Juliette G. D. Goldman).

The third part, "Sexology: Puberty and Adolescence," begins with a general consideration of the sexology of puberty (J. Money and V. G. Lewis) and proceeds to specific issues of preadolescents and adolescents: sexual fantasies (Lester A. Kirkendall

and Leslie G. Mcbride), first sexual intercourse (Herman Musaph), unintended conceptions (L. S. Zabin), and the sexuality of children whose parents live in alternative
lifestyles (Rosalie Chapman and Lee Tead).
The final part, "Sexological Syndromes in Childhood and Adolescence," consists
of articles addressing sensitive, controversial sexual problems of adolescents: eroticized
children (Alayne Yates), incest (Warren Farrell), male juvenile partners in pedophilia
(Theo G. M. Sandfort and Walter T. A. M. Everaerd), adolescent paraphilias (Gregory
K. Lehne), child abuse and prevention (James J. Krívacska), and children with disabilities
(Susan E. Knight). (SGF)

IL,PO
277. Ransohoff, Rita M. **Venus After Forty: Sexual Myths, Men's Fantasies, and
Truths About Middle-Aged Women.** Far Hills, N.J.: New Horizon Press, 1987. 276 p.
Includes bibliographic notes. ISBN 0-88282-034-6.
Psychotherapist Ransohoff focuses her attention primarily on the mid-life anxieties of
women over forty. Because of their treatment by men, these women feel vulnerable and
rejected, lose self-esteem, and become depressed. Basically, there is a double standard of
aging explained by men's attraction to and success with younger women that, while
bolstering the male ego, leaves women feeling angry and abandoned. Ransohoff explores
this phenomenon by searching for the reasons supporting this separation of youth and age.
First, she reveals the myths and fantasies behind men's attitudes toward women, how
they develop from infancy through adolescence, and their impact on male/female relationships in later life. For example, impressions in early childhood about female anatomy and
mother/father interactions generate lasting images that may manifest themselves later in
visions of the "good" mother (fairy godmother) and the "bad" mother (the witch). As boys
mature sexually, these fantasies emerge as myths that later affect men's attitudes as they seek
mates. Also, awareness in later life of the passing of youth and the inevitability of death
causes men to seek comfort, reassurance, and love from younger women.
Attesting to masculine insecurity are certain fantasies and myths: the voracious women
men fear; the battleaxe men shun and banish to asexuality; the small vagina myth leading
men to seek out younger women; and the myths associated with menstruation, pregnancy,
childbirth, and menopause. Symptoms of male stress generated by these fantasies and myths
are often exaggerated dieting, hyperexercise, and the pursuit of young women. Women's
adaptation to male mid-life stress sometimes manifests itself in trying to match the macho
style of men: watching sports on TV, riding behind men on motorcycles, and so forth. Both
men and women, encouraged by the media, become narcissistic in this competitive world of
personal struggle stemming from the double standard of aging.
Ransohoff concludes by recalling successful outcomes to these mid-life crises both
for couples and single women, and discusses the lives of women, some famous, who have
taken charge of their lives and remained sexually attractive beyond mid-life: Marcia
Davenport, Jane Digby, Lou Andreas-Salomé, George Sand, Colette, Isadora Duncan,
and others. (TJW)

PR
277a. Rossi, Alice S., ed. **Sexuality Across the Life Course.** Chicago: University of
Chicago Press, 1994. 418 p. (The John D. and Catherine T. MacArthur Foundation series
on mental health and development. Studies on successful midlife development). Includes
bibliographies and indexes. ISBN 0-226-72833-1.
Distinguished social scientist Rossi is Professor Emerita of Sociology at the
University of Massachusetts, Amherst, and the author of numerous books relating to
gender, politics, development, and family. In this edited volume, she includes articles
addressing the question of what changes in physical health and psychological well-being
take place in sexual functioning across the life course, from adolescence to old age. The
overall emphasis is to present research that demonstrates the power of an integrated,
multidisciplinary model. Rossi articulates the rationale for this model in her opening

essay, "*Eros* and *Caritas*: A Biopsychosocial Approach to Human Sexuality and Reproduction," wherein she draws on findings from evolutionary biology, behavioral genetics, psychological studies of physical attraction and gender differences in personality to show that a "multidisciplinary approach enriches our understanding of sexuality, mate choice, and reproduction" (p. 3).

The thirteen other essays in the book are clustered according to themes into three major parts. One part focuses on history, culture, and lifestyle as aspects of sexual diversity. In "Human Sexuality, Life Histories, and Evolutionary Ecology," Jane B. Lancaster contextualizes specific issues of human sexuality in midlife in the broader framework of the evolution of human reproductive behavior. Tom W. Smith, in "Attitudes Toward Sexual Permissiveness: Trends, Correlates, and Behavioral Connections," examines recent trends in sexual attitudes toward premarital, extramarital, and homosexual relations, analyzing the influential variables, correspondence between actual sexual behavior and attitudes about it, and impact on psychological well-being. Claire Sterk-Elifson ("Sexuality Among African-American Women") and Benjamin P. Bowser ("African-American Male Sexuality Through the Early Life Course") present empirical data on the effects of ethnic background on sexual behavior and attitudes, while Martha R. Fowlkes ("Single Worlds and Homosexual Lifestyles: Patterns of Sexuality and Intimacy") provides an "extensive interpretive review of the major social science literature pertaining to the affective and companionate features, as well as to the patterns of sexual behavior, that characterize the lives of voluntarily single adults and lesbian women and gay men" (p. 151).

Another major part of the book deals with sexuality in selected phases of the life course. J. Richard Udry and Benjamin C. Campbell ("Getting Started on Sexual Behavior") concentrate on understanding the timing of the onset of sexual behavior as well as some of the effects of different ages at onset. Sharon Thompson ("Changing Lives, Changing Genres: Teenage Girls' Narratives About Sex and Romance, 1978-1986"), drawing on a narrative study of 400 teenage girls' sexual, romantic, and reproductive histories, uses feminist and genre analysis to "read" their accounts of sexual and romantic experiences. The impact of age on various aspects of sexuality is the topic of essays by John N. Edwards and Alan Booth ("Sexuality, Marriage, and Well-Being: The Middle Years"), John B. McKinlay and Henry A. Feldman ("Age-Related Variation in Sexual Activity and Interest in Normal Men: Results from the Massachusetts Male Aging Study"), and Judith A. Levy ("Sex and Sexuality in Later Life Stages").

The last part of the book deals with selected health issues. Raul C. Schiavi ("Effect of Chronic Disease and Medication on Sexual Functioning") reviews and summarizes information on the ways that disease and medications affect sexuality. Richard Green ("Sexual Problems and Therapies: A Quarter Century of Developments and Changes") provides an overview of the ways in which revisions in the identification, diagnosis, and treatment of problems in human sexuality have occurred over the past twenty-five years. Richard J. Gelles and Glenn Wolfner ("Sexual Offending and Victimization: A Life Course Perspective") use age-related stages of development to analyze variations in rates of sexual offending and victimization.

Most of the articles bring together concepts and data that cross disciplines to enrich their analyses. Contributors come from a diversity of disciplines (e.g., sociology, anthropology, medicine, psychiatry, comparative literature) and utilize a variety of research methods (e.g., quantitative, qualitative, reviews of the literature, and so on). (SGF)

IL,PO

278. Ruebsaat, Helmut J., and Raymond Hull. **The Male Climacteric.** New York: Hawthorn Books, 1975. 190 p. Includes index. ISBN 0-8015-4810-1.

Chills, temporary lapses of memory, paralysis of the will, and loss of sexual desire were just a few of the ailments that writer Hull experienced over a five-year period that sparked his interest in the male climacteric. His interviews with middle-aged men as well as the creation and distribution of a questionnaire to males and females who expressed some knowledge of the subject in conversation provided preliminary data for collaboration with a physician to write this book. Ruebsaat and Hull identify the male climacteric as "a critical stage, a turning point" in the lives of men somewhere between the ages of forty-five and sixty during which they may undergo major emotional and physical changes. Unlike menopause, the male climacteric is not inevitable and may not affect all men. Nevertheless, it can severely disrupt the health, career, and personal relationships of those affected by it. Part I provides a detailed description of the sexual (e.g., impotence, loss of libido), physical (e.g., swelling, hot flashes, air hunger, headaches), mental and emotional (e.g., fatigue, moodiness, loss of self-confidence) symptoms of the climacteric, and then examines their effects on home life, work, and general social behavior. Part II discusses possible physical, psychological, and social causes of the syndrome. By including basic information on the physiological and sociocultural concomitants of aging, this part defines the broader context within which the symptoms occur. Part III offers practical advice for helping men and their loved ones cope with the unpleasant effects of the climacteric. One section presents a chart that aids men in identifying sexual, physical, and psychological symptoms; other sections provide guidance in dealing with physicians and psychiatrists; and suggests ways in which men can delay or cope with the climacteric. A sprinkling of contemporary cases and historical examples serves to highlight the problems of men who experience this difficult but seldom discussed phase of a man's life. (SGF)

IL,PO
279. Sarrel, Lorna J., and Philip M. Sarrel. **Sexual Turning Points: The Seven Stages of Adult Sexuality.** New York: Macmillan, 1984. 320 p. Includes bibliography and index. ISBN 0-02-606910-5.
   The central theme of this book is that sexuality is a lifelong process of growth and change that responds to the challenges and stresses of interpersonal and social events (having a boyfriend or girlfriend, getting married, parenting, breaking up) and biological changes of the life cycle (puberty, pregnancy, menopause, illness, aging). Sexual turning points are "specific and predictable life events experienced by most people that tend to produce alterations in sexual behavior, attitudes, and feelings" (p. 4). Sarrel and Sarrel not only want to provide a basis for understanding fundamental facts about sex, but also want to convey a sense of what sexuality means at different times in life. Exploration of a range of "normal" human experiences at sexual turning points may engender realistic expectations about sexuality and help prevent some of the problems associated with it. Each section discusses the biological and psychological aspects of seven sexual turning points: sexual unfolding (puberty, peers, love, sexual orientation, masturbation), making or breaking commitments (living together, conflict, abortion), marriage (sex life, sex roles, sex therapy, extramarital sex, dual careers), pregnancy and birth, parenting, divorce and remarriage, and aging (mid-life changes of men and women, medical problems). They show the feedback between psychosocial and biological aspects of sexuality by combining the expertise of their respective fields of social work and obstetrics/gynecology with the psychosomatic, cotherapist approach to the treatment of sexual disorders that they derived from their training with Masters and Johnson. As codirectors of the Yale Sex Counseling Service for fifteen years, they have treated the problems of over 5,000 students, faculty, and employees, and they draw heavily on the life experiences of their clients to highlight the types of attitudes and problems that people have at each sexual turning point. The book provides a basis for sharing anxiety and confusion about sexuality with others and promotes reassurance that much of what people experience and worry about is "normal." (SGF)

PR
280. Schlegel, Alice, and Herbert Barry III. **Adolescence: An Anthropological Inquiry.** New York: The Free Press, 1991. 263 p. Includes bibliography and index. ISBN 0-02-927895-3.
   Anthropologists have paid very little attention to adolescence. Based on codings of measures of adolescent behavior and treatment for a worldwide representative sample

of 186 preindustrial societies, the findings in this book are "a response to the previous neglect" (p. vii). According to anthropologist Schlegel and psychologist Barry, "our work is unique, we believe, because of its scope.... We take a cross-cultural approach and treat adolescence as a universal social and cultural phenomenon" (p. vii). Unlike previous studies of adolescence by psychiatrists, developmental psychologists, and sociologists, this anthropological study is holistic and provides a basis for generalization beyond contemporary society.

Defining adolescence as "a social stage intervening between childhood and adulthood" (p. 8), Schlegel and Barry have as their goal an examination of the "behavior and treatment of adolescents and the concomitant features of culture and social organization that account for variability across cultures" (p. 10). They organize their findings and discussion around eight major issues: (1) families and the natal household, (2) participation in peer groups and the larger community, (3) adolescent sexuality and the regulation of reproduction, (4) marriage, (5) conditions under which pathology arises, (6) preparation for adult life, (7) gender differences, and (8) the timing and length of adolescence.

Central to their analysis of adolescence is an ethnological model of human social organization, that assumes that incest avoidance is a fundamental requirement of the human family and that reproduction is at its core. Drawing on primate research, Schlegel and Barry construct a human ethogram composed of four basic social groups: (1) the dual-sex family that is made up of people of all ages; (2) single-sex adolescent peer groups; (3) adult male groups, that may include adolescents on the periphery, if at all; and (4) adult female groups, that include adolescent girls as participants. They hypothesize that human social organization, like that of other primates, has social mechanisms to prevent close inbreeding. Therefore, the sexes are likely to be sexually separated at puberty with boys associating with males and girls with females; and, the attention of adolescent boys will be directed to persons of their same-sex peer group, away from their natal families. This organization means that adolescence is more likely to be difficult for boys than girls, who experience continuity in their roles with other women. The data in the book test the model.

Overall, Schlegel and Barry conclude that their findings support their hypotheses derived from the model of a human ethogram. They find that subsistence patterns, property ownership, community structure, and anticipation of adult life account for variations in the behavior and treatment of adolescence. Early patterns of socialization result in "proclivities" that can be supported or modified later in life. Of major importance is the difference in the social settings that adolescent boys and girls occupy; girls enter the adult world through cooperation with adult women in the household while boys enter it through their peer groups. The patterns of traditional societies not only apply to industrial ones but also hold important lessons for interpreting adolescence in American society. (SGF)

PR

281.   Sugar, Max, ed. **Atypical Adolescence and Sexuality.** New York: Norton, 1990. 227 p. Includes bibliographies and index. ISBN 0-393-70109-3.

In the opening chapter, Sugar, a clinical professor of psychiatry at Louisiana State University School of Medicine and Tulane University School of Medicine, presents an overview of atypical adolescence and lists statistics that may indicate that "the stereotype of the ideal adolescent boy or girl may be in the minority" (p. 1). This observation is realistic if one considers as atypical those teenagers with emotional disorders, eating disorders, asthma, sensory dysfunction, retardation, chronic severe physical illnesses, and those who are sexually abused, substance abusers, and learning disabled. This collection of essays offers guides to meeting the psychotherapeutic needs of these adolescents as they move through their decade of individualization. Lorna J. Sarrel and Philip M. Sarrel write the next chapter, based on their experiences as counselors with students through the Yale University Health Services. They discuss the process of sexual development of adolescents as an unfolding and identify ten steps in this unfolding, with success being gauged by the capacity to satisfy "sexual and psychological intimacy with another person or persons" (p. 19). The remaining chapters, written by contributors with credentials and affiliations in the fields of psychiatry, psychology, pediatrics or sex counseling, address the various conditions or situations that may affect the sexual development and in turn the emotional and social functioning of the atypical adolescent. The chapters offer a concise introduction to each condition or situation and address the supporting role of the family, the counselor, the physician, and others in the helping professions as these young people cope with the passage from adolescence to adulthood, made more difficult by their atypical condition(s). Reference to the classic research of Erikson, Freud, Kinsey, Masters and Johnson, and others as well as more recent publications are cited in the text. Appropriate cases and suggested therapies are included in most chapters. Topics addressed are adolescent retardates, sensory disabilities of deafness and blindness, gender identity, eating disorders, asthmatic adolescents, critically ill adolescents, pregenital promiscuity, juvenile prostitution, homosexuality, and sexual abuse. (MM)

11

Sexual Functioning and Disorders

IL,PO

282. Boston Women's Health Book Collective. **The New Our Bodies, Ourselves: A Book by and for Women.** New York: Simon & Schuster, 1984. 647 p. Includes bibliographies and index. ISBN 0-671-46088-9.

The Boston Women's Health Book Collective wrote *The New Our Bodies, Ourselves* to "offer some of the basic information we as women need to take care of our health" both as individuals and as users of formal medical services. It emphasizes "what women can do—for ourselves, for each other—in staying healthy, healing ourselves and working for change" (p. 3). This third edition of the original (1973) edition has been expanded and revised to provide more information and cover more topics. The original *Our Bodies, Ourselves* was the outgrowth of a discussion group that explored the experiences of women using the medical establishment, and the activist approach of the original authors is reflected in the current edition. The authors state their intention "to work to create a more just society in which good health is a right, not a luxury" (p. xiii), and this goal gives *The New Our Bodies, Ourselves* a political presence throughout.

The New Our Bodies, Ourselves covers the physical issues most commonly experienced by women. Sections include "Taking Care of Ourselves," including body image, food, alcohol, drugs and smoking, physical movement, alternatives to medical care, psychotherapy, environmental and occupational health, and violence against women; "Relationships and Sexuality," including heterosexual and lesbian relationships; "Controlling Our Fertility," including a description of the anatomy and physiology of sex and reproduction, birth control, sexually transmitted diseases, pregnancy testing, abortion, and new reproductive technologies; "Childbearing," covering pregnancy, birth, the postpartum period, and pregnancy loss; "Women Growing Older," including menopause and aging; "Some Common and Uncommon Health and Medical Problems," ranging from yeast infections to cancer; and "Women and the Medical System," including the politics of medical care and organizing for change.

Throughout, the book calls for self-awareness, education, and positive action. Women's feelings and self-knowledge are frequently ignored or belittled by health care professionals. Women must question these professionals, insist on respect and information, and take an active part in treatment and prevention. The choices each individual makes regarding sexual activities, childbearing, birth control, and other decisions should be based on both personal needs and complete information. Such decisions should be respected by others and must not be the basis for discrimination, resentment, or judgment.

Reference notes follow each chapter and most chapters include footnotes. Resource lists of books, articles, periodicals, catalogs, audiovisual materials, and/or organizations are given at the end of each chapter. (SDH)

BIOMEDICAL ASPECTS. ANATOMY, PHYSIOLOGY

PR

283. Dickinson, Robert Latou. **Human Sex Anatomy: A Topographical Hand Atlas.** Facsimile 2nd ed. Huntington, N.Y.: Krieger, 1971. 145 p., 175 figs. (Medical Aspects of Human Fertility). Includes bibliography and index.

Put forward as a basic contribution to the scientific study of sex and dedicated to Havelock Ellis, *Human Sex Anatomy*, originally published in 1933, grew out of the 1923 program of the National Committee on Maternal Health, Inc., for materials to fill gaps in our knowledge about aspects of marriage and sex life (sterility, birth control, sterilization, abortion, sex experience, and basic anatomy and physiology of sex). In his original foreword, Dickinson called his work "a grouping of pictorial averages, a sketchbook of the framework on which to mould the science—and art—of sex life." By 1949, when the second edition was published, additional anatomical and physiological statistics, including data from Kinsey's *Sexual Behavior in the Human Male* (1948), had been gathered, modifying and amplifying the original material. This folio-sized book is divided into two sections: "Text and Commentary," made up of chapters discussing different facets of female and male sex anatomy ("The Bony Pelvis"; "Uterus, Ovaries and Tubes"; "The Vagina"; "The Vulva and Breast"; "Male Genital Anatomy"; "The Anatomy of Coitus"; and "The Anatomy of the Control of Conception") and "The Atlas Proper," composed of 175 drawings, diagrams, and charts showing the aspects of female and male anatomy discussed in the first section. The figures, closely tied to the written text, are mostly black-and-white sketches drawn from life at full scale. One-half of the figures are based on original drawings and measurements; one-quarter cover novel presentations or assemblages; a significant number of the drawings are by Dickinson. Some of the figures represent numerous tracings of roentgenograms to provide averages of anatomical detail. Sandwiched between the two sections is a near-400-item bibliography identifying the world's literature (mostly German, French, and English works) on the anatomy and physiology of sex. Illustrative of the kinds of anatomical and statistical data found in the atlas are: (1) the appearance, anatomy, and average dimensions of both the flaccid and erect penis; (2) the average location and excursion of the clitoris with respect to the symphysis; and (3) the location of the penis in the vagina in relation to the clitoris in various coital positions. As Dickinson states, his atlas concerns itself "with neglected aspects of form and function, with practical issues, with newer claims and findings, together with programs of study" (p. 2). This atlas seems to be without rival in the anatomical field. Consequently, its continued educational use by students, educators, and medical illustrators is to be expected. (TJW)

IL
284. Durden-Smith, Jo, and Diane deSimone. **Sex and the Brain.** New York: Arbor House, 1983. 298 p. Includes bibliography and index. ISBN 0-87795-484-4.
    To the three major scientific revolutions of the past (Copernican, Darwinian, and Freudian), Durden-Smith and deSimone add a fourth: the new science of the human brain. A product of four years of research (including interviews with prominent scientists in the "new" field), this book counters established "nurture orthodoxy" by suggesting that "nature" plays a more crucial role in shaping the differences between males and females than most of us are willing to grant. Although it may be difficult to admit that psychological states are not purely products of the mind, that the mind and body are not entirely separate, and that gender is not entirely learned, Durden-Smith and deSimone present current research that seems to support these points of view and question the basic assumptions around which most social sciences operate. They recognize that their discussion is not only controversial but may be considered "illiberal," anti-feminist, and anti-scientific; after all, the scientists studying the relationship between the brain and behavior have been accused of doing work that "ought not to be done." After discussing the roots of the nature/nurture debate, Durden-Smith and deSimone concentrate on the relevance of brain research to sexual behavior (the brain, the sexing of the brain, the brain and the body). They provide intriguing discussions of such issues as whether male and female brains are organized differently, why females seem to be more nurturant than males, why depressive disorders affect females more often, why paraphilias and sex-related deviance affect males more, how right and left brain hemispheres affect male and female behavior, and how sex hormones relate to male and female behavior. They integrate their data into a discussion of why sex exists and what its social consequences are. They attempt to counter some prevalent myths (women were liberated by contraception,

singles have the best lives). They point out the merit of considering how biological, social, and cultural factors combine to produce the sexual problems we face today. They emphasize how and why sexuality developed in humans and explore possible differences in the chemistry of male and female bodies and brains. They conclude by reminding us of the possible consequences of technological intervention (the pill, vasectomies, barbiturates prescribed during pregnancy) in sexual and reproductive processes. They synthesize a massive amount of scientific data into a clear, issue-oriented account of how biological, psychological, and social factors may relate to each other, and they provide thought-provoking insights that can contribute to a balanced perspective on sex differences. (SGF)

PR,IL

284a. Hamer, Dean, and Peter Copeland. **The Science of Desire: The Search for the Gay Gene and the Biology of Behavior.** New York: Simon & Schuster, 1994. 272 p. Includes bibliography and index. ISBN 0-671-88724-6.

In *The Science of Desire*, Hamer describes the details of his research that indicates a genetic influence on male sexual orientation. He also describes the events surrounding the publication of this study and speculates on the implications of his results. The research of Hamer and his collaborators was published in *Science*, the journal of the American Association for the Advancement of Science, on July 16, 1993. The title of his article is "A Linkage Between DNA Markers on the X Chromosome and Male Sexual Orientation." A reprint of the paper is included as appendix A in the book.

Hamer points out that because of the political climate and national debate over gays in the military at the time, publication of his article, which would otherwise have been of interest only to researchers in the scientific community, attracted considerable public attention and has led to spirited debate. He relates numerous stories of the criticism that has been directed at him and the efforts that some have used to try to discount the validity of his findings. He counters these arguments by citing the statistical methods used in the study and in many cases demonstrating the implausibility of his critics' suggestions. He states that his goal was never to comment on the morality of homosexuality. He attempts to give the reader a feel for how a researcher designs and conducts a scientific research project. In this case, rather than trying to prove that there is a gene that makes people homosexual, his study relied on scientific methods to determine if there are characteristic features of the genetic makeup of people who are homosexual.

Hamer devotes most of his book to a description of the research design and methods, obviating the need for the layperson to read or understand the intricacies of the scientific article itself. His experiments involved interviewing and taking blood samples from hundreds of gay men and as many other members of their families as possible. A copy of the interview questions is included as appendix B of the book. At each step in the discussion of the design of the experiments, he mentions the possibility of problems in the analysis resulting from incorrect classification of a participant as homosexual or heterosexual. Family tree analysis indicated with some degree of confidence that homosexuality has a genetic component that is passed from mother to son and resides on the X chromosome. The blood samples were used to obtain the DNA of the study subjects for use in linkage analysis. The molecular genetic techniques and the statistical methods of linkage analysis are discussed in enough detail to give the reader a sense of Hamer's reasoning in the interpretation of his results. Thus, Hamer concludes that his experiments indicate, with a high degree of certainty, that a gene influencing sexual orientation can be found near other, known genetic markers to the q28 region of the X chromosome.

In his last chapter, Hamer discusses and speculates on numerous implications of the results of his findings. He describes some of the studies that he and other researchers have used to try to establish a biological mechanism of action of a gene that determines sexual orientation. He discusses the evolutionary implications of a genetic trait that is seemingly contrary to reproduction and hence its own survival. He also discusses the likelihood that other behavioral characteristics, such as alcoholism and mental illnesses, have a genetic component. The final chapter discusses the unresolved ethical and legal issues surrounding this research and homosexuality in general. (FGW)

PR,IL

285. LeVay, Simon. **The Sexual Brain.** Cambridge, Mass.: MIT Press, 1993. 168 p. Includes bibliography, index, and glossary. ISBN 0-262-12178-6.

LeVay, a neurobiologist noted for his 1991 study of the hypothalamus of gay and straight men, states in the introduction that "the aim of this book is to focus more precisely on the brain mechanisms that are responsible for sexual behavior and feelings." He also intends to look for the biological basis for the sexual diversity between men and women and among individuals of the same sex.

At the outset, LeVay distinguishes between the work of psychologists and neuro-biologists in their approach to brain study. Originally pro-Freudian, he later rejected Freud's ideas as unscientific and fossilized. Sexual biology seemed to show the most promise, so he turned to the study of sexuality from a biological standpoint.

LeVay displays his cultural literacy by organizing the book into thirteen chapters, each named or based on a quote from a poem or play by Shakespeare. Chapter 1, "Thou, Nature, Art My Goddess," examines the nature/nurture controversy, pointing out "the relative roles of heredity and environmental factors in sexuality." Chapter 2, "Time's Millioned Accidents," describes from the sociobiologic standpoint the evolutionary forces that made humans sexual and molded their sexual behavior. Chapter 3, "For a Woman Wert Thou First Created," describes how genetically "our bodies develop as males or females." Chapter 4, "What's in the Brain That Ink May Character?" describes the structure of the brain with emphasis on regional specialization and the techniques used to study the brain.

In chapter 5, "The Womby Vaultage," LeVay focuses on the hypothalamus, the small endocrine gland beneath the thalamus, which exerts control over sexual and reproductive matters. Chapter 6, "The Beast with Two Backs," examines the mechanisms of sexual intercourse, noting "that many of the neuronal circuits that mediate coitus lie not in the brain but in the spinal cord," and showing that copulation is a series of reflexes controlled and modulated by the hypothalamus. Chapter 7, "A Joy Proposed," and chapter 8, "The Child-Changed Mother," highlight courtship behavior and maternal behavior respectively, as sex-differentiated traits whose basis in brain function has been studied in animals.

In chapter 9, "The Generation of Still-Breeding Thoughts," LeVay "presents the evidence that sexual behavior typical of males and females depends on the functions of distinct, specialized regions within the hypothalamus" (p. xv). Chapter 10, "My Brain I'll Prove the Female," covers the development of the brain regions in males and females. In chapter 11, "In All Suits Like a Man," LeVay "discusses some of the differences between men and women that fall outside the sphere of sex itself," such as aggressive-ness. Chapter 12, "So Full of Shapes Is Fancy," examines sexual orientation and its development. LeVay discusses "the biological mechanisms that may contribute to making a person gay, straight, or bisexual." He then covers gender identity and transsexuality in chapter 13, "Wrapped in a Woman's Hide."

In the epilogue, "Two Artificial Gods," LeVay states that "the most promising area of exploration is the identification of genes that influence sexual behavior and the study of when, where, and how these genes exert their effects" (p. 137). However, "strong as the influence of genes may be, they do not fully account for the diversity that we see around us." Lastly, LeVay states that "the ultimate challenge will be to establish how the genetic differences among individuals interact with environmental factors to produce the diversity that exists among us." (TJW)

PR

286. Lowry, Thomas Power. **The Classic Clitoris: Historic Contributions to Scientific Sexuality.** Chicago: Nelson-Hall, 1978. 120 p. Includes index. ISBN 0-88229-387-7.

This fundamentally important work on the anatomy and physiology of the clitoris was put together by the president of the Northern California chapter of the American Association of Marriage and Family Counselors. Upon completing his medical educa-tion, Lowry served as a research associate at the Reproductive Biology Research

Foundation in St. Louis, Missouri, otherwise known as the Masters and Johnson Clinic. He prefers "the cognitive scholarly approach to sexuality" to the all-too-common experiential approach and hopes that this book "will fill a critical void in the current education of sex therapists and educators." In his book, Lowry brings together three previously overlooked works published during the past 130 years, and comments upon their significance as contributions to our understanding of the clitoris. The essays in question are: "The Mysterious Origins of the Word 'Clitoris'," by Marcel Cohen, the renowned French philologist; "The Female Sex Organs in Humans and Some Animals," a detailed anatomical and physiological study (which includes a rare and enlarged side view of the clitoris), published in 1844 by the German anatomist, George Ludwig Kobelt; and "Female Cloaca and Copulatory Organs: Comparative Anatomy," Ulrich Gerhardt's comparative study of the sex organs of fish, amphibians, reptiles, birds, and mammals. Finally, a current anatomical and physiological description of the clitoris is given by Kermit E. Krantz, Dean of Clinical Affairs at the University of Kansas, in a paper entitled "Corpus Clitoridis." Lowry comments that Krantz's essay "should further lay to rest the unnecessary and unproductive controversy of 'clitoral' versus 'vaginal orgasm'." (TJW)

PR
287. Money, John, and Herman Musaph, eds. **Handbook of Sexology.** New York: Elsevier, 1978. 5 v. Includes bibliographies and indexes.
      This monumental collection of papers was originally published in 1977. Organized into 17 sections and 108 chapters, it presents current sexological studies and research from a variety of fields, including psychology, sociology, psychiatry, anthropology, urology, gynecology, endocrinology, and venereology. While strongly emphasizing the biomedical disciplines, it nevertheless gives some attention to topics in such areas as history, religion, and law.
      The 1978 edition is a republication of this work. which rearranges the seventeen sections into five conceptually coherent volumes: volume I, "History and Ideology" (containing four sections: "History and Theory of Sexology," "Youth and Sex," "Customs of Family Formation and Marriage," and "Religion, Ideology and Sex"); volume II, "Genetics, Hormones and Behavior" (containing three sections: "Genetics, Cytogenetics, Sex Reversal and Behavior," "Prenatal Hormones and the Central Nervous System," "Hormones and Sexual Behavior in Adulthood"); volume III, "Procreation and Parenthood" (containing three sections: "Regulation of Procreation," "Pregnancy and Childbirth," and "On Parenthood"); volume IV, "Selected Personal and Social Issues" (containing three sections: "Special Issues: Social," "Special Issues: Personal," and "Geriatric Sexual Relationships"); and volume V, "Selected Syndromes and Therapy" (containing four sections: "Psychosexual Impairment," "Sexual Problems of the Chronically Impaired: Selected Syndromes," "Personal and Social Implications of Diseases of the Genital Tract," and "Treatment and Counseling for Sexual Problems").
      This enormous compilation of information and knowledge about human sexuality can be expected to provide a strong foundation for the emerging science of sexology. (TJW)

PR
288. Netter, Frank H. **The CIBA Collection of Medical Illustrations. Volume 2. A Compilation of Paintings on the Normal and Pathologic Anatomy of the Reproductive System.** Edited by Ernst Oppenheimer, M.D. With a foreword by John Rock, M.D. Summit, N.J.: CIBA, 1977. 287 p. Copyrighted in 1954 and 1965. Includes index. ISBN 0-914168-02-9.
      According to the foreword, "in 1950 not less than 363,145 deaths occurred because of our ignorance in matters of reproduction or our failure to apply what little knowledge we had." It goes on to say that the attention of the physician must "be applied to the deep secrets of human sex and its Aristotelian final cause, reproduction," and that what Netter has supplied in this superbly illustrated volume is "an exceedingly compact and inclusive

postgraduate course in both male and female reproductive anatomy, physiology and pathology."

The 233 plates, all painted by Netter, are dispersed throughout the fourteen sections into which this book is organized. The sections are as follows: section I, "Development of the Genital Tracts and Functional Relationships of the Gonads"; section II, "Normal Anatomy of the Male Genital Tract"; section III, "Diseases of the Penis and Urethra"; section IV, "Diseases of the Prostate and Seminal Tract"; section V, "Diseases of the Scrotum and Testis"; section VI, "Normal Anatomy of the Female Genital Tract and Its Functional Relationships"; section VII, "Diseases of the Vulva"; section VIII, "Diseases of the Vagina"; section IX, "Diseases of the Uterus"; section X, "Diseases of the Fallopian Tubes"; section XI, "Diseases of the Ovary"; section XII, "Pregnancy and Its Diseases"; section XIII, "Anatomy and Physiology of the Mammary Gland"; and section XIV, "Intersexes." Accompanying the illustrations are explanatory texts prepared in collaboration with various specialists. This volume can be used in educational, clinical, and scientific contexts. (TJW)

PR
289. Pariser, Stephen F., Stephen B. Levine, and Malcolm L. Gardner, eds. **Clinical Sexuality.** New York: Dekker, 1983. 216 p. (Reproductive Medicine, v. 3). Includes bibliographic references and index. ISBN 0-8247-1895-X.

According to the editors of this volume of papers on clinical sexuality written primarily by doctors, "most physicians today still fail to develop competence in this area" (p. v). The topic of sexual functioning remains a "luxury," relegated to a time when physicians have already mastered "the basic tasks of their specialties." Consequently, many doctors do not respond to opportunities to help sexually distressed patients. The aims of this introductory book are to present a clinical perspective on sexuality and to acquaint the interested physician with different ways that he or she can recognize sexual problems and interact with patients suffering from these symptoms. The initial chapter defines some of the components of a general clinical evaluation of a sexual disorder (e.g., interviewing and problem definition). The next few chapters discuss the identification, possible etiology, and treatment approaches to psychosexual problems, including gender dysphoria and marital conflict. The remainder of the book gives more attention to the anatomical and physiological aspects of sexual disorders. Separate chapters are devoted to problems associated with specific populations: females (gynecological disorders, hysterectomy, sexuality in pregnancy, etc.), males (impotence, vasectomy, priapism, penile prostheses, etc.), people with disabilities, and those suffering from different types of medical illnesses (cancer, myocardial infarction, liver disease, etc.). Other topics include the relation of drug types to sexuality and the symptoms and treatment of sexually transmitted diseases. This overview of the field can acquaint the beginner and reassure the seasoned practitioner of the significant ways in which physicians can help their patients who are experiencing sexually related problems. (SGF)

PR,IL
290. Sevely, Josephine Lowndes. **Eve's Secrets: A New Theory of Female Sexuality.** New York: Random House, 1987. 213 p. Includes bibliography and index. ISBN 0-394-55438-8.

In *Eve's Secrets*, Sevely challenges current beliefs about female sexuality that contend that women require "more physical stimulation than men and . . . play a generally secondary role in the sex act" and that "men ejaculate, women do not" (p. xvi). In addition Sevely questions current knowledge concerning male and female genital anatomy. She presents her own theory as a contribution to the problem of sexual differentiation. She also believes that it "offers women for the first time a way of perceiving how men relate to *them* sexually instead of vice versa," and it "offers men a new awareness of their own sexual anatomy and a greater insight into what it is that excites and pleases women sexually" (p. xxiii).

In chapter 1, Sevely examines the origin of the belief that the penis and clitoris are homologues, or counterparts, by reviewing the divers views of Plato, Aristotle, Galen, Rufus, Avicenna, Vesalius, and Fallopio, concluding that the belief is a "result of an ingrained male perspective that viewed the female as inferior and an unquestioning acceptance of incorrect translations" (p. 16). Sevely's theory proposes that the true counterpart of the clitoris is not the penis but the internal part of the penis, the corpora cavernosa, which she calls the male clitoris. The theory states that (1) there is a male clitoris and (2) the penile glans corresponds to the female glans located below the meatus and above the vagina.

Chapters 2, 3, and 4 present facts about the female urethra, female fluids, and the vagina as support of Sevely's theory of female sexuality. What is disclosed amounts to a reinterpretation of male and female genital anatomy that views the vagina, and not the clitoris, as the counterpart of the penis.

These revelations have implications for sexual activity. Sevely concludes that "no longer will lovemaking tend to fixate on the clitoris, no longer will the urethra be thought of merely as a conduit for the release of urine, and no longer will the vagina be considered a void lacking in sensitivity" (p. 179). She believes that this knowledge can drastically alter the thinking of anatomists and sexologists about female sexuality, improve techniques for lovemaking, and enhance the mutual regard of sexual partners.

Well-illustrated, the book also contains appendixes presenting in tabular form the Musculature of the Sexual Organs, Galen's Homologues of Male and Female Sexual Organs, Arey's Male and Female Homologues, and the Lowndes Crowns Theory of Homologues of Male and Female Sexual Organs. (TJW)

IL,PO,YA
291. Silber, Sherman J. **The Male: From Infancy to Old Age.** New York: Scribner's, 1981. 212 p. Includes index. ISBN 0-684-17664-5.

This practical book on the physical aspects of male sexuality is intended as a guide for men and women who wish to know "just how the male genitalia work, what can go wrong, and what can be done about it" (p. xii). Silber, a well-known urologist, divides his book into four parts: "How the Male Organs Work" deals with the mechanics of erection and orgasm, the role of hormones, especially testosterone, and the concept of seasonal variations in sexual desire; "What Can Go Wrong" covers physical damage to the penis as well as venereal diseases, impotence and corrective surgery, pain in the testicles, and prostate gland problems; "The Little Boy's Problems" explains circumcision in the context of ritual and hygiene, the undescended testicle, bedwetting, and the development of the sex organs before birth, sex differentiation, and ambiguous genitalia; and "Gender Identity and Homosexuality" explores gender confusion relative to homosexuality, transsexualism, transvestism, fetishism, and paraphilia.

In contrast to what is made available to the female, Silber believes that there is little in the popular literature to aid the male who, in the course of his life, is confronted with a variety of genital and sexual problems. He hopes that this guide will fill that gap. (TJW)

Normal Sexual Functioning

Sexual Response Cycle

PO
292. Kline-Graber, Georgia, and Benjamin Graber. **Woman's Orgasm: A Guide to Sexual Satisfaction.** New York: Warner Books, 1975. 240 p. Includes bibliography and index. ISBN 0-446-31329-7.

Concerned about the high incidence of orgasmic dysfunction among women, Kline-Graber and Graber have written this book as a guide to achieving orgasm. It is based on three years of clinical interviews and therapy of over 1,000 patients, and is grounded in the work of such well-known researchers as Joseph LoPiccolo and Arnold

Kegel. The authors, who operate a clinic for the treatment of sexual dysfunctions in Madison, Wisconsin, have developed two sets of instructions for women who wish to learn how to achieve orgasm either alone through masturbation and/or with a partner during intercourse.

Before setting out the procedures to be followed, the authors devote parts 1 and 2 to an explanation of female orgasm physiologically, stressing the effects of stimulating the clitoris and the pubococcygeus muscle. They also describe the stages of actual female orgasm (à la Masters and Johnson), and show the differences between orgasm during intercourse and orgasm achieved by masturbation. In addition, they review the work of several prominent writers (Freud, Kinsey, Mary Jane Sherfey, Seymour Fisher) on female orgasm, focusing on their misconceptions about female orgasm. Clearly, orgasm is a learned behavior. However, the problem is that many women who think they are orgasmic are really not. What they think is orgasm is something else, and until they understand the nature of orgasm and admit their own problems, they will be in need of instruction. Sadly, many women do not understand the nature of orgasm. Kline-Graber and Graber lay the blame on society, parents, and peers who "encourage a seductive, flirtatious, but basically asexual and controlled role during the developing years for the female, and this negative conditioning process, with its subtle reinforcement of the reward of 'being a good girl,' robs women of their basic biological birthright to orgasm" (p. 66).

The heart of the book is part 3, that consists of the instructions women can follow at home to teach themselves how to have orgasms, either alone or with intercourse.

The steps for learning how to have an orgasm by self-stimulation include: (1) self-examination, (2) pubococcygeus muscle exercises, (3) self-sensory examination, (4) beginning masturbation, (5) advanced masturbation, (6) breathing and sounds, (7) auto-suggestion, (8) sexual fantasies, (9) vibrator masturbation, (10) tapering off the vibrator, and (11) adding vaginal pubococcygeal stimulation.

The ten steps for learning to achieve orgasm with intercourse include communication exercise, pleasuring, breathing and sounds, masturbation together, clitoral with vaginal pubococcygeal stimulation, manual clitoral stimulation by a partner, using your vaginal pubococcygeal muscle during intercourse, movements during intercourse, clitoral stimulation during intercourse, and tapering off clitoral stimulation during intercourse.

Ancillary questions dealing with sex education, adult nudity, privacy, sex stereotyping, and the like are discussed in the final part of the book. (TJW)

PR,IL
293. Ladas, Alice Kahn, Beverly Whipple, and John D. Perry. **The G Spot and Other Recent Discoveries About Human Sexuality.** New York: Holt, Rinehart and Winston, 1982. 236 p. Includes bibliography and index. ISBN 0-03-061831-2.

The authors of this tightly written book hope that the findings of recent research will contribute to an understanding of human sexual response. On the basis of reviews of the literature, testimonials from women and men, answers to a questionnaire administered to 198 women analysts (134, all members of the Institute of Bioenergetic Analysis, responded) who had undergone therapy, and the self-reports of women examined by nurses and doctors, the authors affirm: (1) the existence of the G spot (a named effect derived from the investigations of Dr. Ernst Grafenberg, around mid-century), an area situated deep within the anterior wall of the vagina adjacent to the urethra; (2) female ejaculation through the urethra during orgasm as a result of stimulation of the G spot; (3) the contribution of a strong pubococcygeus muscle to orgasm; and (4) the existence of a continuum of orgasmic response. Although the sampling method used in the study conducted by Ladas may be questioned as less than scientific, the intriguing and indicative conclusions definitely add more fuel to the long-standing debate over clitoral versus vaginal orgasm. Neither totally accepting nor wholly rejecting the views of their predecessors, the authors attempt a synthesis of previous knowledge about sexual response (from Aristotle and Galen to Freud, Kinsey, and Masters and Johnson) that incorporates the new information obtained by them within the existing framework. They believe that acceptance of the ideas presented in this book should have a salutary effect on the sex lives of those readers who are receptive to the somewhat startling conclusions presented. In particular, they are confident that their conclusions will contribute to the enhancement of sexual lovemaking and in providing comfort to women who have felt fear, embarrassment, and rejection. Appendixes cover instruments used in pubococcygeus muscle training, a list of referral sources for therapy, and an abstract with tables presenting information from the questionnaire used in the study. (TJW)

PR
294.   Masters, William H., and Virginia E. Johnson. **Human Sexual Response.** Boston: Little, Brown, 1966. 366 p. Includes bibliography and index.

Masters and Johnson present the initial results of their pioneering eleven-year empirical investigation of human sexual response with the goal of providing the scientific community with "physiologic fact rather than phallic fallacy" to replace myths and fears about sexuality. They concentrate their research interest on what people do in response to effective sexual stimulation rather than on what they say they do or should do. Their method follows from this goal: they directly observe, physically measure, and record the gross physical changes that occur during the sexual response cycles of 694 men and women respondents in a controlled setting. They supplement their laboratory observations with medical, social, and psychosexual interviews of their laboratory subjects and clinical research population. They arbitrarily divide the sexual response cycle into four separate phases (excitement, plateau, orgasm, and resolution) in order to provide an effective framework to describe in detail the physiological variants in sexual reaction. Within this framework they establish not only the anatomy of human response to sexual stimulation, but also the physiological variation of individual reaction patterns. Overall, they emphasize the similarities (e.g., myotonia and vasocongestion) rather than the differences between men and women in the anatomy and physiology of their sexual response. Although they admit that their research population is subject to many forms of selectivity (upper socioeconomic status, higher intelligence, heterosexual, primarily white, willing to cooperate), they maintain that they have opened the door to answering a basic question fundamental to the study of human sexual response: What physical reactions develop as the human male and female respond to effective sexual stimulation? Their study is a methodological milestone in establishing sexuality as a legitimate domain for scientific study. Much of what we know about the physiology of human sexual response derives from their work. (SGF)

PR,IL
295.   Reich, Wilhelm. **Genitality in the Theory and Therapy of Neurosis.** Translated by Philip Schmitz. Edited by Mary Higgins and Chester M. Raphael. New York: Farrar Straus Giroux, 1980. 225 p. (Early Writings, v. 2). Includes bibliographic references and index. ISBN 0-374-16112-7.

Originally published in 1927 under the title *Die Funktion des Orgasmus* and revised between 1937 and 1945, this translated edition presents Reich's early thinking on the causal link between neuroses and genital disturbances. For Reich the orgasm occupies the central place in sexual activity; it represents the release of tension that removes the individual from a condition of sexual stasis. He demonstrates his position with a detailed examination and graphing of what happens to men and women during coitus. The cycle described has a sensory phase of excitation followed by a release of tension in the second phase.

The psychoanalytic theory of neuroses stipulates the frustration of sexual drives by the requirements of morality, producing various neurotic symptoms, such as impotence and frigidity. Reich gives a biological basis to neurosis, a hypothesis that separated him from Freud. According to Reich, in addition to repressed ideas, experiences, desires, satisfactions, and so forth underlying neurotic symptoms, the situation also requires dammed-up sex drive energy. In therapy, it is necessary to eliminate the source(s) of the damming-up of the energy that is at the root of the psychic illness (psychosis, perversion, neurotic criminality). Reich describes the various aspects of therapy that are involved in eliminating sexual stasis and restoring balance in the tension/release of energy equation. Reich goes on to explain certain destructive impulses (brutality, sadism) in terms of sexual stasis. Finally, he deals with the social significance of genitality, relating it to sexual satisfaction and the ability to work. He also discusses Freud's theory of vaginal primacy and offers his own explanation of the transformation of clitoral eroticism through "the shift of anal and oral libido to the vagina" (p. 167).

While the psychoanalytic community of the time preferred not to be identified with Reich's view on the function of orgasm, "the whole development of his work flowed out of orgasm research and his conviction that the orgasm function holds the key to the most basic questions in nature" (p. ix). (TJW)

PR
296.   Rosen, Raymond C., and J. Gayle Beck. **Patterns of Sexual Arousal: Psychophysiological Processes and Clinical Applications.** New York: Guilford Press, 1988. 404 p. Includes bibliography and index. ISBN 0-89862-712-5.

Rosen and Beck have produced "the first comprehensive review of theory and data in the emerging field of sexual psychophysiology" (p. vii), a branch of sexual science that deals with the patterns and processes of human sexual arousal.

The book is divided into three sections. The opening section, "Conceptual Foundations and Historical Overview," begins by briefly tracing the history of psychophysiology. One of the major foci of study has been the development of an adequate definition of sexual arousal. Two-, three-, and four-stage models have been proposed, but none are completely viable. A variety of measurement techniques has been developed for use in psychophysiological testing, primarily instruments for measuring vasocongestion. All these have problems with reliability and intrusiveness; also, questions remain about the correspondence between engorgement and subjective arousal. Laboratory study of orgasm has been limited and a comprehensive understanding of this phenomenon remains elusive. Despite Masters and Johnson's emphasis on similarity between male and female orgasm, many researchers find significant differences between them. Research shows great variability in orgasmic experience, and there is no single widely accepted typology of orgasm. The impact of endocrine factors in sexual psychophysiology has only recently been seriously studied. Testosterone and estrogen are necessary for both male and female sexual response, but the levels required show high variability.

In section 2, "Current Applications of Sexual Psychophysiology," Rosen and Beck review laboratory research in sex therapy and sexual dysfunction, including studies on responses to erotica and pornography and to repeated exposure to violent pornography, and laboratory techniques for the assessment and treatment of deviant behavior. Advances in sexual science have led to useful changes in the classification of sexual dysfunction as formalized in DSM-III; however, there is evidence that these classifications need further definition and division. Research on male sexual dysfunction has concentrated on erectile failure and premature and retarded ejaculation; the primary topics for study of female dysfunction have been difficulties in reaching orgasm, penetration problems, and inhibited sexual desire or excitement. Effects of alcohol and other drugs on sexual response are receiving increasing attention; no drug studied to date appears to directly stimulate sexual response.

The final section, "Future Directions in Sexual Psychophysiology," reviews the major themes of the book and outlines areas of future research. The book concludes with an appendix discussing the use of human subjects in sexual research and an extensive bibliography. (SDH)

Reproductive Cycle

IL
297.   Corea, Gena. **The Mother Machine: Reproductive Technologies from Artificial Insemination to Artificial Wombs.** New York: Harper & Row, 1985. 374 p. Includes bibliography and index. ISBN 0-06-091325-8.

Fearful that in our present patriarchal society women's bodies will be reduced to the status of marketable commodities for reproductive purposes, feminist Corea describes the rapid development and use of reproductive technologies. Just as women have sold certain body parts (breasts, vagina, buttocks) for sexual purposes in prostitution, so now they are being persuaded to offer up their wombs, ovaries, and eggs in the interest of scientific progress and the questionable effort of helping infertile women.

Corea explores these technologies, delving into their histories, methods, social effects, and speculating about the future when women will be regarded as "mother machines." She believes that certain groups—men in general, infertile women who look to technology for relief from their special problem, and older women who accept the notion of test-tube babies, as well as those with genetic diseases, endometriosis, hyperthyroid, or a history of miscarriage, who are envisioned as future IVF candidates—will have trouble accepting this book. She believes that the issue is not infertility but rather the exploitation of women by men.

In part I, "Artificial Insemination," Corea discusses "eugenics, the attempt to improve the human race by controlling who is allowed to produce," the threat to patriarchy from artificial insemination by donor sperm (AID), and "how medicine and law have managed . . . to fit AID into the concept of the patriarchal family." In part II, "Embryo Transfer," she describes "the history and procedures involved in embryo transfer in animals" and follows this with the business of embryo transfer in humans. In part III, "In Vitro Fertilization," she "recounts the history of IVF technology and describes the potential uses of IVF technology as foreseen by reproductive engineers, provides an account of iatrogenic (doctor-induced) origins of many forms of infertility and discusses the risks of IVF to woman and child."

Part V deals with related technologies: sex determination, surrogate motherhood, the artificial womb, and cloning.

Corea concludes by discussing what she believes is the control by men of female biological reproductive processes, envisioning reproductive brothels where the reproductive technologies could be used and where women sell wombs, ovaries, and eggs.

Finally, she discusses women's and men's disparate reproductive experience, one continuous, the other discontinuous. She opines that men envy women their closer connection to the human species through birth and then have tried to render their experience their own by developing obstetrics, gynecology, and the new reproductive technologies. Corea says a final word about the "efforts of women from many countries, working together, to deal with the threat posed by this biological revolution." (TJW)

PR,IL,PO,YA,CH
298.   Demarest, Robert J., and John J. Sciarra. **Conception, Birth and Contraception: A Visual Presentation.** Introduction by Mary S. Calderone, M.D. New York: McGraw-Hill, 1969. 129 p. Includes glossary.

The central feature of this book is a set of sixty-one full-color illustrations of the anatomy and physiology that come into play in conception, birth, and contraception; many of the drawings are life-sized. A clearly written, nontechnical text by Sciarra, head of the Department of Obstetrics and Gynecology at the University of Minnesota Medical School, complements the mostly "life-sized" drawings by the prominent medical illustrator Robert Demerest to implement the goal of the book: to present the "fundamentals, the elementary knowledge needed to form the foundation for a mature understanding of human reproduction" and "with a regard to esthetics and human dignity." Demarest and Sciarra present different aspects of reproduction in an illuminating visual and verbal sequence. The first section deals with conception, beginning with general aspects of male and female anatomy and physiology and ending with the particulars of fertilization, implantation, and gestation. The next section describes and illustrates the three stages of labor as well as the process of nursing. The final section discusses natural and artificial methods of contraception: how they prevent conception, how to use them, and factors to consider in evaluating whether to use them (e.g., effectiveness, side effects). This book is a useful tool for sex education for a wide range of audiences—from high school students to parents and physicians. (SGF)

IL,PO
299. Francoeur, Robert T. **Utopian Motherhood: New Trends in Human Reproduction.** Garden City, N.Y.: Doubleday, 1970. 278 p. Includes bibliography.
    "We stand on the brink of a major revolution. . . . The eternal mystiques of masculine and feminine . . . are evaporating . . . their death accelerated by a very short-fused, ready-to-explode biological time bomb," writes Francoeur, a researcher in the field of embryology, in the prologue to this book. He refers to humankind's newly found ability to control and duplicate human reproduction in the laboratory, independent of the timeless male-female sexual union. Francoeur discusses these startling advancements resulting in artificial insemination, frozen sperm cells, test-tube babies, embryo transplants, genetic engineering, and asexual cloning. In addition, he focuses on enormous moral issues: whether the rights to reproduce should be limited to men and women selected for their desirable qualities and intelligence, whether the traditional husband-wife relationship is becoming outdated, and who should decide the course of human evolution now that the power to do so is in our hands. A selected annotated bibliography provides a guide to further reading. (EBS)

IL
300. Greer, Germaine. **Sex and Destiny: The Politics of Human Fertility.** New York: Harper & Row, 1984. 539 p. Includes bibliographic notes and index. ISBN 0-06-015140-4.
    In her introductory "Warning," Greer, the celebrated author of the classic feminist work, *The Female Eunuch*, comments that this book is a "plea for a new intellectual order" (p. xiv), one that respects the social and cultural context within which people in a variety of cultures make decisions about their reproductive lives. The ostensible concern in the West about the problem of overpopulation is manifested in its family planning programs for other societies. However, Greer meticulously and pungently argues that the exportation of contraceptive devices, sterilization techniques, and abortion procedures represents the imposition of a Western anti-child paradigm on groups that value sexuality, reproduction, and children.
    The book begins with Greer's assessment of modern society's departure from the pro-child stance of most societies of the past: "We in the West do not refrain from childbirth because we are concerned about the population explosion or because we feel we cannot afford children, but because we do not like children" (p. 2). Her contrast between pregnancy and birth in the West and in other cultures sets the stage for the numerous cross-cultural and historical comparisons that she uses to substantiate her points in the rest of the text. Her conclusion that "motherhood is virtually meaningless in our society" (p. 29) leads to her next major point: Western society's devaluation of fertility results in an attempt to destroy the fertility of groups who do value it.
    The bulk of the book is a documentation of Western society's anti-child paradigm and the deleterious consequences that it brings to other groups, although the purpose is rationalized as a humanitarian gesture designed to help develop "underdeveloped" countries. She contends that encouraging sterilization in other cultures expresses little faith that these groups know how to manage their own fertility. However, chastity, abortion, infanticide, selective choice of sexual partners, and other forms of social regulation of fertility may depress population as well as consumer-oriented pharmaceutical and mechanical devices. A history of the birth control movement, eugenics, nonreproductive sex, and an emphasis on the nuclear family attest to the low value that

Westerners place on fertility. The family planning movement, including the population lobby, interferes in the support of extended family forms prevalent in other cultures. The consequent government involvement in family planning is "heavy handed, misinformed, [and] haphazard in its methods"; it robs individuals of reproductive control and choice. The danger for the future of fertility lies in "stupidity masked by the professional elite" (p. 468). "False reasoning" and political manipulation threaten to destroy not only respect for human life but also viable beliefs and customs that have persisted through generations in other cultures. Western society's arrogance that the world is theirs is undermining an important dimension of life. As Greer puts it: "Most of the pleasure in the world is still provided by children and not by genital dabbling" (p. 257). After all, "what is our civilization that we should so blithely propagate its discontents?" She concludes that Westerners have no right to define or solve a problem of world overpopulation. (SGF)

PR,IL
301. Rothman, Barbara Katz. **Recreating Motherhood: Ideology and Technology in a Patriarchal Society.** New York: Norton, 1989. 282 p. Includes bibliographic notes and index. ISBN 0-393-02645-0.

Motherhood in all its complexities is explored and analyzed in this challenging study by Rothman, professor of sociology at Baruch College and the City University of New York. Rothman's approach to the major issues of pregnancy, abortion, adoption, infertility, midwifery, medical treatment of premature babies, child care, fatherhood, and surrogacy is from a carefully reasoned feminist viewpoint. Surrounding and affecting all these issues in our society are the ideologies of capitalism, patriarchy, and technology. Rothman's depiction of the detrimental influence of these ideologies on various aspects of motherhood leads her to suggest a new feminist social policy that calls for "economic justice, an end to patriarchy, valuing nurturance."

Specific proposals arising from her analysis include: (1) recognizing that women have full rights of personal privacy, bodily autonomy, and individual decision making in pregnancy; (2) the acceptance of adoption agreements only after the birth of a child; (3) development of effective solutions to infertility, but eschewing radical solutions such as using animal wombs and artificial wombs on the grounds that every child has a right to a human mother; (4) legal recognition of midwifery as a profession; (5) active involvement of men in child care; (6) granting mothers and legally recognized co-parents full medical decision making rights for the care of their newborns and very young children; (7) recognizing the value of child care through parental leave arrangements; (8) granting child-care workers their monetary due and recognizing such special rights as job security; (9) discouraging men's patriarchal attitudes but encouraging their capacity to be caring fathers; (10) granting full parental rights to birth mothers, including rights of custody of the babies they bore; and (11) elimination of the practice of contracting for the ownership of a baby, i.e., surrogacy, or the legal sale of a child.

Each of these proposals derive from Rothman's focus on the real needs of mother, father, and child that, she believes, have been swept aside in an unintentional obedience to the demands of ideology, patriarchy, and technology. (TJW)

Menstruation & Menopause

PR
302. Buckley, Thomas, and Alma Gottlieb, eds. **Blood Magic: The Anthropology of Menstruation.** Berkeley: University of California Press, 1988. 326 p. Includes bibliography and index. ISBN 0-520-06350-3.

According to editors Buckley and Gottlieb, although there has been a fascination with and a recognition of the significance of menstruation as a "staple" topic in anthropology, there are very few substantive findings about it. And, despite the importance attributed to variations in menstrual symbolism, " . . . the study of menstrual symbolism has been limited by a paucity of detail regarding such variations, by imbalances in ethnographic reporting, and by overly reductionistic theoretical frameworks" (p. 4). Buckley and Gottlieb chose the collection of essays in this book to be "representative of the scope and spirit of . . . new cultural-anthropological approaches to menstruation" (p. 5), many of which draw on the fieldwork of women and are open to biocultural themes in symbolic analysis. Overall, there is a recognition that biology and anthropology are cultural subsystems that facilitate the interpretation of menstruation as a form of behavior and focus of symbolic elaboration.

As an introduction to the nine essays in the book, Buckley and Gottlieb devote the first part to a critical appraisal of earlier theories of menstrual symbolism, most of which cluster around three major themes: (1) the equation of menstrual taboos with oppression of women; (2) the psychoanalytic interpretation of menstrual taboos as indicative of neurosis or anxiety about women; and (3) the view that menstrual taboos are an extension of rational responses to practical problems, e.g., menatoxins, menstrual odor. They conclude that the origins of menstrual taboos lie in the symbolic realm. After reviewing the two major types of analyses of menstrual symbolism—symbolic structures focused on pollution and/or sociological correlates of symbolic structures—Buckley and Gottlieb assert that "body, culture, and society are all implicated cybernetically in a single system of highly complex origins and functions" (p. 47).

The nine essays that follow are divided into three sections, each of which is introduced by Buckley and Gottlieb. The analyses in the first two sections focus on the authors' direct observations. The three essays (by Alma Gottlieb, Carol Delaney, and Laura W. R. Appell) in the section, "Menstrual Images, Meanings, and Values," are organized around the variety of cosmologies and semantic categories that apply to menstruation in non-Western cultural systems (Ivory Coast, village Turkey, the Rungus of Borneo). In the next section, "The Sociology of Menstrual Meanings," the essays by Denise L. Lawrence, Vieda Skultans, and Emily Martin focus on the ways in which economic, political, and broader social organizations in Portugal, Wales, and the U.S., respectively, shape the experience, meaning, and behavior associated with menstruation; of particular interest is an exploration of links between menstruation, gender, and power. The last section, "Exploratory Directions: Menses, Culture and Time," is narrower in focus, and the three essays (by Thomas Buckley, Frederick Lamp, and Chris Knight) are largely "deductive, historically reconstructive, and heuristic" (p. 50); all analyze the relevance of Martha McClintock's findings about menstrual synchrony in different cultural contexts (among the Yurok, the Temne, and the Aboriginal Australians). Buckley and Gottlieb hope that these essays will contribute to fruitful analysis and research in the anthropology of menstruation. (SGF)

IL

303.   Delaney, Janice, Mary Jane Lupton, and Emily Toth. **The Curse: A Cultural History of Menstruation.** New York: Dutton, 1976. 276 p. Includes bibliographic notes and index. ISBN 0-87690-222-0.

The Curse is a cultural history of menstruation that examines beliefs about a wide variety of aspects of menstruation, including PMS (premenstrual syndrome), menopause, "male menopause," and the technology and concepts used to deal with it. Because the authors think that menstruation has been an important way in which men have controlled women in ancient and primitive as well as postindustrial societies, this work is offered as a route for dispelling myths and giving women a basis for feeling more respect for themselves as women.

Each of the seven major parts of the book ("The Tabooed Woman," "The Menstrual Cycle in Action," "The Menstruating Woman in the Popular Imagination," "Menstrual Images in Literature," "The Menopause," "Sideshow," and "Men") reveals significant ways in which beliefs about menstruation have constrained the behavior and diminished the self-concept of women. Part 1, "The Tabooed Woman," lays the groundwork for this perspective. By meticulously documenting taboos of social and sexual avoidance during menstruation, probing the reasons for female rites of passage at menarche, tracing the "unclean" history of menstruation in the Judeo-Christian tradition, and pointing out modern ways in which ideas about menstruation are politically and medically manipulated, the authors try to substantiate the "taboo" aura of their subject. Later chapters explore the subtle influence of such factors as advertising, fairy tales, psychoanalytic theory, menstrual jokes, and explanations of PMS on women's evaluations of their bodies and themselves. Others discuss male links to menstruation via vicarious behavior like genital bleeding in male puberty rites and emotional and behavioral rhythms in men's lives.

By sorting out myths from the reality of the menstrual process, the authors hope that their readers will regard menstruation as "Eve's blessing" rather than as a curse. (SGF)

PR
304.   Komnenich, Pauline, Maryellen McSweeney, Janice A. Noack, and Nathalie Elder, eds. **The Menstrual Cycle, Volume 2: Research and Implications for Women's Health.** New York: Springer, 1981. 236 p. Includes bibliographic references and index. ISBN 0-8261-2980-3.

This volume complements its predecessor, *The Menstrual Cycle. Volume 1: A Synthesis of Interdisciplinary Research* (1980) in its concern for dispelling myths that surround menstruation and suggesting fruitful ways to conduct research on the topic. The authors of the twenty articles in this book attempt to counter an orientation of biological determinism by demonstrating the advantages of an interactionist approach, that includes cross-gender, cross-cultural, and in-depth psychological assessments of the menstrual cycle as well as physical ones. The authors of the chapters are drawn from a variety of professions (public health, medicine, education, psychology, biology) and attest to the importance of an interdisciplinary approach that can promote a balanced view of the topic. The contributors grapple with questions of what biases may shape their work; how to evaluate the implications of applying their findings, particularly as they pertain to women's personal lives; and how to design less biased research.

The three parts of the book ("The Menstrual Cycle: A Life Event," "Rights and Responsibilities," and "Implications for Women's Health") indicate the diversity of topics covered in this collection; subjects range from critiques of the design of menstrual cycle research and studies of attitudes about menstruation in this culture and in others to studies of genetic and epidemiological aspects of the menstrual cycle, ethical considerations in the use of hormone therapy or techniques for menstrual regulation, and the implications of menstrual cycle research for women's health care. A special effort was made to include a clinical component in the presentation. The editors hope that this volume "is the second step along a cumbersome path to better science in the interest of women." (SGF)

IL,PO
305.   Sheehy, Gail. **The Silent Passage: Menopause.** New York: Random House, 1991. 161 p. Includes index. ISBN 0-679-41388-X.

Menopause is one of the great taboos. Although it is a natural and inevitable experience for every woman, it is surrounded by fear, ignorance, denial, and secrecy. But when Gail Sheehy found herself in the midst of her own change of life, she decided to investigate it. This book is the result.

Sheehy found that most women approach menopause with insufficient information regarding its physiological and emotional effects, with fear of becoming unloved and unneeded, and with an unspoken hope that, if it is denied, it will not happen to them. Group meetings in California revealed a deep fear of the loss of youth and desirability. It is to be hoped that the generation of women about to enter menopause can change these attitudes by speaking out and approaching the change of life actively and in control of their bodies and lives.

Menopause varies significantly from woman to woman. It involves three phases, not distinctly separated, that cover five to seven years, usually occurring between the ages of 40 and 55. The first phase is perimenopause, when women experience the dramatic fluctuations in hormone levels that can cause hot flashes, irregular periods, heart palpitations, memory lapses, and depression, the beginning of accelerated bone loss and increased risk of coronary heart disease, a decrease in sexual desire, and dryness and thinning of the vaginal tissues. It is sometimes advantageous to begin hormone replacement therapy (HRT) during this period. The second phase, menopause, when the ovaries stop releasing eggs, marks the actual transition. During the final phase, which Sheehy calls "coalescence," women reach a new equilibrium with a restored sense of well-being. Often this is a point of liberation and the beginning of a new life of action and exploration, free from the pressures of reproduction. Menopause can be seen as the beginning of a "Second Adulthood," since the average woman lives 33 years following her menopause.

Hormone replacement therapy (HRT) can ease many of the temporary symptoms of menopause, including hot flashes and memory loss, and more importantly, can decrease the risks of osteoporosis and heart disease—but only while the hormones are being taken. A link between HRT and breast cancer is unconfirmed. The decision of whether or not to use HRT depends on a woman's personal experience and family medical history.

There is a great need for additional study and discussion of menopause. It is important that each woman take control of her life and health, making the transition through menopause with optimism, information, and good health care from a knowledgeable and sympathetic physician. (SDH)

IL

306. Shuttle, Penelope, and Peter Redgrove. **The Wise Wound: Myths, Realities, and Meanings of Menstruation.** Revised edition. Foreword by Margaret Drabble. New York: Grove Press, 1988. 358 p. First published in Great Britain in 1978. Includes bibliography and index. ISBN 0-8021-1136-X.

Drawing information from a wide array of sources—from scholarly analyses and medical journals to the films, literature, mythology, and rituals of folk and popular culture—Shuttle and Redgrove, both of whom are poets and novelists, explore the meaning of menstruation. Rather than focusing on menstruation as a curse, they emphasize its features as an unexplored reservoir of feminine nature—a "wise wound," that taps the inner rhythms, feelings, and potential of women. This perspective requires the reader to let go of negative interpretations of menstruation, which may derive from the fear that men feel when they confront this seemingly dangerous, yet powerful arena of women's physiology. The basic message of the book is that "menstruation is a great and neglected resource . . . an evolutionary force." When it was published in 1978, it was "the first book ever published to show the range of that neglected area."

Shuttle and Redgrove begin with an overview of "the science of bleeding," in which they describe scientific interpretations of menstruation, pointing out some limitations of the medical model (e.g., the assumption that menstruation only relates to reproduction). They convey the dismal ways in which menstruation has been portrayed and counter these images with the suggestion that a positive view of menstruation may open many doors, that it may be a "blessing in disguise." They continue by explaining how the cycle of emotions that accompanies the menstrual cycle may be the basis for psychological integration, not disintegration. Menstruation is an opportunity for women to be in tune with the power of their bodies, with each other, and with broader aspects of the cosmos, e.g., lunar cycles. Ancient cultures wove rituals and beliefs around these rhythms. Menstrual practices of the past have benefited and honored women, but some, like the persecution of witches, have constrained and punished women for their power. Contemporary movies like *The Exorcist* and Christopher Lee's Dracula films illustrate the depth of fear and potential that menstruation expresses in modern society.

Shuttle and Redgrove conclude that the menstrual aspect of women's physiology goes beyond the importance of ovulatory function; it is a conveyor of "imaginative and creative energies," a route for women to be "initiators into creative modes of sexuality." In the last chapter, added to this revised version of the 1978 edition, they suggest a menstrual mandala, from which women can connect one part of their experience to another and draw insight about themselves and the world around them. This means shifting back and forth between domains of mythology and reality, between dreams and waking states. (SGF)

PO

307. Trien, Susan Flamholtz. **Change of Life: The Menopause Handbook.** New York: Fawcett, 1986. 311 p. Includes bibliography and index. ISBN 0-449-90188-2.

Unlike women in previous times, contemporary women can expect to live a third of their lives after menopause. Nevertheless, little attention has been paid to the needs of these older women beyond dry, technical books that give the impression of an impending "dread disease" during middle age. In contrast to cultural myths, most women go through menopause without medical treatment. This situation spurred Trien, a "health writer headed toward her middle years," to write this nontechnical, readable book that addresses not only the traditional medical issues but also the emotional side of the changes that occur in mid-life. Overall, she hopes to "lead women through the menopause experience in a clear and positive way" by informing them of what to expect, how to deal with the changes, and pursue living a full life.

The information contained in the book is based on two years of intensive research; Trien contacted major medical organizations, national women's health groups, experts in the field, and women from age thirty-five to seventy-five in all stages of the menopause experience. Common questions that women have about menopause, such as what it is, when it occurs, its symptoms, its effect on mood and attractiveness, are answered. An explanation of the physiological basis of the menstrual system and menopause precedes a discussion of the physiological basis of hot flashes and ways that women can cope with them. However, menopause, the cessation of the menses, is but a part of an important overall transition in a woman's life. Middle-age blues may stem from a variety of factors (role reversal with aging parents, "empty nest," changes in marital satisfaction). Pointers on sources of stress and stress management as well as a discussion of estrogen therapy may assist a women in coping with these changes. Just as important for overall health are wise eating habits and exercise, to each of which a chapter is devoted. Trien discusses in detail the bodily changes that may occur (skin, pelvic organs, hair, muscles, osteoporosis) that affect appearance and self-confidence. In addition, a chapter is devoted to changes in sexuality. Because sex is a "lifelong affair," it is important to understand these changes and the options available for having a satisfactory sex life. In line with its positive orientation, the book concludes with a gynecological guide to staying healthy and the addresses of agencies that provide information about the topics discussed in the text. (SGF)

IL

308. Weideger, Paula. **Menstruation and Menopause: The Physiology and Psychology, the Myth and the Reality.** Revised and expanded. New York: Dell, 1977. 271 p. Includes bibliography and index. ISBN 0-440-55845-X.

According to Weideger, "the menstrual taboo is still active" in our society and exerts a powerful, negative influence over women's self-esteem. Discussions of menstruation and menopause are shrouded in silence, which she interprets as an indication of the shame associated with them. Nevertheless, she thinks that it is time for women to "reclaim" menstruation and menopause as normal, legitimate parts of their lives, freed from the demeaning moral judgments that have surrounded them. She contends that "as long as women run from the reality of the menstrual cycle, we are refusing to know ourselves and are accepting an external definition of ourselves." The goals of this book are to break the silence about menstruation and menopause, shatter myths about them, and foster a positive sense of community among women by sharing knowledge about the menstrual cycle.

Drawing on the 558 responses to her own questionnaire about women's experiences of the menstrual cycle, scientific research from a variety of fields, case histories, and cross-cultural findings, Weideger examines the many dimensions of the cycle. She describes the anatomy and physiology of the menstrual cycle (including menopause), stressing the wide variety of normal attitudes and physical expressions of it. She also outlines some of the problems (PMS, menopausal syndrome, pain, bleeding abnormalities, and cancer) associated with the cycle and treatments for them.

Cultural aspects and theory are also stressed. Weideger describes the various customs that surround menstruation in other cultures: behavioral proscriptions during menstruation, rites of passage to menarche, religious associations of pollution and impurity with menstrual blood. She also critiques theories about the origin of the taboo, particularly Freud's view that it reflects castration anxiety. Myths about menstruation are often perpetuated in our own society by psychoanalysts and gynecologists, whom Weideger likens to witch-doctors; they enforce the menstrual taboo and fail to acknowledge the reality of women's experiences. Furthermore, the implications of the taboo extend beyond menstruation itself. She examines the association between the menstrual and sexual cycles and asserts that belief in the menstrual taboo can "defile" sex and sexuality. The ambiguous connotations of fertility and impurity associated with menstruation add to the problems that women face during menopause. Menopausal women are "invisible" because society expects them to be and because men no longer regard their sexuality as powerful. Weideger hopes that the information presented here will erase some of the confusion about the cycle and aid women in changing their evaluation of themselves and society's conceptualizations of them. (SGF)

Pregnancy. Infertility

(For related material see also entry 31)

PR
309. Lancaster, Jane B., and Beatrix A. Hamburg, eds. **School-Age Pregnancy and Parenthood: Biosocial Dimensions.** New York: Aldine de Gruyter, 1986. 403 p. Includes bibliographies and index. ISBN 0-202-30321-7.

Under the auspices of the Social Science Research Council, Lancaster and Hamburg attempt to close a gap in systematic research on school-age pregnancy by presenting papers that demonstrate the fruitfulness of a biosocial perspective on this topic. According to Lancaster and Hamburg, the core of a biosocial perspective is a commitment not only to the reciprocal influence of biology and social environments on each other but also to an understanding of how biosocial phenomena fit into the spectrum of expectable behavioral and biological expressions of genetic heritage. Therefore, they view school-age pregnancy and parenthood as part of a range of parent-child patterns, including those that existed in the historical and evolutionary past.

The contributors are drawn from the behavioral, social, and biological sciences and attest to the multidisciplinary orientation of the book. Chapters span a wide range of topics that are organized into four major sections: "The Life Cycle and Biological Development"; "Development: Emotional, Cognitive and Sexual"; "Comparative Dimensions: Species, History, and Culture"; and "The Modern World." Lancaster and Hamburg's introductory chapter establishes some broad themes discussed throughout the volume. Although cross-species and evolutionary evidence indicate that the basic human pattern of adolescence is one of low fertility, the last 150 years have witnessed a shift toward an earlier onset of menstruation and more rapid fertility in the twelve to fourteen age groups. The former controls of adolescent subfertility, lactational amenorrhea, and cultural sexual prohibitions are no longer sufficient to contain births in the younger age categories. Melvin Konner and Marjorie Shostak suggest that teenagers today are biologically different from their predecessors and that American society is in the midst of a major evolutionary change.

Many of the other articles address the biological and social facets associated with a changed onset of menstruation and fertility. The diverse research in each section challenges some popular stereotypes: that "the teenage factor" alone contributes to low birth weight babies, that teenagers in preindustrial societies were preoccupied with pregnancy and childbearing as soon as they were married, and that the outcome of teenage pregnancies is necessarily negative for mother and child. Each article raises questions not only about the complex dimensions of school-age pregnancy and parenthood but also about the need for an appropriate methodology and theoretical orientation in dealing with this socially sensitive topic. (SGF)

PO
310. McCauley, Carole Spearin. **Pregnancy After 35.** Foreword by Dr. Howard Berk. New York: Pocket Books/Simon & Schuster, 1976. 222 p. Includes bibliography and index. ISBN 0-671-44931-1.
    Women over thirty-five years of age give birth to more than 10 percent of the babies born in the United States each year. Medical experts do not agree on the degree of risk involved in pregnancy and birth to older women. Extreme conservatives automatically label women over thirty-five "high risk," while more liberal practitioners think that only 10 percent or less of these potential mothers should be considered high risk. McCauley concurs with the optimists who view pregnancy and birth as normal processes that can be adequately dealt with by positive attitudes, nutrition, and birth training. This book provides guidelines for enhancing the safety and success of pregnancy and birth for women over thirty-five. McCauley, a medical reporter, interviewed or corresponded with a wide range of people to gather information for this book; her sources included older parents, physicians, psychologists, midwives, and members of groups concerned with genetic counseling, safe pregnancy, and the various birth services/practices available to Americans. She blends data from medical studies with accounts of case histories to provide a personal, humanistic approach to issues raised by a decision to have children at a later stage in life. From her review of current studies relating age to complications of pregnancy and birth, she concludes that "only a minority of women over 35 are automatically high risk" (p. 21). Nevertheless, she acknowledges the emotional concerns of expectant parents in older age brackets and addresses their fears by providing up-to-date information on genetic, psychological, and medical topics particularly relevant to them. Topics include: (1) an overview of risk factors, (2) choice of a doctor and hospital, (3) genetics (chromosomal disorders, Down's syndrome, counseling, genetic screening), (4) multiple births, (5) diet and drugs, (6) infertility, (7) the psychology of pregnancy during each trimester, (8) choices of methods of labor and delivery (hypnotherapy, decompression, Lemaze, Leboyer, and Bradley methods), and (9) parenting (including adjustment to family and career demands, fathering, single parenting). Although the book is particularly concerned with topics of interest to older couples, it is "for people who try hard at what is the essence of parenting as well as living—stretching bodies, minds, and hearts far enough to include that very new idea, the next generation" (p. 10). (SGF)

PR,IL
311. Nathanson, Constance A. **Dangerous Passage: The Social Control of Sexuality in Women's Adolescence.** Philadelphia: Temple University, 1991. 286 p. (Health, Society, and Policy). Includes bibliography and index. ISBN 0-87722-824-8.
    One of the basic premises of this book is that "sexuality is both historically and culturally relative" (p. 7); social context shapes the form and meaning of biological sex. Consequently, the emergence of adolescent pregnancy as a social issue is a product of historically specific social conditions, groups, and ideological concerns. Nathanson, Professor of Population Dynamics at Johns Hopkins University School of Hygiene and Public Health and Director of the Hopkins Population Center, addresses this critical question: Why have Americans directed so much social attention at adolescent pregnancy

since the early 1970s? The answers are complex, requiring a journey through social history and analysis of changes framed by sociological theories of deviance, social movements, and social control.

The introduction discusses the connection between sexuality and social control. Not only is the meaning of sexuality socially constructed but also the responses these meanings evoke. Therefore, Nathanson devotes as much attention to the public response to adolescent pregnancy as to its social construction. As Foucault pointed out, sexuality has become an instrument for control over bodies and populations in Western societies. Thus, those individuals or groups who control sexuality wield considerable power. What forms has social control over young people taken and why?

Part II provides demographic background for changes in the social and political contexts that gave rise to concern about adolescent pregnancy. From the nineteenth to the twentieth centuries, the management of reproduction shifted from the private to public domain. Part III demonstrates how cultural conceptions of a young woman's "nature" and the structure of their lives fostered concern about female adolescence and channeled specific strategies for its control. Part IV analyzes contemporary models of sexual and reproductive control, particularly the role of the medical community as an agent of moral reform and the role of family planning agencies in social control. In this section Nathanson draws on empirical data from a study of nurses working in family planning clinics in Maryland.

Nathanson concludes that sexually unorthodox and reproductively uncontrolled adolescent women pose a threat to the foundation of the social order and become a metaphor for a loss of social control. Therefore, social groups attempt to manage this apparent deviance by focusing on individual failures rather than addressing the inadequacy of social institutions. Because pregnancy demonstrates that sex has occurred, it makes private behavior public. In the case of unmarried young women, it makes public a violation of social prescriptions. Such behavior is a threat to the social order because it challenges a patriarchal and gender based definition of the female role. Women who have premarital sex sacrifice their bargaining power for a suitable marriage, and, by implication, that of other women who rely on sex for access to traditional marriage. Therefore, limiting birth control becomes a form of social control for those who wish to retain sex as a route to marriage. Allowing premarital sex for women threatens a system based on a premise that men will support women and children. Until that premise changes, the sexuality of adolescent women will continue to be socially constructed as dangerous. (SGF)

PR,IL

311a. Stephenson, Patricia, and Marsden G. Wagner, eds. **Tough Choices: In Vitro Fertilization and the Reproductive Technologies.** Philadelphia: Temple University Press, 1993. 170 p. (Health, Society, and Policy). Includes bibliographic references. ISBN 1-56639-060-5.

Stephenson and Wagner, in this international collection of papers on modern reproductive technologies—in vitro fertilization (IVF), gamete intrafallopian transfer (GIFT), and others—contend that the medical field, industry, and government have not evaluated these medical technologies sufficiently to merit recommending them for general application. Unfortunately, they are in widespread use throughout the developed countries of the world.

Written primarily for professionals, the papers are also recommended for infertile people and the general public. Stephenson and Wagner, in their introductory essay "Infertility and In Vitro Fertilization," point out the lack of "scientifically valid data" concerning these techniques and warn that this new technology remains "an experimental procedure and its user be guided by all the principles and safeguards covering research on human subjects" (p. 1). They go on to discuss its prevalence, etiology, definitions, success measurements, risks, costs, and prevention as well as fertility management strategies and alternatives to the technology.

Part I, "Options for Infertile Men and Women," presents Joseph G. Schenker's paper on medically assisted conception that is a review of the state-of-the-art clinical practice; and Françoise Laborie's paper on social alternatives to infertility, including adoption, voluntary childlessness, and voluntary waiting.

Part II, "Technology Assessment," offers four papers: H. David Banta's evaluation of new health care technology, such as IVF; a paper on the effectiveness of IVF from an epidemiological perspective by Fiona J. Stanley and Sandra M. Webb; Ditta Bartels's paper on the financial costs of IVF in Australia; and Ger Haan's study of the cost-effectiveness analysis of health care services in the Netherlands.

In part III, three papers deal with "Risk Assessment": Stephenson explains the risks involved in ovulation induction during infertility treatment; Lene Koch evaluates the physiological and psychosocial risks in the new reproductive technologies which she points out are considerable; and the paper "The Neonatologist's Experience of In Vitro Fertilization Risks" by Jean-Pierre Relier, Michele Couchard, and Catherine Huon. Finally, part IV, "Law and Ethics," concludes with Sheila A. M. McLean's paper dealing with the legal aspects of modern reproductive technology, and Per-Gunnar Svensson and Stephenson's paper on "equity in resource allocation for the diagnosis and treatment of infertility" (p. 166). (TJW)

YA

312. Witt, Reni L., and Jeannine Masterson Michael. **Mom, I'm Pregnant.** New York: Stein and Day, 1982. 239 p. Includes bibliography and index. ISBN 0-8128-6173-6.

More than a million teenage girls become pregnant every year (one in ten high school girls), and most high school girls who have intercourse will get pregnant before they graduate. Primarily addressed to the large number of teenage girls who are or think they are pregnant, this supportive, clearly written book provides practical information to aid the pregnant teen in coping with the emotional, physical, and social facets of her situation. Witt and Michael, a counselor and a freelance writer, not only provide straightforward physiological information on teenage sex, pelvic examinations, pregnancy, birth, birth control, and abortion, but also provide information to aid the young women in weighing the alternatives so that she can decide what to do. Each decision point is realistically yet empathetically explored. Based on the experiences of thousands of teenage girls from all over the United States and Canada who came to the Eastern Women's Center in New York City, the book supplements factual information with the hopes and hurts of young women coping with their own pregnancies. Initial chapters confront the immediate questions that a girl may have: Am I as alone as I feel? How did this happen to me? How do I know if I'm really pregnant? How can I tell the important people in my life? Later chapters discuss a variety of options available to deal with the pregnancy: abortion, marriage, adoption, foster care, keeping the baby. The last chapters discuss the long-range repercussions of the option chosen by considering the course of pregnancy and childbirth as well as the adult responsibilities entailed in having a baby and continuing to engage in sexual relations. The book concludes with a sixty-seven page guide to hotlines and agencies in the United States and Canada that can aid a girl in getting a pregnancy test, counseling, and information on birth control. Parents, teenage women considering involvement in a sexual relationship, and boyfriends can all profit from reading this sensitively written book. As Harvey Caplan of the American Society of Educators, Counselors and Therapists points out, the book "should become a classic," and he suggests that "it be required reading for all teenagers whether or not they are sexually active." (SGF)

Birth Control. Contraception

(For related material see also entries 113, 116, 241, 1005, 1022)

IL,PO

313.   Billings, Evelyn, and Ann Westmore. **The Billings Method: Controlling Fertility Without Drugs or Devices.** New York: Random House, 1980. 254 p. Includes bibliographic references, index, and glossary. ISBN 0-394-52120-X.

In the interest of controlling and managing women's fertility, Dr. Evelyn Billings and her husband Dr. John Billings of Australia have developed the Billings Ovulation Method. Dating back to the early 1950s, their method involves recognition of "a stringy, lubricative mucus, produced at about the time of ovulation by the cells lining the cervix" (p. 17). According to them the mechanism starts with action of the hypothalamus on the pituitary and resultant hormones acting on the ovaries and their follicles, that begin to produce primitive eggs and a hormone called estradiol. Estradiol activates the cervix to produce the mucus, which then appears at the vaginal opening, signaling the state of fertility.

A woman's task is to recognize this specific type of mucus as the onset of fertility, and then to identify the basic fertility pattern in the menstrual cycle and the time during which intercourse may take place in order to achieve or avoid pregnancy. It has been shown that "over 90% of women can identify the fertile phase and the peak day of fertility in the first month of observation" (p. 36). After considerable research and testing trials around the world (Tonga, Australia, Korea, India, Ireland, and the United States), the ovulation method has been demonstrated to be a highly effective and superior fertility regulation method, provided women are motivated enough to examine their bodies regularly.

Billings describes her method in great detail, emphasizing the production of mucus in the menstrual cycle. But she also discusses topics related to the method: learning about fertility in adolescence, the pill, breastfeeding, menopause, conception, birth control devices, and the rhythm method of fertility control.

Included are a listing of teaching centers for the Billings Method around the world and a useful glossary of terms. (TJW)

PO

314.   Bullough, Vern L., and Bonnie Bullough. **Contraception: A Guide to Birth Control Methods.** Buffalo, N.Y.: Prometheus Books, 1990. 177 p. Includes bibliographic notes and index. ISBN 0-87975-589-X.

As a practical guide this book by Bullough and Bullough, both registered nurses, provides information on family planning as well as birth control methods. They state in the preface "that the ability of women to plan their pregnancies has been one of the most dramatic developments in human history." This ability "to plan pregnancies, or entirely avoid them," has "challenged the traditional concepts of the role and status of women in society, and has helped to make the relationship between the sexes more equal."

Following a largely historical chapter on aspects of contraception, Bullough and Bullough introduce basic information on male and female human anatomy and physiology. They then devote separate chapters to the various methods of birth control: barrier contraceptives (diaphragms, the cervical cap, the sponge); oral contraceptives; intrauterine devices (IUDs); spermicides; abstinence and the rhythm method; the condom; sterilization (vasectomy, tubal ligation); and abortion which, while not a form of contraception, can be construed as a form of birth control. In each of these methods, Bullough and Bullough discuss function, technique, effectiveness, advantages, risks, side effects, and disadvantages. A chapter on other forms of contraception introduces methods of withdrawal (*coitus interruptus*), *coitus reservatus*, postcoital douching, etc. Here they discuss other forms of sexual intercourse having contraceptive importance (anal intercourse, oral-genital sex, and mutual masturbation) as well as prospective contraceptive methods: the pill RU 486, Depo-Provera, male contraceptives, vaginal rings, progestin implants, injectables, anti-pregnancy vaccine, and electric contraceptives.

They conclude by pointing out that the choice of a birth control method involves the following major considerations: effectiveness of the method, side effects, personal preference, and the method's potential for disease prevention. They also look at the research frontier and identify five areas of importance: precise ovulation prediction, a reliable method of reversing male sterilization, a one-a-month pill for inducing menstruation, an anti-fertility vaccine, and a spermicide with better anti-viral properties. Finally, after calling for more research on contraceptives, they state, "The effect of all the discoveries . . . has been to lessen the importance of the sexual act as simply one of procreation and to emphasize the pleasurable aspects of sex" (p. 168). (TJW)

PO
315.   Everett, Jane, and Walter D. Glanze. **The Condom Book: The Essential Guide for Men and Women.** With an Introduction by Kenneth H. Mayer, M.D. New York: New American Library, 1987. 139 p. ISBN 0-451-15173-9.

Everett, a New York City journalist, and Glanze, a prolific editor of reference works and other books, designed this book to promote the correct, consistent use of condoms. The introduction by Mayer (Chief, Infectious Disease Division, Memorial Hospital, Pawtucket, R.I.) establishes the emphasis of the book: "Barring abstinence, or an enduring and exclusively monogamous relationship antedating the epidemic of AIDS, proper and persistent use of condoms provides the only significant protection against AIDS and other STDs" (p. xv). The F.D.A.'s statement about condoms, which concludes the text of the book, reiterates the need to use condoms as protection against STDs. The dominant theme of the text is that contemporary sexual relations are inherently dangerous because of the health hazards that they pose. Information about types of condoms and their usage provides some control over risks of contracting a STD. A twenty-two-page question and answer primer presents detailed, practical information on the use of condoms; it is designed to facilitate the acceptance of condom usage and to aid in dispelling myths and stereotypes about condoms. Everett and Glanze focus most of their attention on the use of condoms as prophylactics, not as contraceptives.

The bulk of the book is an annotated alphabetical list of over 108 specific brands of condoms. Each annotation has information on the name of the product, its manufacturer or distributor, packaging, description of the condom (e.g., material, shape, lubrication, odor, taste, color), and comments by users of the product. No mention is made of how many people tested each type of condom, nor was there any specification of the sample of users. Personal experience with the products is anecdotal. Additional comments give such information as price, reactions to manufacturers' claims, and caveats about usage. For example, "Despite its tickler feature, Thruster could function as a regular condom. See, however, the entry Ticklers—especially the cautionary words there." (SGF)

PO
316.   Goldstein, Marc, and Michael Feldberg. **The Vasectomy Book: A Complete Guide to Decision Making.** Foreword by C. Wayne Bardin, M.D. Los Angeles: Tarcher, 1982. 190 p. Includes bibliography, index, and glossary. ISBN 0-87477-207-9.

This book is intended not only for single or married men who are trying to decide to have a vasectomy but also for "physicians and family planners who must counsel individuals about the advisability of permanent sterilization." Goldstein and Feldberg provide a history of vasectomy, which was first performed in the United States in 1894; they are careful to identify all the wrong reasons for which the operation was performed (impotence, rejuvenation, control of masturbation, eugenics, and population control). They also provide a detailed description of the male reproductive system, including a discussion of the structure and function of each organ (testicles, epididymis, vas deferens, seminal vesicles, and prostate gland) and point out the effect of vasectomy (the cutting and sealing of the vasa deferentia) on the system. While vasectomy has no overall effect on the production of either sperm or hormones, or on the sensation of orgasm, it does render the person sterile, that is, incapable of procreating through intercourse.

In subsequent chapters Goldstein and Feldberg ask "Is vasectomy right for you?" "What are the emotional aftereffects?" and "What about the medical aftereffects?" Since vasectomy is a form of permanent contraception, a chapter is devoted to the comparison of birth control alternatives, including tubal ligation; hysterectomy; the pill; IUDs; diaphragms; condoms; rhythm; *coitus interruptus*; and gels, foams, and creams. Although 450,000 men have vasectomies in the United States each year, only about 10,000 to 30,000 seek to have the operation reversed. Vasectomy reversal by microsurgical methods is discussed.

Goldstein and Feldberg point out that since there is "no safe, highly effective, easy-to-use male contraceptive . . . on the horizon," men will continue to have vasectomies with a certain percentage continuing to have the operation reversed. However, the search for a male pill goes on, with universities and laboratories concentrating on stages of the male reproductive system: sperm production, sperm maturation, and sperm transport. (TJW)

IL,PO
317. Gordon, Linda. **Woman's Body, Woman's Right: A Social History of Birth Control in America.** New York: Grossman, 1976. 479 p. Includes bibliographic notes and index. ISBN 0-670-77817-6.

Birth control has always been closely associated with economic, moral, and feminist issues in the United States. Gordon's political and social history of the birth control movement in the United States focuses on these relationships.

Until the twentieth century, most of the widely practiced methods of reproductive control in the United States were illegal. The radical perfectionist and utopian reformers of the early nineteenth century provided a basis for the movement toward legal birth control. This movement was dramatically influenced by the American interpretation of British neo-Malthusian beliefs that poverty and its accompanying social ills were caused by overpopulation. The American feminist movement, emerging in the 1840s from the perfectionist background, adopted a neo-Malthusian philosophy along with eugenic concepts of controlling breeding to produce quality offspring. In the 1870s, the feminist movement called for "voluntary motherhood," advocating fewer children, selection of times for pregnancy, and the right of women to refuse intercourse. The voluntary motherhood reformers encouraged abstinence and male continence rather than the use of contraceptive devices. Almost as a backlash, male political leaders raised the issue of "race suicide," accusing women who wished to limit their families of being selfish, unnatural, and responsible for the decline in the birth rate among the upper classes. The medical community identified birth control as harmful, immoral, and dangerous.

Around 1900, progressive medical professionals reversed their stand on birth control. The radical social changes of the early twentieth century, which included sexual permissiveness, resulted in great gains for the birth control movement. The primary organizers, Emma Goldman and Margaret Sanger, became active during this time. Goldman endorsed birth control as part of women's rights, but could not make it a popular cause because of her extremist politics. Sanger, after an early radical period, established the American Birth Control League, which engaged the support of physicians and academicians, argued for a bill to legalize medical distribution of contraceptive devices, and opened birth control clinics across the country. The recurring theme of eugenics led to charges of genocide; however, the growth of the Nazi party and the economic ruin of the Great Depression led birth control leaders to turn to economic issues. The change of name to Planned Parenthood in 1938 marked a change in the organization's emphasis to defense of the family, endorsement of women's independence, and, eventually, a call for worldwide population control.

The historical separation between birth control reform and the feminist movement in the United States weakened both movements. Reproductive freedom can only be achieved as part of a wider movement toward women's freedom. (SDH)

PR,IL
318. Himes, Norman E. **Medical History of Contraception.** With a new preface by Christopher Tietze, M.D. Medical foreword by Robert Latou Dickinson, M.D. New York: Schocken Books, 1970. 521 p. Includes bibliography and index.

First published in 1936, this work remains (according to the preface of the 1970 edition) "the only large-scale effort in the English language, and indeed in any language, to fully document man's attempts to control his fertility from prehistoric to modern times." The book is a readable chronicle of humanity's ageless struggle to achieve "adequate parenthood." The book's scope is wide, touching on the anthropologic, economic, and sociologic aspects of the subject. Described first are some of the ingenious and occasionally successful techniques of various preliterate societies around the world in preventing conception. The account continues chronologically through antiquity (Egyptians, Greeks, Romans, Asians, Islamics, and so forth) through the Middle Ages and up to the modern era of prophylactics and pills. The last part of the book deals with the diffusion, democratization, and socialization of birth control knowledge, an important trend that first became prominent in the nineteenth century and continues to this day, and the effects of this dissemination of knowledge on world population characteristics. The bibliography is extensive. (EBS)

PO,YA
319. Lieberman, E. James, and Ellen Peck. **Sex & Birth Control: A Guide for the Young.** Revised ed. Introduction by Mary S. Calderone. New York: Schocken Books, 1982. 277 p. Includes index. ISBN 0-8052-0701-5.

Lieberman, a physician who specializes in adolescent sexuality, and Peck, a syndicated teen columnist, try to answer practical questions about birth control and to address straightforwardly some general social and psychological issues that surround teenage sexuality. Since parents may not know some essential information about birth control, and sex education courses bypass it by stressing only the anatomy and physiology of sex and reproduction, parents as well as teenagers can benefit from reading this book. Lieberman and Peck think that many young people are physically ready for intercourse before they are emotionally prepared for it; this "sex gap" may lead to the "baby trap"—early marriage and parenthood for which the adolescent is even less prepared. Approximately 10 percent of women in the fifteen-to-twenty-year-old age group get pregnant every year, but most of them did not plan to conceive. Therefore, it is important for teenagers to understand the choices and responsibilities that accompany sexual freedom. Knowledge about birth control is an integral part of this understanding. Lieberman and Peck combine information about why, how, and the extent to which various types of birth control work, with a point of view that stresses the importance of integrating "sex" with respect, affection, and love. Based on the assumption that teenagers are ready to learn about sex and to use information to aid them in coping with relationships, the book is forthright and non-moralistic in its presentation of research on teenage sexuality and of the facts that teenagers want to know about birth control. Answers to questions that teenagers often ask follow most chapters. The concluding chapters grapple with difficult questions about sex education, normality, morality, the future of marriage and parenthood, and overpopulation. Lieberman and Peck do not shirk from giving specific advice. For example, "If you plan to have sex, be prepared; if you're not prepared, wait; if you can't wait, at least don't be caught off guard a second time" (p. 15). In 1973 the first edition of this updated guide for the young was selected by the American Library Association as one of the Best Books for Young Adults. (SGF)

PR,IL

320.   McLaren, Angus. **A History of Contraception: From Antiquity to the Present Day.** Oxford, Eng.: Basil Blackwell, 1990. 275 p. (Family, Sexuality, and Social Relations in Past Times). Includes bibliographic notes and index. ISBN 0-631-16711-0.

In the introduction McLaren states that this study is "the first comprehensive overview of the history of fertility control" since Norman Himes's classic work, *A Medical History of Contraception*, published in 1936. What McLaren attempts is an account of fertility control in the ancient and medieval worlds as well as in the modern world. He devotes separate chapters to Ancient Greece, the Roman Empire, the Christian West, the Middle Ages, early modern Europe, the industrializing West, and the twentieth century.

Rather than concentrating his study on well-known contraceptive devices to limit pregnancies, he covers the full range of fertility control methods that have been used since earliest times, including abstinence, *coitus interruptus*, prolonged breastfeeding, abortion, and infanticide. Rather than providing a straightforward account of the development of birth control methods through the ages, McLaren examines the important social, cultural, religious, and gender factors obtaining in each society or group that affect the fertility control decision making by the men and women concerned.

McLaren debunks "social scientists who argue that the history of family planning is a tale of unalloyed advances" (p. 2) over the past century; they forget that fertility has always been controlled, whether to promote it or curtail it, although not necessarily with modern birth control devices. Indeed, sometimes the modern methods backfire, as in some Third World countries, where older traditional methods have been displaced by modern techniques, and population growth has exploded.

McLaren's examination of the cultural contexts of fertility control in different places at different times reveals the effectiveness of traditional methods used by people in response to societal and cultural pressures. As they promote modern methods of birth control, the birth controllers might be less sanguine about their achievements if they took note of past approaches to fertility control used by people.

For McLaren, "The modern contraceptive 'revolution' is in some senses simply an increase in degree of control available and the percentage of the population exercising such controls" (p. 5). It must be acknowledged that "Fertility control has always been a culturally dependent category" (p. 5). (TJW)

PR,IL

321.   Noonan, John T., Jr. **Contraception: A History of Its Treatment by the Catholic Theologians and Canonists.** Cambridge, Mass.: Belknap Press of Harvard University Press, 1966. 561 p. Includes bibliographic footnotes and index. ISBN 0-674-16853-4.

The stated purpose of this history of the point of view of the Roman Catholic Church toward contraception is met very fully, and the background material employed is so complete that it may also be regarded as a history of Western attitudes and contraceptive practices. It is presented in four phases: Part 1, "Shaping of the Doctrine (50-450)"; part 2, "The Condemnation Ingrained (450-1450)"; part 3, "Innovation and Preservation (1450-1750)"; and part 4, "Development and Controversy (1750-1965)." The Jewish background to early Christian attitudes is discussed mainly on the basis of the Old Testament, but later Jewish attitudes as given in the Babylonian Talmud, the Tosefta, and the Midrash are also considered. Christian attitudes are described from the New Testament and the Apostolic Fathers. Later Catholic material concerns the writings of theologians and canon lawyers.

Although contraception was not formally proclaimed a mortal sin until the High Middle Ages, many relevant distinctions were made very early, such as that between contraceptives and abortifacients. The nature of contraception was broadly conceived. In addition to the use of physical barriers and medicinals, the employment of anaphrodisiacs, sex acts other than coitus, the biblical sin of withdrawal (with or without seminal emission), and sterilization for the sole purpose of avoiding pregnancy also qualified as contraception. Although considered non-sinful, virginity, celibacy, and temporary abstinence were also formally deemed contraceptive acts. Coitus was considered licit only when it had a conscious procreative purpose. Later theological considerations bore heavily on sin and the need for penance. Contraception was seen as injury against the human race (or a particular population), against the family, against the self, against nature, and against God. The penitential acts, however, "were of a fragile spiritual kind, dependent not on courts to enforce, but on hearts to accept." Later Catholic theological consideration of contraception as sin, although based on broader scientific knowledge, retained this attitude of penance based on private individual remorse. (DJS)

PR,IL
322. Raspe, Gerhard, ed. **Schering Workshop on Contraception: The Masculine Gender (Berlin, November 29 to December 2, 1972).** Oxford, Eng.: Pergamon Press, 1973. 332 p. Includes bibliographies and index.
This collection of twenty-four papers from a workshop on male contraception consists primarily of reports and speculations on biological and biochemical research with implications for development of additional forms of male contraception. Lay readers may be most interested in Alfred Jost's paper "Becoming a Male" ("Becoming a male is a prolonged, uneasy, and risky venture; it is a kind of struggle against inherent trends toward femaleness"); Brigitta Linnér's feminist call for equality in society, in family, and in bed; and (above all) Caroline Merula Days and David Malcolm Pott's essay "Condoms and Things," dealing with male involvement in contraception. Days and Pott argue that family planning programs are geared for female contraception when "male methods of contraception have been and remain numerically the most important in nearly all countries." These male methods include *coitus interruptus*, condoms, and vasectomy. In addition, males often take responsibility for female birth control (e.g., seeing that the woman has a supply of birth control pills and takes them regularly). Days and Pott conclude: "Men are in the majority as family-planning users in nearly all countries." The book closes with a "manifesto" of desiderata for new forms of male contraceptives. (**Men's Studies,** 1985)

PR,IL
323. Reed, James. **From Private Vice to Public Virtue: The Birth Control Movement and American Society Since 1830.** New York: Basic Books, 1978. 456 p. Includes bibliographic notes and index. ISBN 0-465-02582-X.
Focusing primarily on the contributions of Margaret Sanger, Robert Latou Dickinson, and Clarence Gamble, Reed traces the development of the American birth control movement from the early part of the nineteenth century to the late twentieth century in this in-depth study. He also pays attention to the efforts of a host of other important figures in the movement, including Emma Goldman, Ben L. Reitman, Katherine B. Davis, Mary Ware Dennett, Katherine Dexter McCormick, John Rock, Min-Cheuh Chang, and Gregory Goodwin Pincus.
An introductory part I, "Birth Control Before Margaret Sanger," examines the declining birth rate in the United States between 1800 and 1940, attributing its causes generally to the transition from a traditional to a modern society and particularly to changes in personal reproductive behavior. The usual methods of birth control throughout the nineteenth century were *coitus interruptus*, douching with spermicides, the pessary, eventually condoms, and abstinence. Early treatises on marriage and the family contain information on birth control methods, e.g., Charles Knowlton's *Fruits of Philosophy*. These marriage manuals assumed singular importance with the rise of the nuclear family, specified sex roles for men and women; and promoted the notion of family limitation. On the other hand, contraception was condemned by the law, public opinion, the church, and organized medicine. Indeed, a high standard of morality was being upheld by purity crusaders and zealous enforcers, such as Anthony Comstock.
Parts II, III, and V analyze the efforts of Sanger, Dickinson, and Gamble to spread contraceptive knowledge. Although they often cooperated, their approaches to the

problem were quite different. Sanger's approach sprang from a "feminist impulse, the desire to give women control over their bodies." From 1914 to 1937 she led a successful campaign "to remove the stigma of obscenity from contraception and to establish a nationwide system of birth control clinics." Indeed, on October 16, 1916, she opened the first American birth control clinic in the Brownsville section of Brooklyn, New York.

Robert Latou Dickinson was a gynecologist, medical advocate of contraception, and author of several important studies on human sexuality. While Sanger's efforts forced changes in the law and demonstrated that birth control worked, Dickinson over the years overcome the reluctance of the medical profession to add contraception to the normal repertoire of medical services. Through his Committee on Maternal Health, founded in 1923, he promoted clinical research on contraception, sterility, abortion, and related issues. He also gave instruction on contraceptives as part of normal premarital advice, promoted cooperation between the birth control movement and organized medicine, and in 1937 brought about the official acceptance of contraception by the American Medical Association.

At the urging of Dickinson, Clarence Gamble, pharmacologist and heir to the Ivory soap fortune, committed himself to the birth control movement. He "concentrated his efforts on a search for alternatives to the doctor-diaphragm-special-clinic regimen" (p. 226). He wanted cheap, but improved contraceptives; he wanted to disseminate these contraceptives widely, especially to the poor, who had no access to either clinics or physicians. By the time of his death in 1966, Gamble had spent a large portion of his wealth promoting the birth control movement.

Reed goes on to discuss the development of the anovulant pill. He relates how Gregory Pincus, a physiologist at Harvard, noted for his *in vitro* fertilization of ova, was introduced to Katherine Dexter McCormick by Margaret Sanger. A philanthropist as well as a fighter for women's rights, McCormick provided financial support to Pincus and his colleagues for hormonal research and the development of a birth control pill. By 1960, the pill Enovid, a progestin/estrogen steroid, was developed, tested in Puerto Rico, and marketed.

Reed's final chapter, "The Trouble with Family Planning," reviews the accomplishments of the population control movement but casts doubt on the claim that it has effectively reduced the rate of fertility in the United States. Moreover, the family planning problem is that it has never been wholeheartedly embraced by the nations of the world or, for that matter, by the United States. (TJW)

PR,IL
323a.   Reilly, Philip R. **The Surgical Solution: A History of Involuntary Sterilization in the United States.** Baltimore: Johns Hopkins University Press, 1991. 190 p. Includes bibliographic notes and index. ISBN 0-8018-4096-1.

Physician and attorney Reilly states in his preface: "During the first six decades of the twentieth century, more than 60,000 mentally retarded or mentally ill individuals, most of them residents of large state institutions, were sterilized for eugenic reasons." Most of this sterilization, begun in the nineteenth century, was involuntary, done in the belief that defective genes were responsible for the antisocial behavior of the feebleminded, the insane, epileptics, paupers, alcoholics, and criminals. If these unfortunates could be effectively sterilized, the nation's gene pool would be cleansed of impurities. Reilly traces "the rise and decline of eugenics sterilization programs in the United States." He shows that the movement developed locally; two-thirds of all states passed laws applying to those residents in state institutions, such as asylums and hospitals.

Reilly also reveals the intellectual justification for sterilization of degenerates on the basis of evolutionary theory, Mendelian genetics, and eugenics. He also points to technical developments achieved between 1898 and 1920: vasectomy (for men), and salpingectomy (for women). The coming together of theory and practice, coupled with fear of the inheritability of degeneracy, gave rise to the belief that the nation should rid itself of degenerates if only laws could be passed enforcing a eugenics program. Backed by wealthy Americans, physicians, and scientists, the movement made progress in eighteen states across the country between 1905 and 1921. In this period, California led the states with 2,558 sterilizations.

In the landmark case *Buck v. Bell*, the Virginia Supreme Court and later the U.S. Supreme Court (1927) upheld a Virginia law allowing involuntary sterilization of "potential parents of socially inadequate offspring" (p. 67). Justice Oliver Wendell Holmes wrote the majority opinion that includes these ringing words: "It is better for all the world if, instead of waiting to execute degenerate offspring for crime, or to let them starve for their imbecility, society can prevent those who are manifestly unfit from continuing their kind" (p. 87). The pace of eugenic sterilization in the United States picked up and did not slacken until World War II when the availability of trained surgeons was curtailed by the war effort.

Reilly makes clear that criticism of eugenic sterilization programs came from many quarters, including leading geneticists, prominent social scientists, physicians, and the Catholic Church. The Nazi's use of sterilization in the interest of creating a master race also caused much concern in the West. In spite of this opposition, many programs persisted. Sterilization increased in North Carolina and Virginia but declined in California. As of 1985, "at least nineteen states had laws that permitted the sterilization of mentally retarded persons" (p. 148). Also, interest in sterilization as a right became an issue in the 1960s; after *Roe v. Wade*, voluntary sterilization, like abortion, became constitutionally protected on the basis of a person's right to privacy.

Finally, in discussing the etiology of mental retardation, Reilly states that "our understanding of the causes of mental retardation does not permit us to conclude that sterilization of retarded persons would significantly alter the prevalence of retardation in future generations." Furthermore, he states that "the era of involuntary sterilization for eugenic reasons seems over" and "the more pressing problem currently is how to assert a retarded person's *right* to be sterilized" (p. 160). (TJW)

IL
324. Shapiro, Howard I. **The New Birth Control Book: A Complete Guide for Women and Men.** New York: Prentice-Hall, 1988. 306 p. Includes bibliography and index. ISBN 0-13-611781-3.

Shapiro, a Connecticut gynecologist, has written this ready-reference book on the subjects of contraception, sterilization, and abortion for women and men who are concerned and confused about the effects of contraception on their bodies. He believes that women have become disenchanted with the medical establishment because of poor advice on birth control they have been given in recent years, and he blames the situation on physicians, manufacturers, and the Food and Drug Administration.

This work, however, is not a polemic on that issue, but rather a compendium of up-to-date, factual information on birth control conceived in the broadest terms. The information, which is generously illustrated with pictures, diagrams, and charts, is presented in a question-and-answer format. Each of the eleven, clearly written chapters covers a distinct topic within the field of birth control: the reproductive system; birth control pills; diaphragms, spermicides, and condoms; *coitus interruptus* and rhythm; postcoital contraception; abortion; vasectomy; tubal ligation; hysterectomy; and the future. Each chapter on birth control methods contains a wealth of technical data and information on procedures, effectiveness, side effects, risks, and possible medical consequences. The last chapter on the future presents modern methods of contraception, sterilization, and abortion. (TJW)

IL
325. Winikoff, Beverly, and Suzanne Wymelenberg. **The Contraceptive Handbook: A Guide to Safe and Effective Choices.** Yonkers, N.Y.: Consumers Union, 1992. 248 p. (Consumer Reports Books). Includes bibliography and index. ISBN 0-89043-430-1.

Covering all types of modern contraceptive methods available in the United States, this compact guide summarizes what is known about each device or treatment. Intended for "men and women of all ages who are sexually active or about to become so," this handbook is designed to help weigh the advantages and disadvantages of each method. Following an illustrated introductory chapter on the anatomy and physiology of sex and reproduction, embracing such topics as ovulation, fertilization, tubal pregnancy, and menstruation as well as sexual intercourse and how contraceptives work, Winikoff and Wymelenberg devote five chapters to the principal methods of birth control. Chapter 1 covers the barrier methods: the condom, the diaphragm, the cervical cap, the contraceptive sponge, and spermicides. In each case advantages and disadvantages, safety concerns, effectiveness, health matters, use, and costs are discussed. Chapter 2 describes the main hormonal methods of birth control. These include birth control pills, or oral contraceptives, which "offer almost complete protection against pregnancy when taken as prescribed" (p. 69). Principal types are the combination pills, containing synthetic estrogen and progestin; the progestin-only minipills; and Norplant, that requires insertion of six flexible and slender rods under the skin of the inner upper arm.

Chapter 3 discusses intrauterine devices (IUDs), usually made of plastic, that are inserted in the uterus. Two types—Progestasert and ParaGard T 380A—are approved by the FDA. Chapter 4 covers the surgical methods of contraception, mainly tubal ligation for females, and vasectomy for males. Standard techniques of performing these operations as well as effectiveness and reversibility, are discussed and illustrated.

Chapter 5 is devoted to other methods of fertility control, such as the calendar rhythm method, the temperature method, the cervical mucus method, the symptothermal method, withdrawal, and morning-after contraception.

Chapter 6 examines other issues in birth control. These include abortion, breast-feeding and contraception, and new contraceptive options (female condoms, vaginal rings, timed-release injectable microspheres, and Depo-Provera, a long-acting injectable progestin). (TJW)

Abortion

(For related material see also entries 726a, 1017, 1018)

IL,PO

326. Baulieu, Etienne-Emile, with Mort Rosenblum. **The "Abortion Pill": RU-486, a Woman's Choice.** New York: Simon & Schuster, 1991. 238 p. Originally published in 1990. Translation of: *Génération pilule.* Includes index. ISBN 0-671-73816-X.

Baulieu, Professor of Biochemistry on the medical faculty of Paris-Sud and Director of INSERM (Institut de la Santé de la Recherche Médicale), prefers to call RU-486 the "unpregnancy pill" rather than the "abortion pill." RU-486, which Baulieu discovered in 1980, is an anti-hormone that neutralizes progesterone, a hormone that maintains pregnancy. It binds to the progesterone receptor and blocks the work of the hormone. In effect, it stops the gestation process by breaking down the embryo bond to the uterine wall. The effectiveness of RU-486 is improved by the administration of prostaglandins, another natural hormone. Baulieu states that the use of RU-486 is a "new method of menstrual regulation, neither contraceptive nor abortive" (p. 27); rather it is contragestive. He reveals that RU-486 has application beyond the field of reproduction, in treating breast cancer, brain tumors, and Cushing's syndrome.

Baulieu tells of the first presentation about RU-486 before the French Academy of Sciences on April 19, 1982, and recalls the massive, unanticipated press coverage that followed, hailing the arrival of a new birth control and abortion pill. He also describes the debates that followed, the international repercussions, and the adverse reactions of the Catholic Church, fundamentalists, and the right-to-life movement. In separate chapters he recounts in detail the French experience with RU-486, the spread of information about it throughout the world, and the reactions in the United States where much of the opposition to RU-486 is based on religious grounds.

After a sobering chapter on world population growth (at the present rate, world population will reach 6.4 billion people by the year 2001 and 10 billion before the year 2050), Baulieu discusses the medical role of RU-486 in fertility control. Baulieu also looks into the future and evaluates the different methods of birth control we have now, the potential for RU-486 in treating a host of human medical problems besides fertility; and the medical, legal, ethical, and religious questions involved in determining when a human being begins to exist. (TJW)

PR,IL
327.   Callahan, Sidney, and Daniel Callahan, eds. **Abortion: Understanding Differences.** New York: Plenum Press, 1984. 338 p. (The Hasting Center Series in Ethics). Includes bibliographic footnotes and index. ISBN 0-306-41640-9.

"Conflicts over abortion reflect various views about how to live a good life in a good society." To explore differences in people's backgrounds that tend to eventuate in pro-life or pro-choice positions, Callahan and Callahan, a married couple with several children, set up a project in which eight selected contributors (four pro-life and four pro-choice) from the fields of philosophy, sociology, social work, psychiatry, and political science were invited to submit articles in four general areas: abortion and the family, childbearing and childrearing, women and abortion, and abortion and the culture. Each article is preceded by an autobiographical introduction, emphasizing particularly those aspects of upbringing and life experience that might be expected to have influenced the contributor's attitude toward abortion. Each article is followed by an extended commentary by another of the contributors holding a differing view. Preceding the eight argumentative articles, two articles by sociologists provide background about the ways people relate the abortion issue to broader values: one analyzes data from public opinion surveys, and the other analyzes the world views of pro-life and pro-choice activists. The two concluding articles are by Sidney Callahan and Daniel Callahan, each followed by a commentary by the other. All of the contributors except Daniel Callahan are women, but this was not deliberate. A disproportionate number come from Catholic backgrounds, but only half of these are practicing Catholics, and a third of them adopt a pro-choice position. The articles necessarily include most of the common arguments involved in the abortion controversy, but the book succeeds in its goal of illustrating some of the personal attitudes leading to a variety of positions on the pro-life/pro-choice spectrum. (DJS)

PR
328.   Connery, John R. **Abortion: The Development of the Roman Catholic Perspective.** Chicago: Loyola University Press, 1977. 336 p. Includes bibliographic notes. ISBN 0-8294-0257-8.

This historical study follows the development of Western Christian attitudes toward abortion up to the Reformation, followed by Roman Catholic attitudes until 1950. The Jewish background is explored in the first chapter, where it is brought out that the only mention of abortion in the Bible occurs in the Hebrew version of the Old Testament, which states that a man whose pregnant wife has been struck by another man so as to cause a miscarriage may demand a fine (Exodus 21:22-25). In the Jewish translation into Greek (Septuagint), this passage is altered to demand a life for a life if the fetus is perfectly formed. The Roman background (chapter 2) completes the coverage of pre-Christian influences.

The period from early Christianity to 1869 (chapters 3-11) comprises the main body of the text, that is followed (chapters 12-15) by an extended discussion of the Catholic Church's last major controversy regarding abortion: this concerned the licitness of craniotomy and dismemberment of the fetus during deliveries that threaten the life of the mother. Because of its emphasis on historical development, the book does not provide an unambiguous statement of the current Roman Catholic doctrine as applied to abortion. Rather it is a record of how the Church viewed abortion issues in the past. The book addresses many specifically religious concerns, including the question of the time at which the embryo or fetus gains its soul, the necessity of baptism before death, and the implications of the dogma of the Immaculate Conception. With minor exceptions, the focus of the book is on deliberate abortion intended to safeguard the life of the mother. (DJS)

PR,IL

329.   Costa, Marie. **Abortion: A Reference Handbook.** Santa Barbara, Calif.: ABC-Clio, 1991. 258 p. (Contemporary World Issues). Includes bibliographies, index, and glossaries. ISBN 0-87436-602-X.

In the United States abortion is a woman's legal right. Nowhere else in the world is this so. The conflict between the pro-choice and pro-life parties over abortion is sometimes viewed as one "between traditional family values and self-expression and fulfillment, between Judeo-Christian ethics and the more amorphous 'situational ethics,' between selflessness and selfishness" (p. xii). So Marie Costa put the issue in her book *Abortion.*

"The purpose of this book," she explains, "is to provide access to available information as well as the full spectrum of thought, on abortion. It is not intended to promulgate any view, except the view that all voices should be heard and listened to" (p. xiv). Intended for activists, historians, journalists, laypersons, researchers, students, and writers, the handbook brings together information from a wide array of sources, covering the history of abortion, biography, statistics, abortion techniques, a directory of resources, a bibliography, and a listing of nonprint materials. In order to maintain an impartial and balanced approach to the material, Costa tries to use the language that the pro-choice and pro-life advocates would use themselves.

The first chapter is a detailed chronology covering significant legislation, court decisions, medical developments, trends, political events, religious proclamations, and other occurrences from 1588 to 1991. Chapter 2 presents twenty-three biographical sketches of key personalities drawn from the pro-choice and pro-life camps of the abortion conflict. Costa includes such figures as Faye Wattleton, Eleanor Smeal, and Molly Yard from the pro-choice side and Judie Brown, Henry Hyde, and Bernard Nathanson from the pro-life side.

In chapter 3, "Facts and Statistics," Costa presents such important information as worldwide laws and policies, abortion statistics, abortion techniques, abortion complications and risks, an overview of embryonic and fetal development, harassment of abortion providers, and public opinion about abortion. Chapter 4 provides an annotated directory of fifty-nine organizations within activist groups, research organizations, educational institutions, legal defense funds, political lobbying groups, and support services that include alternatives to abortion. For each organization she provides address, purpose and goals, membership fees, and a rundown on publications, if any.

Chapter 5 is a fully annotated bibliography of selected print sources: bibliographies, anthologies, books and monographs, periodicals, and subscriber-based news services. The last chapter, "Selected Nonprint Resources," includes detailed descriptions of a computer database search service and numerous films and videocassettes on the subject. (TJW)

PR

330.   Devereux, George. **A Study of Abortion in Primitive Societies: A Typological, Distributional, and Dynamic Analysis of the Prevention of Birth in 400 Preindustrial Societies.** Revised edition. New York: International Universities Press, 1976. 414 p. Original edition published in 1955. Includes bibliography and indexes. ISBN 0-8236-6245-4.

At the outset of his study of abortion in 400 traditional societies, Devereux states the three main purposes of the 1955 edition of the book: (1) "to develop a typology of practices and attitudes pertaining to abortion"; (2) to provide a large body of data to support two theses, one methodological and the other substantive; and (3) to provide relatively exhaustive source material on abortion to support further research on the subject. Therefore, this work uses the subject of abortion (which "was chosen more or less accidentally") to demonstrate the utility and implications of cross-cultural research. Overall, "the chief purpose of this work is to add another inch to the bridge which, one day, will inevitably link the social and the psychological sciences." In the preface to the second edition, Devereux reiterates the contribution of his work—elucidation of abortion as a scientific and human problem—and, he specifically refuses to engage in "complacently hollow rhetoric" about abortion.

The goal of part 1, "Typology" is to demonstrate the plasticity of humans by documenting the range of attitudes and practices related to abortion in a variety of cultural groups. The main categories for clustering the information are: motivation, alternatives, frequency, time, techniques, physical consequences, the aborted fetus, the abortionist, attitudes, and social action. Devereux provides examples of beliefs and customs for each category, all of which are preceded by a brief bibliography of the sources of the information.

The goal of part 2, "Culture and the Unconscious," is to show that in-depth clinical studies as well as broad cross-cultural studies of a single trait may produce similar conclusions. Using the cross-cultural data in part 3, "Source Material," Devereux demonstrates the validity of psychoanalytic hypotheses about the meaning of abortion, thus showing that Freud's conclusions about his middle-class Viennese patients have universal applicability. Devereux maintains that there are unconscious attitudes and fantasies that play a role in explaining the reasons for abortion: "abortion invariably represents a trauma and is actuated by conflicts, which, after the completion of abortion, lead to additional conflicts and stresses." Parents' identification with their children's sibling-rivalry conflicts, their own counteroedipal conflicts, flight from parenthood, or pressure from the prospective father may all prompt abortions.

Devereux selects and lists alphabetically 400 ethnic groups, or primarily traditional societies, in part 3. A great deal of the data is found in the Human Relations Area Files (HRAF) at Yale University. Each entry is accompanied by one or more bibliographic sources with one or more quotations about abortion from each source. From his data Devereux develops seven groups, or categories, useful in the grouping of ethnic traits. These groups are Motive, Involuntary or Forced Abortion, Techniques, Attitudes, Penalties and Consequences, Penalty for Not Aborting, and Abortion as Penalty. Traits are subsumed under each group and finally a set of symbols, or notation, is assigned to the traits. In part 4 he develops a table of traits by matching by symbol each of the tribes with the seven groups, thereby creating a quick method for looking up information about aspects of abortion among the tribes.

In part 5, Devereux concludes that "the psychology of the aborting woman has certain affinities with that of the woman who carries her normal fetus to term." (TJW/SGF)

IL

331. Faux, Marian. **Roe v. Wade: The Untold Story of the Landmark Supreme Court Decision That Made Abortion Legal.** New York: Macmillan, 1988. 370 p. Includes bibliography and index. ISBN 0-02-537151-7.

The *Roe v. Wade* story begins with a meeting in Dallas, Texas, in December 1969 when Norma McCorvey, a pregnant woman seeking an abortion, Linda Coffee, her lawyer, and Sarah Weddington, an assistant city attorney, conferred about the feasibility of challenging the Texas abortion law. McCorvey agreed to assist by suing the state of Texas in order to get the court to allow her to have an abortion. Permission to have an abortion would entitle all women in Texas in similar circumstances to have abortions. The court's ruling in favor of McCorvey could have an impact not only on Texas women seeking abortions but also on women everywhere.

Faux goes on to show how McCorvey (using the pseudonym Jane Roe) and her attorneys sued District Attorney Henry Wade of Dallas County, stating that the abortion statutes of Texas were unconstitutional, and claiming that if law enforcement officials in Texas could not enforce the abortion laws, then Jane Roe should be free to obtain an abortion from a licensed physician. Indeed, before the three-judge Fifth Circuit Court meeting in Dallas, the decision was made on June 17, 1970 in favor of the plaintiff, finding that the Texas abortion law was unconstitutional. The judges wrote: "On the merits, plaintiffs argue as their principal contention that the Texas abortion laws must be declared unconstitutional because they deprive single women and married couples of their right, secured by the Ninth Amendment, to choose whether to have children. We agree." Unfortunately, the judges refused to back up their decision with an injunction to stop enforcing the abortion law, stating that it would be excessive interference in the affairs of a state.

The next step for Coffee and Weddington was to take their case to the United States Supreme Court, which they did, Weddington arguing the case, that was in essence a challenge to the constitutionality of all state abortion laws. Argument took place in December 1971. Weddington placed her case on a constitutional footing, stating that she believed the Ninth and Fourteenth Amendments as the proper places for the abortion right to reside. The justices probed various aspects of abortion: mootness, the impact of pregnancy on a woman's life, when is a fetus protected by the Constitution, fetal rights, and so forth.

Following oral arguments, Justice Blackmun was chosen to write the majority opinion; the Burger court was enlarged by two new appointments by President Nixon; drafts of opinions were circulated among the justices; and reargument (to clarify certain points) was held on October 10, 1972.

The Supreme Court made its decision on January 22, 1973, Justice Blackmun reading an abbreviated version of the opinion before the court. He stated that a woman had a privacy right to abortion, grounded in either the Fourteenth Amendment's concept of liberty or in the Ninth Amendment's reservation of rights to the people. But he went on, the right was not absolute, stating that "the pregnant woman cannot be isolated in her privacy." In certain circumstances the state could intrude: for moral reasons, to protect a woman's health, and to protect potential life. He went on to discuss the difficult question of when life begins and the stages of pregnancy. A scathing dissent from the majority opinion of 8 to 2 came from Justice Byron White and Justice Rehnquist. In any case, the decision struck down all state abortion laws.

Throughout the book Faux describes both the activities of the reform movement and the opposition forces, as well as the reactions to the decisions of the courts. She points out that "Supreme Court decisions generally unite the nation more than divide it." Unfortunately, *Roe v. Wade* would prove to be the rare decision that did not unite the nation. After so many years, abortion remains a great unresolved issue in American society. (TJW)

PR

332.   Glendon, Mary Ann. **Abortion and Divorce in Western Law.** Cambridge, Mass.: Harvard University Press, 1987. 197 p. (Rosenthal lectures; 1986). Includes bibliographic notes and index. ISBN 0-674-00161-3.

In this study, Glendon, Professor of Law, Harvard Law School, makes cross-national comparisons in the areas of abortion law and divorce law in order to better understand Anglo-American law as it pertains to the legal situation on abortion and divorce in the United States. What she discovers as a result of these comparisons is that in the United States "we have less regulation of abortion in the interest of the fetus than any other Western nation, but we provide less public support for maternity and child rearing" (p. 2). As to divorce, "we have been less diligent than most other countries in seeking to integrate the economic casualties of divorce through public assistance or enforcement of private support obligations" (p. 2).

The above conclusions were reached as the result of a comparative analysis of abortion and divorce laws in twenty countries of Western Europe and North America. In two countries (Belgium, Ireland) abortion is illegal; in twelve countries (Portugal, Spain, Switzerland, England, France, Finland, West Germany, Iceland, Italy, Luxembourg, Netherlands) abortion is allowed for cause; and in six countries (Austria, Denmark, Greece, Norway, Sweden, U.S.) there is elective abortion.

Glendon shows that the United States has the most anomalous and liberal abortion and divorce laws of all the countries studied. She asks, "Why . . . is the abortion debate dominated by talk of 'rights'?" "Why did the term 'no fault divorce' arise and take hold of the context of American divorce law reform?" For answers, she delves into the evolution of laws on the European continent, where lawgivers, influenced by the political and educational views of Rousseau, developed civil codes that were concerned with the welfare and improvement of the citizenry. In contrast, Anglo-American law, devoid of a directional basis, developed case by case, is viewed "no more or less than a command backed up by organized coercion" (p. 7). Glendon looks for guidance to a few American scholars who have begun to examine law in new ways, including anthropologist Clifford Geertz, who has "advised comparative lawyers that . . . law is not just an ingenious collection of devices to avoid or adjust disputes and to advance this or that interest, but also a way that a society makes sense of things" (p. 8). From this perspective, legal systems "will differ in the 'stories they tell,' the 'symbols they display,' and the 'visions they project' " (p. 8).

This approach, Glendon believes, should ameliorate legal thinking in America, allowing our lawgivers to pay greater attention to those aspects of abortion (and divorce) law that will bring about (1) accommodation of the opposing views now held by the pro-choice and pro-life factions, and (2) promote greater concern for the consequences of abortion (and divorce), especially the social and financial impact on all family members.

Glendon regrets the fashionable view "within the American legal profession since the late nineteenth century—that moral questions are out of bounds, and that the task of law is to adapt itself to behavior" (p. 140). We can learn from the European continental countries something about "the value of developing life" and "responsibility in personal relationships" (p. 141). (TJW)

PR,IL
333.   Hern, Warren M. **Abortion Practice.** Boulder, CO: Alpenglo Graphics, 1990. 368 p. ISBN 0-9625728-0-2.

Abortion Practice is a medical textbook written by Hern, M.D., M.P.H., Ph.D., who is Director of the Boulder Abortion Clinic in Boulder, Colorado, and who is also Assistant Clinical Professor, Department of Obstetrics and Gynecology, University of Colorado Health Sciences Center in Denver.

Abortion Practice was prepared especially to provide information for physicians, nurses, and other health personnel who are providing abortion services. It takes a broad public health approach to the subject of abortion as well as a focus on the details of clinical practice. The first chapter, for example, is titled "The Epidemiologic Foundations of Abortion Practice." In this chapter, the medical and evolutionary aspects of pregnancy as a medical condition are discussed along with the health risks of pregnancy for the woman. Against this background, the epidemiologic aspects of abortion are discussed, including the interpretation of statistical data to inform treatment choices. Various chapters discuss patient evaluation, abortion counseling, abortion nursing, operative procedures and management of complications, staffing and operation, legal aspects, long-term risks of abortion, program evaluation, and community relations.

This book is meant to be useful for not only health personnel but also counselors, social workers, administrators, policy makers, lawyers, legislators, and social scientists with an interest in abortion. It has become the principal medical text used by those providing abortion services in the United States and elsewhere in the world. (Author)

PR,IL
334.   Luker, Kristin. **Abortion and the Politics of Motherhood.** Berkeley, Calif.: University of California Press, 1984. 324 p. (California Series on Social Choice and Political Economy). Includes bibliography and index. ISBN 0-520-04314-6.

Sociologist Luker's scholarly study of abortion focuses on the rise of the pro-life and pro-choice movements in America, especially in the state of California. For background to the clash between these two opposing forces, Luker traces the issue's early history up through the nineteenth century. In the second half of the century abortion emerged as a social problem, and physicians, with official backing from the American Medical Association, took a strong anti-abortion position, claiming that abortion was wrong because it interfered with pregnancy, that was one unbroken, continuous process from conception to birth. Luker also reveals that by 1900 in the United States all the states had passed anti-abortion laws, and only physicians could legally perform abortions (all other abortions were criminal abortions). Dubbed the first "right-to-life" movement in the country, this medical control over abortion lasted well into the twentieth century, with the Catholic Church's position supporting the movement.

Luker then points out that this control of abortion by physicians began to erode as a result of changing public attitudes and a desire for reform, that was manifested in California with the passage of the Therapeutic Abortion Act of 1962. In the 1960s the challenge to the medical profession's control of abortion came from two bodies: the California Committee on Therapeutic Abortion, that wanted reform, and the Society for Humane Abortion, that wanted repeal of all abortion laws. Women were claiming abortion as a woman's *right*, which put the abortion issue on a new plane, effectively removed abortion decisions from the control of physicians, and eventually led to the repeal of all abortion statutes in the country.

Luker then devotes a chapter to the emergence of the Right-to-Life movement in the wake of the momentous 1973 *Roe v. Wade* Supreme Court decision striking down all previous abortion laws. She summarizes the pro-life and pro-choice systems of values and beliefs, eliciting the profound differences in their positions with respect not only to abortion but also to the deeper questions of morality and motherhood.

Luker concludes her study with a chapter on the future. Despite the 1973 Supreme Court decision, the pro-life movement has grown dramatically; it is now able to confront the pro-choice forces with equal strength and confidence in the correctness of its position. Consequently, in Luker's opinion, "the future of abortion in America remains unpredictable." She further states that "given the history of abortion in America, none of us should be too surprised if, by the turn of the century, technological changes were once again to make abortion a battleground for competing social, ethical, and symbolic values" (p. 245). A final statement in appendix I describes the methodology Luker used in her study.

An earlier work by Luker, *Taking Chances* (1975; reissued 1990), examines the question of why abortion is so prevalent in a society where there is so much contraception. Luker concludes that the women seeking abortion are neither neurotic nor irrational; she believes that pregnancies are deeply rooted in the sexual behavior of women *and* men. (TJW)

PR,IL

335. Mohr, James C. **Abortion in America: The Origins and Evolution of National Policy, 1800-1900.** New York: Oxford University Press, 1978. 331 p. Includes bibliographies and index. ISBN 0-19-502249-1.

In 1800 there was neither state nor federal legislation on abortion in the United States. British common law governed the matter. Complicating the situation was the commonly held belief that a fetus did not exist until quickening occurred around midpoint in gestation. Furthermore, no reliable tests existed for pregnancy at that time. In this highly documented work on abortion in America, Mohr traces the history of abortion and abortion legislation during the nineteenth century. Unfortunately, statistics on the abortion rate do not exist. However, for the first quarter of the century, abortion was not rare, and knowledge of abortion techniques was widespread.

The earliest laws dealing with abortion were passed between 1821 and 1841. Mohr describes these early laws and the circumstances and significance of their passing. The first wave of legislation occurred in ten states and one territory; the statutes invariably punished the person who performed the abortion or administered the abortifacient. Women were not criminally liable.

Between 1840 and 1880 there was a great upsurge in abortion and the use of abortifacients, accounted for by the awareness of the American public that abortion was a common thing and by the increasing use of abortion by white, married, Protestant, native-born women of the middle and upper classes. Prominent abortionists, such as the flamboyant Madame Restell of New York City, performed abortions on a commercial scale; and there was a growing business in abortifacient medicines. While infanticide and abortion after quickening were clearly unacceptable in this period, abortions performed before quickening, like contraception, seemed an appropriate and acceptable method of avoiding unwanted children.

Legal reaction to the situation was cautious. However, the physicians' crusade against abortion, encouraged by the American Medical Association on the grounds that abortion interfered with the production of children and threatened marriage, the family, and the future of society, resulted in the passage of a substantial number of new and revised state laws opposing abortion between 1860 and 1880. These statutes accepted the proposition that "the interruption of gestation at any point in the pregnancy should be a crime and that the state itself should try actively to restrict the practice of abortion" (p. 200).

Mohr's book "has attempted to explain how and why the United States changed during the nineteenth century from a society that tolerated the practice of abortion without written policies to a society that officially proscribed the practice in detailed criminal statutes" (p. 246).

In his afterword, Mohr briefly examines the controversial *Roe v. Wade* decision of 1973, that reversed the abortion policies that prevailed so long in the United States. (TJW)

IL

336. Nathanson, Bernard N., and Richard N. Ostling. **Aborting America.** Garden City, N.Y.: Doubleday, 1979. 320 p. Includes bibliography and index. ISBN 0-385-14461-X.

Aborting America tells the engrossing story of how Bernard N. Nathanson, a well-known gynecologist and abortionist, changed his mind about legalized abortion. As one of the founding fathers of the National Association for Repeal of Abortion Laws (NARAL), he was instrumental in getting the New York State Abortion Statute of 1970 passed and signed into law by Governor Nelson Rockefeller. He then directed the Center for Reproductive and Sexual Health (CRASH) in New York City, the "first—and largest—abortion clinic in the Western world" for a year and a half. During his tenure, CRASH performed 60,000 abortions with no maternal deaths.

In these circumstances, Nathanson, impressed by medicine's growing knowledge of the fetus based on sophisticated technology, began to question his own thinking about abortion. He concluded that human life is a continuum, stretching from the onset of pregnancy to death, and it should be realized that with abortion "human life of a special order is being taken."

Nathanson attempts to shed light on the abortion issues that have polarized the country into two camps: those who are for a liberal abortion policy, the pro-choice group, and those who are striving for a constitutional amendment that would strictly control abortion, the pro-life group. In several chapters, including "The Specious Arguments Against Abortion" and "The Specious Arguments in Favor of Abortion," Nathanson examines over twenty controversial positions assumed by these groups. Arguments such as the one that abortion is dangerous to the mother's health, or the one that women should have control over their own bodies, are carefully critiqued.

Nathanson assigns the term *alpha* to the human life growing in the womb from the moment of implantation and then reviews the state of knowledge about alpha that medicine has gained through ultrasonography, fetoscopy, amniocentesis, etc. Current knowledge about alpha's cardiovascular system, nervous system, sexual identity, biochemistry, and changing bodily features has expanded dramatically, forcing a new understanding and appreciation of human life.

Nathanson also discusses the stages of pregnancy, focusing on such matters as conception, implantation, viability, brain and heart function, and birth. He also reviews the opposing intellectual positions of prominent philosophers bearing on the morality of abortion. His personal position is that alpha is "a distinct organism that, because it is defenseless, needs special protection from mothers, from doctors, and from society" (p. 228). In this context, he critiques the various trivial, social, eugenic, and circumstantial excuses for abortion.

Nathanson also discusses the social context of the abortion issue, linking America's position to the cheapening of life in the world as experienced in such cataclysms as the Holocaust and Hiroshima. What is needed, he believes, is not a new law but rather a greater reverence for that unique creature that begins life at a point earlier than is recognized. An appendix presents the abortion positions of the major churches and religions in the United States. (TJW)

PR,IL
337. Reardon, David C. **Aborted Women: Silent No More.** Foreword by Nancyjo Mann. Chicago: Loyola University Press, 1987. 373 p. Includes bibliography and index. ISBN 0-8294-0579-8.

This three-year study presents the experiences of women who have had abortions. It is based primarily on a detailed questionnaire administered to 252 women in forty-two states by WEBA (Women Exploited by Abortion). The questionnaire, including survey results, appears in the appendix but is discussed in chapter 1.

Reardon claims that "comparatively little has been done to identify and understand the women who have abortions—until now." Moreover, he says, "We need to know *who* these women are, *why* they choose abortion, and perhaps most importantly, *how* abortion changes their lives" (p. 1). This study uses both a subjective approach, examining personal stories and reflections of aborted women, and an objective approach, based on a survey and statistical analyses. Reardon states that pro-choice groups, such as NOW (National Organization for Women), have opposed long-range surveys of aborted women on the grounds that they would be an invasion of privacy. This stance, he further claims, prevents "other women from being warned about the potential physical and psychological risks they face if they, too, choose abortion" (p. 2).

After the statistical analysis of the survey results, that compare the WEBA sample with national statistics in terms of age, marital status, family size, race, and repeat abortions, there follows a discussion of the circumstances leading to abortion, factors influencing the abortion decision, abortion counseling and clinic service, the physical aftereffects of abortion, and the psychological aftermath.

Subsequent chapters examine (1) evidence from the pro-choice side of the question, (2) the physical risks of abortion, (3) the psychological impact of abortion, (4) the so-called "hard" cases (therapeutic abortion, rape, incest), (5) the impact of abortion on later children, (6) abortion as a business, (7) abortion before and after legalization, and (8) the future of abortion in the United States. Personal testimonials from aborted women accompany each of the main chapters of the study. In fact, the story of Nancyjo Mann, the founder of WEBA, is the foreword of this book.

Of the many conclusions to this study, one of the most telling is that "over 95 percent of those surveyed said they would not have chosen abortion" if they had known at the time how the decision to abort would eventually affect their lives. Reardon's anti-abortion stance contributes to the important, ongoing debate between advocates of the pro-choice and pro-life positions. (TJW)

IL,PO
338. Rosenblatt, Roger. **Life Itself: Abortion in the American Mind.** New York: Random House, 1992. 194 p. Includes bibliography. ISBN 0-394-58244-6.

This lengthy essay on the abortion controversy in America calls for a new approach to the debate and presents a possible solution to the conflict. Rosenblatt believes that the public debate on abortion has become so highly politicized and polarized that it does not reflect the ambivalence felt by the American people.

The history of abortion involves an ongoing search for answers to three fundamental questions: When is a fetus a person? What circumstances justify an abortion? and Who decides? Different times and cultures have given varied and contradictory answers to these questions, but most Western societies have been able to accommodate the contradictions without too much difficulty. The United States, however, has seemingly been unable to deal with the conflicting ambiguities of abortion ever since the American Medical Association made it a public issue in 1857.

Rosenblatt feels that the inability of Americans to come to terms with their ambivalence toward abortion stems from our national history and philosophy. Coming from a historically deeply religious society, Americans wrestle with moral questions surrounding diversity and individualism, the public good and the right to privacy, optimism and guilt, and fear of sexuality. Polls show that while 73 percent of Americans feel abortion should be permitted, 77 percent view it as murder. This ambivalence must be recognized before any workable solution can be achieved, but the abortion debate has become so politically polarized that people seem unable to engage in any meaningful discussion of their conflicting feelings that would permit the development of a mutual understanding. In interviews with more than fifty people from the middle American state of Iowa, Rosenblatt explored this conflict and found some common ground that could allow for a possible solution. He proposes a "permit but discourage" policy that would recognize the need for abortion rights while acknowledging the gravity of the action and the importance of providing alternatives and education to reduce its occurrence. (SDH)

PR,IL
339. Sachdev, Paul, ed. **International Handbook on Abortion.** New York: Greenwood Press, 1988. 520 p. Includes bibliographies and index. ISBN 0-313-23463-9.

Following a review of abortion trends around the world, looking at the legal status of abortion and abortion policies in individual nations, the demographics of abortion, the characteristics of abortion seekers, and the phenomenon of repeat abortions, Sachdev provides tabular data on abortion by world regions and individual states.

In separate chapters, leading national experts report on abortion in thirty-one countries and one region (Latin America). Each report surveys in depth such topics as the historical development of abortion policy, abortion research, the legal status of abortion, illegal abortions, abortion among special groups, and the role of such special interests as the medical profession, religious and women's pressure groups in the enactment of legislation. Some reports present detailed demographic data.

Sachdev states that this handbook avoids "arguments concerning the moral and religious aspects of abortion." It should also be noted that while coverage is universal, many countries are not included in this compilation, e.g., the USSR. Arranged alphabetically for easy access, the reports are thoroughly indexed by subject. (TJW)

PR,IL
340. Staggenborg, Suzanne. **The Pro-Choice Movement: Organization and Activism in the Abortion Conflict.** New York: Oxford University Press, 1991. 229 p. Includes bibliography and index. ISBN 0-19-506596-4.

Applying social movement theory to the efforts to extend and maintain the abortion rights movement in the United States, Staggenborg, a professor of sociology at Indiana University, begins in part I by examining the origin and development of the movement before legalization in 1973. She looks first at how the movement came into being and how collective action led to legalization.

In part II, "Surviving the Victory, 1973-1976," Staggenborg describes the impact of the movement on the *Roe v. Wade* decision, the subsequent professionalization and formalization of the movement, and the growth of the anti-abortion countermovement.

Part III, "Countermovement Victories and Movement Expansion, 1977-1983," describes the movement's growth following the passage of the Hyde Amendment that banned Medicaid funding of abortions in 1976. Here she also discusses single-issue politics and the reproductive rights component of the movement.

In part IV, "The Pro-Choice Movement in the 1980s and Beyond," she explains how the movement survived during the 1983-1989 stalemate between pro-choice and pro-life forces. She also looks at the Reagan-Bush positions on abortion, the Missouri anti-abortion statute in *Webster v. Reproductive Health Services*, that is a challenge to *Roe v. Wade.*

Finally, Staggenborg assesses "the implication of the history of the pro-choice movement for theories of social movements" (p. 10). Throughout the study, she refers to six national organizations (National Abortion Rights Action League, Religious Coalition for Abortion Rights, Zero Population Growth, National Organization for Women, the National Women's Health Network, and the Reproductive Rights National Network) and seven local organizations active in Chicago and Illinois. A detailed examination of these organizations appears in appendix A; their organizational newsletters and documents are described in appendix B. Appendix C is a discussion of interviews with pro-choice activists. (TJW)

PR,IL
341. Tribe, Laurence H. **Abortion: The Clash of Absolutes.** New York: Norton, 1990. 270 p. Includes bibliographic notes and index. ISBN 0-393-02845-3.

Stating that "In 1989 the sixteen-year era of judicial protection of legal abortion rights that began with the Supreme Court's 1973 decision in *Roe v. Wade* ended with that Court's five to four decision upholding certain state regulations on abortion in the case of *Webster v. Reproductive Health Services*" (p. 6), Tribe, Tyler Professor of Constitutional Law at Harvard Law School, goes on to ask whether there is a way of reconciling the "clash of absolutes," i.e., the right to life versus the right to liberty that the present controversy over abortion in the United States represents. Tribe hopes that this book will contribute to a solution of the abortion issue by looking for common ground in the pro-choice and pro-life arguments and by going beyond the conflict into the area of social and technological changes. His book is also about constitutional law, especially the constitutionality aspect of privacy that some legal authorities, such as Robert Bork, say does not exist.

For background understanding of the issue, Tribe begins this work by reviewing the Supreme Court's *Roe* opinion and the post-Roe decisions on abortion leading up to *Webster.* He then looks at abortion's history in the United States from the American Revolution to the present, paying attention to such elements as the position of the Roman Catholic Church, social and demographic forces, the concerns of women and physicians, the nineteenth and twentieth centuries' anti-abortion laws, and such factors as poverty, race, and population control. Tribe proceeds to look at abortion politics, past and present, in various societies around the world, including the Soviet Union, China, India, and Western Europe.

Tribe closely examines the Constitution in search of a justification for an abortion right, focusing attention on the "liberty clause" in the Fourteenth Amendment, that reads "No State shall . . . deprive any person of life, liberty, or property, without due process of law" (p. 83). Justice Blackmun used this amendment in writing the majority opinion on *Roe v. Wade.*

Turning to the question of whether a fetus is a person, Tribe looks at the "scientific" claims of the pro-choice and pro-life advocates, concluding that cell biologists and other experts on the anatomy and physiology of the embryo are unable to provide an answer to the question. *Roe v. Wade*, Tribe asserts, did recognize the importance of "both the interest of the fetus and the interest of the pregnant woman" (p. 138).

Tribe devotes two chapters to the consequences of the *Roe* decision: immediate pro-choice and pro-life reactions, single-issue politics, abortion funding, the uneasy alliance of fundamentalist Christians and Roman Catholics, attempts to overturn *Roe*, abortion politics in the 1984 and 1988 presidential elections, the *Webster* decision, and the reactions to *Webster* at both the federal and state levels.

Finally, Tribe explores the grounds for a political compromise beyond the compromise in *Roe* itself. He discusses consent requirements, notification provisions, waiting periods, limiting the reasons for which abortion will be allowed, contraceptive techniques, and other topics. He injects into the dispute ideas about women's sexuality, women's roles in a patriarchal society, and the dangers of government interference in life and death matters as being areas both sides in the abortion clash should explore and evaluate. (TJW)

Childbirth

IL

342. Arms, Suzanne. **Immaculate Deception: A New Look at Women and Childbirth in America.** Boston: Houghton Mifflin, 1975. 318 p. Includes bibliography and index. ISBN 0-3951-9893-3.

"For the midwives," reads Arms's dedication in this chilling analysis of childbirth in America. Barbara Ehrenreich and Deirdre English have written a brief history of the usurpation of the midwife's function at normal births by the medical profession (see their *Witches, Midwives, and Nurses*, 1973). What Arms does in this book is to describe the consequences of this for the childbirth process, for laboring women, and for their babies. The basic question she raises is whether unnecessary medical intervention into the normal birth process has not succeeded in rendering hospital birth more rather than less risky to mother and child than home birth. She offers detailed evidence indicting routine obstetrical use of drugs, fetal monitors, IVs, episiotomies, forceps in deliveries, and hormones to induce or speed up labor. She also presents personal testimonies and other evidence on the harmful effects of hospitals' dehumanizing and inflexible routine on the labor process and the mother, father, and child. This strong indictment of obstetrical practice is continued in her discussion, in the second half of the book, of traditional practices of midwifery in a home birth situation—where obstetrical faith in complex technology and crisis mentality is replaced by the midwife's faith in nature, patience, and caring. Interviews with and statements by mothers, midwives, nurses, and doctors alternate with Arms's own analysis throughout.

Readers might also want to look at Doris Haire's *The Cultural Warping of Childbirth*, originally published in 1972 and included in *The Cultural Crisis of Modern Medicine*, edited by John Ehrenreich (New York: Monthly Review Press, 1978); Jane B. Donegan's *Women and Men Midwives: Medicine, Morality, and Misogyny in Early America* (Westport, Conn.: Greenwood Press, 1978); Judy Barrett Litoff's *American Midwives, 1860 to the Present* (Westport, Conn.: Greenwood Press, 1978); and Nancy Stoller Shaw's *Forced Labor: Maternity Care in the United States* (Elmsford, N.Y.: Pergamon Press, 1974). (**Women's Studies**, 1979)

PR,IL

343. Jordan, Brigitte. **Birth in Four Cultures: A Crosscultural Investigation of Childbirth in Yucatan, Holland, Sweden, and the United States.** 4th ed. Revised and expanded by Robbie Davis-Floyd. Prospect Heights, Ill.: Waveland Press, 1993. 235 p. Includes bibliography. ISBN 0-88133-717-X.

As Davis-Floyd notes in her foreword, "This book was instrumental in defining the field of Anthropology of Birth, as well as establishing some of its primary methods of cross-cultural comparison, analysis, and strategies for planning change; [it has become a] 'classic in the field' for all those interested in birth" (p. ix). In this fourth edition, the first part retains the materials of the original 1978 text with Davis-Floyd's substantial updates of information and references added in the notes. The second part contains three more recent articles on authoritative knowledge by Jordan, all of which elaborate themes established in part 1.

In addition to struggling with ways to conceptualize and research childbirth cross-culturally, medical anthropologist Jordan wanted to determine how "childbirth could be understood as a culturally grounded, biosocially mediated, and interactionally achieved event" (p. xi). Using data collected in four countries during many years of fieldwork, Jordan compares and contrasts their birthing systems with the biomedical obstetrical pattern in the United States. She treats parturition as a biosocial event, jointly produced by the interaction of (universal) biology and (a particular) society and suggests that people everywhere structure birth practices into an acceptable routine that varies little within the society but may vary extensively across societies. Her goal is to "isolate some features of the birth process that recommend themselves as units for cross-cultural comparison within a biosocial framework" (p. 9). Part 1 establishes the need for a biosocial, cross-cultural analysis of ethno-obstetric systems. Jordan provides a detailed account of Yucatan childbirth processes (a significant contrast to a medical model), that normalize childbirth and incorporate a midwife to collaborate with the woman in birthing her child. A comparison of birthing systems in Yucatan, Sweden, Holland, and the United States yields some important features to include in a cross-cultural, biosocial analysis of childbirth: the system-specific definition of the birth process; preparation for parturition; attendants and support systems; birth territory; the use of medication; the technology of birth; and the nature of the decision-making process during labor and delivery. For the benefit of future researchers, Jordan devotes a chapter to the methodological and ethical issues involved in research on an intimate behavior like birth and adds her personal reflections about the process. In the final chapter in part 1, Jordan discusses the utility of a cross-cultural perspective when planning change in developing countries; biomedical approaches and technological sophistication may not result in lower maternal and child mortality. Part 2, "Authoritative Knowledge in Childbirth," continues Jordan's theme that childbirth must be seen in a holistic framework, informed by biosocial, cross-cultural information. She examines the ways in which indigenous and cosmopolitan knowledge form the basis of decisions that guide the production of birth. She concludes that medical technology establishes a "regime of power" that defines authoritative knowledge. By only allowing information consistent with a biomedical model, indigenous practices and beliefs are devalued, often at a high social cost. (SGF)

PR,IL
344. Shorter, Edward. **A History of Women's Bodies.** New York: Basic Books, 1982. 398 p. Includes bibliographic references and index. ISBN 0-465-03029-7.

Shorter believes that the physical basis for equality between the sexes has now been achieved. Until this century women had been victimized by (1) male dominance, that gave men unlimited sexual access to women's bodies, often resulting in unwanted pregnancies; (2) children's demands on their time and energy; and (3) diseases (childbed fever, etc.) over which there was little or no control. However, with better nutrition, certain medical discoveries, and the feminist movement, conditions for women began to improve.

Shorter, a professor of history at the University of Toronto, has brought his considerable scholarship to bear on an aspect of women's studies hitherto neglected, viz., the traditional experience of childbirth by common people. Heavily documented with primarily German, French, and English medical works (books, periodical articles, statistical studies, government documents) and other miscellaneous sources (folk tales, songs, proverbs), this book describes in great detail the customs and practices associated with the discrete stages of childbirth (antenatal care, labor, delivery, postnatal care), emphasizing the central role played by midwives as well as the community of women who cared for the expectant mother. Traditionally, the care of women in childbirth was essentially an activity of women; doctors were called in only in emergencies.

Pain and death resulting from complications and inappropriate care were the frequent fate of women in childbirth until quite recently. Care of pregnant women was based on local custom and superstitions. In many cultures women worked in the fields until the onset of labor; bleeding the expectant mother was another common practice. During delivery midwives' procedures were generally crude and intrusive, often resulting in injury or death to the mother and infant. For example, the practice of removing the umbilical cord and placenta by vigorous tugging and pulling sometimes caused severe hemorrhage or turned the uterus inside out. Postnatal care usually kept women, at least those who could afford it, in bed, sweating profusely, for long periods of time. Infections (peritonitis, bacteremia, septic thrombophlebitis, cellulitis) following delivery were an abiding problem; it was difficult to ascertain their causes, and the issue of home versus hospital delivery was in question.

The shift from midwives to doctors delivering babies and from home to hospital care was gradual, arising apparently from women's and husbands' demands for improvements in childbearing. The advent of caesarian births, the use of anesthetics, and concern for the fetus all contributed to the demise of midwifery and the rise of obstetrics as a field. Concern for women with unwanted pregnancies led to improvements in abortion methods late in the nineteenth century.

In addition to the history of the childbirth experience and midwifery, Shorter explores issues surrounding the differences between men's and women's bodies: the question of longevity and the impact of diseases on women's health; diseases of sexual significance, such as various vaginal discharges and venereal diseases (not important before 1850); injuries sustained at birth (fistulas, lacerations, prolapse of the uterus); and men's diseases.

Shorter's thesis is that women's victimization from men, children, and nature came to an end between 1900 and 1930, and that this has provided a strong basis for the feminist movement in the struggle for personal autonomy. (TJW)

Lactation. Breastfeeding. Breasts

IL

345. Ayalah, Daphna, and Isaac J. Weinstock. **Breasts: Women Speak About Their Breasts and Their Lives.** New York: Summit Books, 1979. 286 p. ISBN 0-671-40021-5.

Recognizing that the images of women's breasts in the media are exaggerated, Ayalah and Weinstock decided "to produce a photographic catalog of the breasts of women of all ages, without makeup or special lighting effects, and without bias toward the preconceived cultural ideal of 'beautiful breasts' " (p. 10). They hope that their efforts will not only serve as an antidote to the standard media images, but also that they might encourage women to accept their own breasts and to appreciate the "uniqueness and dignity of their individual bodies."

Although some women were eager to be photographed, others were reluctant to have their breasts photographed, and many refused. The authors concluded that "women were negatively affected by the ever-present media images of 'ideal breasts' " (p. 13).

Going beyond the objectives of their original project, Ayalah and Weinstock prepared a questionnaire that probed women's attitudes and feelings about their breasts in connection with childhood, puberty and adolescence, present feelings, sex, men, bras and bralessness, clothing, breast exposure, pregnancy and breastfeeding, health, and aging. The detailed responses of 38 women selected from over 200 interviewees to the ninety-five questions asked are frank and revealing. Ranging in age from twenty to seventy-nine, the women came from different backgrounds: housewives, mothers, working women of all kinds, including models and exotic dancers.

Hundreds of black-and-white photographs depict changes in women's breasts during the life cycle from childhood to old age. The frontal and profile views of the breasts of the women interviewed show the great range in size and shape of the human female breast. These straightforward pictures preserve the anonymity of the interviewees by not showing their faces.

Ayalah and Weinstock also prepared three additional questionnaires on puberty and adolescence, breast cancer and mastectomy, and men's feelings about women's breasts, that they said could be obtained by writing to them. (TJW)

PO

346. Halbert, David S. **Your Breast and You.** Abilene, Tex.: Askon Corporation, 1985. 238 p. Includes bibliography and index. ISBN 0-931609-00-3.

Of the women who see physicians, an estimated 25 percent do so because of breast problems. Written by a surgeon who has dealt with patients' breast problems for over twenty years, this book focuses on "what every woman needs to know about breast disease, breast cancer, and cosmetic breast surgery before she has a problem."

The first part of the book deals with a description of the anatomy and physiology of the breast as well as with types of examinations (self-exam, mammogram, thermogram, etc.) that are used to detect breast problems. However, the bulk of the book is devoted to providing information on symptomatology and treatment of noncancerous (benign tumor, fibrocystic disease, pain in the breast, nipple discharge, infections) and cancerous diseases of the breast. Although no more than 9 percent of women are likely to develop breast cancer in their lifetimes, its diagnosis and treatment are emotional and controversial issues. Halbert attempts to present a dispassionate overview of the risk factors in breast cancer (age, sex, race, fat in the diet, location, children, family history), types of primary and metastatic cancers, and the pros and cons of treatments (breast-saving techniques, breast surgery, breast reconstruction). A very brief chapter outlines some of the problems that patients cope with after a diagnosis of breast cancer, such as mate rejection, depression, and lack of a permanent cure. Because women who have had cancer in one breast are five times more at risk for developing cancer in the other breast than other women are, a woman faces a decision about whether to remove the second breast as a prophylactic procedure; subcutaneous mastectomy and reconstruction are options. The last part of the book briefly deals with the reasons for and procedures involved in breast reduction or augmentation.

The primary orientation of this book is to provide a guide to medical and surgical solutions to breast problems rather than to address the psychological responses of women who are dealing with them. Halbert's closing section is in line with this perspective and provides guidelines for selecting a doctor to aid the woman in dealing with the presence of physical problems. (SGF)

IL

347. Love, Susan M., with Karen Lindsey. **Dr. Susan Love's Breast Book.** Illustrations by Marcia Williams. Reading, Pa.: Addison-Wesley, 1992. 455 p. Includes bibliographic notes, index, and glossary. ISBN 0-201-57097-1.

Together with writer and poet Karen Lindsey, Love, physician, Assistant Clinical Professor at Harvard Medical School, and Director of the Faulkner Breast Center in Boston, has written a comprehensive guide to breast care. Women worry about their breasts partly because of their symbolic value in many cultures as "an external badge of our womanhood." However, most women don't know much about their own breasts or even what a normal breast looks like. Since "knowledge is power," Love's goal is "to give readers some of that power" by providing information as well as a psychological context for understanding what is happening to this part of their bodies.

Part 1, "The Healthy Breast," includes information on the anatomy and physiology of the breast, its development, and variations in development. Human breast tissue begins to develop in the sixth week of gestation, and babies are born with some breast tissue. Women's breasts change not only at different stages of life, particularly at puberty and menopause, but also during the sexual response cycle, the menstrual cycle, pregnancy, and breastfeeding. At puberty, women may notice variations in development: the breasts may be too big, too small, or asymmetrical in size; have inverted nipples, no nipple(s), or an extra nipple(s). However, there is nothing abnormal about these features, because "medically speaking," the normal breast is one that is capable of producing milk. It is important for women to do a breast self-examination (BSE) not only for cancer detection but also in order for the woman to become familiar with her own body and what is normal for her. Love explains the different ways of doing a BSE and describes what to look for. And, even though breast size is not related to a woman's ability to produce milk or her vulnerability to breast disease, it may reflect a woman's sense of well-being or sense of attractiveness about herself. Love details the plastic surgery options open to women who want to change the size or structure of their breasts. A detailed chapter discusses the development of the lobules and ducts in the breasts that prepare them for breastfeeding, as well as the intricate feedback between the baby's suckling, the release of prolactin and oxytocin, and the making and let down of milk.

In part 2, Love describes some common problems of the breast, reviewing relevant research about each. She flatly states that "there is no such thing as fibrocystic disease"; it is a "meaningless umbrella term" that masks an array of real symptoms. She suggests that it is more productive to focus on specific symptoms, and then proceeds to describe each of them and what can be done to deal with them: breast pain, breast infection, nipple problems, lumps and lumpiness.

The remaining four parts of the book focus in detail on the risk, prevention of and detection of breast cancer; its diagnosis and treatment; and living with cancer. Aspects of fear, self-image, and practical considerations are dealt with.

Throughout the book, Love confronts the concerns women have about their breasts—their appearance, significance, and functioning—and also describes their physical care. The impact of the culture's beliefs about the breasts is also a consistent theme. Love articulates and corrects many misperceptions about the breasts and breast cancer. The book concludes with appendixes that include a chart on drugs used for systemic treatment of breast cancer; how to lower fat in the diet; resources, references, and additional reading to supplement information in the chapters; regional support organizations for cancer and breast cancer patients; and addresses and telephone numbers of cancer centers. (SGF)

PO

348. Raphael, Dana. **The Tender Gift: Breastfeeding.** New York: Schocken Books, 1976. 200 p. Includes bibliography, index, and glossary. ISBN 0-8052-0519-5.

Recognizing the anguish of modern American women who want to breastfeed their babies but have difficulty in doing so, Raphael, an anthropologist and Director of the Human Lactation Center, presents a sympathetic, readable account of how breastfeeding is accomplished. She asserts that "the woman who wants the intensity that breastfeeding offers can have it" if she understands the process of lactation, remembers the benefits that it produces for herself and her baby, recognizes the cultural constraints that surround it, and makes sure that she receives some mothering herself. The contents of the book address the substance of each of these pieces of advice.

Becoming a mother ("matrescence") is a period of transition. However, emphasis on the baby draws attention from the important emotional and behavioral transitions that the woman undergoes. In many cultures, a woman has the support of people who interact with and aid her during pregnancy, birth, and lactation; Raphael terms them "doulas." In contrast, American women receive good physical care in the hospital but their emotional needs are often neglected. It is essential that a new mother receive emotional support from an experienced woman (or man) who can help her after she leaves the hospital.

However, a woman still has obstacles to overcome in order to breastfeed. Americans are not very supportive of breastfeeding. Raphael explains some of these attitudes by documenting the transition from breastfeeding to bottle feeding in American society. She points out factors to consider in deciding whether to breastfeed or bottle feed. Of particular importance is her straightforward account of the anatomy and physiology of the breast as well as a consideration of the importance of lactation and breastfeeding in other cultures, among other animals, and for the mother and her infant. And, most important, she provides a practical guide to obtaining the support necessary for helping a woman to lactate: how to identify and interact with a doula as well as where to obtain information on childbirth and breastfeeding. A glossary defines technical words used in the text. (SGF)

Disease. Disability. Surgery

(For related material see also entries 191, 1024, 1024a)

PR
349. Schover, Leslie R., and Søren Buus Jensen. **Sexuality and Chronic Illness: A Comprehensive Approach.** New York: Guilford Press, 1988. 357 p. Includes bibliography and index. ISBN 0-89862-715-X.

Intended for physicians, mental health professionals, nurses, and occupational and physical therapists, this text provides an analysis of the difficulties faced by chronically ill men and women in their attempts to live sexually fulfilling lives.

In part 1, "The Integrative Model of Sexuality Assessment and Treatment," clinical psychologist Schover and psychiatrist Jensen develop a concept of sexual health based on the integration of psychological, biological, and social elements to assist in the assessment and treatment of sexual problems in connection with chronic illnesses such as diabetes, cardiovascular disease, cancer, and other illnesses. The range of topics in this part includes couple therapy; a description of sexual behavior across the life cycle with attendant sexual dysfunctions; emotional factors (stress, anger, depression, etc.) generated by chronic illness affecting sexuality; physiological factors (hormonal, neurological, pain, etc.) involved; assessment of sexual problems; counseling techniques; and medical treatments (hormone replacement therapy, penile prosthesis, breast and genital reconstruction).

Part 2, "Specific Illnesses and Sexuality," deals with sexuality and (1) life-threatening crises from cardiovascular disease, cancer, and end-stage renal disease, (2) insidious illnesses, such as diabetes, chronic obstructive pulmonary disease, and chronic pain, and (3) stigmatizing conditions, including major psychiatric disorders, alcoholism, and infertility.

In part 3, "Training and Ethical Issues," Schover and Jensen describe in detail the training of primary care clinicians, who provide brief sexual counseling, and the sexual health care clinicians, who offer intensive sex therapy or medical treatment. They also deal with various ethical and professional issues in treating sexual problems in the chronically ill: staff resistance to a sexuality program; confidentiality; the relationship between the primary care clinician and the patient; sexual freedom in institutions; the prevention of sexual abuse; and coping with the seductive or acting-out patient.

In conclusion, Schover and Jensen express the hope that this book will contribute in a practical way to the development of sound sexual health care programs, that they envision becoming "a standard aspect of medical and psychological care worldwide." (TJW)

PR
350. Wack, Mary Frances. **Lovesickness in the Middle Ages: The *Viaticum* and Its Commentaries.** Philadelphia: University of Pennsylvania Press, 1990. 354 p. (Middle Ages Series). Includes bibliography and index. ISBN 0-8122-8142-X.

This work by Wack, Assistant Professor, Department of English, Stanford University, represents meticulous research on a medieval document known as Constantine's *Viaticum*. Based on a popular medical handbook, *Provisions for the Traveler and the Nourishment of the Settled*, by Ibn al-Jazzār, a physician in the North African city of Qayrawan, the capital of Tunisia, the *Viaticum* is Constantine's Latin translation and adaptation of a single chapter on lovesickness in that Arabic medical treatise. The treatise, divided into seven books, deals with a variety of diseases, including insomnia, frenzy, drunkenness, sneezing, epilepsy, apoplexy, melancholia, lovesickness, and other maladies. Small in size and compact, it was widely disseminated throughout Islamic culture by merchants and travelers.

In part 2, "The Texts," Constantine's *Viaticum* I.20, along with five separate commentaries, or glosses, on it by Gerard of Berry, Giles, Peter of Spain, and Bona Fortuna, are presented side by side in Latin and English.

In the introductory remarks, Wack states that in the Middle Ages "the disease of love became an important part of medieval culture." Unlike the majority of the population, the privileged sufferers could receive treatment from a professional, university educated doctor. Trained to recognize the symptoms of lovesickness, such as loss of appetite, insomnia, or even a suddenly rapid pulse in the presence of a lady, the physician had a range of remedies, including baths, potions, music, sleep, wine, and even therapeutic intercourse. Lovesickness, they believed, was located in the brain.

According to Wack, beliefs about the cause and treatment of diseases, especially the love malady, changed dramatically between the fifth and fifteenth centuries. Much of the change was brought about in the eleventh century by the translation and dissemination of medical texts brought from North Africa to Europe by Constantine the African.

Historically, the break up of the Roman Empire resulted in the loss of Greek and Latin texts; their preservation credited to Arab scholars who translated them; and credit for their movement back to Europe generally given to the likes of Constantine the African. Thus, the medical tradition about lovesickness, passed down over the centuries by Galen, Rufus of Ephesus, and others, was lost to Europe in the early Middle Ages but reestablished in the eleventh century.

The *Viaticum* and the commentaries that followed show that the disease of love became an important part of medical culture in Europe at the same time that courtly love took shape in the vernacular literature. Wack's research further shows how lovesickness, long regarded as a medical entity, became linked to romantic and courtly love and eventually transformed into recognizable social behavior on the part of the upper classes.

Well-illustrated and fully documented, this volume "makes available to modern readers for the first time editions and translations of the chapter on love in the *Viaticum* and of the commentaries on it" (p. xiv). (TJW)

Sexually Transmitted Diseases. AIDS

(For related material see also entries 243, 246)

IL
351. Berk, Richard A., ed. **The Social Impact of AIDS in the U.S.** Cambridge, Mass.: Abt Books, 1988. 143 p. Includes bibliographies. ISBN 0-89011-602-4.

This collection of nine papers by social scientists addresses the social impact of AIDS in the United States. Following an introductory chapter by Berk showing the geographical distribution of AIDS in Los Angeles County from 1982 to 1987, as well as the interplay of human institutions and epidemics, sociologist Beth E. Schneider describes how AIDS has affected gender relations and sexual behavior in terms of sexual talk and behavior for heterosexual men and women in the past seven years, male-centered problems generated by HIV infection among IV drug users and gay men, and social, sexual, and reproductive problems posed for women who are HIV infected.

In an original paper, psychologist Paul Abramson focuses on the impact of AIDS on the pornographic industry in Los Angeles, where most porno films are produced. He points out that this subculture has been pretty much ignored in the concern over the AIDS epidemic. Sociologist Robin Lloyd identifies another under-studied area, namely the social organization of hospitals in their response to AIDS. In a related paper, Howard E. Freeman, Charles Lewis, and Christopher Corey examine the vexing problem of educating physicians about treating people with AIDS.

The reaction of the Catholic Church to AIDS in the Latino community of the Archdiocese of Los Angeles, is the subject of sociologist Alice Horrigan's paper. James Kinsella of the Los Angeles *Herald Examiner* considers how AIDS has been characterized by the media and how in turn AIDS may affect media practices in the future. Psychologist Bernard Weiner then addresses the public's reaction to AIDS, contrasting, for example, the public's attitude toward hemophiliacs with AIDS and homosexuals with AIDS. In the final paper dealing with cross-cultural perspectives on AIDS, anthropologist Francis Paine Conant speculates about the social consequences of AIDS for the Eastern United States as well as implications for East Africa.

The significant public investment in the management of AIDS over the coming years has been the justification for this volume of essays exploring important social aspects of the AIDS epidemic. Berk hopes that this book will help stimulate further research on these aspects. (TJW)

PR,IL
352. Brandt, Allan M. **No Magic Bullet: A Social History of Venereal Disease in the United States Since 1880.** New York: Oxford University Press, 1985. 245 p. Includes bibliographic notes and index. ISBN 0-19-503469-4.

Although cures are available today for syphilis and gonorrhea, their control leaves much to be desired. The reason is not medical but rather lies in certain attitudes, beliefs, and values held by society. *No Magic Bullet* tells the social history of the STDs over the past hundred years. Brandt, an assistant professor of the history of medicine and science at Harvard University, focuses on the battle waged against these diseases in the United States prior to, during, and after the two World Wars. Brandt views venereal disease as a complex medical, social, ethical, and sexual problem. He seeks "to investigate the impact of values on health care, as well as the impact of medicine on social values and behavior" (p. 16).

The late nineteenth and early twentieth centuries in the United States marked the time of progressive medicine and social hygiene: bacterial diseases (diphtheria, tuberculosis, etc.) were being effectively controlled, and corrupt sexuality was being combated via reform of sexual mores. Nevertheless, Prince Morrow, a leading venereologist and supporter of the eugenics movement, had sounded the alarm of the danger of venereal disease to the very fabric of society in his book *Social Diseases and Marriage*, that showed the impact of these diseases on the innocent victims, women and children. But Victorian reticence on the subject hampered efforts to deal with the situation. Brandt considers various important and interrelated aspects of the problem: immigration, prostitution, organizational efforts, purity crusades, sex education, public health regulations, hospital care, scientific discoveries (in 1905 the causative agent of syphilis, *Spirocheta pallida*; in 1909 the magic bullet Salvarsan for the disease's treatment), and the reflection of all this in literature.

In chapter 2, Brandt reviews the efforts of the social and medical reformers on the eve of World War I to improve the moral climate of the nation and to fight venereal disease. Prostitution, rampant in the vicinity of the training camps, became the principal target of the military authorities. Anti-venereal disease programs, stressing sexual continence, were offered the soldiers.

In chapter 3, Brandt reveals the conditions in France that tested the American approach to venereal disease control. French attitudes and values clashed with the American approach to the problem in such ports as Bordeaux and St. Nazaire. Rejecting the regulated houses of prostitution offered by the French, the AEF established prophylactic stations and leave camps with educational programs organized and run by the YMCA. Altogether from April 1917 to December 1919, at home and abroad, "a total of 383,706 soldiers were diagnosed with either syphilis, gonorrhea, or chancroid." Interestingly, "soldiers serving in the United States accounted for 76.6 percent of the venereal infections in the entire Army during the war" (p. 115).

Brandt goes on, in chapter 4, to deal with the efforts of Thomas Parran, Surgeon General of the United States from 1936 to 1948, to eradicate venereal disease. For various reasons, connected with "fear, stigma, and taboo," he did not attain his goal, although he did bring the topic to national attention.

In World War II Parran's practical approach to the control of venereal disease among the troops was highly effective, and with the discovery of penicillin in 1943, it was thought that the magic bullet had been found. The venereal death rate declined rapidly. With venereal disease no longer a health threat, the authorities too soon relaxed their vigilance, and attention was focused on the moral aspects of the problem. The victory over VD proved short-lived. VD rates began to climb in the late 1950s and by 1980 gonorrhea and syphilis were the first and third most prevalent communicable diseases. Brandt states that "the promise of the magic bullet has never been fulfilled," and that today "venereal diseases persist in epidemic proportions in spite of antibiotics." He admits that the magic bullets "cannot combat the social and cultural determinants of these infections." (TJW)

IL

353. Crimp, Douglas, ed. **AIDS: Cultural Analysis/Cultural Activism.** Cambridge, Mass.: MIT Press, 1988. 270 p. Includes bibliographic footnotes. ISBN 0-262-53079-1.

In this collection of papers concerning the sociocultural dimensions of the AIDS epidemic, editor Crimp states in his introduction that "*only* information and mobilization can save lives," that short of the development of a cure for AIDS, society must face up to the difficulties of the AIDS problem, not delude itself, but assume an activist stance and address key issues of communication and understanding. The contributors form a diverse group, including educators, researchers, health professionals, lawyers, and community activists.

Jan Zita Grover examines a host of AIDS-related terms (AIDS test, AIDS virus, bisexual, carrier, condone, family, general population, risk practice, spread, victim) to show how these keywords have been used and misused in the media by politicians, physicians, and the public. Paula A. Treichler states that "the nature of the relationship between language and reality is highly problematic." She traces the evolution of the AIDS vocabulary from its first appearance around 1981 to the present, showing the untoward results of misapprehension and misunderstanding. Simon Watney explains that in Great Britain and the United States reliable AIDS information is not reaching the general public in a situation tantamount to a denial of the human catastrophe unfolding worldwide. Sander L. Gilman compares the development of current visual images of AIDS and persons with AIDS (PWAs) with those of syphilis and syphilitics since the fifteenth century. Martha Gever in "Pictures of Sickness" reviews the coverage of AIDS in special programs for TV viewing; she also examines in depth Stuart Marshall's videotape *Bright Eyes*, an effort that counteracts misleading images on television. Douglas Crimp in "The Second Epidemic" interviews three members of the AIDS Discrimination Unit of the New York City Commission on Human Rights about their work.

Max Navarre tells about the formation of the PWA Coalition in New York in 1985 in his article "Fighting the Victim Label." His paper introduces a number of statements, articles, letters, and photographs under the rubric "PWA Coalition Portfolio." Suki Ports, a community activist, writes about women and children with AIDS and what is needed socially and politically to help them cope with their problems. Carol Leigh in "Further Violations of Our Rights" takes up the cause of prostitutes and describes the impact of AIDS on the institution of prostitution. Gregg Bordowitz writes about a coalition of activist groups combating AIDS-related hysteria. Leo Bersani in his provocative paper, "Is the Rectum a Grave?" philosophizes about the nature of homosexuality in terms of displacement and self-annihilation. In "AIDS in the Two Berlins," John Borneman describes what is being done about AIDS in West Germany and the German Democratic Republic. Finally, editor Crimp writes about educational issues, including critical reviews of Randy Shilts's book *And the Band Played On* and Larry Kramer's play *The Normal Heart.* (TJW)

PR,IL
354. Dalton, Harlon L., and Scott Burris, eds. **AIDS and the Law: A Guide for the Public.** New Haven, Conn.: Yale University Press, 1987. 382 p. Includes bibliography, index, and glossary. ISBN 0-300-04078-4.

Expertise from various fields is applied to the relationship of the law to the AIDS epidemic in this collection of papers gathered by the Yale AIDS Law Project at Yale University. The authors of the various chapters include lawyers, psychiatrists, historians, and physicians, all of whom are cognizant of the unique problems afforded by the AIDS crisis in the United States.

Divided into six parts, this guide provides three papers in part 1, "The Medical Background": "The AIDS Epidemic: Discovery of a New Disease" by June E. Osborn, M.D.; "The Transmission of AIDS" by Richard Green, M.D.; and "A Historical Perspective" by Allan M. Brandt. Part 2, "Government Responses to AIDS," includes four papers: "Traditional Public Health Strategies" by Larry Gostin; "Schoolchildren with AIDS" by Frederic C. Kass, M.D.; "Prostitution as a Public Health Issue" by John F. Decker; and "Education as Prevention" by Jane Harris Aiken.

Part 3, "Private Sector Responses to AIDS," includes Arthur S. Leonard's "AIDS in the Workplace"; Mark A. Rothstein's "Screening Workers for AIDS"; Daniel R. Mandelker's "Housing Issues"; and Donald H. J. Hermann's "Torts: Private Lawsuits About AIDS." Part 4, "AIDS and Health Care," includes Taunya Lovell Banks's "The Right to Medical Treatment"; Mark Scherzer's "Insurance"; Richard Belitsky and Robert A. Solomon's "Doctors and Patients: Responsibilities in a Confidential Relationship"; and Daniel M. Fox's "Physicians Versus Lawyers: A Conflict of Cultures."

Part 5, "AIDS in Institutions," includes "The Military" by Rhonda R. Rivera and "Prisons" by Urvashi Vaid. Part 6, "Confronting AIDS: The Problems of Special Groups" includes "Intravenous Drug Abusers" by Catherine O'Neill; "The Black Community" by Wayne L. Greaves, M.D.; and "The Lesbian and Gay Community" by Mark S. Senak.

Intended for the numerous and varied groups of professionals (educators, counselors, legislators, policy makers, employers, insurers, etc.) who need to come to grips with the legal issues engendered by the AIDS epidemic, this work provides in readable English a comprehensive guide to a pressing national and international problem. (TJW)

PR,IL
355. Farmer, Paul. **AIDS and Accusation: Haiti and the Geography of Blame.** Berkeley, Calif.: University of California Press, 1992. 338 p. (Comparative Studies of Health Systems and Medical Care, No. 33). Includes bibliography and index. ISBN 0-520-07701-6.

AIDS and Accusation is "the first full-length ethnographic study of AIDS in a poor society" (publisher). Its implications for medical anthropology and an understanding of the context of AIDS extend beyond the small, rural Haitian village where anthropologist/physician Farmer conducted fieldwork from 1983-1990. The goal of this book is to enlarge the frames of reference that North American academicians and communities use to respond to HIV; it is "an attempt to constitute an interpretive anthropology of affliction based on complementary ethnographic, historical, epidemiologic, and political-economic analyses" (p. 13). As Farmer puts it, "Although HIV is a very cosmopolitan microbe, AIDS discourse . . . has always been provincial" (p. 16). This book offers a method for medical anthropologists and a perspective for policy makers and theoreticians to expand their interpretation of HIV transmission in the United States and other parts of the world.

Part I is a brief, ethnographic history of Do Kay, a village formed on the "stony backs" of hills after its inhabitants were displaced from their fertile valley when a hydroelectric project flooded it in 1956. Poverty replaced plenty, and other forms of afflictions followed. Farmer tells what happened when the community confronted its first cases of AIDS. Part II focuses on the lived experience of the afflicted: Manno, a young school teacher convinced that his illness was the result of sorcery; Anita, an adolescent driven into sexual servitude following the death of her mother from tuberculosis and malnutrition; Dieudonne, whose reaction to AIDS was cast in the political terms of a violent period in Haitian history. In parts III and IV Farmer links their experiences to large-scale forces that have shaped the incidence and meaning of AIDS by asking such questions as why these villagers were at risk for HIV infection; why they developed their specific folk beliefs about this new disease; whether they were representative of other AIDS victims in Haiti; and how the virus is transmitted in Haiti. Part III examines the socioepidemiological history of HIV in Haiti; part IV probes the historical and economic factors that led to the introduction of the virus in Haiti.

The concluding section stresses the necessity to develop a holistic understanding of HIV infection in order to respond to it in humane, effective ways. Ethnography reveals the significance of individual lives in shaping the "local moral world." But analysis at the village level is incomplete without taking into account the broader historical, economic, and political forces that shaped these individual experiences. Interpreted in this context, the transmission of HIV is only "superficially random"; it is a "misery-seeking missile." Sexual, political, and economic contact in the New World contributed to the current epidemiology of HIV; "the map of HIV in the New World reflects to an important degree the geography of U.S. neocolonialism" (p. 261). It is likely that the virus came to Haiti from the U.S., probably through tourism and trade, *not* from Haiti to the U.S. Poverty puts young adults at risk to contract HIV; racial prejudice and ethnocentrism in theories about HIV transmission not only perpetuate myths and tunnel vision about transmission but also scapegoat Haiti for the political and economic causes of risk that lie in the international arena. (Publisher/SGF)

PR,IL
356. Fee, Elizabeth, and Daniel M. Fox, eds. **AIDS: The Burdens of History.** Berkeley, Calif.: University of California Press, 1988. 362 p. Includes bibliographic references and index. ISBN 0-520-06396-1.

A historical approach to AIDS underlies the papers in this collection. The authors, according to Fee and Fox's introductory paper, share three principles of historical method: social constructionism (historical reality is created by people); skepticism about historicism (that societies evolve toward goals); and wariness about presentism (distorting the past by seeing it only from the standpoint of our time).

Charles E. Rosenberg in "Disease and Social Order in America" examines aspects of the social history of medicine, including the definition of disease, overoptimistic views of the benefit of medicine's response to social diseases in the past, etc. While the AIDS epidemic illustrates our dependence on medicine, it also highlights the importance of social and cultural perspectives.

In "Epidemics and History," Guenter B. Risse, using an ecological model, shows how political and health organizations have historically responded to crises. Responses to the bubonic plague in Rome in 1656 (blamed on the Jews), the cholera epidemic of 1832 (attributed to the Irish), and the 1916 poliomyelitis epidemic in New York City (blamed on the Italians) are provided.

David F. Musto in "Quarantine and the Problem of AIDS" shows that the practices of quarantine in relation to leprosy, yellow fever, cholera, tuberculosis, and drug addiction have never been successful.

In "The Politics of Physicians' Responsibility in Epidemics," David M. Fox argues that most physicians, past and present, have treated patients as the result of negotiations with civic leaders, especially as to who should treat patients of the lowest classes.

In "The Enforcement of Health: The British Debate," Dorothy Porter and Roy Porter trace the debates and struggles around various legal, philosophical, and ethical issues for a century and a half of British history, highlighting the conflicts between individual freedom and public good.

Elizabeth Fee in "Sin Versus Science: Venereal Disease in Twentieth-Century Baltimore" reveals that the black community was held responsible for syphilis, although public health officials campaigned to present syphilis as a disease of the "innocents." In this debate the conflict between the biomedical approach and the moral approach to the disease was emphasized.

In "AIDS: From Social History to Social Policy," Allan M. Brandt discusses the ways that social responses to venereal diseases have expressed cultural anxieties about contagion, contamination, and sexuality. Brandt "urges policy-makers to pay careful attention to the history of sexually transmitted diseases before deciding on the health and social policies necessary to deal with AIDS."

Following a short illustrated paper by Daniel M. Fox and Diane R. Karp on how artists have depicted infectious diseases visually during plague years of the past four centuries, Paula A. Treichler in "AIDS, Gender, and Biomedical Discourse: Current Contests for Meaning," analyzes the language of AIDS from a feminist point of view. The medical discourse, she argues, functions to reinforce entrenched notions about gender. She speaks about the concern for heterosexual transmission that emerged in 1986 and the focus on women as transmitters of the virus.

Gerald M. Oppenheimer's "In the Eye of the Storm" examines scientific studies of the disease. Using an epidemiological model capable of incorporating nonbiological variables, he traces the various steps made by epidemiologists and virologists to disclose the social and biological elements leading to the definition and cause of AIDS.

In "Legitimation Through Disaster: AIDS and the Gay Movement," Dennis Altman shows how epidemiological studies linked AIDS to homosexuality. He reveals how national differences in the United States and Australia affect the AIDS epidemic. He also brings up the positive effect attention to AIDS has had on the gay movement.

The final essay, "AIDS and the American Health Polity," by Daniel M. Fox, uses the response to the AIDS epidemic in the United States as a basis for examining the structure of the American health care system and the health policy process.

Recognizing that this book is an incomplete look at the bearing of history on the AIDS epidemic, editors Fee and Fox identify some serious omissions, especially the historical context of the epidemic in Africa, Asia, the Caribbean, South America, and continental Europe. (TJW)

PR,IL

357. Feldman, Douglas A., ed. **Culture and AIDS.** New York: Praeger, 1990. 216 p. Includes bibliographies and index. ISBN: 0-275-93189-7.

Feldman, a medical anthropologist and founder of the AIDS and Anthropology Research Group, organized and edited this group of essays focused on AIDS as a cultural phenomenon. Rather than providing an introduction to AIDS, the book is "designed to clarify several key domains in AIDS and the social sciences" (preface). Most of the contributors are anthropologists actively involved in AIDS research and activities, and all of the chapters were written specifically for this volume.

The first four chapters place AIDS in broad cultural contexts. Feldman begins the volume with his essay "Culture and AIDS." Pointing out that "a cultural understanding focuses not only on what humans do, nor only upon how we do it, but upon why we do it" (p. 6), he specifies a range of cultural aspects (explanations of origins, public response, heterosexual sexuality, gay pride, etc.) that are relevant to prevention efforts. S. C. McCombie deals with different responses to the advent of AIDS—how it has been described, evolutionary biological implications, origins, controversies, contagion, control, and comparisons with syphilis—in "AIDS in Cultural, Historic, and Epidemiologic Context." In "Assessing Viral, Parasitic, and Sociocultural Cofactors Affecting HIV-1 Transmission in Rwanda," Feldman comments that some of the key epidemiological questions of AIDS have not been answered, e.g., Why is the spread of HIV infection among heterosexuals in east and west Africa so rapid compared with its slow transmission among non-IV drug-using heterosexual men and women in the U.S.? Michael D. Quam discusses the challenge that AIDS poses for interpretation by social scientists. How does the Parsonian paradigm of the sick role apply to AIDS? How do the social psychological principles of stigma attribution apply to AIDS victims? How is the cultural concept of pollution danger experienced by PWAs?

Another set of essays focuses more specifically on symbolic aspects of AIDS-related behavior. Christopher C. Taylor distinguishes between disease as a biomedical concern and illness as a concept that incorporates meaning. In "AIDS and the Pathogenesis of Metaphor" he goes on to discuss how seemingly scientific facts are often judgmental metaphors. Paul Farmer complements Taylor's points in "AIDS and Accusation: Haiti, Haitians, and the Geography of Blame" by discussing methodological and ethical dilemmas posed by the anthropological investigations of AIDS. In "Prostitute Women and the Ideology of Work in London," Sophie Day discusses how anthropological inquiry leads to information not usually considered in HIV transmission, e.g., the symbolic and behavioral distinctions that prostitutes make between their work and their private lives.

The final set of essays centers on the links between cultural beliefs and social responses to AIDS. In "Minority Women and AIDS: Culture, Race, and Gender," Dooley Worth explores the effects of social context and cultural beliefs on black and Latina women, pointing out that survival skills in minority communities may conflict with AIDS prevention, which needs to focus on the collective impact of socialization on sexual behavior. In "Sex, Politics, and Guilt: A Study of Homophobia and the AIDS Phenomenon," Norris Lang shows how system maintaining ideologies ("sham," "blaming the victim") relative to AIDS affect homophobia and the eventual actions that people take in relation to AIDS. Juliet Niehaus demonstrates differential effects of class and status on the utilization of social services for AIDS patients in "Increasing the Cost of Living: Class and Exploitation in the Delivery of Social Services to PWAs." Finally, two essays explore language as a guide to the social reality of AIDS. William L. Leap, in "Language and AIDS," shows the ways in which discourse about AIDS is not neutral, while Peter Nardi in "AIDS and Obituaries: The Perpetuation of Stigma in the Press" points out that stigma leads to a reconstruction of language used to report the death of PWAs.

In the concluding essay, Feldman notes the unique role that anthropologists can play in AIDS-related activities and research by utilizing the ethnographic method. However, the method needs to address problem-oriented issues rather than theoretical ones. (SGF)

PR,IL
358. Flanders, Stephen A., and Carl N. Flanders. **AIDS.** New York: Facts On File, 1991. 248 p. (Library in a Book). Includes bibliographies and index. ISBN 0-8160-1910-X.

This guide to resources on AIDS is intended for the student and researcher. Divided into two parts, part I, "Overview of the Topic," provides a thorough medical discussion of the AIDS epidemic, followed by a detailed chronology of the subject from January 31, 1981 to December 6, 1989, a summary of important court cases involving AIDS, and brief biographical sketches of a cross-section of significant figures who have been involved in the AIDS epidemic.

Part II, "Guide to Further Research," provides suggestions on how to access information about AIDS in libraries, using the card catalog, indexes, government documents, and computerized databases. It also contains a lengthy, annotated bibliography of books, government reports, and periodical articles covering the general, medical, and legal aspects of the subject. A section devoted to organizational resources follows; it lists many national organizations, followed by state and local organizations arranged by states.

In three appendixes are a list of key acronyms and initials, a glossary of useful terms, and an explanation of the United States Public Health System.

As a guide to resources on AIDS, this book covers the most important bibliographic and organizational sources to begin one's research plus information to delve more deeply into the topic. (TJW)

PO
359. Freudberg, Frank. **Herpes: A Complete Guide to Relief & Reassurance.** Introduction by E. Stephen Emanuel, M.D. Philadelphia: Running Press, 1982. 159 p. Includes bibliography, index, and glossary. ISBN 0-89471-188-1.

Because it exists in epidemic proportions and there is no known cure for it, the herpes virus has become one of America's "most dreaded diseases." Classified as a STD (sexually transmitted disease), its likelihood of spreading is practically assured.

In part I of *Herpes*, Freudberg and Emanuel first describe in general terms the "epidemic" sweeping the United States and identify the genital herpes virus. Exploding common myths about the herpes virus and its transmission, they then delve into the anatomy of a virus and describe the five members of the herpes virus group, including *Herpes simplex virus I* (HSV-I) and *Herpes simplex virus II* (HSV-II). They follow this up with a discussion of the immune system.

In part II are discussed victims' psychological reactions, the sort of help available through such organizations as the American Social Health Organization, which created the Herpes Resource Center, and how the problem can be explained to others.

Herpes simplex virus replicates easily and spreads. Part III, "Complications and How to Avoid Them," deals with such diseases as *herpes keratitis*, which affects the eye; cervical cancer and its link to genital herpes; and herpes virus infections in infants contracted during pregnancy and childbirth.

Part IV, "Fighting Back," discusses "cures" that don't work as well as newer treatments and therapies, including the use of Acyclovir (ACV), interferon, and other substances; prevention of the spread of the herpes virus; measures to ease discomfort and reduce the frequency of attacks; stress associated with the infections; and nutrition.

Appendix A to this clearly written book lists local chapters of the Herpes Resource Center, and appendix B discusses various micronutrients (vitamins and minerals) that are relevant to nutrition programs designed to prevent herpes. (TJW)

IL,PO

360.   Gong, Victor, and Norman Rudnick, eds. **AIDS: Facts and Issues.** Foreword by Congressman Ted Weiss. New Brunswick, N.J.: Rutgers University Press, 1986. 388 p. Revised, updated and expanded edition of *Understanding AIDS: A Comprehensive Guide.* Includes bibliography, index, and glossary. ISBN 0-8135-1202-6.

Opening with an indictment of the Reagan administration's lack of response to the number one health crisis of the 1980s, Acquired Immune Deficiency Syndrome (AIDS), this book is a comprehensive guide to the issues raised by AIDS. Recognized experts from many fields contributed to this collection. Gong initially provides an overview, listing facts and fallacies about AIDS, followed by sections on the epidemiology and etiology as they are known. The clinical part covers immunology, signs and symptoms, viral and parasitic infections, bacterial and fungal infections, cancers, and disorders of the blood. One chapter describes certain at-risk groups: children, users of the nation's blood supply, Haitians, and prisoners.

Several contributors outline the social and economic costs of AIDS, noting society's response to the crisis. They discuss ethical issues, economics, and legal aspects, along with a presentation of San Francisco's model Public Health Department's response to the crisis and a statement of the gay perspective from the National Gay and Lesbian Task Force.

The final two parts of the book are most important for those people with AIDS and those close to or working with them. They describe nursing care, psychological and mental health issues, spiritual and religious dimensions, death and dying, and the prevention of AIDS. Ending with a chapter of questions and answers, health resources, referrals, and hotlines, Gong completes his coverage of the situation in the early- to mid-1980s. Contributors are listed at the end of the book with their credits. (NW)

PR

361.   Herdt, Gilbert, and Shirley Lindenbaum, eds. **The Time of AIDS: Social Analysis, Theory, and Method.** Newbury Park, Calif.: Sage Publications, 1992. 341 p. Includes bibliographies. ISBN 0-8039-4373-3.

Based on papers presented at a 1990 conference sponsored by the Wenner-Gren Foundation for Anthropological Research, this volume explores the impact of AIDS, particularly its effect on anthropological theory, method, and practice. As editor Herdt notes, "The AIDS epidemic is forcing us to change the way we think about and study culture" (p. vii) because it challenges our assumptions, conceptualizations, and approaches to culture, cultural groups, and cultural behavior. It also impels other disciplines, e.g., history, sociology, psychology, to change their approaches to social analysis. This book presents the fruits of an interdisciplinary dialogue on the roles of culture, epidemiology, and medicine in understanding AIDS.

Herdt begins part I, "Social History and Representation," with an overview of the conceptual issues with which the authors deal, primarily how social scientists, especially anthropologists, can respond to the changing face of social reality that AIDS has presented. Culture is central to understanding this reality, but questions about its conceptualization and use arise: How is the culture concept relevant to the study of AIDS? How useful are current epidemiological categories and medical perspectives in preventing AIDS? What ethics will govern social scientists engaged in applied research on AIDS? John H. Gagnon ("Epidemics and Researchers: AIDS and the Practice of Social Studies") discusses the interface between research and practice, particularly the issue of authoritative response to the public's applied questions. Virginia Berridge ("AIDS: History and Contemporary History") examines the historian's role in interpreting AIDS and how that role has changed over time. Paula A. Treichler ("AIDS, HIV, and the Cultural Construction of Reality") concludes part I with an exploration of how to plausibly interpret AIDS as a cultural construction.

Part II, "Method and Theory in Western Society," focuses on the methodological issues raised by AIDS research, particularly how to investigate sexual practices and attitudes. Paul R. Abramson ("Sex, Lies, and Ethnography") provides a critique of current anthropological methods that might be used to investigate sexual transmission of HIV, while Ralph Bolton ("Mapping Terra Incognita: Sex Research for AIDS Prevention—An Urgent Agenda for the 1990s") offers some innovative approaches (e.g., participant observation, cognitive mapping, reports of sexual encounters) to finding out what sex means to participants and how to use it for AIDS prevention. Ernest Quimby ("Anthropological Witnessing for African Americans: Power, Responsibility, and Choice in an Age of AIDS") draws attention to the factors that social scientists consider when they attempt to intervene on behalf of people infected with HIV, and Martin P. Levine ("The Implications of Constructionist Theory for Social Research on the AIDS Epidemic Among Gay Men"), after reviewing current research on HIV in gay men, proposes a constructionist approach to AIDS research. Stephanie Kane and Theresa Mason (" 'IV Drug Users' and 'Sex Partners': The Limits of Epidemiological Categories and the Ethnography of Risk") point out the drawbacks of ethnographic research that focuses on social groups for prevention efforts.

In part III, "Cross-Cultural Studies," the authors relate theoretical and methodological issues to specific cultural contexts. Richard G. Parker ("Sexual Diversity, Cultural Analysis, and AIDS Education in Brazil") points out the need to understand the erotic dimensions of sexual experience within their cultural context. By specifying the range and distribution of sexual practices in ethnic groups, Joseph M. Carrier and J. Raúl Magaña ("Use of Ethnosexual Data on Men of Mexican Origin for HIV/AIDS Prevention Programs") think that anthropology can contribute to curbing AIDS. Brooke Grundfest Schoepf ("Women at Risk: Case Studies from Zaire") explores the political ecology of AIDS in Zaire, where HIV is transmitted primarily by heterosexual intercourse and is slightly more prevalent among women. Paul Farmer ("New Disorder, Old Dilemmas: AIDS and Anthropology in Haiti") draws attention to the ethical concerns of anthropologists who conduct AIDS research, who need to balance their professional interests, personal integrity, and the needs of the people whom they study. Editor Lindenbaum ("Knowledge and Action in the Shadow of AIDS") draws the book to a close with a discussion of the five themes that she thinks pervade the thirteen preceding papers: (1) The crossing of disciplinary boundaries; (2) culture, history, and the study of disease;

(3) the relationship of social theory to social life; (4) the creation of scientific knowledge; and (5) the call for both knowledge and practice. (SGF)

PR,IL
362. Institute of Medicine. **Mobilizing Against AIDS: The Unfinished Story of a Virus.** Cambridge, Mass.: Harvard University Press, 1986. 212 p. Includes bibliography, index, and glossary. ISBN 0-674-57761-2.

Based on presentations at the annual meeting of the Institute of Medicine in 1985, this book is aimed at the one method of AIDS control: public education. It begins with a description of how AIDS is transmitted, and how the epidemic developed in the United States, Europe, Africa, and Haiti. Eve Nichols traces the search for and discovery of the HTLV-III/LAV virus (now termed Human Immunodeficiency Virus, or HIV), its isolation, how it functions, its explosive replication, and why this knowledge is important for the development of vaccine(s) and treatments.

Nichols describes the functioning of a healthy immune system, and details in accessible language what goes awry upon HIV infection, including the difficulties associated with the virus when it crosses the blood/brain barrier. In the chapter on prevention and treatment, Nichols puts stress on public education, specifically on risk-reduction programs aimed at high-risk groups, including safe-sex techniques for sexually active bisexual and homosexual men as well as information for safer drug use. The issues surrounding testing for antibody status are politically explosive and complex. They include voluntary versus mandatory testing; contact tracing; confidentiality of records; the availability of appropriate counseling for those tested, whether negative or positive; and the problems of donations of blood, semen, and organs for transplant.

HIV is a difficult target for cure and treatment; it means designing new chemical agents and using drugs that were developed for other purposes. The prospects for a vaccine are complicated greatly by the wily nature of HIV. Current estimates for a prototype vaccine range from one to ten years; mass immunization is not an option in the near term. Health education is the only realistic goal. Two chapters deal with individual and societal stress. AIDS patients face discrimination in many forms, almost always based on ignorance and unfounded fear. The book recommends rational, compassionate, and realistic approaches on the part of society and public health agencies. (NW)

IL,PO
363. Kübler-Ross, Elisabeth. **AIDS: The Ultimate Challenge.** New York: Macmillan, 1987. 329 p. ISBN 0-02-567170-7.

Kübler-Ross, world renowned authority on death and dying and author of *On Death and Dying* (1969), turns her attention in this book to AIDS, which now has reached pandemic proportions. Her concern in this book is not with the AIDS virus itself but rather with the care of AIDS patients, usually young adults and children.

Her work with terminally ill patients over more than twenty years taught her the "stages of dying" experienced by these patients: denial and isolation, anger, bargaining, depression, and acceptance. AIDS patients as well as family and friends, show these same stages in the long up-and-down struggle with AIDS. As the publisher's blurb comments, "She reaches out to them so that they can die with dignity and with their loved ones around them. . . . She makes a special plea for women and children with AIDS and prisoners with AIDS, but most important she pleads for babies with AIDS. Unwanted by their mothers, shunned by foster families and adoption agencies, they are too often left—unmothered, unloved—to die alone in hospitals."

On October 9, 1985 Kübler-Ross convened a public meeting in Monterey, Virginia, about the possibility of having a special AIDS care facility for children from six months to two-and-a-half years old established on her own properly in Highland County. Despite expert medical testimony about AIDS, the questions at the meeting revealed the degree of hostility from the people of the region, who turned down Kübler-Ross's proposal.

Despite such setbacks in the early 1980s, Kübler-Ross continued her work with AIDS patients. She called for the establishment of hospices for AIDS patients, for volunteers to work with AIDS patients and special training for volunteers who must learn that the devotion required is one of unconditional love and service.

An appendix contains a discussion of the rising cost of the AIDS epidemic supplemented by a chart showing the reported cases of AIDS and reported deaths from 1979 to 1986. (TJW)

PO

364. Lumiere, Richard, and Stephani Cook. **Healthy Sex . . . And Keeping It That Way: A Complete Guide to Sexual Infections.** New York: Simon & Schuster, 1983. 206 p. ISBN 0-671-45899-X.

Intended for sexually active persons, this three-part guide provides useful information on sexual infections and what to do about them. Part I discusses the general problem of the increase in venereal disease (10 million new cases reported each year), sexual etiquette for individuals who have contracted a disease, terminology, male and female pelvic organs, and disease symptoms. Part II, organized by type of infection (bacterial, intermediate organism, viral, fungal, infestational, protozoan, and intestinal), provides concrete information about individual diseases: cause, symptoms, diagnosis, treatment, etc. For example, under *Hemophilus vaginalis* (HV), one of the bacterial infections, Lumiere and Cook give general information about the disease, how it is caught, first symptoms, diagnosis, treatment, and outcome. Other bacterial infections similarly dealt with are gonorrhea, syphilis, chancroid, and granuloma inguinale. The section on viral infections provides a discussion of oral herpes simplex virus (HSV-I) and genital herpes simplex virus (HSV-II). Part III, devoted to sexual health, contains a special section for women that covers such topics as the healthy vagina, vaginitis, toxic shock syndrome, contraception, when to see the doctor, and pregnancy; the section for men covers responsibility, symptoms of sexual infection in oneself and in the female partner, hygienic considerations, and contraception. Lumiere and Cook also give suggestions on where to go for help and how to stay healthy. The book concludes with a glossary of useful terms. The authors, a medical doctor specializing in gynecology and a marital counselor and sex therapist, warn that information in this area changes rapidly and that their book should not be taken as a substitute for the attention of one's own physician. (TJW)

PR,IL

365. Quétel, Claude. **History of Syphilis.** Translated by Judith Braddock and Brian Pike. Baltimore, Md.: Johns Hopkins University Press, 1990. 342 p. Translation of: *Le Mal de Naples: Histoire de la Syphilis.* Includes bibliographic notes, index, and chronology. ISBN 0-8018-4089-9.

For four and a half centuries (1495-1943) no very effective treatment for syphilis existed. Known originally as *le mal de Naples*, syphilis was encountered in Naples at the time of the return of sailors from Columbus's second voyage to the New World when the French king Charles VIII conducted his Italian campaign in 1495. The affliction, then dubbed *morbus Gallicus* (the French disease), spread rapidly northward throughout Europe and eventually the world. Quétel reviews the much-disputed origin of the illness, describing the various theories that still occupy the attention of scholars.

While Quétel compares the policies and practices in different Western countries and Japan at different times, he places the greatest emphasis on the history of the disease in France. He describes and illustrates in detail what society learned and did about this venereal scourge in the sixteenth, seventeenth, and eighteenth centuries. Girolamo Fracastoro in his poem "Syphilis sive morbus gallicus" (1530) gave the disease its name, deriving it from the shepherd Syphilus who received the disease from the Sun God as punishment for his evil deeds. Fracastoro later postulated that the disease was caused by "tiny invisible living things"!

In response to the epidemic proportions of this sickness, the French opened hospitals to the afflicted, often mingling them with the insane. Later special hospitals for women and children were established. Conditions in these overcrowded dumping grounds were appalling. Early on treatment also involved the oral administration of compounds of mercury and arsenic. Eventually viewed as a disease rather than pestilence, conflicting theories were advanced as to its nature, numerous medical texts were compiled describing symptoms at various stages, and, aided by the microscope, the search for the microbe causing syphilis begun. Not until 1812, when Hernandez distinguished between syphilis and gonorrhea, was headway made in understanding the disease. The gonococcus microbe was discovered in 1879, but the syphilis spirochete (*treponema pallidum*) not until 1905.

It was the German scientist, Paul Ehrlich, who, while experimenting in 1909 with arsenicals, came upon a compound, which he labeled "606" and dubbed Salvarsan, that proved so effective in treating syphilis that it was called a "magic bullet." The great breakthrough, unrecognized at first, came in 1928 when Alexander Fleming accidentally discovered penicillin. Introduced in 1943, complete success was achieved in treating syphilis. The incidence of syphilis plunged worldwide and many wrongfully concluded that it would disappear altogether.

Quétel has carefully traced the many political, social, medical, and research efforts over the centuries to control syphilis and find a cure for it. He gives emphasis to public policies affecting prostitution, which has traditionally received attention as one of the principal social forces spreading the disease. He points out the resurgence of both syphilis and gonorrhea in the 1960s and concludes by commenting on the relationship between these two diseases and the new scourge, AIDS. While our understanding of syphilis is still not complete, the public needs to be educated about the consequences of ignoring the traditional STDs. (TJW)

PR
366.   Reamer, Frederic G., ed. **AIDS & Ethics.** New York: Columbia University Press, 1991. 317 p. Includes bibliographies and index. ISBN 0-231-07358-5.

Reamer, professor in the School of Social Work, Rhode Island College, raises vexing ethical questions concerning AIDS patients that the diverse scholars and practitioners represented in this collection of papers expertly address. Drawn from the fields of medicine, law, social work, religion, philosophy, and political science, each has some ten years of experience dealing with the AIDS crisis.

In "AIDS: The Relevance of Ethics," editor Reamer states that the AIDS epidemic poses ethical challenges to many segments of society; he believes that applied ethics has much to offer those professionals who must examine their professional commitment to work with the AIDS population. "AIDS, Public Health, and Civil Liberties: Consensus and Conflict in Policy" offers Ronald Bayer's "analysis of the shifting tension . . . between public health and civil liberties advocates," emphasizing the "unstable balance between public health safeguards and civil liberties protections." James Childress in "Mandatory HIV Screening and Testing" focuses on the arguments for and against screening and testing of hospital patients, marriage license applicants, pregnant women, newborns, individuals in the state's custody, and international travelers.

Carol Levine in "AIDS and the Ethics of Human Subjects Research" reviews ethical standards for research, including confidentiality of research data, the ethical aspects of screening, access to unapproved therapies, vaccine-related research, and other ethical issues. "AIDS and the Crisis of Health Insurance" is the topic of a paper by Gerald M. Oppenheimer and Robert Padgug, who argue for universal and uniform health care coverage. In "Ethical Issues in AIDS Education," Nora Kizer Bell calls for "assertive and frank forms of education designed to prevent the spread of AIDS" while opposing coercion to contain transmission of the disease. Courtney S. Campbell critically examines AIDS activism, questioning the extent to which activists have adhered to moral criteria inherent in the tradition of civil disobedience in "Ethics and Militant AIDS Activism." In "AIDS and the Physician-Patient Relationship," Robert J. Levine analyzes the physician-patient relationship, speculating about the ethical components inherent in the question of the duty of physicians to treat AIDS patients. Abigail Zuger addresses the ethical norms within the medical profession and among health care practitioners in "AIDS and the Obligation of Health Care Professionals." Ferdinand Schoemen in "AIDS and Privacy" reviews various privacy issues concerning disclosure of information about sexual activities, drug use, and test results on the part of therapists, the HIV infected individual, health insurers, and the state.

Finally, Donald H. J. Hermann in "AIDS and the Law" reviews the range of legal issues and developments stemming from the AIDS crisis, including mandatory testing, privacy, employment, school-based discrimination, protection of third parties, the duty to treat, the use of quarantine, and civil liability. (TJW)

IL,PO

367. Rosebury, Theodor. **Microbes and Morals: The Strange Story of Venereal Disease.** New York: Viking Press, 1971. 361 p. Includes bibliography and index.

Although he hopes that both the scholar and specialist will find it useful, Rosebury has written this book primarily for the general reader. Because it is considered "dirty," venereal disease has been unpopular as a literary subject. However, the abundant scholarly literature allows Rosebury to deal with the subject historically, medically, and technically.

In part I, "Contagion," Rosebury reviews what is known about the origin of both gonorrhea and syphilis. Evidence for both can be found in ancient texts, but there is a persistent theory about the introduction of syphilis into Europe at the end of the fifteenth century by the sailors from Columbus's ships, which Rosebury opposes. He focuses his attention on the writings of Girolamo Fracastoro, who advanced a surprisingly modern theory about the origin and spread of disease (1530), particularly syphilis, that he dubbed the *morbus Gallicus* (French disease).

Rosebury examines syphilis as a member of a group of nonvenereal diseases called the treponematoses. It includes nonvenereal, or endemic, syphilis, yaws, and pinta. Microscopically, the spirochetes of these diseases are indistinguishable, which makes their investigation difficult; they differ, of course, in the diseases they produce.

In part II, "Literature, Art and Morals," Rosebury traces the treatment of VD in the belles-lettres (the Bible, Rabelais, Shakespeare, Ibsen, etc.) and the graphic arts. He also devotes one chapter to the great personages (kings, popes, etc.) who have been afflicted with VD; and another to society's persistent though outmoded view of sex as sin and venereal disease as punishment for sinful behavior.

Information about the status of venereal disease in modern society is presented in part III, "Facts and Figures," and part IV, "Control: Past, Present, and Future." Identifying the "true" venereal diseases as syphilis, gonorrhea, chancroid, and lymphogranuloma venereum (LGV), Rosebury states that only the first two are of major importance. Common, well-understood, and curable, they have nevertheless resisted worldwide attempts to control them. In fact, VD rates in recent years for syphilis and gonorrhea have increased in many countries, including the United States. Rosebury reviews the VD control problem from the mid-nineteenth century to the late 1960s, concentrating on the problem before and after the penicillin era. He discusses the efforts to control prostitution, sanitary measures, public awareness, and drugs, and highlights the work of Thomas Parran, Surgeon General of the United States before World War II.

Rosebury states that VD is "a product of our habits of life and modes of conduct, and its control is likely to require that such habits and modes be changed" (p. 306). This is what he means by the word "morals" in the title. He wants people who believe that they may have contracted a venereal disease to overcome their fears and bring the situation to the attention of medical personnel as soon as possible. This behavior, he believes, would be a major step in the eventual control of VD. (TJW)

IL,PO
368. Shilts, Randy. **And the Band Played On: Politics, People, and the AIDS Epidemic.** New York: St. Martin's Press, 1987. 630 p. Includes notes on sources and index. ISBN 0-312-00994-1.

Why didn't anyone listen? Why was the response to AIDS so slow? In this dramatic chronicle of the recognition of, response to, and treatment of AIDS from 1976 through 1987, journalist Shilts, a reporter on AIDS for the *San Francisco Chronicle* since 1982, documents with meticulous detail, the intersection of medical, political, media, gay community, commercial, and personal responses to the dilemmas posed by AIDS—a "profoundly threatening medical crisis." Although focused on AIDS, Shilts deals with broader concerns and shows the ways that AIDS became the locus for debate about values and beliefs concerning gay lifestyles, appropriate sexual behavior, funding for research and treatment of a sexually transmitted disease, the role of the media in disseminating accurate information about sex and minorities, political and medical lobbying for funds, and the purity of scientific research.

After identifying the fifty-five dramatis personae—doctors, counselors, epidemiologists, researchers, politicians, administrators, gay activists, people with AIDS—and providing an outline of private and governmental organizations dealing with AIDS, Shilts sets the stage in the first chapter for the fifty-eight chapters that follow. Part I, "Behold, a Pale Horse," marks the development of AIDS symptoms in a female Danish surgeon as well as the interest of another doctor in understanding how pneumocystis carinii pneumonia had killed his friend. Part II, "Before: 1980," describes the apparent sexual liberation that gay activists felt accompanied their political liberation before the specter of death began to haunt the gay community. While symptoms of AIDS were appearing from New York City to San Francisco, there was little understanding of the serious consequences to follow. Part III, "Paving the Road: 1981," shifts the scenes to the Centers for Disease Control, hospitals, and places where doctors and researchers attempt to interpret increasing numbers of cases of Kaposi's Sarcoma, opportunistic infections, hepatitis B, and pneumocystis carinii pneumonia in gay patients. Part IV, "The Gathering Darkness: 1982," details the growing recognition of gays that the new syndrome was quite serious. Some concluded that "the disease is moving even if the government isn't" (p. 121). By April 1982, 300 Americans had been struck by AIDS; 119 had died. The syndrome had no name and only nominal funding was granted for research. Over a year into "the epidemic" NIH had no coordinated AIDS plan. The identification of AIDS as a gay disease would affect how government, the scientific community, health officials, and gays would respond to it. Part V, "Battle Lines: January-June," deals with divisions among gay leaders and political officials in how to handle the crisis. AIDS hysteria and AIDSpeak were developing. Part VI, "Rituals: July-December 1983," documents increasing concern and misinformation about AIDS within the context of the media, politics, research organizations, and hospitals. By Christmas 1983, Dr. Robert Gallo told the director of the National Cancer Institute that he had discovered the retrovirus that caused AIDS. Part VII, "Lights and Tunnels: 1984," focuses on increasing concerns about prevention, including rivalries among scientific researchers to claim credit for discovery of the AIDS virus; international competition to claim credit for breakthroughs; political differences between the gay movement on the East and West coasts; balancing the economic interests of blood banks and bathhouses against health concerns. Meanwhile, there was increasing identification of AIDS in other countries and in other groups, e.g., IV drug users, babies, hemophiliacs. Part VIII, "The Butcher's Bill: 1985," characterizes the arrival of the "future shock of the AIDS epidemic" and the challenge of balancing health policy with individual rights—testing, legal ramifications, changes in the sexual practices in the gay community, acceptance of the enormity of the problem." In the epilogue, Shilts notes that the story of AIDS is a story of bigotry and what it can do to a nation. It is a story of shame.

This is a scientific detective story as well as a sober look at the ways that politics affects scientific research, channels medical treatment of diseases, circumvents funding for minorities, and reinforces traditional sexual values. Yet, the personal stories of those affected by AIDS remain a major aspect of the book, which details the pain and despair of those who confront and experience AIDS. (SGF)

PR,IL
369.   Smith, Joseph Wayne. **AIDS, Philosophy and Beyond: Philosophical Dilemmas of a Modern Pandemic.** Aldershot, Eng.: Avebury, 1991. 341 p. (Avebury Series in Philosophy). Includes bibliography and index. ISBN 1-85628-138-8.

AIDS, and the social and political problems associated with the disease, constitute one of the most pressing and controversial bioethical issues of the late twentieth century. However, to date the full philosophical ramifications of this problem have yet to be explored. The aim of this book is to systematically uncover the deep moral and political dilemmas raised by the AIDS pandemic and to suggest a social alternative to received views on the ethics and politics of AIDS. Topics discussed include controversial epistemological and metascientific questions about AIDS, such as the issue of causality and the social construction of disease categories; social and ethical problems associated with homosexuality, prostitution and the use of IV drugs and more general moral problems such as the issues of state paternalism and public policy, individual freedom and sexual conduct, privacy and medical confidentiality, justice in the health care system and the allocation of scarce medical resources.

This book is both a systematic exploration of the ethics and politics of AIDS, and a passionate plea for rationality, dignity, and social justice for AIDS sufferers. (Author) [N.B. Joseph Wayne Smith is Queen Elizabeth II Research Fellow in Bioethics at the Flinders University of South Australia.]

IL
370.   Sontag, Susan. **AIDS and Its Metaphors.** New York: Farrar, Straus & Giroux, 1989. 95 p. Includes bibliographic footnotes.

Sontag, author of the highly acclaimed essay, *Illness as Metaphor* (1978), has now written a derivative work, *AIDS and Its Metaphors*, presenting her reactions to the metaphorical use of language to characterize this new illness.

Going back to Aristotle for a definition of metaphor and citing examples for and against its use in the literature of antiquity, she demonstrates the effectiveness of metaphors in politics, biology, and medicine. "Military metaphors," she avers, "contribute to the stigmatizing of certain illnesses and, by extension, of those who are ill. It was the discovery of the stigmatization of people who have cancer that led me to write *Illness as Metaphor*" (p. 11-12). She reviews historically the treatment and prevention of such killing diseases as cancer, tuberculosis, syphilis, cholera, and the like, that reached epidemic proportions from time to time.

AIDS is the new affliction that is being subjected to the same sort of stigmatization that characterized society's attitude toward patients with cancer, syphilis, etc. Taking metaphorical examples from the press, which depicts AIDS as a military conflict, Sontag provides a detailed description of the course of AIDS from its first stage of HIV infection, through the onset of symptoms, to the terminal stage when the patient succumbs to one or more diseases. It is this language that she deplores.

Sontag goes on to examine society's views of the reasons why people get some of these dread diseases: generally living unhealthy lives, but also weakness of the will, lack of prudence, and addiction to legal chemicals. With AIDS they are indulgence, delinquency, illegal drug addiction, and deviant sex. For some, the principal metaphor to use to describe the AIDS epidemic is "plague," that is viewed as inflicted, that is, as coming from some outside source, be it some Third World country or God. As Sontag says, "In the twentieth century it has become almost impossible [because of medical progress] to moralize about epidemics—except those which are transmitted sexually" (p. 56), and "Many want to view AIDS metaphorically—as, plague-like, a moral judgment on society" (p. 60).

In the popular view AIDS is deemed an unprecedented menace of world proportions, and people everywhere are frightened. It is necessary therefore to try to defuse the "end-of-the-world rhetoric that AIDS has evoked." Sontag suggests that two important ways to deal with the alarm surrounding the AIDS epidemic are (1) to consider AIDS as just a disease, although one of epidemic proportions, and (2) to skeptically view the metaphorical language being used to describe the epidemic. (TJW)

PR,IL
371. Stuber, Margaret L., ed. **Children and AIDS.** Washington, D.C.: American Psychiatric Press, 1992. 226 p. (Clinical Practice; no. 19). Includes bibliographies. ISBN 0-88048-199-4.

In his inaugural editorial to *Pediatric AIDS and HIV Infection: Fetus to Adolescent* former U.S. Surgeon General C. E. Koop stated that "by 1991, it has been estimated that worldwide most new cases of AIDS will occur in children" (p. xiii). According to the Centers for Disease Control, in 1991, 84 percent of new cases of AIDS in children were a result of vertical transmission from mother to infant. Furthermore, the incidence of AIDS in teenagers, though small (about 1 percent of AIDS cases in the United States in 1989), is increasing. HIV infection and AIDS in children and adolescents present special problems that health care workers, physicians, clinicians, and families must deal with. This book draws from the perspectives of a variety of disciplines—law, social work, nursing, psychology, anthropology, neurology, obstetrics, neuropsychology, neonatology, psychiatry, child psychiatry—to address the clinical issues that arise in dealing with children and adolescents infected with HIV. The twenty-six authors of the thirteen articles, primarily professionals in the fields of medicine, social work, and psychology, "present a gestalt of what clinicians who work with children and AIDS encounter" (p. xiii). Most articles consider how the issues of race, ethnicity, socioeconomic status, and physical/psychological development affect coping with HIV infection in children.

The first section, "The Context of Pediatric HIV and AIDS," begins with Mhairi MacDonald's article, "Vertical Transmission of HIV: Management of the Pregnant Mother and Her Infant," that describes the course of vertically acquired HIV infection as well as a basic plan of care for the mother and infant, including new drug protocols. Other articles discuss the specific developmental (e.g., adolescence), medical (e.g., hemophilia), and/or ethnic (Mexican-Latino, African American) contexts that shape the risk of being infected with HIV as well as the types of appropriate interventions within these contexts.

The second section, "Specific Issues for HIV-Infected Children," deals with the effects of HIV infection on the neurological and psychological development of the child as well as with the social issues (e.g., the right of an HIV-infected child to an education, the interaction between family members) raised by infection. In "The Perspective of Families," psychiatrist Lynn S. Baker points out the real difficulties that families face with an HIV-infected child—the linked stressors of stigma, secrecy, isolation, and lack of support and services; "they know what we often do not: What is *practical*" (p. 148).

The final section, "Providing Care for HIV-Infected Children," concerns the delivery of services from social and medical sources to the child and family members dealing with HIV infection. Editor Stuber's final essay summarizes some of the psychotherapeutic issues presented by pediatric HIV and AIDS and suggests how clinicians can apply their skills to the unique psychological and social problems raised by HIV-infection in children. (SGF)

PR,IL
372. Watstein, Sarah Barbara, and Robert Anthony Laurich. **AIDS and Women: A Sourcebook.** Phoenix, Ariz.: Oryx Press, 1991. 159 p. Includes bibliographies and indexes. ISBN 0-89774-577-9.

In fourteen chapters with numerous statistical tables, the compilers of this reference work focus on the complex and pressing problem of the AIDS epidemic as it spreads among women worldwide. As remarked by Ruthann Bates, the Director of the National AIDS Information Clearinghouse of the Centers for Disease Control, in her foreword: "Through the end of July 1990, a total of 7,965 women had died from their infections. Between 1985 and 1988, the death rate for HIV/AIDS quadrupled. By 1987, AIDS had become one of the ten leading causes of death in U.S. women of reproductive age." This sourcebook brings to women the information they need to understand AIDS and its impact on their lives, whether they be "family, lovers, or friends of persons with AIDS, whether they be professional caregivers or AIDS educators" (p. ix).

Chapters cover many aspects of the subject of AIDS, ranging from "Heterosexually Transmitted AIDS," which discusses the facts on reducing the risk of sexual transmission of AIDS, to "Prevention: Medical Management," which provides advice on AIDS treatment. Each chapter provides a discussion of the topic together with a generous listing of selected bibliographic references to published articles, papers, reports, and books, always annotated, and usually supplemented with statistical tables.

Other chapters are "Transmission Through Intravenous Drug Use," "Transmission Through Blood and Blood Products," "The Risk for the Sexual Partners of Hemophiliacs," "Perinatal Transmission," "Lesbians and AIDS," "Myths and Potential for the Transmission and Spread of AIDS Through Women," "African Women and AIDS," "Other Women of Color and AIDS," "Imprisoned Women and AIDS," "Prostitutes and AIDS," "Women and the AIDS Epidemic: Roles and Impact," and "Prevention: Safer Sex."

Table 15, accompanying the chapter on "African Women and AIDS," provides data on worldwide cases reported as of June 1990. Divided by country under each continent, it shows that Africa has 65,149 cases; the Americas, 162,885 cases; Asia, 655 cases; Europe, 35,353 cases; Oceania, 2,096 cases; for a worldwide total of 266,098 cases.

Appendixes include a listing of audiovisual resources in the United States; a directory of national and state hotlines; a glossary of AIDS-related terms and expressions; and a listing of reference materials that identify resources on AIDS and suggestions on methods for continuing research on AIDS.

Recognizing that information on AIDS changes rapidly, even daily, the compilers nonetheless hope that their sourcebook will "serve as a guide to AIDS information, prevention, research, and understanding." (TJW)

Sex Organ Problems. Castration. Circumcision. Clitoridectomy

PR,IL
373. Cloudsley, Anne. **Women of Omdurman: Life, Love and the Cult of Virginity.** New York: St. Martin's Press, 1984. 181 p. Includes bibliography and glossary. ISBN 0-312-887-558.

From 1960 to 1971 Anne Cloudsley and her husband lived in Khartoum, the capital of Sudan; she organized a physiotherapy department in Omdurman Hospital and initiated a natural childbirth program there. She states that this book "attempts to portray the entirety of my experience of living and working in the Sudan. I have recounted the everyday lives of two extended families whom I came to know intimately through working at Omdurman Hospital" (p. 8). Through this experience she "reveals the ethos of the women of Omdurman, so reflecting the lot of women everywhere in the Sudan" (p. 8).

Cloudsley first describes her work and experience in Omdurman Hospital where she acquires a close-up view of women's problems. Besides her hospital duties she learns about household life from her Sudanese friends. With them she observes and even participates in ceremonies celebrating marriages, circumcisions, purifications, and confinements. She witnesses what happens in families during the Muslim holy month of Ramadan. As a result she begins to comprehend male-female relationships in a patriarchal and religious society.

Cloudsley devotes an entire chapter to the ancient practice of circumcision in the Sudan. Although boys as well as girls are circumcised, she emphasizes female circumcision, or clitoridectomy, excision, and infibulation. Known as "pharaonic circumcision" by the Sudanese, female circumcision involves "excision of the external genitalia and sewing up the sexual orifice" (p. 101). An Islamic religious custom traced back to the Prophet Abraham, the ceremony of circumcision may take place anytime between birth and puberty. Cloudsley states that 99 percent of women are still infibulated in Sudan. Outside Sudan in Africa it is also practiced in Somalia, Ethiopia, Kenya, Egypt, and countries of Central and West Africa.

Cloudsley describes in great detail two pharaonic circumcisions by a trained midwife in the house of a friend. First she gives the step-by-step procedure used on a female child of seven and then on her sister of five. Although sanitary precautions were taken, and novocaine was injected into the labia majora and the root of the clitoris, no general anesthetic was used on the patients.

While such reasons as the preservation of virginity and better sexual relations are advanced for the practice of circumcision, the fact of re-infibulation after a birth seems to discount some of the justification. Cloudsley believes that circumcision is an intractable problem in the Sudan and elsewhere because it is a Muslim tradition and a measure for ensuring a girl's virginity.

In the three appendixes Cloudsley discusses (1) different types of circumcision in Africa and what may be done to eradicate them; (2) the importance of understanding female orgasm; and (3) various projects and policies to combat female circumcision that now affects some 30 to 70 million girls in Africa and elsewhere. (TJW)

IL
374.   Hosken, Fran P. **The Hosken Report: Genital and Sexual Mutilation of Females.** 3rd ed. Lexington, Mass.: Women's International Network News, 1982. 327 p. Includes bibliography. ISBN 0-942096-05-3.

Hosken has campaigned against female genital mutilation since the early 1970s. Here she surveys the nature and extent of the practice in East and West Africa, the Arab peninsula, Asia, Europe, and the United States, viewing it within the context of economic development. Female "circumcision"—that varies from removal of the clitoris to complete excision of the clitoris and labia and stitching of the vaginal opening—is a practice deeply embedded in broader cultural restrictions on women's sexuality and reproduction. As such, it is often defended within the Third World against what is seen as the cultural imperialism of Western feminist criticism. Hosken critically examines "the reasons given" for genital mutilation; compares the practice to male circumcision; indicts the "conspiracy of silence" surrounding the custom; and reviews the outlook for women's health. For a detailed case study of genital mutilation in the Sudan, see *Women, Why Do You Weep? Circumcision and Its Consequences*, by physician Asma el Dareer (Zed Press, 1982). (**Women's Studies**, 1987)

IL
375.   Humana, Charles. **The Keeper of the Bed: The Story of the Eunuch.** London: Arlington Books, 1973. 202 p. Includes bibliography. ISBN 0-8514-0210-0.

As the bibliography in this book suggests, the literature on eunuchism in the English language is sparse. The reasons are not hard to find: the lack of primary source materials, possible repugnance toward the subject, and the demise of the custom of emasculation for the traditional purposes of providing guardians of the harem or creating *castrati* for choirs and opera.

The term eunuch derives from the Greek word *eunuchos*, meaning "guardian or keeper of the couch"; it, together with the term *castrato*, refers to males who have been castrated, either as children or after puberty, voluntarily or forcibly. Removal of the male genitals may be partial or complete; if the latter it is referred to as being "swept clean." In any case, it leaves the victim physically and/or psychologically handicapped.

Humana writes that the custom has been practiced from antiquity until quite recent times in the Near East, the Far East, and in Europe. He gives special attention to customs and practices in the Turkish harem since the early fifteenth century, where and when the eunuchs achieved privileged status as elite guards, soldiers, and responsible officials in the Ottoman court.

In Europe, under the influence of Christianity, the eunuch's position was less reviled than elsewhere; indeed powerful and influential eunuchs were known in the Roman Empire. Particularly in Italy, the *castrato* was appreciated for the beauty of his high-pitched singing voice. During the eighteenth century, some 200 *castrati* sang in the churches of Rome, and operas were written with them in mind. "On the accession of Pope Leo XIII in 1878, the practise of castrating small boys for church choirs came to an end, banned by an edict" (p. 120).

Humana devotes a chapter to the eunuch in China, where his existence may be traced back to about 1100 B.C. Originally engaged in court matters, eunuchs were introduced into the harem about 250 B.C. Humana describes their customs, duties, and status in detail, relating many anecdotes and stories from Chinese literature. He also describes that strange Christian cult, the Skopzis, that persisted in Russia from the eleventh century to the 1917 revolution. In the modern world, according to Humana, a few practices and policies, reminiscent of eunuch castration, obtain: sterilization of criminals in certain societies, voluntary vasectomies in the interest of population control, genocidal experiments, inhuman torture of political prisoners, and even circumcision as a rite.

Humana illuminates his book with poignant stories from literature and explicit photographs, drawings, and paintings of this defunct world of eunuchs and *castrati*. (TJW)

PR,IL

376. Lightfoot-Klein, Hanny. **Prisoners of Ritual: An Odyssey into Female Genital Circumcision in Africa.** New York: Harrington Park Press, 1989. 306 p. Includes bibliography and index. ISBN 0-918393-68-X.

Between 1979 and 1983, social psychologist Lightfoot-Klein made several studies of female sexual circumcision based on fieldwork in Sudan, Egypt, and Kenya. Headquartered in Sudan's capital, Khartoum, she conducted extensive interviews with medical personnel, psychologists, and, most importantly, the girls and women subjected to the age-old customs of clitoridectomy and infibulation. She defines the basic types of female circumcision from the *pharaonic*, that "involves the excision of the clitoris, labia minora, and fleshy inner layers of the labia majora," followed by the suturing over of the loose flesh, leaving a taut pinhole opening for urination, to the *sunna*, that refers to partial or total excision of the clitoris or merely removal of the prepuce of the clitoris. The number of African females of all ages who have been circumcised in these ways ranges from 30 to 90 million. These enormous figures pertain to women found across Africa in a band that stretches from Egypt in the northeast and Tanzania in the southeast to Senegal in the west. Female circumcision also occurs in Nigeria, Mali, Burkina Faso, Ethiopia, and Somalia. In Sudan 85 percent of the women are circumcised.

Intercourse for newlyweds—premarital sex is forbidden in these largely Muslim countries—is extremely painful and may require numerous attempts at penetration over several days or even weeks or longer. Following childbirth the women are resutured.

Opposition to female circumcision is growing among the more educated and urban Sudanese. British law in 1946 forbade female circumcision. Sudan shook off British rule in 1956 and in 1974 passed legislation forbidding the practice. Unfortunately, these laws were ignored, and in Sudan pharaonic circumcision continues unabated. The custom is deeply imbedded in society. Encouraged by mothers and grandmothers, proponents advance numerous rationalizations for the practice. Circumcision is done in the interests of cleanliness and health; it increases male pleasure during coitus; it protects women from male aggressors; it precludes promiscuity and guarantees virginity; it assures women of getting married; and so forth.

Lightfoot-Klein provides a brief history of clitoral excision and infibulation practices in the Western world and a discussion of male circumcision as analogous to female circumcision, which it is not. She also provides impressions of Sudanese life along with summaries of interviews with Sudanese men and women from all walks of life, giving their personal opinions about various aspects of female circumcision and the chances for change in this Muslim country. The text's stark diagrams and photographs of female circumcision impart clear, possibly lasting, impressions of these painful practices whose origins, lost in history, remain obscure. (TJW)

IL,PO
377. Older, Julia. **Endometriosis.** Foreword by Anne B. Ward. New York: Scribner's, 1984. 221 p. Includes bibliographic notes and index. ISBN 0-684-18057-X.
The endometrium is the mucous lining of the inner uterine wall. Endometriosis refers to the presence of endometrial tissue in locations where it does not normally occur, such as in the ovaries, Fallopian tubes, the outer wall of the uterus, the pelvic lining, the cervix, or the vagina. The abnormally located tissue passes through the same periodic changes (including bleeding) as the endometrium does. Endometriosis is one of the major causes of infertility in the United States and other developed countries, but it has been given scant attention in the popular press and is often bypassed by physicians as a source of patients' complaints. The goal of this book is to serve as a source of information on what endometriosis is, how it develops, what its possible symptoms are, how to prevent it, and how to treat it. Several explanations have been offered as to how endometriosis develops: (1) retrograde menstruation, (2) transmission of endometrial tissue to other sites by blood and lymph, and (3) accidental implantation (nonsocial infection). Symptoms associated with endometriosis include difficult and painful menstrual flow (the most frequent symptom), difficult or painful intercourse, backache, painful defecation and/or rectal bleeding, infertility, and menstrual irregularities. Older straightforwardly describes different methods for diagnosis (laparoscopy, biopsy, ultrasound) and the pros and cons of various treatments (hormones, surgery, radiation). She also considers factors that may aid or deter progress of the condition: early detection, sanitary pads, intercourse during menstruation, contraceptive methods (the pill, the IUD, the cervical cap), menstrual extraction, and nutrition. The book goes beyond the specifics of endometriosis by explaining the functioning of a woman's endocrine system, clarifying the diagnosis of infertility, and discussing the relation of endometriosis to lifestyle and stages of life (teenager, post-menopause, career). (SGF)

PR,IL
378. Romberg, Rosemary. **Circumcision: The Painful Dilemma.** South Hadley, Mass.: Bergin & Garvey, 1985. 454 p. Includes bibliography, index, and glossary. ISBN 0-89789-074-4.
Romberg, a childbirth educator and vice-president of INTACT Educational Foundation, says that the findings of her research transformed her initial position of neutrality into a "polemic, strongly opposing infant circumcision." The book's goal is not only to provide an overview of the practice of circumcision but also to empower parents to make "the right decision" about their son's circumcision.
Several chapters recount the history of circumcision. In other cultures, the reasons given for male circumcision are diverse (cosmetic or sexual value; a mark of tribal, social, or sexual status; symbolic castration; menstrual envy; sacrifice). Though less frequent, female circumcision also occurs for a variety of reasons (cleanliness, preservation of virginity, enhancing value). Jews have a long tradition of integrating circumcision into their rituals. Routine circumcision of males in the United States began around the turn of the century as a medical procedure or cure to prevent masturbation. Since then, the rationales for it have changed. A separate chapter is devoted to disproving each of them: sexuality ("Circumcision enhances sensation and body image"), the military ("It is required for entrance into the service"), and disease ("Circumcision reduces the incidence of penile, prostate, and cervical cancer"). Romberg then proceeds to describe (and gradually illustrate) the operation itself, the trauma and pain experienced by the infant, and a variety of complications that can result. Numerous personal accounts of circumcision by men and

parents; opinions of experts on the subject; and pictures of babies, parents, and the procedure itself are presented to emphasize the emotional impact of the operation. The volume concludes with information on the choice for "non-circumcision"—care of the intact penis, problems, and participation in the anti-circumcision movement. Humanistic alternatives to circumcision as well as a list of resources (organizations, magazines, films, support groups) are also provided. Overall, Romberg thinks that the central issue concerning circumcision revolves around the "horrendous complications" that can occur, the sexual advantages of retaining the foreskin, ethical considerations of altering another's body without permission, and maintaining the body in its natural state. An extensive 490-item bibliography follows the text. (SGF)

PO
379. Rowan, Robert L., and Paul J. Gillette. **Your Prostate: What It Is, What It Does, and the Diseases That Affect It.** Garden City, N.Y.: Doubleday, 1973. 147 p. Includes index. ISBN 0-385-06301-6.
The United States Public Health Service statistics indicate that at least half of the American male population will suffer some sort of prostatic disorder by age seventy. At present, prostatic cancer is the third highest cause of cancer deaths among men over fifty-five years of age. The main aim of this book is to provide information and advice on the diagnosis and treatment of prostatic problems. As Rowan and Gillette put it, "the best defense against prostatic disease is knowledge" (p. xv). They begin with a general description of the genito-urinary system and then focus specifically on the anatomy and physiology of the prostate. Other topics discussed include the symptoms, treatment, and prognosis of three major prostate diseases that interrupt or alter the gland's function by changing its chemical composition—prostatitis, cancer of the prostate, and benign prostatic hypertrophy—as well as other problems (trichomonas vaginalis and premature ejaculation) associated with the prostate. Consideration is also given to prostate-like disorders in the female. Patients suffering from prostatic disorders, as well as their families, can benefit from information presented on the diagnosis of prostatic disorders (e.g., by urinalysis, catheterization, x-rays), their treatment by surgical and/or nonsurgical techniques (e.g., with hormones, chemicals, x-radiation), and their effects on sexual functioning. Although the book has no bibliography or documentation of information in the text, case histories provided from Rowan's practice (a urologist who specializes in the field of prostate disorders), line drawings of some prostate problems and treatments, and a glossary of terms clarify the text. (SGF)

IL
380. Walker, Alice, and Pratibha Parmar. **Warrior Marks: Female Genital Mutilation and the Sexual Blinding of Women.** New York: Harcourt Brace, 1993. 373 p. Includes bibliography. ISBN 0-15-100061-1.
Female genital mutilation is a long-standing tradition in certain Muslim countries across the African continent. It is a painful practice, estimated to have been performed on "ninety to one hundred million women in African, Asian, and Middle Eastern countries" (p. 24), that Walker, an American writer (*The Color Purple*), and Pramar, award-winning British documentary filmmaker (*A Place of Rage*), agreed in 1992 to fight by teaming up to produce a documentary exposing this pervasive ritual. Walker ties genital mutilation to "other psychic and physical maimings women endure" around the world to make themselves young and beautiful (p. 12).
In her effort to produce the film *Warrior Marks*, Walker received support and cooperation from many organizations (e.g., Great Britain's Channel 4) and individuals (Efua Dorkenoo, the head of FORWARD International, an organization dedicated to eliminating destructive traditional practices). Walker and the filmmaking team, headed by Parmar, visited several West African countries, including Gambia, Senegal, and Burkino Faso, where different types of mutilation, including clitoridectomy and infibulation, take place.

The book version of *Warrior Marks* unfolds in three parts. Part I, "Alice's Journey," describes Walker's motivation and involvement in the project, from her initial letter to Parmar suggesting the idea for a documentary, to her visit in early February 1993 to Burkino Faso, in the Sahel of Africa, to pay her respects at the grave of Thomas Sankara, who, as president of Burkino Faso, openly opposed genital mutilation. Part II, "Pratibha's Journey," correlated with Walker's story, provides the perspective of an Indian-born woman who is alerted to the horrors of genital mutilation from reading Walker's novel *Possessing the Secret of Joy*, about the experiences of a woman who has been mutilated.

Part III, "Interviews," covers interviews with a variety of people, including Efua Dorkenoo, who wrote the play *Tradition! Tradition!*, which raised the consciousness of women about genital mutilation as a social practice with a health consequence; Aminita Diop, who fled her native Mali to avoid mutilation; Linda Weil-Curiel, an attorney in Paris, who fights genital excision done to Muslim children in France by immigrants; Awa Thiam, a fighter against genital mutilation in Africa, who attributes this practice and others to the domination of women by men throughout the world; Dr. Henriette Kouyate, a practicing gynecologist in Dakar, Senegal, who treats mutilated women, conducts retraining workshops for circumcisers and seminars for people in positions of responsibility on aspects of genital mutilation; three circumcisers, who defend the tradition; and two recently circumcised girls, who give their reactions to this ritual. Parmar interviews Baba Lee, an Islamic scholar who is against female genital mutilation, pointing out that circumcision antedates Islam and that there is nothing in the Koran or any of the hadiths supporting the practice.

In a final interview, Parmar asks Walker about her feelings as they are about to leave Africa. Walker responds: "I would like to feel that this movement to eradicate genital mutilation will grow and that the consciousness of people will change. I hope this will happen quickly, because they don't have a lot of time" (p. 350). (TJW)

IL
381. Wallerstein, Edward. **Circumcision: An American Health Fallacy.** New York: Springer, 1980. 281 p. (Focus on Men, 1). Includes bibliographic references and indexes. ISBN 0-8261-3240-5.

Calling circumcision "a solution in search of a problem," Wallerstein raises important questions about America's obsession with routine circumcision. About 85 percent of all American male children are circumcised. While other Western countries have abandoned routine circumcision, only the United States continues the practice. He debunks past and present rationales for the practice, arguing that circumcision does not prevent masturbation, venereal disease, premature ejaculation, or anything else. The foreskin, he argues, serves as a useful protective shield and has an erotic function. Moreover, the operation can lead to complications, and the pain and trauma of infant circumcision (usually performed without anesthetic) may have unknown harmful effects upon the male psyche. For entirely irrational reasons, the practice of routine circumcision lingers on in America, long after the medical profession should have been discouraging it. Three appendixes cover the details of the surgery, its frequency in U.S. history, and an almost unknown statement against routine circumcision issued in 1975 by the American College of Obstetricians and Gynecologists. (**Men's Studies**, 1985)

Disabilities. Handicaps

PR
382. Cornelius, Debra A., Sophia Chipouras, Elaine Makas, and Susan M. Daniels. **Who Cares? A Handbook on Sex Education and Counseling Services for Disabled People.** 2nd ed. Baltimore, Md.: University Park Press, 1982. 260 p. Includes bibliographies. ISBN 0-8391-1727-2.

This handbook is the product of the Sex and Disability Project at George Washington University, Washington, D.C., which received a grant from the Rehabilitation Services Administration, Department of Health, Education, and Welfare for September 1977-1978. The first edition appeared in looseleaf notebook form in 1979. Intended for use by both consumers and providers of services, the authors, Sex and Disability Project staff, conducted anonymous surveys of theses groups to identify their needs for sex education and counseling services. An extensive literature search produced information on identified needs and existing services.

Organized into five sections, the first section presents an overview of sexuality and disability with chapters on myths, attitudes, and rights; the need and variety of services; situational considerations; who should provide services; training needs and options; accessibility of services including checklists for use; and conclusions and recommendations. Each of these chapters ends with a reference list. The second section, arranged in a question-answer format, addresses issues of consumers, counseling and education, and training and policy-making; it also includes resources relevant to those concerns. The final section, over half of the handbook, contains eight appendixes that cover survey summaries, books and journals, descriptions of service and training programs, and names and addresses of consultants and organizations. One appendix provides literature summaries on hearing and visual impairments, cerebral palsy, spinal cord injury, and mental retardation.

This comprehensive handbook sets forth a wealth of information arranged in a user-friendly manner. Data have been compiled into tables, checklists, and resource lists accompanying a very readable text.

Those interested in both individual and professional views on sexuality and physical disability can refer to the compilation of essays in *Sexuality and Physical Disability: Personal Perspectives*, edited by David Bullard and Susan Knight (St. Louis: Mosby, 1981). Most of the authors are people with disabilities, who contribute their personal perspectives on such topics as spinal cord injury, hearing impairment, surgical and medical conditions, sex education and the development of social skills, sex therapy and counseling, and family planning. (RC)

PR

383. Johnson, Warren R., and Winifred Kempton. **Sex Education and Counseling of Special Groups: The Mentally and Physically Disabled, Ill, and Elderly.** 2nd ed. Springfield, Ill.: Thomas, 1981. 255 p. Includes bibliographic footnotes and index. ISBN 0-398-04501-1.

This book is intended as a primer for people in special groups and those in contact with them. As an introduction to various aspects of special group members (SGM) and their sexuality, its emphasis is upon individuals searching for sexual understanding, adjustment, and enjoyment within the parameters of their particular range of possibilities and constraints. Johnson and Kempton identify a basic problem in this field: "One socially unacceptable phenomenon is difficult enough to deal with, but combine two socially unacceptable phenomena—in this case specialness and sexuality—and there is bound to be real trouble, including avoidance behavior" (p. ix).

Johnson and Kempton, pioneers in this field, contribute their sensitivity and practical wisdom. Johnson, Director of the Children's Health and Developmental Clinic at the University of Maryland for over twenty-five years, became a SGM while writing this book. As a member of the presumably incurably ill, he observed that "sex helps retain contact with life" (p. xi). Kempton, affiliated with Planned Parenthood of Southeastern Pennsylvania and an international consultant on sexuality and special groups, is also a SGM because of rheumatoid arthritis. Her career involved her with children and adults with mental and physical disabilities as well as with their parents. During her training of hundreds of professionals, she developed practical teaching materials. As strong advocates for sexual rights and responsibilities among SGMs, Johnson and Kempton define the sexual revolution as a shift in societal attitudes allowing greater involvement of science, medicine, and education in the exploration of sexuality among all individuals, including SGMs.

The book is arranged in two parts. Part I covers sources of failure to provide adequate sex education and counseling for SGMs; five meanings of the concept of "normality"; problems and qualifications for sexual counselors; and three philosophies of sex education and counseling of SGMs—eliminate it, tolerate or accept it, or cultivate it. Chapter 6 presents thirteen precautions in providing sex education and counseling services, and chapter 7 is devoted to helping parents. Part II contains twenty-one chapters arranged by topic, including masturbation, homosexuality, sexual inadequacy, parenthood, and paid sexual companions. The chapter "Sexual Intercourse and Sex Without Intercourse" provides explicit information on a range of behaviors for attaining sexual satisfaction and gives permission to explore options for sexual expression. Johnson and Kempton note that information pertinent to SGMs is mostly applicable to the rest of the population as well. The text is peppered with anecdotes that enhance its heuristic value. (RC)

PR
384. Kroll, Ken, and Erica Levy Klein. **Enabling Romance: A Guide to Love, Sex, and Relationships for the Disabled (and the People Who Care About Them).** Illustrations by Mark Langeneckert. New York: Harmony Books, 1992. 209 p. Includes bibliography and index. ISBN 0-517-57532-9.

Kroll and Klein, a disabled husband and his nondisabled wife, provide sympathetic guidance for disabled people about enhancing their sexuality as well as information for the nondisabled about disabilities and their limitations. Responses from couples to their questionnaire contribute case studies throughout.

Initial chapters focus on self-acceptance and building romantic relationships: how to talk to a disabled person, how disabled persons can "break the ice" about their disability, how a disabled person can learn to act and feel confident and remain sexual even when disabled. Other chapters focus on a menu of sexual variations and alternatives, masturbation, reproduction and contraception, and coping with lack of privacy when attendants are needed.

Part 2 of the book covers "Living and Loving with Specific Disabilities": spinal cord injuries, blindness and limited vision, deafness and hearing impairments, amputation, and other conditions. Each of these chapters discusses sexuality in the context of that disability. Several appendixes list helpful sexuality, family planning, and independent living organizations; dating, friendship, and pen pal services; and independent living mail order catalogs, magazines, videos, and columns. (MC)

PR,IL
385. Levy, Howard S. **Chinese Footbinding: The History of a Curious Erotic Custom.** Foreword by Arthur Waley. Introduction by Wolfram Eberhard. New York: Walton Rawls, 1966. 352 p. Includes bibliography and index.

Levy's well-documented study of footbinding in China and Taiwan tells the story of the liberation of Chinese women from a painful and grotesque practice. Divided into three parts under the headings "History," "Curious," and "Custom," the book underscores the subordinate roles of women in a bygone patriarchal Chinese society.

Sources suggest that "palace dancers probably originated footbinding in about the tenth century" (p. 29-30). Upper-class ladies adopted the practice. Unable to move about freely, they took to their boudoirs. In due course, footbinding reached all classes of the Chinese people, incapacitating in effect half of the population. Despite sporadic anti-footbinding campaigns over the centuries, it was not abandoned until the twentieth century. The Japanese, while they ruled the island of Taiwan, forbade it, and later governments outlawed it on the mainland.

Reasons given for footbinding include feminine vanity (Is it any different from high heels, eyebrow plucking, or face lifting?); aesthetic approval (the bound foot is beautiful, like a lotus); enhancement of lovemaking; and the crippling of women to prevent their wandering about at will. Chinese men believed footbinding enhanced sexual appeal; it affected a woman's posture and gait, caused hips to swell and undulate provocatively, and the genital region to tighten. Furthermore, they deemed the appearance of the bare, though distorted, foot highly erotic—even to touch it, much less kiss, smell, or suck it, was arousing.

Levy provides detailed drawings showing the steps in binding, the stages of the footbinding process, bone positions in the foot before and after binding, and many examples of the tiny decorated shoes worn by wives, courtesans, and prostitutes. He also illustrates his book with photographs of bare feet that have been bound to show their lotus-like shape.

Although the Manchus tried to abolish footbinding in the seventeenth century, it was not until the 1902 anti-footbinding edict of the Empress Dowager Tz'u-hsi that the combined forces of Western missionaries, liberal reformers, champions of women's rights, and proponents of the natural foot made any headway toward abolition. Successive governments have opposed footbinding. Today the practice is outlawed throughout China, and only vestiges of footbinding remain. (TJW)

PO

386. Manning, Richard B. **Impotence: How to Overcome It.** Farmington Hills, Mich.: HealthProInk Publishing, 1987. 249 p. Includes bibliography and index. ISBN 0-933803-07-9.

Writing pseudonymously, Manning, a fifty-year-old sociologist, reveals in this practical guide his problem with impotence and how he overcame it. In the foreword Philip G. Seven, a urologist, discloses that in the United States about ten million men suffer from impotence. He states that "through rather simple surgery most of these men can be returned to a happy, sexually active life."

Manning, after seven years of declining potency (subsequently attributed to a slight stroke), read a newspaper article with the striking headline "How Penile Implant Helps End Impotence." He investigated the claim and attended meetings of an ISG (Impotence Support Group) that apprised him of ROMP (Recovery of Male Potency), an organization with chapters in many states. Through ROMP, Manning found a urologist/surgeon who performed tests showing that he had diminished blood supply at the base of his penis, which accounted for his impotence. The solution suggested was a penile implant that would restore Manning's erections.

Manning then describes the several penile implants on the market and how he chose the inflatable, silicone penile prosthesis. He also describes his operation in detail, his six-day hospital stay, and the convalescence before he was able to have sexual intercourse. He and his wife report that potency was restored and their sexual relations became totally satisfactory.

The lengthy appendix provides useful information about organizations, such as Impotents Anonymous, causes of impotence, illustrated vendor information about implants and equipment, and selected readings on the subject. (TJW)

PR,IL

387. Mooney, Thomas O., Theodore M. Cole, and Richard A. Chilgren. **Sexual Options for Paraplegics and Quadriplegics.** Foreword by Alex Comfort. Boston: Little, Brown, 1975. 111 p. Includes glossary and index. ISBN 0-316-57937-8.

Written by a person with a spinal cord injury in collaboration with two physicians, this pictorial manual is intended for paraplegics and quadriplegics, their sex partners, and health professionals who are "committed to the rehabilitation and resocialization of adults with spinal cord injuries"; its purpose is to present "practical methods for developing sexual competence" (p. x). The philosophy underlying this work is that the 120,000 paraplegics and quadriplegics living in the United States are as entitled to sexual pleasure as other persons and that it is the obligation of the helping professions to facilitate that process. Unfortunately, the obstacles are great: society's isolation of these people, a reluctance to discuss the problem, embarrassment, lack of available literature, and technical difficulties. However, it is possible for the physically handicapped to experience sexual pleasure, even orgasm, provided the effort is made to overcome "the problems of people who must wear catheters or ileostomy bags and who cannot move their arms or legs, or both."

Copiously illustrated with photographs, the chapters deal with the main areas of concern: preparations for sexual experience, techniques of arousal, intercourse positions, and oral-genital and manual stimulation. As Alex Comfort states in the introduction to this unique book: "Almost all disabled people can be made sexually functional with special counseling and a minimum of physical help . . . virtually nobody is too disabled to derive some satisfaction and personal reinforcement from sex" (p. viii). (TJW)

PR
388.   Robinault, Isabel P. **Sex, Society, and the Disabled: A Developmental Inquiry into Roles, Reactions, and Responsibilities.** Hagerstown, Md.: Harper & Row, 1978. 273 p. Includes bibliography and index. ISBN 0-06-142274-6.

Differences are one characteristic of our society. However, inadequate information and understanding surrounding sexuality and individuals with disabilities may exaggerate differences among people and result in deleterious effects.

This early book uses interdisciplinary resources to present an overview of sexuality in relation to persons with congenital and acquired disabilities. It aims to encourage further study in the field and to connect resources with the needs of this population. A developmental perspective is offered as a means to view individuals, both able-bodied and disabled, and their sexuality throughout the life cycle. This chronological discussion identifies the similarities that exist at each stage among all individuals, points out differences or adjustments that must be considered, and suggests realistic choices. A developmental perspective facilitates understanding of the relationship between physical disability and its impact upon sexuality. This enables professionals to anticipate changes and to provide consumers with appropriate information and counseling that can help them in their adjustment and coping.

Robinault, Project Director of the Research Utilization Laboratory at the ICD Rehabilitation and Research Center in New York, turns her attention to the dynamic nature of individuals, relationships, and society, and cautions against oversimplified solutions. Chapters deal with normal sexual development, the impact of physical disabilities upon normal developmental stages, and societal attitudes toward sexually related behaviors. The six chapters sequentially trace developmental patterns from infancy through maturity and emphasize the context of a whole individual functioning within society.

An advocate for sexuality education for all children and adults, Robinault notes that informed, competent role models are necessary to assist children in attaining mature psychosexual development. She states that it is an active learning process requiring attention and effort. To this end, she incorporates an ambitious appendix. Since this publication, Robinault's goal of generating research has been successful, and the reader may update the resources listed in this work by consulting *Who Cares? A Handbook on Sex Education and Counseling Services for Disabled People* by Cornelius, Chipouras, Makas, and Daniels (University Park Press, 1982). (RC)

BEHAVIORAL ASPECTS

PR
389.   Henslin, James M., and Edward Sagarin, eds. **The Sociology of Sex: An Introductory Reader.** New York: Schocken Books, 1978. 288 p. Includes bibliographic footnotes and index.

After reviewing sociological theory and pointing out that "the control of the individual by the larger social group is a universal social fact," editor Henslin states that what is needed in research "are the specifics of that social control—its mechanisms and its consequences" (p. 2). As an integral part of sociology, the sociology of sex focuses on those mechanisms that channel "the sex drive into acceptable forms." In this reader, Henslin and Sagarin bring together twelve papers by sociologists dealing with different aspects of sexual socialization. Henslin's lead paper, "Toward a Sociology of Sex," identifies the need for research in certain areas, such as cross-cultural comparisons of sexual customs, deviant behavior, rule breaking in sexual conduct, and so forth.

In "The New Sexual Morality," James Moneymaker and Fred Monanino reveal that in the United States in the 1970s, attitudes toward sex became increasingly tolerant. For example, there has been a "downgrading and downfall" of virginity among females and a growing institutionalization of nonmarital cohabitation. George W. Goethals in "Factors Affecting Permissive and Nonpermissive Rules Regarding Premarital Sex," discusses theoretical positions in anthropology and psychoanalysis with regard to the generation of suitable hypotheses for research in the area of premarital sex. In "From an Unfortunate Necessity to a Cult of Mutual Orgasm," Michael Gordon discusses the history of the sex manual in American marital education literature from 1830 to 1940, pointing out that research on the impact of these manuals on the reader is inherently complex and ambiguous.

In "Aspects of the Campus Abortion Search," Peter K. Manning suggests several areas of research resulting from the attempt on a large midwestern college campus to find an abortion by unwed coeds. The paper "Forcible Rape" by Duncan Chappell et al. is a comparative study of offenses known to the police in Boston and Los Angeles; it suggests that what is needed is further research and information on "the relationship between social conditions and criminal offenses." Marvin Cummins in "Police and Petting" discusses the decrease in family control over sexual behavior and law enforcement's role in regulating sexuality in public areas.

In "Dramaturgical Desexualization: The Sociology of the Vaginal Examination," editor Henslin and Mae A. Biggs discuss in great detail the examination room setting, rules of behavior, and the relationship between the doctor and the patient during a vaginal examination. By following well defined rituals the sacredness of the vagina is maintained without violating sexual taboos. James K. Skipper, Jr. and Charles H. McCaghy in their paper, "Teasing, Flashing, and Visual Sex," investigate the sexual aspects of stripteasing, purportedly carried out by some 7,000 women in the United States, and reach several tentative generalizations. Nanette J. Davis's paper, "Prostitution: Identity, Career, and Legal-Economic Enterprise," studies a jail sample of thirty prostitutes from correctional institutions in Minnesota, revealing three stages of prostitution: early casual sex, transitional deviance, and professionalization. She then examines the prostitution subculture as a legal-economic enterprise. Arno Karlen in "Homosexuality: The Scene and Its Students," describes the changing homosexual lifestyle, various homosexual milieus, shortcomings of the sociological literature on homosexuality, and poses some interesting questions that the sociologist needs to answer.

Finally, Sagarin, in "Sex Research and Sociology," provides a thoughtful review of developments in sex research since the late nineteenth century and recognizes the pioneering contributions of Alfred Kinsey in developing a sociological approach to the study of sex. (TJW)

Normal Interactions

(For related material see also entries 150, 151, 155, 156, 161, 169, 214)IL

389a. Buss, David M. **The Evolution of Desire: Strategies of Human Mating.** New York: Basic Books, 1994. 262 p. Includes bibliography and index. ISBN 0-465-07750-1.
How are we to understand the contradiction between the love that humans seek and the conflict that characterizes intimate relationships? This is the major question that Buss,

Professor of Psychology at the University of Michigan, Ann Arbor, addresses. He thinks that the answer lies in the mating strategies developed by men and women in our evolutionary past. The persistence of psychological adaptations from humans' prehistoric past explains the patterns and dilemmas confronted by contemporary men and women who grapple with mating in a modern context. Buss's goal is to "pull back the layers of adaptive problems that men and women have faced in the course of mating and uncover the complex sexual strategies they have evolved for solving them" (p. 6). Central to these adaptive problems are selecting, attracting, keeping, and replacing a mate.

In chapters devoted to such topics as what men and women want, attracting a partner, staying together, casual sex, sexual conflict, and breaking up, Buss uses the theoretical framework of evolutionary psychology, that applies the principles of sexual selection to humans and identifies the underlying psychological mechanisms developed in the course of evolution, to explain the mating strategies of men and women. Since the theory assumes that mate choice and attraction of mates is not random, men's desire for young, beautiful, healthy women and women's desire for older, high status, wealthy men are viewed as persistent elements of men's and women's sexual strategies for obtaining the best mates. Likewise, jealousy, commitment, sex differences in attitudes toward casual sex, reasons for break-ups (e.g., infidelity, infertility, sexual withdrawal, inadequate economic support), and sexual abuse/coercion can be explained in such terms. These explanations are meant to illuminate mating behavior, not prescribe it, and may provide clues to achieving harmony in relationships.

Buss bolsters his theoretical tenets with empirical research drawn from findings of studies in the biological, social, and behavioral sciences, as well as from his own five-year international study on human mating desires ("the largest ever undertaken" [p. 4]), with fifty collaborators in thirty-seven cultures who received surveys from 10,047 people worldwide. Overall, he uses these diverse findings to develop "a unified theory of human mating, based not on romantic notions or outmoded scientific theories, but on current scientific evidence" (p. 5). Much of what he finds is "not nice" and counters conventional thinking. Buss concludes that "we have ignored the truth about human mating for too long. Conflict, competition, and manipulation also pervade human mating, and we must lift our collective heads from the sand to see them if we are to understand life's most engrossing relationships" (p. 18). (SGF)

PO
390. Ellis, Albert. **Sex and the Liberated Man.** Secaucus, N.J.: Lyle Stuart, 1976. 347 p. Includes bibliography and index. ISBN 0-8184-0222-9.

An extensively rewritten and updated version of Ellis's *Sex and the Single Man* (1963), this volume attempts to take into account the dramatic changes in the sexual and social landscape of America since the 1960s. An enthusiastic cheerleader of the "erotic revolution," Ellis gleefully turns the tables on prudes by arguing that abstention from sex can be physically, mentally, and sexually harmful. Writing with gusto, he praises the benefits of masturbation and offers suggestions on avoiding guilt over erotic pleasure. Having listened sympathetically to feminist critics of male sexual attitudes and performance, Ellis transmits their complaints to men, repeatedly warning males not to equate sex simply with coitus. He recognizes, however, that despite women's liberation men will still have to take the initiative sexually most of the time. Discussing techniques of arousing women and of "petting" (noncoital erotic activity), he also suggests how a man can help a woman with sexual problems and how men can help themselves with such problems as fast ejaculation, lack of erection, and so on. Ellis also recognizes that sexual intercourse is still of major importance, and he devotes a chapter to techniques and positions. The concluding chapter, discussing what is and is not a sexual disturbance, reverts to Ellis's major themes of enjoying sex and of modifying one's behavior through the conscious method of rational-emotive therapy. (**Men's Studies**, 1985)

PO
391. Ellis, Albert. **Sex Without Guilt.** New York: Grove Press, 1965. 184 p. Originally copyrighted in 1958. Includes bibliography.

This book is a slightly augmented collection of columns published by Ellis in a liberal monthly newspaper, *The Independent*, from 1956 to 1958, after this material was rejected by other publishers because of its controversial subject matter. Ellis, a pioneering sexologist, dispels myths and inaccurate notions regarding sex. Each chapter, originally a column or combination of columns, deals with a specific aspect of sexual behavior, treated with a heavy dose of Ellis's enlightenment. The primary message of his commentaries, backed by scientific arguments, is that many types of sexual behavior that have been tinged with shame, guilt, and societal deprecation are actually healthy, normal, and even desirable: "New Light on Masturbation," "Thoughts on Petting," "On Premarital Sex Relations," "Adultery: Pros and Cons," "The Justification of Sex Without Love," "Adventure with Sex Censorship," "When Are We Going to Quit Stalling About Sex Education?" "Another Look at Sexual Abnormality," and "The Right to Sex Enjoyment." The other chapters analyze the dysfunctions and social problems that have resulted from social misconceptions about sex and errant behavior patterns: "Why Americans Are So Fearful of Sex," "How Males Contribute to Female Frigidity," "Sexual Inadequacy in the Male," "How American Women Are Driving American Males into Homosexuality," "On the Myths About Love," and "Sex Fascism." (EBS)

PR,IL
391a. McCormick, Naomi B. **Sexual Salvation: Affirming Women's Sexual Rights and Pleasures.** Westport, Conn.: Praeger, 1994. 284 p. Includes bibliography and index. ISBN 0-275-94359-3.

Throughout the twentieth century considerable attention has been paid to women's sexuality. According to McCormick, Distinguished Teaching Professor in the Department of Psychology at the State University in New York at Plattsburgh, five independent sexual revolutions are responsible: the sexualization of the marketplace; the development of unique youth subcultures; the growth of sexual science and the rise of sex therapy; the lesbian and gay rights movement; and feminism. Feminists interpret these distinct revolutions differently: Radical Feminists "emphasize the extent to which girls and women are sexual victims who must be protected from manipulative and coercing men, whereas Liberal Feminists seek to remove any restrictions interfering with women's sexual autonomy and gratification" (p. 9). Many of the debates over such topics as sexual violence, pornography, and prostitution are divisive; according to McCormick, "They have distracted women from working together and working with men on our really important shared goals" (p. 12). Men and women must cooperate and not alienate each other in further argument. Sexual salvation is the affirmation of women's sexuality, a search for sexual fulfillment. McCormick sides with the Liberal Feminists and advocates "greater sexual rights and pleasures for all women" (p. 2).

McCormick believes that people's sexual behavior is scripted, apparent in so many ways: sexual motivation, attracting a partner, initiating sex, refusing sex, and sexual intercourse. Feminists of all stripes are challenging these accepted sexual performance scripts. She also explores the relationship between love and sex, defining several kinds of love and stressing the importance of intimacy in relationships, whether heterosexual, bisexual, or homosexual.

McCormick devotes a chapter to the worldwide institution of prostitution, pointing out, "Economic survival, not psychopathology, may be the major factor in most decisions to enter prostitution" (p. 92). Nevertheless, many prostitutes have positive feelings about their work: empowerment, sexual satisfaction, and economic achievement. She appraises the feminist arguments about women who work in the sex industry. Some believe that pornography is an instrument of the patriarchy while others believe that pornography has a useful place in society. McCormick recommends tolerance toward those women in the sex industry; moreover, we should encourage sex workers to unionize and support women in small business ventures. Indeed, the sex industry provides women with the possibility of enhancing men's sexuality as well as their own. McCormick goes on to critique various models of human sexual fulfillment, including those of Freud, Kinsey, Masters and Johnson, and those of modern sex therapists and others who would change or modify certain aspects of these models to satisfy better the needs of women. In attempting to achieve a woman-affirming sexuality among special groups, including poor women, women of color, lesbians, older women, and physically disabled women, McCormick dwells on the "veneration of the orgasm" and the "tyranny of intercourse." Important to women in a sexual relationship is intimacy (i.e., "having a sensitive, considerate lover who touches, caresses, and cuddles them as much as they want" [p. 213]).

Finally, McCormick describes the work of thirteen feminist researchers and sex therapists—eleven women and two men—who are actively pursuing answers to the problems of women's "sexual rights and pleasures." In *Sexual Salvation*, McCormick has attempted a broad review of what we know about female sexuality, in the hope that it will help chart a course for women seeking sexual fulfillment in the coming century. (TJW)

IL
392. Offit, Avodah K. **Night Thoughts: Reflections of a Sex Therapist.** New York: Congdon & Lattes, 1981. 256 p. Includes index. ISBN 0-312-92575-1.

In twenty-six vividly written essays embracing a broad range of topics in human sexuality, Offit, an experienced sex therapist, reflects on the sex problems encountered in her medical practice. Offit's thoughts on morning sex, female orgasm, extramarital affairs, menstruation, fellatio, male sexuality, ejaculation, sex and pregnancy, sex and nursing, impotence, fantasy, nymphomania, homosexuality, smell, overeating and sex, masturbation, recreational sex, incest, anal sex, cunnilingus, postcoital feelings, and sex medicine bring valuable insights on these abiding concerns of sex that beset people in modern society. All of these essays, written in stunning prose, explore the mystery of love in its sexual dimensions. Even the book jacket, displaying Henri Rousseau's exotic painting *The Snake Charmer*, sharpens one's awareness of carnal love. (TJW)

IL,PO
392a. Ogden, Gina. **Women Who Love Sex.** New York: Pocket Books, 1994. 278 p. Includes bibliography and index. ISBN 0-671-86550-1.

Ogden, a marriage counselor and sex therapist, brings her cumulative wisdom to bear on the question of women's sexuality. Since the mid-1970s, she has developed a new theory of human sexuality based primarily on the views of a special population of women who claim that they love sex. She calls them *easily orgasmic women*. In 1980 she identified fifty such women who were eager to answer questions about their vibrant sex lives.

Dissatisfied with both the liberal male approach to sex research as well as the negativity of feminist investigators writing about sex, Ogden "envisioned research that would allow women to help bridge the gaps between main-line sexology and hard-line feminism by shedding light on the full range of women's positive sexual responses" (p. 15). Ogden focuses her attention on these women who love sex by conducting long interviews with them and presenting their views on different aspects of sexuality.

Alice, trapped in a dull marriage, regains her zest for sex through therapy that helped her to realize how her strict upbringing had limited her understanding of sexuality and affected her marital relationship. She and her husband learned how to communicate about sex and to understand each other's sexual needs. Today they both love sex. Maya's story is the exploration of the pleasure-orgasm-ecstasy continuum of sexual response and satisfaction. Iris tells how it is possible for women to attain orgasm by "extragenital stimulation only, without touching any part of your vulva" (p. 103). Dr. Suzanne's story is about "thinking off" (i.e., attaining orgasm through fantasizing without touching oneself in any way). By means of an elaborate experiment, Ogden shows how such orgasms may be measured in the laboratory. Molly, a lesbian, promotes physical nurturing through cuddling, hugging, massage, etc. She believes that these behaviors are a vital factor in achieving sexual satisfaction. Finally, Rosa talks about intimacy as a key ingredient in sex. By intimacy she refers to an emotional connection with one's partner "that links body, mind, heart, and soul" (p. 192).

Ogden's new theory of human sexuality reveals that for women who love sex, more is involved than the mechanics of sexual intercourse. These women's stories highlight the importance of attaining sexual satisfaction by utilizing a whole range of factors—from openness to intimacy—surrounding the central act of sex. (TJW)

Attraction. Beauty. Body Decoration. Dress

(For related material see also entry 127)

IL
393. Brain, Robert. **The Decorated Body.** New York: Harper & Row, 1979. 192 p. Includes bibliography and index. ISBN 0-06-010458-9.

According to Brain, an anthropologist, "the body is a clay to be remodeled and a canvas to be decorated." One of the main aims of the book is to present a cross-cultural description of body decoration to demonstrate how small a gap separates "primitive" and "civilized" people. Body decoration occurs in all cultures and is a kind of language or code that communicates social and individual needs, aesthetic ideals, and religious beliefs. Euro-American plastic surgery, make-up, and hair styles as well as African cicatrization and scarification, insular Pacific tattooing and body painting, and Native American body modifications are variations on a human theme: endowing the body with meaning by modifying it according to cultural needs rather than according to primarily practical concerns. Beautifully and appropriately illustrated throughout, the book raises and helps to answer questions about the complexity and variety of human body decoration. Each chapter develops a theme around which the body is modified (e.g., the painted body, the tattooed body, the scarred body). Of particular interest for the study of human sexuality are chapter 4, "The Mutilated Body," that includes a discussion of clitoridectomy, and chapter 7, "The Sexual Body." Other chapters demonstrate the diverse decorative ways that males and females express their gender. Brain emphasizes that the symbolism that underlies each type of body decoration is much more complex than a single motif. The beauty of this book is more than skin deep; it is dense with well-described examples that explore the rich tapestry of meaning that underlies how humans modify their bodies. (SGF)

IL,PO
394. Glynn, Prudence. **Skin to Skin: Eroticism in Dress.** New York: Oxford University Press, 1982. 157 p. Includes index. ISBN 0-19-520391-7.

Glynn, fashion editor of *The London Times* since 1966, presents a very personal, idiosyncratic view of erotic dress. Her published work, *In Fashion: Dress in the Twentieth Century* (1978), and her familiarity with the world fashion scene over many years, convey a ring of authority to her opinions about eroticism in dress. To begin with, she categorizes eight areas of sexual arousal that man, but especially woman, has used in observing dress: blatancy, innocence and vulnerability, protective power, overt virility, determination to survive through conformation, the priming of the hunting instinct, and sexual arousal through danger. In any case, pieces of clothing are selected "to provoke the crucial clash of two parties to produce a third." It all began, supposedly, in the Garden of Eden when Adam and Eve donned the fig leaf to cover their genitals; ever since, the curious have become erotically aroused wondering what they concealed. Hence the largely historical slant of this book focuses on "dress which has as its basis the deliberate intention to stimulate—either others or the wearer" (p. 22).

In chapter 2, "The Feminine Ideal," Glynn conducts a grand tour of the erotic zones of feminine fashion, including the waist and foot; the breasts; the legs; the back and the bottom; the neck, shoulders, arms and hands; and the stomach, thighs, and pudenda. Fashion has always highlighted these zones and then enhanced them with make-up and jewelry.

In chapter 3, "The Peacock's Tail," Glynn offers an analogous picture of men's erotic zones. She links men's erotic garb to power, the uniform, a feeling of confidence, and heroism. Additional chapters examine the largely hypocritical relationship between Authority (church and state) and Society (fashion); the role of the media in casting women as sex objects and men as power symbols; women's undergarments, types of body mutilation, and intimacy; the erotic use of fastenings (bows, belts, zippers, etc.), and special attire involved in sadomasochistic activities.

Explanatory paragraphs accompany every black-and-white and color illustration to supplement the text and present a wealth of information about eroticism in men's and women's fashions.

This handsome volume substantiates Glynn's basic premise "that any dress or bodily decoration—paraphernalia—above and beyond that necessary for survival has as its inspiration the desire to gratify the wearer or to inflame the interest of somebody else" (p. 153). (TJW)

IL,PO

395. Morris, Desmond. **Bodywatching: A Field Guide to the Human Species.** New York: Crown, 1985. 256 p. Includes bibliography and index. ISBN 0-517-55814-9.

In this illustrated volume *extraordinaire*, Morris, well-known zoologist and animal behavioralist, takes the reader on a visual journey across the human body's landscape, examining it part by part. Twenty chapters correspond to twenty body parts surveyed to reveal the body's diverse animal and cultural dimensions. He begins with the hair, proceeds to the brow, eyes, nose, ears, cheeks, mouth, beard, neck, shoulders, arms, hands, chest, back, belly, hips, buttocks, genitals, legs, and concludes with the feet. Each chapter briefly considers the anatomy and physiology, function, evolution, and growth of the particular body part. Behavioral activities (movements, postures, expressions, and gestures) undergo scrutiny. Such cultural modifications as adornment (painting, tattooing, jewelry), mutilation, and clothing receive attention. Morris explains how external cultural differences displayed in the body merely disguise the "naked ape's" underlying animal identity.

According to Morris, it benefits *Homo sapiens* to adopt an evolutionary perspective. Theory states that in the distant past a furry, four-footed way of life was replaced with a naked-skinned, bipedal existence. There was also a shift from forest fruit picking to hunting prey. In the process a unique body shape evolved. Also during the evolutionary process, a division of labor occurred, the female specializing in food gathering and childrearing, the male in hunting prey. In an amazingly successful way, the species multiplied and spread throughout the world. It is this background understanding that is needed to appreciate fully the human body in all its dimensions and diversity. Credits and captions for the 256 illustrations appear at the back of the book. (TJW)

PO

396. Paillochet, Claire. **Unmentionables: The Allure of Lingerie.** New York: Delilah Communications, 1983. 125 p. Translated from the French by Anne Collier and Christel Petermann. ISBN 0-933328-79-6.

Erotic dress in the form of women's lingerie is the subject of this largely pictorial work. About 200 black-and-white and color pictures, some full page, illustrate the four sections—"History," "The Movies," "Advertising," and "High Fashion"—into which Paillochet divides her book. Translated from the French, the book has a decidedly international flavor, showing such film stars as Brigitte Bardot, Marilyn Monroe, Sophia

Loren, Joan Collins, Hanna Schygulla, Ursula Andress, and others in various stages of undress.

In the history section, Paillochet makes the point that the Roman leg garter could be considered the progenitor of naughty underwear. She contends that today "underclothing has a completely different context from that of yesterday. It has lost its primary function, which was a stage in dressing, a hidden aspect of womanhood, and has become an outfit unto itself, a piece of clothing primarily to be seen."

Lingerie in the movies is depicted from the time Jane Russell displayed her considerable charms in the censor-baiting western *Outlaw* (1943) to Brooke Shields attired in frothy pantaloons in *Pretty Baby* (1978) and Sigourney Weaver caught in her bikini in *Alien* (1979).

Fancy underwear has become commonplace in advertising. Its allure is used to sell almost anything from kitchen interiors to shoes. And as a high fashion item it is sold by specialty shops, such as Frederick's of Hollywood and Victoria's Secret, that put out extravagant catalogs featuring sexy models wearing fine lingerie. Paillochet's last word is that "sexy underthings have a unique talent for keeping men and women around the world in absolute thrall." (TJW)

PR,IL,PO
397. Saint-Laurent, Cecil. **The Great Book of Lingerie.** New York: Vendome Press, 1986. 280 p. Includes bibliography and glossary. ISBN 0-86565-072-1.

In the realm of erotic relations between the sexes the undergarments of women have long played a fascinating role. Lingerie is the subject of this oversized, profusely illustrated study by Cecil Saint-Laurent, novelist and European fashion expert, whose point of view is that men's erotic fantasies are stimulated by what is concealed—or revealed—by women's underwear. Over 300 illustrations, many in color, ranging from medieval woodcuts to contemporary fashion pictures, embellish this volume, with the beauty of the female body acting as the common denominator.

As history, the book chronicles style itself, bringing out the radical changes in women's intimate attire. Often the changes reflected events in society as when, during the French Revolution, the corset disappeared as young women, in the interest of simplicity, resorted to chemises and petticoats beneath straight dresses. Following World War II women quit wearing stockings and began to dye their legs, and skirts got shorter. During the turbulent sixties, the miniskirt made its sudden appearance, glorifying youth and femininity.

The chapter headings embrace a diversity of topics, including "The Origin of Clothing," "The Disappearance of the Corset," "Drawers and Pantaloons," "The Strictures of Morality," and "The Latest Fashions: 1965-1985." Described in word and picture is a veritable panoply of underclothes: nightgowns, slips, chemises, drawers, panniers, corsets, tutus, brassieres, pantaloons, petticoats, bloomers, knickers, stockings, girdles, garters, suspender belts, panties, tights, bodystockings, G-strings, bikinis, and combinations of these in great variety. Viewed successively, these items of stylized clothing tell the history of women's undergarments. As Saint-Laurent comments: "As long as men and women are mutually attracted, women will always be aware of the importance of undergarments. And they will always know that the game between the sexes is very complex and that nudity is an indispensable part of it" (p. 17).

Photograph credits, a selected bibliography, and a glossary comprise the backmatter of this handsome book. (TJW)

PR,IL
398. Schwartz, Hillel. **Never Satisfied: A Cultural History of Diets, Fantasies and Fat.** New York: Free Press, 1986. 468 p. Includes bibliographic notes and index. ISBN 0-02-929250-6.

Historian Schwartz uses historical information as well as photographs and illustrations to chronicle the ways that "our sense of the body, of its heft and momentum, is shaped more by the theater of our lives than by our costume" (p. 4). Weight, fatness, and food are cultural constructs that link our bodies to our sense of self and to the social context of which we are a part. Underlying diets are the themes of romance and ritual. Dieting romance is impatient, a sort of "moral athleticism," an explosive process that frees up the body from its constraints. Dieting ritual is patient work, an implosive fashioning of the inside by working on the outside.

Spanning a period of over 150 years of American history, the book details the link between the social context and ideas about weight, fat, and the body. Each chapter focuses on a particular era. In the Jacksonian era (1820-1850) health reformer Sylvester Graham ushered in the first generation of American weight watchers by his insistence that a simple, abstinent diet of grains, vegetables, and water would counter the over-stimulation of gluttony, that leads to illness, sexual excess, and civic disorder. In the last third of the nineteenth century, after the social exhaustion of the Civil War, dyspepsia and neurasthenia were characteristic ailments, and gluttony became associated with heaviness and fat. As industrial developments (1880-1920) emphasized physical move-ment and consumption (e.g., powered flight, modern dance, home economics), a bal-anced, slender, light body became ideal. The need for regulating the body paralleled the importance of balancing economic overabundance with individual consumption. Glut-tony became a problem of flow, not just weight; fat symbolized excess, waste, and personal health. Regulation meant virtue, and the body expressed the spirit. Fasting, Fletcherism, calorie counting, and thyroid medication reigned as popular methods of slimming. Newly developed weight scales and other forms of precise measurement of the body became tools for assessing beauty and identity. The body was conceptualized in terms of units that individuated the moral state of its owner. By the 1930s, appetite control became a means of fighting dangerous accumulations of fat, just as adherents of the New Deal worried about patterns of economic consumption. Individuals had to become "brokers of desire," not just regulators of bodily metabolism, excretion, and production. Weight, fat, and form were indicators of personality and psychological states. New psychological theories of the 1940s linked the state of the body with an individual's sense of self. Someone who could take charge of the body was also empowering the self. Fats were differentiated into good and bad forms, and diets specified vigilance over types of fat as well as weight. Vitamins and exercise could transform the self, just as society could overcome the setbacks of the Depression. From the 1930s to 1950s, basic attitudes toward living shifted as did the definitions of basic foods. Parents projected their social fears onto the bodies of their born and unborn children, whose bodies became expressions of the adequacy of parenting and their intrapsychic state.

Schwartz concludes that in a society of abundance, desires are defined and manipulated by the culture, and what the individual really wants is unclear. Ambivalence about desires and the nature of reality is exacerbated by the hope of consuming without consequence; "empty calories"; exercise; and purging. Diet regimens promise relief from a postindustrial, consumer society where demands are "never satisfied." Women fall prey to these rituals as a way of empowering themselves in a society that exacts more precise standards for women's form than for men's. Overzealous attention to the body has become a symptom of late capitalism and dissatisfied individuals. "We are not what we eat. We eat what we are. And how we are" (p. 339). (SGF)

IL

399. Thévoz, Michel. **The Painted Body.** New York: Skira/Rizzoli, 1984. 138 p. (The Illusions of Reality). Translation of: *Le corps peint.* Includes bibliography and index. ISBN 0-8478-0539-5.

Thévoz, director of the Collection de l'Art Brut, Lausanne, Switzerland, concep-tualizes the overall purpose of his analysis and explication of body decoration as a demonstration that "there is no body but the painted body, and no painting but body painting" (p. 7). Because humans are aware of their own image, they compensate for their biological insignificance by revising and renewing their bodies to reflect their culture; thus, there is no body but the painted body. Even printed, impressed, or painted representations of the body revive memories of early impulses to mark human flesh. Consequently, there is no painting but body painting.

The book is divided into four sections, each of which emphasizes and illustrates how the body reflects different states of individual and community identity. "The Prehistoric Body" describes the ways in which early humans imprinted culture on their natural form. The emphasis on genital modifications in cave paintings reflects the importance of the opposition of the sexes in structuring early communities. "The Savage Body" explores the significance of body modification in African, American, Australian, and Polynesian societies. While body and face painting were transitory masks used in defined ceremonial contexts, tattooing, scarification, circumcision, and clitoridectomy were more permanent social stamps on individual identity. Often these markings signified initiation or marriage rules that structured an individual's subsequent sexual relations. "The Mirror Stage" explores treatment of the body in historical and modern state communities such as Japan, Greece, New Guinea, and Europe. Various forms of make-up mime nature and contrive a natural look while others (theater paint, clown faces) depart from the natural. Tattooing becomes a signifier of social class. The final section, "The Resurrection of the Flesh," explores body art, contemporary cosmetics, and frequently degraded representations of the body as an attempt to reconcile life and art.

Overall, Thévoz not only points out the sexual symbolism of body modifications but also shows the relevance of understanding the social, biological, and psychological aspects of body symbolism across cultures and time frames. The book is handsomely and copiously illustrated with photographs of carvings, drawings, engravings, paintings, and prints, many in full color. Much of the body painting presents the works of famous artists such as Blake, Catlin, David, Dürer, Fragonard, Goya, Klee, Klimt, Lichtenstein, and Warhol. The illustrations are systematically listed by culture and artist in an appendix at the end. (SGF/TJW)

IL,PO

400. Wolf, Naomi. **The Beauty Myth: How Images of Beauty Are Used Against Women.** New York: Morrow, 1991. 348 p. Includes bibliography and index. ISBN 0-688-08510-5.

Not a conspiracy exactly, but something akin to it emanating from the male-dominated corporate power structure, has produced the "beauty myth." Wolf claims that it is a backlash against the economic, political, and personal gains made by women over the past two decades. She believes that society is fearful of too much freedom and power concentrated in the hands of women; therefore, the inequality between men and women must be maintained. The best way to accomplish this is by enticing women into excessive body care through such dubious means as brainwashing, diet and exercise programs, skin care schemes, and cosmetic surgery. All of these measures, Wolf avers, are carried to extremes by the concerned industries that profit from the sale of products and services used to achieve a phony, artificial beauty. In detail, Wolf explores six different aspects of the beauty myth: work, culture, religion, sex, hunger, and violence.

In the workplace, women have been compelled to emphasize their beauty in relation to their employment status; the higher they move up the corporate ladder, the more stringent become the rules governing appearance. In reality this undermines their striving and keeps them in place. Wolf worries about a PBQ, or professional beauty qualification (a term she coined), becoming institutionalized as a condition for the hiring and promotion of women.

Certain areas of modern culture foster the beauty myth. For example, women's magazines, with their mass production of beauty images and their written messages glamorizing beauty, promote it. They advise women on various subjects: skin care, diet, exercise, cosmetic surgery, getting ahead on the job, and attaining a satisfying sex life. Running through all these segments of female concerns, is the notion that one must harken to the ideals of currently acceptable standards of beauty; ignoring them leads to feelings of guilt and inferiority.

Calling the beauty myth the gospel of a new religion, Wolf says that women have accepted a belief system that states that beauty is real and holy, and that women should strive to attain it. It uses the most effective mind-altering techniques of prominent cults (Scientology, etc.)—prayer, meditation, chanting, group rituals, psychodrama, and confession—to persuade women that they should pursue the rituals of beauty unquestioningly.

With women achieving a measure of sexual freedom in the 1970s, a development startling to the power structure, the backlash showed itself in a different way: myriads of nude images of women appeared everywhere saturating the mass media. The beauty myth even invaded pornography where women were portrayed as inexhaustible sources of sexual pleasure; conventional pornographic images appeared in advertising, fashion photography, cable TV, and even comic books. Taken in by these sexual images foisted upon them, women displayed themselves accordingly. The overall effects, harmful to both men and women, have falsely eroticized women, and men, deceived, have reacted abusively and violently toward women. Natural female sexuality has become distorted with beauty being equated with sex.

In discussing the last two aspects of the beauty myth, hunger and violence, Wolf describes the way young women, in the pursuit of slimness, generate their own medical problems: anorexia nervosa and bulimia, both caused by starving the body of nutrition in the campaign to eliminate body fat. She also attacks cosmetic surgery and the surgeons who profit from it, pointing out that deaths have occurred in these misguided attempts to turn back the aging process for the sake of beauty.

Wolf calls for a third wave of feminism to generate in women a critical attitude toward all aspects of the beauty myth. She does not want a direct attack on the image makers and their corporate backers, but rather a number of changes including an intergenerational cooperation and understanding among women, a return to the appreciation of natural beauty and female sexuality, and interpersonal efforts among men and women to bypass the beauty myth. (TJW)

Dating. Courtship

PR,IL

401.   Bailey, Beth L. **From Front Porch to Back Seat: Courtship in Twentieth-Century America.** Baltimore, Md.: Johns Hopkins University Press, 1988. 181 p. Includes bibliographic notes and index. ISBN 0-8018-3609-3.

Historian Bailey's book is "a study of national systems of convention that governed American courtship from about 1900 through the mid-1960s." She defines courtship broadly as "wooing," whether or not it leads to marriage. And she examines the conventions ("public codes of behavior and systems of meaning that are both culturally constructed and historically specific") that structure and give meaning to personal experiences of courtship.

What has been the system of logic that governs courtship in America, structuring its historical meaning and implications? Bailey chronicles the answer to this question by documenting the transformation of courtship from a system of calling to one of dating, paying special attention to the etiology, evolution, and demise of the dating system that flourished between about 1920 and 1965.

She begins her history at the turn of the century, when courtship was conducted on front porches and in front parlors, usually with the young woman's parents nearby. Control of calling lay with the woman and her family. As working class women moved to the big cities, where their dwellings often lacked front porches, parlors, and pianos, calling was replaced by dating. The emergence of dating paralleled the development of a national American culture, facilitated by urbanization, industrialization, national systems of communication, the extension of education, and cultural media. With dating, the whole system changed, financially for men, who became hosts, and socially for women, who could now vie for the attention of as many suitors as they could handle. The themes of this new system were popularity and romantic competition among women, particularly in high school and college social activities across the country. Courtship was more public, and men held the seat of power and control.

The Great Depression of the 1930s and World War II in the 1940s resulted in a growing shortage of marriageable men, sparking new ideas about dating. The media and numerous advice books urged women to make themselves attractive and to not be too picky about whom they dated; a date became a commodity and men, in essence, wallets. As dating proceeded in the 1950s, many young people went steady and early marriages became commonplace. By the 1960s, the standards of the 1950s were regarded as part of a demeaning game. Sexual freedom led to the assumption that a couple that dates also has sex together; it provided the basis for dating as a kind of serial monogamy in the 1970s and 1980s. Sex became a mark of the youth culture, and conventions about courtship became even more public as scientists and marriage education courses scrutinized them. In the 1990s, sex is the "medium of contemporary courtship," but its meaning is still unclear. Some claim that today's instant intimacy kills romance, but nostalgia for the past will not cure the problem, because our way of viewing the world has changed. We are in the midst of another change in courtship conventions that have yet to be articulated. (SGF/TJW)

PO

402. Perper, Timothy. **Sex Signals: The Biology of Love.** Philadelphia: ISI Press, 1985. 323 p. Includes bibliography and index. ISBN 0-89495-050-9.

The attraction that people feel toward each other when they first meet is not just "chemistry" or that "ole' black magic." According to biologist Perper, it is part of a courtship sequence that has a profound biological function—reproduction. Perper's goal in this book is "to describe how love, intimacy, and courtship grow from a biological core to affect our entire lives" (p. xi). Using a biosocial perspective, he attempts to explain the behavioral basis of mating within which the emotions of "love" are grounded. A biosocial approach involves an investigation of the reciprocal relations between genetic, evolutionary, psychological, and cultural processes. Recognizing that biologists and social scientists have differing beliefs about biology ("ethnobiology"), Perper takes considerable care in discarding myths about biology (e.g., that it is a fixed and unalterable force) to focus on its "real" dynamics, including change, activity, and functionality of behavior. He concludes that the nature/nurture debate is a useless argument; many aspects of culture fill biological functions.

Using material from the biological and social sciences, literature, and Perper's research, the book weaves together two main themes: the courtship sequence and biological functionality. Based on his own data drawn from behavioral observations of the interaction of men and women, Perper documents the courtship sequence as a form of intimate communication, that is composed of approaching, talking, turning one's body toward the other, touching, and synchronizing body movements. Most often, women initiate the sequence and men respond to women's cues. Initial approach and response may be grounded in a neurophysiological feature, a "template," that is a "prefigured gestalt of the ideal" mate. The reluctance that women may express later on complements their proceptivity (female initiation and maintenance of a sexual interaction) in allowing them to choose an appropriate mate. "Search polygamy" (aka "promiscuity") may also serve this purpose. The dynamics of the courtship sequence help to explain why men and women respond differently to each other and endow sex with different meanings.

The biological functionality of the courtship process is socially and symbolically celebrated at marriage. A close association between sex and religion stems from the parallel between sexual relations and concepts of the sacred and profane. Sex becomes a symbolic path to the sacred, where life is created.

In reviewing the behavior of lovers, Perper concludes that "we have been able to track the operation of profoundly biological processes" (p. 247). An appendix specifies the elements of effective, scientific "people watching." (SGF)

PR,IL

403. Rothman, Ellen K. **Hands and Hearts: A History of Courtship in America.** New York: Basic Books, 1984. 370 p. Includes bibliographic notes and index. ISBN 0-465-02880-2.

This work, aimed at scholars in history, sociology, women's studies, and related fields, traces the social history of courtship in the United States from 1770 to 1920. Rothman examines the stages of courtship and its effect on the thoughts, feelings, and behavior of people through the personal reminiscences, diaries, and letters of 350 American men and women. An epilogue based on current sociological research summarizes data from 1920 to 1980.

Courtship in America followed a fairly consistent pattern from 1770 until the social upheaval of the first two decades of the twentieth century. Young people in the United States have had considerable autonomy in choosing spouses; parents traditionally have offered advice and given approval but rarely interfered with their children's choices. Until after World War II, a man had to possess the means to support a wife and family before he could marry. (The G.I. Bill and other government subsidies, combined with an increasing number of working wives, freed men from these constraints.) Women's attitudes toward marriage altered as the family and community structure changed. While married couples tended to remain in the home community, women approached marriage with joy tempered by nervousness, but as close-knit families and communities dispersed and marriage meant a loss of family and friends, nervousness became fear. By the late eighteenth century, when many women had made the transition to living and working away from home, marriage lost this fearful aspect. Attitudes toward love and passion underwent a gradual change as the Puritan fear of passion gave way to an understanding and acceptance of natural drives and emotions, with the Victorian period providing a brief anomaly. Throughout the period studied, couples advocated mutual openness and honesty. Sexual restraint has been a continual practice; however, the responsibility for such restraint gradually shifted from both partners to rest on the women. A marked increase in premarital sexual activity took place in the late 1910s and early 1920s with the growing acceptance of contraception and the emotional responses to World War I. Since 1920, dating and petting have replaced the traditional forms of courtship. Although sexual intimacy has increased, limits to acceptable behavior continue to be enforced, with "being in love" a determining factor. Cohabitation, an increasingly popular and accepted behavior, has become part of the courtship ritual, but marriage remains the goal. (SDH)

Associated Feelings

Love

For related material see also entries 42, 43, 46, 77, 103, 104, 204, 205, 350, 805, 843)

IL,PO

403a. Ackerman, Diane. **A Natural History of Love.** New York: Random House, 1994. 358 p. Includes bibliography and index. ISBN 0-679-40347-7.

Ackerman, whose critically acclaimed *A Natural History of the Senses* (Vintage, 1991), explores the natural world through the five senses, now focuses her attention on the nature of love. She labels it "the white light of emotion" (p. xvii), a metaphor begging for analysis into its essential elements. In her first section, "A Long Desire: The History of Love," she begins with history and gives an intimate account of love among the Egyptians, Greeks, Romans, and through the Middle Ages and the Renaissance to the present. She comments on major figures of each age (Cleopatra, Abelard and Heloise, Casanova, Franklin, Beethoven) to illustrate her perspectives on love, embellishing their stories with poetry, well-known myths, and works of art. She reveals the sexual practices of each age: incest, masturbation, phallic worship, chivalry, courtly love, and so forth.

She observes that the conditions of modern love, slowly achieved over the tortuous course of history, are the freedom and ability to select a lover, to make love in private, and to read about lovemaking in the world's literature. The second section, "The Heart Is a Lonely Hunter," explores the various ideas about love propounded by Plato, Stendhal, Denis de Rougement, Marcel Proust, and Sigmund Freud. She explains biologically "attachment theory" as developed by John Bowlby, who was inspired by the ideas of Konrad Lorenz and Harry Harlow. Dubbing romantic love a "ballet," she goes on to state, "It is evolution's way of making sure that sexual partners meet and mate, then give their child the care it needs to be healthy and make loving attachments of its own" (p. 135).

In "All Fires the Fire: The Nature of Love," Ackerman delves into neurophysiology, evolution, and the chemistry of love. She discusses the effects of oxytocin, phenylethylamine (PEA), the endorphins, and aphrodisiacs on different kinds of love. She then explores eroticism in "A Necessary Passion: The Erotics of Love," revealing the evolutionary forces underlying this elaborate game of love. As they relate to love and sex, she covers such disparate topics as the face, hair, women and horses, men and cars, flying, men and mermaids, the fashion of perversity, kissing, and looking. "Sex obsesses us," Ackerman explains, "as it must if we are to procreate" (p. 179).

In "Passing Strange and Wonderful: Love's Customs," Ackerman describes and interprets love customs appropriate to courtship and marriage around the world and what happens when the customs are violated. Lastly, she deals with varieties of love in "Points for a Compass Rose: Varieties of Love." She discusses altruism, love of children, love of strangers, religious love, love during therapy, and love of pets.

The book ends with a postscript about a trip Ackerman took to the American Museum of Natural History in New York City. Entranced by the exhibit showing "Lucy" and her mate trekking across Ethiopia three million years ago, she muses about the affection and love they reveal and the legacy of that love passed down to us through evolution. (TJW)

PR,IL
404. Bergmann, Martin S. **The Anatomy of Loving: The Story of Man's Quest to Know What Love Is.** New York: Columbia University Press, 1987. 302 p. Includes bibliography and index. ISBN 0-231-06487-X.

In this work on the phenomenon of love—and its connection with narcissism—Bergmann, psychoanalyst and Professor of Psychology at New York University, looks first at how the concept has been treated in early civilizations and by the most renowned thinkers of the Western world. Bergmann guides the reader through (1) the love poetry of ancient Egypt and Sumer; (2) the vocabulary of love developed in Greek myths and plays (especially Plato's *The Symposium*); (3) the Roman contributions (Ovid, Catullus, etc.); (4) the Jewish and Christian statements on love in the Old Testament and the New Testament; (5) the emergence of romantic love in the Middle Ages; and (6) the notions about love as expressed in philosophy and literature from the seventeenth to the nineteenth centuries.

Throughout this first section of the book Bergmann introduces a host of psychoanalytic terms as used by Sigmund Freud at the turn of the century. He applies Freud's vocabulary (ego, id, superego, libido, narcissism, sublimation, etc.) retrospectively to this vast corpus of literature about love. He shows, too, the importance of looking at the past "through Freud's prism," at the same time recognizing literary and artistic contributions to psychoanalysis.

Bergmann believes that "psychoanalysis is in a position to outline a theory of love" (p. 260). He reaches this conclusion by having first reviewed the persistent quest to understand the nature of love, then showing the direct line of descent from Plato to Freud in key psychoanalytic concepts (e.g., sublimation), and finally by examining in the second half of the book, the development of psychoanalysts' views on love beginning with Freud and his immediate cohorts (K. Abraham, Jung, Reich, etc.), and then going on to the contributions of his numerous modifiers (Hartmann, Klein, etc.) and extenders (Balint, Bak, etc.). Bergmann sums up Freud's basic contributions to understanding love in terms of three theories of love. In the first theory of love, Freud connected infantile sexuality, one of the phases of sexual development, to adult love. In the second theory of love, Freud introduced the term *narcissism* and showed how self-love may be transferred to the object as narcissistic love, that is love of another modeled on love of self. In the third theory, Freud showed how love, where the whole ego is involved, is more than a manifestation of the sexual instinct.

In the final chapter, Bergmann presents different kinds of love beginning with infatuation and going on to love and the proximity of death, triangular love, conflictual love, loveless sexuality, masochistic and sadistic love, hermaphroditic love, Pygmalion love, narcissistic love, primary and anaclitic (i.e., incestuous) love, love addiction, transference love, aim-inhibited love, and ideal love. Recapitulated here, each of these kinds of love has been articulated by Bergmann throughout his text. The book reveals in detail the psychoanalytic contributions made by Freud and his followers to our understanding of love as previously examined by philosophers, artists, and others in the "humanist past." (TJW)

IL

405. Bloom, Allan. **Love and Friendship.** New York: Simon & Schuster, 1993. 590 p. Includes bibliographic notes and index. ISBN 0-671-67336-X.

Bloom, author of the best-selling book *The Closing of the American Mind* and the John U. Nef Distinguished Service Professor on Social Thought at the University of Chicago, has written a work that has been described as the "culmination of a lifetime spent thinking and writing about the most fundamental questions facing human beings," among them love and its close ally friendship. Unfortunately, Bloom believes that these emotions, that he calls *eros*, are withering away under the onslaught of science and a new moralism that promotes individualism and egalitarianism.

Bloom's solution to the crisis that has turned eros into sex, is to reexamine the thoughts of a select group of philosophers and writers, e.g., Jean Jacques Rousseau, the Swiss philosopher and author of such classic works as *The Social Contract* and *Confessions.* Recognized as the founder of the Romantic Movement, Rousseau had an influence on several great novels of the nineteenth century, e.g., Stendhal's *The Red and the Black*, Jane Austen's *Pride and Prejudice*, Flaubert's *Madame Bovary*, and Tolstoy's *Anna Karenina.* These novels reflected the romantic elements that Rousseau espoused in both of his novels *Emile* and *La Nouvelle Héloïse.*

In *Emile*, Rousseau set forth the kind of education, including sex education, that a civilized young man should receive. Emile would be educated in the requirements of eros: an eye for beauty, imagination, and an understanding of the role of sex in love. The key to the nature of eros seems to be the distinction between *amour de soi* (self-love) and *amour-propre.* For his survival, natural man relies on self-love, but as he matures and develops relationships with others, e.g., a woman, he wonders what she thinks of him and what he should think of her. In this awareness, *amour-propre* takes over. The relationship, fraught with danger and uncertainty, is ameliorated through longing, imagination, will, and understanding. Hence the importance of education as propounded in *Emile.* To further strengthen his position on the nature of eros, Bloom turns to the plays of Shakespeare, that teach us more about love and friendship than do the investigations of Freud and Kinsey, or even the Romantic novelists, or the philosophy of Rousseau.

Bloom's final excursion, his attempt to restore eros to its rightful place in modern life, is an examination of Plato's *Symposium.* Here, in traditional Socratic fashion, the nature of love and friendship are explored.

In the epilogue, Bloom's further observations about love and friendship include the following: "The necessity in love and friendship is that of nature. Once entered in this world, we are free of all other constraints, but the power of the beloved or the friend over our whole being does not itself admit of free choice in the usual use of the term, and there seems to be no act of the will involved. We simply walk into a magnetic field and are drawn by it. We are not the movers, we are moved. We may be lucky and attract the one to whom we are attracted" (p. 550). (TJW)

IL
406.   Brain, Robert. **Friends and Lovers.** New York: Basic Books, 1976. 287 p. Includes bibliography and index. ISBN 0-465-02571-4.

In his concluding remarks, Brain, an anthropologist, states, "Friendship must be taken as seriously as sex, aggression, and marriage" (p. 264). Accordingly, he examines friendship and love cross-culturally in various societies, past and present, in order to illuminate present-day attitudes. Unfortunately, friendship has not been thoroughly studied by anthropologists. Believing that friendship is a basic human trait, Brain shows how people in different societies make friends through "gestures, invitations, winking, kissing, shaking hands, gifts," and so forth. Loving friendships are indigenous among primitive peoples; they have little to do with marriage. He also believes that in Western societies today, friendship from late childhood on is viewed with suspicion; therefore, it behooves us to look at other societies and their perspectives on friendship to see if we cannot benefit from these comparisons. Brain also interrelates friendship, love, and sex in a continuum that reveals the incompatibility of friendship and sex. One of the unusual characteristics of Western society is its adherence to romantic love, a fraudulent notion that derives from medieval times when troubadours expressed from afar their undying love for noble ladies. Such tragic stories as those of Tristan and Iseult and Abelard and Heloise are myths and models of romantic love. Curiously, today everyone anticipates romantic love, with its implied chastity, promise of sexual fulfillment, and eternal fidelity, as a prelude to marriage. Brain makes the vital point that loving friendships outside the family are endangered by a misguided search for total satisfaction within the framework of marriage, where the wife assumes various roles as mistress, advisor, companion, playmate, and mother. In recent years, fortunately, this narrow ideal has been slowly eroding. (TJW)

PO
407.   Buscaglia, Leo. **Loving Each Other: The Challenge of Human Relationships.** Thorofare, N.J.: Slack, 1984. 298 p. Includes bibliography. ISBN 0-943432-27-8.

Rather than relegating love, commitment, and cooperation to the recesses of sentimental foolishness, Buscaglia ("Dr. Hug"), the well-known author and lecturer, suggests the cultivation of these traits to enhance individual happiness. The purpose of this book is to examine "the complex nature involved in loving each other (the dynamic and ever-changing nature of two or more unique and whole individuals agreeing to emerge and blend in long-term commitment)" (p. 13). Although Buscaglia says people swallow the myth that loving comes naturally, he asserts that living with and loving others "requires skills as delicate and studied as those of the surgeon, the master builder and the gourmet cook" (p. 18). Based on his background of studying relating for twelve years as well as on the results of his formal survey of the attitudes of 600 people, he presents guidelines to help individuals develop the knowledge and skills necessary for creating and maintaining a loving relationship. Each of the main chapters is devoted to a discussion of one important aspect of the behaviors and qualities that respondents agree enhance all loving relationships: communication, honesty, forgiveness, joy, letting go (overcoming jealousy), and intimacy. Although only one chapter deals directly with sexuality, this popular treatment of loving defines the context within which Buscaglia thinks physical expression should occur. Other books by him on love are *Love* (1972) and *Living, Loving and Learning* (1982). (SGF)

PR
408.   Cancian, Francesca M. **Love in America: Gender and Self-Development.** Cambridge, Eng.: Cambridge University Press, 1987. 210 p. Includes bibliography and index. ISBN 0-521-34202-3.

Since the 1950s, family and gender roles have become much more flexible, allowing both men and women to pursue self-development as a personal goal. However, some observers argue that the pursuit of self-development conflicts with the maintenance of family bonds. Cancian, a sociologist at the University of Washington, suggests that a choice between self-development and family is not the only option. Love and self-development can be mutually reinforcing within the context of an interdependent relationship. The goal of this book is to examine how three ideas about heterosexual love—traditional, independent, and interdependent—developed historically and how they affect contemporary intimate relationships.

The apparent conflict between love and self-development stems from the polarization of gender roles begun in the late nineteenth century with the shift from an agrarian to a capitalist economy. The new division of labor stressed the separate spheres of men and women; economic productivity, individual achievement, work, and the public sphere were masculinized while the home, family, love, and privacy were feminized. At the turn of the century, more women entered the labor force and had fewer children, while men had more leisure time as business became bureaucratized. Both genders focused more on self-development. A transition from the traditional marriage, based on parenting, to the companionate marriage that emphasized emotional and sexual intimacy between husband and wife, occurred. However, love remained feminized and was only part of a man's life.

The economic collapse of the 1930s and the postwar commitment to support males in the workforce reinforced companionate marriage for a while. As more women entered the workforce and the feminist movement gained strength, self-development became more important than conformity to traditional roles. Consequently, ideas about love became more androgynous, stressing both male and female responsibility for love. Individual self-development and openness promotes intimacy in an independent model of love. Interdependent love stresses the importance of mutual self-development through intimacy and support.

Each of these types of love has its costs. Social theorists argue about the implications of family type and love for freedom and equality. The feminization of love overlooks the pragmatic ways in which men love. Illness and marital conflict may result from polarized gender roles in loving. Androgynous love offers more possibilities. Cancian concludes that the pursuit of self-development in an interdependent context is more likely than the independent pursuit of self-development to replace the traditional or companionate marriage, which channels current gender relations into polarized forms of loving. (SGF)

IL

409. De Rougemont, Denis. **Love in the Western World.** Translated by Montgomery Belgion. Revised and augmented ed. New York: Pantheon, 1956. 336 p. First edition published in 1940. Includes bibliographic footnotes and index.

This classic work by one of Europe's leading intellectuals is an exposition of "the inescapable conflict in the West between passion and marriage." De Rougemont details passionate love as first manifested in the twelfth-century poetry of the troubadours of southern France in connection with the practice of courtly love and later symbolized by the medieval myth of Tristan and Iseult. The lofty notion of unconsummated but passionate love became profaned in the course of time. After seeking for the origin of the vocabulary of love in Catharism, the heretical religion of the Church of Love, he traces the secularization of the myth in European literature, beginning with the *Roman de la Rose* (written 1237-1280). Eventually the myth infuses the novel, and we get such exemplars as Flaubert's *Madame Bovary*, Tolstoy's *Anna Karenina*, and Hardy's *Tess of the D'Urbervilles*. A further step takes us to (1) mass-produced novels, popular plays, and films, all permeated by a much distorted myth, as well as (2) a reaction to the superficial romanticizing in our literature from such a writer as D. H. Lawrence. De Rougemont sees the passion myth at work in spheres other than literature: in war, politics, and the institution of marriage. He recognizes the breakdown of marriage in the West and attributes much of it to the false notion people have about passionate love as fundamental to happy marriage. In fact, he believes that the two are incompatible because of the popular profanation of the myth of love, that in its current form is inherently transitory. He believes that the institution of marriage can only be saved by (1) understanding that the present predicament arises partly from misuse of the romantic myth and (2) concentrating attention on the meaning and significance of the marriage vows. (TJW)

PR,IL
410. Fisher, Helen E. **Anatomy of Love: The Natural History of Monogamy, Adultery and Divorce.** New York: Norton, 1992. 431 p. Includes bibliography and index. ISBN 0-393-03423-2.

Why do we marry? Why are some people adulterous? Why do human beings divorce? What is infatuation? When did human love and sex evolve? What is the future of the family? Anthropologist Fisher examines the innate aspects of sex and love and marriage, those traits and tendencies that we inherited from our past. She examines flirting behavior and the other courting postures and vocal tones we use naturally to court. She traces love at first sight to animal attraction and explains, from a Darwinian perspective, why we fall in love with one person rather than another. She explores the brain chemistry of attraction and attachment. And she looks at divorce in sixty-two societies and philandering in forty-two cultures to illustrate several patterns of serial monogamy and clandestine adultery—primary aspects of our human reproductive strategy. Then she traces the evolution of human patterns of courtship, marriage, adultery, divorce, remarriage and the sexual emotions back to their origins on the grasslands of Africa some four million years ago. Women, men and power, the genesis of "teenage," the origin of the human conscience, gender differences in the brain and other aspects of human sexuality are also examined from an anthropological perspective as she traces humankind from our hunting/gathering past in Africa through the agricultural revolution and into contemporary Western social life. In the last chapter, Fisher looks at several modern trends and concludes that many are not new. Instead these family patterns came across the centuries, up from primitives who wandered out of Africa millennia ago. (Author)

PO
411. Forward, Susan, and Joan Torres. **Men Who Hate Women & the Women Who Love Them.** Toronto: Bantam Books, 1986. 294 p. Includes bibliography. ISBN 0-553-05135-0.

Loving may be painful, but a woman does not know why. Her partner seems charming, romantic, and intense, particularly in the beginning of the relationship or in public. However, he behaves as if he wants to destroy her; he criticizes, belittles, blames, isolates, and controls her to such an extent that her self-esteem erodes. Not a sadist, narcissist, or sociopath, this controlling man, who psychologically attacks his partner with his words and moods, can be termed a "misogynist," a "woman hater." There are many indications of involvement with a misogynist. For example, he (1) assumes the right to control how a woman lives and behaves; (2) devalues the woman's opinions, feelings, and accomplishments; (3) yells, threatens, or withdraws in angry silence when the woman displeases him; (4) switches from charm to rage without warning; and (5) blames the woman for everything that goes wrong in the relationship. The woman may try a variety of tactics to win his approval; "walk on eggs" to prevent setting him off; feel inadequate; let herself go physically; and repress feelings, particularly anger.

The first part of this best-seller describes how and why these relationships work. Patterns learned with parents may set the tone for later intimate relationships. The misogynist loves a woman but fears dependency on and abandonment by her; he deals with his anxiety by controlling and belittling his partner. The woman involved with a misogynist may come from a psychologically abusive family; she hopes that she can increase the infrequent love and approval from her partner. The dual "madness" of their relationship involves the woman allowing her partner to express angry feelings for her while she expresses the man's vulnerable feelings of need. The resulting exchange of dependency only heightens the anger, hostility, and stress. The second part of the book presents exercises designed to help the woman change herself and her relationship. Without *doing* something different, the destructive pattern persists. The highly directive therapeutic approach, based on Forward's work with her clients, focuses on engendering self-assertiveness and self-confidence in the woman; the goal is not to change her partner, but to change how she thinks about herself and behaves, as well as to alter the way her partner *treats* her. The decision to leave a misogynist as well as the aftermath of such a decision are also explored. Although the path to change is difficult, Forward reassures the reader of its value; she has experienced it herself. (SGF)

IL
412. Fromm, Erich. **The Art of Loving.** New York: Harper & Row, 1956. 112 p.
This book is based on the premise that love is an art, the mastery of which requires a knowledge of its theory and practice. Fromm, a renowned psychoanalyst, believes that the practice of love calls for discipline, concentration, patience, and a supreme concern for the art. He theorizes that the art of loving affords lonely people the best opportunity for coping with the feeling of separateness or isolation that afflicts everyone from birth. The main problem of human existence is to overcome this separateness; one way is through sexual orgasm. However, for lasting effect this method requires love, which is difficult to obtain. Love implies certain mutually interdependent elements, including care, responsibility, respect, and knowledge. This syndrome of attitudes toward another person is characteristic of the art of loving. In terms of the objects of love, Fromm provides five categories: brotherly love, motherly love, erotic love, self-love, and love of God. He states that erotic love, in contrast to brotherly love and motherly love, is "the craving for complete fusion, for union with another person" (p. 44). He contrasts his view with that of Freud, who viewed sexual desire (i.e., erotic love) as the removal of bodily tension. Fromm looks at sexual desire as a need for love and union to overcome the feeling of separateness. These are the elements of the theory and practice of love as propounded by Fromm in parts II and IV of this closely reasoned book. In part III, Fromm, highly critical of modern capitalism, explores the economic and cultural factors that make loving difficult and account for the disintegration of sacred and profane love in Western society. (TJW)

IL
413. Gaylin, Willard. **Rediscovering Love.** New York: Viking, 1986. 288 p. Includes bibliography and index. ISBN 0-670-81120-3.
Psychoanalyst Gaylin, co-founder and President of the Hastings Center, thinks that each generation—using its own tools, language, philosophy, biases—needs to reexamine the concept of love. Rediscovering love is particularly important in the present era, that extols individualism, rationality, the pursuit of pleasure, psychological fulfillment, and sexuality. Our culture has encouraged people to be narcissistic—self-involved—to the neglect of deep interpersonal connections in the community and with each other. Love has become an "epiphenomenon" when it should be the center of our existence, an affirmation of our humanity.
Social and cultural changes have fostered our current confusion of being loved with loving; lust with passion; and sex with love. The nineteenth century over-evaluated the importance of the individual; gave too much credence to science and rationalism without honoring the validity of emotion; paid too much attention to similarities between humans and other animals; and focused more on the present and future than on traditions of the past. Success was measured by winning in competitive pursuits, despite the attendant anxiety of taking risks; workers provided pieces of products and exchanged mastery of a craft for money that could be exchanged for subsistence and pleasure. Freud's work epitomized many of these trends by focusing on libido and the pleasure

principle. However, Gaylin thinks that Freud's narrow definition of pleasure and an emphasis on the transformation of the libido in development left little room for highlighting the significance of love for humans.

Gaylin draws from literature, personal experience, and professional activities to elucidate the nature of love. Most chapters relate to different facets of love—the need for love; the nature of pleasure; the nature of love; the experience of love; the loss of love; the capacity to love. The biological capacity to love flows from the prolonged dependency period of the infant on the parent; from the human imagination; and from the freedom from instinctual fixation. Love is not sexual gratification; sex is unfulfilling if it is not attached to love. Rather, love involves an expanded view of pleasure—one that involves delight in new experiences, mastery, activity, transcendence. Underlying all forms of love are three major human capacities: sexual passion, caring, and fusion. Parental love involves fusion and caring; romantic love adds passion, that, unlike lust, can be maintained over a long period of time. Idealization of the other allows both individuals to transcend himself or herself. When a loved one is lost—through death, divorce, rejection, abandonment—a person becomes more aware of the need for and magnificence of love. Women, who define themselves more in terms of attachments, suffer more from the loss of love than men, who concentrate their definition of self on pride in work and mastery. People who are autistic, schizophrenic, pathological, and narcissistic cannot love. The rest of us need to move beyond pleasure to community and love. This entails taking the risks of being hurt, identification, commitment, and delayed gratification. Why should people go through this? Love is not the icing on the cake, "It is the cake" (p. 26). (SGF)

IL

414. Harlow, Harry F. **Learning to Love.** San Francisco: Albion, 1971. 116 p. Includes bibliography and index.

Distinguished primate researcher Harry Harlow presents a summary of findings to date on affection, that he and his late wife Peggy derived from almost twenty years of research on primates. As Harlow notes, "objective reports on human love are conspicuously scarce"; scientific studies of affection have been rare. His book is divided into three major sections. The first presents ideas about five forms of love. The second contrasts the behavioral expressions of the positive emotions of affection with the negative ones of fear and anger. The final section discusses some aspects of social behavior in general.

The first section makes up the bulk of the book. Love is defined as affectional feelings for others. Based on his research with rhesus monkeys, Harlow describes five major affectional systems that are interactive and interpersonal. The first two, maternal and infant love, are highly reciprocal and develop from intimate maternal contact in early infancy. Maternal love differs from other love systems in that its full sequence is usually recurrent with each child. Maternal love includes phases of care and comfort, ambivalence, and relative separation. Infant love, which is not recurrent, includes organic affection and reflexive love; comfort and attachment; security and solace; disattachment and environmental exploration; and relative independence. A third affectional system is age-mate or peer love, which is one of the major determinants of social and sexual development; it is more critical than maternal love in fostering adult social and sexual relationships. Harlow regards this system as the most important and pervasive one. Three different kinds of play (creative, free, and formal) set the stage for later interactions. The fourth affectional system, heterosexual love, is characterized by three discrete subsystems: mechanical, secretory, and romantic. Finally, paternal love serves as a secondary protective system for infants; its roots seem to be more experiential than biological.

The second section discusses some of the underpinnings for the "fundamentally antisocial" emotions of fear and anger. These emotions are channeled by maturation of affectional systems; their potential is innate, but learning determines their specific targets. Finally, the section on social behavior considers such processes as socialization, conformity, group processes, and attitude acquisition and change. Perceived similarities are particularly important in determining social attraction between individuals.

This short, readable book provides a basis for examining the link between humans and other primates that can foster an understanding of the biosocial basis for affectional relationships. The research of this pioneer in the study of primate behavior has applications in such areas as adolescent behavior and sexual dysfunction. (SGF)

IL

415.   Johnson, Robert A. **We: Understanding the Psychology of Romantic Love.** San Francisco: Harper & Row, 1983. 204 p. Includes bibliography. ISBN 0-06-250436-3.

Johnson, a Jungian analyst in private practice in San Diego, California, and author of books on masculine and feminine psychology, here interprets the twelfth-century myth of Tristan and Iseult. Likening the dreams of individuals to the myths of cultures and societies, he attempts to show that dreams and myths are real in that they reveal the inner self and the psyche of society.

Using Hilaire Belloc's translation of Joseph Bédier's retelling of *The Romance of Tristan and Isolde*, Johnson alternates in the text between the narrative itself and his interpretation of the tale's dramatic action. The story, he avers, is "a vivid symbolic picture of the huge forces at work in all of us, both men and women, when we are caught up in the experience of romantic love" (p. ix). Since the twelfth century, Tristan has represented Western man in traditional patriarchal society searching for his "lost feminine side," his anima, in the women around him. In Tristan's case, it is Iseult the Fair, the Irish beauty, who embodies all that is desirable in women. It is the love potion, accidentally imbibed, that smote them both, bringing on a period of intense, but transitory, bliss, resolved only by the lovers consciously deciding to separate and return to their socially approved roles.

The tragedy is that, enamored as he is of Iseult the Fair and incapable of pursuing reasonable and desirable goals in a marriage to Iseult of the White Hands, Tristan attempts to rekindle his lost romantic love for Iseult the Fair. Trickery overtakes Tristan and Iseult the Fair, and they perish tragically.

Johnson believes that the myth reveals what is happening today in society. Individuals, increasingly dissatisfied with what they have, fall repeatedly in and out of love. This frantic search for love is, in reality, the male's pursuit of his anima in women and the female's pursuit of her animus in man, in order to complete themselves. It can only end destructively because in time the impermanent romantic love wears off. It is an unsustainable quest based on unrealistic expectations that no one can possibly fulfill.

In the conclusion, Johnson focuses on human love, symbolized by the icons and rituals of Christianity. By pointing out the fallacy underlying romantic love, he hopes to reorient modern people in their pursuit of love. He does not totally renounce romantic love but instead points out the value in providing a balance between the forces of anima and the demands of the real world. Romantic love is, after all, humankind's attempt to get in touch with an inner self. As such, it is to be cherished. (TJW)

PR

416.   Lasky, Judith F., and Helen W. Silverman, eds. **Love: Psychoanalytic Perspectives.** New York: New York University Press, 1988. 235 p. Includes bibliographies and index. ISBN 0-8147-5036-2.

This collection of papers emerged from a conference held in 1986 on the psychoanalytic aspects of love sponsored by the Psychoanalytic Society of the Postdoctoral Program of New York University. The papers present theoretical positions by psychoanalysts on various kinds of love.

The three opening papers—"Eros, Agape, Amor, Libido: Concepts in the History of Love" (Waltraud Ireland); "Love: Transcultural Considerations" (Robert Endleman); "What Is This Thing Called Love? The Popular Ballad as a Framework for Changing Conceptions of Love" (Barbara Cohn Schlachet and Barbara Waxenberg)—discuss respectively the experience of love in terms of "the ideas of love in ancient Greece, early Christianity, the later medieval period, and psychoanalysis"; how "love and the love object are defined in several tribal cultures" and how these views compare with love in Western culture; and the effects of popular music "as one of the most potent disseminators of cultural expectations regarding the learning of love."

How love attachments may prevent current love relationships from being fully satisfactory are explored in three papers: "Love in a Hall of Mirrors: Reciprocal Transference Relationships in Marriage" (Walter Gadlin); "Sibling Relationships and Mature Love" (Judith F. Lasky and Susan F. Mulliken); "Perversion: The Terror of Tenderness" (Leanne Domash).

"Differential Roles of Narcissism in Healthy and Pathological Love Relationships" (Michael P. Varga); "Fantasies of Love and Rescue in Fatherless Adolescent Boys" (Patrick R. Lane); and "Falling in Love and Being in Love: A Developmental and Object-Relations Approach" (Eileen J. Setzman) examine "the attempt to make up in current life for unsatisfying love relationships in the past." "Trust and Testing in Love Relations" (Peter Lawner) and "The Struggle to Love: Reflections and Permutations" (Joan O. Zuckerberg) suggest that the analyst can succeed in helping the patient by providing a different type of experience for the patient. "The Self and Loving" (Harold B. Davis) reviews that controversial area of theoretical and clinical interest, idealization in relation to love, from different theoretical positions, e.g., overestimation of the object.

The last section of the book includes "Aspects of the Erotic Transference" (Helen W. Silverman); "Should Analysts Love Their Patients? The Resolution of Transference Resistance Through Countertransferential Exploration" (Robert S. Weinstein); "Mature Love in the Countertransference" (Irwin Hirsch); and "The Classical Psychoanalytic Stance: What's Love Got to Do With It?" (Andrew B. Druck); which deal with various aspects of the treatment situation and how love affects it.

Lasky and Silverman conclude that the contributors concern themselves with similar issues: the relationship between childhood experience and adult love, the psychological requirements for loving, the feelings encompassed by the experience of love, the appearance of love in psychoanalysis, and the treatment of love problems. They believe that psychoanalysis can help explain these issues and out of this endeavor develop a theory of love that could resolve, for example, the differentiation between carnal love and romantic love. (TJW)

PR,IL
417. Lystra, Karen. **Searching the Heart: Women, Men, and Romantic Love in Nineteenth-Century America.** New York: Oxford University Press, 1989. 336 p. Includes bibliography and index. ISBN 0-19-505817-8.

In this work, Lystra, an American studies scholar, explores the meaning and significance of romantic love in nineteenth century middle-class America. Using the archives of the Henry E. Huntington Library, she chose the love letters of more than 100 single and married people as cultural documents indicative of the nature of romantic relations. Unlike diaries and memoirs, love letters capture a private dimension of the *social* relationship between lovers; they are not merely individual reflections but are meant to be read by the beloved. The letters span a time period coinciding with two Victorian reigns, beginning in the 1830s. Lystra emphasizes the essential role of romantic love at the time: " . . . ideas of romantic love suffused the world view of nineteenth century middle-class Americans and guided their emotional experience and behavior" (p. 7). Throughout the book Lystra uses portions of love letters to corroborate her conclusions. Each of the chapters explores a different theme: (1) the significance of love letters, (2) individualism and the romantic self, (3) sexuality in Victorian courtship and marriage, (4) the integration of public and private life worlds, (5) sex-role boundaries and behavior, (6) Victorian courtship rituals and the dramas of private life, (7) duty-bound roles and unaccountable love, (8) patriarchy, religion, and romantic love.

Lystra challenges some accepted assumptions about Victorian relationships, e.g., that women were not interested in sex and were passionless in their relationships. She points out that purity referred to legitimate sexual expression, not to a *lack* of sex. In addition, expressions of love were of historical importance because they marked a shift from social roles to feelings guiding individual behavior; they reinforced the process of defining the self and establishing individuality. Overall, Lystra shows the dynamic interplay between culture, society and the individual as they focus on the concept and experience of love. As society changed, so too did ideas of love. Consequently, individuals dealt with love quite differently. Lystra seeks to explain how. (SGF)

PO

418. Norwood, Robin. **Women Who Love Too Much: When You Keep Wishing and Hoping He'll Change.** New York: Pocket Books, 1985. 302 p. Includes bibliography and index. ISBN 0-671-62049-5.

Are you a woman who will do anything to keep a relationship from dissolving? Are you willing to wait, hope, and try harder to please the man you are with? Are you willing to take more than your share of the responsibility, guilt, and blame in any relationship? Do you find nice men boring? A woman who loves too much is likely to answer "yes" to these questions. Loving too much means that a woman experiences pain, depression, and a sense of worthlessness; it does *not* mean that she loves too many men, too often, or too deeply. Loving becomes loving too much when a relationship is destructive to a woman's emotional and physical health. Although a woman's partner is "inappropriate, uncaring, or unavailable," she is unable to give him up. Rather, she may want him ever more. It is the purpose of this book to "help women with destructive patterns of relating to men recognize that fact, understand the origin of those patterns, and gain the tools for changing their lives" (pp. xv-xvi).

The basis of loving too much is fear—a fear of being unlovable, ignored, abandoned, or destroyed. Its roots stem from childhood, when a girl denies her needs and cannot distinguish between good and bad experiences. When she chooses a partner, she may feel comfortable with an unloving man because she is recreating past painful patterns in an attempt to master them—to make the unloving, loving. Therefore, a woman wants to save or help (and control) her partner by loving him so much (with selfless, all-accepting love) that he changes. He is attracted to her because her strength, devotion, and help seem to make up for what is missing in his life. Each may become the other's excuse for dysfunctional behavior. Norwood terms such a relationship "addictive." It may actually lead to addiction to food, alcohol, or drugs. Disappointment in the relationship is denied; the relationship hangs on hope, not reality. The woman blames herself, tries to change, and becomes more deeply dependent on the man who has become her "emotional gauge"; rage, loss of self-respect, and stress disorders may follow.

When faced with such a relationship, a woman needs to love herself enough to stop the pain. A ten-point recovery program provides steps to facilitate the growth of self-esteem; self-love and self-acceptance are the antidotes to the obsessive need to earn love through suffering. (SGF)

PR,IL

419. Person, Ethel Spector. **Dreams of Love and Fateful Encounters: The Power of Romantic Passion.** New York: Norton, 1988. 384 p. Includes bibliography and index. ISBN 0-393-02527-6.

Rational, scientific analyses downplay or dismiss the importance of love while the intellectual discourse of poets, lyricists, novelists, and filmmakers extols its relevance. Using a philosophical and cultural perspective, psychoanalyst Person argues that "love serves an important function not only for the individual but also for the culture. It is the narrative thread not just in novels, but in lives" (p. 23). Because a person's sense of self develops in the context of interaction with others, it is always linked to intimate relationships. Above all, love is a creative act, a product of the imagination, that derives its power from its ability to spark the realization, transformation, and transcendence of the self. In a culture particularly focused on material life, love is one of the few areas where individuals can experience spiritual meaning in their lives. Person relies on the testimony of lovers, the stories of people she knows, literary and film artists, biographies and autobiographies, for data about love, because she chooses to stress the normalcy of passionate love. The first two sections describe the experience and aims of romantic love in terms of its role as a context of growth. Love extends beyond pleasure; sex becomes "a sacred rite in the religion of mutual love," an expression of transcendence of the self and merger with the beloved. As the self extends beyond the narrow bounds of the ego from the "I" to the "we," the individual idealizes the beloved and desires to merge with him or her. While this experience may result in growth, the process of loving can be difficult. The last three sections are devoted to the paradoxes and struggles entailed by loving; gender differences in loving; and possible outcomes of loving. Self surrender can lead to dependence rather than to transcendence. Power struggles for dominance and control in the relationship may develop. Partners may be disillusioned by routinization, lack of sexual passion, or low mutuality in the relationship. Triangles generated by envy and desire may threaten the romantic dyad. Furthermore, men and women may experience love differently because of different cultural prescriptions for gender and problems with development. Men are more likely to want power over love while women seek power through love. Love can be an unhappy experience when the lover is rejected, disenchanted, or involved in an empty, hurtful relationship that serves social rather than psychological needs. It can also be enduring and enriching when it "promotes the love's sense of self-worth and liberates him from the strictures of self" (p. 322). However, the unconventional love of adulterers, heterosexuals with greatly different ages, and homosexuals has to face social scorn while conventional lovers wrestle with the transition from passionate love to affectionate bonding. Overall, love is an agent of change—a creative, meaningful, and individually satisfying experience. (SGF)

IL
420.   Reik, Theodor. **Of Love and Lust: On the Psychoanalysis of Romantic and Sexual Emotions.** New York: Farrar, Straus and Cudahy, 1957. 623 p.
Several major writings of Reik, psychoanalyst and early follower of Freud, comprise this collection on the psychoanalysis of romantic and sexual emotions. They include material from works written since 1943 (e.g., *A Psychologist Looks at Love*). In this work, Reik examines the differences between love and sex, concluding that "sex and love are different in origin and nature" (p. 16). While the sex urge seeks out lustful pleasure, love searches for joy and happiness. Sex relates to the domain of biochemistry and physiology; love to the domain of the psychology of emotions. Reik differed with Freud on the nature of love: Freud made love, along with affection and friendship, a part of sex. Psychoanalytically speaking, Reik says that love, like every search for human perfection, is a necessary illusion that helps us escape our loneliness and isolation.
In *Masochism in Modern Man* (1941), Reik proposes a new theory of masochistic behavior that attempts to explain why people strive for physical and psychic pain, deliberately accepting sacrifices, shame, humiliation, and disgrace. The essence of masochism seems to reside in such factors as fantasy, defiance, paradox, and secret rebellion. Reik believes that sadism is inherent in masochism as something turned against the ego. "The masochist aims at the same pleasure we all do but he arrives at it by another road, by a detour. . . . He submits voluntarily to punishment, suffering and humiliations and thus has defiantly purchased the right to enjoy the gratification denied before" (p. 361). Reik extends this concept of masochism to religious groups, that promise rewards in heaven in exchange for sacrifices on earth; and to nations, such as the Jews, who have suffered while believing that they are the chosen people. Detecting the tragic element in these martyr attitudes, Reik believes that it is a "tale of human frailty and sorrow . . . of human force and lust" (p. 366).
The third item in this collection is a short paper on the various factors that make some men and women bypass marriage and family life. Although most women welcome

marriage, most men are marriage-shy. Behind these attitudes are men's fear of duty, obligation, and responsibility; some women's reluctance to marry derives from feelings of inferiority, contempt for the male, and self-hatred.

Reik's final work is on the emotional differences of the sexes and is based on material gathered during his forty-five years of psychoanalytic practice. (TJW)

PR
421. Singer, Irving. **The Nature of Love.** Vol. 1, **Plato to Luther.** 2nd ed. Chicago: University of Chicago Press, 1984. 381 p. First published in 1966. Includes bibliographic notes and index. ISBN 0-226-76094-4.

At the outset, Singer, professor of philosophy at the Massachusetts Institute of Technology, explains his intentions to examine the nature of love from Plato to the present time in terms of two types of valuation, appraisal, and bestowal. He intends to apply these concepts to the writings of major philosophers and thinkers and thereby arrive at a basis for understanding religious love, courtly love, romantic love, and love in the modern world.

In the first part of volume 1, Singer shows that love is a way of valuing something; in personal love relationships, the lover not only appraises the love object, but he or she generates a new value and raises love to a new height. This is bestowal of love over and above objective appraisal. Singer goes on to discuss the love of things, persons, and ideals. He compares these different kinds of love and then focuses on love as an ideal of love in the philosophies of Plato, Santayana, and Freud. In evaluating these views he concludes that the concept of bestowal, that is, the lover's interest in the beloved as an independent and important being, is lacking.

In the interest of constructing a new philosophy of love, Singer explores the concepts of appraisal and bestowal as they have developed in the writings of those exemplars of idealism, Plato, Aristotle, and Plotinus. He also examines the poetry of Ovid and Lucretius, who, in reaction to idealism, regarded love more realistically; they nonetheless developed their own erotic idealization.

In part 3, Singer examines religious love in the Judeo-Christian tradition. He says that the "concept of loving another as a person virtually began with the Old Testament." Christianity, with its roots in Judaism, defines itself as the religion of love, where God and love are the same. Singer then pursues different elements of Christian love: *eros*, *philia*, *nomos*, *agape*, the first two inherited from the Greeks, the latter two from the Jews. In *agape*, God's love is bestowed on everything. Although Singer shows that religious love reached its height in attempts to harmonize *eros* and *agape* during the Middle Ages (the achievements of St. Augustine and St. Thomas Aquinas), reaction to the narrowness of medieval religious idealization set in; first, with the rejection of Catholic notions of love (*caritas*) by Martin Luther, who returned to the single notion of God's love (*agape*) for man, and, second, with the beginnings of courtly and romantic love. (TJW)

PR
422. Singer, Irving. **The Nature of Love.** Vol. 2, **Courtly and Romantic.** Chicago: University of Chicago Press, 1984. 513 p. Includes bibliographic notes and index. ISBN 0-226-76096-0.

Interested in discovering the origins of our current ideas about sexual love insofar as they have been determined by works of philosophy and literature, Singer, in volume 2, "focuses on concepts of love between men and women that developed continuously from the eleventh or twelfth centuries through the nineteenth."

Pointing out that courtly and romantic love derive from different philosophical traditions, Singer distinguishes between "realist" and "idealist" approaches to love. He discusses the concept of courtly love in the *eros* tradition, concentrating on the love of the troubadours, the writings of Andreas Capellanus, and the medieval romance of Abelard and Heloise, all of which exemplify the split between human and religious love.

He goes on to show "how medieval humanism's failure to achieve an adequate synthesis between naturalistic and religious love was followed by relatively more stressful attempts in later centuries." Illustrative of this are the philosophy of Marsilio Ficino and the writings of John Milton. The plays of Shakespeare, however, suggest "a major synthesis of ideas about love that are characteristic of the modern world."

Singer also examines types of romantic love, suggesting that "the concept of Romantic love arose as a response to reactions against the Renaissance and Puritan syntheses." In the chapters on Rousseau, Sade, and Stendhal, he examines three different attitudes toward passion. He then explores the differences between benign romanticism, which is "optimistic about man's capacity to achieve on earth a heterosexual love that will be comparable to religious love and able to maintain itself in a permanent union such as marriage," and Romantic pessimism, which "finds the world too vile for any such hopes to be realized." These aspects of the ideology create the "background for all twentieth century thinking about the nature of love." (TJW)

PR

423. Singer, Irving. **The Nature of Love.** Vol. 3, **The Modern World.** Chicago: University of Chicago Press, 1987. 473 p. Includes bibliographic notes and index. ISBN 0-226-76098-7.

Philosophical historian Singer states that this third volume of *The Nature of Love* "investigates attempts by thinkers in the modern world to elucidate the attitude or state of mind which is love" (p. xiii). These past and present thinkers are philosophers, writers, and scientists working in the Western tradition.

In part I, Singer relates his conclusions from the earlier volumes "to our present condition in the post-Romantic era that we inhabit" (p. x). Nineteenth-century thinkers (Kierkegaard, Tolstoy, Nietzsche) rejected the idealistic courtly and Romantic ideologies as being utterly unrealistic.

Singer devotes part II to thinkers who have contributed to the analysis of love in the twentieth century. These philosophers and creative writers are in the realistic tradition and include Freud; Proust; D. H. Lawrence and G. B. Shaw, whom he identifies as representing the extremes of twentieth-century Puritanism; Santayana; and Sartre, together with other existentialists.

Part III covers relevant scientific endeavors in psychoanalytic theory, ethology, sociobiology, plus other specialized areas of the life sciences. Singer refers to the works of John Bowlby, Harry F. Harlow, Melanie Klein, Konrad Lorenz, Edward O. Wilson, Margaret Mead, William J. Goode, and others, all of whom attempted to understand the concept of love.

In conclusion Singer sketches his philosophy as it presently exists. Here he touches "on issues in both feminist theory and ideology, in order to test the parameters of my anti-reductivist approach" (p. xi). Throughout the book the term "idealization"—by which Singer means "the making of ideals through the bestowal of value"—is manipulated in diverse ways. Singer analyzed appraisal and bestowal in the first volume; here he states that "lovers create a value in one another that exceeds the individual or objective value each may also be appraised to have" (p. xii).

Finally, after an analysis of sexual love, Singer suggests "a distinction between falling in love, being in love, and staying in love," and then sketches developments in his thinking about "appraisal and bestowal, merging, and the various objects of love" (p. 438). The chances of finding happiness in the three stages of love are improved, Singer believes, through the harmonization of both the idealistic aspects and the realistic aspects of love. (TJW)

PR,IL

424. Solomon, Robert C. **Love: Emotion, Myth, and Metaphor.** Buffalo, N.Y.: Prometheus Books, 1990. 347 p. Originally published in 1981. Includes index. ISBN: 0-87975-569-5.

Solomon, a philosopher, addresses both conceptual and experiential aspects of love in this book. In the first part he identifies and assesses the wide range of myths and metaphors that have been associated with love. He notes that the choice of a metaphor is significant because "choosing one's metaphor is, in fact, choosing one's love life as well" (p. 32). Metaphors for love relate to a variety of domains, e.g., economic ("love as an exchange of affection"), work ("make it work"), communication ("feedback and input from the beloved"), medicine ("love is a disease"), biology ("love is natural"). In his philosophical analysis of what he characterizes as popular myths of love, Solomon tries to aid in unraveling the confusing and often contradictory meanings linked to love. For example, he asserts that love is not a feeling. Rather, it is "an emotion, nothing else" (p. 34). Because love is an emotion, it is an active way through which people structure their experience. It follows that people do not "fall" in love; they choose to love. After analyzing the conceptual aspects of love, Solomon turns to the experience of love. He argues that the essence of love resides in the "loveworld" created by lovers themselves. The second part of the book explores this domain. "Fastasy is the food of love" (p. 178), and loveworlds have their own internal dynamic, structure, rituals, and language.

Love is a creative process during which individuals develop a shared self that is mutual and reciprocal. They select and idealize characteristics of each other in a context of freedom and fantasy and then act out their chosen love roles, apart from their social roles. In this sense, love transforms the self and the beloved into unique players in the love world. However, ingredients of public roles such as respect, commitment, honesty, promises, and peaceful coexistence are not realistic expectations for love. Love involves tension, rebellion, and rejection of public canons of behavior. Its rewards include support, bolstered self-esteem, and an enhanced sense of self. (SGF)

IL

425. Stendhal. **On Love.** Translated by Philip Sidney Woolf and Cecil N. Sidney Woolf. With decorative drawings by Robert Greco. Mount Vernon, N.Y.: Peter Pauper Press, [1950]. 261 p. Translation of: De l'Amour. First edition appeared in 1822.

Stendhal is the pen name of Henri Beyle, author of the classic French novel The Red and the Black. His abiding interest in the topic of love derives from his days spent in the salons of Europe, especially Milan and Paris, where, he says, the only "business of life is pleasure" and good conversation. On the basis of his experiences and observations, Stendhal formed a theory that regards love as a disease of many stages culminating in what he called crystallization.

Basically there are four kinds of love: (1) passion-love, the kind that overcame Abelard and Heloise; (2) gallant love, a type of love that prevailed in the salons of Paris before the revolution; (3) physical love, that is common to all from about the age of sixteen on; and (4) vanity love, involving mistresses and which may or may not include physical love. Stendhal admits that there are many shades of differences among these dominant forms of love.

Stendhal takes the reader through the seven stages leading to love's crystallization. These are: (1) at first, admiration for another; (2) a recognition of the pleasure attending kissing, etc.; (3) hope; (4) the birth of love; (5) first crystallization, a mental state confirming love; (6) the onset of doubt, which demands proof of the love; and (7) a second crystallization based on the discovery of new perfections and charms in the beloved. He proceeds to discuss such factors as beauty, modesty, infatuation, feminine pride, courage, and jealousy as they relate to the kinds and stages of love.

With anecdotes, the reflections of philosophers, and the opinions of great lovers, Stendhal takes the reader on a tour of love in the principal cities and countries of the world, including France, Italy, Rome, England, Spain, Germany, Florence, Paris, Provence, Arabia, and even the United States. He also discusses special topics, such as the education of women, marriage, virtue, and divorce.

Stendhal finally assembles a series of what he calls "scattered fragments" and offers them as observations on love. A few plucked from the text are as follows:

Love, such as it exists in smart society, is the love of battle, the love of gambling. Nothing kills gallant love like gusts of passion-love from the other side. Sappho saw in love only sensual intoxication or physical pleasure made sublime by crystallization.

As to the poor reception his book on love received, Standhal laments, "I found no more than seventeen readers between 1822 and 1833; it is doubtful whether the Essay on Love has been understood after twenty years of existence by a hundred connoisseurs" (p. 7). (TJW)

PR,IL
426. Sternberg, Robert J., and Michael L. Barnes, eds. **The Psychology of Love.** New Haven, Conn.: Yale University Press, 1988. 383 p. Includes bibliographies and index. ISBN 0-300-04589-1.

Despite an increase in psychological studies of love, Zick Rubin notes in the preface that "the science of love is still in its infancy" (p. viii) and suggests some paths that future researchers might pursue, e.g., developing a common vocabulary, investigating love's connection with sex, studying environmental/demographic contexts, and relating love to other social support systems. Sternberg, Professor of Psychology and Education at Yale University, and Barnes, a graduate student in psychology, state that this book "presents the attempts of contemporary psychologists whose field of expertise is the study of love and close relationships to figure out just what love is" (p. 3). They divide the sixteen chapters into five parts, the first of which is the introduction.

The seven chapters in part 2, "Global Theories of Love," focus on love as a whole. Bernard I. Murstein analyzes different classifications of the nature of love, including ideas about its origins, its modes, "its primary intended beneficiary," and its developmental stages. John Alan Lee identifies different love styles and suggests how people can find partners whose love styles match their preferred styles. Phillip Shaver, Cindy Hazan, and Donna Bradshaw investigate the role of attachment, care giving, and sexuality in the definition and meaning of romantic love. David Buss presents an analysis of the evolutionary biology of love, followed by Robert Sternberg's triangular theory of love, composed of passion, decision/commitment, and intimacy. George Levinger considers the question of whether we can translate Sternberg's components of love into visual images of a love relationship. Stanton Peele's chapter on psychological approaches to love concludes part 2 with a discussion of romantic love as obsessive attachment, psychologists' views about it, and the model of addictive love.

Part 3 focuses on theories of romantic love. Elaine Hatfield compares passionate and companionate love and concludes that a good loving relationship entails partners capable of both intimacy and independence. Nathaniel Branden's analysis of the twentieth-century North American vision of romantic love leads him to conclude that a positive sense of self is necessary for maintaining romantic love; "its success over time is a triumph of psychological maturity" (p. 231). Sharon Brehm focuses on the function of passionate love, comparing Stendhal's views with those of the Christian mystics; she thinks that passionate love functions as an "intense combination of imagination and emotion [that] serves to motivate human beings to construct a vision of a better world...." (p. 260). In the final chapter of part 3, Kenneth L. Dion and Karen K. Dion present some of the findings of their research on the role of personality in romantic love and also review cross-cultural perspectives on love; they suggest that individualism-collectivism "plays a critical role vis-a-vis romantic love in the culture of the United States and elsewhere in the world" (p. 287).

Part 4, "Theories of Love and Relationship Maintenance," begins with Donn Byrne and Sara Murnen's analysis of how to maintain loving relationships; they find that habituation, similarity, and evaluation are key realms to explore to understand this process. Wendy M. Williams and Michael L. Barnes propose that three kinds of boundaries—between partners' internal worlds, between their external lives, and between the external world and the internal world of the relationship—affect the viability of love relationships. Steven R. H. Beach and Abraham Tesser end this part with a discussion of components that most people associate with love, using a cognitive theoretical perspective.

Part 5 ties the previous parts of the book together, presenting an overview of some of the issues raised by the other chapters. Ellen Berscheid makes three major observations about the study of romantic love. Understanding emotional experiences that underlie romantic love as well as how lovers interpret them are both necessary for understanding romantic love. Finally, researchers need to pay more attention to the role of sexual desire in romantic love. (SGF)

IL

427. Tennov, Dorothy. **Love and Limerence: The Experience of Being in Love.** New York: Stein and Day, 1980. 324 p. Includes bibliography and index. ISBN 0-8128-2328-1.

What is it like to experience "being in love?" Some experts regard it as intense pleasure, others classify it as a symptom of low self-esteem, and yet others construe it as "fancy," a culturally invented product. Tennov, an experimental psychologist, systematically investigates romantic love as a normal condition. Using unstructured interviews, volunteered reports of love experiences, diaries, letters, anonymous phone calls, specially prepared written material, and other scholarly studies, she tries to find out why people fall in love, the incidence of unhappy love, and how to help people who are unhappy because of love. She coins the term *limerence* to refer to the mental state of "being in love." While limerence has elements of liking, affection, love (caring for the happiness, safety, and well-being of another), and sexual attraction, it is not synonymous with any of these states. Some of its distinctive components are intrusive thinking about the object of passionate desire (LO=limerant object), an intense longing for reciprocation, a need for exclusivity, fear of rejection, priority of the LO over everything else, and an extraordinary ability to emphasize only the positive attributes of the LO. Drawing on a variety of interesting case histories, 400 unstructured interviews, and a vast literature on love, Tennov captivatingly describes some of the positive and negative aspects of individuals' limerant experiences. She probes the differences in male and female responses to limerence, its social effects, and its relation to biology. After investigating the possible causes and effects of limerence, she questions the extent to which it can be controlled. She hopes that her preliminary report will open the door to other serious and thorough considerations of what limerence means. (SGF)

PR,IL

428. Walsh, Anthony. **The Science of Love: Understanding Love & Its Effects on Mind & Body.** Buffalo, N.Y.: Prometheus Books, 1991. 276 p. Includes bibliography and index. ISBN 0-87975-648-9.

Walsh brings evidence to bear from a number of sciences that the satisfaction of the need to love is basic to the physical, psychological, and social health of human beings. The first section is devoted to "skin love." Drawing mainly from the neurosciences, Walsh shows that initial messages of love received during infancy come in the form of tactile stimulation, which has an important influence on brain development. He then explores the chemistry of mother love and how love is related to the three broad areas of the "triune" brain. Among the topics dealt with in this section are genetic/environmental interplay in brain development, brain hemisphericity, the hormonal basis of parenting differences between men and women, and breast feeding. It is Walsh's contention that an infant's early experience lays down a neurophysiological template that strongly influences the rest of its life.

The second section deals with "kin love"—relationships with others and how they affect physical and psychological well-being. Walsh shows how love deprivation affects such disease syndromes as hypertension, multiple sclerosis, deprivation dwarfism, schizophrenia, depression, and substance abuse. A chapter on "Lovelessness and Lawlessness" explores the effects of negative love experience on cognitive development, autonomic nervous system functioning, and psychopathy. A chapter on "Love and

Society" looks at love across various cultures and political systems and examines the importance of democracy for romantic love. The final section—"In Love"—deals with romantic love. Its three chapters deal with the origin of love, the chemistry of falling in love, evidence for a hormonal theory of homosexuality, monogamy/promiscuity, sexual strategies of men and women, the objectification of love, love styles, jealousy, and extramarital love. Walsh postulates that romantic love is a direct progression from "skin love to kin love to in love." That is, the way we experience romantic love and sexuality is directly related to other nonromantic love relationship experiences in infancy, childhood, adolescence, and adulthood. (Author)

[N.B. Professor Walsh is in the Department of Sociology, Anthropology, and Criminal Justice at Boise State University in Idaho.]

Pleasure

IL,PO
429. Masters, William H., and Virginia E. Johnson. **The Pleasure Bond: A New Look at Sexuality and Commitment.** Boston: Little, Brown, 1974. 268 p. ISBN 0-316-54981-0.

Many couples wonder if it is possible to maintain the physical attraction that first brought them together; they often assume that sex loses its power to arouse passion as its novelty diminishes. Masters and Johnson directly address these concerns in a readable, interesting manner. They accentuate the psychosocial aspects of sexual functioning by focusing on three major elements that they think contribute to effective sexual functioning: knowledge, comfort, and choice. An understanding of these elements allows couples to overcome their fears and establish a "pleasure bond." Pleasure not only derives from tension release and sensual gratification but also from the wider experience of responsibility for one's feelings and from commitment to another person. Recognition of individuality not only brings satisfaction but makes possible mutual, sustained pleasure. The feedback between mutual concern and pleasure creates a bond between loving couples. Much of the text derives from eleven symposia that Masters and Johnson conducted between May 1971 and June 1972. They asked a small number of couples who were satisfied with their relationships or were successfully coping with dissatisfaction to discuss any concerns they had about sex. They include the edited versions of five of the symposia in the book. The book is a mixture of dialogue and commentary. Chapters cover major concerns related to the establishment and continuation of intimacy: young marriages, what men stand to gain from women's liberation, why working at sex won't work, extramarital sex, swinging sex, what sexual fidelity means in a marriage, second marriages, touching, and how pretending makes sexual pleasure impossible. (SGF)

PO
430. Rueger, Russ A. **The Pleasure Book.** Photographs by Trudy Schlachter. New York: Pocket Books, 1984. 176 p. Includes bibliography. ISBN 0-671-50493-2.

The needs-based psychology of Abraham Maslow (*Toward a Psychology of Being*) underlies the approach to pleasure expressed in this book. According to Maslow, the basic human needs (life, safety, security, belongingness, affection, respect, self-respect, and self-actualization) may be arranged in a hierarchy, each level of which must be satisfied before moving on to the next level. Rueger states that the first three needs are preconditions for pleasure; the next four needs are different aspects of the pleasure experience; and the highest level, self-actualization, is only attained by psychologically fit persons. He believes that people are inhibited from becoming "self-actualizers" by various cultural restraints, or "pleasure prohibitions," a prime example of which is "erotic inhibition," introduced into civilization to control the sex drive. An outgrowth of erotic inhibition is "another set of prohibitions called the 'touch taboos.' These extended the ban on sexual expression to sensuality and touching. Nudity was forbidden, as well as bodily contact, whether alone or with others" (pp. 23-24). All of these prohibitions are misplaced, says Rueger, because "pleasure is your birthright. Your biology was built for it, and it makes little sense to deny what God has given you. You deserve as much enjoyment as you can get, and don't let any person, social institution or cultural norm try to convince you otherwise" (p. 27). The pleasure philosophy then "is a modern alternative to outmoded pleasure prohibitions" (p. 27). The chapters of this book are devoted to the expression of pleasure in all aspects of life. The healthy hedonist should pursue pleasure at work as well as at play, seeking pleasure in mental effort and in associations with friends and lovers. Experiencing psychic, spiritual, sensual, and sexual pleasure is a must. Finally, a hedonist should understand that there is a politics of pleasure that depends on the type of society one inhabits. It is essential to try to understand those forces that are inimical to the pursuit of pleasure and oppose them, and also to appreciate those forces that tolerate the pleasure seeker. Throughout the book numerous black-and-white photographs of a bright-eyed, heterosexual couple demonstrate the various realms of pleasure. (TJW)

IL
431.   Tiger, Lionel. **The Pursuit of Pleasure.** Boston: Little, Brown, 1992. 330 p. Includes bibliographic notes and index. ISBN 0-316-84543-4.
        Written by the distinguished Charles Darwin Professor of Anthropology at Rutgers University, *The Pursuit of Pleasure* offers a sweeping examination of pleasure in its manifold expressions in sex, food, travel, pets, drugs, and power. Tiger's systematic approach identifies four broad categories of pleasure: physiopleasure, sociopleasure, psychopleasure, and ideopleasure. In Tiger's view, all the particular pleasures may be subsumed under these categories. Particular pleasures developed as the human species evolved during its long struggle to survive. Along with pain, which informed the evolving species what was dangerous and to be avoided, pleasure served as a directional beacon toward what to embrace. He concludes that pleasure is an "evolutionary entitlement" to be accepted and enjoyed.
        Beginning with physiopleasure, Tiger examines sex, food, and drugs as highly sought-after pleasures. Eventually pleasure becomes a matter for government and institutions, that, out of fear usually, introduce restrictions for the control of pleasure. Pleasure becomes a political issue. As Tiger explains it, "Powerful people enjoy it when they are able to define and restrict the pleasure of others" (p. 14). Throughout the book, Tiger maintains "a clear focus on the physiological elements of pleasure, the possible evolution of our human pleasure systems, and the specific social, economic, and political activities involved in sustaining human pleasure" (p. 15). He states that we need pleasure in the same way we need vitamins, carbohydrates, sugar, water, and warmth.
        Tiger deepens his study of pleasure by examining the causes, both proximate and ultimate, of people's sexual behavior. Men generally "seek sexual relationships with a wide array of women," which "maximizes their opportunity for successful reproduction" (p. 85). Women's situation is different: they are more hesitant to become involved because of the numerous risks entailed. Their behavior becomes coy. Evidence indicates that this is a cross-cultural reproductive phenomenon.
        Tiger's final words echo his belief that pleasure is an evolutionary entitlement: "Pleasure resonates as an imperative. There is no choice but to expect it, experience it, enjoy it. We could not have survived the dark nights and bright days of our immense story without it" (p. 299). (TJW)

Jealousy

PR,IL
432.   Dingwall, Eric John. **The Girdle of Chastity: A Fascinating History of Chastity Belts.** New York: Clarion Press, 1959. 171 p. Includes bibliographic footnotes and indexes.

Jealousy, according to Dingwall, seems to be the motivating force behind the introduction and use of chastity belts throughout Europe over about the past five hundred years. Believed to have originated in the Orient and brought to Europe by the Crusaders, the girdle of chastity developed in a variety of ways. Dingwall documents seven basic types of girdles, including the simple, one-piece girdle with a longitudinal oval, often dentated, opening in a convex plate snugly covering the vulva to allow for urination. A more complicated two-piece girdle contains openings both front and back for urination and defecation. The plates attach to a locking device that requires a key to open. Most other belts seem to be variations on these two basic types.

The provenance of most girdles of chastity is somewhat uncertain, but it is thought that fourteenth- and fifteenth-century Italian culture was conducive to their introduction. In due course, the idea spread to France, Germany, and other countries. Dingwall devotes a long historical chapter to the subject, emphasizing European developments up to the twentieth century. Widespread as these belts were, their use was probably confined to the upper classes. Here jealous husbands and lovers, especially those who traveled widely, imposed the belts on wives and mistresses, locking up the *pudendum muliebre* and taking the key until their return. This was supposed to guarantee the woman's fidelity as well as assure the husband that any subsequent offspring were his own.

Dingwall devotes a chapter to cases brought before a court of law by women who complained that wearing a chastity belt was cruel and punitive. They often won their cases.

A chapter on witty and satirical allusions to the chastity belt in literature concludes this study. Clear photographic plates and art works illustrate this specialized book. (TJW)

IL,PO

433. Friday, Nancy. **Jealousy.** New York: Morrow, 1985. 539 p. Includes bibliography. ISBN 0-688-04321-6.

By her own admission, all of Friday's writing has had the personal goal of sorting through central issues and paradoxes in her own life. *Jealousy* is no different. Blunt descriptions of her own experiences with jealousy as well as long conversations with her psychiatrist friend, Richard Robertiello, provide intriguing narrative around which the major themes of the book are woven. Friday's admission that she is jealous combined with her questions to Richard about whether he is jealous engender further questions about the definition of jealousy, its origins, and how it manifests itself among men and women.

The theory of Melanie Klein, a prominent psychoanalyst during the first part of the century, emerges as a persuasive framework for Friday's understanding of the origin and process of jealousy. In *Envy and Gratitude* (New York: Basic Books, 1957) Klein suggests that envy, established in the first weeks of life, leads to jealousy. The infant loves and resents the mother's breast due to the power it has to provide or deny pleasure; he or she envies it. Denial, devaluation, and idealization are defenses against it. The appearance of a rival (father or sibling) may lead the infant to think that a third party is responsible for the mother withdrawing her attention; the scene is set for jealousy. However, envy can be the first step in a process that opens the door to love. Envy may produce guilt about negative feelings toward the mother, but may ultimately give way to reparation (atonement for malice felt) and gratitude for the positive behavior (holding, giving milk) of the mother. Adult experiences with jealousy (fear of someone displacing your beloved) and envy (a desire to have what someone else has) are not unusual emotions and do not mean weakness (even though psychiatrists, counselors, and the media avoid the subject); coming to terms with them by acknowledging their presence, dealing with guilt, and allowing for gratitude aids in developing love, which involves acknowledging the exchanging dependencies, and leads to healthy integration of positive and negative aspects of personality.

In her journey to understand the elements of jealousy, Friday examines such topics as self-esteem, betrayal, competition, definitions of masculinity and femininity, male and female sexuality, and the much neglected subject of sibling rivalry. She presents personal, in-depth interviews of specific individuals (including author Erica Jong) on feelings about jealousy, weaves them together with the comments of experts (Segal, Kohut, and Brazelton), and deepens them with quotes from literature as well as findings from contemporary works on the relationship between males and females. Therefore, the book becomes a statement about much more than jealousy; it becomes the focus for a discussion of the state of love, sex, and power in contemporary society. (SGF)

IL,PO
434. Pines, Ayala M. **Romantic Jealousy: Understanding and Conquering the Shadow of Love.** New York: St. Martin's Press, 1992. 300 p. Includes bibliography and index. ISBN 0-312-07106-X.

Drawing on extensive research, clinical work, questionnaires, and workshop experience, Pines, a couples therapist and research associate in the Department of Psychology, University of California, Berkeley, wrote this book as a practical guide for persons with jealousy problems. At the outset, Pines defines "romantic jealousy" as "the jealousy that emerges in the context of a romantic relationship" (p. 2). She also distinguishes between jealousy and envy, and between normal and abnormal jealousy.

To the question "Are you a jealous person?" 54 percent of 728 people in three separate studies responded "yes" and 46 percent said "no." Pines includes questions the reader can use to compare himself/herself with the respondents in the surveys.

Pines identifies five approaches used to explore and explain jealousy. These include (1) the *psychodynamic approach*, that stresses the unconscious forces at work in jealousy, especially unresolved childhood conflicts; (2) the *systems approach*, that focuses on a couple's immediate problems; eschews the historical component; examines the emotions, actions, and thoughts of the persons involved; and recommends disrupting those destructive patterns of behavior that evoke jealousy; (3) the *sociobiological approach*, that views jealousy as innate in everyone—indeed human jealousy is akin to animal jealousy—"the result of evolutionary processes that are different for men and women" (p. xii); (4) the *behavioral approach*, that recognizes jealousy as a learned response that can be unlearned; and (5) the *social psychological approach*, that looks upon jealousy as the result of cultural dynamics.

Pines incorporates all five approaches in her own views about jealousy. She focuses on those aspects in each approach that are most relevant for coping with jealousy. She believes that there is no single way to deal with jealousy—depending on the situation, one should use "the most effective strategy or combination of strategies" (p. 245). A lengthy questionnaire in the appendix may be used by the reader to explore his/her romantic jealousy problems. (TJW)

Partner Choice

Marital

(For related material see also entries 148, 168)

PO
435. Botwin, Carol. **Is There Sex After Marriage?** Foreword by Harold I. Lief, M.D. New York: Pocket Books, 1986. 287 p. Includes bibliography and index. ISBN 0-671-60778-2.

Inhibited sexual desire is not only a problem in the general population but also is one of the leading sexual problems in marriages today. With the assumption that the perception of a problem goes a long way in helping to solve it, Botwin describes common behavior that hinders sex and fulfillment in relationships with the hope that couples can recognize the points in their relationships that are particularly susceptible to sexual problems.

The first part of the book describes the "natural history of a marriage"—a series of stages that are common to most marriages. Predictable variations in sexual interest occur at each stage: (1) the sharp drop in sexual activity during the early years after the initial romance; (2) the anxiety and frustration that are associated with conception and pregnancy; (3) the pressures of child-rearing on a sexual relationship; (4) the repercussions of defining the self during middle age; (5) the emotional and physical issues that couples confront after children leave home; and (6) the importance of good health and a receptive partner for good sex during the "golden years."

While part 1 concentrates on normal stress points in marriage, part 2 concentrates on specific psychological attitudes and emotional pitfalls that can affect sexual desire at any stage of marriage. Sexual boredom usually accompanies unconscious hostility stemming from such issues as unrealistic expectations, guilt, and inhibitions. Positive views of parents projected onto spouses may become negative ones over time. Fear of intimacy and anger (one of the major sources of sexual inhibition) may also stifle desire in an ongoing sexual relationship. Stress, power issues, and coping with success may also inhibit sexual expression.

Drawing heavily on surveys, statistics, and clinical studies of sexual behavior and marriage, the book presents a highly readable guide to coping with sex and emotional stress in long-term relationships. In the process, Botwin provides a series of guidelines for resolving some of these problems. An appendix contains a directory of sex clinics in the United States for readers who think that they may need the assistance of professionals in sorting out their sexual problems. (SGF)

IL
436. Derenski, Arlene, and Sally B. Landsburg. **The Age Taboo: Older Women— Younger Men Relationships.** Boston: Little, Brown, 1981. 262 p. Includes bibliography and index. ISBN 0-316-51366-0.

Based primarily on fifty two- to three-hour tape-recorded interviews of older woman/younger man couples in addition to Derenski and Landsburg's observations of couples in therapy, the book focuses on understanding what younger men and older women are looking for when they form a committed relationship (marriage or long-term living together) with each other. A wider goal is to examine how two people with differing social and sexual upbringing can live together and improve the quality of their relationship. Derenski and Landsburg, both licensed family therapists and spouses of men considerably younger than themselves, concentrate on healthy, long-term relationships rather than on brief encounters popularized by the press, and examine how age assists or hinders problems entailed by the changing roles of men and women. Older women are defined as six or more years older than their mates. However, the age difference between most respondents ranged from six to eighteen years. Average duration of a relationship was one to ten years; nearly all the women and half the men were previously married; three-quarters of the women had children from a previous marriage; and most respondents live on the West Coast. The book begins by addressing issues specific to couples who have broken the age taboo: (1) going public, (2) private fears about the viability of the relationship, and (3) the social consequences of breaking the age taboo. Other chapters relate to questions that concern all committed relationships: (1) power and dominance, (2) money and status, (3) sex, and (4) children.

The concluding chapters sum up the advantages of an older woman/younger man relationship, outline some common denominators of relationships that have persisted, and discuss what features of these relationships can aid any couple in forging a successful interaction. The multifaceted approach not only contributes information on couples who have crossed the age barrier but also provides more general insight into the nature of cultural taboos, social pressure, and the components of an intimate relationship. (SGF)

PO
437. Dolesh, Daniel J., and Sherelynn Lehman. **Love Me, Love Me Not: How to Survive Infidelity.** New York: McGraw-Hill, 1985. 192 p. Includes index. ISBN 0-07-017394-X.

This book concentrates on the experiences of partners betrayed by sexual infidelity. It provides advice for dealing with their feelings, easing their pain, and responding to the situation. Dolesh and Lehman, both therapists and married to each other, derive their advice from research on the dynamics of infidelity based on interviews with over 500 people. They find that most people go through similar emotional stages when reacting to infidelity (or other situations of betrayal). They suggest that identification of these stages is beneficial to structuring avenues for individual growth in the face of betrayal.

The first chapters explore the signs and causes of infidelity. Loneliness, excitement, and turmoil at home may lead to an affair. An attentive partner can find signs of betrayal that a person engaged in an affair usually inadvertently provides, such as working or traveling more, developing a new body or wardrobe, and mood swings. Calming yourself and taking control of your own life and aspects of the relationship are productive initial reactions.

Five common emotional stages characterize the reactions of betrayed partners: (1) a feeling of betrayal ("a devastating, life-changing experience . . . one of the most painful experiences in life"), (2) denial and rationalization of the betrayal, (3) fear of abandonment and overcompensation, (4) depression and anger, and (5) action.

The final chapters provide concrete information on the variety of goals and options that the betrayed person can choose: rebuild, let go, or choose an alternate lifestyle. Guidelines for evaluation of what to do, how to marshal inner resources as well as how to use legal, community, and religious resources, are also included. Finally, there is advice about how to deal with the children. Composite case histories of seven individuals who experienced and dealt with infidelity in their own way are used throughout the book to illustrate the variety of ways in which this emotionally laden experience can be expressed. (SGF)

PR,IL,PO

438. Lindsay, Jeanne Warren. **Teens Look at Marriage: Rainbows, Roles, and Realities.** Buena Park, Calif.: Morning Glory Press, 1985. 256 p. Includes bibliography and index. ISBN 0-930934-16-4.

Although a great deal of attention has been paid to the problem of teenage pregnancy, very little has been given to the nature of the relationships of teenage couples, for whom sex and pregnancy are only part of a wider context of interaction. This book tries to fill the gap by serving as a resource that "is meant to provide insight into the culture of teenage couples, thereby helping teachers, other professionals, students, and parents increase their understanding of teenagers' attitudes toward marriage and to learn of the realities of teenage partnerships" (p. 23).

Lindsay, an anthropologist who developed and coordinates a Teen Mother Program in southern California, draws on two types of data to describe the culture of teen couples. The first is derived from the results of a questionnaire administered to a nationwide sample of 3,118 teenagers still in high school; it taps the ideals of teenagers about marriage. The other examines the realities of teenage relationships on the basis of results of questionnaires administered to 359 teenagers married or living together, questionnaires answered by eighty-two alumnae of the Teen Mother Program, and in-depth, personal interviews with seventy-six teenagers married or living together. The contrast between the results of these data portray a world in which expectations are often at variance with reality. Although most teenagers want marriage to last forever, many divorce soon after the wedding or within a few years. Although few expect major changes after marriage, almost 80 percent drop out of school, many lose friends, and quite a few experience the Lost Adolescence Syndrome. Spouse abuse, jealousy, living with parents or friends, unequal distribution of domestic tasks, problems in communication, and differences in sexual desire are issues with which these young people must cope. Lindsay concludes that it is appropriate to advise against early marriage and parenthood, but she provides suggestions for helping those already in one of those situations. Since 20 percent of babies born in the United States are born to teenage mothers, the way in which these situations are dealt with will have important repercussions on the next generations. (SGF)

PR,IL,PO

439. Scarf, Maggie. **Intimate Partners: Patterns in Love and Marriage.** New York: Random House, 1987. 428 p. Includes bibliography and index. ISBN 0-394-55485-X.

Scarf, a writer notable for her book *Unfinished Business* (Doubleday, 1980), which probed for the causes of women's depression, was prompted to write this book after noticing that there is a plethora of interpretations about divorce but very few about marriage. The assumption seems to be that working out a satisfactory relationship with an intimate partner does not require much learning; most of it probably occurs naturally. In preparation for her analysis of the complex emotional patterns in love and marriage, she participated in courses and a program on marital family therapy and talked with therapists (Nadelson, Kaplan, Offit, Katchadourian, and particularly Stuart Johnson, Director of Family Therapy at Yale Psychiatric Institute).

The book is based on in-depth interviews with thirty-two couples (selected from a list of 200) in a variety of geographic regions who volunteered to participate in the project. It chronicles the marital history of five couples whose lives seem to best exemplify the types of problems and tasks that couples face in working out an intimate partnership at a particular phase in life or during a specific phase of the relationship. As Scarf puts it: "This book is about the basic way in which marriages are made: the basic materials that are used in their construction and how these affect the structure of the relationship that develops" (p. 12).

The chapters of each of the six parts of the book focus on different phases of a marital relationship: (1) becoming a couple, (2) emotional triangles that involve lovers or other third parties, (3) marital problems and solutions, (4) sexuality, (5) transformation when children leave home, and (6) adjustment to later life after the parenting phase. Each part blends the absorbing marital histories of the five couples with reviews of relevant psychological theory (particularly drawing on object relations theorists and family systems theorists, such as Bowen, Haley, and Minuchen). Common problems that couples experience include reconciling needs for autonomy and intimacy, participation in a less than satisfactory intimate system (caretaker/wounded bird, infidelity), projection of individual conflicts onto the partner, and splitting off from negative aspects of the self. Throughout, Scarf emphasizes the impact of past intimate relationships, particularly those experienced as a child, on current relational problems. When relationships are unhappy, they tend to involve power struggles and attempts to resolve conflicts established in earlier intimate relationships. Couples often collude in producing their particular brand of dissatisfaction. When each member of a couple can acknowledge his or her individual contribution to marital conflict, maintain differences (or autonomy) within an intimate context, and establish dialogue with each other, both are on the path to becoming intimate partners. (SGF)

IL,PO

440. Stopes, Marie Carmichael. **Married Love: A New Contribution to the Solution of Sex Difficulties.** Authorized ed., newly reset and revised. With a preface by Dr. Jessie Murray. New York: Putnam, 1939. 177 p. Includes bibliography.

First published in England in 1918, this classic work, "dedicated to young husbands and all those who are betrothed in love," has proved inspiring to many generations of couples. Stopes is famous for her pioneering work in the birth control movement in England, where she and her husband opened the first birth control clinic in London in March 1921. This book was published at a time when very little literature on sexual relations was available, owing primarily to the prevalent taboo concerning the public discussion of sex. Based on years of listening to women's complaints about sexual difficulties in marriage, Stopes concluded that for various reasons both men and women were abysmally ignorant of the facts of life. At the time of marriage, women were often unaware of what the marriage bed implied. Invariably men and women lacked sound knowledge of the anatomy and physiology of sex; usually they harbored erroneous notions about the opposite sex. Her book, then, was written to inform those about to marry or those already married about the true nature of the sexual relationship. Two of

Stopes principal points in her platform for improving sexual relations are the ideas, startling at the time, that (1) there should be mutuality of the sex act between men and women and (2) there should be a balance between the lower and higher parts of life, between the body and the relationship. She noted that women are subject to a periodic recurrence of desire that can be identified within the menstrual cycle. If men understood this basic fact and were observant of their wives' behavior, improvements in the physical side of marriage could occur in terms of timing and frequency of intercourse. This realization led Stopes to write this pioneering work that provided for the time a frank discussion of the physiological as well as the spiritual side of sex. Other topics relating to sex between married people are examined: sleep, modesty and romance, abstinence, contraception, children, and social relations. The guidance provided is surprisingly modern in its approach. Because of the pall cast over sexual matters by the infamous Comstock legislation, this book was not published in the United States until 1931. (TJW)

PR,IL

441. Van de Velde, Theodoor H. **Ideal Marriage: Its Physiology and Technique.** Translated by Stella Browne. Introduction by J. Johnston Abraham. New York: Random House, 1930. 323 p. Includes bibliography.

Van de Velde was one of the major writers on human sexuality during the early twentieth century. This book presents his beliefs and research on techniques for good sexual relationships in marriage, based on his experience as a practicing gynecologist in the Netherlands. First published in 1926, the book is significant in its articulation of values that encourage both men and women to enjoy the physical and spiritual aspects of their marriage. It is divided into sections on human sexual physiology, describing both male and female organs and responses as well as sensory stimuli; sexual intercourse, including descriptions of ten accepted positions; and bodily, psychic, and mental hygiene. Van de Velde believed that rewarding sexual relationships are very important for both partners in a marriage for reasons of mental, emotional, and physical health. Understanding and knowledge, especially on the part of the husband, are necessary to achieve such relationships. Therefore, the human sexual function is explained in detail, including the woman's physical and hormonal cycle and the production of sperm by the male. The sexual act itself should begin with the prelude, or activities that encourage readiness for intercourse, then develop into love-play and culminate in "communion" or coitus. The act should be followed by a period of afterplay and relaxation. The husband is responsible for bringing the wife to simultaneous orgasm through his technique and patience. Therefore, this book is addressed both to the doctor who needs to impart definite and accurate information to husbands and to the husband who should be the initiator, teacher, and leader during intercourse. Bodily hygiene, including both cleanliness and good health, is most important, as is a positive mental attitude toward conjugal relations. However, the most important factor in the Ideal Marriage is spiritual love between the partners. Consultation with religious authorities indicates that Ideal Marriage is compatible with the teachings of the major Western religions except those that demand an ascetic life. The book concludes with eight color plates depicting the male and female genitalia and data concerning ovarian function, menstruation, and pregnancy. (SDH)

PO

442. Westheimer, Ruth. **Dr. Ruth's Guide for Married Lovers.** New York: Warner Books, 1986. 244 p. Includes index. ISBN 0-446-51282-6.

Despite the plethora of sex manuals on the market, very few deal specifically with sex between partners living in a marital (or stable) relationship. Rather, they seem to focus on "glorious fun" apart from marriage. The few marriage manuals that exist, such as Van de Velde's *Ideal Marriage*, are out-of-date. Dr. Ruth offers a manual geared specifically to people in the present generation who are interested in monogamous behavior. She writes with "post-Kinsey, post-Masters and Johnson, post-sex revolution insight and information." Armed with views that "sex is a good binder in a marriage" and "it is better to vary the sex a little than the sex partner," America's popular interpreter of sexual problems and issues guides the reader through a very readable, uncomplicated description of the phases and dimensions of marital life, from the beginning of a serious relationship, with its concomitant expectations and fantasies, through the honeymoon and into the realities of contraception, pregnancy, birth, children, aging, and sexual difficulties.

At the outset, it is important for a person to define his or her own sexuality as well as define realistic expectations of a marriage in order to understand what she or he wants from a relationship. Practical advice about the honeymoon (a time for joy and intimacy more than a sexual marathon), openness in a relationship (how much to reveal about the past), and how to talk about sex dovetails with information about the genitals (private and shared aspects), orgasms (the clitoral/vaginal controversy), positions, and taking care of the body. Enhancements of the relationship can occur through fantasies, masturbation, sexy films, books and music, and love in the morning. Problems may occur in the life of a marriage when expectations clash with reality or when partners experience sexual difficulties (a man experiences erectile problems, premature ejaculation, or retarded ejaculation; a woman experiences vaginismus, preorgasm, or is unresponsive). Strategies for dealing with these problems as well as guidelines for selecting a therapist are provided. The advice is presented with the goal of helping a couple to "care for and nurture the lasting closeness they want." As usual, Dr. Ruth comes directly to the point with humor and compassion. (SGF)

Premarital. Extramarital. Postmarital

(For related material see also entry 164)

PR,IL
443.   Atwater, Lynn. **The Extramarital Connection: Sex, Intimacy, and Identity.** New York: Irvington, 1982. 263 p. Includes bibliography and index. ISBN 0-8290-0770-2.

According to Atwater, a sociologist and editor-at-large for *Forum* magazine, "The evidence suggests that we are sexual schizophrenics." Although most Americans say they disapprove of extramarital sex, at least half of all married men and close to 40 percent of married women engage in an extramarital relationship (EMR) sometime during the course of their married life. What accounts for the chasm between belief and behavior? What are the meanings and consequences of an EMR for the participants? How do EMRs relate to the "sexual revolution," and what do they indicate about future trends in marriage and the family? These are a few of the global questions that transcend the text of this book written for scholars, researchers, and clinicians as well as for college students studying gender roles and for men and women interested in the area of intimate relations. Atwater limits her study of the "extramarital connection" to women who have or are currently engaged in an EMR because women seem to be in the vanguard of change in marital roles and because very little attention has been focused on women who have had extramarital liaisons. Since she is particularly interested in the meaning of an EMR, she chose to conduct in-depth interviews with 50 of 300 respondents to an ad placed in *Ms.* magazine. Respondents were selected for wide variation in background and spanned (1) ages twenty-three to fifty-nine; (2) high school to postgraduate education; and (3) homemaking, clerical/secretarial, and managerial occupations. Most interviewees were urban, middle-class women who had participated in more than one EMR (67 percent), had children (70 percent), and had intact marriages at the time of the interview (65 percent). Interviews lasted about three hours, were conducted either with Atwater (thirty) or by a taped self-interview (twenty), and were based on a nine-page interview schedule covering personal data; marital data; feminist attitudes and behavior; explanation of involvement; EMR activity; EMR with women, marriage, and family relationships; outcomes; and attitudes toward marriage, EMR, and female sexuality. Findings are based on the interviews; Atwater's personal conversations with men and women at professional meetings, lectures, etc.; and works published on EMR through the first part of 1980. They are organized into the following chapters: "Extramarital Relationships," "Getting Involved," "Extramarital Intimacy," "Open Marriage," "Sexual Scripts and Sexual Behavior," "After Involvement: Identities and Attitudes," "Extramarital Relationships with Other Women," and "The Extramarital Connection." Using a sociological, feminist perspective, Atwater concludes that changes in the family and sexual lifestyles in the last two decades are irreversible and that Americans need to free themselves of past mythologies and the blinders of traditional moral condemnation in order to achieve an understanding of the increasingly common experience of an extramarital relationship. (SGF)

PO

444. Brown, Helen Gurley. **Sex and the Single Girl.** New York: Bernard Geis Associates, 1962. 267 p.

In a sassy, conversational style, Brown, editor of *Cosmopolitan* magazine, presents her personal view of "how to stay single—in superlative style." The book is addressed to women who are not married "but who are not necessarily planning to join a nunnery." Achieving happiness while single does not require great beauty, money, a magnetic personality, or supreme organizational skills, but rather developing the "raw material" that a woman has. As Brown puts it, "You have to work like a son of a bitch" (p. 8). The book is full of practical ways to accomplish that "work."

Brown first characterizes and assesses the eligibility of available men in a single woman's life (e.g., Don Juans, married and separated men, younger men) and then proceeds to detail where to meet them (e.g., at work, clubs, vacations, or in men's departments in stores). She gives tips on how to be sexy, both in general (accept yourself as a woman and be able to enjoy sex) and in particular (e.g., flirt, have clean hair, don't talk too much). An outline of sensible nutritional habits designed to maintain good health, a guide on how to diet and exercise to stay in shape, pointers on how to select a wardrobe, and advice on how to apply makeup are resources presented to enhance the single woman's fitness and appearance. The ambiance of the woman's apartment is not neglected; ways to decorate tastefully, but at a reasonable cost, are also noted. Domestic skills like cooking and managing money are also important aspects of maintaining a satisfactory single life. Finally, routes to job satisfaction and to coping with the phases of a relationship are suggested.

Although a good deal of attention is paid to developing a pleasing appearance and meeting men, the point of the book is to encourage single women to feel good about themselves and their lifestyles. Brown endorses a view of the single woman as the "newest glamor girl of our times," not "a creature to be pitied and patronized" (p. 5). The view that a single woman can have a rich, full life challenged the marriage and family orientation of the preceding decade of the 1950s. (SGF)

IL,PO

445. Heyn, Dalma. **The Erotic Silence of the American Wife.** New York: Turtle Bay Books, 1992. 304 p. ISBN 0-679-41339-1.

Much of this book consists of interviews that Heyn conducted with women who came forward to discuss their extramarital affairs with men. These women express a deep dissatisfaction with their marriages and affirm that extramarital sex has been a welcome relief from the burdens of marriage and, on the whole, beneficial.

On the basis of this testimony, diverse scholarly studies, and impressions garnered from world literature—Tolstoy's *Anna Karenina*, Flaubert's *Madame Bovary*, Hawthorne's *The Scarlet Letter*, Hardy's *Tess of the D'Urbervilles*, and others—Heyn probes the nature of adultery and its consequences.

The trouble lies, it seems, with the institution of marriage. Up to this moment, young women are energetic, expressive, ebullient, and free, on a par with young men. Then, overnight, their lives change: married, they are expected to subordinate their interests to those of their spouses. Somehow, in this patriarchal process they lose their spontaneity, even their sexuality. As Heyn points out, "A married man keeps his sexuality while opting for sexual exclusivity; a married woman is supposed to become inherently monogamous, as though her sexuality were easily transferred elsewhere because it is not really her own; and as though sexual exclusivity were a deeply ingrained, biological female personality trait" (p. 109).

Not surprisingly, many women respond by seeking relationships and sexual ful-fillment outside marriage. It is this behavior—its complications and consequences, and even its justification—that Heyn explores. In the United States, Heyn believes, the Perfect Wife, as embodied in Donna Reed, a television personality who is "beautiful, smiling, supportive, contented, giving, feminine," has been offered as a model for American women to emulate. The ideal, supposed to last forever, has been undermined in recent years. Women are speaking up, challenging the ideal. Issues of sexuality once responded to by silence are now being addressed openly: orgasm, premarital sex, homosexuality, oral sex, abortion, and so forth.

What Heyn seems to be saying is that the erotic life of many married women has been stifled in marriage; that the extramarital affairs, despite the risks inherent in such relationships, seem both to satisfy these women's pursuit of pleasure and their desire to break the Donna Reed-like ideal of goodness. (TJW)

IL

446. Hunt, Morton M. **The Affair: A Portrait of Extra-Marital Love in Contempo-rary America.** New York: World, 1969. 317 p. Includes bibliography and index.

The goal of this book is to paint a "portrait of the extramarital affair in American society today," especially as it applies to white middle-class patterns of behavior. Hunt derives his information from ninety-one tape-recorded, in-depth interviews with men and women still having affairs; a small number of diaries kept by the interviewees; forty interviews and correspondences with professionals who have special knowledge of the subject; and previously published data on the subject.

Our culture's view of affairs stems from a blend of two different traditions: (1) the pagan, courtly one in which marriage is a practical arrangement and affairs are tolerated as a part of a full life, and (2) the Puritan bourgeois one in which marriage is an all-encompassing, romantic, idealistic relationship, and affairs are regarded as its enemy. Affairs are complex relationships that may be defined differently by men and women, may be experienced differently, and may manifest themselves in a variety of forms.

Hunt describes several phases of affairs, each of which is a chapter in the book: desire, temptation, consummation, flourishing, decaying, and aftermath. He gives his portrait life by presenting archetypal histories as well as relevant research findings about each phase. Most people have fantasies of more than one partner and have a deeply rooted desire for variety. People generally have affairs because of sexual and/or emotional boredom, not because they are "in love." Usually the partner is close at hand and well-known. Partners' responses to an affair vary and may depend upon whether they follow a more "pagan" or "Puritan" tradition. The idea of overwhelming passion is more mythical than real; many people seek merely fun and satisfaction. The practicalities of how to conduct this primarily concealed activity include how to communicate with each other, where and when to meet, and how to behave. Affairs are experienced differently and may range from low to high involvement; they can have variable effects on a marriage (result in divorce, make little difference, make it tolerable).

Spouses' reactions to finding out about an affair are most likely to include rage, jealousy, humiliation, and depression rather than tolerance and understanding. The aftermath of an affair is likely to be commensurate with the degree of involvement of the partners in it. With low emotional commitment, the aftermath can be mild; but with high involvement, the consequences can be highly charged. The majority of men and the minority of women continue having affairs after they have experienced one. Only half of the affairs that result in marriage are successful. The portrait that emerges from this very readable book is one of complexity—in terms of motivation, levels of involvement, consequences, and differential gender responses to affairs. (SGF)

PR
447. Kirkendall, Lester A. **Premarital Intercourse and Interpersonal Relationships.** Foreword by Brock Chisholm. New York: Gramercy, 1961. 302 p. Includes bibliography.

For this study, Kirkendall, Professor of Family Life at Oregon State University, interviewed 200 college-level males about their sexual behavior. The purpose was to provide data concerning the effects of premarital sexual intercourse upon the personal interrelationships of the participants. Does premarital sex tend to strengthen or weaken these relationships? Is premarital sex right or wrong? To answer these and related questions, Kirkendall establishes a value framework based on interpersonal relationships, one in which the moral decisions made "work toward the creation of trust, confidence, and integrity in relationships," "increase the capacity of individuals to cooperate," and "enhance the sense of self-respect in the individual" (p. 6).

Kirkendall selected subjects who were "white, college students, primarily middle-class, Protestant, and in their late teens or early-to-middle twenties" (pp. 9-10). He organized the female partners of the subjects on six levels according to the degree of increasing attachment. These levels are: (1) prostitutes; (2) pick-ups; (3) casual acquaintances; (4) dating partners; (5) partners with whom a relationship of some strength exists; and (6) fiancées. Using the interview-case history approach, he determined for each level of liaison (1) the motivation of the subjects and partners; (2) the degree to which they communicated with each other; (3) what protective measures (use of condoms, confidentiality, etc.) the subjects and their partners took; (4) the attitudes of the subjects and partners toward responsibility; and (5) the feelings of satisfaction or dissatisfaction resulting from the subjects' sexual experiences. Kirkendall established a category analysis system on the five relationship characteristics in order to secure statistical data.

Kirkendall also addresses the question of the effects of premarital intercourse upon marital adjustment. He states that they "range from positive, strengthening consequences for the relationship to very damaging and disruptive ones" (p. 226). He also identifies both the impeding forces and the facilitating forces affecting the integration of sex into interpersonal relationships.

As a result of the study's suggestions and conclusions, Kirkendall hopes that "our culture may move toward a more responsible, satisfying, and a more fulfilling use of sex, not only in the premarital period but throughout life" (p. 252). (TJW)

IL
448. Lampe, Philip E., ed. **Adultery in the United States: Close Encounters of the Sixth (or Seventh) Kind.** Buffalo, N.Y.: Prometheus Books, 1987. 224 p. Includes bibliographies and index. ISBN 0-87975-375-7.

Lampe, Professor of Sociology at Incarnate Word College, San Antonio, Texas, says that the theme of this book is to examine adultery in the United States from colonial times to the present. This theme has wider implications: (1) it facilitates a recognition of the difference between real and ideal culture; (2) it provides a basis to understand American society and how it has changed; and (3) it provides an integrated perspective for understanding the complexity of factors that contribute to adultery, which is often regarded as a social problem. Using a "general historical or developmental approach," Lampe begins with an initial chapter that provides an overview of the cultural heritage of the United States as it relates to the foundations for the aspects of adultery discussed in subsequent chapters (law, religion, literature, philosophy, science). The backgrounds that make up American traditions are not necessarily consistent with each other and may be contradictory. Consequently, "a wide range of behavior, together with the reactions which such behavior evokes, is to be expected—including adultery" (p. 39). Lampe defines and explores the dimensions of adultery as a type of social behavior, considering it in terms of three major perspectives about sexual behavior: (1) moralizing (i.e., judgments within the scope of religion and morality) including apotheosizing (i.e., exalting and glorifying sexual behavior); (2) medicalizing (i.e., judgments in terms of health and sickness); and (3) normalizing (i.e., as a type of social behavior or interaction).

Attorney Sue M. Hall and Philip A. Hall, Associate Professor of Social Work, evaluate the current legal status of adultery in the United States, documenting the large number of changes in the law as it applies to adultery; they also discuss the link between legality and legitimacy. In his discussion of religion and adultery, Tarcisio Beal, Professor of History and Religious Studies, concludes that "one can expect that the majority of the Christian churches will continue to see adultery as an abomination, even while increasing numbers of individual Christians see it as morally justifiable" (p. 102). In her chapter on adultery in American literature, Rose Marie Cutting, Professor of English and Communication Arts, contrasts the centrality of adultery as a literary theme in nineteenth-century literature with its relative absence in American novels until the twentieth, except for nineteenth-century verse written by women and the works of a few novelists (Nathaniel Hawthorne, Henry James, Kate Chopin). Twentieth-century novels contain adultery as a theme but regard it as less shocking because "they see the successful marriage as the exception not the rule" (p. 128). Professor of Philosophy Robert J. Connelly's survey of the literature on adultery and sex reveals that very few philosophical publications in the United States had addressed the topic until the late 1950s. In contrast, Lampe shows that behavioral and social scientists have paid more attention to adultery, increasingly using a normalizing perspective. Lampe concludes the book by summarizing some of the salient conclusions of the preceding overviews and suggests that the normalizing perspective will continue to prevail and that adultery will "begin a moderate but general decline" (p. 215). (SGF)

PR,IL
449. Lawson, Annette. **Adultery: An Analysis of Love and Betrayal.** New York: Basic Books, 1988. 440 p. Includes bibliography and index. ISBN 0-465-00075-4.

According to British sociologist Lawson, an unhappy marriage does not adequately explain the occurrence of adultery. The relevance of affairs extends beyond marriage to include gender relations and the nature of society. Based on 579 completed questionnaires and 100 in-depth interviews from a middle-class, well-educated, white British sample, Lawson's study focuses on adultery as a social phenomenon. Expectations about love, sex, and marriage are contained in cultural myths. The myth of "me" (individuals develop a liberating sense of self through their lives) currently conflicts with the myth of romantic marriage (love and sex are bound together in an exclusive marriage), and much of the conflict differs according to gender.

The first part of the book explores what adultery is. It is "all about the setting, breaking, or maintaining and the creation of boundaries" (p. 32). Love is the major publicly stated reason for marriage, and much of the identity of a married couple relies on sexual exclusivity and open, honest communication. Adultery removes the traditional boundaries of marriage. Couples who share a story, an "imagined projection," as well as sex are more likely to be content with their marriages and not become involved in affairs.

Part 2 examines the nature of liaisons in which many individuals involve themselves. The experience is likely to vary according to gender. Women engage in a process of self-discovery, where they shift into a different emotional world. Their myth of romantic love is at odds with their myth of me. In contrast, men do not perceive a conflict between their marital needs and their individual needs for self-fulfillment; they engage in affairs because they are curious about sex with another woman or do not think that an involvement will harm their marriage. Both men and women choose friends or neighbors as lovers and are likely to meet their first lovers at work. Generally affairs are carried out in a space not associated with the marital pair, although one-third of the women interviewed had invited lovers into their homes. Women are less likely than in the past to wait to become involved. Particularly for women, drama and a sense of being alive are prime pleasures of an affair; males rate sexual fulfillment more highly. However, women suffer from more guilt, jealousy, and a greater risk of losing their spouses than men do. Men and women also differ in their reasons for revealing or hiding the affair from a spouse. Discussing an affair can lead to renegotiation of the assumptions of the marriage. However, women are less likely to tell their husbands for fear of hurting them and their reputations. Men have no such concern about women's reputations. While women are more likely to be hurt by the deceit of an affair, men are more offended by sexual betrayal. Although lovers may think that they have control over their affairs, they may not be able to control their emotions; males may enjoy a sense of power while women take pleasure in self-discovery. Love affairs have their own dynamic, part of which is maintained by secrecy. Apparent control in an otherwise chaotic life as well as the significance of experiences at work may also be important elements.

Part 3 deals with the end of an affair. Divorce is more likely for people who have affairs. The consequences can be more serious for women than men because they have less economic and social flexibility in their lives. Nevertheless, gender scripts constrain both men and women. If people continue to believe that marriage is the main place where good, loving, strong, erotic feelings are expressed, the conflict between the myths of me and romantic marriage will continue, as will affairs. (SGF)

PR,IL

450. Reiss, Ira L. **Premarital Sexual Standards in America: A Sociological Investigation of the Relative Social and Cultural Integration of American Sexual Standards.** Glencoe, Ill.: Free Press, 1960. 286 p. Includes bibliography and index.

In times of profound social change, when old patterns of sexual behavior are being questioned and new forms adopted, it is helpful to understand prevailing sexual standards. A dozen years in the making, this book by a sociologist identifies and analyzes premarital sexual standards in America at the beginning of the 1960s. After discussing the physiological and cultural bases of sexual codes and making interspecies and cross-cultural comparisons, Reiss examines Hebrew, Greek, and Roman cultures for customs that we have inherited. He also looks briefly at the romantic love, urban-industrial, and feminist revolutions in terms of their impact on sexual standards. Focusing on premarital sexual standards, he identifies and analyzes each of the following sexual standards: (1) abstinence, (2) double standard, (3) permissiveness without affection, and (4) permissiveness with affection. Each of these contains within it subtypes of standards. The double standard, for example, embraces two subtypes, orthodox and transitional. Standards, in Reiss's view, derive from a balancing of values: love, pleasure, security, respectability, independence, religion, safety, and so forth. The standards are usually not formally declared but informally understood. One formal standard is abstinence, closely tied to religion: it forbids intercourse outside of marriage for both men and women. The double standard, on the other hand, is acceptable for men but wrong and unacceptable for women. Reiss also proposes that on a continuum there are two basic types of sexual behavior: body-centered, that stresses the physical aspects of the act, and person-centered, that takes place in the context of a love relationship with emphasis on the other person. For each standard, Reiss explores both negative-value consequences (pregnancy, venereal disease, social condemnation, guilt feelings, weakening of marriage) and positive-value consequences (physical satisfaction, psychic satisfaction, aid to marital sexual adjustment). One of the interesting trends identified by Reiss is that permissiveness with affection is gaining headway, allowing "for the first time in thousands of years . . . sex standards which tend to unify rather than divide men and women" (p. 245). Data for this study came from the extensive research studies undertaken by Kinsey, Ehrmann, Burgess and Wallin, Terman, and Reiss himself. Information from the Institute of Sex Research was also helpful. (TJW)

PR

451. Reiss, Ira L. **The Social Context of Premarital Sexual Permissiveness.** New York: Holt, Rinehart and Winston, 1967. 256 p. Includes bibliography and index.

This empirical study of premarital sexual attitudes complements Reiss's earlier theoretical work, *Premarital Sexual Standards in America.* Like its precursor, the overall intent is to contribute to sociological theory, that is, explaining social facts via other social facts rather than by individual characteristics and motivations. Reiss, a distinguished sociologist, claims that "this is the first systematic sociological study of a national probability sample in the area of premarital sexual attitudes" (p. vii). The research (conducted between 1960 and 1964) uses seven different samples, and its 2,734 respondents include adults, college and high school students, and blacks and whites.

The study revolves around two major sets of variables. Premarital permissiveness is the dependent variable, which is measured by a Guttman scale rather than indicated by an overall typology; the rankings then become a basis for determining what sexual standard an individual holds—abstinence, a double standard, permissiveness without affection, or permissiveness with affection. The other set of variables are the hypothesized sociocultural correlates of premarital permissiveness, that comprise the independent variables: general background factors (class, religion, region, city size, age, gender); dating experiences and love conceptions; sexual behavior and guilt reactions; perceived permissiveness of parents, peers, and close friends; and family characteristics (size, gender and age of children, number of parents).

Seven chapters present the empirical findings of the study in addition to findings from previous, relevant research of other investigators; each chapter concludes with a proposition about the findings. The final chapter reviews, summarizes, and integrates these propositions into a theoretical formulation of the broad relationships that exist between them. A sociological framework pervades the theory, that posits that courtship and family institutions directly determine the norms of premarital sexual permissiveness. As Reiss summarizes his theory: "The degree of acceptable premarital sexual permissiveness in a courtship group varies directly with the degree of autonomy of the courtship group and with the degree of acceptable premarital sexual permissiveness in the social and cultural setting outside the group" (p. 167).

The book is aimed at graduate students and researchers who may benefit from its methodological approach as well as its substantive findings. (SGF)

IL,PO
452. Schickel, Richard. **Singled Out: A Civilized Guide to Sex and Sensibility for the Suddenly Single Man—or Woman.** New York: Viking Press, 1981. 115 p. ISBN 0-670-64710-1.

Relations between the sexes might have turned out differently had the leisure classes of Rome, schooled as they were in Ovid's *Ars amatoria*, been privileged to read Schickel's *Singled Out*. While chiefly tendering advice to males, both books include pointers in romantic dalliance that women might find rewarding.

Ars amatoria is concerned primarily with how first to acquire a mate and then how to maintain that relationship. *Singled Out* is about how to function socially and sexually following a broken marriage. In this sensitive, urbane, witty, and autobiographical work, Schickel, a film critic for *Time* magazine, provides insights into a host of postmarital activities and situations: dating, playing the field, coping with boredom, spotting the *femme fatale* and avoiding wimpdom, dealing with children (hers), being just good friends, brief encounters, and sexual quick fixes.

Obviously, this brief work offers no pat solution to the problem of being singled out; it does, however, provide some unconventional advice and guidance to the recently divorced that could aid them in getting through their present crises and finding new relationships. As Gloria Vanderbilt said, "I hope every man in the world not only reads it but thinks about it—a lot." (TJW)

PR,IL
453. Strean, Herbert S. **The Extramarital Affair.** New York: Free Press, 1980. 222 p. Includes bibliography and index. ISBN 0-02-932180-8.

Strean, psychoanalyst and Distinguished Professor at the Graduate School of Social Work at Rutgers University, examines the extramarital affair from a psychoanalytic perspective. This approach, he states, will enable the reader "to appreciate not just the rationales that people offer for their extramarital activity but its deeper and more significant unconscious meaning to them" (p. xiv). The subjects that Strean has studied over a ten-year period are seventy-five men and women attempting to sustain their marriages while conducting affairs of from a few months to several years' duration. Strean does not attempt to consider the brief "one-night stands" and other expressions of casual sex.

Human beings are conflicted, according to Freud, because the pleasure principle, seeking constant gratification, is opposed by the reality principle, that recognizes self-preservation and "the voice of the superego, or conscience." In other words, fantasies about extramarital affairs are not always carried out. The 50 percent of the married men and women who do have affairs are really fleeing from the difficult, complex, and demanding requirements of modern marriage. "Why some individuals chose to react to the conflicts of marriage by becoming involved in an extramarital sexual relationship is the major concern of this book" (p. xvi).

Strean begins with an examination of marriage and its discontents, pointing to the frustration, anger, competition, and self-centeredness in twentieth-century culture. The realities of marriage do not match the expectations. One of the reasons is society's overidealization of romantic love; when romance fails in marriage, the extramarital affair becomes an option. According to Strean, the "happy marriage is composed of two happy people" (p. 14). They have "overcome childish narcissism and feelings of omnipotence and strive to achieve what is realistically possible" (p. 17).

For a satisfactory marriage, Strean claims that it is necessary to resolve certain "psychosocial tasks." In Freudian parlance, conflicts arising during the psychosexual stages of development (oral, anal, phallic, oedipal, latency, pubertal, adolescent, and genital) are the root causes of marital problems manifesting themselves in extramarital affairs. It is the satisfactory resolution of these conflicts as one matures that leads to the happy marriage, and the unsatisfactory resolution of them that engenders the extramarital affair.

In several chapters Strean uses case history examples to discuss various types of conflicted marriages and demonstrates why an extramarital affair seems the solution. He concludes "that an extramarital affair is *never* a healthy or mature act" (p. 202). He believes that "many people who get married are psychologically still children, seeking gratification of childish wishes" (p. 203). Only when people resolve their psychosocial, or psychosexual, wishes, will they enjoy loving a person of the opposite sex and commit themselves to a happy monogamous marriage, that then renders unnecessary the extramarital affair. (TJW)

PO

454. Wolfe, Linda. **Playing Around: Women and Extramarital Sex.** New York: Morrow, 1975. 248 p. Includes bibliography. ISBN 0-688-00290-0.

Recognizing that beneath the orderly surface of married life in her Manhattan neighborhood there flowed an extensive undercurrent of extramarital affairs, Wolfe conceived the idea of writing a book about female extramarital sex. All the signs of the times—statistical surveys, public revelations, professional opinion—seemed to support her feelings about extramarital sex among women in the mid-1960s, that indicated a radical break with the double standard. In order to find who the women are who engage in extramarital affairs, she approached the problem in a twofold manner. Part I of *Playing Around* reviews both the treatment of the adulterous woman in history and her portrayal in classical and contemporary fiction. Wolfe points out that in contrast to the great novels of the past on the subject written by men (Tolstoy's *Anna Karenina*, Flaubert's *Madame Bovary*, and Lawrence's *Lady Chatterley's Lover*), we have today the writings of many women authors (Lessing, Jong, Rossner, Birstein, Oates, etc.) who, feeling free to explore the subject for the first time, seem preoccupied with the adulteress. Parts II and III consist of the results of lengthy interviews "with sixty-six women . . . selected from a preliminary list of a hundred." Hardly reflecting a cross-section of the population, the accounts were mainly gathered in the Manhattan area from women distantly linked to Wolfe through friends and acquaintances. By guaranteeing anonymity through the use of fictitious names and promising to be as nonjudgmental as possible, Wolfe was able to elicit intimate information about the marriages of sometimes shy and embarrassed women. The interviews are organized under two headings: "Marriage" and "Experimental Marriage." The former gives accounts of women "who attempt to be secretive about extramarital sexual experiences." Discussed are long-term affairs, sporadic affairs, romances, and brief encounters of women who remained married as well as the circumstances that led others to break up their marriages. "Experimental Marriage" presents the experiences of women "who are committed to acknowledging such experiences to their husbands." Open marriages, group sex, and mate swapping are some of the topics considered in this section. Because we are living at a time when more people are able to pursue emotional aspirations than ever before, Wolfe says that "extramarital sex is simply another one of the innumerable activities engaged in by people preoccupied with personal happiness. This happiness is our society's prime ethic" (p. 240). She also sides with Simone de Beauvoir in thinking that women's adultery is in itself a response to the inequities of the female condition, "an angry time-tested response" (p. 241). Wolfe concludes that "women are as disparate in their motivations and capacities for extramarital sex as they are in their appearance, and that affairs . . . are absolutely unique and individual" (p. 243). She believes that the time is propitious to attempt to understand the phenomenon of extramarital sex through the eyes of women themselves. (TJW)

IL
455. Yablonsky, Lewis. **The Extra-Sex Factor: Why Over Half of America's Married Men Play Around.** New York: Times Books, 1979. 239 p. ISBN 0-8129-0796-5.
More than half of American married men engage in extramarital sex—or *extra sex*, in Yablonsky's terminology. Drawing upon in-depth interviews with more than 50 men, 16 women, and upon 771 responses from married men to a brief general survey questionnaire, Yablonsky argues that the motives for extrasexual activities are complex. Nevertheless, he makes the following generalizations: "Total monogamy for most married people in contemporary society is a myth"; about 80 percent of married men who engage in extra sex are satisfied with their wives and their marriages; and about 80 percent of these men have a strong "homing drive" and have no intention of leaving their home situation; most extra sex is clandestine and is not discovered by the wife; most often it is of brief duration; and most men participate in extra sex for the companionship of other women and not simply for sex. The excerpts from the in-depth interviews that form most of the book's contents suggest that extra sex grows out of and creates considerable emotional turmoil. (**Men's Studies**, 1985)

Homosexual

(For related material see also entries 4, 14, 109, 138, 159, 166, 824, 828, 851, 966, 1027-1031)

IL
456. Abelove, Henry, Michele Aina Barale, and David M. Halperin, eds. **The Lesbian and Gay Studies Reader.** New York: Routledge, 1993. 666 p. Includes bibliographic notes and essay. ISBN 0-415-90518-4.
This reader presents for the first time an array of lesbian and gay studies, some from well-known scholars, others from new writers, from an expansive variety of traditional disciplines, such as philosophy, classics, history, anthropology, sociology, psychology, and politics as well as such newer fields as African-American studies, Latino studies, ethnic studies, cultural studies, and AIDS and the gay community. The book is intended to do for sex and sexuality what analogous women's studies readers have done for gender; that is, explore the interests of gays and lesbians in the structures of more historically established disciplines, and to contribute to the study and development of contemporary gay and lesbian culture.

The forty-two essays gathered here constitute the largest and most comprehensive collection compiled to date concerning lesbian and gay studies. It is designed to meet the academic needs of the growing number of gay and lesbian survey courses being taught at American institutions of higher learning. The reader intentionally omits personal testimonies, artistic representations, specific literary studies, and creative writings, which have been anthologized in other published works.

The text is divided into seven sections: politics and representation; spectacular logic; subjectivity, discipline, resistance; the uses of the erotic; collective identities/dissident identities; and between the pages. The "User's Guide" includes an arrangement of the essays according to discipline. The reader concludes with "Suggestions for Further Readings," meant as a guide for continuing studies, divided by type of material, selected disciplines, and broad subjects. Among the well-known names contributing articles are Eve Kosofsky Sedgwick, Teresa de Lauretis, Adrienne Rich, Audre Lorde, John D'Emilio, Yvonne Yarbro-Bejarano, and Catherine R. Stimpson. (JPC)

IL
457. Altman, Dennis. **The Homosexualization of America.** Boston: Beacon Press, 1982. 246 p. Includes bibliography and index. ISBN 0-8070-4143-2.

Australian sociologist and writer Altman presents two themes in this book: the emergence of homosexuals as a new minority with their own culture, lifestyles, political movement, and claim to legitimacy, and the impact of this minority on the larger society.

The first part outlines the explosion of gay and lesbian culture that has come about since the late 1960s as a result of social change made possible by living in a liberal capitalist democracy. This began with the "new homosexual," one whose homosexual identity was perceived as fundamentally positive now rather than sick or criminal or sinful. Concomitant to this new self-assertion has been the flowering of gay culture in arts, letters, dance, styles and fashion, modes of living, relationships, and even in politics and economics. Gay churches; gay legal and counseling programs; separate gay information centers; bookstores; libraries; academic and professional caucuses and societies; organized gay sporting events and rodeos; gay businesses such as travel agencies, restaurants, baths, bars, and guest-houses; and gay business guilds have all arisen in recent years. These wield increasing economic and political influence, all made possible by a distinct gay market. Recognized minority status is being achieved, albeit slowly, through movements to include homosexuals in various antidiscrimination and human rights ordinances, as well as through extension of legal protection to homosexuals at all legal levels.

Altman also looks at homosexuality from a cross-cultural perspective, along with discussions of gender and sex roles, and the distinction between homosexual behavior and identity. He presents an analysis of homophobia as a result of repressed homosexual desire, and he deals with the formation of gay tribalism as a product of advanced urban society.

The economic, political, and cultural impact of this new homosexual identity on America, and therefore on the world, follows in the second half of the book. Altman's thesis is that the recognition of group identity allows minorities to influence the larger culture, and that consumer capitalism allows for the opportunity for unprecedented varieties of lifestyles. Altman concludes by predicting that the minority status of homosexuals will gain strength, that gay contributions to society will have increasingly greater impact, and that sexuality will continue to remain a political battleground. (NW)

PR,IL
458. Bell, Alan P., and Martin S. Weinberg. **Homosexualities: A Study of Diversity Among Men and Women.** New York: Simon & Schuster, 1978. 505 p. Includes bibliography and index. ISBN 0-671-24212-1.

Commissioned by the National Institute of Mental Health, this volume, an official publication of the Institute for Sex Research, contains the most comprehensive study of homosexuality since Kinsey. On the basis of face-to-face interviews with nearly 1,500 people, two-thirds black and white men and one-third black and white women over a period of ten years, Bell and Weinberg's work will have a lasting impact on our society's changing views of homosexuality.

The bulk of the text deals with three areas, each investigated in depth: (1) the dimensions of sexual experience, including homosexual behaviors and feelings as they relate to the Kinsey scale, levels of sexual interest, activity and overtness, the incidence of cruising, sexual and affectional partnerships, sexual techniques and problems, degrees of self-acceptance, and a five-category typology of sexual experience; (2) social adjustments of homosexuals as indicated by job and career issues, religious, political, and social activities, incidence of marriages and friendships, and an exploration of social difficulties; and (3) psychological adjustments of homosexuals as measured by such factors as general health, happiness, psychosomatic symptoms, and self-acceptance, loneliness, tension, depression, exuberance, and others.

Bell and Weinberg suggest that their findings concerning the widely diverse homosexual population should be used by legislators involved in decriminalization of homosexual behavior, by community leaders dealing with civil rights issues of gays, by personnel heads in government and business, and by sex educators, clergy, and counselors. "The present investigation amply demonstrates that relatively few homosexual men and women conform to the hideous stereotypes most people have of them." "Homosexuality is not necessarily related to pathology." They hope that their work will help eliminate bigotry against homosexuals based on fear and ignorance, and that this will be replaced by respect and appreciation for homosexuals. (NW)

PR
459.   Bell, Alan P., Martin S. Weinberg, and Sue Kiefer Hammersmith. **Sexual Preference: Its Development in Men and Women.** Bloomington, Ind.: Indiana University Press, 1981. 242 p. Supplementary 321-page volume, *Statistical Appendix*, published separately in 1981. Includes bibliography. ISBN 0-253-16673-X; 0-253-16674-8 supp.

This study is the culmination of a series of books including *Homosexuality: An Annotated Bibliography* and *Homosexualities: A Study of Diversity Among Men and Women*. The object of *Sexual Preference* is to chart the development of sexual orientation among males and females while statistically challenging the accepted theories concerning the "cause" of homosexuality. In face-to-face interviews with around 1,500 individuals the researchers have sought to relate adult sexual preference to many different variables, primarily those having to do with familial constellations (mother-son relationships, father-daughter relationships) and adolescent-peer relationships.

Among the authors' conclusions are the fact that parents are not responsible for the sexual orientation of their children, nor are societal influences such as rape or seduction, or name-calling or bad experiences with the opposite sex. The evidence points rather to a (possibly biological) correlation between very early gender identification and later adult sexuality. The authors state, "Boys and girls who do not conform to stereotypical notions of what it means to be male or female are more likely to become homosexual" (p. 221). Furthermore, change or reversal of orientation for either homosexuals or heterosexuals is virtually out of the question. Finally, they conclude that it is possible for homosexuals to enjoy mature, constructive, and rewarding lives; they express the hope that homosexuals will be regarded in the light of scientific facts, and not on the basis of prejudice or moralism, since homosexuality is neither a willed choice nor is it per se pathological. (NW)

PR,IL
459a.   Bérubé, Allan. **Coming Out Under Fire: The History of Gay Men and Women in World War Two.** New York: Free Press, 1990. 377 p. Includes bibliographic notes and index. ISBN 0-02-903100-1.

Writer and lecturer Bérubé recounts in this meticulously documented study the story of gay and lesbian GIs in World War II. Sixteen million GIs served in the war; it is estimated that from 650,000 to 1.5 million males were homosexual. Based on letters between GIs, interviews with seventy-one gay men and lesbians, and declassified archival documents, the study (1) shows how the military mobilization for war forced soldiers to confront their homosexuality and (2) reconstructs "the rich social and personal lives of gay GIs during the war" (p. xi). Under the peacetime mobilization of 1940-1941, the armed forces, believing that certain groups would make poor soldiers, excluded women, blacks in the Marines and Army Air Corps, and homosexuals. Bérubé recalls that after the Revolutionary War individuals in the Army and Navy were criminalized for acts of sodomy, but in World War II "the concept of the homosexual as a personality type unfit for military service and combat" was introduced. This policy shift from the act of sodomy to the individual had far-reaching consequences. But after Pearl Harbor on December 7, 1941, the pressure to mobilize great numbers of men made it difficult to identify and disqualify all homosexual inductees.

During the 1930s and 1940s gay men and women had difficulty coming out; but in World War II many had to confront their homosexuality and adjust to the military's expanded antihomosexual policies. When identified, gays and lesbians were given undesirable discharges. Their reactions was to fight with the military over gay rights, justice, and the upgrading of discharges.

Bérubé describes how gay and lesbian GIs survived the screening process during induction. They adjusted and adapted to military life in various ways: forming buddy systems; learning and using a special lingo and body language; developing a live-and-let-live attitude toward others; adopting useful roles for coping with barracks life; banding together in cliques; taking jobs as male typists, stenographers, chaplain's assistants, hospital corpsmen, male nurses; performing in male shows to entertain themselves. Complementing the USO shows, which utilized well-known entertainers, GIs in drag were a big hit throughout the war. Off-base, life for gay GIs explored the intimacy of civilian parties and the public world of commercial bars, nightclubs, and bathhouses.

Bérubé examines the conflicts among psychiatrists and the military over homosexuality and how to cope with it. At one point they decided that it was a mental illness deserving discharge rather than imprisonment. Most homosexual GIs fulfilled their military service undetected and honorably; others were identified, tried, and imprisoned. They subsequently received undesirable, "blue discharges," making it difficult to adjust to civilian life.

Bérubé also discusses homosexual behavior in combat; the realization on the part of homosexuals that they were fighting two wars—one against the enemy, the other against military policy that was determined to give them "blue discharges"; the postwar struggle for gay and lesbian rights in the peacetime economy; the response of the nation and its people to changes in the attitudes of homosexuals after the war; and the acknowledgment that homosexuals are a definable minority coping openly with a variety of abiding problems. (TJW)

PR,IL
460. Bieber, Irving, et al. **Homosexuality: A Psychoanalytic Study.** New York: Random House, 1962. 358 p. Includes bibliography and index.
This work represents an important phase in the scientific investigation of homosexuality. Begun in 1952 and lasting nine years, this systematic study of 106 male homosexuals and 100 male heterosexuals was undertaken by a research committee consisting of eight psychoanalysts and one clinical psychologist, chaired by Bieber. The heterosexual group was used as a comparison sample; both groups were receiving psychoanalytic treatment and were white, middle-class, and resided in the New York City area.
The first chapter, "Concepts of Male Homosexuality," reviews briefly the various theories propounded by Sigmund Freud, Karen Horney, Harry Stack Sullivan, and others.

In chapter 2, "Chronology and Methodology," the authors explain their aim of going beyond the narrow and flawed confines of the case history method used by previous researchers, to use, instead, a significantly large sample to perform a statistical study using questionnaires.

The researchers qualify the limitations of their approach, namely that it does not test the association of controlled variables and that the variables are selected for most probable relevance, allowing the testing of some current psychoanalytic hypotheses. They disclaim any à priori convictions, except that fathers are hostile to their homosexual sons (borne out in the findings). The investigators also divulge their unanimous theoretical bias that minimizes attention in the study to a hereditary, chemical, or organic-genetic etiology of homosexuality. "We assumed that the dominant sexual pattern of the adult is the adaptive consequence of life experiences interpenetrating with a basic biological tendency toward heterosexuality." Topics covered by an extensive series of questionnaires (filled out by psychoanalysts) include patients' sexual experiences, relations with various family members and with women outside of the family, homosexual practices, adaptational responses, psychosomatic disorders, and attitudes regarding treatment.

The remaining chapters explicate findings of different sections of the questionnaires: "Mother-Son Relationship," "Father-Son Relationship," "Siblings," "The Triangular System," "Developmental Aspects of the Prehomosexual Child," "Homosexuality in Adolescence," "The Sexual Adaptation of the Male Homosexual," " 'Latent' Homosexuality," "The Results of Treatment." The final chapter summarizes the overall conclusions reached from the study. The questionnaire is reproduced in the appendix.

Under "Conclusions," the authors state that "the study provides convincing support for a fundamental contribution by [Sandor] Rado on the subject of male homosexuality: a homosexual adaptation is a result of 'hidden but incapacitating fears of the opposite sex.' " The role of the parents in the homosexual outcome is emphasized throughout the study, with various types of disturbed parent-child relationships that promote these fears of heterosexuality being described. Differing with Kinsey, Ford, Beach, and others, the Bieber team concludes that homosexuality, as a fear-induced adaptation, is "necessarily pathologic" and not a variant of normal sexual behavior or genetically caused. (EBS)

PR
461. Blackwood, Evelyn, ed. **The Many Faces of Homosexuality: Anthropological Approaches to Homosexual Behavior.** New York: Harrington Park Press, 1986. 217 p. Includes bibliographies and index. ISBN 0-918393-20-5.

As Joseph Carrier comments in the foreword, "Few anthropologists to date have had the courage to study human sexual behavior in other cultures as a major focus of their research; even fewer have had the courage to study highly stigmatized homosexual behavior" (p. xii). Each of the thirteen articles in this collection is based on empirical data gathered in the field by the contributor. Not only does this collection represent some of the past decade's best anthropological research on homosexuality but it is also the first collection of articles dealing with homosexual behavior in different culture areas.

Editor Blackwood's article, "Breaking the Mirror: The Construction of Lesbianism and the Anthropological Discourse on Homosexuality," points out that anthropology has not developed an adequate theory about the cultural construction of homosexual behavior, partly because the discipline has focused on male homosexual behavior to the exclusion of female homosexual behavior and partly because little cross-cultural research has been done to highlight the larger cultural context that shapes the behavior. Barry Adam contributes to the definition of social contexts that channel homosexuality in "Age, Structure, and Sexuality: Reflections on the Anthropological Evidence on Homosexual Relations." He argues that same-sex eroticism is a predictable outcome of particular combinations of age, gender, and kinship. In "The Hijras of India: Cultural and Individual Dimensions of an Institutionalized Third Gender Role," Serena Nanda explores the institutionalized third gender role in India—the role of the Hijras, who contain elements of both male and female but are not defined as either. J. Patrick Gray investigates the domains of meaning associated with Kimam ritualized homosexual behavior in terms of rituals and ceremonies that relate to successful control of fertility in his article "Growing Yams and Men: An Interpretation of Kimam Male Ritualized Homosexual Behavior." Andrea Sankar examines the ways in which members of a sisterhood in Hong Kong structure their relationships in "Sisters and Brothers, Lovers and Enemies: Marriage Resistance in Southern Kwangtung," while Denyse Lockard defines the U.S. lesbian community in her article "The Lesbian Community: An Anthropological Approach." Institutionalized friendship among adolescent girls and young women in South Africa is Judith Gay's theme in "Mummies and Babies and Friends and Lovers in Lesotho." The next three articles deal with homosexuality in Central and South America. Clark Taylor uses game theory to show how homosexual interaction problems in Mexico are dealt with in heterogeneous situations in "Mexican Male Homosexual Interaction in Public Contexts"; Peter Fry examines the relationship between Afro-Brazilian possession cults and male homosexuality in "Male Homosexuality and Spirit Possession in Brazil"; and Richard Parker builds on Fry's analysis by suggesting how these cultural domains relate to the wider context of sexual meanings in Brazil in "Masculinity, Femininity, and Homosexuality: On the Anthropological Interpretation of Sexual Meanings in Brazil." The final three articles relate to gender-mixing statuses, particularly the berdache. Charles Callender and Lee M. Kochems explain that gender mixing statuses should not be equated with homosexuality in "Men and Not-Men: Male Gender-Mixing Statuses and Homosexuality." In "Why Was the Berdache Ridiculed?" David F. Greenberg disputes the idea that berdaches were laughed at because of negative views about homosexuality; rather, they were laughed at in the context of traditional joking relationships. Finally, Walter L. Williams, in "Persistence and Change in the Berdache Tradition Among Contemporary Lakota Indians," discusses the continuation of the berdache tradition among the Lakota, pointing out that the role entails more sexual contact with men than had been previously thought.

Overall, the contributors emphasize the importance of cultural context in understanding both male and female homosexual behavior. As John DeCecco says in the preface, the volume may "help stem the tide of biological reductionism by showing the many cultural faces of homosexuality" (p. ix). (SGF)

PR,IL

462. Boswell, John. **Christianity, Social Tolerance, and Homosexuality: Gay People in Western Europe from the Beginning of the Christian Era to the Fourteenth Century.** Chicago: University of Chicago Press, 1980. 424 p. Includes bibliography and index. ISBN 0-226-06710-6.

This scholarly study, by a professor of history at Yale University, examines European attitudes toward gay people from the Roman Empire through the High Middle Ages. Neither ancient Rome nor early Christianity appears to have stigmatized homosexual behavior. Boswell examines biblical texts and early Christian writings for allegedly anti-homosexual injunctions—and finds none. During the disintegration of the Roman state, however, hostility toward gays became manifest, but from civil authorities rather than the church. During the early Middle Ages a gay subculture was tolerated, and by the eleventh century gays were prominent at many levels of society in Europe. But during the latter half of the twelfth century, hostility toward gays and homosexuality again reappeared as part of a rise of general intolerance throughout Western society. Embedded in theological, moral, and legal complications of the later Middle Ages, this hostility influenced Western thought for centuries to come. In appendix I, Boswell discusses lexicographic problems connected with St. Paul's epistles; appendix II contains texts and translations of key works. An "Index of Greek Terms" facilitates the reading of the text. (**Men's Studies**, 1985)

PR,IL
463. Comstock, Gary David. **Violence Against Lesbians and Gay Men.** New York: Columbia University Press, 1991. 319 p. (Between Men—Between Women). Includes bibliography and index. ISBN 0-231-07330-5.

This is the first book to study the social problem of anti-gay/lesbian violence. Beginning with a historical overview of such violence from 1945 to the late 1970s, Comstock documents the emergence of lesbian/gay neighborhoods in major U.S. cities after World War II and describes how the increased visibility of lesbians and gay men was followed by physical attacks that were illegal but socially sanctioned.

He then presents results from his 1986 national survey of lesbians and gay men by detailing the frequency and types of physical assaults, incidents of murder, and settings in which these incidents occur, and he compares his data with national crime statistics. He also studies the perpetrators by using information supplied by his survey participants as well as reports from the media, court records, personal interviews, and the statements of school officials, police officers, and district attorneys.

Comstock then proposes a sociological explanation for the fact that adolescent males are most prone to perpetrate violence against lesbian/gay people. Within a patriarchal socioeconomic system, he suggests, the lower status assigned to adolescent men is offset by permission and encouragement to demonstrate physically their power over those who occupy even lower rungs of the ladder. Lacking the universal patriarchal privilege of "owning" a wife, and being denied access to meaningful employment, young men may attack lesbians and gay men.

Comstock concludes by finding similar compensatory violence expressed within Judeo-Christian scripture. The only explicit prescription of physical punishment for homosexual activity is promulgated by a ruling class in Israel that has fallen and been granted some measure of autonomy by a dominant Persian empire. Although this prescription has been used in the Christian West to influence public policy against lesbians and gay men, an examination of the social and political context in which it took shape reveals its shortcomings in contributing to a Judeo-Christian ethical norm of responding to and transforming suffering. (Author)

(N.B. Gary David Comstock is the University Protestant Chaplain and Visiting Assistant Professor of Religion at Wesleyan University, Middletown, Connecticut.)

PR,IL
464. D'Emilio, John. **Sexual Politics, Sexual Communities: The Making of a Homosexual Minority in the United States, 1940-1970.** Chicago: University of Chicago Press, 1983. 257 p. Includes bibliographic footnotes and index. ISBN 0-226-14265-5.

This scholarly and readable study portrays the forces and events in America between 1940 and 1970 that led to gay liberation. In the opening chapter, D'Emilio surveys homosexuality in America from its beginnings to the 1930s; in later chapters he provides more detailed accounts of homosexual awareness during World War II, the formation of gay urban cultures, the crackdown on gays during the McCarthy period, and the uneven fortunes of gay organizations like the Mattachine Society. During the 1960s, important legal decisions coincided with the rise of gay activism on both the East and West coasts, culminating in the Stonewall riots of 1969. In a concluding chapter, D'Emilio, a professor of history at the University of North Carolina, surveys the post-Stonewall scene. (**Men's Studies**, 1985)

PR,IL
465. Dover, Kenneth J. **Greek Homosexuality.** New York: Vintage Books/Random House, 1980. 244 p. Originally published by Harvard University Press in 1978. Includes bibliography and index. ISBN 0-394-74224-9.

Hailed as a landmark study, this work by British classical scholar Dover, covers homosexual behavior manifested in Greek art and literature between the eighth and second centuries B.C. Homosexuality in much of ancient Greece was overt and unrepressed, accepted as a normal facet of sexuality (in fact, the Greek vocabulary made no distinction between homosexuality and heterosexuality).

The first section, "Problems, Sources and Methods," discusses the status and nature of homosexuality in Greek society. Dover admits that scholarship is unable to explain the how, when, and why of the emergence of homosexuality as a conspicuous feature of Greek culture. Summarized are the main sources of scholarly information on Greek homosexuality: the visual arts (chiefly vase paintings depicting homosexual scenes), literature—poetry and plays (particularly the comedies of Aristophanes), a courtroom speech, and the dialogues of Plato.

Section 2, "The Prosecution of Timarkhos," examines a unique piece of documentation, a speech made by a prosecutor at the trial of Timarkhos, a politician accused of once having prostituted himself homosexually. The speech is a rich revelation of Athenian mores, which Dover carefully dissects within the Greek legalistic framework of hubris and legitimate/nonlegitimate eros.

The next section, "Special Aspects and Developments," contains a large selection of photographs of vases whose scenes of varying degrees of explicitness Dover explicates and related to such aspects of homosexuality as courtship, domination and submission, and copulation.

The remainder of the book deals with the treatment of homosexuality in various poems, plays, and philosophical discourses. The matter of female homosexuality is also discussed, although very little on the subject is mentioned in the extant literature and art of the Hellenistic world, an exception being in the works of the female poet Sappho.

Dover believes that the sentiment "It's impossible to understand how the Greeks could have tolerated homosexuality" is one "of a culture which has inherited a religious prohibition of homosexuality. . . . The Greeks neither inherited nor developed a belief that a divine power had revealed to mankind a code of laws for the regulation of sexual behaviour; they had no religious institution possessed of the authority to enforce sexual prohibitions" (p. 203). Consequently, they "felt free to select, adapt, develop and—above all—innovate." A comprehensive appendix contains a list of vases mentioned in the book, a bibliography, an index of Greek texts and documents, an index of Greek words, and a general index. (EBS)

IL
466.   Duberman, Martin Bauml, Martha Vicinus, and George Chauncey, Jr., eds. **Hidden from History: Reclaiming the Gay and Lesbian Past.** New York: New American Library, 1989. 579 p. Includes bibliographic notes.

Four years in the making, *Hidden from History* is a collection of twenty-nine papers intended to fill gaps in the history of homosexuality, both gay and lesbian. Written by some of the foremost writers and scholars of our day, the essays are arranged chronologically under broad headings: "The Ancient World," "Preindustrial Societies," "The Nineteenth Century," "Early Twentieth Century," and "World War II and the Postwar Era."

The editors claim that the outpouring of scholarship on the gay and lesbian past may be attributed to (1) a more tolerant climate for this kind of historical research than before and (2) the belated acceptance by historians generally of the legitimacy of the social history approach in this area. Contributions include essays by John Boswell, David Halperin, Judith Brown, James Saslow, Martin Duberman, Jeffrey Weeks, Carroll Smith-Rosenberg, Erwin Haeberle, John D'Emilio, and others.

Since homosexuality until recently has been neglected, even suppressed, as a field for legitimate research, the editors, in their selection of papers, have made a conscious effort to provide a broad perspective through time and place. About one-third of the material pertains to the lesbian past, a number of papers are histories of homosexuality in Third World societies, several papers deal biographically with respected historical figures, others delve into the history of homosexual repression and resistance in different countries, and still others are the result of oral history research "to recuperate the lives of those who left few written documents."

The proposition that gay identity and gay people can be found throughout history, as proposed by John Boswell, receives criticism from Jeffrey Weeks and Jonathan Katz, who argue that "sexual categories and identities are socially constructed and historically specific."

Other subjects treated in this volume include arguments about the appearance of "the homosexual" in history, some focusing on the early eighteenth century, others the end of the nineteenth century; homosexuality in both industrial and nonindustrial societies; and the study of homosexuality in such places as the South African gold mines; the lesbian community in Buffalo, New York; Cuba; and San Francisco.

The editors contend that "gay people's hunger for knowledge of their past is strong," and hope that their compilation will contribute to the reclamation of the homosexual past. (TJW)

PR
467. Friedman, Richard. **Male Homosexuality: A Contemporary Psychoanalytic Perspective.** With a foreword by Roger A. MacKinnon. New Haven, Conn.: Yale University Press, 1988. 296 p. Includes bibliography and index. ISBN 0-300-03963-8.

Friedman's study is a four-part comprehensive, psychoanalytical examination of male homosexuality. In part 1, "Biopsychosocial Research and Male Homosexuality," Friedman presents and examines the biological literature concerning homosexuality, including studies of twins, childhood gender identity, and a review of Freudian interpretations. The next section, "Psychopathology and Sexual Orientation in Males," examines the relationships between psychopathology and male sexual orientation. Case studies are introduced while studying ego and superego and their effects on the total mental state of a person. Part 3, "Developmental Considerations," discusses the onset of gender role identity and the development of defined sexual orientation as well as the initial aspects of erotic life. The final section is dedicated to theoretical issues, that evolve into a holistic approach that might seem controversial to some readers.

Friedman's thesis states that differentiation in sexual gender identification between homosexuals and heterosexuals differs in content but not in process. Exclusivity of sexual orientation does not presuppose unconscious tendencies in the opposite direction. Friedman questions the earlier beliefs that passivity is the same as femininity and equal to homosexual behavior, and that homoerotic imagery symbolizes damage to the male and his self-esteem. (JPC)

PR
468. Gonsiorek, John C., and James D. Weinrich, eds. **Homosexuality: Research Implications for Public Policy.** Newbury Park, Calif.: Sage Publications, 1991. 295 p. Includes bibliography and index. ISBN 0-8039-3764-4.

This volume is a revision of the 1982 book *Homosexuality: Social, Psychological, and Biological Issues*, the goal of which was to summarize scientific knowledge about homosexuality up to that time. In response to the burgeoning research and theory on homosexuality in the 1980s, Gonsiorek and Weinrich once again sought the sponsorship of the American Psychological Association's Society for the Psychological Study of Social Issues to produce this book, that attempts to summarize "what science knows about homosexuality and its relevance for public policy" (p. ix). Rather than attempting to span all of the topics that relate to homosexuality as a social issue, Gonsiorek and Weinrich chose to focus on topics crucial for the general public's understanding of information presented in public policy debates about homosexuality. They believe that a scholarly explanation of what science knows about these topics can clarify the "ignorance, distortion, and prejudice" that often characterize these debates.

The first four chapters ("The Definition and Scope of Sexual Orientation" by Gonsiorek and Weinrich; "Homosexuality, Nature, and Biology: Is Homosexuality Natural? Does It Matter?" by John A. W. Kirsch and Weinrich; "Masculinity and Femininity in Homosexuality: Inversion Revisited" by Richard C. Pillard; "Strange

Customs, Familiar Lives: Homosexualities in Other Cultures") deal with the nature and causes of sexual orientation. The next two chapters ("Stigma, Prejudice, and Violence Against Lesbians and Gay Men" by Gregory M. Herek and "Sexual Orientation and the Law" by Rhonda R. Rivera) examine the types and effects of social and legal discrimination against lesbians and gays. "Psychological and Medical Treatments of Homosexuality" by Charles Silverstein, "The Empirical Basis for the Demise of the Illness Model of Homosexuality" by Gonsiorek, "Constructionism and Morality in Therapy for Homosexuality" by Gerald C. Davison, and "Sexual Orientation Conversion Therapy for Gay Men and Lesbians: A Scientific Examination" by Douglas C. Haldeman consider the reasons why homosexuality is not a mental illness and the ethics of mental health approaches to therapy for homosexuality. "Homosexual Identity: Coming Out and Other Developmental Events" by Gonsiorek and James R. Rudolph, "Lesbian and Gay Relationships" by Letita Anne Peplau, and "Lesbian Mothers and Gay Fathers" by G. Dorsey Green and Frederick W. Bozett discuss homosexuality within the contexts of the normal developmental cycle, relationships, and the family. The concluding chapters ("Partner Notification as an Instrument for HIV Control" by Edmund F. Dejowski, Lidia Dengelegi, Stephen Crystal, and Pearl Beck, and "AIDS Prevention and Public Policy: The Experience of Gay Males" by Gonsiorek and Michael Shernoff) deal with the implications of AIDS for the homosexual community.

Editor Gonsiorek notes some basic themes that run through the chapters: (1) scientists have been biased in their attempts to understand homosexuality; (2) homosexuals and heterosexuals are alike in many ways; (3) cross-cultural research can elucidate ethnocentric assumptions and document the wide range of human behavior; and (4) multidisciplinary approaches are valuable. He concludes, "Homosexuality is as biologically natural as heterosexuality . . . [and] sexual orientation . . . is not merely a culturally constructed artifact but an enduring aspect of humanity" (p. 246). (SGF)

PR,IL
469.   Great Britain. Committee on Homosexual Offenses and Prostitution. **The Wolfenden Report: Report of the Committee on Homosexual Offences and Prostitution.** Authorized American ed. Introduction by Karl Menninger, M.D. New York: Stein and Day, 1963. 243 p.

In August 1954 Parliament appointed the Committee on Homosexual Offences and Prostitution to consider the law and practice relating to homosexual offenses and prostitution in England, Scotland, and Wales and to report what changes, if any, were desirable. The committee met in private for sixty-two days, thirty-two of which were devoted to hearing witnesses representing such diverse fields as law enforcement, penology, medicine, psychiatry, psychology, religion, government, and public welfare. It took as its primary duty the consideration of "the extent to which homosexual behavior and female prostitution should come under the condemnation of the criminal law." The committee's report, named after its chair, Sir John Wolfenden, is divided into four parts. Part 1, "Introductory," is concerned with the committee's procedures and approach to the problems. Part 2, "Homosexual Offenses," is about homosexuality generally, the extent of the issues and the lack of statistical information, the present law and practice, the treatment of offenders, preventive measures, and the need for research. Part 3, "Prostitution," is concerned with street offenses; living on the earnings of prostitutes; premises used for the purposes of prostitution; procuration; and refreshment houses, aliens, and the punishment of offenses. Part 4 consists of the "Summary of Recommendations" and "Reservations" on the part of certain committee members. Key recommendations of the committee in regard to homosexuality were (1) that homosexual behavior between consenting adults in private be no longer a criminal offense; (2) that buggery (sodomy), previously classified as a felony, be reclassified as a misdemeanor; (3) that male persons charged with importuning for immoral purposes be entitled to claim trial by jury; and (4) that research be instituted into the etiology of homosexuality and the effects of various forms of treatment. The committee's deliberations in regard to prostitution concerned the fact that the law "should confine itself to those activities which offend against public order and decency or expose the ordinary citizen to what is offensive or injurious" (p. 143). Consequently, the recommendations of the committee were primarily limited to matters of annoyance, solicitation, premises used for prostitution, and procuring. It also recommended that research be instituted into the etiology of prostitution. The Wolfenden Report was completed on August 12, 1957. Recommendations made by the Wolfenden Report were made British law in 1967 by the Sexual Offences Act. (TJW)

PR,IL
470. Green, Richard. **The "Sissy Boy Syndrome" and the Development of Homosexuality.** New Haven, Conn.: Yale University Press, 1987. 416 p. Includes bibliography and index. ISBN 0-300-03696-5.

Green's book represents a fifteen-year study of two behavior groups, each consisting of sixty-six boys, one group described as "feminine boys" and the other as "masculine boys." The results are contrasted in an attempt to gain a better understanding of fundamental sexual identity. The purpose of the study is to determine why some boys demonstrate cross-gender behavior and others do not, and to understand the relationship of early gender-based behavior to adult sexuality. Studying the boys from age four to nineteen, Green investigates the "feminine boys" desires to be female; preferences for toys, playmates, and behavior traditionally considered female; and aversion to sports. Green's methodology includes detailed conversations with the boys and their parents (singularly and together), behavior observation, psychological testing, and interviews with some of the boys as young men concerning their sexual histories and preferences.

Green analyzes his findings and prepares a synopsis of earlier relevant studies. Three-quarters of the "feminine boys" interviewed as young men acknowledged gay or bisexual desires, whereas only one of the "masculine boys" turned out to be gay. Green warns against drawing simple, direct conclusions from his study, and identifies other important, complementary variables revealed by his study concerning the development of sexuality. (JPC)

PR,IL
471. Greenberg, David F. **The Construction of Homosexuality.** Chicago: University of Chicago Press, 1988. 635 p. Includes bibliography and index. ISBN 0-226-30627-5.

This massive tome studies various conceptions of homosexuality and the responses to these conceptions in various cultures in different historical periods. The study extends *labeling theory*, that is, a shift from focusing on the reasons for specific behaviors to the reasons for societal disapproval of specific behaviors, into the realm of sexuality. It examines why some societies are hostile to homosexuality, while others tolerate, approve, and even institutionalize it. Greenberg is also concerned with the conceptualization of homosexuality, that is, differing views of sexual typologies, images, and changing definitions.

This study suggests that the contemporary advances of the gay movement have allowed such a study to take place. Greenberg discusses the role of *moral entrepreneurs* as agents attempting to change public perceptions of a moral concern, often resulting in defining groups with different moral values as *deviant*. Homosexual prohibitions are quite different since they are represented in all classes, races, nationalities, and other groups. The discussion is further complicated by the fact that not all societies have recognized homosexuals as a distinct social group. Thus conventional social strategies inadequately address the question of homosexuality. Greenberg's study attempts to outline the social history of homosexuality by examining the fundamental beliefs of sexuality in the daily lives of societal members and the in-place concepts and structures used by societies to interpret these experiences, given that ideologies must seem compatible with the already accepted beliefs of a given society. Results are never static, because sexual socialization is constantly changing with the evolution of social structures and ideological change.

The study is divided into two broad sections. The first, "Before Homosexuality," begins with an examination of transgenerational, transgenderal, and egalitarian homosexuality in kinship societies; and homosexuality in archaic, early, and feudal civilizations. The study encompasses surveys of dozens of civilizations from the Zuni to the Kaluli, from ancient China to the ancient Celts. In all these studies, Greenberg examines reports from outside visitors, legal codes, literature, artistic representations, religious writings, and mythologies, in an attempt to reveal the forms homosexuality took and the responses, negative and positive, it generated in early societies. Part 2, "The Construction of Modern Homosexuality," begins with the appearance of homosexual subcultures in Renaissance Europe and continues to the modern period. Greenberg examines efforts of repression, the enforcement of laws, the effects of the Reformation and the Counter-Reformation, market economies, and the emergence of modern science and governmental bureaucracies on homosexuality. The study ends with a discussion of gay liberation and the appearance of AIDS.

This study is truly encyclopedic, the bibliography alone covers 113 pages, but Greenberg cautions readers that his work is intended as a sociological investigation and not a historical text. Greenberg is a professor of sociology at New York University and holds a Ph.D. in physics. (JPC)

IL
472. Herdt, Gilbert, ed. **Gay Culture in America: Essays from the Field.** Boston: Beacon Press, 1992. 255 p. Includes bibliographic notes. ISBN 0-8070-7914-6.

This collection of essays focuses on the study of "the legitimacy of the gay experience and the authenticity of gay culture." The studies are developed from a social scientist's point of view. In their "Introduction: Culture, History, and the Life Course of Gay Men," Herdt and Andrew Boxer set the stage for the essays by preparing a review of the emergence of gay culture in America from the 1960s to the present.

Herdt's " 'Coming Out' as a Rite of Passage: A Chicago Study" examines the anthropological significance of self-declared homosexuality by reviewing earlier literature on the topic and studying a group of 200 gay and lesbian adolescent members of the Horizon coming-out groups in Northside Chicago. Martin P. Levine's "The Life and Death of Gay Clones" studies the socialization of gay men as it compares and contrasts with society at large. This constructionist study focuses on the "gay clone" as a dominant social type that emerged in urban American gay ghettos during the 1970s, symbolizing the liberated gay male. Data were gathered in New York City's West Village, from which Levine examines social context, sociocultural organizations, and the significant effects of the advent of AIDS on this social type. "The Pursuit of the Wish: An Anthropological Perspective on Gay Male Subculture in Los Angeles," by E. Michael Gorman, inspects the development of the gay community in Los Angeles, its movement away from a persistent preoccupation with eternalizing youth to a more politically participatory community of significant economic force, expanding in demographic and cultural diversity. Stephen O. Murray surveys the "Components of Gay Community in San Francisco," including sociocultural characteristics, education, migration, education, and identity. Murray concludes that gay migrations to San Francisco do not necessarily imply downward economic and employment mobility. The study does recognize differences in perceptions of gay culture in different ethnic and age groups.

John L. Peterson's "Black Men and Their Same-Sex Desires and Behaviors" acknowledges the lacuna of research conducted concerning black gay men. This introductory study discusses identity, behavior, dual identities (black versus gay), and relationships in the African-American gay community. Frederick R. Lynch's four-year study examines suburban California gay men in "Nonghetto Gays: An Ethnography of Suburban Homosexuals." Lynch confirms earlier findings that suburban homosexuals were less socially involved in the gay community and more circumspect and fearful of exposure. The study concludes that geographical selection of middle-class homosexuals is based on employment requirements rather than sexual lifestyle. Joseph Carrier describes the tragic life of one east Los Angeles gay Latino man in "Miguel—Sexual Life

History of a Gay Mexican American." Miguel's story highlights differing variables impeding social acceptance of gay identity in Latino communities, the tragic results of oppression, and the stereotyping of ethnic groups within the dominant white homosexual community. Finally, Richard K. Herrell studies the Chicago Gay and Lesbian Pride Gay Parade, basing his methodology on the semiotic poetics of Kenneth Burke. The parade is modeled after the ethnic parades also held in Chicago. Herrell shows its similarities to these other parades, but also identifies where it diverges. He compares the confrontational 1979 sexually-centered parade to the more assimilating, love-based parade of 1987 in order to reveal the parade's development. He believes that the parade will continue to communicate "the community's own unsettled and conflicting social definitions and the struggle of gays and lesbians to find a place of equality in the polity and respect in the society." (JPC)

PR,IL
473. Humphreys, Laud. **Tearoom Trade: Impersonal Sex in Public Places.** Enlarged ed. Chicago: Aldine, 1975. 238 p. (Observations). Includes bibliographic footnotes and index. ISBN 0-202-30283-0.

Roundly criticized on ethical grounds when *Tearoom Trade* was originally published in 1970, Humphreys defends his sociological methods with a "Retrospect" in the 1975 edition. Individuals objected to his voyeuristic approach to studying the sexual behavior of men in public toilets (known as tearooms) located in city parks of major U.S. cities.

Under the direction of Lee Rainwater of Harvard University, Humphreys, a sociologist and former divinity student, undertook the difficult task of researching the homosexual subculture pursuing impersonal sex in public places. In the foreword, Rainwater states that *Tearoom Trade* makes "an important contribution to our understanding of one particular form of deviant sexual behavior" and explodes the "many myths on which police moral enterprise directed toward tearooms and other homosexual gathering places is based."

According to Humphreys the homosexuals frequenting tearooms are engaged in a game of chance, a risk-taking type of action. The players seek maximum rewards in situations of minimum risk by following recognized rules of the game. Humphreys participated in the game by assuming the role of "watchqueen," a lookout who warns participants of impending danger. His position enabled him to function as a voyeur, observing the players' silent communication (gestures, facial expressions, touch signals). Over a period of time, he made 50 systematic observations involving 173 participants who engaged in the sexual act of fellatio. He was able to categorize these individuals as trade, ambisexual, gay, and closet queens. By means of a complicated, disguised, and effective procedure, he was able to gather extensive data about the lives of a special group of twelve men away from the tearooms. He discovered that 54 percent of these subjects were married and living with their wives in stable relationships. These men from different walks in life seek "instant sex" generally on the way to work in the morning or on the way home in the evening. Humphreys speculates that visits to public restrooms, apparently a widespread phenomenon on the American scene, replaces the visits to "twenty-minute" whorehouses of a former time.

In conclusion, Humphreys states that only where it constitutes an obvious public nuisance should there be a need to drive this harmless activity underground. The effort would be ineffective anyway and would be feasible only in a total police state. (TJW)

IL
474. Hyde, H. Montgomery. **The Love That Dared Not Speak Its Name: A Candid History of Homosexuality in Britain.** Boston: Little, Brown, 1970. 323 p. First published in England under the title *The Other Love*. Includes bibliography and index.

Written by a member of the British House of Commons who was influential in the creation and implementation of the Wolfenden Report (that led to the decriminalization of homosexuality in England in 1967), this book traces the incidence of homosexuality from Norman times to the present. A mixture of fact, opinion, gossip, court records, rumor, and literary allusions, this volume constitutes an "apologia" for homosexuality and the fact that it has existed and even thrived for centuries in spite of Britain's repressive legal and religious atmosphere.

Opening with a chapter on popular misconceptions regarding homosexuality, Hyde then moves to a description of the "sodomitical character of the Norman Court" and then historically forward to a discussion of the first trial for homosexual offense in England, that of the Earl of Castlehaven, that represented a shift in public opinion from homosexuality as sin to homosexuality as crime. Next comes a catalog of convictions during the Georgian era, followed by a peering look into the lives of some Victorian homosexuals. The contributions of sexology pioneers Havelock Ellis and John Addington Symonds are then set against the actual "monstrous martyrdoms" (Wilde) or witch hunts of the day. The trials of Oscar Wilde are dealt with only briefly since such material was already available, including work of Hyde himself who is a noted authority on Wilde.

The next chapter sets the scene for the next sixty years, spanning Bloomsbury and both world wars, and is followed by a discussion of the provenance and implementation of the Wolfenden Report. The book ends with an analysis of the directions that homosexuality seems to assume in modern Britain as a result of decriminalization. Hyde's plea is that homosexuality must in time "come into its own without fear and without reproach as the expression of a satisfying and socially acceptable human relationship." (NW)

PR,IL
475. Karlen, Arno. **Sexuality and Homosexuality: A New View.** New York: Norton, 1971. 666 p. Includes bibliography and index.

This book is a comprehensive overview of homosexuality from a historical, transcultural, and multidisciplinary perspective. By focusing on homosexuality as one aspect of sexual behavior, Karlen evaluates the meaning of "the sexual revolution" of the 1920s and 1960s. He dispels long-standing misconceptions about homosexuality and explores research findings that shed light on arguments such as the biological versus social causes of homosexuality and how family structure and childrearing affect sexual behavior. The book includes interviews with researchers, homosexuals, and college students to reveal a variety of attitudes, experiences, and perceptions relating to homosexuality. The first part devotes much discussion to what is known about homosexuality in the ancient world. Karlen contends that homosexuality's presence in Babylonian, Greek, and Roman civilizations was predated by other cultures in the Mediterranean world. Homosexuality in the dawn of history was often integrated in religion, as in the form of priests who were eunuchs and transvestites, and in the form of male temple prostitutes, homosexual intercourse functioning as part of the religious rites. Homosexuality was both extolled and condemned in these various cultures. Separate chapters deal with homosexuality in Greek, Roman, Judeo-Christian, and Victorian milieus. In delving into the Judeo-Christian roots of sexual morality, Karlen notes that the Jews were not the first to equate flesh with evil. The Old Testament makes only vague allusions to homosexuality. Similarly, our perceptions of homosexuality in Greek, Puritan, and Victorian times have been oversimplified and distorted. Karlen also discusses the various sociopolitical theories advanced throughout the last few centuries that explain the status of homosexuality according to the matriarchal or patriarchal orientation of the society. He dismisses these theories of Bachofen, Engels, Graves, de Beauvoir, Briffault, et al., stating that "it is difficult to believe that a value as deep as the approval or disapproval of homosexuality could change on political grounds." In discussing the modern scientific literature on homosexuality, he states flatly, "the evidence is overwhelming that genes do not cause homosexuality." Instead he embraces the etiology of a "complex, multifactor" explanation that includes chemical deficiencies and hormonal imbalances. At the same time, while he believes that "homosexuality is not a sickness," he allows in another part of the book that it "probably does originate in emotional conflict or developmental distortion." He supports the conclusions of Irving Bieber's monumental collection of psychoanalytical research that suggests psychological causation. The book explores the modern methods of treating homosexuality. Psychoanalysis has been shown to be ineffective in this regard. In a chapter on transsexuals, he notes that "there is no record of an adult transsexual being cured by psychotherapy." However, he cites claims of behaviorist therapists that show significant success rates in effecting cures of homosexuality. These claims are countered by psychoanalysts, who suspect that the "cure" deceptively means that one neurotic symptom (i.e., homosexuality) has probably been displaced by another. (EBS)

PR,IL

476. Katz, Jonathan. **Gay American History: Lesbians and Gay Men in the U.S.A.** New York: Crowell, 1976. 690 p. Includes bibliographies and index. ISBN 0-690-01164-4.

"Documents of our history, the history of Lesbians and Gay men in the United States—including related heterosexual attitudes and acts—are for the first time brought together in this anthology," announces Katz in his introduction. This book brings to the fore hundreds of letters, diaries, interviews, and legal documents previously buried in libraries and archives. Chronicled is a 400-year period of gay relationships within a landscape of conflict between homosexuals and American society as well as the struggles of the homosexual emancipation movement.

Part I, "Trouble: 1566-1966," reconstructs the repression and persecution suffered by gays, starting with the dawn of American history, exemplified by the execution of a French interpreter by the Spanish in Florida, and executions in the Virginia Colony and in New England. The unceasing string of maltreatment carries through to the 1950s and 1960s in the form of latter day witch hunts and trials for "unnatural carnal copulation." Part II, "Treatment: 1884-1974," reviews some of the varied efforts of medicine and psychology to cure or modify homosexuality, including anaphrodisiac measures, abstinence, castration, hypnosis, psychoanalysis, hormone medication, electric shock, aversion therapy, and lobotomy. Although lesbianism is given ample attention throughout the entire book, part III, "Passing Women: 1782-1920," focuses on some notable case histories of the unfairly stereotyped distaff side of homosexuality. Part IV, "Native Americans/Gay Americans: 1528-1976," sheds light on the little-known presence of homosexuality among American Indians. Although the Indian attitudes toward homosexuality varied, homosexuality was often institutionalized and respected. Part V, "Resistance: 1859-1972," documents a long but little-known tradition of gay resistance manifested in various forms: letters, poems, essays, treatises, novels, and political action groups. The final part, "Love: 1779-1932," relates cases of homosexual attraction and relationships as evidenced by letters, journals, and novels. The book contains an extensive bibliography and notes. (EBS)

IL

477. Kayal, Philip M. **Bearing Witness: Gay Men's Health Crisis and the Politics of AIDS.** Boulder, Colo.: Westview Press, 1993. 275 p. Includes bibliography and index. ISBN 0-8133-1728-2.

Bearing Witness is concerned with the sociology of AIDS, a book that views the effects of AIDS on the gay community and the resultant rise of volunteerism. The first mobilization began in the early 1980s, in New York City, with the emergence of an organization called the Gay Men's Health Crisis (GMHC), in which Kayal participated. Kayal traces the effects of AIDS on the gay community and documents and comments on the development of community services as a new phenomenon by, for, and among members of the gay community. The rise of volunteerism was in direct response to the lack of response to the epidemic by the country at large. Kayal investigates the relationship of AIDS volunteerism and the restoration of empowerment to the gay community.

The text is divided into three parts. Part 1, "AIDS: The Issues," discusses fundamental issues that have arisen due to the evolution of the AIDS epidemic in the United States. These include religion, morals, medicine, volunteerism, democratization, and minority responses. Part 2, "Ideology: Volunteerism and AIDS," focuses on the rise of volunteerism in the gay community and its educational, political, altruistic, and ideological implications. This section also investigates volunteerism and women, African-Americans, and Latinos. The final part, "The Significance of Gay/AIDS Volunteerism," measures the effects that volunteerism, focusing on GMHC, has had on the gay community and its contributions to community building, political cohesion, self-acceptance, healing, and social change. (JPC)

PR,IL
478. Lewes, Kenneth. **The Psychoanalytic Theory of Male Homosexuality.** New York: Simon & Schuster, 1988. 301 p. Includes bibliography and index. ISBN 0-671-62391-5.

Lewes is a clinical psychologist who practices psychoanalytic therapy. This book is an important historical, cultural, and theoretical account of how male homosexuality has been viewed—and sometimes misconstrued—by the psychoanalytic tradition, from Freud through the 1980s.

In this study, Lewes reveals how the original psychoanalytic ideals of understanding and compassion have been betrayed by clinicians and theorists behaving less like healers than like moralistic upholders of the status quo. Viewing Freud and his early followers in a new light, Lewes shows how they posited a surprisingly wide variety of "normal" outcomes of psychosexual development, including homosexuality. But on this issue psychoanalysis soon changed from an open-minded and humane discipline into an insular and calcified orthodoxy. And by the time of the *Kinsey Report*, as Lewes demonstrates, the psychoanalytic establishment had little interest in the fresh attempts by other disciplines to understand homosexuality and human sexuality in general.

Lewes chronicles the efforts within psychoanalysis to define homosexuality as a disease, as well as the changes in the larger society that eventually led to the decision by the American Psychiatric Association to delete homosexuality from its list of psychiatric disorders. Exposing the basis of the acrimony and alienation that have characterized the relationship between homosexuals and psychoanalysis, *Psychoanalytic Theory* is a sometimes shocking account of intolerance and hostility. But it is also the story of unexpected compassion on the part of relatively unheralded thinkers and practitioners whose contributions to psychoanalysis are achievements of the highest order.

This study explores the limits—and the possibilities—of psychoanalysis as a humane science. (Publisher permission received to use book jacket statement as an abstract.)

PR,IL
479. Licata, Salvatore J., and Robert P. Petersen, eds. **Historical Perspectives on Homosexuality.** New York: Haworth Press/Stein and Day, 1981. 224 p. (Research on Homosexuality, v. 2). Reprint of volume 6, nos. 1/2, of the *Journey of Homosexuality.* Includes bibliographic footnotes and index. ISBN 0-8128-2810-0.

Because of the stigma attached, homosexuality as a viable area of historical research has only recently become a possibility. Considered a seminal work of a new discipline, this volume comprises works by scholars who used primary and secondary sources that were collected in part by gay activist groups such as The Homosexual Information Center and the Lesbian Herstory Archives, in part from individual libraries and special collections, as well as from ecclesiastical, legal, and medical records.

Topics covered include the myth of lesbian impunity (from persecution), trial records of a lesbian execution in Germany in 1721, the connection between sodomy and heresy in Switzerland, male prostitution in Victorian England, sodomy in Stuart England and Colonial Massachusetts, stigmata and persecution of homosexuals in Nazi Germany, and the Gay Rights Movement in the United States, in addition to other areas of historical interest. Lists of accessible archives and libraries, and appropriate bibliography have been included. (NW)

PR
480. Marmor, Judd, ed. **Sexual Inversion: The Multiple Roots of Homosexuality.**
New York: Basic Books, 1965. 358 p. Includes bibliographies and index.

Divided into three parts, this collection of papers by psychologists, psychiatrists, psychoanalysts, and physiologists attempts to shed light on the psychodynamic, sociocultural, biological, and situational factors determining homosexuality.

In the biological section Rollin H. Denniston surveys ambisexuality in animals, demonstrating that homosexuality is not unique to humans; William H. Perloff shows that homosexuality is not dependent on hormones nor amenable to change by hormonal substances; and C. M. B. Pare deals with the etiology of homosexuality by examining genetic and chromosomal aspects.

In part two on the sociocultural perspective, Evelyn Hooker focuses on the "importance of both personality and social or cultural variables in producing and shaping adult patterns of male, overt homosexual behavior" (p. 84); Marvin K. Opler concentrates on anthropological and cross-cultural aspects of homosexuality; Thomas S. Szasz looks at the legal and moral aspects; Gordon Rattray Taylor reviews the historical and mythological aspects, pointing out that there is no culture from which homosexuality has not been reported; Saul H. Fisher comments on the widespread male homosexuality, especially pederasty, in ancient Greece as well as the degraded status of women.

In part three the clinical view on homosexuality is presented: Sandor Rado critically examines the concept of bisexuality; Robert J. Stoller deals with gender identity and cross-gender impulses; Lionel Ovesey considers pseudohomosexuality and homosexuality, focusing on the psychodynamics of treatment; Leon Salzman comments on the use and abuse of the expression "latent homosexuality"; Irving Bieber focuses his attention on clinical aspects of homosexuality; Cornelia B. Wilbur deals with the clinical aspects of female homosexuality; May E. Romm, lamenting that female sexuality is a neglected subject, discusses the background and problems that affect the passage from homosexuality to heterosexuality; and Peter Mayerson and Harold I. Lief present a follow-up study of nineteen cases of homosexuals undergoing psychotherapy.

In his introduction, Marmor states that "this volume presents convincing evidence that homosexuality is a potentially reversible condition" and that it contributes toward the "recognition that homosexuality is a disorder of adaptation." (TJW)

PR
481. McWhirter, David P., Stephanie A. Sanders, and June Machover Reinisch, eds. **Homosexuality/Heterosexuality: Concepts of Sexual Orientation.** New York: Oxford University Press, 1990. 423 p. (The Kinsey Institute Series). Includes bibliographic references and index. ISBN 0-19-505205-6.

This collection of twenty-two articles, produced by twenty-nine recognized professionals in the field, is intended to represent "the state of the art" at the end of the 1980s. These essays present a multidisciplinary overview of the study of sexual orientation, the variables that affect it, and assumptions that influence research findings. The text warns against dichotomous distinctions, such as homosexual/heterosexual, and unidimensional sexual orientation models, for such rigid categories do not adequately reflect the complexities of sexual orientation or the myriad of possibilities of sexual behavior. The essays investigate in depth sexual orientation, gender identity and gender roles, variable meanings for femininity and masculinity as well as cultural, contextual, biological, and sociocultural factors that contribute to sexuality.

The findings suggest that there is no single, biological or socioenvironmental cause of sexual orientation. Sexual orientation is described as multidimensional and affected by many factors. Research must concentrate on expressed behavior rather than conventional labels that misguide and skew results.

The text is divided into seven parts each addressing a particular "perspective." These perspectives include historical and religious, psychobiological, evolutionary, cultural and sociological, identity development, relational, and conceptional and theoretical. The collection is volume two of the Kinsey Institute Series. (JPC)

IL
482. McWhirter, David P., and Andrew M. Mattison. **The Male Couple: How Relationships Develop.** Englewood Cliffs, N.J.: Prentice-Hall, 1984. 341 p. Includes bibliography and index. ISBN 0-13-547661-5.

This longitudinal study of 156 couples whose relationships have lasted from one to thirty-seven years is the first empirical book-length treatment of male-male coupling. McWhirter and Mattison, a psychologist and a psychiatrist (and a couple of many years), laid the groundwork and carried out interviews over a period of eight years. Thoroughly documented, this book sheds light on the requisites for stable, long-term love relationships between men. The researchers have assigned six stages to these relationships: blending, nesting, maintaining, building, releasing, and renewing, with each stage lasting from one to several years.

Perhaps the one myth that this study explodes is that gay male relationships do not last. Close to one-third of the studied relationships were of ten years duration or longer, up to over thirty years. Among other salient findings was that the single most important factor in keeping relationships together is establishing compatibility through complementarity in the first decade, and lack of possessiveness in the second. In addition, it was found that while most gay male couples expect mutual emotional dependability, sexual exclusivity is not expected. Also, couples with the greatest longevity have the widest differences in age. The book concludes with recommendations, speculations, and possible directions for future research. (NW)

PR,IL
483. Money, John. **Gay, Straight, and In-Between: The Sexology of Erotic Orientation.** New York: Oxford University Press, 1988. 267 p. Includes bibliography, indexes, and glossary. ISBN 0-19-505407-5.

In addition to being Professor of Medical Psychology and Professor of Pediatrics at The Johns Hopkins Hospital and School of Medicine, distinguished sexologist John Money was the founder of the University's Gender Identity Clinic, founder and director of the Office of Psychohormonal Research, and the first (in 1955) to conceptualize and define "gender role" and "gender identity." Drawing on over thirty-five years of research in his clinic as well as on his extensive knowledge of history, culture, psychology, physiology, and medicine, Money evaluates many of his findings, comparing them with each other and those of other researchers, and then draws conclusions about the nature of sexual orientation, i.e., a pattern of sexual attraction and eroticism based on gender. He states that "this book is addressed to those who would like to know the present state of knowledge regarding what determines that some children grow up to become homosexual, whereas others become bisexual or heterosexual . . . it is designed to explain homosexuality to homosexuals themselves, as well as to other people, and likewise for heterosexuality and bisexuality" (p. 6). One of his major conclusions is that people develop their sexual orientation partly because of their prenatal history and partly because of their postnatal history. Each of the four major chapters discusses what influences the development and expression of sexual orientation.

Chapter 1, "Prenatal Hormones and Brain Dimorphism," is an overview of the available research on prenatal influences on sexual orientation, particularly hormonal and neurological factors. Using long-term, follow-up studies of "people born with defective sex organs" (e.g., a micropenis, a penis and scrotum instead of a vulva) Money concludes, "There is no option, no plan. . . . One either is or is not bisexual, homosexual, or heterosexual" (p. 11); it is not a matter of preference. The criteria for defining sexual orientation are the body's sexual morphology, the gender of the person's mentality, and the gender of his or her behavior, not the internal organs, gonads, or chromosomes. Heterosexuality and homosexuality derive from a primary bisexual or ambisexual potential during fetal development, but there is no evidence that prenatal hormones alone, independent of postnatal social communication and learning, determine orientation.

In chapter 2, "Gender Coding," Money discusses different kinds (e.g., sex-irreducible, sex-derivative, sex-shared) of gender coding, which is "both multivariate and sequential" and a product of both biological and social factors; "there are no absolute criteria of what is male and what is female in gender coding" (p. 120).Of major importance in gender coding are the processes of identification and complementation that shape gender differentiation during childhood. In addition, other gender differences may be encoded in the brain through the senses at critical times in postnatal life. Chapter 3, "Gender Crosscoding," considers the etiology of transsexualism, transvestism, homosexuality, and bisexuality and the degree to which they become fixed or easily changed. Money concludes that cultural factors reinforce prenatal proclivities and "are incorporated into childhood gender crosscoding when it occurs" (p. 120). The basic principle underlying sexual orientation is "developmental determinism," not nature versus nurture; it develops in stages and may have more than one cause. The most critical years for the formation of orientation are late infancy and prepubertal childhood, not puberty and adolescence. The final chapter, "Lovemaps and Paraphilia," explains how lovemaps can develop normally or become vandalized, resulting in paraphilias, regardless of sexual orientation. A forty-five-page glossary follows the text, explicating most technical terms used in the book. (SGF)

PR

484. Murray, Stephen O., ed. **Male Homosexuality in Central and South America.** New York: GAU-NY, 1987. 199 p. (Gai Saber Monograph 5). Includes bibliographies and lexicons.

The division between masculine and feminine types of behavior is basic to Latino views of sex and gender and serves as an organizing principle for the definition of homosexuality. Masculine insertors ("activos") are not regarded as homosexual whereas feminine insertees ("pasivos") are. Murray notes that the "actual flux and uncertainty of sexual expression is ignored 'by the culture' " (p. 198), and individual identity and behavior may vary quite a bit from these ideal types. This book provides three kinds of resources for identifying and assessing variations in male homosexuality in Central and South America: (1) papers on homosexuality in contemporary Latin America and among indigenous peoples in South America; (2) bibliographies of books and articles on homosexuality in Mesoamerica, Brazil, indigenous South America, and Western South America; and (3) Spanish, Portuguese, and Aymara homosexual lexicons.

Organized into two major sections, one focuses on Latin American groups and the other on those in "tribal America." In section 1, Latin America, articles relate primarily to Mexico, Brazil, Haiti, and Peru. Clark L. Taylor discusses variation in attitudes toward homosexuals in pre-Columbian and Colonial Mexico and then relates them to current attitudes about homosexuality in contemporary Mexico. In pre-Columbian Mexico, homosexuality was not only accepted in private life in many Mesoamerican cultures but also played an important role in Mexican religious life; however, ruling Aztecs and the Spaniards held similar "prudish," rigid, and repressive views toward homosexual behavior. Currently, Mexican Mestizos identify with Spanish or Aztec views but not with those of the "weak" people who seem to condone sodomy. In another article, Murray addresses the ways in which the Mesoamerican family limits the growth of a gay subculture. Because the family is a major unit of economic production and emotional support for its members, and the revelation of homosexual behavior can result in expulsion from the home, homosexually active Mesoamerican men are reluctant to admit their sexual orientation. Focusing on Brazilian homosexuality, Frederick L. Whitam describes gay life in Sao Paulo, the largest gay community in Latin America, while Manuel Arboleda G. describes social attitudes and sexual variation in Lima, Peru. Peter Fry analyzes an Afro-Brazilian possession cult in which homosexual cult leaders have high status. Murray suggests that Haitians regard homosexuality with "bemused tolerance" rather than condemnation as Ford and Beach concluded. Murray and Manuel Arboleda G. conclude the section with a discussion of the meaning of the label "gay" in Latin America.

Section 2, "Tribal America," contains papers by Murray that deal with the methods and labels used to characterize homosexuality among indigenous Latin American peoples. He discusses how ethnographers and missionaries interpreted same-sex genital contact among peoples of Upper Amazonia and the status of cross-dressing Araucanian shamans in southern South America. In another paper he notes how "experts" often ignore dubious or unexpected results in their fieldwork or publications.

Other Gai Saber Monographs assess aspects of homosexuality, including *Reflections on the American Homosexual Rights Movement* (1983) by Jim Levin; *Social Theory, Homosexual Realities* (1984) by Stephen O. Murray; *Homolexis: A Historical and Cultural Lexicon of Homosexuality* (1985) by Wayne Dynes; and *Homosexuality, Intolerance and Christianity: A Critical Examination of John Boswell's Work* (1986, 2nd edition) by Warren Johansson, Wayne Dynes, and John Lauritsen. (SGF)

PR,IL

485. Porter, Kevin, and Jeffrey Weeks, eds. **Between the Acts: Lives of Homosexual Men, 1885-1967.** London: Routledge, 1991. 153 p. Includes index. ISBN 0-415-00944-8.

"Between the acts" refers to the years between 1885 and 1967 when all forms of male homosexual behavior were illegal in Britain. The 1885 Labouchère Amendment to the Criminal Law Amendment Act, a "blackmailer's charter," made all private and public acts of homosexuality illegal—subject to criminal law. This continued until 1967 when the Sexual Offences Act excluded some homosexual activities as criminal: private acts occurring between those over age twenty-one, living in England and Wales (but excluding people in the armed services and merchant navy). This eighty-two year period "formed a crucible in which lesbian and gay identities were forged." In an atmosphere of illegality, social hostility, and prejudice, how did people with a homosexual orientation come to terms with their desires and construct their personal and social identities?

This book presents the personal stories of fifteen homosexual men, born between 1880 and 1920, who lived through this "twilight world." Unlike published biographies that deal with the lives of well-known public figures, this collection documents how ordinary men lived under very difficult circumstances. Each chapter encapsulates how males expressed their homosexuality within different social roles—soldier, teacher, priest, academician, dancer, public servant, prostitute, in London, in South Africa. In some cases the life was respectable or remodeled; in others, it was lonely, exiled. Co-editor Weeks, author of *Coming Out: Homosexual Politics in Britain from the Nineteenth Century to the Present* and *Sexuality and Its Discontents*, interviewed twenty-five older homosexual men during 1978-1979, from whose interviews fifteen were chosen for this compilation. Although the interviews are not representative of the whole range of male homosexual experience, they "present a vivid impression of male homosexual life in the earlier part of this century as it was revealed in later life by active participants" (p. viii). (SGF)

IL,PO

486. Rowse, Alfred Leslie. **Homosexuals in History: A Study of Ambivalence in Society, Literature and the Arts.** New York: Dorset Press, 1983. 346 p. Reprint of the 1977 edition published by Macmillan Publishing Company. Includes index. ISBN 0-88029-011-0.

Penetrating sketches of the lives of eminent homosexuals from the Renaissance to the present by the Oxford historian and self-proclaimed authority on Shakespeare, A. L. Rowse, are the subject of this fascinating book. Advertised by the publisher as the "first serious study of the problems and contributions of the homosexual through the ages," the work embraces men of genius who were homosexuals: philosophers and kings, artists and musicians, writers and thinkers. Confessing a lack of knowledge of lesbianism, Rowse limits himself to male homosexuals. He also eschews the ancient and medieval worlds by admitting that his expertise begins with the Renaissance. He states in the preface that his "purpose is not theoretical discussion but the more enlightening one of the study of concrete fact, the way men actually are and behave." A brief list of some of the famous male homosexuals Rowse writes so perceptively about includes Erasmus, Leonardo da Vinci, Michelangelo, Francis Bacon, Christopher Marlowe, Lord Byron,

Frederick the Great, King Ludwig II of Bavaria, Oscar Wilde, Tschaikovsky, T. E. Lawrence, Noel Coward, W. Somerset Maugham, and Yukio Mishima. Americans he writes about are Walt Whitman, Herman Melville, Nathaniel Hawthorne, and Henry James. Rowse shows that many of these individuals were sexually repressed in early life, often had dominating mothers whom they loved, and, not caring to reveal their natures to family or society, responded by creating some of the greatest works of art and literature. (TJW)

IL,PO
487. Shilts, Randy. **Conduct Unbecoming: Lesbians and Gays in the U.S. Military, Vietnam to the Persian Gulf.** New York: St. Martin's Press, 1993. 784 p. Includes bibliographic notes and index. ISBN 0-312-09261-X.

Shilts, author of the best-selling book *And the Band Played On* (1987), exposes in this monumental investigative report, the anti-gay and lesbian policies of the U.S. military from Vietnam to the Persian Gulf. By way of prologue, he examines homosexuality in the military from 1778 to 1984, revealing that the German military genius Baron Friedrich von Steuben, who trained General Washington's troops at Valley Forge in 1778 and wrote the first drill instruction manual for the army, was gay, as was Stephen Decatur, the first American naval hero, commander of the *USS United States* during the War of 1812.

Shilts moves forward to the 1950s and the impending war in Vietnam. Although medical officer Lt. Thomas Dooley, hero to the Vietnamese people who, beginning in 1954, had fled North Vietnam for the south and needed medical care, never fought the anti-gay policy of the U.S. military, he did become a symbol of all that was wrong with the military's anti-gay and lesbian policies. Despite Dooley's heroic work, the Navy, after discovering he was a homosexual, quietly gave him an "Undesirable Discharge" in March 1956. Dooley resigned from the service to achieve even greater fame by establishing a network of medical clinics throughout Southeast Asia and elsewhere. Not until 1961, when he was dying of cancer, did Dooley receive his honorable discharge.

Shilts uncovers his revelations about the treatment of gays and lesbians in the military by telling the personal stories of dozens of individuals caught up in the military purges of homosexuals starting with the Vietnam War. These accounts, threaded through the entire text of the book, inform the reader about the military's stubborn, although sometimes ambivalent, position toward gays and lesbians. Most homosexuals had to be ferreted out by such agencies as the U.S. Navy Intelligence Service. The grounds for discharge are contained in the Uniform Code of Military Justice, that forbids "conduct unbecoming an officer and a gentleman" and, according to article 125, outlaws sodomy. However, the UCMJ also forbids the military from forcing soldiers to incriminate themselves. Throughout the book Shilts details the many investigations of gays and lesbians, showing how ruthlessly the NIS and others pursued their investigations. A new anti-gay policy was achieved in January 1981 by the revision of DoD Directive 1332.14. This 123-word statement begins: "Homosexuality is incompatible with military service." Used to defend the Pentagon's policies on homosexuality, it had a devastating effect on homosexuals in the military during the 1980s.

One of the poignant stories told by Shilts is that of Bronze Star holder Tech Sergeant Leonard Matlovich, Jr., who, in 1975, challenged the military's ban on gays and, after his discharge, became an activist in gay causes until his death from AIDS in 1988. Matlovich's tombstone epigraph reads: "When I was in the military they gave me a medal for killing two men and a discharge for loving one."

Based on some 11,000 interviews plus thousands of documents obtained through the Freedom of Information Act, this book exposes the hypocrisy of the military's position on homosexuals. It also reveals the existence of a vast subculture of gays and lesbians distributed throughout the U.S. armed forces. Reading this book should remove all doubt about how the military treats gays and lesbians in all the American armed services. (TJW)

PO
488. Silverstein, Charles, and Edmund White. **The Joy of Gay Sex: An Intimate Guide for Gay Men to the Pleasures of a Gay Lifestyle.** Illustrated by Michael Leonard, Ian Beck, and Julian Graddon. New York: Simon & Schuster, 1977. 207 p. Includes bibliography and index. ISBN 0-671-24079-X.

This handbook, similar in format to *The Joy of Sex* by Alex Comfort, is a graphically illustrated reference and guide "by gays and for gays, about the gay subculture that comes equipped with its own rituals, its own agonies and ecstasies, its own argot" (p. 16).

The contents of this guide cover a wide-ranging span of subjects extending from aspects of making love (e.g., kissing, frottage, nibbling, etc.), to more general subjects of the gay lifestyle, like androgyny, bisexuality, coming out, emotional problems, friendship, married gay men, and stereotypes. The book focuses on how to have a fulfilling life as a gay man, with emphases on play, pleasure, sex technique, sensuality, and many other aspects of gay relationships.

Silverstein and White have striven to use simple, straightforward language in the construct of definitions that are significant for many gay readers as well as for the general reader and the professional. The text is supplemented by numerous clear and detailed illustrations showing men enjoying the pleasures of this lifestyle. (RL)

PR,IL
489. Tripp, Clarence A. **The Homosexual Matrix.** New York: McGraw-Hill, 1975. 314 p. Includes bibliography and index. ISBN 0-07-065201-5.

The result of ten years of work by a psychotherapist, sex researcher, and colleague of Alfred Kinsey, some consider this book to be the most influential and enlightening work on homosexuality in the modern literature. Tripp first explores the popular and historical attitudes toward sex in light of the post-1960s liberalization of sexual mores. He discusses biological considerations in sexuality and inquires into the origins of homosexuality as well as into the origins of heterosexuality. Tripp contends that sexuality develops through a matrix of positive attractions in homosexuals (as well as in heterosexuals) and not as had heretofore been believed, that is, through negative reactions to such things as fear of castration, hostile fathers, or close-binding mothers. Next he discusses homosexual sex techniques in relation to physiology, eroticized violation of taboo, situational sex, the psychology of sexual interest, and the function of resistance. He also discusses the ubiquitousness of homosexuality; the adaptive mechanisms by which homosexuals deal with the world (tribe, town, city); and the mechanisms by which some homosexuals avoid dealing with their homosexuality through denial, gender role, "personal innocence," only-for-now claims, or "special friendships." Tripp deals with the manifold variations of short- to long-term relationships. A lively discussion of the psychology of effeminacy, which does not relate to homosexuality, follows. He distinguishes among nelly, swish, queenly, and camp lifestyles.

In the politics of homosexuality Tripp summarizes the many ways that homosexuality can become politically significant, locally and even internationally. He covers such related issues as blackmail, the role of privilege, homosexuality in diplomacy and espionage, the mass media, and publishing.

The major issue in the book is the question of psychotherapy. Tripp attacks his professional colleagues who try to "cure" something for which, he thinks, there is neither need nor reason for "cure." Indeed, Tripp states that there are no cures for homosexuality. He believes that psychotherapy should direct its efforts at effecting smooth adaptation to one's discovered homosexuality. In his final analysis he views homosexuality as a fact of life, and in his opinion this is where the questions and answers ought to begin and end. (NW)

Lesbian

(For related material see also entries 111, 882)

IL
490. Brown, Judith C. **Immodest Acts: The Life of a Lesbian Nun in Renaissance Italy.** New York: Oxford University Press, 1986. 214 p. (Studies in the History of Sexuality). Includes bibliographic notes and index. ISBN 0-19-503675-1.

Drawing upon an impressive array of primary sources from the State Archives of Florence and Pisa, from the Vatican Archives, and from unpublished manuscripts, Brown has recreated the life story of Sister Benedetta Carlini, Abbess of the Theatine Convent of the Mother of God.

In a small village near Florence early in the seventeenth century, Sister Benedetta's story unfolds. Her parents sent her to a convent when she was nine. In her early twenties she began to have religious and erotic visions and subsequently suffered great physical pain. She claimed to have supernatural contacts with Christ. Some years after Sister Benedetta had been elevated to the position of Abbess at age thirty, ecclesiastical inquests, ordered because of doubts about her claims of miracles, mystical experiences, and visions, turned up allegations about her involvement in a sexual relationship with a young nun assigned to care for her in her years of illness. The narration moves quickly to reveal prophetic warnings, trances, the appearance of stigmata, a mystical marriage, apparent death, and return to life, and describes in considerable detail the series of investigations that preceded Benedetta's imprisonment for thirty-five years in solitary confinement in the convent before death released her from the torment and unresolved conflict of her life. With scholarly attention to detail, Brown leads readers through scenes of high drama as she brings the story to life and extends the story with astute hypotheses. But she stops short of explaining all, artfully leaving readers to judge whether they are witnesses to manipulation or self-delusion.

Brown includes key portions of her sources in the twenty-five page appendix. This work is a unique documentation of gender relations and attitudes toward women and lesbianism in Renaissance Europe. It provides a rare and authentic glimpse of an obscure period in women's sexual and religious history. (LF)

IL,PO
491. Curb, Rosemary, and Nancy Manahan, eds. **Lesbian Nuns: Breaking Silence.** Tallahassee, Fla.: Naiad Press, 1985. 383 p. Includes bibliography and glossary. ISBN 0-930044-62-2.

"This is the first book published on the subject" of "erotic love between women in religious life" (p. xxxv). So states Manahan who, together with Curb, has edited this collection of testimonials from forty-nine present and former nuns who have broken silence about their sexual orientation. As former nuns and declared lesbians, they explain that the term "Lesbian nun" is used "for Lesbians still in religious communities as well as for those who left several decades ago" (p. xx). In her introductory article, "What Is a Lesbian Nun?" Curb relates her own experience and acts as spokeswoman for the other contributors. Lesbian nuns, she says, range in age from their late twenties to the mid-sixties and on the average have spent eight years in religious life. Although a few are converts, most grew up in Catholic families. While affording them an opportunity for a sound education, the religious life also served "as a refuge from heterosexuality, a Catholic marriage, and exhausting motherhood." Convent life enabled them to develop positive personality traits; it also, unfortunately, fostered others: blind obedience, self-denial, custody of the senses, and perfect self-control. They also discovered the great taboo of convent life—particular friendships (p.f.s.) with other nuns. The struggle with p.f.s. stemmed from the unspoken belief that they could lead to lesbian relationships. In one poignant tale after another, the nuns reveal how sexually ignorant they were on entering the convent, how they developed particular friendships that grew into sexual relationships, how dissatisfied they became with the stifling life, and how anguished they became on making the decision to leave. In some cases, without explanations, they were asked to leave. Most of the ex-nuns are now living with lovers, are politically active, and in one way or another have made spirituality the center of their lives. Some have forsaken their religion; others have turned to witchcraft. Curb believes that the book is dangerous in the sense that our patriarchal society "values only women who relate to men" and that the "very existence of autonomous communities of women threatens patriarchal arrogance." Hence, "a collection of autobiographical stories from Lesbian nuns not only violates patriarchal taboo, it is unimaginable in our polarized society" (p. xx). Photographs of the nuns, showing them in their religious habits and later in secular garb, accompany many of the stories. A glossary of terms bearing on the religious life appears at the end of the text. (TJW)

IL
492. Faderman, Lillian. **Odd Girls and Twilight Lovers: A History of Lesbian Life in Twentieth-Century America.** New York: Columbia University Press, 1991. 373 p. (Between Men—Between Women). Includes bibliographic notes and index. ISBN 0-231-07488-3.

This book traces the evolution of lesbian identity and subcultures from the late nineteenth century to the late twentieth century. Drawing on a variety of sources—journals, unpublished manuscripts, songs, news accounts, novels, medical literature, and numerous personal interviews with lesbians of all ages, races, and classes—Faderman weaves together a narrative of lesbian life and the metamorphoses it has undergone since the sexologists first defined the "female sexual invert" in the nineteenth century.

Faderman traces the development of the category "lesbian" from the era when "romantic friendship" between women was socially condoned to late nineteenth century attitudes toward romantic friendship, which were influenced both by medical literature and the increasing successes of the feminist movement that made it possible for women to make their lives with other women. The sexologists supplied the concept of "the lesbian" and the women's movement helped women establish economic independence. Thus a lesbian subculture could be formed such as had not previously existed. That subculture was affected in various ways through twentieth century developments such as the sexual experimentation that characterized the 1920s, the depression of the 1930s that forced many women out of the careers that had recently been opened to them, World War II that required womenpower and thus made possible once again women's economic freedom as well as casting them in situations in which bonding between them was encouraged, the McCarthy era in which homosexuals were viewed as a threat to national security, the hippy movement, the second wave of feminism, the New Left, and finally the Stonewall riots of the 1960s, that all served to make possible a militant lesbian feminist movement throughout the 1970s, and the evolution of that militancy in the 1980s. The book concludes with speculations about the future of lesbian life in the 1990s. (Author)

IL
493. Faderman, Lillian. **Surpassing the Love of Men: Romantic Friendship and Love Between Women from the Renaissance to the Present.** New York: Morrow, 1981. 415 p. Includes bibliographic notes. ISBN 0-688-03733-X.

This volume had its beginning in a study of Emily Dickinson's poems and love letters to Sue Gilbert. The fact that Dickinson evidenced no anxiety or guilt about expressing her feelings about that relationship conflicted with Faderman's assumptions about attitudes toward homosexuality in the centuries before the sexual revolution and led her to look at the work of other nineteenth-century female writers. To her surprise, she found evidence to suggest that sometime during the life span of virtually every educated nineteenth-century woman there was a love relationship with another woman. Such liaisons were variously described as "Boston marriage," "the love of kindred spirits," or "sentimental friends." They appeared in correspondence, fiction, and biography, typically without any implications of abnormality or wrongdoing.

Assuming that such romantic attachments were related to Victorian constraints on heterosexuality, Faderman sought to test that hypothesis by investigating earlier literature. It became evident that in the eighteenth century the term *romantic friendship* was common and described a love relationship between females that was looked upon as virtuous and noble. Similar references in seventeenth-century literature led Faderman back to the Renaissance where she identified beginnings of romantic friendship.

Faderman struggles with the question of why such relationships were condoned in earlier times and more recently were persecuted, at least until the 1960s and the feminist movement. She traces the "outlaw status" of female same-sex love to the end of World War I and links it with changes in women's status and with new medical pronouncements by Freud and disciples of Krafft-Ebing, a theme of censure quickly picked up in twentieth-century literature and popular media.

Faderman cites great changes in patterns of human sexuality over the centuries and sees the increase in male and female sexual activity in both heterosexual and homosexual relationships as an explanation of the infrequent references to sexual contact between women in early writings.

Skipping across centuries and drawing skillfully on literary references from diverse sources, Faderman answers questions as she puzzles them out for herself. The bibliographic notes provide a rich source of material. (LF)

IL,PO

494. Loulan, JoAnn. **Lesbian Sex.** San Francisco: Spinsters Book Company, 1984. 309 p. Includes bibliography. ISBN 0-933216-13-0.

Loulan states the goal of this book from the outset: "This is a book about lesbian sex, written by a lesbian counselor, for lesbians . . . to help you achieve the kind of sex life you want" (p. xi). It is aimed at individuals, not couples, and is meant to provide a practical, comprehensive look at the ways in which sexuality is an integral part of lesbian lives. Therefore, sexual technique is only one facet of the book. Major concerns include a range of psychological, social, and cultural issues that lesbians confront and that affect their sexuality.

Drawing on her training as a marriage and family counselor who has been counseling lesbians since 1977, Loulan begins the first section with a discussion of the barriers that lesbians face in defining and accepting their sexuality: the definition of sex by men, homophobia, and sexual trauma. Living in a culture that fears homosexuality as well as dealing with internalized homophobia affects lesbian sexuality in many ways—from the anxiety of initiating dates to restraints on expressing affection, attraction, and sexuality in a heterosexual society. Overcoming negative messages about being a lesbian is the first step in developing a healthy life. Being knowledgeable about your own body—its sexual anatomy and physiology—as well as about erotic fantasies and behaviors are routes to a satisfying sex life. Loulan devotes the second section to this topic, including a new interpretation of the female sexual response cycle, which consists of feedback between willingness, desire, emotional excitement, physical engorgement, orgasm, pleasure, and/or shutdown. She discusses the specifics of "what we do in bed," activities that range from massage, breathing, holding, touching, kissing, licking, and sucking to stimulating the G-spot, using sex toys, and fantasizing.

However, the course of sexual interaction may not run smooth, and Loulan addresses some of these difficulties in the third section: orgasmic problems and concerns (e.g., not having an orgasm, focusing on orgasm too much, irregular orgasms, partner differences in responsivity); desire issues; linking different sexual behaviors; and sexual addiction. Other issues in lesbians' lives that affect sexuality are also discussed in the fourth section: the long process of coming out and defining herself as a lesbian; being single; changes in sexuality in long term relationships; dealing with disabilities; motherhood; excessive use of drugs and alcohol; aging; and youth.

Throughout the text, Loulan quotes many women who comment on the issues at hand, and she suggests appropriate homework for working on a specific area. The final lengthy section is devoted to a wide range of homework exercises that are meant to help the reader deal with the physical and psychological issues raised in the book. Appendixes provide information on sex and disability, sexually transmitted diseases and problems, and drug and alcohol abuse. Overall, Loulan stresses the importance of knowledge about and acceptance of yourself as a lesbian and the appreciation of the diversity of others around you. (SGF)

IL
495. Martin, Del, and Phyllis Lyon. **Lesbian/Woman.** Volcano, Calif.: Volcano Press, 1991. 428 p. Twentieth anniversary edition. ISBN 0-912078-91-X.
Originally published in 1972, this edition of *Lesbian/Woman* contains the complete 1972 text as well as an extensive "Lesbian/Woman Update, 1991." Martin and Lyon, the leading founders in 1955 of the Daughters of Bilitis (DOB), the first lesbian organization in the United States, begin the book with this defining statement: "A Lesbian is a woman whose primary erotic, psychological, emotional and social interest is in a member of her own sex, even though that interest may not be overtly expressed." They go on to dispel the myths surrounding lesbians and their lifestyle. They examine the importance of the lesbian's self image and "how she feels about herself on hearing of her homosexuality, how she confronts those societal attitudes that proclaim her less than human because of a state of being" (p. 60). In addition to lifestyle, they also discuss sexual behavior and sex roles, pointing out the inhibiting effects of cultural conditioning, religious persuasion, family ties, and economic dependence on the status quo. Martin and Lyon offer their personal reflections about growing up gay, lesbian motherhood, and the fears, real and imagined, that plague the lives of lesbians.
In the chapter "Lesbians United," they describe the first meeting of the Daughters of Bilitis on October 19, 1955. They intended it to be a "Lesbian social club with parties and discussion groups" (p. 220). DOB began publishing *The Ladder*, a newsletter/magazine in October 1956. It spelled out the purpose of DOB as a women's organization helping the lesbian to discover "her potential and her place in society" (p. 223). In time, the DOB explored all the problems faced by lesbians, how they managed their personal lives, and how they dealt with individuals and the public. Major problems included dealing with male homosexuals and their organizations and with the women's movement, especially as exemplified by the National Organization for Women (NOW).
In "Lesbian/Woman Update, 1991," Martin and Lyon recapitulate what has happened in the lesbian movement since 1972. They begin by discussing major problems faced by individual lesbians, such as discrimination in employment, in education, and in government and military service. Then more positively they point out the contributions of lesbians in such diverse fields as music, creative writing, the theater, films, and video. They discuss advances made in the attitudes of health professionals toward lesbians, in facing the AIDS epidemic; in women's health care, teaching, relations with the church, media coverage, and conference participation; in international activities, immigration, and human rights violations; and in sex laws (especially concerning sodomy).
Martin and Lyon emphasize the impact of the Washington March of October 17, 1987 when more than 500,000 men and women of various persuasions marched together in the capitol "to underscore demands for Lesbian/Gay rights" (p. 386). The book concludes with a "Lesbian Agenda for the 90s," that puts family issues at the top of the list and avers that for lesbians "there is no better time than now to organize and stand up for their rights" (p. 425). (TJW)

PO
496. Sisley, Emily L., and Bertha Harris. **The Joy of Lesbian Sex: A Tender and Liberated Guide to the Pleasures and Problems of a Lesbian Lifestyle.** Illustrated by Yvonne Gilbert, Charles Raymond, and Patricia Faulkner. New York: Crown, 1977. 223 p. Includes bibliography and index. ISBN 0-517-53159-3.

The introduction to this illustrated guide to a lesbian lifestyle sets the tone for the rest of the book. Sisley and Harris present their interpretation of why lesbians have been portrayed as terrifying, evil, and mysterious: lesbians seem to threaten patriarchal structures by refusing to limit their eroticism according to the constraints of socialization or to confine their sexual activity to the "heterosexual reality" of penile/vaginal intercourse. Lesbian sexuality links mind, body, and spirit by focusing on pleasure and equality between partners; it is about re-creation, an impulse toward erotic freedom. As they put it, "the joy of sex for lesbians is that sex is not just screwing but all the other delicious components of communicating sensuality in a framework that combines tenderness and passion not bounded by the crotch." The contents of this book cover a broad spectrum of topics ranging from making love to more general concerns about a lesbian lifestyle (butch/femme, children of lesbians, civil rights, growing older, married lesbians, etc.). The book concentrates on how to have a rich and rewarding life as a lesbian by focusing on caring (making love as distinct from having sex), sex play and playfulness, and pleasure. By dispelling some widely held myths about lesbians, Sisley and Harris hope to communicate the idea that a women is an integrated person who is free to be a lesbian. For a "woman is not free to be anything unless she is free to be a lesbian." Numerous illustrations complement the text by portraying women enjoying the pleasures of their lifestyles. The book encourages women to feel secure in their lesbianism and to realize that their lifestyle can be a component in the overall process of becoming a total being. (SGF)

PR,PO

497. Vida, Ginny, ed. **Our Right to Love: A Lesbian Resource Book.** Produced in cooperation with Women of the National Gay Task Force. Englewood Cliffs, N.J.: Prentice-Hall, 1978. 318 p. Includes bibliography. ISBN 0-13-644401-6.

Rita Mae Brown, a "Mother of the Movement," anticipates one of the objectives of this lesbian resource book in her foreword: "Maybe it's time America grows up and learns to value difference instead of trying to homogenize all of us like so much pasteurized milk." She hopes that this book will foster a respect for lesbians' right to love, regardless of the reader's sexual or philosophical orientation. Vida, media director of the National Gay Task Force, elaborates the theme of encouraging communication about lesbians in order to improve public attitudes and alleviate some of the pain and repression lesbians experience because of ignorance. Accordingly, the forty articles by well-known women, forty personal testimonies, and eighty photographs that make up the text represent a wide range of thinking within the lesbian community. Each section exposes the reader to major issues of concern: lesbian identity, relationships, research and therapy, sexuality, health, activism, visions of the future, legal problems and remedies, and the media. Chapters on lesbian culture and the spectrum of lesbian experience provide an overview of the development of the movement and the diversity of lives that relate to it. By dispelling myths and stereotypes, the contributors provide a basis for understanding the nature and scope of lesbian lifestyles. They hope that this comprehensive resource guide will become a practical aid to survival for lesbians whose concerns seem to be overshadowed by "a culture where women's activities have been regarded as a footnote to male history." The appendix provides useful information for women just making contact with the movement. It contains a bibliography of 200 titles of pamphlets, nonfiction, fiction, periodicals, bibliographies, and biographies as well as a national listing of movement organizations, religious groups, services, coffee houses, feminist retreats, women's centers, and other helpful contacts. Esther Stineman, compiler of the core bibliography *Women's Studies*, considers this "a definitive source on lesbianism . . . essential for reference collections." (SGF)

Bisexual

PR,IL
498.   Cantarella, Eva. **Bisexuality in the Ancient World.** Translated by Cormac
Ó Cuilleanáin. New Haven, Conn.: Yale University Press, 1992. 284 p. Includes bibliography and index. Translation of: *Secondo natura.* ISBN 0-300-04844-0.
       Bisexuality was intrinsic to the cultures of the ancient world. In both Greece and
Rome, same gender sexual relationships were acknowledged, and those between men
were not only tolerated but widely celebrated in literature and art. Nor for Greeks and
Romans was homosexuality an exclusive choice, but alternative to and sometimes
concurrent with the love of the opposite sex.
       While exploring aspects of the female condition in Classical antiquity, Cantarella
came to understand that the sheer ubiquity of male homosexuality had a fundamental
impact on relationships between men and women. Drawing on the full range of surviving
sources—legal texts, inscriptions, medical documents, poetry and philosophical literature—she now reconstructs the homosexual cultures of Greece and Rome and provides
a history of bisexuality in the Classical age.
       Cantarella explores the psychological, social, and cultural mechanisms that deter-
mined sexual choice and considers the extent to which that choice was free, directed, or
coerced in each civilization. In Greece the relationship between adults and young boys
was deemed the noblest of associations, a means of education and spiritual exhaltation.
Cantarella reveals that such relationships, although highly regulated and never left to
individual spontaneity, were more than pedagogic and platonic: they were fully carnal.
In Imperial Rome, however, the sexual ethic mirrored the political, and males were
cruelly domineering in love as in war. The critical sexual distinction was that between
active and passive, the victims commonly being slaves or defeated enemies, rather than
young Roman freemen.
       In terms of female bisexuality, accounts of love between Roman women were
transmitted exclusively by men. In Greece, however, women had Sappho to give them
voice. Cantarella examines the activities of the *thiasoi*—Greek communities of women—
and reveals that their ritual ceremonies also embraced passionate love.
       Explained also is how the etiquette of bisexuality was corrupted over time and
how, influenced by pagan and Judeo-Christian traditions, homosexuality came to be
regarded as an unnatural act. Cantarella's interpretation claims not only that homosexuality was common, but that for Greeks of both genders it constituted true love. (Publisher
permission granted to use material from the book jacket.)
       [N.B. Eva Cantarella is professor in the Institute of Roman Law at the University
of Milan.]

PR,IL
499.   Hill, Ivan, ed. **The Bisexual Spouse: Different Dimensions in Human Sexuality.**
McLean, Va.: Barlina Books, 1987. 264 p. ISBN 0-937525-01-4.
       Hill of the Ethics Resource Center in Washington, D.C. points out in the preface
that the magnitude of bisexuality in marriage today would "have been astounding to us
a few years ago, and disbelieved a few decades ago."
       The first part of the study consists of six in-depth interviews with bisexual couples
and with four women and four men who experienced bisexuality within the context of
their marriages. In general, these stories demonstrate how couples who seem to represent
the ideally happy heterosexual couple, after years of marriage, gradually became aware
of the existence of same-sex love in their lives, and they reveal how this knowledge
affected their marriages.
       Part 2 consists of a nationwide sexuality survey of psychiatrists and sex therapists,
conducted by the Opinion Research Corporation of Princeton, New Jersey, to obtain
viewpoints on some ten questions pertaining to the cause and modifiability of homosexuality, the existence and incidence of bisexuality in American society, and, in view of

AIDS and other sexually related issues, the status of male homosexual activity, female homosexuality activity, monogamy, and celibacy. The results of the psychiatrists' and sex therapists' answers to the questions are presented in detail, including written added observations made by those interviewed.

In the final part of the book, Judd Marmor, past president of the American Psychiatric Association, points out that "the issue of bisexuality has long been a subject of dispute among psychiatrists and sex therapists," some denying that such a classification exists and believing that "all bisexuals are really closet homosexuals taking refuge behind a heterosexual façade," and others claiming "that all people are bisexual but that the original alternative impulses have been repressed, either by societal pressures (in heterosexuals) or by certain early life experiences (in homosexuals)" (p. 253). He also comments on the sexuality survey itself, addressing (1) the causes of homosexuality, (2) the modification of homosexuality toward heterosexuality, (3) bisexuality as a bona fide classification and the incidence of bisexuality, (4) the incidence of bisexuality or homosexuality among married people, (5) trends in incidences of homosexuality, and (6) changes in social and sexual behavior related to AIDS and other factors. He concludes that "an enlightened society must ultimately be able to accept . . . the millions of men and women who, through no fault of their own, find themselves erotically responsive to members of their own sex" (p. 264). (TJW)

IL

500.   Klein, Fred. **The Bisexual Option: A Concept of One-Hundred Percent Intimacy.** New York: Arbor House, 1978. 221 p. Includes bibliography. ISBN 0-87795-179-9.

Klein, a practicing psychiatrist and director of the Institute of Sexual Behavior, makes a strong case for bisexuality by (1) referring his position to the Heterosexual-Homosexual Rating Scale developed by Alfred Kinsey and (2) buttressing his argument with case histories of men and women who have come to him for help. In part I, "What Is Bisexuality," he discusses the Kinsey sexuality continuum; Anna Freud's contention that heterosexuality, homosexuality, and bisexuality may be determined by an examination of one's dream fantasies; the levels of emotional and sexual intimacy between individuals; and his own view of how homosexuals and bisexuals are able to resolve the Oedipus Complex. In part II, "Bisexuality and Health," following a definition of neuroses, case history profiles of the neurotic bisexual and the healthy bisexual are given. In part III, "The Bisexual in Society," Klein explains the lack of a bisexual community or subculture; lists and comments on such renowned bisexuals as Alexander the Great, Joan Baez, Tallulah Bankhead, Colette, André Gide, W. Somerset Maugham, Kate Millett, Socrates, Oscar Wilde, and Virginia Woolf; and discusses three literary works: Virginia Woolf's *Orlando*, Ursula K. Le Guin's *The Left Hand of Darkness*, and D. H. Lawrence's *Women in Love*, in which bisexuality is portrayed. Klein says that the cultural stereotypes of masculinity and femininity are changing, as are people's perceptions of sexuality, monogamy and the family, and feminism and the women's movement. The premise of this book, in Klein's words, is: "Bisexuality is now staking its claim upon our serious consideration as a real force for bringing about that bright future." (TJW)

PR

500a.   Weinberg, Martin S., Colin J. Williams, and Douglas W. Pryor. **Dual Attraction: Understanding Bisexuality.** New York: Oxford University Press, 1994. 437 p. Includes bibliographic notes and index. ISBN 0-19-508482-9.

Although research indicates that bisexuality may be quite widespread, almost nothing was known about it in the early 1980s. The authors—all sociologists—began their long-term study of bisexuality in 1983 in San Francisco. Their goals were to examine how people with a dual sexual preference construct their sex lives and to assess society's impact in shaping individuals' choices about their desires. (They deliberately use the term "sexual preference" to emphasize the active role that people play in developing their own sexuality, in contrast with "sexual orientation," which assumes a biologically based, fixed basis for sexual desire).

The authors gathered their data from fieldwork: detailed questionnaires sent to members of bisexual, homosexual, and heterosexual organizations; and in-depth interviews with members of the Bisexual Xenter, one of the largest bisexual organizations in the country.

Part I, "Bisexual Lives," includes testimonials of bisexuals who portray their world and the attitudes, relationships, feelings, and behavior of those who inhabit it. The authors find that the majority of bisexuals establish heterosexuality first and become bisexual over time. Men and women experience bisexuality in different ways, and there are at least five types of bisexuals. Appendix A contains statistical data from the 1983 interview survey on a variety of topics discussed in part I, including sexual activities, significant others, marriages, jealousy, and being "out."

In part II, "Bisexuality, Heterosexuality, and Homosexuality," the authors use the results of the questionnaire surveys to compare the sociosexual lives of people who define themselves as bisexuals, homosexuals, and heterosexuals. Bisexuals experience discrimination and rejection, and they are more circumspect in disclosing their bisexual identity than are homosexuals. Further, sexual preferences may change over time. The part also addresses issues of how sexual preference develops, its dimensions, managing multiple identities, and engaging in intimate relationships. Appendix B presents tabulations of the 1984-1985 questionnaire survey of bisexuals, homosexuals, and heterosexuals.

Part III, "After AIDS," presents the results of the authors' return to San Francisco in 1988 to study the impact of AIDS on bisexuals. Issues examined include changes in sexual preference, sexuality, and relationships; change and the transsexual bisexual; psychological responses; and types of adaptations to a changed social context. The results of the 1988 follow-up study are presented in appendix C.

The authors conclude that "Learning plays a significant part in helping people traverse sexual boundaries, past and present intimate relationships influence a change in sexual preference, and that bisexual activity is inseparable from a social environment that provides varied sexual opportunities. . . . Our research finds that sexual preference is much less fixed and much more complicated and fascinating than most current thinking holds" (p. 9). (TJW/SGF)

PR,IL
501. Wolff, Charlotte. **Bisexuality: A Study.** London: Quartet Books, 1979. 262 p. Includes bibliography, index, and glossary. ISBN 0-7043-3253-1.

Intended for the layperson as well as the professional, this book is an attempt to define bisexuality and distinguish it from androgyny (a question examined in detail in appendix 1). In her first chapter, Wolff provides a review of the literature on bisexuality, going back to Greek myth for the origin of the concept of hermaphroditism (that there is a third sex partaking of the nature of both sexes) and linking the concept to the investigations of C. G. Jung, W. Fliess, S. Freud, and R. von Krafft-Ebing in the nineteenth century and of Melanie Klein, Helene Deutsch, Karen Horney, John Money, and Robert Stoller in the twentieth century.

Wolff examines the biological factor in bisexuality in light of advances in genetics, brain research, and endocrinology. Research seems to indicate that the female is "biologically the more primitive sex," and that psychosexual characteristics of individuals depend largely, but not entirely, on hormonal secretions.

Wolff distinguishes between sexual identity (belonging to either male or female sex) and gender identity, that develops with the growth of personality. The latter is strongly affected by environmental factors and is "either consciously male or female or a mixture of both. The latter situation represents the natural human condition" (p. 52). Wolff hopes to replace the terms *masculinity* and *femininity* with the expressions "sense of maleness" and "sense of femaleness," that she says reside in all individuals.

Following a discussion of the methodology used in her study of 150 bisexuals (75 men and 75 women, all volunteers, who answered a questionnaire and were interviewed),

Wolff recounts in "Early Influences" and "Later Relationships," the experiences of the participants, stressing the influence of the family, environmental conditions, casual sexual contacts, sexual dreams and fantasies, and so forth on individuals' sexual orientations. The statistical data concerning these influences and others are found in an appendix. Sample interviews with three participants and lengthy autobiographical statements from five women and four men who write about their emotional and sexual experiences and offer their personal ideas about bisexuality are found in later chapters. In conclusion, Wolff provides her own definition of bisexuality: it is the "root of human sexuality and the matrix of all bio-psychical reactions, be they passive or active" (p. 1). (TJW)

Group. Swinging

PR,IL
502. Bartell, Gilbert D. **Group Sex: A Scientist's Eyewitness Report on the American Way of Swinging.** New York: Peter H. Wyden, 1971. 298 p. Includes bibliography and index.
Group sex, popularly known as swinging, was the subject of a three-year investigation undertaken in the late 1960s by Bartell, an associate professor of anthropology at Northern Illinois University. Recognizing the dearth of literature available on the subject, he, with assistance from his wife, decided to research systematically what they "had always believed to be largely a myth." Popularly defined, swinging is "having sexual relations as a couple with at least one other individual" (p. 4). The book views mate-swapping, or swinging, from an anthropological standpoint; it examines attitudes and behavior, shows how individual patterns are transferred to group sex, and draws conclusions about the viability of this subculture in the United States.
The Bartells interviewed 350 informants from the Chicago metropolitan area, bolstered by an additional group of swingers in Texas and Louisiana. They also participated as observers in swingers' parties, taking notes and using a tape recorder. They compiled numerous case histories, a number of which are included in the book. The sample population consisted of predominantly white middle-class suburbanites ranging in age "from eighteen to the mid-fifties for the women and from twenty-one to seventy for the men" (p. 25). One-tenth of the couples interviewed admitted to being unmarried; 87 percent had children. Further data were gathered on educational backgrounds, occupations, religious preference, reading habits, racial prejudices, drug use, and bodily appearance.
The Bartells explored other aspects of the swinging scene as well: the reasons why swingers swing; the publications and organizations involved in promoting contacts between interested parties, both singles and couples; the mechanics of getting together; etiquette and behavior of novices and experienced swingers; what actually takes place during swinging sessions; and the dropout rate among swingers.
The popularity of private parties and the extent of organization-sponsored parties are discussed. Bartell estimates that 8 million couples swing in America and that about 1 percent of the population is involved in swinging in one way or another. He also explores the negative and positive aspects of swinging, concluding that swinging, while a relatively recent phenomenon in America, is not a fad but is likely to find accommodation under the conditions of open sexuality so noticeable in society since the 1960s. (TJW)

PR
503. Gilmartin, Brian G. **The Gilmartin Report.** Secaucus, N.J.: Citadel Press, 1978. 492 p. Includes bibliography and index.
Funded by a grant from the National Science Foundation, this book focuses on that form of unconventional sexual behavior variously known as swinging, mate sharing, wife swapping, and group sex. It is a form of extramarital sex or adultery, and is recognized

as prevalent in areas of middle- and upper-middle-class suburbia. It is not of a criminal nature, although sociologists look upon it as deviant behavior. Scholarly estimates put its frequency "at about 2 percent of all married couples," which translates into a very large number in American society. Interestingly, at least 80 percent of swingers have children.

Gilmartin defines swinging as "that form of extramarital sexual behavior which involves legally married couples sharing coitus and other sexual behaviors with other legally married couples in a social context defined by all participants as constituting a kind of recreation-convivial play" (p. 16). Types of swingers include egotistical swingers, those who avoid emotional involvement with their partners; recreational swingers who emphasize the social aspects of swinging; and interpersonal swingers who develop close emotional ties with partners.

In this California study based on questionnaires and interviews, 100 middle-class swinging couples and 100 middle-class nonswinging couples and their children are compared and contrasted on a variety of background characteristics, attitudes, beliefs, experiences, and so forth. Gilmartin discusses the many aspects of the swinging phenomenon. Following an introductory chapter explaining the study, he goes on to discuss mate-swapping from the cross-cultural and historical perspectives. Chapter 3 presents the methodology of the study and chapters 4 through 8 deal with questions concerning how and why middle-class people decide to become involved with swinging (relationships with parents and kin, relationships with neighbors and friends, political and religious philosophies, premarital dating and courtship, pornographic literature). Later chapters focus on the degree of contentment swingers have with their lives and marriage, what actually goes on at swinging parties, some of the deviant and bizarre sexual behavior practiced by some swingers, and a summary discussion of sexual mate-swapping in America, including a discussion of the psychological and marital consequences of swinging, and whether swinging poses a threat to the institution of marriage in the United States. (TJW)

PR,IL
504. Karlen, Arno. **Threesomes: Studies in Sex, Power, and Intimacy.** New York: Morrow, 1988. 370 p. Includes bibliography. ISBN 0-688-06536-8.

Defined as "three people in one bed or in one *ménage* [literally, a household], with more than a sexual dyad among them" (p. 44), threesomes are neither rare (about 5 percent of the population has engaged in them) nor carried out as most people imagine them to be. Researcher and writer Karlen began with this basic behavioral definition of threesomes and decided to find out who made up threesomes; what their social, family, and sexual histories were; and how the threesomes began, proceeded, and resolved themselves. To do this, he conducted 50 brief life histories, long, open-ended interviews and detailed sex histories of members of threesomes; obtained partial information from another 200 informants; and received responses from 150 completed questionnaires of people actively engaged in swinging.

People involved in threesomes are rather conventional in some ways: most are white, middle-class, and conservative to moderate in their political views. Many are not swingers although most swingers will eventually engage in threesomes. However, because such behavior is not generally socially acceptable, others exaggerate their involvement in nonacceptable activities such as drug use and politically liberal activism.

No one pattern characterizes threesomes. Rather, there are many kinds of triads, motives for being involved in them, sexual patterns, and types of lifestyles. Two men and a man are more likely to make up a threesome than two men and a woman or three men or three women. Despite their diversity, some common feelings and conflicts emerge: intimacy, flight from intimacy, conquest, submission, jealousy, abandon, narcissism, homosexuality, Oedipal reenactment, magical fantasy, reality testing, and ecstasy. As Karlen notes, " . . . although threes involve only a minority, they illuminate what all of us do and feel" (p. 31). Members of triads were often late starters or very active early starters in their sexual behavior. The most pervasive psychological dynamics involved the search for power and/or intimacy. Men and women had very distinctive ways of experiencing relationships and eroticism; women are more likely to engage in sex together without feeling that their heterosexual orientation is threatened. Jealousy can be an issue in triads as is conflict. The most successful triads maintain clear, acceptable roles; "a threesome often requires not abandon but the timing and tact of ballet" (p. 29). Descriptions of sets of triads and commentary by the participants demonstrate the living context of Karlen's theoretical points. (SGF)

Celibate

PO
505. Brown, Gabrielle. **The New Celibacy: Why More Men and Women Are Abstaining from Sex—and Enjoying It.** New York: McGraw-Hill, 1980. 200 p. Includes bibliography. ISBN 0-07-008430-0.

Brown, an educational psychologist, introduces the concept of the "new celibacy" as a freely chosen, positive outgrowth of the sexual revolution. She argues that celibacy and sex are independent since they both express the human quality of being able to choose the path of one's actions. Therefore, celibacy is not antithetical to sex but is a potential basis for sexual fulfillment. In contrast to the "old celibacy," based on repression and fear of sex, the new celibacy may provide a much-needed antidote for individuals in a culture that has placed too much emphasis on sex as a basis for relationships, mental health, and general well-being. Primarily addressed to those who might choose celibacy as a positive life experience (although not necessarily for a lifetime), the book explores the value of celibacy in enhancing intimate relationships. Two chapters investigate the physical, psychological, and social dimensions of celibacy for both men and women and include case material to illustrate how different individuals have experienced celibacy. Later chapters discuss the specifics of celibacy as a part of marriage, as a mode of consciousness raising, and as a kind of attitude. Although focused on celibacy, the book deals with general issues associated with the link between sex and relationships: the nature of love, the role of sex in marriage and other intimate relationships, and the way sex affects one's self-image. (SGF)

Noncoital Sexual Stimulation

Fantasy

(For related material see also entry 941)

IL,PO
506. Fox, Siv Cedering. **Joys of Fantasy: The Book for Loving Couples.** Photographs by Joseph Del Valle. New York: Bell, 1982. unpaged. Originally published in 1977 by Stein and Day. ISBN 0-517-362473.

Sexual fantasies are a normal part of everyone's lives and can play a positive role in sexual experience. They express Fox's point of view that the "mind is the main erogenous zone. It is there sense becomes sensuality." Fox, Erica Jong, and Joel Oppenheimer are some of the writers who wrote the main parts of this text—a series of poetic and prose expressions of sexual fantasies. Almost every page is covered with soft-focus, sepia-toned photographs of nude individuals, couples (both heterosexual and homosexual), and groups acting out the erotic fantasies described in the text. Since many sexual fantasies invade culturally taboo areas, their depictions may seem shocking to some readers. Group sex, transvestism, incest, homosexuality, rape, masturbation, intercourse with a teacher or a member of the clergy, and close-ups of male and female sex organs are some of the taboo fantasies that are pictured with appropriately dream-like photographs. The point of this book for "loving couples" is to emphasize that fantasizing is universal and acceptable. The text guides the reader into an appreciation of the kinds of stimulation fantasies can provide if people allow their minds to expand and include the input from their imaginations. By showing and describing such scenes as pretending to be an animal, undressing a woman, saying "taboo" words, imagining the vagina as an open rose or a penis as a rosebud, Fox encourages the reader to feel okay about his or her individual fantasies, however bizarre and forbidden they may seem; they are shared although not often acknowledged by many other people. The book's emphasis on imagination helps to balance the often one-sided, physical, and mechanical approaches to sexuality; the mind plays an integral role in sexual expression. (SGF)

PO
507. Friday, Nancy. **Men in Love: Male Sexual Fantasies: The Triumph of Love over Rage.** New York: Delacorte Press, 1980. 527 p. ISBN 0-440-05264-5.

After examining women's sexual fantasies in *My Secret Garden* (1973) and *Forbidden Flowers* (1975), journalist Friday turned her attention to men's sexual fantasies. Even though the sexual fantasies of men and women have a common goal—sexual excitement—their content has very different themes. For example, the female daydream of being sexually dominated by a male is not mirrored by a similar desire of the male to dominate; men rarely fantasize about overpowering a woman against her will. A man's "secret garden" is not like a woman's. Women who acknowledge this fact put themselves in a better position to perceive men as people, like themselves, who are struggling for love and sexual satisfaction. Fantasy is "a map of desire, mastery, escape, and obscuration; the navigational path we invent to steer ourselves between the reefs and shoals of anxiety, guilt, and inhibition" (p. 1). It is not necessarily a frustrated wish but rather a vehicle for helping to resolve conflicts and inconsistencies that may or may not be conscious. The central thesis of the book is that men's love of women is filled with rage derived from early ambivalence engendered by a mother who was the child's first erotic object and his first inhibitor. The "denied little boy," who Friday concludes is a part of every male, works out part of his rage through fantasy and demonstrates how love triumphs over rage. Therefore, fantasies express thoughts of men who love women. The fantasies described and analyzed were sent to Friday in response to a note at the end of *Forbidden Flowers* requesting information on male fantasies. Out of 3,000 men who responded to her request, she selected 200 who she felt were most representative of the group. Over two-thirds of the respondents were under forty; most were college graduates or had attended college; the majority lived in the East, primarily in New York; and slightly more respondents were married than single. Written in consultation with prominent psychiatric authorities, the book seeks to explain the reasons behind men's fantasies in psychoanalytic terms. Although not representative of all men's fantasies, those presented relate a complex and varied set of topics, including masturbation, water games, anal sex, oral sex, and sadomasochism. Friday's analysis of the fantasies includes a discussion of its general theme, thus providing background information on various aspects of sexuality. (SGF)

PO
508. Friday, Nancy. **Women on Top: How Real Life Has Changed Women's Sexual Fantasies.** New York: Simon & Schuster, 1991. 460 p. ISBN 0-671-64844-6.

Women on Top is a follow-up to *My Secret Garden*, Friday's popular book about women's sexual fantasies, published in 1973. Friday claims that women's fantasies and even their sexual behavior have changed markedly since the early 1970s. Basically, many women have shed their guilt about the sexual fantasies they were having, fantasies that included forcible rape by faceless men. The guilt women experience, according to Friday, comes from two main sources, mother and church. Helping to overcome that guilt have been the sexual revolution, the women's movement, and a deeper knowledge of women's sexuality. Claiming that women's sexual fantasies were an unacknowledged component of female sexuality before 1973, Friday presents these current fantasies as the product of women who admit their anger and desire to be in control of their sex relationships with men.

Friday recognizes a "close kinship between masturbation and fantasy" (p. 32). Masturbation, she observes, is a natural, externally physical act; fantasy is an interior image-structuring phenomenon. Women began in the 1970s to rid themselves of masturbatory guilt as the activity came to be viewed as "normal" by therapists, sexologists, and even the American Medical Association. Books were written and classes conducted on how to masturbate. Friday believes that the benefits from masturbation for females are considerable, helping women to establish their sexual identity, to distinguish between love and sex, to become sexually proficient, and to achieve sexual pleasure.

Taking masturbation as basic to women's sexual fantasies, Friday arranges the material in her book in three chapters that reflect the themes that turn up in women's fantasies: women in control, women with women, and sexually insatiable women. These fantasies represent a selection made from thousands of fantasies women, mostly in their twenties, submitted to Friday on the basis of a request printed in *My Secret Garden* and its sequel, *Forbidden Flowers.*

While the included fantasies run the gamut of sexual activities—sexual intercourse, oral and anal sex, bestiality, homosexuality, group sex, sadomasochism—it is clear that they remain fantasies and do not necessarily transfer directly into actual behavior. Nevertheless, they show, according to Friday, that the fantasies appearing since 1973 have become sexier and oriented in the direction of the control that women now anticipate. (TJW)

PR,IL
509. Kronhausen, Phyllis, and Eberhard Kronhausen. **Erotic Fantasies: A Study of the Sexual Imagination.** New York: Grove Press, 1981. 429 p. First Evergreen Black Cat Edition 1970. ISBN 0-8021-4205-2.

This book is the result of a literary investigation of sexual fantasies by two psychoanalysts well known for their efforts to liberalize censorship laws and expand the scope of sex education. They believe that erotic fantasies "serve as mental aphrodisiacs and psychological stimulants, underlying 'normal' sexual behavior," and act as "safety valves for bottled-up sex feelings, strivings, and wishes that are socially unacceptable." They do not think that sexual fantasies lead to abnormal or socially dangerous behavior. Recognizing the difficulty of collecting empirical data on the subject, they turned to a rich source of such information, i.e., underground erotic literature, past and present, from around the world. They collected about 100 erotic writings, starting with literature available in the seventeenth century. They present representative excerpts followed by comments on the significance of the particular works. The selections are organized by categories of sexual fantasies: homosexuality, transsexualism, bondage, sadomasochism, incest, juveniles, and bizarre fantasies involving animals, fetishes, and sex aids. A chapter on erotic folklore is also included. When Samuel Pepys was in a bookstore in 1668, he saw a copy of *L'Ecole des filles*, a rather mild sex manual by contemporary standards; he quickly pronounced it "the most bawdy, lewd book that I ever saw." Nevertheless, he bought it, took it home, and read it. He then burned it. In contrast, the authors of this unusual collection of erotic works suggest that "those who are easily offended in their moral sensibilities or who are disturbed by the unusual" think twice before reading it. (TJW)

Touching

PO
510. Kennedy, Adele P., and Susan Dean. **Touching for Pleasure: A 12 Step Program for Sexual Enhancement.** Illustrated by Joann Daley. Chatsworth, Calif.: Chatsworth Press, 1988. 119 p. Includes as a supplement *Safer Choices* by Susan Perry. ISBN 0-917181-11-5.

Based on years of experience, sex surrogacy expert Kennedy and sex researcher Dean have produced a practical manual on the art of touching for sexual pleasure. They believe that touching for many people is a lost art in America. Written in a very personal style for both male and female readers, this book and its program are intended to reacquaint individuals with their sensual responses to tactile stimulation.

Chapters cover the need for touching; the hand caress, face caress, and foot caress; body image exercises done by a couple in the nude; the back caress, the front caress, the sensual shower; sexploration (i.e., self-exploration of the genitals by each partner); pleasuring (i.e., undertaking such foreplay activities as kissing and oral lovemaking); and sexual intercourse. A chapter on touching as its own reward concludes this practical book. Throughout, explicit drawings by Joann Daley enhance the text. Supplementing the text is Susan Perry's short statement *Safer Choices*, a guide on how to minimize contracting sexually transmitted diseases. (TJW)

PR,IL

511. Montagu, Ashley. **Touching: The Human Significance of the Skin.** 3rd ed. New York: Harper & Row, 1986. 494 p. Includes bibliographic references and index. ISBN 0-06-096028-0.

The skin, the largest organ of the body, is the sensory receptor organ responding to touch. This book concentrates on the roles that skin plays in the physical and behavioral growth and development of the individual. The main question that it seeks to answer is: "What influence do the various kinds of cutaneous experiences which the organism undergoes, especially in early life, have on its development?" (p. 19). The approach used to explore the answers to this question is somatopsychic (not psychosomatic), which focuses on how the presence or absence of tactile experience affects behavioral development. Touching may take many forms—holding, licking, stroking, caressing, patting with the hand, simple body contact, pinching, kissing—or it may involve the massive tactile stimulation characteristics of sexual intercourse. This book covers touching in many important arenas of existence: gestation and birth, growth and development, human sexuality, aging, and cultural variation. Topics include the implications of infant immaturity in humans; breastfeeding; the relevance of cradles, clothes, music, rocking, and dance to tactile stimulation; the relationship of touch with communication and tactile deprivation with violence. Montagu makes a strong case for stimulation in human infants in the belief, supported by much evidence, that adult behavior can often be traced back to infant care. Of particular interest is the chapter "Skin and Sex" in which Montagu attempts to answer the basic question, "Do individuals who are maternally adequately cared for differ from those who are not, in the manner in which they respond to cutaneous stimulation in sex relations, in petting, and coitus?" He investigates each topic by drawing on cross-species, cross-cultural, and developmental studies. He gives thorough coverage to the scientific investigations of tactuality, to the literature about touching, and to the varying customs of different cultures. The interdisciplinary approach of the book makes it appropriate for use in various academic disciplines, particularly anthropology and psychology. The clarity of the text makes the information accessible to a popular audience as well. (TJW/SGF)

PO

512. Rueger, Russ A. **The Joy of Touch.** Photographs by Trudy Schlachter. New York: Simon & Schuster, 1981. 176 p. Includes bibliography. ISBN 0-671-42469-6.

Having written several articles on related topics such as tickling and cuddling, Rueger, a trained psychologist, came up with the idea of doing a work on touching in general. This practical guide to touch techniques for stimulation, relaxation, health, and well-being is the result. Part I discusses the touch taboos in modern society as well as the inherent human need to touch and be touched. Part II, devoted to the "touching tools" of the body, focuses on the skin, hands, head, nose, and sensitive spots, including the erogenous zones. Part III emphasizes the actual touch techniques for stimulation and relaxation, including sensitivity strokes as applied to numerous areas of the body. Massage techniques for two as well as self-massage and group massage are covered. Part

IV covers reflexology massage, Shiatsu massage, bodywork, and touch techniques in psychic healing. Part V deals with drugs (alcohol, depressants, marijuana, etc.) and devices (hot tubs, saunas, waterbeds, womb-boxes, etc.) as touch enhancers. Part VI discusses sensuous cuddling, erotic tickling, and sexual touch. Copiously illustrated with black-and-white photographs of a young nude couple demonstrating the various touch techniques, the book is a straightforward presentation of the theory and practice of touching. (TJW)

Massage

PO
513. Downing, George. **The Massage Book.** Illustrated by Anne Kent Rush. Berkeley, Calif.: Random House-The Bookworks, 1972. 183 p. (The Original Holistic Health Series). 183 p. Includes bibliography. ISBN 0-394-70770-2.

According to Downing, massage "when practiced by lovers . . . can be a beautiful extension of sexuality." However, it is basically a healing art; erotic massage is only a part of it. Massage is also "a unique way of communicating without words." The approach to massage employed in this book was developed at the Esalen Institute in Big Sur and San Francisco and is a variation on the time-honored Swedish massage.

The first part of the book contains practical information about supplies, equipment, and conditions as well as how to prepare someone for a massage and how to use the hands for massage. The second part provides illustrated instructions on how to give a complete massage, using some eighty strokes applied to different parts of the body, starting with the head and neck, and going on to the chest and stomach, the arm, the hand, front of the leg, the foot, back of the leg, the buttocks, and the back. Alternate sequences are also suggested. Further comments are given on body tension, discomfort and nervousness on the part of the subject, massaging to music, the limitations of self-message, massaging animals, and erotic massage.

The third part of the book is for the person already familiar with massage who is interested in developing a unique personal style. Downing's approach to style rests philosophically on body awareness achieved through breathing exercises and a concept called "centering": focusing one's attention on the center of one's body, the abdomen. Helpful also are meditation and the Chinese method of moving meditation, or Tai Chi Chuan. Downing also provides brief comments about other methods of massage, knowledge of which should prove useful to the would-be masseur or masseuse; they are zone therapy, or reflexology, Reichian massage, rolfing, Proskauer massage, Shiatsu, and the massage accompanying acupuncture. Downing also provides information about the professional aspects of massage and some anatomical drawings of the skeleton and the body musculature. (TJW)

PO
514. Inkeles, Gordon, and Murray Todris. **The Art of Sensual Massage.** With photographs by Robert Footherap. New York: Simon & Schuster, 1972. 161 p. ISBN 0-671-02022-6.

Written by people with many years of experience, this practical manual covers the entire range of sensual massage, a concept Inkeles and Todris place somewhere between the "poles of therapy and sex." The first section, devoted to preparations for massage, discusses the various oils and essences used in massage as well as the environment for massage: soft lighting, quiet, warmth, incense, and the preferences of the person being massaged. The second section systematically covers the parts of the body included in a complete massage: abdomen and chest, neck and head, the arms, the hands, the front of the legs, the feet, the back of the legs, and finally the back. The touches and strokes deemed most useful for each section of the body are carefully explained in words complemented with many black-and-white photographs of nude couples demonstrating the positions and strokes used for sensual massage. The photographs and text capture the pleasure and sensuality of this type of massage. A chapter on special effects includes neck stretching, back twisting and stretching, arm flexing, and leg pressing. A final chapter is devoted to erotic massage, that embraces various gentle techniques of touching and stroking recommended for lovers. Accessories and a brief history of massage are included.

Inkeles's new version of this practical guide is entitled *The New Sensual Massage* (New York: Bantam Books, 1992). Divided into three parts ("Start Massaging Tonight," "A Complete Body Massage," and "Massage Specialties"), the book is replete with many color photographs; nude couples demonstrating the massage positions and strokes; and anatomical illustrations of bones, muscles, and nerves. (TJW)

Masturbation

IL,PO
515. Dodson, Betty. **Sex for One: The Joy of Selfloving.** New York: Harmony Books, 1987. 178 p. Previously published under the titles *Liberating Masturbation* (1974) and *Selflove and Orgasm* (1983). ISBN 0-517-56676-1.

Sex for One is an expansion of Dodson's views on masturbation expressed in earlier versions of this work. In 1973 Dodson began her Bodysex workshops for women who wished to learn more about their own sexuality. The idea for this erotic project grew out of consciousness-raising experiences she shared with other feminists. Her idea, emerging from her personal struggle with her own sexuality, is that women's liberation is inextricably bound up with sexual liberation. One way to achieve the latter is through masturbation, in the past an oft-condemned sexual practice.

Bodysex workshops, successfully conducted over a period of years, involve small groups of women willing to meet weekly in Dodson's erotically appointed living room. As she describes it, the women disrobed on arrival, sat in circles, discussed and displayed their genitals, exercised, and used vibrators to achieve orgasm. As a result, these women overcame their sexual inhibitions and guilt feelings through masturbation. In similar fashion, Dodson conducted Bodysex workshops for men.

Dodson actively participated in the women's liberation movement, helping to plan a women's sexuality conference in New York in 1973, promoting the Equal Orgasm Amendment, and, as an artist, exhibiting her erotic paintings in art galleries. Throughout *Sex for One*, Dodson's explicit art illustrates the sexual practices discussed.

Eventually Dodson became involved in transcendental meditation and now contends that masturbation is an active form of meditation. The final chapter is a collection of letters to Dodson from men and women relating their masturbatory experiences and expressing appreciation for the help and guidance provided by her books. (TJW)

PR
516. Marcus, Irwin M., and John J. Francis, eds. **Masturbation: From Infancy to Senescence.** New York: International Universities Press, 1975. 502 p. Includes bibliographies and index. ISBN 0-8236-3150-8.

This compilation of papers by psychiatrists provides a broad psychoanalytic perspective on the subject of masturbation. In their introduction, Marcus and Francis comment that "the increasing momentum for self-realization, self-awareness, and acceptance of one's own uniqueness is exploding the remnants of social taboos concerning sexuality, stemming from our Puritan heritage." They note that humanity has held a belief in the harmful effects of masturbation for over 5,000 years; that only recently has this taboo been exorcised, especially as a consequence of the Freudian approach to sexuality.

The editors' introductory paper is a general treatment of the developmental view of masturbation, considering definition, phases of masturbation in childhood, pubertal activities, the relation of masturbation to psychopathology, and psychoanalytic technique. Isidor Bernstein discusses the integrative aspects of masturbatory activities and fantasies; James A. Kleeman writes about genital self-stimulation in infant and toddler girls; Virginia L. Clower examines the significance of masturbation in female sexual development and fixation; and Frances K. Millican, et al., deal with oral autoerotic, autoaggressive behavior, and oral fixation.

Edith Buxbaum deals with anal masturbation and object loss; Erna Furman describes some aspects of a young boy's masturbation conflict; Leon Ferber writes on beating fantasies; Robert A. Furman provides an excerpt from the analysis of a prepubertal boy; and William T. Moore examines some economic functions of genital masturbation during adolescent development.

Charles A. Sarnoff examines narcissism, adolescent masturbation fantasies, and the search for reality; Sidney Levin describes the relation of various affects to masturbation conflicts; Marc H. Hollander probes women's use of fantasy during sexual intercourse; Martin A. Berezin writes on masturbation and old age; and Charles N. Sarlin takes a cross-cultural look at masturbation and psychosexual development.

René A. Spitz provides some remarks on a bibliographical investigation of the relationship of authority to masturbation; Dale R. Meers examines precocious heterosexuality and masturbation in the ghetto; Harold Kolansky and William T. Moore investigate marijuana use and autoerotic activity; and Norman Kiell reviews the subject of masturbation in the literature with his paper, "Ay, There's the Rub." (TJW)

IL
517. Sarnoff, Suzanne, and Irving Sarnoff. **Masturbation and Adult Sexuality.** New York: Evans, 1979. 319 p. Previously published as *Sexual Excitement/Sexual Peace.* Includes bibliographic notes and index. ISBN 0-87131-469-X.

Based on personal experience, interviews, research results, and feedback from teaching a course on human sexual love, this book by an education specialist, and her husband, a professor of psychology at New York University, begins by identifying the pleasures and problems (anxiety, fear, guilt, ambivalence) of masturbation as they normally unfold in childhood and later years. Everyone engages in physical and/or mental masturbation, but gratification from solitary sexual experience may be problematic, depending upon how the mind is used during that activity. This book attempts to present a thorough integration of the experiential, developmental, and interpersonal aspects of masturbation.

In part I, "The Experience of Masturbation," the authors deal first with the physiological and psychological dimensions of masturbatory orgasm (stages; solitary orgasm; responsibility; substitutes; repression; overcoming repression through psychotherapeutic, bioenergetic, and sex therapy; and self-help) and then with the erotic and nonsexual fantasies associated with masturbation.

Believing that masturbation is a natural expression of the need for love and that boys and girls have an equivalent need to give themselves sexual gratification, Sarnoff and Sarnoff, in part II, "Masturbation and Child Development," trace the masturbatory reactions of children to a variety of challenges at different stages in their development. From infancy through childhood to adolescence, masturbatory activity serves to relieve the tensions engendered by such stressful situations as weaning, toilet training, separation from one's parents, coping with school and competition, and the onset of puberty. Brought under self-control and properly expressed, masturbation can smooth the transition of those sexual activities characteristic of loving and productive adults.

Part III, "Masturbation and Adult Fulfillment," brings the Sarnoffs's positive views to bear on the masturbatory behavior of adults, both married and single. Recognizing that unresolved conflicts about masturbation may affect the personality of the individual in adulthood, couples are advised to communicate their secret involvements in masturbation, taking the time to share their fantasies. Various techniques designed to heighten erotic satisfaction in lovemaking and suggestions to use masturbatory fantasies to resolve ambivalence about forming sexual relationships are also described.

Throughout the book the Sarnoffs share their own quite different masturbatory histories and behavior. This approach to a rather taboo subject imparts a ring of authenticity to the theoretical parts of the book. In the epilogue, "From Confusion to

Understanding," they review the history of change in expert opinion about masturbation and examine trends in pornography and sex education as they relate to masturbation. They conclude that despite the problematic nature of masturbation, people can hope to understand its role in life and by using it properly can succeed in "making desirable changes in their personalities and in their loving relationships." (TJW)

Kissing

PR,IL
518. Perella, Nicholas James. **The Kiss Sacred and Profane: An Interpretative History of Kiss Symbolism and Related Religio-erotic Themes.** Berkeley, Calif.: University of California Press, 1969. 356 p. Includes bibliography and index. ISBN 0-520-01392-1.

The subtitle is a good summary of the book, which concentrates on the European tradition from the New Testament to the Baroque period. Parella, a professor of Italian at the University of California, examines the divine kiss, the courtly kiss, the kiss as union of two souls, the kiss of peace, the kiss of betrayal, the kiss of death, and the erotic kiss. Although he views the kiss from theological, philosophical, literary, and erotic aspects, the book consists mainly of critical, textual analysis of references to the kiss in the Bible, in medieval love lyrics, in neo-Platonic philosophy of the Renaissance, and in poetry of the Renaissance and Baroque periods. The basic symbolism of the kiss is union, or spiritual exchange and love, particularly in the sense of divine love and of the meeting of souls in the human kiss. Kissing is traced through the transformation into religious metaphor that love and the kiss achieve to the later evolution of their expression in courtly love where ecstasy and eroticism were transmuted into a pure union of the spirit. In the later philosophy of the neo-Platonists the concept of "the soul-in-the-kiss" conceit is fully developed as a symbol with mystical significance. It is only in the late Renaissance-Baroque period that poets give full expression to the physical, erotic delights of the kiss. The book has a small number of illustrations in sepia that add little to the convincing scholarly presentation. (JA)

Oragenitalism

PO
519. Franklin, Jacqueline, and Steven Franklin. **The Ultimate Kiss: A Guide to Oral Sex.** Los Angeles: Media Publications, 1982. 113 p.

Because of its delicate and controversial subject matter, the Franklins have written this guide to oral sex under pseudonyms. They consider themselves "among the most expert of the few couples currently writing books dealing with sexual subject matter drawn from their own experience," and they "treat the topic of oral sex from the standpoint of delight." Every page of the text is illustrated: over 200 black-and-white photographs show a young couple engaged in various kinds of genital and anal stimulation. The text explains in detail just what is being demonstrated. Thoroughly covered are the fundamental techniques of cunnilingus, fellatio, analingus, and the use of sexual toys, such as vibrators, to enhance the pleasures of oral sex. The book is instructionally explicit and erotic. (TJW)

PO
520. Grant, Susan, and Donald Grant. **Joys of Oral Love.** Edited by Bernhardt J. Hurwood. With a preface by Emily Coleman. Illustrated by Jon Gregory. New York: Carlyle Communications, 1983. 224 p. Originally copyrighted in 1975. Includes bibliography. ISBN 0-503-07003-3.

Emily Coleman sets the tone of this book in the preface by introducing oral sex as a venerable activity, something complete in itself, and an inherent part of our biological and emotional heritage. As an expression of love, oral sex is a way to use the mouth to be good to yourself and others. Grant and Grant present the text in three chapters designed to explode myths and eradicate fears about oral love. The first surveys oral love "from the dawn of history through the present day through the eyes of novelists, poets, historians, social scientists, entertainers and just plain folks" (p. 17). It gives a variety of perspectives on oral love: historical, cross-cultural, psychological, religious, literary, legal, and secular. The long second chapter is a verbatim account of the comments of a panel of twelve experienced and uninhibited men and women enthusiastically discussing, and sometimes disagreeing on, the particulars of oral sex. Included on the panel were several erotic artists, an expert on massage parlors, a trained sex surrogate, an actress in X-rated motion pictures, a mother and daughter, and several writers and editors. The principal chapter is a detailed description of the techniques and artistry of oral love in its broadest dimensions with emphasis on cunnilingus and fellatio. Attractive sepia and black stippled drawings display the diverse acts of oral love. (TJW)

IL
521. Legman, Gershon. **Oragenitalism: Oral Techniques in Genital Excitation.** New York: Bell, 1979. 319 p. Reprint of the 1969 edition published by Julian Press, New York. ISBN 0-517-30807-X.

Author of a string of books on censorship, erotic folklore, and sexual humor, Legman turns his attention to a previously highly taboo subject: oral excitation of the male and female genitalia, or, to use his own term, oragenitalism. The surprising lack of illustrations in the book is balanced by Legman's flowery and expansive prose, that reflects his erudition and delight in written expression. The book has four parts: "Cunnilinctus," "Fellation," "Irrumation," and "The Sixty-nine." In each part technique is emphasized. A special part, "A Practical Treatise," is a translation of a hitherto unpublished French work on fellation. Although male-oriented assumptions underlie this work, it provides detailed descriptions of oragenitalism. The text is replete with references to related literature but lacks footnotes and a bibliography. Content accessibility to this informative work is seriously compromised by the lack of a detailed subject index. (TJW)

Intercourse

Genital

IL
522. Eichel, Edward, and Philip Nobile. **The Perfect Fit: How to Achieve Mutual Fulfillment and Monogamous Passion Through the New Intercourse.** New York: Donald I. Fine, 1992. 192 p. Includes index. ISBN 1-55611-320-X.

In this short book, Eichel and Nobile join forces to introduce a new position for sexual intercourse, that is achieved by means of the Coital Alignment Technique (CAT), developed by Eichel over a fifteen-year period. They claim that with this new method sexual partners easily experience orgasmic satisfaction.

The first two chapters critically review the achievements of such sexology pioneers as Sigmund Freud, who started the debate over the relative merits of the vagina and clitoris as the "dominant erotogenic zone." Also, the contributions of Wilhelm Reich, Havelock Ellis, Alfred Kinsey, and the team of Masters and Johnson are noted. The work of Shere Hite, John Perry, and the Brauers also come in for critical attention. Eichel believes that their work has contributed immensely to our understanding of human sexuality.

According to Eichel, the clitoris has long been recognized as the key female sex organ for producing sexual pleasure. While so recognized, in the traditional sexual position, the clitoris usually does not receive direct stimulation. This is not really an anatomical difficulty, but rather lies in the inability to bring penis and clitoris into close contact during normal intercourse, regardless of sexual position adopted. The CAT attaches paramount importance to sexual position, preferring the man on top position to all others. For the CAT to be effective, the man must avoid placing his weight on his elbows. Rather he should evenly distribute his weight over the woman's body. Also his body must be higher up over the woman's in what is referred to as "pelvic override." With man and woman in tight coordination, small, slow, smooth pelvic movements should follow. In theory, the result should be intense orgasmic satisfaction for the partners. Line drawings illustrate the basic features of the CAT.

Eichel's supporting data for the CAT, provided in the appendix, originally appeared in the summer 1988 issue of the *Journal of Sex and Marital Therapy*. They are based on a questionnaire sent to fifty-eight members of an encounter group already familiar with the technique. Eichel also matched his forty-three replies with a control group of couples untrained in the technique. The results of this comparison supported Eichel's contention that the CAT is an effective method for enhancing sexual intercourse and that a mutually fulfilling new sexual position has been found. (TJW)

PO
523. Wilson, Glenn. **Sexual Positions: A Photographic Guide to Pleasure and Love.** Photography by Peter Barry. New York: Arlington House, 1984. unpaged. ISBN 0-517-554879.

A short, clearly written, sometimes humorous text by Wilson, Senior Lecturer at the Institute of Psychiatry, London, complements the soft-focus photographs of the popular photographer Peter Barry in this guide to foreplay, sexual intercourse, and oral sex. Altogether 224 full-color photographs depict couples posed in a variety of often gymnastic sexual positions. Wilson's text, using information from sex surveys and the conclusions of sex researchers, is logically organized under various headings: "Preparations for Sex" (creating the mood, foreplay, oral sex, bedroom manners), "Positions for Sex" (standard and variational), "Erotic Settings," "Sociable Sex" (group sex), "Erotic Fantasies," "Enhancements" (erotica, clothing, equipment, S-M, aphrodisiacs), "Men: How to Seduce a Woman" (eight pieces of advice), "Women: How to Seduce a Man" (ditto), and "How to Be Loved" (learn how to bestow love if you wish to be loved). Barry's photographs are meant to fulfill much of what Wilson recommends, but the text and photographs seem divorced from each other, as if they were independently produced and subsequently blended. (TJW)

Anal

IL
524. Morin, Jack. **Anal Pleasure & Health: A Guide for Men and Women.** 2nd ed. Burlingame, Calif.: Yes Press, 1986. 269 p. Includes bibliography and index. ISBN 0-940208-08-3.

In many places sodomy is deemed a "crime against nature," anal intercourse is recognized as a taboo, and the anus and rectum are viewed solely as channels for the elimination of bodily wastes. Nevertheless, there are those individuals who look upon anal sex as a legitimate avenue of pleasure. The purpose of this book by Morin, a therapist in private practice in San Francisco and an educator who regularly conducts anal awareness and relaxation workshops, is to legitimize anal sex and to provide a guide to anal techniques for those wanting to go beyond customary sexual activities. The information presented is "based on the experiences of dozens of men and women who have actively sought to rediscover the anal area as a positive part of themselves—a part to be known intimately and enjoyed" (p. 6). Following introductory chapters on anal pleasure and the anal taboo, Morin gradually explores the physical aspects, varieties, and methods of anal pleasure: visual and tactile exploration of the anus, the anatomy and physiology of the anal canal, muscle awareness and control, anal eroticism through self-pleasuring techniques, and anal pleasure with a partner, involving analingus and anal intercourse. Crucial to satisfactory sexual relations through anal pleasure is honest communication with one's partner. This chapter and one on sex roles and power dynamics in anal sexual relations are especially noteworthy. Two appendixes supplement the text: one on "Common Problems of the Anus and Rectum," that focuses on sexually transmitted diseases (STDs) and other diseases affecting the anus and rectum; and the second on a detailed discussion of the "Research Process and Findings" on which this book is based. (TJW)

Orgasm

(For related material see also entry 581)

PO
525. Brauer, Alan P., and Donna Brauer. **ESO: How You and Your Lover Can Give Each Other Hours of Extended Sexual Orgasm.** New York: Warner Books, 1983. 226 p. Includes bibliography and index. ISBN 0-446-51270-2.

Alan Brauer is a practicing psychiatrist, founder of the Stanford Medical Center Biofeedback and Stress Reduction Clinic and of the Brauer Stress and Pain Control Medical Center in Palo Alto, California, and Donna Brauer is a trained psychotherapist. Their book derives from extensive work in the "treatment of sexual problems and in developing and teaching methods of enhancing sexual pleasure." By 1982, they "had trained some sixty couples and forty individuals" in Extended Sexual Orgasm (ESO); approximately 15 percent of those attending weekend seminars on ESO reported progress in the technique. Their work is summed up in two charts labeled "Female Orgasmic Responses" and "Male Orgasmic Responses," that detail the three stages of orgasm as experienced uniquely by women and men. Capitalizing on what is known about clitoral orgasm from the research of Masters and Johnson and on the published claim for the existence of a G-spot in the vagina by Ladas, Whipple, and Perry, the Brauers promote a sexual technique that is intended and designed to produce a type of orgasm that manifests itself in the female, for example, after bursts of rapid vaginal muscle contractions characteristic of the single orgasm but also eventually by continuous slow contractions of deeper pelvic muscles that permit extended orgasm. ESO, characterized by ever increasing arousal, may last from thirty minutes to an hour or more. Sharp line drawings of the male and female sexual anatomy and of partners in position for stimulation render clear the anatomical basis and techniques most useful in bringing one's partner to a state of ESO. The book also contains many helpful suggestions about sexual functioning in general. (TJW)

PO
526. Britton, Bryce, and Belinda Dumont. **The Love Muscle: Every Woman's Guide to Intensifying Sexual Pleasure.** Illustrated by Bonnie Hofkin. New York: New American Library, 1982. 211 p. Includes bibliography. ISBN 0-452-25382-9.

The main purpose of this book, written in a popular style by an experienced sex therapist, is to teach women how to achieve (and to provide) intense sexual pleasure by means of skillful use of the PC (pubococcygeus or "love") muscle. For those women who are dissatisfied with their sexual performance or desirous of improving it, the route to the attainment of satisfying sex is by following several prescribed six-week schedules of PC muscle exercises; these depend on one's level of sexuality, which is determined by taking a series of tests, such as the "Twentieth Century Orgasm Quiz," the "Your Love Muscle Condition Test," and "Your Love Muscle Control Test." In addition, the entire armamentarium of sexual stimulation is discussed in terms of its contribution to lovemaking: erogenous zones, massage, clitoral stimulation, the Grafenberg spot, oral sex, masturbation, and sexual aids. A secondary aim of this book is to present what is called "An Intimacy Code," that is proclaimed as a code of sexual morality for sex partners. Honesty about oneself, frank communication, accepting responsibility for one's own orgasm, and concern for one's partner's feelings are among the points that make for successful intimacy between lovers. This aim is subsidiary to the major goal of intensification of sexual pleasure for women through expert use of the love muscle. (TJW)

PR,IL
527.   Fisher, Seymour. **The Female Orgasm: Psychology, Physiology, Fantasy.** New York: Basic Books, 1973. 590 p. Includes bibliography and indexes.

The Female Orgasm and *Understanding the Female Orgasm* (1973) are two versions of the same work. While the former attempted to "review and make sense of all available scientific literature concerning the nature of femininity and sexual responsiveness in women" as well as to describe Fisher's empirical findings about what factors contribute to a woman's ability to have orgasm, the latter condenses the scientific version with the intent of discussing in nontechnical language, "what we know about sexual behavior and sexual responsiveness in women." These goals make it clear that both of these books examine a wide range of behavior related to the nature of female sexuality, although the ostensible focus is an explanation of female orgasmic behavior. They supplement the findings of Kinsey and Masters and Johnson by attempting to understand the psychological aspects of sexual behavior investigated by these pioneers in sex research. They consider not only how a woman's personality influences her sexual responsiveness but also how "a basic drive" becomes a part of her life.

Part I contains a massive literature review of what is known about female sexual responsiveness, including such topics as the establishment of female identity, body experiences that characterize womanhood, adaptations to pregnancy and menstruation, and fantasies associated with sexual arousal. Based on previous studies, Fisher concludes that "many widely held ideas about female sexuality are erroneous." For example, he finds that a woman's sexual responsiveness is not an index to her emotional stability, practice has little effect on a woman's ability to be orgasmic, orgasm is not likely to be impaired by traumatic sexual experiences, a woman's attitude toward her father may be more related to her sexual responsiveness than those toward her mother, and it is difficult to find any traits that predict a woman's orgasmic potential.

Part II presents the findings of seven empirical studies conducted by Fisher in which he sought to determine how psychological factors influence a woman's sexual responsiveness and her adaptation to the structure of the female role. Using questionnaires, interviews, laboratory procedures (including physiological measurements) and a large battery of psychological tests, he evaluated the sexual behavior of these multiple samples of women. He concluded that a woman's sexual behavior is very complex; it is difficult to predict one aspect from another. One of his major findings is that the lack of dependability of love objects is associated with a woman's difficulty in reaching orgasm. Other findings that he deemed significant are that clitoral rather than vaginal stimulation contributes more to sexual arousal and that there is an experiential difference between them, and that women who experience a lot of menstrual discomfort are not particularly psychologically disturbed. His thorough investigations also sought information on topics such as the relationship between personality and frequency of masturbation, clothing preferences and sexual behavior, degree of femininity and sexual responsiveness, and body image and orgasmic potential.

The conclusions reached in *The Female Orgasm* are also those presented in *Understanding the Female Orgasm.* It is risky to generalize about the nature of female sexual responsiveness. Research in this area is in its elementary phase. (SGF)

PO
528.   Hartman, William, and Marilyn Fithian. **Any Man Can: The Multiple Orgasmic Technique for Every Loving Man.** New York: St. Martin's Press, 1984. 177 p. Includes bibliography and index. ISBN 0-312-04520-4.

A method for developing in men the ability to have multiple orgasms during intercourse is the subject of this book by Hartman and Fithian, co-directors of the Center for Marital and Sexual Studies in Long Beach, California. Central to the multi-orgasmic technique is the recognition that orgasm and ejaculation are separate phenomena, a notion that contradicts the popular belief that they always occur together.

Hartman and Fithian began doing research on sexual behavior in the laboratory and providing treatment for sexual dysfunctions in the late 1960s. They claim that their methods have benefited several thousand single, married, aged, and disabled people who came to them for help in coping with impotence, premature ejaculation, and other disorders. Believing that good sexual performance is largely a matter of shared and balanced intimacy, they have worked out a series of exercises that will provide men with the ability to control both orgasm and ejaculation, thereby creating the means for men and women to balance out the inherent disparate sexual responses during intercourse.

Three steps are generally needed before a man can incorporate the multi-orgasmic technique into his sexual repertoire. The first requirement is to strengthen the pelvic muscles (pubococcygeus and associated muscles) through prescribed exercises. Then it is necessary to learn the "squeeze" technique during masturbation to control ejaculation. Finally, couples should learn the "nondemand pleasuring" technique that involves two people pleasuring each other without intercourse.

Hartman and Fithian present the evidence for multi-orgasmic capability in men and women in the appendix. Using a Beckman R411 dynograph, they studied heart rate during orgasm: 120 beats per minute occurred at the peak of orgasm. Women have discrete multiple orgasms, characterized by peaks and valleys, as well as continuous multiple orgasms where the heart rate remains high. Research findings showed that "multi-orgasmic male patterns are similar to that of the female" (p. 165). In their research they "observed 740 volunteer research subjects, 282 of them males. Of that number 33 were multi-orgasmic" (p. 157). (TJW)

PO

529. Heiman, Julia, Leslie LoPiccolo, and Joseph LoPiccolo. **Becoming Orgasmic: A Sexual Growth Program for Women.** Englewood Cliffs, N.J.: Prentice-Hall, 1976. 219 p. (The Self Management Psychology Series). Includes bibliography and index. ISBN 0-13-072652-4.

Although specifically designed to help women who are inorgasmic or have difficulty experiencing orgasm, this book presents a general framework for sexual growth for a wide range of women who want to learn more about their sexual feelings, explore their potential, and change their current sexual behavior. Based on the results of successful sex therapy, the authors (all associated with the Department of Psychiatric and Behavioral Science, School of Medicine, SUNY-Stony Brook) present guidelines to facilitate a process of sexual growth that can be adapted to individual needs. Many of the procedures were developed by Joseph LoPiccolo, who derived much of his theoretical orientation from the Kinsey reports and Masters and Johnson and formed ideas about therapeutic orientation from Donald Hastings and Arnold Lazarus. Overall, the program stresses the uniqueness of each individual and emphasizes the theme that sexual growth is one part of personal growth. Chapter 1 explores the ambivalence and fears that often accompany getting involved in a program for changing sexual response; it gives reassurance about what to expect from the experience. Chapters 2 to 7 present exercises and learning experiences that a woman can undertake on her own. Subject matter includes guidance in compiling a personal sex history; information on facets of female sexual response; the relationship of body image to sexual functioning; and self-pleasuring exercises that include touching, masturbation, using a vibrator, and hints on increasing arousal and triggering orgasm. Chapters 8 through 11 focus on improving sexual relations with a partner. Both sexual and nonsexual dynamics of sharing pleasure are discussed. Topics include how to take responsibility for your own sexuality, ways to avoid putting pressure on yourself or your partner, information on male sexual response, and ways to give sexual pleasure via intercourse and noncoital expression as well as to enhance it with oral and anal stimulation. This sensitively written work recommends rather than dictates avenues to sexual growth and does not promise any easy solutions. The authors are consistent in their emphasis on a program that acknowledges individual needs, fears, and potential. They raise a variety of questions about sexuality that stimulate individual awareness and encourage answers that facilitate change. (SGF)

PO

530. Kassorla, Irene. **Nice Girls Do—And Now You Can Too!** Los Angeles: Stratford Press, 1980. 237 p. Includes bibliography. ISBN 0-936906-01-4.

Guilt about sex is a burden imposed upon many of us in childhood. Kassorla, a successful psychologist and sex therapist, has developed a step-by-step approach, the "Pleasure Process," that she claims enables women to overcome their fears and guilt feelings about sex and learn to enjoy sexual loving to the fullest. The ultimate reward for those completing the six-step process is the ability to easily experience the maxi-orgasm, a seemingly endless series of orgasms over a period of hours. The six vital steps include hugging, fingertipping, verbalizing, recalling erotic childhood images, granting one's lover the license to stimulate one's erogenous zones and focusing one's attention on the pleasure received, and last, intercourse, a sharing of orgasms with another loving person. Although written for women, the philosophy underlying the process and the process itself are likely to interest men as well. (TJW)

IL,PO

531. Meshorer, Mark, and Judith Meshorer. **Ultimate Pleasure: The Secrets of Easily Orgasmic Women.** Foreword by Beverly Whipple, Ph.D. New York: St. Martin's Press, 1986. 230 p. ISBN 0-312-82826-8.

Although this book was written specifically for women who desire to enhance their sexual pleasure through orgasm, it should also benefit men who enjoy pleasuring their partners. It is about the experiences of "easily orgasmic women," that is, women who achieve "orgasm during at least 75% of sexual contacts" (the women in this study were orgasmic in over 90% of their sexual contacts); orgasms were triggered by sexual intercourse and/or other stimulation, such as oral and anal sex.

The data on which this study (conducted by a married couple who are attorneys and sexologists) is based were collected by means of a pre-interview questionnaire and in-depth interview (presented in appendixes) from sixty voluntary participants representing a cross-section of heterosexual American women. Married, widowed, divorced, separated, and single, they ranged in age from twenty-one to fifty-nine. Religiously diverse, fifty-four were Caucasian and six black. Most of them went to college; their occupations varied widely from homemakers to teachers. The average woman might be characterized as "middle-class." Thirty-five were mothers. On average, the women in this study obtained three orgasms per contact, and three sexual encounters per week was average. Forty-four women often experienced multiple orgasms, and a few "ultra-orgasmic" women achieved from six to a dozen orgasms per contact.

This book is largely about how these women pursue pleasure in their lovemaking, eventually reaching orgasm, the ultimate pleasure. The women stress the importance of such crucial elements as the basic attitudes of sexual partners toward sex and pleasure, the necessity of partners communicating their desires and appreciation during lovemaking, focusing one's attention on the lovemaking act, and appreciating the physical and mental attributes of one's partner.

Through the words of the participants, the Meshorers describe many facets of orgasmic sex, including the intensity and quality of orgasms. They present a whole range of mental and physical arousal techniques. They discuss the G spot, the PC muscles, and female ejaculation. Interestingly, only 15 percent of the women reported orgasms that could be attributable to the G spot. The women discuss mental stimuli, such as self-appreciation, fantasy, roles, and body-part imaging, that help in one's arousal and approach to orgasm. Finally, they describe the moments before orgasm and the orgasm itself. The portrait of the easily orgasmic woman that emerges from this study is one who accepts herself, has a caring and communicative partner, and has a positive attitude toward pleasure. (TJW)

Sex Aids: Aphrodisiacs, Dildoes, Drugs, Exercise, Games, Hypnosis, Lubricants, Vibrators

(For related material see also entries 1020, 1021)

PR,IL
532. Araoz, Daniel L., and Robert T. Bleck. **Hypnosex: Sexual Joy Through Self-Hypnosis.** New York: Arbor House, 1982. 222 p. ISBN 0-87795-367-8.

Araoz and Bleck, professors of psychology at C. W. Post University and affiliates of the Hypnosex Program of Dynamic Imagery Associates, present a sexual self-help program using the methods of hypnosex—the application of the principles of self-hypnosis to sexual functioning. In the first four chapters, they establish a basic link between sexual functioning and hypnosis; both depend upon using the mind in a "natural, healthy and creative way" to enhance personal enjoyment. They are careful to define and discuss the nature of hypnosis as well as to attempt to dispel some common myths about it, such as "I'll lose control" or "I can't be hypnotized." They then introduce the five phases of self-hypnosis (natural rhythmic breathing, scientific body relaxation, positive inner-mind imagery, self-suggestion, and re-entry) and provide some basic scripts to facilitate the process. A brief chapter on human sexuality serves as an orientation to the complex interaction of the mind and body in sexual functioning and suggests ways in which thoughts about sex can be a source of sexual problems or enhancement. Chapters 5 to 10 demonstrate how to adapt self-hypnosis to a variety of sexual situations—to enhance sexual pleasure, to deal with sexual dysfunction, to share sexual fantasies, to share hypnotic experiences, and to contribute to holistic sex. Each of these chapters includes a variety of innovative scripts that counselors may find useful if they use hypnosis as part of sex therapy. The final chapter discusses some other ways that hypnosis can apply to many aspects of our lives. They advocate hypnosex as a viable adjunct to sex therapy and regard it as a valuable tool to help the layperson enhance his or her sexuality and develop positive "inner-mind" thinking. (SGF)

PO
533. Blank, Joani. **Good Vibrations: The Complete Guide to Vibrators.** Burlingame, Calif." Down There Press, 1982. 44 p. Includes bibliography. ISBN 0-940208-05-9.

Since it first appeared in 1975, this little book on vibrators and their use has enjoyed a remarkable popularity. Intended for both men and women, it provides a brief history of the use of vibrators for sexual gratification, descriptions of various kinds of vibrators (coil-operated, motor-driven, battery-operated, the Swedish massager, eggs and Ben-Wa balls), suggestions on how to buy a vibrator, information on use of the vibrator in self-gratification, mutual masturbation, and anal/rectal stimulation. The myth of addiction to vibrators is dispelled and health matters (cleanliness, use during pregnancy) are considered. Blank believes that where there is love, vibrators "may enhance or liven up the sex by augmenting verbal and physical communication and contact" (p. 41). (TJW)

PO
534. Herrin, Kym, and Richard Benyo. **The Sexercise Book.** Mountain View, Calif.: Anderson World Books, 1982. 220 p. ISBN 0-89037-226-8.

The assumption underlying the material in this book is that exercise stressing primarily the neck, arms, chest, abdomen, hips, legs, back, buttocks, and spine muscles promotes flexibility, strength, endurance, and body tone that in turn enhance sexual performance. Hence the appellation "sexercise." Herrin, an avid exerciser and former *Playboy* playmate, has written this book for women to increase not only their ability to express love physically but also their comfort and enjoyment in doing so. The exercises, 120 in all, are organized into three categories according to degree of difficulty: casual, intimate, and intense. Each exercise is described and accompanied by a photographic sequence of two or three pictures of Herrin scantily clad or nude demonstrating the exercise. Benefits from each exercise are indicated, sometimes with reference to sexual activities. Additional chapters include material on female organs and associated muscles, exercises that one may do with one's lover, massage with a male partner, and exercising to music. In using this book it will be necessary for the reader to make up her own selection of exercises and manage her own exercise program. Herrin hopes that sexercises will not only help women to appreciate the sexual aspect of their own bodies but also to enhance their love lives by channeling the fruits of exercise and physical fitness into sexual activity, thus increasing sexual desire. (TJW)

PO
535. Lance, Kathryn, and Maria Agardy. **Total Sexual Fitness for Women.** New York: Rawson, Wade, 1981. 224 p. Includes bibliography and index. ISBN 0-89256-176-9.

In the spirit of *Our Bodies, Ourselves*, this exercise book was written by two women for women. Based on the fitness program of Agardy, the routines concentrate on the muscles surrounding the pelvis, although they do include exercises to improve the strength and flexibility of the entire body.

Part 1, "Feminine Fitness," describes the particular fitness needs of women. Because women bear children, their pelvic area differs from that of men and requires specific, direct exercises to maintain its fitness. Of particular importance are the abdominal muscles, the muscles of the lower back, and the PC (pubococcygeus) muscle ("the least discussed muscle of your body"), that serves as the floor to the abdominal cavity and controls the flow of urine as well as the contractions of the vagina and anal sphincter.

Part 2, "Getting Started," details the components of the exercise program. Each set of abdominal, pelvic, and lower back exercises is divided into levels suitable for women at different stages of fitness. Helpful chapters on how to stick with exercise, answers to common questions about the program, and relaxation exercises are included.

Part 3, "Lifelong Pelvic Fitness," focuses on addressing specific concerns of women at different stages of the life cycle: PC control in children; dealing with PMS and cramps; pregnancy, delivery, and recovery from childbirth; infertility; sexual dysfunction and decreased vaginal tone and sensitivity; and involuntary leakage of urine.

Pelvic fitness not only offers specialized benefits for different aspects of the reproductive system but also holds out the prospect of a more pleasurable sex life for all women. The program requires no special equipment and only a short investment of time. This clearly written book is intended for women of all ages and degrees of physical fitness. (SGF)

PO
536. Milonas, Rolf. **Fantasex: A Book of Erotic Games for the Adult Couple.** Revised ed. New York: Perigee Books/Putnam, 1983. unpaged. Originally copyrighted in 1975 by Grosset & Dunlap, Inc. ISBN 0-399-50839-2.

Fantasex is a practical book for those who wish to play erotic games. Cleverly illustrated with line sketches of couples engaged in sex in a host of positions, it provides instructions on how to play two games: Role Fantasex and Situation Fantasex. Male roles (Playboy, Gynecologist, Nazi Officer, etc.) and female roles (A Rich Widow, Bride, Branch Librarian, etc.) are chosen randomly by number. Following one of four game plans—Cooperative Plan in which decisions are made by mutual consent, Male Dominant Plan in which he makes all the decisions, Female Dominant Plan in which she makes all the decisions, and Pure Chance Plan in which randomly chosen numbers determine the decisions—the players proceed to select from the "Plays" section of the book the game variants they want to play. Thirty plays for use when playing either role or situation fantasex are described and illustrated. Furthermore, twenty-two illustrated "Positions" may be used when playing either role or situation fantasex. A final section describing forty fantasies allows couples to play Situation Fantasex. Fantasy 39, for example, is described thus: "While studying the habits of a remote jungle tribe, she finds herself all alone with the ruling prince. They play together curiously." A position is chosen for use according to one of the game plans, and the couple play Situation Fantasex. The sixty-two roles, thirty plays, twenty-two positions, and forty erotic fantasies provide the basis for exploring variety in a playful, sexual atmosphere. (TJW)

IL

537. Scott, Gini Graham. **Erotic Power: An Exploration of Dominance and Submission.** Secaucus, N.J.: Citadel Press, 1983. 257 p. First published under the title *Dominant Women Submissive Men.* ISBN 0-8065-0968-6.

Dominance and submission refer to practices of consensual power exchange in which one partner, usually the female, plays a dominant role, while the other, usually the male, assumes a submissive role; although it encompasses sadism and masochism as well as bondage and discipline, it is not restricted to those more extreme arenas. For two years, sociologist Scott was a participant/observer in two San Francisco Bay organizations that were composed of D&Sers. On the basis of her research, she introduces the general reader to the world of dominance and submission. Unlike past research by psychologists and psychiatrists, that have focused on case studies of troubled individuals, Scott describes the typical participant in D&S, a practice that cross-cuts most social categories.

Each part of the book explores one aspect of the cultural and social organization of D&S. Part I is devoted to how and why people become involved in it. Most participants find female dominance erotically stimulating and emotionally satisfying. Most males are attracted to sexual submission as a way to counterbalance a primarily dominant lifestyle. Likewise, females may find sexual dominance appealing as a balance to an overall submissive lifestyle. A predisposition to D&S stemming from fantasies of submission in childhood and/or emotional and situational factors account for the pull of individuals into these practices.

Part III describes the psychological and sexual dynamics of a D&S power exchange. D&S relationships have much in common with other types of sexual interaction in terms of duration, frequency, kinds of erotic exchanges, and variety. Parts III, IV, and V describe the activities and behavior of the relatively small number of people (20,000) who explore D&S publicly and seriously. Part III, "Joining the Scene," focuses on the workshops, foursomes, organized groups, and parties that allow individuals to become more comfortable about assuming unconventional sex roles. Part IV deals with the psychological dynamics of the power exchange. In order for the power exchange to work, the dominant must maintain control, but the submissive must set limits. It is within this context that fantasies, toys, pain, bondage, humiliation, and other facets of power manipulation associated with eroticism are discussed. The final part discusses the commercial aspects of D&S: professional mistresses, the professional session, and magazines and books.

Scott concludes that, unlike the social stereotypes of D&S, at the core of D&S communities are "mostly sensible, rational, respectable, otherwise quite ordinary people, for whom D&S is a way of playing with unique, bizarre, unusual, and often taboo forms of fantasy and erotic expression, as a release from the everyday world"; they "avoid truly dangerous or harmful activities" (p. 253). Since between 15 and 75 million adults are estimated to engage in some form of erotic activity in which the female is dominant and the male submissive, D&S can be considered to be part of the continuum of "normal" sexual behavior. (SGF)

PR,IL

538. Stark, Raymond. **The Book of Aphrodisiacs.** New York: Stein and Day, 1982. 195 p. Originally published in 1981. Includes bibliography and index. ISBN 0-8128-6164-7.

This book attempts to fill the gap in descriptions of sexual substances rarely noticed by the medical community. Based on folklore and naturopathic experience, it provides a ready-reference guide to drugs affecting sexuality. It lists over 500 different substances in three separate sections: (1) "Aphrodisiacs, Potency Aids and Sexual Enhancers"; (2) "Contraceptives, Abortifacients, Medications of Fertility, Anaphrodisiacs, Menstrual Medicines";

and (3) "Miscellaneous." Substances are arranged alphabetically under common name followed by double scientific name (e.g., Jimson Weed, *Datura stramonium*). Insofar as possible, Stark notes the geographic distribution of each plant or organism; describes myths and legends that surround its use; and provides details about preparation and dosage, reactions, warnings, etc. The substances listed are not necessarily acceptable medicinal agents employed by the medical community, and their purchase may be illegal in some countries. Stark, a trained naturopath and recognized authority on herbology, confines the term "aphrodisiac" to "those substances which heighten the sexual senses in a relatively short time, say, in no more than one or two hours." He explains that aphrodisiacs "give rise to sexual sensations by increasing blood flow, producing cerebral excitation, stimulating the lower spinal area, or causing urethral irritation." An interesting section, "Ancient Texts on Love and Sex," explores such works as Vatsyayana's *Kama Sutra*; another Indian sex manual, the *Ananga-Ranga*; and the Chinese *Tao Te Ching*, for information about medicinal plants used as aphrodisiacs and sexual enhancers. A list of places where some of the substances described may be purchased is provided. (TJW)

PR,IL

539. Taberner, Peter V. **Aphrodisiacs: The Science and the Myth.** Philadelphia: University of Pennsylvania Press, 1985. 276 p. Includes bibliography and index. ISBN 0-8122-7994-8.

Rather than simply listing aphrodisiacs and describing their properties and effects, Taberner, a lecturer in pharmacology at the University of Bristol, England, attempts to dispel the myths surrounding aphrodisiacs as well as to provide a scientific basis for their study. He begins by reviewing the definitions of aphrodisiacs, the state of the law with respect to them, and the ways in which they are advertised. Following a chapter on the use of drugs as aphrodisiacs in ancient cultures—Indian, Chinese, Greek, Roman, and Arab—he discusses magic charms, potions, and philters used in attempts to influence the course of events. He then distinguishes between herbalism and quackery, discussing, in particular, vegetable aphrodisiacs, ginseng, and secret remedies. Taberner selects four classical aphrodisiacs and explains their widespread use historically: rhinoceros horn, Spanish flies, the mandrake, and alcohol. He points out that alcohol is "undoubtedly the most widely used drug in western society" and that "no drug is completely safe."

An important chapter on the scientific approach to the study of sex and aphrodisiacs follows. It examines sex hormones, or steroids, in terms of release, dosage, and therapeutic use and discusses types of sexual inadequacy, erection, and ejaculation. He provides a discussion of scientific method in the investigation of sex hormones and aphrodisiacs. A lengthy chapter on drugs of abuse follows in which are discussed the nature and use of amphetamines, cannabis, cocaine, opium, nicotine, nitrites, nutmeg, LSD and the psychedelic drugs, hypnotics and sedatives, and also such stimulants as kola and khat. Taberner then describes drugs used clinically as aphrodisiacs, including yohimbine, strychnine, luteinizing hormone releasing hormone (LHRH), dopamine (especially its regulation of sexual function and libido), serotonin, and drugs with aphrodisiac and anaphrodisiac side-effects. A final chapter on sex stimulants points to the future use of pheromones, perfumes, bodily secretions, brain stimulation, and subliminal stimulation.

Taberner states that "there can be little doubt that there will always be a future for aphrodisiacs," especially in medical science, but "for the healthy normal subject who seeks only to add new dimensions of pleasure to his or her sex life, the quacks will be ever ready with their nostrums and remedies for separating the credulous from their money." (TJW)

PO

540. Wells, Carol G. **Right-Brain Sex: Using Creative Visualization to Enhance Sexual Pleasure.** New York: Prentice Hall Press, 1989. 238 p. Includes bibliography and index. ISBN 0-13-780818-6.

Sex therapist Wells's how-to-do-it book of sex instruction bases its approach on recent understanding of the bicameral brain, which contains a left hemisphere responsible for more practical, analytical thinking and a right hemisphere given over to the more imaginative mental processes, including the storing of sex images garnered over a lifetime. Wells urges readers to learn how to use the right brain to enhance sexual pleasure and solve a variety of sexual problems. One can accomplish this by using a goal-directed process known as visualization that has been used successfully in business and sports.

Visualization, that uses "mental rehearsal in anticipation of the real-life experience" (p. xv), is "part imagination, part meditation, and part analogy" used to facilitate change. Initially one practices this three-part process to get used to visualization by exercising first the imagination (selecting the image), then meditating, or concentrating deeply on the image, and finally drawing comparisons to similar images. Wells uses this simple technique in connection with particular problems encountered in trying to cope with sexual problems. Wells also notes the inherent differences between fantasy and visualization and hypnosis and visualization.

Crucial to successful visualization are three right-brain processes that one must master: change, transition, and concentration. The ability to make basic changes in sexual routines (behavior patterns, the use of time, practicing, and motivation); the ability to cross bridges from the nonerotic state to the erotic state; and mastering the technique of concentration must be learned for the successful use of visualization in the solution of sexual problems.

Building on this background, Wells introduces a series of chapters about concrete areas of sexuality, including touching, masturbation, the lustful attitude, play, and pleasure. She concludes with chapters on the relation of love to sex and the achievement of orgasm and erection.

For those in need of help, Wells recommends consulting a licensed sex therapist. Of course, not all professionals use visualization as a technique for solving sex problems, but one should ask about it if one is interested in working further with this successful technique. (TJW)

Sexual Variations

PR
541. Hirschfeld, Magnus. **Sexual Anomalies and Perversions: Physical and Psychological Development, Diagnosis and Treatment. A Summary of the Works of the Late Professor Dr. Magnus Hirschfeld.** Edited by Norman Haire. New and revised ed. London: Encyclopaedic Press, 1966. 630 p. Originally published in 1938.

Reprinted many times since it was originally published in 1938, this book is a compilation of Hirschfeld's writings by his pupils who wished to memorialize their teacher and mentor in a text reflecting his thinking on the subject of sexual variations.

In the introduction, Norman Haire takes issue with the use of the word *perversions* in the title, castigating it as old-fashioned and out-of-date, and proceeds to compare it with the terms *aberration* and *variation*. The text is divided into five books. Book I, "Normal Development of Sexuality," deals with sexuality in its several stages from the embryonic stage through puberty to death, emphasizing physical development, the effect of hormones, and psychological factors. Book II, "Irregular Sexual Development," describes such anomalies as infantilism, premature sexual development, castration, and hypererotism largely in terms of glandular functioning and development. Book III, "Deflections of the Sexual Impulse," discusses deviations from the normal direction of the sexual impulse: masturbation, narcissism, hermaphroditism, androgyny, transvestism, and homosexuality. Books IV and V deal with variations arising from fixations on component impulses of the sexual impulse. These include sadomasochism, sexual murder, necrophilia, fetishism, exhibitionism, and scopophilia.

This work reflects several of Hirschfeld's key achievements as a sexologist: that sex hormones "exercise a decisive influence on the development of the entire sexual personality" and "that all sexual anomalies are caused by irregularities in development" (p. 24). (TJW)

IL
542. Masters, R. E. L. **Forbidden Sexual Behavior and Morality: An Objective Reexamination of Perverse Sex Practices in Different Cultures.** New York: Julian Press, 1964. 431 p. Includes bibliography and index.

The forbidden sexual practices covered in this volume include bestiality, a variety of homosexual acts, miscegenation, the use of so-called aphrodisiacs, and pedophilia. Written from the point of view of an "objective" and "scientific" approach as opposed to the views of those who take rigid moralistic and legal positions, Masters hopes to shed light on those subjects about which either little has been written and/or much misinformation is available. As Harry Benjamin comments in the introduction: "Nowhere in the scientific or semi-scientific . . . literature is anything found that can . . . be compared to the first part of Masters's book dealing with 'Bestiality.' It may well be the 'Bible' of this subject" (p. x).

The lengthy section on bestiality is a survey and analysis of the "meaning and content of the sexual relations of humans with beasts." As such, Masters gives a historical review of bestiality among primitive peoples, in Greek and Roman mythology, and in modern times (covering the religious, legal, and medical aspects of the subject). Examining bestiality in the context of mythology, folklore, fiction, and art, he muses about the connection between love and lust, and deals with bestiality as perversion, alluding to the contributions of Krafft-Ebing, Freud, and Albert Ellis.

The section on homosexual (including lesbian) acts deals with the physiological and psychological foundations of masturbation, fellatio, cunnilingus, and sodomy. It examines the roles of dominance and submission in homosexual relationships as well as special environments (prison, military, etc.) as occasions for homosexual acts, and also discusses these acts in heterosexual contexts.

A short essay on miscegenation, presenting Norman Mailer's views on the superiority of black sexuality, followed by another short essay on the use of mescaline and other drugs as aphrodisiacs are included. An essay on adult-child sex relationships takes as its point of departure the novel *Lolita* by Vladimir Nabokov. It examines such aspects of the problem as age of consent, pedophilia in primitive societies, child prostitution, nymphophilia (the love of an adult for a female child), and pedophilia.

Masters concludes with the following statements: "My purpose . . . in this volume has been, first of all, to make clear the inadequacy of moralistic absolutes and the laws derived from them where human sexual practices and compelling—and compulsive— human sexual cravings are concerned," and "contemporary antisexual legislation is so outmoded both in terms of contemporary sexual behavior and current scientific knowledge as to reduce that legislation to absurdity" (p. 403). (TJW)

PR,IL
543. Thompson, William E., and Alan J. Buttell. **Sexual Deviance in America.** Emporia, Kans.: The School of Graduate and Professional Studies, Emporia State University, 1984. 48 p. (The Emporia State Research Studies, Vol. XXXIII, no. 1). Includes bibliography and glossary.

Combining their backgrounds in sociology and law, Thompson and Buttell review the literature on sexual deviance in the United States. Initially, they examine the issue from a cross-cultural perspective, focusing on societal taboos that influence the many definitions of sexual deviance. Since no sexual act is inherently deviant, it is difficult to construct a definition of sexual deviance satisfactory to everyone. However, two factors seem to determine deviant sexual behavior: societal reaction to a particular act and the "social visibility" of the act. Pointing out that "the literature suggests that American attitudes about sex and sexual deviance have changed over the past few decades and they continue to change," Thompson and Buttell review sex law enforcement, which varies from region to region and from offense to offense. "Sex laws are, for the most part, more symbolic than functional, and despite opinions to the contrary, are rarely enforced in a rigid manner" (p. 40). Many sex offenders are deviant only in the area of sexual behavior; the rapist, however, commits crimes of violence and his offense is against a person rather than just an illegal act. So-called victimless crimes committed by sex offenders are in the areas of homosexuality, voyeurism, transvestism, exhibitionism, and others.

Research to explain the causes of sexual deviance is inconclusive. The evidence suggests that "different types of deviant sexual acts are probably caused by different factors, and different acts are committed by different types of people" (p. 40). Methods of treating offenders are reviewed; it is apparent that no one method is satisfactory. Because sexual deviance has many causes, there probably should be a multi-treatment approach. Decriminalization of many so-called deviant acts seems to be a feasible and even a necessary approach to the problem of sexual deviance. The authors conclude that "it may be that the spectrum of human sexuality is too broad to ever be contained within human normative structures. If this conclusion is found to be valid, society's efforts might be productively geared to expanding the social definitions, interpretations, and range of tolerance, to accommodate the broadest possible spectrum of human sexuality" (p. 41). (TJW)

IL,PO
544. Ullerstam, Lars. **The Erotic Minorities.** Introduction by Yves de Saint-Agnès. Translated by Anselm Hollo. New York: Grove Press, 1966. 172 p. Includes glossary.

Ullerstam's position with respect to sexual minorities—homosexuals, exhibitionists, fetishists, etc.—is that these sexually eccentric individuals are not psychopathic but are deserving of humane consideration that would allow them their sexual satisfactions. As a basis for this position, he accepts "Kinsey's *valuation* that 'perversions' are phenomena in the realm of normal biology" (p. 39), and not necessarily pathological. Indeed, these variant behaviors occur in the animal world and even in some other human societies.

Ullerstam discusses the state of our knowledge in regard to incest, exhibitionism, pedophilia, saliromania, algolagnia (sadism and masochism), homosexuality, scopophilia, and other sexual deviations. Scientifically speaking, we know next to nothing about them; there has been practically no research on them. We do know, Ullerstam claims, that they all have "a great potential for happiness."

Reviewing the sex and pornography laws in Sweden, Ullerstam claims that they have mainly benefited the coital propensities of heterosexuals but, excepting homosexuals, have come down hard on the sexual minorities. Thus, he calls for the sexually handicapped to unite and for others more fortunate to assist them in their struggle for a sexual bill of rights. He proposes a nine-point sexual reform program consisting of (1) sex education starting in the family, (2) support from religion, (3) sex information and referral centers, (4) open advertising in the press, (5) clubs for exhibitionists, (6) medical treatment of impotent and frigid handicapped people, (7) pornography services, (8) instructional literature for homosexuals and others, and (9) the establishment of brothels.

Ullerstam believes that an enlightened attitude toward the sexually disenfranchised will go a long way toward reducing violent crime, combating venereal disease, and making life happier for those thousands of so-called perverts who joylessly exist in the shadow of society. (TJW)

Psychosexual Disorders. Sex Therapy

PR
545. Chasseguet-Smirgel, Janine. **Sexuality and Mind: The Role of the Father and the Mother in the Psyche.** New York: New York University Press, 1986. 167 p. (Psychoanalytic Crosscurrents). Includes bibliography and index. ISBN 0-8147-1400-5.

What did Freud say about female sexuality? What is the role of the father in the psychological development of the person? Are there differences between "male" love and "female" love? Eminent French analyst Chasseguet-Smirgel carefully explores these and other questions in *Sexuality and Mind.* Based on her vast clinical experience, the book confronts issues that, until recently, had been ignored by traditional psychoanalytic thinkers.

She tries to grasp the unconscious motives that can lead men (and women as well) to stifle the powers of women. She also describes how the unconscious image of the mother—that she calls "almighty and dangerous"—can arouse not only fear and aggression but also fascination, and how this position can lead to a wish to eradicate the father and his derivatives. A "fatherless" universe, she contends, is one in which thought processes are deeply altered, resulting in "an Orwellian world where words may mean anything and its opposite."

"A world where women (representing the mother) have no rights, where they are 'insulted and injured,' " she suggests, "reveals its deep insecurity connected with the fear of being annihilated by the overwhelming power of the primitive mother. A world where the father has disappeared is a world where the very ability to think has been annihilated. The reunion of father and mother not only gives birth to the child but to the mind with its full capacities of functioning."

With essays on Freud and female sexuality, submissive daughters, utopias, the Green movement in Germany, and apocalyptic fantasies, *Sexuality and Mind* offers important new insights to analysts on the psychodynamic nature of the father and of its extension to the social and political world. (Author)

[N.B. Janine Chasseguet-Smirgel is currently a Professor at the Charles de Gaulle University in Lille, France.]

PR

546. Kaplan, Helen Singer. **The Evaluation of Sexual Disorders: Psychological and Medical Aspects.** New York: Brunner/Mazel, 1983. 289 p. Includes bibliographies and index. ISBN 0-87630-210-X.

In the introduction, Kaplan says that "diagnosis is the single most important function of the clinician who deals with sexual complaints" (p. 3). Unfortunately, traditional methods of assessment were not developed to diagnose sexual disorders, and the principles of psychosexual medicine are poorly understood. The goal of this book is to present a method of evaluation that integrates psychological and medical aspects of the diagnosis of sexual problems.

The book is divided into three sections. In the first section, "Psychosexual Evaluation," Kaplan explains the rationale behind, and the elements of, the data gathering sequence and assessment process. Of particular importance is the use of a "specially structured, problem-centered diagnostic interview" that allows the clinician to distinguish between organic, psychological, and marital aspects of psychosexual disorders. The interview elicits information about the patient's current sexual experience, deeper roots of the sexual difficulty, and the role of the couple's interaction. All of these data become the basis for forming a treatment plan that includes behavioral intervention as well as psychodynamic and systems components.

In the second section, physicians who are authorities in gynecology, urology, and endocrinology provide a foundation for the medical evaluation of sexual disorders. Each contributor reviews the anatomy and physiology related to a problem, describes diseases and drugs that may cause the pathology, and suggests guidelines for diagnosis. Kaplan points out the importance of recognizing the existence of disorders as separate disease states in a triphasic conceptualization of sexuality and considering male and female disorders as separate clinical entities. Problems discussed in this section include disorders of male and female orgasmic excitement, desire phases, and dyspareunia.

In the final section, Kaplan attempts to integrate comprehensively the medical and psychological concepts and diagnostic procedures presented in the first two sections. She describes the diagnostic criteria and clinical features of the psychosexual syndromes (gender identity disorders; psychosexual dysfunctions, including sexual pain, spasms, and disorders of orgasm, excitement, and desire phases; sexual phobias and avoidance; unconsummated marriage) and then summarizes the medical and psychological aspects of evaluation for each. Tables summarizing information as well as case studies complement the text. (SGF)

PR,IL
547. Kaplan, Louise J. **Female Perversions: The Temptations of Emma Bovary.** New York: Doubleday, 1991. 580 p. Includes bibliographic notes and index. ISBN 0-385-26233-7.

In the world of perversions, nothing is what it seems to be, because perversions are elaborate cover-stories, screens for the unconscious motives that lie beneath them—unfulfilled infantile rage and desire to abolish the differences between generations, between male and female, between body parts and the whole body. Consequently, female perversions have been neglected because they are so well disguised; analysts have looked for them in the wrong places—in the expressions of male perversions like fetishism, transvestism, exhibitionism, voyeurism, masochism, sadism, and pedophilia. True, women engage in less than 1 percent of these perversions. However, women's perversions take a different form, related to the dominant female stereotypes of Western, industrialized society. It is no accident that the emergence of rigid gender stereotypes and concern with gender conformity occurred in tandem with industrialization and commercialization. Kleptomania, homovestism, extreme submissiveness (the "slave of love"), mutilations, female impersonation *by women*, child abuse, and anorexia are the perverse scenarios of females that dovetail with these stereotypes. Drawing from classical works of literature, particularly Flaubert's *Madame Bovary*, the lives of well-known writers and other professionals, psychoanalytic theory, history, and her experience as a therapist in New York City, Kaplan attempts to "scrutinize the world of perversion, penetrate the surface, and lay bare the deceptions that are hidden beneath" (p. 6).

Infantile gender ideals that frame the world in scenes of either/or collaborate with rigid gender stereotypes to produce perversion; "socially normalized gender stereotypes are the crucibles of perversion" (p. 14). Perversion demands performance, and the perverse strategy is a psychological process that uses social stereotypes of masculinity and femininity to deceive the onlooker, and often the performer, about the unconscious motives of the perversity—to control in adulthood what seemed uncontrollable in infancy or childhood. In this sense, a perversion becomes a safety valve for the individual—a means to quell anxiety and fear—a way to stave off sinking into madness. The goal of the perversion is to keep everyone focused on the deception. Despite differences in expression, male and female perversions share the art of disguise—deception about the real meaning of the behavior.

The seeds of perversion are sown in childhood, when the child attempts to make sense of body integrity and changes, sex differences, and the behavior of others, particularly the sexual relationship between Mom and Dad. In attempts to understand their development, girls have experiences and fantasies that family members and society at large tell them are in the domain of males. How, then, do males and females come to terms with their cross-gender strivings? Males may disguise their feminine desires with hyper-masculinity, fetishism, and sadism. Females, particularly those who acknowledge their sexual sensations and intellectual power, may deal with these "masculine" characteristics by masquerading as a hyper-feminine woman; by denying male/female differences in anorexia; by mutilating themselves with cosmetic surgery or delicate self-cutting to establish control over their bodies; by becoming ultra-fashionable; by stealing; or by becoming a fetish, like Marilyn Monroe.

The text details the origin and elaboration of perverse scenarios and concludes that gender stereotypes are social straight-jackets that contribute to twisting the fantasies and polymorphous sexuality that are a normal part of human sexuality and distinguish it from that of other animals. For example, it is not surprising that commercialization and industrialization combine with women's inferior role to produce perversions like kleptomania and compulsive shopping. Like Emma Bovary, Western society at the end of the twentieth century engages in a masquerade of sexual freedom. Beneath the veneer of commercialized, available sex, counter-culture feminism, essentialist doctrines of masculinity and femininity, lie the treasures and power of polymorphous sexuality that contains the potential for both men and women to fashion their own lives. The social script as well as individual responses to it have to change. (SGF)

PR
548. Schnarch, David M. **Constructing the Sexual Crucible: An Integration of Sexual and Marital Therapy.** New York: Norton, 1991. 636 p. Includes bibliography and index. ISBN 0-393-70102-6.

According to Schnarch, Associate Professor of Psychiatry and Urology at Louisiana State University School of Medicine, a paradigm shift in the conceptualization and practice of sexual and marital therapy is necessary. Modern sex therapy, based primarily on Masters and Johnson's or Kaplan's concepts of the sexual response cycle, focuses on producing "functional" physiological sexual responses that become equated with sexual fulfillment. Unfortunately, neither sex nor marital therapists include much about intimacy, eroticism, or desire as continuing passion in their therapeutic models. Schnarch's book presents a new paradigm, the sexual crucible, that is an elicitation approach that uses consistent links between intimacy, sexuality, and individual differentiation to facilitate positive development in all three areas; fundamental goals are "profound personal growth in nonsexual areas," access to sexual potential, and emphasis on health rather than on dysfunction. The sexual crucible is a nonreactive therapeutic context within which a couple's relationship and their sense of self can become transformed. The therapist uses the couples' sexual style as a window into the functioning of the individuals and their relationship. The process becomes a confrontation with each participant's self rather than a matter of negotiation, communication, homework assignments, developing paradoxes, or sexual technique. Therefore, therapy involves an examination of the individuals, the dyad, and the systems in which they have grown up. The marriage is "the crucible of adult human development," and sexual interaction becomes part of intimacy, which goes beyond orgasm to enhance sexual potential.

A critique of the models for modern sex therapy (e.g., Masters and Johnson, Kaplan), shows why a new paradigm is needed. The second chapter presents the first component of Schnarch's new paradigm—a quantum model of sexual functioning that integrates its physiological and psychological aspects. The third chapter introduces the concept of sexual potential as a way of examining phenomenological intensity and salience in sexual response. Two chapters define intimacy as "the recursive experience and disclosure of self in the presence of the partner" (p. 109) and present a clinical model for it. Unlike definitions of intimacy that require reciprocal disclosure or a reflected sense of self, Schnarch's clinical model focuses on intimacy as a product of self-validated, self-soothing, differentiated individuals who have accepted their existential loneliness. "I" contact, not "fusion-delusion," is a necessary prelude to the development of intimacy. Common notions that marriage is a fusion of selves into "we" or that love automatically brings deep intimacy and intense eroticism can undermine a marriage. Conflict and stress can be bases for developing intimacy, not harbingers of disaster. Couples need to confront, not bypass, individual and relationship issues when they encounter sexual difficulties, and therapists need to view sexual dysfunction in a wider context. Using the approach of the sexual crucible can lead to a profound interface between sexuality and spirituality. (SGF)

PR,IL
549. Schoenewolf, Gerald. **Sexual Animosity Between Men and Women.** Northvale, N.J.: Jason Aronson, 1989. 249 p. Includes bibliography and index. ISBN 0-87668-933-0.

Schoenewolf, a psychoanalyst in private practice in New York, believes that a great deal of disharmony between the sexes, in the family, and in society may be traced to early childhood experiences, especially to the relations between parents and child. This is where the sexual animosity begins as a result of the narcissism engendered by the attitudes and behavior of mother and father toward the child. The Freudian explanation is found in penis envy on the part of the little girl and castration fear on the part of the little boy. If these feelings are not resolved, male and female narcissism result, and the consequences of narcissism affect sexual relationships, the family, and society.

After exploring in detail the etiology of sexual animosity, Schoenewolf examines female narcissism and male narcissism in turn, pointing out the characteristics and types of narcissism in both sexes and describing their manifestations in behavior. He then looks at sexual animosity in society and in the family. He concludes the theoretical part of his study with a brief look at the harmonic couple, those fortunate people who have resolved the problems of the Oedipus complex, the Electra complex, penis envy, and castration fears. He defines such a couple as a genital couple, a couple "interested in finding ways in which to cooperate rather than compete, ways to make each other feel good rather than ways to control or destroy each other, and ways to unite with rather than separate from each other" (p. 113). In such a couple "sexual animosity is minimal, and what animosity does exist is mitigated through their sexual unions" (p. 114).

The second part of the study is taken up with five case studies. In "Lizzie the Brat," "The Loner," "Animosity in Africa: The Martyrdom of Dian Fossey," "An Analysis of *A Streetcar Named Desire*," and "In a Rooftop in New York," different manifestations of sexual animosity, including rape and murder, from various types of narcissists are described and analyzed. Each of these case studies supports the psychoanalytic interpretation of sexual animosity advanced by Schoenewolf in the first part of the book.

In a postscript he states that in the act of mating "man and woman become one, simultaneously satisfying both Eros . . . and Thanatos. . . . When man and woman are in tune with each other, their movements, feelings, and thoughts intertwined, animosity and separatism dissolve. Each wave of masculinity meets a wave of femininity, culminating in release, in death, and in rebirth. Each feels connected and powerful in relation to the other. Each feels whole and in harmony with their dualities. Each feels fully alive." (TJW)

PR,IL

550. Showalter, Elaine. **The Female Malady: Women, Madness, and English Culture, 1830-1980.** New York: Pantheon Books, 1985. 312 p. Includes bibliography and index. ISBN 0-394-42021-1.

According to Showalter, a professor of English at Princeton University, few histories of psychiatry have paid much attention to questions of gender. This book is a "feminist history of psychiatry and a cultural history of madness as a female malady" (p. 6). Complemented by many historic photographs, the detailed narrative traces how cultural conceptions of gender influence the definition and treatment of mental disorders. Of particular interest is why madness is aligned conceptually with femininity.

Using England as the social context for her analysis, Showalter identifies three major historic periods associated with specific brands of psychiatry. Victorian Psychiatry (1830-1870), hailed as the first psychiatric revolution, ushered in a time for moral management of the insane; "asylums," architecturally modeled after country homes, replaced madhouses, that were little more than hideaways for the "beastly" insane. Victorian psychiatrists sought to domesticate the insane by replacing physical restraint and harsh treatment with close supervision and re-education into socially acceptable behavior. Believing that insanity was caused by "worry, want, and wickedness," therapists sought to inculcate the virtues of industry, self-control, and perseverance. Women's insanity was attributed to weakening of the mind from the "biological crises" of puberty, pregnancy, childbirth, and menopause. Uncontrolled sexuality became a major symptom. Treatments such as clitoridectomies or leeches applied to the cervix and labia seemed like "an attempt to postpone or extirpate female sexuality" (p. 75). Although Conolly demonstrated that an asylum could be managed without physical restraints, the close supervision by male managers and psychiatrists did little to free women from the imposition of male definitions of appropriate female behavior. As asylums became overcrowded, and their staffs demoralized, a new psychiatric theme emerged: Psychiatric Darwinism (1870-1920). With its emphasis on the congenital inferiority of the insane and the hereditary disposition of the impotent and unfit to become insane came a continued tendency to label women as insane. Their nervous disorders included anorexia, hysteria, and neurasthenia. Maudsley conceded that women would be better off at home than in asylums. However, the social theories of Spencer and the biological ones of Geddes and Thompson reinforced Victorian constraints on femininity as scientifically sound. Female reproductive physiology precluded mental development. Women who rebelled against their sex roles were labeled insane. However, Freud and Breuer established that repressed emotions could cause hysteria and paved the way for a more socially sensitive view of mental illness.

Psychiatric Modernism (1920-1980) developed in response to the recognition that the symptoms of shell-shocked men were similar to those of hysterical women. Yealland's authoritarian treatments contrasted with the humane approaches of W. H. R. Rivers. Yealland disbelieved that males could behave so femininely while Rivers acknowledged that shell-shock, like hysteria, has an emotional cause. The disorder challenged current assumptions about appropriate male/female behavior as well as the etiology of hysteria in the female reproductive system. Yet postwar conservatism reinstated some of the established beliefs about sex roles. With a decline in the incidence of hysteria, schizophrenia ascended as the culturally defined female malady. "Schizophrenia offers a remarkable example of the cultural conflation of femininity and insanity" (p. 204). Although neither clinically nor statistically a female disorder, the schizophrenic woman became as "central a cultural figure for the twentieth century as the hysteric was for the nineteenth." Disproportionately diagnosed as schizophrenics, women were subjected to treatments of insulin shock, electroshock, and lobotomies. Esterson and Laing shifted the burden of causation from the woman to her family and to psychiatry itself. Women mirrored some of their own society's fragmentation. Despite giving credence to women's thoughts and social context, antipsychiatrists had "no coherent analysis to offer women." The feminist therapy movement offers hope for the future. "Until women break them for themselves, the chains that make madness a female malady, like Blake's 'mind-forg'd manacles,' will simply forge themselves anew" (p. 250). (SGF)

PR

551. Weeks, Gerald R., and Larry Hof, eds. **Integrating Sex and Marital Therapy: A Clinical Guide.** New York: Brunner/Mazel, 1987. 255 p. Includes bibliographies and indexes. ISBN 0-87630-447-1.

Recognizing the limitations of the growing field of sex therapy—brief, problem-centered, specific treatment formats and techniques, homework assignments—many experts consider the field isolated, compartmentalized, even stagnant and technologically rigid. Thus, in the interest of revitalization, Weeks and Hof suggest a systems perspective that integrates the artificially separated fields of sex and marital therapies. This broadened view, then, will address such problems as family sexuality; love, intimacy, and affection; geriatric sexuality; the effects of rape on marriage; and infertility as well as the usual topics of inhibited sexual desire, impotence, inorgasmia, sexual fantasies, etc. The results should bring about enhancement and enrichment of the two fields in an integrated manner.

Part I, using a systems perspective, brings together contributions on theoretical issues involving the evaluation of the marital relationship of clients with sexual complaints (Larry Hof); and the interrelationships of love, intimacy, and sex (Luciano L'Abate and William C. Talmadge). It also addresses practical applications, such as a process of understanding sexual problems within an intergenerational framework (Ellen M. Berman and Larry Hof); in-office techniques that can be used to enhance a couple's sexuality (Stephen R. Treat); counseling couples to deal with the sexual concerns of their children (Maggi Ruth P. Boyer); and the uses of sex hypnotherapy in teaching couples how to develop a positive stance toward sexuality (Daniel L. Araoz and Ellen Kalinsky). Part II, devoted to special problems, covers (1) a couple's reaction to infertility as a life crisis (Patricia P. Mahlstedt); (2) therapeutic techniques in helping couples cope with extramarital sexual relationships (Frederick G. Humphrey); (3) the effects of rape on marital relationships (William R. Miller); (4) the systematic treatment of inhibited sexual desire (Gerald R. Weeks); (5) the analysis and treatment of hypersexuality in men and women (Martin Goldberg); and (6) marital and sexual counseling of elderly couples (Jacob D. Stone). (TJW)

Gender Identity Disorders. Transsexualism

(For related material see also entry 100)

PR
552. Arndt, William B., Jr. **Gender Disorders and the Paraphilias.** Madison, Conn.: International Universities Press, 1991. 488 p. Includes bibliography and indexes. ISBN 0-8236-2150-2.

Compiled here is a comprehensive overview of the subject matter and literature pertaining to gender disorders and the paraphilias. In the preface Arndt points out that the information about these subjects "comes from such diverse fields as endocrinology, general psychiatry, psychoanalysis, forensic medicine, psychology, sociology, and social work." He also states that he is guided by the principle of "constructive alternativism," meaning that he examines the subjects from various perspectives. Arndt covers all the gender disorders and paraphilias mentioned in the 1987 edition of *Diagnostic and Statistical Manual of Mental Disorders* (DSM-III-R). He limits his sources to Western cultures, does not review therapeutic procedures, and confines his reviews on the literature to males only.

In part I, definitions and historical trends, Arndt points out that sexual acts lie on a continuum from normal to deviant, with such factors as intercourse, heterosexuality, statistical prevalence, cross-cultural data, morality, and what is considered natural being used to define deviance. After proposing the concept of ideal sexuality ("an expression of the psychologically healthy person") as a basis for determining deviancy, he proceeds to examine the contributions to sexuality made by Richard von Krafft-Ebing, Albert Moll, August Forel, Iwan Bloch, Magnus Hirschfeld, Havelock Ellis, and Sigmund Freud.

In "Sex, Gender, and Sexuality" Arndt shows that "the paths to adult sexuality, straight or deviant, begin at the moment of conception" (p. 17). In connection with the determination of masculinity, he discusses biological sex, sex differentiation, gender identity, Freudian psychoanalysis, gender role acquisition, the components of sexual behavior, and sexual behavior in childhood and adolescence.

In part II, "The Gender Identity/Role Disorder," Arndt covers childhood gender disorders, especially the cross-gender problem of masculine identity and discusses such influencing factors as biology, parental contribution, and peer relations. He also fully reviews the subject matter and literature of transvestism and transsexualism.

In part III, "The Paraphilias," he states that the term *paraphilia* stands for the outmoded expressions of sexual perversion and sexual deviation. He describes the paraphiliac as someone "attracted either to something or someone other than an adult and/or relates to his partner in an incomplete or nonegalitarian fashion" (p. 173). In contrast, "the sexually ideal male not only is certain of his masculinity, he is also attracted to a person to whom he can relate as an equal in a warm and loving way" (p. 173). Alluding to the Freudian dichotomy of sex object and sex aim, Arndt characterizes paraphilias as "disturbances of partner preference and distortions in mode of relating to that partner" (p. 174). In turn, he discusses in detail the following paraphilias: fetishism, pedophilia, father-daughter incest, exhibitionism, sadism, masochism, and such adjunctive paraphilias as voyeurism, sexual asphyxia, piercing, klismaphilia (erotic use of enemas), and infantilism.

Arndt derives a number of conclusions from his survey: there are "more cases of males than females with gender disorders and paraphilias"; "all males have a feminine aspect, and attenuated forms of paraphilias exist in all men"; "many more men have strong gender disordered and deviant inclinations and fantasies than those who act them out"; and probably there is a prenatal hormonal influence affecting the masculinization of the male baby. Arndt also highlights the itineraries leading toward ideal sexuality and deviant sexuality. (TJW)

PR,IL
553. Benjamin, Harry. **The Transsexual Phenomenon.** New York: Julian Press, 1966. 286 p. Includes bibliography and index.

In this classic work, Benjamin provides a state-of-the-art review of transsexualism in the mid-1960s. He recognizes that without the attention brought to the subject by the Christine Jorgensen case in the early 1950s, very little attention would have been given to the subject in the medical literature. As a practicing physician with a strong interest in sexological problems, he clinically observed over the years men and women who were dissatisfied with their anatomical sex. Not to be confused with transvestites (a term used by Magnus Hirschfeld in his classic work *Die Transvestiten*), these individuals feel that their identity is different from that of their biological sex; thus, they desire to have their sex organs altered surgically in order to transform themselves into their perceived sexual identity. The majority of these individuals are males wanting their sense of femaleness confirmed anatomically. In his first paper on the subject, which appeared in 1953, Benjamin coined the term *transsexualism*, that is now recognized internationally.

Following his introductory remarks, Benjamin attempts to define, diagnose, and classify transvestism, transsexualism, and homosexuality. He establishes a Sex Orientation Scale (SOS), suggested by the Kinsey Scale, in which he hypothesizes six different types of the transvestism-transsexualism syndrome, ranging from the pseudo-transvestite, who dresses in the clothes of the opposite sex only sporadically (and would be placed at the heterosexual end of the Kinsey Scale), to the true transsexual who urgently needs (or believes he or she needs) a sex change operation and hormone treatment. Although at the opposite end of the Kinsey Scale, this person is not a homosexual, but does desire a relation with a member of his or her own sex, but only as a member of the opposite sex.

Although Benjamin explores transvestism, his main focus is on transsexualism. He examines the possible causes (etiology) of transsexualism: genetic, endocrine, and psychological. He also discusses the nonsurgical management of transsexuals, the conversion operation, the results of fifty-one operations, and legal aspects in transvestism and transsexualism. A chapter on female transsexuals completes the volume.

Benjamin concludes: "The etiology of the transsexual state is still largely obscure, but a light seems to blink here and there in publications from the laboratories of brain physiologists. . . . From the therapeutic end, it cannot be doubted or denied that surgery and hormone treatment can change a miserable and maladjusted person of one sex into a happier and more adequate, although by no means neurosis-free, personality of the opposite sex" (pp. 163-64).

Several papers are in the appendixes: "Complementarity of Human Sexes" by Gobind Behari Lal; "Transsexualism: Mythological, Historical, and Cross-cultural" by Richard Green; and "Transsexuals' Lives" by R. E. L. Masters, that provides transsexual autobiographies and biographical profiles of transsexuals. A supplement showing before and after photographs of transsexuals concludes the book. (TJW)

PR
554. Blanchard, Ray, and Betty W. Steiner, eds. **Clinical Management of Gender Identity Disorders in Children and Adults.** Washington, D.C.: American Psychiatric Press, 1990. 199 p. (Clinical Practice, no. 14). Includes bibliographies. ISBN 0-88048-187-0.

This book is part of the series Clinical Practice that focuses on bringing current, empirical, and theoretical material about psychiatric problems to the clinician (e.g., psychiatrist, mental health professional) working outside of a hospital setting. The emphasis is practical, drawing from cases, suggesting treatment approaches, and providing up-to-date literature reviews. The goal of this volume is to "acquaint the reader with various syndromes of gender identity disturbance in males and females, the different types of social circumstances in which patients find themselves, and the range of treatment options" (p. xiii). Most of the contributors are associated with the Gender Identity Clinic at Clarke Institute of Psychiatry in Toronto, Ontario, Canada. As Blanchard, a research psychologist at the clinic notes in the preface, gender identity disorders are a "heterogeneous collection of conditions" (e.g., homosexual dysphoria, transvestism, transsexualism) that vary in degree and kind as well as in etiology. Consequently, options for clinical management of the variety of manifestations of "gender identity disorders" can vary considerably.

Kenneth J. Zucker, Head of the Child and Adolescent Gender Identity Clinic at Clarke, introduces the reader to the assessment, diagnosis, and treatment of children who may be experiencing problems in gender identity development, typically indicated by a "strong identification with, and preference for, the sex-typed characteristics of the opposite sex" (p. 4). Blanchard describes the types of men and women that are likely to seek treatment for gender identity disorders; for men these include transvestism and heterosexual, homosexual, asexual, analloerotic, or bisexual gender dysphoria, and for women they include heterosexual and homosexual gender dysphoria. Steiner outlines the complexity, demands, and pressures of undertaking an assessment and clinical management of gender-dysphoric patients. Lana Stermac suggests options for clinical management of nontranssexual gender dysphoric patients, e.g., hormonal management, marital counseling, group therapy, individual psychotherapy. Leonard H. Clemmensen discusses the elements of the "real life test" (i.e., a trial period of living in the cross-gender role) for patients diagnosed as transsexuals who are considering medical and/or surgical intervention for sex-reassignment. Robert Dickey and Steiner provide a detailed description of hormonal treatment and sex-reassignment surgery, which they think is the most effective treatment for selected transsexuals. The final chapters discuss the psychological and social consequences of gender dysphoria and its treatment—Blanchard and Peter M. Sheridan focus on gender reorientation and psychosocial adjustment while Robert Dickey examines the association between gender dysphoria and antisocial behavior. (SGF)

PR,IL,PO
555. Bolin, Anne. **In Search of Eve: Transsexual Rites of Passage**. South Hadley, Mass.: Bergin & Garvey, 1987. 160 p. Includes bibliography and index. ISBN 0-89789-082-5.

This study focuses on sixteen male transsexuals in the process of becoming women. Bolin, an anthropologist, relied on participant observation as the primary method of investigation, supplemented by life histories, questionnaires, and masculinity-femininity indexes. In addition, attendance at weekly meetings of the Berdache Society, a transsexual support group, and immersion in transsexuals' everyday lives was included in the research strategy. Distinct as the only anthropological study of contemporary Western transsexualism, it is intended for an academic as well as a lay audience.

The transsexual's metamorphosis is viewed as a patterned development that has the characteristics of a rite of passage. The rite of passage is dramatized by important stages and events that punctuate the progress toward the sex change surgery. The medical profession, transsexual intragroup interaction, stigma, and transsexuals' perceptions of women are the salient factors shaping the passage to womanhood.

In the investigation, transsexuals were followed as they separated themselves from their former male lives; as they began therapy, including female hormone treatment; as they prepared for and actually adopted the female role; and as they were finally incorporated into society as women following surgery. The approach taken here did not assume that transsexuals began their rite of passage with fully crystallized feminine identities, but rather regarded these identities as gradually emerging in conjunction with changes in social identity and physical appearance.

Several findings of this study refute commonly held notions about transsexuals. Transsexuals are not shown to have family histories with dominant mothers and absent fathers, exclusive homosexual orientation, effeminate childhoods, nor did they view their penises as organs of hate and disgust. In addition, contrary to reports in the literature, transsexuals generally are not hyperfeminine in gender identity or role. These findings contribute to the study of gender dysphoria and to a growing body of anthropological work on secular ritual and symbol in contemporary America. (Author)

IL,PO

556.   Feinbloom, Deborah Heller. **Transvestites & Transsexuals: Mixed Views.** New York: Delacorte Press, 1976. 303 p. Includes bibliography and index. ISBN 0-440-08513-6.

In a literature dominated by psychological and medical perspectives, *Transvestites & Transsexuals* offers a sociocultural orientation to the field of gender dysphoria. Feinbloom's goal is to provide a readable work that captures the complexity of transvestism and transsexualism (primarily male-to-female).

Feinbloom's sociological training is evident in her theoretical perspective as well as in the research method of participant observation. The research represents two distinct field experiences, and the book recapitulates this in its organization with heterosexual transvestites the subject of the first half of the book and transsexuals the second half.

Feinbloom sets the stage by defining the sometimes confusing and superficially similar phenomena of heterosexual transvestites, gay female impersonators, and transsexuals. The theoretical approach that combines ethnomethodology with symbolic interaction is offered as relevant for understanding both transvestism and transsexualism. For Feinbloom, transvestism and transsexualism are natural field experiments whereby gender is made problematic; because of this, they reveal a dominant societally held substrate of beliefs about gender. Transvestism is presented through case histories with an interpretation of the subjects and their wives' "accounts" or explanations of being transvestites as a manifestation of the inner self. A general background of transsexualism is also presented. Transsexual coping strategies and passing are given a great deal of attention. A major point woven throughout the book but especially salient in the transsexual chapter on passing, is the importance of gender as a learned and socially negotiated system manifested in the presentation of self in everyday life.

A concluding chapter reiterates and integrates the subjects of transvestism and transsexualism with musing on the meaning of cross-dressing vis-à-vis rigid sex role dichotomization (e.g., would there be transvestism if sex roles were more fluid?). Two appendixes conclude the book: one focuses on the ethical implications of fieldwork with "deviant" populations and the other includes letters and comments from the research population about the book. (AB)

PR

557.   Green, Richard, and John Money, eds. **Transsexualism and Sex Reassignment.** Baltimore, Md.: Johns Hopkins University Press, 1975. 512 p. Originally published in 1969. Includes bibliography, index, and glossary. ISBN 0-8018-1038-8.

This work is the first collection of articles on the subject of male-to-female and female-to-male transsexualism written for health care practitioners and researchers. It represents a major effort to present systematically collected data that cover various topical areas. Green and Money have specifically avoided debates on the controversial aspect of the sex change surgery, although the conclusion suggests that surgical reassignment remains the most viable solution for the assimilation of transsexuals into society.

The collection includes the work of thirty-two contributors, most of whom are drawn from the medical profession. The book begins with an introduction by Harry Benjamin, who first applied the term *transsexual* and who pioneered research in his now classic *The Transsexual Phenomenon* (New York: Julian, 1966). Aimed at the treating community of clinicians, this collection is divided into five parts. Part I, "Social and Clinical Aspects of Transsexualism," defines the syndrome developmentally, socially, and cross-culturally in articles by Green and Pauly. Part II, "Psychological Aspects of Transsexualism," includes an impressive array of articles by Money and coworkers Stoller, Guze, Pomeroy, and Doorbar, covering such topics as psychological adjustment, family history, and sexual behavior. Part III, "Somatic Aspects of Transsexualism," broadly addresses physical but nonsurgical aspects of the syndrome, including among other articles the impact of estrogen therapy on male-to-female transsexuals and a preliminary finding of a possible association of temporal lobe disorders and gender dysphoria. Part IV, "Treatment Aspects of Transsexualism," the largest section of the book, focuses on various treatment issues. Treatment is construed broadly and includes articles spanning topics from psychological evaluations to surgical reassignment. Part V, "Medicolegal Aspects of Transsexualism," includes medical and legal issues and problems encountered in the United States, England, Denmark, and Sweden. Green concludes the book with a call for continued research on the subject of transsexualism and its heuristic value for understanding larger areas of gender research such as the nature-nurture debate. (AB)

PR
558. Lothstein, Leslie Martin. **Female-to-Male Transsexualism: Historical, Clinical and Theoretical Issues.** Boston: Routledge and Kegal Paul, 1983. 336 p. Includes bibliography and index. ISBN 0-7100-9476-0.
    As Co-Director of the Case Western Reserve University Gender Identity Clinic, Lothstein, a psychoanalytically oriented psychotherapist, worked intensively for eight years with over 200 male and female transsexual patients (fifty-three women). He became increasingly aware not only of the personal anguish of female transsexuals but also of the degree to which they were neglected or misunderstood by mental health professionals. Most research and therapy dealing with transsexuals has focused on male-to-female rather than female-to-male transsexuals. Lothstein's work "represents the first attempt to organize the body of literature on female transsexualism and to devote an entire book to the condition of female transsexualism."
    Because so little is known about female transsexuals, myths and half-truths about them persist, e.g., that female transsexualism is a new phenomenon, is so rare that it isn't worth investigating, is solely a physiological disorder, is a sexual disorder, is an alternative lifestyle. This book articulates what is known about female transsexuals and what remains to be known, particularly in the context of treatment. Chapters deal with historical, psychological, and medical issues; diagnostic issues, including the contributions of Krafft-Ebing, Freud, Hirschfeld, and Benjamin as well as an analysis of the DSM's definition of the "disorder"; psychobiological issues, particularly whether there is a direct biological cause of female transsexualism; psychological issues and theories, especially the need for a clear typology of gender pathology that distinguishes different degrees of disturbance; and a review of strategies and recommendations for the evaluation and psychological (counseling and psychotherapy) and biological (hormones and surgery) treatment approaches. More than one-quarter of the book consists of descriptions of clinical cases that elucidate the phenomenology of the female transsexual experience.
    Lothstein concludes that "female transsexualism is a universal phenomenon . . . which has historical, cultural, literary, and mythological roots." However, transsexualism poses social and medical problems for which the legal, medical, and therapeutic professions are not fully prepared. Family dynamics seem to explain the evolution of nonbiological aspects of female transsexualism. Because of female transsexuals' underlying ego deficits, intensive, long-term psychotherapy is the treatment of choice for them,

although sexual reassignment surgery may be desirable for a small number. Overall, "until proven otherwise, female transsexualism must be viewed as a psychological disorder." (MC/SGF)

IL

559. Raymond, Janice C. **The Transsexual Empire: The Making of the She-Male.** Boston: Beacon Press, 1979. 220 p. Includes bibliographic references and index. ISBN 0-8070-2164-4.

Presented in this provocative study is a feminist analysis of transsexualism and its context. Raymond's argument is that the medical practice of transforming men into women and women into men by hormone treatment, behavior modification, and surgery is basically an attempt to strengthen patriarchal domination of women by perpetuating stereotypical roles of feminine and masculine behavior. According to Raymond, most of the operations transform men—men who claim they are women "trapped in male bodies"—into transsexually constructed females. Transsexual women are a minority; Raymond calls them token transsexuals.

Raymond argues that transsexualism is an enterprise of the "transsexual empire," an expression for the medical conglomerate of urologists, gynecologists, endocrinologists, plastic surgeons, and the like, in collusion with psychiatrists, psychologists, drug companies, and hospitals that has highlighted the "need" of transsexuals for a solution to his/her "gender dysphoria." These groups have a vested interest in the expansion of the empire. At its core, the primary cause of transsexualism is a patriarchal society that produces sex role stereotypes.

"Everything You Always Wanted to Know About Transsexualism" provides information about the history of transsexualism, the major figures and institutions involved in its development, research efforts, costs, individual reactions of transsexuals to the change, medical procedures and problems, and legal aspects of sex conversion. Raymond also examines the medical model at the core of the transsexual empire, a world that transforms many moral issues and sociopolitical and environmental problems into technical problems. She opposes this medical model, which she claims "de-ethicalizes" problems and behavior, with an "ethic of integrity," defined as the preservation rather than the disintegration of the individual's wholeness. Transsexual surgery destroys this wholeness; transcendence, the key concept of integrity, takes the individual contemplating a sex change and guides him/her to an acceptance of their given sexual identity. In the conclusion Raymond offers solutions to the transsexual problem through legal measures and public education. (TJW)

PR

560. Stoller, Robert J. **Perversion: The Erotic Form of Hatred.** Washington, D.C.: American Psychiatric Press, 1986. 256 p. Includes bibliographic footnotes and index. ISBN 0-88048-262-1.

From his ongoing work on sex and gender identity, Stoller presents observations about perversion. He acknowledges objections that may be made in today's society to his use of the term, but defends his point of view that perversion does exist and can be defined. The essential task of this volume is to define perversion and to examine its clinical components. Stoller draws careful distinctions between "variants," "aberrations," and "perversions" and demonstrates that hostility is the dominant force in perversion. He uses case material to illustrate how childhood conflicts and traumas are transformed into erotic fantasies designed to turn victim into victor.

As in his earlier volumes that dealt with the development of masculinity and femininity, Stoller stresses the significance of mother-infant symbiosis and family dynamics in gender development. He hypothesizes that perversion develops as an attempt to cope with threats to gender identity. Further, he suggests that the greater frequency and bizarreness of perversion found in males occurs because the task of separation for the male child from his mother's femaleness is more complex and fraught with greater possibility of failure than the female child experiences in forming her gender identity. Variously describing perversion as dehumanization of one's sex objects, "an erotic neurosis" (p. 163), "the erotic form of hatred" (p. 4) and labeling it as "exclusively human" (p. 53), Stoller builds his argument that "the more gross the hostility, the less question that one is dealing with perversion" (p. 56). Thorough discussions of various psychic motivations presented throughout the book prepare the reader for the brief final chapter, in which Stoller voices his view on the usefulness of perversions to society and his own note of hope for the future. (LF)

PR
561. Stoller, Robert J. **Sex and Gender: On the Development of Masculinity and Femininity.** New York: Science House, 1968. 383 p. Includes bibliography and index.

This volume, which Stoller describes as a "preliminary clinical report," grew out of a ten-year research project that included the psychoanalysis of eighty-five patients with attention to developing methods of observation that would minimize bias and reveal the dynamics of sexual behavior and identity development. From the psychoanalytical perspective, Stoller presents cases representative of patients with and without "biological abnormalities" and discusses issues in treatment. For the purposes of this research, sex is defined as biological, determined by physical characteristics. Gender identity is portrayed as a psychological phenomenon. Gender is shown to be "primarily culturally determined—learned postnatally," but also influenced by biological forces.

Stoller offers conclusions based on research, and he also advances arguments and speculations that he acknowledges lack conclusive evidence, but which he considers important and worthy of more scientific investigation. His data point to the powerful influence of parents (especially mothers) on gender development. Symbiosis and separation are the issues around which psychopathology in gender development is seen to occur. Stoller speculates that if this is the pattern in gender identity development, it is likely to be repeated in other areas of personality development as well.

In discussing the development of choice as it relates to gender, Stoller builds on Freud's concept that repression and biological factors diminish free will, and goes on to suggest that a third factor also operates to limit choice. That factor is described by Stoller as a kind of learning that occurs in a nontraumatic interchange with the environment (especially with the mother)—"changes which occur without conflict and are as impelling a source of behavior as are many prenatal constitutional factors." Consistently, Stoller urges other researchers, including fellow psychoanalysts, to tie their speculation to scientific methodology. Throughout this book, Stoller can be seen to follow his own advice, moving from hypothesis to data gathering/treatment, to assessment and on to new hypotheses, all the while solidly grounded in theory. In the appendix he provides extensive data on transsexualism, including verbatim interviews with mothers. (LF)

PR
562. Stoller, Robert J. **Sex and Gender. Volume II: The Transsexual Experiment.** New York: Jason Aronson, 1975. 316 p. Includes bibliographic references and index. ISBN 0-87668-243-3.

Focusing on male transsexualism as a way of understanding more about the psychological origins of masculinity and femininity, Stoller makes two key assumptions. The first is that clinical method is useful as a tool of scientific inquiry. The second is that close examination of a specific gender aberration, its dynamics and etiology, will provide clearer understanding of gender development and gender identity.

Background material on bisexuality and homosexuality from biological and psychoanalytical perspectives sets the stage for development of hypotheses about development of extreme femininity in males, and detailed reporting of evaluation and treatment of Stoller's patients and of information about their family members.

From his case material and from the published works of other analysts and therapists, Stoller identifies similarities and parallels in family dynamics and parental influence on transsexuals and examines the applicability of psychoanalytic concepts like castration anxiety, penis envy, and Oedipal conflict to their situations.

Stoller attaches great importance to the mother's handling of the child and believes the degree of femininity in the male child will vary in precise and predictable ways according to conditions in very early childhood. He characterizes transsexualism as one way among many that "we can grow to misperceive ourselves and the outside world" (p. 19) and delineates ways in which the transsexual differs from other feminine men. He differentiates transsexualism clinically from "perversion," which by his definition always includes fetishization while transsexualism does not. (LF)

PR
563. Stoller, Robert J. **Splitting: A Case of Female Masculinity.** New York: Quadrangle/New York Times Book, 1973. 395 p. Includes bibliographic references. ISBN 0-8129-0338-2.

This volume illustrates Stoller's single case study research method. He carefully develops a chronology that covers fourteen years of Mrs. G's life, seven of which she spent in treatment and analysis with Stoller. Mrs. G. was a very masculine woman who broke most of society's rules in her attempt to survive and maintain a sense of self. Transcripts and case notes detail her antisocial and self-destructive behavior, the separation of affect and awareness, her belief that she had a penis, other delusions and hallucinations, the amnesias for psychotic episodes, and the multiple personalities that developed.

Throughout the study, in chapters devoted to mothering, homosexuality, Mrs. G's parents, and the characters produced by splitting, Stoller traces the origins in childhood of this disturbed woman's gender identity.

Stoller reviews the factors that he believes contribute to gender identity before presenting eight parental factors (early and nontraumatic) that he sees as contributing to the development of femininity in females. Stoller moves away from classical analytic hypotheses about the development of femininity, stressing nonconflictual learning and negating the Freudian notion that women are fundamentally inferior. He suggests that we know too little about the etiologies and varieties of homosexuality to define it. Further, he hypothesizes that some noninstinctual behaviors fixed early in life are immutable and discusses the question of to what extent children are shaped by conscious and unconscious parental fantasies.

Stoller assists the reader with explanatory material in notes and references and in four appendixes that enrich the text without cluttering it. (LF)

PR
564. Yates, Alayne, ed. **Sexual and Gender Identity Disorders.** Philadelphia: Saunders, 1993. P. 356-562. (Child and Adolescent Psychiatric Clinics of North America, Vol. 2, No. 3). Includes bibliographic references and index. ISSN 1056-4993.

Yates, Chief of Child and Adolescent Psychiatry at the University of Arizona College of Medicine, notes in the preface, "The literature on child and adolescent sexuality has tended to focus on sexually transmitted diseases (STDs), gender identity, and homosexuality," not on such "adult" issues as desire or arousal. Yates hopes that this book will contribute to a greater understanding of childhood sexuality and suggest ways that the development of adult sexual dysfunctions can be prevented. This volume of papers, authored by professionals from a variety of disciplines (history, anthropology, sociology, law, medicine, psychology, psychiatry), broadens the scope of inquiry to include three major foci, around which the fourteen articles are organized.

The first section, "Differentiating Normal from Pathologic Sexual Development," the most general of the three, is designed to highlight the contexts and phases of healthy sexual growth among children and adolescents. Historian Stevi Jackson explores the historical context of childhood sexuality while anthropologist Suzanne G. Frayser concentrates on a cross-cultural perspective. Eleanor Galenson reviews current views of psychosexual development from birth through age three; Alvin A. Rosenfeld and Saul Wasserman discuss normal children's sexual development from age five until puberty. Max Sugar presents information on adolescent sexuality as part of a developmental period. Mary Jane Rotheramp-Borus and Marya Gwadz review patterns and consequences of sexual risk behavior among youths.

The second section, "Sexual Disorders," addresses "heightened, diminished, and problematic sexual responsiveness together with associated intrapsychic and behavioral changes." Toni Cavanagh Johnson presents a schema for distinguishing between pathologic hypersexual behavior from normal, intense sexual play among preschool-aged and latency-aged children. Alayne Yates discusses the emergence of hypoactive sexual desire disorder in childhood and adolescence. John Money and Galdino F. Pranzarone explain how paraphilias are induced by negative nonsexual as well as sexual child-rearing experiences during childhood and adolescence. Judith V. Becker and John A. Hunter provide a brief review of the research literature on adolescent sex offenders, particularly offenses that involve aggression.

The last section, "Gender Identity, Role and Orientation," concentrates on reviews of recent research on gender identity, role, and orientation. Heino F. L. Meyer-Bahlburg contributes two papers, one on new genetic, endocrine, and neuroanatomic findings relevant to a psychobiologic theory of sexual orientation, and the other on the course of gender identity development in intersex patients. Kenneth J. Zucker and Richard Green review the diagnosis, family and psychological characteristics, and treatment issues of children with gender identity disorders. The volume concludes with Zella Luria and Carol Nagly Jacklin's consideration of ways that biomedical interpretations of sexuality have been challenged by recent findings in the social sciences as well as by feminist and gay critiques. (SGF)

Paraphilias: Bestiality, Exhibitionism, Fetishism, Flagellation, Masochism, Pedophilia, Sadism, Transvestism, Voyeurism

(For related material see also entries 18, 80, 105, 108, 420)

PR
565. Bullough, Vern L., and Bonnie Bullough. **Cross Dressing, Sex, and Gender.** Philadelphia: University of Pennsylvania Press, 1993. 382 p. Includes bibliographic essay and index. ISBN 0-8122-3163-5.

As the distinguished authors state in the introduction, "Cross dressing is a simple term for a complex set of phenomena" (p. vii) that may range from occasionally wearing a couple of items of clothing of the opposite sex to an attempt to live an entire life as a member of the opposite sex. The practice and meaning of cross-dressing have varied according to culture and time period as have professional interpretations of its etiology. The goal of this book is to provide a comprehensive examination of cross-dressing that highlights its complexity rather than offering simple explanations for it.

The first part of the book emphasizes different views of cross-dressing in different cultural contexts and during different historical periods. In many cultures, gender is not an ascribed status, based purely on the appearance of the genitals, but is an achieved status, based on behavior, tasks performed, clothing, anatomy, and other factors. Gender categories go beyond the binary divisions of the genders in the United States and point to the significance of social and cultural factors in shaping the interpretation of anatomy, identity, sexual behavior, and definitions of gender. The hijras of India, the xaniths of Islam, the mahu in Tahiti, and the bayot in the Philippines are just a few examples of the range of gender variations worldwide. The Bulloughs trace traditions of cross-dressing from mythology and history in the ancient world (e.g., when Judaism and early Christianity were reflected through the negative Neoplatonic interpretation of sex); the Middle Ages (e.g., when women cross-dressed to elevate their status); the sixteenth and seventeenth centuries (e.g., when "playing with gender," particularly during festivals and recreational times was popular); in the eighteenth century (e.g., when men became concerned about cross-dressing as a threat to masculinity); and in the nineteenth and twentieth centuries (e.g., when definitions of masculinity and femininity began to change and transvestism became a threat to the maintenance of separate spheres). Throughout these periods, cross-dressing was not necessarily linked to sexual behavior; cross-dressers could be homosexual, heterosexual, bisexual, or asexual.

The second part focuses on the twentieth century and modern perspectives about cross-dressing, beginning with the development of the medical model and its effect on the interpretation of cross-dressing; contemporary psychotherapists concentrate on childhood experiences to explain cross-dressing, unlike earlier theorists who related it to heredity. The interpretation of cross-dressing also changed as heterosexual transvestism was distinguished from homosexuals' dressing as drag queens. Transsexualism and sex reassignment surgery became additional factors to consider in understanding cross-dressing and sparked further interest in studies of gender identity and sexual orientation. Victoria Prince's organization of cross-dressers' clubs added to the emergence of organized transvestism in the late twentieth century. At present, probably 1 percent of the adult male population cross-dresses. Current theories emphasize the relevance of a genetic predisposition for cross-gendered identity. In conclusion, the Bulloughs offer some practical advice to cross-dressers, their families, and their friends about how to deal with cross-dressing. A guide to further reading follows the main text.

The Bulloughs conclude that "cross dressing and gender-blending have been ubiquitous throughout history. . . . Much of what we believe to be feminine and masculine behavior is socially and culturally derived" (p. 360). Cross-dressing leads us to consider the broader question of what gender is and to rethink the gender "boxes" in which we live. (SGF)

IL

566. Caplan, Paula J. **The Myth of Women's Masochism.** London: Methuen, 1986. 280 p. Includes bibliography and index. ISBN 0-413-41850-2.

Caplan (teacher of psychology, psychiatry, and women's studies in Canada) argues that the attribution of masochism to woman is an unfortunate myth. Much of its origin can be traced to such pioneering psychoanalysts as Sigmund Freud and his followers, including some women psychoanalysts. Helene Deutsch averred that women are naturally masochistic, narcissistic, and passive; and Marie Bonaparte viewed heterosexual intercourse as a kind of beating, with the female ovum accepting this masochistically. Furthermore, latter-day analysts, including Alan Parkin, Natalie Shainess, and Kurt Eissler, as well as such diverse groups as sociobiologists, some feminists, and psychologists, provide support for women's innate masochism.

In Caplan's detailed examination of the subject, much of it anecdotal, an abundance of evidence is gathered to show that what often passes as masochism is really reasonable reaction to intolerable situations, a way of avoiding confrontation in the interest of peace. The book is organized around important areas of female involvement: motherhood, childrearing, male/female relationships, care of the body, violence, work, and therapy. In these areas, women's activities often appear to be naturalistic, self-sacrificing, hedonistic, narcissistic, provocative, and long suffering. Society's response to these perceptions tends to produce varying kinds and degrees of suffering in women, which often convert to guilt as a woman reflects upon her feelings and behavior.

Caplan believes that society nurtures the false notion of women's masochism. She concludes that women's masochism has, in reality, been a manifestation of women's abilities to delay gratification, to put other people's needs ahead of their own, and to try to earn happiness through effort; the scarcity (real or feared) of better alternatives; or their effort to *avoid* pain" (pp. 219-20).

In denying the very concept of masochism (p. 220), Caplan asks about the "real causes of women's unhappiness." She argues that they are: (1) lack of political, economic, and social power; (2) poor self-esteem derived from the "feminine" stereotype of not being particularly strong intellectually, physically, emotionally, or morally; (3) sex-role stereotypes that tend to place women "into one of the two basic kinds of myths about women—that they are either cold, rejecting, or castrating, or overemotional, irrational, and emotionally smothering and draining" (p. 225). Only by removing the externally imposed sources of suffering and guilt—the myth of masochism and the sex-role stereotypes—will women be able to cope fully with the world around them and be able to "celebrate their strengths and their joy" (p. 226). (TJW)

IL
567. Dekker, Rudolf M., and Lotte C. van de Pol. **The Tradition of Female Transvestism in Early Modern Europe.** Foreword by Peter Burke. New York: St. Martin's Press, 1989. 128 p. Includes bibliographic notes and index. ISBN 0-312-02367-7.
      In the seventeenth and eighteenth centuries, when the Dutch Republic possessed a large army, formidable navy, and the Dutch East Indies Company, the phenomenon of female cross-dressing manifested itself in surprising ways. Dekker and van de Pol, of Erasmus University, Rotterdam, examine extant records of 119 women living as men in the army, navy, and overseas merchant fleet between 1550 and 1839. Strongest in the Netherlands, England, and Germany, the tradition of cross-dressing existed throughout Europe, although the phenomenon seems not to have appeared until the late sixteenth century and to have pretty much vanished by the mid-nineteenth century. While the image of female transvestism appeared widespread in contemporary popular songs, novels, plays, and operas of the period, this study derives its conclusions primarily from an examination of Dutch judicial archives, the archives of the Dutch East Indies Company, newspaper accounts, travel reports, and medical reports.
      The records reveal various motives for the women living a disguised existence, ranging from proclaimed patriotism and an inherent urge to cross-dress to more immediate and pressing reasons: to avoid poverty at home, to do a man's work, to travel and see the world, to leave Holland and settle elsewhere, to escape from the law or other untenable situations, to follow a husband or lover, and so forth.
      Besides searching for the motives of women wishing to live as men, Dekker and van de Pol relate many poignant stories of individual women whose testimonies provide fascinating accounts of how they lived and fared as disguised sailors and soldiers. The story of Maria van Antwerpen is particularly pertinent: she lived as a man for thirteen years and in an autobiography left a record of her experiences.
      In addition to discussing sexuality and intersexuality in a theoretical way to account for transvestism, transsexualism, and lesbianism, Dekker and van de Pol examine legislation, religion, public opinion, folklore, and literature as they relate to the praise or condemnation of transvestism.
      They account for the decline of cross-dressing in the nineteenth century by stating that "after 1800, the Netherlands no longer offered a good matrix for female transvestism. The country had lost much of its attraction to immigrants, the VOC [Dutch East Indies Company] was dead and buried, and Holland entered a long period of economic decline and peace" (p. 103). (TJW)

IL
568. Deleuze, Gilles. **Masochism: An Interpretation of Coldness and Cruelty.** Together with the entire text of *Venus in Furs* by Leopold von Sacher-Masoch. New York: Braziller, 1971. 248 p. Translation of: *Presentation de Sacher-Masoch*.
      Deleuze begins this study of masochism and sadism by explaining the role of language and style in the writings of Leopold von Sacher-Masoch and the Marquis de Sade. Pointing out that the words *masochism* and *sadism*, as coined by Richard von Krafft-Ebing, are clinical terms providing accurate descriptions of certain types of

behavior, Deleuze argues that the writings of Masoch and Sade depicting those behaviors are serious explications of the masochistic and sadistic states and should not be construed as pornographic. Furthermore, the styles of writing are also different: while both are descriptive, that of Masoch is didactic and that of Sade demonstrative. Moreover, Masoch's descriptions are inoffensive, while those of Sade are patently obscene.

Sadism, Deleuze says, represents a negative approach to life with disorder, destruction, and death integral to its results. Masochism is essentially positive, employing such fetishistic devices as furs, shoes, whips, helmets, and the like to achieve an ideal state of exaltation.

Deleuze examines the complementarity of sadism and masochism, and while not denying a connection between the two, avers that they are fundamentally analogous only. For example, in a masochistic situation, the one who wields the whip is not a sadist, but rather someone who must be persuaded in the masochistic act. Similarly, the recipient of sadism is not a masochist. In order to discount the existence of a sadomasochistic entity, Deleuze differentiates between sadism and masochism in a series of chapters each focusing in turn on a subject: the types of women in Masoch's novels; mothers' and fathers' roles in sadism and masochism; the contrasting attitudes of Sade and Masoch toward art and aesthetics, and toward humor, irony, and the law; opposing views of written contracts and rituals; and the primacy of the superego in sadism and that of ego and idealization in masochism.

Deleuze provides Freudian interpretations of sadism and masochism, pain and pleasure, linking them to the life and death instincts (Eros and Thanatos). In the final chapter, Deleuze has this to say about sadomasochism: "Sado-masochism is one of these misbegotten names, a semiological howler" (p. 115). He avers that sadism and masochism are totally different, which not only accounts for their peculiar sexual behaviors but also for the two styles of writing that Sade and Masoch display.

As an important addendum to this theoretical work, Deleuze has included the complete text of Masoch's famous novel, *Venus in Furs*. (TJW)

PR

569. Docter, Richard F. **Transvestites and Transsexuals: Toward a Theory of Cross-Gender Behavior.** New York: Plenum Press, 1988. 251 p. (Perspectives in Sexuality: Behavior, Research, and Therapy). Includes bibliography and index. ISBN 0-306-42878-4.

The objective of this work is to propose a theory of transvestism and secondary transsexualism (transsexualism as an outgrowth of either transvestism or homosexuality) and to provide information concerning these behaviors. The study underlying the work is based upon survey and test data from 110 heterosexual transvestites and some of their wives, together with follow-up correspondence over a five-year period. Docter also followed forty transvestites more closely over those five years, interviewing and observing them regularly and attending their meetings.

Docter assumes that "cognitive determinants" (beliefs, perceptions, self-appraisals, sexual scripts) are critical factors in the structuring of behavior, and that transvestism and secondary transsexualism can be studied only through a developmental perspective or life span view. The book includes descriptive information and an introduction to gender issues and the spectrum of cross-dressing; a review of the literature; material on self and identity, sexual excitement, and fetishism; and survey results. Docter proposes a five-stage theory about the process of transvestism, beginning with childhood antecedent conditions, progressing through adolescence with the formation of fetishistic behaviors involving women's clothing. Further stages lead to complete cross-dressing, culminating in either stable transvestism or going on still further to transsexualism. Docter maintains that how well the individual self is able to manage the cross-gender identity will determine whether a stable pattern of transvestism develops and continues. In the rare cases where the integration and management of this cross-gender identity is not resolved, anxiety and—for some—transsexual urges become intense. This differs, however, from the pattern of primary transsexualism, that shows gender dysphoria early in childhood, non-fetishistic cross-dressing, and often homosexual orientation. (MC)

PR
570. Feierman, Jay R., ed. **Pedophilia: Biosocial Dimensions.** New York: Springer-Verlag, 1990. 594 p. Includes bibliographies and indexes. ISBN 0-387-97243-9.

Most of the twenty-two articles in this volume are the product of an intense examination of adult-child sexual interaction at a one-week retreat in 1987 of fifty invited experts from seven countries at the residence of the Servants of the Paraclete in Jemez Springs, New Mexico. The program was sponsored by the International Society for Human Ethology.

According to Feierman (Department of Psychiatry, University of New Mexico), the lay and professional literature on child sexual abuse is "anthropo-, ethno-, and chronocentric," i.e., based on assumptions that such abuse occurs only among humans, only in Western society, and only recently. The goal of this book is to complement some of the best contributions in the child abuse literature (primarily in sociology and social psychology) with new biosocial contributions from history, political science, sexology, primatology, anthropology, psychiatry, and experimental and developmental psychology to develop a transspecies, transcultural, and transhistorical perspective on "the roots of pedophilia as the phenomenon is found in contemporary industrialized societies." The scope of the work goes beyond abuse to consider a broader issue—the basis for erotic age orientation. What are the biosocial determining and regulating factors among humans that lead to pedophilia (sexual attraction to prepubertal children) and ephebophilia (sexual attraction to adolescents)? Unlike the perspective of "victimological thinking," the biosocial approach considers the role of the child or adolescent as an "active interactant," although both views converge in their judgment that the person in power should accept legal and moral responsibility for such interactions. The thesis that underlies the biosocial perspective is that "aspects of the behavior [adult sexual behavior with children] result from an interaction of genetic and nongenetic determinants and that in many instances, there is strong support that some of the genetic determinants were subjected to positive selective pressures or were by-products of selective pressures in our evolutionary past."

Feierman organized the articles, written by distinguished researchers from a variety of fields (e.g., Vern L. Bullough, Irënaus Eibl-Eibesfeldt, David M. Taub, Milton Diamond, John Money) in six sections, the core of which are concepts that ethologist Tinbergen has suggested are crucial in understanding any behavior: (1) evolution, (2) cause, (3) function, and (4) development. Feierman wraps these sections with an introduction and conclusion that provide the theoretical continuity of the volume—a biosocial perspective. Careful to provide operational definitions of all concepts used, Feierman develops a model of brain masculinization and defeminization that locates pedophiles and ephebophiles in a context of parent/child interaction and male/female attraction. He concludes that "pedophilia and ephebophilia are not functionally adaptive in the individual pedo- or ephebophile per se but, rather, are the by-products of natural and sexual selection for adult-male and adult-female heterosexuality in their male and female kin." Beyond its consideration of pedophilia, the volume presents data on biosocial determinants of sexual behavior in general, particularly the ways in which sexual behavior is context-dependent in humans. (SGF)

PR,IL
571. Garber, Marjorie. **Vested Interests: Cross-Dressing & Cultural Anxiety.** New York: Routledge, 1992. 443 p. Includes bibliographic notes and index. ISBN 0-415-90072-7.

The International Foundation for Gender Education estimates that 6 percent of the U.S. population are cross-dressers and 1 percent are transsexuals. Cross-dressing has a rich historical tradition, and transsexualism may be one twentieth century manifestation

of an ancient theme of cross-dressing—a means of transcending the dual gender categories dominant in Western culture. Garber, Professor of English and Director of the Center
for Literary and Cultural Studies at Harvard, says that "this book is an attempt to explore
the nature and significance both of the 'fact' of cross-dressing and of the historically
recurrent fascination with it" (p. 3). Rather than analyzing cross-dressing as a process of
imitating or trying to become the "opposite" sex, she looks *at* it as a special category of
behavior that challenges binary gender categories of male and female. Not knowing
whether someone is or can be classified as male or female creates anxiety that becomes
"a battleground for competing vested interests" (p. 16).

Garber claims that the role of the cross-dresser is "interruption, [the] disruptive
act of putting in question" (p. 13) and that "transvestism is a space of possibility
structuring and confounding culture . . . the crisis of category itself" (p. 17). The first
six chapters describe "transvestite logics," the ways in which transvestism creates
culture. Garber explores the meaning of the link between cross-dressing, sumptuary laws,
and theatricality in the medieval and early modern periods; how clothing defines gender
and gender differentiation; transvestism, power relations, and career paths; transvestism
and gay identity; gender transition surgery; and fetishism. The last seven chapters
examine "transvestite effects," how culture creates transvestites. Plays, opera, TV,
music, religion, fashion, and fiction are some of the arenas in which transvestism is
displayed. Garber concludes that transvestism needs to be understood for what it is, not
for what it isn't. "The compelling force of transvestism in literature and culture comes
not, or not only from these effects, but also from its instatement of metaphor itself, not
as that for which a literal meaning must be found, but precisely as that without which
there would be no such thing as meaning in the first place" (p. 390). The book is profusely
illustrated with black-and-white and color photographs of examples of cross-dressing.
(SGF)

IL

572.   Gibson, Ian. **The English Vice: Beating, Sex and Shame in Victorian England
and After.** London: Duckworth, 1978. 364 p. Includes bibliography and index. ISBN
0-7156-1264-4.

Thoroughly documented and illustrated, Gibson's study is about widespread beating (flogging and flagellation) in Victorian England and Wales. He first reviews the
literature on the subject, going back to the work of the seventeenth century physician
Johann Heinrich Meibom, who published a short study in 1629, explaining that flagellation applied to the buttocks is a sexual stimulant. Other writers, among them J. J.
Rousseau, the Marquis de Sade, and Richard von Krafft-Ebing, discoursed on flagellation. The latter in his classic study *Psychopathia Sexualis* (1886), stated that one of the
forms of sadism is flagellation.

Gibson documents the different manifestations of flagellomania pervading British
society. Parental beating was commonplace, and the entire school system accepted
beating, known as the "lower discipline" because it focused on the naked buttocks.
Birching prevailed in the preparatory schools and in the public schools, such as Eton,
Rugby, Winchester, Harrow, and others. Gibson quotes Winston Churchill's comments
on the brutality of the birchings he received and witnessed at St. George's preparatory
school. Other testimony came from the poet Swinburne, who apparently embraced the
practice of birching at Eton, writing flaggelant poetry and pornography, and secretly
visiting flagellant brothels.

Gibson devotes a chapter to the judicial flogging of adults as well as flogging in
prisons, the army, and the navy. He also covers flagellant correspondence in the media,
flagellant prostitution, and flagellant fantasies.

In England the practice of birching was supported by quotations from scripture
(Proverbs mainly) and also by such shibboleths as "Spare the rod and spoil the child,"
that appeared in Samuel Butler's satirical poem *Hudibras* (1664). By way of understanding sexual flagellation, Gibson discusses different explanatory theories, some

psychoanalytic, and one advocated by Desmond Morris called female rump-presentation theory. Morris connects this theory with flagellation of the upturned buttocks. Gibson summarizes as follows: "The English Vice began in the home, spread to the home's most obvious extension, the school (particularly the boarding school), and thence to the courts, the prisons, the Army and Navy, the colonies—and the brothels. The British Empire, it might be argued, was founded on the lash" (p. 64). (TJW)

PR,IL

573. Gosselin, Chris, and Glenn Wilson. **Sexual Variations: Fetishism, Sadomasochism and Transvestism.** New York: Simon & Schuster, 1980. 191 p. Includes bibliography and index. ISBN 0-671-24624-0.

Very little is known about the characteristics of the range of people who engage in sexual variations, despite "deviant" and "abnormal" labels applied to them by the medical community and sensationalized accounts of them in newspapers and pornographic literature. Gosselin and Wilson, two psychologists from London's Maudsley Hospital, hope that their findings will provide a broad, "natural" context within which to interpret these patterns.

This book presents the results of a carefully researched study of three types of sexual variations: sadomasochism, fetishism, and transvestism. Gosselin and Wilson compiled much of their data from questionnaires distributed to members of correspondence and social clubs (in England and abroad) catering to adherents of sexual variations (e.g., the Mackintosh Society and the Beaumont Society). Over 600 subjects agreed to complete two questionnaires. One, the Eysenck Personality Questionnaire, measures three aspects of personality: extraversion, neuroticism, and psychotism. The other was designed to collect background information on such characteristics as age, marital status, occupation, upbringing, and sexual history, and to examine sexual fantasies and behavior. Seventy-five of the respondents constituted control groups of "normal" men (fifty) and women (twenty-five) whose answers to the questionnaire could be compared with those of the "variants." The three years of research also included conversations and interviews with clinicians, crisis-intervention groups, and counselors who provide help for people with sexual problems. After describing the activities in which each variant group engages, Gosselin and Wilson compare fantasies and activities of sexual variations with each other and with "normals." They then relate each variant to aspects of personality, mental health, and family background. Some attention is given to preliminary results of research on transsexuals and "sexually adventurous women." The concluding chapter presents a cogent, thought-provoking interpretation of people who participate in sexual variations as "script-writers and actors in rather specialized plays, put on in the theater of fantasy which all of us possess" (p. 154). The majority of fetishists, transvestites, and sadomasochists do not resemble classical models of the neurotic, psychopath, or psychotic, and many of their fantasies overlap with those of "normals." Their fantasies and behavior patterns raise some complex questions about who and what is "sexually normal." (SGF)

PO

574. Greene, Gerald, and Caroline Greene. **S-M: The Last Taboo.** New York: Grove Press, 1974. 345 p. ISBN 0-8021-0064-3.

Although the "sexual revolution" was in progress when this book was written, the Greenes could find very little attention being paid to sadomasochism, except in a derogatory way. Ignorance and fear contribute to the stereotypes of sadomasochism as a violent, harsh, and inhuman activity. In contrast, they suggest that sadomasochism is the "ultimate Venusberg of our senses," "a lost romanticism" that transcends social barriers and depends upon total trust. Sadomasochism depends more upon imagination than on genital linkage and frees its participants from a primarily biological expression of sexuality.

The labeling of sadomasochism as an arena for intellectual discussion began with Richard von Krafft-Ebing's portrayal of sadism as sexual pleasure in inflicting pain and masochism as sexual pleasure in the receipt of pain. Havelock Ellis was a pioneer in interpreting sadomasochism with interest and sympathy.

After a journey into the historical roots of the study of sadomasochism, the Greenes delve into the realities of the sadomasochistic experience itself: how to meet partners, sadomasochism in marriage, the variations of preferences in love play within the sadomasochistic context, the general sadomasochistic scenario characterized by mutual control of erotic activities, the dynamics of water sports and B and D, and the use of sadomasochistic materials.

After confronting areas of the human subconscious regarded as "taboo, disgusting, inaccessible, and dangerous," the Greenes point out the positive aspects of this stereotypically "heinous" activity as a "way to love, based on the most intimate knowledge of the human soul," that tries to "calm violence by love."

Appendixes supplement the text with excerpts from literary works by such notables as Charles Baudelaire, Aubrey Beardsley, and Pauline Reage, who express aspects of the "last taboo." Overall, this discursive work is regarded by some as a "pioneer volume" that presents the case *for* sadomasochism. (SGF)

PR,IL

575. Krafft-Ebing, Richard von. **Psychopathia Sexualis, with Especial Reference to the Antipathic Sexual Instinct: A Medico-Forensic Study.** Translated from the twelfth German ed. and with an introduction by Franklin S. Klaf. Foreword by Daniel Blain. New York: Stein and Day, 1978. 434 p. Published by Stein and Day in 1965. Includes index. ISBN 0-8128-6011-X.

Krafft-Ebing's youthful interest in criminal cases of sexual deviance prompted him to study medicine so that he could qualify as a neurologist and psychiatrist; his interests in law, sexual deviation, and medicine converged in what Edward Brecher calls his "powerful and terrifying masterpiece," *Psychopathia Sexualis*, published when he was forty-six. Despite his attempts to orient this work to a professional audience of lawyers, doctors, and judges, Krafft-Ebing and his book became well known beyond these circles. Paul Robinson terms him a "transitional figure between Victorian and modern styles of sexual theorizing," a person who was probably the "most influential sex psychologist of the last quarter of the nineteenth century."

Krafft-Ebing's aim was to "record the various psychopathological manifestations of sexual life in man and to reduce them to their lawful conditions" (pp. xiii-xiv). He thought that scientific research was warranted in this area because of its "forensic bearing" and influence on the well-being of society. The first three chapters—"Fragments of a System of Psychology of Sexual Life," "Physiological Facts," and "Anthropological Facts"—present background material. They are heavily influenced by nineteenth-century assumptions about the nature of men, women, and sexuality, and are of historical interest in their articulation of these themes, such as that women are passive and uninterested in nonprocreative sex, that shame and modesty underlie morality, and that masturbation contaminates higher ideals. Chapter 4 defines general sexual pathology, which is both neurological and psychological. Krafft-Ebing classifies most pathological states as cerebral neuroses and proceeds to concentrate his attention on paraesthesias (perversions of the sexual instinct): sadism, masochism, fetishism, and antipathic sexuality (inversion or homosexuality). Chapter 5 deals with special pathologies, for example, satyriasis, epilepsy, and hysteria. Themes of pathology and danger permeate the discussions in these chapters. By drawing on over 200 cases collected from his own patients, other doctors, earlier medical literature, and defendants in criminal courts, Krafft-Ebing provides testimony for his view that unbridled sex can undermine the health and honor of individuals as well as the very foundations of society. By mixing extreme cases (e.g., murder and cannibalism) with seemingly innocuous deviations, he gives the overall impression that *all* sex is dangerous. Masturbation is particularly singled out as a probable cause for most sexual deviation. Underlying most of the material in these chapters is the assumption that sexual deviation from the monogamous norm is the result of a mentally perverse disposition that was probably inherited but might have been acquired. He claims that this is not surprising since the generative organs are so closely associated with other aspects of the central nervous system. The tension between morality and the "sexual instinct" is an ever-present concern in his discussion. The final chapter considers the legal implications of pathological sexuality and recommends that the court needs to consider the mental condition of the perpetrator of a sex crime rather than concentrating on the act itself, if it is to render a just verdict. This work puts sexuality in the context of pathology and disease and sets the stage for both the scientific examination and public discussion of sexual matters. (SGF)

PR,IL
576. Money, John. **Lovemaps: Clinical Concepts of Sexual/Erotic Health and Pathology, Paraphilia, and Gender Transposition in Childhood, Adolescence, and Maturity.** New York: Irvington, 1986. 331 p. Includes bibliography, indexes, and glossary. ISBN 0-8290-1589-2.

Sexologist Money, Professor of Medical Psychology and Pediatrics at Johns Hopkins University and Hospital, presents the "first book about lovemaps." He introduces "lovemaps" as a principle that can help to explain the development of both healthy and pathological sexuality and eroticism ("sexuoeroticism"). According to Money, everyone has a lovemap—a template (or representation in a person's brain/mind) that depicts an idealized version of erotic attraction and genital arousal. Lovemaps develop early in life and usually develop normally as uncomplicated, heterosexual images that are manifested after puberty. Juvenile sex rehearsal play is a prerequisite for such healthy development. However, pathological lovemaps can develop if the child is deprived of or neglects sex rehearsal play; is subject to prohibitions, abusive punishments, and severe discipline; or is traumatized by abrupt exposure to socially tabooed sexuoeroticism.

Pathology can express itself in three forms: hypophilia (sexual dysfunction), hyperphilia (erotomania), and paraphilias ("perversions"). All of these pathologies manifest a split between love and lust, which reflects a philosophy of sex derived from religion. Money concentrates a lot of attention on the description and explanation of paraphilias that express "vandalized or redesigned" lovemaps. Arousal, genital response, and orgasm only occur when the paraphilic fantasy is carried out in practice. Over forty paraphilias fall into six major categories (sacrificial/expiatory, marauding/predatory, mercantile/venal, fetishistic/talismanic, stigmatic/eligibilic, solicitational/allurative), all of which attempt to turn the "tragedy" of lovemap distortion into a "triumph" of lust. Each has an individual and species-determined component ("phylism"). In addition, lovemaps can be gender transposed so that there is a disjunction between the sexual dimorphism of the body and gender behavior; bisexuality, homosexuality, transsexuality, and transvestism are examples of this.

Money also turns his attention to social censure of paraphilias. He points out that paraphilias are not contagious and that such ideas are rooted in outmoded degeneracy theories. Treatments are available. Depo-Provera, a form of antiandrogenic therapy, has provided some relief of social tension and agitation associated with paraphilias.

Five detailed case histories provide concrete examples of the concepts presented. A vocabulary of the paraphilias illustrates the variety of forms that lovemap disorders may take. (SGF)

PR,IL
577. Rossi, William A. **The Sex Life of the Foot and Shoe.** New York: Saturday Review Press, 1976. 265 p. Includes bibliography and index. ISBN 0-8415-0417-2.

Former podiatrist and editor of footwear and industry publications William A. Rossi has written a fully documented and illustrated study of foot and shoe eroticism. He begins by stating, "The foot is an erotic organ and the shoe its sexual covering." He claims that about 80 percent of footwear is designed, produced, fitted, and sold primarily for sex attraction" (p. 1).

Rossi takes a long look back in history and reveals how Chinese women bound their feet for sexual purposes, a practice that prevailed for about 1,000 years. From early childhood, girls had their feet bound by bringing toes and heel close together to achieve the lotus foot, a configuration much adored by men. Rossi believes that the foot possesses "sexual nerves" that, when stimulated, cause sexual arousal. This accounts for the popularity of such behavior as foot tickling, foot massaging, foot biting, toe sucking, and foot kissing. Furthermore, Rossi believes that the evolution of the foot enhanced human sexuality by enabling man "to stand and walk upright by virtue of his unique foot." This contributed to humankind's sexual versatility as in being able to assume various coital positions.

Additionally, of the basic motives for wearing shoes—modesty, protection, status—sexual attraction is the most important. The fashion industry recognizes the foot as an erotic structure that needs a sexualized covering. Hence the efforts of the industry to design alluring footwear, e.g., shoes with high heels. Such footwear eroticizes the legs, the hips and buttocks, the posture, and the gait.

In "Cinderella Was a Sexpot," Rossi tells an amusing story illustrating women's concerns about having the most attractive shoes to wear. The Cinderella fable about the glass slipper hinges on small foot size, which only Cinderella had. As Cinderella slipped her foot into the glass slipper, the prince exclaimed, "Ah! the perfect fit!" But Cinderella replied, "Yes, I know. But do you have it in red, a smaller size, a higher heel, and a pointed toe?" Cinderella was interested more in looks than in fit.

Rossi includes chapters, sprinkled with amusing anecdotes and stories, on foot love and shoe love, foot lovers, foot fetishes and shoe fetishes, the popularity of leather footwear, ornamental footwear, and the taboo of the naked foot. He concludes with a series of questions: "Why don't we wear sensible shoes? Why can't they make fashionable shoes that are comfortable? Why do so many people wear those silly styles? Why do we stuff our feet into tight or pointed-toed shoes, or shoes so small? Why do we neglect or abuse our feet? Why do we let vanity rule our feet?" The answer to these questions is always the same: "the foot is an erotic organ and the shoe is its sexual covering" (p. 253). (TJW)

PR,IL

578. Weinberg, Thomas, and G. W. Levi Kamel, eds. **S and M: Studies in Sadomaso-chism.** New York: Prometheus Books, 1983. 211 p. (New Concepts in Human Sexuality). Includes bibliographic references and index. ISBN 0-87975-218-1.

Therapists usually look upon sadism and masochism as manifestations of individual psychopathology. However, Vern Bullough, in the preface to this edited volume on studies in sadomasochism, states that "this perspective gives a distorted view of a widespread phenomenon by ignoring the sociological and cultural factors that encourage and support the existence of sadomasochism" (p. 9). The emphasis in this collection is to provide a comprehensive overvieew about what is known about the social and psychosocial aspects of sadomasochism.

Classical perspectives on sadomasochism introduce the volume and provide a historical context for the materials that follow. Richard von Krafft-Ebing introduced the concepts of sadism and masochism into the literature and interpreted them as forms of psychopathology. Sigmund Freud suggested that they were two forms of the same entity. Havelock Ellis modified the broad definition of sadomasochism to an erotically motivated pain that might be spurred on by love. Paul Gebhard introduced the notion that sadomasochism is subcultural social behavior—a product of culture.

The articles that follow the introduction to the section on S&M focus on the ways that individuals act in the subcultural context of sadomasochism. Of particular interest is Andreas Spengler's empirical study of sadomasochism in roles, that uses qualitative and quantitative data to link the subculture of sadomasochism with the identity formation of its participants. One article points out the limitation of a psychoanalytic view of sadomasochism stages in the acquisition of a leatherman identity and another gives a personal account of a dominatrix. A section on S&M interaction describes the "scenes" of sadomasochistic interaction. Thomas Weinberg's paper draws on Erving Goffman's frame analysis (i.e., social definitions give behavior specific meaning) in his attempt to understand the characteristics of sadomasochistic interaction. Four biographies illustrate the diversity of sadomasochistic experience, while a paper by Pat Califia portrays the lesbian experience. Gerhard Falk and Thomas Weinberg point out that sadomasochistic themes are not limited to the secret world of the "velvet underground"; recreational facets of Western culture play on these themes. The last section describes the "structures," the social organization of sadomasochism. G. W. Levi Kamel points out that sadism and masochism are meaningful behaviors for their participants, bound by rules, control, and rationality.

The picture of sadomasochism that emerges from these studies challenges stereotypes of sadomasochism as an activity steeped in cruelty, violence, and irrationality. Rather, it is part of an organized world of social behavior. (SGF)

PR
579.   Wilson, Glenn D., ed. **Variant Sexuality: Research and Theory.** Baltimore: Johns Hopkins University Press, 1987. 268 p. Includes bibliographies and indexes. ISBN 0-8018-3464-3.

This collection of papers, presumably of interest to psychologists, biologists, and psychiatrists, deals with recent contributions to an understanding of variant sexuality and sexual deviation.

Alex Comfort focuses his attention on definition, deviance, and variation, giving special attention to bonding and sadomasochism and showing that sexual behavior must be understood in the context of its meaning for the individual. Raymond Goodman reviews the evolution of sexuality by concentrating on the role of chromosomes, genes, hormones, etc. in determining both normal and aberrant behavior. Pierre Flor-Henry reviews the research on neurological factors in deviant sexuality and gives evidence on how deviants can be distinguished from normal persons on the basis of EEG testing. Editor Wilson highlights the male preponderance in sexual deviation and suggests that it may be attributed to competition for access to reproductive females and the target-seeking nature of the male libido. Vaclav Pinkava's paper concerns the application of the mathematical theory of logical nets to sexual variation.

Arthur Epstein examines fetishism by comparing the behavior of human and nonhuman primates. Paul Kline reviews Freudian psychoanalytic theories of sexual deviation; he finds Freudian theories in this area difficult to confirm scientifically. Frederick Whitam favors a biological rather than a social explanation for the behavior of gays and lesbians in the United States, Brazil, and the Philippines. Ron Langevin and Reuben Lang examine correlations between voyeurism, exhibitionism, obscene calls, toucherism, and rape while questioning the validity of the concept of "courtship disorders." Christopher Gosselin states that an anthropological study of sadomasochistic practices that takes account of their meaning to the individuals involved is essential to full understanding of the variation.

Wilson believes that the ten papers in this collection cover the most important developments in the understanding of variant sexuality in recent years. (TJW)

Psychosexual Dysfunctions: Addiction, Dyspareunia, Impotence, Inhibited Sexual Desire, Anorgasmia, Premature Ejaculation, Vaginismus

(For related material see also entry 295)

PR
580.   Arentewicz, Gerd, and Gunter Schmidt, eds. **The Treatment of Sexual Disorders: Concepts and Techniques of Couple Therapy.** Translated by Tom Todd. New York: Basic Books, 1983. 350 p. Translation of: *Sexuell gestörte Beziehungen.* Includes bibliography and indexes. ISBN 0-465-08748-5.

This book is the product of a research project carried out between 1972 and 1979 by the Division of Sex Research in the Department of Psychiatry at the University of Hamburg. The aim of the project was to design and evaluate a modification and extension of Masters and Johnson's treatment techniques for a wide variety of sexual problems, including lack of desire, premature ejaculation, and orgasmic dysfunction. Two hundred sixty-two couples with sexual dysfunctions were treated in two sessions per week in outpatient settings, sometimes by one therapist, or, much less often, in groups of couples. Assessment of the short- and long-term outcomes of this treatment program forms the core of the book.

The book is divided into three sections with chapters contributed by the editors, Arentewicz (Senior Scientist, Clinical Psychology, at the Institute for Psychology, University of Kiel) and Schmidt (Senior Researcher and Professor in the Division of Sex Research, Department of Psychiatry, University of Hamburg), as well as by other psychotherapists (psychiatrists and psychologists trained in client-centered or behavior therapy as well as physicians and psychologists trained in psychoanalysis) who participated in the project. Part I, "Causes and Treatment," provides a theoretical overview of the behavioral symptoms of sexual dysfunctions, their organic and psychosocial etiologies, and a couple-oriented psychotherapeutic program for treatment. Arentewicz and Schmidt suggest that symptoms of sexual dysfunction be integrated into an overall treatment plan that may address neurotic conflict and marital distress. Such a program should strive to resolve the self-reinforcement mechanism, compensate for learning defects, understand the meaning of the sexual dysfunction to the couple, and understand psychodynamic conflicts and anxiety.

Part II, "Couple Therapy: Research and Results," evaluates how well couple therapy modified the symptoms, sexual behavior, and general psychological state of the clients. Overall, the authors regard their therapeutic program as a success, gauged by both short- and long-term (one to four and a half years) effects. While 75 percent of the couples showed permanent improvement, 25 percent did not. Chapters also discuss difficult cases, unintended side effects of therapy, and drop-outs. The formal setting of the therapy seemed to make little difference in therapeutic outcomes. However, therapy in groups was less successful than single-couple therapy.

The final section presents a manual of couple therapy for sexual dysfunction. It is intended for use by qualified psychotherapists, not as a self-help guide. The authors stress the need for an integrated approach to the treatment of sexual dysfunctions. Their findings substantiate the feasibility of modifying Masters and Johnson's techniques and demonstrate their applicability in another cultural setting. (SGF)

PR,IL
581. Barbach, Lonnie. **Women Discover Orgasm: A Therapist's Guide to a New Treatment Approach.** New York: Free Press, 1980. 237 p. Includes bibliography and index. ISBN 0-02-901800-5.

According to major sex surveys (Kinsey 1953, Hunt 1974, and Hite 1976), roughly "10 percent of married American women and 30 percent of sexually active unmarried women never experienced orgasm" (p. 15). In the 1970s sex therapist Barbach, using a "behaviorally oriented psychotherapeutic approach," developed a systematic group therapy program for anorgasmic women. This guide, intended for sex therapists, describes in detail the ten-week program that Barbach believes "helps women to achieve orgasm, alone or with a partner."

After defining orgasm from the physiological and psychological standpoints and reviewing the literature on the subject, Barbach attributes orgasmic dysfunction to a basic lack of sex information and negative attitudes acquired from parents, society, and religion. She delves into the nature of orgasm, contrasting the Freudian position on clitoral versus vaginal orgasm with Masters and Johnson's conclusions about the validity of clitoral stimulation.

Barbach points out that Alfred Kinsey "laid the foundation for the important assumption that orgasm can be considered a learned response and that failure to achieve it is not necessarily a sign of neurosis but, rather, a possible result of faulty or inadequate learning" (p. 6). Rejecting the psychoanalytic approach in favor of a behavioral approach to solving the problem of orgasmic dysfunction, Barbach has designed a program that "involves groups of six or seven women who meet together for 10 sessions of about two hours each." Central to the program are participants' homework assignments and progress reports to the class. For these assignments, Barbach relies heavily on a nine-step masturbation scheme as a learning technique to help women achieve orgasm. "The overall concept is to approach new goals through small behavioral steps. By gradual stages, the woman learns to gain control over and feel good about her body; then she learns to take responsibility for her own orgasm through masturbation; finally she learns to ask for or to do what feels best with her partner" (p. 21).

Basically, this guide describes the different aspects of the treatment program, covering such topics as setting up a group, selecting participants, the therapist's role, issues that arise during the sessions, individualizing the homework in the later sessions, involving one's sexual partner, couple assignments, ethical issues in group treatment, and so forth. In the final sessions, Barbach discusses with the participants the success of the program and provides suggestions for continuing the pursuit of stated sexual goals. (TJW)

IL,PO
582. Carnes, Patrick J. **Don't Call It Love: Recovery from Sexual Addiction.** New York: Bantam Books, 1991. 439 p. Includes index. ISBN 0-553-07236-6.

Carnes, a pioneer in the field of sexual addiction, encompasses two topics in *Don't Call It Love*: sexual addiction itself and the rehabilitation of sex addicts. The work is based on a study begun in 1986 by a team of twelve people who worked on it for three years. They developed two surveys, one for sex addicts, and the other for coaddicts. From the 1,500 survey copies given to addicts, 289 were completed; from the 500 copies given to coaddicts, 99 were completed; in other words, 20 percent of the surveys were returned. The survey group "tended to be white, educated, and professional" (p. 3). Nineteen percent of the participants were women. A project to supplement the surveys involved interviewing 89 recovering sex addicts and 37 coaddicts.

In part I, "Anatomy of an Addiction," Carnes explains the nature of sex addiction. While recognizing the importance of sex in people's lives, he identifies ten signs indicating the presence of sexual addiction, including "a pattern of out-of-control behavior," "inability to stop despite adverse consequences," "ongoing desire or effort to limit sexual behavior," "severe mood changes around sexual activity," and "neglect of important social, occupational, or recreational activities because of sexual behavior" (p. 11-12). Carnes discusses each of the ten signs of sex addiction in depth. He goes on to explain the feeling of powerlessness among eleven behavioral types of sex addicts; he also deals with the costs and consequences of sexual addiction, the vulnerability of children involved, and the addictive partners of sex addicts.

In part II, "Transformation of an Illness," Carnes, using as a model the twelve-step program of Alcoholics Anonymous, describes the stages of recovery and the tasks imposed on addicts over three plus years of striving to conquer sex addiction, attain a healthy sex life, overcome the effects of child abuse, if any, and move on to renewal of a normal life. Organizations helpful in sex addiction recovery include Sex Addicts Anonymous (SAA), Sex and Love Addicts Anonymous (SLAA), Sexaholics Anonymous (SA), and Sexual Compulsives Anonymous (SCA).

The appendix presents several self-assessment surveys: the original survey used in this study, an abuse survey, a coaddiction inventory, and a coaddict consequences survey. Also included are selected data sets derived from this study pertaining to sexual activity. (TJW)

PR,IL
583. Hall, Lesley A. **Hidden Anxieties: Male Sexuality, 1900-1950.** Cambridge, Eng.: Polity Press, 1991. 218 p. (Family Life Series). Includes bibliography and index. ISBN 0-7456-0741-1.

Based on correspondence placed in the Contemporary Medical Archives Centre of the Wellcome Institute for the History of Medicine in London by birth control pioneer Marie Stopes, this study by Senior Assistant Archivist Hall analyzes the sexual anxieties of men who wrote to Dr. Stopes, author of the popular book *Married Love*, for advice and guidance.

In the introductory chapters on male sexuality, Hall refers to the major foci of scholarly sexological interest at the turn of the century: deviant sexual behavior, childhood sexuality, female sexuality, and marital sexual relations. Overlooked in this equation, because deemed normal and unchanging, male sexuality had remained a relatively unknown entity. Males were simplistically perceived as "forceful, aggressive, promiscuous, 'instrumental' " (p. 2). Furthermore, the normal male was described as one who is "heterosexual, wants to marry and lead a conventional conjugal life, and has no 'deviations of object' in his sexual life" (p. 3). Because of these assumptions, male sexuality had often been ignored. However, anxieties of many kinds plagued men at that time; they contradicted the belief in the focused, single-minded, lustful male.

As background for her study, Hall examines the attitudes toward sexuality prevalent in Victorian times and well into the twentieth century as revealed in the writings of such disparate groups as the medical professions, the proponents of social purity, and quacks. Hall draws attention to the efforts of William Acton, Havelock Ellis, Sigmund Freud, and those who were interested in the twin problems of prostitution and disease. Before examining the letters received by Stopes, Hall devotes a chapter to the evolution of the marriage manual and the changing concept of marriage. She points out that Havelock Ellis introduced "the concept of conjugal love as an act" that had to be learned. His pamphlets *The Objects of Marriage* (1918), *The Erotic Rights of Women* (1918), and *The Play-Function of Sex* (1921) propounded a new and higher ideal of marriage. Hall also points out that Marie Stopes's *Married Love* (1918) gave such ideas "wide currency instead of being confined to a small group of the sexually progressive" (p. 66).

A chapter on men's sexual problems in marriage precedes the reactions and remarks of men who had read Stopes's book. Hall quotes widely from the readers' correspondence and brings out the main problems men were facing in their sexual lives: premature ejaculation and retarded ejaculation, which were clearly dysfunctions affecting the actual sexual union. Others, including nocturnal emissions, masturbation, circumcision, and organ size had more to do with fears of unfitness for marriage. A chapter on the problems men encountered in the medical consulting room—essentially physicians' inability to deal with male sexual problems, concludes Hall's study. Marie Stopes presumably answered all these letters.

Hall states in her conclusions that as of 1950, despite less anxiety concerning such problems as nocturnal emissions, masturbation, and venereal diseases, "the existence of the common male dysfunctions and their prevalence in the community continue to be a well-kept secret" (p. 171). Marie Stopes's correspondence reveals the advice men received about their sexual anxieties; many of these anxieties still exist, and will continue to obtain so long as the medical profession is reluctant to cope with them and so long as males are perceived as healthy in their currently aggressive sexual behavior. (TJW)

PR,IL
584. Hartman, William E., and Marilyn A. Fithian. **Treatment of Sexual Dysfunction: A Bio-Psycho-Social Approach.** Long Beach, Calif.: Center for Marital and Sexual Studies, 1972. 282 p. Includes bibliography and index. ISBN 0-9600626-1-0.

Published as an outgrowth of work begun in 1964, this book provides the background and procedures for a two-week intensive sexual therapy program given at the Center for Marital and Sexual Studies in Long Beach, California. It focuses on sex therapy for those individuals and couples with such problems as impotence, premature ejaculation, painful intercourse, failure to respond orgasmically, and so forth. Hartman and Fithian, who form a dual-sex therapy team, contend that their course helps those whose goal is satisfactory penile-vaginal orgasmic response. They have worked with 1,167 different individuals in sexual functioning over a seven-year period.

Using a bio-psycho-social approach, Hartman and Fithian begin by giving a battery of psychological, physical, and sexological exams and acquiring a detailed sex history of each client. These help determine the subject's fitness for the program and provide the therapists with various data on personality, client's self-conception, symptoms of dysfunction, and sexual goals.

At the center clients are taught how to caress the foot, the face, and the body, which they practice in privacy. They become involved in body imagery through careful examination of the body from head to toe in front of a mirror, and are soon ready for sexual caresses leading to coitus. Therapists teach the clients several techniques used to correct specific copulatory problems: (1) the "squeeze technique" whereby the woman squeezes the penis at the point of imminent ejaculation, stopping this response for several seconds, and then repeating this maneuver until the man learns how to control his ejaculation; (2) the "quiet vagina" technique involving inserting the erect penis in the vagina and keeping it there without movement for twenty to thirty minutes (this benefits men who have trouble maintaining erections); and (3) the use of nondemand body positions for men and women in order to pleasure themselves and become familiar with, for example, the responsive areas in the vagina.

Videotapes and films showing coital positions and intercourse facilitate the behavioral modification pursued in this program. Toward the end of the program there is an evaluation of progress, scheduling of follow-ups, and sometimes additional assignments for those who seem to require further therapy. Hartman and Fithian conclude with comments on group workshops lasting from one to six days that would be mini-versions of the two-week program. (TJW)

PR,IL

585. Kaplan, Helen Singer. **Disorders of Sexual Desire: And Other New Concepts and Techniques in Sex Therapy.** New York: Simon & Schuster, 1979. 237 p. Includes bibliography and index. ISBN 0-671-25362-X.

"Sexual desire is an appetite or drive which is produced by the activation of a specific neural system in the brain, while the excitement and orgasm phases involve the genital organs" (p. 9). Desire problems (e.g., loss of interest in sexual activity, refusal to pursue sexual gratification) constitute a separate clinical subgroup of sexual dysfunctions that have a distinctive pattern of pathogenesis and special therapeutic requirements. Like other sexual dysfunctions, desire phase disorders relate to sexual anxiety but differ from them in that they involve deeper, more intense anxiety, more hostility to partners, more tenacious defenses, and are rarely responsive to standard sex therapy. Use of the biphasic model of human sexual response and dysfunction is inadequate to deal with these disorders.

On the basis of a five-year study of 1,000 patients treated for sexual complaints by 12 members of a therapist group, Kaplan presents comparative data on treatment failures and successes in an effort to refine theoretical constructs and suggests improved therapeutic techniques to deal with sexual problems, particularly disorders of sexual desire. Three theoretical themes pervade the material presented: (1) the psychosomatic concept of sexual dysfunction, (2) identification of remote and immediate causes of sexual dysfunction, and (3) the integration of behavioral and psychodynamic concepts and treatment methods.

Area I of the book presents a triphasic conceptualization of human sexuality and discusses the physiology, clinical features, psychopathology, etiology, treatment, and prognosis of each phase (i.e., desire, excitement, and orgasm). Area II focuses specifically on the description and treatment of desire phase disorders of males and females. Twelve case histories illustrate typical clinical and psychodynamic features of clients and trace their positive or negative responses to treatment. Area III discusses insights derived from the treatment of sexual dysfunction and suggests some new therapeutic strategies that may improve existing treatment modalities. The appendix contains extensive tables that detail the effects of different types of illnesses and drugs on each of the three phases of sexual response.(SGF)

PR
586. Kaplan, Helen Singer. **The Illustrated Manual of Sex Therapy.** Drawings by David Passalacqua. New York: Times Books, 1975. 181 p. ISBN 0-8129-0545-8.

The purpose of this book is to describe and illustrate the sensuous interactions commonly structured for couples in sex therapy; it serves as a supplement to Kaplan's well-known book, *The New Sex Therapy* (1974), that integrates erotic experience with psychotherapy. The core of the *Illustrated Manual* is an interplay between Kaplan's descriptions of therapeutic erotic techniques and their portrayal in thirty-nine drawings by Passalacqua. Kaplan bypasses a description of the concepts of psychoanalysis, marital therapy, and behavior modification (with which practitioners should be familiar before treating sexual dysfunction) and concentrates on conveying information that will aid the therapist, teacher, student, and client in understanding the experiential dynamics of sex therapy. After providing a summary of the nature of sexual response in males and females and the dynamics of sexual dysfunction and basic concepts of causality, Kaplan describes erotic techniques that can be used for various sexual dysfunctions as well as those designed for specific problems (frigidity, female orgastic dysfunction, vaginismus, impotence, retarded ejaculation, and premature ejaculation). She formulates hypotheses about the rationale and operation of these techniques and is careful to point out that they are not mechanical, inhumane exercises. She explores the emotional impact that these techniques are likely to evoke in the couple, and suggests therapeutic strategies for dealing with them. Kaplan's highly individualized, flexible approach to sex therapy draws on her considerable experience as a psychoanalyst, sex therapist, and educator. (SGF)

PR
587. Kaplan, Helen Singer. **The New Sex Therapy: Active Treatment of Sexual Dysfunctions.** New York: Times Books, 1974. 544 p. Includes bibliographies and index. ISBN 0-8129-0502-4.

Traditional approaches (marital therapy, psychotherapy) to sexual dysfunction have focused on symptoms as a manifestation of a serious underlying conflict and problem; treatment is comprehensive and based on the assumption that symptoms are not necessarily a reflection of pathology but can be caused by simpler, more immediate problems amenable to brief rather than lengthy therapeutic intervention; it is limited to the goal of relieving the dysfunction so that sexual functioning can be improved. Its distinctive feature is the use of structured sexual experiences and communicative tasks at home in conjunction with therapeutic sessions as an integral part of treatment. The subject matter of this volume "is concerned solely with conceptualizing and describing the process of sex therapy." Kaplan, a distinguished psychiatrist and sex therapist, draws her perspective from her experience in treating sexual disorders since 1964.

This classic, clearly written book is organized into six areas, each of which addresses a major facet of sex therapy. Area I is devoted to basic concepts—the biological data that are the foundation of the rational treatment of sexual disorders; such treatment is based on understanding how normal physiology and pathogenesis operate. Included in this area is information on the anatomy and physiology of sexual response (primarily drawn from Masters and Johnson's research) as well as the relationship of the brain and hormones to sexual functioning. Area II focuses on the etiology of sexual dysfunctions, which have multiple determinants. The major types of explanations for sexual dysfunctions are surveyed and placed in a theoretical framework that rests on the hypothesis that sexual dysfunctions can be viewed as psychosomatic disorders that can be treated by modifying the immediate sources of stress on sexual functioning. Biological determinants, such as the effects of illness, drugs, and age on sexual response, as well as psychological determinants, such as intrapsychic, dyadic, and learned causes are reviewed. The third area, treatment, lays out the theoretical basis for the treatment of specific sexual dysfunctions (erectile dysfunction, premature ejaculation, retarded ejaculation in males, and general sexual dysfunction, orgastic dysfunction, and vaginismus in the female), which are addressed in area IV. Couples are generally treated together with a combination of prescribed sexual experiences and psychotherapy. "Deep" intervention is used only to the extent that broader issues impede the cure of sexual symptoms. Relieving the symptoms of sexual dysfunctions that make it difficult to have or enjoy intercourse is the main object of sex therapy. Area V concentrates on special clinical problems such as dealing with couples, each of whom has a sexual dysfunction or who are in the midst of marital discord and also how to deal with individuals who have psychiatric disorders.

Area VI, "Results," and the epilogue sum up Kaplan's impressions about the efficacy and impact of sex therapy. Like other forms of therapy, very few outcomes have been tested in a controlled way. Nevertheless, the results seem promising. Furthermore, the brief intervention format has implications beyond sex therapy; it indicates the usefulness of setting a limited goal of dealing with immediate causes. In this framework, the client's experience rather than the therapist's direction alone can have a powerful impact on relieving the symptoms.

Numerous case studies, cross-references to other parts of the text, and short selected bibliographies aid the reader in broadening the information base and helping the sex therapy student in developing an individual style. (SGF)

PR,IL
588. Kasl, Charlotte Davis. **Women, Sex, and Addiction: A Search for Love and Power.** New York: Ticknor & Fields, 1989. 401 p. Includes bibliography and index. ISBN 0-89919-519-9.

For most women, sexually addictive and sexually codependent behavior are intertwined. Sexually codependent behavior reflects basic female conditioning in our society—we are taught that a women's power is in her sexuality, yet her sexuality is often controlled by men. Thus, sex can easily become a basic form of barter: it is the price many women pay for love and the illusion of security. The addicted woman, seeking a sense of personal power and an escape from pain, may use sex and romance as a high or as a way to feel in control, just as an alcoholic uses alcohol. Either way, however, sex never satisfies her longing for love and self-worth.

Combining candid case histories with cultural analysis, Kasl dramatically evokes both the experience of addiction and the process of recovery. She illuminates the relationship between adult addiction and early abuse or neglect and explores the connections between all forms of addiction. Her guide to recovery is backed by a discussion of healthy love and spiritual awareness. With this book, women can learn to experience their sexuality as a source of love and positive power, and sex as an expression that honors the soul as well as the body. (From book jacket description by permission of the publisher, Tickner & Fields/Houghton Mifflin Co.) (TJW)

[N.B. Charlotte Davis Kasl, Ph.D., works as a psychological counselor and healer in Minneapolis, Minnesota.]

PR
589. LoPiccolo, Joseph, and Leslie LoPiccolo, eds. **Handbook of Sex Therapy.** New York: Plenum Press, 1978. 531 p. (Perspectives in Sexuality: Behavior, Research, and Therapy). Includes bibliographies and index. ISBN 0-306-31074-0.

Until Masters and Johnson's 1970 publication of *Human Sexual Inadequacy*, that focused on symptom removal of sexual dysfunction by brief directive counseling of a couple, sexual dysfunctions were regarded as an indication of profound personality disorders, rooted in the psychosexual stages conceptualized by Freud. Since then, there has been "an information explosion on sex therapy" that is difficult to keep up with, particularly since sex therapists and researchers come from a variety of professions. The goal of this book is to "pull together the most definitive information available on sexual dysfunctions" (p. ix). In the opinion of the LoPiccolos, both of whom are members of the Department of Psychiatry and Behavioral Science in the School of Medicine at the State University of New York at Stony Brook, each of the forty-three articles in this volume "represents the best available material on a particular topic." The seventy-one contributors are drawn primarily from the professions of psychology and medicine, particularly psychiatry. The book is divided into ten parts, each of which addresses a specific dimension of the field of sex therapy. Part I presents an overview of sex therapy that includes a summary of some of the types of sex problems and treatments as well as a review of the literature on the effectiveness of sex therapy. Part II deals with the assessment of sexual function and dysfunction and provides information on clinical, sexual, psychophysiological, and historical assessment techniques. Part III considers the determinants and types of female orgasmic dysfunction as well as the analysis and treatment of these problems by such techniques as masturbation, desensitization, and pubococcygeal therapy, while part IV concerns the diagnosis and treatment of dyspareunia and vaginismus. Parts V and VI deal with issues of treatment for male orgasmic dysfunction (e.g., the use of group treatment, written materials, deconditioning anxiety, mechanical aids) and erectile dysfunction. Part VII concerns sexual dysfunction in special populations, including the elderly, pregnant women, blacks, postcoronary patients, people with spinal cord injuries, chronic renal failure, and diabetes. Parts VIII and IX deal with group procedures and other therapeutic approaches to sexual dysfunction (e.g., individual sex therapy, psychiatry, and the use of surrogates). The volume concludes with a consideration of professional issues. The status of sex therapy, its identification as a legitimate form of psychotherapy, and standards for training and licensing sex therapists are particularly salient concerns. (SGF)

PR
590.   Masters, William H., and Virginia E. Johnson. **Human Sexual Inadequacy.** Boston: Little, Brown, 1970. 467 p. Includes bibliography and index.

Human Sexual Inadequacy follows from the research presented in *Human Sexual Response* (1966) as a clinical report that melds the fruits of fifteen years of laboratory data on human sexual response and eleven years of therapeutic "trial and error" in dealing with sexual dysfunction. By paying particular attention to the psychological and physiological dimensions of human sexual response, Masters and Johnson encourage clinicians to follow a multidisciplinary approach to treating dysfunction with the hope of preventing further sexual dysfunction. The therapeutic format is grounded in two basic premises: (1) sexual functioning (or dysfunction) is a product of a couple in interaction, and (2) sexual response is a "natural," malleable form of physical expression highly subject to distortion by learning. Therefore the client is the relationship rather than an individual, and sexual dysfunction stems from taking sex out of its natural context. Therapy attempts to restore it to that context.

The book outlines a general therapy format (including dual sex therapy teams, principles for communication within the treatment unit, sex history taking, dealing with fears of performance) and discusses its application to such dysfunctions as premature ejaculation, ejaculatory incompetence, primary and secondary impotence, orgasmic dysfunction, vaginismus, dyspareunia, and sexual inadequacy in the aging male and female. Masters and Johnson claim an impressive 80 percent average success rate in treating 510 marital units. A case is a "success" if the presenting symptoms do not return after five years or more. The two-week rapid treatment format for sexual dysfunctions has become the model for many current sex therapy programs. (SGF)

IL
591.   Offit, Avodah K. **The Sexual Self.** Revised ed. New York: Congdon & Weed, 1983. 316 p. Includes index. ISBN 0-86553-079-3.

Drawing on her extensive experience as a psychosexual therapist, Offit wrote this book to help people understand their sexuality. Her approach is to relate psychosexual disorders to the approximately eight basic character traits identified by the American Psychiatric Association: dependence, aggressiveness, passive-aggressiveness, paranoia, schizoid withdrawal, histrionic display, compulsiveness, and narcissism. She does not survey the consequences of such traits in all spheres of life but limits the discussion to their sexual manifestations. The assumption behind this approach is that "character shapes sexuality and especially sexual difficulties." Offit thinks that "how we act, think, dream, and feel sexually" tells us "who we are and what we believe." In other words, our "sexual self" sums up our personalities. Moreover, "our fundamental sexual feelings and attitudes are based on early life experiences"; therefore, the best guarantees for healthy sexuality in an individual are salutary body contact and trust experienced by children.

Part I, "Being and Becoming," is concerned with the establishment of sexual feelings through "touch bonding" and with the attachment to and separation from loved ones; part II relates the several personality traits and sexual behavior; part III discusses both female and male psychosexual disorders, such as impaired orgasm and ejaculation; part IV deals with psychosexual therapy in theory and practice; and part V turns to the larger issues of female sexual liberation and the "New Sexuality." (TJW)

PR,IL
592. Sarrel, Lorna J., and Philip M. Sarrel. **Sexual Unfolding: Sexual Development and Sex Therapies in Late Adolescence.** Boston: Little, Brown, 1979. 354 p. Includes bibliographic notes and index.

The Sarrels, whose background includes running the Sex Counseling Service at Yale from 1969 to 1979 and teaching human sexuality courses at the college level, describe the process of sexual unfolding, by which one becomes aware of oneself as a sexual being who relates to others in a sexual way. The book is designed to assist other therapists and medical personnel active in sex education, counseling, or therapy for college-aged people.

Sexual unfolding involves a complex web of physical, emotional, and social growth and experience and is a gradual, uneven process that varies greatly from person to person. Its success requires time, trust, communication, and mutually enjoyable exploration with a caring partner. Competitiveness, anxiety, peer pressure, and unrealistic personal goals, as well as ignorance and misunderstanding, can lead to unsuccessful or painful sexual experiences for both men and women (e.g., vaginismus, premature ejaculation, and ejaculatory inhibition).

Sex counseling in the university setting is primarily educative and symptom-focused. Although they are fairly sophisticated, some students lack knowledge in significant areas concerning sex. Sex therapy, based on Masters and Johnson's approach, involves longer-term (generally seven to fifteen visits), more structured treatment. It focuses on the couple and usually consists of a consultation, medical exam, roundtable discussion, sex education, instruction in interpersonal communication, sensate-focus touching, and other applicable techniques. Therapists work in male-female teams, each of which deals with the client of the same sex.

Other features of sex education at the Yale campus include a booklet for students, a student-run counseling center, and a noncredit course on human sexuality. Topics covered include male and female sexuality; communication, trust, self-assertion, and vulnerability between partners; contraception and abortion; pregnancy and birth; and subjects requested by the students. (SDH)

PR
593. Stekel, Wilhelm. **Frigidity in Woman in Relation to Her Love Life.** Authorized English version by James S. Van Teslaar. New York: Liveright, 1943. 2 v. (Disorders of the Instincts and the Emotions). Copyright 1926. Includes bibliographic notes.

The prolific and imaginative Viennese physician Wilhelm Stekel (1868-1941), a psychoanalyst who was one of Freud's early followers, explains the scope of this two-volume work: "This work treats of the psychic disorders of love which manifest themselves in women as sexual frigidity (dyspareunia) and in men under the form of absolute or relative impotence" (p. 1). (*Impotence in the Male*, published in 1927, is the companion work to these volumes.) Stekel's theoretical goal is to show that mental experiences, not physical constitution, are responsible for neuroses and psychoses; further, the latter may be brought about by refinements in culture that repress instincts. Using 93 cases from his clinical practice, literary examples, and analytical concepts of his own as well as many derived from Freud, he demonstrates that women's ideas about love as well as their experiences in relationships affect their ability or willingness to have orgasms.

Stekel thinks that everyone's sex life, including love and falling in love, begins at birth, not at puberty, and that children's erotic impressions persist in adulthood, often craving repetition. A fixation of infantile impressions, particularly of idealized parents, may account for "love attractions" later on; a rift between infantile and adult requirements for love may produce physical and psychological disorders in a person's love life. An intricate mind/body relationship is responsible for the outcome. A woman's psychological flexibility as well as the ties she has to her family affect the prognosis of her disorder. First sexual experiences can shape the entire course of a person's adult sex life; "the first (traumatic) sexual experience is the touchstone which tests one's mind power" (p. 76).

In Stekel's clinical practice, 50 percent of the women suffered from sexual anesthesia (i.e., frigidity, dyspareunia); they were absolutely (not much forepleasure, orgasm), relatively (rare forepleasure, weak orgasm), or passionately (great longing and forepleasure, no orgasm) frigid. The detailed analyses of the ninety-three cases he presents suggest a number of reasons for frigidity, among which are fear of pregnancy, infection, or discovery; guilt; sinful thoughts; anxiety; too much attachment to the past, particularly to family members; lack of love, imagined love, or hatred of a partner; childhood trauma; gratification from "unpleasure"; a need to remain in power.

Nevertheless, "no woman is absolutely anaesthetic" (p. 117); rather, she has not found an adequate form of sexual gratification and/or someone that she truly loves. Neuroses and paraphilias limit rather than expand a person's ability to enjoy the full range of their sexuality. Society also limits sexual response by constraining women's options to be free to express themselves without social censure; "dyspareunia is a social problem; it is one of women's weapons in the universal struggle of the sexes" (Vol. 2, p. 62). By having an orgasm, a woman may feel that she is being submissive; frigidity enables her to "triumph" over the man. Like other neuroses, sexual anesthesia is an attempt to deal with conflict. Stekel concludes that the prevention of dyspareunia is chiefly an educational problem; "the woman of the future is not a 'she-man;' she is a 'full-woman' " (Vol. 2, p. 301). (SGF)

PR

594.   Stoller, Robert J. **Observing the Erotic Imagination.** New Haven, Conn.: Yale University Press, 1985. 228 p. Includes bibliography and index. ISBN 0-300-03424-5.

This work, the sixth in a series on gender identity—masculinity and femininity—and erotic excitement, presents Stoller's hypothesis that the desire to humiliate is an element in eroticism. Stoller is quick to acknowledge that his approach to his work is psychoanalytical and his observations are based on life histories. He devotes a chapter to detailed reporting of the analysis of a single homosexual woman, Lisa. He reports on her "I am crazy" (p. 191) theme, on her relationship with parents, lovers, and the transference relationship with him as her therapist. He advances the idea that her homosexuality is an erotic neurosis, the eroticism energized by hostility. In a shorter account of his work with a young male pedophile and his use of pornographic materials to access associations and unconscious scripts, Stoller reports again a strong theme of humiliation in the young man's life experience and in his erotic arousal. Secrets, risk-taking, revenge, and use of fetishes in daydreaming are described as manifestations of traumas, frustrations and conflicts in childhood, later expressed as anger or hatred.

In his on-going study of erotic excitement, Stoller began to question why he found the same dynamics present in perversions and in the erotic experience of patients he considered "nonperverse." Covered also are the dynamics of erotic behavior. Excitement is explained as energy that comes from opposite poles, from two possibilities, from uncertainty. In erotic excitement, he adds the element of wishing, consciously or unconsciously, to harm or humiliate the object of one's erotic excitement. Some conclusions that Stoller offers are that erotic impulses are ingenious, wondrous constructions, that just about any body function or object can be eroticized, and that we still have more to learn about eroticism. (LF)

PR

595. Stoller, Robert J. **Sexual Excitement: Dynamics of Erotic Life.** New York: Pantheon, 1979. 281 p. Includes bibliographic notes and index. ISBN 0-394-49778-3.

Sexual excitement, both perverse and normal, is the subject of this work, the fifth in a series of books on masculinity and femininity. Stoller hypothesizes that "hostility—the urge to harm one's sexual object—was the central dynamic in the sexual excitement I called 'perverse' " (p. xii). The hostility stems from "childhood traumas and frustration that threatened the development of one's masculinity or femininity" (p. 6). A key mechanism in manifesting this hostility is fetishization (or dehumanization) through fantasies of someone by means of, say, an inanimate object or a bodily function (defecation, urination), that induces sexual excitement. Hostility is blatant in such perversions as sadomasochism but less apparent in, say, exhibitionism.

Stoller, psychoanalyst and professor of psychiatry at UCLA, relates the treatment of Belle, whose sexual fantasies and scripts were examined for content and function. Over a period of years, Belle, outwardly normal in appearance and behavior, had her fantasies brought to the surface and carefully analyzed. Part 1, "Hypotheses on Sexuality," focusing on the role of hostility, secrecy, fetishization, etc., in producing sexual excitement, provides the theoretical underpinnings of this book. Part 2, "Data: Belle," presents the details of Belle's psychoanalysis, dealing with her erotic daydreaming, anality, sadomasochism, exhibitionism, and her "lovely," a term used to capture Belle's sense of herself. Part 3, "Theories of the Mind," first explores Stoller's understanding of mental processes, that he calls microdotting, and then answers the question, "Who is Belle?" Part 4, "Conclusion," discusses Belle's treatment. Basically, Belle's sexual excitement was caused by her fantasies, peopled by characters drawn from traumatic childhood experiences.

Stoller concludes by stating that "when analysis reduces patients' hatred, . . . people do not find their pleasure diminished. Instead, erotic activities—excitement and gratification—get more tender. . . . For Belle, with her lifelong focus on femininity and eroticism to express what meant most to her, the crucial issues of her existence were best condensed in an erotic daydream" (pp. 222-23). (TJW)

IL

596. Valins, Linda. **When a Woman's Body Says No to Sex: Understanding and Overcoming Vaginismus.** New York: Viking, 1992. 360 p. Includes bibliography and index. ISBN 0-670-84355-5.

Written by a woman who has experienced the pain and anguish of the female disorder called vaginismus, this study serves all those who hope to overcome that malady and have a happy sex life. Valins has researched her subject since 1986, and in 1990 founded Resolve, a support group for women with vaginismus. She defines vaginismus as "an involuntary spasm of the muscles surrounding the vaginal entrance which occurs whenever an attempt is made to introduce any object, including a penis, into the vagina" (p. 9). However, she believes vaginismus is "an emotional condition, the causes of which are psychological" (p. 10).

Valins recognizes two types of vaginismus: (1) an inherent inability to tolerate penetration, and (2) a type that is acquired. She points out that vaginismus is different from dyspareunia—a medical term for painful intercourse—in that dyspareunia allows penetration. Valins rejects the idea that vaginismus is a sexual problem. Vaginismus, she believes, may be caused by several factors: fear of intimacy, fear of dependence, lack of self-love, poor self-esteem, lack of trust, and feeling unentitled to needs. Since these fears and anxieties are deep-seated and psychosomatic, Freudian psychoanalysis has relevance in their treatment.

Valins describes her own background from childhood, explaining her long-standing fear of intercourse. She then proceeds to explain vaginismus, what causes it, how to seek help, treatments available, and speculates on how it can be prevented. She focuses on three distinct systems of treatment: psychodynamic/psychoanalytic therapy, essentially based on the theories of Freud; behavioral/sex therapy that delves into conditioning and learned behavior; and humanistic/growth therapy, that concentrates on the body as well as the mind through such techniques as Gestalt, psychodramatic encounter, and transpersonal approaches. Valins also explains Freudian and Jungian analytical techniques and their relationship to social and cultural factors.

The text of this study closes with a personal statement by Valins referring to her sexual relationship with her lover, her relationship with her parents, and her relationship with herself. The resolution of her vaginismus involved satisfactory solutions to the problems coming out of unresolved conflicts in each of these areas. Primarily a personal statement rather than a scholarly work, her views on vaginismus provide information and guidance for the layperson. Various programs, centers, and individuals treating vaginismus in the United Kingdom and the United States are listed and discussed in the appendix. (TJW)

Sexual Aggression. Sexual Coercion. Sex Crimes

(For related material see also entries 28, 32, 730)

PR
597. Dolan, Yvonne M. **Resolving Sexual Abuse: Solution-Focused Therapy and Ericksonian Hypnosis for Survivors.** New York: Norton, 1991. 237 p. Includes bibliographic notes and index. ISBN 0-393-70112-3.

Dolan, a psychotherapist, provides specific and practical techniques for the treatment of adult survivors of sexual abuse. At the outset she provides an overview of the symptomatology associated with sexual abuse and the variables that influence the severity of trauma it induces.

Derived from solution-focused therapy and Ericksonian hypnosis, this two-pronged approach focuses on helping patients find relief from symptoms stemming from or related to sexual abuse, to alter feelings associated with memories of trauma so that flashbacks of the trauma become less intrusive, and to develop a positive, practical and healthy future orientation. In this approach, patients are encouraged to trust themselves, to move at their own pace, and to recognize and build on tiny signs of healing.

Specific strategies are offered for treatment of post-traumatic amnesia, sexual dysfunctions, self-mutilation, memory problems, and related Post Traumatic Stress Disorder symptoms such as low self-esteem, concentration difficulties, and irrational guilt. Case examples illustrate how clinicians may tailor the techniques described to meet the needs of individual patients.

It is Dolan's underlying assumption that, despite the traumas they have endured, patients have the inner resources to create uniquely effective solutions to their problems. Both solution-focused and hypnotic techniques are presented to address patient resources in the context of a safe, respectful relationship. (Author)

PR,IL,PO
598. Gelles, Richard J., and Murray A. Straus. **Intimate Violence.** New York: Simon & Schuster, 1989. 297 p. Includes bibliographic notes and index. ISBN 0-671-68296-2.

Violence occurs where we least expect it—in the home among family members, where we expect a safe haven of love and support. Nearly twenty years of research, including a 1985 national survey of over 6,000 people, conducted by sociologists Gelles and Straus points to "structural properties of the family as a social institution that makes it our most violent institution with the exception of the military in time of war" (p. 51). Part I discusses the characteristics of violent homes, and part II addresses the impact of intimate violence on family members and different approaches to coping with it (i.e., legal, medical, social, and personal). Gelles and Straus assume that a social pattern lies beneath what seems to be a very specific problem within individual families.

According to them, it is a myth that violence and love cannot coexist in the same family. Intimate violence includes sexual victimization, emotional abuse, neglect, and physical violence. Although the media focus on abuse to women and children, violence to siblings is the most common form. Other hidden victims include teenagers, parents beaten by teenagers, elders, and courting couples. Furthermore, as many women hit men as men hit women, although three-quarters of violence by women is done in self-defense. Three major factors contribute to the incidence of intimate violence: (1) the rewards of being violent outweigh the costs; (2) few effective social controls over family relations exist; and (3) the structural properties of the family, i.e., acceptance of family violence, privacy, sexual inequality, foster violence. Confrontation over power underlies most intimate violence. According to the results of their 1985 national study of over 6,000 people, there seems to have been a decline in abuse to women and children (19/1000 parents report violence to children; 30/1000 women report severe beatings). Gelles and Straus attribute this change to changes in the American family in the last decade, e.g., more alternatives for women's lives, less stress with more family planning, fewer children.

Whatever the reasons for intimate violence, "people are not for hitting," and no one desires to be hit or sexually abused. Almost one-third of victims will recreate the violence as adults and almost one-half suffer severe psychological repercussions, e.g., depression, despair, low self-esteem. Victims *do* try to cope with the violence; most do not succumb to learned helplessness. Social factors rather than masochism "entrap them." More than specific techniques, a conviction and determination expressed by the victim that violence must stop is likely to be effective in terminating it. Unfortunately, the criminal justice system and the medical community have provided little help to victims. Other professionals, particularly social service providers, are divided on whether to provide compassion for the participants or control of the situation. Gelles and Straus suggest three ways to prevent intimate violence: (1) eliminate cultural norms that support the acceptance of violence as an appropriate way of resolving family conflicts and problems; (2) develop programs that reduce stress and inequality, especially sexism, in families; and (3) revoke the "hitting license" that allows hitting family members, particularly children, to discipline, train, or punish them. (SGF)

PR

599. Grauerholz, Elizabeth, and Mary A. Koralewski, eds. **Sexual Coercion: A Sourcebook on Its Nature, Causes, and Prevention.** Lexington, Mass.: Lexington Books, 1991. 240 p. Includes bibliography and index. ISBN 0-669-21786-7.

Accepting the widely held belief that sexual coercion (being forced or pressured into unwanted sexual acts) is commonplace in American society, beginning in childhood and continuing into adulthood, Grauerholz and Koralewski in this fourteen-paper collection, have assembled the views of researchers drawn from many fields, including anthropology, sociology, psychology, women's studies, and biology. These experts examine the nature, causes, and prevention of sexual coercion.

Part I, "The Nature of Coercion," consists of four papers. Patricia A. Harney and Charlene L. Muehlenhard look at the legal, psychological, and sociological literature on rape, dealing specifically with definitions, the incidence and prevalence of rape, the characteristics of rapists, and the consequences of rape. Dean D. Knudsen reviews the research on child abuse and suggests avenues for future research. Kathleen McKinney and Nick Maroules cover the literature on sexual harassment in academe and the workplace, and JoAnn L. Miller examines studies on prostitution in contemporary American society.

In part II, "The Causes of Sexual Coercion," Wendy Stock examines feminist explanations of sexual coercion, including male dominance and hostility toward women as the means of controlling women. Barry Burkhart and Mary Ellen Fromuth explore individual psychological and social psychological understandings of sexual coercion and reveal the extent to which sexual coercion is embedded in the structure and processes of culture. Randy Thornhill and Nancy Wilmsen Thornhill focus on men's motivations in rape and whether men have psychologically adapted to rape as a result of evolution by selection.

In part III, "Preventing Sexual Coercion," Martha E. Thompson examines the theory, research, and practice of women and children's self-defense against sexual coercion. Andrea Parrot considers the role of parenting in preventing sexual coercion, and Elizabeth Rice Allgeier and Betty J. Turner Royster focus their attention on dating and how couples may cope with their desire to have sex. Janet Lynne Enke and Lori K. Sudderth concentrate on sex education and how ideas about sexual coercion may be introduced into programs. Jo Dixon deals with feminist reforms of sexual coercion laws, and Heidi Gottfried presents a paper on preventing sexual coercion through economic changes that give women equal work opportunities, help with child care services, family and medical leave, and so forth.

In part IV. "Conclusion," Grauerholz and Koralewski review what is known and not known about the nature, causes, and prevention of sexual coercion. (TJW)

IL

600. Holmes, Ronald M. **Sex Crimes.** Newbury Park, Calif.: Sage Publications, 1991. 146 p. Includes bibliography, index, and glossary. ISBN 0-8039-3953-1.

Criminologist Holmes has written this primer about sex crimes for the layperson. He provides an overview of sex crimes in the United States and contrasts normal sex with the sexual behavior of deviants. He itemizes sex standards that people use to determine their sexual conduct: statistical (what most people do), religious (what one's religion permits or prohibits), cultural (what one's culture encourages or discourages), and subjective (persons judging their own behavior). Holmes finds that the common elements in both normal and deviant sex are fantasy, symbolism (what people see in the media), ritualism, and compulsion. Possessed by sex offenders, these elements may lead to serious crime. He comments that one's religion and family background—whether it be Hebrew, Greek, Roman, or Christian—have a great influence on sexual behavior.

Noting that sex offenders in prison currently number over 62,000 in the United States, Holmes states that many of these offenders manifest nuisance behaviors, which he identifies as voyeurism, exhibitionism, transvestism, obscene telephone calls, frottage, bestiality, pygmalionism (falling in love with a statue, doll, or mannequin), gerontophilia, and mysophilia (an erotic interest in filth). These behaviors are often associated with the perpetration of serious sex crimes, such as incest, rape, and pedophilia.

Following a chapter on homosexuality that deals with institutional homosexuality, the homosexual prostitute, and the homosexual pedophile, Holmes takes up such dangerous sex crimes as necrophilia, infibulation, autoeroticism, pyromania, and lust murder. For each type of sex crime, Holmes examines its etiology, the sex offenders' characteristics, the effects on victims, and treatment of sex offenders. He then looks at the victims, both primary and secondary, of sexual assault and how to deal with their victimization. Here he relates the impact of Ted Bundy's lust murders on the families of the victims.

Holmes concludes by stating that changing the "sex offenders sexual value system and propensity for violence" through "early identification of those persons who may become sexually violent as they age into adulthood," and by giving "serious consideration to identification, isolation, and effective change of those who are dangerous," we may be able to provide the protection that society demands (p. 114). (TJW)

PR
601. Marshall, W. L., D. R. Laws, and H. E. Barbaree, eds. **Handbook of Sexual Assault: Issues, Theories, and Treatment of the Offender.** New York: Plenum Press, 1990. 405 p. (Applied Clinical Psychology). Includes bibliographic references and index. ISBN 0-306-43272-2.

This edited collection of papers from many clinicians/researchers is designed to bring readers up to date on current knowledge and thinking about sexual assault, understood here to mean offensive male sexual aggression against women and children. While prevention of sexual assault and the treatment of victims are areas needing attention, the focus in this work is on the evaluation and treatment of the perpetrators of the assault.

Twenty-two chapters cover topics within five major divisions. Part I is an introduction to sexual assault, its nature and extent, and classification of the offenders. Part II deals with research about possible factors influencing sexual assault: sexual gratification as a primary motivation, power and humiliation, pornography, androgenic hormones, brain damage/dysfunction, sexual arousal, social and cultural factors and cognition factors (beliefs, attitudes, perceptions, and emotions). Part III discusses theories of sexual assault, including a feminist perspective, the concept of "courtship disorder," conditioning theory, and an integrative theory of the etiology of sexual offending. A chapter in this section reviews recent studies pertaining specifically to incestuous fathers.

The penultimate section summarizes treatment modes. Some of these include sexual preference modification, hormonal treatment, social skills enhancement, modification of cognitive distortions, relapse prevention, and a summary of the outcome of comprehensive cognitive behavioral treatment programs. Areas are highlighted that the editors believe deserve greater research attention: selection of offenders for treatment, self-management and prevention of relapse, early onset of sexual offending, misuse of measurement technology, and the measurement/characterization of "sexual assault."

The editors conclude that while improved treatment of offenders is important, it is not the solution to the problem. What remains is the development of courageous prevention strategies, such as the implementation of social change that empowers women and children. (MC)

PR
602. Prentky, Robert A., and Vernon L. Quinsey, eds. **Human Sexual Aggression: Current Perspectives.** New York: New York Academy of Sciences, 1988. 407 p. (Annals of the New York Academy of Sciences, v. 528). Includes bibliographic references and indexes. ISBN 0-89766-451-5.

Central issues in sexual aggression are dealt with in this compilation of papers presented at a conference entitled Human Sexual Aggression: Current Perspectives, held by the New York Academy of Sciences in New York City in 1987. In the preface, Prentky and Quinsey state that "the overriding mission of this conference was to give research on human sexual aggression a priority that is commensurate with the magnitude of the problem and the depth of public concern." The work addresses issues in five distinct areas of sexual aggression.

In part I, "Psychological and Typological Issues," the papers examine taxonomic systems for the classification of child molesters and rapists, aberrant sexual offenders, phallometric assessments of sexual preference, and clinical reflections on sexual aggression. Part II, "Social and Cross-Cultural Issues," shifts the focus with papers on child molestation, cultural spillover theory, child sexual abuse and adolescent sexual functioning, causes of sexual aggression as explained by cultural and individual measures, and sexual aggression among male college students. Part III, "Biological Issues," contains papers on sexual aggression in the Great Apes, the correlation of sadistic behavior with endocrinological factors and brain abnormalities, courtship disorders (voyeurism, frotteurism, etc.), biological drives and the will, and organic treatment of biological drives.

In part IV, "Treatment and Prevention," researchers present papers on programs for outpatient treatment for child molesters, measuring the effectiveness of treatment for the aggressive adolescent sexual offender, predicting child molesters' response to treatment, California's New Outcome Study on sex offender treatment and evaluation, relapse prevention of sexual aggression, and advancements in physiological evaluation of assessment and treatment of the sexual aggressor. Part V, "Victim Issues," examines serial rapists and their victims, immediate and delayed treatment of rape victims, the effects of sexual abuse on children, long-term clinical correlation of childhood sexual victimization, rape in marriage and date rape, and coping strategies and recovery from rape. Part VI, "Social Policy," deals with the impact of forensic issues on women's rights, ethical issues in the treatment and maltreatment of sexual offenders, Canadian responses to law reform, social policy and criminal sexual violence, legislative remedies for rape, and a social policy perspective on human sexual aggression.

Prentky and Quinsey claim that there has been very little empirical research on human sexual aggression, that treatment has been largely experiential. But now with increased scholarly attention being given to the subject there is a need for a state of the art appraisal of recent advances. They believe that for the present this publication will satisfy that need. (TJW)

PR

603. Schlesinger, Louis B., and Eugene Revitch, eds. **Sexual Dynamics of Anti-Social Behavior.** With a foreword by Robert L. Sadoff. Springfield, Ill.: Thomas, 1983. 317 p. Includes bibliographic references and index. ISBN 0-398-04802-9.

The purpose of this collection is "to examine various types of anti-social behaviors that are sexually motivated or that have distinct sexual dynamics" (p. xi). Written by psychiatrists, psychologists, sociologists, and criminologists, most, but not all, of the papers have a decidedly psychoanalytic bias. The book is divided into three sections along a hypothetical spectrum of increasing antisocial behaviors. An understanding of how a particular pathology in the spectrum functions, operates, and develops is the goal of each paper.

In section I, "Socially Tolerated Acts," Edward Sagarin and Robert William Jolly, Jr., look at prostitution as a profession and a pathology. A paper reporting the research of Edward Donnerstein and Neil Malamuth follows, relating the effects of aggressive pornography to individuals' sexual responsiveness. Natalie Shainess gives a psychoanalytic interpretation of the abnormal pursuit of sexual encounters by men and women, laying some of the blame on the doorstep of Masters and Johnson. Harry Gershman in his paper wonders about the consequences of sexual permissiveness today, and Richard C. Stuntz reviews research on gender dysphoria and surgical sex reassignment.

Section II, "Non-Tolerated Offenses," starts off with a paper on genital exhibitionism in men and women by Marc H. Hollender, followed by George Zavitzianos's paper relating kleptomania and female criminality. T. Nicholas Groth and William F. Hobson examine the dynamics of sexual assault and its impact, conceptualizing rape as the sexual expression of aggression. Using the case history method, Eugene Revitch explores the topic of compulsive burglaries with covert sexual motivation, and Ivan Fras examines pyromania and its relationship to sexuality.

In section III, "Rare and Bizarre Behaviors," Schlesinger and Revitch explore the sexual dynamics in homicide and assault, concluding that certain types of behavior may presage a dangerous assault; Harvey L. P. Resnik considers eroticized repetitive hangings in his article; Selwyn M. Smith and John Dimock review the psychopathology of necrophilia; Robert E. Litman deals with bondage and sadomasochism; and André Bourguignon focuses on the pathological relationship of men with blood, sexuality, and death in his paper on vampirism and autovampirism. Each paper in this collection provides a review of the literature along with a list of references. (TJW)

IL

604. Walkowitz, Judith R. **City of Dreadful Delight: Narratives of Sexual Danger in Late-Victorian London.** Chicago: University of Chicago Press, 1992. 353 p. (Women in Culture and Society). Includes bibliography and index. ISBN 0-226-87145-2.

Walkowitz, a professor of history and director of women's studies at Johns Hopkins University, explores in this book the social and cultural milieu of London in the last half of the nineteenth century. Written from a feminist perspective, she focuses attention on certain events of the 1880s, highlighting the sexual danger that women faced daily when they ventured out of their own private worlds into the increasingly available but dangerous public spaces. These women, whether from the wealthier or more destitute parts of London, risked being stared at, accosted, harmed, kidnapped, and even murdered.

London at that time, with eight million inhabitants, was the largest city in the world. The fruits of Empire were being brought to it on many levels—for example, the first department stores were being established to make shopping available and comfortable for women, who desired to sample exotic goods from around the world.

Walkowitz begins by examining the London urban landscape that featured "the tradition of the urban male spectatorship" and the bifurcation of London into East End and West End as "a backdrop for personal adventure and self-creation" (p. 11). She selects events that show the sexual dangers increasingly encountered by women in Victorian London. Through the media readers were apprised of events that made women wary about entering certain spaces. For example, W. T. Stead's exposé of child prostitution that appeared in the *Pall Mall Gazette* in 1885, entitled "Maiden Tribute to Modern Babylon," told about the traffic in girls. It ran for several days and shocked the nation. Public demonstrations resulted and Parliament reacted by enacting age-of-consent legislation. Also, the frightful Jack the Ripper sex murders between August 31 and November 9, 1888 of five prostitutes in the Whitechapel area of London offered no witnesses and few clues. These brutal murders have never been solved.

Emphasizing the growing participation of women in the social and cultural life of London, Walkowitz describes the founding in 1885 of the Men and Women's Club by the socialist and mathematician Karl Pearson. Encouraging members to address sexual issues at monthly meetings, Pearson led discussions and heard reports on child prostitution, homosexuality, pornography, marriage, eugenics, the "new sexuality," and the "woman's question." Olive Schreiner, Maria Sharpe, and Elizabeth Cobb were members of the club, which lasted four years.

Further exploring the arena of sexual danger for women, Walkowitz examines Georgina Weldon's "campaign against her husband, Henry, and a mad-doctor alienist, L. Forbes Winslow, for conspiring to intern her in an insane asylum because she was a spiritualist." Recognizing a parallel to the original ripper murders, Walkowitz examines the crimes of the Yorkshire Ripper, a serial killer, who in 1975 in Leeds killed thirteen prostitutes. This case suggests that despite the passage of years, nothing has altered the environment of sexual danger for women in public areas.

Walkowitz concludes with this statement: "Today, as in the past, feminists struggle to devise an effective strategy to combat sexual violence and humiliation in our society, where violent misogyny seems so deep rooted. Similarly, the media continues to amplify the terror of male violence, as it did during the sexual scandals of the 1880s, persuading women that they are helpless victims" (p. 244). (TJW)

Incest

(For related material see also entries 91, 94, 953, 1036)

PR,IL

605. Arens, W. **The Original Sin: Incest and Its Meaning.** New York: Oxford University Press, 1986. 190 p. Includes bibliography and index. ISBN 0-19-503754-5.

The goal of this book stems from a gap in the literature on the incest taboo. "The literature suggests quite clearly that as a rule intellectuals have either ignored or unintentionally denied the existence of incest in propounding their theories about the universality of the prohibition" (p. vii). Discussions of incest have been equated with discussions of the incest taboo. They are not the same. Consequently, the importance of incest has been overshadowed by an emphasis on the taboo. The book examines the practice, meaning, and significance of incest in order to provide a clearer statement of the problem that incest poses for science.

Arens begins by tracing the history of thought on the incest taboo. The search for the meaning of incest has centered on questions about the origin and functions of the incest taboo. Morgan, Tylor, McLennan, Freud, and Lévi-Strauss addressed the link between the incest taboo, exogamy, and the emergence of culture, assuming that incest indicated a more primitive state of nature; the origins of the taboo were cultural. Westermarck suggested that a natural aversion to incest may lie at the basis of the taboo. Malinowski focused on contemporary functions of the incest taboo, concluding that it prevented social chaos that could result from incest. Sociologists analyzed incest as deviant behavior while other investigators labeled it as inherently pathological.

Arens presents a range of research findings that aid in the assessment of theories about the incest taboo and provide guidance in dealing with views about incest itself. For example, empirical data suggest that incest is not necessarily disruptive, confusing, or pathological. Theorists may have neglected the possible positive results of incestuous relationships. Also, primate field data indicate that noncultural animals share a tendency to outbreed, not inbreed. The fact that incest occurs regularly in human populations deserves explanation.

Arens analyzes the cultural complexity of incest by looking at both sanctioned cases of royal incest and unsanctioned cases in American society. The symbolic role of incest cannot be reduced to sociobiological formulae or sociological functions. "The practice or suggestion of incest is an artifact of culture, rather than nature" (p. 100). However, acknowledging that incest itself rather than its avoidance is more uniquely human entails a shift in assumptions about human nature and the supposed superiority of culture over nature. "Arriving at this unsavory conclusion has involved coming to terms with the messages of traditional . . . social science" (p. 153). (SGF)

PR,IL

606.   Fox, Robin. **The Red Lamp of Incest.** New York: Dutton, 1980. 271 p. Includes bibliography and index. ISBN 0-525-18943-2.

Like the small, bright red Chinese lantern that quickly illuminates when the correct switch is triggered, so too does anthropologist Fox attempt to shed some light on the issue of incest. Using the insights of his "pantheon of savants" (Darwin, Marx, Freud, and Lévi-Strauss) about the transformation into a human state, Fox weaves them together with contemporary findings from various disciplines to attempt a "biosocial synthesis" that rewrites Freud's *Totem and Taboo* "with half a century of hindsight." Freud argued that the sons of a primal horde engaged in incest with their mothers and killed their fathers. Overcome with guilt, they instituted the rule of the incest taboo and established their fathers as a totem, to be revered and respected.

Fox argues that something like the primal horde must have occurred and left its mark on subsequent generations in the form of avoidance rules and behavior between parents and children. He first turns to the primate evidence and equilibrational theory to establish the basis for his point of view. Primates are divided into three groups: females with their young, elder males, and peripheral males. Control of sexual access to females by elder males is a recurring theme among primate species; it is not unlike the father/son conflict of the wife/mother that Freud describes. However, humans departed from the breeding pattern of their primate kin. Pressures to equilibrate (balance alternatives) occurred as the frontal lobes of the brain developed. Through a process of feedback between brain development and equilibration the brain continued to increase in size. Humans achieved the ability to formulate rules to govern their behavior and supersede emotional responses to situations. In the process, the incest taboo, exogamy, and initiation ceremonies served to reinforce the right of elder males to have control over younger males' reproductive access to females. Kinship systems came into being as relationships within which groups exchange mates according to given rules. Consequently, uneasiness about incestuous relationships in contemporary societies is less due to rules and more to the "kinds of creatures we are." (SGF)

PR
607.   Goodwin, Jean. **Sexual Abuse: Incest Victims and Their Families.** 2nd ed. Chicago: Year Book Medical Publishers, 1989. 269 p. Includes bibliographies and index. ISBN 0-8151-3537-8.
Several investigators join psychiatrist Goodwin in writing twenty-one papers for the second edition of her book on incest and sexual abuse. They present numerous case studies stemming from Goodwin's work with over 300 incest victims and their families. Most of these cases were referrals from protective service agencies, including instances of ongoing child sexual abuse as well as examples of abusive parents who had been abused themselves in childhood. Although Goodwin's experience has been mainly with extreme and difficult cases, she incorporates those ideas of colleagues, friends, and patients "for an understanding of those incest situations that leave minimal scars" (p. xiii).
The book is logically organized: in section I, "Evaluation and Treatment Planning," are (1) a description of a systematic five-point approach to investigating an allegation of incest; (2) a discussion of errors that professionals dread in incest cases, e.g., incorrect diagnosis of sexual abuse or overlooking actual incest based on a family's denial; (3) an examination of drawings done by victimized and nonparticipant children as clinical clues to incest; (4) a consideration of paranoia found in some incest fathers; and (5) the realization of how the needs of incest victims vary with the victim's developmental stage in life.
Section II, "The Sequelae of Incest," covers some of the late sequelae of the incest experience, describing "girls and women whose incest experiences usually were not recognized or treated in childhood, but who came to medical attention months or years later with complaints that could be understood as delayed reaction to incest" (p. xiv). Some of the reactions dealt with include hysterical seizures, suicide attempts, female homosexuality, pregnancy, Multiple Personality Disorder (MPD), and dissociative symptoms. In their search for a syndrome definition in survivors of extreme incestuous abuse, Goodwin and colleagues have identified five types of common sequelae: (1) fears, (2) ego constriction, (3) anger dyscontrol, (4) repetitions (in nightmares or flashbacks), and (5) sadness with sleep disturbance.
Section III, "Forensic and Social Implications of Research in Sexual Abuse," addresses three areas of the problem: the need for physicians to report child abuse, cross-cultural perspectives on clinical problems of incest, and the many obstacles to controlling incest in our society.
Survey results show that 15 percent of women in the general population have experienced incest with a relative, and 1 to 4 percent have experienced father-daughter incest; consequently, the child sexual abuse problem has been brought to center stage in present-day society. (TJW)

PR,IL
608.   Herman, Judith Lewis, with Lisa Hirschmen. **Father-Daughter Incest.** Cambridge, Mass.: Harvard University Press, 1981. 282 p. Includes bibliography and index. ISBN 0-6742-9505-6.
Addressing victims of incest and the professionals who work with them, Herman develops a feminist analysis of father-daughter incest and examines the possibilities for healing and prevention. Part 1, "The Incest Secret," evaluates existing theories about the causes and effects of incest, sharply diverging from the viewpoints of Freud and Kinsey

by asserting that incest is real and inflicts lasting damage. Part 2, "Daughters' Lives," draws on interviews with incest victims and with women whose fathers were seductive but stopped short of genital contact. Part 3, "Breaking Secrecy," reports on legal, clinical, and self-help approaches to dealing with incest. Herman's study contains extensive documentation, including case histories and interviews. Florence Rush's *The Best Kept Secret: Sexual Abuse of Children* and Jean Renvoize's *Incest: A Family Pattern* (Boston, Routledge & Kegan Paul, 1982) present other overviews of both theoretical and practical concerns. (**Women's Studies**, 1987)

PO
609. Kosof, Anna. **Incest: Families in Crisis.** New York: Franklin Watts, 1985. 101 p. Includes index. ISBN 0-531-10071-5.

It is estimated that one in three girls and one in eight boys have experienced some form of sexual abuse by the time they are eighteen. Written for the layperson in a discursive style, this nontechnical book focuses on one form of sexual abuse—incest—that Kosof, an anthropologist, broadly defines as "any sexual relationship between a child and an adult with parental responsibilities; or between two siblings." This definition goes beyond the legal specification of incest as sexual intercourse between relatives to include fondling, touching, oral sex, or any other physical activity that has to be kept a secret.

Although based on interviews with victims, family members, mental health professionals, and personnel of counseling centers and social service agencies in the United States, this is not a scientific study of incest but rather an exploration of its facets and a search for an explanation of its existence. Incest is portrayed as "adultery, child abuse, betrayal, the breaking of a universal taboo, a crime." Psychological and social explanations of the incest taboo seem to make more sense than biological ones; the taboo regulates sexual conflicts and rivalries and sets an appropriate background for socializing children. The most common form of incest is father-daughter, although brother-sister and mother-son occur more frequently than reported. The repercussions of breaking the taboo are different for the participants. The victim feels guilt, anger, and isolation. The mother, who often says that she does not know of the incest, plays a role in the behavior; her submission to a dominant husband or difficulty in talking about intimate issues may perpetuate the problem. The father often denies the problem, finds it difficult to stop his behavior, and frequently will not go for treatment unless forced to.

Treatment of incest involves breaking the secret and being prepared for the legal, psychological, and family consequences of the disclosure. Males may need to be jailed and/or receive counseling to experience the consequences of their actions. Some experts say that the family system can be restored in half of the cases seen. However, nonlegal routes to change may be less harmful for the victim. Concern for teaching a child to prevent incest may be the most viable route for dealing with the problem. Two valuable appendixes provide further information for people coping with incestuous behavior. Appendix I, compiled by the National Center on Child Abuse and Neglect, lists incest programs in the United States. Appendix II, compiled by Parents United, Inc., lists child sexual abuse treatment programs. (SGF)

PR
610. Meiselman, Karin C. **Incest: A Psychological Study of Causes and Effects with Treatment Recommendations.** San Francisco: Jossey-Bass, 1978. 366 p. (Jossey-Bass Social and Behavioral Science Series). Includes bibliography and index. ISBN 0-87589-380-5.

Meiselman, a clinical psychologist, addresses this book primarily to mental health professionals. Her goal is to provide "accumulated observations and hypotheses of numerous clinicians and researchers over the past fifty years" (p. xii), that can aid practitioners in the evaluation and treatment of incest cases. After an initial summary of anthropological and sociological views of the origin and function of the incest taboo, Meiselman suggests that social conditions, cultural prohibitions, and psychological factors present in the nuclear family context may account for the maintenance of the taboo. She then points out some of the pros and cons of different research strategies for studying incest and summarizes both American and foreign studies of incest behavior, particularly all of those with a sample of five or more. Throughout the book she integrates the findings of previous psychological studies with those of her own research on incest, that compares a psychotherapy sample of fifty-eight cases with a control group of nonincestuous patients at a Los Angeles psychiatric clinic.

Most of the book focuses on the presentation of findings about the psychological causes, development, characteristics, and effects of incest. She pays particular attention to father-daughter incest, the most common form of incest in her sample. She also discusses the dimensions of other types of heterosexual incest, cases of same gender incest, and situations of multiple incest. She points out that no single personality characteristic or family pattern causes incest. Many of the findings challenge popular stereotypes about incestuous behavior, such as that daughters seduce their fathers and enjoy it, that incestuous fathers are psychotic men from rural or lower class backgrounds, and that mothers "set up" their daughters for incest.

Meiselman concludes that "incest is usually a negative life event that is followed by adjustive difficulties" (p. 331). The final chapter provides recommendations to professionals for the detection, treatment, and prevention of incest cases. Acknowledging the truth of incest reports as well as the dynamics of families in which incest occurs are steps in this direction. (SGF)

PR

611. Russell, Diana E. H. **The Secret Trauma: Incest in the Lives of Girls and Women.** New York: Basic Books, 1986. 426 p. Includes bibliography and index. ISBN 0-465-07595-9.

The research on which this book and two previous ones by Russell, *Rape in Marriage* (1982) and *Sexual Exploitation: Rape, Childhood Sexual Abuse, and Workplace Harassment* (1984), are based began in 1977. The findings are derived from interviews with a nonclinical, representative sample of 930 women in the San Francisco area. Russell claims that these results provide the "soundest data base yet available for making tentative national estimates" (p. 10) about issues related to incest.

The twenty-four chapters are divided into five parts. The first part describes the distinctiveness of the method used and details the study's definition of incestuous abuse as "any kind of exploitive sexual contact or attempted contact that occurred between relatives, no matter how distant the relationship, before the victim turned eighteen years old" (p. 41). The second part concentrates on the magnitude of the problem and its characteristics. Russell comments that one of the "most shocking" findings of the study was that 16 percent of the women had been abused by a relative before they were eighteen. She estimates that the real incidence of incest may have increased in the United States in this century. Estimates of prevalence may be too low because few incest victims report sexual abuse. Incest rarely involves physical violence and may occur only once in many cases. The research reveals that women at high risk are likely to come from *higher* income families, be raised by a stepfather, and have mothers with a high school education. Having a working mother or a rural background does *not* increase vulnerability to incest.

Part 3 describes the social characteristics of victims, their perceptions of the trauma they experienced (79 percent report negative reactions), and their ways of coping with it (some were quite assertive). Later in life, incest victims are more likely to be separated or divorced, defect from their religion, have children at an early age, or become other types of victims. Part 4 focuses on the characteristics of the perpetrators, who include a range of relatives. Contact with uncles is a "serious and widespread" problem, and sexual contacts with brothers are not "harmless." Incest with stepfathers is more likely to be severe and longer-lasting than with biological fathers.

Part 5 considers the roles of other family members in the incestuous context. In 72 percent of the cases where the mother did not know about the incest, the victims had experienced more severe forms of incest. Therefore, it is "crucial that we as a society stop participating in the conspiracy of silence that has kept incest one of the best-kept secrets for so long" (p. 13). (SGF)

PR

612.   Shepher, Joseph. **Incest: A Biosocial View.** New York: Academic Press, 1983. 213 p. (Studies in Anthropology). Includes bibliography, indexes, and glossary. ISBN 0-12-639460-1.

According to Shepher, a professor of anthropology and sociology at the University of Haifa, the extensive literature on incest has never been systematically surveyed nor synthesized in light of one theory. He proposes to fill these gaps by presenting "a sociobiological view of incest and a comprehensive survey of the theoretical literature on incest" (p. 5).

Following Edward O. Wilson's lead, Shepher first summarizes some of the basic tenets of sociobiology that are important elements of his own view of incest (e.g., epigenetic rules, parental investment). He then reviews methodological issues relevant to the study of the incest taboo (e.g., a definition of incest, the relevance of animal behavior, conceptualization of the regulation, origin, persistence, and functions of incest) and concludes that a definition of incest as "heterosexual intercourse between persons whose genetic relatedness is 1/4-1/2" is appropriate for his inquiry.

Several theories and research findings set the stage for a sociobiological approach. Shepher thinks that the sexual indifference of boys and girls in Kibbutz peer groups and of the bride and groom in Taiwanese *sim pua* marriages confirms Westermarck's view of innate aversion as one basis of the incest taboo's origin and demonstrates that sibling incest is "preculturally avoided by a biophysical mechanism" (p. 67). Fox, Bischof, Burnham, Parker, and Bateson have recognized these elements while Aberle, Lindzey, and Ember have noted the importance of inbreeding as a factor. All point to a sociobiological theory that Shepher codifies in a series of eight propositions. He presents evidence to show that incest regulations have evolved to prevent inbreeding through mechanisms of inhibition, prevention, and prohibition. Other evidence in line with his propositions shows that (1) father-daughter incest is most common, (2) females are likely to resist more than males, (3) incest occurs more often in cases of actual or socially imposed isolation, and (4) cultural variability of the taboo increases as relationships are further removed from core dyads. Secondary functions explain the persistence of the taboo. The classical theories of the family socialization school (Freud, Malinowski, Seligman, Murdock, Parsons) and those of the alliance school (Tylor, Fortune, White, Lévi-Strauss) address these concerns. Shepher evaluates previous theories in terms of their explanatory strength and coherence with a sociobiological view of incest. He concludes that his study shows the coevolution of culture and biology; cultural rules follow basic biological predispositions. (SGF)

IL

613.   Twitchell, James B. **Forbidden Partners: The Incest Taboo in Modern Culture.** New York: Columbia University Press, 1987. 311 p. Includes bibliography and index. ISBN 0-231-06412-8.

Despite indications that interest in incest "is almost plague-like in our collective imagination," the dynamic themes of incest presented in modern literature have been ignored. Twitchell, a professor of English at the University of Florida, proposes to correct that oversight by exploring Anglo-American attitudes toward incest as they are reflected in art, literature, and popular culture. Although incest has been conceptualized as an "unnatural act," Twitchell argues that it is an "uncultural act." Art and literature converge in promoting the message: "avoid incest." Anxiety about incest is expressed in fictional family structures.

Twitchell begins by documenting the degree of concern that modern society has in explaining "the enigma of incest." Implications of father-daughter incest in advertising;

themes of brother-sister (*Cat People*), father-daughter (*Chinatown*), and mother-daughter (*Luna*) incest in films; and scientific theories about incest (fully described in the appendix) reinforce this point of view. Horror, the "acceptable" social response to incest, is reflected in some of the art of Klee, Ruppert, Goya, Munch, and Kubin; in obscene language; in children's stories such as "Little Red Riding Hood" and "Beauty and the Beast"; and in horror tales of monsters and vampires.

Twitchell then traces modern interest in the incest taboo from the late nineteenth century to the present. He discusses how major works of the Romantic poets Shelley, Byron, and Wordsworth explored the limits of natural boundaries by portraying resignation, escape, or narcissism as responses to incestuous fantasies. While Gothic novels characterized the shocking, grotesque aspects of incest, pornographic materials supplied "voyeuristic titillation." Prose works of American writers Poe, Hawthorne, and Melville reiterate incestuous themes. After Melville, literary interest turned to realism and naturalism. Overall, the literary and artistic themes of the last century and a half reveal "deep-seated anxieties not only about sex, but about the family structure itself" (p. 239). (SGF)

IL

614. Ward, Elizabeth. **Father-Daughter Rape.** New York: Grove Press, 1985. 247 p. Includes bibliography and index. ISBN 0-394-62032-1.

The title of this book expresses Ward's feminist interpretation of the widespread phenomenon of sexual child abuse. Rather than limiting her discussion to incest, which focuses attention on the relation of the participants in sexual interaction, she tries to draw attention to the dynamics of the situation by using the term *rape*, because she concludes that childhood sexual abuse generally feels like rape. "Father" refers to offenders as a group, whether they be fathers, uncles, father-figures, or trusted males; "daughter" refers to girl children sexually abused by the fathers. Rape includes intercourse or molestation of girl children (daughters) by trusted males (fathers).

Ward, born in Australia, interviewed a potpourri of Australian friends and acquaintances who had been sexually abused by male family members while they were children. The first section consists of nine personal accounts of childhood abuse chosen from the range of those interviewed. Ward believes that several themes emerge from these accounts: fathers as rapists; mothers who seem blind to what has happened; daughters who feel helpless, hopeless, passive, and angry.

The second part presents a theoretical interpretation of the experiences recounted in the first section. Rape ideology is interpreted as an attitude and practice that keeps women isolated and dependent on men. It is part of capitalist patriarchy that plays on competition and distrust and uses sex and violence to promote susceptibility to these aims. Freudianism, often used as a basis for therapy in these cases, perpetuates male supremacist ideals and reinforces rape ideology. It serves to blame the victim, who is viewed as desirous of having intercourse with her father. Using such theories, social and behavioral scientists have exonerated fathers from their roles in raping daughters.

Ward reviews a wide range of current theories about why people participate in childhood sexual abuse. Overall, she interprets the data and research on father-daughter rape, the fathers, daughters, mothers, and sons in terms of their embeddedness in a patriarchal social structure. Her own view is that fathers who rape girl children do so because they have access to powerless females. She concludes that theories support a mythology that labels the daughter as precocious and blames her or her mother for the situation, thus dismissing the profound damage to the daughter's further development. The cycle perpetuates itself in sons who reject their mothers and gain access to their own daughters.

The last section addresses the ultimate aim of this book—how to effect prompt action after the silence is broken about the dynamics of father-daughter rape. (SGF)

Rape

(For related material see also entries 1042, 1043)

PR,IL
615.   Allison, Julie A., and Lawrence S. Wrightsman. **Rape: The Misunderstood Crime.** Newbury Park, Calif.: Sage Publications, 1993. 307 p. Includes bibliography and indexes. ISBN 0-8039-3706-7.

Allison, a professor at Pittsburg State University, Pittsburg, Kansas, and Wrightsman, a professor at the University of Kansas, Lawrence, Kansas, have written a comprehensive study of rape as a misunderstood crime in the United States. Misunderstood because not all rapes are alike; there are many different types; reporting in the media is often confusing; statistics about rape are frequently misleading; and the public's image of the rapist is too often stereotypical—a sex-starved and/or insane stranger. The goals of this book are "to document and illustrate the multiple motivations for rape"; to clarify the statistics on the incidence of rape; to provide an up-to-date review of the crime of rape from a psychological perspective."

By way of background, Allison and Wrightsman present three theories of rape identified by sociologist Lee Ellis in 1989: the feminist theory of rape, that claims women are "viewed by men as little more than property," and "rape is seen as the use of sexuality to establish and maintain dominance and control of women by men" (p. 16); the social learning theory of rape, that would see rape "as an aggressive behavior that was learned from observing acts in real life or the mass media, especially aggressive acts that go unpunished" (p. 16); and finally an evolutionary theory of rape that emphasizes the biological sex roles of men and women, giving the females the task of caring for offspring while the males invest their time in securing as many sex partners as possible.

Allison and Wrightsman allocate the chapters of their book as follows: chapter 2 examines the rapist and the feminist belief that exposure to pornography contributes to rape; chapters 3, 4, and 5 concern particular kinds of rape: stranger rape, date and acquaintance rape, and marital rape; chapters 6 and 7 consider "the acceptance of rape myths in the general populace, callous attitudes toward sex, and the phenomenon of 'blaming the victim' " (p. 19), and offer different explanations for "the prevalence of negative reactions to rape victims" (p. 19). Chapter 8 includes victims' reactions to rape; chapter 9 discusses the treatment of rape victims by trial courts, and chapter 10 reviews the extensive recent legislation that has revolutionized the legal system's reaction to rape. Chapter 11 takes up the question of punishment and treatment for rapists, and chapter 12 describes various ways of preventing rape.

In conclusion Allison and Wrightsman reiterate that "rape is a crime, it is an act of violence, and its consequences are dramatic" (p. 259). The perpetrators need to be held responsible for their behavior. "Society must recognize that all violence, including rape, is unacceptable behavior" (p. 259). (TJW)

PR
616.   Amir, Menachem. **Patterns in Forcible Rape.** Chicago: University of Chicago Press, 1971. 394 p. Includes bibliography and index. ISBN 0-226-01734-6.

In this pioneering study, Amir, a sociologist, presents the first statistical, in-depth investigation of the nature of rape and rapists. As Marvin Wolfgang, a leading American criminologist, says in the foreword, this is "the most thorough, rigorous, and detailed study in the literature," and "no important study of rape in the future can ignore this work." Part I introduces the general orientation and background of the study. A broad phenomenological approach is adopted to study rape; it emphasizes the analysis of interactional ingredients of the crime itself in order to reveal the patterns that underlie it. Therefore, data collection focused on gathering information about the social characteristics of the individuals involved as well as the situational factors related to the commission of the crime. The immediate aim of the study, begun in 1961, was to analyze forcible rape in the Philadelphia area. Forcible rape is defined as "the carnal knowledge of a women by a man, carried out against her will and without her consent, extorted by threat or fraudulence" (p. 17). The database includes all cases of forcible rape listed by the Philadelphia police in the years 1958 and 1960: a total of 646 cases and 1,392 known offenders. Parts II, III, and IV present and analyze the primary phenomenological factors that Amir thinks determine the concept of rape. Part II profiles the victim and offender in the rape situation according to racial differences, age patterns, marital status, employment and occupation, temporal and spatial patterns, the use of alcohol, and previous criminal record. Part III describes the characteristics of the rape situation (felony rape, group rape) as well as phases of the modus operandi of a rape. Part IV focuses on the characteristics of the victim in forcible rape; the degree of interpersonal relations between the victim and the offender, the potential victim and a vulnerable rape situation, and victim-precipitated forcible rape. The findings in these three parts shatter a major myth about rape: that a woman is attacked without warning by an unknown assailant. Amir found that most rapes are planned, many occur indoors, many involve a group of offenders, and they often include offenders known to the victim. In part V, Amir suggests a social rather than a psychological explanation for the patterns of forcible rape that he revealed. The data point to the importance of a subculture of violence in which situations are more likely to be perceived as calling for violence, including forcible rape. A succinct final chapter summarizes the conclusions. Throughout the book, findings are compared with other studies on the subject. An extensive thirty-page bibliography is a rich resource of materials on relevant literature on rape prior to this study. (SGF)

PR

617. Baron, Larry, and Murray A. Straus. **Four Theories of Rape in American Society: A State-level Analysis.** New Haven, Conn.: Yale University Press, 1989. 250 p. Includes bibliography and index. ISBN 0-300-04519-0.

This book is a publication of the Family Violence Research Program and the State and Regional Indicators Archive of the University of New Hampshire in Durham, New Hampshire. Baron and Straus's interest in doing research on rape was influenced by the fact that rape is a persistent and growing social problem; between 1960 and 1987 the number of reported rapes escalated from 16,860 to 91,111, an increase of approximately 440 percent over the 28-year period. Because of the focus on rape at the state level, "the present study uses a macrosociological approach and empirically assesses theories that might explain the wide variations among states in the incidence of rape" (p. 4).

Four theories of rape are examined in this study: (1) the gender inequality theory that proposes that rape functions as a mechanism of social control in patriarchal societies where men assert their power over women and maintain the existing system of gender stratification; (2) the theory that pornography causes rape because it reflects and promotes male dominance in society, sexually objectifies women, and depicts physical assaults against women that serve as behavioral models; (3) the social disorganization theory that claims that the erosion of institutional and informal forces of social control undermines social constraints and frees individuals to engage in nonconforming behavior; and (4) the legitimate violence theory that purports to show where violent cultural norms (violent television viewing, violent magazines, violent sports, corporal punishment, lynchings, etc.) are strongest, there is likely to be a spillover or carryover into illegitimate or illegal areas, such as rape.

Data on rape for this study are taken from the *Uniform Crime Reports* of the Federal Bureau of Investigation and examined by state and region. State-level data on indicators of gender equality, legitimate violence, and social disorganization, for example, are also used for presentation in tables and charts. Indexes such as the Gender Equality Index, the Sex Magazine Circulation Index, etc. are introduced. Definitions of pornography are presented and discussed while an alternative definition is formulated.

Baron and Straus, believing that the four theories of rape are complementary parts of a more comprehensive theory, introduce a theoretical model of variables antecedent to rape that provide an integrated theory of rape leading to hypotheses concerning the rape rate, such as "the higher the circulation rate of sexually explicit magazines, the higher the rape rate" (p. 174). They conclude by dealing with the social origins of rape, restriction of pornography as a rape reduction policy, and the primary prevention of rape. (TJW)

PR

618. Bourque, Linda Brookover. **Defining Rape.** Durham, N.C.: Duke University Press, 1989. 428 p. Includes bibliography and index. ISBN 0-8223-0901-7.

Bourque describes how definitions of rape relate to social structures, research in sociology and psychology, and the law. She reviews the research on rape, compares research designs, and examines how an individual's social roles affect that person's decision on whether a given encounter constitutes an act of rape.

With the increase in the visibility of rape and society's response to it, there has been a vast increase in the number of persons deciding whether a rape has occurred. There is little consensus regarding what information is used in this decision, and the subsequent decision on whether to report a rape, or how various subgroups in contemporary Western society arrive at definitions of rape.

Bourque first illustrates the variability of rape definitions used in court cases and by professionals, victims, perpetrators, and laypeople. She evaluates existing research on women victims and male assailants, social-psychological findings based on attribution theory, changing legal definitions of and punishments for the crime of rape, and studies of community attitudes toward rape.

She then describes the design, findings, and conclusions of her study of data gathered from previous studies of Los Angeles County residents, which used traditional surveys and first-person "vignettes." This material was analyzed in the light of standard demographic characteristics, crime statistics, perceptions of vulnerability, and defense measures of the respondents. The instrument used to collect data and summary correlation matrices is included. Groups choosing different definitions are profiled by variables including their demographic characteristics and attitudes about rape. The relationship between victim and assailant, location, amount of force, and amount of resistance were important criteria in respondents' definitions. The study results are compared with previous research, showing the implications for theory and practice.

Bourque concludes that more detailed and varied studies are needed to assess how rape relates to measures of personality, sexuality, and violence as well as to the dynamics of male-female relationships, and the extent to which such characteristics are amenable to increased public education and to social change. A clear and consistent terminology also must be developed. This book is primarily geared toward researchers and other professionals in the fields of sociology, psychology, criminology, social welfare, and public health. (Author)

[N.B. Professor Bourque is in the School of Public health of the University of California, Los Angeles.]

IL,PO

619. Brownmiller, Susan. **Against Our Will: Men, Women and Rape.** New York: Simon & Schuster, 1975. 472 p. Includes bibliographic references and index. ISBN 0-671-22062-4.

Discussions of women's experiences in rape speak-outs prompted Brownmiller to confront her own fears, past, and intellectual defenses and motivated her to write this book—a work that has played a prominent role in bringing the issue of rape to national attention. The major purpose of this meticulously researched and well-documented book is to demonstrate that rape has a history that illuminates its characteristics and enhances understanding of its role in contemporary society. The title of the book derives from a female-oriented definition of rape: "If a woman chooses not to have intercourse with a specific man and the man chooses to proceed against her will, that is a criminal act of rape" (p. 18). The initial chapters analyze the function and meaning of rape through a range of time periods. They speculate about the prehistoric origins of rape, discuss the roots of its property-oriented legal definition, and trace its history in war (World Wars I and II, Bangladesh, Vietnam), riots, pogroms, revolutions (the American Revolution), Mormon persecution, KKK mob violence against blacks, Congo mob violence against whites, and in white interaction with native Americans and slaves. The theme that pervades this overview is that rape functions as a "conscious process of intimidation by which all men keep all women in a state of fear" (p. 15). The rest of the book concentrates on documenting the characteristics and role of rape in contemporary American society. It addresses a variety of topics: (1) profiles of the typical ("police-blotter") rapist, (2) different types of rapes (interracial, homosexual, juvenile, police, marital), and (3) the myths (e.g., she asked for it, she wanted it, etc.) and realities that surround the victim. The final chapter, "Women Fight Back," suggests avenues for legal reform and stresses the point that the threat, use, and implicit cultural support for rape affect everyone, because the basic issues involve pervasive attitudes about male/female relationships, sex, power, and strength. The powerful, disturbing facts cited in this complex book encourage readers to confront their own fears and defenses in an effort to deny rape a future. (SGF)

PR,IL
620. Estrich, Susan. **Real Rape.** Cambridge, Mass.: Harvard University Press, 1987. 160 p. Includes bibliographic notes and indexes. ISBN 0-674-74943-X.

This in-depth analysis of Anglo-American law governing rape begins by describing Estrich's (an attorney) own rape: how she reacted, what she did, and what she experienced at the hands of the police. After distinguishing between stranger, or aggravated rape (of which hers was a typical example) and simple rape, she points out that "the law says that it is rape to force a woman 'not your wife' to engage in intercourse against her will and without her consent" (p. 4). However, while the law deals sternly with stranger cases like hers, it is wary of simple rape cases in which the victim "claims to have been raped by a friend or neighbor or acquaintance."

It's Estrich's purpose to analyze the law as it pertains to simple rape in order to demonstrate, in the interest of fairness to the female victim, that simple rape cases should be taken seriously and viewed as "real rape." The legal system seems to conspire in refusing to blame the men who commit a simple rape. As far back as the seventeenth century, English Lord Chief Justice Matthew Hale warned that rape is a charge "easily to be made and hard to be proved, and harder to be defended by the party accused, tho' never so innocent" (p. 5). The approach of the law ever since has been to demand that the female victim convincingly prove her side of the case. She might say that she did not consent to intercourse, that she used physical resistance, that the man used force, that her account can be corroborated, that she complained promptly, and that her prior history of sexual behavior was not unchaste. Other factors that may affect the outcome of a rape case include the circumstances of the alleged rape, the presumption that women have rape fantasies, that they are inherent liars, and that they mean yes when they say no.

In two important chapters Estrich reviews the common law approach to rape by examining major cases in many of the states from the nineteenth century to the mid-1970s, and then from the mid-1970s to 1985. She points out, "Every state has courts of appeal which review convictions in criminal cases to ensure that they are supported by substantial evidence and consistent with the law" (p. 27). Appellate opinions are most important in that they help determine the limits of the common law.

Reform of rape law in the states has come largely at the urging of feminists. The Model Penal Code of the American Law Institute has also contributed by proposing a new definition of rape and shifting the focus from the victim to the defendant. Nevertheless, despite these apparent improvements in the law, the modern law still contains within it distrust of the alleged rape victim. Wives of defendants are especially suspect.

Estrich hopes that positive male attitudinal changes toward women have come about in recent decades. Transferred into a public attitude affecting the law, this improvement in male/female relationships could bring about a more sensitive treatment of women in simple rape cases. In such cases of real rape, there should be no built-in biases with respect to defendant and victim. (TJW)

PR,IL
620a. Fairstein, Linda. **Sexual Violence: Our War Against Rape.** New York: Morrow, 1993. 288 p. Includes index. ISBN 0-688-06715-8.

District Attorney Fairstein, Director of the Sex Crimes Prosecution Unit (SCPU) of the Manhattan District Attorney's office, describes her experiences in dealing with various rape cases occurring in New York City. She views rape as an act of physical, emotional, psychological, and sexual violence. It flourishes in our society and is the most unreported crime within the criminal justice system.

Fairstein, a graduate of the University of Virginia School of Law, explains her attraction to public service and desire to be an assistant district attorney. She details her progress up the ladder of the criminal justice system of New York County, including full descriptions of the several bureaus into which the D.A.'s office is organized: Complaint Bureau, Indictment Bureau, Supreme Court Bureau. She also shows how the NYPD and the D.A.'s office coordinate their efforts to make the system work.

Fairstein discusses many individual cases, emphasizing rape cases that eventually get to court. The case of the Midtown Rapist, who physically violated and raped a number of women working in commercial buildings in Manhattan, is the main focus of her description of the police work and legal work leading to the capture and conviction of this serial rapist.

She also draws attention to three legislative achievements that allow attorneys to bring rape cases to trial with a reasonable expectation of winning. These reforms, accomplished only within recent decades, include the elimination of the corroboration requirement that once prevented many rape cases from ever coming to trial; the introduction of rape shield laws that prevent defense counsels from prying into a plaintiff's prior sexual history; and repeal of the "earnest resistance" rule, which many victims found hard to demonstrate.

In textbook fashion, Fairstein discusses the myriad topics encountered in the legal work related to sexual violence: complaints, indictments, arraignment, work with grand juries, bail, plea bargaining, stranger and date rape, physical appearance of plaintiff and defendant in court, prostitution rape, DNA identification, sexual scams, false reports of rape, the identification of the rapist, sentencing, and so forth.

Fairstein attributes a great deal of the success the SCPU has had in successfully prosecuting these sex crimes to the reorganization of the D.A.'s office undertaken in 1976 by District Attorney Robert Morgenthau. (TJW)

PR,IL
621. Finkelhor, David, and Kersti Yllo. **License to Rape: Sexual Abuse of Wives.** New York: Holt, Rinehart and Winston, 1985. 258 p. Includes bibliographic notes and index. ISBN 0-03-059474-X.

The laws covering marital rape vary widely across the United States. In most states, a man cannot be prosecuted for raping his wife, for the marriage license gives men and women access to their spouses' bodies. This doctrine may be traced back to the seventeenth century when Matthew Hale, a prominent English legal scholar, wrote, "The husband cannot be guilty of rape committed by himself upon his lawful wife, for by their mutual matrimonial consent and contract, the wife hath given up herself in this kind unto her husband, which she cannot retract" (p. 2). Although feminists have opposed this doctrine, Hale's pronouncement has been incorporated into laws around the English-speaking world with enduring impact.

The purpose of this book is to present scientific information on marital rape, a subject largely ignored in the literature. The data are based on a questionnaire administered to 323 women in spring 1981; the sample is "only representative of Boston area women who had a child between the ages of six and fourteen living with them" (p. 204).

This limitation derives from the fact that the survey was part of a larger investigation dealing with child sexual abuse. Further data on spousal rape comes from the National Clearinghouse on Marital Rape (NCMR), which collected statistics in California after that state changed its law in January 1980 and removed the spousal exemption.

North Americans have traditionally regarded marital rape as a trivial event; many are startled by the idea of criminalizing marital rape. The women interviewed by Finkelhor and Yllo were mainly at local family planning agencies and battered women's shelters. Their case histories form a major part of this study. The women talked about "humiliation, degradation, anger, and resentment. Women were left, if not physically disabled, then psychologically traumatized for a long time" (p. 18).

A chapter is devoted to explaining three types of marital rape: battering rape, where forced sex is combined with beatings; force-only rape, where wives are coerced but not beaten; and obsessive rape, where the sexual interest is strange and perverse, either with or without battering. Finkelhor and Yllo follow this with chapters on the kinds of men who rape their wives, marital rape and sexuality, resisting marital rape, and the impact of marital rape. They present a chapter on marital rape and the law, emphasizing state statutes and public opinion, followed by a chapter on the debate over criminalizing marital rape.

They also advance a program for ending marital rape. It involves expanding self-help, social service, and criminal justice resources for victims, and changing people's attitudes that presently "keep marital rape victims locked in their shame and isolation" (p. 186), and changing the law to eliminate the spousal exemption that still exists in twenty-seven states (1985). Appendixes contain the statistical data on the research study and the information gathered by the NCMR. (TJW)

PR,IL
622. Groth, A. Nicholas, with H. Jean Birnbaum. **Men Who Rape: The Psychology of the Offender.** New York: Plenum Press, 1979. 227 p. Includes bibliographic notes and index.

Based on data from 500 offenders, this study examines the "myths" and realities of rape and the men (and women) who commit it. Groth defines rape as a "pseudo-sexual act," indicating that from a clinical viewpoint any form of sexual assault should be included. Among the "myths" surrounding rape is the idea that pornography causes it. Groth distinguishes among anger rape, power rape, and sadistic rape, discusses possible methods of resistance, and examines the multiple motives underlying rape. He notes sexual dysfunctioning of offenders, their subjective responses, and the effects of intoxication. Remarking that the majority of men are not rapists, Groth indicates that rape "appears to be the result of a core group of highly repetitive or chronic offenders." Many of these offenders had suffered sexual trauma in childhood, often some form of sexual abuse. Patterns of rape, including gang rape, are discussed. Using information from twenty offenders and seven victims, Groth explores rape of males, noting the likely under-reporting of such offenses. "Women victims do not report that they feel less of a woman for having been raped," he writes, "but men victims do often state that they feel the offender took their manhood." The under-reporting of sexual assaults upon boys is also indicated, with Groth estimating that boys and girls are probably equally the victims of such assaults. The female offender, he notes after discussing one such case, "remains an incompletely studied and insufficiently understood subject." (**Men's Studies**, 1985)

PR,IL
623. Mezey, Gillian C., and Michael B. King, eds. **Male Victims of Sexual Assault.** Oxford, Eng.: Oxford University Press, 1992. 149 p. Includes bibliographies and index. ISBN 0-19-261871-7.

In the preface Mezey and King state that they are attempting "to open the debate on male sexual assault, bringing together existing data, theoretical perspectives, and implications for future practice and policy." The seven papers in this collection include

Michael B. King's observation that the sexual assault of adult men, usually by other males, is widely recognized in such community institutions as prisons. However, information on sexual assault in the general community is scarce, attributable to the legal definition of rape, which is "restricted to forced penile penetration of the vagina" (p. 1). King includes the results of a survey of twenty-two men assaulted in the community and makes several suggestions to rectify the lack of information and understanding of the problem.

"Homophobia: Covert and Overt," by D. J. West, "challenges the prevailing stereotype of homosexuals as perpetrators of attacks on heterosexual men" (p. v). He adds that there is a long way to go in order to "afford persons of minority sexual orientation the same respect that heterosexuals enjoy" (p. 25). In "Male Children and Adolescents as Victims," Bill Watkins and Arnon Bentovim review current knowledge on the subject, dispelling myths and examining the links between early victimization and later sexual offending. Editor King, in "Male Rape in Institutional Settings," discusses the violent nature of sexual encounters in prison and the military setting, pointing out that such violence is not likely to be reduced until humanitarian changes occur in these institutions.

In "Surviving Sexual Assault and Sexual Torture," Stuart Turner writes about psychological reactions to male sexual assault in the context of torture and about the post-traumatic stress disorder that results. In "Male Co-Survivors: The Shared Trauma of Rape," Daniel C. Silverman informs us that friends and family of the assault victim "may experience distress and, by their reactions, influence the victim's recovery" (p. vi).

Ivor H. Jones in "Cultural and Historical Aspects of Male Sexual Assault" surveys the record to reveal how such assault was treated in Rome and Greece, under early and medieval Christianity, Islam, in China, and in eighteenth-century Europe. Zsuzsanna Adler deals with legal issues faced by male victims of sexual assault. She points out that "men and women have an equal right to care and concern after an assault."

"Treatment for Male Victims of Rape" by editor Mezey addresses the type of help a victim of sexual assault needs, "who should provide that help, and how effective are current treatments in assisting victims to make a full recovery" (p. vi). (TJW)

PR,IL

624. Russell, Diana E. H. **Rape in Marriage.** New York: Macmillan, 1982. 412 p. Includes bibliography and index. ISBN 0-02-606190-2.

Before the 1970s, little research was carried out on rape, much less on rape by intimates. This work is the "first book . . . on the violent sexual abuse of women by their husbands . . . and the only study of wife rape in the United States to be based on interviews with a random sample of women" (p. 1). The goal of this book is to establish the magnitude of the problem of rape in marriage, to provide a basis for understanding why the problem exists, to demonstrate its connection to other forms of abuse, and to suggest some solutions to the problem. Russell's orientation is to view wife rape within the context of a patriarchal system where the imbalance of power between men and women increases the likelihood that men will abuse women. She presents her findings from the women's perspective of abuse and uses lengthy quotes from eighty-nine interviews to reinforce her points.

The twenty-five chapters of this book are arranged in nine parts. The first part establishes the legal position toward rape in marriage; most states dismiss it with a "marital rape exemption." The second part describes the methodology and concepts used in the research. The definition of rape includes intercourse that was forced, obtained by threat of force or when consent was impossible, and forced oral and anal sex or digital penetration. The third part presents general statistics and theory on the prevalence of rape in marriage and its relation to other forms of abuse. Of 644 married women interviewed, 14 percent admitted that they had been raped by their husbands. Russell acknowledges the difficulty of defining rape within a continuum of sexual relations but warns that merely regarding it as a part of family violence submerges its significance.

Parts 4 and 5 describe the characteristics of the participants. Men who rape their wives come from various social classes, are primarily white, and cannot be classified as "clinically insane." It is not clear why men rape their wives, although factors such as power, anger, attitudes toward women and sex, and drugs may play a role. Wives who are raped are less easily identified as a social group than rapists. Most women report some trauma from rape in marriage but remain in the marriage because they blame themselves for the rape or are in an economically disadvantaged position. Findings in part 8 indicate that the most traumatized victims are ones who report marital rape to the police or end the marriage.

Parts 6, 7, and 9 present some general interpretations of the findings: rape reflects an abuse of power where men regard women as property; tactics used by rapists are similar to those employed in other forms of torture; and research in other countries shows the similarity in problems that women face. Russell concludes by suggesting that wife rape should be made illegal and that the power imbalance underlying rape in marriage should be equalized. For, "to continue to see rape in marriage as a husband's privilege is not only an insult, but a danger to all women" (p. 361). (SGF)

IL
625. Scacco, Anthony M., Jr., ed. **Male Rape: A Casebook of Sexual Aggressions.** New York: AMS Press, 1982. 326 p. (AMS Studies in Modern Society: Political and Social Issues, no. 15). Includes bibliographies and index. ISBN 0-404-61621-6.

Most of the twenty-six essays in this collection are concerned with sexual violence in which males are victims, especially in prison. As Scacco notes in the preface: "In today's world the judge who sentences a young person to reform school or prison passes male rape on him as surely as the sentence." The anthology contains both previously printed and original articles. Wilbert Rideau and Billy Sinclair's opening essay describing prison as a sexual jungle is followed by a harrowing account of the 1973 prison gang rape of peace activist Donald Tucker—which is followed by an even more harrowing essay written by Tucker nearly a decade later that reveals all too clearly the psychosexual damage that he sustained. Later essays analyze racial factors involved in such attacks. Also studied is sexual violence in other institutions, such as juvenile correctional facilities, mental wards, military prisons, and women's prisons (Dorothy West's account of rape by female inmates is as terrifying as Tucker's story). Later sections of the volume present psychological profiles of sexual offenders, and suggest treatment and methods of reducing sexual violence in American society. (**Men's Studies**, 1985)

Child Abuse

(For related material see also entries 93a, 910, 1055, 1057)

PR,IL
626. Bierker, Susan B. **About Sexual Abuse.** Springfield, Ill.: Charles C. Thomas, 1989. 222 p. Includes index. ISBN 0-398-05565-3.

Bierker, a social worker in Devon, Pennsylvania, has written this book "to educate the general public about sexual abuse" (p. 3). Noting that taboos against the sexual abuse of children exist, it is paradoxical that taboos against discussing the subject also prevail. It is the taboo against the latter that she insists "must be broken and discarded."

Bierker begins by defining sexual abuse as a "sexual activity perpetuated on a child by an older person using coercion" (p. 4). She presents a history of sexual abuse, including biblical citations on the subject. She discusses the attention given the subject by Sigmund Freud in his seduction theory, John Henry Wigmore in *The Treatise on Evidence*, and Alfred Kinsey's *Sexual Behavior in the Human Female.*

Bierker advocates honesty in dealing with sexual abuse. She urges all parents to admit that they "have felt some degree of incestuous feeling toward our children" (p. 11). Although she has not documented her statements about the subject, she goes on to state that "it's normal to have these feelings." She provides some information on the question of the increase or decrease of sexual abuse in society as well as observations about the characteristics of sexual abusers, such as the fact that approximately 90 percent of all perpetrators are men. She also provides information about groups that encourage child sexual abuse, "kiddy porn" rings, cults, and a vocabulary of terms and expressions relating to sexually abusive activities.

Chapters on the "Signs of Sexual Abuse" (in children), "Sexual Abuse Education and Prevention," "Adult Survivors of Sexual Abuse," "Special Characteristics of Sexual Abuse Victims," and "The Psychological Characteristics of the Perpetuators" follow. A long chapter on "Incest" and a final chapter on "Sexual Abuse and the Law" conclude this succinct, practical guide, that, unfortunately, lacks a bibliography. (TJW)

PR
627. Campagna, Daniel S., and Donald L. Poffenberger. **The Sexual Trafficking in Children: An Investigation of the Child Sex Trade.** Dover, Mass.: Auburn House, 1988. 250 p. Includes bibliography and index. ISBN 0-86569-154-1.

Sexual trafficking in children, defined as "the sexual exploitation of a person under the age of eighteen for pleasure or financial gain," includes crimes as diverse as "child pornography, prostitution, sex rings, molestation (outside the family), sex tourism industry, white slavery, bogus adoption schemes, nude dancing or modeling, apprenticeship or recruitment for prostitution, procuring, and indenturing" (p. 5). Campagna and Poffenberger's five-year study is based on taped interviews of victims, exploiters, and agency practitioners; a nationwide survey of police; field observation studies in select American cities; case studies; informant observations; and a survey of relevant literature dating back to 1900. Written for practitioners in the criminal justice system and in social organizations, it provides information about commercial sexual exploitation as a pressing national and international problem.

At the root of sexual trafficking in children is pedophilia, "an adult's sexual preference for, or attraction to, underage persons." Campagna and Poffenberger examine pedophiliac behavior, victim/offender relationships, pedophile sex rings, offender therapy, and pedophile organizations and publications. They also devote separate chapters to juvenile prostitution, pimping, child pornography, and the international child sex trade.

In the last section of the book they explore different avenues to cope with the sexual exploitation of children. One chapter looks at the prospects of reform in the context of state and federal intervention in the form of statutes or such legislation as the Child Abuse and Pornography Act of 1986. Another chapter examines (1) the cycle of victimization in relation to the sexual and psychological disorders of dysfunctional families, and (2) the intervention role of state service and criminal justice agencies to help and guide families susceptible to sexual trafficking. Another chapter deals with victim advocacy at the regional or local level through community-based programs as the key "to providing investigative, prosecutorial, and treatment services that either reduce the level of trafficking or extend direct and immediate assistance to its victims" (p. 215).

A final chapter provides recommendations for action to help end the sexual trafficking in children. Various investigative and prosecutorial strategies are suggested, such as establishing a pimp file and a pornography index data bank, a criminal history review, sting operations, a child witness protection sanctuary, polygraph examinations, and so forth.

Campagna and Poffenberger's final words are: "No child knowingly volunteers for the role of victim in a sexually exploitive situation. The circumstances are complex. Exploiters take advantage not only of the victim's weakness, ignorance, and distress but also of certain characteristics of our society" (p. 227). Further, "the victim must be provided with a choice. When real alternatives exist, the vast majority of victims choose the positive situation of an independent, yet nurturing and supportive environment, thereby breaking the vicious cycle of victimization. Herein lies our best hope for the future" (p. 227). (TJW)

PR,IL

628.   Clark, Robin E., and Judith Freeman Clark. **The Encyclopedia of Child Abuse.** Introduction by Richard J. Gelles. New York: Facts on File, 1989. 328 p. Includes bibliography and index. ISBN 0-8160-1584-8.

An overview of child abuse by Richard J. Gelles introduces the content of this encyclopedia. It discusses historical evidence of child abuse and neglect, the difficult problem of defining "abuse," the extent of child abuse and neglect as revealed by statistics, patterns and causes of child abuse, models for exploring abuse, the consequences of maltreatment, and future trends.

Some 500 descriptive entries, alphabetically arranged, include the names of relevant organizations and individuals, abstract concepts (compliance), practices (clitoridectomy, castration), injuries (retinal hemorrhage), diseases (gonorrhea), place names (Hong Kong), perversions (sadism), types of sexual abuse (rape, genital touching, incest), legal cases (*Wisconsin v. Yoder*), and the like.

Numerous useful appendixes round out the book, including data on organizations, resource centers, state child abuse statistics, and the text of the 1959 United Nations *Declaration of the Rights of the Child*, and so forth.

This work reflects a range of disciplines that contribute to an understanding of child maltreatment. Clearly written and well organized, it should satisfy the informational needs of a wide variety of users. (TJW)

IL,PO

629.   Crewdson, John. **By Silence Betrayed: Sexual Abuse of Children in America.** Boston: Little, Brown, 1988. 267 p. Includes bibliographic notes and index. ISBN 0-316-16094-6.

Crewdson, an editor and sometime correspondent for the *Chicago Tribune*, states that "little is known about why adults have sex with children and how victims should be treated" (p. 223). Nevertheless, he attempts to provide an overview of what is known about child sexual abuse in America. His interest in the subject, triggered by the reaction to the showing of a made-for-television movie called *Something About Amelia*, detailing the story of the incestuous relationship of a teenage girl with her father, led him to attend the Third International Conference on the Sexual Victimization of Children, held in Washington, D.C. in 1984, and then to visit Los Angeles, where he looked into the bizarre McMartin case.

Crewdson's sources of information are varied and include conversations with sexually abused men and women and abusing men and women. Two unusual cases examined by him are (1) the Jordan, Minnesota case, which attracted widespread attention from 1983 to 1986, and (2) the Manhattan Beach, California case involving the Virginia McMartin Pre-School, which has remained in the news since the fall of 1983. Both of these cases attest to the difficulty of criminally investigating child sexual abuse in institutional settings: the large number of people involved; the unreliability of children's testimony in which exaggeration, lies, and recantings are common; and the lack of recognized procedures for either prosecuting or defending such cases.

In his search for answers to the cause and cure of child sexual abuse, Crewdson reviews and points out the limitations of surveys conducted by Finkelhor (1979), Russell (1983), and Brad Lewis of the *Los Angeles Times* (1985). Outside the United States, Canada, and a few West European countries, very little information on the extent of sexual abuse of children is known. Crewdson goes on to review Freud's contribution to the subject: the seduction theory and the Oedipus complex.

In a series of chapters devoted to victims, abusers, families, pedophiles, and caretakers, Crewdson shows that a typical child abuser cannot be characterized. Many believe, however, that the behavior is learned. The most prominent theory, attributable to Freud, is that an abuser is narcissistic. Pedophiles, for example, swept up in their own self-image, often strive to have sex with children legalized; persistent in their pursuit of children, they often insinuate themselves into day-care centers, the Boy Scouts, churches, etc. In his concluding chapters Crewdson deals with the subjects of justice, therapy, prevention, and society. He believes that certain social measures—keeping abusers away from children, improved licensing of day-care center workers, clamping down on child pornography—can be employed to reduce the incidence of child sexual abuse. (TJW)

PR
630. Finkelhor, David. **Child Sexual Abuse: New Theory and Research.** New York: Free Press, 1984. 260 p. Includes bibliography and index. ISBN 0-02-910020-8.

The goal of this book is to fill a need for theory and research about child sexual abuse by identifying important theoretical issues, presenting findings that contribute to a baseline of good research in the field, and suggesting ways to deal with methodological problems. In the first part of the book, Finkelhor, Associate Director of the Family Violence Research Program at the University of New Hampshire, presents his ideas about subjects that he thinks have been neglected or confounded: child sexual abuse as a social problem; ethical concerns about adult-child sexual interaction, which he suggests are founded in the belief that children are incapable of true consent to such acts; and a specification of factors that make some children more at risk for sexual abuse than others. Finkelhor then integrates much of what is known about sexual abuse into a four preconditions model developed to understand why abuse occurs. The first precondition is that perpetrators need to be motivated to abuse. Emotional congruence between the adult's needs and the child's characteristics, sexual arousal by children, and blockage in having social and emotional needs met by adults can each contribute to that motivation. The second and third preconditions are that the perpetrator has to overcome internal as well as external inhibitions about sexual abuse of children. Finally, the perpetrator has to overcome the child's resistance. The model demonstrates the complexity of the problem and the danger of single-factor explanations.

The rest of the book is devoted to a presentation of new research findings from several studies conducted by Finkelhor. The findings of one study were derived from a population survey of 521 parents interviewed in the Boston area in 1981. The object of the research was to find out how parents respond to issues of child abuse. The findings indicate that although the public is relatively knowledgeable and concerned about child abuse, parents poorly communicate their concerns to their children. Surprisingly, the relationship between the child and the perpetrator was not deemed as important in evaluating the seriousness of abuse as the age difference between the child and adult or the types of sexual contact in which they engaged. Other research presented includes a review of the literature on the relatively ignored topics of boys as victims and women as perpetrators of sexual abuse. Another study, based on a sample of 790 professionals in the Boston area, reveals the problems that plague the field of treatment. In his concluding chapter, Finkelhor suggests that theory can be strengthened by borrowing concepts from appropriate fields (e.g., social psychology), integrating theories about offenders with those focused on family systems, and intensifying research efforts in such areas as prevalence, incidence, reporting, offender treatment, longitudinal studies of a cohort of abused children, and prevention. (SGF)

PR,IL
631. Finkelhor, David. **Sexually Victimized Children.** New York: Free Press, 1981. 228 p. Includes bibliography and index. ISBN 0-02-910400-9.

In this exploratory study, sociologist Finkelhor presents findings from a questionnaire survey of 796 students drawn from a nonrandom yet diverse sample of six New England colleges and universities. He hopes to provide an empirically based description of the main features of child sexual abuse and to substantiate concern about the social problem of sexually victimized children.

Finkelhor takes great care in assessing the relevance of child sexual abuse as a social problem and in clearly defining its unique features, that distinguish it from rape and physical abuse. An overview and critique of thirteen theories about why children are sexually victimized (e.g., about the offender, the victim, the family context, sociocultural norms) indicates that "knowledge on this subject is still in a primitive state" (p. 20) and establishes the rationale for the survey results that form the core of the book. The definition of child sexual victimization is based on two criteria: type of sexual activities (simulated, attempted, or actual intercourse; genital fondling; exhibitionistic display of genitals; sexual kissing, hugging, or fondling; overt and frightening sexual overtures) and age discrepancy between the child and adult. According to these criteria, such experiences occur among one in five girls and one in eleven boys. Detailed findings are presented on the following topics: characteristics of the experience (prevalence, relation to partner, duration, types of sexual behavior, initiation, force, reporting), attributes of older partners, incest, sources of trauma, distinctive background features of sexual victims, social and demographic features, and family structure and composition. A comparison of selected findings from this study with those of earlier studies or those focused only on reported cases points out the distinctiveness of the current research.

Among the significant findings of this research are that a large number of children are sexually abused; preadolescent children are most vulnerable; offenders are usually men; females generally regard the experience as traumatic, especially if force is used or the partner is older; sexual victimization has *not* increased in the last thirty years; and the family plays a crucial role in creating vulnerability to victimization. Finkelhor concludes that the majority of adult-child sexual experiences are abusive and that priority should be given to the problem of victimization. (SGF)

PR

632. Finkelhor, David, with Sharon Araji, Larry Baron, Angela Browne, Stefanie Doyle Peters, and Gail Elizabeth Wyatt. **A Sourcebook on Child Sexual Abuse.** Beverly Hills, Calif.: Sage Publications, 1986. 276 p. Includes bibliography and index. ISBN 0-8039-2749-5.

The field of child sexual abuse has expanded rapidly since the mid-1970s. However, the accumulation of knowledge in the field has been hampered by the difficulty of obtaining accurate data on sexual abuse, limited dissemination of information on the subject, and the diffusion of research in a variety of disciplines. In an effort to consolidate current and older studies, both published and unpublished, Finkelhor and his associates present "a decade review of scientific knowledge about the problem of child sexual abuse" (p. 11). Rather than assessing research on a study-by-study basis, the authors characterize the total body of research on a particular topic by summarizing the patterns that emerge from it. In addition, they offer suggestions for the improvement of research in the area.

The eight chapters of the book center on five main topics: the prevalence of sexual abuse, children at high risk, offenders, initial and long-term effects, and prevention. Survey estimates of the prevalence of child abuse range from 6 to 62 percent for females and 3 to 31 percent for males, a disparity in findings that may be plausibly explained in terms of the methodology used. In contrast, most studies converge in their identification of factors that place children at high risk for abuse, for example, a female gender, girls with few friends, a preadolescent, and specific types of parental roles. Theories and findings about offenders indicate that four major factors contribute to molesting behavior: emotional congruence, sexual arousal, blockage, and disinhibition. A critique of the literature on offenders indicates that single-factor theories are deficient in explanatory power. A review of the initial and long-term effects of abuse reveals a few salient variables (e.g., the impact is worse if the abuse occurred over a longer length of time, if the victim's family was unsupportive of her, and if the behavior involved a father or stepfather). In an effort to provide a basis for research that fills in the sketchy findings in this area, Finkelhor and Browne propose a conceptual framework of "4 traumogenic dynamics" (traumatic sexualization, betrayal, powerlessness, stigmatization) that relates sexual abuse to outcomes. Finkelhor then considers methodological issues (definition of abuse, study design, sampling, ethics) that could aid in gathering more information on effects. The book concludes with a summary of the rationale for and content of prevention problems. The authors hope that their efforts will become a foundation for better research in the area of child abuse. (SGF)

PR
633. Haugaard, Jeffrey J., and N. Dickon Reppucci. **The Sexual Abuse of Children: A Comprehensive Guide to Current Knowledge and Intervention Strategies.** San Francisco: Jossey-Bass, 1988. 432 p. (The Jossey-Bass Social and Behavioral Science Series). Includes bibliography and indexes. ISBN 1-55542-077-X.

Today increasing attention is being paid to all forms of sexual abuse, especially the sexual abuse of children by adults. This compilation attempts "to integrate the accumulated knowledge from the research, treatment, and legal literature" and to provide a framework for those concerned with child sexual abuse, including service providers, researchers, teachers, counselors, members of the clergy, and others.

Following an introductory chapter describing how society has dealt with child sexual abuse in the past and the problems encountered today, Haugaard and Reppucci present in part 1 basic information about the topic: definitions, extent of the problem, consequences for victims, and incest and incestuous families. In part 2 they identify the victims of child sexual abuse by diagnosing sexual abuse in therapy and evaluating the accusations of alleged victims. Part 3 focuses on clinical interventions used with victims and their families with a discussion of basic issues in treatment; crisis intervention and treatment planning; individual, group, and family treatments; and preventing child sexual abuse. Part 4 discusses relevant legal issues by dealing with the child and the helping professionals as witnesses in child abuse trials and with the legal and clinical arguments concerning procedures in the courtroom.

A final chapter highlights the major themes presented in the book and suggests directions for future research and action. Haugaard and Reppucci conclude that there is "much to learn in order to understand this vague phenomenon labeled child sexual abuse," that "our knowledge will always be flawed," and that "few statements should ever be accepted as representing a truth about this field" (p. 376). They hope that their review of the literature in this dynamic field will assist others in the pursuit of further knowledge and understanding and aid in decision making. (TJW)

PR
634. Korbin, Jill E., ed. **Child Abuse and Neglect: Cross-Cultural Perspectives.** Berkeley, Calif.: University of California Press, 1981. 217 p. Includes bibliographies and index. ISBN 0-520-04432-0.

In the first foreword, anthropologist Robert B. Edgerton states that "Dr. Jill Korbin is the first anthropologist to make child abuse a topic of concerted study" (p. vii). And, in the second foreword, C. Henry Kempe, a pioneer in the field of child abuse and neglect, comments, "Cross-cultural perspectives in the field of child abuse and neglect are largely lacking and therefore this book fills a very important void" (p. ix). In the introduction, Korbin emphasizes the importance of cross-cultural research in answering such basic questions as whether child abuse and neglect are universal and whether they occur under specific conditions. Because most information on child abuse and neglect is derived from research and clinical experience in Western countries, and because most anthropologists have focused on normative child-rearing in other cultural contexts, there has been little comparative data from which to assess the role of culture in increasing or decreasing the probability of child abuse and neglect. Nine of the eleven chapters concentrate on investigators' examination of definitions of and conditions for child abuse and neglect in nine different cultural contexts: (1) New Guinea (L. L. Langness), (2) Sub-Saharan Africa (Sarah and Robert LeVine), (3) native South America (Orna R. Johnson), (4) rural India (Thomas Poffenberger), (5) Turkey (Emelie A. Olson), (6) Japan (Hiroshi Wagatsuma), (7) Taiwan (David K. H. Wu), (8) People's Republic of China (Jill E. Korbin), and (9) Polynesia (James and Jane Ritchie). The chapters do not single out child sexual abuse for particular emphasis but consider the context for various forms of child abuse and neglect.

Part of the difficulty in examining child abuse and neglect in different cultural contexts is to assess three different levels at which cultural factors affect the definition of abuse and neglect: (1) different cultures regard the same behavior in different ways—acceptable in one, abusive in another; (2) each group has criteria to identify behavior outside of acceptable bounds; and (3) entire groups may engage in societal abuse and neglect of children. In the final chapter, Korbin concludes that a consideration of cross-cultural variation in definitions and contexts of child abuse and neglect points to several factors that can increase or decrease the probability of maltreatment of children: (1) the cultural value of children; (2) beliefs about specific categories of children; (3) beliefs about age capabilities and developmental stages of children; and (4) embeddedness of child rearing in kin and community networks. Although the data in the chapters lead to the conclusion that there is no universal, acceptable standard for child-rearing or for deciding what is abusive, they do suggest that "a network of concerned individuals beyond the biological parents is a powerful deterrent to child abuse and neglect" (p. 208). (SGF)

PO

635. Rush, Florence. **The Best Kept Secret: Sexual Abuse of Children.** Englewood Cliffs, N.J.: Prentice-Hall, 1980. 226 p. Includes bibliographic notes and index. ISBN 0-13-074781-5.

In the introduction, Susan Brownmiller characterizes Rush as the "first theorist on the subject who does not blame the child in any way" and the "first thinker to see child sexual abuse not as an isolated incident but as a pervasive pattern with antecedents of social acceptance that reach far back in history" (p. ix). This book is a documentation of those antecedents as well as a commentary on the sociocultural factors that perpetuate them.

Rush, a feminist writer and activist who was sexually abused once as a child, first establishes the immense scope and social, emotional, and medical consequences of the problem of child sexual abuse. However, the problem is not a new one. Rush points to the religious traditions of Christianity and Judaism as well as practices in other cultures such as India and ancient Greece, that have perpetuated one or more varieties of child sexual abuse by condoning child marriage, child rape, or child prostitution. She notes that even in Victorian times older men seemed to have a predilection for little girls. Child prostitution, white slavery, and pornography were not uncommon.

In addition to these historical and cultural traditions, other social and cultural factors have allowed or even encouraged child sexual abuse to continue. Freud's formulation of the Oedipus complex, which discredits women's reports of incest as fantasies, lingers on as a basis for blaming the victim. Fairy tales, films, and literature perpetuate the view that women should submit to men and that little girls are either in love with their fathers or are "bad" girls (seductresses like Lolita). Cultural support of male sexual expression can serve to rationalize pedophiles as "harmless" or incestuous fathers as "misunderstood." The law adds to the problem by failing to establish sexual abuse as a serious offense, blaming the victim, forgiving the molester, and making prosecution of sex offenders difficult. Dismissal of kiddy porn and child prostitution as serious problems provides tacit support for their continuation. Calls for the sexual freedom of children, as in the man/boy movement, are veiled excuses for sexual exploitation.

Rush concludes that the scope of sexual abuse is "overwhelming" when it is placed in its historical context. However, culture is malleable, and "once we perceive, question and challenge the existence of the sexual abuse of children, we have taken the first crucial step toward the elimination of the degradation, humiliation and corrosion of our most valuable human resource—our young" (p. 195). People need to deal with the "best kept secret." (SGF)

Sex Murder

PR
636. Ressler, Robert K., Ann W. Burgess, and John E. Douglas. **Sexual Homicide: Patterns and Motives.** Lexington, Mass.: Lexington Books, 1988. 234 p. Includes bibliographic references and index. ISBN 0-669-16559-X.

Ressler is program manager of the FBI's Violent Crime Apprehension Program (VICAP). Along with Burgess, of the Pennsylvania School of Nursing, and FBI agent Douglas, he has written this well-documented book on sexual homicide. Based on a study of thirty-six convicted and incarcerated male sex murderers, all white, who were interviewed in prison, the book provides data on the characteristics of this group of criminals, the manner in which their crimes were committed, and information on the scenes of their crimes.

The first six chapters reveal the subjects' social backgrounds and formative events in their lives; their preoccupation with murder and what triggered their first murder; the act of murder itself, including antecedent behavior and post-murder behavior and problems, such as how to dispose of the body; and an analysis of motivation, including an in-depth examination or case study of a sex murder.

Chapter 7 deals with the establishment in 1984 by President Reagan of the National Center for the Analysis of Violent Crime (NCAVC), which has four programs: Research and Development, Training, Profiling and Consultation, and VICAP. Administered by the FBI's Behavioral Science Unit, the aim of the Center is to have a single national resource center collecting and making information available nationwide to the entire law enforcement community.

Subsequent chapters cover other aspects of sexual homicide: crime scene and profile characteristics of organized and disorganized murderers; criminal profiling from crime scene analysis; the role of forensic pathology in criminal profiling (written by James L. Luke); interviewing convicted murderers; the police artist and composite drawings (written by Horace J. Heafner); the victim's family and its response to trauma; victims: lessons learned for responses to sexual violence (written by Daniel L. Carter, Robert A. Prentky, and Ann W. Burgess).

In the final chapter, "Murderers: A Postscript," the authors tell what eventually happened to the thirty-six murderers in the study. They also discuss important areas of investigation: childhood sexual trauma and deviant fantasies. They add that "basic research in biological and psychosocial factors are necessary to explore the biochemical hormonal sensory levels associated with deviant fantasies of both youth and adults" (p. 216).

The entire VICAP Crime Analysis Report is given in the appendix. It embraces under 9 categories 186 items of information that may be used as a guide for the crime scene investigator. (TJW)

PR
637. Revitch, Eugene, and Louis B. Schlesinger. **Sex Murder and Sex Aggression: Phenomenology, Psychopathology, Psychodynamics and Prognosis.** Springfield, Ill.: Charles C. Thomas, 1989. 137 p. Includes bibliography and index. ISBN 0-398-05556-4.

This work on homicide by two distinguished professors of psychiatry discusses "sexually motivated gynocide (that is, the killing of women), as well as various forms of sexual aggression that may not have resulted in death" (p. ix). Revitch and Schlesinger believe that sexual victimization of women far exceeds that of the sexual victimization of men.

In a continuum of sexual aggression they explain gynocide in terms of anger directed at the mother but displaced toward another female that results in sexual homicide. Their classification, reflected in the organization of the book, shows catathymic gynocide and compulsive gynocide as two main classes. After reviewing existing classifications of crime, they propose the concept of "motivational stimuli" leading to the offense as their principle of classification. This results in a motivational spectrum divided into (1) social, (2) situational, (3) impulsive, (4) catathymic, and (5) compulsive offenses, with most of the cases of sexual aggression occupying the fourth and fifth divisions.

After describing catathymic attacks as "activated by a sudden impression that floods consciousness with repressed conflicts and disrupts controls and logical thinking," Revitch and Schlesinger identify three stages of catathymia: (1) incubation, (2) violent act, and (3) relief (p. 8). They then present and discuss twelve cases of catathymic gynocide and nine cases of compulsive gynocide and assault. They describe compulsive offenses as at the extreme end of the motivational spectrum: the offenders are under extreme pressure to commit the act, sometimes struggling against the impulse, which may induce extreme tensions with somatic manifestations (headaches, sweating). They mention such well-known offenders as serial killers William Heirens, Richard Speck, and the Boston Strangler. Some instances are collaborations, as was the case of Charles Starkweather and Carol Ann Fugate. Although sexual violence against children, cannibalism, vampirism, and necrophilia are rare, they do occur, attracting wide attention in the press. The primary method of killing is strangulation often accompanied by rape either before or after the victim's death.

Revitch and Schlesinger devote a chapter to the psychodynamics, psychopathology, and diagnosis of gynocide. Revitch has noted "that men who assault or kill women have at least some of the following characteristics: hostility to women, preoccupation with maternal sexual conduct, overt or covert incestuous preoccupation, guilt over and rejection of sex as impure, sexual inferiority, and occasionally a need to completely possess the victim or whatever she may represent" (p. 109).

In a final chapter of prognostic considerations (always important at time of parole), the authors point out that most sex offenders are not psychotic, and most mental patients do not commit crimes. Also, the majority of known sex offenders (exhibitionists, voyeurs, pedophilic offenders, and purveyors of pornography) are not violent. Moreover, compulsive sex offenders seem to lack "a sense of ethics, a capacity for empathy, or an ability to feel guilt or remorse; in other words, they are incapable of distinguishing between right and wrong" (p. 114).

Predictive indicators, according to Revitch and Schlesinger, include: (1) a history of unprovoked attacks on women; (2) expressions of hatred and contempt for women; (3) breaking and entering in bizarre circumstances and a history of voyeurism; (4) fetishism of female undergarments and destruction of female clothes, particularly during breaking and entering; (5) sadistic fantasies and fantasies of rape or other aggressive acts against women; (6) confusion of sexual identity as revealed by projective tests; and (7) torture and killing of animals, particularly cats" (p. 116). The authors hope that their modest volume will increase awareness of the problem of sexually motivated gynocide and sexual aggression. (TJW)

Prostitution

(For related material see also entries 90, 92, 97, 102, 604, 875, 885, 1040, 1041, 1041a)

PR,IL

638. Barry, Kathleen. **Female Sexual Slavery.** New York: New York University Press, 1984. 325 p. Originally copyrighted in 1979. Includes bibliographic notes and index. ISBN 0-8147-1069-7.

Rejecting the notions that women are driven to prostitution by economic conditions, feeblemindedness, or an innate desire for unlimited pleasure, feminist writer Barry (Assistant Professor of Sociology at Brandeis University) claims that local prostitution, the international traffic in women, and the women and children who are sexually dominated by trusted males in the home are part of what she calls "female sexual slavery." As such they are expressive of male dominated societies worldwide.

Written with a view to raising women's consciousness, Barry begins with a discussion of prostitution as "an indication of an unjust social order and an institution that economically exploits women" (p. 9). She reviews the work of the English feminist Josephine Butler, who fought the effects of the Contagious Diseases Acts in England in the nineteenth century, that regulated, localized, and legalized prostitution. She marshalls impressive data to show how young women are swept into the international slave traffic, taken to places like Zanzibar, and sold at auction as prostitutes and/or servants for Arab harems, eros centers, and households. Although the United Nations approved a "Convention for the Suppression of Traffic in Persons and of the Exploitation States" in 1949, little has been done to suppress the traffic, and it apparently continues to flourish.

Barry presents an in-depth analysis of prostitution worldwide, using the difficult-to-obtain INTERPOL report of 1974 on trends in the traffic of women in thirty-seven countries, prepared for the United Nations Division of Human Rights, as a basis for her disclosures.

In her search for explanations of why men impose prostitution (slavery) on women, she states that "*sex is power* is the foundation of patriarchy, and patriarchy is *rule by male right*" (p. 194). In the family men dominate women on a one-to-one basis, and male authority becomes a part of the larger social, political, and economic order. The outcome is female sexual slavery on a grand scale. Pornography is one of the salient and visible manifestations of male domination and sexual violence against women, which Barry labels a "practice of cultural sadism" (p. 206).

In her search for the ideological roots of cultural sadism, she turns to the eighteenth century and examines the sexual practices of the Marquis de Sade; follows this up with a consideration of the Freudian notions of the unconscious, the sex instinct (libido), and sadomasochism; and finally brings in the genetic determinism of the sociobiologists. Thus, a common belief is engendered that explains why men can't help doing what they do to women—hence, all the evil practices of cultural sadism.

Barry does not despair, however, but believes that the feminist movement can turn things around by fostering sexual relations between the sexes that are based on new values of sexual intimacy: warmth, affection, love, and caring. (TJW)

IL
639. Bristow, Edward J. **Prostitution and Prejudice: The Jewish Fight Against White Slavery, 1870-1939.** New York: Schocken Books, 1983. 340 p. Includes bibliography and index. ISBN 0-8052-3866-2.

In this well-documented study Bristow recounts the sordid details of Jewish white slavery from about 1870 to 1939 and the Jewish fight against this singular phenomenon. He begins by describing the negligible Jewish involvement with prostitution before the great social, economic, and cultural changes of the nineteenth century. He then traces the origins of Jewish commercial prostitution in central and Eastern Europe, especially in the Russian Pale of Settlement, Germany, Rumania, Poland, including Galicia and Bukovina. The principal factors contributing to prostitution were widespread destitution, pogroms, massive migrations, overcrowded living conditions, and the weakening of traditional social, religious, and parental controls. In these circumstances, a subculture of Jewish pimps, prostitutes, and brothelkeepers sprang up and fanned out across five continents.

Although Jews hardly accounted for all activity in the white slavery networks that emerged, they did maintain an important position in brothelkeeping and procuring in parts of Europe, South America, South Africa, North America, and the Far East. They dominated the international traffic out of eastern Europe, especially in Jewish women. Bristow describes some of the methods used by the Jewish procurers, including marriage, false promises of a better life abroad, kidnapping, intercepting women at railway stations and ports of entry, and simply escorting women to their supposed destinations. Terminal points for the deceived women include some of the largest cities in the world: Warsaw, Paris, Odessa, Constantinople, Johannesburg, Manila, and New York, where they were placed in brothels or sold in slave markets. Bristow cites and documents many examples of the tragic fate of these unfortunate Jewish girls and women. He also details the activities of their Jewish procurers, pimps, and keepers, many of whom achieved a fame of sorts worldwide as white slavers. Proud of their activities, these "unclean ones," as they were dubbed by their more respectable Jewish opponents, even formed a fraternal body, the Zwi Migdal Society, that survived for over forty years.

The Jewish response to the appalling state of affairs worldwide involved a variety of courageous individuals and organizations. Prominent Jewish leaders—rabbis, philanthropists, social workers—worked on strategies involving legal, political, social, and religious measures and, for example, formed special groups to combat the phenomenon in the field with travelers' aid at key locations along the main routes to foreign destinations. Individual organizations, such as the Independent Benevolent Association, the Jewish Association for the Protection of Girls and Women, the B'nai B'rith, interdenominational groups, special vice commissions, and even the League of Nations participated at different times in the white slavery struggle.

Bristow has chronicled the long Jewish fight against white slavery both before and after World War I and concludes it just prior to the beginning of World War II in September 1939. (TJW)

PO

640. Bullough, Vern, and Bonnie Bullough. **Prostitution: An Illustrated Social History.** New York: Crown, 1978. 336 p. Includes bibliographic notes and index. ISBN 0-517-52957-2.

In order to write a comprehensive history of prostitution, the Bulloughs have adopted a broad definition derived from Iwan Bloch which states that prostitution is "a distinct form of extramarital sexual activity characterized by being more or less promiscuous, was seldom without reward, and was a form of professional commercialism for the purpose either of intercourse or of other forms of sexual activities and allurement, resulting in due time in the formation of a special type" (p. xi).

The Bulloughs organize this study chronologically and examine the economic, social, psychological, religious, and other aspects obtaining at a given time. They attribute the rise of prostitution to the double standard and to the subordinate roles played by women in the earliest patriarchal societies.

The fourteen chapters on prostitution into which this generously illustrated book is divided discuss origins; sacred and profane prostitution in the ancient Near East; Greek and Roman prostitution; the sexual morality of Christians and Moslems; sexual views and customs in India and China as they affected prostitutes; the approach to prostitution in Western Europe in the early Middle Ages; the impact of the Reformation and venereal diseases on the institution; how kings and commoners dealt with prostitution in the seventeenth and eighteenth centuries; widespread regulation, including medical inspection of prostitutes in nineteenth-century Europe; the spread of prostitution in America from colonial times to the twentieth century; attitudinal changes toward sex and prostitution in the nineteenth century; medical views affecting sexual behavior in the nineteenth century and the changing status of women; the legal struggle, especially in England and the United States, affecting the status and conduct of prostitutes; and the changing sexual relations between men and women that impinge on the system of prostitution worldwide.

The Bulloughs conclude their social history with the recommendation that prostitution be decriminalized, that the activity be conducted discreetly, so that "those who wanted prostitutes would find them, and those who did not could avoid them" (p. 295). They hope that ultimately society will "eliminate the double standard of sexuality that remains the bulwark of prostitution in all societies."

A valuable bibliographic essay surveying the literature of the field ends this study. In 1987 Prometheus Books reissued this study without the illustrations as *Prostitution: A Social History.* (TJW)

PR

641. Davis, Nanette J., ed. **Prostitution: An International Handbook on Trends, Problems, and Policies.** Westport, Conn.: Greenwood Press, 1993. 403 p. Includes bibliography and indexes. ISBN 0-313-25754-X.

Prostitution in sixteen countries—from Australia to Yugoslavia—is the subject of this collection of papers by scholars on the subject. Editor Davis points out in the preface that, in contrast to viewing prostitution traditionally as an issue of poverty and deprivation, the current focus is on newer issues, including (1) the AIDS epidemic, (2) child prostitution, (3) female prostitute victimization, (4) self-help movements among prostitutes, (5) international tourism, and (6) changes in social policy. She also states that prostitution today is considered part of the sex industry and prostitutes as sex workers. Indeed, new forms of prostitution have emerged, such as escort services, eros centers, sex holidays, sex therapy centers, telephone sex calls, and dating services. Moreover, in some nations, social control of prostitution has moved in the direction of decriminalization and/or legalization.

This study "represents a partial effort to explore prostitution in a wide range of societies that differ in their cultural, political, religious, social, and legal systems" (p. viii). The pattern of themes for investigating prostitution in each country includes: "(1) social and legal definitions of prostitution, (2) history and trends for each society, (3) social organization of prostitution, (4) theories of prostitution, (5) contemporary status and life-styles of prostitutes, (6) law enforcement, (7) politics of prostitution, (8) intervention, and (9) social policy" (p. ix). Variations in each of these themes obtain for the countries covered. For example, social policies among these countries embrace criminalization, decriminalization, legalization, abolition, tolerance, intolerance, permissiveness, restrictiveness, quotas, and free trade. None seem to work well for long. National upheavals, such as German reunification or the Yugoslav civil war, have radically disturbed the practice of prostitution. Experience has shown, however, that once an area is stabilized, the old patterns of prostitution return. In many societies, "penalizing prostitutes costs the state huge sums of money for little more than a 'revolving door' situation, whereby offenders are merely recycled through the system and are out on the streets within hours. Critics emphasize that such money would be better spent in services for the women, such as providing food, shelter, counseling, and job training" (p. 3).

Davis believes that conventional thinking about prostitution needs to change. A solution to the problem might be found in the Cuban experience, that embraced "social, economic, and political equality and the cessation of the violence against women" (p. 10). She states finally, "The primary obligation for international, national, and local endeavors to transform the prostitute-as-victim into the woman-as-survivor is to help relieve human suffering without strings attached" (p. 10). She hopes that this handbook will fill "a significant gap in understanding prostitution in multicultural terms" (p. vii). (TJW)

PR

642. Decker, John F. **Prostitution: Regulation and Control.** Littleton, Colo.: Fred B. Rothman, 1979. 572 p. (Publication of the Comparative Law Project, Vol. 13). Includes bibliography and index.

Professor Decker, of De Paul University, focuses on the regulation and control of prostitution in Western societies in this study. In the light of rapid social change, significantly impelled by the women's movement, Decker puts forth a reform program featuring legalization and decriminalization of the "oldest profession." This comprehensive work can be viewed as a contribution to the legislative reform movement promoting "humanistic recommendations in the area of the legal regulation of sexual conduct" (p. xviii).

Following an introductory chapter devoted to the size of the problem, its definition, and the reasons why prostitution has been suppressed in society, Decker reviews the evolution of prostitution control from primitive societies and the ancient societies of the Near East, Greece, Rome, and early Christianity, through the Middle Ages and the

Reformation, to present-day Europe and the United States, concluding that prostitution was developed "to meet the sexual needs of those persons who do not have access to or receive satisfaction from more typical sexual relationships" (p. 74), and that the legal responses to traditional prostitution have been three: laissez-faireism, repression, and regulation.

In two chapters Decker discusses legal controls and their implementation in the United States, and compares the controls used in Great Britain, Canada, France, Netherlands, Sweden, and West Germany. He devotes a chapter to the principal focus of prohibition, the prostitute; and another to the supporters and beneficiaries of the prostitute's work: patrons, pimps, panderers, and other promoters.

Decker next examines nine motives for controlling prostitution, including protection of public morality, a humanistic concern for the prostitute, and prevention of venereal disease. He also tackles the constitutional problems with prostitution control that embrace the topics of cruel and unusual punishment, right to privacy, equal protection under the law, and others.

The last chapter looks at alternatives to repressive controls of prostitution. These are essentially legalization and decriminalization. He then presents his ten-point prostitution control model as a useful and effective policy for dealing with prostitutes. This program allows the prostitute to practice her profession legally, but acts as a social contract placing certain restrictions and responsibilities squarely on her shoulders. In this way, prostitution can be acceptable to society.

The appendixes include the prostitution regulations of Paris (1878) and Berlin (1911); the Lyon County (Nevada) Code of 1978; and the Model Prostitution Control Act. In addition to an extensive bibliography on prostitution, the study includes a comprehensive listing of cases on prostitution. (TJW)

PR,IL

643. Delacoste, Frederique, and Priscilla Alexander, eds. **Sex Work: Writings by Women in the Sex Industry.** Pittsburgh, Pa.: Cleis Press, 1987. 349 p. Includes bibliography. ISBN 0-939416-11-5.

That prostitution should be decriminalized and legitimized seems to be the message of this compilation of testimonials, essays, and documents assembled by the editors, both committed to the public recognition of sex work. While the overall reach of this book is prostitution in general, there are various other activities that are embraced as well: stripteasing, nude dancing, nude modeling, sexual massage, and pornographic film acting. The latter activities, it seems, are sometimes covers or fronts for prostitution.

In her introductory remarks Alexander states, "Prostitution will remain a crime in this country, and in other countries which criminalize it, so long as there is no identifiable voting bloc that clamors for changes in the law." She identifies three organizations that are fighting to have the laws repealed: COYOTE (Cast Off Your Old Tired Ethics), founded in 1973; U.S. PROS (U.S. Prostitutes' Collective), that basically wants prostitution to disappear; and WHISPER (Women Hurt in Systems of Prostitution Engaged in Revolt), that sees prostitutes as victims of patriarchy.

Part I, "In the Life," consists of forty-five statements from streetwalkers, call girls, strippers, models, masseuses, porno stars, and others who tell their stories in vivid and explicit language. Some seem to like the life, describing it as lucrative and rewarding in many ways; others deplore what they are doing by pointing to the degrading and dangerous aspects of sex work.

Part II, "Connections," consists of Alexander's lengthy discourse on prostitution in general, followed by three essays on special aspects of the subject: the unchaste nature of whore's work, lesbians as prostitutes, and the scapegoating of prostitutes in the AIDS epidemic.

Part III, "United We Stand, Divided We Die: Sex Workers Organized," describes not only the work of the three organizations mentioned above but also the whores' movement in Holland. It also includes such basic documents as the World Charter of the

International Committee for Prostitutes' Rights and draft statements from the Second World Whores' Congress held in 1986. (TJW)

PO

644.   Evans, Hilary. **Harlots, Whores & Hookers: A History of Prostitution.** New York: Dorset Press, 1979. 255 p. Includes bibliography and index. ISBN 0-88029-029-3.

In 1929, speaking before the Sexual Reform Congress in London, William J. Robinson stated: "If in spite of all the humiliations, risks, obstacles, atrocious punishments, ostracisms and fears of hell, prostitution has continued unabated up to the present time, it is fair to presume that it will continue to persist in the future. But it will persist not because it always has: it will persist because it satisfies a definite and important biologic need, and answers it in a way that no other present arrangement does" (p. 245). That quote also reflects the view of Evans, whose historical survey of prostitution does convey a sense of inevitability about prostitution. Despite its clamorous title, *Harlots, Whores & Hookers* is a well-written overview of prostitution from ancient times to the present. Evans, a British author, is a social historian who writes about "significant minorities"; he believes that a sound historical background in the subject of prostitution should be of inestimable value to those who are attempting to cope with prostitution as a social problem. He further believes that we must learn "to see the prostitute both as a social component and as an individual, recognising what we want from her and also why she is willing to supply what we want" (p. 15). In this history, intended for the general reader rather than the scholar, Evans begins with a general discussion of "The Oldest Profession," the reasons for its persistence throughout history despite the universal taboo on sexual promiscuity, the view of prostitution as a lively exchange of sexual favors for money, the special appeal of prostitution to women, why men turn to prostitutes for sex, and the act of prostitution itself, with its colorful cast of characters and time-honored rituals. In succeeding chapters Evans deftly surveys the history of prostitution, beginning with religious and secular prostitution in the earliest civilizations and ending with a status report on prostitution and vice in modern societies, especially England, Japan, and the United States. While the emphasis is overwhelmingly on heterosexual prostitution, some attention is given to homosexual prostitution. Evans liberally quotes from primary sources, especially the testimonials of prostitutes and madams, to capture the spirit of prostitution at particular times in history. The work is well illustrated with historical prints and book illustrations, photographs, portraits, and documents, many taken from the Mary Evans Picture Library. (TJW)

PO

645.   **Fille de Joie: The Book of Courtesans, Sporting Girls, Ladies of the Evening, Madams, a Few Occasionals, & Some Royal Favorites.** New York: Grove Press, 1967. 448 p.

This oversized book is a collection of stories and pictures depicting the role of the prostitute in societies throughout history. In the foreword the publisher states that under the heading *fille de joie* have been "included not only professionals, but also royal favorites, concubines, courtesans, ladies of the evening, call girls, amateurs, and occasionals." The spirits of two schools of thought on the question of prostitution—"Those who favor regulation and control . . . and . . . those who in an excess of moral zeal advocate legislation destined to destroy that which is daily re-sown by society itself"—pervade this profusely illustrated book.

Fiction and nonfiction are included, ranging from personal statements by whores and madams (e.g., "New York Call Girl" by Virginia McManus and "New York Madam" by Polly Adler) to excerpts from famous autobiographies (e.g., Giacomo Casanova's "My Short and Lively Stay in Ancona" and Henry Miller's "Four Filles de Paris") as well as stories by Frank Harris, Nelson Algren, Guy de Maupassant, James Sherwood, Alexander Woollcott, and others.

Ten picture essays focus on different aspects of the life: "Harems and Baths," "Maisons," "Royal Mistresses," "Street Scenes," and others. And each story or essay is illustrated with portraits of prostitutes and paintings and sketches by some of the world's great artists: Goya, Toulouse-Lautrec, Beardsley, Degas, Rowlandson, Renoir, and others. Photographs of memorabilia, such as book illustrations, pages from the New Orleans *Blue Book* (a guide to the famous Storeyville district), advertisements, brothel coins, brass checks, and so forth are shown.

Because of its rich mixture of words and pictures, *Fille de Joie* provides a perspective different from other studies on prostitutes and prostitution. (TJW)

PR,IL
646. Greenwald, Harold. **The Elegant Prostitute: A Social and Psychoanalytic Study.** New York: Walker, 1970. 305 p. Includes bibliography and index. ISBN 0-8027-0093-4.

Originally published as *The Call Girl* (1958), this revised edition presents new material on the social and professional life of the call girl, her pimp, and her clients, or "Johns." Psychoanalyst Greenwald has retitled this book, *The Elegant Prostitute* in order to emphasize the fact that the call girl is generally better looking, better educated, more articulate, and more appealing than her street walking sisters. She lives in a more refined environment and receives correspondingly higher rewards for her time and talents. Greenwald states that this facet of prostitution has never received any serious professional attention, so he hopes that his psychoanalytic study will at least partially fill that gap.

In part 1 Greenwald describes the social and professional life of the call girl in terms of income, expenses, sources of clients, the variety of sexual services, working hours, special vocabulary, status, associations, and amusements.

Part 2 presents the results of Greenwald's psychoanalytic study of three call girls who had voluntarily come to him for treatment: Sandra, Stella, and Rose. In Rose's case he used hypnosis to delve into the deep-seated causes of Rose's acceptance of life as a prostitute. Generally speaking, Greenwald believes that early in life these girls were deprived of first motherly and then fatherly affection, so that they turned to self-debasement and self-degradation in order to punish their parents, especially their mothers. They also entered the life in order to "search for someone who would take care of them in the way that they had not been cared for originally. For that reason it was extremely difficult for the girls to mature emotionally and become independent human beings" (p. 148). He reports that of "six girls seen for psychoanalytic therapy, five eventually left the profession."

Part 3 is a survey of twenty call girls who were interviewed in depth to discover the psychological and social factors influencing the choice of profession. Questions were asked pertaining to the relationship between the parents of the girls, the behavioral symptoms of the girls, the defenses put up by the girls to justify their choices, and various social factors (economic, personal attractiveness, attitude toward work). Part 4 deals with the men in the lives of the call girls: the pimps and the clients.

Greenwald concludes by expressing his opinion on the regulation and abolition of prostitution. Finding it hard "to understand how an ethical society can condemn some of its members to the kind of degradation to which even the aristocrats of prostitution, the call girls, are subjected," he opts for a therapeutic treatment of prostitutes, including group therapy. (TJW)

PR,IL
647. Henriques, Fernando. **Prostitution and Society.** New York: Citadel Press, 1963-68. 3 v. Vol. 1, *Primitive, Classical and Oriental*, 1963. 438 p.; Vol. 2, *Prostitution in Europe and the Americas*, 1965, 438 p.; Vol. 3, *Modern Sexuality*, 1968. 349 p. Includes bibliographies and indexes.

Puzzled by the lack of literature on prostitution and the almost total neglect of the subject by British historians, Henriques, Lecturer on Social Anthropology at Leeds University, presents the student and the general reader with a survey of prostitution since earliest times based on a selection of significant periods in the history of prostitution.

In the preface to volume 1 Henriques dwells on the definitional situation in prostitution studies, pointing out the difficulties scholars have had attempting to define prostitution. He believes that a definition should encompass "the whole of venal sexual activity" and not just sexual intercourse. As to the dearth of literature, he notes that it has been over a century since the American, William Sanger, produced his history of prostitution. In *Prostitution and Society*, Henriques hopes to establish "a general hypothesis regarding the nature and function of prostitution in human society." Another objective is to test Havelock Ellis's idea that "wherever the free union of young people is impeded under conditions in which early marriage is also difficult, prostitution must certainly arise."

The survey begins with a chapter on sacred, or theological, prostitution, which in antiquity was widespread throughout the Mediterranean, Asia Minor, West Africa, and northern India. A most intriguing question examined is the transformation of sacred prostitution into secular prostitution. Prostitution in society is dealt with in depth in subsequent chapters devoted to classical Greece; Rome; classical India; India under British rule; China; Japan; the Near East, including Egypt; Africa; the New World; and the Pacific. Fully documented and amply illustrated with forty plates and numerous line drawings, this first volume of Henriques's *magnum opus* provides the opening chapter of the first comprehensive treatment of the subject in English in over a century.

Volume 2 continues his investigation of prostitution in several societies of the Western world. Following chapters on early Christian sexuality and the medieval whore, Henriques focuses on seventeenth and eighteenth century prostitution in Russia, France, and London. He then goes on to prostitution in the Caribbean and Brazil, followed by five chapters on various aspects of illicit sex in the United States, attributing the features of American prostitution to "the essentially material civilization of the affluent society" (p. 366).

In the third and concluding volume of this work, Henriques devotes several chapters to prostitution in nineteenth-century London and Edinburgh, and shows the close link between the liquor trade (beer and spirits) and prostitution. He looks at the real working conditions of the prostitute, her relations with clients, and dissects Victorian sexual morality. White slavery as a worldwide phenomenon receives close attention. Finally, Henriques reviews contemporary sexuality and advances the hypothesis that prostitution is a valid social institution tied to the economic setting. His concluding words are "Whether sexual permissiveness is accepted for adolescents or not, whether the incidence of extra-marital sexual activity increases or not, the certain, hard core demand for the prostitute will continue. Our society has produced that demand. Prostitution remains the responsibility of our society" (p. 341). (TJW)

PR,IL

648. Hobson, Barbara Meil. **Uneasy Virtue: The Politics of Prostitution and the American Reform Movement.** New York: Basic Books, 1987. 275 p. Includes bibliographic notes and indexes. ISBN 0-465-08868-6.

Unlike most books on the subject, Hobson's study of prostitution is about policy and politics. A research associate at the Center for the Study of Industrial Societies, University of Chicago, historian Hobson draws heavily on archival materials, e.g., court and prison records; interviews with prostitutes, police, prosecutors, and social workers; and the existing literature. While concentrating on prostitution in the United States from 1820 to the present, she highlights, for purposes of comparison, prostitution policies in several European countries, including Sweden, England, Holland, and Germany.

This work is not about the prostitution culture or the lives of prostitutes. In it Hobson defines prostitution as "a social institution that embodies the relations between the sexes and classes; as a body of laws and legal practices; as a reform movement linked to other movements; and as a phenomenon with historical and cultural traditions that frame the discourse and guide the search for alternatives" (p. 4). Dividing her work into four parts, she begins locally with the evolution of prostitution policy, focusing on one city, Boston, which, in response to community pressure, conducted a full-scale campaign against vice starting in the 1820s.

Among the powerful groups espousing reform were the self-appointed moral reformers, temperance and purity groups, prison reformers, and suffragists. Advocating the rescue and protection of prostitutes rather than their punishment, these groups, Hobson concludes, failed to understand that prostitution was a viable alternative to low wages and the lack of employment opportunities. These feminists also sought stricter enforcement of laws against pimps, brothelkeepers, and customers.

In the second part of the book, "Prostitutes and Their Keepers," Hobson "explores the social reality of prostitutes—their motivations, economic options, and possible futures," that are "set against the prevailing medical and legal analyses of prostitution as pathology and sexual deviance" (p. 6).

In part 3, "A National Crusade and Its Aftermath, 1900-1939," Hobson discusses the nationwide campaign to rid American cities of commercialized prostitution. In this period questions were raised about the sex relationship between prostitute and patrons, between lovers, and between wife and husband. The prostitute was not necessarily "the fallen woman" but rather "the unadjusted girl," a delinquent type, evaluated by psychologists, social workers, and penologists.

In the final part, "Recent Challenges and Debates, 1970- ," Hobson focuses on the "unsuccessful challenges of feminist groups, civil liberties lawyers, and prostitutes themselves to change the course of prostitution policies in the United States" (p. 7). She contrasts the prostitution policies in Holland, Germany, and Sweden with the American anti-legalization policies, concluding that the Dutch model promotes a legitimate prostitution work culture while the Swedish model, that "favors repression against sex commerce as a business enterprise and offers social work remedies for prostitutes," has been the most influential in the United States. (TJW)

PR,IL

649. Horn, Pierre L., and Mary Beth Pringle, eds. **The Image of the Prostitute in Modern Literature.** New York: Frederick Ungar, 1984. 147 p. Includes bibliography. ISBN 0-8044-2702-X.

The ten essays in this collection provide criticism about the image of the prostitute in different literatures and cultures around the world. This criticism, written by men and women, shows by and large the prostitute as an object and literary symbol reflecting patriarchal themes and values.

As Horn and Pringle point out in their introduction, the fictional prostitute exists in many guises: the *bitch-witch*, who leads others to ruin or death (Emile Zola's Nana in the novel by that name); the *femme fatale* in stories emphasizing the prostitute's seductive qualities; the *weak-but-wonderful* prostitute, i.e., the "whore-with-a-heart-of-gold" (Nancy in Dickens's *Oliver Twist*); the *saved prostitute* (Carrie in William Faulkner's *The Reivers*); the *sinner-but-survivor* type, such as Becky Sharp in Thackeray's *Vanity Fair*; the *seduced-and-abandoned* prostitute (Little Emily in *David Copperfield*); the *hapless harlot*, who never has a moment of enjoyment, depicted in modern Latin American literature; the *proud pro* (Mrs. Warren in Bernard Shaw's *Mrs. Warren's Profession*); and finally those numberless prostitutes who act as foils in literature.

The papers include Bonnie Hoover Braendlin's examination of the character Mildred in Somerset Maugham's *Of Human Bondage*; Amy Millstone's "French Feminist Theater and the Subject of Prostitution, 1870-1914"; Jill Warren's perspective on Nana as reflecting Emile Zola's view of prostitution; Thomas Whissen's "The Magic Circle: The Role of the Prostitute in Isak Dinesen's Gothic Tales"; Nicholas Moravcevich's "The Romantization of the Prostitute in Dostoevsky's Fiction"; Evelyne Accad's "The Prostitute in Arab and North African Fiction"; Ann Lowry Weir's "Courtesans and Prostitutes in South Asian Literature"; Lawrence E. Hussman, Jr.'s "The Fate of the Fallen Woman in *Maggie* and *Sister Carrie*"; James M. Hughes's "The Uncommon Prostitute: The Contemporary Image in an American Age of Pornography"; and Amy Katz Kaminsky's "Women Writing About Prostitutes: Amalis Jamilis and Luisa Valenzuela."

Horn and Pringle believe that the female contributors to this collection bring a fresh perspective to the examination of a topic so close to feminist interests. (TJW)

IL

650. Murphy, Emmett. **Great Bordellos of the World: An Illustrated History.** London: Quartet Books, 1983. 254 p. Includes bibliography and index. ISBN 0-7043-2395-8.

This handsomely illustrated book is an entertaining, informative, and somewhat anecdotal history of the bordello from earliest times to the present. After briefly surveying the largely temple-associated prostitution of the oldest civilizations (Sumeria, Babylon, and Egypt), Murphy focuses attention first on Greece, where the municipal bordello, the *dicterion*, unconnected with religion, was created by Solon, a wise statesman primarily interested in tax revenues; and then on Rome, which developed the *lupanarium*, a series of cells separated by a wide corridor, murals above the doorways indicating the kinds of sex to be obtained within. Brothels of this sort, identified by phallic symbols displayed outside, have been preserved in Pompeii and Herculaneum. Murphy also discusses the Dark Ages, when the lupanars fairly disappeared to be replaced by more barbaric activities, such as rape and slaughter. He describes how the Crusades provided an impetus for the development of traveling brothels and discusses twelfth-century developments in England, showing how the stewhouses, ostensibly bathhouses, were formalized with court and church approval. This long-lived institution thrived in London until the Black Death of 1665 and the Great Fire of 1666 greatly reduced its influence, the inhabitants scattering to the Continent and the New World. He dwells on the highly cultivated whoredom flourishing in Italy during the Renaissance, its tendrils reaching deep within the Vatican, and includes a chapter on the establishment of seraglios and harems as an outgrowth of Arab conquests and the slave trade in North Africa and the Near East. Another chapter discusses the unique contributions by India, China, and Japan to the evolution of the bordello. By showing how the colonies were the dumping ground for undesirables, many of whom became prostitutes, he does not neglect the New World. Murphy informs us that prostitution was flourishing in England in 1857: 6,000 brothels and 60,000 strumpets were reported in London alone, one woman in every sixteen a whore. Child brothels and flagellant houses were not uncommon in Victorian England. As the United States expanded westward, New York, New Orleans, Chicago, and San Francisco became notorious centers of vice and corruption. Then in the early part of the twentieth century, reaction set in and by 1917 most of the sporting clubs across the land were closed. But prostitution, like the weather, prevails. It is legal in Nevada and appears in many disguised forms elsewhere. Murphy's well-written and well-researched book makes one keenly aware of the durability of "the oldest profession." (TJW)

PO

651. O'Brien, Martin. **All the Girls.** New York: St. Martin's Press/Marek, 1982. 336 p. ISBN 0-312-02003-1.

O'Brien, an English journalist and travel writer, sets out on a personal odyssey to find out how prostitutes behave worldwide. As he states in the beginning of this travelogue: "It is, quite simply, the record of a journey that lasted several months during which time I deliberately sought out and allowed myself to be drawn into any professional sexual situation which offered itself." It is also "a story about a particular type of people—the way they live and work, rather than the place they live and work in" (p. 9). His stops included brief stays in Buenos Aires, Rio de Janiero, Caracas, Sydney, Melbourne, Honolulu, Tokyo, Hong Kong, Bangkok, Tel Aviv, Budapest, Munich, Frankfurt-am-Main, Berlin, Moscow, Leningrad, Amsterdam, Paris, Los Angeles, the famous Mustang Ranch in Nevada, Las Vegas, Chicago, and New York. Not a fastidious fornicator, he strikes up an acquaintance with the first hooker who comes along. He experiences a wide range of sexual practices for which he pays liberally. Unfortunately, O'Brien draws no conclusions when his journey is over about what he has seen or done. He hoists that task onto the reader who has been given a truly intimate and possibly unique look within the world of whoredom. Engagingly told, this unidimensional view of prostitution contributes to one's understanding of the oldest profession. (TJW)

PR,IL
652. Pheterson, Gail, ed. **A Vindication of the Rights of Whores.** Preface by Margo St. James. Seattle, Wash.: Seal Press, 1989. 293 p. Includes bibliographic references. ISBN 0-931188-73-3.
    This anthology begins with Pheterson's history of the prostitutes' rights movement over the past fifteen years, essentially in the United States, but also including developments around the world. She pays particular attention to Margo St. James's organization, COYOTE (Call Off Your Old Tired Ethics), which was founded in 1973 in the United States to stand up for prostitutes' rights. She also notes the establishment in 1975-1985 of similar organizations in other parts of the country, such as HIRE (Hooking Is Real Employment) in Atlanta, Georgia; and other places abroad, including Canada's CORP (Canadian Organization for the Rights of Prostitutes), England's PLAN (Prostitution Laws Are Nonsense), and the National Network of Prostitutes in Brazil.
    This self-organization gained headway slowly; by the mid-eighties it was strong enough to convene the First World Whores' Congress in Amsterdam, Netherlands, in 1985. The main achievement of this conference was to found the International Committee for Prostitutes' Rights (ICPR), which drafted a world charter of demands. The main thrust of the charter was embodied in the first clause of the document: "Decriminalize all aspects of adult prostitution resulting from individual decision." Other features of the charter addressed human rights, working conditions, health, services, taxes, public opinion, and organization. Participants included prostitutes and ex-prostitutes from the Netherlands, France, Switzerland, Germany, England, Sweden, the United States, and Canada.
    In 1986 the second Congress was held at the European Parliament in Brussels, Belgium. Prostitute participants from around the world addressed the Congress on the status of prostitutes in their respective countries, which included Italy, Australia, Austria, Thailand, France, West Germany, England, Canada, the United States, Switzerland, Netherlands, Morocco, Ecuador, India, Sweden, Vietnam, and Belgium. The ICPR issued three major statements: Prostitution and Human Rights, Prostitution and Health, and Prostitution and Feminism. The Congress also took up the vexing question of migrant prostitutes and their rights.
    The last part of this anthology includes reports from prostitutes in Burkina Faso, Kenya, Indonesia, Israel, Madrid, and Sao Paulo, in which Pheterson writes: "The range of speakers in this book testifies both to the commonality of struggle among prostitutes around the world and also to the widely diverse circumstances that determine their lives. . . . This anthology is meant to be an historical document and an impetus for a new politics of prostitution. This is meant to invite, not exclude, those who are absent. The ICPR is a young organization which began in the West. Different cultural settings point to different specific needs and different strategies for change. Those strategies include everything from literacy training to health care to legal reform to public education. This is a movement in need of many allies" (p. 259). (TJW)

IL
653. Sanger, William W. **The History of Prostitution: Its Extent, Causes and Effects Throughout the World.** New York: Eugenics, 1937. 708 p. Originally published in 1858. Republished with appendix in 1895. Includes index.

Sanger, resident physician at Blackwell's Island, New York City, spent about seven years, two of them abroad, in the preparation of the monumental *The History of Prostitution*. Completed in 1858 as an expanded response to the original request of the Board of Governors of the Alms-House of the City and County of New York to report on prostitution and the incidence of syphilis in New York City, Sanger's classic report, replete with scholarly detail and documentation, goes back to the origins of prostitution in the pre-Christian era, focusing on customs among the Jews, Syrians, Egyptians, Persians, Greeks, and Romans. It then deals with the morals, manners, and institutions involved with prostitution in France, Italy, and Spain from the Middle Ages to the mid-nineteenth century. It has chapters on conditions in Portugal, Algeria, Bulgaria, Denmark, Switzerland, Russia, Sweden, Norway, Great Britain, Mexico, and Central and South America. It also covers sexual customs among the North American Indians and peoples in other nations. Although written from a mid-nineteenth-century Victorian point of view that denounced prostitution as a dreadful vice, Sanger's work is still recognized as one of the most complete histories of prostitution in the English language.

The work concludes with a thorough examination of prostitution in New York City. The investigation is based on a detailed questionnaire administered by the New York City police to 2,000 prostitutes located in the twenty-two wards of the city. Thirty-seven questions covering many aspects of their lives were asked (age, where born, how long in the country, immigration details, marital status, children, how long a prostitute, diseases, reasons for becoming a prostitute, earnings, habits, religion). The resultant statistics are given in tabular form following each question.

In the report Sanger stated that there were 6,000 public prostitutes in New York City (out of a population of about 700,000); the majority were from fifteen to twenty-five years old; three-eights were born in the United States; one-fifth of them were married; one-half of them had children; one-half admitted to having had syphilis; etc.). He also concluded that "prohibitory measures have signally failed to suppress or check prostitutes" (p. 676). An appendix to Sanger's report attempts to update the situation in New York City to the late 1890s. Both documents seem to "favor some system of regulation and inspection as the only means of checking and controlling syphilis" (p. 698). (TJW)

PR,IL

654. Symanski, Richard. **The Immoral Landscape: Female Prostitution in Western Societies.** Toronto: Butterworths, 1981. 349 p. Includes bibliographies and indexes. ISBN 0-409-87130-3.

In this well-documented study of prostitution in Western societies, Symanski presents his argument that prostitution is a biosocial problem. To begin with, "men proscribe the sexual behavior of females and support an essentially monogamous mating system, yet they often behave promiscuously. Female prostitutes constitute one of several outlets for male behavior" (p. 1). Second, prostitution, especially street prostitution, is a highly visible activity that is considered repugnant by society and needs to be somehow controlled. It must be dealt with geopolitically. Confinement to a particular place is the usual solution; and mobility is the prostitute's reaction to this measure.

By means of police records, personal testimonials, and observers' comments as well as detailed statistical tables, diagrams, and charts, Symanski shows the prevalence of prostitution in cities, states, and countries worldwide. In a series of chapters, he describes and analyzes (1) the urban setting for prostitution and how it is perceived by people; (2) the costs of prostitution to the prison system, the courts, and the taxpayer; (3) the attitudes and sexual preferences of prostitutes and their customers; (4) the development and application of laws aimed at prostitution; (5) the heavy hand of the state where prostitution is legalized; (6) the status of prostitution in Nevada; (7) problems of race, class, and space in the structure of prostitution; (8) the world of the pimp and other human predators; (9) street prostitution in big cities such as New York City; (10) the mobility of prostitutes as a survival strategy; (11) the story of the closing of brothels and the clearing of the streets in such places as Chicago and London; and (12) the modern alternatives to brothel prostitution: massage parlors, escort services, encounter studios, and so forth. Finally, Symanski discusses the quest for solutions to the problem of prostitution, concluding that decriminalization of the activity seems to be a valid one.

In a lengthy appendix, Nancy Burley and Symanski present a cross-cultural perspective on prostitution. On the basis of the Human Relations Area Files (HRAF), they identify all societies in which prostitution has been noted by ethnographers and provide in a series of tables information on different aspects of prostitution, such as how and why women become prostitutes. (TJW)

Asia & Africa

IL
655.   De Becker, Joseph Ernest. **The Nightless City: Or the "History of the Yoshi-wara Yūkwaku."** 3rd ed. revised. Yokohama: Max Nossler, [1905]. 386 p.

Written by a twenty-year resident of Japan, this study, first published in 1899, contains voluminous data about the establishment, development, control, and regulation of large areas of land set aside for licensed prostitution, known as the Yoshiwara Yūkwaku (Yoshiwara District). These districts were generally fenced in and moated, provided with large gateways, and guarded.

Prior to the late sixteenth and early seventeenth centuries there were no fixed places for brothels and assignation houses in Japanese cities. Then around 1612 it was proposed that brothels and assignation houses in the city of Yedo (present-day Tokyo) be gathered together in one place. By 1617 this idea was approved and, although it was not completed until 1626, the district was open for business in 1617. The district attracted brothels from several cities, including Kyoto, Osaka, and Nara. Gutted by fire in 1667, the Yedo Yoshiwara was established anew on about eighteen acres of land. It was still flourishing in the early twentieth century.

De Becker provides a detailed description and history of the Yoshiwara Yūkwaku, covering such diverse topics as the layout, buildings, and architecture of the place; the classes of brothels and prostitutes; the dress and coiffures of the courtesans; fees charged customers; examinations for venereal diseases; the day and night engagements of the inhabitants; leaving the Yoshiwara after years of service; death and suicide; burial; and the lives of famous courtesans. He also examines the laws regulating prostitution, paying close attention to the contracts between the brothels and the prostitutes. He discusses the problem of medical inspection and provides statistical data on prostitution in Japan in 1898.

The book contains numerous illustrations depicting various aspects of the prosti-tutes' lives as well as detailed maps and plans of the Yoshiwara Yūkwaku as of 1846. Curiously, specific sexual practices of the courtesans are ignored completely in this lengthy, scholarly study. Cognizant of the prevailing view that prostitution is a "social evil," De Becker focuses on presenting data of use to sociologists, physicians, and others. (TJW)

[N.B. As a result of the 1957 antiprostitution laws of Japan, Tokyo's Yoshiwara district, after more than three hundred years of operation, is closed.]

IL
656.   Gronewold, Sue. **Beautiful Merchandise: Prostitution in China 1860-1936.** New York: Harrington Park Press, 1985. 114 p. Originally published in 1982 by The Haworth Press. Includes bibliography and index. ISBN 0-918393-15-9.

A lecturer on Asia at the American Museum of Natural History, Gronewold presents in this short volume a study of prostitution in prerevolutionary China. Using primary sources (newspapers, magazines, government documents, law codes, missionary reports, the firsthand descriptions of foreigners) as well as literature and biographies, she reconstructs the daily lives of prostitutes (euphemistically called "beautiful merchan-dise") at various times between 1860 and 1936. She describes "an economy in which women and female children were regularly sold, traded, pawned, and adopted as servants, slaves, brides, foster daughters, concubines—and prostitutes" (p. x). She argues that this sexual economy, not qualitatively different from the gin trade, remained unchanged during such upheavals as the fall of the Empire and despite attempts at reform, urbanization, and Western cultural influences.

In the first chapter, Gronewold covers prostitution during the latter years of the Ch'ing Dynasty, 1860-1911. Because of censorship and prudery during this period, she had to rely principally on foreign sources of information. She describes the classes of brothels and their inmates; how they were organized; costs of visits; how brothels recruited young girls; how the girls were raised, educated, and given instruction in the "Art of the Bedchamber"; occupational hazards; possibilities for upward mobility within the brothel structure; and the eventual fate of prostitutes. Prostitution was an integral part of the social system, that "functioned according to a highly developed body of beliefs in propriety, called *li*, that regulated social behavior and granted or took away 'face.' " Never condemned by statute in Ch'ing China, prostitution was permitted, regulated, and taxed.

Gronewold enlarges her study by examining the economic fate of women in China, describing the traffic in women, and what happens to women in times of famine. She also devotes a chapter to the transformation of Chinese society between 1911 and 1936, a period of sweeping changes in all sectors of society. In prostitution the major change involved the manner in which prostitutes were procured: purchase gave way to pawning and this put the family in a position to profit from the work of daughters and other disposable females. This also better insured women's survival and was preferable to infanticide. Incidentally, the Chinese Revolution brought an end to this whole system of prostitution: "there would be no traffic in sexual commodities and no place for 'beautiful merchandise.' " (TJW)

PR,IL

656a.   Odzer, Cleo. **Patpong Sisters: An American Woman's View of the Bangkok Sex World.** New York: Blue Moon Books/Arcade, 1994. 313 p. Includes bibliography. ISBN 1-55970-281-8.

Although prostitution is illegal in Thailand, the government has for many years winked at the thriving Thai sex industry. In Bangkok three streets named Patpong 1, 2, and 3, are the focal points of a variety of establishments catering to the sexual needs and wants of foreigners ("farangs"), mostly men but some women, who flock as sex tourists to Thailand in pursuit of excitement and sexual pleasure. Also, many are ex-GIs, veterans of the Vietnam War, who prefer the Thai lifestyle to what they might encounter back home.

Odzer, an anthropologist whose doctoral dissertation at the New School of Social Research in New York City, became the basis for *Patpong Sisters*, describes in detail the vibrant lifestyle of those who work in Patpong. Establishing a close rapport with bar girls, pimps, and others, she gathered information about commercial sex in Bangkok and elsewhere. Ordinarily Thai women are expected to be passive in their relationships with men; those Thai women recruited at an early age into prostitution learn quickly how to be assertive and self-reliant. Enamored of these beautiful young women, the farangs pay generously for sexual favors—they sometimes even marry them. The Patpong sisters' goals are basically related to their need for money to support themselves, their parents, and others living in the poverty-stricken hinterland. On occasion Odzer accompanied a bar girl on a visit to her family in a small village, thus coming to know intimately the lives and motivations of these prostitutes. She even had an affair with a particularly appealing pimp.

Odzer carefully describes the three streets of Patpong with their numerous establishments and teeming life, pointing out that Patpong 3 caters exclusively to homosexual activities. She provides diagrams showing the locations of bars, restaurants, massage parlors, and other attractions. Places with such colorful names as Pussy Galore, Playgirl, Baby Go-Go, and Goldfinger line the crowded streets. Layouts of individual bars, such as the Queen's Castle Bar and the Rose Bar, along with pictures of bar girls in action, give a sense of the charged atmosphere of these places.

Odzer, who did her research in Patpong in 1988, points out that AIDS, a taboo subject for discussion until recently, is now spreading rapidly throughout the country. The government, for long fearful of losing revenue from sex tourism, has belatedly admitted that there is a problem. Although VD clinics exist in Patpong, the bar girls knew nothing of the epidemic until the late 1980s.

During her stay in Thailand, Odzer came to recognize, except for the elite classes, the lowly status of women in the male-dominated Thai society. As for the bar girls, she states that "the prostitutes are pioneers in advancing women's autonomy by breaking from the mold of suppressed and passive females" (p. 307). (TJW)

IL

657. Sturdevant, Saundra Pollock, and Brenda Stoltzfus. **Let the Good Times Roll: Prostitution and the U.S. Military in Asia.** New York: New Press, 1992. 343 p. Includes bibliography and glossary. ISBN 1-56584-049-6.

Well-documented and copiously illustrated with photographs, this work is a study of prostitution in cities surrounding U.S. military bases in the Philippines, South Korea, and Okinawa. Sturdevant, a photographer with a Ph.D. in modern Chinese history from the University of Chicago, and Stoltzfus, a member of the Mennonite Central Committee charged with befriending the women working in the bars near Subic Naval Base, investigate the sale of women's sexual labors outside these bases using information they gathered in the 1980s about the lives, motivations, and working conditions of these women. The book includes, in addition to general information about prostitution in these countries, personal stories from those who became bar girls.

After lengthy and critical discussion of the American military presence in the Pacific and the elaborate agreements between the bases and the local authorities regarding off-base entertainment of military and naval personnel, the book focuses on the work of the prostitutes themselves.

The first section is devoted to the Philippines, where the principal bases are Clark Air Base and Subic Naval Base. Sturdevant and Stoltzfus describe the entertainment system in Olongapo and neighboring towns where there are 15,000 to 17,000 registered and unregistered "hospitality women," who work in some 330 bars, massage parlors, and tailor shops, and on the street. A joint project of the Olongapo City Health Department and the U.S. Navy is the Social Hygiene Clinic (SHC) where the sex workers are registered. Prostitution is illegal in the Philippines and unregistered prostitutes may be arrested and imprisoned. The hospitality women report regularly to the SHC for medical checkups.

After gaining the confidence of several bar girls, Sturdevant and Stoltzfus let them tell their own stories of involvement in prostitution, either as waitresses, go-go dancers, cashiers, or entertainment/hostesses. They believe that these stories present a complicated picture of poverty, degradation, and helplessness on the part of the Filipina women.

Sturdevant and Stoltzfus encounter a similar system in the southern part of Korea, at Tong Dan Chun and Uijongbu near Seoul, where the American G.I. finds entertainment provided by "club women." In Okinawa the bar system is somewhat different in that most of the bar girls servicing Americans are contract labor recruited in the Philippines.

The study concludes with a general critique of female sexual labor and the worldwide effort to organize prostitutes into an effective force struggling for social acceptance and betterment. The authors also examine various aspects of the military's attitudes, policy, and role in relation to the communities adjacent to the military and naval bases. They fully realize the supporting role played by sexual labor in support of the local economy, and they appreciate the attitude of American G.I.s in their need for entertainment after spending grueling days in the field maintaining their state of readiness. (TJW)

Europe

IL

658. Burford, E. J. **Bawds and Lodgings: A History of the London Bankside Brothels, c.100-1675.** London: Peter Owen, 1976. 206 p. Includes bibliography and index. ISBN 0-7206-0144-4.

Against a background of British history from the second to the seventeenth centuries, this book provides a scholarly study of prostitution in Britian along the south bank of the Thames River at the first permanent Roman settlement, eventually known as Southwark. Here the Romans erected *lupanaria* (brothels) for the use of the soldiers who, according to their terms of service, were not allowed to marry. The Roman occupation, lasting until the fifth century, "gave Britain and the Britons not only Roman order and civilization but also organized, legal, and institutionalized prostitution—and as a sort of bonus, venereal disease" (p. 23).

The record concerning prostitution during the Anglo-Saxon period is sparse for several centuries. Apparently, tolerance of prostitution allowed the Bankside brothels to survive the major events leading up to the Norman conquest: St. Augustine's attempt to Christianize pagan Britain in the late sixth century; the ascendancy of Canute to the throne of England in 1016; and the reign of Edward the Confessor (1042-1066).

It is said that William the Conqueror owned brothels in Rouen; the Bankside stewhouses (brothels) had nothing to fear either from him or successive kings for several centuries. The Crusades, begun in 1097, depleted the number of Englishmen and swelled the ranks of prostitutes. Henry II, the first Plantagenet and the first Norman king to speak English, issued in 1161 a detailed ordinance governing the Bankside stewhouses and putting them under the direction of the Bishop of Winchester, who benefited from stewhouse rentals up to the time of Charles II in the seventeenth century. King Edward II founded the Lock Hospital of Southwark in 1321; such places came to deal with sufferers from venereal diseases, especially following the epidemic that befell England in 1498.

The stewhouses had distinctive names, an old Roman custom. *The Barge*, owned by the nuns of Stratford, was popular in 1337 and still flourished in 1466. Burford provides a list of eighteen Bankside brothels as of the end of the fifteenth century; he also traces their ownership through the centuries and provides sketches of their relative locations from the vantage point of London.

Under the Tudor rulers Henry VII, Henry VIII, Edward VI, Mary I, and Elizabeth I prostitution received uneven treatment. Henry VIII, a lapsed Catholic, besides determining the religious fate of the English people, came down hard on prostitution and buggery, ordering Cardinal Wolsey to purge both London and Southwark.

Although Parliament in 1640 "enacted that prostitution was no longer a crime but only a nuisance" (p. 179), the sale of the Bishop of Winchester's land between 1647 and 1649 to private developers spelled the beginning of the end of the Bankside brothels. The Great Plague of 1665 as well as the Great Fire finished off the brothels, scattering their inmates to the four corners of the earth. (TJW)

PR,IL

659. Corbin, Alain. **Women for Hire: Prostitution and Sexuality in France After 1850.** Translated by Alan Sheridan. Cambridge, Mass.: Harvard University Press, 1990. 478 p. First published as *Les filles de noce: Misère sexuelle et prostitution aux 19e et 20e siècles.* Includes bibliography and index. ISBN 0-674-95543-9.

Although this scholarly study of prostitution in France focuses on the period 1871 to 1914, historian Corbin also encompasses the period from 1850 to 1871 and the contemporary period beginning in 1914. This work is "an attempt to discern the coherence between [men's] sexual need on the one hand and, on the other, the structural, behavioral, discursive, and political aspects of prostitution" (p. xvii).

In the 1850s the architect of the "French system" of prostitution was the physician Alex. Parent-Duchâtelet, who describes the system in his book *De la prostitution dans la ville de Paris considérée sous la rapport de l'hygiène publique, de la morale et de l'administration.* While realizing that prostitution was not legal, he nevertheless recognized the necessity of providing for men's sexual appetites and therefore promoted the establishment of the regulated and supervised *maison de tolérance*, the predominant type of brothel for registered prostitutes.

Believing that prostitutes are marginal people who reject "work in favor of pleasure," avoid "the need to settle down," and run the risk of becoming lesbians, Parent-Duchâtelet nonetheless stated that prostitution must be tolerated rather than prohibited. His system featured the enclosed milieu, supervision, and a hierarchical and compartmentalized structure. The focus of the system was the *maison de tolérance*, located in certain urban districts. Its inhabitants remained enclosed there, prohibited from venturing outside, and admitted only to other enclosed spaces, such as the hospital, the prison, and the convent-like centers for reform and rehabilitation. In effect, the system was established to concentrate vice and channelize male sexuality.

Alongside prostitutes confined to brothels were the freelance prostitutes working out of the *maisons de passe*, low-class unregistered establishments, and later the *maisons de rendezvous*, catering to men higher in the social ladder.

Corbin shows statistically the gradual decline of the enclosed system of prostitution. He emphasizes the impact of changing social, economic, and cultural factors on the system. Fear of the spread of venereal disease, the desire to protect society from what was considered a social evil, and the worldwide concern for the prostitute as a person in need of rescue and reform, contributed to the decline of the system.

According to Corbin, the twentieth century displays a new constellation of ideas relating to prostitutes and sexuality. Male sexual sensibility evolved: "turning to a prostitute was felt more and more to be a last resort, and during such encounters men would try to satisfy the deep need for fully relational sexuality that was developing in urban society; in relations with prostitutes, too, the erotic was gaining ground over the genital" (p. 331).

By World War I little remained of the regulationist system with its innumerable restrictions. Prostitutes were breaking free of their confinement, and they "could now sell themselves and get treatment without being locked up" (p. 336). The *maison de rendezvous* proliferated and prostitutional behavior spread throughout French society. While fear of the liberated female vanished, at the same time, in the interest of public hygiene, police surveillance and supervision remained. (TJW)

PR,IL
660. Finnegan, Frances. **Poverty and Prostitution: A Study of Victorian Prostitutes in York.** Cambridge, Eng.: Cambridge University Press, 1979. 231 p. Includes bibliography and index. ISBN 0-521-22447-0.

In the Victorian city of York, England, between 1837, the opening year of Queen Victoria's reign, and 1887, prostitution flourished in the midst of poverty. This study details the plight of low-class prostitutes in a nonindustrial town where opportunities for work were limited primarily to domestic service, laundry work, and dressmaking. Unable to find legitimate work young women turned to prostitution. Prostitution, however, provided few rewards and drove many to seek help from the York Penitentiary Society, which operated the Refuge, a home where girls could try to reform themselves over a two-year period.

Primary sources for this study include local newspapers and various archival records, such as the Annual Reports of the York Penitentiary Society. The study begins with a description of the areas in York where brothels were located. Ironically, these houses of ill fame began close to the York Minister, the great Anglican cathedral, and spread southward within the city walls. Unsanitary and overcrowded, these areas consisted of narrow lanes and alleys, as shown by the numerous illustrations sprinkled throughout the book.

Following this description of the houses and haunts of prostitutes, Finnegan peruses extant records to identify some 1,400 prostitutes and brothel-keepers operating in York over the fifty-year period. The records provide names, ages, addresses, and personal histories of individuals, and traces their turbulent lives from time of recruitment until their careers ended, often by death at an early age.

Following a chapter on prostitutes' clients, who came from all walks of life in York and surrounding areas in Yorkshire, and even from Scotland and Ireland, Finnegan describes various aspects of prostitutes' lives, such as disease, drunkenness, and criminality. A final chapter deals with efforts at rescue and reform. "By 1887, out of the total of 412 formally admitted to the Refuge since it had been opened in 1845, the Annual Reports reveal that only 142 girls were placed in service" (p. 167). Many of these lapsed into their old way of life, so it cannot be said that the rescue and reform effort was significantly successful.

Finnegan believes that the accepted opinion about prostitutes' lives, derived essentially from the studies by the English physician William Acton and A. J. B. Parent-Duchâtelet in France, are misleading. In their views individual prostitutes, after a brief experience at their trade, reentered society and assumed a normal life. They had also suggested that prostitutes were healthier than their peers in respectable society. Finnegan believes that her study gives the lie to such optimistic speculations and that in reality the prostitute gradually sank to the lowest depths of misery and degradation, and only in exceptional cases did they ever escape from their desperate situation.

Finnegan calls for further study of prostitution, research based on primary records rather than on secondary sources. This is required to dispel the myths that have arisen around the daily lives of prostitutes. (TJW)

PR,IL

661.   Flexner, Abraham. **Prostitution in Europe.** Introduction by John D. Rockefeller, Jr. Montclair, N.J.: Patterson Smith, 1969. 455 p. (Patterson Smith Reprint Series in Criminology, Law Enforcement, and Social Problems, No. 30). Copyright 1914 by the Century Co. Includes bibliographic footnotes and index.

Flexner, well-remembered for his critical studies of American higher education, especially medical education, and for the founding of the Institute for Advanced Study (Princeton, N.J.) undertook this study of prostitution in Europe under the auspices of the Bureau of Social Hygiene, a private organization established in 1911 and headed by John D. Rockefeller, Jr. The study followed on the heels of another major endeavor, George J. Kneeland's *Commercialized Prostitution in New York City*, published in 1913.

Flexner examines the state of prostitution in the larger cities of England, Scotland, France, Italy, Belgium, Switzerland, Holland, Denmark, Norway, Sweden, Germany, and Austria-Hungary. He visited twenty-eight cities, including London, Edinburgh, Paris, Rome, Berlin, Munich, Amsterdam, Copenhagen, Stockholm, Geneva, Vienna, and Budapest. He found that "prostitution is an urban problem, its precise character largely dependent on the size of the town" (p. 5). Recognizing that in the huge urban metropolitan areas prostitution is a matter of "barter, promiscuity, and emotional indifference," Flexner finds prostitution objectionable because of the associated demoralization, waste, disease, and crime. In general, this study touches on various aspects of prostitution: "the factors determining demand, the sources of supply, the various methods used in its regulation or control, their operation and value, the effect of abolishing regulation, and the general outcome of the European experience" (p. ix).

The official regulations for prostitution in Paris (1878), Berlin (1911), Hamburg (1909), and Vienna (1911) are included as appendixes. Another relevant study of prostitution sponsored by the Bureau of Social Hygiene is Howard B. Woolston's *Prostitution in the United States: Prior to the Entrance of the United States in the World War* (1921). The Kneeland, Flexner, and Woolston studies were reprinted in 1969 in Patterson Smith Reprint Series in Criminology, Law Enforcement, and Social Problems. (TJW)

PR

662. Gibson, Mary. **Prostitution and the State in Italy, 1860-1915.** New Brunswick, N.J.: Rutgers University Press, 1986. 297 p. (Crime, Law, and Deviance Series). Includes bibliography and index. ISBN 0-8135-1172-0.

Gibson's study of prostitution as an aspect of Italian social history stems from her recognition of the importance of the Italian policy of regulation from the time of unification in Italy to World War I. While prohibition and decriminalization are also important ways of dealing with prostitution, the Italian experience with legalization over a protracted period of time has value for historians, scholars, policymakers, and students.

Divided into two major sections, dealing with the state and the with the prostitutes, section 1 "examines chronologically the policy of regulation as embodied in Italian law and as implemented by bureaucrats in the Ministry of the Interior in Rome." Opposition to regulation came from various leftist groups, including feminists, to replace regulation with a policy of abolition. Section 2 examines closely the lives of Italian prostitutes in relation to the state. With data extracted from official records in major cities of Italy (Bologna, Naples, Milan, Rome, Turin, Palermo, Florence, Genoa, and Venice), Gibson presents a social profile of prostitutes as compared to Italian women in general.

In examining the interaction of prostitutes with police and public health doctors on the streets, in police stations, and in *sifilicomi* (hospitals for prostitutes), Gibson reveals the repressiveness of the system and the resistance to regulation from the prostitutes. She claims that this interaction between state and prostitutes profoundly affected both parties; it is this that explains "the etiology, form, and extent of prostitution in late nineteenth- and early twentieth-century Italy." Such tension between oppressed prostitutes and the bureaucrats crippled government policy.

After detailing the gradual failure of regulationist policies under the Cavour Law of 1860, the Crispi Law of 1888, and the Nicotera Law of 1891, as well as the Fascist statutes of 1923, 1931, and 1940, Gibson examines the various movements and forces that led to the Merlin Law of 1958, that abolished decriminalized prostitution in Italy. The latter forbade the establishment of houses of prostitution, and it ordered the closing of existing brothels. The act of prostitution was not criminalized "if carried out privately and without the interference of a third party" (p. 229). This implies that prostitution was not abolished, only its regulation. While prostitution was decriminalized, its solicitation was not.

While focusing on prostitution in Italy between 1860 and 1915, Gibson's added comments on subsequent periods in Italian history round out the course of the repressive policy of legalization that lasted for a period of one hundred years. (TJW)

PR,IL

663. Harsin, Jill. **Policing Prostitution in Nineteenth-Century Paris.** Princeton, N.J.: Princeton University Press, 1985. 417 p. Includes bibliography and index. ISBN 0-691-05439-8.

Harsin's study of prostitution in Paris embraces the entire nineteenth century but also includes observations on prostitution during the Revolution and the early years of the twentieth century. Remarkably, during this period none of the governments (Revolution, Empire, Restoration, July Monarchy, etc.) ever passed a law outlawing prostitution. Nevertheless, the message from society was always to do something about prostitutes, who, it was believed, brought moral decay, disorder, and disease to society. By default, prostitution became a matter for the Prefecture of Police of Paris, which set up the Morals Brigade (Brigade des moeurs) to control and contain prostitution.

Throughout Europe in the early nineteenth century there was a fervent interest in public hygiene and sanitation, and this concern extended to prostitution as well. Police control began with "a simple administrative decision in 1802 to provide facilities for examining public prostitutes for venereal disease" (p. xvi), that shortly became mandatory and led to the inscription of all prostitutes. In the main, this system of prostitution control prevailed in Paris for about 100 years. It was a system that tolerated prostitution but controlled it to a remarkable degree through a large developing police bureaucracy, given over to apprehending prostitutes who got out of line.

Harsin devotes a chapter to Dr. Alexandre-Jean-Baptiste Parent-Duchâtelet, an expert on "clogged sewers, polluted rivers [and] dead horses"; he became famous for his book *De la prostitution dans la ville de Paris*, which provided the theoretical support for the system of prostitution that the police favored.

This nonlegal regulatory system featured the confinement of prostitutes in a type of bordello called the *maison de tolérance*, although other locations, such as back rooms of taverns and lodging houses, also accommodated prostitutes and their clients. One of the main problems confronting the morals police was clandestine prostitution and its unregistered prostitutes, who resided in some of the foulest areas of Paris.

Harsin traces the evolution of this system, devoting part 1 of the book to the administrative structure and legal basis for the regulatory system. In part 2, she examines the practical functioning of the system and its effects on the women involved in it. Here she observes the denial of civil rights to prostitutes in a country where women had few rights. Part 3 examines the main problems of the regulatory system: the clandestine prostitute and the rise of the *maison de rendezvous* as a rival to the *maison de tolérance*. Essentially, the old system of strict regulation gave way to a more open, even more tolerant, system of prostitution control.

Harsin employs extensive statistical material—gathered both by Parent-Duchâtelet and the Prefecture of Police—to support her scholarly examination of nineteenth-century prostitution in Paris. (TJW)

IL

664. Lawner, Lynne. **Lives of the Courtesans: Portraits of the Renaissance.** New York: Rizzoli, 1987. 215 p. Includes bibliography and index. ISBN 0-8478-0738-X.

One of the striking features about court life in Italy in the sixteenth century was the colorful presence of courtesans (together with courtiers and princes), a caste of ambitious women created by society to serve the social, cultural, and sexual needs of the court. As such these "honest courtesans," as they were called, emerged in Rome at the papal court toward the end of the fifteenth century. This work, based on primary sources in art and literature of the times, shows how Renaissance artists and writers depicted and represented the courtesan in their work.

Lawner points out that in 1490 in Rome, with a population of about 50,000, men greatly outnumbered women and, although the men were chiefly celebates, the women were mainly prostitutes, numbering about 6,800. The higher-class prostitutes, the courtesans, educated in the arts and letters, made lively companions for princes, prelates, ambassadors, bankers, and merchants. Not confined to Rome, courtesanship flourished in Florence, Venice, and other Italian cities as well as spreading northward into France, Germany, the Netherlands, and elsewhere. The cult of the courtesan lasted another two centuries.

On the basis of novellas, plays, poems, letters, and other documents, we know that the courtesans were of humble origin and lived in luxury in palaces and villas. The following quote from a novella by Matteo Bandello reveals how they lived: "There is a custom in Venice . . . namely that a courtesan takes six or seven lovers, assigning to each a certain night of the week when she dines and sleeps with him. During the day she is free to entertain whomever she wishes so that her mill never lies idle and does not rust from lack of the opportunity to grind grain" (*Novelle* II, 31).

Many of these courtesans answered to such pretentious names as Imperia, Fiammeta, Beatrice of Ferrara, and Leda. Pietro Aretino identified many of them in his scandalous sonnets accompanying Giulio Romano's drawings in *I Modi*, an Italian Renaissance work of erotic art. Many artists were drawn to Rome and other great Italian cities. Their talents were often lavished on painting courtesans, depicting them in portraits, as reclining nudes, and in classical, mythological, and erotic settings.

While the emphasis in Lawner's study is almost wholly on the Italian courtesan, some attention is paid to her counterparts in France, Germany, and the Netherlands. Her chapters on "The Courtesan in Rome and Venice," "The Courtesan in Literature," "The Courtesan Image in Art," and "The Courtesan in Venetian, French, and Northern Painting," each illustrated with beautiful paintings by some of the greatest artists of the sixteenth century (Raphael, Titian, Carpaccio, Bellini, Giorgone, Veronese, Tintoretto, and others), provide a solid understanding of the unique role of courtesans in European history. (TJW)

IL
665. McLeod, Eileen. **Women Working: Prostitution Now.** London: Croom Helm, 1982. 177 p. Includes bibliography and index. ISBN 0-7099-1717-1.

McLeod is in the Department of Applied Social Studies at the University of Warwick; she is also a founding member of PROS (Programme for Reform of the Law on Soliciting), an organization of prostitutes and others concerned with decriminalizing offenses specifically relating to prostitution. In discussing her methodology for this study, McLeod states that this book "was written as part of the effort to secure better treatment for prostitutes by presenting a more authentic account of their activities and the social circumstances relating to them" (p. 148). Prostitutes cooperated fully in the interviews conducted by McLeod in Birmingham, Manchester, and other towns in the English Midlands.

Although the Wolfenden Report of 1957 stated that "prostitution is an evil of which any society which claims to be civilised should seek to rid itself," prostitution thrives in England today. It is not illegal, but there are laws that forbid soliciting, such as The Street Offences Act of 1959. Fines went from forty shillings to twenty-five pounds Sterling and imprisonment increased from fourteen days to three months under the law. It is generally agreed that the laws relating to prostitution inflict particularly heavy penalties on street prostitutes, protect prostitution in a paternalistic way, attempt to rehabilitate and punish at the same time, and discriminate against women.

For her study, limited mainly to street prostitution, McLeod interviewed thirty prostitutes and twenty clients, the former ranging in age from late teens to early forties, single and married, some with children. She also acquired similar data on the male clients. The interviews averaged one and one-half hours, covering a set of topics, including personal circumstances, working conditions, services provided, conducting business, clients, and attitudes toward the law.

This interview-based study shows that prostitutes are the most stigmatized group in society; that for some women sex is their most valuable commodity; that male clients are seeking relief from insufficiencies of marriage and other aspects of male sexuality; the law's injustice and futility makes a good case for decriminalization; and prostitutes' campaigns for reforms are tied in with feminist efforts to improve the conditions in which women exist and work.

McLeod does not suggest that prostitution be eradicated, but rather that its acceptance be based on a better understanding of the problems faced by prostitutes, and a recognition of the untenable situation they find themselves in, vis-à-vis the law. (TJW)

PR,IL
666. Otis, Leah Lydia. **Prostitution in Medieval Society: The History of an Urban Institution in Languedoc.** Chicago: University of Chicago Press, 1985. 240 p. (Women in Culture and Society). Includes bibliography and index. ISBN 0-226-64032-9.

In presenting this history of prostitution in the region of Languedoc in southern France between the twelfth and sixteenth centuries, Otis, a lecturer at the University of Montpellier I, relates how the activity, barely tolerated in the twelfth and thirteenth centuries, became institutionalized in the fourteenth and fifteenth centuries, and eventually condemned in the sixteenth century. Basing her investigation primarily on a thorough examination of the archival records of the principal towns of the region (Toulouse, Montpellier, Carcassone, etc.), municipal codes and statutes, royal documents, current scholarly literature, and general histories of prostitution, Otis discusses the various social, economic, demographic, and cultural factors affecting prostitution in the area. Keeping in mind the historical events in Europe that had an impact on prostitution—the spread of venereal diseases, the plague, the Reformation and the Counter-Revolution—she also examines the conflict between the secular mores and the church-imposed sexual morality in regard to adultery, concubinage, and fornication. Therefore, while the nucleus of the book is a regional case study of medieval prostitution, the study explores the wider context of how prostitution developed in Western Europe as a whole.

Otis carefully examines the varying circumstances of the lives of the prostitutes in the private and public brothels in the Languedocian municipalities, showing how the "hot streets" and red-light districts came to be established; how many prostitutes came to run their own houses; how the city fathers eventually municipalized the brothels, choosing the sites most suitable for them, and contracting (farming) for their operation with interested parties; how the meager civil rights of prostitutes gradually increased, permitting them to participate in urban celebrations; how repentant prostitutes were provided for; how prostitutes, procurers, and even customers were punished, and so forth. Lacking only personal views of the prostitutes about their work, this richly documented book affords a rare perspective on "the oldest profession" during a period of change when "secular authorities, both municipal and royal," attempted through the municipalization and protection of brothels, "to impose a uniform standard of sexual conduct on lay society" (p. 110).

As Catherine Simpson states in the foreword, Otis's research "weaves the history of women with the histories of several vast phenomena: sexuality; the growth of urban economies; the contest among municipal, state, and religious authorities for the power to define public morality and order; and the struggle within Christianity between Catholicism and an emerging Protestantism" (p. ix). It serves as a much-needed scholarly exploration of a period for which there are few clear studies of prostitution. (TJW)

PR,IL

667. Walkowitz, Judith R. **Prostitution and Victorian Society: Women, Class, and the State.** Cambridge, Eng.: Cambridge University Press, 1980. 347 p. Includes bibliography and index. ISBN 0-521-22334-2.

In this social history of prostitution in Victorian Britain, Walkowitz (Department of History, Rutgers University), focuses her attention on the Contagious Diseases Acts of 1864, 1866, and 1869. Intended as controls over the spread of venereal diseases among garrison personnel in towns and ports, they had a profound effect on the working-class women who, for economic reasons, had turned to prostitution for a livelihood. Inasmuch as the acts were discriminatory, bearing down more heavily on the prostitutes than on their customers, a powerful, and eventually effective, revolt occurred, resulting in the repeal of the acts between 1870 and 1886.

The study, based on archival sources, unpublished theses and papers, annual reports, and various published sources, is divided into three parts. An introductory part I, "prostitution, Social Science, and Venereal Disease," analyzes the lifestyle of the common prostitute in Victorian Britain; characterizes the "Great Social Evil" and describes the individual and institutional efforts at moral reform; and then reveals the prevalence of venereal diseases, especially syphilis and gonorrhea, among prostitutes, and their treatment in medical facilities, such as lock hospitals (for disciplinary confinement), where conditions were generally unsanitary.

Part II, "The Contagious Diseases Acts, Regulationists, and Repealers," discusses the origin and establishment of the acts; the emergence of organized opposition from feminists; and the work of the Ladies' National Association, under the leadership of Josephine Butler, in the repeal movement. Walkowitz points out that LNA's "leaders rejected the prevailing social view of prostitutes as pollutants of men, and instead depicted them as the *victims* of male pollution, as women who had been invaded by men's bodies, men's laws, and by that 'steel penis,' the speculum" (p. 146).

Part III, "Two Case Studies: Plymouth and Southampton Under the Contagious Diseases Acts," concentrates on efforts in two southern ports to repeal the acts and the opposition to those efforts from the regulationists. The local and national debates that raged over this repeal issue encompassed a wide range of social, medical, and political issues: "the double standard of sexual morality; the participation of women in political activity; the control of women by male doctors; and the role of the state in enforcing sexual and social discipline among the poor" (p. 3).

The aftermath of the defeat of the acts witnessed the rise of social purity crusades focusing upon youthful sexuality as a dangerous activity. The crusades against child prostitution and the traffic in female sexual slaves, coupled with the scandals centering on "the sale of 'five pound' virgins to aristocratic old rakes" electrified public opinion, which brought about the passage of the Criminal Law Amendment of 1885, raising the age of consent for girls to sixteen. (TJW)

North America

IL
668. Barnhart, Jacqueline Baker. **The Fair But Frail: Prostitution in San Francisco, 1849-1900.** Reno, Nev.: University of Nevada Press, 1986. 136 p. (Nevada Studies in History and Political Science; No. 23). Includes bibliography and index. ISBN 0-87417-102-4.

Based on historian Barnhart's Ph.D. thesis, this book presents the engrossing story of prostitution in San Francisco from the heyday of the gold-rush years to the turn of the century. Barnhart views prostitutes as "working women, often self-employed, and in great demand in a society temporarily free of condemnation of them" (p. 2). She examines the history of their public acceptance and explains how in the years 1849 to 1851, the prostitute, who made up the bulk of San Francisco's female population, was greatly admired and respected by the miners, gamblers, speculators, and other entrepreneurs of the city. But with changes in the composition of the population and under the growing influence of Victorian cultural values, the prostitute fell from total acceptance to tolerance of her behavior to social ostracization by the end of the century.

As early as 1852, when the number of San Francisco prostitutes was about 2,000, a hierarchy was established among them, ranging from parlor-house residents, brothel prostitutes, dance hall harlots, to streetwalkers. Euphemistically they were called the *fair but frail* or *ladies in full bloom*. They met their customers in dance halls, hotels, boarding houses, and cribs built exclusively for prostitution, the latter found chiefly in the Barbary Coast. Ethnically, besides the native Anglo-Americans, the prostitutes were drawn from Mexico, other Latin American nations, Europe, and China. The elegant French prostitutes were the most highly regarded while the least respected were the Chinese, who came to San Francisco under an indenture system.

Barnhart goes on to describe the changing economic, political, social, and cultural climate affecting the development of prostitution in San Francisco. She attributes the decline of wide-open prostitution in the city to the influx of people with different moral values, forcing the activity into less noticeable channels where it now resides. (TJW)

IL
669. Benjamin, Harry, and R. E. L. Masters. **Prostitution and Morality: A Definitive Report on the Prostitute in Contemporary Society and an Analysis of the Causes and Effects of the Suppression of Prostitution.** Introduction by Walter C. Alvarez. New York: Julian Press, 1964. 495 p. Includes bibliography and index.

Almost every aspect of prostitution is covered in this in-depth study undertaken in an effort to enlighten people on the value of prostitution as a legitimate sex service and on the futile attempts to suppress it. Basing their study on both the existing literature and on personal contact with the people most involved in prostitution (judges, lawyers, police, urologists, madams, and prostitutes), Benjamin and Masters first provide thoughtful comments on the vexing problem of definition, concluding that a concise definition of prostitution remains to be formulated. They then present a brief historical account of prostitution from the earliest times to the present. They argue that prostitution is not immoral or degrading in itself, but that current punitive policies toward it are damaging and need to be modified.

Concentrating on prostitution in the United States, they ask "Why does a woman become a prostitute?" and go on to examine various psychological, economic, sociological, and other theories for an explanation, while paying attention to the advantages and disadvantages of "the life." They delineate the various types of prostitutes, how they operate, and the services they provide. They devote chapters to the customer, the pimp, the madams and brothels, and homosexual prostitution.

After examining prostitution from the economic, legal, and health standpoints, they discuss the usefulness of prostitution in medical practice, espionage, penology, the armed forces, and sex education. Benjamin and Masters state that their study clearly shows that the price society pays for the suppression of prostitution includes moral damage to the courts and police, an increase in crimes and criminals, the encouragement of homosexuality, the weakening of venereal disease control, psychosexual conflicts, and harm to the prostitute.

In the last chapter, "Sex as Service," they conclude that "prostitution, sanely dealt with, is a useful institution that could be made far more useful still" (p. 473); furthermore, prostitutes "should be freed of any feelings of guilt and inadequacy, and should be able to conduct their chosen work with safety and under decent conditions." (TJW)

IL
670. Butler, Anne M. **Daughters of Joy, Sisters of Misery: Prostitutes in the American West, 1865-90.** Urbana, Ill.: University of Illinois Press, 1985. 179 p. Includes bibliography and index. ISBN 0-252-01139-2.

Butler researched this book on frontier prostitution in the American West following the Civil War by traveling extensively throughout the Western states examining original documents and records located in courthouses, libraries, archives, historical societies and museums, and by reading widely in the relevant published and unpublished literature. The result is a well-documented social history describing "the quality of life for prostitutes who lived in various locations on the post-Civil War frontier" (p. xviii). Curiously, the prostitutes themselves left no personal accounts of their lives, so that little is known about how they felt about their work or why they chose it. Nevertheless, Butler has managed to piece together the evidence to reveal the living conditions of the frontier prostitute in scattered locations throughout the West, including San Antonio, Deadwood, Cheyenne, Laramie, Denver, Boise, Fort Union, New Mexico, and elsewhere.

Chapter 1 describes the various levels of prostitution ranging from conditions in brothels and saloons to the seamier life in cribs and on the street. Prostitution is depicted as a barely viable way of life at a time when few occupations were open to women on the frontier. Chapter 2 looks at the physical and emotional problems facing prostitutes on a daily basis, depending on where they worked, their marital status, and whether or not they had children to support. Chapter 3 explores the relationships and problems of prostitutes with customers, the desperate plight of some prostitutes that led to suicide, and the feeble efforts of churches to provide help for those desiring to abandon the profession. Only the Sisters of the Good Shepherd in St. Paul, Minnesota, provided an effective rescue operation for prostitutes. Chapters 4, 5, and 6 reveal the ties between prostitutes on the one hand and law enforcement, the legal profession, and the military on the other. Although prostitution was illegal, the efforts of the law and the military were not suppression but rather accommodation of a societal force that seemed a natural accompaniment to the pioneering endeavors of the settlers of the West.

Butler concludes that despite their peripheral status in society prostitutes participated in the institutional development of the frontier. Their contributions stemmed from their interactions with surrounding institutions: the criminal justice system, the legal profession, the military, the press, and public bodies, whose scope, attitudes, and functioning they helped to define. Illustrated with photographs of prostitutes and their abodes, this book provides glimpses of frontier life from an unusual perspective. (TJW)

IL
671.   Carmen, Arlene, and Howard Moody. **Working Women: The Subterranean World of Street Prostitution.** New York: Harper & Row, 1985. 208 p. Includes glossary. ISBN 0-06-039040-9.

Carmen and Moody describe an outreach program for prostitutes in New York City conducted by the Judson Memorial Church. Originally established in 1975 as a gynecological service for prostitutes, the Judson Prostitution Program soon expanded its scope, and members of the congregation went into the streets to acquaint themselves with the work of prostitutes. Gradually rapport was established with the street prostitutes in the Times Square area; then in 1978 Judson introduced its mobile unit as a locally available haven for girls when they needed to avoid the police, or had a need for rest, advice, emergency help, or a bit of nourishment. In time, as they earned the trust of the girls, Carmen and Moody learned how the street prostitutes lived, how they worked with their pimps, how they dealt with the johns, how they coped with the police and the courts. Out of this experience the goals of the project emerged. Already certain myths about prostitution had evaporated (e.g., the general belief that prostitutes pass along venereal diseases at an alarming rate when actually, because of the widespread use of condoms insisted upon by the prostitutes, the opposite is true).

The project focused on such goals as recognizing prostitutes as professionals who provide a service to the community. The prostitutes themselves believe that they provide men with an outlet for sexual frustrations; they look upon themselves as sex surrogates working in a sex industry already established in society. More important, the ultimate goal of the project's work became the elimination of all laws that make prostitutes criminals. Basically, three laws dealing with disorderly conduct, loitering, and soliciting are used against the girls. Carmen and Moody contend that the 1976 solicitation law aimed at prostitutes is "a fundamental denial of a woman's right to exercise her sexual autonomy" (p. 191). In addition, because enforcement of the law is ineffectual society is faced with a "glaring example of the worst cost-effective law enforcement in the nation." Approximately 20,000 prostitutes are arrested, detained, and prosecuted in New York City each year; at a cost of $2,500 each arrest, this means a total cost of $50 million a year to the public.

Carmen and Moody reflect the position of the Judson Memorial Church when they say that "one can't deal with a prostitute's pain and frustration very long without realizing that her situation is an effect caused by social relations, laws, expectations, and other norms that make her what she is" (p. 181). After examining the pros and cons of legalized prostitution, they come out for "the simple act of decriminalization—through repeal of all laws which regulate sex between consenting adults, regardless of the form it takes or whether money changes hands" (p. 201).

Although not a scholarly work, and admittedly existential, parochial, and impressionistic, *Working Women* presents the authors' strongly held position that the solution to many of the private and public problems of prostitutes will only be found in the decriminalization of their work and the development of respect for them as professional working women. (TJW)

PR,IL
672.   Connelly, Mark Thomas. **The Response to Prostitution in the Progressive Era.** Chapel Hill, N.C.: University of North Carolina Press, 1980. 261 p. Includes bibliography and index. ISBN 0-8078-1424-5.

The Progressive Era, defined as a period of profound social transformation in American society in the first two decades of the present century, witnessed an antiprostitution movement that at times reached rather shrill proportions. Perceiving the blatant prostitution of the time "as one of the grosser manifestations of industrial America," elements within the progressive generation paradoxically focused on prostitution as a symbol of what was wrong in a changing society.

This well-documented book attempts to deal with the problem of prostitution in these years by examining two underlying factors: the problem of women in industrial

America (their migration from the country into the city, their working conditions, and the alleged threat to them from pimps and white slavers); and the concern over immigration as a source of females for urban brothels. Connelly also explores the links between prostitution and venereal diseases, appraising the attitudes and approaches of American medicine with respect to venereal diseases. He describes the efforts of vice commissions in many American cities to investigate the great "social evil." The Chicago Vice Commission Report, *The Social Evil in Chicago* (1911), was especially thorough: it became the model for the reports of twenty-seven other cities, including Cleveland, Syracuse, Philadelphia, and Denver. He also describes the abundant literature dealing with the so-called white-slavery scare, and examines closely the federal legislation (White Slave Traffic Act of 1910, better known as the Mann Act) intended to control it.

Connelly also deals with the culmination of the antiprostitution movement during World War I. The antiprostitution measures (suppression of vice in training areas, venereal disease treatment, recreational programs, and moral instruction stressing the value of sexual continence and the idealization of women) taken by the military both at the training camps in the United States and later in Europe were remarkably successful in keeping venereal disease under control. These measures also reflected the beliefs of those who throughout the Progressive Era urged the repression of vice, waged unremitting war on clandestine sexual immorality among young single women, fought the spread of venereal diseases, campaigned for the destruction of urban vice districts, and promoted the value of sexual continence.

Without the war to sustain interest in the suppression of vice the antiprostitution movement in America quickly dissipated in the postwar years. Connelly attributes this collapse to "the triumph of a secular and technical approach to social problems, which supplanted the older moralistic approach" (p. 153). The Progressive Era was over. (TJW)

PR,IL

673. Gilfoyle, Timothy J. **City of Eros: New York City, Prostitution, and the Commercialization of Sex, 1790-1920.** New York: Norton, 1992. 462 p. Includes bibliography and index. ISBN 0-393-02800-3.

Gilfoyle, Assistant Professor of History at Loyola University in Chicago, has documented and supported his research on the history of prostitution in New York City from 1790 to 1920 with maps of Manhattan, tables of statistics, numerous illustrations, substantial notes, and an extensive bibliography of primary and secondary sources. His research reveals that in the period 1790 to 1820, prostitution was confined to the lower end of Manhattan, in what has been called the "Holy Ground" near St. Paul's Chapel, and in areas close to the docks and wharves. Essentially, prostitution was invisible, confined to taverns and lodgings, and primarily served visitors to the city. But from 1820 on, prostitution became commercialized and directed by economic and market forces. As Gilfoyle says, the promoters of prostitution "turned sexuality into something to be sold, displayed, and utilized to yield income. Sex became a profitmaking venture" (p. 20).

As the city grew and expanded, it "experienced a kind of sexual revolution after 1820" (p. 29). In a series of maps, Gilfoyle depicts this expansion spatially by showing the wide distribution of blocks and individual houses of prostitution from 1820 to 1859 along such key streets as Chapel Street, Broadway, and the Bowery. Because of the dynamic movement of prostitution northward, attributed to the windfall profits from real estate transactions, "the geography of prostitution . . . was fragmentary, dispersed, and short-lived" (p. 36). Gilfoyle describes sexual activity in select districts, such as Five Points, the West Side, Water and Cherry Streets, and the Hook. One George Templeton Strong labeled the prostitute-infested streets of New York a "whorearchy." The renowned Dr. William Sanger gave the primary cause of prostitution as destitution; "prostitution was mostly a function of low wages and irregular employment" (p. 59).

In post-Civil War New York, the sex industry grew in step with the city itself. Prostitution permeated most city neighborhoods from the Bowery to Harlem. Situated not only in brothels and along the streets, but also in tenement flats, hotels, music halls, and saloons, prostitution provided the customer with a variety of choices. From this geographic expansion and structure, prominent families realized enormous profits from renting houses to madams and prostitutes at inflated rates. Corrupt politicians and the police participated in this economic enterprise by demanding payoffs and bribes.

Efforts to stamp out commercial sex, such as the antebellum brothel riots, proved futile. Gilfoyle traces the shift in power from prostitutes to pimps in response to the brothel riots. He also draws attention to the vice campaigns, the efforts of Anthony Comstock, the rise of concert halls and French balls as venues for prostitution, the Raines law hotels, the syndicates, and finally, to how, after the crusades of the likes of Charles Parkhurst, Clarence Lexow, and others, and the victorious results of the work of the Committee of Fourteen, prostitution, as the prime component of the wide-open sex industry, changed in character and became an underground economy.

Gilfoyle shows that such visible reminders of prostitution as buildings became a thing of the past. "Just as the skyscraper epitomizes the new metropolis, the dearth of physical structures from a past New York exemplify a former sexuality now gone" (p. 315). (TJW)

PR,IL
674. Goldman, Marion S. **Gold Diggers & Silver Miners: Prostitution and Social Life on the Comstock Lode.** Ann Arbor, Mich.: University of Michigan Press, 1981. 214 p. (Women and Culture Series). Includes bibliography and index. ISBN 0-472-09332-0.

The height of the Comstock Lode silver rush near Gold Hill and Virginia City, Nevada, occurred between 1860 and 1880. Collectively known as the Comstock, the area accommodated some 25,000 transient and ethnically diverse people at the peak of activity in 1873. With the decline in mining beginning in 1880, only about 3,600 people resided there by 1900. In a table giving the occupations of females eighteen years of age and older at the Comstock in 1875, Goldman shows that out of a total of 3,572 females, 9 were madams and 298 prostitutes. There were more prostitutes than servants, laundresses, and seamstresses combined. Goldman examines the contrasting gender roles of respectable women and prostitutes at the Comstock in terms of chastity, courtship, marriage, homemaking, leisure-time activity, and work.

She also provides a general overview of prostitution in the Comstock with information about the local argot, residential patterns, social customs, and data concerning the age, ethnicity and race, and marital status of prostitutes. She then examines the stratification of prostitutes, identifying five general groups: madams; elite prostitutes, or adventuresses; the middle rank of women living alone in cottages and working in melodeons, saloons, or in the best brothels; working women who labored alone in small brothels, or in one- or two-women bawdy saloons; and prostitutes of the lowest order, outcast slatterns and Chinese slaves. In the irregular marketplace of prostitution, the customers remained anonymous; their relationships with prostitutes were brief and impersonal. Other men involved in Comstock prostitution were the pimps, profiteers (owners of buildings, etc.), saloonkeepers, and lawmen.

Recognizing that prostitution "is so compelling a topic because it combines nothing more and nothing less than the most basic elements of life—work and sexuality" and that "prostitution sex and work are one" (p. 152), Goldman concludes by sketching some theoretical considerations about prostitution. She proposes a sociological definition of prostitution; reveals through the Comstock experience the depth and scope of the relationship between prostitutes and social structure; and relates prostitution to individual psychosexual development and the material forces determining the supply of sellers and buyers of sex.

A map of Storey County, Nevada; a plan of Virginia City; and pictures of prominent prostitutes illustrate this study. Included also is an appendix listing 137 prostitutes by name and address. (TJW)

PR,IL
675. Hill, Marilynn Wood. **Their Sisters' Keepers: Prostitution in New York City, 1830-1870.** Berkeley, Calif.: University of California Press, 1993. 434 p. Includes bibliography and index. ISBN 0-520-07834-9.

Hill, a visiting scholar at the Schlesinger Library at Harvard-Radcliffe, has written an intimate study of the life and work of prostitutes in New York City between 1830 and 1870. Using primary source materials from newspapers and tax and court records to brothel guidebooks and personal correspondence, she illuminates the private as well as public lives of this group of women. The study reveals that in spite of the limited economic, social, and legal options available to women at the time, the New York prostitute was able to create a life for herself that, although fraught with difficulties, was open to possibilities. Without neglecting the dangers and hardships of prostitution that traditional histories emphasize, this study also offers an analysis of the profession's positive attractions. New York prostitution was at a unique juncture in its history during the middle decades of the nineteenth century because some of the women involved were able to establish a significant degree of control over the business, and because the more fortunate ones were able to reap meaningful economic rewards.

By the 1830s, prostitution in New York was no longer hidden in back streets and the dock areas but was visible throughout the city. Although officially outside the law, it was well integrated into the city's urban life, and in spite of the discrimination and legal harassment prostitutes suffered, they repeatedly asserted their rights as citizens before the police and courts to protect themselves and their property. Nineteenth-century tax records reveal that not only might a woman improve her economic situation through prostitution, but the more long-term career-oriented prostitutes networked with each other as businesswomen to take advantage of the possibilities of their marketplace. By the 1870s, the city's political machine gained control of the trade, thus circumscribing both the occupational independence of New York's prostitutes and a female-managed opportunity-structure that had existed for several decades.

In exploring the private as well as public aspects of prostitutes' lives, Hill demonstrates that, despite a wide range of personal motives, most nineteenth-century women chose prostitution from the limited occupational options available because they wished to provide as well as possible for themselves, their children, and other loved ones. In addition to economic rewards unavailable in other occupations, prostitution offered social freedoms that traditional employment and familial restrictions did not allow. Although most people judged the profession unrespectable, this status was not unredeemable: many moved on to other, respectable occupations, or to marriage. Hill emphasizes the common concerns prostitutes shared with women outside the profession. Like other nineteenth-century women, they depended on family and friendship networks to help them cope with the difficulties of daily life. As mothers, sisters, daughters, wives, and laborers, trapped by circumstances, they sought a way to create a life and work culture for themselves and those they cared about.

The book includes numerous statistical tables and illustrations as well as extensive notes and bibliographical sources that demonstrate the depth of the research. (Author)

PR,IL
676. Reynolds, Helen. **The Economics of Prostitution.** Springfield, Ill.: Charles C. Thomas, 1986. 206 p. Includes bibliography and index. ISBN 0-398-05161-5.

Reynolds, visiting scholar at the Institute of Criminology, Cambridge University, uses four models of legal and political constraints to describe and analyze the environments of prostitution in the United States. In these models the major common environmental elements are identified: (1) the written laws, statutes, and codes affecting prostitution; (2) the degree to which the police enforce the laws; and (3) community attitudes toward prostitution and law enforcement. Obviously, these elements vary from community to community; their combination determines what transpires in a community's prostitution market.

Reynolds identifies certain communities as close but not rigid exemplars of these models: San Francisco for the Laissez Faire Model; the brothels of Nevada as a Regulation Model; Boston's Combat Zone as a Zoning Model; and two neighborhoods in Dallas for the Control Model. In each of the chosen communities the environmental variables of prostitution are examined: the state and local statutes affecting prostitution; the economic incentives (high earnings, tips, tax-free income) and disincentives (fees, payoffs, clothing costs, pimps); the types of prostitutes and services encountered; the role of pimps; the location (on maps) of the activities in question; and other special factors, such as police corruption, organized crime, and community reaction.

From her study, Reynolds draws five fundamental conclusions about prostitution markets: "1. Prostitution will continue to exist, indeed thrive, even if it is prohibited by law. 2. Citizens, lawmakers, and law enforcers can, to some extent, set limits on the kinds of prostitution activities that take place in their community. 3. Within whatever limits apply, prostitution will still exist, but its character and outward appearance will be qualified by those limits. 4. The models presented in this book present a useful way of thinking about the varieties of legal environments and prostitution markets in the United States today. 5. Current public policies constituting the prohibition of prostitution should be changed for the good of society itself" (p. 181).

After reviewing what is inherently wrong morally, socially, and legally with prostitution and what is good sexually and economically about prostitution, Reynolds presents four suggestions for "changes in public policy that will decrease the social costs and increase the social benefits of prostitution." These relate to decriminalization of prostitution, reassignment of police priorities, penalties for prostitution, and neighborhood measures to exclude prostitution. (TJW)

IL

677. Rose, Al. **Storyville, New Orleans: Being an Authentic Illustrated Account of the Notorious Red-Light District.** Tuscaloosa, Ala.: University of Alabama Press, 1988. 225 p. Includes bibliographic notes and index. Originally published in 1974. ISBN 0-8173-4403-9.

In New Orleans between 1898 and 1917 there flourished a legally established red-light district called Storyville. It got its name from Alderman Sidney Story who wrote the legislation creating the district just outside the French Quarter. Rose tells the story of Storyville by tracing the history of prostitution in Louisiana back to the arrival of women under royal French auspices in the early eighteenth century. The institution flourished, especially after the American accession to power in 1803 when Mississippi River commerce increased, bringing to New Orleans rivermen, gamblers, prostitutes, and soon thereafter, soldiers. The social and economic impact of prostitution offended the law-abiding, so New Orleans in 1857 passed an ordinance to license and tax the profession. Unfortunately, the ordinance did not pass its first legal test. By the late nineteenth century prostitution and its attendant evils had created for the inhabitants of the city an intolerable moral situation. Alderman Story came up with legislation that specified "a certain district outside of which it will be unlawful for prostitution to be carried on." The ordinance was enacted on July 6, 1897, became effective on January 1, 1899, and prevailed until February 7, 1917, when open prostitution was banned within five miles of any United States military installation by order of the Secretary of War and the Secretary of the Navy.

Rose states that his purpose in undertaking this study was to paint a vivid picture of Storyville from various perspectives: historical, legal, social, and cultural. Relying on original source materials—pictures, newspaper accounts, personal interviews, and miscellaneous legal and social documents—Rose devotes separate chapters to such topics as the experiences of well-known madams, prostitutes, and politicians; a walking tour of Basin Street with its saloons, cabarets, brothels, and the like; the music and jazz musicians, mainly black, that gave Storyville its luster; the press, especially those newspapers, *The Mascot* and the *Sunday Sun*, which chronicled the doings of the demimonde; and seven taped personal accounts of survivors of Storyville who tell their sometimes shocking stories in stark detail.

In its heydey Storyville, the first legally established prostitution district in the United States, employed some 2,000 prostitutes, many of whom were black and segregated, working in 230 houses, cabarets, houses of assignation, and cribs. The overall result of the closure of Storyville was the dispersal of vice throughout New Orleans, which weakened control of the activity.

The appendixes to this fully illustrated book include copies of early legislation pertaining to prostitution in New Orleans, a directory of Storyville's jazz musicians, and a typical issue of the *Sunday Sun* for February 25, 1906. (TJW)

PO
678. Sheehy, Gail. **Hustling: Prostitution in Our Wide-open Society.** New York: Dell, 1974. 254 p. ISBN 0-440-13800-0.

Based on two years of street research in the early 1970s, *Hustling* is a systematic exposé of prostitution in New York City. Journalist Sheehy (*Passages*, 1976; *Pathfinders*, 1981) explains her study as curiosity about the "boom" in prostitution resulting from a negative male reaction to the liberated woman. According to Sheehy the entire enterprise of prostitution, aside from satisfying the sexual needs of lonely men, seems to be financial profit for a range of people and institutions, including street hookers, pimps, predatory street bums, hotel operators, madams, lawyers, politicians, landlords, and organized criminal factions. She estimates that in the United States, the earnings from 200,000 to 250,000 prostitutes amount to some $7.9 billion annually. Those who profit least from the system are the prostitutes themselves who, driven by dreams of upward mobility, are "old at thirty, bitter, and broke."

The bulk of her book, based primarily but not exclusively on interviews with street people, consists of a number of stories she wrote for the *New York* magazine, portraying different rungs of the prostitution ladder from the hooker to the courtesan. These include "Redpants and Sugarman," the poignant tale of a hooker and her pimp; "Minnesota Marsha," an account of how a lovely Polish girl from Minneapolis got swept up into prostitution; and "The Landlords of Hell's Bedroom," which exposed the hidden profiteers of prostitution. Sheehy does not reveal any remedies for prostitution. She does, however, comment resignedly on the overall situation by saying that only in America is the prostitute punished for prostitution per se and that little effort is being made either to tackle the real profiteers or to rehabilitate the prostitute. (TJW)

PR,IL
679. Vice Commission of Chicago. **The Social Evil in Chicago: A Study of Existing Conditions.** With recommendations by the Vice Commission of Chicago. Chicago: Vice Commission of Chicago, 1911. 399 p. Includes index.

Asked by a federation of churches to undertake a study of the "social evil" (prostitution) in Chicago, the mayor established the Vice Commission of Chicago, which was then authorized on June 27, 1910 by the City Council to undertake and produce a study of vice conditions in the city. Under the direction of a thirty-member Commission, the chairman appointed ten subcommittees to systematically study these conditions. George J. Kneeland became principal investigator. Numerous meetings were held and field investigations carried out. After a little over nine months, on April 5, 1911, the Commission submitted its report to the mayor and City Council.

The report consists of a detailed outline of the study with questions, an introduction and summary, a proposed ordinance creating a Morals Commission of the City of Chicago, and a long list of recommendations addressed to federal, state, county, and city officials; parents; organizations; and the press. In seven chapters the Commission addresses the main facets of the problem: the existing conditions in the city, the social evil and the saloon, the police, sources of supply of prostitutes, child protection and education, rescue and reform, and the medical aspects of prostitution. Appendixes include the revised statutes of Illinois and ordinances of the City of Chicago relevant to prostitution, statistical tables, and exhibits.

The goal of the Commission was the immediate repression and ultimate elimination of prostitution in the limits of the city of Chicago. The study showed prostitution in Chicago to be a commercialized business "of large proportions with tremendous profits of more than Fifteen Million Dollars per year, controlled largely by men, not women" (p. 32). Furthermore, present laws affecting prostitution were not enforced, and certain sections of the city had become restricted districts. The number of prostitutes in the city was estimated to be over 5,000, young women who worked out of assignation houses, saloons, brothels, and hotels. Generally these were immigrant women, women from broken families, and girls from rural areas.

The Commission found that among the causes that influenced girls and women to enter upon a life of prostitution were lack of ethical teaching and religious instruction, the economic stress of industrial life on unskilled workers, unhappy home conditions, careless and ignorant parents, love of ease and luxury, the craving for excitement and change, and ignorance of hygiene. Many other aspects of prostitution are analyzed in this groundbreaking study that became the model for similar studies of prostitution in municipalities across the country. (TJW)

PR,IL
680. Winick, Charles, and Paul M. Kinsie. **The Lively Commerce: Prostitution in the United States.** Chicago: Quadrangle Books, 1971. 320 p. Includes bibliographic references and index.

For the most part this book is based on over 2,000 interviews conducted by Winick and Kinsie or their assistants over a ten-year period in the United States with "all elements in the social system of prostitution and of those in the community who attempt to cope with it" (p. v). Winick, a professor of Sociology at the City University of New York, and Kinsie, a longtime student of the subject and one-time director for the League of Nations Committee on Experts for the Traffic in Women and Children, explore legal, social, and moral perspectives of prostitution in chapter I; chapters II-V explore the attitudes, behavior, and practices of the chief actors in the social system of prostitution: the prostitute, the madam, the pimp, and the bit players (taxi drivers, bellboys, and other go-betweens). How prostitutes have plied their trade in the major cities of the United States in the first half of the century is the subject of chapter VI, which carefully examines the techniques and procedures practiced in different urban settings (red-light districts, brothels, massage parlors, taxi-dance halls, street walking, hotels and motels, bars, and call houses). Winick and Kinsie examine the attitudes of clients in chapter VII. In chapters VIII-X they consider the problem of prostitution in relation to the law, the military, and international control. In a final chapter, "The Future," they identify those forces in American society contributing to a possible increase in prostitution and to those countervailing trends that are likely to cause a decrease in the institution. Finally, they speak hopefully for an enlightened attitude and more rreasonable public policy toward the long-standing social problem of prostitution. (TJW)

Latin America & the Caribbean

PR,IL
681. Guy, Donna J. **Sex & Danger in Buenos Aires: Prostitution, Family, and Nation in Argentina.** Lincoln, Neb.: University of Nebraska Press, 1991. 260 p. (Engendering Latin America: A Series). Includes bibliography and index. ISBN 0-8032-2139-8.

This in-depth study of prostitution in Buenos Aires and, by extension, Argentina from the middle of the nineteenth century to the waning days of the rule of Juan Peron, embraces many aspects of the subject. It deals with legal ordinances, white slavery, bordellos, venereal disease, and the tango. It also relates prostitution to broader topics, such as politics, the Catholic Church, the family, patriarchy, urban growth, employment, and the image of Argentina generally.

Argentina, with a Catholic heritage, did not find prostitution especially repugnant; the church acknowledged it philosophically, citing St. Augustine and St. Thomas Aquinas who considered it a necessary evil. To them prostitution was "a sewer whose removal would pollute the palace." Reformers, on the other hand, preached sexual self-control, believing that "female prostitution must be suppressed" (p. 13).

Newly established in 1853, Argentina attracted European immigrants, including prostitutes. Guy notes that at the end of the nineteenth century Argentina had the reputation "as the port of missing women," attributable primarily to the work of white slavers, Jews, who rounded up European Jewish girls with promises of marriage in Argentina and elsewhere. The efforts of these Jewish pimps were widespread in the years between 1870 and World War I; they took advantage of pogroms, poverty, and unemployment in Eastern Europe to build a distribution network of white slavery. Guy tells this story in considerable detail, including the efforts of Jewish organizations and international bodies to combat the evil traffic.

In 1875 the Buenos Aires municipal authorities legalized prostitution, which had never been a criminal offense, although earlier, unemployment and poverty were deemed criminal and punishable by law. Municipal control of prostitutes became necessary in the interest of public order. Bordellos were established; prostitutes were registered, taxed, and given regular medical checks. Moreover, clandestine prostitution flourished. By 1889, 2,007 prostitutes registered for the first time, and the *sifilicomio*, a hospital dedicated solely to the treatment of venereal disease among prostitutes opened. The new system of legalized prostitution in Buenos Aires took on a structural resemblance to its counterparts in Europe.

Guy traces the many periodic efforts to reform bordello ordinances. As a result of these changes bordellos opened and closed, prostitutes moved to practice their trade in cabarets, or entered the clandestine world of prostitution. Following a period of compromise after 1919, municipally regulated prostitution in Buenos Aires was abolished in 1934. This came about as the result of a program supported by the socialists advocating "the abolition of legalized prostitution, the formation of a system of free medical treatment for all venereal disease patients, absolute divorce, reform of paternity laws, improved working conditions for mothers and children, sex education in primary and secondary schools, and the closing of obscene forms of entertainment" (p. 97).

Guy points out that, according to the 1871 civil code, "the role of good women was to marry and bear future generations. Mothers and children in turn were to obey the male patriarch who would select their occupations" (p. 3). She states that many Argentine men believed that "all independent working women essentially destroyed male authority and female life" (p. 135). Working women, such as waitresses, should withdraw from the labor force or else be equated with whores. Under the rule of Juan Peron, a renewed attempt was made to legalize prostitution in the military and civilian sectors of the Argentine economy. His decree of December 30, 1954, reestablishing the old system, had as its purpose "to defend family, society, and nation through medically supervised municipal bordellos" (p. 181). It was a reaction against blatant homosexuality, drunkenness, and tango dancing, which, according to the homophobic Peronists, were endangering the lives of men. However, Peron was ousted in 1955; his "overthrow marked the definitive end of legalized prostitution and municipally regulated bordellos in Argentina" (p. 207). (TJW)

12
Social and Cultural Aspects of Human Sexuality

GENDER ROLES AND CONCEPTUALIZATION OF THE SEXES

(For related material see also entries 256, 566, 962, 980, 1053, 1054)

PR
682. Adler, Lenore Loeb, ed. **International Handbook on Gender Roles.** Westport, Conn.: Greenwood Press, 1993. 525 p. Includes bibliography and index. ISBN 0-313-28336-2.

Adler, Professor of Psychology and Director of the Institute for Cross-Cultural and Cross-Ethnic Studies at Molloy College, has focused much of her career on gender roles and cross-cultural psychology; among her fourteen books are *Women in Cross-Cultural Perspective* (1991), *Cross-Cultural Research in Human Development* (1989), and *Cross-Cultural Topics in Psychology* (in press). All of the fifty-six contributors, most of whom are women and psychologists, lived and worked in the countries about which they have written. One of the main goals of this reference work is "to gain greater insight into people's customs and manners, while providing the opportunity to achieve a better understanding of men's and women's gender roles" (p. xxii). In addition, as Nancy Felipe Russo says in the foreword, "It is hoped that this handbook will stimulate looking beyond cultural and national boundaries and encourage increased collaboration among scholars across cultures and countries" (p. xiv).

Each of the thirty-one chapters focuses on gender roles in particular, representative countries from six continents, e.g., Australia, Finland, India, Japan, Mexico, New Zealand, Portugal, Tanzania, and the United States. Chapters are organized alphabetically by country. To facilitate the comparison of men's and women's roles in various ecological settings, each of the chapters follows the same format: (1) introduction; (2) overview; (3) comparisons of gender roles during phases (infancy, early childhood, school years, young adulthood, adulthood, old age) of the life cycles of men and women; (4) summary and conclusions; and (5) references. Readers can compare information about similar topics across different countries by drawing on information from the same sections in different chapters; or, they can compare gender roles in different aspects of the life cycle by comparing specific sections within the chapters.

In the introduction, Adler notes that differences between countries are often easier to see than the similarities—the prevalence of traditional customs in rural areas, similar effects of modernization (e.g., monogamy in modern and Westernized countries, a lessened role for matchmakers, the continued traditional role of women as caretakers of the household and children), the high status of men. Comparisons of such areas as men's and women's attitudes, the relative workloads of men and women, adjustments in old age, the types of laws in effect to ensure equality of roles, and educational opportunities for the genders allow readers to assess the contemporary situation of the genders worldwide. Adler concludes that "women in the modern world aspire to equality with men, yet truly androgynous gender roles are still beyond reach, since the traditional sex stereotypes still prevail" (p. xix). (SGF)

IL

683. Allgeier, Elizabeth Rice, and Naomi B. McCormick, eds. **Changing Boundaries: Gender Roles and Sexual Behavior.** Palo Alto, Calif.: Mayfield, 1983. 347 p. Includes bibliography, index, and glossary. ISBN 0-87484-536-X.

Allgeier, Professor of Psychology at Bowling Green State University who co-authored the text *Sexual Interactions* (D. C. Heath and Co., 1984) and is on the board of the Society for the Scientific Study of Sex, teams up with McCormick, who is on the faculty of the psychology department at the State University of New York at Plattsburgh and is director of the Psychological Services Clinic there, to edit a volume of papers that explores how changing gender roles affect how satisfied men and women feel about their relationships and themselves. Overall, their goal is to "synthesize what is known about the relationship of gender roles, differences, and similarities with information about sexual attitudes and experiences" (p. ix). They assume that gender roles establish some expectations for how to be sexual and that social rules about masculinity and femininity define boundaries for expected sexual behavior.

The essays of the seventeen contributors, most of whom are psychologists who teach at universities, are clustered into two parts. Part 1, "Developmental Perspective," focuses on gender role socialization through the life cycle and its effect on sexual expression. Developmental changes in gender role socialization and sexuality during childhood, youth, and young adulthood demonstrate that the young adhere to relatively strict rules of gender role and sexual behavior. A much greater set of options and more flexible guidelines for behavior are open to older adults. Specific topics in this part include childhood sexual socialization, becoming sexual in adolescence, courtship, gender role and sexual response, male and female expectations of love and sex, and sex in the second half of life.

Part 2, "Contemporary Perspectives," focuses on the impact of social change on gender roles and sexual behavior. Issues discussed include alterations in gender roles in response to modern contraceptive technology; sex in the workplace; being single; gay and lesbian lifestyles; and sexual violence and erotica.

In the epilogue, Allgeier and McCormick conclude that a current trend toward more variation in gender roles may mean that individual needs, rather than strict gender roles, will structure sexual expression in the future. (SGF)

IL

684. Archer, John, and Barbara Lloyd. **Sex and Gender.** Cambridge, England: Cambridge University Press, 1985. 355 p. Includes bibliography and indexes. ISBN 0-521-31921-8.

Using the perspective of attribution theory, which investigates human behavior in terms of commonsense explanations of their causes and effects, Archer and Lloyd, both psychologists, concentrate on describing the complex attributes of gender. They use *gender* to refer to male/female distinctions based on social criteria, while *sex* is reserved for those based on biological criteria.

The issues raised in the first two chapters set the tone for the overview and evaluation of psychological research on gender that follows. Archer and Lloyd argue that commonsense reasoning about differences between men and women (e.g., that men and women are fundamentally different) has influenced psychological research on gender differences, first, by emphasizing difference and, second, by guiding the description, analysis, and explanation of differences. For example, researchers may rely on common-sense ideas to define concepts in psychometric or demographic research.

The remainder of the book is a detailed examination of research on specific topics relevant to an adequate understanding of sex and gender. One chapter focuses on physical differences between the sexes (their evolutionary origin, their development in boys and girls, their cultural significance) while another looks at the human sexual experience from the point of view of psychobiology, psychoanalysis, and sociology. A host of scientific studies assess the validity of popular stereotypes that categorize men as more aggressive, violent, powerful, and fearless than women and those that characterize women as more anxious, fearful, moody, and depressed than men. Archer and Lloyd also evaluate the evidence presented to explain why the family, particularly responsibility for child care, has been regarded as a woman's domain and why a man's domain is likely to include occupation of the most prestigious and highly valued positions in the world of work. Their discussion also includes an examination of why characteristics such as nurturance and attachment are associated with women while intelligence and achievement are associated with men.

In summing up their conclusions, they go beyond everyday notions of nature/nurture to present a more complex, interactionist view of the development of male/female differences, for example, perspectives that consider prenatal hormones and the brain, the imitation of role models, and developmental pathways. They end with the suggestion that an emphasis on the social construction of gender opens the door for change in a variety of directions, particularly when viewed within the framework of intergroup relations. (SGF)

IL
685. Beauvoir, Simone de. **The Second Sex.** Translated and edited by H. M. Parshley. New York: Knopf, 1964. 732 p. Originally published in France in 1949 under the title *Le Deuxième Sexe.* Includes index.

This classic text of the feminist movement is built on existentialist philosophy and the belief that, since ancient times, women have been forced to occupy a secondary position in a primarily masculine world. As Beauvoir writes in the introduction, "humanity is male and man defines woman not in herself but as relative to him." The work is divided into two parts. Book 1 covers the definition of woman, her social and economic history, and myths and images. In order to define woman, it is necessary to view the female organism within the society. Woman is trapped between the role of object or "Other" assigned her by society and her desire for liberty and transcendence. She has been confined to a secondary position in society since primitive times, primarily because of her passive submission to her biological fate. Religion, especially Judeo-Christian tradition, treats her as both evil and holy and mandates masculine superiority and control. The patriarchal society gives children an image of male superiority that leads girls to believe in their natural inferiority. Various myths and images such as virgin, coquette, wife, mistress, sorceress, Eve, and Mary Magdelene demonstrate ways man views woman. These images are examined in works by five male authors: Montherlant, D. H. Lawrence, Claudel, Breton, and Stendhal.

Book 2 treats woman's life in the modern world. Woman is taught from childhood to accept her passive, inferior role. Any natural rebellion is overcome when menstruation confirms her destiny. The young woman desires intimacy and dreams of love, but her first experience of intercourse is usually traumatic and disappointing. Whether in rape or marriage, intercourse involves physical penetration and therefore is a violation. Lesbianism allows a woman to reconcile an active, independent personality and her sexual role; however, the lesbian may feel that she has lost her femininity without gaining the virility she seeks. In marriage, woman gains an identity through her husband, but becomes his vassal. Sex in marriage is a service owed by the wife to the husband and sexual love, if initially present, soon disappears. The wife does no work directly useful to society and is therefore recognized as a parasite. Her biological destiny of continuing the species, though necessary, is unrewarding, and her children suffer from her bitterness and frustration. The menopause presents woman with the prospect of years of useless life ahead and may precipitate physical and emotional crises before a cynical serenity is reached. Woman's social and economic situation leads to ambiguous feelings toward her life, man, and her body. She may seek to justify her existence through religious mysticism, self-love, or devotion to a man, but these are vain pursuits of her true being. It is only through independent, meaningful, productive activity that woman can affirm her status as subject rather than object, and such activity will only be possible in a socialist world. (SDH)

IL
686. Brooks-Gunn, Jeanne, and Wendy Schempp Matthews. **He & She: How Children Develop Their Sex-Role Identity.** Englewood Cliffs, N.J.: Prentice-Hall, 1979. 388 p. Includes bibliography and index. ISBN 0-13-384388-2.

Brooks-Gunn is Associate Director of the Institute for the Study of Exceptional Children and a professor of clinical pediatric psychology at Columbia University; Matthews is a child psychologist and a consultant for the Training Institute for Sex Desegregation of the Public Schools at Rutgers University. They have combined their expertise to produce an easy-to-read, clearly presented developmental account of sex-role socialization, which is oriented toward parents, educators, nurses, child-care workers, and child development students.

The authors use Block's definition of sex roles as "a constellation of qualities an individual understands to characterize males and females in his [or her] culture" (p. 3). Sex role identity, one aspect of self-identity, is the product of culturally based sex roles, socialization practices, and personal beliefs and attitudes. While biology channels the sequence of prenatal events that produce gender identity (i.e., biological sex or the sex of rearing) of the child, it does not determine the child's sex-role identity. Rather, social, cultural, and psychological factors account for a great deal of its development. The relative roles of these factors are discussed in a chapter that evaluates three major theories of sex-role development: identification, social learning, and cognitive developmental. Another chapter points out their general contribution to sex-role behavior. The core of the book discusses the relevance of these factors and theoretical formulations to each developmental period: infancy (origin of sex roles), early childhood (emergence of sex roles), middle childhood (consolidation of sex roles), pubescence (coming of age and sex roles), and adolescence (toward an adult sex role). For each period, Brooks-Gunn and Matthews present empirical evidence about differences between boys and girls, explain the influence of sex-role mediators (e.g., school, parents, media, peers), and describe the child's active and changing perception of sex roles. They conclude that children are more alike than different and are subject to a multiplicity of influences on their sex-role identity. "While the world continues to divide them into he and she, we must remember that they are individuals first" (p. 299). (SGF)

IL
687. Cox, Sue, ed. **Female Psychology: The Emerging Self.** 2nd ed. New York: St. Martin's Press, 1981. 494 p. Includes bibliography. ISBN 0-3122-8742-9.

Using quotations, cartoons, poetry, and artwork to enhance the text, this popular anthology goes beyond a psychology of white, middle-class, heterosexual women. Twenty-seven articles—many new to this edition—are gathered in seven thematic sections: "Biological and Cultural Perspectives"; "Psychological Sex Differences"; "Ethnic Diversity of Female Experience" (including black, Asian-American, Chicana, and Native American women); "Psychological Oppression"; "Relationships: Sexuality and Intimacy"; "Mental Illness or Social Problem?"; and "Toward Change and Liberation." Such scholars as Eleanor Emmons Maccoby, Carol Nagy Jacklin, Jeanne H. Block, Nancy Henley, Jo Freeman, Nancy Felipe Russo, and Phyllis Chesler contribute to the volume. Cox provides a substantial introduction and briefer introductions to each section. Another valuable reader for the undergraduate psychology classroom is Juanita H. Williams's *Psychology of Women: Selected Readings* (2nd ed. New York: Norton, 1985), designed to accompany Williams's introductory text, *Psychology of Women: Behavior in a Biosocial Context* (2nd ed. New York: Norton, 1983). (**Women's Studies,** 1987)

PR,IL,PO
688. Ehrenreich, Barbara. **The Hearts of Men: American Dreams and the Flight from Commitment.** New York: Anchor, 1984. 206 p. Includes bibliographic notes and index. ISBN 0-385-17615-5.

According to Ehrenreich, the asymmetry of male and female economic needs in the family has shaped the "battle of the sexes" and underlies central themes in men's liberation, feminism, antifeminism, and the new right—marriage, monogamy, sexual and reproductive freedom, homosexuality, and gender autonomy. "This book is about the ideology that shaped the breadwinner ethic and how that ideology collapsed, as a pervasive set of expectations, just the last thirty years" (p. 11).

Ehrenreich begins with an analysis of the traditional companionate marriage, characterized by the male as the breadwinner and the female as the homemaker. In the 1950s a man was supposed to grow up, marry, and support his wife and children. Deviants from this role were regarded as not fully adult, as irresponsible, or as possibly homosexual.

The rest of the book chronicles and analyzes the changes that eroded traditional expectations about men and women's roles. It is a story of male revolt against the breadwinner role. In the 1950s, "grey flannel dissidents" lamented their male discontent as "conformity" and malaise at work; home was more of a burden. *Playboy* became a forum for male rebellion against sharing earnings in a traditional marriage. Hefner's magazine articulated the message that men could be single and use wealth as a means for personal pleasure—to buy consumer goods and attract women for a sexual relationship without a long-term commitment. The focus on sex legitimized the playboy's deviance; " ... a playboy didn't have to be a husband to be a man" (p. 51).

Beatniks rejected both jobs and marriage, and medical research suggested that the stress of the male role could lead to coronary heart failure. Psychology emphasized growth rather than conformity. Maslow's self-actualization involved exploration in work, in sex, and at home. Marriage was viewed as financially burdensome and sexually repressive. The androgynous ideal of the 1960s counter-culture tapped men's and women's desires for more financial and sexual flexibility.

By the 1970s, the ideology of male liberation articulated past male discontent. A break from the breadwinner role was held up as liberal, middle-class reform with rewards of more authentic male/female relationships, better sex, less guilt, and more personal growth. The concurrent development of a gay culture and identity removed the sanction of accusations of homosexuality against men who chose not to marry or share their wages with women. Feminists and male liberationists converged in their desires to see women earn an independent wage. However, antifeminists and the new right opposed this trend on the grounds that it undermines the family by legitimizing men's freedom to forego supporting the family.

Ehrenreich concludes that "there is no going back to the companionate family"; it fosters sexism, sexual manipulation, and dependence of women. Rather, women need to be paid better wages; receive social support for independent wage-earning; and cooperate with men in forming a new human family, where both men and women have access to good wages, sexual variety, and respect. (SGF)

PO

689. Ehrenreich, Barbara, Elizabeth Hess, and Gloria Jacobs. **Re-making Love: The Feminization of Sex.** Garden City, N.Y.: Anchor Press/Doubleday, 1986. 228 p. ISBN 0-385-18498-0.

In *Re-making Love*, the authors argue that there has been a sexual revolution in attitudes that was initiated by women, not men. They document the revolution by showing how changes have occurred in sexual behavior and the meaning of sex in our lives. They trace the development of the revolution from its antecedents (the teenage response to Frank Sinatra and Elvis Presley) through the early 1960s to the present. The uncontrolled response of American girls in the early 1960s to the performances of the Beatles signaled one of the first dramatic expressions of the sexual revolution. The authors contend that the girls viewed the Beatles as sex objects and themselves as pursuers, a major departure from the repressive norms of the 1950s. They then focus upon other factors that contributed to the revolution: the writings of Betty Friedan and Helen Gurley Brown, the sexy novels of Jacqueline Susann and others, the sex surveys of women's magazines (*Redbook, Cosmopolitan*) and other investigators, and the sex research of Masters and

Johnson, which led to widespread concern about the nature of that elusive phenomenon, the orgasm.

They also identify the then prevailing social conditions of women: sexual discontent within traditional marriage, isolation and conformity in suburbia, and the concentration of young, single women in cities. In addition, certain medical advances of the day, especially the contraceptive pill, had an impact on female sexuality. According to the authors, the broader feminist movement, which emerged in 1968, owes its genesis to the women's sexual revolution. One of the major issues today is the role of the sexual revolution within the women's liberation movement.

Measured and validated by the "vast increase in women's extra- and premarital experience that occurred in the sixties and seventies," the sexual revolution continued unabated into the 1980s. An information explosion in the literature of human sexuality occurred; the burgeoning sex therapy industry prospered; and an awakening of the possibilities, or joy, of sex, transpired. Seemingly, women were beginning to enjoy sex as much as men.

Commercial manifestations of the women's sexual revolution in the 1980s are examined: the marketing of sex paraphernalia exclusively for women, the prevalence of male strip joints, the availability of women's sex magazines, pornography tailor-made for women, and S/M viewed as a sexual option for women. Also described is the impact of current sexual values on religious fundamentalism. Such figures as Marabel Morgan, author of *Total Woman* and *Total Joy*, who advocate sexual adventures within the bonds of marriage, have stirred up a great deal of controversy in the fundamentalist communities about the role of women.

Although statistics and other evidence point to a continuation of the women's sexual revolution in the 1980s, the authors have noted a negative reaction to the sexual revolution from a number of quarters in America, which threatens to undo the changes of the past. (TJW)

IL

690. Filene, Peter Gabriel. **Him/Her/Self: Sex Roles in Modern America.** Baltimore: Johns Hopkins University Press, 1986. 323 p. Includes bibliographic notes and index. ISBN 0-8018-2893-7.

Sex roles define the behavior expected of an individual as a member of his or her gender. Filene's book traces the history and changes in male and female sex roles in America since 1890. It is an attempt to understand "how and why these roles have been prescribed and thereby to learn how men and women might go beyond 'masculine' and 'feminine' into roles that exclude as little as possible of their personalities" (p. xv).

At the end of the nineteenth century, Americans still taught the ideal Victorian sex roles. In reality, the ideals did not exist and were getting more difficult to support. As women, longing for individual freedom, began organizing for the suffrage battle, men faced their own difficulties in balancing between aggression and chivalry and finding an appropriate arena for "manly" accomplishment in an increasingly civilized society. This male conflict has continued through the years since the turn of the century. The two World Wars and the Depression provided new opportunities for women, but prejudices remained and women made little advancement toward equality. In the 1950s, although female employment continued to rise, the ideal life remained marriage, home, children, and security. Men found their jobs increasing calling for "feminine" attributes such as personal relation skills, appeasement and negotiation, rather than "manly" aggression and risk-taking. Home life echoed this with the sharing of housework, child care, and sexual satisfaction. Still, the stereotypes of breadwinner and housewife governed individual thought and behavior. The dichotomy between role and reality resulted in both internal and interpersonal conflicts that were seldom understood. It was the children who came of age in the 1960s who realized the limitations of existing sex roles and were able to break out of the stereotypes. The political movements of the sixties led directly to the new women's movement and its revolutionary class, cultural, and legislative changes. Men associated with activist women were also forced to reconsider and redefine their own roles. Those who did so faced peer resistance and personal anxiety even as they found greater self-fulfillment. Despite the gains made since the 1960s, extensive cultural and personal changes are required before new sex roles that allow full individual realization can be generally accepted.

In the latest edition of *Him/Her/Self*, Filene gives more attention to the antifeminists at the end of the century as well as in the 1970s, pointing out that "equalization has threatened traditionalists' need for social order"; the satisfaction women find in domesticity; the women's movement in the 1960s and 1970s, emphasizing the part played by middle-aged professional women and the National Organization for Women (NOW). In the interest of further progress in the women's movement, Filene recommends (1) reduced discriminization against women, and (2) changes in attitude and behavior of men toward women and also toward themselves. (SDH/TJW)

IL

691. Friedan, Betty. **The Feminine Mystique.** New York: Norton, 1963. 378 p. Includes bibliographic notes and index.

This work is a response to Friedan's realization that a discrepancy exists in America between the reality of life for women and the image to which they are trying to conform. Friedan's research and experience led to her study of "the problem that has no name," a general, unfocused feeling of dissatisfaction with life. Despite the rights and freedom won by the feminists earlier in this century, the vast majority of women gave up their education and careers and returned to the home in the late 1940s and the 1950s. They were encouraged to be passive and dependent, to give up careers and intellectual pursuits, to devote themselves to home and family—in short, to comply with the "feminine mystique." College students, avoiding intellectual commitment, used their college years to find husbands. The average age at marriage dropped to below twenty and the average number of children increased as women sought happiness, fulfillment, and identity in marriage and family. Popular psychology reinforced this movement by stressing woman's biological function and publicizing an apparent conflict between education and femininity. College administrators responded by revising the curriculum to emphasize "marriage and the family" studies. The media, recognizing the undercurrent of discontent, advocated hobbies, volunteer work, and "togetherness" as solutions. Studies by and for the advertising industry identified the emptiness of the housewife's life; the industry responded by using women's unfulfilled needs and feelings of guilt to enhance sales. Sexual orgasm became a prime goal, but lost much of its pleasure as women unsuccessfully sought personal identity and relief from boredom in sex both in and out of marriage.

According to Friedan, "the problem that has no name" facing women in America is a lack of self-identity due to poor education, lack of personal ambitions, and discouragement from any intellectual effort. American children, often overcontrolled and overprotected, have absorbed the same passive mentality, resulting in low assertiveness, low self-esteem, lack of ambition, and widespread promiscuity. The high death rate and low morale of U.S. prisoners in Korea is seen as a direct result. Despite the general belief that ambition, education, and career will destroy a woman's femininity, studies by psychologists and sociologists, including Maslow, Kinsey, Burgess, and Cottrell, indicate that both sexual and personal satisfaction increase with self-actualization, level of education, and career success.

Friedan postulates that the only cure for "the problem that has no name" is an aggressive pursuit of a "life plan" combining purposeful education, professional career goals, marriage, and motherhood. She proposes a new educational funding program similar to the G.I. Bill and alternative college schedules that would enable women to complete their education while meeting other commitments. Only by achieving personal identity through education and career goals will women be able to fulfill their human potential, thus freeing their husbands and children to strive for and realize their own identities.

According to *Women's Studies* (1987), in *The Second Stage* (1982) Friedan addresses "the daughters," whom she thinks are burdened by the legacy of feminist expectations, the "feminist mystique" (p. 27). Friedan argues that the "first stage" of the women's movement accepted the male model of success. In the "second stage," a movement of men *and* women must fight to "restructure institutions and transform the nature of power itself" (p. 28). (SDH)

IL
692. Friedl, Ernestine. **Women and Men: An Anthropologist's View.** New York: Holt, Rinehart and Winston, 1975. 148 p. Includes bibliography and glossary. ISBN 0-03-091529-5.

Friedl, a professor in the Department of Anthropology at Duke University and President of the American Anthropological Association, uses an ecological and structural/functional theoretical orientation to explore the impact of subsistence modes on sex roles. In her introduction, she reviews the arguments for biological or sociocultural determination of sex roles and concludes that social conditioning, not biology, is of major importance in channeling the direction of sex roles; biology is a baseline, not a limitation, upon which social structures are built. The overall goal of this book is to examine the degree of diversity that exists in sex roles across different types of societies. Of particular concern is an examination of the social, cultural, and physical environmental conditions within which variation exists; the types of constraints placed on such variation; and the degree of dominance that each sex expresses.

Friedl begins with an articulation of basic propositions that guide her presentation of sex roles. First, subsistence technology as well as a group's political and social organization have important consequences for the sexual division of labor, the allocation of power and prestige to men and women, and the quality of male-female relationships. Second, the work women usually perform affects the spacing of children and the pattern of child-rearing. Third, extradomestic distribution of goods and services confers power and prestige. Fourth, control over the distribution of goods and the organization of labor for extradomestic exchanges affects the nature of sex roles. Finally, rituals and symbols express significant aspects of the relationship between men and women.

The bulk of the book describes hunting and gathering (part I) and horticultural (part II) societies; subsistence techniques, control of resources, control over sexual access and reproduction, involvement in ritual, and sex role changes with age are some consistent topics for discussion. Numerous cross-cultural examples pervade these discussions.

In the epilogue, Friedl summarizes the findings about sex roles among hunter-gatherers and horticulturists to demonstrate their value in understanding sex roles in industrial society. She suggests that control over the production and distribution of resources is a major route to power in most societies. "Relevant Case Studies" annotates fourteen ethnographies that contain material relevant to the study of sex roles. (SGF)

IL
693. Greer, Germaine. **The Female Eunuch.** New York: McGraw-Hill, 1971. 349 p. Includes bibliographic notes. ISBN 0-07-024375-1.

This work is one of the books basic to the women's liberation movement of the 1970s. As Greer explains in the introduction, this "second feminist wave" is a call for revolution, a call for women to free themselves from a demeaning and restrictive system. The work is divided into five sections: body, soul, love, hate, and revolution. It examines the situation of women, including upbringing, stereotypes, needs, beliefs, and emotions. Greer believes that women have equal or greater potential than men, but have been "castrated" through socialization to be soft, weak, passive, timid individuals whose purpose is to exist as sexual objects and servants for men. The combination of these characteristics forms a stereotype that embodies the accepted image of femininity in Western culture. In an attempt to become this image, women subvert their energy and initiative and deny their own ambitions, desires, and abilities. The primary goal for girls and women is love and marriage, a perverted and distorted ideal based on romantic fantasies and male objectification of the female stereotype. The nuclear family is seen as abnormal and detrimental to all members, and alternatives such as extended or communal families are suggested.

The response to the perverted image of love is hate, both among men, who express it through sadism, guilt, abuse, and ridicule, and among women, who respond with misery, bitter resentment, and rebellion against men. Revolution is presented as perhaps the only method to correct the situation. Women must harness and use their skills and energy to liberate themselves. Women's liberation is seen as a means to liberate all people and bring civilization to maturity. Through this movement, sex can become a form of communication between mutually equal, strong, tender individuals. Revolution will demand extreme changes in existing conventions such as marriage and family life, but these are necessary to achieve true freedom. Various methods to precipitate revolution are possible, including the powerful weapons of economic boycott and withdrawal of labor, sexual activity, support for violence, and support for the government.

The second edition (1981) includes an introduction that summarizes the changes seen in the intervening ten years. The most important development is the growth of women's support groups, which allow women to share experiences and plan strategies to achieve liberation. (SDH)

PR,IL
694. Illich, Ivan. **Gender.** New York: Pantheon Books, 1982. 192 p. Includes bibliographic notes and index. ISBN 0-394-71587-X.

Illich, an educator residing in Cuernavaca, Mexico, applies his analytic abilities to a consideration of the problem of the destruction and loss of gender and its replacement by a rampant sexism over the past several hundred years. The distinction between gender and sexism is like that between vernacular language and taught mother tongue: the former is natural, the latter cultural. Illich says that gender "distinguishes places, times, tools, tasks, forms of speech, gestures, and perceptions that are associated with men from those associated with women" (p. 3).

According to Illich, instead of having tasks, tools, trades and crafts based on gender we have a society genderless in its particulars, featuring economic man in a competitive struggle. This genderless behavior helps to account for "the rise of capitalism and a lifestyle that depends on industrially produced commodities." In these circumstances it is inevitable that women suffer from discrimination. Economically, their earnings will always lag behind those of men. Indeed, the belief in a "non-sexist" economy, in which equality will prevail, is a myth, as is the belief in the sexual ancestry of society. Illich believes that we should disabuse ourselves of these myths, recognize our "sexist" circumstances, restore gender to its proper historical context, and do what we can to promote in our lives and homes a style that is not sexist and competitive but comprehends the inherent gender differences, which have largely disappeared. Almost everything today—language, jobs, goals, aspirations—is genderless; only biological sex remains to distinguish men from women. The price society pays for this increasingly unisex world is sex discrimination in the workplace and attendant criminal behavior (rape, prostitution, pornography). Indeed, it is a bleak picture that Illich paints of modern industrial society, especially for women.

Illich believes that historians have neglected gender in their economic histories of Western civilization. He seems to lament the loss of gender, not because society based on gender was especially idyllic (it was not), but rather because our present genderless society, so depressingly sexist in character, seems to be striving for economic goals that are unattainable. Throughout this book, Illich comments in titled footnotes on key words and literature that could take his thesis into fresh areas of exploration. (TJW)

PR
695. Morgen, Sandra, ed. **Gender and Anthropology: Critical Reviews for Research and Teaching.** Washington, D.C.: American Anthropological Association, 1989. 462 p. Includes bibliographies. ISBN 0-913167-33-9.

Representing the "culmination of a three-year project which is built on the strong foundation of feminist scholarship and activity in the field of anthropology" (p. v), this book draws on the work of feminist anthropologists to demonstrate the ways in which the insights of new research on gender and women's lives are relevant to the teaching of anthropology in all subfields of the discipline and can be "mainstreamed" into the curriculum. In her introductory essay, Morgen emphasizes that "this book is about both *women* and *gender*, and about the particular historical relationship between scholarship on women (i.e., the anthropology of women) and theories about gender" (p. 1). Morgen's introduction traces the development of different anthropological approaches to women and gender from the 1970s, when most material about women was located in discussions about personality, sex roles, marriage, family, and kinship, to the current wealth of new research on women and gender that can be applied beyond the previous constraints of past categories.

The eighteen chapters, written almost exclusively by women anthropologists with expertise in the subject area (e.g., Adrienne L. Zilhman on the role of women in early hominid evolution, Jane B. Lancaster on women in biosocial perspective, June Nash on gender studies in Latin America, Ruth Borker and Daniel N. Maltz on anthropological perspectives on gender and language) are organized by culture region (aboriginal Australia, American Indians, Caribbean, sub-Saharan Africa, Latin America, Middle East, Hindu societies, Southeast Asia, modern China, United States) and selected subfields (biological anthropology, primatology, archaeology, sociocultural anthropology, linguistics). To facilitate the use of new research scholarship in undergraduate teaching, each chapter is organized according to a similar format: (1) an introductory conceptual overview of the significant themes, debates, literature, and background information that characterize the context of the culture region or subfield; (2) two specific suggestions for inclusion in the curriculum; (3) the author's recommendation of resources (films, readings, exercises) to be included in introductory courses; and (4) an annotated bibliography of particularly useful references.

Throughout, the contributors challenge androcentric and Eurocentric assumptions about gender, ethnicity, power, history, social institutions, and cultural constructs with a variety of theoretical perspectives that focus on the importance of women's lives and gender as a basic category of identity and social organization in anthropological research and teaching. Of particular interest for those interested in human sexuality is the concluding article by Sue-Ellen Jacobs and Christine Roberts, "Sex, Sexuality, Gender, and Gender Variance," in which they adopt a biosocial perspective in presenting their conceptual and ethnographic overview of sex, sexuality, gender, and gender variances. Morgen notes that the guide tries to "provide the widest possible coverage of culture areas and subdisciplinary specialization . . . [as well as to] represent the diversity of theoretical perspectives most current in feminist anthropology" (p. 14). (SGF)

PR,IL
696. Muir, Edward, and Guido Ruggiero, eds. **Sex and Gender in Historical Perspective.** Translated by Margaret A. Gallucci with Mary M. Gallucci and Carole C. Gallucci. Baltimore: Johns Hopkins University Press, 1990. 234 p. (Selections from *Quaderni Storici*). Includes bibliographic notes. ISBN 0-8018-4072-4.

This collection, translated from the Italian, consists of articles taken from the Italian journal *Quaderni Storici*, revealing various sex roles lived by women in history as well as aspects of sexuality affecting those roles. Most of the articles reflect the approach of the new social history, that uses the individual to elucidate broader social structures.

The first article, " 'Menstruum Quasi Monstruum': Monstrous Births and Menstrual Taboo in the Sixteenth Century," by Octavia Niccoli, discloses the relationship between female sexuality, menstruation, and the monstrous existing in the minds of those who decried carnal excesses, believing "these births as resulting from transgressing the sexual ethic." Anna Roa, in "The New and the Old: The Spread of Syphilis (1494-1530)," explains "how Europe encountered and integrated into its cultural world the new and highly disturbing disease of syphilis." Her article focuses on its cultural causes, explained by *fabulae* (tales) in a myth-making process that related syphilis to leprosy and monstrous sexual relations.

Lucia Ferrante's article, "Honor Regained: Women in the Casa del Soccorso di San Paolo in Sixteenth-Century Bologna," describes "the institutions that early modern Bologna used to attempt to control what were defined as errant female bodies," those bodies "that did not fit within the accepted parameters for women—family and convent." In the same vein, Sandra Cavallo and Simona Cerutti write about the intimate relationship between woman's body and honor, using documents collected by ecclesiastical judges involved in marital disputes, in "Female Honor and the Social Control of Reproduction in Piedmont Between 1600 and 1800."

Luisa Accati used individual case histories reconstructed from court documents gathered by the Inquisition to disclose the carnal power of the female body that balances and competes with the priest's spiritual power in "The Spirit of Fornication: Virtue of the Soul and Virtue of the Body in Friuli, 1600-1800." In "One Saint Less: The Story of Angela Mellini, a Bolognese Seamstress (1667-17[?])," Luisa Ciammitti tells about an Ursuline nun who attempts "to lead a saint-like life with the help of her male spiritual advisors." Her story exposes the tension between individual women and the Church and provides the powerful sexual imagery of relations between God and a woman.

Flaviana Zanolla in "Mothers-in-Law and Daughters-in-Law at the Beginning of the Twentieth Century in P. of Friuli" analyzes "interviews with peasant women to reconstruct the power dynamics of peasant families at the turn of the century. Her analysis reveals women's networks of power within the family that redounded to the benefit of women in relation to their husbands. Finally, Giulia Calvi discusses women's networks in the American factory in "Women in the Factory: Women's Networks and Social Life in America (1900-1915)." It focuses on women "formed and disciplined within the family" [but] "socialized beyond its confines." (TJW)

IL,PO

697. Neely, James C. **Gender: The Myth of Equality.** New York: Simon & Schuster, 1981. 322 p. Includes bibliographic references and index. ISBN 0-671-41542-5.

Neely, physician and surgeon, believes that an unnatural rift has developed between the sexes in recent years, disrupting families and tearing the social fabric apart. This book, dealing with inherent sex differences, is his response to this crisis. Certain that an understanding of these biological and psychological gender differences is essential if men and women are to overcome the social forces dividing them, he takes the reader on a journey through the various stages of male and female development from birth and adolescence through adulthood and old age. Initially, he explains in the chapter "Separate, Not Equal" how the female is the basic sex of humankind in that all the chromosomes in the egg are female and half of those in the sperm are too. The male hormone, testosterone, however, is the hormone that causes the sexual differentiation into two distinct dimorphic sexes. Later, in the chapter "Only Connect," he gives a precise physical explanation of the sexual act in terms of the relationship between the hypothalamus and the sympathetic and para-sympathetic nervous systems. But it is this precise understanding of what actually occurs between the two sexes physically during intercourse that is the mechanism for promoting mutual connection or, as it were, love. The biological basis for mutual understanding and love is an intriguing argument and Neely provides observations on such issues as abortion, careers and mothering, male aggressiveness, and middle-age marriage.

Neely buttresses his positions with quotations from philosophy and the belles-lettres rather than from the scientific literature. One of the forces militating against better relations between the sexes is embodied in the extreme feminists, those women who have been characterized by the psychiatrists as having had "an unfortunate or unsatisfactory relationship with the male of the species that derives originally from the young girl's relationship to her father" (p. 45). Neely's position is that "we are in this life together and need each other terribly. As with the generations, so with the sexes—the similarities are eventually much greater than the differences and we are all headed for the same place, a fact we might lose sight of in the adversary atmosphere many young women are creating" (p. 45). (TJW)

IL
698. Yorburg, Betty. **Sexual Identity: Sex Roles and Social Change.** New York: John Wiley & Sons, 1974. 227 p. Includes bibliographic notes and index. ISBN 0-471-97810-8.

Sexual identity is "the image of the self as a male or a female and convictions about what membership in that group implies" (p. 1); it is learned as a part of roles individuals play in social life. Therefore, it is possible to infer some of the makeup of sexual identity by examining sex-typed roles. In an effort to understand the anxiety and problems associated with issues of changing sex roles in the early 1970s, Yorburg examines different aspects of sex roles as they relate to variations in sexual identity. Each chapter provides a broad sketch of one perspective that could contribute to this effort.

An introductory chapter looks at the biological basis of sexual identity, while another uses a historical perspective to explore why and how sex-role concepts have changed in nonliterate, hunting and gathering, and agricultural societies. Yorburg suggests that the development of science and technology helps to explain some of this change. A similar model is used to understand cross-cultural variations in sex roles and self-images in contemporary societies. A brief set of descriptions of sex-typed roles and values in China, Japan, Arab Middle East, sub-Saharan Africa, the Soviet Union, Spain, and Latin America not only demonstrate variation but consistency, despite the encroachment of modern technology. Despite major changes, much from the traditional value systems persist. Yorburg also discusses how variation in sex-typed roles occurs within the context of the United States. Personality differences between men and women as well as class, ethnic, and life cycle differences in sexual identity testify to the importance of learning in producing variation. Yorburg concludes that women are a minority whose true liberation will occur when both men and women can tolerate and value individuality, equality, and humanity. (SGF)

Masculinity/Femininity. Androgyny

IL,PO
699. Bly, Robert. **Iron John: A Book About Men.** Reading, Mass.: Addison-Wesley, 1990. 268 p. Includes bibliographic notes. ISBN 0-201-51720-5.

According to poet Bly, "the images of adult manhood given by the popular culture are worn out" (p. ix) and the grief in men, which has steadily increased since the Industrial Revolution, "has reached a depth now that cannot be ignored" (p. x). It is time for men to reclaim the "Wild Man," variously portrayed in traditional stories as a priest, shaman, or lord of the animals. Bly uses the story of Iron John (first articulated by the Grimm brothers in about 1820 and recounted in its entirety in the epilogue) as a metaphor for an initiatory path that men may take if they wish to discover a new way for males to become men. He divides the story into eight segments, each of which he discusses as a phase in the transition to manhood.

The first step is for a male to acknowledge, welcome, and reclaim Iron John, the "deep male" part of his psyche, a "primitive being covered with hair down to his feet" (p. 7). Iron John carries the boy (the initiate) away from his parents into the forest, where he learns to face the wounds of childhood, expand his consciousness, and gather the courage to proceed on his journey alone. During the third phase, the boy moves his "love energy" from his mother to his father, all the while protected by male gods, and in the fourth phase, he comes to terms with the craving he has to be with his father. The next challenge is to deal with feminine energy—his mother's, his own, his lover's—by experiencing it and learning from it how to honor his own soul and become a lover. The sixth task for the boy is to define and awaken his inner warriors, that defend the boundaries of the self and fight for eternal, sacred causes. The crux of the boy's initiation into manhood occurs in the seventh phase, when he rides into combat as a red, white, and black knight, whose colors mark a masculine sequence from one state of being to another. The red symbolizes goodness and virtue, on which the boy focuses after having suffered through the difficulties of the red period. Finally, the black means a recognition of a man's shadow qualities, his dark side, which he'd most like to hide. The boy's complete transition into manhood comes when the wound received by the black knight becomes a sign for his acceptance as the groom of a princess; his reconciliation with his parents; and public recognition of his masculine soul, including his dark side.

The boy's development allows the Wild Man to present himself as the lord that he really is, not the animal-like being that the boy originally befriended. Bly concludes that the Wild Man comes to life "after thought, after discipline imposed on ourselves, after grief" (p. 226). The point of the story is that a man needs to be in touch with the Wild Man, who can guide him into a rich sense of self and enable him to cope with past wounds, confront new challenges, and reconcile masculine and feminine principles. Throughout his discussion of each phase, Bly draws on other myths; psychological concepts, particularly those of Freud and Jung; anthropological analyses of initiation ceremonies in other cultures; and research on male/female relationships to clarify the significance of his analysis to contemporary men. (SGF)

IL
700. Brownmiller, Susan. **Femininity**. New York: Linden Press/Simon & Schuster, 1984. 270 p. Includes bibliography and index. ISBN 0-671-24692-5.

Femininity extends beyond biological femaleness and always demands more definition because it must constantly reassure males and females of their differences. It is, in essence, "a romantic sentiment, a nostalgic tradition of imposed limitations" (p. 19). Brownmiller, author of *Against Our Will*, once again defines and explores an issue that she thinks is central to male/female relationships and perpetuates inequality between the sexes. She attempts to stimulate awareness and examination of multiple facets of femininity (biological, cultural, social, psychological, and historical) in an effort to demonstrate that its origins and perpetuation illustrate the ways in which it circumscribes a woman's choices about her life and limits her possibilities for success. Extreme commitment to the canons of femininity harms women who fulfill roles of symbolic aristocrats, humble servants, and glamorous playthings.

The book is organized around a series of concrete, "pragmatic" topics (hair, clothes, voice, skin, movement, emotion, ambition) in order to avoid irrational digressions into mystical associations with the subject. By linking feminine principles to these topics, Brownmiller shows the degree to which they mirror or diverge from "basic biology." Drawing on a wealth of cross-cultural, contemporary, and historical data as well as on personal experience, she describes an array of social and cultural elaborations of "femininity." Corsets, foot binding, images of movie stars, fictional characters, dress codes, and make-up are just a few of the items that are grist for Brownmiller's analytical mill. She considers a variety of themes: (1) the origins of femininity from an upper-class perspective, (2) femininity as part of the historic subjugation of women, and (3) the seductive glamour of femininity. She also places major emphasis on an underexamined aspect of femininity: the competition between women that it entails. She encourages an examination of femininity in terms of our culture and times. Is it healthy or useful? The reader must decide. (SGF)

PR,IL
701. Clatterbaugh, Kenneth. **Contemporary Perspectives on Masculinity: Men, Women, and Politics in Modern Society**. Boulder, Colo.: Westview Press, 1990. 182 p. Includes bibliographic references and index. ISBN 0-8133-0991-3.

Clatterbaugh is Associate Professor of Philosophy at the University of Washington. This book surveys the major perspectives on masculinity, perspectives that offer a definition of masculinity, an account of how it is created and maintained, and an evaluation of masculinity. The perspectives examined are biological and classical conservatism, radical and liberal profeminism, men's rights' perspectives, mythopoetic perspectives, socialism, and black and gay perspectives. Each perspective's relationship to feminism is also explored. The book brings out the philosophical assumptions on which these perspectives depend and offers the criticisms with which each must contend. The conclusion indicates some new directions for research and for philosophical inquiry.

This is the first book to survey the range of responses to feminism that men have made, and it is also the first to put political theory at the center of men's awareness of their own masculinity. Clatterbaugh attempts to treat all views with fairness as he develops and defends a vision of men and masculinity consistent with feminist ideals and a just society. (Author)

IL,PO

702. Farrell, Warren. **The Myth of Male Power: Why Men Are the Disposable Sex.** New York: Simon & Schuster, 1993. 446 p. Includes bibliography and index. ISBN 0-671-79349-7.

According to best-selling author (*The Liberated Male, Why Men Are the Way They Are*) and political scientist Farrell, power is "having control over one's own life." By that definition, contemporary conceptions of male power are myths. The goal of *The Myth of Male Power* is to demonstrate why and how men are really the "disposable sex," with the hope that an articulation of men's plight will balance the rhetoric of feminism to create growth and understanding between men and women. Eschewing a stance that claims either sex is the oppressed sex, Farrell ultimately favors a gender transition movement. However, a men's movement may be necessary to voice men's perspective before an integrated outlook can be attained. The key to relationships is to "listen, listen, listen" and to take responsibility for one's own life rather than blaming, being a victim, and feeling entitled to being rescued.

Part I lays out the conceptual questions of the book. Is male power a myth, and why do we have difficulty believing it is? Underlying the answers to these questions is the recognition of a shift in expectations for relationships from Stage I to Stage II. Traditional Stage I marriages required role mates for survival, i.e., men who were providers and protectors, women who were domestic and caretakers. Stage II marriages require more than survival; they need soul mates for personal and mutual fulfillment. Neither sex had power in Stage I. The current challenge is to interpret and change Stage I institutions so they are functional in Stage II. What has been labeled "power," "patriarchy," "dominance," and "sexism" are often vehicles for males to serve the needs of females—by dying as heroes, by becoming successful enough to earn the love of beautiful females, by paying for a home but having little time to participate in it.

Part II descends to the "glass cellar," "the invisible barrier that keeps men in jobs with the most hazards," where men feel powerless and disposable. Death professions like fire fighting, logging, construction, and coal mining are almost exclusively male. Men are trained to be violent protectors in war; violent with each other in domestic life; and violent to themselves if they do not fulfill the demands of the traditional male role. Men commit suicide more often than women; have a seven-year shorter life span than women; and are homeless more than women. However, few people seem to care about protecting men.

Part III, "Government as Substitute Husband," contends that when divorces left women without "husband-as-savior," women found a "substitute savior" in the government, which provided special legal protection for women. This "legal bias . . . has begun to wreak havoc with the Constitution's guarantee of equal protection." "Female-only" defenses, e.g., PMS, "battered woman syndrome," mothers don't kill, harm both sexes and engender further feelings of powerlessness, which may lay at the root of abuse. Sexual harassment legislation protects women's role as victim, blames men, and doesn't facilitate recognition of a woman's role in the "sexual dance." Rape laws give women the power of false accusation and neglect the rape of men in prisons. Welfare programs focus on the needs of women and children, not men.

Farrell concludes that the journey of Stage II is to give "both sexes survival skills and self-actualization skills." And, "the challenge of *The Myth of Male Power* . . . is to care enough about men to spend as much of the next quarter century helping men become Stage II men as we did the last quarter century helping women become Stage II women . . . to go beyond women as sex objects and men as success objects to both sexes as objects of love." (SGF)

PR
703. Gilmore, David D. **Manhood in the Making: Cultural Concepts of Masculinity.** New Haven, Conn.: Yale University Press, 1990. 258 p. Includes bibliography and index. ISBN 0-300-04646-4.

Gilmore, a professor of anthropology at the State University of New York, Stony Brook, provides a cross-cultural examination of masculinity in various societies, including several in the circum-Mediterranean area, as well as in Micronesia, Melanesia, equatorial Africa, South America, and South and East Asia. He explores the cult of manhood among hunter-gatherers, horticultural and pastoral tribes, and postindustrial civilizations. Some of these societies are militant, others peaceful; some hierarchically organized, others egalitarian; some feature matrilineal kinship systems, others patrilineal.

Gilmore shows that "ideas and anxieties about masculinity as a special-status category of achievement are widespread in societies around the world"; on the other hand, there are exceptions where manhood is of minimal interest. Examples of the macho image are the Spaniards of Andalusia in southern Spain, the Trukese of Micronesia, the Samburu of Africa, the Sambia of New Guinea, the Mehinaku of Brazil, and the American he-man; representatives of the latter are the Tahitians and the Semai people of Malaysia.

Gilmore aspires in his investigation of these societies to determine (1) if masculine behavior is culturally determined or (2) if there is such a thing as innate masculinity, biologically determined, and supportive of Freud's notion that "anatomy is destiny." Most of the societies studied seem to indicate that male rituals, male testing, and male behavior are culturally constructed. However, he shows that macho behavior is not quite universal; there are puzzling exceptions (e.g., the Tahitians and the Semai). Certain environmental and economic factors seem to promote macho masculine behavior in both primitive societies and modern industrial societies. As Gilmore surmises: "The harsher the environment and the scarcer the resources, the more manhood is stressed as inspiration and goal. This correlation could not be more clear, concrete, or compelling; and although it does not prove anything about causal relations, it does indicate a systematic relationship in which gender ideology reflects the material conditions of life" (pp. 224-25). Gilmore reaches the conclusion that "to be a man in most of the societies we have looked at, one must impregnate women, protect dependents from danger, and provision kith and kin" (pp. 222-23). In competitive circumstances, these behaviors bring forth a heroic quality in males that ranges in different societies from extreme machoism to manly confidence and self-assuredness in industrial and postindustrial societies. (TJW)

IL
704. Heilbrun, Carolyn G. **Toward a Recognition of Androgyny.** New York: Harper & Row, 1973. 195 p. Includes bibliographic notes and index. ISBN 0-06-090378-3.

Androgyny in world myth and literature are explored by Heilbrun, a professor of English literature at Columbia University. She that many of the barriers between men and women would crumble if the androgynous nature of humans was generally recognized. The abundant but often hidden evidence for this belief is presented in the three essays that comprise the book. Heilbrun questions the old sexual order of rigidly defined roles for men and women; the polarization of the sexes must be changed in the interest of survival. Individuals must realize the ideals of androgyny whereby individual roles and modes of behavior are freely chosen. Recognizing the difficulties many people have in acknowledging profound social change, she assures us that androgynous behavior has been with us a long time, as the evidence in myth and literature attests.

The first essay, "The Hidden River of Androgyny," begins historically by noting the shift from goddess worship to patriarchy in ancient Greece; by contrasting the strongly masculine spirit pervading the *Iliad* with that of the *Odyssey*, where the feminine impulse dominates; and then by identifying the central role played by androgynous women in Greek drama (*Eumenides, Antigone, Oedipus Rex, Medea, The Trojan Women, Lysistrata*). The essay goes on to a consideration of the strong patriarchal tone in the literature of the Judeo-Christian tradition, which nevertheless showed certain ambivalence toward patriarchy in biblical stories. Medieval civilization engendered several remarkable alternatives to the patriarchal spirit: the rise of romantic love and the cult of the Virgin Mary. The love story of Abelard and Heloise epitomizes for all time the tragic clash of sex roles. Androgyny in the literature of the Renaissance is exemplified by Spenser's *The Faerie Queene* and by many of Shakespeare's plays.

The second essay, "The Woman as Hero," examines the novel "as a form astonishingly imbued with the ideal of androgyny" (p. xx). Heilbrun shows that in the novels of Richardson (*Clarissa*), Thackeray (*Vanity Fair*), and Hawthorne (*The Scarlet Letter*) women characters occupy an especially important place. She discusses the major female novelists of the nineteenth century: George Eliot, Jane Austen, and the Brontë sisters. Finally, she looks closely at the period 1880-1920, in which women played androgynous roles in the work of male writers: G. B. Shaw, D. H. Lawrence, Henry James, and E. M. Forster. Heilbrun states that male novelists used women as heroes in that period for reasons that stemmed "not out of any urge to fight the feminist battle, but because woman's place in the universe provided the proper metaphor for the place of the heroic in the work of literary art" (p. 92). She identifies novelists whose females were devoid of androgynous qualities: Conrad, Joyce, Tolstoy, Flaubert, and others. Woman as hero vanishes after World War II; indeed most of the postwar novelists (Roth, Malamud, Mailer, Bellow, Dickey) "picture the universe as one in which men are escaping women, demeaning them, or exploiting them" (p. 111). Sadly, female novelists have hardly done better.

In the third essay, "The Bloomsbury Group," Heilbrun examines the key figures of this influential British literary school, especially its guiding light, Virginia Woolf, and Lytton Strachey, famous for his *Eminent Victorians*. She looks upon this group as embodying and courageously practicing the androgynous spirit.

Heilbrun concludes with this hopeful remark: "I am confident that great androgynous works will soon be written." However, she has given up on modern male novelists, and sees women novelists still exploring female consciousness, "particularly the consciousness of being victimized by men, and by that personal beauty through which today's female characters are so often betrayed, or betray themselves" (p. 171). (TJW)

PR

704a. Herdt, Gilbert, ed. **Third Sex, Third Gender: Beyond Sexual Dimorphism in Culture and History.** New York: Zone Books, 1994. 614 p. Includes bibliographic notes and index. ISBN 0-942299-81-7.

Anthropologist Herdt, Professor of Human Development at the University of Chicago, says that the central question pervading this volume is whether two sexes or genders are natural or inevitable across history, culture, time, and space. The essays address three crucial areas in understanding sexual and gender variation: (1) description and documentation of third sex/third gender categories and roles as well as the cultural/historical contexts in which they have appeared; (2) description of the sexual activities and rules that may affect how third sex and gender categories are developed; and (3) transmission of third sex roles and categories through cultural and historical processes. Herdt remarks, "To the best of our knowledge, this volume is the first of its kind to address these issues from the complementary perspectives of anthropology and social history" (p. 18).

Herdt's introduction reiterates the importance of transcending dimorphic sexual and gender categories, and provides an historical and conceptual overview of how third sexes and genders have been interpreted. At the core of the Western paradigm of sex and gender since the nineteenth century lies a reproductive model, based on the inevitability of two sexes. What is needed are descriptions of the "lived realities of the people themselves" (p. 81). Ten chapters are divided into two parts: historical contributions and anthropological contributions. The historical section begins with Kathryn M. Ringrose's exploration of the social and cultural placement of eunuchs in Byzantine society. Definitions of sex and gender changed as Byzantine society did, which spark questions about the stability of contemporary definitions of sex and gender. Ralph Trumbach considers the impact of an emerging, modern two-gendered paradigm on the categorization of London's sapphists, "ambiguously gendered women" of the eighteenth century. Theo van der Meer examines changing views of homosexuality from the seventeenth through the nineteenth centuries, particularly how popular beliefs in a third sex became incorporated into nineteenth century medical discourse on the nature and origins of homosexuality. Gert Hekma questions the extent to which hypotheses about sexual inversion during the second half of the nineteenth century can be regarded as a third gender. René Grémaux inquires whether some Balkan women, who wore men's clothing and weapons, performed their roles, and were somewhat socially acknowledged as men, could be considered a third gender.

Niko Basnier begins the anthropological contributions by analyzing the link between social and cultural processes in Polynesian societies and the prevalence of "intermediate" gender categories throughout the region. Will Roscoe reviews anthropological research on North American berdaches to generate a new theoretical approach to understanding berdache roles and developing an integrated analysis of gender diversity. Serena Nanda's discussion of hijras in India provides a model of cultural diversity and demonstrates that Western dichotomies of sex and gender are not universal. Herdt discusses the categorization of a rare form of hermaphroditism (i.e., boys are mistaken for girls because of their small penises but take on a male gender identity at puberty) in the Dominican Republic and in New Guinea. The availability of a third gender category rather than a biomedical explanation accounts for this transition. Anne Bolin discusses cultural change in gender variant social identities, particularly among male-to-female transsexuals. Because transgenderists challenge the strict correlation of gender with genitals, body, social status, and/or role, they demonstrate that gender is socially, not biologically produced.

Overall, the detailed descriptions and conceptual analyses of the contributors create a cross-disciplinary dialogue about the development, stability, and implications of dimorphic conceptualizations of sex and gender. They offer new interpretations of the roles, codes, identities and lives of people experiencing diverse sexual and gendered natures in many different contexts and suggest alternate ontologies and epistemologies. (SGF)

IL
705. Horney, Karen. **Feminine Psychology.** New York: Norton, 1967. 269 p. Includes bibliographic references.

Edited and with an introduction by Harold Kelman, this volume brings together Horney's articles on the psychology of women, spanning the period from 1922 to 1936. Horney was important as one of the early Freudian revisionists and was path-breaking as a feminist critic of Freud. Her psychoanalytic approach emphasized human plasticity and potentiality for growth. She sought explanation for repression and blockage in the social context as well as in family history. This theoretical perspective is particularly apparent in her writings on women. Attacking orthodox psychoanalysis for its assumption of a male model of development and a male viewpoint, Horney makes a major departure in attributing much of female neurosis and of male fear and dislike of women to patriarchal culture. Included in this collection are: "The Flight from Womanhood," "Inhibited Femininity" (on the problem of frigidity), "The Problem of the Monogamous Ideal," "The Distrust Between the Sexes," "Problems of Marriage," "The Dread of Woman," "The Denial of the Vagina," "Maternal Conflicts," "The Overvaluation of Love," "The Problem of Feminine Masochism," and "The Neurotic Need for Love." (**Women's Studies**, 1979)

IL,PO

706.   Keen, Sam. **Fire in the Belly: On Being a Man.** New York: Bantam Books, 1991. 272 p. Includes bibliographic notes. ISBN 0-553-07188-2.

In the face of criticism and questions about the nature and role of men in contemporary society, there are few books that address the issues of "questing" men. Keen (M.A., Harvard Divinity School; Ph.D., Princeton University) says, "This book is an attempt to fill this lack. . . . It is for a new kind of man who is being forged in the crucible of the chaos of our time. It is for men who are willing to undertake a spiritual journey . . . to celebrate a new vision of manhood—a vision of man with fire in his belly and passion in his heart" (pp. 6-7). Keen invites men to begin this journey with him and encourages both men and women to enter a conversation about manhood. Drawing on insights from his own life, enduring friendships with a few men, and participation in a group of twelve men who have met every week since 1978 to discuss men's issues, he organizes the contents of the book into a verbal rite of passage that describes a journey of separation from what is known; movement through a frightening and confusing labyrinth of roles, feelings, and perceptions that can lead to a new way of being; and reintegration into ordinary life.

The first step in a man's spiritual journey is to separate himself from the world of women, around which much of his life has centered, and then to examine the roles he has played in other sectors of his life. Manhood has been linked to protection, procreation, and providing for others, and modern myths encourage men to be warriors, lovers, and workers. However, war entails wounds, violence, and pain; sex is one of the few ways that men are allowed to feel; and economic roles imply that manhood can be purchased by success. Men need to demythologize these ideals of manhood by considering other ways of defining authentic manhood. Past ideas of manhood (e.g., man as hunter, as planter, as warrior, as thinker, as Dionysian, as prophet, as image of God, as power, as scientific-technological, as self-made, as postmodern) as well as the conditions that gave rise to them have contributed to current definitions of manhood and demonstrate that men have creatively responded to the times in which they have lived; they can do so now by becoming "fierce gentlemen," able to be gentle, earthy, and powerful without being violent.

The core of the book, "A Primer for Now and Future Heroes," describes the "soulful quest," the often painful "pilgrimage into the self" where a man examines such familiar traits of masculinity as artificial toughness, having all of the answers, false optimism, pragmatism, and activity, and then considers feelings of fear, doubt, despair, fantasy, and waiting. Separation from and the death of these familiar, damaging traits leads to the birth of comfort with new virtues, among which are wonder, empathy, moral outrage, friendship, enjoyment, and wildness. The basis of manhood becomes care, wisdom, and delight, not being alone. Entry into these experiences is a homecoming that also prepares men to "come together" with women. Love, intimacy, marriage, and family are contexts within which men and women can be together. The final chapter provides some "travel tips for pilgrims," the most important of which is to begin where you are, not travel according to someone else's itinerary. (SGF)

IL,PO

707.   Levine, Linda, and Lonnie Barbach. **The Intimate Male: Candid Discussions About Women, Sex, and Relationships.** Garden City, N.Y.: Anchor Press/Doubleday, 1983. 364 p. Includes bibliography and index. ISBN 0-385-17612-0.

The co-authors of *Shared Intimacies: Women's Sexual Experiences* (Anchor Press/Doubleday, 1980), social worker Levine and sex therapist Barbach, once again combine their talents to explore the range of thoughts, attitudes, experiences, and problem-solving techniques of a sample of 120 men who are college-educated, career-oriented, middle class, and feel good about their sexuality. The findings of this research are based on in-depth interviews (lasting at least two hours) with heterosexual men who volunteered, were recommended, or were purposely selected for the study. Levine and Barbach were surprised to find that these men, regardless of their ages or lifestyles, wanted more intimacy, particularly sexual intimacy, in their lives. Each chapter incorporates lengthy quotes from the men interviewed with scientific data on male/female relationships and sexuality to describe consistent issues in men's lives: fulfilling sociocultural and personal expectations of masculinity; being a good lover; developing the components of good sex; enhancing gourmet lovemaking; courtship; communicating with a partner; dealing with sexual problems; coping with sex without a partner; having sex before, during, and after the birth of a baby; and sex and aging.

Overall, these men suggest that traditional role scripts for masculinity are incompatible with the development of intimacy, particularly sexual intimacy. Rather than the pursuit of an enduring erection, unfailing ejaculation, unmitigated and overpowering sexual desire, and consistent expertise in and knowledge of lovemaking, these men suggest that it is okay to be monogamous, masturbate, communicate feelings, be anxious, allow a woman to take the initiative, and plan for sex. In essence, these men want the flexibility to experience their innermost selves with their partners. (SGF)

IL
708. Petras, John W., ed. **Sex: Male/Gender: Masculine: Readings in Male Sexuality.** Port Washington, N.Y.: Alfred, 1975. 256 p. Includes bibliographic references. ISBN 0-88284-019-3.

Twenty-four previously published items examining the physiology of maleness and the cultural roles of masculinity make up this anthology. Part I, "The Individualistic Perspective," includes essays on the biological imperatives of maleness, as well as a nineteenth-century discourse on the hideous effects of masturbation and early twentieth-century views of how the "real boy" ought to behave. In part II, "The Socio-Cultural Perspective," the socialization of males is presented. Two comical boyhood memoirs by Julius Lester and Bill Cosby are followed by portraits of executive males and blue-collar working-class men at home. Mirra Komarovsky explores contradictions in the masculine role as experienced by college students. Part III, "Masculinity/Femininity," includes Jack O. Balswick and Charles W. Peek on the inexpressive male, Norman Mailer on women's liberation, and Michael Korda on the domestic chauvinist. Part IV, "Male Liberation and the New Masculinity," explores new directions for men, including Keith Olstad's "basis for discussion" of brave new men, and essays on breaking away from mainstream American masculine roles. (**Men's Studies**, 1985)

IL
709. Singer, June. **Androgyny: Toward a New Theory of Sexuality.** Introduction by Sheldon S. Hendler. Garden City, N.Y.: Anchor Press/Doubleday, 1976. 375 p. Includes bibliography and index. ISBN 0-385-11025-1.

The purpose of this book is to help one become conscious of the different aspects of himself or herself and to gain awareness of the dualities that mold the psyche, particularly the male-female duality. Singer, a Jungian psychologist, begins by tracing the development of religion in primitive societies and exploring the similarities among various mythologies. Each of the mythologies considered includes a time before creation in which an all-encompassing whole containing all potentiality existed. This "One" split into "Two," making creation possible. The Two symbolizes all polar opposites, including the masculine-feminine split within the psyche that prevents most individuals from achieving their true potential. Various philosophies and religions have attempted to integrate these opposites through study, discipline, and the practice of mental, physical, or sexual techniques. The Western world, however, has reinforced the psychic division through the patriarchal Judeo-Christian tradition and the emphasis on scientific method.

In part II Singer explores the ideal of androgyny, the full integration of the self or "the rhythmic interplay of Masculine and Feminine within the psyche of one individual" (p. 266). This integration is the result of an "evolution of consciousness" based on the acceptance of the universe as an open system in which energy can be created, enhanced, and exchanged. Acceptance of one's androgynous being is necessary for the development of both the creative woman and the feeling man. By developing the androgyne self, an individual can separate sex and gender roles, enabling one to form well-functioning interdependent relationships with others. Such an individual does not need to exploit a partner to fill voids in his or her personality. The androgyne accepts his or her own heterosexual, bisexual, and homosexual natures without guilt or confusion. Masturbation and celibacy can express life energy and inner fulfillment, although sexual intercourse holds the greatest potential for true androgynous experience through the dissolution of gender identity. The guiding principle of life for the androgyne is union, with the understanding and acceptance of its opposite, separation. (SDH)

Male/Female Relationships. Misogyny

(For related material see also entries 93, 411, 418, 963)

PR,IL
710. Banner, Lois W. **In Full Flower: Aging Women, Power, and Sexuality.** New York: Alfred A. Knopf, 1992. 422 p. Includes bibliographic notes and index. ISBN 0-394-57943-7.

When she was forty-eight, historian Banner "chanced into a relationship" with a thirty-year-old man. Her feeling that something was wrong about their being together surprised her and prompted her to think about cross-age relationships. Her personal odyssey led her to investigate aging in a more general way, particularly the link between power, sexuality, and gender, "central to all relationships." The interconnections between the topics of age-disparate relationships and aging "provide elucidation of the key matter of how, whether young or old, we make our way through the journey of life, to attain a respected, joyous maturity, to grow to the point that we are in 'full flower.' "

Statistics show that there is a rise in the number of marriages between older women and younger men; in 1983, nearly 40 percent of women aged 35-44 married younger men. Nevertheless, information about such relationships seems to be "forgotten history." Banner's goal in this book is "to reclaim this history of aging women, to find other stories hidden beneath the accepted narratives of the past" that reveal the contexts and themes that relate to aging women. Economic, demographic, and psychological interpretations of cross-age relationships are insufficient to explain the cultural and individual factors that enhance an older woman's power and allure. Therefore, a history of age-disparate relationships becomes a "history of the personal," of the factors that apply to relationships in general—love, sex, spirituality, power, autonomy, friendship, gender construction, and self-definition. In contrast to Simone de Beauvoir's *Coming of Age*, Banner goes beyond a discussion of oppression to discuss themes of resistance and independence among aging women.

In part 1, Banner demonstrates and articulates some of the main themes by analyzing the content and production of *Sunset Boulevard*, the 1950 film starring Gloria Swanson as an aging movie star of fifty and William Holden as a younger screenwriter who agrees to live with her. She uses the film as an historical text from which to explore the meaning of aging women from the ancient world to the present. Part 2 traces the history of aging women from the goddesses of ancient Greece and Rome with their younger male god-consorts and Penelope's young suitors in Homer's *Odyssey* to the emergence of dualistic Western concepts that categorize women as either spiritual or sexual. Part 3 explores the context of relationships from the medieval and early modern European centuries. Banner discusses courtly love in the eleventh century, the wife of Bath in Chaucer's fourteenth century *The Canterbury Tales*, and the persecution of witches in the seventeenth century. Part 4 considers women in more modern eras (the nineteenth and twentieth centuries). Definitions of gender shifted until the "domesticated, patriarchal family became a haven of security" and the spiritual, "sentimentalized, domestic woman" was at its core. The cross-age relationships of American writer Margaret Fuller and French novelist Colette are foci for a discussion of the nineteenth century while research and attitudes about menopause are indicative of attitudes about aging women in the twentieth century. Banner ends her study in part 5 with a discussion of the contemporary context of aging women. black women's experience shows that aging need not imply a lack of sexuality or fervor for life. However, research shows that patriarchy operates to maintain gender hierarchies. Negative periods of women's experience seem to coincide with periods of male dominance, particularly when women contest it. Nevertheless, "new definitions are being devised for the life-cycle categories of youth, middle age, and old age." (SGF)

IL
711. Barker-Benfield, G. J. **The Horrors of the Half-Known Life: Male Attitudes Toward Women and Sexuality in Nineteenth-Century America.** New York: Harper & Row, 1976. 352 p. Includes bibliographic references and index. ISBN 0-06-010224-1.
  Barker-Benfield, in this scholarly psychoanalytic examination of sex roles in nineteenth-century America, has drawn on the writings of Melville, from whose *Moby Dick* the title of this volume was taken; Alexis de Tocqueville; and John Todd, a prominent New England divine who wrote prolifically and prescriptively and on the history of medicine.
  This work is in four parts. Part I develops a composite picture of the pressures and effects of early American democracy on men. The theme of extreme separation of the sexes was developed by Tocqueville from his carefully documented observations of human behavior in the American wilderness. He described the American male as closed off from emotions and exploitative of nature, women, and Native Americans. The split between the sexes, inescapable and deplorable, was a recurring theme in Melville's work. Part II chronicles the campaign of American medicine against midwives and the concurrent development of obstetrics and gynecological surgery. Control of women (particularly their childbearing capacity and sexuality) by male gynecologists is presented as a variation on the sexual separation theme. Sexual surgery was promoted as a cure for masturbation and insanity. Vignettes of celebrated obstetricians and gynecologists portray them as monomaniacal, anxious, competitive men eager to parade their surgical virtuosity. Part III is devoted to analysis of the writings of the Reverend John Todd (1800-1873), whose *Student Manual* was intended to guide the conduct and personal development of young men. Masturbation was Todd's principal target. He developed the theme of a "spermatic economy" in which books, words, sperm, and money were seen as interchangeable resources to be hoarded or expended. He argued that subordination of women and separation of the sexes were required for full expression of male identity and power. Part IV profiles Augustus Kinsley Gardner, gynecologist and medical writer, who shared Todd's masturbation phobia, belief in a "spermatic economy," and attitudes toward women. His work addressed the political and social meanings of reproduction.
  Throughout the volume, Barker-Benfield looks at nineteenth-century man in historical context, building support for the thesis that pressures of democratic society on males shaped their sexual beliefs and attitudes toward women. (LF)

PR,IL,PO
712. Beck, Aaron T. **Love Is Never Enough: How Couples Can Overcome Misunderstandings, Resolve Conflicts, and Solve Relationship Problems Through Cognitive Therapy.** New York: Harper & Row, 1989. 415 p. Includes bibliography and index. ISBN 0-06-091604-4.
  Although love is a powerful force in a marriage, "it does not in itself create the substance of the relationship—the personal qualities and skills that are crucial to sustain it and make it grow" (p. 5). In this book designed to educate and provide guidelines for dealing with partnership problems, Beck, University Professor of Psychiatry at the University of Pennsylvania, applies the principles of cognitive therapy to difficulties in intimate relationships. Cognitive therapy is based on the assumption that the way a person thinks about another's actions determines how he or she reacts emotionally to the person. By correcting

misinterpretations, clarifying miscommunication, and altering self-defeating ways of thinking, housemates, roommates, and bedmates of the same or different genders can improve communication and develop a more enjoyable and fulfilling relationship. The first nine chapters address some of the most common problems in thinking and communication that affect relationships: (1) the power of negative thinking; (2) the shift from idealization and positive framing "in love" to disillusionment in longer term relationships; (3) the clash of differing perspectives; (4) the imposition of rigid expectations and rules; (5) static in communication; (6) conflicts over important decision-making; (7) the role of automatic thoughts that precede anger and self-defeating behavior; (8) thinking disorders and biases; (9) hostility. The next nine chapters provide helpful suggestions for showing couples how each partner can take responsibility for his/her role in the relationship and choose to change it by such techniques as redefining the problem; reinforcing commitment, trust, goodwill, loyalty, and fidelity; keeping track of positive behaviors; changing personal distortions; clarifying conversation; working together; and understanding the partner's perspective. The last chapter addresses special problems such as reduction of sexual desire; sexual problems; and infidelity.

Copious examples and self-help exercises at the end of many of the chapters supplement the theoretical framework of the book to facilitate its use as a self-help book. Beck "walks" the reader through the principles of each chapter with the expectation that many couples' problems can be solved by adjusting cognitions and practicing new ways of processing information about partners. (SGF)

PR

713. Bloch, R. Howard. **Medieval Misogyny and the Invention of Western Romantic Love.** Chicago: University of Chicago Press, 1991. 298 p. Includes bibliography and index. ISBN 0-226-05972-3.

Bloch defines misogyny as "a speech act in which woman is the subject and the predicate a more general term," that is, the transformation of "woman" to a universalized object that removes individual woman from history. Only by examining antifeminist writing—and its clichés—can its internal incoherence be exposed, allowing misogyny to be deconstructed and exposed as both wrong and inconsistent.

A persistent repetitive discourse of misogyny permeated writing during the medieval period and governed the way women were perceived through the nineteenth century. Even the literature of courtly love, sometimes seen to oppose misogyny, is closely related to this antifeminism. Medieval misogyny stems from the writings of the Church fathers and is based on the association of the feminine with the corporeal and the masculine with the mind or soul; the association of women with the cosmetic, decorative, and false; and the theological condemnation of simulation, aesthetics, or pleasure in material embodiment. Simultaneously, Christianity teaches equality of the sexes and idealizes women martyrs. This creates a polarized, marginalized, contradictory definition of the feminine that traps women in both the Fall and the Redemption of humanity. Within this paradox, the only route to salvation or equality is through perfection, defined as virginity; but true virginity denies corporeality. Virginity is a pure, abstract, and negative idea, which is destroyed by its embodiment or even its perception; in literature, this leads to the death of the virgin.

The theme of love lost through indiscretion, which permeates the literature of courtly love, is an extension of this medieval obsession with virginity. However, an analysis of love lyrics reveals that they deal primarily with the (male) poet's perception of himself. Possession of the idealized virgin is necessary to the completion of the male identity, but can never be achieved. Historically, courtly love appeared at the beginning of the twelfth century, just when women were gaining power to hold and dispose of real property and to make their own marriage choices. The idealization of women through courtly love mirrored misogyny as an antifeminist reduction and disenfranchisement that served to remove women from public life. (SDH)

IL

714. Bloom, Allan. **The Closing of the American Mind.** New York: Simon & Schuster, 1987. 392 p. Includes index. ISBN 0-671-47990-3.

Although the central concern of this book is higher education, it includes valuable subjective descriptions of the sexual attitudes and behavior of an important group in American society: "the kind of young persons who populate the twenty or thirty best universities." Bloom's "sample" thus "consists of thousands of students of comparatively high intelligence, materially and spiritually free to do pretty much what they want with the few years of college they are privileged to have."

The burden of his presentation on sexuality is given in a single chapter, "Relationships" (pp. 82-137), which includes subsections entitled "Sex," "Separateness," "Divorce," "Love," and "Eros" (interspersed with subsections on self-centeredness, equality, and race, minimally related to sexuality). He draws a picture of sexual behavior almost untouched by love (owing to an inability to make serious commitments) or by eros (there is no divine madness, there are no Dantes yearning for Beatrice and "the easy sex of teen-agers snips the golden thread linking eros to education").

Another chapter, "Music" (pp. 68-81), argues that listening to rock music is a form of masturbation based on the rhythm of copulation, and that it is agreeable to the youth culture's desire for free sexual expression, anarchism, and the "mining of the irrational unconscious and giving it free rein." Although these two chapters are self-contained, the two chapters preceding them illuminate the attitudes underlying student sexuality. (DJS)

PO

715. Cassell, Carol. **Swept Away: Why Women Fear Their Own Sexuality.** New York: Simon & Schuster, 1984. 206 p. Includes bibliography. ISBN 0-671-45238-X.

Women today are concerned about their roles in male/female relationships. Understandably, many of them still cling to certain romantic notions about love, about being "swept away" by Mr. Right, who will lead them confidently into a blissful future composed of devoted husband, charming offspring, and cozy home. Unfortunately and increasingly, Mr. Right is failing to live up to expectations. Typically in the current environment, our vulnerable young women, after falling hopelessly in love and succumbing to their lovers' persistent blandishments, are inexplicably abandoned. The problem stems from women's inability to separate myth from reality. Men and women are operating on different planes. Women view love as a concomitant part of sex: "love + sex = LOVE"; men use love (and words of love) to get sex: "sex + love = sex." Cassell uses the expression "Swept Away" to describe "a sexual strategy, a coping mechanism, that allows women to be sexual in a society that is, at best, still ambivalent about, and at worst, condemnatory of female sexuality. It is a tactic, employed unconsciously by women to get what they want—a man, sexual pleasure—without having to pay the price of being labeled wanton or promiscuous. Swept Away is, consequently, a counterfeit emotion, a fraud, a disguide of our true erotic feelings which we've been socialized to describe as romance" (p. 25). Hoping to take advantage of the social and sexual gains chalked up in the 1960s, women are looking for solutions to problems inherent in their precarious relations with men. Is there, for example, an approach to dating that is not fraught with fears and dangers? Cassell, President of the American Association of Sex Educators, Counselors and Therapists, thinks so; she uses her extensive background and experience derived from serious discussions with women across the country, to arrive at an effective strategy for women to cope with the often disastrous "Swept Away" syndrome. Essentially, it involves looking at sex realistically; embracing it as a legitimate source of pleasure; being responsible for one's contraceptive needs; acting independently, knowledgeably, and discriminatingly in the face of one's admitted sexuality; and not taking foolish chances in so-called romantic situations. In this way, women may overcome the fear of their own sexuality in their relations with men. (TJW)

IL
716. Dinnerstein, Dorothy. **The Mermaid and the Minotaur: Sexual Arrangements and Human Malaise.** New York: Harper & Row, 1976. 288 p. Includes bibliography. ISBN 0-06-090587-5.

Dinnerstein uses the myth images of half-human beasts to underscore the ambiguity of the human position in the animal kingdom and to symbolize female seductiveness and male lust for power. She develops the thesis that, in our society, women are offered immunity from risks and efforts related to achievement and that both males and females foster and make use of that female immunity. She decries what she views as the morbidity of our "sexual arrangements." Defining "sexual arrangements" as "the division of responsibility, opportunity and privilege that prevails between male and female humans and the patterns of psychological interdependence that are implicit in this division," she paints our gender arrangement as a no-win situation for both men and women. She sees women as bearing life-long parenting responsibility that is accompanied by real authority only when their children are very young. In their relationships with males, Dinnerstein believes women have power only to withdraw love; all other economic and social powers rest with men. The female is portrayed as embodying parental responsibility and childlike powerlessness.

Dinnerstein draws skillfully from literature, philosophy, anthropology, psychology, and a deep sense of self as she traces the origins of gender separation to predominant female care of the young and to gender roles that govern the reliving and reworking of the original infant/parent relationship. She argues that a gender-based division of responsibility locks us into a self-destructive stance which she believes threatens our collective survival, and she poses the question of why this semihuman, monstrous mermaid and minotaur collaboration is perpetuated. (LF)

PO
717. Farrell, Warren. **Why Men Are the Way They Are.** New York: McGraw-Hill, 1986. 403 p. Includes bibliography and index. ISBN 0-07-019974-4.

This book is meant to complement Farrell's earlier work, *The Liberated Man* (1975), in which he explained for men how women construe the significance of independence. It articulates how men experience male-female relationships. The themes discussed were generated in over 300 workshops that Farrell conducted with men and a similar number with women. He deals with such questions as why love, intimacy, and commitment mean different things to men and women; why men are so preoccupied with success; and how a woman can get a man to express his feelings or how she can change him for the better.

Central to an understanding of men's experiences is the role that primary fantasies play for both men and women. A man's primary fantasy is sexual access to many beautiful women, while a woman's is obtaining economic and emotional security through marriage. Men pursue success to be accepted by beautiful women, while women cultivate beauty to capture the attention and commitment of successful men. In the process, men become women's "success objects" while women become men's "sex objects." Many of the conflicts and dilemmas that men and women face in relating to each other stem from the implications of pursuing different fantasies. Serious social problems such as rape and spouse abuse are also related to these themes. An emphasis on women's sense of powerlessness has led to a "new sexism" that discounts men's feelings of powerlessness. If power is defined to include control over one's life, then both men and women experience their own brand of frustration and impotence.

Farrell draws on numerous portrayals of men and women in the media to support his point of view. He details the logical implications of a male's pursuit of success and a female's of beauty, to explain a wide variety of problems of and between men and women. For example, the distancing required for attaining success can alienate a man from the skills needed to develop intimacy. Farrell explodes many myths about why men are the way they are and provides guidelines that both men and women can use to better understand each other. He concludes that equality involves taking responsibility for what does or does not happen, not blaming the other. Accepting mutual responsibility can pave the way for truly loving behavior, not love based on destructive fantasies. (SGF)

PR

718.   Fisher, Seymour. **Sexual Images of the Self: The Psychology of Erotic Sensa- tions and Illusions.** Hillsdale, N.J.: Lawrence Erlbaum Associates, 1989. 345 p. Includes bibliography and indexes. ISBN 0-8058-0439-0.

Fisher builds on two aspects of his previous research—one on "how people construct ideas about their body space" (p. x) (e.g., *Body Experience in Fantasy and Behavior*, 1970; *Body Consciousness*, 1973; *Development and Structure of the Body Image*, 1986) and the other on "factors contributing to sexual responsiveness in women (e.g., *The Female Orgasm*, 1973)" (p. x)—to examine the interface between body image and sexuality. His goals are twofold: (1) to "trace how sexual practices and fictions infiltrate and, in turn, are influenced by our body attitudes" (p. ix) and (2) "to provide up-to-date analyses of the literature dealing with a range of topics (e.g., orgasm consistency, clitoral-vaginal preference, erectile dysfunction in men, the etiology of homosexuality) that have long been a matter of puzzled concern to sex researchers" (p. x). The seven chapters, replete with references to relevant research, present hypotheses about how sexuality shapes body image and how body image affects sexual behavior as they apply to child development; male and female sexual awareness and response; the origins of homosexuality, cross-dressing, and transsexuality; and the psychological response of women to changes in their bodies as a result of pregnancy, menstruation, contraception, and birth. The final chapter presents an overview of "strategies and illusions mediating sexual tuning" (p. 255).

Fisher asserts that most of us construct a "body map," but most cultures are uncomfortable with the "natural" body. Parents socialize their children to believe "sexual fictions," e.g., that sex does not exist, which conflict with children's own genital sensations. This Western tradition of distorting the role and experience of sexuality results in confusion about the body; and, it hampers a child's development, which depends upon establishing a clear definition and boundary for his/her body. As an adult, a person's socialization about his/her body may affect sexual response. Orgasmic women have a clear sense of their body's boundaries and are assertive, confident, and able to provide feedback about sexual stimulation. Men with erectile difficulties are often socialized to perceive their bodies in a negative way and to be unaware of their bodies' responses. Fisher thinks that a child's early experience of trying to reconcile the physical differences between males and females into an acceptable form may result in problems that contribute to homosexuality. Transvestism and transsexualism may be very human expressions of body dissatisfaction, similar to those of people who desire to alter their bodies, and their identities, with plastic surgery. Overall, it is relatively easy for a person to create illusions about his/her body, particularly since the culture often engenders unrealistic ideas about the body. Women, in particular, face reproductive changes in their bodies (e.g., menstruation, contraception, pregnancy, birth), that require consistent, periodic adjustments to changes in body image. Fisher explores how they deal with these alterations.

In the final chapter, Fisher notes that "sexuality is a prime pathway for the culture to transmit body meanings" (p. 287). He relates his findings to Freud's formulations, refuting Freud's view that sexual problems are signs of general psychological disturbance. (SGF)

PO

719.   Goldberg, Herb. **The New Male: From Self-Destruction to Self-Care.** New York: Morrow, 1979. 321 p. Includes bibliographic references and index. ISBN 0-688-03526-4.

In this energetic exhortation, Goldberg sees the modern male in crisis, and offers advice on how to replace his self-destructive tendencies with positive changes that will include self-care, spontaneity, and personal fulfillment. The book's first section, analyzing the present male dilemma, depicts modern American men as cardboard Goliaths, compulsively proving their masculinity, running from failure, and facing mid-life burnout. In section II, Goldberg explores how different kinds of women can place men in difficult binds. Especially interesting is his account of the Actor-Reactor syndrome, in which the man's role as the initiating and responsible partner inevitably leads to accusations that he is an oppressor and exploiter. Conversely, Goldberg also analyzes the binds which men can place women in by their conflicting demands. In section III, he explores men's reactions to the women's movement, discussing how men's timid responses can result in their getting the worst of both sides of the liberation crunch. He castigates the willingness of present society to accept and perpetuate negative and sexist stereotypes of men: he advises men that the women's movement can save their lives—but only if they stop reacting with guilt-laden accommodation and start refashioning their lives to meet their own needs. The final section offers advice to help men emerge from the restrictions of past gender roles. It urges them to become aware of antimale sexist vocabulary, learn to feed themselves, cultivate buddyships, avoid "earth mother" women, and "custom-make" their own lives. (**Men's Studies**, 1985)

PO
720. Goldberg, Herb. **What Men Really Want.** New York: Signet, 1991. 224 p. ISBN 0-451-16972-7.
　　Clinical psychologist Goldberg's intent is to "provide a psychological map for the development of a realistic and authentic relationship" (p. 15) . . . by "bringing the reality of men to women and women's negative responses to a neutral starting point so that accurate, objective listening can replace the defensively filtered distortions that now occur . . ." (p. 30). Understanding, listening, and acceptance of a man as he really is are all routes to a loving relationship. Blame, anger, resentment, crying, overdependency, and accusations in response to men impede a satisfying relationship and may prompt withdrawal.
　　The first half of the book is an introduction to men's reality, which explains why men withdraw, need to control, seem aggressive, seem to have "cold" logic, are so interested in sex, and won't open up. Goldberg offers practical advice to women who want to cope with men's defensive behaviors by discussing why men have the behavior; its effect on the man; its effect on the woman; and what the woman can do about it. Underlying his advice are several themes. Not only is it important for a woman to hear what the man is communicating with his behavior but also to develop her own inner strength, boundaries, and sense of self, regardless of whether she is in or out of a relationship. Ultimately, Goldberg thinks that men want self-assured women, not dependent ones. Relationships involve a give and take as well as a willingness to accept responsibility for one's own actions and work through conflict. Support means honest communication, not just enthusiasm and encouragement.
　　The second half of the book is focused on three areas. First, answering questions that women have about men. For example, why does he hate it when I cry? Why is he afraid to commit? Why do men have extramarital affairs? Why isn't he as interested in sex as he was in the beginning of the relationship? Why doesn't he have any close friends? Why does he feel so insecure, even though he's so successful? Second, explaining the polarities that harm a relationship. A basic theme is that "whatever women struggle with, men struggle with the opposite" (p. 149) because men and women do not share the same view of the world and therefore, the same reality. Dealing with conflict becomes a matter of looking at one's own defenses and recognizing one's own role in relationship struggles. Whether and how to make a man over is the subject of an entire chapter. Goldberg concludes with suggestions for how to relate to a man realistically and develop intimacy with him. Key themes in these suggestions are maintaining your own identity and self-esteem; not assuming that someone can fulfill all of your needs or make you happy; dealing with conflict; and recognizing and understanding the defenses of one's role. (SGF)

PO

721. Lerner, Harriet Goldhor. **The Dance of Intimacy: A Woman's Guide to Coura-geous Acts of Change in Key Relationships.** New York: Harper & Row, 1989. 255 p. Includes bibliographic notes and index.

Lerner, a staff psychologist and psychotherapist at the Menninger Clinic, directs her attention to facilitating intimacy, broadening the scope of her analysis from the subject of her previous best-selling book, *The Dance of Anger.* Intimacy means being who we are and letting others be the same; staying emotionally connected even though we are different from our partner; and being able to express personal strengths and weaknesses in a balanced way. The goal of the book is to develop guidelines for change so that "we have relationships with both men and women that do not operate at the expense of the self, and to have a self that does not operate at the expense of the other. . . . it is the heart and soul of intimacy" (p. 4).

Drawing on a theoretical framework of family systems, psychoanalysis, and feminism, Lerner emphasizes those aspects that she has found "empowering, theoreti-cally sound, and useful in my personal life and professional work." At the core of these concerns is a focus on the self and the family. Without a well-grounded sense of self, intimacy cannot occur. Defining the self occurs in the process of interacting with others. Anxiety, conflict, and anger are clues to "hot" emotional issues that need to be resolved. Often these "negative emotions" stem from unresolved problems in the family of origin and express themselves in current relationships. The path to intimacy includes identifying the original pattern and confronting family members about them. Relatives usually resist efforts to change so that the family system stays intact. Thinking rather than reacting to resistance; being persistent, calm, and defining a "bottom line"; and maintaining a self-focus rather than a critical one aid in changing negative patterns. Change is difficult, particularly because individuals are embedded in systems of relationships. Because culture shapes definitions of the family and intimacy, "personal change is inseparable from social and political change." This book provides information for individuals who want to effect a change. (SGF)

IL

722. Masters, R. E. L., and Eduard Lea, comps. **The Anti-Sex: The Belief in the Natural Inferiority of Women: Studies in Male Frustration and Sexual Conflict.** New York: Julian Press, 1964. 492 p.

Masters and Lea have assembled this anthology of writings by fifteen male authors of the past to show the widely held belief in the inferiority of women. Masters provides an introductory review of the literature from antiquity to the present and thus tries to explain this worldwide hatred of women throughout history.

These selections represent but a small sampling of this large genre of literature. Following the paper by Masters, they include "A Note on Misogyny in the East" by well-known Arabist and Orientalist Allen Edwardes; a selection from a classic of Arab erotology, *The Perfumed Garden,* by Sheikh Nefzawi; an excerpt from the Marquis de Sade's famous novel *Juliette*; an essay, *On Women,* by the great German philosopher Arthur Schopenhauer; a comedy, *The Thesmophoriazusae,* by the Greek dramatist Aristophanes; a John Dryden translation of Roman satirist Juvenal's *Sixth Satire*; a selection from the infamous *Malleus Maleficarum* (The Witches' Hammer) by the Dominicans James Sprenger and Heinrich Kramer concerning the behavior of witches; and Joseph Swetnam's seventeenth-century pamphlet *The Arraignment of Lewde, Idle, Froward and Inconstant Women.*

Further selections include the sixteenth-century anonymous catalog in verse of male grievances against women, entitled *Against Women*; Jonathan Swift's *A Letter to a Young Lady on Her Marriage,* published in 1727; another anonymous work *Man Superior to Woman,* first published in 1739, concerning woman's inferior intellectual capacity; a selection from O. F. Adams's *The Presumption of Sex,* published in 1892, attacking woman's alleged lack of compassion, cruelty, and ruthlessness; selections from Edouard de Beaumont's *The Sword and Womankind,* published in 1882, holding woman responsible for much that is regrettable in human history; a selection from August Strindberg's autobiographical novel, *The Confessions of a Fool*, describing an unhappy marriage; Otto Weininger's philosophical reflections concerning womankind in his book *Sex and Character*; and finally John Philip Lundin's book *Women*, published in 1963, describing the good and bad feminine traits that make women desirable to men.

These writings contain material sufficient for an understanding of misogyny throughout the world over a vast span of time; nevertheless they only suggest the extent of this type of material in the world's literature. (TJW)

PO

723. Packard, Vance. **The Sexual Wilderness: The Contemporary Upheaval in Male-Female Relationships.** New York: David McKay, 1968. 557 p. Includes bibliographic notes and index.

Shunning the term *sexual revolution* as accurately descriptive of the changing sexual scene in the 1960s, Packard, whose keen observations of social phenomena appear in such works as *The Hidden Persuaders* (1957) and *The Waste Makers* (1960), christened this fractious period of confrontation the "sexual wilderness" and used this expression for the title of his book. In it he labors at understanding the stresses and strains of faltering male-female relationships in a host of economic, social, moral, and technological contexts. For four years, Packard read extensively, traveled widely, and studied intensively the whole question of sexual relations between men and women in contemporary Western society, especially the United States. In part I, "Changes and New Problems," he uses surveys conducted since World War I bearing on sex roles, women's liberation, courtship, premarital sex, marriage, extramarital sex, swinging, and so forth in an attempt to understand the rapid changes occurring in sexual attitudes and behavior. He identifies six environmental forces that have contributed to a change in male-female relationships in the 1960s: (1) the development of new contraceptives, (2) technological innovation in the home, (3) the impact of increased life expectancy for both men and women and shifts in age distribution within the population, (4) expansion of higher education, (5) changes in personal and religious beliefs, and (6) lifestyle changes produced by war and international tensions.

In light of the seemingly dramatic increases in sexual freedom and uninhibited behavior, Packard devotes part II, "Assessments and Possible Directions," to an analysis of these trends and a demonstration of the directions society might take in future male-female relationships. He first examines a spectrum of sexual attitudes and behaviors in three dissimilar countries: the Soviet Union, Israel, and Sweden, and then reviews the opinions and conclusions of anthropologists (J. D. Unwin, G. Murdock), sociologists (C. C. Zimmerman, P. Sorokin), psychologists (S. Freud, O. Sternbach), sexologists (A. Ellis, A. Kinsey), and historian A. J. Toynbee on whether sexual freedom should be encouraged or made a matter of social concern. Packard confesses to being "more impressed by the cautionary views of Toynbee, Unwin, Freud, and Sternbach than by those calling for still greater permissiveness and naturalism" (p. 396). Finally, he turns his attention to the features of a code of sex standards appropriate for the modern world, and then looks at the prospects for sound marriages and enjoyable unions in the twenty-first century. He concludes on a positive note with a discussion of seven characteristics that he thinks contribute to a successful marriage: (1) a large capacity for affection, (2) emotional maturity, (3) effective communication, (4) a zest for life, (5) the capacity to handle tensions constructively, (6) a playful approach to sex, and (7) acceptance of a partner as he or she is. (TJW)

PR,IL,PO

724. Tannen, Deborah. **You Just Don't Understand: Women and Men in Conversation.** New York: Morrow, 1990. 330 p. Includes bibliography and index. ISBN 0-688-07822-2.

Men and women can interpret the same conversation differently and contribute to misunderstandings in a relationship. Tannen, Professor of Linguistics at Georgetown University, thinks that gender differences in ways of speaking, "genderlects," underlie some of this miscommunication. By using a sociolinguistic approach to male/female communication, she identifies gender patterns in communication and seeks to understand them.

Gendered communication styles derive from the different ways that men and women participate in and perceive their worlds. Men engage in a hierarchical social order that requires competition, negotiation, achievement, and protection. "Life . . . is a contest, a struggle to preserve independence and avoid failure" (p. 25). In contrast, women are involved in a social network of connection that calls for negotiation, balance, support, and consensus. "Life . . . is a community, a struggle to preserve intimacy and avoid isolation" (p. 25). For men, status (and familiarity with asymmetry) is of primary concern, whereas for women, intimacy (and familiarity with symmetry) is the focus. Conversations between men and women reflect these world views; these metamessages engender different interpretations of conversations.

For example, a woman is not feeling well and tells her husband. He responds by offering to take her to the doctor. She feels slighted and angry because she did not receive what she wanted. For her, the process of talking about her problem is reassuring and establishes a connection. For him, her ailment is a problem to be solved and requires action. He thinks he is being effective by helping remove the source of her problem, and she feels that he does not care about her feelings. Tannen offers numerous other examples to demonstrate common types of differences in interpretation of conversations by men and women. She addresses the following issues: Why men are so absorbed by reading the newspaper and gathering information; why women share secrets and converse more with their female friends; why men seem to lecture rather than listen; why men engage in what appears to be competitive talk while women make "nice" talk; why women's talk seems cooperative and polite while men's seems punctuated by interruptions. Problems arise when women try to interpret men's conversation by women's standards, and vice versa. By understanding the world view that shapes the conversational styles of men and women and keying into the metamessages common to each world, men and women can begin to bridge the communication gap. (SGF)

SOCIAL EXPECTATIONS EXPRESSED IN SOCIAL INSTITUTIONS

Law. Criminal Justice System

(For related material see also entries 354, 620, 642, 933)

PR,IL
725. Barnett, Walter. **Sexual Freedom and the Constitution: An Inquiry into the Constitutionality of Repressive Sex Laws.** Albuquerque, N. Mex.: University of New Mexico Press, 1973. 333 p. Includes bibliographic notes and index. ISBN 0-8263-0255-6.

Barnett, a professor of law, believes that the sodomy statutes in American states are unconstitutional because they discourage individuals, especially homosexuals, from pursuing happiness in their own way. Individuals who fornicate, commit adultery, or engage in so-called unnatural sex acts or homosexual acts can be prosecuted for criminal behavior under the sodomy statutes of a number of states, despite the fact that these are usually private and victimless acts between consenting adults.

Barnett presents arguments that attack these so-called morals laws on constitutional grounds. The particular laws in question are those that prohibit "unnatural" sex acts (commonly referred to as "sodomy" laws), often embracing, besides sodomy, such related sexual practices as fellatio and cunnilingus. The arguments selected to support his position that these laws are unconstitutional include the void-for-vagueness doctrine (many statutes use the vague and undefined expression "crimes against nature"); the right-of-privacy doctrine; the establishment of religion clause of the first amendment (sodomy laws have a demonstrably religious origin); the independent rights doctrine (arguing that sexual fulfillment, although not provided for in the Bill of Rights, is a fundamental human right); the use of scientific knowledge in judging the criminality of deviational sexual behavior, and its relevance to the "sickness theory" and the prospects for "cure"; equal protection under the law (there is discrimination against minorities, e.g., homosexuals); and cruel and unusual punishment (referring to lengthy felony sentences for sodomy in certain states). Each of these arguments, exemplified by decisions rendered in numerous cases, includes a discussion of the Constitution and relevant state laws.

Barnett believes that changes in the majority's attitude toward minorities can be brought about through the political process, as has been the experience of blacks in the United States. However, their lack of visibility makes this a difficult route for homosexuals. He hopes that the judiciary will exhibit "enough human sympathy to apply these arguments and *compel* reform," and with reform "the state would finally be expelled from a sanctuary to which it should never have been admitted in the first place—the intimate private lives of its citizens" (p. 313). (TJW)

PR

726. Brundage, James A. **Law, Sex, and Christian Society in Medieval Europe.** Chicago: University of Chicago Press, 1987. 674 p. Includes bibliography and indexes. ISBN 0-226-07783-7.

In the preface to this monumental work, Brundage, Professor of History at the University of Wisconsin, Milwaukee, states that the book's focus is "on the triangular relationship between sexual practices, theological values, and law" (p. xx). Furthermore, he intends to show that medieval canon law was crucial to the development of modern sex laws in the West, and that the canonists had based their thinking upon the earlier work of patristic writers and theologians, transforming moral teachings into law. Secularization of medieval canon law began after 1300 with the Reformation.

Brundage begins historically by reviewing sexual behavior and the law in the ancient world (Near East, Greece, Rome), in Judaism and early Christianity, and in the Christian Empire from Constantine to Justinian. Similarly he reviews law and sex in early medieval Europe from the sixth to the eleventh centuries. And finally he examines canon law, sexual behavior, and the era of church reform in the twelfth century. In each of these chapters Brundage discusses the law concerning certain topics, including marriage, divorce, remarriage, adultery, prostitution, concubinage, rape, and sexual deviations.

The core of the book (chapters 6 to 9) deals first with sex and marriage as systematically expressed in a twelfth century textbook of canon law entitled *Decretum* by the jurist Gratian; then with sexual behavior as treated by the early decretists (canon law teachers) from Paucapalea to Huguccio; followed by sex and marriage in canon law from Pope Alexander to Pope Gregory IX, a period lasting from 1190 to 1234, which produced numerous commentaries on canon law; and finally sex, marriage, and the legal commentators from 1234 to 1348.

In chapters 10-12, Brundage surveys sex, marriage, and the law from the Black Death, when between a quarter and a third of Europe's population perished, to the Reformation, at the beginning of the sixteenth century. It was a stable period during which little change took place in the law and theology of sex and marriage. He continues dealing with the usual sexual issues in the Age of the Reformation, the efforts of the Protestant reformers, Luther, Calvin, and others. Catholic reforms and counter-reforms, the Council of Trent, and so forth. Distinguishing between sex law in Protestant societies and Catholic societies, Brundage brings out the similarities and differences between Protestant and Catholic attitudes toward sex, and how both have been affected by medieval sex law.

Brundage concludes by reflecting on the relationship between medieval sex law and modern society, citing three factors—the socioeconomic environment, the identification of the erotic with the sacred, and the inertia of the law and its institutions—to help explain the prevalence of medieval sexual teaching in the legal systems of Western societies today. He points out that "legislative bodies and courts have begun to eliminate some vestiges of the medieval Christian view from the secular laws" (p. 587). Appendix 3 discusses "Survivals of Medieval Sex Law in the United States and the Western World." (TJW)

PR,IL

726a. Garrow, David J. **Liberty and Sexuality: The Right to Privacy and the Making of** *Roe v. Wade*. New York: Macmillan, 1994. 981 p. Includes bibliography and index. ISBN 0-02-542755-5.

Pulitzer Prize winner and author of *Bearing the Cross*, the highly acclaimed biography of civil rights leader Martin Luther King, Jr., Garrow, in *Liberty and Sexuality*, traces the legal history of two separate though related reproductive rights movements in the United States: birth control and abortion. He holds that the birth control movement had its legal origin in an 1879 Connecticut criminal law that prohibited not only the actual use of contraceptives but also declared such devices obscene and forbade any discussion about them. Connecticut birth control advocates, including at one time Katherine Houghton Hepburn (the mother of the actress), took over eighty years to overcome opposition to birth control. On June 7, 1965, the U.S. Supreme Court in *Griswold v. Connecticut* ruled by a 7 to 2 vote that the Connecticut birth control law was unconstitutional, that it infringed upon privacy rights within the family. Connecticut's defense was based on the belief that the law prevented sexual immorality by forbidding contraceptives to married couples.

Garrow, recently Visiting Distinguished Professor of History at The Cooper Union, conducted hundreds of interviews and researched the extensive archival materials in order to understand the struggle to make abortion a woman's private reproductive right. Believing that "The right to privacy is inherent in the right to liberty" (p. 705), Garrow traces the history of the abortion movement, linking it to the birth control movement. He examines the challenges to and the defenses of both the Texas and Georgia antiabortion statutes. In great detail he reveals the U.S. Supreme Court's deliberations concerning *Roe v. Wade* and *Doe v. Bolton*. On January 22, 1973, the U.S. Supreme Court ruled by a 7 to 2 vote that the Texas and Georgia statutes were unconstitutional and declared abortion a woman's constitutional right.

Garrow also discusses legislation subsequent to *Roe v. Wade*. In a series of decisions the Court had ruled that unmarried adults and teenagers had rights to privacy in their sexual activity. But the Court also began to narrow its understanding of the right to privacy, as in its decision in *Bowers v. Hardwick* (1986) when it denied the right to privacy to same-sex couples to have consensual sex in private.

Garrow considers these landmark court decisions made in the late 1960s and early 1970s, as setting the legal boundaries of the sexual revolution. His monumental study of the legal history of the birth control and abortion movements in the United States lays the groundwork for future investigations of the right to privacy issue. (TJW)

PR

727. Gebhard, Paul H., John H. Gagnon, Wardell B. Pomeroy, and Cornelia V. Christenson. **Sex Offenders: An Analysis of Types.** New York: Harper & Row, 1965. 923 p. Includes bibliography and indexes.

This study of sex offenders and sex offenses, conducted by the staff of the Institute for Sex Research, relies on data gathered from books, official records, and interviews with men incarcerated in American penal institutions, supplemented with help from consultants and penal authorities. The authors state: "Our primary purpose in making this study has been to determine if and how persons who have been convicted of various types of sex offenses differ from those who have not, and how they differ from one another" (p. 12). The study consists largely of statistical tables of data and descriptive text derived from interviews of over 1,500 men convicted of a wide variety of sex offenses, whether in prison or not. For control purposes, these data are compared with similar data taken from the sexual histories of thousands of persons never convicted of a sex offense that were available from the files of the Institute.

Various definitions of sex offenders and sex offenses—legal, cultural, and psychiatric—are examined in order to arrive at workable definitions. For the purposes of the study, "a sex offender is a person who has been legally convicted as the result of an overt act, committed by him for his own immediate sexual gratification, which is contrary to the prevailing sexual mores of the society in which he lives and/or is legally punishable" (p. 9). Because women are "rarely charged with, and still more rarely convicted of, sex offenses other than prostitution," this study is limited to "white" men and to sex offenders sixteen years of age and over.

The types of sex offenses into which the sample is divided are based on three independent variables: (1) whether the offense was homosexual or heterosexual in nature; (2) whether the offense was consensual or forced; and (3) whether the object of the offense was a child, a minor, or adult. A typical category is "heterosexual, forced, with an adult." In addition, peeping, genital exhibition, and three types of incest are included among the fourteen types of sex offenses established. Chapters 2 and 3 cover methodology, terminology, and sample descriptions used in the study.

Sex offenders, prison, and control groups are compared with respect to a large number of variables, including masturbation, sex dreams, marriage, extramarital coitus, homosexual activity, animal contacts, and criminality. The data on various types of sex offenders are presented first in a series of descriptive chapters; subsequent chapters deal mainly with the variables used in describing and comparing the types of sex offenders.

In the epilogue the authors state that "it is impossible to summarize in any adequate way the enormous and highly diverse amount of data on which this sex offender study is based" (p. 873), and they claim that "given the data in this present volume and life histories of individuals comparable to the histories we took, one could predict with an accuracy better than chance what sort of sex offense an individual would commit were he to commit one" (p. 874). Commenting on the law, the authors suggest that there will be no "great reduction in the number of sex offenders unless our laws are changed to an unlikely degree." They also support the widespread belief that "what two or more consenting adults do sexually in private should not be governed by statute law." Undoubtedly, such a belief, if carried out within the law, would reduce the number of sex offenders. (TJW)

PR

728. Green, Richard. **Sexual Science and the Law.** Cambridge, Mass.: Harvard University Press, 1992. 323 p. Includes bibliographic notes and index. ISBN 0-674-80268-3.

Green is Professor of Psychiatry at the University of California, Los Angeles. Bringing a sexual science perspective to his work, he has testified in dozens of legal cases. He also has a law degree. In his introduction to this text, Green points out that sexual science data has been accumulating at a great rate since the Kinsey Reports of 1948 and 1953, the work of Masters and Johnson in the 1960s and 1970s, and the explosion of sex research in the 1980s. It is now possible to use this information to inform lawyers and the courts of its relevance to legal cases covering a wide variety of sexual issues.

The need for this book stems from the explosion of information on such topics as child sexual abuse, abortion, transsexualism, and the like, and the need to apprise lawyers and judges of this vast new knowledge derived from research and study of human sexuality. In a series of chapters, Green deals with such issues as fornication, child custody and homosexual parents, homosexuality as a fundamental right, immigration and homosexuality, transsexualism, pornography, intergenerational sexuality, sex education, prostitution, abortion, surgical or chemical castration of sex offenders, sex-linked defenses to criminal behavior, and sexual science and sexual privacy.

In each of the chapters, Green generally asks a series of pertinent questions, explains what is known about the subject on the basis of sex research, reviews the law bearing on the subject, and then shows how sexual science information has been brought to bear in legal cases in order to bring about an informed decision. For example, in the chapter on fornication, he refers back to the landmark outcome in the *Griswold v. Connecticut* case where Connecticut law prohibited the use of contraceptives. In 1967 the Connecticut legislature repealed the law. Fornication, defined as sexual intercourse between consenting unmarried persons, raised the issue of sexual privacy. Green testified in a New Jersey case on fornication, *State v. Saunders.* Using data from the work of Masters and Johnson to support his position, he testified to the "emotional and behavioral consequences of its proscription" (p. 6).

Green concludes with some general comments about human sexuality and states, "whatever sexuality cases do come to court, philosophical and legal scholars will continue to argue over the relative weight to be given to the desires of the individual, the standards of society, and the powers of the state in limiting sexual autonomy. The relevance of sexual science to these considerations of law is underscored by the nature of human sexuality" (p. 266). (TJW)

PR

729. Holmes, Ronald M. **The Sex Offender and the Criminal Justice System.** Springfield, Ill.: Charles C. Thomas, 1983. 236 p. Includes bibliography and index. ISBN 0-398-04884-3.

Intended for use in classrooms, police departments, and social service agencies, Holmes's book examines a variety of sex offenses and analyzes their impact on victims and society. First, he discusses the role of society in forming sexual ideas and preferences, the concept of normalcy, the evolution of sex roles in the United States, and theoretical models of sex deviance. The majority of the book discusses various sex offenses in terms of their danger to society. Nuisance offenders "do not endanger the very existence of society, but they do cause some discomfort and a general level of alarm and suspicion" (p. 27). Their crimes fall into the sexual areas of fetishism, partialism (erotic attachment to body parts), voyeurism, exhibitionism, triolism, kleptomania (where the stolen object has some form of sexual overtones), frottage, bestiality, coprolagnia, and pygmalionism (sexual desire for a statue, doll, or mannequin). At the other extreme are dangerous sex crimes: the usual outcome of these crimes is physical harm or death, either to the perpetrator or the victim. The dangerous sex crimes dealt with are rape, necrophilia, piquerism (lust murders), erotic hanging, pyromania, vampirism, cannibalism, and sadism/masochism. Several chapters are devoted to assessing the nature and social impact of transvestism, transsexualism, homosexuality, pedophilia, incest, child pornography, and pornography. Holmes examines each type of sex offense in terms of typology, etiology, and treatment. Although emphasis is on the sex offender, he does provide useful information for the criminal investigator who deals with victims and their problems. Holmes also examines group therapy as a treatment for sex offenders. Aware of the difficulties inherent in trying to distinguish between normal and abnormal sexual behavior, and cognizant of the necessity of endeavoring to rehabilitate the sex offender, he suggests a systems approach to sex crimes and proposes the formation of a sex crime unit made up of generalists and specialists within the criminal justice system to deal holistically with the sex offender. A glossary of sex crime terms and expressions is included. (TJW)

PR

730. MacNamara, Donal E. J., and Edward Sagarin. **Sex, Crime, and the Law.** New York: Free Press, 1977. 291 p. Includes bibliography, index, and glossary. ISBN 0-02-919680-9.

Believing that there is a "yawning gap" in the literature dealing with the relationships among sex, crime, and the law, MacNamara and Sagarin attempt to bridge that gap by summarizing the state of knowledge in this area with attention to past developments, current trends, and future directions. Before examining specific areas of offenses, they discuss (1) the need for social and legal control of sexual behavior; (2) the scope of the law with respect to social conduct; (3) the typologies and categories of sex crimes; (4) the sexual content of nonsexual crimes (e.g., homicides); (5) certain tangential issues such as illegitimacy, abortion, and venereal disease; (6) the relationship of issues of sexuality to crimes and the law; and (7) the question of sex crimes as a logical concept. Here sex crime is defined as "behavior that is illegal in a given jurisdiction, that is explicitly sexual, or that has been declared criminal because it exploits, caters to, makes possible, or is dependent upon explicit sexual behavior" (p. 19).

The areas of offenses explored are rape; pedophilia; homosexuality; prostitution; offenses against the public order, e.g., exhibitionism; peripheral crimes, such as fornication, seduction, adultery, cohabitation, and miscegenation; and pornography. MacNamara and Sagarin analyze each of these areas systematically with definitions, the characteristics of the area, pertinent laws, etc. In the chapter on prostitution, for example, they discuss the various definitions, the nature of prostitution in the United States, the law and the process of arrest, prostitution and concomitant crime, white slavery, and legal and social policy in terms of the proposed Model Penal Code and the issues of regulation, abolition, and decriminalization.

In "Legal Reactions and Legal Reform" they have tried to distinguish among sex acts that are patently harmful to the victims, those that would be better tolerated, and those that are victimless. They state the "need for systematic examination of the evidence with regard to rehabilitation of sex offenders, rates of recidivism," and therapeutic treatment. There must also be an examination of sex psychopathic laws in the United States as well as attention to the need for decriminalization of adult consensual sex acts, the legality of which forms the basis of the Model Penal Code of the American Law Institute.

They conclude that "a transformation has taken place in American society with regard to sex," and that it is possible for American law in the last quarter of the twentieth century both to reflect and to mold attitudes that are rational, that do not challenge the central place of the family as a desirable institution but will allow it to develop in a flexible manner with legal restriction, and that are tolerant and nonpunitive in regard to harmless sexual conduct while freeing police and courts to pursue serious criminals." (TJW)

PR,IL

731. Posner, Richard A. **Sex and Reason.** Cambridge, Mass.: Harvard University Press, 1992. 458 p. Includes bibliographic footnotes and index. ISBN 0-674-80279-9.

Posner, a judge in the U.S. Court of Appeals as well as a senior lecturer at the University of Chicago Law School, noted that Americans, including lawyers, are not well-informed about sex; consequently, there is little solid basis upon which sound judgments affecting social policy can be made. His immediate goal in this book is to summarize the principal findings of the vast multidisciplinary literature on sexuality— from medicine, biology, psychology, psychiatry, medicine, theology, philosophy, anthropology, sociology, economics, jurisprudence—"as far as they bear on law, in a form accessible to the legal profession" (p. 2). His broader goal is to "present a theory of sexuality that both explains the principal regularities in the practice of sex and in its social, including legal, regulation and points the way toward reforms in that regulation— thus a theory at once positive (descriptive) and normative (ethical)" (p. 3). To find unity in the diversity of sexual behaviors, attitudes, and means of controlling them, Posner applies economic analysis to sexuality and its regulation.

Part 1 ("The History of Sexuality") provides background information on the history of scholarship on sexuality; historical and cross-cultural variations in human sexual customs and regulations; and ways that the law, particularly in the United States, has regulated sex. Part 2, "A Theory of Sexuality," is the theoretical core of the book. It begins with a discussion of the biology of sex, primarily from a sociobiological point of view, in which Posner articulates some of the main assumptions that underlie the economic analysis that follows. For example, he assumes that women have a weaker sex drive than men and that men seek to limit women's sexual activity to establish paternity; that biological and developmental factors largely determine the range of possible and potentially desired sex acts; and that the decision to engage in a particular sex act is a matter of choice. Analysis of the biology of sex permits a distinction between determined and chosen aspects of sex; their interface shapes the nature of sexual variation. The next few chapters develop Posner's economic view of sexuality which he thinks can explain the type and frequency of different sexual practices as rational responses to opportunities and constraints. In contrast to the sex drive and sexual preference, sexual practices are rational, i.e., well adapted to the actor's ends, whether conscious or not, and can be analyzed in terms of means and ends, costs and benefits. The beneficial ends of sex are procreative, hedonistic, and sociable, but the means to attain them are not interchangeable. The costs of sex compared to its benefits determine the frequency of specific practices, e.g., adultery, rape, prostitution, teenage sex, sex education, incest, abortion, and homosexual behavior. Much of the variation in sexual attitudes and practices can be explained by a few economic variables: the effective sex ratio, the extent of urbanization, and the changing occupational role of women. Part 3 applies the economic theory of sexuality to the regulation of sexuality in specific areas, e.g., marriage, pregnancy, homosexuality, erotic art, pornography, nudity, coercive sex, and parenthood. Posner concludes that "economics can retain the baton of the multidisciplinary orchestra" (p. 436). (SGF)

PR
732. Slovenko, Ralph, ed. **Sexual Behavior and the Law.** Springfield, Ill.: Charles C. Thomas, 1965. 886 p. Includes bibliographic footnotes and index.
    In the preface Harry Golden says that "the point made by the scholars in this volume is that the law is ambiguous and vacillating for the simple reason that our attitudes toward sex are ambiguous and vacillating." Lloyd W. McCorkle adds to that in the foreword by pointing out that the law is "only one part of a larger normative system which forbids some acts and prescribes others," and that human sexual behavior and the law offer a cardinal illustration of the tension between enlightened opinion and legal practice.
    The forty-seven contributors to this major work are primarily lawyers, psychiatrists, and psychoanalysts as well as several criminologists, philosophers, sociologists, and writers. Slovenko is a professor at the Tulane School of Law, New Orleans, Louisiana, who provides the lengthy introductory paper, "A Panoramic View: Sexual Behavior and the Law" in part 1. Part 2 is also a general paper, "Psychoanalytic Theory of Sexuality," by Reuben Fine. Part 3, "Social Structure and Sexual Behavior," relates various topics—ideology, sex crimes, and behavior—to the law. Part 4, "Domestic Relations," has five papers covering marriage, divorce, polygamy, unmarried mothers, and abortion. Part 5, "Psychodynamics of Sexual Deviations and the Law," contains thirteen separate papers on sex offenders, homosexuality, and various paraphilias. Part 6, "Sexual Relations in Non-Sexual Offenses," offers two contributions. Prostitution receives consideration in part 7, "Commercialized Vice." Two papers explore victimization in part 8, "Victims of Sex Offenses." Part 9, "Recidivism and Preventive Detention," discusses sex offenses, sex offenders, sexual psychopath laws, and sex offenders in prison. Part 10 presents three papers on the dissemination of sex information and the law, the mass media and sex deviation, and pornography.
    In the epilogue, Gene L. Usdin states: "Laws regarding sexual conduct are rooted in antiquity and nurtured too frequently by myths, superstition and fundamentalist religious concepts. The adoption of laws (and more importantly their interpretation), which are realistic in their views of sex and human nature, is basic in the development of a more mature society that provides dignity for the individual and the society." (TJW)

IL
733. Tong, Rosemarie. **Women, Sex, and the Law.** Totowa, N.J.: Rowman & Allanheld, 1984. 216 p. (New Feminist Perspectives Series). Includes bibliographic notes and index. ISBN 0-8476-7230-1.
    The aim of this book is to ask why "women have suffered in different sorts of ways at the hands of Anglo-American law for the same reason: their sexuality" (p. 1). Tong

believes that there is an inherent bias, stemming from the nature of patriarchal society, against women in the execution of the law, which supposes that the "battered woman had it coming, the raped woman wanted it, and the harassed woman encouraged it" (p. 3). The image of woman in the law is that of a lying temptress whose testimony is suspect. Despite recognized ambiguities in the concept of sexuality, Tong says that Anglo-American law assumes the code of compulsory heterosexuality, which adversely affects the position of women before the law and redounds to the benefit of men. Nonetheless, women are using the legal system to redress the wrongs they bear; presently, Tong claims, they are making headway in reforming the law so that they do not suffer on account of their sexuality.

A chapter is devoted to each of the following areas in which women are looked upon as victims: pornography, prostitution, sexual harassment, rape, and battering. Tong reviews the traditional Anglo-American law pertaining to each area as it affects women and examines the various opinions and viewpoints of groups as they relate to legal remedies and reform. She then discusses these same five areas of female victimization from the perspectives of blacks and lesbians.

Tong identifies links between the five areas. One such link is the good girl/bad girl syndrome that pervades Western culture; largely a product of male imagination, many women have internalized it and allowed it to dominate their thinking. She also concludes that while the law is a woman's ally in redressing past inequities, it is limited in what it can do to effect change in society's view of women, especially their sexuality. (TJW)

Politics. Sexism. Feminism

(For related material see also entries 464, 825, 909, 1059)

PR,IL
734. Blanchard, William H. **Revolutionary Morality: A Psychosexual Analysis of Twelve Revolutionists.** Santa Barbara, Calif.: ABC-Clio Information Services, 1984. 281 p. Includes bibliography and index. ISBN 0-87436-032-3.

This study is a penetrating look at twelve renowned revolutionists from a classic Freudian psychoanalytic standpoint for the purpose of establishing a typology of the rebel-cum-revolutionary. The case studies are divided into four types of revolutionists: type I consists of those who were never "conscious revolutionaries," the rebels without a world mission (T. E. Lawrence, J. J. Rousseau, and Leo Tolstoy); type II are those who believed themselves capable of bringing about revolutionary change but whose vision was limited to their own countries (Prince Kropotkin, Mahatma Gandhi, and Karl Marx); type III are those theoreticians and activists who, even after victory, found it difficult to take over and administer the revolution (Sun Yat-sen, Leon Trotsky, and Che Guevara); and type IV, the victorious revolutionaries who have no scruples about the exercise of power (Fidel Castro, V. I. Lenin, and Mao Tse-tung). The four parts into which the book is divided correspond to each of these four revolutionary types.

Blanchard's thesis is that masochism underlies the revolutionary behavior and morality of these twelve individuals. To prove his point, he examines the role played by masochism in the lives of the revolutionists by showing how each expressed "the sensuality and the virtuous thrill derived from suffering"; he then emphasizes "the importance of attention-getting behavior as a child and the need for some demonstration of love for and love from the masses as an adult"; he finally places them in a "four-stage continuum of revolutionary development from the primitive masochist to the successful revolutionary" (p. x). All of these individuals perceived and protested a lack of equity in society. They became morally indignant and attempted to do something about it. In order to be effective, they established a revolutionary morality and willingly subjected themselves to a great deal of personal hardship in the interest of the noble cause. Between the sexual masochist (Rousseau, Lawrence) at one end of the spectrum and the martyr for a cause (Gandhi, Guevara, among others) at the other end, there is, according to Blanchard, a common pleasure in suffering. The Gandhis and Guevaras transcend their personal masochism and derive their satisfaction by suffering for others. The psychosexual theory that masochism accounts for much in the revolutionary behavior of the twelve revolutionists discussed is amply supported only in the cases of the early revolutionists (Rousseau, Lawrence, Tolstoy). For the successful revolutionaries, especially Lenin and Mao Tse-tung, the claim seems tenuous because of a dearth of pertinent evidence about their personal lives in support of the argument. Blanchard provides a great deal of documentation in his study. A selected bibliography organized according to the names of the twelve revolutionists concludes this work. (TJW)

IL
735. Daly, Mary. **Gyn/Ecology: The Metaethics of Radical Feminism.** Boston: Beacon Press, 1978. 424 p. Includes index. ISBN 0-8070-1511-3.
   The title of this book expresses Daly's support of Françoise d'Eaubonne's thesis that "the fate of the human species and of the planet is at stake, and that no male-led 'revolution' will counteract the horrors of overpopulation and destruction of natural resources." Although Daly is concerned with all forms of pollution, the "mind/spirit/body pollution inflicted through patriarchal myth and language" is her particular target in this volume. She finds the English language to be in need of new words (or sometimes new meanings for old words) for her purposes of breaking through "the Male Maze." She uses hyphens and capitalization in ways intended to conform to her meaning rather than to standard usage. Using the language tools that she creates, Daly charts the journey of radical feminism.
   The "Journey," as it is detailed, involves exorcism of the "internalized Godfather," confrontations with manifestations of "evil" used to victimize women, "spinning" into new perceptions and new freedoms, a transforming of self. The "Journey" is portrayed in three "Passages," each with different style, movement, and language. The first passage reveals clearing vision and the excitement of discovery. The second is more somber, intense, and analytical. The third is creative, inventive, and empowering.
   A short quotation may best present the challenging nature of this work:

> At our Un-Conventions, Crones cackle at the crude Deceptions of the Demons who persist in trying to blend their voices into our Hearings. A-musing Amazons unravel the twisted tales of androcratic "argonauts" who allegedly sailed with Jason on a ship named *Argo* in quest of the Golden Fleece. (p. 418)

Daly assists her readers with generous notes and an index of new words with page numbers to indicate where in this volume the words are first defined or used. (LF)

IL
736. Dworkin, Andrea. **Intercourse.** New York: Free Press, 1987. 257 p. Includes bibliography and index. ISBN 0-02-907970-5.
   Using powerful images from life and literature (Count Leo Tolstoy and wife, Stanley Kowalski and Blanche Du Bois, St. Joan of Arc, and Madame Bovary), Dworkin, well-known for her earlier book, *Pornography: Men Possessing Women*, presents in *Intercourse* another frightful landscape in her appraisal of male/female relationships. As she perceives it, women are being brutally dominated by men through sexual intercourse. Apparently, it is the forceful entry and penetration without accompanying tenderness or consideration of needs that women find repellent and a violation of their bodies.
   While this ubiquitous activity has the seal of approval of both the American Right and Left, it is generally performed in such a crude and perfunctory manner as to leave women dissatisfied sexually (Hite reported that only three in ten women experience orgasm in intercourse), embarrassed, and degraded. Women in such circumstances are second-class citizens, deprived of their freedom, shorn of their dignity, and regarded as the playthings, or slaves, of men. Intercourse so conducted is of interest to the state, for

"gender is what the state seeks to control: who is the man here? which is the woman? how to keep the man on top, how to keep the man the man; how to render the woman inferior in fucking so that she cannot recover herself from the carnal experience of her own subjugation. Intercourse is supposed to be natural and in it a man and a woman are supposed to show and do what each is by nature. Society justifies its civil subordination of women by virtue of what it articulates as the 'natural' roles of men and women in intercourse; the 'natural' subjugation of women to men in the act" (pp. 148-49).

And the law conspires in this subjugation. "Laws create male dominance, and maintain it, as a social environment. . . . The purpose of laws on intercourse in a world of male dominance is to promote the power of men over women and to keep women sexually subjugated (accessible) to men. These laws—great and small—work. They work by creating gender itself" (p. 150). Dworkin asserts, "Marriage is the legal ownership of women, the legal intercourse that is the foundation of male authority" (p. 158).

Dworkin suggests some solutions or at least palliatives to issues she has articulated. She recalls the efforts of the nineteenth-century feminist Victoria Woodhull who proposed a female-first model of intercourse. Woodhull proposed that women have "real and absolute control in each and every act of intercourse, which would be, each and every time, chosen by the woman" (p. 136). Dworkin does not outline a program for reform of the act of sexual intercourse; rather, she emphasizes the importance of recognizing the disturbing implications of the act of intercourse. (TJW)

IL,PO

737. Faludi, Susan. **Backlash: The Undeclared War Against American Women.** New York: Crown, 1991. 552 p. Includes bibliographic notes and index.

According to Pulitzer prize-winning journalist Faludi, United States women are currently experiencing an antifeminist backlash, triggered "not by women's achievement of full equality but by the increased possibility that they might win it." Though not a conspiracy, contemporary cultural and social trends are pushing women back into "acceptable" roles, silencing, infantilizing, commercializing them into believing that "feminism's achievements, not society's resistance to these partial achievements" are causing them pain. Faludi contends that "to blame feminism for women's 'lesser life' is to miss entirely the point of feminism, which is to win women a wider range of experience . . . [to be] free to define themselves— instead of having their identity defined for them . . . by their culture and their men."

At the root of the backlash against women's search for equality are some basic myths: (1) a man shortage, (2) a plunge in the economic status of women who were divorced under no-fault divorce laws, (3) an "infertility epidemic" that has particularly affected professional women who have postponed childbearing, and (4) a "great emotional depression" affecting single women and "burnout" affecting career women. Faludi argues that all of these purported "facts" are false and provides evidence to explain why. Such backlash has historical precedents in the United States, appearing each time that women seem to have progressed toward greater equality—in the mid-nineteenth century, the early 1900s, the 1940s, and the early 1970s.

Examples of backlash abound in popular culture. Media first popularized the themes of backlash, giving credence to mythical or traditional ideas: momism, new traditionalism, cocooning, infertility, spinster boom. Films of the 1980s portrayed backlash themes in which women opposed other women, anger at circumstances became depression, and family life conflicted with women's independence. Television shows gave prime time to nesters, patriarchs, married women, mothers, and cheerleaders instead of to single women, careers, and self-reflection. Clothes made the woman as fashion emphasized restrictive, superfluous, and frilly garments. The beauty industry capped off the backlash with a "return to femininity," a.k.a. the traditional look.

Faludi thinks that the origins of backlash stem from the "pro-family" strategies of new Right men with their female "intermediaries." Ostracism, hostility, and ridicule of women's rights advocates by policymakers in the Capitol discouraged many women. And, scholarly/popular thinkers like George Gilder, Alan Bloom, Robert Bly, and Sylvia Ann Hewlett added more thoughtful relationales to antifeminist arguments.

The effect of backlash has been destructive for women. Popular psychology locates the effects of backlash pressure in women's minds—as their problem. Myths about women's improvements in the workforce covered up impediments in employment, promotions, and pay. And "improvements" in health care place fetal rights about women's rights. The hope is that women will recognize the force of their own power and effectively resist the pressures of backlash. (SGF)

IL,PO
738. Gilder, George. **Men and Marriage.** Revised ed. Gretna, La.: Pelican, 1986. 219 p. Includes bibliographic notes. ISBN 0-88289-444-7.

A revised and expanded edition of *Sexual Suicide* (1973), *Men and Marriage* restates Gilder's conservative vision of modern gender changes and argues that the intervening years have demonstrated the accuracy of that vision. He points out that republication of his book was temporarily blocked by militant feminists. Linking sex roles closely with physiology, Gilder sees the enemy as "sexual liberals" who attempt to alter or reverse those roles as if they are solely cultural creations and hence arbitrary. On the contrary, Gilder argues that traditional roles represent a crucial form of human adaptation: civilization has been made possible by the subordination of male sexual impulses to female rhythms of procreation. Most young males, as Gilder depicts them, are randy barbarians needing to be tamed by madonnas. When the male's traditional role of protector and provider for women is eroded, both the family and civilization disintegrate. The current sexual revolution favors younger, pretty women and older, successful males; it victimizes younger males (who are not socialized toward constructive behavior) and middle-aged women (who are devalued and discarded). Gilder targets for criticism affirmative action schemes, gay liberationists, feminists, advocates of androgyny, utopian socialists, and the welfare system. He praises Phyllis Schlafly's efforts to defeat the ERA in the face of what seemed like its certain victory. He defends capitalism and the traditional family, arguing that the alternative to men and marriage is men and misogyny. The ghetto, he says, demonstrates what society will be like if sexual liberals have their way: the families will be headed by single females, and the males will travel in predatory packs. (ERA)

IL
739. Gordon, John. **The Myth of the Monstrous Male and Other Feminist Fables.** New York: Playboy Press, 1982. 253 p. Includes bibliography.

In this lively polemic, Gordon takes issue with some trends of militant feminism. Describing himself as a feminist who supports equal rights opportunities, Gordon offers a riposte to such feminists as Susan Brownmiller (*Against Our Will*), Marilyn French (*The Women's Room*), Kate Millett (*Sexual Politics*), Adrienne Rich (*Of Woman Born*), Mary Daly (*Gyn/Ecology*), and Ashley Montagu (*The Natural Superiority of Women*). He contends that the women's liberation movement has become sexually repressive, linking itself to the antisex elements of earlier women's movements. He regards the men-are-oppressors stereotypes of some modern feminists as variants of the men-are-sexual-beasts stereotypes of older feminists. In the past, he argues, women pretended to be asexual creatures; they granted sex to the hungry male only in exchange for marriage (which included the male's commitment to lifetime financial support). The women's movement, which initially promised to liberate women from hypocritical bargaining, is now becoming reluctant to surrender the power such bargaining confers on women. "As for men," Gordon concludes, "their need right now is not for the much-vaunted right to cry, but simply for the capacity to get very damned angry at what is being said about them as a sex, and at the everywhere-manifest consequences of the propaganda." (**Men's Studies**, 1985)

IL,PO
740. Mailer, Norman. **The Prisoner of Sex.** New York: New American Library, 1971. 175 p. Authorized reprint of an edition published by Little, Brown and Company. Includes bibliographic notes. ISBN 0-917657-59-4.

This book is Mailer's defense of male sexuality as portrayed in the writings of Henry Miller, D. H. Lawrence, Jean Genet, and himself. These worthies had been attacked by the radical feminist, Kate Millett, in her book *Sexual Politics*. Mailer believes that she should have been erecting monuments to these individuals for their contributions to the sexual revolution. Fundamentally, though, Mailer's adversary in this book is the movement known as women's liberation, or more precisely, the ideas and programs favored and fostered by such organizations as the National Organization for Women (NOW) and the Society for Cutting Up Men (SCUM). Mailer believes that these movements hold to a mechanistic, technological view of women. His understanding of the goals and objectives of women's liberation is derived primarily from reading a quantity of feminist literature. His ideas of what women want stem from the writings and thoughts of Gloria Steinem, Bella Abzug, Germaine Greer (*The Female Eunuch*), Betty Friedan (*The Feminine Mystique*), and Kate Millett (*Sexual Politics*), as well as the pronouncements and manifestos of NOW and SCUM, random contributions appearing in such radical publications as *Rat* and *Off Our Backs*, and miscellaneous pieces appearing in the collection *Sisterhood Is Powerful*. Mailer believes that in its efforts to promote the sexual revolution the movement has turned to scientists and technologists for salvation in the form of technological fixes designed to remove from women's backs the onus of childbearing and other inconveniences occasioned by their sexuality, thus allowing their exploited selves to compete in the working world on an equal footing with men. To achieve its goals the movement seems to want "a permissive single standard of sexual freedom" (Millett, *Sexual Politics*, p. 62); continued scientific and technical advances in contraception and abortion, the development of a reliable method of "extra-uterine conception and incubation" (Ti-Grace Atkinson, *Women's Liberation*, p. 45); and ultimately use of clever operations to eliminate the physical differences between men and women. As Mailer sees it, this is the direction the movement is taking. In protest Mailer takes us on a tour of human sexuality, examining our biological origins and espousing the rationale behind the literary outpourings of Miller, Lawrence, Genet, and himself, who he thinks have a better understanding of the nature of love and sex than the disgruntled feminists. (TJW)

IL
741. Millett, Kate. **Sexual Politics**. New York: Doubleday, 1970. 393 p. Includes bibliography and index.
    Literary criticism is a tool used by a number of feminist writers, most notably Simone de Beauvoir in *The Second Sex*. In *Sexual Politics*, Millett uses it to illustrate the politics of power and domination in contemporary sexual relationships. Millett defines politics as "power-structured relationships . . . whereby one group of persons is controlled by another" (p. 23). In Western society, the male control of females is a cultural birthright. The family raises boys as members of a powerful, violent elite while preparing girls to join a parasitic, dependent class. Myth and religion reinforce the view of women as impure, inferior, and ignorant. Women demonstrate psychological traits common to repressed minority groups, such as self-contempt and group hatred.
    Tracing the history of the sexual revolution in America, Millett points out that what began as revolutionary social change fell short of its promise. Following the successful suffrage battle, the feminist movement collapsed. The major weaknesses of feminism were the concentration on the franchise issue, the movement's bourgeois character, and its failure to challenge the patriarchal ideology. Male writers responded to the early sexual revolution in three ways: a realistic, revolutionary approach, shown by Mill and Engels; a sentimental, chivalrous view, such as Ruskin's; and an ambivalent treatment of masculine fantasy, shown by Tennyson. The period also provided a forum for female authors such as the Brontës, George Eliot, and Virginia Woolf.
    This period of reform was followed by a counterrevolution. The Nazi regime dealt with feminism by controlling feminist groups, strengthening the patriarchy, and idealizing women as mothers. The Soviet Union, after a failed attempt to eliminate patriarchy and the family unit, restored the paternal government and family authority. In the United

States, the status of women declined due to the economic situation, public reaction to war, and the pervasive antifeminism of Freudianism.

Among those responsible for the antifeminist reaction were contemporary writers such as D. H. Lawrence, Henry Miller, and Norman Mailer. All three endorse male supremacy in religious or spiritual terms. Miller and Mailer present women as objects of contempt and stress the violence that is equated with sex in American male culture. In comparison, the feminine characters of Jean Genet share traits of submission, weakness, inferiority, and servitude, but are also artistic, intelligent, and triumphant in their despair and martyrdom. Male violence toward women is due to the male's fear of the feminine within himself. Millett emphasizes Genet's theme that "all prisoners of definitions imposed on them by others, most . . . find freedom by an angry assertion of selfhood and solidarity" (p. 354). (SDH)

PR,IL,PO
742. Morgan, Robin. **Sisterhood Is Global: The International Women's Movement Anthology.** Compiled, edited, and with an introduction by Robin Morgan. Garden City, N.Y.: Anchor Press/Doubleday, 1984. 815 p. Includes bibliography, index, and glossary. ISBN 0-385-17797-6.

Unlike Morgan's earlier collection of essays and poems, *Sisterhood Is Powerful*, *Sisterhood Is Global* is a reference work "meant to be a broadly representative, energetic, and varied assemblage of facts and articles by women" (p. xiv). Seventy countries and the United Nations are covered, with the Third World heavily represented. Under each country are two sections: a statistical preface and an essay by one or more native women residents. At the end of each essay is a short suggested reading list. Statistics include demography, government, economy, and "gynography," or social statistics such as marriage, divorce, welfare, contraception, abortion, incest, rape, battery, prostitution, and crisis centers. All statistics, where possible, are broken down by sex. The "gynography" section is further divided into "policy" and "practice," which compare official policy or laws (with citations) with the actual deviations from these. The prefaces also include short women's history summaries entitled "Herstory" and religious or mythological notes concerning women. The statistics demonstrate the economic, social, and legal liabilities faced by women worldwide, including lower wages and repressive, discriminatory social and legal systems. The essays that follow the statistical prefaces vary in length, tone, and subjects covered. Although the contributors were given guidelines, no attempt was made by Morgan to make the material reflect a consistent approach, philosophy, or political stance. In general, the essays present personal views of the historical, legal, and social positions of women in each country and the problems facing them. Common themes include seeing possibilities for positive change, taking power within the existing systems, coordinating action on a national and international level, and working outside of existing governments and organizations on a person-to-person level. (SDH)

IL,PO
743. Morgan, Robin, ed. **Sisterhood Is Powerful: An Anthology of Writings from the Women's Liberation Movement.** New York: Vantage Books, 1970. 648 p.

"What we have tried to put together," Morgan writes in the introduction to this anthology, "is a sort of introduction to the movement: why we are, what we are, what we have done, where we might be going, but told in our own words, not those of the distorting mass media." The women's movement is presented as a genuine radical movement against the oppression of racism, sexism, class and caste systems, capitalism, and the family structure. The anthology includes an introduction and historical perspective, five sections on issues and the movement, and a final section of excerpts from movement documents. The five sections include "The Oppressed Majority: The Way It Is" on women and the workplace, welfare, church and the law; "The Invisible Woman: Psychological and Sexual Repression" on the social, psychological, and medical issues including birth control, images of women, prostitution, lesbianism, and women in literature; "Go Tell It in the Valley: Changing Consciousness" on the women's movement among black, Hispanic, and high school women; "Up from Sexism: Emerging Ideologies," a selection of movement views; and "The Hand That Cradles the Rock: Protest and Revolt," a collection of poetry.

Many common experiences and opinions of woman are voiced in this anthology: oppression, lack of advancement and below-average wages in the workplace, the demeaning attitudes of those in positions of authority toward women, the social expectations and insidious images of the feminine. The sexual revolution, although it freed women from the Victorian repression of their sexuality, changed the emphasis to performance rather than personal fulfillment. Birth control is creating a revolutionary separation between sexuality and reproduction, but the continuing existence of the nuclear family reinforces women's menial role. Black and Hispanic women are involved in two revolutions, combining the women's movement with their battle for racial equality. Even women in the peace movement and in organizations such as SDS and SNCC faced both overt and hidden sexism. Sexism is institutionalized within the capitalistic culture and cannot be overcome until a truly egalitarian, socialistic society is established and the family unit, which ties women to housework and childbearing, is destroyed. Seen in its broadest context, the women's liberation movement is one part of a continuing, worldwide struggle for human liberation. (SDH)

IL,PO

743a. Paglia, Camille. **Vamps & Tramps: New Essays.** New York: Vintage Books, 1994. 531 p. Includes index. ISBN 0-679-75120-3.

In this sequel to her book *Sex, Art, and American Culture* (1992), Paglia writes about sexuality, feminism, education, and pop culture. In the introduction, in addition to describing the book's organization and the types of documents it contains, Paglia presents her theoretical, practical, and libertarian approaches to the many issues and personalities in these private and public arenas. She justifies her aggressive and confrontational attitudes toward feminists on the basis of her belief that they are sapping the vigor of American education and destroying the spirit and independence of American women. She aims to set things right in *Vamps & Tramps*, and to lead a movement for sexual and educational reform in the nation, and eventually, the world. She wants "to change the climate of ideas *around* the academic and feminist establishment" (p. xv).

Paglia begins with a TV skit, "The Penis Unsheathed," in the first section titled "The Year of the Penis," that reveals how phallocentric past civilizations—Greece and Rome—were, and adds that we seem to be making a new beginning in this direction today, as witness the case in which Lorena Bobbitt cut off her husband's penis. This skit melds into her major essay, "No Law in the Arena: A Pagan Theory of Sexuality," in which she "systematically presents [her] libertarian views of rape, abortion, battering, sexual harassment, prostitution, stripping, pornography, homosexuality, pedophilia, and transvestism" (p. xiv). Subsequent essays and TV productions appear under the rubric "The Culture Wars," dealing with such topics as oppressive campus politics, political correctness, victimization, the anti-pornography efforts of Catherine MacKinnon and Andrea Dworkin, and censorship.

Next, Paglia explores pop culture, citing the cases of Woody Allen, Amy Fisher, Sandra Bernhard, Barbra Streisand, and Vladimir Nabakov's novel *Lolita*, which redefined the relationship between childhood and adult sexuality. In the same vein, she considers other personae: Princess Di, Hillary Clinton, Anita Hill, Paula Jones, and Jacqueline Kennedy Onassis. In the section "Memoirs and Adventures," Paglia reveals the intimate aspects of her own persona: her friendships with gay men, her sexuality, her opposition to establishment feminism, her ventures into disclosures with Loren Hutton and drag queen Glennda Orgasm.

"On Literature and Art" offers Paglia's idiosyncratic views on the opera *Carmen*, the character of Alice in Lewis Carroll's children's classics, D. H. Lawrence's novel *Women in Love*, and a denunciation of Susan Sontag in "Sontag, Bloody Sontag."

The balance of the book has a collection of book reviews (Madonna's *Sex*, Warren Farrell's *The Myth of Male Power*, David Shipman's *Judy Garland*); miscellaneous writings (an advice column for the lovelorn for *Spy* magazine); cartoons about Paglia herself; and a chronicle of events since her last book. (TJW)

PR,IL
744.   Pateman, Carole. **The Sexual Contract.** Stanford, Calif.: Stanford University Press, 1988. 264 p. Includes bibliographic notes and index. ISBN 0-8047-1477-0.

In this . . . original work of political philosophy, one of today's foremost feminist theorists challenges the way contemporary society functions by questioning the standard interpretation of an idea that is deeply imbedded in American and British political thought: that our rights and freedoms derive from the social contract explicated by Locke, Hobbes, and Rousseau and interpreted in the United States by the Founding Fathers.

The author shows how we are told only half of the story of the original contract that establishes modern patriarchy. The sexual contract is ignored and thus men's patriarchal right over women is also glossed over. No attention is paid to the problems that arise when women are excluded from the original contract but incorporated into the new contractual order.

One of the main targets of the book is those who try to turn contractarian theory to progressive use, and a major thesis of the book is that this is not possible. Thus those feminists who have looked to a more "proper" contract—one between genuinely equal partners, or one entered into without any coercion—are misleading themselves. In the author's words, "In contract theory universal freedom is always a hypothesis, a story, a political fiction. Contract always generates political right in the forms of domination and subordination." Thus the book is also aimed at mainstream political theorists, and socialist and other critics of contract theory.

The author offers a sweeping challenge to conventional understandings—of both left and right—of actual contracts in everyday life: the marriage contract, the employment contract, the prostitution contract, and the new surrogate mother contract. By bringing a feminist perspective to bear on the contradictions and paradoxes surrounding women and the contract, and the relation between the sexes, she is able to shed new light on fundamental political problems of freedom and subordination. (Permission to use book cover abstract granted by publisher.)

IL,PO
744a.   Roiphe, Katie. **The Morning After: Sex, Fear, and Feminism on Campus.** Boston: Little, Brown, 1993. 180 p. Includes bibliographic notes. ISBN 0-316-75431-5.

Roiphe, a Harvard alumna doing graduate work at Princeton University, observed the feminist scene on campuses during the late 1980s and early 1990s. What she saw were manifestations of a feminism she did not like: ritualistic Take-Back-the-Night marches, sexual harassment peer-counseling groups, male bashing, faculty intimidation, and a strident campus "speak code" that blocked legitimate criticism and disagreement. Most distressing to Roiphe was the image of women as victims, as frail creatures who must be protected from date rape, sexual harassment, and sexist vocabulary. Her motivation for writing this book "comes out of frustration, out of anger, out of the names I've been called, out of all the times I didn't say something I was thinking because it might offend the current feminist sensibility" (p. 7).

The campus atmosphere Roiphe describes may be characterized as follows: blue lights illuminate the campus after dark; warnings such as "Since you cannot tell who has the potential for rape by simply looking, be on your guard with every man" (p. 9); students being provided with whistles to ward off rapists; feminist activists interrupting campus tours by parents and students to warn incoming freshmen of sexual dangers; and so on. These images contrast sharply with conditions that once prevailed on campuses across America. She believes that a brand of feminism is creating an atmosphere of danger, suspicion, and distrust on American campuses.

Roiphe devotes separate chapters to campus safety, the so-called "rape crisis," the "dangers of dating," sexual harassment, and the influential Catherine MacKinnon, whom she dubs the "antiporn star." Throughout the book, she addresses various questions affecting women students on campus: AIDS and other STDs, safe sex, condom use, anorexia nervosa, speakouts against sexual violence, and so forth. Roiphe laments the fact that the women's movement, by focusing on these issues within a framework of patriarchy and domination, is creating an intolerant culture "captivated by victimization." The movement is producing a generation of women "yearning for regulation, fearful of its sexuality, and animated by a nostalgia for days of greater sexual control." She says that campus feminism has given us the "sensitive female, pinched, leered at, assaulted daily by sexual advances, encroached upon, kept down, bruised by harsh reality" (p. 172). This brand of feminism represents "sexual thoughts and images censored, behavior checked, fantasies regulated" (p. 171). Roiphe wants none of this; she attacks feminists who are "on the front lines of sexual regulation." Campus feminism, as she experienced it, "was not about rebellion, but rules; it was not about setting loose, as it once was, it was about reining in" (p. 171). (TJW)

IL
745. Snitow, Ann, Christine Stansell, and Sharon Thompson, eds. **Powers of Desire: The Politics of Sexuality.** New York: Monthly Review Press, 1983. 489 p. Includes bibliographic notes. ISBN 0-85345-610-0.

In the introductory essay, the editors present the issues that pervade the rest of the volume. They assert that sexuality is a social construct, not a natural force, which feminists have generally avoided discussing. Nevertheless, sexuality is very much alive as a political issue. They suggest that it is time that feminists explore both the origin and types of desire and begin to integrate sexuality into the "project of human liberation." However, the approach cannot be simplistic. As one contributor (Benjamin) puts it, "a politics . . . that tries to sanitize or rationalize the erotic, fantastic components of human life, will not defeat domination but only vacate the field" (p. 297). The editors suggest that the political struggle is over "who is going to make sex and in what form" (p. 12). As background to the effort of developing a political theory of sex, they present a political and intellectual history of sex within feminist and socialist thought over the last 200 years.

The rest of the volume is divided into sex sections, each of which expands on themes presented in the introduction and is linked to major issues by a brief, initial synopsis of its contents. The articles in the first section look at ways in which sexual mores have changed with the rise of industrial capitalism, while those in the second try to explain the forces that underlie sexual revolutions, especially the transition from 1880 to 1930. A third section examines the boundaries of the institution of heterosexuality and ultimately the categories that underlie the definition of gender. A fourth section addresses questions about the relation of erotic roles to gender and power, while a fifth examines the dimensions of sexual openness, particularly in relation to changing social definitions of sexual practices. The volume concludes with discussions of current controversies, such as prostitution, pornography, abortion, and general issues of sexual victimization.

The thirty-three contributors are a diverse group of feminist writers and activists drawn from the fields of history, sociology, journalism, fiction, and poetry. Their provocative comments raise basic questions about the nature of women's experience of sex, how sexuality is political, the effect of the "sex revolution" on women's lives, and the foundations of gender. (SGF)

PR,IL
745a. Sommers, Christina Hoff. **Who Stole Feminism? How Women Have Betrayed Women.** New York: Simon & Schuster, 1994. 320 p. Includes bibliographic notes and index. ISBN 0-671-79424-8.

Sommers, Associate Professor of Philosophy at Clark University, points out in the preface the erroneous figures concerning anorexia, birth defects, and domestic battery that have been used by feminist theorists to persuade women that "our society is best described as a patriarchy, a 'male hegemony,' a 'sex/gender system' in which the dominant gender works to keep women cowering and submissive" (p. 16). Dubbing the women who have broadcast these untruths "gender/feminists," Sommers states that she will "evaluate here the views of such feminists as Gloria Steinem, Patricia Ireland, Susan Faludi, Marilyn French, Naomi Wolf, and Catherine MacKinnon and the findings that inform them" (p. 17), as well as the organizations that support them. She has written this book because she is "a feminist who does not like what feminism has become" (p. 18).

Sommers contrasts the "classically liberal, humanistic feminism," which succeeded in achieving many of the same legal rights that men enjoyed, such as the right to vote, the right to hold property, to divorce, to equal education, with present-day feminism. Equity feminism, Sommers states, goes back to Elizabeth Cady Stanton and the Seneca Falls convention in 1848. Modern "Second Wave" feminism is led by gynocentric ideologues who believe that women are "in thrall to a system of male dominance" (p. 22). She believes that this group, despite its influence in education and politics, is not reaching the majority of American women—it actually lacks a constituency.

Motivated by anger, resentment, and a belief that males as a group are responsible for women's subordination, the New Feminists, Sommers avers, have set about to change the workplace and the academy. In education they have altered curricula, influenced speech on campus, intimidated faculty, and confused students. Their efforts are "affecting the American classroom at every level, from the primary grades to graduate school" (p. 53). Sommers attacks the thinking underlying these efforts, particularly the feminist goal of "transforming the knowledge base" (p. 76) in all its dimensions. As a result, in the feminist classroom, where a political perspective is being imposed, women are receiving an education inferior to that of men.

After criticizing such organizations as the Association of American Colleges (AAC) for supporting the gender/feminists' educational agenda, Sommers goes on to examine thoroughly two studies sponsored by the American Association of University Women (AAUW): the 1991 study that showed that adolescent girls suffered a dramatic drop in self-esteem between the ages of eleven and sixteen as compared with boys; and the 1992 Wellesley Report, which showed that gender bias—in sexual harassment, discrimination in the curriculum, and lack of attention from teachers—is favoring boys and shortchanging girls. Sommers faults both of the AAUW-sponsored reports on the basis of underlying philosophies, misinterpretation of data, and as examples of advocacy research.

Sommers identifies and criticizes other promotions of the gender/feminists: the nonexistent March of Dimes report on the cause of birth defects, the January 1993 Super Bowl hoax on domestic battery, and the 1993 Louis Harris and Associates report on women's' physical and mental well-being. While data in the Harris study clearly showed that American women were enjoying life, the interpretation released to the public claimed that women suffered severe depression and low self-esteem.

As Sommers sees it, gender/feminists "regard most women as men's dupes" (p. 258). She doubts that their misandrist approach will get them very far—reaction is already setting in. "Mainstream feminists," she declares, "are only just becoming aware of the fact that the Faludis and the Steinems speak in the name of women *but do not represent them*. With the new awareness that the feminist leaders and theorists are patronizing them, there is a very real possibility that the mainstream is the tide of the not-too-distant future" (p. 274). Sommers believes "the public has learned that academic feminism has been playing a leading role in promoting the illiberal movement known as 'PC' in the nation's colleges. Now it is beginning to realize that the New Feminism is socially divisive and that it generally lacks a constituency in the population at large" (p. 274). (TJW)

IL

746. Vance, Carole S., ed. **Pleasure and Danger: Exploring Female Sexuality.** Boston: Routledge & Kegan Paul, 1984. 462 p. Includes bibliographies and index. ISBN 0-7102-0248-2.

The papers, imagery, and poetry contained in this volume were drawn from "The Scholar and the Feminist" IX Conference (held at Barnard College in 1982). Entitled "Towards a Politics of Sexuality," this controversial conference was designed to address "women's sexual pleasure, choice, and autonomy, acknowledging that sexuality is simultaneously a domain of restriction, repression, and danger, as well as a domain of exploration, pleasure, and agency" (p. 443). However, the "prosex" orientation of the conference sparked opposition from antipornography groups, who labeled it "anti-feminist." The vociferous protests against the conference resulted in the confiscation of copies of its major text and withdrawal of foundation support for the 1983 meeting.

Vance's introductory essay addresses not only the theme of the conference but also reaction to it. She argues that sexuality is a complex phenomenon that women need to confront honestly. Discussions of pleasure are not meant to weaken arguments about sexual danger but to allow women to hear a full range of expression about sexual experience and its diversity. Examination of the social construction of sexuality and its link to gender are important parts of this process. Vance concludes that "it is not enough to move women away from danger and oppression; it is necessary to move toward something: toward pleasure, agency, self-definition. Feminism must increase women's pleasure and joy, not just decrease our misery" (p. 24).

Thirty professionals and activists from a variety of fields (history, psychology, anthropology, poetry, literature, art, and film criticism) offer discussions that focus on the relevance of sexual exploration as a political and personal goal. For example, Ellen Carol DuBois and Linda Gordon examine feminists' conceptualization of sexual danger in the social purity politics of the nineteenth century, while Alice Echols critiques the relatively recent development of cultural feminism. Meryl Altman examines sex manuals as a form of popular literature expressive of the meaning of sex to women in the 1960s and 1970s. Sharon Thompson questions how much impact feminist ideology has made on teenagers who continue to pursue sex in the context of romance. Esther Newton and Shirley Walton argue for a more precise sexual vocabulary that acknowledges sexual variety. Gayle Rubin offers thoughts for a radical theory of the politics of sexuality, which she argues must identify, describe, explain, and denounce erotic injustice and sexual oppression. Overall, these and other essays and expressions in the volume explore the question of what women want from sex and how to deal with it. (SGF)

PR,IL

747. Weeks, Jeffrey. **Sexuality and Its Discontents: Meanings, Myths & Modern Sexualities.** London: Routledge & Kegal Paul, 1985. 324 p. Includes bibliographic notes and index. ISBN 0-7102-0565-1.

Weeks, a research fellow in the Social Work Studies Department at the University of Southampton, comments that this is the final book in an "unplanned, informal trilogy of works" that pertains to the social organization of sexuality. The first, *Coming Out: Homosexual Politics in Britain from the 19th Century to the Present* (1977) dealt with issues of sexual identity, particularly the historical variation and change in gay identity. Weeks concluded that there is no essence that characterizes sexual identity but rather "changing patterns in the organization of desire." The second book, *Sex, Politics and Society: The Regulation of Sexuality Since 1800* (1981) explored the link between the social control of sexuality and the emergence of industrial capitalism. *Sexuality and Its Discontents* examines in detail the categories, concepts, and languages that have been used to articulate sexual meaning and values.

The aim of this book is to "show the historical, theoretical and political forces that have created the framework of . . . [the current] crisis in sexual meanings" (p. ix). Weeks adopts the view that history is politics and that the present is historical. He then argues that present discontents about sexuality are rooted in a tradition that has inflated the importance of sexuality. In the first part of the book, he establishes four types of changes that have shaped the emergence of the "new moralism," that is based on fear and dogmatic proscriptions: the commercialization and commodification of sex, a shift in male/female relations, changes in the way sexuality is regulated, and restructuring of old sexual antagonisms and the development of new political movements. The second part analyzes the sexual tradition that contains the ideas that have structured and legitimized contemporary attitudes. Of particular relevance are the sexologists, whose privileged status has allowed them to influence concepts of male and female sexuality and to define boundaries of the normal and abnormal. However, Weeks thinks that their emphasis on an essential sexual nature is misdirected and sets up an unfortunate opposition between sexual energy and social constraint. A third part of the book is a critical examination of psychoanalysis. Weeks points out that psychoanalytic formulations lead the way to seeing sexual identity as a social product, not an expression of an essential nature. The last section covers dilemmas of identity, desire, and choice by discussing the theory and practice of new social movements (e.g., feminists, lesbians, gays) that have challenged the tenets of social tradition. He uses the themes identified in this part to develop a "radical pluralist" position that advocates a range of sexual possibilities rather than one based on restriction and denial. He argues that neither patriarchy, racism, nor capitalism is the sole source of sexual discontent. A common cause directed at democratizing contemporary society could foster a vision of sexuality that includes pleasure and choice. (SGF)

Religion. Morality. Sexual Ethics

For related material see also entries 40, 89, 134, 157, 366, 854, 855, 978)

IL
748. Bailey, Sherwin. **Sexual Ethics: A Christian View.** New York: Macmillan, 1963. 159 p.
    This work deals with the moral principles governing the mutual relations of men and women, especially sexual relations, including the marriage bond, sexual behavior, and contraception. Anglican preacher Bailey looks at the historical, personal, and moral aspects of these mutual relations. He attempts to present a "cogent view of the nature and ethical obligations of sexual relationship as seen by a Christian who believes that the Church of the twentieth century is being called to undertake a radical reconsideration of God's will for men and women" (p. 8).
    In part I, "The Historical Background to Sexual Ethics," Bailey concerns himself with an account of Western sexual ideas and attitudes. He points out that the Christian sexual tradition as developed in the six centuries after Christ, while owing a great deal to its Jewish heritage and the influence of Hellenistic asceticism, emerged primarily from the writings of St. Paul on marriage and the single state and woman's subservience to man, as well as on the ascetical views of the Church fathers (Tertullian, Jerome, Augustine, etc.) who preached on the subjugation of the body, virginity as the ideal state, the sinfulness of man, and the continent life. He also examines in succession (1) the contribution of Thomas Aquinas in the thirteenth century to the systematization of the Christian sexual tradition; (2) the work of the reformers of the sixteenth century, especially Martin Luther and John Calvin, in establishing the state of marriage as being no less honorable than virginity; and (3) the feeling in the twentieth century that the inherited sexual ideas and attitudes need to be modified in the light of our present knowledge and experience.
    In part II, "The Principles of Sexual Ethics," Bailey points out that man is not a single entity but rather a sexual duality with man and woman at opposite relational poles, manifesting many different kinds of sexual relations, as friends, partners, lovers, husbands, associates, etc. This sexual relationship signifies "the free and equal association of man and woman in all the manifold interests and enterprises of social, political, and ecclesiastical life" (p. 82). It also calls into question such social stereotypes foisted on men and women, and other features of inequality.
    Bailey then argues Christian perspectives on coition, love, and marriage, pointing out that sexual ethics should "guide husband and wife in the right ordering of their coital relationship as a whole" (p. 94). Love, a special form of sexual relation, should prevail in the marital state, bringing forth such relational factors as self-giving, desire, friendship, affection, and the act of coition.

In the final part of this book, Bailey deals with three ethical issues: chastity, contraception, and divorce and remarriage. As to the first, he argues for premarital continence. On the second he believes that contraception may be used responsibly and respectfully for family planning. As to the third, he attempts to refute the position of the Catholic Church on its stand on the indissolubility of marriage.

Bailey's thoughts on the theology and ecclesiastical history of sexual relations were examined in greater depth in his earlier work *Sexual Relation in Christian Thought* (Harper, 1959). (TJW)

PR,IL
748a.   Baldwin, John W. **The Language of Sex: Five Voices from Northern France Around 1200.** Chicago: University of Chicago Press, 1994. 331 p. (The Chicago Series on Sexuality, History, and Society). Includes bibliography and index. ISBN 0-226-03613-8.

In the decades surrounding the year 1200 five works of diverse content were produced in northern France that, according to Baldwin, the Charles Homer Haskins Professor of History at Johns Hopkins University, provide historians and modern readers with a good idea of the main issues of medieval sexuality. Baldwin places each of these works in a particular tradition: (1) the work of Pierre the Chanter (d. 1197) represents the theological-canonistic tradition of Augustine; (2) the anonymous *Prose Salernitan Questions*, addressing medical problems, supports the tradition handed down by Galen; (3) Ovid's classical tradition is articulated by André, chaplain of the French king, through his Latin treatise *De amore*, intended for clerics; (4) Jean Renart's writings, such as *Le roman de la rose*, intended for royalty, knights, and ladies, that highlights the vernacular tradition of romance; and (5) Jean Bodel's fabliaux, intended for townspeople and the lower aristocracy, that depict the racy folklore tradition.

Baldwin points out that the "predominant Christian ideology harbored a negative evaluation of sexuality as inherently evil, appraised the act itself as shameful, and raised inhibitions over the expression of the subject except to condemn it" (p. xiv). Four of the five discourses he analyzes offer different perspectives on the official sexual morality. He examines these perspectives in a series of chapters in terms of the sociology of sexuality, the sexual body, sexual desire, coitus, children, and gender.

Baldwin's conclusions concern sexual relations between individuals around 1200, a time when the church's traditional views on sexuality were being openly challenged or ignored in such areas as the biology of sex, marriage, fornication, adultery, and gender relations. Baldwin also concludes that the best sources for studying sexual behavior in the twelfth century are such writings as those examined in this book. (TJW)

PR,IL
749.   Biale, David. **Eros and the Jews: From Biblical Israel to Contemporary America.** New York: Basic Books, 1992. 319 p. Includes bibliography and index. ISBN 0-465-02033-X.

Award-winning Jewish historian Biale presents a detailed study of Jewish practices, beliefs, and attitudes relating to procreation, sexuality, and eroticism from biblical times to the modern period. His goal is to investigate how Jews have "constructed notions of sexuality, how they have thought about it and struggled with it in the texts they produced" (p. 6), not so much to discover what past Jewish behavior actually was. Texts reflect and shape experience, and "discourse defines desire." Using texts produced by the "cultural elite"—priests, rabbis, philosophers, mystics, Hasidic masters, Enlightenment literati, Zionist ideologists, and others—Biale closely interprets the written literature of the Bible, the Talmud, and medieval scholars. He recognizes that the history of Jewish sexuality must go beyond an elitist, male-oriented perspective to include the experiences of women, ordinary people, and the interaction of this cultural system with other cultures. One aspect of history that he examines is the political dimension of sexual practices. Conflicts in God's commands relating to exogamy (a rule to marry outside of the community) versus endogamy (a rule to marry inside of the community) were directed to the preservation of a minority culture. Biale also traces through history the effects of the sexual customs of the surrounding, politically dominant culture on the practices of the Jews. Drawing on current literature such as Philip Roth's *Portnoy's Complaint* and current films such as Woody Allen's work, Biale concludes the study with a consideration of Zionism as an erotic revolution, an identification of sexual stereotypes in American Jewish culture, and the suggestion that Jewish sexuality needs to move beyond traditional male definitions. This first overall history of Jewish sexuality reveals dilemmas of desire, in which Jews have struggled with contradictory attractions, embedded in their culture. Biale maintains that the Jewish culture of which Jewish sexuality is a part has always had to deal with issues of conflicting values of fertility/procreation/gratification and asceticism. Far from being a static culture devoted to "monolithic dogma," the story of Jewish sexuality is one of a "profoundly ambivalent culture." (JA/SGF)

PR,IL
750. Brown, Peter. **The Body and Society: Men, Women, and Sexual Renunciation in Early Christianity.** New York: Columbia University Press, 1988. 504 p. (Lectures on the History of Religions, New Series, No. 13). Includes bibliography and index. ISBN 0-231-06100-5.

Brown, Rollins Professor of History at Princeton University, widely known for the biography *Augustine of Hippo* (1967), traces in this well-documented study the development of sexual renunciation in the first six centuries of Christianity, i.e., from St. Paul to Pope Gregory I. Sexual renunciation refers to permanent "continence, celibacy, life-long virginity" among men and women as preached by a host of Christian teachers who lived in various places in the circum-Mediterranean world—Europe, northern Africa, Egypt, the Near East, Anatolia, and Mesopotamia.

Brown divides his study into three parts. Part I, "From Paul to Anthony," begins with an account of the pagan world in the second century A.D., "where Christianity had begun to achieve a certain measure of public visibility" (p. xiii). He discusses the writings of such major contributors to the notions of abstinence, continence, and virginity as Paul of Tarsus, Plutarch, Soranus, Valentinus, Justin Martyr, Irenaeus, Galen, Clement of Alexandria, Tertullian, Marcus Aurelius, Origen, Plotinus, Mani, Porphyry, Athanasius, Anthony, and others. Sexual renunciation, advanced as an alternative to the sexual attitudes in the Roman world, had many variations among the wandering Christian preachers, depending on the time and the location.

By the time of the conversion of Emperor Constantine in A.D. 312, "Total sexual renunciation [although confined to a restricted group] had become a widely acclaimed feature of the Christian life" (p. 208). In part II, "Asceticism and Society in the Eastern Empire," Brown traces the development of asceticism from the emergence of the Desert Fathers (Anthony, John Climacus) living isolated in caves and monasteries on the fringe of the fertile Nile Valley; through asceticism's impact on the clergy, laypersons, and devout women in the cities and villages of Egypt; through female asceticism growing out of upper-class Christian households and guided by clergymen and such prominent and wealthy women as Olympias of Constantinople and Macrina; to the efforts of such charismatic figures as Gregory of Nyssa and John Chrysostom in Antioch who wrote and preached about sexuality, marriage, and the virgin life. At the same time, in the late fourth century, Ephraim the Syrian produced hymns addressing the same ascetic topics.

In part III, "Ambrose to Augustine: The Making of the Latin Tradition," Brown focuses attention on contributions from three great Catholic teachers: St. Ambrose, St. Jerome, and St. Augustine. Ambrose became bishop of Milan in 374; a man of action, he recognized the burden of sexuality. He preached the cleansing effect of baptism and extolled continence and virginity. He established firm boundaries between the Catholic Church and the secular world.

Jerome, ousted from Rome by the Roman clergy, settled in Bethlehem in 385. Though an erudite ascetic, he favored female companionship. Nevertheless, he recognized the sexual dangers within the body, adopted the Paulist view of marriage, and held out the hope to men and women of companionable life in heaven without the burden of sex.

In Milan in 386, Augustine reluctantly rejected sexual pleasures, adopting an ascetic, eventually monastic, lifestyle and becoming, by 395, the Catholic bishop of the north African seaport town of Hippo. According to Brown, Augustine modified the strict views of the Church fathers with respect to continence, marriage, and virginity and revised the story of Adam and Eve by endowing the pair with physicality and sexuality before the Fall. Augustine's views, apparently more acceptable to the faithful, forever mitigated, but did not totally eliminate, the austere views on sexual renunciation held by the early Christian fathers. Today an uneasiness about sex continues to linger as a heritage from those early Christian efforts to cope with the sexual impulse. (TJW)

PR,IL
751. Bullough, Vern L., and James Brundage. **Sexual Practices & the Medieval Church.** Buffalo, N.Y.: Prometheus Books, 1982. 289 p. Includes bibliography and index. ISBN 0-87975-141-X.
This collection of papers presents the scholarship of several medievalists on the subject of sexual attitudes and practices in the Middle Ages as disclosed in the writings of theologians, philosophers, canon lawyers, and other scholars. According to the chief authors, Bullough and Brundage, there is a dearth of available information concerning medieval sex.
The introductory paper by Bullough describes the Christian inheritance as reflected in the opinions of those Greek and Latin church fathers active between the first and seventh centuries, which includes various figures from St. Paul to St. Augustine. It examines Christian teachings on such topics as fornication, adultery, celibacy, castration, marriage, homosexuality, and the like.
The first section of the book presents seven papers on Christian theory, practice, and attitudes: "Formation of Medieval Ideals: Christian Theory and Christian Practice" (Bullough); "Chaste Marriage and Clerical Celibacy" (Jo Ann McNamara); "The Prostitute in the Early Middle Ages" (Bullough); "Transvestism in the Middle Ages" (Bullough); "The Sin Against Nature and Homosexuality" (Bullough); and "Sexual Irregularities in Medieval Scandinavia" (Grethe Jacobsen).
The second section, focusing on the legal aspects of sex, also contains seven papers: "Sex and Canon Law: A Statistical Analysis of Samples of Canon and Civil Law" (Brundage); "The Marriage of Mary and Joseph in the Twelfth-Century Ideology of Marriage" (Penny S. Gold); "Concubinage and Marriage in Medieval Canon Law" (Brundage); "Adultery and Fornication: A Study in Legal Theology" (Brundage); "The Problem of Impotence" (Brundage); "Rape and Seduction in the Medieval Canon Law" (Brundage); and "Prostitution in the Medieval Canon Law" (Brundage).
The last section includes four papers: "Sex in the Literature of the Middle Ages: The Fabliaux" (Sidney E. Berger); "Prostitution in the Later Middle Ages" (Bullough); "Human Sexuality in Twelfth Through Fifteenth-Century Scientific Writings" (Helen Rodnite Lemay); and "Postscript: Heresy, Witchcraft, and Sexuality" (Bullough).
An appendix discussing "Medieval Canon Law and Its Sources" with an examination of the six works comprising the *Corpus iuris canonici*, concludes this valuable work. (TJW)

IL
752. Durkin, Mary G. **Feast of Love: Pope John Paul II on Human Intimacy.** Chicago: Loyola University Press, 1983. 248 p. Includes bibliography and index. ISBN 0-8294-0443-0.
Between September 5, 1979 and April 8, 1981, Pope John Paul II gave fifty-six Wednesday general audience talks dealing with sexuality and the body. These talks then appeared in translation in the English edition of *L'Osservatore Romano* (the appendix gives a listing of the addresses with date of delivery and date of their newspaper appearance). Subsequently, Father Andrew M. Greeley, the popular American novelist and philanthropist, asked Mary G. Durkin, a pastoral theologian, to summarize the contents of these addresses

and comment upon them. The result is *Feast of Love: Pope John Paul II on Human Intimacy.*

The papal talks are grouped under eighteen headings that form the chapters of this book and present a theology of sexuality and the body. Each chapter begins with one or more biblical quotations followed by Durkin's summary of the Pope's address and ending with her "Spiritual Reflection" on the topic, which attempts to integrate the Pope's thoughts with a contemporary scientific perspective.

Chapter topics include the "Beginning," an account of human creation and fall that appear in the first chapters of Genesis; "Original Solitude"; "Original Unity"; "Original Nakedness"; "Nuptial Meaning of the Body"; "Original Innocence"; "Knowledge and Procreation"; "Shame and Lust"; "Appropriation"; "Adultery in the Body"; "Desire"; "Adultery in the Heart"; "Appeal to Goodness"; "*Eros, Ethos,* and Spontaneity"; "Redemption of the Body"; "The Flesh and the Spirit"; "Purity and Life According to the Spirit"; and "Purity of Heart."

Durkin believes that "Pope John Paul II's theology of the body and of sexuality provides a vision that challenges us to recognize that our encounters with Mystery, which we experience in the extraordinary dimensions of our human sexuality, are actually invitations to participate in the feast that God had originally planned for man and woman. This vision gives the basis for a spirituality of sexuality, a spirituality that will allow us to recognize the extraordinary dimension of our sexuality" (p. xvi).

Durkin's reflections attempt to integrate the papal vision with current thinking on many related topics, including masculinity and femininity, fantasy, nudity, male/female relationships, sexual intercourse, procreation, sex roles, premarital and extramarital sex, and erotic behavior. Thus, this book is intended to help those confused by the baffling signals emanating from our sex-oriented society to better cope with the problems of their own sexuality and to understand religiously the inherent spirituality of that sexuality. This book is a powerful statement on the vision of the head of the Roman Catholic Church concerning topics of great moment with the Church today. (TJW)

IL

753.   Epstein, Louis M. **Sex Laws and Customs in Judaism.** Introduction by Ari Kiev. New York: KTAV Publishing House, 1967. 251 p. Includes bibliography and index.

This volume deals primarily with Jewish sex laws and customs outside the normal marriage relationship. The totality of laws and their interpretation yields "a code of sex morality . . . blending legal precepts and ethical ideals and aiming not only at rectitude but at saintliness (which) must regard purity of mind both as elemental in stimulating proper conduct and at the same time as the goal and objective of proper conduct." The code attempts to regulate both actions and thoughts. Modesty is primary to avoid tempting oneself as well as others into improper thought and acts.

The positive injunction is to be fruitful and multiply. Celibacy is not acceptable. "The sex impulse . . . is a holy urge . . . if expressed in loving union between man and wife." Epstein compares prebiblical and biblical law, talmudic law, and post-talmudic law and practice regarding modesty, sex segregation, flirting and familiarity, perversion, prostitution, rape and seduction (primarily in terms of property rights), adultery, and jealousy. He finds that "it is the purpose of law to supersede primitive tribal usages and to regulate human affairs by standards of equity." Although it is apparent that Jewish customs have been influenced by the surrounding society in areas including dress, modesty, and prostitution there remains the conviction that "sex morality is a discipline and ideal which reaches out into the remotest avenues of social and personal conduct." (JA)

IL,PO

754.   Feuerstein, Georg. **Sacred Sexuality: Living the Vision of the Erotic Spirit.** Los Angeles, Calif.: Jeremy P. Tarcher, 1992. 239 p. Includes bibliography and index. ISBN 0-87477-683-X.

Surveying a vast diversity of religions and spiritual traditions—including Christianity, Judaism, goddess worship, Taoism, and Hinduism—Feuerstein uncovers the deeply spiritual hidden messages about sexuality at the core of all of these great teachings: spirituality is in essence erotic, and sexuality is in essence spiritual.

Beyond the freedoms provided by the sexual revolution, there is another, more rewarding, challenging, and creative option: experiencing sexuality as a transformative vehicle of spirituality—sacred sexuality. Sacred sexuality is about recovering the bliss and delight beyond pleasure, the immortal energy locked within our bodies. Sacred sexuality is about the reenchantment of our lives, about embracing the imponderable mystery of existence.

Sacred sex is above love, not merely the positive feelings between intimates, but an overwhelming reverence for all embodied life. Through sacred sex, we directly participate in the vastness of being. It fills us with wonder and stillness.

In spite of recent liberalizations in our culture's views and practices relative to sexuality, most of us continue to feel a gnawing and vague dissatisfaction with our sex lives. We continue to hunt down the orgasm and even seek to prolong it, but for most of us it is still little more than a brief, if intense, sensation that leaves us hungering for some greater release of which it seems a mere shadow.

Feuerstein presents the view that we cannot live fully as human beings without first recovering the spiritual depth of our sexuality. Yet our sexuality can help us get in touch with that depth, serving as a gateway to the spiritual dimension. This book is intended to expand the understanding and experience of sex and open new horizons that allow us to realize the full potential of lovemaking. Sacred sexuality is the *real* sexual revolution. (Author)

PR,IL

755. Foster, Lawrence. **Religion and Sexuality: The Shakers, the Mormons, and the Oneida Community.** Urbana, Ill.: University of Illinois Press, 1984. 363 p. Includes bibliographic essay and index. ISBN 0-252-01119-8.

Many radical religious groups originated and developed in western New York State in the 1830s and 1840s during a period of rapid social change; the revivalist fervor was so intense that the area was called the "Burned-Over District." Historian Foster utilizes primary manuscripts and printed materials in a narrative style to focus on understanding the origin and development of alternative sexual and family forms in three of these groups: the Shakers, the Oneida Perfectionists, and the Mormons. Of particular interest is the way in which religious ideology and social context interacted to produce new forms of male/female relationships in a religious setting. Core chapters explore the experiences of the founders, the appeal and formation of each religious community, and the ways in which each group approached marriage and family relations. Foster argues that rapid economic changes (greater geographic mobility, the concentration of male occupations in the highly competitive "outside world," and the segregation of females in their management of the domestic sphere) before the Civil War placed strains on the existing family system and on male/female roles. Consequently, there was a need to structure these changes. The wider society adjusted by adhering to Victorian tenets of idealization of the family, sexual restraint, and the "cult of womanhood." The Shakers, Perfectionists, and Mormons responded by developing communal religious communities, distinctive in terms of their sexual and family arrangements. Sexual arrangements became a means to wider aims of restoring order to a fragmented social life and conforming to communal and divine goals. The Shakers instituted norms of celibacy; the Perfectionists developed "complex marriage" (akin to group marriage) and coitus reservatus; and the Mormons advocated plural marriage in the Church's formative years. Rather than looking at each of these groups as cultural side shows, Foster tries to understand them not only as innovative strategies for coping with a crisis of transition but also as radical experiments that may provide some insight into the struggle to deal with dissatisfaction with sexuality and marriage. Therefore, this study is relevant not only for historians but also for sociologists, anthropologists, students of religion, and sexologists. (SGF)

IL

756. Gardella, Peter. **Innocent Ecstasy: How Christianity Gave America an Ethic of Sexual Pleasure.** New York: Oxford University Press, 1985. 202 p. Includes bibliography and index. ISBN 0-19-503612-3.

The ethics of sexual pleasure enjoyed by Americans today has, according to Gardella, Assistant Professor of Religion at Manhattanville College, a long history going back to Puritan times and linked to varying religious attitudes toward sex. Basically it derives from the eagerness of American Christians of many persuasions to overcome original sin, a centuries-old burden that has hampered the faithful, especially women, in their enjoyment of sexual pleasure.

Gardella traces the transformation of religious attitudes toward sex from one that equated sex with sin to one that he characterizes as "innocent ecstasy," that is, innocent in the sense that sex is not sinful, and ecstatic in that men and women are encouraged to extract the highest pleasure possible from their sexual activity. He shows that evolving doctrines and positions in American Christian religions has brought about this remarkable transformation.

The separate trends of thought contributing to this transformation include (1) Catholic sensuality stemming from basic doctrine dealing with orgasm, passion, and sin; (2) Protestant reactions to Catholic attitudes and teaching that led to unanticipated involvement in sexual matters; (3) the medical community's evolving concerns linking sin, health, and sexual behavior; (4) evangelical Christianity's promotion of emotional experiences transforming the personality from the inside out; (5) the widespread experiences of visions of the Virgin Mary by Catholic girls, giving the Romantic ideal of woman a Christian form; and (6) the sexual views of Margaret Sanger and others that surfaced during the birth control movement.

In Gardella's view, all these converging strands of thought about sex and sin have resulted in a new sexual ethic that the majority of Americans, as indicated by many sex surveys, have embraced. Those Americans in the evangelical mold, such as Marabel Morgan, have disavowed any connection between original sin and sex; Catholics, such as Father Andrew Greeley and others, have promoted a sacramental quality in sexuality. Gardella comments, "Feminist theology . . . carries on the Victorian feminist crusade to sanctify the body, to establish a religion of health, and finally to abolish the disharmony between body and soul, or nature and God" (p. 154). The numerous trends that have redeemed sex, that is, have removed sex as a source of guilt, have apparently also elevated sex to a level of sacredness, to a position where ecstatic sex is tantamount to worship, a religious experience welcomed by many individuals. (TJW)

IL

757. Ginder, Richard. **Binding with Briars: Sex and Sin in the Catholic Church.** Englewood Cliffs, N.J.: Prentice-Hall, 1975. 251 p. Includes bibliography and index. ISBN 0-13-076299-7.

A Roman Catholic priest of the Pittsburgh diocese, Father Ginder says that he has been writing this book for twenty-five years; the process transformed him from a sexual conservative to a liberal. Author of the controversial column, "Right or Wrong," in *Our Sunday Visitor*, a Catholic periodical with over a million subscribers, Ginder presents here his views on various aspects of human sexuality as dealt with by the Catholic Church.

He believes that the Church has not kept pace with changes in the sexual behavior of Catholics and as a result has lost its hold on many of the faithful. He attributes much of this to the rigidity of the tradition-bound hierarchy in the Church and to their reluctance to pay attention to advances in sexual knowledge since the time of Sigmund Freud, Havelock Ellis, Richard von Krafft-Ebing, and others who pioneered in the new field of sexual science around the turn of the century. Furthermore, he believes that the Church fosters anti-sexual attitudes stemming from the teachings of St. Paul and the Church fathers. It imparts this anti-sexuality to the faithful from infancy through adulthood by means of its moral teachings on such subjects as masturbation, premarital sex, homosexuality, birth control, sadomasochism, and the like. The result has been wholesale disobedience of the faithful, declining membership in the Church, and the Vatican's loss of credibility.

To understand the momentous changes that have occurred in personal sexual morality in the twentieth century and the Church's failure to adjust to these changes, Father Ginder examines each of several areas of conflict. He lays particular stress on the papal encyclicals *Casti conubii* (1930), which was the first papal denunciation of birth control, and *Humanae vitae*, which reaffirmed the position of the earlier statement. Ginder points out that "Pope John convoked Vatican Council II [1965-1966] because he could see that the modern age had far outstripped the Church" (p. 2). But Pope Paul VI's decision against sex in the 1968 encyclical on birth control, which was promulgated despite an almost unanimous recommendation for birth control from a commission of sixty-five knowledgeable laypeople and clergy, dashed the hopes of many Catholics for an enlightened sexual outlook and called into question the notion of papal infallibility in matters of faith and morals.

Besides examining the Church's rigid position on contraception, Ginder also illuminates views on homosexuality; the development of conscience and its relation to morality; masturbation and the Church's focus on the notion of sex as strictly reproductive; and the pursuit of pleasure as a legitimate goal in human sexuality.

Finally, he admits to having driven "a Mack truck through one taboo after another—birth control, fornication, masturbation, sodomy, 'bad thoughts and desires,' kinky sex" (p. 224). He believes that most Catholics agree with his positions on these taboos; what bothers him is the failure of the Church hierarchy to understand the situation. He adds that "we Catholics are witnessing the breakdown of casuistry within the Church—and casuistry is the method by which Catholics have lived since the sixteenth century" (p. 224).

Ginder believes that in response to the growing consensus for positive change within the Church, a revised sexual morality touching upon the several areas dealt with in this book will inevitably emerge. It is literally a question of the survival of the Catholic Church in the modern world. (TJW)

IL
758.   Johnson, Edwin Clark. **In Search of God in the Sexual Underworld: A Mystical Journey.** New York: Quill, 1983. 238 p. Includes bibliography. ISBN 0-688-02046-1.

An ex-monk, psychotherapist, countercultural product of the 1960s, Johnson tries to reconcile two of the major issues of the modern world, sexuality and spirituality, while attempting to pull together the diverse strands of his own life into a meaningful whole. He generalizes his personal experiences into a broader framework from which he hopes everyone will profit. What began as a research assignment on male juvenile prostitution for a government consulting organization becomes the catalyst for a mystical journey exploring the meaning of God in terms of the modern world. Drawing upon Joseph Campbell's concept of the hero in *The Hero with a Thousand Faces*, Johnson interprets his research experience as a heroic quest for his own identity and for God. Everything in his world is symbolic. The young prostitutes, pimps, and hustlers with whom he lived and interacted in San Francisco's Tenderloin District became an underworld, a mythical realm full of demons, with whom he, as hero, must wrestle and cope in order to re-emerge with a transformed identity and greater sense of understanding about the world. He perceives himself in the role of a *bodhisativa*, a compassionate person who participates in the world's salvation. He draws from an eclectic array of myths, stories, and spiritual traditions to reach some bold conclusions about the relationship between God, sex, and meaning. He casts aside old labels and focuses on the transcendence of different experiences. He hopes that the positive conclusions he reaches about his experience can benefit others by demonstrating how a change in consciousness can contribute to changes in the world. (SGF)

IL
759.   Kardiner, Abram. **Sex and Morality.** London: Routledge & Kegan Paul, 1955. 274 p. Includes bibliographic notes and index.

Acknowledging his debt to Freud, Briffault, Rado, Spitz, Linton, and Du Bois, Kardiner, Professor of Clinical Psychiatry at Columbia University, in a carefully reasoned argument, presents his views on sex and morality in society.

Defining morality as "what people *should* do," Kardiner goes on to point out that it is an ideal that people often have difficulty living up to. Inculcated into children at an early age, primarily by parents and the church, morality becomes customary. Studied by anthropologists as "the way we do things," these customs (e.g., marriage) become "binding, persistent, and difficult to change." Furthermore, they vary from one culture to another.

Sex customs, often practiced in secrecy, are a special case. Because of the pressure to alter sex morality, Kardiner believes that it is necessary to examine these sex customs, identifying their sources and learning how they are taught. In successful cultures, the patterns of morality, including sex morality, have a high degree of effectiveness.

Kardiner compares and criticizes the contributions of Sigmund Freud and Alfred Kinsey to an understanding of sexual behavior. While Freud showed the significance of sex in relation to human happiness, Kinsey revealed the discrepancies between sex conventions and actual practice. Using a different approach, Kardiner presents "sex customs in relation to the total social context" (p. 24). Intending to provide a much-needed synthesis concerning sexual behavior, he examines such topics as nineteenth century liberalism, Darwin's evolutionary thought, the feminist movement, the Freudian doctrine, and advances in medicine and technology, stressing their impact on sexual behavior and morality.

He meticulously examines human sexual nature and its social control; the price paid by society for a restrictive sexual morality in terms of educating children; the age-old conflicts over masturbation and homosexuality; feminism; the decline of the family; and the deterioration of parent/child relationships.

Kardiner concludes with a final question: "How can we regulate sex custom so that it serves the ends of social expediency and does not jeopardize personal happiness?" He believes that "the family is the place where we can exert the greatest influence on sex morality and all other morality" (p. 263), and that parents, aided by psychiatry, are in the best position to undertake the task. (TJW)

PR,IL

760. Kosnik, Anthony, et al. **Human Sexuality: New Directions in American Catholic Thought.** New York: Paulist Press, 1977. 322 p. Includes bibliography and index. ISBN 0-7091-0223-4.

Commissioned by the Catholic Theological Society of America in 1972, this in-depth study of human sexuality is the report of a committee chaired by Kosnik, a priest and professor of moral theology at Saints Cyril and Methodius Seminary, Orchard Lake, Michigan. It was undertaken in order to arrive at "helpful and illuminating guidelines in the present confusion" in regard to "the adequacy of traditional Catholic formulations and pastoral responses to sexual matters." The result is a work addressed to theologians and other professionals, to those doing pastoral work, and to concerned Catholic laypersons. The authors initially provide the reader with a biblical perspective on human sexuality by thoroughly reviewing the Old and New Testaments with particular attention to passages dealing with sex and cautioning that the Bible is an historical document and does not offer a systematic presentation of sexuality. (Indeed, there is no word for the concept of sexuality in the biblical Hebrew or Greek.) The largely historical second chapter covers first the thinking of the early Church Fathers, such as St. Augustine, from the second to the fifth centuries, followed by developments from the sixth to the tenth centuries, the eleventh to the fourteenth centuries, the fifteenth to the nineteenth centuries, and finally the twentieth century. For this span of time, the Catholic Christian tradition with respect to human sexuality is explained. In chapter III, the authors carefully critique many of the conclusions of the major surveys of sexual behavior and the contemporary views of leading sexologists and therapists. In chapter IV they attempt "to integrate the biblical, historical, and anthropological data into a theological synthesis" and arrive at a theology of human sexuality. The authors also provide guidelines sought for in this study and deal with many aspects of marital sexuality, nonmarital sexuality, homosexuality, and special questions, such as masturbation, sexual variants, sex clinics, transsexualism, pornography and obscenity, and programs of sex education. The study is thoroughly documented and contains in the appendixes full texts of important documents, including the papal "Declaration on Certain Questions Concerning Sexual Ethics," which appeared in *L'Osservatore Romano* on January 22, 1976. The pastoral recommendations of this report were rejected and condemned by the Vatican's Sacred Congregation for the Doctrine of the Faith, a department of the Curia that deals with doctrinal deviation, because the authors "failed to accept the established Catholic view that procreation is the central purpose of human sexual activity" (*New York Times*, December 9, 1979, p. 21). (TJW)

IL
761. Kramer, Heinrich, and James Sprenger. **The Malleus Maleficarum.** Translated with introductions, bibliography and notes by Rev. Montague Summers. New York: Dover, 1971. 277 p. Unabridged republication of the 1928 edition. Includes bibliography. ISBN 0-486-22802-9.

The Bull of Pope Innocent VIII, *Summis desiderantes affectibus*, dated December 9, 1484, expressed deep concern about the widespread practice of witchcraft in Northern Germany whereby, it was alleged, all sorts of horrors, including many of a sexual nature, were being perpetuated by means of incantations, spells, conjurations, and so forth. It delegated two energetic Dominicans, Father Henry Kramer and Father James Sprenger, the responsibility for investigating as Inquisitors these charges of witchcraft and heresy and empowered them with authority to correct, imprison, and punish any persons found guilty of these offenses.

The Malleus Maleficarum (*The Witches' Hammer*), jointly written by Kramer and Sprenger as a guide to facilitate the work of judges in witch trials, includes the papal Bull as its preface. For about three centuries the *Malleus* was the principal document for combating witchcraft throughout Europe and it "lay on the bench of every judge, or the desk of every magistrate." It came to be accepted by Protestants as well as Catholics as the ultimate authority on the subject.

In the introduction to the 1928 edition of the *Malleus*, Montague Summers states that the practice of witchcraft was "a vast political movement, an organized society which was anti-social and anarchical, a world-wide plot against civilization" (p. xviii). The Inquisition dealt with it as a heresy and used the *Malleus* and similar documents as instruments in the struggle.

The sexual aspect of witchcraft is exposed in the *Malleus* by a number of the questions that are addressed: "Whether Children Can Be Generated by Incubi and Succubi," "Concerning Witches Who Copulate with Devils," "Whether Witches May Work Some Prestidigitatory Illusion So That the Male Organ Appears to Be Entirely Removed and Separate from the Body," "How Witches Impede and Prevent the Power of Procreation," and so forth.

The final part concerns judicial proceedings in both civil and ecclesiastical courts against witches and heretics. In order to extract confessions torture was used, as the following quotation reveals: "But if neither threats nor such promises will induce her to confess the truth, then the officers must proceed with the sentence. . . . And while she is being questioned about each several point, let her be often and frequently exposed to torture, beginning with the more gentle of them; for the Judge should not be too hasty to proceed to the graver kind" (p. 226). It is not surprising that many feminists see the *Malleus* as a particularly virulent form of patriarchal repression. (TJW)

IL
762. Larue, Gerald. **Sex and the Bible.** Buffalo, N.Y.: Prometheus Books, 1983. 173 p. Includes bibliography. ISBN 0-87975-206-8.

First as a university professor of biblical history, literature, and archaeology, and then as a certified marriage, family, and child counselor, Larue became increasingly concerned with the effect of biblical writings on the sexual behavior and feelings of contemporary people. The central aim of this book is to "explore some of the ways in which biblical attitudes toward human sexuality impinge on our culture and have an impact on our lives" (p. 13). To what extent do materials written over 2,000 years ago have relevance to the sexual issues with which people today are coping? Drawing primarily on his own translations of biblical passages from 1100 B.C.E. (Before the Common Era) to about 150 C.E., Larue presents the biblical view of a wide variety of topics, each of which is addressed in a separate chapter. The contents focus on three major subject areas: (1) marriage and the family, including the controversial topics of sex education, surrogate parents, wide age differences in mates, adultery, incest, and illegitimacy; (2) sexual anatomy and physiology, for example, testicles, menstruation; and (3) specific sexual norms and practices, for example, virginity, celibacy, rape, prostitution, masturbation, and circumcision.

It is clear that the Bible has quite a bit to say about sex, much of which is neither punitive nor negative. By juxtaposing what the Bible says with current sexual practices and needs, Larue raises the question of how teachings that applied to a very different social and cultural organization are helpful or appropriate to twentieth-century society. In the process, he draws on psychological, sociological, and therapeutic work associated with sexuality to provide a brief overview of contemporary sexual issues. He concludes that analyses of biblical passages need to leave room for common sense in their application to current problems; some edicts are clearly outmoded and downright harmful. The Song of Songs clearly shows that sexual pleasure was and can continue to be a joyful experience throughout life. (SGF)

PR,IL

763. Lawrence, Raymond J., Jr. **The Poisoning of Eros: Sexual Values in Conflict.** New York: Augustine Moore Press, 1989. 280 p. Includes bibliographic footnotes. ISBN 0-9623310-0-7.

According to Lawrence, a minister in the Methodist and Episcopal churches for thirty-two years, "The history of Western sexual values is profoundly equivocal; the tradition is divided against itself" (p. 1). These antithetical traditions are the Platonic dualist philosophy of the Greco-Roman empire, which separated the spirit and flesh, extolling spiritual pursuits above material ones; and Hebraic theology which affirmed a unity of the human creature, both spirit and flesh. Lawrence argues that the meaning of the Jesus movement and early Christianity was distorted through a Greco-Roman philosophy and political structure, resulting in 1500 years of repudiation of Jewish roots. The book is "an attempt to restore our collective memory." *The Poisoning of Eros*, winner of the 1989 book award of the World Congress of Sexology, explores in detail the way in which a Hebraic, sex-affirmative biblical tradition was transformed into a sex-negating Christian philosophy and later reclaimed during the Prostestant Reformation and its aftermath. The "sexual revolution" was consistent with early Christian teachings.

Lawrence begins with portraying the roots of Christianity in the Jesus movement. Jesus was dynamic, sensuous, and politically radical; he criticized the patriarchal institution of marriage and favored the equality of women. Paul was no ascetic, but a sex-affirming Jew who was not negative about sex or marriage. Both affirmed sexual desire and fulfillment as a gift of the creator, not as a defilement of the body. However, after 400 years, the early ecstatic religion was institutionalized into a syncretistic religion, the central ethical issue of which was sexual purity rather than idolatry. Augustine, Jerome, and Ambrose articulated the philosophy of the Roman Church and promoted the view that sex is the root of evil.

During the Middle Ages, the 1,000 years between Augustine and Luther, monasticism flourished and marriage was incorporated into the Church as a liturgical event, under the Church's authority. Aquinas wrote the major theological document of the time—*Summa theologica*—attempting to synthesize Aristotilian philosophy and Christian theology. Nevertheless, the Middle Ages remained a time of extremes—from renunciation to worldliness.

By the sixteenth century, the autocracy of Rome crumbled and the Hebraic roots of Christianity resurfaced. More emphasis was placed on the teachings of the Bible; monasticism diminished; and marriage was possible for the clergy. Luther, head of the German reformation, focused on the importance of faith, not righteous living, as a way of validating the Christian life. Sex and the erotic were integral, valued parts of living. After the Reformation, sex became privatized, no longer a matter of religious or ethical supervision.

After the sixteenth century, prominent secular figures, e.g., Rousseau, Boswell, Marx, Nietsche, Kant, and Freud, were significant in shaping sexual values. Historians have been reluctant to acknowledge the sexual activities of famous Americans such as Franklin, Washington, and Jefferson; they cling to unrealistic portraits of their sexual purity. By the 1920s and 1930s, the twentieth century's greatest theologians, Tillich and Barth, lived and espoused a sex-affirmative philosophy. By the last quarter of the twentieth century, views that emphasize the restriction of sex to marriage are no longer credible.

After identifying numerous myths and distortions about Christian views of sexuality and tracing the poisoning of Eros in this carefully documented work, Lawrence proposes a new ethics of "carnal reciprocity"—"an ethics rooted in an affirmation of sexuality that permits, even asserts that sexual self-actualization is preferable to sexual innocence, abstinence, and self-denial" (p. 247). (SGF)

PR

764. Levin, Eve. **Sex and Society in the World of the Orthodox Slavs, 900-1700.** Ithaca, N.Y.: Cornell University Press, 1989. 326 p. Includes bibliography and index. ISBN 0-8014-2260-4.

Levin states that her study of sex among the Orthodox Slavs—Serbians, Bulgarians, Russians—from A.D. 900 to 1700 opens for scholars "a hitherto unexplored area of inquiry." She observes that these peoples, despite national differences, displayed remarkable cultural affinities during the medieval period, strengthened by Orthodox Christianity. In this long period these peoples "shared a common Byzantine inheritance in religion, literary heritage, the arts, and teaching on sexuality" (p. 14). This inheritance was shared only marginally with the Slavic peoples to the north—Poles, Czechs, Slovaks—who received their cultural influences from the Roman tradition of the West.

Levin informs the reader about the ecclesiastical image of sexuality, an image that "promoted a view of sexuality as something alien to Christian life" (p. 36). This view, derived from the Greek Church, had been elaborated over nine centuries from the time of the Crucifixion. It regarded sex as evil, unhealthy, and abnormal. The Orthodox position on the origin of sex states that in the nonsexual Garden of Eden "through greed, intemperance, and disobedience, sin entered the world, and sexual desire was born" (p. 46). Levin provides further explanation of the Orthodox Slavs' position on sexuality in chapters on marriage, incest, illicit sex, rape, and the role of the clergy, along with the secular powers, in molding sexual conduct. The Orthodox considered sex a public rather than a private matter, and so were willing to talk about it rather than keep its manifestations secret.

This in-depth study has led Levin to the following observations and conclusions: (1) regulations established by church and state spelled out the sexual interrelationships of families to individual members and servants, men to women, and clergy to parishioners; (2) the states granted complete authority over morality and interfamilial matters to the church; (3) secular authorities concerned themselves with sexual behavior only where it directly threatened peace and order, as in rape cases; (4) religious and secular authorities had the same goal of restricting uninhibited sexual expression that they believed threatened both spiritual well-being and the social order; (5) the church developed and enforced a sexual standard that was compatible with popular sensibilities; (6) the community took an active interest in the sexual behavior of its members, with neighbors reporting violations to authorities; (7) the penance for sexual sins was public and observable; and (8) the Orthodox Slavs, in contrast to their Western neighbors, paid scant attention to the emotional component of sexual relations.

Finally, Levin observes that "the laity accepted the church's teachings on what constituted sexual sin and its perception of proper sexual conduct as essential to spiritual well-being." This adherence to Orthodox sexual standards attests to the fact that over the centuries "harmony between ecclesiastical and popular attitudes was extraordinarily stable, lasting through periods of political upheavals and foreign conquest." Illustrations of religious icons, frescoes, woodcuts, and miniatures illuminate the Orthodox views on sexuality. (TJW)

IL

765. Nelson, James B. **Embodiment: An Approach to Sexuality and Christian Theology.** New York: Pilgrim Press, 1978. 303 p. Includes bibliographic notes and indexes. ISBN 0-8066-1655-5.

Embodiment literally refers to the incarnation of God in Jesus Christ, the way in which the Word became flesh. Consequently, Christianity needs to take seriously the meaning of the link between the spiritual and the physical. Given the questions raised by the sexual revolution, Nelson, a professor of Christian ethics at the United Theological Seminary (Twin Cities), thinks that Christians need to ask not only the usual question of what Christianity says about individuals' lives as sexual beings but also what human sexual experiences mean for the way in which individuals live their faith. This two-way perspective permeates the materials discussed in this book. Nelson views sexuality in broad terms as a language and as "the physiological and psychological grounding of our capacity to love" (p. 8).

One part of the book deals with embodiment in sexual theology and the ways in which the body/spirit dichotomy has been dealt with. Two kinds of dualism manifest in the great religions of the world (Hinduism, Buddhism, Christianity) have resulted in sexual alienation, for example, rejection of the body with its inherent sexuality. These include spiritualistic dualism, the separation of mind from body, with the body in a degraded position, resulting in human sexuality being regarded at best as a regrettable necessity; and sexist dualism, or the systematic subordination of women to men, who consider themselves in possession of superior qualities and capacities. In the chapter on sexual alienation, Nelson traces the development of these dualisms from early Hebrew, classical Greek, Roman, and early Christian history through the fateful musings about sex of the Church Fathers (Tertullian, Jerome, Augustine) and St. Thomas Aquinas, to the conservative positions of Reformation thinkers (Luther, Calvin). He concludes that both spiritualistic and sexist dualisms are integral parts of the Christian past. One answer to the sexual alienation experienced by many of the faithful is reconciliation through "resurrection of the sexual body" (p. 70). In successive chapters entitled "Love and Sexual Ethics," "Marriage and Fidelity," "The Morality of Sexual Variations" (fantasy, erotic and pornographic literature, masturbation, oragenitalism, anal intercourse), "Gayness and Homosexuality," "The Sexually Disenfranchised" (the physically disabled, the seriously ill, the aging, and the mentally retarded), Nelson deals with the concrete issues of human sexuality, with how Christians might reacquaint themselves with their sexual selves, and with the embodiment of God in the sexuality of Jesus Christ and humankind. (TJW)

IL,PO

766. Pagels, Elaine. **Adam, Eve, and the Serpent.** New York: Random House, 1988. 189 p. Includes bibliographic notes and index. ISBN 0-394-52140-4.

How did traditional patterns of gender and sexual relationships that are so familiar in Christian societies arise to begin with? According to Pagels, a professor of religion at Princeton University and author of *The Gnostic Gospels* (1979), the evolution of sexual attitudes currently associated with Christianity began in the first four centuries, when the Christian movement was gradually transformed into a religion of the Roman Empire. To understand this transition, it is necessary to analyze differing interpretations of creation that reveal the attitudes and values of the day. First-century writers used Adam, Eve, and the Serpent as metaphors for their concerns about marriage, divorce, and gender. Therefore, this book investigates four centuries of Christian interpretations of Genesis as a process of intellectual history, focusing on issues of sexuality, freedom, and marriage. How was the story of Adam, Eve, and the Serpent used to justify established beliefs? How did it reflect the social situation of the people who were interpreting its meaning?

The development of early Christianity was marked by contention over interpretation of the strictures of Jesus and the apostle Paul concerning sexual behavior. Since these strictures were stated rather than explained, and since they introduced new restrictions beyond those of Judaism, they engendered many theological arguments. These arguments occupied the four centuries from the death of Christ until the Church adopted the interpretations of Augustine, Bishop of Hippo.

Each chapter discusses a theme that Christians tried to understand or justify by their interpretation of the story of Creation. Adam and Eve's behavior in the Garden of Eden was initially explained as an instance of disobedience, not a sexual violation; moral freedom and responsibility prevailed. Clement of Alexandria (c. A.D. 180) emphasized that God created humans "in his image" and therefore humans were innately good. Gnostics later questioned whether Genesis implied that humans were endowed with free will and were morally free. Later, however, Augustine of Hippo (A.D. 354-430) altered the Church's view by showing that the disobedience was an indication of humans' inherent depravity and humans, through their free will, are generators of endless sin. Many of the Church Fathers (Methodius, Jerome, Tertullian, Ambrose) regarded sexual intercourse as unclean, a view that pervaded Western thought for some 1,600 years. Celibacy and abstention from intercourse within marriage are the aspects of sexuality most closely identified with the era, but Pagels also gives considerable attention to procreation, marriage, divorce, and adultery, as well as to prostitution, abortion, and the subordination of women. (DJS, TJW, SGF)

IL

767. Parrinder, Geoffrey. **Sex in the World's Religions.** New York: Oxford University Press, 1980. 263 p. Includes bibliography and index. ISBN 0-19-520202-3.

Parrinder, Professor Emeritus of the Comparative Study of Religions, London University, has written a score of books on various aspects of religion. In this work, he ventures into the relatively unexplored area of sex in the world's major living religions. As a comparative study, it examines factually and systematically the sexual attitudes, beliefs, customs, and practices found in Hinduism, Buddhism, Confucianism, Taoism, Shintoism, Islam, Judaism, Christianity, and the indigenous religious beliefs of Africa. Included among the common topics discussed are religious myths, fertility, chastity, marriage, sacred rituals, taboos, prostitution, sex manuals, sex in art, the status of women, and male/female relationships.

The study begins with a consideration of sacred sex in India, follows through with the Buddhist renunciation of Indian eroticism, and investigates other Indian religious traditions (Jainism, Sikh beliefs, Parsi customs, and tribal beliefs). A chapter on Japan's Shinto myths and the floating world of the Geishas follows one on Chinese Yin and Yang and Confucian morality. Parrinder, who spent many years studying African religions, writes about the myths, phallicism, initiation rites, marriage customs, and taboos of the native religions as well as of the effects of Christian and Muslim religious influences. Then, in separate chapters, he examines sex in the three great Semitic or exclusively monotheistic religions: Judaism, Christianity, and Islam.

In a final chapter, he considers the impact of advances in medicine, psychology, and the emancipation of women on religion in the modern world. He concludes by suggesting that one can gain an understanding of sex from a study of religion that, with reform, adjustment, and more respect to women, "may contribute to new sexual ethics" (p. 247). (TJW)

PR,IL

768.   Payer, Pierre J. **Sex and the Penitentials: The Development of a Sexual Code, 550-1150.** Toronto: University of Toronto Press, 1984. 219 p. Includes bibliography and index. ISBN 0-8020-5649-0.

Payer traces the rise and demise of the penitential literature between A.D. 550 and 1150. He also analyzes the penitentials for their sexual content, which was a substantial part of these confessional manuals. The underlying assumption of the penitentials was that "sexual intercourse was permissible only between a man and a woman who were legitimately married to one another and then only done for the sake of procreation" (p. 3). Emanating from the teachings of St. Augustine, this approach considered all other forms of sexual activity immoral and sinful. In the medieval world, the penitentials, through the imposition of penances for various acts of sexual misconduct, encouraged chastity, promoted celibacy, discouraged second marriages for widows, and fostered monasticism. The need for penitentials arose with the transformation from public to private penance, which required a close relationship between priest and sinner.

The numerous penitentials had their origin in Ireland in the sixth century with the *Penitential of Vinnian*, the *Penitential of Columbanus*, and the *Penitential of Cummean*. They spread to Anglo-Saxon England (*Penitential of Bede*), and then to the Frankish world (*Burgundian Penitential*), thus providing a relatively homogeneous code of sexual conduct lasting about 500 years. Apparently the impetus for these manuals did not flow from Rome.

Payer analyzes the sexual content of representative penitential texts created in the period prior to A.D. 813. Sexual topics dealt with in the penitentials generally include adultery, periods of sexual abstinence, positions of sexual intercourse, incest, aphrodisiacs, fornication, homosexuality, bestiality, masturbation, and sexual pollution. In connection with each of these topics penances to be completed over stated periods of time were meted out by priest-confessors to the sinners. For example, in the *Penitential of Cummean*, the base penance for adultery with a neighbor's wife was sexual abstinence for one year; with a vowed virgin resulting in a child, three years. Length of penance was usually a function of the gravity of the offense.

Objections to the system of penitentials emerged in the ninth century, reflecting the lack of documented authority in many of these handbooks. Alternative canonical works in which the penitential canons were incorporated into collections of canon law were promulgated. Eventually a science of canon law developed that led to the abandonment of the penitentials as a practical tool. But for many years, the penitentials "provided for the day-to-day failings of Christians, which could be most varied" (p. 116).

Payer includes several appendixes covering such matters as general areas of sexual behavior covered in the penitentials, periods of sexual abstinence, penances as measures of gravity, homosexuality and the penitentials, and notes on the language of the penitentials. (TJW)

IL

769.   Ranke-Heinemann, Uta. **Eunuchs for Heaven: The Catholic Church and Sexuality.** London: Andre Deutsch, 1990. 326 p. Includes bibliography and index. Translation of: *Eunuchen für das Himmelreich*. ISBN 0-233-98553-0.

German Catholic theologian Ranke-Heinemann has taken a passage from Matthew 19:12 about men becoming eunuchs "for the sake of the kingdom of heaven" in order to give prominence to celibatarian attitudes toward such topics as marriage, women, virginity, sexual pleasure, and various other phenomena and practices relating to belief and behavior.

In thirty chapters Ranke-Heinemann ranges over the centuries starting with an account of the non-Christian roots of Christian sexual pessimism, and continuing with the enumeration of anti-sexual statements of the Church Fathers before Augustine, including Justin Martyr, Clement of Alexandria, Origen, John Chrysostom, Ambrose, and Jerome. She then examines the anti-sexual views of Augustine; the growth of celibacy; the role of penitentials; and the celibatarian fear and repression of women. She also covers the views of famous scholastics, such as Albertus Magnus; the contrary views of Peter Abelard; the notions of restrained sexual intercourse held by Huguccio; Thomas Aquinas's distortions of Aristotle's thoughts on the nature of man and beast; the sexual ethic of Thomas Aquinas; the medieval campaign against contraception; the ban on incest; and witchcraft-induced impotence and demonic intercourse. According to Ranke-Heinemann, Catholic theology attained its zenith in Thomas Aquinas whose *Summa theologica* solidified Catholic sexual morality in the thirteenth century.

Subsequently, a number of moral theologians, e.g., Martin Le Maistre (d. 1481), expressed views on marital intercourse, contraception, sexual pleasure, among other things, more liberal than those of their predecessors. However, their influence was short-lived. Even today their views are rigorously ignored. The Roman Catechism, commissioned by the Council of Trent and published in 1566, signaled a return to the old sexual pessimism of the scholastics. Ranke-Heinemann also discusses Martin Luther's emphasis on divine forgiveness and mercy which resulted in a moderating effect on Catholic sexual ethics. She then reviews Jansenist and Jesuit views on sexual morality, the attitudes toward contraception between 1500 and 1750, as well as the birth control issue in the nineteenth and twentieth centuries. In three final chapters she explores the Catholic Church's positions on abortion, masturbation, and homosexuality.

In sum, Ranke-Heinemann has critically examined the Catholic Church's long-standing positions on various subjects of a sexual nature, bringing out the numerous anti-sexual views of a host of celibatarian figures who renounced sexual pleasure, denigrated marriage as being inferior to celibacy, placed women in a subordinate position with respect to men, and adopted negative positions on such subjects as abortion, birth control, masturbation, and homosexuality. She places responsibility for these negative, often nonsensical, views squarely on the shoulders of celibatarian theologians, popes, and clergy who, she claims, should have known better. (TJW)

PR,IL

770. Rosner, Fred. **Sex Ethics in the Writings of Moses Maimonides.** New York: Bloch, 1974. 129 p. Includes bibliographic references and index.

Maimonides (1135/8-1204), renowned Talmudist, philosopher, and physician, and leader of the Jewish community in Egypt, authored significant works in religion, philosophy, and medicine. Rosner's book contains translations of one complete work and excerpts from other works dealing with various aspects of human sexuality. Completely translated is Maimonides's *Treatise on Cohabitation*, written in Arabic for Al-Malik, the Sultan of Hamat, Syria, and providing recipes for foods and drugs, aphrodisiac in effect, to enhance erections and improve sexual intercourse.

Rosner also includes statements on sex excerpted from several of Maimonides's medical writings, such as the *Treatise on Hemorrhoids, Treatise on the Regimen of Health, Commentary on the Aphorisms of Hippocrates, Treatise on Asthma, Medical Answers,* and *Medical Aphorisms.*

Maimonides's *magnum opus*, the *Mishneh Torah* (Code of Maimonides) presents in a systematic manner all of biblical and Talmudic law. Rosner discusses several books of this work, such as the *Book of Holiness* and the *Book of Women*, both dealing with topics of sexuality. In the former, Maimonides lists thirty-seven commandments concerning illicit intercourse and provides detailed explanations of each. He also emphasizes "the disciplinary intent of the laws, which counteract the worldly tendency to regard pleasure as the purpose of man's existence" (p. 95). In the *Book of Women*, "Maimonides discusses laws of marriage, levirate marriage, the virgin maiden and the wayward woman" (p. 110).

Maimonides's philosophical masterpiece, *Guide for the Perplexed*, also deals with sex, lust, and morality. He indicates that "the perfect man must have complete control over his lust for food, drink and sex." He expresses the abhorrence of Judaism of harlotry and prostitution and comments on crossbreeding, circumcision, adultery, and other sexual matters.

Finally, Rosner presents excerpts from Maimonides's *Commentary on the Mishnah*, which discusses forbidden unions, bestiality, lesbianism, homosexuality, and so forth. At one point he comments, "For since the true design of intercourse is to propagate the race and not only for sexual pleasure, then the pleasurable part of coitus was only given to stimulate human beings towards the major goal of the sexual act which is to maintain the seed (of humanity). Clear evidence for this contention is the fact that lust ceases and sensual delight subsides after the emission of the semen." (p. 121). (TJW)

IL

771. Sabbah, Fatna A. **Woman in the Muslim Unconscious.** Translated by Mary Jo Lakeland. New York: Pergamon Press, 1984. 132 p. (The Athene Series). Translation of: *La Femme dans l'Inconscient Musulman.* Includes bibliographic notes and index. ISBN 0-08-031625-5.

This book, written pseudonymously by an educated Muslim woman, offers a feminist perspective on Islam, sexuality, and male/female relationships. It presents the criteria by which the ideally desirable woman is judged in Islamic culture: silence, immobility, and obedience. By way of explanation, Sabbah quotes, analyzes, and interprets various sacred Islamic texts, including the Koran and the Sunnas. These documents provide the legal (i.e., orthodox) basis for the Muslim conceptions of love, desire, and the ideal woman. The views expressed become ingrained in the Muslim unconscious and account for men's dominant attitude toward women.

In Sabbah's mind a major question is establishing the relationship between the world of order (provided by the legal discourse) and the world of disorder (the erotic discourse). A different perspective from the one perpetuated by the sacred texts is provided by various erotic works (e.g., *The Perfumed Garden* by Shaykh Nefzawi), treatises on woman as an object of love, works describing Paradise, and wedding manuals for Muslim men. All are widely available in the Arabic language in Muslim countries today; in the main, they discuss erotic techniques, medical aspects of copulation, and sensuality in the hereafter. This material, listed in the text, contributes to the religious discourse because it provides answers to the questions of how men should conduct themselves sexually. Woman is viewed as an omnisexual creature, "a voracious crack . . . whose most prominent attribute . . . is her sexual organs" (p. 24). As such, she vigorously pursues man, longing for the penis to satisfy her basic need for orgasm.

Another major question is what evokes the female body as an object of love, desire, and male concern. And what puts women in the submissive role vis à vis Muslim men? Underlying these perceptions and questions of male and female sexuality is an official view of the universe: it is organized hierarchically and occupied by divine, human, and other beings, each having a specific sex. At the apex is God who speaks directly or indirectly through his prophet to believing man who, in turn, applies to believing woman what he has received from God. This hierarchy determines the power structure among all beings. The divine word, embodied in the Koran, is passed down the hierarchy so that everyone knows his or her place with respect to the divine will, which is clear and unambiguous. Paradise, characterized by an abundance of riches, is the reward of the believers; in it they repose on couches, eating and drinking in the company of placid sexual partners, the houris, created by God for the delectation of men. Houris are faultless, young, loving, virginal, and devoid of uteri. Although earthly women attain Paradise too, they have been replaced by the houris in the affections of men.

Sabbah explains that in the Muslim scheme of things, the divine will is paramount; it is man's task to comprehend that will as expressed in the Koran. The system allows for no deviations from the stated tenets of the religion. Men's and women's roles are fixed and immutable. In accordance with the sacred texts the ideal woman follows the paths of obedience, silence, and seclusion. Women are exclusively sexual beings; economically and politically they are obliged to remain subservient to men.

Closely related to Sabbah's book is *Beyond the Veil: Male-Female Dynamics in a Modern Muslim Society* (New York: Schenkman, 1975) by Fatima Mernissi, which deals with the traditional institutions that embody the inequality between the sexes in Muslim countries. (TJW)

IL
772.   **Sexual Symbolism: A History of Phallic Worship.** Includes *A Discourse on the Worship of Priapus* by Richard Payne Knight and *The Worship of the Generative Powers* by Thomas Wright. Introduction by Ashley Montagu. New York: Julian Press, 1957. 217, 196 p. Includes bibliographic footnotes.

Knight's *Worship of Priapus*, a seminal study of phallic worship, shocked elements of English society when it was first printed in 1786. The work is based on the examination of various artifacts in museums and collections throughout Europe; these include amulets, bronzes, coins, medals, and stone carvings displaying phallic symbols. Common throughout the civilizations of Greece, Egypt, and India, the organs of generation, both male and female, did not convey any impure or licentious meanings but were rather intended to reflect the creative powers of such as the Greek gods Bacchus and Pan or the Egyptian deities Isis and Osiris. Knight observes that the generative attribute of the Creator is often joined with such animals as goats, bulls, cows, and serpents; and female generative organs are often associated with nature and represented by the shell.

In addition to discoursing on Greek and Egyptian mythology, Knight also examines the religion of the Hindus and the prominence that phallicism plays in it. Furthermore, he comments on the phallic symbolism and rites in the Jewish and Christian religions, even showing the remnants of such symbolism at the end of the eighteenth century in the Kingdom of Naples.

Wright's study, *The Worship of the Generative Powers* (1866), complements the earlier work by Knight. It concentrates on the spread of priapic worship throughout Western Europe during the Middle Ages up to about the fifteenth century. Like Knight, Wright identifies and describes a variety of artifacts, including amulets, medals, statues, bronzes, pottery, and altars dedicated to Priapus. Located in Britain, the southern part of France, and elsewhere, these objects and structures attest to widespread worship of the generative organs. In Ireland, for example, stone carvings over church doorways, intended as protection against the evil eye, show females exposing themselves in an unequivocal way.

Wright also describes such Roman festivals as the Liberalia and the Floralia, noted for their licentiousness, which evolved into medieval festivals typified by a parade led by someone bearing a huge phallus. May festivals, held in town squares, often featured the phallic May pole around which people frolicked into the night.

Wright also delves into secret societies and witchcraft that flourished during the Middle Ages. He describes the Church's reaction to these movements, referring to the inquisition and its treatment of witches. Both Knight's and Wright's studies are well illustrated with line drawings of typical priapic artifacts. (TJW)

PR,IL
773.   Shafer, Ingrid H. **Eros and the Womanliness of God: Andrew Greeley's Romances of Renewal.** Chicago: Loyola University Press, 1986. 284 p. Includes bibliography and index. ISBN 0-8294-0519-4.

In this study Shafer addresses and unpacks the following questions: Why does Father Andrew Greeley refer to God as "She" as well as "He" and write best-selling novels (with erotic scenes) that he calls "parables of grace?" What are the theological leitmotifs of Greeley's fiction? How do these themes fit into universal archetypal mythic structures in general and the Catholic imaginative universe in particular? What can the feminine and erotic dimensions of experience tell us about ourselves, our relationship to others, our attitude toward the world, and our response to death? What can they teach us about God and the Church?

The Catholic imagination, especially in its popular manifestation, has an intuitive understanding that God can be known through the objects and experiences of the world.

Nevertheless, ever since its Jewish birth into the declining Greco-Roman milieu, Christianity has been vitiated by dualism and patriarchal androcentrism. Both make it impossible to fully grasp the theological implications of the Incarnation: the sacramental potential of the erotic, celibacy based not on denigration but appreciation of sexuality, God as Mother-Father and passionate Lover, and a church fueled by unconditional caring instead of judgmental authority. The intellectual climate of the twentieth century permits us to exonerate women and sexuality after millennia of magisterial calumny.

Through citation and interpretation of passages from fifteen Greeley novels, Shafer shows how Greeley illuminates God's androgyny and passion by utilizing the mode of the literary romance and braiding such popular medieval themes as the quest for the Holy Grail or magic princess into contemporary plot-strands. Greeley's stories suggest that the human journey toward God is simultaneously a quest for psychic integration, and that once Eros has been recovered, the chrysalis of the human tragedy breaks open to reveal the over-arching divine comedy of grace. (Author)

PR,IL,PO
774. Spong, John Shelby. **Living in Sin? A Bishop Rethinks Human Sexuality.** San Francisco: Harper & Row, 1988. 256 p. Includes bibliography and index. ISBN 0-06-067505-5.

Living in Sin? grew out of the controversy occasioned by the publication in late 1986 of the *Report of the Task Force in Changing Patterns of Sexuality and Family Life* that was distributed to lay and clergy delegates to the 113th Annual Convention of the Episcopal Diocese of Newark. Originally initiated by John Shelby Spong, Bishop of Newark, New Jersey, as a member of the Standing Commission on Human Affairs and Health of the Episcopal Church, the report touched on several sensitive issues of human sexuality, including cohabitation by the unmarried; single persons and sex; and homosexual couples.

Bishop Spong not only addresses these issues but also goes beyond them to examine some fundamental problems faced by mainline Christian churches, such as grasping the significance for the Church of the radical economic, political, scientific, and cultural changes that have occurred in recent decades. There is cause, particularly in the area of human sexuality, for a reexamination of the Church's stance on specific issues.

According to Spong the opposition to changes in our way of thinking about human sexuality is prejudice, which precludes rational discussion of sexual matters. Unfortunately, the Bible is used by some to support their belief that no changes are needed in the realm of present attitudes toward sex. These literalists fail to recognize that the Bible is full of "contradictions, of expressions of prejudice, and of attitudes that have long been abandoned" (p. 25).

In addition to a careful examination of the Bible historically in order to show its shortcomings as a source for argument, Spong also looks at aspects of the sexual revolution that have swept over the West in recent years: the feminist movement, patriarchy, the environmental movement (resisting the rape of Mother Earth), women in the workforce and the professions, challenges to the institution of marriage, and scientific and technical breakthroughs. While all these point to a diminution of the old patriarchal controls, they also raise new concerns about morality and sexual ethics.

Spong discusses sexual issues in human sexuality, including divorce, homosexuality, the biblical attitudes toward women and homosexuality, and celibacy. His program for renewal of faith and confidence in the Christian Church includes the old idea of betrothal, a ritual for separating people, blessing gay and lesbian commitments, the approval of sex for singles, and the ordination of women in the Church.

Rather than a call to immorality, as many in the Church will claim, Spong believes that his book is "a call to a new and rigorous morality inside a set of parameters different from those of the past." He goes on to say that "sexuality is designed by the Creator not just for procreation but also for the enhancement of human life" (p. 226). (TJW)

PR,IL
775. Valente, Michael F. **Sex: The Radical View of a Catholic Theologian.** New York: Bruce, 1970. 158 p.

Catholic theologian Valente argues in this book that the Roman Catholic Church needs to revise its doctrine of sexual ethics, especially those aspects concerning birth control, marriage, and sexual behavior. The pressure to change the traditional positions of the Church in the area of sexuality has come from revisionist theologians who recognize the need for change in a modern technological world whose population growth is out of control. Valente describes the Church's position of relying on natural law doctrine as a basis for its unchanging views.

Viewing natural law "as being the eternal law of God for man," analogous to the physical laws of nature, the Church has decreed that man must conform to it. The trouble, as Valente sees it, is that man has freedom of choice, which allows him to pursue his own options. The revisionists' opposition to traditional natural law derives from an understanding different from the official understanding of sexuality, man's sexual needs, and developments in psychology.

Viewing sexuality in human life from a strictly theological point of view, Valente's argument rejects the natural law sexual morality while it pursues a new fundamental view of sexuality that is a "more truthful description of what human life—which is sexed life—requires for the ethical use of one's sexual potential" (p. 26). A new morality should be based on "reasonable conclusions grounded in human logic and vastly improved science" (p. 31).

Valente delves into the historical background of the traditional morality, examining the thinking of St. Paul and St. Augustine. He also analyzes the reasoning of St. Thomas Aquinas on the development of the doctrine of natural law in the area of sexual morality, which stipulated that all sexual acts, including coitus, must be natural. Valente believes that because man is able to alter "the natural" in the universe, that the notion of what is natural is not static, fixed, determined, or final, "but as far as man is concerned— is nonexistent" (p. 57). He also draws attention to some of the early revisionists, especially Martin Le Maistre (1432-1481) who pitted reason against tradition, rejected the Augustinian belief that sexual pleasure is evil, and spoke about the several uses of intercourse, such as to clear one's mind, to maintain one's health, and to enjoy sexual pleasure.

The revisionists in recent decades have rejected the notion that procreation is an *absolute* good, have pointed to the Church's ambivalence about birth control, i.e., its approval of the rhythm method of birth control, with its implied rejection of "natural law," recognized the need for a greater role of sexuality in human life, and promoted the idea of love as the most fundamental element in personal relations.

Today, Valente states, one has a choice: to follow the Church's unrealistic orthodox interpretation of sexual ethics or "to opt for the revisionist tack on contraception and with it arrive at the destruction of the natural law doctrine and the recognition of the need to rethink the *whole* of sexual ethics" (p. 115). (TJW)

Economy. Labor Force, Workplace. Sexual Harassment

(For related material see also entry 1056)

IL,PO
776. Brock, David. **The Real Anita Hill: The Untold Story.** New York: The Free Press, 1993. 438 p. Includes bibliographic notes and index. ISBN 0-02-904655-6.

On assignment from *American Spectator* magazine, investigative reporter Brock in *The Real Anita Hill* presents an in-depth analysis of the Thomas-Hill confrontation before the Senate Judiciary Committee in October 1991. Anita Hill, a law professor at the University of Oklahoma School of Law, alleged that Clarence Thomas, a sitting federal judge and a Supreme Court nominee awaiting confirmation, had sexually harassed her ten years earlier when she worked for him at the U.S. Department of Education and the Equal Employment Opportunity Commission (EEOC0, which polices sexual discrimination in the workplace. Judge Thomas categorically denied the charges, baffled as to why Anita Hill, whom he had consistently helped over the years, would bring such career-threatening charges.

For several days the televised hearings were heard throughout the nation, the Republican committee members staunchly supporting Thomas and the Democratic committee members siding with Hill. In the end, the Senate confirmed Judge Thomas's nomination by a vote of 52 to 48.

Brock's investigation, limited to verifying the allegations of sexual harassment against Thomas, "shows that while there may indeed be no way of knowing exactly what transpired between Thomas and Hill, a great many things *can* be known about Anita Hill that were not previously disclosed which sharply contradict her public image and raise serious doubts about her credibility." Brock examines the official record of the Senate hearings and brings forth evidence never disclosed to the public. In chapter 6, for example, he shows damaging discrepancies in the testimony of Hill's chief corroborating witness Susan Hoerchner, who unwittingly disclosed that the time (spring 1981) of Hill's complaint to her about Thomas's harassment, Hill had not yet gone to work for Thomas. Brock labels this chapter "Judge Hoerchner's Amnesia."

After carefully reviewing the evidence in the case, Brock concludes that "in the absence of a confession from either Thomas or Hill . . . the weight of the evidence is such that no reasonable person could believe that sexual harassment occurred in this case" (p. 381).

The result of the Thomas-Hill hearings: Clarence Thomas is on the U.S. Supreme Court; Anita Hill, despite her unsubstantiated charges, is the center of attention and catalyst for discussing sexual harassment; and the sexual harassment issue is on the national agenda as "a symbol of the feminist and civil rights movements." (TJW)

IL
777.   Department of Defense. Office of the Inspector General. **The Tailhook Report: The Official Inquiry into the Events of Tailhook '91.** New York: St. Martin's Press, 1993. 250 p. First edition June 1993. ISBN 0-312-10392-8.

This is the official report of the Office of the Inspector General of the U.S. Defense Department on the activities that took place at the 35th Annual Tailhook Symposium in Las Vegas, Nevada, between September 8-12, 1991. Called Tailhook '91, the meeting involved officers of the U.S. Navy and Marine Corps and members of a private, nonprofit social/professional organization of naval aviators, contractors, and others, called the Tailhook Association. Over 4,000 active and retired officers and civilians attended the weekend meeting, that consisted, on the one hand, of serious exchanges of information through speeches, discussions, debriefings, and exhibits, and on the other, of social activities that occurred in various suites, corridors, and pool patio areas of the Las Vegas Hilton.

The nation was shocked when certain events caught the attention of the press and the Congress. Lt. Paula Coughlin, an admiral's aide, lodged an official complaint of assault, stating that she was pinched and grabbed by the buttocks, had her breasts fondled under her clothes, and had her crotch grabbed. Altogether the Inspector General identified ninety victims of indecent assault, a significant number of incidents of indecent exposure, and other types of sexual misconduct. Appendix F provides individual victim/assault summaries for the ninety victims, who include besides the female naval officers, seven male officers, students from the nearby University of Nevada, spouses of officers, hotel employees, and others.

Chapter 6, "Indecent Assaults," describes the so-called "gauntlet," that occurred in a crowded hallway where drunken naval officers assaulted unsuspecting female officers who attempted to pass through. These women were apparently "fondled, grabbed, groped, pinched, or otherwise consensually assaulted" (p. 37). Examples of indecent exposure occurred, including streaking, "mooning," and "ballwalking" (an activity where officers exposed their testicles while parading around in mixed company). Other improper behavior included leg shaving, "butt biting," "zapping" (placing squadron logos on women's buttocks, breasts, and crotches), and public and paid sex.

In the last chapter, the Inspector General states that there was a "breakdown of leadership at Tailhook '91," that the harassing activities "deviated from the standards of behavior that the Nation expects of its military," that the officers involved "must bear a major portion of the blame," and that "leaders in naval aviation, ranging from the squadron commanders to flag officers who tolerated a culture that engendered the misconduct also bear a portion of the blame" (p. 95). Confident that the "Navy will address the causes and conduct that combined to produce the disgrace of Tailhook '91," the Inspector General offers no recommendations. (TJW)

PR,IL
778. Dziech, Billie Wright, and Linda Weiner. **The Lecherous Professor: Sexual Harassment on Campus.** 2nd edition. Urbana, Ill.: University of Illinois Press, 1990. 251 p. Includes bibliography and index. ISBN 0-252-06118-7.

The impetus for this book came from Dziech and Weiner's experiences and observations in academia, and their belief that "silence is part of the problem (of sexual harassment), that ignoring the issue only makes it worse" (p. 1). Throughout the book, Dziech and Weiner present vignettes of professor/student interactions that illustrate their discussion of the issues involved in sexual harassment on campus. Their thesis is that misuse of power by faculty is the central issue. They identify and proceed to discredit a variety of myths about the role of college women in sexual harassment issues. The vulnerability of women students to harassers is described. Checklists of behaviors and common roles assumed by harassers are presented in a chapter devoted to detailing developmental variables in the male experience that contribute to the lifestyle of "the lecherous professor." Attention is given to institutional politics and roles of administrators, non-harasser male and women faculty in relation to sexual harassment of students. Dziech and Weiner conclude by making detailed suggestions for solving what they show to be a sensitive and serious campus problem. Solutions include efforts by students, parents, chief administrators, deans, department heads, and faculty. Appended are Title VII Guidelines on Sexual Harassment, a student's guide to legal remedies for sexual harassment, the American Council on Education's statement on sexual harassment, presidential and university policies on sexual harassment, an institutional committee statement and college policy on sexual harassment and a university sexual harassment survey.

This edition, published six years after the original, documents progress and changes that have occurred in relation to sexual harassment in academe. In separate authors' notes Dziech and Weiner reflect personal reactions to change in institutional climate and evolution of their thinking about the problem of sexual harassment. Both are powerful statements of belief that strengthen this frank and intense document. The book presents helpful insights into the complex issues of sexual harassment and the newer concept of peer harassment. It offers challenges to all who are connected with the academic world. (LF)

PR
779. Edelwich, Jerry, and Archie Brodsky. **Sexual Dilemmas for the Helping Professional.** Revised and expanded edition. New York: Brunner/Mazel, 1991. 272 p. Includes bibliography and index. ISBN 0-87630-628-8.

Transference and countertransference, positive and negative, between therapist and client are subjects commonly taught to aspiring professionals and discussed in the professional literature. Recently the sexual dynamics of the relationship has become a more specific area of concern and discussion. This book brings to the forefront the "sexual dilemmas" faced by those in the helping professions (psychiatry, psychology, medicine, social work, education), including not only practicing professionals and trainees, but also those who serve as administrators or supervisors or coworkers of helping professionals.

Following the introductory chapter, and using brief cases and examples gathered from interviews, the early chapters explore five major dimensions of sexuality that affect the client and the professional. These dimensions are: seduction, therapeutic and antitherapeutic; power and opportunity for both client and clinician; self-interest of the clinician with ethical implications of sexual acting out with clients, incidence and relations with former clients; and morality, exploring ethics, limits of involvement and the role of supervisors. The emphasis in the remaining chapters relates to the practice of "referring out" clients, which is not always the best solution, or specializing to avoid difficult clients.

Edelwich and Brodsky then examine other sexual dilemmas in relationships: liaisons between staff members and sexual harassment. They look at the increased liabilities of the work, including malpractice, criminal prosecution, professional sanctions and, if a professional is affiliated with an institution, organizational liability. The concluding chapter suggests specific guidelines presented in a question and answer format with references to the preceding chapters. The information and guidelines offered would be appropriate for clinicians, social workers, correctional officers, educators, and those training for such roles. They suggest more training and education programs for all helping professionals to prepare for what may be considered the inevitable dilemma. Serving the best interests of the client, making the responsible choice, using a network of peers and colleagues, and intervention by administrators or supervisors are common themes, providing "practical and ethical benchmarks for coping with the daily challenges of working with people" (p. xxiv).

Edelwich is Assistant Professor of Drug and Alcohol Rehabilitation Counseling at Manchester Community College in Connecticut and involved with training and workshops; Brodsky is a writer and senior research associate at the Program in Psychiatry and Law, Massachusetts Mental Health Center, Harvard Medical School. Their emphasis in this book is on fostering training and networking with a "viewpoint . . . not from psychoanalytic theory, with its emphasis on past determinants of present behavior, but from Reality Therapy and Rational-Emotive Therapy" (p. xxiv). (MM)

PR,IL

780. Gutek, Barbara A. **Sex and the Workplace: The Impact of Sexual Behavior and Harassment on Women, Men, and Organizations.** San Francisco: Jossey-Bass, 1985. 216 p. (Jossey-Bass Social and Behavioral Science Series). Includes bibliography and index. ISBN 0-87589-656-1.

The principal research reported in this volume was based on a large random sample of working women and men in Los Angeles County. Findings from several other studies are also included. Gutek looks broadly at sex in the workplace, addressing such issues as the dynamics of social interaction, problematic sex, sex segregation of jobs and pay differentials, frequency of social-sexual behavior in various work settings, the gender gap in attitudes about sexuality, and the increasing visibility of harassment and harassers.

Gutek's theoretical tools include a model of "sex role spillover" that she and her research colleagues developed to explain how gender expectations are carried over into the workplace and have an impact on work roles. She reports a striking gender gap in attitudes, with men consistently reporting they are flattered by sexual approaches by women and women consistently reporting they are insulted by sexual overtures from men. Education was found to be the variable that most strongly modified women's attitudes about sex in the workplace, but was found not to modify men's attitudes at all. Both employees and employers were found to recognize symptoms of sex role spillover. However, both groups tended to attribute problematic sex to individual behavior rather than to spillover.

Sexually integrated work settings were found to be relatively rare, but where they exist, women were found to gain more benefits from the integration than men, and less social-sexual activity was reported. Considerable variation was found in the extent to which workplaces are sexualized. Work tends to be trivialized in settings where physical attractiveness is emphasized.

Gutek provides a helpful summary of the common themes that run through her research and outlines comprehensive recommendations to managers for eliminating sexual harassment in the workplace. (LF)

PO
781. Horn, Patrice D., and Jack C. Horn. **Sex in the Office.** Reading, Mass.: Addison-Wesley, 1982. 168 p. Includes index. ISBN 0-201-10264-1.

According to the authors, a former senior editor of *Psychology Today* and *Self* and a current senior editor of *Psychology Today*, sex in the office is not new, but the revolutions of the 1970s and 1980s (the women's movement, sexual liberation, the restructured American family) have changed the attitudes and atmosphere surrounding it. This book aims to examine impartially the many aspects of office sex in the 1980s and deal with the question of "whether the office will become the new battleground of the sexes or the spawning ground for better-than-ever sexual relationships" (p. 19). Beginning with the social and cultural changes in women's roles and sexual mores over the last decade (more educated women in the work force for a longer period, sexual freedom, etc.), the Horns explore the ways in which both individuals and businesses are attempting to cope with the impact of these changes. After categorizing the range of activities included in sex in the office (flirting, one-night stand, casual date, affair, sexual harassment, commitment) and exploring why "the office is a sexy place," they discuss the motives underlying most romantic relationships, how people conduct their relationships in the office, co-workers' and corporate response to involvements, and some speculation about the hope for male/female relationships based on equality rather than exploitation. The chapter on sexual harassment is particularly useful in providing information about laws and techniques for coping with harassment. Although the Horns refer to a number of surveys and psychological studies, they do not document their sources nor do they indicate how and why they obtained the case material that they quote throughout the text. Consequently, it is difficult to know the degree to which the opinions expressed throughout the book can be generalized. The assertions seem to be a mixture of the Horns' experiences, findings from studies they have read, and a selection of quotes from people they interviewed. (SGF)

IL
782. Noble, David F. **A World Without Women: The Christian Clerical Culture of Western Science.** New York: Alfred A. Knopf, 1992. 327 p. Includes bibliographic notes and index. ISBN 0-394-55650-X.

The exclusion of women from the sciences has a long, though cyclical, history in the Western world. In this survey and analysis covering the early Christian church through the nineteenth century, Noble shows that it has been closely related to the development of clerical society and higher education.

Although the homosocial scholastic culture of ancient Greece is sometimes seen as the basis for Christian misogyny, early Christian culture taught an androgynous ideal and recognized the importance of women and families in the society. However, by the thirteenth century, fear of sexuality and the rise of clerical asceticism, accompanied by the struggle by leaders of the church to establish their authority, resulted in the creation of the ascetic male clergy as a powerful social force. Celibacy became a requirement for all clergy, the sexes were separated in religious houses, and women religious were stripped of authority and relegated to dependence upon male priests. Ecclesiastical schools, restricted to male students, became the primary institutions for education, and universities developed as all-male, celibate centers for clerical education. These thirteenth- and fourteenth-century universities shaped European education well into the nineteenth century. With the rediscovery of Aristotle, scientific thought flourished in the universities. Natural philosophers and alchemists attempted to prove the existence of

God and to create life without female intervention. This pursuit, with its religious overtones, emphasized the importance of the celibate, ascetic, and homosocial life.

The religious reform movements of the sixteenth and seventeenth centuries provided opportunities for many lower- and middle-class women to speak out and attract followings as mystics and prophets; in the wake of the Reformation, however, they were persecuted as heretics and witches. The dissolution of strict social controls during this period also gave upper-class women access to private education and to scientific and philosophical circles, although formal membership in such organizations remained restricted to men.

It was in the United States, with its tradition of radical religious movements and community-based education, that formal scientific and technical education was first made available to women. This was primarily due to the practical need for trained workers in an industrial society. Women's colleges and coeducational institutions flourished in the nineteenth century, many of them founded and funded by leading industrialists. But as women gained knowledge and career skills, male control over professional standards and organizations grew, limiting access and advancement. By the end of the nineteenth century, women found themselves relegated to the margins of the professions and their participation in science and technology again declined. (SDH)

PO

783. Rutter, Peter. **Sex in the Forbidden Zone: When Men in Power—Therapists, Doctors, Clergy, Teachers, and Others—Betray Women's Trust.** New York: Fawcett Crest, 1989. 288 p. Includes bibliography. ISBN 0-449-14727-4.

Sex in the forbidden zone is "sexual behavior between a man and a woman who have a professional relationship based on trust, specifically when the man is the woman's doctor, psychotherapist, pastor, lawyer, teacher, or workplace mentor." Until he felt tempted to involve himself with one of his clients, psychiatrist Rutter had believed in the myth of the beneficent doctor and thought that the sexual exploitation of clients was rare. His brush with a relationship in the forbidden zone prompted him to investigate the psychological dynamics behind such taboo relationships by finding out their prevalence and the stories of those involved in them. He was surprised to find that they are "quite common," and 96 percent of them involve exploitation of a woman by a man. Consequently, he focused his research on this pattern of a male professional exploiting a female.

When he began his research in 1984, there was very little written on the subject. The silence surrounding the topic derived from men's fantasies and envy of others engaged in forbidden relationships as well as women's shame about them. Rutter draws his conclusions from 1,000 case reports of male professionals involved in sex in the forbidden zone, whose histories he obtained from his sixteen years of practice, from other professionals, from reports and conferences, and from open-ended interviews with the male and female participants.

Using Jungian concepts and approaches, Rutter describes his findings about why and how men and women become involved in such relationships and then suggests routes for prevention and recovery. Women often become involved to maintain an important relationship that gives her hope for healing past wounds and awakening and recognizing her true self. Men also use the relationship to aid them in healing past inner wounds, but also draw on myths and fantasies of women as deferential, sexual, and destructive. Women continue in the relationship because it offers them the chance to fulfill their deepest expression of themselves; they do not distinguish between the sexual and nonsexual aspects of the relationship. Men go through a process of testing their fantasies, redefining behavior so that it fits with their fantasies, and then continue with the relationship or end it.

The consequences of such relationships are destructive to the participants, cutting them off from the very purposes that they thought the relationship would serve—healing and self-enhancement. Ironically, Rutter says that healing for men and women comes when they relinquish such relationships. Women can acknowledge their desire, even though they do not act upon it. However, they need to guard their boundaries by recognizing, monitoring, shaping, and defending themselves. Men need to recognize the harm that can occur if they act out their fantasies and use their fantasies as a catalyst for beginning to heal past wounds in other ways. Both men and women can use their experience to teach their children how to avoid sex in the forbidden zone. Ultimately, turning away from sex in the forbidden zone becomes part of the process of healing. Rutter ends the book with a list of organizations and books that are resources for those who want more information on the topic. (SGF)

IL
784.   Wooden, Wayne S., and Jay Parker. **Men Behind Bars: Sexual Exploitation in Prison.** New York: Plenum Press, 1982. 264 p. Includes bibliographic references and index. ISBN 0-306-41074-5.
       Sexual exploitation of men in prisons is a recognized but unacknowledged and inadequately addressed problem. Based upon more than 200 interviews and questionnaire responses from a California prison, Wooden and Parker examine the prison setting, the dynamics of sexual exploitation, and the factors contributing to it. Among such factors are race or ethnic group (black, white, Chicano) and sexual orientation (heterosexual, bisexual, homosexual). They describe the sexual roles (jockers, punks, sissies) and the situation of homosexuals in prison. Nine percent of the heterosexual males were sexually assaulted in prison; 41 percent of the homosexuals were pressured into sex. Some solutions to alleviate the problem are offered, including policy changes in placement of prisoners, personnel requirements, and protection for inmates who complain about abuse. The appendixes provide the questionnaire and statistical tables. (**Men's Studies**, 1985)

Marriage. Family. Divorce

(For related material see also entries 66, 81, 439, 445, 453, 551, 1049)

PR,IL
785.   Briffault, Robert. **The Mothers: A Study of the Origins of Sentiments and Institutions.** New York: Macmillan, 1927. 3 v. (Landmarks in Anthropology). Reprint: New York: Johnson Reprint, 1969. Includes bibliography in volume 3.
       Briffault's *The Mothers* is one of the classic works in the old and continuing debate over the matriarchal or patriarchal character of earliest human societies (other key figures in this debate are Lewis Morgan, Friedrich Engels, Johann Bachofen, and, more recently, Helen Diner and Elizabeth Gould Davis). Briffault writes in his preface that his research led him to conclude that "the social characters of the human mind are, one and all, traceable to the operation of instincts that are related to the functions of the female and not to those of the male. That the mind of women should have exercised so fundamental an influence upon human development in the conditions of historical patriarchal societies, is inconceivable. I was thus led to reconsider the early development of human society, or its fundamental institutions and traditions, in the light of the matriarchal theory of social evolution."
       Among the many topics he discusses are the evolution of motherhood, the origin of love, the matriarchal phase in civilized societies, primitive division of labor between the sexes, the institution of marriage, group marriage and sexual communism, promiscuity and individual marriage, primitive jealousy and love, the social evolution of monogamous marriage, taboo, the witch and the priestess, the great mothers, modesty, purity, and romance. There is also an abridged edition of *The Mothers*, edited by Gordon Taylor (New York: Atheneum, 1977). (**Women's Studies**, 1979)

PO
786.   Brook, Bryan. **Design Your Love Life: A Guide to Marriage and Relationships in the '90s.** New York: Walker, 1989. 170 p. Includes bibliography. ISBN 0-8027-1092-1.
       As Brook puts it, "today's interpersonal landscape resembles more a minefield than a field of flowers" (p. 12). Brook, who earned a doctorate in social work and specializes

in marital crisis intervention, sexual therapy, and divorce mediation in his private practice, draws on divorce statistics and trends in contemporary relationships to support his views. The average marriage lasts 6.9 years; 45 percent of new marriages are not first marriages; few men or women wait for sexual activity before marriage; women file for divorce twice as often as men. In addition, conflict has increased within marriages, and the genders are polarized. The question that pervades the book is how couples can have intimacy with independence and commitment without confinement. Brook's answer is a "designer marriage," a nonresidential, sexclusive, committed relationship that preserves each partner's independence and responsibility for his or her own life. He comes to this conclusion after assessing the results of a survey of men's and women's concerns about the opposite gender.

Conclusions drawn from the responses of 450 men and 450 women in the Denver area, 30 percent of whom are married and 70 percent divorced, reveal areas of tension between the genders. Men's concerns center on themes of being dominated and mistrusted by their marital partners. For example, they think that women want more security; are materialistic; try to change men according to a rigid plan; don't respect men's feelings; don't give men credit for the services they perform; and expect men to be responsible for their maintenance and well-being. In contrast, the women express "restrained defensiveness" about men with their concerns. Among other things, women say that men prefer dependent women; care more about money than emotional loyalty; have a double standard; prefer women with no children; and are their own worst enemies in getting empathy from women. Just as women were trying to figure out how they fit into the workforce in the 1960s, men are now trying to discern how they fit into marriage and the family.

Brook thinks that marriages can benefit from redesign. Rather than relying on trial and error to organize a marriage, couples can introduce positive change by design that is sensitive to the four major issues in contemporary loving relationships: intimacy, independence, commitment, confinement. Using numerous examples from couples who have designed their love lives by time sharing, social architecture, and conflict resolution by well thought out legalities, Brook makes the case for rethinking individual options for personal commitment and interpersonal love. He believes that these sorts of relationships offer positive options for the future. Rather than facing personal frustration and interpersonal decline, couples and families can benefit from the personal freedom and interpersonal growth that designer relationships provide. (SGF)

PR,IL
787. DeLora, Joann S., and Jack R. DeLora, eds. **Intimate Life Styles: Marriage and Its Alternatives.** Pacific Palisades, Calif.: Goodyear Publishing Co., 1972. 421 p. Includes bibliographic references. ISBN 0-87620-447-7.

Put together by two social scientists, this collection of fifty papers on intimate lifestyles in the United States uses a social systems approach to the subject. It posits a continuum of social systems ranging from the two-person system (a couple dating for emotional satisfaction and companionship) to a large-scale industrial bureaucracy whose ends are production and profit. Between these extremes lie other systems, such as interacting cocktail lounge habitués, communes, and families. Requirements for the viability and sustainability of social systems include performing useful functions for the overall society, serving its members satisfactorily, recruiting and socializing new members, and integrating all elements of the system with each other.

Mindful of the overriding theme of marriage and its alternatives, the DeLoras describe the various ways in which many Americans are challenging the traditional systems in the realm of sexual interaction. In the 1960s and early 1970s there appeared an "extensive number of rapidly changing patterns of erotic behavior" (p. 245). The book delineates these changes and also looks to the future for alternatives to those basic institutions (systems) of marriage and the family.

Divided into seven parts, the book covers dating and male selection (seven papers); sex as a social concern (six papers); sex as a personal and interpersonal concern (seven papers); the structure and stress of the contemporary family in a changing society (nine papers); voices of protest from gay and lesbian sources (five papers); current alternatives to traditional marriage (eight papers); and future intimate lifestyles (eight papers). A theoretical statement by the editors on the concept of the social system closes out the contributions of the many authors whose papers appeared mostly in scholarly journals and popular magazines. (TJW)

IL

788.   DiCanio, Margaret. **The Encyclopedia of Marriage, Divorce and the Family.** New York: Facts on File, 1989. 607 p. Includes bibliography and index. ISBN 0-8160-1695-X.

Trained as a medical sociologist, freelance writer DiCanio introduces her encyclopedia of marriage, divorce, and the family with a brief summary of the changes that have taken place in these major institutions over the past twenty-five years. The desirability of marriage can no longer be assumed. Career women have postponed marriage and/or children. Divorces have become commonplace; stepfamilies and single-parent families have increased, bringing with them their own unique dilemmas for adequate functioning. Changes in gender roles, medical technology, and availability of housing have affected the nature of marriage and the family. Nevertheless, marriage remains a core concept around which lifestyle and family are defined. Marriage is central to arrangements for living in a home. The family is a group within which children are born and raised.

This encyclopedia includes over 500 alphabetically arranged entries that incorporate many of the facets of change affecting marriage and the family. New terms and concepts (e.g., flextime, baby boomers, genetic counseling, Bradley's childbirth) as well as shifts in the meaning of older ones (e.g., fatherhood, motherhood, couples, divorce) reflect these changes. Topics covered include medical procedures (e.g., amniocentesis, fetoscopy), practical advice (e.g., child-proofing, death education, genetic counseling, credit rating, buying a home, weddings), cross-cultural practices (e.g., types of marriage, couvade, multi-parent families, residence patterns), controversies (e.g., sex education, infant sleeping practices, teenage pregnancy), aspects of the family cycle (e.g., romantic love, death, the elderly), and problems affecting the family (e.g., drugs, eating disorders). The clearly written entries often take the form of brief essays that review current literature on the topic or give a brief history of the concept (e.g., abortion, couples, adoption, birth control). Nine appendixes (e.g., consumer guides to family counseling and mental health services or to divorce procedures; sample antenuptial agreements; resources related to such concerns as adoption, elder services, family violence, disabilities, health, housing, drug abuse) supplement some of the practical information included with the entries. (SGF)

IL,PO

789.   Greeley, Andrew. **Faithful Attraction: Discovering Intimacy, Love, and Fidelity in American Marriage.** New York: Tom Doherty Associates, 1991. 287 p. Includes bibliography. ISBN 0-312-85109-X.

This book reports on an analysis of national sample data collected by Gallup of married Americans. Eighty-seven percent of the respondents say their spouse is their best friend, 75 percent that they would marry the same person again, and 67 percent that their marriage is "very happy." A quarter report that divorce was once a serious possibility in their marriage but only 2 percent say that it is now a serious possibility. More than nine out of ten say that they have been faithful to their spouse for the duration of their married life (similar patterns have been found in data collected by the National Opinion Research Center). The strongest predicator of marital adjustment and fulfillment are agreement on basic values, agreement on sexuality, and a mix of frequent joint prayer and frequent erotic playfulness. One out of six respondents said that they were in the "falling in love" phase of the marriage cycle, a proportion that is invariant with both age and duration of marriage and correlates with ecstatic descriptions of the spouse and a very active sexual life even when one is over sixty years old. Romantic love, it would seem, need not vanish with age or duration of marriage. Sexual play was more important for men under forty but more important for women over forty. Two-thirds of American spouses say that they never totally abandon all their sexual inhibitions. (Author)

IL

790.   Haeri, Shahla. **Law of Desire: Temporary Marriage in Shi'i Iran.** Syracuse, N.Y.: Syracuse University Press, 1989. 256 p. Includes bibliography, index, and glossary. ISBN 0-8156-2465-4.

In 1978 and again in 1981-82 Haeri, a cultural anthropologist, spent time in Iran interviewing Iranian men and women about the institution of temporary marriage (*mut'a*) in Iranian society. Temporary marriage according to Shi'i law is a legal contract of exchange approved by the religious establishment, the ayatollahs, other divinely inspired religious leaders, and religious scholars. Since the Khomeini revolution of 1979, it has become commonplace.

Historically, *mut'a* marriage is a centuries old custom, sanctioned by the Qur'an, permitted by the Prophet Muhammad, but in the seventh century outlawed by the second caliph, 'Umar, whose view of it is ignored by the Shi'ites. It remains a point of chronic dispute between the two great branches of Islam, the Sunnis and the Shi'ites.

In current practice, temporary marriage occurs during pilgrimages, long-distance travel associated with trade, and at other times when men are absent from their families. Religious shrines in large cities are where the men and unmarried women, be they virgins, divorced, or widowed, generally meet and agree on the period that the marriage shall last (an hour, several days, or for longer periods) and how much money the man is willing to pay the woman. No witnesses are required, the marriage may not be registered, and the parties separate at the end of the specified period.

Temporary marriage is distinguished from permanent marriage in that the object of the former is sexual enjoyment for the man while for the latter it is financial support and procreation for the woman. Haeri's interviewees, however, point out that temporary marriage for women may also be one of gaining a degree of autonomy in their personal lives as well as a source of sexual pleasure. Islamic law does not recognize sexual pleasure for women as a marriage goal. Women are expected to be passive, silent, and obedient, and not necessarily sexual.

In the Muslim view male and female sexuality are radically different. Women are perceived as a source of energy; they are reactive to men, who are propelled by their sex drives. "If men are not present, women have presumably no need to sex (they are in possession of it, or are *it*), but in the presence of men, women are perceived to become sexually insatiable. In other words, in each other's presence a man cannot help but want to have sex, while a woman cannot help but yield. This may partly explain the obsession with veiling and covering women: to disguise, veil, disfigure, and cover this simultaneously fascinating and frightful being before whom men are presumably reduced to their bare instincts" (p. 203).

Haeri further points out the "overwhelming desire of Iranian men and women to be married. It is the most significant rite of passage in Iran, and not only does it confer status and prestige on men and women, it also establishes the only legitimate channel for association between the sexes, erotic or nonerotic" (p. 208). Furthermore, she states that "challenged by secularly educated urban Iranian women and men and by the West, the contemporary ulama have been called upon to address themselves to the implications of this custom for modern Iranian society, to respond to the charges that *mut'a* is legally equivalent to hire or lease, that it is abusive of women, and that it is in fact legalized prostitution" (p. 209).

Haeri believes that segregated Iranian society today is ambivalent about male/female relations. Despite official and religious approval of temporary marriage, there is a stigma attached to it stemming from traditional notions of sexuality in permanent marriage and from its close ties to prostitution. (TJW)

IL
791.   Lindsey, Ben B., and Wainwright Evens. **The Companionate Marriage.** New York: Boni & Liveright, 1927. 396 p.

In the preface, Lindsey, a judge for the Juvenile and Family Court of Denver, states: "Companionate Marriage is legal marriage, with legalized Birth Control, and with the right to divorce by mutual consent for childless couples, usually without payment of alimony." In 1927, when the book was published, birth control was illegal in the United States; there was no divorce by mutual consent. Indeed, divorce was difficult to obtain; usually it meant collusion and perjury by the parties concerned, including the lawyers and the court. Not to be confused with free love or trial marriage, companionate marriage (a term Lindsey attributes to sociologists) is for people who seriously wish to make a life together. In order to make a go of it, however, they wish to postpone parenthood. Hence the need for knowledge about contraceptives. If, after a reasonable period of adjustment, the married couple decides to divorce because of incompatibility, they could do so by mutual consent before a judge without the benefit of lawyers, and there would be no alimony payments. Lindsey's position derived from his many years of experience in the juvenile and family court that he pioneered in Denver. In solving the problems of married and unmarried people who came to him seeking counsel, he attempted to cope with the startling rise in the divorce rate in America. Throughout the book Lindsey and Evans recount interesting anecdotes to illustrate the variety of marital situations commonly encountered, and explain the difficulties inherent in trying to reform existing marriage laws. Other components of Lindsey's companionate marriage system include compulsory physical examination for venereal disease and other possible defects prior to marriage as well as a system of sex education as an antidote to the abysmal ignorance of newlyweds concerning prophylaxis and as a way of promoting lasting marriages through a happier sex life. Lindsey believed that if his approach to marriage were adopted, the sexual conduct of young people would improve and the worry and guilt associated with illicit sex, practicing birth control, and abortion would be precluded. This book made a significant contribution toward changes in the divorce laws of the United States. It may also have had an impact on the sexual ethics of the American people. (TJW)

IL
792.   Malinowski, Bronislaw. **Sex, Culture, and Myth.** New York: Harcourt, Brace & World, 1962. 346 p. Includes bibliography and index.

This work is basic reading in the structure and history of the family and the sexual division of labor imposed by family structure. Malinowski has written the anthropological primer of marriage, parenting, kinship, and sexual patterns. His analysis affirms that marriage and the family are society's fundamental, permanent units. "But, with all due deference to traditional morality I see forces in the modern world which will demand an independent and just treatment of unmarried love and perhaps homosexual love side by side with the standardized institutions," Malinowski writes in the persona of Anthropologist in dialogue with Man of the World. A particularly intriguing chapter entitled "Pioneers in the Study of Sex and Marriage" reviews the work of Freud, Edward Westermarck, Robert Briffault, Earnest Crawley, and Havelock Ellis. In this chapter, Malinowski finds Freud's theories of libido and infantile sexuality inadequate in the face of evidence from cross-cultural research, affirms Westermarck's analysis of the primacy of the marriage union, indicts Briffault's conclusions in *The Mothers*, and praises Havelock Ellis as a mentor and a genius of "common-sense and prophetic intuition" in his theories on social ethics and human sexuality. (**Women's Studies**, 1979)

PR
793.   Murdock, George Peter. **Social Structure.** New York: Macmillan, 1949. 387 p. Includes bibliography and index.

In this classic anthropological monograph on social organization, Murdock draws on the approaches of sociology, American historical anthropology, behavioral psychology, and psychoanalysis to focus on the relation of family and kinship organization to sex and marriage. Using social and cultural data from the Institute of Human Relations at Yale University and from library sources, he establishes a worldwide sample of 250 societies with which he statistically tests hypotheses to establish scientifically valid generalizations about social structure. His analysis stresses the importance of the postulational method of scientific inquiry as well as the use of the cross-cultural method to shed light on and put aspects of American society into perspective.

Most of the book systematically defines and discusses basic units of social organization: the nuclear family and its composite forms, i.e., extended families, polygamous and monogamous families; consanguineal kin groups and clans; the community; basics of kinship; and the determinants of kinship terminology. A synthetic chapter on the evolution of social organization demonstrates the links between kinship, terminology, social units, and families.

The last three chapters focus on the components of social structure analyzed in the text and their relationship to aspects of human sexuality. In "The Regulation of Sex" Murdock examines the forms of sexual regulation as they relate to marital status, kinship, social structure, social status, particular events and circumstances, and sex in general. Sexual permissiveness is *not* characteristic of "primitive" societies, and few societies lack any sexual restrictions. "Societies cannot remain indifferent to sex but must seek to keep it under control" (p. 260). Otherwise, the sexual drive could elicit "behavior which may imperil the cooperative relations upon which social life depends" (p. 260). His chapter "Incest Taboos and Their Extensions" reveals eight major attributes of incest taboos, including their application to all non-marital cross-sex relationships in the nuclear family; their failure to coincide with nearness of biological kin; and their high correlation with conventional kin groups. His cross-cultural analysis demonstrates that patterns of sexual behavior are not the result of historical accident or a closed system but are "everywhere molded and directed by prevailing forms of social organization" (p. 313). The final chapter, "The Social Law of Sexual Choice," points to categories of people who will be preferred sexual and marital partners. There is a negative gradient of choice related to ethnocentrism, exogamy, adultery, homosexuality, propinquity, appropriate age, and kinship. The regularities of social organization and sexual behavior that this meticulous, ambitious study reveal lead Murdock to conclude that "sexual behavior and the forms of social organization in our own society exhibit the same regularities and conform to the same scientific principles as do comparable phenomena among the simpler people of the earth" (p. 322). (SGF)

IL,PO
794. O'Neill, Nena, and George O'Neill. **Open Marriage: A New Life Style for Couples.** New York: Evans, 1972. 287 p. Includes bibliography. ISBN 0-87131-438-X.

The O'Neills, husband-and-wife anthropologists, present their best-selling articulation of an alternative and seemingly revolutionary form of marriage to help remedy the high percentage of divorces and ailing marriages. The problem, they contend, is that "the patriarchal marriage of the Judeo-Christian tradition based on an agrarian economy is simply outmoded." The new, complex lifestyles of contemporary society require a new type of marriage. They term their innovative option for today's couples "open marriage," an "honest and open relationship between two people, based on the equal freedom and identity of both partners. It involves a verbal, intellectual, and emotional commitment to the right of each to grow as an individual within the marriage."

The O'Neills recommend rewriting the old, rigid, restrictive traditional marriage contract with an "open contract" that breaks preconceived molds and allows a free and spontaneous relationship based on real mutual needs, autonomy, equality, role flexibility, and role reversals. Possessiveness and subservience to rigid role models are replaced by "independent living." Romantic love is depicted as irrational; its unrealistic expectations can choke a marriage to death. Likewise, jealousy is a negative learned response that can and should be eliminated for a healthy marriage. Illustrative scenarios relate those conceptual points to everyday situations.

Although the main emphasis in the book is on growth in the marriage via better communication, role flexibility, adjustment of expectations, individual identity, privacy, and trust, the open marriage philosophy also extends to the bedroom. The O'Neills demystify sex as something that can mean many things to many people and that can be legitimately separated from love. Open marriage also redefines sexual fidelity, which is "the false god of closed marriage." Although they do not recommend extramarital sex, they do not say that couples should avoid it either; it should be an available option when trust and maturity will allow it.

The final chapter uses the concept of synergy to show how the guidelines for an open marriage are associated with each other as part of a dynamic process. If the tenets of this book are followed, the O'Neills believe that readers will experience the synergy of an open marriage in which they combine to produce a beneficial effect that is greater than the sum of their separate, individual actions. (EBS)

PR
795. Phillips, Roderick. **Putting Asunder: A History of Divorce in Western Society.** New York: Cambridge University Press, 1988. 672 p. Includes bibliography and index. ISBN 0-521-32434-3.

This is the only general history of marriage breakdown and divorce in Western society. It covers Great Britain, Europe, and Scandinavia from the Middle Ages, North America from the seventeenth century, and Australasia from the nineteenth century. Phillips has drawn on a wide range of primary and secondary sources to chart the evolution of marriage breakdown and divorce, and to place their histories within broader social, economic, demographic, political, and cultural trends.

One feature of the book is its description and analysis of changes in divorce laws and policies, from the Middle Ages and the development of the doctrine of the indissolubility of marriage, through the changes during the Reformation, the legalization of divorce in the American colonies and during the French Revolution, to the liberalization of divorce laws in the nineteenth century and the development of no-fault divorce from the 1960s. Changes in law and policy are placed firmly in their contexts, from the English Civil War to the Russian Revolution and the rise of Nazism, divorce is treated as part of broader social, family, and sexual policies.

Putting Asunder is distinguished by going beyond legal history and linking marriage breakdown and divorce. It asks whether rising divorce rates since the nineteenth century indicate increasing marriage breakdown or, alternatively, an increasing proportion of broken marriages being dissolved. Phillips concludes that because of specific social, economic, and cultural conditions in the past, expectations of marriage were flexible and low. For this reason, marriages were more stable and less likely to end in separation or dissolution than in the past hundred years. (Author)

[N.B.: Roderick Phillips is Professor of History at Carleton University in Ottawa, Canada. His book has also been abridged as *Untying the Knot: A Short History of Divorce* (Cambridge University Press, 1991).]

IL,PO
796. Russell, Bertrand. **Marriage and Morals.** New York: Liveright, 1929. 320 p.

Russell, eminent philosopher, mathematician, and pacifist, focuses his attention on a search for the kind of sexual morality needed in the modern world. He justifies his quest by claiming that conventional sexual morality is grounded in senseless superstition and hidebound traditions that ensure the unhappiness of many men and women. He assumes that sex is natural; that it involves more than the sex act; and that it is an instinct to be trained, not thwarted by excessive self-control. "Fear, prohibition, and mutual interference with freedom" (p. 212) only serve to hinder the attainment of the good life. His approach is to trace the origin of sexual morality by examining sexual systems, past and present, in terms of questions pertaining to personal behavior, relations between men and women, marriage, extramarital relations, family, and population. Two major bases for morality lie in the desire for certainty of paternity and the ascetic belief that sex is wicked. Against this background of Christian sexual ethics, modified by the Catholic and Protestant churches, Russell examines a series of diverse but interrelated questions, including romantic love, contraception, the liberation of women, marriage, extramarital sex, prostitution, trial marriage, the family and the state, divorce, population, and eugenics. The sexual ethic that emerges from this wide-ranging examination of sexual issues in Western society is based on a couple of basic principles: (1) a "deep, serious love between man and woman which embraces the whole personality of both and leads to a fusion by which each is enriched and enhanced" (p. 212); and (2) adequate physical and psychological care of children. Russell concludes that "the essence of a good marriage is respect for each other's personality combined with that deep intimacy, physical, mental, and spiritual, which makes a serious love between man and woman the most fructifying of all human experiences" (p. 215). (TJW)

PR,IL
797. Shorter, Edward. **The Making of the Modern Family.** New York: Basic Books, 1975. 369 p. Includes bibliography and index. ISBN 0-465-04327-5.

The family as we know it is a modern social unit, shaped by historical developments in Western industrialized societies over the last 300 years. Using data from individuals familiar with the lives of ordinary people (local medical doctors, minor bureaucrats, antiquarian scholars), Shorter chronicles the transformation of the traditional family, embedded in a larger social order, into the modern family, marked by privacy and self-realization of the participants. At its core, the story is one of a shift in the relationship between the nuclear family and the surrounding community; of the development of "sentiments" that emotionally bound couples to each other, linked mothers to their infants, and stressed affective rather than instrumental chords in the family.

The composition of the traditional European household was larger and more complex in its functions than that of the modern family. In contrast to idealized notions of the extended family (which was not important in rural life until the nineteenth century), traditional rural domestic groups might include children from previous marriages, family relatives, servants, lodgers, and orphans. Such arrangements affected how people thought and acted toward each other. Numerous people could observe and disrupt options for sexual privacy and emotional intimacy. Community activities such as local secular and religious rituals as well as a strict segregation of labor and sex roles gave little scope for the development of intimacy. Marriage was usually affectionless and held together by considerations of kinship and property. "It would never have occurred to them [married couples] to ask if they were happy."

Two sexual revolutions jarred the traditional organization. First, by the end of the eighteenth century, young people gave more credence to their "inner feelings" in courtship and markedly increased their premarital sexual involvement. Community controls over individual behavior began to slip away. By 1850, truly traditional society had broken up. Between 1850 and 1940, "almost all couples were eroticized." By the twentieth century, premarital sex was more common than at any time since the Middle Ages. The second sexual revolution occurred in the 1950s and 1960s, when adolescents focused more on eroticism and sex than on sentiment. Overall, there was a close connection between changes in sexual and emotional patterns.

Likewise, the degree of attachment between mother and child began to change from parental indifference to maternal love. Infants were less likely to be abandoned or relegated to mercenary wet nurses; they were more likely to be breast-fed by their own mothers. The household became a home, a "sentimental nest for the modern family."

Romance, maternal love, and sentimental beliefs about the unity and privacy of the family served to reinforce the separation of the nuclear family from the surrounding community. As pressure from surrounding social networks became less effective, intercourse was separated from lifelong monogamy. Although occurring at different rates in different countries and social strata, the emergence of the modern family occurred in response to the development of market capitalism which demands individualism. The tenets of the changing economy—a competitive market, individual choice, private gratification, and a wish to be free—provided the cultural context for the importance of sentiment. "The free market was like an acid bath for the traditional village and small town." Freed from the constraints of community controls, intimacy between individuals—courting couples, spouses, mother and child—could develop. That special sense of solidarity—"a state of mind" and private sense of emotional solidarity—sets the modern family apart from its predecessors. (SGF)

PR,IL
798. Spurlock, John C. **Free Love: Marriage and Middle-Class Radicalism in America, 1825-1860.** New York: New York University Press, 1988. 277 p. (The American Social Experience Series; 13). Includes bibliographic essay and index. ISBN 0-8147-7883-6.
In this study, Spurlock, who teaches at Rutgers University, provides an in-depth examination of the "free love" movement in the United States. Beginning with an analysis of middle-class development in the early decades of the nineteenth century, he goes on to explain the challenges to the most cherished middle-class values of the time: marriage, sexual purity, individuality, and social equality. Inspiration for opposition to features of those values came from such European thinkers as Robert Owen and Charles Fourier, who inspired many Americans to work toward reform. One feature of reform was the communitarian approach to restructuring society. Such communities as New Harmony, for example, attempted in the 1820s to implement the notions of Owen. Amid the full social life of the community were frequent discussions about courtship, marriage, and sexual relations.
Besides Owenism, other movements committed to individuality were examining basic social institutions. Transcendentalism was one; another was Fourierism. Sharp attacks on marriage came from still other groups: the perfectionists, who used a revivalist approach to inspire their followers; and the harmonialists, who, motivated by the likes of Emanuel Swedenborg, Henry James, and Andrew Jackson Davis, looked for super-natural enlightenment through mesmerism.
Spurlock turns his attention in chapter 4 to the first free love community in the United States. Growing out of the harmonialist philosophies and Fourierist socialism, the approach of the free lovers stressed individual sovereignty, which meant a new attitude toward marriage. Led by Stephen Pearl Andrews and Josiah Warner, a new community called Modern Times was established about forty miles east of New York City. It was an economic experiment, intended "to unburden society from the inessential or harmful accretions of superstition, authority, and custom" (p. 114). It would ensure equity to all, yet guarantee the sovereignty of the individual. In 1852, through the efforts of Marx Edgeworth Lazarus, the theory and practice of free love made considerable headway at Modern Times. Other adherents to free love were Thomas and Mary Nichols; through their writings they advocated "variety in love and sexual union without external constraints" (p. 130), together with a healthy lifestyle. They did place limits upon sexual indulgence, which became a means of freeing women from the sexual demands of men.
According to Spurlock, "The ultimate expression of middle-class radicalism was free love—the repudiation of any relations between man and woman that violated the individual sovereignty of either" (p. 139). The philosophy spread through a network of communities and organizations across the northern states and "seemed to merge with antislavery, feminism and spiritualism."
Spurlock discusses the lives of those who became free lovers: Stephen P. Andrews, Marx E. Lazarus, James A. Clay, Austin Kent, and Mary Gove Nichols. In the final chapter, he traces the decline of the free love movement as a radical element within the American middle class, several of whose mainstream values it opposed. One of the last influential free lovers was Victoria C. Woodhull; however, her strong views alienated the public, which now considered free love as a sinister movement. (TJW)

PR,IL
799. Stone, Lawrence. **The Family, Sex and Marriage in England 1500-1800.** New York: Harper & Row, 1977. 800 p. Includes bibliography and index. ISBN 0-06-014142-5.

This book is a work of enormous scope, tracing the history of the family in England over three centuries from 1500 to 1800. Written by the distinguished historian Lawrence Stone, Dodge Professor of History at Princeton University, it contains a wealth of detail as well as suggested typology of changes in family structure during that period. Stone argues that the "open-lineage family"—a wide kin network placing scant importance on privacy—gave rise to a transitional form he calls the "restricted, patriarchal, nuclear family"—a narrower domestic circle under the authority of the father—to culminate in the "closed, domesticated, nuclear family"—an even narrower and more private circle, but characterized by warmer and more egalitarian family relations. This last form he identifies as possessing the basic characteristics of the modern family, which, he asserts, was well established by 1750 in the middle and upper classes of England. He attributes these changes in the family to the emergence of "affective individualism," but it should not be assumed that the "end-product of affective individualism, namely the intensely self-centered, inwardly turned, emotionally bonded, sexually liberated, child-oriented family type of the third quarter of the twentieth century is any more permanent an institution than were the many family types which preceded it" (p. 683).

Sexual conditions, attitudes, and behavior affecting the family are discussed in part V, "Sex." Disincentives to sexual activity at all levels of society included an appalling state of personal hygiene, rampant venereal disease, and a lack of privacy as well as such psychological factors as prudery and religious scruples. Certain features relating to sexual behavior of Western man were evident during these centuries: a reluctance to marry early, the hostility of Christianity to sex as pleasure or play, and the imposition of romantic love on the sexual desire. Nevertheless marriage among the upper classes flourished, sexual passion was admitted and encouraged, wives were often viewed as mistresses, extramarital liaisons were tolerated, and the introduction of sex aids into sexual activity was encouraged. The double standard also persisted. Stone concludes this part of the book by contrasting plebeian sexuality and upper class sexuality and explaining their psychological impact on the institution of marriage. (TJW)

PR,IL

800. Vaughan, Diane. **Uncoupling: Turning Points in Intimate Relationships.** New York: Vintage, 1990. 250 p. Includes bibliography and index. ISBN 0-679-73002-8.

Although professionals have focused a lot of attention on the consequences of a divorce for couples and their children, they have sidestepped concentration on the process that couples go through in leaving an intimate relationship. The goal of this book is to examine how couples make transitions out of intimate relationships. Sociologist Vaughan highlights the "social rhythm" that underlies what seems to be a chaotic and disruptive experience. She maintains that uncoupling occurs in a uniform way, whether the participants are married or not. After obtaining 103 interviews with a diversity of middle-class individuals going through some phase of the uncoupling process, she identifies twenty-six turning points and 120 categories and subcategories of the transition, around which she structured the text of this book. Each chapter deals with a major phase or issue relevant to the phases of uncoupling.

An initiator and a partner participate in the uncoupling process. Initiators first sense that something is wrong and begin to psychologically separate and form a different identity from the relationship. Partners become involved in the process later, after the initiator has confronted the partner about his/her negative feelings toward him/her and his/her desire to end the relationship. The beginning of uncoupling is a secret—the perceptions of the initiator that the relationship is a source of discomfort. Discontent continues until the initiator sees the relationship as unsalvageable. Disillusionment encourages the initiator to focus on the partner's faults and to reorder a history of the relationship in more negative terms to himself/herself and to others. By "mid-transition," the initiator feels pushed from the older context and pulled to a new one; he/she is developing a new identity, partially by cumulative dissociation from the partner, friends, and activities that link them together. Despite this dissociation, the discontent may not be clearly communicated to the partner. Signals are easy to dismiss, because they are obscured by the trust and routine of daily life. However, when the initiator is sure of his/her feelings, he/she confronts the partner with both negative feelings and a desire to end the relationship, which now seems to detract from the person that the initiator has become. The acknowledgment of a deeply troubled relationship encourages the partner to try to change the situation by focusing on the positive aspects of the relationship and changing to offset termination. The partner is at a disadvantage because the initiator has already dealt with the first stages of leaving. Separation may occur and become a public statement of the dissipation of the couple's identity. Friends, relatives, and associates may also begin to mourn the loss of the relationship. The partner tries to put order into chaos by engaging in self-help programs; going to counseling; becoming involved in a new relationship or religion. He/she begins to forge a new identity, just as the initiator did earlier. Uncoupling occurs when the participants and others define the initiator and partner as separate, independent of each other. Separation and divorce are rarely the final stages of uncoupling. The relationship changes but does not usually end; common property, children, and lifestyles still bind the participants to their relationship. Reconciliation is possible if the partners reveal the initial secret of discontent early enough.

Although information on forming relationships is full, little is known about the intimate environment that people form with one another. Furthermore, uncoupling is not ritualized the way that coupling is. Despite formal recognition of the rituals of uncoupling, Vaughan details the psychological and social concomitants of the process. (SGF)

PR,IL,PO

801. Wallerstein, Judith S., and Sandra Blakeslee. **Second Chances: Men, Women and Children a Decade After Divorce.** New York: Ticknor and Fields, 1989. 329 p. Includes bibliographic notes and index. ISBN 0-89919-648-9.

In this book, "the first ever written on the long-term consequences of divorce on the American family" (p. x), Wallerstein and Blakeslee weave findings on the experiences of spouses and children ten years after divorce with three in-depth case studies of families that highlight some of the complex problems and opportunities for parents and children in dealing with divorce.

Wallerstein and her associates began their study of 60 families (including 131 children) going through divorce in 1971, a time when little was known about how to cope psychologically with divorce. Middle-class families rather than a clinical group undergoing treatment were chosen to tap the long-term consequences for "normal" people who were doing reasonably well. What is divorce like under the best of circumstances? The authors attempt to portray the hearts and minds of respondents, each of whom was interviewed in a succession of lengthy, in-depth, face-to-face interviews. All members of the family were interviewed. By contacting the same sample five and ten years later, researchers were able to evaluate whether divorce is a "brief crisis" or one with salient long-term effects on parents and children.

The results are surprising and fly in the face of commonly held assumptions that divorce allows spouses to escape an intolerable marriage and build a new life. Although divorce is a single legal event, it is a continuing psychological process that affects all of the family members. Its overall effects relate to the long-term adjustment of the postdivorce family, not just to short-term responses to the legal event. "Divorce does not wipe the slate clean. . . . Our second chances are not created equal" (p. 4). Furthermore, "children do not perceive divorce as a second chance, and this is part of their suffering" (p. 14).

Adults and children react differently to the situation. While many adults feel that they are better off after divorce, divorce is a major turning point in their lives—one that entails a series of external and internal changes, many of which were not anticipated. Divorce usually results in a diminished capacity to parent; continued coping with unresolved marital issues; anger; depression; and economic shifts. In a sense, it is the reverse of marriage and reveals our fundamental values about the worth of human relationships. Adults enter uncharted territory where their trust is shaken about relationships; they feel anxiety about new relationships; and they wonder if anyone will want them.

Divorce is almost always more devastating for children. Children's development occurs "in the shadow of divorce" (p. 297). They may observe violence between their parents; continued anger between their parents; a severe drop in their standard of living; rejection by at least one parent; and a second divorce over a ten-year period. Almost half of the children in this study entered adulthood "worried, underachieving, self-deprecating" and sometimes angry individuals. Effects may differ by gender, and adolescence is a period of major stress. Of particular importance to children's "proper development" is a continuing link with parents who cooperate with each other. Contact with both fathers and mothers is essential. Wallerstein and Blakeslee hope that the book will "prevent, or at least substantially reduce, the casualty list by providing an accurate map of the roads' windings, the mistakes that can be avoided and the obstacles that need to be overcome" (p. xxi). (SGF)

IL
802. Watson, Mary Ann, and Flint Whitlock. **Breaking the Bonds: The Realities of Sexually Open Relationships.** Denver, Colo.: Tudor House Press, 1982. 203 p. Includes bibliography.

Psychologist Watson and her husband, illustrator Whitlock, explore the realities of sexually open relationships by presenting findings from their interviews with 100 people who have been or currently are involved in such relationships. People included in the interview process were not randomly chosen but were referred by word of mouth. They are mostly well educated, financially secure, middle-class thirty- to forty-year-olds who work in psychology-related professions. Therefore, the results of the study cannot be regarded as representative of those who would choose this lifestyle. Nevertheless, this study is an attempt to fill a "huge gap" in the literature—"to present open relationships as they are dealt with by actual, living people who have gone through the hell and/or have experienced the heights," not merely outlined in their ideal forms in a book such as *Open Marriage* by the O'Neills.

The disjunction between the ideals and realities of monogamy (almost half of all marriages end in divorce; many husbands and wives have engaged in extramarital sex; individuals may desire multiple sexual partners) opens the door for open relationships, those based on the freedom and identity of both partners. Rather than resorting to clandestine affairs, these couples negotiate the meaning of commitment for each of them.

However, the disjunction between the ideals and realities of open relationships can also create problems: jealousy, decisions about ground rules, communication strategies with spouse and secondary, the role of children, the role of the secondary. These problems are not "sugar coated" in order to advocate open relationships. Some relationships do not survive. Case histories, pertinent illustrations, and sound caveats surround descriptions of the three main groups of people interviewed; those in the process of opening their marriages, the secondaries who relate to those in open marriages, and those who were involved in open marriages but are now separated or divorced. In the preface, Will Mahoney, Executive Director of Beyond Monogamy, Inc., of Denver, Colorado, recommends several of the chapters as "required reading" for anyone considering this lifestyle; Watson and Whitlock's "treatment of pitfalls should help people look before they leap into the challenging waters of alternative lifestyles." (SGF)

PR,IL
803. Westermarck, Edward. **A Short History of Marriage.** London: Macmillan, 1926. 325 p. Includes index.

This short history is based on the fifth edition of Westermarck's monumental classic, *History of Human Marriage* (1921). It deals with the evolution of marriage as a social institution. In chapter I, Westermarck defines marriage "as a relation of one or more men to one or more women which is recognized by custom or law and involves certain rights and duties both in the case of the parties entering the union and in the case of children born of it"; it "always implies the right of sexual intercourse." In addition to being a regulated sexual relation, marriage is also an economic institution involving the support of the wife and children by the husband and their duty to work for him. Westermarck delves into the origin of marriage by examining the behavior of lower animals and primitive peoples, concluding that marriage evolved in the family through custom and habit.

In chapter II, he points out the indispensability of marriage among many primitive peoples and the contempt with which the unmarried are viewed. In contrast, in civilized Christian societies, where celibacy is highly valued, the marriage ratio is declining. In chapter III, he discusses the rules of racial endogamy and the origin of castes and classes in India and elsewhere. Chapter IV explains the rules and regulations against endogamous (i.e., incestuous) marriage. It advances a theory of exogamy based on the absence of erotic feelings between relatives who grow up together, a psychological fact recognized by the Church when it prohibited marriage between close relatives. He points out the harmful effects of inbreeding in support of his theory.

Chapters V, VI, and VII describe various circumstances of marriage: (1) marriage by capture, and traces of this early practice in modern marriage; (2) arranged marriages, the idea of consent, and the decline of parental power; and (3) marriage through property considerations, including purchase, gift, and dowry.

Chapter VIII explores the variety of marriage rites signifying betrothal, the sexual consummation of the marriage, the fruitfulness of the union, the protection and preservation of the marriage, etc., all viewed as survivals of earlier methods of concluding a marriage. In two chapters, Westermarck reviews the causes and effects of monogamy, polygyny, polyandry, and group marriage. In the final chapter, he examines the duration of marriage and the right to dissolve it. Throughout the book, Westermarck supports his arguments on the origin and nature of marriage with a great amount of cross-cultural data. Documentation for this work is found in the original study on which this short account is based. (TJW)

CULTURAL EXPRESSIONS AND ISSUES. EROTIC ARTS. COMMUNICATION

PR,IL

804. Dijkstra, Bram. **Idols of Perversity: Fantasies of Feminine Evil in Fin-de-Sièle Culture.** New York: Oxford University Press, 1986. 453 p. Includes bibliography and index. ISBN 0-19-503779-0.

According to Dijkstra, Professor of Comparative Literature at the University of California, San Diego, the intellectual assumptions of the second half of the nineteenth century produced a "cultural war on women" and artwork that seems recognizable as a "veritable iconography of misogyny." The focus of this book is "what and how, during the second half of the nineteenth century, men came to think about women—and why" (p. vii). Using an historical perspective, Dijkstra selected over 300 illustrations that are useful as historical documents and reflective of materials popular among a wide range of viewers at the turn of the century. Each chapter of the text links specific cultural themes with their artistic expression—a visual and verbal interplay that reinforces Dijkstra's contention that artistic renderings of women were symbolic projections of men's anger at and fears of women's sexual and social changes. Using scholarly and popular literature of the time to establish individual themes, he documents a shift from images of women as pure, obedient beings to evil, devouring victimizers of men.

The humble, obedient "household nun" guarded a man's soul; her pale, hollow-cheeked complexion and affinity for flowers reveal her frail, sensitive nature. As she became more virtuous from self-sacrifice, spiritual purity, and lack of sex, her physicality degenerated; female invalids, floating women, and women "safely dead" became objects of erotic fascination for men in the 1860s. By the 1870s, men began to fear the sexual and physical excitement of women; sexual passion was not part of the definition of decent women. Pictures of collapsing or exhausted women implied that solitary sensuality (masturbation) had a degenerative effect on women. Such sexuality should be absorbed by reproduction. Flowers in abundance paralleled the emphasis on women's fertility. By the 1890s, female sensuality was too apparent to be contained. Her erotic abandonment in languid poses seemed to invite rape. Images of sex forced on women pulled men into fantasies of former times when women made no demands on male sexuality. Depiction of women in circles; viewing themselves in mirrors; basking in moonlight—reinforced the idea that women have no originality or individual identity; they gain a meager identity by reflecting aspects of men. Portrayals of lesbianism deflected any threats of sexual demands on males. Children, much less threatening than strong women, became the new erotic objects. Women who did not conform to masculine ideals of femininity became viewed as hindrances to progress: heavily muscled, active, and self-indulgent, these "women" looked like savage beasts. By 1900, dancing women with beautiful bodies lured unsuspecting males to join them in their uncontrolled desires, the result of which was the men's deaths. Females are identified with animals and abundant vegetation, as if to further cement the tie between women and devolution; they are closer to animals than men. As women became more vocal about their rights, their images became more graphically evil and destructive. Sphinxes, vampires, and demons deceived, enervated, and killed men. As consumerism developed in the early 1900s, productive men felt marginal. Women's devouring nature was an apt metaphor and scapegoat for men's economic demise. A man's love of women could mean his destruction. In the end, Salome becomes a dominant metaphor for women's ultimate transformation from the household nun. By severing John the Baptist's head, she echoes nineteenth century men's fears that trusting bodily sensations and their emotions to women brings with it the danger of losing their rationality and possibly their lives. (SGF)

PR,IL

805. Hagstrum, Jean H. **Sex and Sensibility: Ideal and Erotic Love from Milton to Mozart.** Chicago: University of Chicago Press, 1980. 350 p. Includes bibliographic footnotes and index. ISBN 0-226-31289-5.

The eighteenth century, often portrayed as an era of cold reason and prudence, is characterized by Hagstrum as a time in which a dramatic increase in familial affection and personal warmth occurred. In this scholarly work which builds on the social history of Lawrence Stone, Hagstrum delineates the development of affective individualism as it is portrayed in literature, music, and the visual arts. His focus is neither on sex per se nor on sensibility per se, but on their intersection. To the *Oxford English Dictionary*'s definition of sensibility (capacity for refined emotion; delicate sensitiveness of taste, also readiness to feel compassion for suffering, and to be moved by the pathetic in literature and art) Hagstrum adds "the emotion of tender sexual love." He presents a gallery of eighteenth-century fictional characters, women and men, who represent permanent human images and skillfully weaves them into chapters that illustrate ideals like hetero-sexual friendship or sentimental love and marriage.

Heroes and heroines of Mozart's *Magic Flute*, Beethoven's *Fidelio*, Gluck's *Orfeo* and *Alceste*, and literary heroines like Pope's Eloisa and Belinda, Fielding's Amelia, and Rousseau's Julie represent for Hagstrum the union of Eros and sensibility. Watteau and Greuze are the eighteenth-century painters who Hagstrum believes most forcefully present combinations of the erotic and the delicate, the sensual and the sentimental, the voluptuous and the melancholy. More than thirty illustrations of paintings and etchings enrich the text. Hagstrum presents art forms not simply as the data of historical change but as "a part of reality—cause as well as effect."

This disciplined and sharply honed study makes a convincing case for modifying beliefs about late seventeenth-century and eighteenth-century life and demonstrates the ways in which the eighteenth century served as a bridge between the Puritan and the Romantic. (LF)

IL,PO

806. Paglia, Camille. **Sex, Art, and American Culture: Essays.** New York: Random House, 1992. 337 p. Includes bibliography and index. ISBN 0-679-74101-1.

Various newspaper and magazine pieces, book reviews, interviews, and previously unpublished materials comprise this collection of materials offering Paglia's views on issues of moment in the areas of sex, art, and culture. Paglia, Professor of Humanities at the University of the Arts in Philadelphia, explains in the introduction that her main concerns are American popular culture, date rape, education and academe, sex in America, and feminism. She hopes that an examination of these areas of thought in the style of the sixties can revitalize American culture.

The first two essays review Madonna's pop star image, which so offends the feminists, but is the "future of feminism." A laudatory *Penthouse* magazine article on Elizabeth Taylor, called by Paglia a "pre-feminist," follows. "Rock as Art," the next essay, extols rock music but warns the rock musicians that being a slave to their audiences is detrimental to their careers. Following is a short essay on male homosexual drive, described as an attempt at a "civilization-forging movement away from the mother." In "The Joy of Presbyterian Sex" Paglia gives the reader a long negative review of a report entitled *Keeping Body and Soul Together,* issued by the Special Committee on Human Sexuality of the Presbyterian Church (USA). Paglia then praises the artistry of Robert Mapplethorpe in "The Beautiful Decadence of Robert Mapplethorpe." A brief essay, "The Strange Case of Clarence Thomas and Anita Hill," follows. Another essay, "Rape and Modern Sex War," along with several interviews with the media on rape, comes next.

Six critical and largely negative reviews of books give Paglia's perspectives on such diverse topics as Cleopatra, bodybuilders, women, Marlon Brando, and cross dressing. The canceled preface of Paglia's book *Sexual Personae* comes next, followed by a memoir devoted to her most inspirational teacher, Milton Kessler. She then provides an outline of the content to a course on multiculturalism that she and Lily Yeh taught at the University of the Arts. A very long negative review of two books, entitled "Junk Bonds and Corporate Raiders: Academe in the Hour of the Wolf," allows Paglia to vent her spleen on American higher education. A long M.I.T. lecture on the crisis in American education ends the essay section, although some relevant appendixes, including a bibliography of articles about Paglia, end the book. (TJW)

IL,PO

807. Paglia, Camille. **Sexual Personae: Art and Decadence from Nefertiti to Emily Dickinson.** New York: Vintage Books, 1990. 718 p. Includes bibliographic notes and index. ISBN 0-679-73579-8.

On the basis of a comprehensive system of thought concerning nature and society, Paglia, Professor of Humanities at the University of the Arts in Philadelphia, has undertaken in *Sexual Personae* to examine decadence in art and literature from Egyptian times to the twentieth century. She states that "decadence is a *disease of the eye,* a sexual intensification of artistic voyeurism" (p. 16). Society, she says, is a bulwark erected by man against the encroachments on life by indifferent natural forces. Throughout civilization males, using their talent for defining, categorizing, and hierarchizing things, have been the principal builders of this social edifice. From these male efforts females have benefited greatly.

Paglia believes that women are closer to nature than men, that women express themselves more in conformity with the flow of nature. Consequently, their roles have not been empire building but rather ones of perpetuating the status quo by absorbing, weakening, or thwarting male endeavors. The vital link between male and female (society and nature) is sex. In early historical times there were earth-cults, symbolized by mother goddesses, worshipped for their fertility. At some point in history, the earth-cults gave way to sky-cults, principally the Judeo-Christian religion, which adopted an anti-sexual stance aimed at eradicating nature-oriented pagan rituals, a struggle that Paglia avers is still being waged by the Church.

Support for her view is to be found in a close examination of mythology, art, and literature. Here she identifies the sexual personae who emerge as finished products from the interplay of author and subject, artist and model. These personae, or masks, represent attitudes and behaviors that society accepts as typical. They are essentially sexual in nature, often portraying decadence in art and literature. Prominent sexual personae include the fertility figure, the androgyne, the femme fatale, and the beautiful boy. Specific examples are the Venus of Willendorf, a commonly found fertility figurine dispersed across Europe about 30,000 B.C.; the bust of Nefertiti whose profile introduces a sharp androgynous Apollonian image; and Botticelli's *St. Sebastian*, a Renaissance beautiful boy.

The well-ordered Apollonian approach to art begins in Egypt and continues unabated to the present. It is the approach of the Western eye, defining architecture, painting, sculpture, and beauty. Too, it is the eye of eros relentlessly appraising the female figure. Paglia opposes the Apollonian approach with the Dionysian, which rises from the recognition of the turmoil of nature and women's role within it. This role she characterizes as ecstactic, hysterical, promiscuous, and emotional.

Paglia's cosmos reveals the unending battle of the sexes. Feminism's attempt to modify this conflict by making men behave more like women is doomed to failure. Feminists need to study their mythology, art, and literature to comprehend the extent of the gulf between men and women, who stand for different worlds. She shows the way by examining decadence in art and literature of ancient Greece and Rome, the Renaissance, and Romanticism. Three influential figures informing Paglia include the Marquis de Sade, Friedrich Nietzsche, and Sigmund Freud. They understood the opposition of nature to society, and in individual ways imbued their writings with a recognition of this discontinuity.

Paglia ranges over a wide panorama, focusing on the sexual personae in art and literature from ancient Egypt to the nineteenth century, or as she puts it in the title of her book, from Nefertiti to Emily Dickinson. There is a great deal on specific topics in this book: cats, rape, urination, pornography, prostitution, cinema, capitalism, and so forth. All these individual topics are integrated into this holistic view of society and nature. It is a "sensational" view intended to provoke emotional reaction and controversy. (TJW)

PR,IL

808.   Suleiman, Susan Rubin, ed. **The Female Body in Western Culture: Contemporary Perspectives.** Cambridge, Mass.: Harvard University Press, 1986. 389 p. Includes bibliographies. ISBN 0-674-29871-3.

The essays appearing in this collection are taken from two 1985 issues of *Poetics Today.* To the question "What 'place(s)' has the female body occupied in the Western imagination, and in the symbolic productions of Western culture, over the past two thousand years?" the editor, Harvard professor Suleiman, provides answers by offering various perspectives on the question from twenty-three feminist authors.

In her introduction, Suleiman states, "The cultural significance of the female body is not only . . . that of a flesh-and-blood entity, but that of a *symbolic construct.*" Eschewing the images of the pornographic industry, she has grouped the essays under six thematic subheadings: Eros, Death, Mothers, Illness, Images, and Difference. From these six perspectives emerges an awareness of the "significant convergence of all the essays around a limited number of problems and questions," subsumed under the general opposition of male versus female. It is apparent that sexuality pervades, either explicitly or in muted fashion, the content of these essays. Suleiman's own paper "(Re)Writing the Body: The Politics and Poetics of Female Eroticism," begins the section on Eros, followed by "The Somograms of Gertrude Stein" by Catherine R. Stimpson, and Thomas G. Pavel's "In Praise of the Ear." The section on Death contains Eva Cantarella's "Dangling Virgins: Myth, Ritual, and the Place of Women in Ancient Greece," Margaret Higonnet's "Speaking Silences: Women's Suicide," and Alice Jardine's "Death Sentences: Writing Couples and Ideology." The Mothers section includes Julia Kristeva's "Stabat Mater" and Nancy Huston's "The Matrix of War: Mothers and Heroes." The Illness section contains Ellen L. Bassuk's "The Rest Cure: Repetition or Resolution of Victorian Women's Conflicts?" Mary Ann Doane's "The Clinical Eye: Medical Discourses in the 'Woman's Film'," and Noelle Caskey's "Interpreting Anorexia Nervosa." Six papers in the Images section include Margaret R. Miles's "The Virgin's One Bare

Breast: Female Nudity and Religious Meaning in Tuscan Early Renaissance Culture," Nancy J. Vickers's "This Heraldry in Lucrece' Face," Carol M. Armstrong's "Edgar Degas and the Representation of the Female Body," Janet Bergstrom's "Sexuality at a Loss: The Films of F. W. Murnau," Mary Ann Caws's "Ladies Shot and Painted: Female Embodiment in Surrealist Art," and Alicia Borinsky's "Jean Rhys: Poses of a Woman as Guest." Six essays in the final section, Difference, are Christine Brooke-Rose's "Woman as a Semiotic Object," Mieke Bal's "Sexuality, Sin, and Sorrow: The Emergence of Female Character," Monique Canto's "The Politics of Women's Bodies: Reflections on Plato," Nancy K. Miller's "Rereading as a Woman: The Body in Practice," Naomi Schor's "Female Fetishism: The Case of George Sand," and Charles Bernheimer's "Huysmans: Writing Against (Female) Nature."

The contributors have given a penetrating view of the female body as depicted in the past and present male-dominated discourses characteristic of art, literature, language, law, philosophy, psychiatry, and theology. Suleiman's vision of the future "lies somewhere in the direction of blurred gender boundaries, that is, in a critique of traditional, absolute male/female oppositions." (TJW)

PR,IL

809. Webb, Peter. **The Erotic Arts.** Revised ed. New York: Farrar Straus Giroux, 1983. 569 p. First published by Martin Secker & Warburg Limited, London, 1975. Includes bibliography and index. ISBN 0-374-14863-5.

According to Webb, Senior Lecturer in the History of Art in the Faculty of Art and Design at Middlesex Polytechnic in London, the erotic arts include expressions of sexual themes that are related specifically to the emotions and/or justified on esthetic grounds. The artistic manifestations of eroticism in painting, sculpture, drawing, photography, literature, film, and the performing arts constitute the subject matter of this comprehensive treatise, now revised from the well-received 1975 edition. Webb comments in the preface that the book is an art book with a difference because it is "essentially about attitudes—a record of the attitudes of various people at various times and various places to the uses of sexual imagery, whether in paintings, sculpture, films, plays, novels, or music" (p. xxi). Chapter 1 deals with the differences between erotic art and pornography and probes the problem of satisfactory definitions. The next five chapters examine eroticism in ancient and primitive art, Oriental art and religion, Western art, Victorian art and literature, and twentieth-century art. Chapters 7 through 10 explore the erotic novel, eroticism in films, eroticism in the performing arts, and eroticism in the theater. The book not only includes over 300 black-and-white erotic illustrations, but also has several appendixes that round out and update the main text. Appendix I concerns the *Sonnets* or *Postures* of the sixteenth-century writer Pietro Aretino, illustrated by the engravings of Marcontonio Raimondi. Appendix II is an informative discussion of the restricted collections of the British Museum and the Victoria and Albert Museum. Appendix III includes interviews with four contemporary artists (Hans Bellmer, Allen Jones, David Hockney, and Henry Moore) on the nature of eroticism in twentieth-century art. Appendix IV covers censorship in the cinema worldwide, tracing in some detail its development in the United States and Great Britain. Appendix V is a brief survey of pornography covering magazines, films, and photography. Webb points out that the experience in Denmark, where in 1967 restrictions on pornography were abolished, has alleviated fears that children would be corrupted morally and that there would be an increase in sex crimes. Since then, other countries—Sweden and West Germany notably—have followed Denmark's example. Appendix VI updates the basic text in the erotic arts from 1975 through 1983. Finally, a vital part of the book is a critical bibliography, systematically arranged and highly valued by the author. (TJW)

Literature. Folklore

(For related material see also entry 1025)

IL
810.   Allen, Virginia M. **The Femme Fatale: Erotic Icon.** Troy, N.Y.: Whitston, 1983. 209 p. + 48 photographic prints. Includes bibliographic notes and index. ISBN 0-87875-267-6.

One of the images of women in the visual arts is the femme fatale. Allen's book, based on her doctoral thesis, is about that image as it evolved in nineteenth-century literature and art to become a stereotype in the twentieth century. While the image, which grew out of men's fear of women who demand the right to control their own desires, their bodies, and their reproductive tracts, derives mostly from the nineteenth century, the label itself is of twentieth-century origin (possibly first applied by George Bernard Shaw at the turn of the century).

Essentially a femme fatale "is a woman who lures men into danger, destruction, and even death by means of overwhelmingly seductive charms" (preface). Allen also characterizes her as one who "does not conceive. Sin alone may feed at her luscious breast. She was construed as the woman who controlled her own sexuality, who seduced men and drained them of their 'vital powers,' in an exercise of eroticism that had no issue" (p. 4). She is often depicted with long flowing hair, full and parting lips, long full throat, a heavy-lidded gaze, a striking facial pallor.

Early examples in the evolution of the femme fatale in art include works by Henry Fuseli (*The Nightmare, Daughter of Herodias*), Dante Gabriel Rossetti (*Astarte Syriaca, Mrs. William Morris*), and Edvard Munch (*Madonna, The Vampire*). In literature, Goethe's plays (*Götz von Berlichingen* and *Faust*) contain the prototypically destructive woman as does John Keats's ballad *La Belle Dame sans Merci*. The notion of the "Eternal Feminine," or Mary/Eve dichotomy, was probably Goethe's invention.

In her central chapters, Allen focuses on the development of the idea of a femme fatale in the life and writing or art of Theophilé Gautier (*Mademoiselle de Maupin*), Charles Baudelaire (*Les Fleurs de Mal*), Gustave Moreau (*Jason and Medea*) in France, and Dante Gabriel Rossetti (*St. Cecilia, Lady Lilith*), Algernon Swinburne (*Poems and Ballads*), and Edward Burne-Jones (*The Beguiling of Merlin, The Tree of Forgiveness*) in England. Of these men she says: "Not only did they create femmes fatales; they created *more* of them than others around them" (preface).

The stereotypical image produced by these writers and artists spread rapidly around the world, appearing on the stage, in opera, as the vamp of cinema, and in graphic advertising. Throughout the text, Allen demonstrates in various ways the connection between the femme fatale and the growth of feminism. Although created by men who felt threatened "by the escape of some actual women from male dominance," these images can be seen to represent female freedom from male domination as well as rejection of maternity and female control of her own body and sexuality. (TJW)

IL
811.   Atkins, John. **Sex in Literature.** London: Calder and Boyars, 1970-1978. 3 v. Vol. 1, **The Erotic Impulse in Literature**, 1970, 411 p.; Vol. 2, **The Classical Experience of the Sexual Impulse**, 1973, 348 p.; Vol. 3, **The Medieval Experience**, 1978, 378 p. Includes bibliographies and index. ISBN 0-7145-0919-1 (v. 2); 0-7145-3668-7 (v. 3).

Eroticism in literature is the subject of the first volume of Atkins's comprehensive *Sex in Literature*. He limits his comments to works (folktales, letters, novels, poetry, nonfiction, translations) available in the English language and read by the nonspecialist, an important distinction inasmuch as he views "erotic literature as writing about sexual activity and the erogenous zones" (p. 12). Thus he eliminates scientific literature (with exceptions) from consideration. He also refrains from tracing the publishing history of a particular item, although he recognizes the bibliographic importance of the *Index Librorum Prohibitorum* by Henry Spencer Ashbee in any serious study of erotica. In his introduction, Atkins deals with the vexing problem of definitions, emphasizing the futility of distinguishing among erotic literature, pornography, and obscenity, and pointing out that erotic literature, rather than being a genre in its own right, fits into the total literary pattern, sometimes as a wholly erotic work (e.g., *My Secret Life*), sometimes as part of a larger work (e.g., *Lady Chatterley's Lover*).

Atkins's book is a discussion of the occurrence of different aspects of sex in erotic literature: erotic language, the prevalence and frequency of sexual activity, personal views of sex, the female body, male virility, the mechanism of lust, kissing, the orgasm, masturbation, dildoes. He supports his comments with choice quotations from literature apropos the subject. The literature discussed ranges from *The Arabian Nights* to the novels of Norman Mailer.

Pursuing his goal to cover the subject of sex in literature, Atkins, in his second volume, examines chronologically the Greek and Roman experience. Part I first reviews the markedly heterosexual Greek love poetry appearing in *The Palatine Anthology*, compiled in the tenth century; it then discusses the lives and erotic writings of the Romans Catullus, Ovid, Juvenal, Martial, Petronius, and Apuleius. Part II devotes individual chapters to practices generally associated with the Greeks (homosexuality, lesbianism, buggery, and impotence) and the Romans (phallic worship and love as madness). Throughout the book, Atkins makes pertinent associations between eroticism in the literature of antiquity and similar phenomena in contemporary writing.

In the third volume of *Sex in Literature*, Atkins concentrates in a series of chapters on the belles-lettres of the medieval period with additional chapters on the Elizabethans and the Renaissance. Following a general chapter on courtly love, the *fabliaux*, and such classics as the *Roman de la Rose* and *The Heptameron*, Atkins, with quotations and comments, analyzes such renowned erotic works as Boccaccio's *The Decameron*, *The Arabian Nights* (especially the Burton translation), and Rabelais's *The Histories of Gargantua and Pantagruel*. He also has chapters dealing with cuckoldry; metaphors for sex in military, hunting, agricultural, nautical, musical, sporting, and lock-and-key terminology; English folk songs; and the ideas of incubus and succubus.

An appendix, "Postures and Groups," identifies and discusses a series of works having to do with the number and suitability of sexual positions, including the *Ananga Ranga*, *The Perfumed Garden*, Aretino's *Ragionamenti*, *Tableaux Vivants*, Forberg's *De Figuris Veneris*, Van de Velde's *Ideal Marriage*, and the works of the Marquis de Sade, Frank Harris, Angela Pearson, and Jean Genet. As in the earlier volumes, Atkins relates the eroticism encountered in this literature to analogous situations in modern writing. (TJW)

PO

812. Barbach, Lonnie, ed. **Pleasures: Women Write Erotica.** Garden City, N.Y.: Doubleday, 1984. 246 p. ISBN 0-385-18811-0.

As stated by Barbach, a well-known sex therapist who has written extensively about women's sexuality, her motivation in putting together this book is the recognition of "a tremendous need for written material that could assist women in creating an erotic frame of mind, not only to help them become orgasmic but also to increase their level of desire" (p. viii). Accordingly, she asked dozens of women to write about their "real sexual experiences that would be arousing to women and would give them permission to feel good about their sexuality and sexual activities" (p. ix). Contributions came from "straight women, lesbian women, married, single, conservative and liberal women" (p. ix), many of whom remained anonymous or pseudonymous. A surprising number of the frankest testimonials are signed by women whose brief biographies at the end of the book disclose that they are either experienced writers (journalists, editors, poets, playwrights, novelists) or professionals (teachers, therapists, psychologists, consultants). What the prospective woman reader is exposed to is a collection of thirty-one first person accounts of specific sexual episodes that center on important aspects of sexuality in a relationship with a partner, such as first experiences of sex, brief encounters, recreational sex, power in sex, group sex, and lesbian sex. Vivid descriptions of sex acts, calculated to arouse the most blasè reader, abound in this unique, entertaining, and intimate collection of confessions bravely put forward by women wanting to help women. They not only document these experiences but also give women permission to feel good about them. (TJW)

PR,IL

812a.   Charney, Maurice. **Sexual Fiction.** Dubuque, Ia.: Kendall Hunt, 1990. 180 p. (New Accents). Originally copyrighted in 1981. Includes bibliography and index. ISBN 0-8403-6323-0.

Charney, Distinguished Professor of English at Rutgers University, proposes the category "sexual fiction" to replace what has usually been dismissed as pornographic literature. It embraces such well-known titles as *Portnoy's Complaint* and *Lolita*, as well as great quantities of inferior materials that could not win approval from the literary critics. Elevating sexual fiction to the same specialized level with science fiction and detective novels, Charney believes that the usual canons of criticism should apply as much to sexual fiction as to the other fictional genres. Pointing out that the central theme of sexual fiction is sexual activity, just as the solution of murder is the focus of detective novels, Charney advances his thesis by examining a series of recognized titles from the world's literature.

Charney introduces his subject by examining Nancy Friday's *My Secret Garden* (1973), a work on women's sexual fantasies that provides an overview of the subject matter, or preoccupation, of the sexual fiction genre. He begins his exploration of sexual fiction with the novels of the infamous Marquis de Sade, the eighteenth-century philosopher who sexualized all of reality and whose sexual fantasies are expressed in *Justine* and *The 120 Days of Sodom* through "pain, oppression, torture and victimization" (p. 33).

Charney then compares, analyzes, and interprets recognized pairs of novels: Pauline Réage's *Story of O* (1954) and Jean de Berg's *The Image* (1956), both sadomasochistic expressions of the sexual impulse; two classics of English sexual fiction, John Cleland's *Memoirs of a Woman of Pleasure* (1749), popularly known as *Fanny Hill*, and, though technically not a work of fiction, the anonymous Victorian autobiography *My Secret Life,* that reads like sexual fiction. Both books are about people who immerse themselves in endless rounds of sexual experiences. Charney next discusses D. H. Lawrence's *Lady Chatterley's Lover* (1928) and Henry Miller's *Tropic of Cancer* (1934), both highly individualized expressions of sexual freedom; Philip Roth's *Portnoy's Complaint* (1969) and Erica Jong's *Fear of Flying* (1973), whose principal characters pursue the good life in terms of sex; and those concisely written novels of sexual fantasies, Gael Greene's *Blue Skies, No Candy* (1976), Terry Southern and Mason Hoffenberg's *Candy* (1958), and Vladimir Nabokov's *Lolita* (1955), all of which explore sexual behavior and values in a consumerist society, and served as satirical vehicles "for cultural mythology, expressing it, confirming it and making fun of it at the same time" (p. 14).

Of the sexually explicit works examined, Charney admits that "[n]ot all are acclaimed masterpieces, even of sexual writing, but they all represent attitudes or positions essential for our discussion. . . . At its worst, sexual fiction is preprogrammed and prepackaged according to popular formulas; at its best, it is moving, teasing, provocative, cathartic and transcendent. We are challenged to confront our secret selves in all of our splendor and degradation" (p. 163). (TJW)

IL

813.   Coffin, Tristram Potter. **The Proper Book of Sexual Folklore.** New York: Seabury Press, 1978. 145 p. ISBN 0-8164-9337-5.

Coffin, a professor of English and Folklore at the University of Pennsylvania, explores in this short volume the sexual content of a wide range of folklore. He examines cross-culturally and historically various myths, ballads, sexual obscenities, poems, limericks, songs, rituals, jokes, sayings, proverbs, riddles, and the like. He acknowledges that, in the interest of propriety, most folklore has changed from its original version to something more acceptable. Although folklore is much concerned with love, many of the themes deal bluntly with role reversals, homosexuality, lesbianism, bestiality, necrophilism, and incest. These are themes that run counter to society's major commitment to monogamous relationships. They become the subject of songs, poems, jokes, and the like. In original form they are often crude and shocking, but as they evolve their content gradually changes, and finally they become "something a decently brought up young chap might give to his mother to read although he might well refuse to read it to her aloud" (p. ix).

As Coffin states: "Man likes order. Once mating customs and sex roles have been established, variations are not welcome," adding, "Moreover, sex with its ability to generate, defy death, and control so many aspects of human behavior is particularly explosive" (p. 4).

How the folklorist treats his specialty is important. Coffin notes that Gershon Legman, whom he calls "Moses of all things pornographic," in his *Rationale of the Dirty Joke*, tells "the reader more than he cares to know" (p. 58). Coffin believes that taste and wit are key elements in "proper" folklore—hence the way much folklore has been modified over the years. It is here, he believes, that the work of Legman and other pornographers falls short. To them, wit and taste are irrelevant. (TJW)

PR,IL
814.   Frantz, David O. **Festum Voluptatis: A Study of Renaissance Erotica.** Columbus, Ohio: Ohio State University Press, 1989. 275 p. Includes bibliography and index. ISBN 0-8142-0463-5.

Scholars have dealt with erotica in literature in various ways. Primarily, it has been banned, bowdlerized, and ignored; on occasion, specific authors or works have been studied in isolation. In *Festum Voluptatis*, Frantz attempts to bring the Italian and English Renaissance tradition of erotica into context.

The Italian tradition forms the basis for much of English erotica. Italian erotica can be divided into two broad categories, learned and popular. The learned material, reflecting the humanist background of highly educated men, focuses on wit and rhetorical argument with extensive use of symbolism and parody. Leading writers include Giovanni Francesco, Poggio Bracciolini (author of the first known joke book), Francesco Berni, Annibale Caro, and Antonio Vignale. Popular erotica is designed to arouse the reader's desire rather than titillate the mind. Pietro Aretino, a flamboyant, prolific, and successful commercial author, is the best-known of the popular writers. Among other works, he wrote a series of descriptive sonnets to accompany Giulio Romano's drawings of sexual positions, a book that was seized and destroyed almost as soon as it was published. The work of Aretino and his followers is highly graphic and marked by the use of earthy language.

English Renaissance writers were acquainted with Italian erotica. Their feeling toward it reflected their ambivalence toward Italy itself, which they viewed as a land of culture, learning, literary freedom, lewd living, corruption, and evil. Thomas Nashe, a self-styled disciple of Aretino, adopted the Italian tradition and style of popular erotica in poetry, prose and letters; his work shows genius but was not commercially successful. Other Elizabethan writers also used erotic language and approaches, especially in jests and epigrams. The major authors of the period worked within this erotic tradition, as Frantz shows in a study of Marston, Donne, Shakespeare, and Spenser.

Distinct differences exist between Italian and English erotica, but a knowledge of and appreciation for the range of erotica and the context in which it developed and flourished will enrich our understanding of Renaissance literature and culture. (SDH)

IL

815.   Ginzburg, Ralph. **An Unhurried View of Erotica.** Introduction by Dr. Theodor Reik and preface by George Jean Nathan. New York: Polyglot Press, 1958. 128 p. Includes bibliography and index.

"This treatise is concerned with the hard core of some 2,000 titles of classical erotica in the English language. They are the works which repose today in the Rare Book Rooms and on Restricted Shelves of the world's dozen-or-so leading libraries" (p. 20). As a seasoned publisher of erotica himself (e.g., the ill-fated magazine *Eros*), Ginzburg begins his seven-part work with a discussion of the "Precursors of English Erotica," choosing and providing substantial excerpts from such ancient texts as Ovid's *The Art of Love*, which he calls "a matter-of-fact manual for the hedonistic enjoyment of a woman's body" (p. 23). The gallant and comedic notions of Ovid's work were to reappear later in English erotica, beginning with the Anglo-Saxon *Exeter Book* and Chaucer's *Canterbury Tales*. He goes on to say that genuine erotica and pornography did not appear in England until the Restoration in the latter part of the seventeenth century. Among the early works are the ballads, such as *Young Coridon and Phillis* by Sir Charles Sedley and the anonymous *The Widow That Keeps the Cock Inn*. Of greater renown are the lubric tales of Daniel Defoe (*Roxana* and *Moll Flanders*). Two themes permeated the erotica of the eighteenth and nineteenth centuries: flagellation and the defloration of virgins, "which reflected the ubiquity of these perversions in real life" (p. 54). Translations of foreign erotica (*The Perfumed Garden*, Sade's *120 Journees de Sodome*, Vatsyayana's *Kama Sutra*) made their appearance in the nineteenth century, and London became the world capital for the production of erotica and pornographic works. Best-sellers included *The Merry Muses of Caledonia*, a compilation of Scots songs by Robert Burns, and John Cleland's *Fanny Hill*, still a popular favorite. According to Ginzburg, *Fanny Hill* was involved in America's first prosecution on obscene literature in 1821, and it was "the first work brought out by America's earliest publisher of domestic erotica, William Haynes, a New Yorker." Although many cheap erotic works were produced in the post-Civil War period, America did not produce a great erotic work or a great author of such material until 1876, when Mark Twain penned his scatological masterpiece *1601 . . . Conversation as It Was by the Social Fireside in the Time of the Tudors*. The twentieth century witnessed the appearance of the finest erotic novel ever written, D. H. Lawrence's *Lady Chatterley's Lover*, as well as the infamous autobiography, *My Life and Loves*, by Frank Harris. In his chapter on reference works, Ginzburg discusses the foremost bibliographers and bibliographies of erotica as well as the major collectors and collections of erotica. Finally, in defense of erotic literature, he quotes the opinions of a number of prominent booksellers, lawyers, and psychiatrists. A "Bibliography of One Hundred Titles" of erotic works concludes this thoughtful volume. (TJW)

PR,IL

816.   Goldstein, Laurence, ed. **The Female Body: Figures, Styles, Speculations.** Ann Arbor, Mich.: University of Michigan Press, 1991. 317 p. Includes bibliographic references. ISBN 0-472-06477-0.

This collection consists of fourteen poems, three works of fiction, a book review, and fourteen articles and essays, taken from the Fall 1990 and Winter 1991 issues of the *Michigan Quarterly Review*, edited by Laurence Goldstein.

Margaret Atwood, in the anthology's initial paper, writes that the female body is "a hot topic," describes her own, and urges a man to acquire one. Novelist John Updike in "Venus and Others" says that for most men "a naked woman is the most beautiful thing they will ever see" (p. 5) and suggests that both sexes be realistic about each other's bodies.

The female body permeates practically every field of human endeavor with concerns about "rights and violations of the female body" in abortion, rape, pornography, and new modes of reproduction. Consequently, the female body has become a central focus in much of "contemporary academic scholarship."

Goldstein recognizes that the female body has been "identified as an erotic object, canonized in the nudes of high art and the sex symbols of popular culture" (p. vii). Feminists are hard at work looking for alternative images of the body or as Andrea

Dworkin claims in her fictional story "In October 1973" trying to escape the fear imposed on women by the leering dominant male.

Several authors, such as Carol Gilligan, envision themselves as "subjects of desire," reversing the popular image and making themselves—supported by their female bodies—the engine of aggressive sexuality. But Susan Bordo in "'Material Girl': The Effacements of Postmodern Culture," suggests a counter-resistance to the second generation of feminists is occurring and showing how "white women and women of color have reacted negatively to the moralism (as they see it) of an older feminism that stigmatizes the traditional arts of 'feminine beauty' and enhancement" (p. viii).

Averring that the "female body is not just an anatomical object but a cultural construction" as well, many authors have focused their attention on "language of posture, gesture, movement, dress, and cosmetic alteration." This is not surprising at a time when "gender identity is a topic of energetic attention."

Judith Fryer shows the submission of the female body to the dominant male in her analysis of Thomas Eakins's two paintings, *The Agnew Clinic* and *The Gross Clinic*. And, as editor Goldstein wonders, how are women to react to "the stages of pop singer Madonna's self-creation?"

Goldstein concludes by stating that fortunately the "perspectives on the female body collected here are provisional and contemporary. They do not render earlier readings obsolete or foreclose future discoveries" (p. x). (TJW)

PR,IL
817. Kearney, Patrick J. **A History of Erotic Literature.** London: Macmillan, 1982. 192 p. Reprint edition distributed by Bookthrift, New York. Includes bibliography and index. ISBN 0-333-34126-0.

Gershon Legman's introduction to the anonymous classic *My Secret Life* (New York: Grove Press, 1966) sparked Kearney's interest in the field of erotica and stimulated him to write this history of erotic literature. Limited to works of fiction, verse, and drama that were printed clandestinely from the seventeenth to the mid-twentieth centuries, this book examines how some of the most remarkable erotic works of all time were first published, and received by the public, and have endured to the present. These underground books, produced mainly in western Europe, include such well-known titles as John Cleland's *Memoirs of a Woman of Pleasure*, the Marquis de Sade's *La Nouvelle Justine*, the anonymous *My Secret Life*, and many others. In the introduction, Kearney reviews the works of the major bibliographers of erotic literature, including Henry Spencer Ashbee, Alfred Rose, Jules Gay, Louis Perceau, and Pascal Pia. Their compilations, along with many other valuable sources, are described in detail in the bibliography. The major part of the book guides the reader step by step through the changes that occurred in erotica publishing, primarily in England, France, and Germany, from the late seventeenth century through the first half of the twentieth century. Kearney points out that publishers have now reached a point where they "are free to put out just about anything, although sensitive areas still exist" (p. 181). The book is well illustrated with facsimiles of title pages and plates from the original editions of many of the works discussed. (TJW)

PR,IL
818. Legman, Gershon. **The Horn Book: Studies in Erotic Folklore and Bibliography.** New Hyde Park, N.Y.: University Books, 1964. 565 p. Includes index.

This work on erotic bibliography gains its title from a crudely written sex manual published in 1899 entitled *The Horn Book: A Girl's Guide to the Knowledge of Good and Evil*, the bibliographic history and authorship of which are analyzed in the second paper of this collection. Representing miscellaneous writings of Legman, who served for a time as official bibliographer of the Kinsey Institute, there are three sections to this *omnium gatherum*. The first is "Studies in Erotic Bibliography," including "The Bibliography of Prohibited Books: Pisanus Fraxi," a study of the major three-volume,

English-language, annotated bibliography of erotica compiled by H. Spencer Ashbee under the pseudonym Pisanus Fraxi and published with Latin titles in 1877, 1879, and 1885; "The Horn Book . . ." (mentioned above); and a wide-ranging paper on "Great Collectors of Erotica," including Alfred Kinsey. The second is "The Rediscovery of Burns's *Merry Muses of Caledonia*," an essay that explains how Robert Burns's erotic folksongs in the *Merry Muses* were expurgated by Allan Cunningham, its editor. The third section, "Problems of Erotic Folklore," discusses such erotic types of folklore as bawdy songs, the limerick, and folksongs. Legman is also the author of *Oragenitalism*, *Love and Death: A Study in Censorship* (1949), *Rationale of the Dirty Joke*, and is also editor of *The Limerick*, a collection of 1,700 erotic limericks. (TJW)

PO
819. Lewis, Roy Harley. **The Browser's Guide to Erotica.** New York: St. Martin's Press, 1981. 199 p. Includes bibliography and index. ISBN 0-312-10672-6.
　　This entertaining book is a cursory look at erotica, the literature of love that either horrifies or titillates, depending on one's persuasion. Lewis, a recognized London bibliophile and antiquarian book dealer, draws on his experience and wisdom to trace the origin, development, and flowering of this genre of literature throughout the world from antiquity to the present. He discusses and quotes from individual works, comments on public reaction to their appearance, and examines the impact of censorship on literature at different times and places. For those who are interested in collecting this type of material, there are chapters on what and how to collect, publishers, illustrators, distinguished collectors (J. Pierpont Morgan, Henry E. Huntington, Alfred Kinsey), and remarkable collections (the Arcana collection in the British Library, the L'Enfer collection in the Bibliothèque Nationale, the Delta collection of the Library of Congress, and the largest of them all in the Vatican Library). A bibliography of scarce titles and editions is given as well as a bibliography of books about erotica. (TJW)

IL
820. Palumbo, Donald, ed. **Erotic Universe: Sexuality and Fantastic Literature.** New York: Greenwood Press, 1986. 305 p. (Contributions to the Study of Science Fiction and Fantasy, No. 18). Includes bibliographies and index. ISBN 0-313-24101-5.
　　Erotic Universe, which consists of fifteen essays reflecting theory, themes, feminist views, and fanzines (amateur fan magazines), conducts the reader through the world of sex in fantastic literature. It is a companion to another study on sex and fantasy, also edited by Palumbo, entitled *Eros in the Mind's Eye*, which focuses on sex and fantasy in art and film.
　　In part I of this collection, "Theory," Palumbo traces the relationship between sexuality and the death and resurrection theme in certain classic works, including *The Odyssey*, Joyce's *Ulysses*, and Kesey's *One Flew Over the Cuckoo's Nest*. Judith Bogert's essay "Survival" is a literary search in science fiction for ethical codes for individuals and moral codes for society in a changing world. In William M. Schuyler, Jr.'s "Sexes, Genders, and Discrimination," science fiction offers areas of sex and gender experimentation not possible in mainstream literature. In his essay, "Eve at the End of the World," Brooks Landon analyzes the unusual methods of treating sex roles in the novels of Joanna Russ (*We Who Are About To*), Angela Carter (*Heroes and Villains*), and Thomas Berger (*Regiment of Women*).
　　The first essay in part II, "Themes," is Ann Morris's "The Dialectic of Sex and Death in Fantasy," that examines sexual fantasy relative to death as depicted in many well-known works, including Eliot's "Sweeney Agonistes," Mann's *Death in Venice*, and Irving's *The World According to Garp*. Another theme examined by Judith Bogert is sexual comedy in science fiction and fantasy in "From Barsoom to Giffard." Valerie Broege investigates technological intervention into the arena of sex for pleasure in "Technology and Sexuality in Science Fiction." Leonard C. Heldreth looks at sex with aliens in science fiction in "Close Encounters of the Carnal Kind." James D. Reimer's essay "Homosexuality in Science Fiction and Fantasy" depicts homosexuality in a distant environment, allowing readers to accept the reality of homosexuality over the myths.

In part III, "Feminist Views," the lead essay by Virginia Allen and Terri Paul compares the scientific method with the techniques of science fiction, indicating that science fiction themes can be viewed as hypotheses for innovative gender arrangements. Marleen Barr in her essay analyzes utopian themes in feminist fantastic fiction, presenting perfect societies in contrast to the patriarchal societies in the real world. Judith Spector examines sexuality in the stories of Joanna Russ, Marge Piercy, and Ursula K. Le Guin, feminist writers whose utopian worlds are inhabited by sexy women who decry violence (having experienced it or are aware of it in other worlds) and who are unconcerned with power or wealth. In her essay on other worlds peopled by men and women, Lillian M. Heldreth speculates on heterosexual equality and love as found in the science fiction of feminists Janet Morris, Anne McCaffrey, and Ursula K. Le Guin. Le Guin's novel *The Left Hand of Darkness* (1969) is the subject of an essay by Patricia Frazer Lamb and Diana L. Veith. The story relates the dire consequences of a visit by a young human male to an androgynous society where the people are biologically neuter and asexual except during a few days of the month.

Lamb and Veith also analyze *Star Trek* zines to explain male-male bonding, as exemplified by Captain Kirk and his Vulcan buddy Spock. While the authors state that overt sexuality is absent in most amateur fan magazines, overt heterosexuality and homosexuality abound in some. As they comment, in the vast arena of fantasy and science fiction, anything is possible. (TJW)

PR
821.   Sissa, Giulia. **Greek Virginity.** Translated by Arthur Goldhammer. Cambridge, Mass.: Harvard University Press, 1990. 240 p. Includes bibliographic notes and index. Translation of: *Le corps virginal.* ISBN 0-674-36320-5.

Sissa's intent in this book is to explore the meaning of the female body in the ancient world through analysis of art and literature. The Pythia, the woman who served as the voice of the oracle at Delphi, is the starting point in this exploration. How is one to interpret this image of a virgin possessed by the spirit of the god, which rises from the earth beneath her to enter her body and emerge through the mouth? This implicitly sexual image is also self-contradictory within Greek tradition, for the virgin body was supposedly sealed from entrance, and the virgin herself was silent in the presence of men.

We must turn to the Greek definition of virginity to understand the image. The virgin, or *parthenos*, was not necessarily a woman without sexual experience. Any unmarried woman, or one whose husband was apart from the household for an extended time, was termed *parthenos.* Although the Greek marriage song is the *hymenaios*, the Greeks did not recognize the existence of the hymen as a membrane destroyed by intercourse; the only real physical sign of sexual experience was pregnancy. Even this was questionable; as Greek myth repeatedly shows, pregnancy did not always require physical intercourse. There was even a word for the child of a virgin: *parthenios* (or *parthenias*). However, sexual experience (or its lack) could be discovered by divine signs or visions; it was a mystery that could be revealed by ritual.

The female body was viewed in terms of alternate opening and closing. The sealed virgin body opened to receive the husband, then closed around the seed; that Pythia, a *parthenos* dedicated to the god, opened to receive the spirit of the god; in doing so she closed off her own self-awareness. The allegory of carrying water in a sieve, or filling a perforated jar, symbolized the woman who experienced penetration, or opening of the body, but failed to conceive by not completing closure of the womb. (SDH)

PR
822.   Stewart, Philip. **Engraven Desire: Eros, Image, and Text in the French Eighteenth Century.** Durham, N.C.: Duke University Press, 1992. 380 p. Includes bibliography and index. ISBN 0-8223-1177-1.

Erotic engravings embellished eighteenth century erotic literary texts. According to Stewart, Professor of French at Duke University, North Carolina, such works as

Voltaire's *La pucelle d'Orleans* (Maid of Orleans), Giovanni Boccaccio's *Il Decamerone* (The Decameron), and many others were richly illustrated by the foremost engravers of the time. Objectifying naked or partially clad women, these texts and their supporting engravings reinforced male attitudes toward females. Women were regarded as objects of beauty worth looking at, capturing, and protecting.

Stewart attempts three analyses in *Engraven Desire*: examining the ways engravings are "coded and read"; relating similar kinds of engravings to each other; and interpreting the interplay between text and illustration. He finds that several regular patterns, or motifs, abound in these illustrations. *Voyeurism*, a common theme, is in Laborde's "Le berger fidele," where one Colin, preoccupied by love, accidentally stumbles upon three young women cavorting naked in a stream and beholds "a thousand beauties worthy of heaven." The accompanying engraving corresponds closely to the text. Other patterns found in illustrative engravings include woman as *passive vessel*, usually in a vulnerable reclining position and totally or partially nude; *exploitation*, suggested by the alluring woman in distress being rescued, e.g., Roland rescuing Olympia in Ariosto's *Roland furieux*; and *decency and indecency*, where the erotic is handled in "subdued, witty, or covert ways." Thus, in Voltaire's *La princesse de Babylone*, Formosante, a princess, catches up with her beloved Amazon only to find him in bed embracing a *fille d'opera*. Sometimes engravings bordered on the indecent, as in the illustration "Jupiter and Io" from Ovid's *Metamorphoses*; here a voluptuous Io, displaying full frontal nudity, is seized by Jupiter. In all these examples, Stewart quotes the original text and then provides an English translation followed by interpretation and analysis.

The eighteenth century produced a flood of erotic and pornographic materials. Women, the assumed object of men's lust and desire, exposed in various degrees of *deshabille*, were presented in stories and illustrations in standardized attitudes, settings, and postures. In this scholarly study Stewart has examined both the literature and the engravings to reveal a vital and exciting relationship between the two forms of presentation. (TJW)

PR

823. Thurston, Carol. **The Romance Revolution: Erotic Novels for Women and the Quest for a New Sexual Identity.** Urbana, Ill.: University of Illinois Press, 1987. 259 p. Includes bibliography and index. ISBN 0-252-01247-X.

Recognizing the significance of the erotic romance as "a uniquely female form of American popular culture," Thurston, writer and market research consultant with a Ph.D. in mass communications, focuses her skills and knowledge on the analysis of women's romance novels over the period 1972-1985. For her research, she surveyed a random sample of romance readers in 1982 and 1985; did a content analysis of over 100 romance novels published between 1972 and 1985; and collected numerous publishers' guidelines and tip sheets for romance authors.

Her results show a marked evolution of these novels from depicting only passive innocent heroines and mysterious brutal men to featuring more feisty, assertive women, egalitarian relationships with sensitive men, and romantically described explicit sexual episodes. Eventually the genre split into two basic types: the "sweet romance," continuing in the traditional sex-role portrayals and values, and the erotic romance with explicit sexual activities and more balanced power alignment between heroine and hero. Thurston attributes this evolution to both a broader shift in the general culture toward new women's roles and equality of the sexes, and specific feedback from romance readers to publishers concerning preferences.

She concludes that these erotic romances constitute a type of true female erotica and are sexually stimulating to many readers. In addition, contrary to the claim that romance novels "keep women in their place" by reinforcing stereotypes, romance readers have been spurred by the newer types of romance stories to seek positive change in their own lives.

An appendix provides the publishers' tip sheets for authors of series romance novels, plus further details of Thurston's surveys of romance readers. (MC)

Art

(For related material see also entries 393, 399, 664, 969, 975, 991, 1008)

IL,PO

824.   Beurdeley, Cecile. **L'Amour Bleu**. Translated from the French by Michael Taylor. New York: Rizzoli, 1978. 304 p. Includes bibliography. ISBN 0-8478-0129-2.

In prose, poetry, and painting, this book surveys "the different attitudes towards male homosexuality, from the authors of Antiquity, through the artists of the Renaissance, to the writers and painters of the seventeenth, eighteenth and nineteenth centuries in Europe and America," and "selections from contemporary authors . . . speak openly about matters their ancestors often had to veil" (preface). Beurdeley has also written two works on eroticism in China and Japan. A student of the art and cultures of many lands, she has selected for this impressive study 290 illustrations, many of them in color, to complement a dazzling array of texts from the world's classics. Alternating with the writings of Aristophanes, Plato, Xenophon, Marlowe, Shakespeare, Voltaire, Rousseau, Goethe, Balzac, Wilde, Whitman, James, Mann, Proust, Garcia Lorca, Gide, Genet, Vidal, and Williams are major works of art: Greek statues, Beardsley's erotic drawings, Gauguin's paintings. Together these tell the intriguing history of homosexuality in art and literature. Commentaries by Beurdeley often explain the circumstances underlying a given text or illustration. "Homosexuality" was considered a superior form of love in ancient Greece and Rome but with the spread of Judaism and Christianity all sexual activity not aimed at procreation was banned. Homosexuality came to be viewed as "a vice, a perversion, an act against nature" in the laws of church and state. Nevertheless it has inspired many masterpieces in art and literature. (TJW)

IL

825.   Chicago, Judy. **The Dinner Party: A Symbol of Our Heritage**. Garden City, N.Y.: Anchor Press/Doubleday, 1979. 255 p. Includes index. ISBN 0-385-14566-7.

Over a period of five years (1973-1978), with skills in needlework and enamel painting, artist and feminist Judy Chicago conceived, organized, and directed a project to create a unique memorial to 1,038 women from mythological times to the present. She designed a dinner table in the form of an open equilateral triangle, seating thirteen famous women along each side, set on a porcelain tile floor bearing 999 hand painted names.

The Dinner Party is "a symbolic history of women's achievements and women's struggles" from earliest times. In addition to biographical sketches of each woman (from Primordial Goddess to Anna Pavlova), the book includes thirty-nine colored plates painted with individual butterfly images that have vaginas "so they'll be female butterflies and at the same time be shells, flowers, flesh, forest—all kinds of things simultaneously" (p. 22). Running across the top of each page in cursive is a continuous statement equivalent to a feminist manifesto that concludes with the following words: "Sadly, most of the 1,038 women included in *The Dinner Party* are unfamiliar, their lives and achievements unknown to most of us. To make people feel worthless, society robs them of their pride; this has happened to women. All the institutions of our culture tell us—through words, deeds, and, even worse, silence—that we are insignificant. But our heritage is our power; we can know ourselves and our capacities by seeing that other women have been strong. To reclaim our past and insist that it become a part of human history is the task that lies before us, for the future requires that women, as well as men, shape the world's destiny" (pp. 241-55).

Profusely illustrated, the book includes entries in a dairy kept by Chicago from March 6, 1973 until February 17, 1978, that describes how the project evolved with the help of some 250 women and men skilled in various aspects of the work. The finished product—table, plates, runners, settings—has been developed as a traveling show that Chicago hopes to make permanent.

She has also published *The Birth Project* (Doubleday, 1985), an analogous undertaking focusing on childbirth and containing in its needlework an iconography similar to what was created for *The Dinner Party*. (TJW)

IL,PO

826. Clark, Kenneth. **Feminine Beauty.** London: Weidenfeld & Nicolson, 1980. 100 p. Includes index. ISBN 0-297-776770.

Clark, the late art historian and critic, provides an interesting and provocative contribution to human sensuality by assembling a representative collection of "feminine beauty" from the world's art in this handsome volume. He decided "to concentrate on beauty as we know it in a Mediterranean and Western European world" and discovered "that there had always been two kinds of beauty, which I may call classic and characteristic." The former is represented by ancient Greek art and "depends on symmetry, established proportion and regular features"; the latter treats features with a great deal of freedom. In the course of time the two became mingled so that it is quite difficult today to divide art into the two types. Clark's long essay discusses each of the 175 items in this essentially black-and-white collection of prints, ranging from a slate carving of *King Mycerinus Between Hathor and the Local Deity of Diospolis Parva* (Eygpt, 2590-247 B.C.) and the brown quartzite *Head of Queen Nefertiti* (1373-57 B.C.) to photographs of Greta Garbo, Marlene Dietrich, and Marilyn Monroe. In between, the reader is introduced to the artworks of Crete, Rome, and Western Europe. While the emphasis throughout is on beauty in the face, attention is gradually paid to the breasts and buttocks, and eventually to the entire female form. Suggestions of sexuality are seen in the figures of King Mycerinus's companions, in the stone carving of the *Sky Goddess Nut* (1320-1200 B.C.), and in the *Ludovisi Throne* (fifth century B.C.), depicting a nude Aphrodite rising from the sea. The classic Greek female torso is represented by the *Venus de Milo*. Variations in facial beauty are fully exemplified by the many paintings and stone carvings of the madonna and child. Total nudity as sensual beauty does not seem to have appeared until the fifteenth century, when we have, for example, Giorgione's *Sleeping Venus*, Titian's reclining nudes, Raphael's *The Three Graces*, as well as the erotic *Venus, Cupid, Time and Folly* by Bronzino. Continuing the theme of sensuous female nudity, the seventeenth century is represented by the paintings of Rubens (*The Garden of Love, Andromeda, The Rape of the Sabines*), Rembrandt (*Danae, Bathsheba*), Velázquez (*The Toilet of Venus*); the eighteenth century by Goya (*Maja Desnuda*), Boucher (*Diana Resting After Her Bath, Louise O'Murphy*); the nineteenth century by Ingres (*La Grand Odalisque*), Chasseriau (*Esther, La Source, Le Bain Turc*), Couture (*Odalisque*). The twentieth century (at least the early part) seems to have returned to more fully clothed women and a re-emphasis on facial beauty. (TJW)

PR,IL

827. Clark, Kenneth. **The Nude: A Study in Ideal Form.** The A. W. Mellon Lectures in the Fine Arts, 1953, National Gallery of Art, Washington, D.C. Princeton, N.J.: Princeton University Press, 1956. 458 p. (Bollingen Series XXXV, 2). Includes bibliography and index. ISBN 0-691-09792-5.

After distinguishing between nakedness (being deprived of clothes) and nudity ("the body re-formed"), Clark, the late art historian, goes on to say that the nude "is an art form invented by the Greeks in the fifth century" (p. 4) that should never "fail to arouse in the spectator some vestige of erotic feeling . . . and if it does not do so, it is bad art and false morals" (p. 8). Such provocative statements abound in *The Nude*, an amplification of six lectures that Clark presented in 1953 as the A. W. Mellon Lectures in the Fine Arts at the National Gallery of Art, in Washington, D.C. Alluding to the paucity of written materials on the subject of the nude in sculpture and painting, Clark proposes to show, by examining the nude through the ages, "how the naked body has been given memorable shapes by the wish to communicate certain ideas or states of feeling" (p. 348). The 298 illustrations in black-and-white are woven into the text; an extensive notes section at the end expands textual comments about the illustrations.

An introductory chapter ("The Naked and the Nude"), elaborating the notions of ideal beauty and divine proportions, is followed by three chapters ("Apollo," "Venus I," and "Venus II") tracing the development of the ideal nude form, as depicted in the sculpture and paintings of Apollo and Venus, from antiquity to modern times. A different look is provided by the three chapters ("Energy," "Pathos," and "Ecstasy") showing the nude as the embodiment of energy in heroes and athletes; pathos, exemplarily showing the defeat of heroes; and ecstasy, depicting physical abandonment and spiritual libera- tion. Chapter VIII, "The Alternative Convention," shows the nude as the rejection of physical beauty in the classical sense and alternatively as an object of humiliation and shame. This reaction to antique art emerged following the collapse of paganism and the ascendancy of Christian ascetic values.

In his final chapter ("The Nude as an End in Itself"), Clark examines the nude "as an end in itself and as a source of independent plastic construction." He discusses nudes that do not express energy, pathos, or ecstasy; nor are they representations of antique classical forms. They are, as in the works of Picasso and Henry Moore, independent artistic expressions, yet somehow linked to the earliest works of Greek sculpture. The transformation is represented by four of the eighteen stages of Picasso's *Les Deux Femmes Nues* (p. 367). (TJW)

PR,IL

828. Cooper, Emmanuel. **The Sexual Perspective: Homosexuality and Art in the Last 100 Years in the West.** London: Routledge & Kegan Paul, 1986. 324 p. Includes bibliographic notes and index. ISBN 0-7100-9635-6.

This is the first book to address homosexuality in the visual arts comprehensively. It is an attempt to bring together the work of artists who were or are homosexual with an analysis of how homosexuality is expressed in their art. In the context of social, legal, economic, and artistic bounds, this volume documents the lives and work of Western male homosexual and lesbian artists.

Three issues of importance to these visual arts are: To what extent has the artists' own awareness of their homosexuality influenced their work? In view of the artists' culture and society, how have they achieved self-representation and questioning of their sexuality. Who among the artists presented are or are not homosexual?

This book explores these topics in relation to representational (not abstract) painting, sculpture, and photography produced in Europe and the United States in the last 100 years. Cooper's point is the importance of a lesbian-feminist and a male homosexual presence in art, rather than separate categories of "women's art" or "gay art."

The book opens with background information on homosexuality and art in Renais- sance Italy, much of which has only recently come to light after centuries of deliberate distortion and suppression. An enlightening thread of commentary runs throughout the book that represents a lesbian-feminist point of view that challenges the dominant patriarchal analyses of art.

Some of the artists and their works represented include the male figures of John Singer Sargent, the classical Arcadian scenes of Thomas Eakins, the comradeship expressed by Winslow Homer, the "contrasexuality" of Rosa Bonheur, Harriet Goodhue Hosmer with her monumental sculptures of women, and other women artists of the "Rome Circle." Also covered are David Hockney and his "confessional" paintings, Romaine Brooks, the Bloomsbury artists, Gertrude Stein's Paris Salon, Marsden Hartley, and J. C. Leyendecker, who created the ultimate in American masculine imagery. Further discussion covers Jean Cocteau, Max Jacob, and Christopher Wood and others of the Parisian avant-garde, the artists of the lesbian "New Woman" clubs of Paris and Berlin in the 1920s and 1930s, and more recently such artists as Arthur Tress, Paul Cadmus, George Platt Lynes, Duane Michals, Robert Mapplethorpe; the early gay men's magazines with erotic drawings by Quaintance, later carried on by Tom of Finland; and artists and works appearing in the contemporary journals of gay liberation and feminism, such as the *Advocate* and *Heresies*. (NW)

IL

829. Elisofon, Eliot, and Alan Watts. **The Temple of Konarak: Erotic Spirituality.** London: Thames and Hudson, 1971. 125 p. ISBN 0-500-23140-0.

With photographs by Elisofon and text by Watts, this book describes the Sun Temple of Konarak, located south of Calcutta in the modern state of Bhuraneswar, formerly Orissa. Built in the thirteenth century on the shore of the Bay of Bengal in the classical Indian style of architecture, Konarak has an erotic quality provided by a huge number of erotic sculptures carved into the terraced surfaces. The central structure, about a hundred feet tall, resembles a huge chariot pulled by life-sized horses accompanied by two elephants; it is dedicated to Surya, the Sun God. Twelve-foot-high stone wheels, six on the south side and six on the north side, simulate mechanical movement. In its interior, Konarak, like most Hindu temples, reportedly has a large lingam, or stone phallus, centrally positioned as a sacred shrine.

The erotic sandstone carvings that adorn the surface of the Temple of Konarak are extraordinarily detailed; they depict standing figures of men and women engaged in various sexual acts, including sexual intercourse, masturbation, fellatio, cunnilingus, and so forth. There are also many subordinate figures in attendance, including musicians, children, and animals.

Watts's text on erotic spirituality is an attempt to explain Hinduism. The ancient erotic temples are a source of embarrassment to the upper-class Hindu brahmins, who do not pursue the practices of Tantric yoga, a form of worship no longer the dominant doctrine in India. Watts states that his purpose is to describe "a context and perspective in which these simultaneously erotic and spiritual manifestations of ancient Indian culture may be understood . . . as expressions of a philosophy of enormous importance . . . to the modern world" (p. 59). Hinduism, as exemplified in Yoga, focuses on immediate experience as a way of perceiving reality. Yoga is a sensuous undertaking leading to ecstasy, with sexual union being a way of "attaining unclouded awareness of reality" (p. 74). The carved images at Konarak depict the Tantric emphasis on sexuality and the fusion of phallus and vulva in an act of attaining full enlightenment through the transcendence of opposites. Watts believes that this is "the principal contribution of India to human wisdom" (p. 97).

A few hours drive from the Taj Mahal at Agra is another Hindu temple, Khajuraho, built in the same architectural style and possessing the same erotic quality as Konarak, but better preserved. Photographs of the architectural splendor of Khajuraho conclude the volume.

A more recent work on Konarak and Khajuraho is Richard Lannoy's *The Eye of Love in the Temple Sculpture of India* (Grove Press, 1976). (TJW)

IL,PO

830. Ferrero, Carlo Scipione. **Eros: An Erotic Journey Through the Senses.** New York: Crescent Books, 1988. 271 p. Includes bibliography. ISBN 0-517-66997-8.

The approximately 400 illustrations in this book are a miscellany of diverse erotic works, the products primarily of the nineteenth and twentieth centuries. These minor artistic works, many selected from Ferrero's private collection, represent the kind of art that received restrictive, though pervasive, distribution in Europe and America.

Much of the erotic art appeared on calendars, matchboxes, tobacco boxes, playing cards, and bookplates. Erotic pictures also appeared as advertising, promoting beauty products, candy, and tobacco. Postcards, photographs, oleographs, comic books, silhouettes, and picture cards circulated widely as did prints of drawings, engravings, etchings, and watercolors, which were produced in great volume. Although the creators of this fugitive art are relatively unknown today, the art of a few is widely recognized, e.g., the woodcuts of Albrecht Dürer, the drawings of Aubrey Beardsley, and the engravings of A. von Bayros.

Ferrero organizes his pictures around the five senses—sight, hearing, smell, taste, and touch—and provides an autobiographical introduction to each. How these senses are utilized in erotic pictures, that focus on the genitalia and secondary sex organs of both sexes, is the subject matter of this book. The appeal of this genre of titillating art was widespread among a broad segment of the population; this aspect of erotic art, however, is not examined by Ferrero. But a strong impression of what the European and American publics have been exposed to is communicated by this sense-organized work.

The book ends with a bibliography of the mainly Italian, French, and German sources used in its compilation, as well as a list of illustrators. (TJW)

IL
831. Gerdts, William H. **The Great American Nude.** New York: Praeger, 1974. 224 p. ISBN 0-275-43510-5.

Gerdts, a professor of Art History at Brooklyn College, examines the nude in American art and the interrelationship of social attitudes and art. Although historically the nude was considered "the supreme vehicle of aesthetic expression," the American colonies rejected the nude as a suitable artistic subject because of puritanical social values and their view of it as typical of European decadence. The earliest examples of the naked figure portrayed the Native American as nude, no matter what the usual costume, contrasted to the fully clothed, and therefore civilized, settler or explorer.

By the late eighteenth century America had developed its own professional artists who looked to the classical and European traditions for training and inspiration. Since life drawing was unacceptable, they learned anatomy from etchings after the old masters, from the few nude paintings imported from Europe, and from plaster casts of classic sculpture. Something was usually lost in the process, and there were many anatomically peculiar nodes as a result. American artists began a long tradition of study in Paris and London, adopting the conventions of a formal art that used the nude as metaphor for the ideal and in portraying classic mythology. Among the foreign-trained American artists who created notable nudes were Benjamin West, Gilbert Stuart, and John Singleton Copley.

During the early nineteenth century the nude was found acceptable only when the inspiration was scriptural and moral but the public, and indeed many artists, were uneasy with these portrayals. Increasing exposure made public opinion more favorable. The male nude portrayed nobility, as seen in Greenough's sculpture of George Washington. The female nude implied spiritual qualities. Slowly eroticism was permitted, usually in coy mythological scenes. A natural evolution to popular culture led to the bathing beauty, the barroom nude, and the fire engine cutie.

At century's end Thomas Eakins's realistic portrayal of the unclothed figure in true situations created a new sensibility. Eakins insisted on life drawing for all his students, provoking a public outcry, but the life class became an accepted part of the American artist's curriculum. The nudes of the first decades of the twentieth century by Luks, Bellows, Prendergast, Glackens, and Henri show a technical ease and a freedom to portray the nude in natural situations.

Twentieth-century artists have explored the expressive qualities of the nude. There has been a frank depiction of sexuality, as in the sculpture of Gaston Lachaise. More recently artists, including Betty Dodson and Gerald Gooch, have rendered actual couplings, heterosexual and homosexual, in sensitive graphics and paintings. Others have exploited the expressionistic impact of the naked human to portray angst, decay, loneliness, and the dignity and sadness of old age. This handsome volume is replete with pictures of paintings, drawings, and sculpture. (JA)

PR,IL
832. Gill, Michael. **Image of the Body: Aspects of the Nude.** New York: Doubleday, 1989. 476 p. Includes bibliography.

"[A]rt helps reconcile us with ourselves" (p. 425), and, as Gill concludes in his afterword, "The image of art clothes our imagination and gives us a vocabulary to express the drama in our own lives" (p. 430). Consequently, Gill's description of the roles that the human image has filled since its original depiction in caves 20,000 years ago is not only a chronology of changes in portrayal of the nude but an analysis of the social and cultural contexts in which they are developed. The changing place of artistic expression as well as vignettes of the lives of artists are also components of Gill's massive characterization of changes in creative themes focused on the human body. Through the 302 pictures of art—from the cave paintings at Altamira, Neolithic sculptures, reliefs and drawings from the Old and New Kingdoms of Egypt; through sensual portrayals of men and women in ancient Greece, Rome, Japan, and India; to the agony of Christian experiences of bodily pain, the creativity of the Renaissance and the Romantics; to contemporary confrontations of life's conflicts and power—and the historical and aesthetic perspective of the text, Gill demonstrates the interplay between artistic expression and the issues of contemporary life.

The first chapter, "Ideal Beauty," characterizes the tone and approach that follows in the more specific chapters. Gill describes his concern with universal themes by asking whether there is an enduring appreciation of certain proportions built into the human psyche. Is there a classical, pervasive beauty? To what extent does the sweep of history show a consistent concern? His description of the process of developing a cover photograph for the book with Robert Mapplethorpe reflects the interplay between classical and contemporary themes. Each era interprets the body in its unique way. Each of the chapters probes a different theme, in roughly chronological order.

The Paleolithic artists saw themselves as secondary to the animals upon whom they depended. Religious feelings and the importance of fertility are portrayed in scenes of teeming animals and variations on sexual symbols. Energy, power, and beauty find expression in these images. However, the art of the Egyptians suggests a shift in the role of the sexes, that seems well-defined and categorized. The male ruler dominates the female image during this time of seeming transition. The Egyptians were notable in turning the body into a work of art. The ancient Greeks portrayed the body in a hedonistic light—to be "exercised, cherished, admired." Erotic scenes with bodies link the art of the ancient Greeks and Asians, although the Greeks seemed to be involved in more frenzied interaction than the calm of Hindu lovers. Even the rigidly formalized society of the ancient Japanese found sensual expression in pillow books that reflected activities in "separate quarters" of the cities.

Christian portrayals of the body express much of the pain that accompanied the formation of the Church. In a departure from Asian and Greek themes of sensuality, Christian themes focused on death, pain, and the natural evil in humans. Only bits of saints and martyrs were cherished parts of the body. However, following the constraints of the Dark Ages, new light and beauty in art emerged in the Renaissance. Greater appreciation and support of artists like Donatello and Michelangelo allowed for a burst of creative expression and a renewed enthusiasm for the naked form. Artists like Dürer, Michelangelo, and Leonardo de Vinci transcended the constraints of their time to express transcendent aspects of the human condition. The body became the "visible sphere of the soul." After a hiatus in creative imagination in the eighteenth century, the Romantics of the nineteenth century chose the body as a vehicle for expressing unprecedented feelings. Artistic expression included the personal feelings of the artist as well as a response to the times. Contradictions of the social order as well as individual frustrations were part of the "uncompromising realism" of the time. Rodin typified the times in his attempt to show movement in progress as well as a blending of creativity and sexuality.

The twentieth century has made its own mark on art. Old traditions slipped away as individuals sought to confront the realities impinging closely upon them—war, technology, social change. Picasso said that "a picture is a sum of destructions." Futurists, surrealists, artists like Miro, Picasso, Matisse, and Dali showed some of the fragmentation. In the second half of the twentieth century artists like Giacometti, Moore, Kahlo, Matta, Frank, and Matisse reflect themes of metamorphosis. We continue to be in a process of redefinition during which the body will continue to manifest some of our deepest feelings. (SGF)

PO

833.   Goude, Jean-Paul. **Jungle Fever.** Edited by Harold Hayes. New York: Xavier Moreau, 1981. 144 p. ISBN 0-937950-01-7.

This collection presents the work of Goude, artist, dancer, illustrator, set designer, stage director, and photographer. It expresses his development and interests from early childhood to 1981. Drawings, sketches, designs, castings, and photographs depict his strong interest in dark-skinned people, especially blacks and Puerto Ricans. His associations with certain black females—Radiah, Toukie, Grace Jones—were attempts to promote their talents as models and performers. Another talent was Kellie Everts, an evangelist, muscle builder, and stripper whose pictures Goude did for *Playboy* and *Esquire*. Most of Goude's drawings and photographs of these people are outrageous and funny (as the nude Grace Jones caged like an animal devouring raw meat, or Miss Kellie pushing barbells until her bra and G-string break). Some of them emphasize the genitals, particularly the series of so-called beaver shots, including "Trained Pussy," "The Pussy Singers," "Acrobat," and "Juggler." These and many others suggest the strong sexual flavor of this noteworthy collection of graphic art in which Goude expresses his "jungle fever" and tries to bring nature into conformity with his fantasies. (TJW)

IL

834.   Grant, Michael. **Eros in Pompeii: The Secret Rooms of the National Museum of Naples.** With photographs by Antonia Mulas and a description of the collection by Antonio de Simone and Maria Teresa Merella. New York: Bonanza Books, 1982. 171 p. Includes bibliography and index. ISBN 0-517-17747-1.

Grant, historian of all things Greek and Roman, and Mulas, photographer, have combined their talents to produce a colorful portrayal of the erotic art uncovered in the ruins of Pompeii. A short history of the Raccolta Pornografica (Pornographic Collection) of the National Museum of Naples follows the main section of the book, which is a descriptive catalog of some of the principal erotic items in the special collection. Each item, clearly captioned and described, is represented by a color photograph, some full page. Inventory numbers and locations of each work are provided. Over seventy statues, wall paintings, bronzes, and household objects out of the collection of more than 250 works are depicted in this eye-catching work. Grant's contribution is a seventy-four-page illustrated introduction to the history and life of Pompeii, with emphasis on the catastrophic event that in A.D. 79 overtook and destroyed this thriving commercial city, which was under the special patronage of the goddess Venus. (TJW)

IL

835.   Hess, Thomas B., and Linda Nochlin, eds. **Woman as Sex Object: Studies in Erotic Art, 1730-1970.** London: Allen Lane/Newsweek, 1973. 257 p. Includes bibliographic notes and index. ISBN 0-7139-0662-6.

The investigations in this study are a series of essays by historians on a variety of themes dealing with the erotic use of women in art of the European tradition. Erotic art has always presented woman as the possession of the male voyeur. Even in the case of homosexual art the viewer-possessor is male. It is typical, according to Nochlin, that "the male image is one of power, possession, and domination, the female one of submission, passivity and availability." The unattainability of the erotic ideal in Ingres's nudes, the psychosexual appeal of the theme of the lactating woman nourishing her imprisoned father, and the fascination and fetishism of the corset are all given serious consideration. The woman in ecstasy and/or terror seen in the art of Fuseli, in Bernini's *St. Theresa*, and other orgasmic art reveal the relation of pleasure and pain, eroticism and nightmare. Several of the essays analyze the relation of popular art and high art.

The erotic prints and pornographic photographs of the nineteenth century used poses and themes of the masters, notably scenes of the beauty of her toilette with admiring maids, beaux, and corset makers in attendance. Courbet and Manet borrowed their nudes from popular imagery. "The Femme Fatale and Her Sisters" shows that the sultry sexual tormentor of Munch and Klimt is also the "Gibson Girl" with her dominating posture and passionate glances from downcast eyes. This image is now common in glossy advertising art. The ultimate "woman as object" is in the pin-up who evolved into De Kooning's iconic *Woman* and the pop art images of Ramos, Lichtenstein, and Wesselmann. The interpretation of Picasso's erotic *Suite 347*, a series of engravings reveal that to him "painting, lovemaking, and 'generation' become literally one." Numerous black-and-white illustrations amplify the text. (JA)

IL,PO

836. Hobhouse, Janet. **The Bride Stripped Bare: The Artist and the Female Nude in the Twentieth Century.** New York: Weidenfeld & Nicolson, 1988. 288 p. Includes bibliography and index. ISBN 1-55584-217-8.

Hobhouse offers in this collection selected works by thirteen artists: Aristide Maillol, Pierre Bonnard, Egon Schiele, Henri Matisse, Pablo Picasso, Amedeo Modigliani, Jules Pascin, Gaston Lachaise, Stanley Spencer, Lucian Freud, Balthus, Willem de Kooning, and Philip Pearlstein. She believes that their representations of the female nude are "some of the most famous and beautiful images of this century: Matisse's odalisques, Picasso's *demoiselles*, Bonnard's bathers, Modigliani's madonnas, Balthus's Lolitas, de Kooning's harpies," as well as "venuses, courtesans, caryatids, street urchins, whores, virgins, nymphs and dancers." In stressing the relationship between the artists and their models, Hobhouse says that the painted or sculpted nude "is the metaphor of their relationship." She is "conjured out of memory and desire and fabricated by a process of subtraction and addition." Hence we get her presented in a great variety of ways depending on the artist's painting or sculpting style.

Hobhouse devotes a chapter to each of her chosen artists. She begins with the classical bronze nudes of Maillol, discussing both his style and vision of pure beauty and bringing out his relationships with his models. The illustrations include his magnificent bronze torso *Ile de France*, done in 1921, as well as other bronzes, reliefs, and drawings. She submits the twelve remaining artists to the same severe scrutiny and analysis that she lavishes on Maillol.

In the preface Hobhouse states, "This is a book about the bachelor as much as the bride, the artist as well as the nude, because art comes not just from other art but from lives as they are actually lived, and affected by weather and illness, money and politics, sexual excess and domestic strife. At times the life of the nude is so close to the life of the artist that her form becomes his involuntary autobiography; at times a confession, a description of self in the form of the ideal other. At other times the nude may be a refuge from the facts of the artist's life, what he creates *instead*. At such times she is born not out of what is there but out of what is missing."

Generous in her illustrations of each artist's work, Hobhouse also fully documents her book chapter by chapter and provides a selected bibliography organized by artist. (TJW)

PR,IL

837. Johns, Catherine. **Sex or Symbol: Erotic Images of Greece and Rome.** London: British Museum Publications, 1982. 160 p. Includes bibliography and index. ISBN 0-7141-8042-4.

Sex or Symbol, written by an archaeologist on the staff of the British Museum and based on her lectures given at Exeter University, contends that it is a mistaken notion that the erotic art of ancient Greece and Rome was intended solely for "the purpose of sexual titillation." Unfortunately, Victorian prudery did assume just that, acting accordingly and imposing its notions on museums, which felt obliged to hide many erotic objects in locked cases, thereby handicapping scholars in their studies of the past.

Johns's aim in this book is "to illustrate some of the many examples of sexual imagery in the art of the classical cultures of Greece and Rome," to elicit sexual imagery's significance and purpose in antiquity, and to use it to draw inferences about those societies (p. 9). Places and times covered range from sixth century B.C. Athens to the Roman Empire of the late fourth and early fifth centuries A.D. The book is generously illustrated with photographs (black-and-white and some color) of erotic objects (vases, medallions, herms, wall carvings, lamps, mirror covers, paintings, vessels, statuettes, tintinnabula, etc.), located in museums around the world (London, Naples, Munich, Paris, Athens, Boston, Berlin, and elsewhere).

Chapter I, "Collectors and Prudes," reveals the collection philosophy of the British Museum in the late eighteenth and nineteenth centuries, when donations of erotica from such benefactors as Richard Payne Knight and George Witt were segregated in the Museum Secretum. Johns comments that the "separate treatment which erotic antiquities have received has been damaging to scholarship, and even now, when the trend at last is moving in the opposite direction, the effects are far from forgotten" (p. 35). Subsequent chapters illustrate the meaning and use to which these erotic objects were put. Chapter II deals with objects that relate to fertility and religion. Here the reader encounters images of nursing goddesses, attacking satyrs, likenesses of Pan and Priapus, and so forth. In chapter III, "The Phallus and the Evil Eye," Johns shows the hostile and aggressive aspects of nature gods. For example, common images on Greek pottery are phalluses with the evil eye painted on the glans.

Chapter IV discusses numerous erotic objects in relation to the cult of Dionysos (Bacchus) as a fertility god. But chapter V, "Men and Beasts," emphasizes images and objects that are genuinely erotic and divorced from any religious significance: men and women copulating with various animals, a typical example of which is Leda and the Swan. And chapter VI, "Men and Women," depicts a wide range of heterosexual activity in Greek and Roman art that is clearly erotic.

Johns concludes that the erotica of antiquity should be interpreted in terms of its own time, not according to current categories of eroticism. Furthermore, in studying the past, it is foolish to ignore a whole segment of the record, however distasteful; only by acquiring the fullest picture possible of past behavior can we truly understand our forebears. (TJW)

IL
838. Kronhausen, Phyllis, and Eberhard Kronhausen, comps. **The Complete Book of Erotic Art. Erotic Art, Volumes 1 and 2. A Survey of Erotic Fact and Fancy in the Fine Arts.** New York: Bell, 1978. 312, xiv, 270 p. Originally published in two separate volumes as *Erotic Art* and *Erotic Art 2*. Includes index. ISBN 0-517-24893-X.

Erotic art was exhibited publicly for the first time in 1968 in Lund, Sweden, at the First International Exhibition of Erotic Art. It was moved to Aarhus, Denmark, in 1969. The compilers of this two-volume work assembled the collection in the belief that "erotic art, neglected, suppressed, and persecuted for centuries, has an important contribution to make to the understanding of art, the social history of mankind, and human happiness and progress." Both volumes cover Western art, primitive art, and the erotic art of India, China, and Japan; they bring together the work of classical artists chiefly from the seventeenth, eighteenth, and nineteenth centuries as well as contemporary artists such as Karel Appel, Jean Jacques Lebel, Betty Dodson, George Grosz, Andre Masson, Boris Vansier, and Frederic Pardo. Representative types of art include Japanese and Chinese painted scrolls, miniatures, oils on wood and canvas, pencil and ink drawings, watercolors, engravings, etchings, lithographs, and numerous three-dimensional forms such as collages, carvings, bronzes, pottery, and temple friezes. Interesting introductory material includes a statement, "How Nice People Like Us Got Involved in Erotic Art," in which the intrepid compilers relate the trials and tribulations of preparing for a first in art. Believing that their exhibition will be a contribution to the sexual freedom movement in the world and the battle against censorship by affecting the public's attitude toward sex, they try to show that "important artists of all times and all countries have done erotic work and that some of their erotic works are the best they have done." Interviews with random visitors to the exhibition, including children, are given as well as revealing exchanges with such artists as Larry Rivers and Andy Warhol on the nature of erotic art. Pictures show visitor reaction to the exhibits and several depict Phyllis Kronhausen emerging from Ferdi's "Womb Tomb" on opening day. Much of the art is now on permanent display in The International Museum of Erotic Art in San Francisco, reputed to be the only museum of its kind in the world. (TJW)

PO
839. Kronhausen, Phyllis, and Eberhard Kronhausen, eds. **Erotic Bookplates.** New York: Bell, 1970. 213 p.

Collectors of erotic books in the eighteenth, nineteenth, and early twentieth centuries had a penchant for personalized erotic bookplates to enhance the appearance of their private collections. The Kronhausens have assembled a selection of such miniature artworks taken from The International Museum of Erotic Art in San Francisco, where the displayed items are considered favorites by the viewing public. Likening erotic bookplates to rare postage stamps, they point out that most of the 109 examples in this collection are from Europe, mainly Germany and Austria, although a good many are from Czechoslovakia, Poland, and Hungary, with a few from France and England. Oddly enough, there are no representatives from collections in the United States although it is known that there are many private collections of erotic books in America. The subject matter of erotic bookplates covers the full range of human sexuality, with human sex organs, nudes, intercourse, oral sex, masturbation, homosexuality, bestiality, and such special subjects as "Woman and Satyr," "Leda and the Swan," "Adam and Eve," and "Sex and Death" forming the most popular themes. According to the Kronhausens, the "best part about erotic bookplates . . . is . . . their sense of humor. They resemble in that respect the sexual limerick, and, best of all, without slipping into the kind of vulgarity which, alas, mars the vast majority of the latter." (TJW)

PR,IL
840. Kuryluk, Ewa. **Salome and Judas in the Cave of Sex: The Grotesque: Origins, Iconography, Techniques.** Evanston, Ill.: Northwestern University Press, 1987. 371 p. Includes bibliographic references and index. ISBN 0-8101-0740-6.

Kuryluk, Polish artist and art historian, presents in this well-illustrated study, her interpretation of the grotesque in art. Starting with the discovery at the end of the Renaissance of unusual frescoes in Roman grottoes in the vicinity of Rome and Pompeii—on which occasion the term "grotesque" was applied—she goes on to strive for a general understanding of the grotesque, which depicts a variety of anti-worlds, such as, among others, "the anti-world of femininity as opposed to the world controlled by men," or "the anti-world of sin, flesh, and death as divided from the cosmos of virtue, spirit, and the eternal life." Kuryluk defines the grotesque "as a subculture that emerged at the end of the Renaissance and functioned in opposition to the official culture until the beginning of the twentieth century" (p. 4). Today it is no longer with us, having been rendered unnecessary by the uprooting of old standards and traditions.

Chapter 1 begins with the statement: "The meaning of the grotesque is constituted by the norm which it contradicts: the order it destroys, the values it upsets, the authority and morality it derides, the religion it ridicules, the harmony it breaks up, the heaven it brings down to earth, the position of classes, races, and sexes it reverses, the beauty and goodness it questions." Erroneously, the Roman grottoes were originally thought to be caves, and their frescoes suggested an erotically permissive world. Kuryluk opines, "Because of the association with womb and the cave, all closed spaces tend to be perceived as female" (p. 20). She adds, "Because of the nature of human anatomy, with the genitals situated next to the anus and the urinary tract, even the most sublimated fantasies of the mystical interiors of love are constantly threatened by the shadowy presence of the dirty, obscene, and ridiculous" (p. 21). While Kuryluk shows in grotesque art the many kinds of enclosed spaces depicted (eggs, globes, shells, etc.), she regards the womb as the ultimate cave. Hieronymous Bosch, the fifteenth-century artist, produced grotesque paintings of an anti-Christian world characterized by numerous enclosed spaces and the carnal activities within them.

But Kuryluk focuses her attention on the grotesque drawings of Aubrey Beardsley, the young Englishman, invalid, and fin-de-siècle artist, who dedicated himself to formulating "with ironic clarity the erotic obsessions of his times." Among other things, Beardsley concentrated on the erotic motifs in the stories of Tannhauser, Salome, and Judas.

Beardsley's unfinished novel, *The Story of Venus and Tannhauser*, offers a parody of ancient cave mythology, making "fun of lovers, poets, artists, and aristocrats who in the depth of the earth search for muses and nymphs" for "poetic inspiration and unlimited pleasure" (p. 98).

Kuryluk next examines Beardsley's drawings illustrating Oscar Wilde's play, *Salome*, including "The Dancer's Reward," that shows Salome staring fixedly at John the Baptist's severed head, her reward for dancing before Herod and his guests. This biblical legend, suffused with sexuality, offered Beardsley the opportunity to present his grotesque perspective on female psychology.

In "The Kiss of Judas," Beardsley sacrilegiously depicts "one of Christianity's most dramatic moments, the betrayal of Christ by Judas Iscariot" (p. 260). The shocking drawing shows a naked dwarf "kissing the hand of a hermaphroditic youth who, leaning against an obscenely mutilated tree, has fallen asleep" (p. 261).

Kuryluk finally states, "The image of the cave can be viewed as an archetype resulting from the predominantly male erotic reverie . . . that compared the earth with the female body and its cavities with the female genitals. Thus one understands why the grotesque became associated with a particularly suspect part of the past, and with sex, the forbidden zone of Christianity. The symbolism of the cave suited heterosexual as well as homosexual men because the grotto could function not only as a vagina and a uterus but also as an anus. Dreams of penetration, incest, and regression could be projected onto this sexualized landscape" (p. 317).

In the last part of her study Kuryluk surveys the techniques—debasement, distortion, displacement, and heterogeneity—used by artists of the grotesque. (TJW)

PO

841.   Lahr, Jane, and Lena Tabori, eds. **Love: A Celebration in Art and Literature.** New York: Stewart, Tabori & Chang, 1982. 239 p. Includes index. ISBN 0-041434-20-6.

The experience of broken marriages has motivated the editors to create a stunning literary and artistic tribute to the emotion of love. Throughout the pages of this oversized work, the poetry, short stories, plays, letters, and other writings of literary giants alternate with colorful works of art, each in some remarkable way affirming, describing, explaining, or extolling love. The writings of Shakespeare, Marlowe, Marvell, Nabokov, Colette, e. e. cummings, Eliot, Whitman, Millay, Joyce, Rilke, and others are interwoven with the paintings of Toulouse-Lautrec, Chagall, Picasso, Rubens, Renoir, Whistler, Sargent, Ingres, and Rembrandt, as well as with selections from Egyptian, Persian, Hindu, Greek, and Japanese art and literature. Setting the tone of this eclectic collection is the opening work: *The Diary of Adam and Eve* by Mark Twain. Aspects and stages of love—young love, courting, celebration, passion, commitment, enduring love, meditation—are attested to by such literary gems as Willa Cather's short story, *Coming, Aphrodite!*; an excerpt from D. H. Lawrence's *Lady Chatterley's Lover*; Cole Porter's *You're the Top*; and the delightful play, *The Apollo of Bellac*, by Jean Giraudoux. While sex is not an overt topic in this beautiful book, it does seem to suffuse each and every selection. A brief index of titles, authors and artists is provided at the end. Bibliographic acknowledgment of the literary and artistic sources of the selected works concludes this compilation. (TJW)

PR,IL

842.   Lawner, Lynne, ed. and tr. *I Modi*: **The Sixteen Pleasures: An Erotic Album of the Italian Renaissance.** Giulio Romano, Marcantonio Raimondi, Pietro Aretino, and Count Jean-Frederic-Maximilien de Waldeck. Evanston, Ill.: Northwestern University Press, 1988. 132 p. Translated from the Italian. ISBN 0-8101-0804-6.

I modi, an early Italian Renaissance work of erotic art, edited, translated, and interpreted by art historian Lawner, consists of eighteen imaginative drawings depicting the art of physical lovemaking, done by Giulio Romano, a pupil of Raphael, accompanied by sonnets (*Sonetti Lussuriosi*) composed by the well-known art critic and satirical poet, Pietro Aretino. The drawings inspired Marcantonio Raimondi, a prominent artist, to create copper engravings of them from which prints were made and widely disseminated in Roman society, including the Vatican court. Romano's lascivious drawings and Aretino's erotic sonnets so enraged Pope Clement VII that he had the entire first edition destroyed.

According to art historian George Szabo, writing in the preface, the "*I modi*, published here for the first time in English . . . is possibly one of the very few [copies] that survived the extreme and vicious suppression that this work and its various editions elicited and suffered from the time of its creation in the first decades of the sixteenth century." This edition also includes the recreation of *I modi* done in the 1850s by Count Maximilien de Waldeck, an amateur who embellished but did not distort unnecessarily the original work.

In the text Aretino's sonnets are presented both in the original Italian type beneath each posture and in Lawner's deft translations accompanying the drawings. In her analysis of this work, Lawner points out the social significance of both drawings and poems. She believes that *I modi* "constitutes a gallery in album form of sixteen different courtesans (with their noble lovers) each with a name and a special art" (p. 26), and that such documents (catalogs, lists of courtesans, portraits, and positions) were common in Italy at that time. She also avers that the combined engravings and sonnets constitute a form of social criticism aimed at (1) the corrupt and hypocritical attitudes of the clergy toward deviant sexual behavior, especially fornication and sodomy; (2) revealing the explosion of pagan enthusiasm that had been pent up for centuries, especially for that ancient Roman demi-god of fertility, Priapus; and (3) showing the "absolute beauty of the naked human body, particularly as captured in the moment of lovemaking in the configuration of the couple" (p. 34), a tabooed practice throughout medieval times.

Filtering northward, *I modi* influenced every field of figurative and decorative arts from 1530 on. Romano's images and Aretino's poetry began to appear everywhere. (TJW)

PO

843. Lawrence, Mary, comp. **Lovers: 100 Works of Art Celebrating Romantic Love.** With commentaries by the distinguished and the great. Foreword by Sophia Loren. New York: A&W Publishers, 1982. 219 p. Includes index. ISBN 0-89479-116-8.

"Learn the secret of love and you will discover the secret of death and believe in life eternal." That poignant quotation is taken from the statement of Maria Mestrovic that accompanies her father's famous bronze *Well of Life*, done in 1905 and located outside the Mestrovic Museum in Zagreb, Yugoslavia. All of the lovers so colorfully depicted in this tastefully chosen collection of 101 artworks seem to have learned the secret of love. The compiler has matched the works of Oskar Kokoschka (*The Tempest*), Pablo Picasso (*The Lovers*), Gustav Klimt (*The Kiss*), Henry Moore (*Interlocking*), Jack Culiner (*Love Cycle*), and others with observations on each of the works by distinguished people. Deborah Kerr, for example, quotes a poem by Robert Bridges, to express her interpretation of Francesco Hayez's painting *The Kiss*. Eleanor Harris Howard remarks about Gaston Lachaise, whose bronze *Passion* is included, that "he worked 'like a man possessed' to create his voluptuous work of art." Rumer Godden comments on the anonymous fifteenth-century silver *Embracing Tantric Deities* that "we in the West turn increasingly to India for wisdom in religion and philosophy. She could also teach us a great deal about the art of love." Henry Fonda asks: "Am I, maybe, just a little jealous of a god's life?" as he responds to Jacques-Louis David's *Cupid and Psyche*. Sir John Pope-Hennessy says of Riccio's bronze statuette *Satyr and Satyress*, that in the Paduan Renaissance the satyr assumes the character "of a benign primitive being at the mercy of its own sensual appetites, reflecting, in its instinctive actions, the emotional responses of a more sophisticated form of live." Sexuality occasionally, sensuality abundantly, love always pervades this sweeping, eclectic display of the world's greatest art on the subject of lovers. At the end of this well-designed, oversized book are indexes of artists and commentators. In the front is a listing of the works in the order of their appearance. (TJW)

IL
844. Louville, François de. **The Male Nude: A Modern View.** Edited and with an introduction by Edward Lucie-Smith. New York: Rizzoli, 1985. 174 p. Includes index. ISBN 0-8478-0581-6.

This book is a retrospective catalog of a very popular exhibition in London organized by de Louville, in his words, "to explore a surprisingly neglected topic—the place of the male, as opposed to the female, nude in contemporary art." Representing the work of nearly fifty contemporary artists, this book of pictures of naked men is an attempt to fill that gap in modern art history.

The book opens with a short discussion of the male nude as portrayed in traditional art and pin-ups along with an analysis of the innovations of contemporary artists and the "re-eroticization" of the male nude in art, given that the artistic eroticization of bodies, both male and female, had been usurped by the invention of photography in recent times.

The door to this new approach was opened by David Hockney's homoerotic Pop Art renderings, and this has been carried forward not only by other homosexual artists, but also by numerous feminist artists whose use of irony and objectification of the male body is their statement. Further, it has been carried on by heterosexual women artists who choose to portray naked male individuals as opposed to traditional pornographic representations.

The fine quality reproductions of the pictures range from raunchy and blatantly homoerotic works to meaningful personal representations to the humorous and even to the spiritually inspired devotional depiction of the male nude. A short biographical statement is provided for each artist. (NW)

IL
845. Lucie-Smith, Edward. **The Body: Images of the Nude.** London: Thames and Hudson, 1981. 176 p., 102 plates. ISBN 0-500-23339-X.

In this collection of nude images, the well-known British art critic, Lucie-Smith, presents the development of nude painting from antiquity to the present. Depending on style and intent, he categorizes nudes as rational, uneasy, fleshy, romantic, classical, and so forth and devotes a chapter to each type. In the first chapter, The Rational Nude, the examples chosen for comment are the *Egyptian Acrobatic Dancer* (c. 1305-1080 B.C.), Onesimos's *Girl Preparing to Wash* (c. 480 B.C.), painted on a cup, and the Roman mosaic, *Girl Gymnasts* (fourth century A.D.). Highly stylized, they "give a glimpse of the origins and progress of classicism in painting."

Renaissance painters, inspired by the works of classical Greek sculptors, added measure and balance to their work as, for example, in Raphael's *The Three Graces* (c. 1500), taken directly from a Greco-Roman marble group. Anatomically faithful nudes appear: Albrecht Dürer's *Adam* (c. 1507) is a case in point. Conversely, we get groups of female figures, such as Palma Vecchio's *Diana and Callisto* (c. 1525) in which the sumptuous nudes are less logically constructed than *Adam*. Mannerism, which injected special attributes into the classical style of nude painting, supersedes High Renaissance painting. Michelangelo's classically proportioned but aggressive nudes afford an example, as do the nudes of Hieronymous Bosch in his *The Garden of Earthly Delights*, where we get the so-called "'Gothic' proportions—long legs, wide hips, rounded bellies, small breasts, narrow shoulders."

In the seventeenth century the realism in Mannerism is transferred to the early Baroque and reflected in paintings of the nude, which became more sensual. Titian with his *Venus Anadyomene* (c. 1520) and Coreggio with *The Sleep of Antiope* (c. 1525) anticipate this transformation, while Rubens's fleshy nudes in *Angelica and the Hermit* (c. 1625-28) and Rembrandt's *Bathsheba* (1654) exemplify it. These paintings also foreshadow the Rococo style of the early eighteenth century represented by Boucher's *Toilet of Venus* (1751).

Rival styles of neoclassicism and romanticism, hungering for the past, display their characteristics by mid-eighteenth-century in such works as Tiepolo's *Apollo Pursuing Daphne* (c. 1755-60) and David's *Cupid and Psyche* (1817). The nineteenth century brought to the fore such realistic painters of the nude as Lawrence Alma-Tadema (*In the Tepidarium*, 1881), Jean-Léon Gerôme (*Moorish Bath*), and Adolphe-William Bouguereau (*A Young Girl Defending Herself Against Eros*), who presented their exotic nudes in mythological or historical disguise.

Indicating the transition from Romantic to Symbolist art are the nudes of Delacroix, Chasseriau, and Maclise. These appeared at a time when, as Lucie-Smith comments, "the society of the period was prudish but it nevertheless found sex a subject of overwhelming interest." Continuing the symbolist tradition are the erotic paintings of the nude by Moreau, Picasso, Klimt, and others.

Finally, the diversity and fragmentation of Modernism in paintings of the nude is presented in which the nudes range from the realistic but breathtaking *Half-length Nude* (1929) by Christian Schad to *Woman I* (1950-52) by Willem De Kooning.

Toward the end of this imaginative compilation of nude images, presented in 102 plates, Lucie-Smith states that "the group of modern nudes presented here is only a small section of the available material, but it does demonstrate how fertile our own century has been in its creation of this type of image" (p. 138). It has been "an exploration through pictures of a labyrinth of ideas and feelings . . . about nakedness and nudity in western painting." Furthermore, "painted nudes were always more candid about sexual feeling than anything written, simply because the conventions for verbal description, the actual terminology, did not then exist" (p. 30). (TJW)

PR,IL

846. Lucie-Smith, Edward. **Eroticism in Western Art.** New York: Oxford University Press, 1972. 287 p. (The World of Art). Includes index. ISBN 0-500-20121-8.

Lucie-Smith, art historian and poet, states that this book "is intended to trace the history, and describe the functions, of erotic art in a single culture—that which has its origin in Western Europe" (p. 7). The work is divided into two parts. Part 1, "Contexts," provides a historical approach to erotic works of art by attempting "to place them in the context of culture, the social situations, and the prevailing aesthetic beliefs of the epoch when they were produced" (p. 8). Eight chapters range from the time of Paleolithic art, when the erotic was tied to the notion of fertility, and Greek and Roman art, that gradually secularized eroticism in art; through the reactionary church-dominated medieval period; the later revival of pagan art in the Renaissance; the realistic movement of the late sixteenth century; Romanticism; to the various movements of the late nineteenth and twentieth centuries (Symbolism, Impressionism, Surrealism, Art Nouveau, Expressionism, Cubism, Hedonism, and Abstractionism).

In part 2, "Symbols" (chapters 9-15), Lucie-Smith uses a different approach to erotic works of art. He organizes text and illustrations according to subject matter and "conscious and unconscious symbolism." In addition to being hedonistic, erotic art "seems to serve as an act of exorcism," as in primitive erotic art, and, in modern cultures, as a device to allay men's fears of women. Topics chosen for examination in erotic artworks include voyeurism, sexual intercourse, deviations, cruelty, castration, bestiality, and sexual symbolism (dagger, snake, the head, armor, the horned satyr, the unicorn, the mermaid). A final chapter, "Eroticism and Modernism," attempts to explain contemporary attitudes to sexual imagery in advertising (posters, calendars, etc.), photography, and the cinema, as well as in painting and sculpture. Lucie-Smith believes that erotic art in the European tradition is coming to a close.

The text is illustrated with 273 well-chosen plates, 29 in color, by some of the foremost artists of the past and present. A list of illustrations at the end informs the reader where the particular erotic works of art are located. (TJW)

IL

847. Mullins, Edwin. **The Painted Witch: How Western Artists Have Viewed the Sexuality of Women.** New York: Carroll & Graf, 1985. 230 p. Includes index. ISBN 0-88184-200-1.

Shocked by the remark made by Germaine Greer in *The Female Eunuch* that "women have very little idea of how much men hate them," British art critic and novelist Mullins sets about in *The Painted Witch* to test the truth of Greer's belief by examining paintings by men of women in the Western art tradition. On the assumption that "art does us good simply because it is art" (p. 2), he endeavors to ascertain if art does demonstrate a hatred for women. If so, where is the public good? Have we publicly enshrined misogyny? The consequence conceivably could be the wholesale destruction of masterpieces in the world's galleries.

In London Mullins visits the National Gallery, looking at paintings afresh with his eye alert to catch the visible signs of hatred that might tilt him in Greer's direction. He finds, however, other passions and affections represented—grief, jealousy, worship, lust—that weigh heavily against Greer's thesis.

In the course of his investigation, Mullins establishes a typology of paintings of women. Chapters in the book, replete with illustrations of classic paintings, are devoted to wise and foolish virgins, man-eaters, sinners, mistresses, clothes-pegs, mothers and heroines, married couples, and those upon whom love has been directed, including whores.

Paintings of virgins include Titian's *Sacred and Profane Love* and Lotto's disturbing *The Triumph of Chastity*; those of man-eaters are David's *Death of Marat* and Picasso's *Women with Stiletto*. Sinners feature Rubens's *Bathsheba* and Correggio's *Danaë*, while Giorgione's *Sleeping Venus* and Gauguin's *Two Tahitian Women* represent mistresses. Typical clothes-pegs are Bronzino's *Eleonora of Toledo with Her Son* and Botticelli's *Primavera*. Beloved lepers are Titain's *Noli me tangere*, Delacroix's *Death of Sardanapalus*, and Manet's *Déjeuner sur l'herbe*. Van Eyck's *Madonna and Child* and Renoir's *Maternité* represent mothers and heroines, while Gainsborough's *Mr. and Mrs. Andrews* and Seurat's *A Sunday Afternoon on the Island of La Grande Jatte* show typical married couples. Finally, Mullins's last category—those upon whom love has been imposed—include Rembrandt's *Bathsheba*, Goya's *Naked Maja*, Toulouse-Lautrec's *Jane Avril Leaving the Moulin Route*, and Watteau's *The Shepherds*.

Mullins interprets these great paintings of women (143 of them), explaining as well the motivations of the men who created them. He shows that these men were not all woman-haters, but usually reflected the wishes of patrons—often a ruler—who considered women and their images as possessions to be publicly and proudly displayed. Because women's sexuality has often been deemed a threat to men's power, it became necessary to control, negate, or condemn women. All this is revealed in the paintings discussed in this book. According to Mullins, only a few painters do not show in their work the need to denigrate women's sexuality.

To counteract Germaine Greer's remark, Mullins makes it "abundantly clear from any study of the work of great painters . . . that a banquet of emotions towards women has fed man's creativity" (p. 223). Closely scrutinizing the paintings, the observer can detect love, desire, affection, need, tenderness, admiration, longing, and friendship, but also fear, that sometimes finds expression as hatred—"women depicted as destroyers of man, as voluptuous sacks of evil, helpless fodder for sadists, rapturous victims of martyrdom" (p. 224). Mullins has shown "the over-riding need, poured over the inventions of western art, to corral her, cosset her, control her, reduce her to manageable stereotypes. Viewed from this standpoint, so much art comes to look like magnificent camouflage behind which the dominant sex hides horrible doubts about his fitness to dominate" (p. 224). (TJW)

IL

848.   Nead, Lynda. **Myths of Sexuality: Representations of Women in Victorian Britain.** Oxford: Basil Blackwell, 1988. 228 p. Includes bibliography and index. ISBN 0-631-15502-3.

Putting herself squarely in the middle of the Foucauldian doctrine on the development of discourses of sexuality, art historian Nead describes how in the middle decades of the nineteenth-century British female sexuality became a critical issue. She poses the question: "What role did visual culture play in the categorization of normal and deviant forms of female sexuality and how did a painting of a prostitute displayed on the wall of a London art exhibition relate to representations of prostitution produced elsewhere in society, through medicine, religion or the law" (p. 2)? She thus attempts to establish art as one of the discourses on sexuality, adding to the thesis that while there was antisexual public morality in Victorian England, there was also in art as well as in other areas, a dynamic sexual discourse taking place by means of painting and the graphic arts.

Myths of Sexuality, then, is about the discourse in art that emerged at mid-century and that manifested itself in cultural institutions, certain publics, the language of visual images, and art criticism. Norms of sexual and moral behavior reflecting class hegemony were thus established. For example, in England the ruling class—a diverse but powerful middle class—maintained power over other social classes, with the shared notions of morality and respectability helping to maintain class coherence.

This book explores the ways in which particular areas of sexuality (masculinity, femininity, gender roles, the double standard, female chastity, adultery, and prostitution) were manifested, and depicted as part of the effort to control and regulate sexual behavior. In a series of chapters it examines the paintings of popular artists widely shown at exhibitions and galleries on such topics as respectable roles for women (wife, mother, sister) and deviant roles for women (divorcée, adulteress, prostitute). In the light of official acts, current events, public morality, and philanthropy, Nead examines the criticism of and popular reaction to these depictions.

Nead points out that this book is "an examination of the role of visual culture in the definition of femininity and respectability in the mid-Victorian period but it is framed by the recognition that we are still part of this history of discourses and representations" (p. 10). The book is illustrated with fifty representations of paintings and prints done by popular artists primarily around mid-century. (TJW)

PR,IL

849.   Peckham, Morse. **Art and Pornography: An Experiment in Explanation.** New York: Basic Books, 1969. 306 p. (Studies in Sex and Society).

Peckham, a professor of English, states, "I have called this study in the interdependence of art, pornography and sexual behavior, and in the function of pornography in the various modes of human behavior we name personality, culture, and society, an experiment in explanation." His study of pornography draws on philosophy and logical analysis, linguistics, and sociology to determine the possibility of logically verifying the arguments on either side of the ongoing debate. Inasmuch as many students and critics deny that the aesthetic value of a work of art has any dependence or connection with its subject, art cannot be devalued on the ground that it is pornographic. Art and pornography are not mutually exclusive terms. The positions of intellectuals and anti-intellectuals toward pornography reflect the tension of social attitudes valuing innovation as opposed to social stability. "Change in sexual behavior ordinarily occurs during a revolutionary situation." There is an extended discussion of pornography and its relative sophistication in various visual formats including film, photography, and comic books as well as art at the highest cultural levels. Peckham concludes by stating that "since pornographic art is in its formal function indistinguishable from art in the full stylistic and cultural range of the European culture area, since there is no uniqueness in the formal aspect of pornographic art, there is nothing to be said about it that cannot be said about nonpornographic art." (JA)

IL
850.   Rawson, Philip, ed. **Primitive Erotic Art**. London: Weidenfeld & Nicolson, 1973. 310 p. (World History of Erotic Art). Includes bibliography and index. ISBN 0-297-76537-X.
   Rawson is an art historian; contributors to this volume have varying backgrounds in art and anthropology. "Primitive" in this text refers to pre-literate and proto-literate societies, covering the span from Paleolithic culture to the high pre-Columbian civilizations. Rawson explains that the primitive is characterized by the use of metaphor rather than abstract symbols. "Concrete realities or their representations combined into metaphors convey complex ideas; by relating, in ritual and art, those concrete realities or their images, ideas are related. This is how ritual acts and how works of art gain their meaning."
   The arts of Paleolithic and Neolithic Europe, of the Celts, the Americas, Africa, and the Pacific Equatorial Islands are examined and related to the anthropological interpretation of their rituals and totems. The art always has a social function and is explicated in its content. It is not created for its own sake or for its aesthetic value and cannot be understood independent of its symbolism. Sexuality is just an aspect of the life force that is embodied in the gods and/or ancestor totems.
   The phallus is the central, recurring symbol. "The generic male power is, of course, universally represented by the penis, either in the form of a stylized emblem or as a naturalistic part of a male body, the part analogically symbolizing the whole. . . . On the cosmic scale it symbolizes that which generates the world and all its phenomena."
   The vulva symbol evolved from cup-shaped hollows in Paleolithic art to various triangle symbols to the lucky horseshoe. Later abstraction led to meander and spiral patterns used to represent the essential female. Many phallic symbols survived in Catholic churches through the Middle Ages.
   The beautiful reproductions of artifacts from the various cultures surveyed demonstrate a real diversity of style and theme, but they all relate to a common human concern with fertility, food supply, and continuity of culture and clan. (JA)

IL
851.   Saslow, James M. **Ganymede in the Renaissance: Homosexuality in Art and Society**. New Haven, Conn.: Yale University Press, 1986. 265 p. Includes bibliography and index. ISBN 0-300-03423-7.
   This book, a revision of a doctoral thesis by Saslow, a professor of Renaissance Art at Vassar College, and the first detailed study of homosexuality in the Renaissance, analyzes the wide presence of Ganymede in European art of the mid-fifteenth through the mid-seventeenth centuries, principally in Italy. Ganymede was the beautiful boy in classical Greek mythology who was abducted by Jupiter and pressed into service of the king of gods as a wine-pourer and lover. The resurgence of Ganymede's popularity with aritsts and writers paralleled the revival of the Renaissance interest in classical art and thought. Saslow's intent in this study is to supplement "earlier interpretations of Ganymede as a spiritual metaphor with a more detailed investigation of the sexual, emotional, and social issues he also symbolized, from pederasty to misogyny to conventions of marriage and gender roles."
   Ganymede was variously rendered by the Renaissance artists in the form of three personae: the chaste victim of rape; the honored attendant of the Olympian ruler; and after death, the immortal constellation Aquarius. The artists of northern Italy reacted in different ways to the keenly felt moral contradictions of the classical Ganymede in a setting of Christianity. Chapter 1 delineates how Michelangelo took the approach shared by most of Western culture at that time—synthesizing classical and Christian values, tensely suppressing sexual passion. Chapters 2 and 3 analyze three artists—Correggio, Parmigianino, and Giulio Romano—who, in part reflecting their hedonistic patrons, did not inhibit erotic stimulation, an openness that was not untypical in northern Italy. Chapter 4 examines the sculptor Benvenuto Cellini, whose early homoerotic works became toned down in adaptation to a later moral social austerity.

The artistic transformation and decline of Ganymede and classical mythology in the seventeenth century is outlined in chapter 5. As a subject of art Ganymede spread north of the Alps, but "in the hands of Rubens, Rembrandt, and others, the attractive adolescent of tradition was often reduced to a child, adapted to a more heterosexual version of his myth, or expressly banished from civilized society." (EBS)

IL

852. Saunders, Gill. **The Nude: A New Perspective.** Cambridge: Harper & Row, 1989. 144 p. Includes bibliography and index. ISBN 0-06-430189-3.

From a feminist perspective of the 1980s, Saunders, curator in the Department of Design, Prints and Drawings of the Victoria and Albert Museum, London, looks at the nude in the arts as it has evolved since classical antiquity. While acknowledging the feminist attacks on our current visual culture, which systematically exploits female nakedness as it ignores the male body, Saunders contends that there is legitimacy in portraying the nude, whether male or female. She states, "The naked body in art is the focus for a variety of meanings" (p. 7); this study examines those meanings as they have been articulated in the past and as they are being expressed today.

Except for the Gothic Period (twelfth to sixteenth centuries), when naked bodies appeared only in religious representations, the painting, drawing, and sculpting of the nude have been a central feature of Western art. However, while the Greeks idealized the nude as noble and inspiriting, the Christians made nudity a symbol of shame and guilt. Saunders draws the conclusion that the naked body is "in art ambiguous, and nudity subject to conflicting interpretations" (p. 10).

In search of meaning in the nude art form, Saunders observes that "women have been consistently presented in word and image as innately passive" (p. 22), while men have usually been cast in active roles. This is borne out by such famous paintings as Rubens's *Bathsheba* and Tintoretto's *Susannah and the Elders*. In advertising today such images perpetuate this view of passive, desirable, and available women being actively viewed by potential male customers.

Another meaning derived from an examination of the female nude is the fetishization, mutilation, and fragmentation of women's bodies in art. Saunders exemplifies this by examining a range of artwork from the *Venus de Milo* to Edvard Munch's *Madonna*, Tom Wesselmann's *Pink Breast*, and Allen Jones's *Desire Me*. She believes that "the disabling or distorting of the female nude in certain images indicates a fear of women's autonomous uncontrolled sexuality" (p. 73); moreover, the female nude presents "a male fantasy of women's sexuality," objectifying it "by rendering it anonymous and fragmentary" (p. 74).

From another perspective, artists have grounded the female nude in nature while granting the male a controlling, cultural role. Witness the paintings of female nudes in landscapes, such as Simon Vouet's *Ceres and Harvesting Cupid* and William Etty's *Deluge*. The nature/culture opposition is clearly expressed in Manet's *Déjeuner sur l'Herbe*, which shows the men completely clothed and in control but the women naked and immersed in the landscape. Similar oppositions are seen in paintings of the rescued and the rescuer and the hero and the victim.

According to Saunders, the "female nude was devised as a category of secular art with no purpose beyond the more or less erotic depiction of nakedness" (p. 116). Feminist artists today are attempting to modify this approach by reclaiming nude art from masculine fantasy. They are doing this by the "reworking of myths, the deconstruction of dominant visual codes, parody, role-reversal, and the re-representation of specifically female body experience and imagery" (pp. 117-18). Current examples are Gwen Hardie's *Venus with Spikes* and Eileen Cooper's *Tickling the Trout.* (TJW)

IL
853.   Smith, Bradley. **Erotic Art of the Masters: The 18th, 19th & 20th Centuries.**
New York: Galley Press, [1974]. 207 p. Includes bibliography and index. ISBN 0-8317-
2953-8.
Watteau, Boucher, Fragonard, and Rowlandson from the eighteenth century;
Manet, Ingres, Daumier, Courbet, Degas, Toulouse-Lautrec, Gauguin, Millet, Beardsley,
and Renoir from the nineteenth century; and Masson, Rouault, Courbet, Chagall, Dali,
Picasso, Grosz, Klimt, Wunderlich, Ovenden, Tice, Rivers, de Kooning, and Warhol
from the twentieth century—these are some of the artists whose works are tastefully
reproduced in this colorful gallery of erotic paintings and who, according to Smith,
"devoted themselves to recording humanity's most useful and pleasurable pursuit."
Represented also among the eighteenth- and nineteenth-century paintings are the artists
of China, Mongolia, Japan, Persia, and India. More than 140 separate artworks, located
in the great museums of the world or in private collections, are found here, most of them
in full color. An informative commentary on the cultural backgrounds of the artists
admirably complements the pictorial representations included in the book. All the
paintings are described and their provenance indicated in the back of the book under the
listing "Works of Art." In the opinion of Smith, erotic art, as distinguished from
pornography, "means art that depicts sexual love or sexual desire" and describes "the
dominance of the life instinct over the death instinct." The late Henry Miller in his
perceptive introduction points out that erotic art, always accessible to monarchs, aristocrats, millionaires, the clergy, and censors, is still not fully available to the general public.
There is still fear that ordinary individuals will not know how to handle it, and consequently we have among us self-appointed custodians of the public morality. This
collection of paintings by the masters contributes to public awareness and appreciation
of erotic art. (TJW)

IL
854.   Soulié, Bernard. **Tantra: Erotic Figures in Indian Art.** [London]: Miller Graphics, 1982. 96 p. ISBN 0-517-40290-4.
In this brief work tantric art is expressed in paintings and sculpture of a highly
erotic nature, amplified by a text explaining the origin, development, and artistic
expression of Tantrism, a religious sex cult founded about the third century A.D. in an
explosive reaction against the traditional and repressive Brahmanic Hinduism. The
colorful reproductions, some full page, are credited to various archives, museums, and
private collections, including the Kinsey Institute for Sex Research. Soulié does not
comment on the artworks themselves, but it is apparent that many are on public buildings
and hence anonymous. Tantrism is a religion of sex, apparently still practiced by groups
in India in a limited way. It is concerned with sexual methods of achieving a state of
supreme Revelation, wherein Knowledge and Truth are realized. The positions of yoga
(e.g., the lotus) are the basis of the sexual postures assumed by the Tantrikas, or faithful,
during intercourse; they are intended to facilitate a transfer of energy from the woman
to the man in the form of a primordial fluid that will bring one's partner to the desired
state. Intense and frequent intercourse in the recommended positions, much enhanced by
chanted prayers, or mantras, and controlled breathing bring the participants to a state of
ecstasy, or oneness with the universe. The woman seeks repeated orgasms; the man
exercises control over his ejaculation. The textual basis for these practices is found in
the *Upanishads* and the *Bhagavad-Gita*, metaphysical works that provide guidance for
all Hindus. Soulié attempts to link the mysticism of Tantrism to the ascetic practices of
the early Jesuits, the psychoanalysis of Sigmund Freud, and the counterculture movement
of the 1960s. Despite attempts at explanation, the emphasis in the book is on the ritual
copulations of the figures depicted in the artworks. (TJW)

PR,IL

855. Steinberg, Leo. **The Sexuality of Christ in Renaissance Art and in Modern Oblivion.** New York: Pantheon Books, 1983. 222 p. Includes bibliography and index. ISBN 0-394-72267-1.

According to Steinberg, a distinguished art historian, the representations of Christ's sexuality in Renaissance art have been banished to the corridors of modern oblivion, which is characterized by a "profound, willed, and sophisticated" incomprehension of Renaissance symbols. The major question that he raises is whether the time has come to confront rather than suppress these clearly sexual expressions. Related issues include explaining these representations in theological and symbolic terms. The 123 photographs of art that accompany the main text are introduced to support Steinberg's claim that Renaissance artists produced devotional images emphasizing the sexuality of Christ: people look at as well as touch the Christ child's genitals, Mary draws attention to them by covering them with her hand, the Christ child playfully exposes his genitals, the dead Christ cups his genitals with his hand, an erect penis seems to lie under Christ's covering on the cross and under his shroud after his death. What accounts for the sexual component of these kinds of devotional images? To interpret them as merely naturalistic representations is to deny their importance and complexity. Steinberg claims that Renaissance art "became the first Christian art in a thousand years to confront the Incarnation entire, the upper and lower body together, not excluding even the body's sexual component" (p. 72). He develops a cogent argument to show that sexual representations attest to the "utter carnality of God's humanation in Christ." He leads the reader through a fascinating discussion of possible theological and symbolic interpretations of the pictures and sculptures he includes. Anticipating the disbelief that some readers may feel about even acknowledging Christ as a sexual being, Steinberg devotes the last half of the book to a lengthy, scholarly section of Excursuses on statements in the text; it contains another 123 photographs of artworks to corroborate his central themes. The postscript on Renaissance religious art, by John W. O'Malley, S.J., lends strong support for Steinberg's thesis. (SGF)

IL

856. Stewart, Alison G. **Unequal Lovers: A Study of Unequal Couples in Northern Art.** New York: Abaris Books, 1977. 208 p. Includes bibliography and index. ISBN 0-913870-44-7.

The theme of unequal lovers, i.e., love between the old and the young, is a theme that has interested artists and audiences since antiquity. Stewart limits this study primarily to the fifteenth and sixteenth centuries, periods in which the theme attained popularity and independent representation in the visual arts, especially in northern Europe.

Stewart catalogs these representations in a hand-list of 106 works, describing each work in detail. Arranged in rough chronological order, each entry includes caption of item, such as "Old Fool and Young Woman" or "Love Triangle with Chastity Belt and Key"; artist's name, if known; date of work, if known; type of representation (engraving, drypoint, woodcut, chiaroscuro drawing, etc.); size; and source data.

The text with eighty-two illustrations preceding the hand-list examines the history of unequal lovers in literature and art, beginning with the comedies of the Roman Plautus in the third century B.C. and discussing such later works as *Roman de la Rose* (thirteenth century), Boccaccio's *Decameron* (fourteenth century), Chaucer's *Canterbury Tales* (fourteenth century), and Hans Sachs's *Zweierlei Ungleiche Ehen* (sixteenth century).

Stewart interprets the theme of unequal lovers as representing in the fifteenth century a turning away from the courtly ideal of love to the negative role of women as temptresses and men as fools. Indeed, in courtly love woman was placed on a pedestal and idealized; in the unequal lovers theme she is "brought solidly down to earth where she can be resented for a power which is viewed as too strong, even as out of control" (p. 101). The popularity of the theme of unequal lovers in the visual arts around 1500 may be attributed, so Stewart believes, to the "tendency in engraving to satirize the follies of love." This popularity may also be attributed to such social, economic, and political factors as the growth of towns, a sex ratio favoring women, the rise of the burghers as a class, and the emphasis on money instead of land. (TJW)

PR,IL
857. Thomson, Richard. **Degas: The Nudes.** London: Thames and Hudson, 1988. 240 p. Includes bibliography, index, and list of illustrations. ISBN 0-500-23509-0.

Thomson is a British art historian who is a highly regarded critic/commentator on nineteenth-century art, especially the Impressionist Movement. In this study he examines Degas's nudes, which amounted to at least 20 percent of his oeuvre. His analysis traces the artist's development technically and expressively, but also sees Degas's art as an insight into the French upper-class male assumptions about sexuality and women.

As a student, following the traditional training, Degas developed his skills with exercises in life drawing as a basis for depicting the human figure, clothed and unclothed. The old tradition, that regarded history painting as the highest art, used the nude figure as allegorical symbol and as the representation of "beauty in its purist form."

During the 1860s, as Degas's career developed, history painting declined into trite, sometimes prurient scenes, which did not appeal to the growing middle-class who preferred genre scenes and art that related to the changed socioeconomic realities. The serious artist, such as Manet, influenced by literature's turning to Naturalism, found new expression in scenes of contemporary life and a focus on urban society. Degas was central to the depiction of "this Naturalist insistence on what might happen—on people removing their clothes in likely circumstances or setting, on the greater plausibility of the undressed or partially clad, the 'déshabillée,' than the entirely naked—cut across the academic convention of the nude's imaginary, idealized embodiment of purity of form."

In his forties Degas found lithograph and monotype as the perfect medium for his "predominantly linear, graphic style." Over the next decade he produced the series of bathers that explored the female body in natural, often awkward, poses. Although the genitalia were not explicit, there was an implied erotic element in these works. Also dating from this period were the brothel monotypes that had a more lubricious, caricatural attitude. It is evident that Degas regarded women from the lower classes with less respect and dignity than those shown in secure bourgeois boudoirs. His interest may have stemmed from his own experience, but seemed more of an expression of a topic very current in the day's novels (e.g., Zola) and in the current interest over the socioeconomic problem of prostitution.

During the 1880s, Degas turned to pastels for nude studies that exploited his superb draughtsmanship to show the muscular tension of limbs and back in stretched, balancing or working modes. His suite of bathing nudes from this period showed the use of color and light as well as line in modeling contours.

Thomson agrees that the critics who have accused Degas of voyeurism may have some degree of truth but he feels that the motive force for Degas's nude studies was "an artist's obsession with forms in movement." His use of the same themes and poses throughout his career are evidence of his lifelong consideration of technical artistic problems. Thomson concludes that in the late pastels "grand, strong images, so personal and so modern . . . distantly echo a pose he had copied as a student . . . they have all the dynamic power of a Michelangelo." (JA)

IL,PO
858. Tilly, Andrew. **Erotic Drawings.** New York: Rizzoli, 1986. 80 p. Includes bibliography. ISBN 0-8478-0696-0.

In his opening remarks, Tilly points out that "drawing occupies a central place in Western erotic art." In it "artists give being to aspects of the imagination that find no place in their public, finished work. Drawings can be private or experimental; the erotic drawing is the archetypal underground image."

Of the few erotic Renaissance drawings extant, Tilly highlights Titian's *A Couple in Embrace*, a charcoal and black chalk drawing on blue paper; the anonymous black chalk and pen drawing, *The Rape of Ganymede*; and Parmigianino's etching *Witches'*

Sabbath. The thirty-two erotic drawings and watercolors in the main section of this compilation all date from the eighteenth century onward. They include a few eighteenth-century works: Boucher's *Sleeping Girl*, Fragonard's *The Sacrifice of the Race*, and the anonymous *Samson and Delilah*; many nineteenth century drawings by Fuseli, Rowland-son, Gericault, Daumier, Degas, Beardsley, and others; and numerous twentieth century works by Rodin, Munch, Klimt, Schiele, Modigliani, Grosz, Picasso, De Kooning, Wesselmann, Hockney, and others.

Each drawing is described, analyzed, and interpreted by Tilly. The diverse nature of these drawings leads him to conclude: "One cannot talk meaningfully . . . about a Western tradition of erotic drawing; kinds of erotic art are as disparate as kinds of human sexuality." If there is unity in these works, it stems from "their origins in the West, and their production within a male-dominated artistic culture" (p. 15). (TJW)

IL
859.   Walters, Margaret. **The Nude Male: A New Perspective.** New York: Paddington Press, 1978. 352 p. Includes bibliography and index. ISBN 0-448-23168-9.

Walters, a journalist, uses the nude male in Western art as a basis for a feminist analysis of social and psychological attitudes. Tracing the idealized male figure devel-oped in classical Greece and embraced in the Renaissance, she states: "It is the male and not the female body that becomes a symbol of order and harmony between human and divine, the male that embodies man's supreme cultural values."

The fusion of physical and philosophical virtues exemplified by the idealized male nude was characteristic of societies at the height of political and military power: ancient Greece, the high Renaissance, and Nazi Germany. During periods of stress and political decline art tends more to express pathos, vulnerability, and self-consciousness in the depiction of the nude, as evidenced in Hellenistic, Mannerist, and modern art.

Sexuality is not as overt a theme in depicting the male as in the female nude. This is partially because the man has been the active participant in society and religion, while woman represented passive, domestic, and erotic themes. Another important reason is that most of our artists were males who expressed their own self-image, ideals, and code of behavior. The phallicism inherent in the nude male is more a presentation of power than eroticism. Much of this naked art, however, deals with covert and subconscious efforts of the artist to deal with homosexuality or lack of sexual confidence.

It is only in our time that women have been free to create from male models. Walters examines the art of several and notes that their images of naked men are more objective and realistic. She also notes that when the male becomes the sex object the male/female roles do not really change—the woman must still please the man.

The small black-and-white illustrations reproduce many of the works of the long list of artists discussed in the text. They are selected to illustrate the themes, which include "The Naked Christian," "The Well-Mannered Nude," "Revolutionary Eros," "The Disappearing Male," "The Nude Disembodied," and "Newsstand Nudes." (JA)

IL
860.   Westheimer, Ruth. **The Art of Arousal.** New York: Abbeville Press, 1993. 180 p. Includes index. ISBN 1-55859-330-6.

Westheimer, the popular sex therapist, states in the preface of *The Art of Arousal* that she and an art historian-friend "spent days giggling and choosing the illustrations" for this book. Excluding pictures with a brutal or negative content, they selected some 120 outstanding artworks "to illustrate the progress of an erotic relationship from the first glance to postcoital bliss." Westheimer's unidentified friend does the art history while Westheimer takes responsibility for the sexual content. This combination of talent results in a "book with something for everyone."

Organized into seven chapters, the collection, which is "multicultural and mul-tisexual," begins with a chapter on "Elements of Eroticism" and ends with a chapter on "Blissful Exhaustion." Each colorful chapter presents the authors' interpretations of several famous artworks, mainly paintings, but also sculpture, drawings, and prints.

Among the works chosen to demonstrate the elements of eroticism are Titian's *The Venus of Urbino* (1538) and Velasquez's *The Toilet of Venus* (1599-1660), both reclining nudes displaying respectively front and back views of total nudity. To show the "Pleasures of Looking," one of the pictures chosen is Felix Valbotton's *The White and the Black* (1913), which features a black woman, cigarette in mouth, gazing fixedly at the charms of the nude white woman reclining in sleep before her.

For the chapter "Flirtation and Seduction," the authors invite the reader/viewers to consider Rembrandt's *The Jewish Bride* (c. 1665), which shows a suitor intimately embracing his bride-to-be; and Renoir's *Dance in the Country* (1883). For the chapter focusing on "Kisses and Other Foreplay," numerous examples are offered: *The Stolen Kiss* (1785-1790) by Marguerite Gerard and Jean-Honore Fragonard and Gustav Klimt's 1908 oil on canvas *The Kiss*. They chose for the chapter "The Embrace," Correggio's *Jupiter and Io* (c. 1532) and Indian temple carvings showing the great range of sex positions possible in the embrace.

The chapter "Solitary and Group Pleasures" shows Rodin's drawing *Woman Masturbating* (1879) and the provocative Japanese woodblock print *A Pearl Diver and Two Octopuses* (c. 1814). Finally for "Blissful Exhaustion" the authors chose Botticelli's *Venus and Mars* (1483-1484) and Courbet's *The Sleepers* (1866).

The preface includes some final words about arousal from Westheimer: "After you look at the pictures and read the texts in this book—and maybe make love to your partner, having been stimulated by the material between these two covers—you will recognize the delights of sexual and artistic variety that await your discovery." (TJW)

IL

861.   Zatlin, Linda Gertner. **Aubrey Beardsley and Victorian Sexual Politics.** Oxford: Clarendon Press, 1990. 234 p. (Clarendon Studies in the History of Art). Includes bibliography and indexes. ISBN 0-19-817505-X.

According to Zatlin, Professor of English, Morehouse College, Atlanta, Georgia, Aubrey Beardsley (1872-1898) was a potent critic of Victorian sexual attitudes and conventions through his drawings that appeared in magazines and books. His brief career, during which he produced some 1,100 drawings, peaked at the end of the Victorian age. William Butler Yeats admired his work, stating that Beardsley's life was a "fantastic protest against a society [he] could not remake" (p. 2). In Zatlin's view, Beardsley promoted sex education and sexual exploration.

The most daring artist of the 1890s, Beardsley executed original drawings for the journals *The Savoy* and *The Yellow Book* as well as for such classics as Ben Jonson's *Volpone*, Oscar Wilde's *Salome*, and Alexander Pope's *The Rape of the Lock*. Eroticism cropped out in many of his drawings, and some were flagrantly erotic, such as *The Lacedaemonian Ambassadors*, an illustration for Aristophanes's *Lysistrata*. Sexuality, regulated in Victorian England by the Obscene Publications Act of 1857, was excluded from mainstream art and literature. Nudity in art was limited to classical themes. Challenges to this limiting framework in the 1890s include Oscar Wilde flaunting his homosexuality and Aubrey Beardsley testing the waters with his erotic drawings. As a result both suffered—Wilde incarcerated and Beardsley out of work.

As Zatlin observes, Beardsley "was the first Victorian artist to be explicitly sexual outside of pornography and in a nonpornographic way" (p. 8), and "When Beardsley drew men, he unclothed their lust for power over women. When he drew women, he portrayed their intelligence and their sexuality, in bold defiance of Victorian convention" (p. 8).

Chapter 1 of Zaitlin's study provides a detailed examination of Victorian sexual politics in the 1890s. Chapter 2 focuses on men's dependence on money, position, and sex to affirm their identity as males. Chapter 3 examines Beardsley's women, including those who are dominated by masculine notions of femininity and those who view themselves as intelligent and sexual beings. Chapter 4 explores Beardsley's "use of allusions to Japanese erotica and Western pornography in order to create an erotic art which challenged public sexual morality" (p. 9).

In this fully illustrated study, Zatlin views Beardsley's artistry as social commentary promoting a healthier sexuality for men and women. Beardsley's perspectives on sexual matters are also revealed in his poems "The Ballad of a Barber" and "Three Musicians" included in the appendix. (TJW)

Photography

(For related material see also entry 523)

IL

862.   Booth, Pat. **Self Portrait.** With an introduction by Allen Jones. London: Quartet Books, 1983. 115 p. ISBN 0-7043-2398-2.

In the tradition of the artist painting a self-portrait, Booth, former model become photographer, presents a photo album of self-portraits taken from various angles in a series of indoor and outdoor settings. Speaking of the advantages of using herself as subject, she states that "at any hour of the day or night the model was readily available, enthusiastic, endlessly cooperative." She states that the "body, like my camera, is a tool used to create an image." Her images, she adds, may be "an erotic symbol, sometimes disembodied, dismembered, surreal. Sometimes it is symbolic of sybaritic hedonism." Narcissistic aspects might also enter the mind of the viewer.

The mostly black-and-white photographs and the few in color have been shot beside a pool, on a patio, inside a home, among foliage, in the water, on a tiled floor, in rooms, and on stairways. In some Booth is scantily attired, in others she wears a plastic torso, but most of the time she is nude. Some photographs are close-ups of legs, breasts, buttocks, and the mons, while others are reflected images of herself in a mirror, that result in a self-portrait of a self-portrait! Religious and feminist symbolism are particularly striking in the portrait of her body supine upon a tiled floor against a shadow cast in the form of a cross, with her feet tied together and her arms outstretched.

The approximately seventy-five photographs that make up this volume could prompt one to agree with Allen Jones, who says in his introduction that "photography has largely overtaken painting as a means of portraiture." (TJW)

IL,PO

863.   Clergue, Lucien. **Nude Workshop.** New York: Viking Press, 1982. 108 p. (A Studio Book). ISBN 0-670-51824-7.

The framework for this album by the renowned French photographer Clergue, consists of a progression of photographs of the nude arranged under headings descriptive of the various locations where the photographs were taken: the sea, desert and forest, the quarry, the urban nude, Venetian suite, and the ocean. The album contains eighty-two black-and-white photographs of nude women with a sprinkling of men. In his introduction, Clergue states that "as a rule I don't do many nude studies of men. Women, in my opinion, are more exhibitionistic than men; they are more comfortable in their bodies. Besides, women's bodies are more complex, and the possibilities entailed in photographing them are more abundant" (p. 11). In many of his photographs only the torso is visible. He explains his "beheading" of women and not men as follows: "The virility of a man is often best expressed in his shoulders and back, and in his sex, of course. There is something not quite right about showing the shoulders of a man without his head; a woman's breasts define her and physically 'finish' her" (p. 11).

The individually dated photographs range from as early as 1956 to 1981; they were taken in widely scattered locations: in France on the Camargue; at California's Death Valley, Pebble Beach, and Yosemite National Park; at the famous Les Baux marble quarry in Arles, France, where Clergue was born; in urban settings in New York City, Lausanne, Cholet (France), Chicago, Paris, and Seattle; indoor settings in Venice, Italy; and finally Port Lobos, Carmel, California, and Rockport, Maine, for the ocean series. The natural, honest style of the photographs is strongly reminiscent of the work of the eminent American photographer, Edward Weston, and of Ansel Adams, to whom the book is dedicated. (TJW)

PR,IL
864. Davis, Melody D. **The Male Nude in Contemporary Photography.** Philadelphia: Temple University Press, 1991. 185 p. (Visual Studies). Includes bibliography and index. ISBN 0-87722-839-6.

In contrast to the "omnipresent" female nude, the male nude is conspicuous by his near absence in contemporary photography; and when he appears, he is "quickly covered by silence, suppression and outrage" (p. 3). This trend prevailed in both painting and photography from the nineteenth century onward. In the introduction Davis provides an answer to the question of why there is differential photographic treatment of male and female nudes.

Photography's detail threatens the current definition of masculinity, because it scrutinizes the penis, which symbolizes the "metonymic fantasy" of manhood. Also, dramatic portrayals of nude men in action challenge the action ideal of masculinity, because they appear stilted and are the object of others' gazes, leaving men in the passive position of being the spectacle rather than the spectators. Finally, photographs of the male body may look less like Grecian sculptured marble and more "natural," thus reversing the identification of men with culture and women with nature. In sum, photographs can show the "naked truth," a body unadorned by fashionable ideas or presuppositions about gender. Fear of losing the mystery of the powerful phallus and the manly action ideal leads to censure of male nude photographs. Female nudes function as generators of "libidinous energy," passive objects to be actively viewed by a male audience; they are encouraged rather than censured, at least by males.

The photographers of male nudes face the challenge of confronting a tradition that equates males with aggression and nudity with loss of dignity. Yet to ignore the male nude is "to be, more than ignorant, an accomplice to values that successfully limit our view" (p. 19), many of which are expressed in pornography and in advertising. Davis's intent is to "introduce the social history of the photographed male nude and to present an overview of some of its genres..." (p. 20).

The first genre Davis considers is self-portraiture, illustrated by the photographs of Coplans and the Polaroids of Lucas Samaras. Coplans's self-portraits are not narcissistic whereas Samaras's exhibitionism is autoerotic and narcissistic. The true portraits (or photographs of others), the second genre, are illustrated by the work of Dureau and Mapplethorpe. Mapplethorpe's photographs from *Black Book* fetishize the well-muscled black men into icons of the phallus, full of power and strength. Dureau's photographs present portraits of nude black and white men that are "confrontational and unconventional." The allegorical nudes of the third genre are expressed by Makavejev's film *W.R.: Mysteries of the Organism* and Witkin's photographs. *W.R.* "reveals the mechanisms of political phallocentrism" (p. 125), while Witkin "attempts to make perversion into a metaphor" (p. 24). Throughout, Davis compares and contrasts the work of each pair of photographers in each genre in terms of the visual dynamics of narcissism, aggregate identity, fetishization, abjection, sadism, and phallocentrism. The photographs show that "the naked truth" and the "dressed nude" of ideals are not irreconcilable. (SGF)

IL
865. Donovan, Terence. **Glances.** London: Michael Joseph, 1983. unpaged. ISBN 0-7181-2375-1.

Of the seventy or so black-and-white plates of beautiful women appearing in this photo album, fashion photographer Donovan states: "Every photographer is continually bombarded with evasive images. These are evident briefly, then skitter away untrapped. I have tried to reconstruct moments that escaped my camera but not my memory. Here are my glances from a life."

With each picture Donovan makes statements about his models, who pose for him nude or in various stages of dress and undress. The very first plate shows a woman lying on her tummy across a well-made bed clad only in dark stockings and garter belt. Donovan's comment reads: "Across the road from this room in Paris sat an Italian man repairing violins, his radio playing slightly distorted rock music." A picture of a standing nude soaping herself in a lavatory has this statement: "When the craftsman installed the marble, did he think about the things it would see?" Still another picture shows a nude prone on a carpet in a large room supplied with many pictures, books, and comfortable furniture. Donovan comments, "This house belongs to a man I know. It is full of good taste and wonderful textures. Everything seems placed with mathematical precision. The girl was soft and random." (TJW)

PR,IL
866.   Dunas, Jeff. **Voyeur.** Los Angeles: Melrose, 1983. unpaged. ISBN 0-394-53348-8.

Dunas, a photographer of international reputation, presents his work in this collection of fifty-three photographs of nude and seminude young women taken in from 1979 to 1983. Photographed in various locales in England, France, and the United States, the album has a decided international flavor. All of the models are exquisitely posed in a variety of indoor and outdoor settings (lake, park, window, bedchamber, porch, staircase, decorative apartment, bathhouse) in which their soft-textured bodies contrast sharply with the harsher surroundings. Dunas, whose earlier albums *Captured Women* (1981) and *Mademoiselle, Mademoiselle* (1982) won critical acclaim, has with *Voyeur* managed to evoke the beauty inherent in the female form. (TJW)

IL
866a.   Ewing, William A. **The Body: Photographs of the Human Form.** San Francisco: Chronicle Books, 1994. 432 p. Includes bibliographic notes and index. ISBN 0-8118-0762-2.

Ewing, author of several books on photography and curator of exhibitions at such museums as the Museum of Modern Art (New York City), the Centre Pompidou (Paris), the National Museum of American Art (Washington, D.C.), and the Palazzo Fortuny (Venice), has assembled over 350 color and black-and-white photographic images of the human body, selected from the museums, libraries, archives, and private collections in North America, Europe, and Japan. Photographs of men, women, and children, clothed and nude; of people from different cultures and historical eras; of portions of bodies, inside (cells, embryos, skeletons) and out (toes, feet, upper and lower torsos, ears, eyes, throats, breasts); and abstract compositions infuse the book. Represented are photographs of some of the world's eminent photographers.

Ewing's text frames the photographs in each chapter, which explores the significance of a specific theme that ties the photographs together: (1) fragments (the body "in part"), (2) figures (the tradition of the full-figure nude), (3) probes (the realm of scientific exploration), (4) flesh (the "vulnerable, mortal body" with an "emphasis on corporeality"), (5) prowess (dance and sports with the body at its peak physical condition), (6) eros (the body as an object of sexual desire), (7) estrangement (the oppressed and victimized body), (8) idols (the idealized body), (9) mirror (the camera turned on the photographer's own body), (10) politic (the body as a site of contended meaning and value), (11) metamorphosis (the body transformed), and (12) mind (the body in the realm of dream, fantasy, and obsession). The overarching questions of why there is so much concern with the body and how photography has influenced conceptions of the body for more than a century pervade each chapter.

In the process of delving into the assumptions, beliefs, and conceptions that underlie photographs of the human body, Ewing presents a history of photographic philosophy, technology, techniques, and practitioners from the mid-1800s to the present, pointing out how the attitudes of each era influenced the types of images produced and the social responses to them. From the early nineteenth century, medical photographs of patients, daguerreotypes of criminals, and photographs of the nude by Pictorialists or Impressionist photographers to the photographic illustrations of ordinary people and high-fashion models for mass-circulation magazines in the 1920s; from the sculptured images of bodies by Edward Steichen, Alfred Stieglitz's renderings of the body as reflective of the photographer's emotional state, and Imogen Cunningham and Edward Weston's abstract, geometrical explorations of the body as subject to European Surrealist and constructivist montage and collage, reflecting a world in psychological distress; from a continuation of social anxiety reflected in photographs after World War II to the present with its refinements in the techniques and types of photographic expression—photographs of the body are reflective of the tenor of the times in which they occur and the basis for many different interpretations of its images. (SGF)

PO

867. Farber, Robert. **Farber Nudes.** New York: Amphoto, 1983. 148 p. ISBN 0-8174-3851-3.

About this photo album Farber says: "I've tried to capture the diverse spectrum of ways in which the naked human being can be beautiful—comic, peaceful, erotic, stark, mysterious—and to offer some of the thinking and technique which can make that beauty happen in a photograph." To that end he has divided his photographs of nude women and a few men into "The Elegant Nude," "The Romantic Nude," and "The Graphic Nude." The album contains over eighty color plates and eighty-four black-and-white photographs of professional models who were encouraged to relax and express a sense of joy in informal settings on the beach, in the woods, or in a studio.

The description of Farber's photographs as "painterly" is not far off the mark, for his photographs are impressionistic, expressing "harmony, the easy interaction of model and background." To his own question—"Why are the majority of these photographs of women?"—he responds: "I love how women look, act, and move. I've also had a good deal of experience photographing women, both nude and clothed, and I'm continually fascinated by how the female form 'adapts' to its surroundings." In explaining the men in his photographs, Farber says that "a man photographed with a woman can seem, again, like a strong object around which the female flows. I'm fascinated by the visual 'support' a man can give a woman." Included in the album is a special technical section in which Farber explains how he produced each nude photograph: he provides his original notes about lighting, camera settings, type of camera and film used, the model, where photographed, and for what purpose. (TJW)

PO

868. Hamilton, David. **David Hamilton's Private Collection.** New York: Morrow Quill Paperbacks, 1980. 125 p. Copyright 1976 Swan Productions, Switzerland. ISBN 0-688-03053-X.

A blending of innocence and eroticism characterizes Hamilton's photography, beautifully expressed in this collection of some eighty color plates, halftones, and sepia photographs. He frankly portrays pubescent girls in various revealing indoor and outdoor poses, using natural light to illuminate their nudity. His choice of models (slender, leggy, and small-breasted) stresses their innocence. The soft-focus imagery, subdued coloring, and sepia tones almost transform his photographs into paintings. Recognized worldwide as an outstanding photographer of young girls, Hamilton has assembled other photo books on the same theme, including *Dreams of a Young Girl* (1971), *Sisters* (1973), *Tender Cousins* (1981, also a motion picture), and *A Summer in Saint Tropez* (1982), all available from William Morrow and Company. (TJW)

PR,IL,PO

869. Hedgecoe, John. **John Hedgecoe's Nude Photography.** New York: Simon & Schuster, 1984. 223 p. ISBN 0-671-52326-0.

Hedgecoe, a professor of Photography at the Royal College of Art in London, has assembled, organized, and commented on some 150 nude photographs representative of his work. The black-and-white and color prints of mostly female nudes express the themes into which this volume is organized: "Form and Expression," "Mood and Atmosphere," "Perception and Response," and "Fantasy and Illusion." Each picture is captioned, dated, and described; usually the models are identified by name. The accompanying text delves into the essentials that make clear the relationship between the photographs and the perceptions of the photographer. Hedgecoe's photography seems philosophically linked to the ideas expressed by the late Kenneth Clark in his book *The Nude*. He traces the development of nude photography from its imitative beginnings in 1840 to the present, bringing out the similarities and differences between photography and painting, and revealing that much of photography today is tied to advertising and products of the market. Like Clark, he believes that eroticism is inherent in the better depictions of the nude. A practical section on cameras and accessories, lighting equipment, the studio, the model, and photographic techniques used in taking each picture in this collection concludes this handsome volume. He thus provides guidance for the amateur photographer who wishes to take beautiful pictures of the nude. (TJW)

PR,IL
870. Hester, George M. **The Classic Nude.** Garden City, N.Y.: Amphoto, 1973. unpaged. ISBN 0-8174-0554-2.
     This photo album of nudes is the creation of Hester, a well-known New York fashion photographer with a penchant for artistic expression. Made up of 10 color and an estimated 140 black-and-white photographs, the album "attempts to show the body simply, beautifully, and expressively, coupling freedom of spirit with love of the human figure." The figures are all presented against a uniform, plain background in an identical setting and illuminated by a strobe light in front. The chiaroscuro effects and sculptural qualities thus produced are emphasized. The subjects are men, women, and children. Hester used both professional models and amateurs (friends and neighbors) for his subjects and photographed them either singly or in groups. The results are deliberately classical with the focus on the essential, universal qualities of the human body. (TJW)

IL
871. Jones, Terry, ed. **Private Viewing: Contemporary Erotic Photography.** Introduction by Jack Schofield. London: Sphere Books, 1983. 220 p. [est.]. ISBN 0-7221-6351-7.
     Private Viewing presents the work of thirty-five recognized photographers, including such stalwarts as Robert Mapplethorpe, Jean-Paul Goode, and Christian Vogt. Jones includes information about each contributor in a special section in the back of the book where such questions as "What do you feel about erotic photography today?" and "What is your idea of eroticism?" are addressed. The answers, of course, are embodied in their work which, as Jack Schofield points out in the introduction, shows a wide range of erotic attitudes and perspectives from the bondage images of Nobuyoshi Araki's strikingly Japanese pictures to the French endeavors of Jeanloup Sieff, Patrick Demarchelier, and Jean-François Jonvelle.
     Erotic photography as used in this collection "is just a handy term for the pictures produced by the many thousands of photographers who, in different ways and in different fields, under various social and moral codes, use sexuality as an integral part of their images." Much of it is openly commercial, including advertising and newspaper photographs, those for men's magazines, but also embracing photographs for the photographers' own enjoyment, and those intended for exhibition in a gallery.
     Portraiture (Gilles Larrain); fashion (Laurence Sackman); advertising (Cheyco Leidmann); exhibitionism (Albert Watson); classic nudity (Fabrizio Ferri); surrealism (Jeffrey Silverthorne, Occhiomagico, Bob Carlos Clarke); humor (Marcia Reznick); mystery (Olivier Poivre, James Wedge); underwear (Chico Bialas); the unexpected (Andrea Blanch, Chikako Oyama); and the cute (Roberto Carra) are all served by the highly personal and contemporary women in this collection. (TJW)

PO
872. Jonville, Jean-François. **Mistress.** Foreword by Bernard Chapuis. Los Angeles: Melrose, 1983. unpaged. ISBN 0-394-53687-8.

In this photo album of seminude females, Jonville, one of France's foremost fashion photographers and commercial directors, has provided the viewer with an assemblage of over seventy-five black-and-white candidly erotic snapshots of his favorite friends and "loves." In the introduction, Bernard Chapuis characterizes these scenes as "domestic eroticism," in which the photographer glimpses intimate moments usually reserved for a lover; the exposed breasts, buttocks, and pudenda of subjects are informal aspects of carrying out their mundane activities. Most of the shots are taken in an apartment; the young women seem unposed, even surprised at the picture taking, as they are captured in the process of engaging in an ordinary activity—taking off or putting on clothing, washing while seated on a bidet, kissing, lounging, sleeping, primping, looking through windows, reading, and so forth. Viewers are likely to be pleased by the informality, familiarity, and intimacy that the book expresses. As Jonville comments, "the most beautiful thing imaginable is to live with somebody you love, to share all the little things together, share confidences, share yourself." It is interesting to note that he touchingly sandwiches these seminude shots of his loves between the clothed photographs of his mother and grandmother, who are portrayed separately on the endpapers of the book. (TJW)

IL
873. Kaleya, Tana. **Les Hommes.** New York: Harmony Books, 1974. unpaged. ISBN 0-517-52437-6.

Kaleya, Polish artist/photographer, presents her interpretation of masculine virility and sensuality in this photographic collection celebrating the male body. Her artistically moody poses of young boys and men are accompanied by text from the sonnets of Michelangelo, the great Italian painter and sculptor of the fifteenth and sixteenth centuries whose models also were primarily male. In forty-seven plates representing the upper body and nudes in halftones and sepia, Kaleya tries to capture the pensive moods of men at different stages in their physical development from youth to maturity.

In 1980, continuing her use of mood-capturing soft light, Kaleya published her second album, *Women*, a collection of fifty photographs that attempt to answer the eternal question: "Who am I?" (TJW)

PR,IL
874. Kelly, Jain, ed. **Nude: Theory.** New York: Lustrum Press, 1979. 175 p. ISBN 0-912810-24-6.

Eight internationally recognized photographers—Manuel Alvarez Bravo, Harry Callahan, Lucien Clergue, Ralph Gibson, Kenneth Josephson, André Kertész, Duane Michals, and Helmut Newton—present their views of nude photography in this volume of essays and black-and-white pictures. Although nude photography is only one of the genres in which several of these photographers work, they all seem to enjoy working with the nude, some even specializing in it. The essays reveal the likes and dislikes each photographer has for certain types of models and particular settings as well as their preferences in cameras, equipment, and printing techniques. The result is an intimate look at the interesting ways these masters accomplish their work and view this unique form of photography.

Lucien Clergue, influenced by sculpture, believes that "nudes in the sea represent an affirmation of life"; Ralph Gibson likes to photograph parts or sections of the nude (buttocks, breasts) to produce abstractions; André Kertész tries to add the human touch to everything he photographs, including his mirror-distorted nudes; for his work, fashion photographer Helmut Newton, whose ideal nude is erotic, prefers large women with good legs. Since the 1930s, Manuel Alvarez Bravo has used bandages on his nudes to produce surrealistic effects; Harry Callahan, whose favorite model is obviously his wife, characteristically double-exposes photographs of the nude against a sylvan background; Kenneth

Josephson uses an "images-within-images" technique on faceless models to compile his oblique view of the history of photography; and Duane Michals prefers women who are not too voluptuous and men who are not too muscular in his search for the perfect classical nude. A biographical sketch with accompanying portrait of each photographer is included at the end of the book. (TJW)

IL

875.   Mark, Mary Ellen. **Falkland Road.** London: Thames and Hudson, 1981. 17 p. + 65 plates. ISBN 0-500-54072-1.
        The sixty-five color photographs in this album were taken between October 1978 and January 1979, under difficult circumstances, by Mary Ellen Mark, a Fulbright scholar and photographer of note. She had tried to photograph the prostitutes of Falkland Road for ten years but was usually rebuffed on each occasion; eventually, she was able to earn the respect of prostitutes and transvestites, who now invited her into their cages and rooms to take their pictures.
        Falkland Road, in the slums of Bombay, India, is renowned as a street of brothels; it is lined with wooden buildings. As Mark points out in the introduction: "On the ground floor there are cage-like structures with girls inside them. Above these cages the buildings rise three or four stories, and at every window there are more girls—combing their hair, sitting in clusters on the windowsills, beckoning to potential customers. They vary in age from eleven-year-old prostitutes to sixty-five-year-old ex-madams" (p. 11). From dawn until dusk, customers, young and old, walk up and down the busy street, surveying the girls, who "do everything to attract the men: they beckon and shout and grab at them; sometimes they pull up their skirts and make obscene gestures" (p. 11).
        The pictures vividly portray the life of the prostitutes, madams, and transvestites, who are shown in their ordinary colorful attire as well as in the nude, and sometimes in bed with their customers. Photographer Mark got to know some of them quite well; where they came from, their hopes and dreams, and their realistic attitudes toward life.
        Mark's persistent efforts have resulted in an unusual photographic work that gives in words and pictures an intimate and unforgettable glimpse not of the world of fancy brothels or expensive call girls but of the everyday world of prostitution that is Falkland Road. (TJW)

PR,IL

876.   Marshall, Richard. **Robert Mapplethorpe.** With Essays by Richard Howard and Ingrid Sischy. New York: Whitney Museum of American Art, 1988. 216 p. Includes bibliography. ISBN 0-87427-060-X.
        Published in conjunction with the Whitney Museum of American Art's 1988 retrospective of Mapplethorpe's work, this book presents 130 photographs, 45 in color, that provide a comprehensive overview of the themes and subjects that he covered for two decades, until his death in 1989. The Museum's director describes Mapplethorpe as "one of the most astonishing talents to enliven art of the past decade" (p. 7).
        Mapplethorpe's still lifes, portraits, and figures elicit admiration, discomfort, disgust, and almost always controversy. He applies a medium of light, the camera, to subjects often shrouded in darkness—sexuality and eroticism. Images of sensuality, homoeroticism, intimacy, sadomasochism, and danger are among his central themes. Three essays included in the book provide insight into Mapplethorpe's work.
        Richard Marshall, Associate Curator of Exhibits at the Whitney, notes that Mapplethorpe expanded both the technical and aesthetic boundaries of traditional photography. He attempted to reconcile the figurative/emotive/intuitive with the abstract/geometrical/logical. In addition, he used sexually charged images to confront and elicit viewers' participation in his art.
        Ingrid Sischy, former editor of *Artforum*, comments that Mapplethorpe's ability to transgress categories of nature and culture accounts for some of the "shock" and "magic" of his photographs. Images of female bodybuilders express the strength of the "weaker sex," light rather than darkness reflects on the faces of two nude males kissing each other;

black males display their nudity without shame. Sischy comments, "This is work that is ultimately about no coverup, no censorship, no shameful secrets, no burial of what should be seen and what must be remembered" (p. 88). The explosion of sexual secrets may be the source of some viewers' outrage. The intimacy, that "runs through it (his work) like a hidden zipper," closes the distance between the viewer and the image; the artist and his subject; the "real world" and the studio.

Richard Howard, Professor of Comparative Literature at the University of Cincinnati, says that Mapplethorpe's photographs show the "contradictions of organic life in their aspiration to ecstasy" (p. 159). Flowers, the sex organs of plants, suggest analogies to human genitals and aspects of gender. Faces express the power of the flesh, as do photographs of nude bodies in austere, often bare settings.

Mapplethorpe said, "My work is about seeing—seeing things like they haven't been seen before." His photographs are expressions of his intention as well as vehicles for confronting contemporary fears about socially taboo subjects, particularly sexuality. (SGF)

PO

877. **Masterpieces of Erotic Photography.** New York: Greenwich House, 1977. 175 p. ISBN 0-517-38865-0.

Twelve internationally known photographers present a sampling of their work in this collection of erotic photographs. All of the artists are men; practically all of their subjects are women exuding sexuality in one form or another. Each artist presents a variation of a theme: "images of women and sexuality as seen through men's eyes . . . [expressing] what men hold to be erotic in the female form." For example, Jeanloup Sieff, the Parisian photographer, is represented by eleven black-and-white plates of attractive nudes suggestively exposing their derrieres and pudenda. It is stated that "his women stand doubly bared, for he reveals not only their bodies, but also their private passions." Kishin Shinoyama, a well-known Japanese photographer, presents a set of portraits of identical sisters "which expresses a profound insight into the nature of eroticism and underlines the narcissism of self-love inherent in such relationships." Christian Vogt is quoted as saying "eroticism is the intellectual way of enjoying sex"; his sequence of pictures, captioned *Bathroom Fantasy*, "elicits erotic feelings by the use of opposing symbols, creating a play of tensions between the hard and the soft, the cold and the warm." This collection seems to bear out that dictum. An introduction by the photographer Michael Pellerin describes the collection as a whole and makes no apologies for the claim that the items chosen for it have been labeled masterpieces of erotic photography. (TJW)

PR,IL

878. Minkkinen, Arno Rafael, ed. **New American Nudes: Recent Trends and Attitudes.** Dobbs Ferry, N.Y.: Morgan & Morgan, 1981. 109 plates. ISBN 0-87100-178-0.

In this collection of nude photographs, seventy-four photographers present work that was shown at the Creative Photography Gallery at the Massachusetts Institute of Technology in 1981. It is composed of male and female nude photographs selected from a submission of 3,500 photographs taken over the previous five years by 450 photographers.

Minkkinen has attempted to present "a cross-section of approaches and attitudes in contemporary nude photography." Gone, says Minkkinen, are the canons of nudity recognized by Kenneth Clark in his book *The Nude: A Study in Ideal Form*. Clark stated that the nude, which he distinguished from the naked, carries the vague mental image "not of a huddled and defenseless body, but of a balanced, prosperous and confident body; the body re-formed." Minkkinen maintains that "contemporary photography has little patience with theories of art that cannot accept our wrinkles, imperfections, and unruly pubic hairs."

In contrast to most anthologies of the nude, the 110 mostly black-and-white photographs in this selection represent a striking effort to include a balanced ratio of male and female nudes. The different photographs embrace a remarkable variety of styles. Except for Robert Mapplethorpe's portraits of Lisa Lyons and a few others, most of the photographs were taken in a studio environment. The collection includes frontal shots that sharply highlight details (George Dureau's *Short Sonny*), visual experimentation with complexity

(Vahe Guzelimian's *Climbing the Matterform*), background material directing attention to the subject (Minkkinen's own *Self-Portrait*), innovative lighting in the color photographs (Paul Light's *Nude: Linda*), pictures incorporating rather than avoiding the face (Minnette Lehmann's *Henry W.* and Judith Black's haunting *Self-Portrait*), examples of honest eroticism (Sarah Putnam's untitled nude with slightly parted knees), and group nudes (Lynn Kellner's lovely *Lily and Her Three Girls* and Harvey Stein's humorously erotic *"Miss Nude America"* lineup).

One could agree with Minkkinen that in viewing these new-style nudes one experiences a shared intimacy, even affinity, with many of these everyday bodies and faces. (TJW)

IL

879. Nazarieff, Serge. **The Stereoscopic Nude, 1850-1930.** Preface by Jacques Cellard. Berlin: Benedikt Taschen Verlag, 1990. 160 p. Includes footnotes to photographs. Text in German, English, and French.

This unusual collection consists mainly of 214 photographic prints of nude and seminude women from the early days of stereoscopic photography. Some are stereoscopic daguerreotypes; others are stereoscopic images on paper or glass. Viewing these nudes is accomplished by using a viewing glass (provided by the publisher) that gives a striking three-dimensional effect. In his introduction, Nazarieff presents a history of the development and application of the stereoscope in photography. He also comments on the work of the early photographers using the stereoscopic technique.

Nazarieff has organized the collection into four periods: "The Birth of an Art Form (1850-1855)"; "The Second Empire (1852-1870)," that introduced formal (academic) nude study and pornography; "The Belle Epoque (1885-1910)," that focused on voyeurism; and "The Roaring Twenties (1920-1935)," that is characterized by the appearance of fetishism. This book "summarizes an important chapter in the history of nude photography over a period of nearly a hundred years" (p. 13).

The volume concludes with a section devoted to biographical notes on the early photographers and a final section of information on each of the photographs in the collection. (TJW)

PO

880. Newton, Helmut. **Big Nudes.** Introduction by Karl Lagerfeld. New York: Xavier Moreau, 1982. unpaged. Includes bibliography. ISBN 0-937950-02-5.

Despite the fact that the thirty-nine full-page, black-and-white photographs in this album were taken in France (Paris, Nice, Saint Tropez), Italy (Brescia), Monte Carlo, and the United States (Los Angeles, Beverly Hills, Venice), there is a teutonic quality about them that perhaps may be attributed to Newton's apprenticeship as a photographer in Berlin in the 1930s. Two of his models, Gayle Olinekova and Lisa Lyon, display strength and agility; the remainder are statuesque types who convey a sense of size and monumentality. The introduction to Newton's work, written by Karl Lagerfeld, is entitled "Nordfleisch," a term Newton himself has used to characterize his work. Moreover, the world of fashion, characterized by the "artificiality" that Newton loves, has affected his style. Although setting and decor are important in his work, so is time. This is exemplified by the pairs of photographs taken in Brescia, Italy. These show first a fully clothed model and then, perhaps an hour later, the same model posed in precisely the same way, but naked. This approach brings out the uniqueness of the moment, the contrasting photographs highlighting the differences time and clothing impose on the model. The expression "big nudes" probably derives from the gallery of photographs of tall, nude women posed against white backgrounds either standing or stepping, their arms positioned variously: akimbo, folded overhead, swinging, and so forth. Props are kept to a minimum: cowboy boots, taut chain held overhead, plastic mattress, fur coat, and almost invariably spike heels accentuating the models' heights. The nudity depicted is basically frontal, whether hanging from a trapeze, leaning against a tree or wall, or descending a stairway.

A sadness at the momentariness in Newton's work is conveyed by the quote from Shakespeare's *Cymbeline* appearing at the front of the album beneath an x-ray photograph of a woman's skull above an elaborate necklace: "Golden lads and girls all must, as chimney-sweepers, come to dust." (TJW)

IL,PO

881. Newton, Helmut. **White Women.** Designed by Bea Feitler. New York: Stonehill, 1976. 107 p. ISBN 0-88373-053-7.

Newton is noteworthy as a high-fashion photographer who developed a new style of erotic (and often shocking) fashion photography. He presents about eighty selections of his works in this photo album that he says contains what he calls his "erotic pictures and everyday portraits." Here he depicts nude or seminude women in an assortment of precise, formal settings (hotel rooms, gardens, swimming pools) in such places as Saint Tropez, Nice, Cannes, and Arles in France and in other scattered locations around the world. In one series of colorful pictures taken at Villa d'Este, Lake Como, Italy, Newton's models pose stiffly yet erotically in elegant formal settings. Some of his pictures are startling and bizarre: the series of scenes of men slain by distraught women, or the formally attired giant lifting the veil of the naked pocket Venus seated on an outsized plain table. Themes of control over subjects coupled with a sense of mischief pervade his work, as in the erotic scene in the reclining seat of a black limousine captioned "Eiffel Tower." Newton says: "There must be a certain look of availability in the women I photograph. I think the woman who gives the appearance of being available is sexually much more exciting than a woman who's completely distant. This sense of availability I find erotic." One night Newton found the actress Charlotte Rampling in a hotel room in Arles and there photographed her in the nude gracefully seated on a table. (TJW)

PO

882. Sappho. **The Art of Loving Women: The Poetry of Sappho.** Photography by J. Frederick Smith. New York: Chelsea House, 1975. 159 p. ISBN 0-87754-255-4.

In this photo album, artist/photographer Smith devotes his talent to extolling the beauty of young women in moments of shared intimacy. The soft-focus color photographs of nude and loosely attired females, in pairs and triplets, exemplify the accompanying poetry of Sappho, the famed poetess of ancient Greece. *The Art of Loving Women* is obviously not a single poem but rather surviving fragments of Sappho's immoral verse and represents different aspects of love between women. A fair example is

> You have come—it is well—
> How I longed for you!
> And once more you add fire
> To the fire of love in my heart!
> Blessings, many blessings, fall
> On us for as long as we were apart! (p. 101)

Such moving poetry, blended with artistic photography, abounds in this attractive volume. Sappho's translators are listed on the last page and include such renowned poets as Swinburne, Ben Jonson, Rossetti, and Ezra Pound. (TJW)

PR,IL,PO

883. Steinberg, David, ed. **Erotic by Nature: A Celebration of Life, of Love, and of Our Wonderful Bodies.** San Juan, Calif.: Shakti Press/Red Alder Books, 1988. 212 p. ISBN 0-933211-03-1.

The goal of this work is to offer "an alternative to pornography, one that encourages us all to be fully erotic, fully sexual beings, without alienating ourselves, our deepest human values, or the people with whom we are most intimately involved. It represents only the beginning of what is possible when erotic and sexual themes are addressed ethically and artfully" (p. iv).

In his five years of preparation for this book, editor/author Steinberg confronted a number of cultural issues about the representation of sex in American society. He wanted to choose quality erotica, not materials that reduce sex to "the silly clichés and grand exaggerations of locker room humor." However, he found that even the "best" of pornography trivializes relationships and sex; it does not connect with the ordinary person's experience. In conducting his workshops on pornography, erotica, and sexual fantasy, Steinberg found that men enjoy an "unapologetic focus on sex" while women expressed a theoretical interest in erotic images and stories. However, the legitimate media portray sex as "titillating, simplified, and superficial." Artists avoid sexual themes for fear of ridicule. Respectable galleries or publishers rarely display directly erotic materials. Consequently, the sex phobia of American society allows few vehicles for presenting an alternative to pornography. In this book, Steinberg hopes to remedy this deficiency.

Drawing on the works of 36 women and 25 men of all ages and from all sections of the country, Steinberg compiles 122 duotone photographs, 17 drawings, 15 short stories, and 38 poems that he thinks celebrate the positive, life-affirming, joyous and powerful aspects of sex. Stories and poems alternate with photographs clustered around twelve themes: body forms, connections, men and women, awakening, sex play, male nudes, women in nature, close-ups, introspections, for love, metawomen, and surrender. Homosexual and heterosexual couples are shown in these sections as well as interpretations of male and female sexuality. Images range from graphic pictures of couples engaging in sex play and intercourse to almost abstract depictions of sexuality. Steinberg hopes that the collection will encourage us "to expand our erotic sensibilities to include everything from light-hearted play to confronting the deepest aspects of personal identity and interpersonal communication" (p. iv). (SGF)

IL

884. Sullivan, Constance, ed. **Nude Photographs: 1860-1980.** New York: Harper & Row, 1980. 203 p. Includes bibliographic references.

As Sullivan emphasizes in the foreword, the 134 mostly black-and-white photographs of nudes—mostly female—in this album display an inherent eroticism that emerges regardless of the artistic, documentary, or commercial circumstances of the photographs. She culled the collections of art galleries, museums, libraries, public and private collections throughout Europe and the United States to assemble these examplars of the history of Western nude photography.

From the anonymous prints of circa 1850-1855 through the early classic work of Thomas Eakins, Alfred Stieglitz, Edward Steichen, Edward Weston, and Man Ray, to the experimental efforts of André Kertész, Manuel Alvarez Bravo, Harry Callahan, David Hockney, Sheila Metzner, among others, the pleasure of viewing beautiful bodies proceeds unwaveringly.

Supporting the spirit and intention of this work are two lengthy essays: Robert Sobieszek's *Addressing the Erotic: Reflections on the Nude Photograph*, that examines closely the notion of eroticism in nude photography; and Ben Maddow's *Nude in a Social Landscape*, that extols nudity and nakedness both in literature and art and comments on individual works of photographers in this collection. (TJW)

PR,IL

885. Szarkowski, John, ed. **E. J. Bellocq: Storyville Portraits: Photographs from the New Orleans Red-Light District, Circa 1912.** Preface by Lee Friedlander. Edited by John Szarkowski. New York: Museum of Modern Art, 1979. 88 p., 34 plates. Copyright 1970 The Museum of Modern Art. ISBN 0-87070-250-5.

Thirty-four duotone pictures of prostitutes who worked in the Storyville district of New Orleans around 1912 make up the body of this volume. They represent the only extant work of the little-known commercial photographer, E. J. Bellocq, a small, misshapen man (reminiscent of Toulouse-Lautrec), who plied his trade for about forty-five years in New Orleans. The pictures, reproduced from prints made from glass plates found in Bellocq's desk after his death, are selections from a total of eighty-nine prints. They depict both clothed and nude women posing in their living quarters. Several prints are defaced and others reveal defects in the glass plates.

The lengthy dialogue in the front of the album with Bellocq's acquaintances—a prostitute, a musician, and a photographer—and the editor and others provides a remarkable portrait of the eccentric Bellocq as well as his unique relationship with the Storyville prostitutes.

Lee Friedlander, the photographer who made the prints for this collection and arranged for their publication by the Museum of Modern Art, gives this appraisal of Bellocq's prostitutes: "[T]hey are all beautiful. Beautiful innocently or tenderly or wickedly or joyfully or obscenely, but all beautiful, in the sense that they are present, unique, irreplaceable, believable, receptive. Each of these pictures is the product of a successful alliance" (p. 16).

These rare photographs of prostitutes in one of the few legalized red-light districts in the United States, reveal Bellocq "as an artist of considerable skill and uncultivated but compelling sensibility." (TJW)

PO
886. Weston, Edward. **Edward Weston Nudes.** Remembrance by Charis Wilson. His photographs accompanied by excerpts from the Daybooks & Letters. Millerton, N.Y.: Aperture, 1977. 116 p. ISBN 0-89381-026-6.

Weston's nude photographs comprise the largest category of his work. About fifty of these, taken over the years from as early as 1918, have been tastefully assembled in this glossy album. Charis Wilson, his principal model, partner, and eventually wife, writes in her remembrance about her first encounter, in 1934, with Weston's nude photographs, that "nothing could have been farther from 'Art Poses' than Edward's nudes, and I was fascinated by their strong individuality as body portraits. At first I had the same trouble with the peppers, dead birds, and eroded plants—I couldn't get past the simple amazement at how *real* they were" (p. 7). Impressed by the realism of his pictures, Wilson agreed to pose in the nude for him; between the years 1934 and 1945 she was his favorite model and helper. She is the subject of most of the photographs in this album. Several photographs do feature other models, including Weston's young son Neil, the only male nude in the collection. In his search for the "vital essence of things," Weston focused on the nude body rather than on the personality of the model. Even faces are often covered, averted, or entirely omitted. This technique rarely allowed for anything either in the foreground or background, which are kept starkly simple, to not detract from the nude. Edward Weston (1886-1958) was a preeminent American photographer whose work is reminiscent of the style made popular by Alfred Stieglitz and Ansel Adams. (TJW)

Music. Dance. Burlesque

PR,IL
887. Allen, Robert C. **Horrible Prettiness: Burlesque and American Culture.** Chapel Hill, N.C.: University of North Carolina Press, 1991. 350 p. (Cultural Studies in the United States). Includes bibliography and index. ISBN 0-8078-4316-4.

Allen's book examines burlesque not only as popular entertainment but also as a complex and transforming cultural phenomenon. When Lydia Thompson and her controversial female troupe of "British Blondes" brought modern burlesque to the United States in 1868, the result was electric. Their impertinent humor, streetwise manner, and provocative parodies of masculinity brought them enormous popular success—and the condemnation of critics, cultural commentators, and even women's rights campaigners.

Burlesque was a cultural threat, Allen argues, because it inverted the "normal" world of middle-class social relations and transgressed norms of "proper" feminine behavior and appearance. Initially playing to respectable middle-class audiences, burlesque was quickly relegated to the shadow-world of working-class male leisure. In this process the burlesque performer "lost" her voice, as burlesque increasingly revolved around the display of her body.

Locating burlesque within the context of both the social transformation of American theater and its patterns of gender representation, Allen concludes that burlesque represents a fascinating example of the potential transgressiveness of popular entertainment forms, as well as the strategies by which they have been contained and their threats defused.

Allen is Professor of Radio, Television, and Motion Pictures and Associate Dean of the College of Arts and Sciences at the University of North Carolina at Chapel Hill. (Author)

PR,IL

888. Hanna, Judith Lynne. **Dance, Sex and Gender: Signs of Identity, Dominance, Defiance, and Desire.** Chicago: University of Chicago Press, 1988. 311 p. Includes bibliography and index. ISBN 0-226-31551-7.

Anthropologist and dancer Hanna observes, "Sexuality and dance share the same instrument—the human body . . ." (p. xiii), and the medium is part of the message in an important nonverbal communication system. Yet there has been very little attention paid to the meaningful relationship between dance and society, particularly its implications for gender roles and sexuality. Hanna's goal in this book is "to enrich the discourse on male/female body images and social change by spotlighting and clarifying how gender is socially and culturally constructed and transformed in a critical medium of human communication—the dance" (p. 241).

Part 1 focuses on the conceptual links between dance, sex, and gender. Dancers communicate meaning to others by using common signs and symbols, many of which relate to sex and gender. On stage, dancers may express gender and sexual themes by modeling, which conveys power by being captivating, language-like, open-ended, multisensory, persuasive, and accessible. Dance may reinforce, challenge or expand current attitudes about gender. Behind the scenes, dance production and management reflect sexual and gender patterns. Using her own observations and participation in dance; the descriptions of dancers, producers, directors, critics, audiences, scholars, particularly anthropologists and historians; and visuals; Hanna "takes the gender gap issue and places it within the context of an unexplored realm of expressive culture" (p. 42).

Part 2 provides a worldwide overview of erotic and sex-role themes in dances that have occurred in different times and places. Motifs covered are aphrodisiac dancing for licit procreation and illicit prostitution; premarital and extramarital entertainment; love, life, death, and divinity; sex-role scripting; transvestite parody and adulation; sexual sublimation; and coping with sex-role performances. India's complex dance heritage of divine sexuality, eroticism, and fantasy expresses many of the previous themes and is a prelude to the consideration of Western theater dance in part 3.

Male and female patterns of dominance in twentieth-century Western theater dance have fluctuated according to social context. The history of dance as a business which produces dance images and provides an occupation for dancers is instructive. As women developed modern dance, away from the strictures of ballet, men entered the domain and increasingly took over production and performance roles. Hanna focuses on the dance images themselves as they relate to sexuality, spotlighted performances of gender and sexual stories, and choreography. New dance images for women express complexity rather than unilateral views of women while those of men express more themes of sexual conflict and taboo topics such as homosexuality. Hanna concludes that "through their kinetic discourse of moving reality and illusion, dancers, as social beings, create knowledge" (p. 241). Dance taps five dimensions—three spatial ones, one temporal, and one in the imagination. Dance images about sexuality and gender reveal broader aspects of communication, dominance patterns, and social and cultural change, which may affirm or challenge the existing social order. Many black-and-white photographic illustrations complement the text. (SGF)

Media: Magazines, Newspapers, Radio, Television, Film, Video

(For related material see also entries 926, 1023)

IL
889. Durkin, Kevin. **Television, Sex Roles and Children: A Developmental Social Psychological Account.** Philadelphia: Open University Press, 1985. 148 p. Includes bibliography and indexes. ISBN 0-335-15069-1.

Given the primacy of television as a form of mass communication and the sex-role stereotyping included in many programs, there has been increasing concern about the impact of television on the development of sex roles in children. Written from the perspective of social psychology, this book proposes to "assemble and to evaluate the main findings of recent work on television and sex-role acquisition, to point to gaps and limitations in present enquiry, and to sketch a framework around which future research might usefully address some of the remaining questions" (p. 3). It is directed toward students of social science and mass communications.

Durkin begins by defining some key terms (*sex roles, sex-role stereotypes, sexism*) and theories about the mass media (models of cultural ratification, effects, uses and gratification, and scripts). Sex role refers to behavior that society regards as more appropriate to one sex than the other. Based on a review of a large number of analyses of the sex-role content of television, Durkin confirms that television presents a high degree of stereotyped and distorted images of men and women. However, he does not conclude that the influence is necessarily a bad one. After reviewing the evidence for some major theories of sex-role acquisition (biological, environmental, cognitive developmental), he points out the importance of the child's cognition in understanding the world around him or her. Durkin suggests that studying how children interpret what they see on television is probably a fruitful way of understanding the link between television and sex-role development. A review of studies that test the hypothesis that the effect of sex-role stereotyping on children is more intense as more television is watched, shows that such an explanation is too simplistic and that evidence for it is deficient. Furthermore, empirical studies of children's responses to counterstereotyped programs have mixed results. However, they indicate that a combination of such programs with instruction may be an effective way to develop nontraditional views. In conclusion, Durkin suggests that developmental social psychology is a promising orientation for research of this type because it does not merely look at unilinear effects; it acknowledges the active role of the child's cognitive process, differential stages of development, the role of the family, and the influence of the overall sociocultural context. (SGF)

IL
890. Dyer, Richard. **Heavenly Bodies: Film Stars and Society.** New York: St. Martin's Press, 1986. 208 p. Includes bibliography and index. ISBN 0-312-36649-3.

In this study, Dyer examines the images of three Hollywood stars as read by audiences both during their careers and subsequently. Each projected different values: Marilyn Monroe sexuality, Paul Robeson blackness, and Judy Garland's appeal to the male gay community.

The images stars evoke derive from many sources: the star's films and the promotion of those films with pin-ups, public appearances, studio handouts, and interviews. Also, biographies, press coverage, criticism, and image use in novels, songs, and everyday speech assist greatly in the image making.

The individualism of Monroe, Robeson, and Garland was appealing to audiences everywhere. Their star images were not entirely concocted, but rather sprang from such inherent qualities as sexiness, black manliness, and, in Garland's case, of coping with adversity, which so attracted the gay community. Dyer's analysis of Monroe's image illustrates his approach. It takes account of "the ideas about sexuality that circulated in the fifties," one represented by the philosophy promoted by *Playboy* magazine, the other concerned with understanding female sexuality. Monroe, Dyer says, started as a sexual image, specifically the pin-up, and remained so throughout her prolific career until her death. She was always "set up as an object of male sexual gaze." Witness the *Golden Dreams* calendar, picked up by *Playboy* and made the centerfold of the first issue of the magazine in 1953. This image plus what she projected in her many films (*Bus Stop, The Seven Year Itch, The Prince and the Showgirl*, etc.) imprinted notions of her desirability, vulnerability, and innocence on the minds of her admirers. This image, according to Dyer, is an image of female sexuality for men. Linking psychoanalytic concepts of female sexuality with images of Marilyn Monroe, Dyer goes on to argue that Monroe's extraordinary body represents an orgasmic formlessness of unusual appeal. He believes that the meaning of Monroe for us today, decades after her death, must take into account changes that have occurred in the way society now thinks about sex. (TJW)

IL,PO
891. Ellis, Albert. **The Folklore of Sex.** New York: Grove Press, 1961. 255 p.

In contrast to the stress on sexual behavior in the Kinsey reports, Ellis concentrates on the scientific investigation of contemporary American attitudes toward love, sex, and marriage as they are expressed in the mass media. The first editions of *The Folklore of Sex* and its companion volume, *The American Sexual Tragedy* (1962), were based on Ellis's clinical experience with hundreds of clients and an examination of a near 100 percent sample of the mass media (popular magazines, newspapers, radio and television shows, movies, stage shows, popular songs, best-selling novels, and nonfiction books) extant on January 1, 1950. He assumed that the media reflect and influence sexual attitudes. The second editions of these works benefit from an examination of these media extant on January 1, 1960, and the analysis of changes that had occurred in the decade between the research for each edition. Written in a lively, conversational style, these studies consider the possible reasons for contemporary American attitudes toward a variety of topics linked to the broad themes of love, sex, and marriage. *The Folklore of Sex* discusses such issues as the components of sexual behavior (kissing, petting, nudity, masturbation), nonmarital sex, sex crimes, venereal disease, pregnancy, birth control, and social and cultural expressions of sexual attitudes (sex education, romanticism and Puritanism, obscenity, censorship). *The American Sex Tragedy* concentrates more on themes relevant to courtship and marriage: beauty and dress, romantic love, jealousy, weddings, divorce, family relations. Both books are packed with anecdotes and examples from cases and the media that illustrate the attitudes discussed. For example, Ellis comments on adultery: "To live the happy adulterous life and then to be guilty about or punished for being so sublimely happy—this is the American wish and reality today. A great formula . . . for supplying a steady flow of patients for my psychotherapeutic practice. But a little rough . . . on some of my best customers" (*The Folklore of Sex*, p. 51). The trend from 1950 to 1960 was one of increasingly liberal views toward such topics as sexual relations leading to pregnancy, sex organs, desires and expression, sex perversions and crime, and sex control and censorship. Overall, both books graphically demonstrate the inconsistencies, chaos, and conflicts inherent in American sex mores. (SGF)

PR,IL
892. Eysenck, Hans Jurgen, and D. K. B. Nias. **Sex, Violence, and the Media.** New York: St. Martin's Press, 1978. 306 p. Includes index. ISBN 0-312-71340-1.

In addressing the concerns that reading and viewing violent and overtly pornographic materials may influence behavior, Eysenck and Nias present numerous arguments in the controversy and cite studies illustrating four methods of investigation. Single case studies are presented, but their usefulness is dismissed as an approach that lacks power of proof. Field studies, experimental field studies, and laboratory experiments are discussed at length in the three chapters devoted to them. Relevant variables, personality, and other individual differences like libido, gender, and genetic and environmental factors are given extensive treatment.

In presenting their findings Eysenck and Nias distinguish between violence in the media and pornography. All studies, regardless of the method of investigation, demonstrated association between viewing violence in the media and subsequent aggression. They found the evidence convincing enough to recommend social action. They recommend that filmmakers, producers, and others involved in the portrayal of violence be required to become familiar with the literature of research on aggression and that some form of censorship be imposed to ensure "social responsibility." The effects of pornography on readers and viewers can be demonstrated but they are more variable than the effects of violence in the media. Some of the reported effects are efficacious when the material is used in conjunction with marital or sex therapy. In other cases pornography has been shown to trigger guilt, stimulate antisocial sexual behavior, or result in a myriad of other changes both subtle and overt. Eysenck and Nias make a distinction between erotica and sexual material that portrays violence, perversion (sadism, rape, incest), or degradation of women. They recommend censorship of the latter and rewriting of laws dealing with pornography to permit greater objectivity of interpretation. (LF)

PO

893. Gabor, Mark. **The Illustrated History of the Girlie Magazines: From** *National Police Gazette* **to the Present.** New York: Harmony Books, 1984. 181 p. Includes index. ISBN 0-517-54997-2.

In the preface to this profusely illustrated history of "girlie" magazines, Gabor, already well-known for his earlier work, *The Pin-Up: A Modest History* (1972), states that his purpose is "to show, with historical accuracy, the way magazines have presented women's bodies (not women per se) through the years." Girlie magazines essentially contain "sexy" pictures of women that are produced for a male audience. In words and pictures, Gabor presents the history of such magazines, from the weekly *National Police Gazette* (1845-1932) to the current crop of some 100-odd monthlies worldwide. Chapter 1 gives an overview of the industry, stating that the North American audience reached by these magazines is estimated at 80 million monthly. The big three—*Playboy, Penthouse,* and *Hustler*—have circulations of 4.5 million, 3.8 million, and over 1 million respectively. The remaining chapters trace in fascinating detail the growth and development of girlie magazines decade by decade. The 300 black-and-white and full color pictures of women, many shown on original magazine covers, are clearly reproduced and attractively arranged. They range from the demure nudes of an earlier period to the starkly explicit and erotically provocative displays of the present. According to Gabor, the major truth underlying the success of girlie magazines is that "men are endlessly fascinated by sexy pictures of women. That's the truth. That's the way it is" (p. ix). (TJW)

IL,PO

894. Gabor, Mark. **The Pin-Up: A Modest History.** New York: Bell, 1984. 270 p. Originally published in 1972 in New York by Universe Books. Includes bibliography and index. ISBN 0-517-14435-2.

Pin-up art appears in a variety of forms. In *The Pin-Up*, Gabor attempts to present a history of theses erotic art forms from around the time of the *National Police Gazette* to the present. The pin-up, which may not end up on a wall, can be any kind of image that the viewer admires, but it is commonly that of a sexually alluring woman. Gabor defines a pin-up as a "sexually evocative image, reproduced in multiple copies, in which either the expression or the attitude of the subject invites the viewer to participate vicariously in or fantasize about a personal involvement with the subject" (p. 23). The classic style of pin-up, suitable for pinning up on the wall, was dubbed "cheesecake" in 1915. It is found most often in girlie magazines, such as *Playboy*, in movie fan magazines; on wall calendars; or on posters for display in home or office.

Gabor contends that the first true pin-ups were pictures of show girls, dancers, and actresses working in burlesque. These little-known performers exhibited their charms on playing cards, cigarette cards, tobacco cards, and in popular magazines, such as *Munsey's,*

Broadway Magazine, and others. Over the years famous pin-ups have been the Gibson Girl, the Petty Girl, and the Varga Girl, stylized representations of ideal types that appeared in such magazines as the early *Life* and *Esquire*.

Gabor devotes one chapter to the so-called art magazines (*Gay Parisienne, Paris Nights*) and another chapter to girlie magazines proper (*Esquire, Playboy*). He goes on to describe the more popular American fan magazines (*Screen Fun, Film Fun*, etc.) and their genre of pin-up art, including the "sex goddesses" (Clara Bow, Jean Harlow, Mae West, Betty Grable, and others) as well as the heroes of the screen (Rudolph Valentino, Douglas Fairbanks, Sr., Clark Gable, Cary Grant). Calendar pin-ups and poster pin-ups are fully treated in separate chapters. In his final chapter, "Beyond the Cheesecake Tradition," Gabor describes what he calls "quasi-pin-ups" and "pseudo-pin-ups," forms derived from the pin-up idea. Many of these fall into the categories of nudist photography, fetish themes, bondage themes, soft-core pornography, "beaver" poses, and even pin-ups of musclemen.

The 550 or so pictures that complement the text are fully documented. The frontispiece is a color plate of the famous 1951 Marilyn Monroe nude calendar pose *Golden Dreams*. The foreword by Joan Nicholson, entitled "The Packaging of Rape: A Feminist Indictment," presents a feminist perspective on the cheesecake tradition as one of the most exploitative examples of sexism in the media. (TJW)

PR,IL

895. Gellatly, Peter, ed. **Sex Magazines in the Library Collection: A Scholarly Study of Sex in Serials and Periodicals.** New York: Haworth Press, 1981. 142 p. A monographic supplement to *The Serials Librarian*, Vol. 4, 1979, 1980. ISBN 0-917724-16-X.

More than a guide on how to acquire, organize, store, and display sex magazines in the library, this collection of eleven papers, contributed by librarians, law professors, and scholars, examines a variety of legal, historical, organizational, and management questions bearing on the use of this material. For example, Lawrence S. Thompson, a professor of Classics, University of Kentucky, surveys the literary and practical treatment of sexuality in ancient Greece and Rome; Richard C. Dahl, a professor and Director of the Law Library, Arizona State University, in "Sex, Serials and the Law," writes about the legal uncertainties surrounding the definition of obscenity and the determination of what is pornographic in the library; Barrett W. Elcano and Vern Bullough provide a listing of sex serials in "Sexology: A Personal Guide to the Sexual Literature"; and Sanford Berman, a cataloger, has indexed twelve sex periodicals for a hypothetical sex index in the manner of a typical H. W. Wilson Company index. Other papers include "Sex Magazines"; "Sex Magazines: Problems of Acquisition, Retention, Display, and Defense in Public and Academic Libraries"; "Treatment of Sexually Oriented Magazines by Libraries"; "Erotic Magazines and the Law"; "Children's Rights in the Library: A Personal View"; "Sex Themes in Federal Serials"; and "A Select Annotated Bibliography of Gay and Lesbian Periodicals." The contributions are well written and frequently witty; they provide helpful perspectives for librarians pondering not only how to deal with sexual materials in the library but also how to satisfy their social responsibility in providing the public with material it wants to read. (TJW)

IL,PO

896. Haskell, Molly. **From Reverence to Rape: The Treatment of Women in the Movies.** 2nd edition. Chicago: University of Chicago Press, 1987. 425 p. Includes index. ISBN 0-226-31885-0.

In this new edition of her 1974 book (Holt, Rinehart and Winston, 1974), Haskell adds another chapter, "The Age of Ambivalence," that discusses developments in film from 1974 to 1987. She supplements the themes begun in the first edition, that traces the treatment of women in the movies from the 1920s through the 1960s. The last chapter becomes part of a "historical study of the images of women in film as mostly defined and elaborated by men but with many glorious challenges by the presumed female victims" (p. vii).

A film reviewer for the *Village Voice*, a member of the National Society of Film Critics, and a feminist, Haskell discusses films as a film critic first and a feminist second. Basing her interpretations of movies on the link between films and their cultural context, she attempts to show how "movies are one of the clearest and most accessible of looking glasses into the past, being both cultural artifacts and mirrors" (p. xviii). Her witty and opinionated rendition of women's roles in films chronicles changes in attitudes about male/female heterosexual relationships and cultural expectations about the images that women should project in "real life." Haskell argues that the film industry perpetuates the "big lie" of Western society that women are inferior as well as reinforces myths that function to keep women in their place. Overall, she suggests that "a woman's intelligence (is) the equivalent of a man's penis: something to be kept out of sight" (p. 4). Films of the 1920s expressed a vamp/virgin theme, revered the "sex goddess," and emphasized the fantasy qualities of the star. Films of the 1930s followed the restrictive tenets of the Production Code and demonstrated the virtues of self-sacrifice and matrimony, thus reinforcing "the instincts latent in the American psyche at its most romantic, puritanical, immature, energetic, and self-deluding" (p. 21). As women became a potential economic threat to the jobs of men in the 1940s, "movie heroines had to be brought down to fictional size, domesticated or defanged" (p. 8). The postwar films of the 1950s were "about sex but without sex," while the 1960s ushered in a decade of violent and sexual themes torn from the erotic context of romance. In the 1970s and 1980s, the proportion of women directors increased tenfold, but there were still few "positive role models" of women, although there is evidence of more participation of women in the "male-female business of life."

Haskell drew on both scholarly and popular materials to create this book. Her well-written journey into the world of film examines a complex array of subjects: why images of males and females in movies have changed over time, how the star system has been altered, the orientation and impact of critics' comments on audiences, how films express cultural dictates and provide models for how women should behave, and a critique of the film industry. She concludes that for "every stereotype there's a counter-stereotype and the story of women can no longer be reduced to a recitation of evils. . . . We want nothing less, on or off the screen, than the wide variety and dazzling diversity of male options" (p. 402). (SGF)

PO

897.   Lenne, Gérard. **Sex on the Screen: Eroticism in Film.** Translated from the French by D. Jacobs. New York: St. Martin's Press, 1985. 245 p. Translation of: *Le sexe à l'écran.* Includes index. ISBN 0-312-71335-5.

French film critic Lenne states the theme of this book in the beginning: "The state of the cinema echoes the state of mind of the society that produces it" (p. 2). Therefore, the study of eroticism in the cinema can indicate a good deal about contemporary attitudes about sex, particularly in relation to what is acceptable or not (taboos, inhibitions, censorship). The distinction between eroticism (what we think, what we desire) and pornography (what we do) disappears in the cinema, where representation and imagination coincide. The evaluation of a film as erotic, obscene, or pornographic has less to do with the subject matter and more to do with the director's choices of how to portray the content of the film.

Drawing primarily from European and American films from 1895 through 1981, Lenne provides an overview of and commentary on sex in the cinema by categorizing it according to several themes. One theme focuses on the issue of what is natural and what is not. Although nudity is natural and not intrinsically obscene, its portrayal is strictly regulated. In dealing with content that could be interpreted as abnormal or obscene, how does the film-maker avoid censorship and provide enough popular appeal to make money? Some films (*Bringing Up Baby, Bride of Frankenstein, Baby Doll, Splendor in the Grass*) deal with the boundary between thoughts and sensuality, rules and behavior, and science and feeling. Others contain more specific depictions of masturbation (*Portnoy's Complaint, Class of '44*), homosexuality (*Left Handed Gun, Sunday, Bloody*

Sunday, Boys in the Band, Midnight Cowboy, The Damned), rape (*Clockwork Orange, Straw Dogs*), submission (*Belle du Jour*), infantile eroticism (*Lord of the Flies, Lipstick*), sadomasochism (*Johnny Guitar, Shanghai Express*), transvestism (*Some Like It Hot, Rocky Horror Picture Show*), pedophilia (*Taxi Driver*), incest (*Through a Glass Darkly*), and zoophilia.

Another theme is the sacredness of sex; although it is appealing, it is also regarded as untouchable, unreal. However, the "cinema, more than any other medium, served to fetishize sexuality" (p. 94). The star system and myths perpetuated in film about sexuality only enhance its power. Early films portray sex as evil (*Salome, The Vampire, The Blue Angel*) or corrupting. When freed from rules (*King Kong*), sexual interest has a tragic ending. Sex was the driving force of melodrama, and initiation into sexual experience enhances eroticism. Even popular films such as westerns, thrillers, and fantasies have their sexual elements. Although comedies can demystify or negate eroticism, the films of Mae West, the Marx Brothers, Jerry Lewis, and Woody Allen contain a sexual undertone. Like humor, stark realism can demystify sex; age differences (*Harold and Maude*) and death (*Romeo and Juliet*) are expressions of such realism.

A third theme is freedom of expression and the manner in which society has attempted to curtail portrayals of sexuality. Censorship has resulted in two types of cinema—the general and the underground or clandestine; this bifurcation has reinforced the idea that sex is subversive. The Hays Code institutionalized self-regulation of film, but it was difficult to sustain by World War II. Further suppression occurred with investigations by the House Un-American Activities Committee. Nevertheless, the Code began to collapse in the 1960s with the advent of nudity and sexploitation in films. By the 1970s, hard core films proliferated. Cinéma vérité became popular in the 1960s, and female film directors attempted to overcome clichés about women's sexuality by presenting a more authentic version of sexuality. Swinging, initiation into sexual activities, men's experiences of sexuality, nonmarital sex, and passion outside of social approval were often portrayed. More recently, specialized themes have been exploited because of their popular appeal. Unfortunately, both the regular and specialized cinema often show lovemaking with little imagination. Sexism persists, and violence against women is shown more in the regular than specialized cinema. At times, the camera becomes a mechanical voyeur. Lenne characterizes the period between 1978 and 1981 a time of regression. (SGF)

IL

898.   Palumbo, Donald, ed. **Eros in the Mind's Eye: Sexuality and the Fantastic in Art and Film.** New York: Greenwood Press, 1986. 290 p. (Contributions to the Study of Science Fiction and Fantasy, No. 21). Includes bibliography, filmography, and index. ISBN 0-313-24102-3.

As a companion volume to *Erotic Universe: Sexuality and Fantastic Literature* (1986), editor Palumbo states in the preface that this collection of eighteen scholarly papers explores the depiction of sexuality in two-dimensional fantastic art and film. It ranges from medieval woodcuts to horror classics of the 1930s and recent slasher films. Despite the large number of works and the great variety of formats dealt with, the study reveals a surprisingly consistent range of interests, symbols, and themes in these media.

Paul Grootkerk examines occult eroticism in the art of the fifteenth and sixteenth centuries, especially that of the Germanic and Netherlandish nations, interpreting the works of such artists as Hans Baldung Grün, Albrecht Dürer, and Hieronymus Bosch. Liana Cheney provides interpretations of disguised eroticism and sexual fantasy in sixteenth and seventeenth century art using as examples the cinquecento painters (Bronzino, Titian, Correggio) who worked with classical and mythological themes as well as the more restrained versions of the same themes in, say, the Dutch art of Rembrandt and Steen. Kathleen Russo delves into the erotic art of the eighteenth century and the provocative work of Henri Fuseli, William Blake, and Fragonard. Gwendolyn Layne looks at sexuality as represented in the Victorian fantasy illustrations done by such artists as Edward Burne-Jones, Gustave Doré, Dante Gabriel Rossetti, and John Tenniel. Francine Koslow takes on surrealist art with the creations of Salvador Dali, René

Magritte, and Paul Delvaux. Sylvie Pantalucci continues with surrealist sexual themes, discussing the work of Joan Miro and René Magritte.

Gwendolyn Layne brings out the subliminal seduction in contemporary fantasy illustrations and compares it to what is done in advertising. Sarah Clemens analyzes erotic imagery in contemporary movie poster art.

In "The Beast Within," Leonard Heldreth argues that the metamorphoses of the werewolf in film symbolize the physical changes and psychological consequences of puberty. Anthony Ambrogio explains Fay Wray's role in the horror film *King Kong*, and Martin Norden comments on the sexual references in *Bride of Frankenstein*. John Kilgore discusses sexuality and identity in *The Rocky Horror Picture Show* and Raymond Ruble gives a Freudian interpretation of the same film. Another Freudian interpretation is found in Anthony Ambrogio's analysis of *Alien*. Jim Holte explains the puritan ideology in the American science fiction film.

Anthony Gordon looks at the power of the "force" in the *Star Wars* trilogy from a sexual standpoint, and Mary Jo Deegan reveals the sexism and Freudian formula in the same film. Finally, Sam Umland looks at sexual freaks and stereotypes in recent science fiction and fantasy films.

Recognizing that sexuality in fantastic art and film is a subject with many dimensions, Palumbo refers the reader to the extensive bibliography, filmography, and list of artworks at the back of the volume. (TJW)

PO

899.   Rimmer, Robert H. **The X-rated Videotape Guide.** New York: Arlington House, 1984. 408 p. Includes index. ISBN 0-517-54899-2.

Over the last ten years, the combination of filmmaking with videotape distribution has led to a burgeoning adult film industry, which has "laid the groundwork for erotic art for the masses" (p. 11). This book is essentially a guide to videotapes of X-rated and pornographic films usually available from a local distributor. Rimmer, well known for his novel *The Harrad Experiment* (1967), wrote and compiled this book because he thinks that "the sexvid explosion . . . will eventually set the stage for a new kind of visual sex" (p. 9). In this work Rimmer reviews, categorizes, and rates 650 sexvids (as he dubs the X-rated videotapes) produced between 1970 and 1983, all of which he has viewed, and adds a supplemental listing of some 2,000 adult films he has not seen. Most of the sexvids included are produced for male audiences and emphasize heterosexual and bisexual activities; no homosexual materials are covered. Rimmer introduces a useful rating system that divides the films into Normal (N) and Deviational (D), each division further subdivided according to the character of the particular films. For example, NL means Normal—laughing and bawdy sex; NR, Romantic or deeply caring sex; DS, Deviational sadistic, violent and victimized sex; and so forth. He also has a Collector's Choice (CC) rating, reserved for more than 100 of his favorites. Rimmer's comments are descriptive rather than critical evaluations of the films.

The sexvids, in the main filmography, are organized into thirteen categories, including "Classics," "The Education of a Virgin," "Comedies," "Historical," "Travelogues," "Supernatural," "Star Vehicles," "Cops and Robbers," "Family Sagas," "Role Playing," "Fetishes," "Vignettes," and "Current Releases." Rimmer introduces the book with five opinionated essays: "The Coming Sexvid Explosion"; "A Quick Look at the Adult Film Industry"; "Plots, Conventions and Hang-ups of Sexvids"; "Uncloistering Virtues . . . or Rating the Sexvids"; and "Making Your Own Sexvids." A center section features photographs of favorite male and female performers; a special section lists the names and addresses of distributors of adult films in the United States. (TJW)

IL,PO

900.   Robinson, Phillip, and Nancy Tamosaitis. With Peter Spear and Virginia Soper. **The Joy of CyberSex: The Underground Guide to Electronic Erotica.** New York: Brady, 1993. 331 p. Includes bibliography and index. ISBN 1-56686-107-1.

Tamosaitis and Robinson have teamed up to write a comprehensive guide to the burgeoning world of cybersex. This book's four sections include a user's guide, a tour of online adult bulletin boards, a review of erotic CD-ROMs and disks, and an examination of the new field of interaction in the artificial worlds of virtual reality.

Since most cybersex requires a computer, section 1 explains what kind of computer is best, how to set it up, and then how to use the various resources described in later sections. In section 2, husband and wife team Peter Spear and Virginia Soper take a decidedly irreverent look at the field of erotic disks. CD-ROMs, that look just like the popular audio CD disk, are optical disks that contain digitized information with graphics and sounds. There are now hundreds of CD-ROMs packed with adult images, ranging from French postcards of the 1920s to models in lingerie, to interactive nude photo shoots.

In section 3, Tamosaitis leads the reader on a tour of thirty of the most lively adult bulletin board services (BBS). BBSs are computer forums set for computer users to call into and exchange messages and pictures. There are thousands of such boards, and many of them have adult areas or are entirely devoted to adult topics. This chapter describes how they work, what kind of people you'll run into there, what kind of erotic images can be found online, and how you can actually meet, or avoid meeting, bulletin board folks in the flesh.

The final chapter is devoted to exploring cybersex visions, an exploration of the whole new virtual universe. This section of the book explains what virtual reality is and how it may change the way sex is experienced by many in the future. Robinson looks at who is creating and monitoring the new media, and talks with men and women at a new breed of magazines, cinema companies, and software development companies who are striving to turn fantasy into reality. (Author)

IL,PO

901. Rosen, Marjorie. **Popcorn Venus.** New York: Avon, 1974. 448 p. Includes bibliography and index. ISBN 0-380-00177-2.

Images in the movies are molded by the audience's attitudes; they are not imposed on a passive public. But how do the public's will, the film industry's agenda, and women's views intersect in films? Does art reflect life or vice versa? How have women chosen or been encouraged to view themselves in films? In charting the course of women in film from the beginning of movies through the early 1970s, avid film buff Rosen addresses these questions, beginning with the premise that "the Cinema Woman is a Popcorn Venus, a delectable but insubstantial hybrid of cultural distortions" (p. 10).

Each part of her chronicle of women in film, which proceeds decade by decade, demonstrates the link between the significant social and cultural developments in the decade and images of women in film. Part 1, "Emerging from Victorianism," describes how the birth of the movies coincided with and hastened the genesis of the modern woman. Women, who made up a little more than 18 percent of the working population in 1900, were drawn to the cinema by glimpses of the male world. Until 1920 Mary Pickford became the darling of the working class and Victorianism. By 1919, when the nineteenth amendment granted women the right to vote, women were not very tolerant of male oriented themes. Part 2, "Wet Dreams in a Dry Land," describes how women, who made up 25 percent of the workforce, made the 1920s roar. However, the image of women in films was divorced from reality. Images of freedom were at odds with the reality of women earning 60 percent of male wages and other constraints on their roles. By the 1930s, after the collapse of the stock market in 1929, women were in desperate straits; 2 million (20 percent) women would soon be out of jobs. Films of the 1930s did not show existing conditions. Instead, they portrayed supposed independent women whose underlying agenda was marriage. Women became "celluloid aphrodisiacs." Part 3, "The Thirties—Sacrificial Lambs and the Politics of Fantasy," shows how "blondes had the most fun"; Jean Harlow became the "Number One Bad Girl," and other blondes, e.g., Mae West, Ginger Rogers, Marion Davies, Carole Lombard, Miriam Hopkins, enjoyed popularity. Garbo, Dietrich, Davis, Shearer, Stanwyck, and Hepburn also rose in importance. However, when the Japanese bombed Pearl Harbor on December 7, 1941, social roles shifted dramatically. Part 4, "The Forties—Necessity as the Mother of

Emancipation," focuses on the changes. Women took over men's jobs. Women's pictures portraying the sacrifices of love dominated in the early 1940s. When men returned from the war in 1945, film noir reigned, depicting women in roles that accentuated the evil of assertive women and the ambivalence of other women. Part 5, "The Fifties—Losing Ground," asserts that only segments of women's complexity were shown by the 1950s, an era dominated by "mammary madness," e.g., Marilyn Monroe, and greater recognition of the growing influence of adolescents. By the 1960s and early 1970s, singles, flower children, and thrillers became the foci of films. Part 6, "Sixties into Seventies—Revolution and Renaissance?" discusses the final demise of the star system and the ascendance of foreign films that portrayed women as integrated personalities. Rosen thinks the time has come for women to participate in film production and direction in a more substantial way. "It is time to start utilizing feminine resources. And reinterpreting the American Dream" (p. 404). (SGF)

PO

902. Smith, Kent, Darrell W. Moore, and Merl Reagle. **Adult Movies: Rating Hundreds of the Best Films for Home Video & Cable.** New York: Beekman House, 1982. 252 p. ISBN 0-517-39871-0.

Over 8,000 adult films have been made over the years, about 2,000 of which are on videocassette. In this guide 205 of the best films are reviewed and rated, including films for general distribution to the public: Fellini's *Satyricon* (1969), Kubrick's *A Clockwork Orange* (1971), and Bertolucci's *Last Tango in Paris* (1973). As masterpieces these films were awarded four stars by the editors. Other adult films deemed masterpieces are *The Devil in Miss Jones* (1972) and *The Opening of Misty Beethoven* (1976), which received their distribution through the porno theaters. The rating for the oldest adult film in this compilation, *The Immoral Mr. Teas* (1959) is only one star (watchable), while that for the most renowned adult film of all time, *Deep Throat* (1959), is only two stars (recommended).

According to the introduction, "an adult film is a feature-length film that shows, with varying degrees of candor, human lovemaking. It may be a comedy, a drama, or even a documentary." Again, "an adult film is not pornography. Pornography is a work that is obscene, that transcends the moral codes of its society. Our society has changed such in recent years that works once considered obscene are no longer" (p. 10). The editors evaluate these films in terms of acting, casting, script, production values, directing, theme, and humor. On the basis of subject matter they also categorize the films as graphic, erotic, or taboo. The arrangement of the reviews is alphabetical by movie title interspersed with brief sketches of the characteristics and background of thirty-three porno stars. Included in these portraits are such personalities as Marilyn Chambers, Annette Haven, Veronica Hart, Seka, John Holmes, and Harry Reems. Linda Lovelace is conspicuously absent from the group. Looking toward the future, the editors say that the "new trend now is towards subtler treatment of the sex acts. The semi-ridiculous orgasm shots are dying out. The cinematography is less gynecological and more erotic" (p. 11). So it goes. (TJW)

PR,IL

903. Studlar, Gaylyn. **In the Realm of Pleasure: Von Sternberg, Dietrich, and the Masochistic Aesthetic.** Urbana, Ill.: University of Illinois Press, 1988. 247 p. Includes bibliographic notes and index. ISBN 0-252-01536-3.

Studlar, a professor of film studies at Emory University, offers an alternative to Freudian and Lacanian theories of visual pleasure that conventionally have aligned dominant cinema's pleasures with sadistic voyeurism and the satisfaction of male spectatorial needs. Using as its chief example the von Sternberg/Dietrich films produced at Paramount between 1930 and 1935, this study begins with a consideration of Gilles Deleuze's *Masochism: An Interpretation of Coldness and Cruelty.* Studlar develops a model incorporating Deleuze's account of masochism but also relying on contemporary object-relations theory that focuses on the role of pre-Oedipality in the formation of perverse fantasies. From this perspective, Studlar seeks to illuminate a broad range of questions about cinematic pleasure for both male and female spectators. That pleasure, it is argued, has been too narrowly conceived within psychoanalytic theories of film that often reduce spectatorial response to the terms of an either/other binary opposition and that inadvertently duplicate the phallocentrism of their psychoanalytic sources.

Through an exploration of films that demonstrate the creative transformation of a masochistic fantasy into art, *In the Realm of Pleasure* describes visual and narrative strategies that evoke the polymorphous possibilities of film experience. To that end, Charles S. Peirce's notion of iconicity is employed to demonstrate how von Sternberg's ambiguously anti-illusionist masochistic heterocosm presents actress Marlene Dietrich in a masquerade of femininity offering sexually subversive pleasures to viewers of both genders.

Finally, the structural similarity of masochistic object relations to the spectator/screen relationship is addressed within the framework of the cinematic apparatus and the concept of the "dream screen." Thus, while *In the Realm of Pleasure* suggests that certain pleasures may be fundamentally inherent in the cinema as a process, the model defined around the "masochistic aesthetic" also opens specific avenues for close textual analysis as it points to the need to reconsider more generally the psychoanalytic and stylistic complexities of Hollywood film practice. (Author)

PR,IL
903a.   Wexman, Virginia Wright. **Creating the Couple: Love, Marriage, and Hollywood Performance.** Princeton, N.J.: Princeton University Press, 1993. 288 p. Includes bibliography and index. ISBN 0-691-01535-X.

The secondary plot of approximately 95 percent of all Hollywood films made before 1960 centered on heterosexual love, relying on the convention of "creating the couple" (i.e., boy meets girl, boy loses girl, boy gets girl). Focusing on this major Hollywood theme of creating the couple, Wexman, Professor of English at the University of Illinois at Chicago, uses a method akin to sociological poetics (i.e., the examination of the relation between textual reading and social history), to "suggest a new strategy for the textual analysis of Hollywood cinema..." (p. xi). Throughout, she grounds her views in detailed analyses of specific films that were influential and/or illustrative of the themes she explores.

The first of four sections introduces the theoretical framework of the study. Viewing movies as social ritual, Wexman draws on concepts from film and literary criticism, history, cultural anthropology, feminism, philosophy, psychology, and political science to link film texts with social history. She asserts that movie stars function as romantic ideals whose portrayals shift with the social contexts to which they relate. Conventions of acting as well as the appearance (e.g., clothing, body type and movement, physical beauty, make-up) and behavior of actors are expressive of shifting norms about gender, sexuality, romantic love, and marriage. A detailed analysis and comparison of *The Maltese Falcon* with *The Big Sleep* illustrate how the films' narrative patterns and the stars' personae and acting techniques express ideologies of love and marriage epitomized in the process of creating the couple.

Other sections of the book further illustrate the ways that various styles of film performance relate to shifting social norms. In "Patriarchal Marriage and Traditional Gender Identities," Wexman demonstrates how traditional norms of patriarchal marriage and gender are expressed in directing style and genre. D. W. Griffith's direction of Lillian Gish in such silent films as *Way Down East* and *Orphans of the Storm* epitomizes women as helpless victims in need of men's protection, particularly in marriage. The films of the quintessential Western hero, John Wayne, show the genre of Western films expressing a property-centered view of relationships with dynastic marriage at its core. In "Companionate Marriage and Changing Constructions of Gender and Sexuality," Wexman examines gender distinctions in film, particularly the role of beauty and glamour in female performances (e.g., Gloria Swanson in *Sunset Boulevard*) and the role of method acting in portrayals of conflicted masculinity (e.g., Marlon Brando in *On the Waterfront*). In the last section, "Beyond the Couple," Wexman analyzes *Nashville*, *House of Games*, and *Do the Right Thing* as illustrations of the link between Hollywood's self-reflexive acting styles and a social context in which the monogamous marriages of couples are breaking apart and expanding into new modes of relating. (SGF)

Advertising

PR,IL
904. Goffman, Erving. **Gender Advertisements.** Introduction by Vivian Gornick. New York: Harper & Row, 1979. 84 p. Includes bibliographies. ISBN 0-06-090633-0.

Noted sociologist Goffman tackles the task of understanding gender advertisements by viewing them in the broader context of rituals that maintain social life and contribute to an individual's sense of self. Three essays precede the presentation of photographs that Goffman collected from newspapers and current popular magazines easily available to him. The first, "Gender Display," establishes the overall theoretical perspective of the work. Display, part of expressive behavior, can be viewed as a ritual (a single fixed element of a ceremony) that contributes to affirming social arrangements and presents broad views of the relationship between humans and their world. Gender displays can then be interpreted as conventionalized portrayals of gender ("the culturally established correlates of sex") that guide perceptions about the way gender should be. The sources of images for gender displays are cultural and include not only the animal world but also parent-child relations; they do not express any inherent biological difference between male and female behavior. "What characterizes persons as sex-class members is their competence and willingness to sustain an appropriate schedule of display: only the content of the displays distinguishes the classes" (p. 9).

The second essay, "Picture Frames," examines the process of portraiture as a ritual that translates opaque messages into articulated areas of social importance. Both the "natural" uncontrived pictures and the commercial ads draw on the human ability to switch from reality to fantasy and to draw conclusions about other people's lives from brief glimpses of their behavior.

Finally, "Gender Commercials" describes the rationale behind the presentation of the photographs that follow. Photographs are chosen to fit into sets that illustrate gender display related to a particular theme—relative size, feminine touch, functional ranking, family, ritualized subordination, and licensed withdrawal. Concentration on subtler dimensions of gender portraiture and pictures of one gender in the stereotypic poses of the other are meant to jar the reader into considering the meaning behind the stereotypes. Goffman concludes that ads are merely hyper-ritualization of displays common to people who participate in social situations. They portray not only an ideal view of masculinity and femininity but also an articulation of some aspects of how males and females actually relate to each other. (SGF)

IL
905. Key, Wilson Bryan. **Media Sexploitation.** Introduction by Richard D. Zakia. New York: New American Library, 1977. 234 p. Includes bibliography and index. ISBN 0-451-07537-4.

This book is the sequel to *Subliminal Seduction*, Key's first presentation of how subliminal perception is used in mass communication to manipulate the unconscious of consumers in the interest of selling products. While *Subliminal Seduction* dealt with forms of subliminal manipulation of a variety of emotions, this book deals with visual, auditory, and olfactory techniques of subconsciously arousing and manipulating sexual feelings. Key titles the volume *Media Sexploitation* because he thinks that the technology and expertise of the media employed are engaged in "deceitful seduction" used to "mind rape" a naive public. The book is an attempt to heuristically illustrate the observable ways in which magazines, newspapers, television ads, and the design of products themselves are permeated with subliminal techniques. Forty-nine images are included as references for the points made in the text. No experimental techniques are used to test hypotheses, though the results of other forms of research are referred to.

Very few areas of advertising are left unscathed by Key's hypotheses of sexploitation. Fixations developed as a child may be played upon. *Playboy* and *Playgirl* seem to be linked to unresolved Oedipal conflicts and latent homosexuality. Odors, which are often a basis of reproductive and social behavior in other species, may be subconsciously manipulated. Pitches to the cleanliness cult of America may include a fresh lemon scent that is similar to the smell of seminal fluid. Sounds may also be exploited. The lyrics of rock songs, like those of the Beatles, may serve to legitimize hallucinogens. Key thinks that the overall danger of public unawareness of such techniques is that it is "not at all improbable that under intensive, repetitive, long-term subliminal bombardment, entire value systems could be rearranged" (p. 14). (SGF)

IL

906. Key, Wilson Bryan. **Subliminal Seduction: Ad Media's Manipulation of a Not So Innocent America.** New York: New American Library, 1974. 220 p. Includes bibliography and index. ISBN 0-451-09887-0.

It is Key's contention that "every person reading this book has been victimized and manipulated by the use of subliminal stimuli directed into his unconscious mind by the mass merchandisers of media" (p. 1). The federal government, corporations, public relations and ad agencies, and the mass media use subliminal techniques to persuade. However, very little has been written on the subject. The public seems not only unaware of this phenomenon but also unwilling to believe that it exists. The purpose of this book is to establish the existence of subliminal perception and to demonstrate how subliminal techniques are used in mass communication to manipulate and control human behavior for economic ends. Key uses examples from the media rather than experimental techniques to bolster his point of view.

Subliminal perception includes sensory inputs that communicate directly with the unconscious and circumvent conscious awareness. The first few chapters introduce the reader to the principles on which subliminal perception is based. Areas of human behavior in which subliminal phenomena have been demonstrated to exist include dreams, memory, value norm anchor points, conscious perception, verbal behavior, and emotions. Perceptual defenses such as repression, isolation, regression, fantasy formation, sublimation, denial, projection, and introjection highlight the difference between the conscious and unconscious and become the basis upon which subliminal messages are sent to and received by the public. The rest of the book is filled with explanations of subliminal techniques and illustrations of how they are used in the media. A sixteen-page insert of photographs is used to graphically illustrate the existence of subliminal techniques.

Sex is a major theme exploited in these forms of communication. Embedded trigger devices, such as words or images related to sex, may be included on the photoengraving plate and not appear clearly to the conscious eye, but may be perceived by the unconscious. Airbrushed ice cubes in liquor ads may depict graphic sexual scenes. Magazines such as *Playboy, Vogue,* and *Cosmopolitan* play upon deep emotional conflicts about male and female roles; and television ads express a preoccupation with erogenous zones.

Key directs his writing to the public whom he believes needs to be aware of the media manipulation to which they are subject. Marshall McLuhan's interpretative introduction to this book enhances the reader's appreciation of deception present in advertising. Those who want a more scientific presentation of subliminal perception can read N. F. Dixon's *Subliminal Perception* (London: McGraw-Hill, 1971). (SGF)

PR

907. Millum, Trevor. **Images of Woman: Advertising in Women's Magazines.** Totowa, N.J.: Rowman and Littlefield, 1975. 206 p. Includes bibliography and indexes. ISBN 0-87471-628-4.

Magazines are not only influential sources of information about products but also purveyors of images and messages about the society and culture in which they occur. The goal of this academic study is to examine ads in women's magazines in order to (1) understand the social and cultural meanings contained in them beyond product messages and (2) develop a systematic method of analysis for understanding meaning in ads. The work focuses on a survey and analysis of the visual aspects of all of the large display ads (830) published in six extremely popular English women's magazines during the months of March and September 1969; however, its findings can be applied to other time periods and media.

Millum provides background for analyzing the ads by first discussing advertising and visual communication in general, the process of making an ad, and concepts of femininity. He then suggests a classification of the form and content of ads in terms of four constituent parts of an ad illustration: actors, product, setting, and stage props. The development of the broad classification is then used to classify, correlate, and analyze the ads. He finds that there are remarkably coherent patterns both within and between the categories he establishes. For example, simplicity of the content of ads is not paralleled by simplicity of form; crowdedness in settings correlates with familiar, everyday themes; plain actors are in crowded settings. Attributes in some ads cluster and contrast with those in others.

The information on ads, visual communication, women, and classification provides a guide to the world of meaning of women depicted in ad illustrations. Four images of women emerge: hostess, mannequin, wife/mother, and self-involved woman. Noticeably absent are images of career women.

Millum concludes that ads confirm ideal types and stereotypes but do not promote a world of fantasy; they legitimize the status quo. The discovery of systematic patterns shows that visual vocabulary is limited not only by the ethos and mechanics of business but also by sociocultural assumptions. The patterns also demonstrate that the study of visual communication can proceed "in a way which is not merely selective and intuitive" (p. 181). (SGF)

Pornography. Obscenity. Censorship. Expurgation

(For related material see also entries 12, 99, 106, 849)

IL
908. Baird, Robert M., and Stuart E. Rosenbaum, eds. **Pornography: Private Right or Public Menace?** Buffalo, N.Y.: Prometheus Books, 1991. 248 p. (Contemporary Issues). Includes bibliography. ISBN 0-87975-690-X.

The statements that make up this collection explore the gulf separating those who believe that pornography should be regulated and those who believe that restrictions on the availability of this material would be a violation of free speech. The book's aim is to improve "our perspectives on the relevant issues" by examining the effects of pornography on individuals and society and determining what can and should be done about the situation.

Part 1 focuses on two major government reports on pornography. First, *The Report of the Commission on Obscenity and Pornography* (1970) concluded that empirical research "has found no evidence to date that exposure to explicit sexual materials plays a significant role in the causation of delinquent or criminal behavior among youth or adults" (p. 24). One dissenting voice to the report, by Charles Keating, Jr., rejected the findings of the President's Commission. In her paper, Susan Brownmiller joins the fight against pornography, noting, however, that the cause unites feminists and right-wing, religious conservatives. The 1986 report of the Attorney General's Commission on Pornography rejected the conclusions of the 1970 report, pointing out that there should be different treatments for sexually violent material; nonviolent materials depicting degradation, domination, subordination or humiliation; and nonviolent and nondegrading materials. It recommended prosecution of materials that portray sexual violence, a less strong approach to the second category, and still more restraint with respect to the last category.

Part 2 provides several feminist perspectives on pornography. Gloria Steinem's paper attempts to distinguish between erotica and pornography. Andrea Dworkin's paper defines and explores various facets of pornography in connection with the Human Rights Ordinance of the City of Minneapolis which she wrote with Catherine MacKinnon. Judith M. Hill examines the nature of degradation, which characterizes what she calls victim pornography. Harry Brod in his paper argues "that pornography's image of male sexuality works to the detriment of men personally even as its image of female sexuality enhances the power of patriarchy . . ." (p. 76). Helen E. Longino then argues that pornography is immoral because it harms people. Finally, philosopher Alan Soble discusses defamation and the endorsement of degradation in certain pornographic materials.

Part 3 presents five papers on libertarian perspectives on pornography, including Barbara Dority's defense of sexual representation and expression on the basis of the position stated in the First Amendment of the Constitution that "Congress shall make no law . . . abridging the freedom of speech or of the press. . . ." Theodor A. Gracyk's paper takes issue with the "arguments and ordinances against pornography" by challenging the anti-pornographers over their understanding of pornography. Then William A. Linsley warns of the dangers inherent in the censorship of pornography, and Rita C. Manning grapples with the definition of pornography as it appeals to the "harmfulness of some sexually explicit material," especially harm to women. Finally, Ronald Dworkin's paper struggles with the attempt to justify "censorship within the constitutional scheme that assigns a preeminent place to free speech" (p. 172).

Part 4 provides three religious perspectives on pornography. One is from Tim LaHaye, who argues that pornography is mental poison that should be eliminated, if only to reduce the number of forcible rapes in this country. Thomas Parker, of the Dallas Baptist Theological Seminary, stresses the harmful impact of pornography on marriage. Mary Jo Weaver, Professor of Religious Studies at Indiana University, presents her scholarly opinion about process theology, which shows that religion can welcome eros, thus undermining pornography and "the tyrannizing tradition of conservative Christianity" (p. 208).

Part 5 presents two papers on the causes of America's moral decline. George P. Will's "America's Slide into the Sewer" draws attention to the rap lyrics of 2 Live Crew, and F. M. Christensen's paper discusses the uncertain anecdotal, statistical, and experimental evidence concerning the causal links between violence and depictions of violence and sex in pornographic materials. (TJW)

PR,IL

909. Berger, Ronald J., Patricia Searles, and Charles E. Cottle. **Feminism and Pornography.** New York: Praeger, 1991. 178 p. Includes bibliography and index. ISBN 0-275-93819-0.

The purpose of this book is to "synthesize the literature on pornography that has been written from a *feminist* perspective." Intended for both graduate and undergraduate students as well as for scholars, the book presents the views of differing schools of feminist thought on the issue of pornography. Also examined are traditional views of pornography derived from public opinion surveys and from conclusions reached by government commissions, such as the 1970 Commission on Obscenity and Pornography and the 1986 Attorney General's Commission on Pornography.

The authors then analyze the debate on pornography, elucidating the positions of the radical feminists (Andrea Dworkin, Catherine MacKinnon, Kathleen Barry) and the libertarian feminists (Ann Barr Snitow, Carole Vance, Lisa Duggan). From the debates between these groups, feminist antipornography and anticensorship positions emerged. Other feminist perspectives on pornography are explained by the authors, including those of liberal feminism, Marxist feminism, socialist feminism, and black feminism. Among these competing groups, liberal feminists constitute the dominant group within feminism.

The authors then turn to men's perspectives on pornography and men's responses to the feminist debate, where we hear the voices of Michael S. Kimmel, Harry Brod, Philip Weiss, and Timothy Beneke. They also cover men's feelings about censorship, liberation, and responsibility as they relate to pornography. A chapter is devoted to reviewing various kinds of "studies that assess the quantity and quality (type) of available pornography, the correlation between pornography and rape, and the experimental effects of exposure to pornography" (p. 94). They conclude with criticisms of pornography research in terms of systematically collected evidence, behavioristic assumptions, bias, and other methodological shortcomings. They note that to date there is little evidence linking either directly or indirectly the use of pornography with rape.

In the legal context, they note that "antipornography feminists were attracted to the promise of a new and innovative civil rights approach to pornography" (p. 129). In contrast, "some feminists have called for a renewed focus on remedies that are available in existing law" (p. 130). The former approach implies censorship, which is anathema to the libertarian feminists.

The final chapter of this cogently written book covers nonlegal alternatives for coping with the pornography issue, including political-economic and educational approaches that could in due course modify the violent and degrading elements of pornography. (TJW)

PR,IL

910. Burgess, Ann Wolbert, ed. **Child Pornography and Sex Rings.** Lexington, Mass.: Lexington Books, 1984. 221 p. Includes bibliographic references and index. ISBN 0-669-06741-5.

A highly publicized moral crusade against child pornography in the United States brought about the passage in 1978 of Public Law 95-225, forbidding the use of children in sexually explicit materials. The research summarized in this book is the first systematic study on child pornography in the United States. It was funded by the U.S. Department of Health and Human Services' Office of Human Development Services in 1980 in response to the 1977-1978 crusade. Written by persons involved in the research study, the book is intended "for people whose work brings them into contact with either victims or perpetrators of sex crimes against children" (p. 3).

The research concentrates on sex rings and youth prostitution. Sex rings fall into three categories. Solo rings, in which individual adults work with groups of children, usually involve a male adult with legitimate access to children through work, sports, or social or familial activities. Transition rings involve multiple adults sexually involved with children and often include the exchange or sale of pornographic photographs of children. Syndicated rings are highly organized business operations that recruit children, produce and distribute pornographic materials, deliver sexual services, and establish and maintain customer contacts. Analysis of sex rings shows that offenders are usually male, middle- or upper-class, thirty to fifty-nine years old; more than half of the children involved are boys; the most common activities are fondling and oral sex, with vaginal and anal sex occurring in approximately 60 percent of the rings; and, in 73 percent of the cases, sexual activity takes place in the offender's home. Most offenders are also compulsive collectors of child pornography and child erotica. Children remain in sex rings because of peer group dynamics, threats of retaliation, blackmail, and material rewards.

Teenage prostitution involves both male and female youths. Male prostitutes are usually white, bisexual, and involved in drug use. They work alone. Female prostitutes include a larger percentage of minorities, use fewer drugs, work with pimps, and are more often physically abused than their male counterparts. A study of young male prostitutes indicates a high proportion of early, coercive sexual experiences, including forced incest by male relatives.

Sexual exploitation of children has been found to adversely affect the child's emotional development. The child may become unable to respond emotionally, may learn to use sex to acquire recognition or attention, or may learn that sex is "wrong" and must be hidden. Children's reactions to disclosure of sex ring activity include denial, withdrawal, excessive risk taking, nightmares, and/or identification with the exploiter. Parental responses include rationalization, minimizing the event, avoidance of facts, and secrecy. Therapy should be made available to the child and family as soon as involvement is discovered.

Recommendations for community responses to child pornography and sexual exploitation include the use of interagency task forces, development of victim advocacy and community mental health center outreach programs, and national availability of information concerning convicted sex offenders. (SDH)

IL

911. Carter, Angela. **The Sadeian Woman: And the Ideology of Pornography.** New York: Pantheon Books, 1978. 154 p. Includes bibliography. ISBN 0-394-50575-1.

Carter's *The Sadeian Woman* is an interpretation of the thoughts of the Marquis de Sade as expressed in his major novels: *Justine, or the Misfortunes of Virtue*; *Juliette, or the Prosperities of Vice*; *The Hundred and Twenty Days of Sodom*; and *Philosophy of the Boudoir*. Carter relates this thought to the denigration of male and female sexuality found in bathroom graffiti, porno movies, and Hollywood productions featuring macho men and sex goddesses. Usually, these are increasingly complicated icons of female sexuality, ranging from the unidimensional "fringed hole" in the bathroom stall to the innocent dumb blondes (Marilyn Monroe, etc.) encountered on the screen. Carter's feminist perspective is that all these abstract representations of women confronting us daily, result in an unrealistic view of women as purely sexual objects.

Carter devotes an entire chapter to the picaresque tale of Justine, giving the reader a blow-by-blow account of the rapings, beatings, and other degradations to which the heroine is subjected. Through it all, until her sudden death, Justine remains true, but shaken, to her creed of virtue. Carter dubs her the patroness of the modern screen heroine as exemplified by Marilyn Monroe and others. Unlike her sister, Juliette, to whom Carter devotes a full chapter, Justine does not choose the path of vice. On the other hand, Juliette's goals are financial profit and libidinal gratification. She stands for the good old virtues of self-help and self-reliance. Juliette does not suffer; she causes suffering. Carter envisions her in a boardroom of glamorous and sexy lady executives. She is the *Cosmopolitan* girl—hard, bright, dazzling, meritricious, playing to win. Carter in effect makes the two sisters of the Sadeian world the models for modern sex goddesses and career women.

Carter concludes her polemical preface with a poignant statement that might have come from the lips of the Marquis himself: "Charming sex, you will be free; just as men do, you shall enjoy all the pleasures that Nature makes your duty, do not withhold yourselves from one. Must the more divine half of mankind be kept in chains by the others? Ah, break those bonds: nature wills it." (TJW)

PR,IL

912. Commission on Obscenity and Pornography. **The Report of the Commission on Obscenity and Pornography.** Washington, D.C.: Government Printing Office, 1970. 646 p.

"The Congress finds that the traffic in obscenity and pornography is a matter of national concern." That statement in Public Law 90-100, dated October 3, 1967, was the basis for creating the advisory Commission on Obscenity and Pornography, which over a period of two years (1968-1970) investigated (1) the laws pertaining to the control of sexual obscenity and pornography; (2) the distribution and volume of obscene and pornographic materials; and (3) the effect of sexual obscenity and pornography on the public, particularly minors. Given the task of making recommendations, the Commission prepared drafts of proposed legislation, both federal and state.

As a result of panel reports and hearings, including two public hearings held in Los Angeles and Washington, D.C., in May 1970, the Commission presented its findings and recommendations in the form of this *Report* to the President of the United States on September 30, 1970. Prepared under the direction of Chairman William B. Lockhart, Dean and Professor of Law, University of Minnesota, the *Report* is divided into four parts.

Part 1, "Overview of Findings," deals with (1) the volume of traffic and patterns of distribution of sexually oriented materials; (2) the effects of explicit sexual materials;

(3) positive approaches to sex education, industry self-regulation, and citizens' action groups; and (4) law and law enforcement.

In part 2, "Recommendations of the Commission," the Commission recommended in the nonlegislative area the launching of a massive sex education program, open discussion in regard to obscenity and pornography, the development of factual information, and citizen involvement in promoting these recommendations. The Commission then recommended the repeal of federal, state, and local legislation prohibiting the sale, exhibition, and distribution of sexual materials to consenting adults; the adoption by states of legislation prohibiting the commercial distribution or display for sale of certain sexual materials to young persons; the enactment of legislation prohibiting public displays of sexually explicit pictorial materials; and against adoption of any legislation limiting or abolishing the jurisdiction of the Supreme Court of the United States or of other federal judges and courts in obscenity cases.

Part 3, "Reports of the Panels," includes reports on (1) the traffic and distribution of sexually oriented materials in the United States, (2) the impact of erotica, (3) positive approaches to the development of healthy attitudes toward sexuality, and (4) legal considerations relating to erotica.

Part 4 contains separate statements of Commission members, and the appendices include a copy of Public Law 90-100, biographies of Commission members, a list of contractors, and a list of witnesses at the public hearings.

Three Commissioners dissented from the recommendations of the majority of the Commission and wrote minority reports explaining their positions and vehemently attacking the *Report.* Both the U.S. Senate and President Nixon rejected the report. (TJW)

PR,IL
913. Commission on Obscenity and Pornography. **Technical Report of the Commission on Obscenity and Pornography.** Washington, D.C.: Government Printing Office, 1971-1972. 9v.

These volumes of research supplement the *Report of the Commission on Obscenity and Pornography*. They report on "(a) constitutional and definitional problems relating to obscenity controls, (b) traffic in and distribution of obscene and pornographic materials, and (c) effects of such materials, particularly on youth, and their relationship to crime and other antisocial conduct." According to W. Cody Wilson, the Executive Director and Director of Research for these reports, "these volumes share two characteristics: a focus on empirical description and a lack of refinement in presentation." Produced by independent contractors working under severe time limitations, the reports were not thoroughly reviewed or edited.

Volume I, *Preliminary Studies* (198 p.), includes literature reviews on sex censorship, human sexual arousal, and the role of pornography in the causation of juvenile delinquency; theoretical analyses of pornography and erotic materials; and preliminary empirical observations on moral reasoning about sexual dilemmas, the relationship between pornography and juvenile delinquency, attitudes toward pornography, and the effect of the mass media on sexual behavior.

Volume II, *Legal Analysis* (241 p.), concerns itself with the definition of obscenity law in the United States as well as with historical, philosophical, and comparative perspectives on obscenity laws. Specific chapters are devoted to obscenity in various societies, including Argentina, Australia, Denmark, France, Hungary and the Soviet Union, Israel, Italy, Japan, Mexico, United Kingdom, West Germany, and Yugoslavia.

Volume III, *The Marketplace: The Industry* (208 p.), focuses on commercial traffic in sex-oriented materials in the United States, while volume IV, *The Marketplace: Empirical Studies* (288 p.), concentrates on consumers of sex-oriented materials as well as specific studies of trafficking sex-oriented materials in different settings (e.g., Denver, Boston, San Francisco).

Volume V, *Societal Control Mechanisms* (378 p.), is concerned with such topics as law enforcement, citizen action groups, industry self-regulation, and sex education. Volume VI, *National Survey* (256 p.), presents the findings of a national survey of public attitudes toward and experience with erotic materials. Volume VII, *Erotica and Antisocial Behavior*, and volume VIII, *Erotica and Social Behavior* (379 p.), continue the theme of understanding the social impact of erotic materials.

Volume IX, *The Consumer and the Community* (480 p.), explores the ways in which erotic materials relate to the individual and his or her social context. How does the individual form judgments about sexual stimuli? How do communities form standards about erotica? How do sex-oriented materials affect adolescents? How variable are the standards for modesty and obscenity cross-culturally? These are some of the topics dealt with in this volume.

Much of the research in each of these nine volumes is original. Therefore, the reports are a rich source of materials for further investigation. (TJW/SGF)

IL

914. Commission on Pornography. **Attorney General's Commission on Pornography. Final Report, July 1986.** Washington, D.C.: Government Printing Office, 1986. 2v. (1960 p.).

Chaired by Henry E. Hudson, a Virginia attorney, Edwin Meese's Commission on Pornography, pursuant to the provisions of the Federal Advisory Committee Act of 1972 and the Charter of the Attorney General's Commission on Pornography, dated March 29, 1985, undertook "to determine the nature, extent, and impact of pornography in the United States, and to make specific recommendations to the Attorney General concerning more effective ways in which the spread of pornography could be contained, consistent with constitutional guarantees." In its investigation, which held public hearings and meetings in Washington, D.C., Chicago, Houston, Los Angeles, Miami, and New York City from June 18, 1985 to January 1986, the Commission, focusing its attention on visual and graphic pornography, examined the following facets of the pornography industry: law, law enforcement, and the constraints of the First Amendment; the relationship between pornography and human behavior; the production, distribution, and marketing of pornographic materials; the creation, consequences, and legal control of child pornography; and the role of organized crime in the pornography industry.

Recognizing that society has noticeably changed technologically, socially, culturally, and in other ways in the sixteen years since the President's Commission on Obscenity and Pornography made its report, the Commission believes that the present report will provide an up-to-date and realistic view of the pornography industry today.

The *Final Report* is divided into six parts and an appendix containing the Commission's Charter. The significant data in part 1 are the individual commissioners' statements, including the dissenting statements of Judith Becker and Ellen Levine. Part 2 does several things: (1) discusses the formation and work of the Commission, reviews the work of the 1970 Commission on Obscenity and Pornography, and attempts to define central terms; (2) reviews the history of pornography; (3) discusses the constraints of the First Amendment relative to free speech and the press; (4) examines the market for pornography, the industry as a whole, and organized crime; (5) explores the question of whether pornography is harmful, and categorizes sexually explicit pornographic materials as (a) sexually violent material; (b) nonviolent materials depicting degradation, domination, subordination, or humiliation, and (c) nonviolent and nondegrading materials; (6) discusses the law and law enforcement with respect to pornography and obscenity; (7) inquires into child pornography; and (8) addresses the role of private action in the war on pornography.

Part 3 lists the ninety-two recommendations of the Commission, and follows through with a discussion of their relationship to obscenity laws, child pornography, victimization, civil rights, nuisance laws, and antidisplay laws. The recommendations concern changes in federal and state law; federal, state and local law enforcement agencies; the U.S. Department of Justice; the Judiciary; the Federal Communications Commission; the regulation of child pornography; correctional facilities; and public and private social service agencies.

Part 4 deals with a variety of questions, including the performers in pornographic films, organized crime, and the imagery found in magazines, books, and films. It provides long lists of these materials, and even gives detailed descriptions of specific materials (e.g., *Tri-Sexual Lust*, a magazine; *Tying Up Rebecca*, a book; and *Deep Throat*, a motion picture and videotape cassette). This part also lists the witnesses testifying before the Commission and persons submitting written statements.

Part 5 consists of an extensive bibliography and a listing of the Commission's staff; part 6 consists of photographs, usually of Commission members and testifying witnesses.

According to the chairman, there was disagreement among the members with respect to those materials encompassing imagery depicting sexual activity without violence, submission, degradation, or humiliation. He states that there is "no cogent evidence that materials in this class have a predominantly negative behavioral effect" (p. 28), but they do "tend to promote the notion that women are inherently promiscuous and enjoy sexual exploitation. This type of imagery conveys the impression that women are fundamentally immoral and hedonistic" (p. 29). It appears "to impact adversely on the family concept and its value to society."

The conclusions of this report are embodied in the ninety-two recommendations in part 3, that essentially are of a legislative and law enforcement nature. (TJW)

PR,IL

915. Cornog, Martha, ed. **Libraries, Erotica, Pornography.** Phoenix, Ariz.: Oryx Press, 1991. 314 p. Includes bibliographies and index. ISBN 0-89774-474-8.

Cornog, editor of this seventeen-chapter collection of papers, has brought together a group of contributors from different walks of life to present views on how libraries might cope with the flow of sexually explicit materials—books, periodicals, videotapes and cassettes, etc.—and the censorship problems accompanying that flow.

In the introductory chapter, Cornog and Timothy Perper review the history of censorship since the 1920s, observing how librarians reacted to objections to the presence of certain books in library collections, how the liberating 1960s resulted in new challenges to librarians' acquisition policies, and how the secularizing and politicizing of sex have brought a torrent of sexual materials into the library on a great number of issues: pornography, AIDS, abortion, sexual abuse, etc. A background paper by Gershon Legman waxes eloquent on the history of pornographic materials and reveals interesting facts about the major writers, collectors, and collections of pornography in the West. In chapter 3, Cornog and Perper tackle the problems of distinguishing between and defining erotica and pornography. In chapters 4 and 5 Bill Katz and Will Manley discourse on the pros and cons of having pornographic materials in the library. Vern Bullough, in chapter 6, examines the question of the research and archival value of having erotica and pornography in the library. Christine Jenkins, in chapter 7, discusses the vexing question of feminism, pornography, and libraries. Then, in chapter 8, Elizabeth M. McKenzie examines the feminist-sponsored Minneapolis, Minnesota, and Indianapolis, Indiana, porn ordinances and similar laws, which to date have been rejected.

Cornog writes two articles on *Playboy* magazine—one on the congressional effort to have the Library of Congress braille edition of the magazine discontinued and the other on how libraries have handled the acquisition, preservation, and availability of the magazine. She also addresses, in chapter 11, the integration of sexuality materials into the collections, the many problems associated with internal cataloging/classification disputes, vandalism, and community and staff controversies over the handling of these materials.

In chapter 12 Gwendolyn L. Pershing describes major erotica research collections, including the Kinsey Institute and others. Similarly, Daniel C. Tsang describes homosexuality research library collections. Chapters 14 through 16 are bibliographies, including an annotated selective bibliography on pornography and censorship by Evelyn Apterbach et al.; an annotated list of quality erotica by David Steinberg; and Robert Rimmer's "A Connoisseur's Selection of X-Rated Videotapes for the Library."

Finally, Timothy Perper concludes this collection with a summary and bibliographic essay on the sexual content of literature as it affects society, the library, and its readers. He also provides a list of nonfiction books on sexuality and another list of aids to book selection for librarians and others. (TJW)

IL

916.   Dworkin, Andrea. **Pornography: Men Possessing Women.** New York: Perigee Books, 1981. 300 p. Includes bibliography and index.

"Male domination of the female body is the basic material reality of women's lives" writes feminist Dworkin. Her book focuses on "the power of men in pornography" which she defines as "the graphic depiction of whores" (p. 9) in a society that sees all women as whores. Men have power and the attributes of power; women are powerless and thus are denied humanity; they exist solely for male sexual domination. Pornography is the graphic representation of male power through the conquest and degradation of women.

As boys grow from infancy, they see the powerlessness and humiliation of their mothers and choose to become men, the holders of power. They adopt violent behavior out of fear at appearing feminine. Women, while powerless, are seen as dangerous in their sexuality and threatening in their weakness. Force is accepted by men as the appropriate means of controlling this danger. The use of violence against women is approved, both as the man's right and as something desired by the woman. Female protests or resistance at forced sex are seen either as teasing or dishonest or as evidence that the woman does not know her true, lustful sexual nature, which desires pain, humiliation, and repeated, forceful penetration. The ultimate male sex act involves the death of the woman.

Pornography teaches, reinforces, and glorifies these violent, male-supremacist beliefs and behaviors. It supports racism, portraying minority men, like women, as bestial, masochistic, degraded, and/or weak. Much pornography, ranging from the life of the Marquis de Sade to "erotic" literature and art, is interpreted by the political Left as liberating. In reality, pornography is a tool used to justify the enslavement of women. (SDH)

IL

917.   Faust, Beatrice. **Women, Sex, and Pornography: A Controversial and Unique Study.** New York: Macmillan, 1980. 239 p. Includes bibliographic notes and index. ISBN 0-02-537050-2.

This witty book explores sex differences by focusing on two questions that Faust deems central to the problem of pornography: How important is the seeming difference between men's and women's attitudes toward it? and Is it harmful? Faust, an Australian writer and social reformer, establishes a working definition of pornography as a genre with its own conventions: it is primarily characterized by its manner of presentation, that is, an extremely literal, often unreal documentation of sexual activity that emphasizes content at the expense of all other considerations. In line with Kinsey's finding that most women are less responsive to visual stimuli than most men, Fault hypothesizes that the sexual psychology of females and males is different. Drawing on a wide range of scientific studies, she points to some major differences between the sexes: males are performance-oriented, more quickly aroused, conditioned to a wider range of stimuli, and are genitally focused while women are more process-oriented, conditioned to tactile stimuli, and focus on the contextual nature of the relationship. She then examines the implications of these differences for understanding contemporary expressions of masculinity and femininity from the media to the bedroom: the popularity of "sweet savagery," *Cosmopolitan* magazine, and *The Total Woman*; the demise of the magazine *Viva*; the appeal of cosmetics and fashion for women; the relationship between sex and aggression; the different attitudes that men and women seem to have about rape; and the repercussions of different attitudes toward sex for healthy sexual relationships between men and women. She tries to answer the tantalizing question of why a woman can't be more like a man. Her orientation is to regard sex differences as an interaction between social and biological factors, and her hope is to encourage others to examine in detail the consequences of these differences. (SGF)

IL

918. Griffin, Susan. **Pornography and Silence: Culture's Revenge Against Nature.** New York: Harper & Row, 1981. 277 p. Includes bibliographic notes. ISBN 0-06-090915-3.

What is pornography? What effect does it have on the pornographer and his object? In this book, Griffin argues that "pornography is an expression not of human erotic feeling and desire, and not of a love of the life of the body, but of a fear of bodily knowledge, and a desire to silence eros" (p. 1). She attempts to define the pornographic mind and examine the influence of pornography on society. She views pornography as a result of the long-term division in Western culture between mind and body, culture and nature, and sees the pornographer as an individual attempting to deny and destroy that emotional and feeling part of the self that represents "body" or "nature." In the pornographer's mind, these attributes, which have been labeled "feminine" by our culture, are transferred to the image of woman. By humiliating, raping, torturing, and ultimately murdering this image, the pornographer attempts to destroy the feminine part of the self. Griffin associates pornography with racism and anti-Semitism and demonstrates the similarity between pornographic literature and the propaganda of the Third Reich. The attempted extermination of European Jews was a natural outgrowth of Germany's mass delusion; since any attempt to destroy the feared and unwanted parts of oneself through literature or film is bound to fail, the pornographer will finally turn against actual living beings who resemble this pornographic image and seek to destroy them.

The effects of pornography on women, other than such violence by men, include a gradual loss of self-identity as women attempt to make themselves into the "sex goddess," the pornographic image that is accepted by society as "feminine." This is an unreal image of passivity, submissiveness, cupidity, lack of intellect, and victimization that denies the energy, intelligence, and individuality of women. Just as pornography destroys the individuals involved, it also destroys the erotic relationship. Only by complete acceptance of feelings and emotions and by sharing strengths and vulnerabilities can a true erotic, rather than pornographic, relationship exist. (SDH)

IL

919. Gubar, Susan, and Joan Hoff, eds. **For Adult Users Only: The Dilemma of Violent Pornography.** Bloomington, Ind.: Indiana University Press, 1989. 248 p. (Everywoman: Studies in History, Literature, and Culture). Includes bibliographies and index. ISBN 0-253-20508-5.

This is a collection of papers given at the multidisciplinary faculty seminar on violent pornography held at the Kinsey Institute at Indiana University in the 1985-1986 academic year. The first paper, by editor Hoff, "Why Is There No History of Pornography?" responds to the question by noting that in the past today's social history techniques were missing as also was a Foucauldian view of sexuality. Part of the problem, Hoff claims, is the thorny matter of definitions of such basic terms as obscenity, pornography and erotica, and their impact on law, the arts, the feminist movement, and even male/female relationships. What is needed, she asserts, is a gender analysis; without it, no convincing history of pornography will emerge.

In "Representing Pornography," editor Gubar emphasizes the violence against women in pornographic art (especially the surrealistic art of René Magritte), literature, and film, and discusses camps of feminist interpretation and criticism. Mary Jo Weaver in "Pornography and the Religious Imagination," probes the religious underpinnings of pornography and discovers that traditional Christianity, wherein "the male inherits the lordly qualities of God the Father, while the female is enjoined to be submissive to God's rule as it is enacted by the male" (p. 70), provides the rationale for the subordination of women and the pornographic imagination.

Edna E. Einsield in "Social Science and Public Policy," contrasts the conclusions of the report of the 1970 Commission on Obscenity and Pornography with those of the 1986 report of the Commission on Pornography. In "Pornography as a Legal Text," Robin West elicits the notion that women "live under the rule of two political sovereigns—the state and men—rather than one" (p. 111), which defines patriarchy, and that pornography is the legal text of patriarchy, which renders women powerless before the onslaught of violent pornography.

Switching from past debates to contemporary aspects of pornography, Gubar and Hoff present first a paper by Doris-Jean Burton, "Public Opinion and Pornography Policy," that presents the results of a public opinion poll on public attitudes toward pornography and the impact, if any, on public policy. Then Richard B. Miller shows in "Violent Pornography" that violent pornography is essentially nihilistic "because it suggests a flagrant violation of customary attitudes and practices" and in extreme form, thanatic, because it depicts the annihilation of others as a source of amusement.

In "Beyond the Meese Report," David Pritchard shows that pornography regulation is determined by variable cultural, social, and political factors. Lauren Robel in "Pornography and Existing Law" addresses the question of the redress existing law offers to pornography's victims.

In "Fetishism and Hard Core," Linda Williams examines the major aspect of hard core pornography, the "money shot," or "come shot," and assigns it the status of a "fetish substitute for the reality of a male-female sexual connection" and then interprets it in terms of Marx and Freud. Finally, in "Mitigating the Effects of Violent Pornography," Margaret Intons-Peterson and Beverly Roskos-Ewoldsen first review both the literature of nonviolent pornography and violent pornography and then "consider various techniques that might be used to mitigate the effects of violent pornography," which include (1) prohibitive legislation, (2) teaching critical viewing skills, (3) debriefing after exposure, and (4) briefing before exposure. (TJW)

PR,IL

920. Haight, Anne Lyon. **Banned Books, 387 B.C. to 1978 A.D.** 4th ed. Updated and enlarged by Chandler B. Grannis. With an opening essay by Charles Rembar, Esq. New York: Bowker, 1978. 196 p. Includes bibliography and index. ISBN 0-8352-1078-2.

The main section of this book is a chronological listing and discussion of "book bannings over the centuries, worldwide, but with emphasis on recent U.S. episodes." The subject matter ranges from Plato's suggestion in 387 B.C. that Homer's *Odyssey* be expurgated to the banning of an anthology of poems from a Massachusetts high school library in 1977. In between are listed bannings, censorship acts and actions, court decisions, and the like affecting the works of such renowned authors as Oscar Wilde, James Joyce, D. H. Lawrence, Havelock Ellis, Marie Stopes, Margaret Sanger, Bertrand Russell, Henry Miller, Alfred Kinsey, and many others whose works were banned for sexual content. Authors whose works are of a religious or political nature—Martin Luther, Voltaire, Thomas Paine, Adolf Hitler—are also listed.

The book contains an introductory historical essay entitled "Censorship in America: The Legal Picture," by Charles Rembar. Five appendixes cover miscellaneous documents and comments: "Trends in Censorship," "Statement on Freedom of the Press," "Excerpts from Important Court Decisions," excerpts from the *Report* of the Commission on Obscenity and Pornography, and "Selected U.S. Laws and Regulations."

Overall, *Banned Books* provides pertinent information about how censorship has been applied to many of the books abstracted in this reference work. (TJW)

PR,IL

921. Hawkins, Gordon, and Franklin E. Zimring. **Pornography in a Free Society.** Cambridge: Cambridge University Press, 1988. 236 p. Includes bibliography and index. ISBN 0-521-36317-9.

The twenty years between the mid-1960s and the mid-1980s could be called the Era of the Pornography Commissions. Within those twenty years, four nationally chartered commissions were established to investigate the problems of pornography: in the United States in 1968, in Great Britain in 1977, in Canada in 1985, and in the United States again in 1985.

In the United States, the report of the first commission was denounced as a charter for pornographers and that of the second as a reflection of the moral militancy of the Reagan counterrevolution. The immediate stimulus for this book was the publication of the final report of Attorney General Edwin Meese's Commission on Pornography in July 1986. In it Hawkins and Zimring attempt to view the problem of pornography in a wider perspective than that of partisan political debate.

To that end, in part I of the book, Hawkins and Zimring compare the two American reports with the report to the British Committee on Obscenity and Film Censorship that appeared during the years between the American reports. The comparison deals with the approach of each of them to the definition of the field of inquiry, the nature and distribution of pornography, the existing evidence on the behavioral effects of pornography, and to the issues that arise when a society that values free expression is also concerned about pornographic communication.

In part II, Hawkins and Zimring address four topics that have become significant to the understanding of pornography as a social issue with the increased availability of sexually explicit material since the 1960s, but were not considered in detail by the commissions. They discuss the radical feminist challenge to pornography, pornography and child protection, the social control of pornography without censorship, and likely future developments. Arguing that the furor over pornography and the commissions themselves is part of a "ceremony of adjustment" to the widespread availability of sexually explicit material, they predict less social concern about pornography as time passes. (Authors)

PR,IL
922. Hurwitz, Leon. **Historical Dictionary of Censorship in the United States.** Westport, Conn.: Greenwood Press, 1985. 584 p. Includes bibliography, index, and chronology. ISBN 0-313-23878-2.

In the preface Hurwitz states that this compilation "attempts to present an overview of the types of censorship and the types of speech and press that have been subjected to censorship, repression, and punishment" in the United States. Then, in a lengthy introductory essay, he provides a historical overview of the four main categories into which most government censorship activities fall: political censorship (speech, press, and national security); community censorship (speech, press, and public order/safety); constitutional censorship (speech, press, and conflicting rights); and moral censorship (speech, press, and sin).

Alphabetically arranged and cross-referenced, the content of this work consists of a wealth of information relating to the historical background presented in the introduction. Various types of entries cover organizations (Women Against Pornography, American Civil Liberties Union); court cases (*Griswold v. Connecticut, United States v. One Book Entitled Ulysses*); tests used in obscenity cases (Hicklin Rule, Roth Standard); publications (*Tropic of Cancer, Married Love*); federal and state statutes (Tariff Act, Anti-Evolution Statute of Arkansas); movies (*Caligula, Blue Movie/Fuck*); and general concepts (obscenity, pandering, privacy). For each topic, Hurwitz provides an in-depth historical and descriptive analysis. Several useful appendices include a chronology for the period 1644 to 1984, a long alphabetical list of legal cases, a selected bibliography, and an index. (TJW)

IL
923. Kappeler, Susanne. **The Pornography of Representation.** Minneapolis: University of Minnesota Press, 1986. 248 p. (Feminist Perspectives). Includes bibliographic notes and index. ISBN 0-8166-1544-6.

This feminist critique of pornography and patriarchal culture moves away from traditional arguments against pornography that deal with content and usually include a component of concern that somehow the behavior that is represented in the pornographic expression is going to turn into human behavior in real life. Kappeler defines pornography as "representational practices" and makes it clear that she is not examining a special case of sexuality, but rather the political, cultural, and economic contexts of word- or image-based representations.

Thirteen "Problems," each presented in chapter form, comprise the body of the book. The first, "Fact and Fiction," deals with a sadistic, racist murder in Namibia. The second problem, "Human Rights," explains pornography in its relation to the civil rights of women, focusing on an illustrative ordinance approved by the Minneapolis City Council. Problem three, "Obscenity and Censorship," looks at pornography as a phenomenon of "popular culture." "Porn versus Erotica," problem four, further illustrates the difficulties of dealing with pornography in a politically effective way. The remaining problems, "Subjects, Objects, and Equal Opportunities," "Why Look at Women?" "Art and Pornography," "The Literary and the Production of Value," "The Book Business," "Playing in the Literary Sanctuary," "Collaboration," "Communication," and "Sex/Sexuality" continue to probe the responsibility of the producers of pornography, the idealogy of publishing interests, the subjectification of men and the objectification of women, the powerlessness of consumers, the silence of women and the "monologuization" of communication. Each problem introduces new illustrations, but the arguments in each problem artfully pyramid on the illustrations of arguments already presented in earlier problems. Kappeler presents the powerful argument that women, ethnic minorities, and working-class citizens cannot hope, given current cultural values, to have full human democratic rights or freedom, and she pleads that a strategy be evolved to ensure a kind of collectivity that is not defined by "male bonding over commodities and enemies" (p. 219) and to ensure communication that is an exchange of meaning and not an ego trip. One understands better the implications of changing consciousness. (LF)

IL

924. Kendrick, Walter. **The Secret Museum: Pornography in Modern Culture.** New York: Viking, 1987. 288 p. Includes bibliography and index. ISBN 0-670-81363-X.

Kendrick, a professor of English at Fordham University, examines the origin and development of pornography in modern culture. He first evaluates the various dictionary definitions of pornography, showing how the term has changed from something that meant writing about prostitutes and prostitution to our modern understanding of the term. Pornography began to take on its present meaning as early as 1758 when certain artifacts of a "lascivious" kind (vases, lamps, everyday utensils, furniture, etc.), having been unearthed from the ruins of Pompeii, were placed under lock and key as being unsuitable to display to visitors, especially women and children. These artifacts were placed in a Secret Museum, identified as pornography, systematically cataloged, and listed in a printed catalog. In England, a similar museum was established at the British Museum to house such artifacts; also, erotic books were stored in a locked case in the library of the Museum.

Having disposed of definition and origin as basic to an understanding of pornography in modern culture, Kendrick begins his main task of tracing the idea of pornography in the modern sense over the past 2,000 years from classical Greek culture to the nineteenth century, a period he designates as the prepornographic era. He discusses the work of nineteenth-century British bibliophiles who assiduously collected what we would call pornography today. He goes on to establish a hypothetical Young Person who in the fantasies of the guardians of public morality should be shielded from erotic literature lest he or she be corrupted. These same individuals, fearful that women, children, and the poor might gain access to the reviled literature, initiated measures to thwart the supposedly anarchical threats emanating from the Young Person presumably seeking forbidden knowledge.

The entire armamentarium of suppression was brought to bear on the problems of obscene literature through legal measures, public trials, censorship of novels, bowdlerization of the classics, and so on. Kendrick examines the important legal arguments and decisions concerning the nature of obscenity in such landmark cases as the trial of *Madame Bovary* in France, the case of *Regina vs. Hicklin* in England, and the cases brought to court in the United States because of the relentless efforts of Anthony Comstock, a special agent for the Post Office.

Liberation from the legal constraints on the written word took place gradually in the United States until the 1960s, when the courts granted total freedom in this regard. A landmark decision was made in 1933 by John M. Woolsey, a United States district court judge in New York, who exonerated James Joyce's *Ulysses* from the charge of obscenity, stating also that it was not pornographic. The final blows to antiobscenity efforts came in the 1950s and 1960s when the Supreme Court redefined obscenity, the "hard core" of pornography was isolated, and anything written with even a small amount of redeeming social value was permitted.

Kendrick's Young Person, now "no longer the girl or boy about to be debauched by a book," became a more sinister figure who wallowed in hard-core pornography. He "had no taste for art, literature, or anything of 'social importance' " (p. 208). Society demanded protection from him.

Kendrick takes 1970 as the end of the pornographic era. In his final chapter, he examines the highlights of the struggle against hard-core pornography. In turn, he discusses the conclusions of the Commission on Pornography and Obscenity and President Nixon's reaction to them; and the efforts of feminist organizations to combat "a sexual tyranny that fostered violence against the minds and bodies of women" (p. 228). With pornography looked upon as the cause of violence against women and children, the 1985 Commission on Pornography issued its *Final Report* aimed at regulating the activities of the distributors of pictorial hard-core pornography. In the postpornographic era, Kendrick sees violence rather than sex as the target of the antipornographers, and that the issue is now one of politics rather than morals. (TJW)

IL

925. Lederer, Laura, ed. **Take Back the Night.** New York: Morrow, 1980. 369 p. Includes bibliographies and index. ISBN 0-688-03728-3.

A collection of essays, interviews, book excerpts, and research papers by prominent feminists, *Take Back the Night* challenges the pervasive apathy toward pornography in the United States. Adrienne Rich describes the book as a microcosm of the American feminist movement at the beginning of the 1980s.

Helen Longino explains that pornography invites social, economic, and cultural oppression of women; it is implicated in the committing of violent crimes against women; and it is a vehicle for dissemination of lies about women and their sexuality. Gloria Steinem distinguishes between erotica and pornography; in pornography, "there is no sense of equal choice or equal power . . . erotica is about sexuality, but pornography is about power and sex-as-weapon." Susan Brownmiller and other contributors compare television violence with pornography. They argue that both glorify violence and have a direct relationship to the rising crime rate.

Many of the articles center around pornography and the First Amendment. Attorney Wendy Kaminer emphasizes the need "to fully understand the legal process while shaping an effective anti-pornography movement." In her article, "For Men, Freedom of Speech; for Women, Silence Please," written in response to editorials characterizing feminists as "overwrought" and "strident," Andrea Dworkin challenges the motives of men who use the First Amendment as an argument to preserve pornography.

Another important group of articles presents those harmed by pornography and those that benefit from the pornography industry. Robin Morgan and others explain that pornography perpetuates myths about women, such as that all women want and enjoy being raped, that it is always the woman's fault (she asked for it), and that women don't really mean "no." Children, especially in recent years, are used in pornography that promotes sexual abuse of children. Some believe that the growing independence of many women, as a result of the women's liberation movement, has made men more attracted to the innocence and helplessness of children.

Pornography publishers, filmmakers, and their distributors are the main beneficiaries and promoters of pornography. *Playboy* and other pornographic magazines work at gradually breaking down past taboos to expand their industry and create variety for their users.

In her short story, "Coming Apart," Alice Walker illustrates the effects of pornography on blacks. Susan Lurie contributes a psychoanalytical piece, refuting Freud and offering a new reading of the Oedipus myth. She argues that pornography exists to combat a fear of women and their sexuality. In another section, "Research on the Effects of Pornography," Irene Diamond states that the 1970 Commission on Pornography and Obscenity's decision that pornography is harmless was not warranted on the basis of the data available to it. In the "Taking Action" section, Beverly LaBelle describes the highly publicized movie *Snuff*, purported to show the actual murder and dismemberment of a woman, as the ultimate in woman hating. (DP)

PR,IL

926. Leff, Leonard J., and Jerold L. Simmons. **The Dame in the Kimono: Hollywood, Censorship, and the Production Code from the 1920s to the 1960s.** New York: Doubleday, 1990. 350 p. Includes bibliography, filmography, and index. ISBN 0-385-41722-5.

In a censored scene from *The Maltese Falcon* Iva Archer asks Sam Spade about the woman in the bedroom: "Who is that dame wearin' my kimono?" Such scenes as these were subject to the scrutiny of the Production Code Administration, that was charged with the task of upholding both the principles and particular applications of the 1930 Production Code. In response to increasing state censorship of films, public protests, proposed congressional legislation, and the Wall Street crash, movie moguls approved the Quigley/Lord Code to protect their investments. Although Postmaster Will Hays had been head of Hollywood's trade association, the Motion Picture Producers and Distributors of America, since 1922, it was not until his appointment of Joe Breen as his assistant and de facto head of West Coast operations that systematic enforcement of guidelines for visual and scripted content occurred.

The three basic principles of the 1930 Production Code were: "(1) No picture shall be produced which will lower the moral standards of those who see it. Hence the sympathy of the audience should never be thrown to the side of crime, wrongdoing, evil or sin. (2) Correct standards of life, subject only to the requirements of drama and entertainment, shall be presented. (3) Law, natural or human, shall not be ridiculed, nor shall sympathy be created for its violation." Sexual behavior, language and innuendo were central targets for modification or elimination in films.

Leff (who teaches film history and screenwriting at Oklahoma State University) and Simmons (who teaches American constitutional history at the University of Nebraska at Omaha) describe the controversies surrounding Code approval of twelve films, including *She Done Him Wrong, Gone with the Wind, The Outlaw, The Postman Always Rings Twice, The Moon Is Blue, Lolita,* and *Who's Afraid of Virginia Woolf?* Reactions to these films provide a "kaleidoscope of shifting values, an extraordinary body of case law that traces the relationship between Hollywood, the Code, and American culture" (p. xiv).

The Production Code Administration was as much a history of Joe Breen's career as it was of censorship of films. Breen and his colleagues read scripts, screened pictures, and prepared letters to producers about the delicate feedback between the film, the media, and the script. The power struggles between the producers, writers, and distributors over the application of moral principles to film; shifts in American culture and audience demands; how rules were made and applied; and changes in the studio system all relate to discussions about the acceptability of dialogue, homosexuality, nudity, non-marital relationships, sexual perversions, and bedroom scenes. Questions of art versus entertainment, principles versus money, realism versus fantasy pervaded decision-making about appropriate material for films.

By 1968 Breen had died and the Production Code faded into a Rating System for films. By 1973 screen sex was so popular that *The Devil in Miss Jones* and *Deep Throat* were among the twelve top-grossing films of the year. Formal censorship of movies by the industry had eroded. (SGF)

PR

927. Malamuth, Neil M., and Edward Donnerstein. **Pornography and Sexual Aggression.** Orlando, Fla.: Academic Press, 1984. 333 p. Includes bibliographies and indexes. ISBN 0-12-466280-3.

The eleven papers that comprise this compilation on pornography and aggression are organized into five parts. Following an introduction by Donn Byrne and Kathryn Kelley giving a historical perspective on pornography research past and present, Malamuth and Donnerstein in part I present papers dealing with the causes of aggression against women (Malamuth) and with the effect of pornography on violence against women (Donnerstein).

Part II presents one paper by Barry S. Sapolsky on experimental research covering the impact of pornography that is not primarily violent in content, and another by Dolf Zillmann and Jennings Bryant on the impact of long-term exposure to pornography on arousal and on attitudes. In part III, John H. Court examines correlational data from the United States and other parts of the world suggesting that legalizing pornography has been associated with an increase in the incidence of rape in several countries. On the other hand, Paul R. Abramson and Haruo Hayashi report data from another country showing that pornography, even violent pornography, does not seem to have an effect on the incidence of rape. Then Larry Baron and Murray A. Straus report a significant association between the sales of pornography magazines in the United States and the rates of reported crimes against women.

Part IV contains two papers discussing possible causes of sexual aggression other than pornography. Mary P. Koss and Kenneth Leonard identify sexually aggressive men who commit rape and review the literature on the subject. Jacqueline D. Goodchilds and Gail L. Zellman concern themselves in their paper with sexual signaling between young couples and with sexual aggression in adolescent relationships. Part V examines the legal implications of research on pornography and sexual aggression. Steven Penrod and Daniel Linz explain the use of psychological research findings in effecting legislative change on the regulation of pornography and obscenity. Then Daniel Linz, Charles W. Turner, and Bradford W. Hesse discuss the basis of liability for injuries produced by media portrayals of violent pornography.

In the afterword on sex, violence, and the media, H. J. Eysenck concludes (1) that the portrayal of sex and violence in the media does have important effects on at least some people; (2) that it is possible to formulate general theories that explain the findings, and that indeed have predicted most of them; and (3) that these results present problems for society that go far beyond the realm of social psychology, and involve sociologists, philosophers, lawgivers, and politicians in general, as well, of course, as the community at large, whose voices cannot in this context be disregarded. (TJW)

PR,IL

928. Marcus, Steven. **The Other Victorians: A Study of Sexuality and Pornography in Mid-Nineteenth-Century England.** New York: Basic Books, 1966. 292 p. (Studies in Sex and Society). Includes index.

Using the techniques of literary criticism and historical analysis, Marcus examines significant medical, bibliographical, autobiographical, and pornographic writings from the Victorian era in order to present both the official and unofficial views of sexuality prevailing at the time.

For the official view, Marcus analyzes two works by William Acton—his surprisingly forward-looking book, entitled *Prostitution* (1870) and his popular text, *The Functions and Disorders of the Reproductive Organs* (1857). The latter, Marcus says, conveys "the notion that sex is a curse and a torture, and that the only hope of salvation for man lies in marriage to a woman who has no sexual desires and who will therefore make no sexual demands on her husband" (p. 32). It also contends that children are asexual creatures until puberty, that masturbation is harmful, and that the sexual feelings of the unmarried should be suppressed until marriage.

Another glimpse of the Victorian period is obtained by considering the grand undertakings of Henry Spencer Ashbee who, under the fairly scatological pseudonym Pisanus Fraxi, compiled the "first bibliography in the English language devoted to writings of a pornographic or sexual character" (p. 35). In three volumes (*Index Librorum Prohibitorum, Centuria Librorum Absconditorum,* and *Catena Librorum Tacendorum*) Ashbee listed thousands of items he had collected on his journeys across Europe. A meticulous bibliographer and true Victorian, he warns that the carefully described items should "be used with caution even by the mature" (p. 48).

Still another view of Victorian times is provided by that anonymous classic *My Secret Life,* that chronicles the lifetime sexual experiences of a Victorian gentleman. Marcus's analysis of this work "shows us that amid and underneath that world of Victorian England as we know it . . . a real, secret social life was being conducted, the secret life of sexuality" (p. 100).

Marcus then probes the content of four typical nineteenth-century pornographic novels (*The Lustful Turk, Rosa Fielding, The Amatory Experience of a Surgeon, Randiana*), identifying those characteristics that define them as pornography. The final, substantive chapter reviews the extensive literature of flagellation.

By way of summarizing the elements of pornographic writings and fantasies, Marcus presents in a concluding chapter his conception of pornotopia, a pornographic fantasy land where "reality is conceived as the scene of exclusively sexual activities and human and social institutions are understood to exist only insofar as they are conducive to further sexual play" (pp. 194-195). That is the world that the "other Victorians" recorded, described, and made known. (TJW)

IL,PO

929. Nobile, Philip, and Eric Nadler. **United States of America vs. Sex: How the Meese Commission Lied About Pornography.** New York: Minotaur Press, 1986. 370 p. ISBN 0-89110-020-2.

Nobile and Nadler, authors of this polemic leveled against the work of the Attorney General's Commission on Pornography, are editors of *Forum,* a popular magazine devoted to spreading sexological knowledge. In *United States of America v. Sex,* published shortly after the release of the Commission's *Final Report* in July 1986, they interpret the work of the Meese Commission as it conducted open hearings and executive meetings in major cities of the country.

Handicapped by underfunding and the requirement to produce a report within a year, the Commission produced a document that merited the skepticism of many. What Nobile and Nadler report exposes the suspect features of the Commission's work: the selection of commissioners whose conservative positions were known beforehand; unwillingness and perhaps inability to define pornography; no provision for research on aspects of pornography; limitation of recommendations almost wholly to legal and law enforcement steps to control pornography, ignoring such important issues as sex education; blatant desire to tie pornography, whether hard-core or soft-core, to antisocial behavior; and rejection of the conclusions of the better-funded, research-oriented 1970 Presidential Commission which stated that "empirical research designed to clarify the question has found no reliable evidence to date that exposure to explicit sexual materials plays a significant role in the causation of delinquent or criminal sexual behavior among youth or adults."

Nobile and Nadler also provide sketches of the careers of the Commission members: Chairman Henry Hudson, a Virginia attorney; Father Bruce Ritter, a Franciscan priest who directs Covenant House in New York City; James Dobson, president of Focus on the Family, a publishing and broadcast organization; Frederick Schauer, a professor of law at the University of Michigan; Park Eliot Dietz, a psychiatrist/sociologist at the University of Virginia; Edward Garcia, a federal judge from California; Diane Cusack, a councilwoman from Scottsdale, Arizona; Judith Becker, an expert on sex offenders; Deanne Tilton, head of the California Consortium on Child Abuse Councils; and Ellen Levine, editor of *Woman's Day.* They also include a chronology of events of the

Commission's work; a selection of letters to the chairman of the Commission from recognized writers who "expressed serious reservations about the censorious impulses of the Commission," including John Updike, John Irving, William F. Buckley, Jr., and William Kennedy; and finally the opinions of members of a "Shadow Commission" consisting of Betty Friedan, ACLU's Barry Lynn, Barbara Ehrenreich, Hendrik Hertzberg, Dr. John Money, Marcia Pally, Dr. Bernie Zilbergeld, and others, who reach conclusions quite different from those of the Commission. (TJW)

IL,PO
930. Oboler, Eli M. **The Fear of the Word: Censorship and Sex.** Metuchen, N.J.: Scarecrow Press, 1974. 362 p. Includes bibliography and index. ISBN 0-8108-0724-6.

In his search for explanations of censorship in society, Oboler, late librarian of Idaho State University at Pocatello, Idaho, and champion of free expression, has written a well-documented analysis of sex censorship from the earliest times to the present. Using various perspectives—anthropological, linguistic, psychological, religious—he speculates on the origins of censorship in prehistory, examines the nature of taboos in primitive societies, reviews the importance and "sacredness" of the Word in both Testaments, extols the freedom of speech in the Age of Pericles, and describes the beginnings of censorship in early Rome. He closely examines the Judeo-Christian influence on censorship, focusing on the notions of sex, sin, women, and censorship as viewed by the church fathers (St. Paul, Tertullian, St. Jerome, St. Augustine, St. Thomas Aquinas), the founders of religious orders (St. Benedict, Gregory the Great), the Council of Trent (1545-1563), Savanarola, the Catholic *Index Expurgatorius*, and Martin Luther. Oboler discusses the Puritan attitude toward sex and censorship in Calvin's time, English and American Puritanism, and the Irish censorship experience since 1929. He appraises current viewpoints among prominent Protestant and Catholic thinkers, concluding that there is today a more liberal attitude toward sexuality than ever before, especially in the Protestant camp.

In a series of chapters, Oboler considers (1) the psychological basis of censorship (i.e., what motivates the censor to attempt to guide public morality), (2) censorial attitudes that focus attention on the work of the creative artist, (3) censorship practices at the community level, (4) legal censorship in England and America from 1727 onward, (5) the librarian's task in book selection in view of the "new morality," (6) the official reaction to the *Report of the Commission on Obscenity and Pornography*, (7) the relationship between individual morality and censorship, and (8) recent decisions (1957-1973) of the U.S. Supreme Court affecting censorship.

Several appendices supplementing the text include a collection of anticensorship quotations, the recommendations of the Commission on Obscenity and Pornography, and statements on and about the Commission's *Report*.

On the basis of his wide-ranging investigation, Oboler concludes that "censorship has no basis in reason," that it is "neither essential nor inevitable for man's progress or well-being—only customary." (TJW)

IL
931. Perrin, Noel. **Dr. Bowdler's Legacy: A History of Expurgated Books in England and America.** New York: Atheneum, 1969. 296 p. Includes bibliographic notes and index.

Bowdlerism may be defined as a conscious, voluntary act of editing done by private individuals, usually for moral reasons, in order to remove from texts words or ideas that may be considered embarrassing or pernicious, such as sexual or religious allusions. The term is derived from the efforts of the best-known expurgator of the nineteenth century, Thomas Bowdler, a retired physician and country gentleman who, along with his sister Harriet and in the cause of Christianity, bowdlerized—a term that was soon accepted for the expurgation process—twenty of Shakespeare's plays to produce in 1807 the *Family Shakespeare*, the popularity of which kept it in print for over a hundred years.

Perrin presents several causes for this literary expurgation which originated in the eighteenth century and became prevalent in the nineteenth: the vogue of sentiment and delicacy accounting for the manners and morals of polite society that took hold at the turn of the nineteenth century, the rise of evangelical religion in eighteenth-century England, working relations of the sexes resulting from the industrial revolution, and the rise of a general reading public. Just before the Victorian age, a new literary morality appeared in England that concentrated on what was unseemly in poetry and prose. Anything derogatory of religion or containing sexual allusions was bound to be expurgated. Self-appointed guardians of public morality deleted from texts all that was considered obscene and judged likely to offend the delicate sensibilities of high-minded people, especially women, who should be protected from unsavory influences.

During Victorian times expurgation increased dramatically in England. Besides Shakespeare, the busy expurgators turned their attention to the Bible; the novels of Fielding, Sterne, Smollett, Richardson, Defoe, and others; the poetry of Byron, Burns, Donne, Herrick, and others; and the classic works of Chaucer and Pepys. In America, where the movement lagged behind the English experience, the Bible, Franklin's *Autobiography*, Whitman's *Leaves of Grass*, and Melville's *Moby Dick* received attention. One of America's purifiers was Noah Webster, who kept the "dirty words" out of his dictionary.

In the last chapter, Perrin discusses the decline of bowdlerism. He asserts that the movement for literary purity became a casualty of World War I. Varied reasons are advanced for its demise: the rise of Freudian psychology, the women's rights movement, the appearance of mass media other than the book, and the reaction that had set in against the excesses of bowdlerism toward the end of the century. Perrin points out that the movement died quickly. Nevertheless its vestiges are detectable still, and a return to a similar effort, even today, is always possible. (TJW)

PR,IL

932. Randall, Richard S. **Freedom and Taboo: Pornography and the Politics of a Self Divided.** Berkeley, Calif.: University of California Press, 1989. 340 p. Includes bibliography and index. ISBN 0-520-06379-1.

Randall, Professor of Political Science at New York University, in this study of pornography, takes a broad, systematic approach to the subject in order "to understand why pornography has been a persistent problem for human beings everywhere" (p. ix). His perspective is that the pornographic is "both a universal social category . . . and a psychological one." Pornography's themes "invite and repel," a paradox whose roots may be found deep within the mind. Thus Randall bases much of his examination on psychoanalytic insights that aid in understanding the "pornographic within." He is also interested in society's ambivalent attitudes toward "transgressive sexual expression," which he believes reflect both the inner self and the external controls that prevail.

Randall's study begins by distinguishing between the pornographic within (erotic fantasies violating sexual taboos, norms, conventions, and the like) and the pornographic without (representations in the real world of images, language, gesture, and sound). In part I, he examines the nature of the pornographic animal (Homo sexualis) with his forbidden wishes and fantasies reflecting humanity's unique sexuality; and then the way societies have regulated sexual works and images. In part II, he delves into the nature of the pornographic imagination as manifested in both aesthetic literature and in the "I know it when I see it" category. He also assesses the substantial research literature on the effect of pornography on individuals and society, concluding that the research has not provided a conclusive answer to whether pornography is causally linked to antisocial or criminal behavior. In part III, Randall deals with pornography as a social institution, especially its ties with libertarian doctrine, and the difficulties encountered in coping with it in a liberal democratic society.

In part IV Randall examines our highly sexualized communications environment that has brought about remarkable changes in the technical quality, variety, and availability of pornographic materials. Then he reviews the evolution of changes in American law affecting obscenity and pornography, making more precise what is and is not obscene and pornographic. He concludes that in a free speech, mass democratic society, pornography will continue to be an abiding problem because frustrated sexual behavior, inherent in civilized society, results in sexual fantasies that lead inevitably to expression of those fantasies in pornographic media. (TJW)

PR,IL

933. Rembar, Charles. **The End of Obscenity: The Trials of** *Lady Chatterley, Tropic of Cancer,* **and** *Fanny Hill.* New York: Harper & Row, 1986. 528 p. Hardcover edition published in 1968 by Random House. Includes index. ISBN 0-06-097061-8.

In the 1986 preface to *The End of Obscenity* (1968), attorney Rembar states that the law dealing with obscenity has not changed since the landmark 1966 Supreme Court decision on John Cleland's *Memoirs of a Woman of Pleasure*, a.k.a. *Fanny Hill.* He says that the three obscenity tests still obtain: To be judged obscene a work must be (1) predominantly prurient, (2) patently offensive, and (3) utterly devoid of redeeming social value. The three tests were regarded as established for all media; however, since 1966 no books have been successfully prosecuted, but there have been successful prosecutions of other forms of expression, such as film, picture magazines, television, radio, and videocassettes. Prosecutors are reluctant to press charges against books because "pursuing obscenity is no longer popular" (p. xii).

Victorian obscenity laws prevailed in the United States through the middle of the twentieth century. Deemed obscene had been Theodore Dreiser's *An American Tragedy*, Lillian Smith's *Strange Fruit*, and Edmund Wilson's *Memoirs of Hecate County.* On the other hand, in 1934 New York federal courts held that James Joyce's *Ulysses* was not obscene.

Rembar states that this book is about an idea, a legal concept, that "the government could not suppress a book if it had merit as literature" (p. 4). If so, the First Amendment, which guarantees free expression, was applied. Attempts by government to stop the publication of D. H. Lawrence's *Lady Chatterley's Lover*, Henry Miller's *Tropic of Cancer*, and John Cleland's *Fanny Hill* are explored. If these works were obscene (i.e., if the writings were lustful [prurient]), exciting a sexual response from the reader, which was all that was required under existing law, then they would be banned and author and publisher jailed.

The legal background against which Rembar argued his cases was the importance of the 1957 Roth and Alberts cases in which the Supreme Court stated that obscenity is not protected by the First Amendment and ruled that existing federal and state anti-obscenity statutes were valid. This book describes the exciting obscenity trials of the three books in question, which culminated in the Supreme Court's decision on the *Fanny Hill* case in 1966. Justice Brennan's majority opinion on *Fanny Hill* sums up the significance of these trials:

> ... a book cannot be proscribed unless it is found to be *utterly* without redeeming social value. This is so even though the book is found to possess the requisite prurient appeal and to be patently offensive. Each of the three federal constitutional criteria is to be applied independently; the social value of the book can neither be weighed against nor canceled by its prurient appeal or patent offensiveness ... (p. 480).

On this basis, Rembar speculates that "obscenity as the term has been commonly understood—the impermissible description of sex in literature—approaches its end. So far as writing is concerned ... there is no longer any law of obscenity" and "not only in our law but in our culture, obscenity will soon be gone" (p. 493). (TJW)

PR,IL

934. Russell, Diana E. H., ed. **Making Violence Sexy: Feminist Views on Pornography.** New York: Teachers College Press, 1993. 302 p. (Athene Series). Includes bibliography and index. ISBN 0-8077-62689-5.

This anthology of some twenty-five papers and statements summarizes the current stance of feminists against pornography in the United States and Canada. In the introduction, Russell defines male heterosexual pornography "as material created for heterosexual males that combines sex and/or the exposure of genitals with the abuse or degradation of females in a manner that appears to endorse, condone, or encourage such behavior" (p. 3). She distinguishes it from erotica, which she characterizes as "sexually suggestive or arousing material that is free of sexism, racism, or homophobia, and respectful of all human beings and animals portrayed" (p. 3). Pornographic material is thus deemed abusive and degrading to women, objectifying them "as amazons, panting playthings, adult toys, dehumanized objects to be used, abused, broken, and discarded" (Brownmiller, *Against Our Will*, 1975, p. 394).

Russell tells the story of how the women's antipornography movement got started and how it eventually split over the issue of censorship. She also describes the impact the work of the Attorney General's Commission on Pornography had in 1986 and how feminists Catherine MacKinnon and Andrea Dworkin made pornography a civil rights issue.

Part I, "Survivors of Pornography," provides several first-person accounts of experiences with pornography by such notables as Gloria Steinem (the sad story of abused wife Linda Lovelace); Bebe Moore Campbell (telling the life of Angel, a porn star); Eveline Giobbe (a prostitute); Katherine Brody (incest survivor); and the Rev. Susan Wilhelm (pornography and marital brutality). In part II, "Overview," statements from John Stoltenberg, Patricia Hill Collins, Van F. White, and Martin Dufresne, and a "Question and Answer" section by Catherine MacKinnon and Andrea Dworkin cover the theoretical foundation of the feminist anti-pornography position. In part III, "Feminist Research on Pornography," Russell presents six papers on the work of feminists investigating different facets of the pornography problem, such as sexual abuse of women, rape, and racism.

In part IV, "Feminist Strategies and Actions Against Pornography," Russell presents several testimonials from feminists about practical actions taken against porn shops, booksellers, publishers, and individual writers. One such target of feminist ire is Bret Easton Ellis whose book *American Psycho* depicts the degradation, brutalization, and evisceration of women. (TJW)

PR

935. Stoller, Robert J. **Porn: Myths for the Twentieth Century.** New Haven, Conn.: Yale University Press, 1991. 228 p. Includes bibliography. ISBN 0-300-05092-5.

For this investigation of the porn industry, psychoanalyst Stoller dons the methodological garb of an ethnographer in the hope of fathoming the dynamics of sexual excitement, and also to give ethnographers something to ponder over in their interviews with identified participants in ethnographic studies. Stoller believes that the "subjectivity" of participants' views should not be ignored; in fact, he believes that it should be given prominent consideration, just as a psychoanalyst, in trying to find truth in an analysand's statements, pays rapt attention to subjective material.

In this book Stoller investigates ethnographically the subculture of the porn industry by interviewing individuals who have first-hand knowledge of that industry: Bill Margold, a pornographer/performer/director; Happy, a would-be porn queen who has just been recruited by Bill; Kay Parker, a popular porn star for ten years and now public relations director for a major X-rated producer and distributor; Nina Hartley, a porn star; Jim Holliday, generally regarded as the historian and bibliographer of pornography; Merlin, a S&M pornographer; and Ron, a scriptwriter.

From his perspective as a psychoanalyst interviewing participants in the porn industry, Stoller reaches several conclusions that have an impact on his own thinking about sexual excitement and those who devote themselves to producing that excitement. He believes that porn—"the product—films and videotapes—produced primarily for men who identify themselves, by means of what gives them an erection, as erotically interested in women"—does little harm and little good, either to performers or viewers. He further believes that the pornographers interviewed are suffering from Oedipal rage, which blinds them to the shoddiness of the porn industry. They are thumbing their noses at society, men as well as women, parents, institutions, and mores. Furthermore, Stoller distrusts the anti-pornographers who claim that pornography is man's game, for they don't realize that there are pornographies for women, gays, and lesbians. Then Stoller refutes the present legal tactic that states that pornography is prostitution. He suggests that a rigorously logical approach to the anti-porn scholarship should reveal the weaknesses of that scholarship.

Finally, Stoller points out that the battle over pornography is not a "showdown between good and evil." We should concern ourselves with "the real world of hatred, not the theatre of pornography" (p. 225). In fact, Stoller finds that "the precise details of erotic life—fantasies and action" are a good way to examine "the dynamics of rage, useful as long as I do not do as pornhaters: equate fantasizing with realizing" (p. 225). (TJW)

PO

936. Weatherford, Jack McIver. **Porn Row.** New York: Arbor House, 1986. 248 p. Includes bibliography. ISBN 0-87795-798-3.

The Strip, where many sex-oriented businesses are centered, is located on a few well-defined blocks on 14th Street in northwest Washington, D.C., a stone's throw from the White House. Weatherford, Assistant Professor of Anthropology at Macalester College, worked as a clerk/flunky at a porn shop called the Pink Pussy. Not only did the shop sell magazines (soft-core, hard-core, gay, transvestite, B&D, and S/M, etc.); sex aids (body oils, lubricants, dolls, dildoes, drug paraphernalia, etc.); and soft- and hard-core films and videos; it was also equipped with small booths that provided peep shows and a place where men could watch sixteen-minute pornographic films, simultaneously masturbating or being fellated by prostitutes. Weatherford's main purpose in working there was to study the pornographic subculture by using the time-honored anthropological technique of participating in and observing the setting that he hoped to understand.

From his strategically located post at the cash register at the front of this sex emporium, Weatherford was able to watch the flow of characters into and out of the Pink Pussy. They consisted of those who made a living off the Strip—pimps, prostitutes (male and female), drug pushers, and other unsavory types—as well as the sex-starved visitors—by day, construction workers, government employees, addicts, and tourists; by night, teenagers from the suburbs, women in search of midnight cowboys, and other thrill-seeking habituees. Businesses catering to their needs included massage parlors, strip joints, bars and restaurants with live shows, and other sex-oriented businesses, such as the Pink Pussy. Although Weatherford describes the activities at the Pink Pussy in great detail, he also gives a more general picture of what goes on along the Strip, including the use of the various fast-food restaurants as meeting places for those engaged in running the Strip. Over coffee, managers meet with their helpers, prostitutes hash over the previous night's experiences, pimps instruct their girls, and so on. When Weatherford's job became hazardous because of the competition between rival companies to gain control of the business, he quit. To his dismay, he found the world outside the Strip differed little in terms of matters sexual—advertising, fashion, magazines, television, the news—all seemed hell-bent on catering to a popular yearning for sex.

Weatherford makes cross-cultural comparisons of sexual behavior in numerous societies with that of the Strip. He concludes that American sexual behavior is exceedingly strange. Despite the gawdy display of sex in such places as the Strip, created to satisfy the sexual wants of sex hungry men and women, modern society seems to provide less opportunity for the manifestation of sexuality than many other cultures. (TJW)

Humor: Satire, Quotations, Jokes, Comics, Puns, Limericks

(For related material see also entry 19)

PO
937. Chieger, Bob. **Was It Good for You, Too? Quotations on Love and Sex.** New York: Atheneum, 1983. 258 p. Includes index. ISBN 0-689-70650-2.

With such one-liners as "A lover teaches a wife all that her husband has concealed from her" (Honoré de Balzac) in section 1 ("Adultery") and "When women go wrong, men go right after them" (Mae West) in section 32 ("Women on Men"), Chieger has assembled some pithy, witty, and provocative comments on love and sex. Literature, film, television, radio, and lectures provide the sources of these sayings, which are arranged chronologically within thirty-two subjects. Most of the phrase spinners in this collection are our contemporaries from the entertainment world (Joan Rivers, Zsa Zsa Gabor, Woody Allen), the literary world (Fran Lebowitz, Gore Vidal, Norman Mailer), the political world (Henry Kissinger, Ayatollah Khomeini), and the world of pundits and satirists (H. L. Mencken, Pauline Kael). Even a few scientists (Albert Einstein, Marie Curie, Margaret Mead) have said some marvelous things about love and sex. Earlier contributions come from such perceptive observers as Ovid, Socrates, Lord Chesterfield, Voltaire, Oscar Wilde, and Mark Twain. Of the 2,000 quotations in this delightful work, perhaps none is more haughty than Henry Miller's "Sex is one of the nine reasons for reincarnation. The other eight are unimportant." (TJW)

PO
938. King, Florence. **He: An Irreverent Look at the American Male.** New York: Stein and Day, 1978. 204 p. ISBN 0-8128-2513-6.

King describes herself as neither a "total woman" nor a women's liberationist. (The most readable section of *Ms.* magazine, she notes, is the "No Comment" department.) With a sharp eye and ear, King skewers the foibles of American males—and females—in recent times. After regaling readers with salty recollections of her teenage sexual experiments in the 1950s, King goes on to characterize various male types in the 1970s. Not to be missed is her send-up of the male feminist, whom she dubs Jonathan Stuart Mill. Ever trendy, Jonathan has lost interest in the black causes and is now (he explains with a straight face) "into women." King also exposes the literary sins of recent male writers, and she portrays the new misogynist, who got that way (she confesses) partly from too many encounters with strident feminists. Although she professes a passion for the polished Alistair Cooke types, one suspects that in reality they would be too tepid for her. Despite her "irreverent look at the American male," many readers will sense King's delight in him, foibles and all. (**Men's Studies**, 1985)

PO
939. Legman, Gershon, ed. **The Limerick: 1700 Examples with Notes, Variants and Index.** New York: Bell, 1969. 511 p. Includes bibliography and index. ISBN 0-517-13911-1.

The authors of most limericks, especially the erotic ones, are unknown. Legman derived the 1,739 limericks in this collection from various anthologies, going as far back as *Cythera's Hymnal*, published in 1870. Other basic sources, such as Norman Douglas's *Some Limericks* (1928) and certain oral collections existing only in manuscript, provided examples of both the truly bawdy limericks characteristic of the nineteenth century and the more typically scatological ones of today. Legman defines the limerick as basically an indecent verse-form ("a gruelling combination of sick sex and sadistic scatology") of five anapestic lines usually having a rhyme scheme of *aabba*. The clean limerick (one without erotic content) has "never been of the slightest real interest to anyone, since the end of its brief fad in the 1860's" (p. vii). The bawdy limericks in this compilation are categorized under eighteen headings, such as "Little Romances," "Organs," "Strange Intercourse," "Oral Irregularity," "Buggery," and so forth. Each limerick is dated, tying it into its source. A typical limerick is the following:

There was a dentist named Stone
Who saw all his patients alone.
In a fit of depravity
He filled the wrong cavity,
And my, how his practice has grown!

Legman's long introduction traces the prehistory of the limerick (a word derived from the Irish town of Limerick) as far back as 1300, and even makes a case for its appearance in the plays of Shakespeare and Ben Jonson. The modern limerick appears to have originated in 1863 with the reprinting of Edward Lear's *Book of Nonsense*, first published in 1846. Writing limericks became a fad. About the limerick, Arnold Bennett said, "the best ones are entirely unprintable"; George Bernard Shaw stated, "they must be left for oral tradition"; and Arthur Wimperis claimed that the ones "of any literary merit are distinctly Rabelaisian" (p. xi). The present collection bears out what these worthies have said about the character and tone of this enduring verse-form.

Legman winds up his remarks by claiming that the limerick "is not only the fixed poetic form original to the English language, but the bawdy limerick in particular is today the only kind of newly-composed poetry in English, or song, which has the slightest chance whatever of survival" (p. lxxii). (TJW)

IL,PO

940. Legman, Gershon. **Rationale of the Dirty Joke: An Analysis of Sexual Humor.** First Series. New York: Grove Press, 1968. 811 p.

This book analyzes the structure of erotic jokes within a historical, psychological, and sociological framework. Based on the premise that jokes are not invented, but evolve, Legman traces recurring thematic similarities and variations over time and relates them to cultural factors. Legman, considered to be the leading authority on erotic folklore and literature, states that erotic humor is the most popular of all types in all centuries and cultures. In Freudian fashion he explains that jokes are an expression of hostility and aggression (sometimes self-directed) and the teller negates his feelings of fear and uneasiness about the subject matter by exposing the listener to the same feelings. In consideration of the reader, the jokes most likely to offend are placed at the end of the chapters, and the more offensive chapters and themes increase as one approaches the end of the book. According to Legman, erotic and scatological jokes can be divided into fifteen subject groupings. This book covers nine of those fifteen subjects, each treated in a separate lengthy chapter: "Children," "Fools," "Animals," "The Male Approach," "The Sadistic Concept," "Women," "Premarital Sexual Acts," "Marriage," and "Adultery." The remaining subjects (homosexuality, prostitution, venereal disease, castration, dysphemism and cursing, and scatology) are "presumably of less ordinary occurrence or of greater psychological danger or violence, and are therefore theoretically of greater anxiety-content than those in this First Series" (p. 11). These he covers in a second, already completed book (*No Laughing Matter*, distributed in 1975 by Breaking Point, New York). At the end of the First Series there is an outline of subjects and motifs that details all fifteen subject fields and their subcategories in both series. Although Legman notes that he draws on older folklore collections, *novellieri*, European jest books, research in the field (the urban milieu of parlor, bedroom, and beer joints), tales of raconteur friends, and excerpts from the popular press, he does not include a bibliography with the First Series. However, the Second Series does conclude with a bibliography and index. (EBS)

PO

941.   Madonna. **Sex.** Photographed by Stephen Meisel. Art directed by Fabien Baron. Edited by Glenn O'Brien. New York: Warner Books, 1992. 128 p. ISBN 0-446-51732-1.

Metal covered, spiral bound, and plastic wrapped, this latest production by Madonna is a revelation of her sexual fantasies. That's all it is, she says. "Everything you are about to see and read is a fantasy, a dream, pretend." She adds "Nothing in this book is true. I made it all up."

Following a brief introduction in which Madonna encourages safe sex with condoms, a poetic statement introduces herself as Dita, a sort of love technician and guide, who boasts of her sexual prowess. Illustrations follow: the first shows Madonna naked, sucking her middle finger while placing her right hand toyingly in her crotch. Batches of S&M pictures follow, interspersed with explicit sexual musings by Madonna as Dita. Clever use of the Christian cross supports Dita's efforts to distinguish between benign S&M and sexual abuse.

Colorful, full-page illustrations depict various simulated sexual acts, including oral sex (cunnilingus and fellatio), sex with teens, analingus, masturbation, narcissistic "pussy" love, sex with an old man, gay and lesbian sex, interracial sex, exhibitionism, bestiality, and group sex.

Intermittently, throughout the book, a series of love letters from Dita to her lover Johnny punctuates the text, but ends with Dita disgusted to discover that Ben is going down on Johnny. Concerning people's assumed desire to improve their sexual repertoires, Dita remarks, "A lot of people are afraid to say what they want. That's why they don't get what they want."

Two special features supplement this book: a comic book insert about an orgy involving Dita and her friends; and a compact disc carrying a vocal by Madonna from *Erotica*, her latest disc collection.

In a final word Madonna thanks her friends, including Isabella Rossellini, Naomi Campbell, Tatiana von Furstenburg, Ingrid Casaras, Big Daddy Lane, Vanilla Ice, and others for their willingness to take off their clothes and perform as ordered. A bare-breasted Madonna appears on almost every page. One very striking pose shows Madonna hitchhiking boldly and provocatively (into the future?) along a Miami thoroughfare without a stitch on. (TJW)

IL

942.   Redfern, Walter. **Puns.** Oxford, Eng.: Basil Blackwood, 1985. 234 p. First published in 1984. Includes bibliographic notes and index. ISBN 0-631-13793-9.

As valid as but subtler than the limerick is the pun. Difficult to define, the pun is "the coupling of things that do not customarily cohabit" (p. 173). For example, on the cover of Redfern's book *Puns* is Man Ray's famous photograph *Violon d'Ingres* (1924), that depicts a seated naked woman, back to the viewer, with two painted scrolls ornamenting her flesh, giving the impression of a musical instrument. Contrast with this visual pun the following: "There's a vas deferens between children and no children" (p. 18). Confident that these delightful visual and verbal puns are bound to titillate, trigger guffaws, or at least bring a knowing smile to the face, Redfern, a teacher of French studies in England, takes the reader on a journey through the tangled world of puns and punning from the ancients to such modern-day punsters as James Joyce and Vladimir Nabokov.

The wordplay that punning affords seems limitless. Erotica, particularly, is a fruitful area for generating puns. For the world of erotic puns, the reader must consult the index where, under the headings eroticism, obscenity, pornography, and scatology, one will find numerous references to discussions of puns. One reference exposes the following: "Your mother's like a police station—dicks going in and out all the time" (p. 92). Or this one: "A pornographer is one who offers vice to the lovelorn" (p. 18). Finally, this eyecatcher from Irish writer Brigid Brophy: "It is a very daycent class of fellatio you meet travelling Aer Cunnilingus" (p. 170). (TJW)

II,PO,YA

943. Sherman, Allan. **The Rape of the A*P*E*: The Official History of the Sex Revolution, 1945-1973: The Obscening of America: An R*S*V*P* Document.** Chicago: Playboy Press, 1975. 448 p. (*** American Puritan Ethic; **** Redeeming Social Value Pornography). Includes chronology.

This book is Sherman's idiosyncratic history of sex in general and the American Sex Revolution in particular. Famous for his recording of the song "Hello Muddah, Hello Faddah," Sherman has now written the funny story of sex, dedicated "to the dirty-minded Americans who made the sex revolution possible; and to the clean-minded ones who made it necessary." Before launching into this *tour de force* on sex, Sherman clears the decks by exorcising the "dirtiest" word in the English language: *fuck*. He accomplishes this formidable task by typing the word 504 times on one sheet of paper! The American Sex Revolution, he asserts, "was as inevitable and as seriously motivated as any revolution in history."

It became necessary to overthrow the American Puritan Ethic (APE) before we could enjoy unfettered sexuality. Inspired by FDR's statement, "This generation of Americans has a rendezvous with history," young Americans and their dirty-minded parents did just that—they devastated the morality of the APE that had characterized America before World War II.

Sherman backtracks to the beginnings of life on Earth in order to explain how sex and later religion, marriage, sin, guilt, and shame originated, and how, when, and where sex got mixed up. A turning point in the story comes when Dawg-muh, the religion man; Posh, the society man; and Flagg, the government man; try to recruit Sap, the hero of this story, along with his companion, Lala, and teach them all about the sins, taboos, and rules and regulations their puritanical institutions imposed on the sex lives of people. As a result of these ethical restrictions, the sex life of Sap and Lala, which had been so free and idyllic for hundreds of thousands of years, slowly collapsed under the weight of civilization.

Sherman identifies the early rumblings of the revolution, as in World War II when, in countries around the world, the American serviceman underwent an unparalleled sex education provided free of charge by the U.S. Armed Forces. He precisely dates it as occurring on November 10, 1945 in Long Beach, California, when "a pimply-faced 16-year-old boy," Ellsworth "Sonny" Wisecarver and beautiful 25-year-old Mrs. E.D., who had been shacking up with Sonny, appeared in court and accepted the judge's pronouncement that Sonny was "an incorrigible sexual delinquent," a judgment based on Sonny's record of affairs with married women ever since he was fourteen. Bob Hope joked about Sonny on his Tuesday night Pepsodent radio show, and before long the entire country, except the followers of APE, were laughing and savoring the story.

Sherman provides a chronological itemization of events from 1945 on that reveal the unfolding sex revolution in the United States. A sampling of events: the publication in 1948 of Alfred Kinsey's *Sexual Behavior of the American Male*, a major scandal; in 1952 an ex-GI named George Jorgensen traveled to Copenhagen, Denmark, but never came back: Christine Jorgensen returned, having left his/her name and penis in a Copenhagen operating room; in 1953 the first issue of *Playboy* magazine was published; in 1959 young girls appeared on American beaches wearing a new kind of swimsuit, the bikini.

On and on, year by year, Sherman chronicles the American sex revolution. By 1973, Americans had reached a point where only one obstacle remained: achieving The Magic F**k (MF), an experience that will solve all one's problems. He also speculates about such possibilities as electrofantasex, simulgasm, and so on. Sherman closes with a reminder that the APE, unfortunately, never rests. In praise of his seriocomic book about sex, comedian Steve Allen gushed, "It's outrageous . . . witty . . . wild . . . enlightening . . . hysterically funny." (TJW)

PO
944. Simons, G. L. **The Illustrated Book of Sexual Records.** New York: Bell, 1984. 192 p. ISBN 0-517-44899-8.

Simons's book may be used as a handy reference work to find famous (or infamous) first facts about sexuality, human or otherwise, many of which are both amusing and informative. The material, presented in the form of paragraph-length responses to such superlative statements as "Oldest sex manual," "Earliest contraceptives," "First sex institute," "Largest penis in the animal kingdom," "First reclining nude in European erotic art," and "Earliest sex laws," is organized into eight sections: "Human Physiology"; "Sex Technique & Performance"; "The Arts"; "Aberrant Sex & Deviation"; "Animals & Plants"; "Contraception & Castration"; "Sexology"; and "Prudery, Superstition & the Law."

Many of the entries within these sections are illustrated with black-and-white photographs and humorous cartoons. Unfortunately, the book lacks an index to the wealth of seemingly well-researched information. (TJW)

PO
945. Thurber, James, and E. B. White. **Is Sex Necessary? or, Why You Feel the Way You Do.** New York: Blue Ribbon Books, 1929. 197 p. Includes glossary.

This parody on human sexuality has the earmarks of a scholarly study: a foreword, a preface, substantive footnotes, and numerous illustrations. It even has a glossary explaining the sex jargon of the day. For example, back in the 1920s it was difficult to understand the term *psychoneurosis*, but Thurber's glossary took care of the matter neatly: "Psycho-neurosis: Same as neurosis, only worse."

Intended primarily for the puzzled average American, this book adopts a serious tone in its apparent study of male/female relationships during the sexual revolution in the 1920s. Because they are not sexologists themselves, Thurber and White say they rely for astute opinion on those well-known professionals, Drs. Walter Tithridge and Karl Zaner, whom they address as the "deans of American sex" (p. xv).

In order to explain the deteriorating relations between the sexes then going on, the authors examine such phenomena as the rise of pedestalism, or the American male's amazing worship of the female; the period of *Übertragung* (transition) in which men transfer their ardor for women to games; and women's reaction to sudden male interest called Diversion Subterfuge, which manifested itself in fudge-making.

In later chapters Thurber and White deal with ways to tell love from passion; feminine types (Quiet Type, Outdoors Type, Clinging Vine); the Sexual Revolution, or women's sudden awareness that they had the "right to be sexual" and not simply amiable, resulting in the woman spending "all her time admiring herself in mirrors, and Man, discouraged, devoting himself to raising begonias" (pp. 84-85). So in places like New York City love atrophied.

Continuing their satire, they present three chapters entitled "What Should Children Tell Parents?" "Claustrophobia, or What Every Young Wife Should Know," and "Frigidity in Men." They also have a special section, "Answers to Hard Questions," turning their attention to such puzzlers as the following: "Should a woman live with her husband if they are separated?" (TJW)

PO
945a. Zacks, Richard. **History Laid Bare: Love, Sex, and Perversity from the Ancient Etruscans to Warren G. Harding.** New York: HarperCollins, 1994. 463 p. Includes bibliography.

Zacks arranges this history of sex chronologically beginning with an Assyrian law tablet dated 1450 B.C. about kissing, abortion, and rape, and ending with an A.D. 1921 entry about President Warren G. Harding's affair with Nan Britton, carried out in an anteroom closet adjacent to the Cabinet Room of the White House. The book is divided into eight parts: The Ancient World, Late Classical and Early Middle Ages, The Middle

Ages, The Renaissance, The Seventeenth Century, The Eighteenth Century, The Nineteenth Century, and Early Twentieth Century.

Zacks's purpose is to restore to history the sex stories that were omitted from studies by Victorians and other scholarly prudes. The source material for these "stories, fragments, vignettes" is available, and one needs only to probe beneath the surface. The book "aims to amuse, enlighten, and to fill a gap" (p. xv). Each entry is captioned (e.g., "Cleopatra Seduces Mark Antony, 42 B.C.," "Pauline Bonaparte's Gynecological Report, 1807"). Zacks's comments in italics follow and introduce the subject matter, often in translation. Entries close with source notes.

Intended for bedtime reading, this collection of anecdotes offers a wealth of amusing material not readily available in the typical history of sex. (TJW)

Nonverbal Communication. Body Language. Nudism

(For related material see also entry 395)

PO
946. Clapham, Adam, and Robin Constable. **As Nature Intended: A Pictorial History of the Nudists.** Los Angeles, Calif.: Elysium Growth Press, 1986. 118 p. Includes bibliography. ISBN 1-55599-007-X.

Written by Clapham, a television documentary producer with the BBC, with the assistance of photographer Constable, the history of nudism presented in this profusely illustrated book goes back to the beginnings of the nudist movement in Germany around the turn of the century. Nudists recognize Richard Ungewitter as the father of the nudist movement. A German intellectual, he proposed in a slim illustrated volume published in 1905 that a utopian nudist society be created for everyone regardless of age or sex. His society was short-lived, but the idea caught on and spread rapidly. In Switzerland, Werner Zimmerman advocated nakedness in schools and wrote extensively about nudism. In Germany, Paul Zimmermann established the world's first nudist resort north of Hamburg and called it *Freilichipark* (Open Air Park), which lasted until 1981. Frances and Mason Merrill, enthusiastic Americans, helped spread the movement to America with their classic work, *Among the Nudists* (1931). The movement continued to flourish in Germany as *Nacktkultur* until the Nazis banned all nudist activity in 1933. In England the movement was called gymnosophy; the New Gymnosophy Society was formed and a magazine launched.

In 1929 Maurice Parmalee published *Nudism in Modern Life*; in it he tackled the thorny question of sex and nakedness. He states: "Sex feeling and curiosity . . . characterise practically all adults who enter the gymnosophic movement. After becoming habituated, sex stimulus through vision usually falls to normal, and the initial curiosity is satisfied."

The nudist movement caught on quickly in the United States where, under the influence of Bernarr MacFadden, editor of *Physical Culture* magazine, the first nudist group, the American League for Physical Culture, was born. After its demise in the early 1930s, it was replaced by the American Sunbathing Association, which today has 25,000 members.

The remainder of the book is devoted to a discussion of the modern movement in several European countries, especially West Germany, England, France, Denmark, and Yugoslavia, identifying the principal European nude beaches. Singled out for description is the *Zone Naturiste* at Cap d'Agde in the south of France, which has become very popular with Europeans in general and is symbolic of today's "phenomenal growth of nudity on the beaches of Europe." (TJW)

PR,IL
947. Henley, Nancy M. **Body Politics: Power, Sex, and Nonverbal Communication.** Drawings by Deirdre Patrick. Englewood Cliffs, N.J.: Prentice-Hall, 1977. 214 p. (The Patterns of Social Behavior Series). Includes bibliographic references and index. ISBN 0-13-079632-8.

While a great deal of attention has been given to the horizontal dimension of nonverbal communication (e.g., closeness, intimacy, sexuality, and emotional expression), very little has focused on the vertical dimension (e.g., status, power, dominance, and superiority). This book attempts to remedy that oversight by examining the intersection between sex, power, and nonverbal communication. Henley asserts that power is the context within which we live our lives. Nonverbal behavior plays a crucial role in the power continuum as a link between covert and overt control of others; it is a microstructure that supports the political/economic macrostructure of society. Rather than attributing sex differences in nonverbal behavior to biological differences, Henley tries to demonstrate that these differences are learned responses to differences in power that serve to maintain the current power structure. By using a systems perspective (i.e., considering individual units of behavior in the context of the total communication situation) and a perspective significantly influenced by Goffman, Brown, Birdwhistell, O'Connor, and Anthony, the book reviews nonverbal behavior in several areas of study—from general considerations of male/female differences in the use of time (women's time is regarded as at the disposal of others while men have more control over theirs), space (women have control over less territory and less desirable spaces than men), environment (women are more restricted in their personal space and the territory they occupy), and language (males have instrumental language while females have more expressive language) to more specific aspects of interpersonal communication such as demeanor, touch (more touching is associated with superiors asserting dominance over subordinates, not necessarily because males are more oversexed than females), eye contact (women may look at males more because they feel positively toward them and because they want their approval), and facial expression (a man's emotional display is limited while a woman's has more range).

Based on a presentation of numerous research findings in each of these areas of study, Henley concludes that power rather than inherent gender difference is the most parsimonious explanation of male/female differences in nonverbal communication; such differences are "not sex differences, they are power differences" (p. 192). Helpful pointers on conducting research on nonverbal communication lace this innovative approach to nonverbal communication between males and females. (SGF)

PR,IL

948. Mayo, Clara, Alexandra Weiss, and Nancy Henley, eds. **Gender and Nonverbal Behavior.** New York: Springer-Verlag, 1981. 284 p. Includes bibliography and index. ISBN 0-3879-0601-0.

The thirteen papers in this anthology review past research on various aspects of sex differences in nonverbal behavior, report new findings, and point to theoretical implications and areas requiring further study. Among the topics addressed are gender patterns in touch, space, gaze, and movement; androgyny and nonverbal communication; the role of socialization and other factors in the acquisition of nonverbal skills

For a more thorough review of existing data, see *Nonverbal Sex Differences* by Judith A. Hall (Baltimore, Md.: Johns Hopkins University Press, 1984). Hall systematically draws together the vast research literature on gender differences in nonverbal behavior, analyzes it statistically, and evaluates significant theories and hypotheses. She looks at accuracy of judgment of nonverbal messages, and accuracy of expression, plus specific sources of cues: face, gaze, interpersonal distance and orientation, touch, body movement and position, and voice. (**Women's Studies**, 1987)

IL

949. Thorne, Barrie, Nancy Henley, and Cheris Kramarae, eds. **Language, Gender, and Society.** Rowley, Mass.: Newhouse House, 1983. 342 p. Includes bibliography and index. ISBN 0-8837-7268-X.

Eight years after their groundbreaking volume *Language and Sex: Difference and Dominance*, sociolinguist Thorne and psycholinguist Henley are joined by speech communication specialist Cheris Kramarae to produce a second anthology. Like its predecessor, the present volume features a hefty annotated bibliography. Although selective, it is the most thorough guide available to published materials on gender marking and sex bias in language structure and content, stereotypes and perceptions of language use, sex differences and similarities in language use, conversational interaction among men and women, genre and style, children and language, language varieties in American English, and nonverbal aspects of communication. The ten papers that precede the bibliography follow a similar outline of topics, beginning with a survey of recent research by the editors. Other pieces address gender bias (the "he/man approach" and the "pronoun problem"), rural black women's linguistic options and choices, female intonation, women and men in conversational interactions, genre and style in women's writing, and men's speech to young children. (**Women's Studies**, 1987)

Cross-Cultural, Ethnographic, and Area Studies

(For related material see also entries 330, 343, 654, 703, 704a, 1051)

PR,IL

950. Caplan, Pat, ed. **The Cultural Construction of Sexuality.** London: Tavistock, 1987. 304 p. Includes bibliographies and indexes. ISBN 0-422-60880-7.

Caplan, anthropologist of Goldsmiths' College, London, and editor of this collection of ten diverse papers by anthropologists, sociologists, and social historians, states in the preface that the aim of this work is "an understanding of how and why sexuality is constructed the way it is" in societies around the world. Caplan's introduction provides the cultural underpinnings for this collection with a sweeping review of the history of sexuality in the West, the politics of sex, the contribution of social anthropology to the study of sexuality, the relationship of sex to gender and the concept of sexual identity.

The first three papers are by social historians who consider sexuality in Western society. Jeffery Weeks examines the viability of sexual identity as a concept in terms of resistance, choice, and relationships. Margaret Jackson, writing from a feminist perspective, discusses sexology and the social construction of heterosexuality with emphasis on the eroticization of women's oppression. Victor J. Seidler writes about male sexual identity and its links to rationality, providing also a critique of the power aspects of Michel Foucault's writings on sexuality.

The politics of sex, signified by the feminist slogan, "The personal is political," is exemplified in Shirley Anderer's paper on vaginal iconography in African tribal behavior and on such symbolic expressions as Judy Chicago's striking depiction of the female genitalia of important women in civilization in *The Dinner Table*, both the exhibition and the book.

Carol P. MacCormack and Alizon Draper's paper concentrates on the social and cognitive aspects of female sexuality in Jamaica. Victoria Goddard examines the control of women and their sexuality through honor and shame in Naples, Italy. Allen Abramson looks at the history of sexuality on the island of Fiji, recalling Margaret Mead's Samoan work on the sexuality of adolescent females and its rejection by D. Freeman. Nici Nelson deals with Kikuyu notions of sexuality, especially the aspect of commercialized sexual relationships in Mathare Valley, Kenya. Gill Shepherd focuses on male and female homosexuality among the Swahili Muslims of Mombasa. Pat Caplan, in the final paper in the collection, views the options women have, besides lesbianism and masturbation, in the search for sexual outlets. She suggests celibacy as a possible solution, using the ideas of Gandhi, an advocate of *brahmacharya*, or celibacy for all, to the problem of dangerous heterosexuality and sexual servitude. (TJW)

PR,IL

951. Ford, Clellan S., and Frank A. Beach. **Patterns of Sexual Behavior.** With a foreword by Robert Latou Dickinson. New York: Harper & Row, 1972. 307 p. Originally published in 1951. Includes bibliography and index.

Although originally published in 1951, this book remains a valuable source of findings about patterns of sexual behavior. Ford, a professor of anthropology at Yale University, and Beach, professor of psychology at Yale University, collaborated to produce a threefold frame of reference that serves as a general background within which they describe and attempt to understand human sexual behavior. The first component of this framework is a cross-cultural perspective. Similarities and differences between cultures need to be examined to formulate valid comprehensive statements about human sexuality. No one culture can serve as a representative of the span of human sexual behavior. In order to achieve this perspective, Ford and Beach draw on anthropological data on 190 primarily preliterate societies contained within the Human Relations Area Files. In addition to the United States, societies described include those in Oceania, Eurasia, Africa, North America, and South America. The second perspective is evolutionary or zoological. By comparing humans and lower animals it is possible to elucidate elements of sexual behavior common to many species. Books, technical articles, reports by zoologists, and field studies by naturalists, as well as fifteen years of personal research by Beach provide the data for this perspective. Finally, Ford and Beach develop a physiological perspective that examines the relationship between sexual behavior and physiology. They admit that they consciously avoid moral evaluations or an emphasis on sexual symbolism. Since they define sexual behavior as "behavior involving stimulation and excitation of the sex organs," copulation between the sexes comprises the core of the book. Chapters dealing specifically with coitus are "The Nature of Coitus," "Types of Sexual Stimulation," "Circumstances for Coitus," "Attracting a Sex Partner," and "Sexual Partnerships." Other forms of sexual stimulation form the basis for other chapters: "Homosexual Behavior," "Relations Between Different Species," and "Self-stimulation." While three-quarters of the book deals with cross-species, cross-cultural dimensions of sexual behavior, the last quarter considers physiological factors. The final chapter summarizes some of the major similarities in the sexual behavior of humans and other animals. (SGF)

PR,IL
952. Frayser, Suzanne G. **Varieties of Sexual Experience: An Anthropological Perspective on Human Sexuality.** New Haven, Conn.: HRAF Press, 1985. 546 p. Includes bibliographies and indexes. ISBN 0-87536-342-3.

The goal of this book is to present and demonstrate the fruitfulness of an integrated model of human sexuality. Frayser, an anthropologist and sexologist, asserts that human sexuality is a system in its own right, related to but not subsumed by social, cultural, psychological, and biological factors. The book concentrates on four main themes: (1) a systematic description of the extent and types of variation in human sexuality; (2) confirmation that aspects of sexuality are related to each other and form patterns; (3) explanation of identified patterns; and (4) application of the findings to an understanding of sexual issues in American society. Each of the chapters elaborates one of these themes. The information presented in the book is drawn from a variety of fields (anthropology, sociology, psychology, biology, sexology, history) as well as from Frayser's cross-cultural research, based on a representative sample of sixty-two of the world's cultures.

"Our Human Heritage" reviews cross-species research and evolutionary theory to establish the similarities and differences between human and nonhuman sexuality. In order to highlight the distinctiveness of humans as animals that engage in a lot of nonreproductive and reproductive sexual behavior, Frayser divides her description of the extent and types of human sexual variation into two chapters: "The Sexual Cycle" and "The Reproductive Cycle." "The Sexual Cycle" includes discussions of prenatal sexuality, genital dimorphism, bases of sexual differentiation (division of labor, child training, incest taboos), puberty and adolescence, rules pertaining to the choice of sexual partners, types of sexual interaction, and the role of hormones. "The Reproductive Cycle" concentrates on marriage as the major form of identifiable reproductive relationship across cultures and discusses data on spouse selection, forms of marriage, divorce, widowhood, conception, pregnancy, birth, lactation, and preferences for children.

The detailed descriptive material on the sexual and reproductive cycles forms a framework for exploring the links within and between the cycles. "Patterns of Human Sexuality" goes beyond description to establish a highly significant set of associations that point to clusters of variables that define restrictive and permissive patterns of sexual behavior as well as differential sexual patterns for men and women. The restrictive pattern is identified by such customs as monogamy, prohibitions on premarital and extramarital sex, and elaborate marriage celebrations, that emphasize the importance of containing sexual behavior within a reproductive relationship; the permissive pattern is identified by the converse of these traits.

In conclusion Frayser provides a historical overview of sexual patterns and ideas in the United States over the last 100 years and demonstrates how the sexual paradigm has shifted from a relatively restrictive to a permissive pattern. Her emphasis on the contribution that a variety of factors make to the sexual system within American culture and across cultures is in line with an anthropological emphasis on wholism.

Several lengthy appendixes explicate aspects of the cross-cultural method used to produce many of the findings in this book. An extensive ethnographic bibliography follows the appendixes and documents sources that Frayser found most useful in gathering information on sex and reproduction in sixty-two societies. (Author)

PR

953. Freud, Sigmund. **Totem and Taboo: Some Points of Agreement Between the Mental Lives of Savages and Neurotics.** New York: W. W. Norton, 1950. 172 p. Includes bibliography and index. ISBN 0-393-00143-1.

Originally published between 1912 and 1913 in the periodical *Imago* (Vienna), the four essays in this volume represent Freud's first attempt to use a psychoanalytic framework to address issues in social psychology as well as to forge a link between the fields of psychoanalysis and social anthropology.

Freud uses his concept of the Oedipus complex (a psychosexual stage of development in which a boy desires his mother and wishes to destroy his father, who represents competition for his mother's affection) to explain the close association between belief in taboos and in totemism (a system of beliefs that stresses a mystical relationship between an individual or group and a plant or animal). Drawing on a variety of theoretical and ethnographic works in anthropology, Freud suggests that the incest taboo originated during a period in human history when sons of a primal horde banded together, killed their father, and had sexual access to their mother. The guilt produced by their actions was so overpowering that they instituted the incest taboo to prevent a recurrence of their crime; totemism helped them atone for their actions by symbolically worshipping their father. Thus, the roots of cultural rules and primitive religion began with these events.

Freud supports his hypothesis by explaining that an extensive incest taboo is found among the Australian Aborigines, whom he regards as the "direct heirs and representatives" of "primitive" humans; the intensity of their horror of incest is related to their proximity to the origins of the taboo. Therefore, they defend against incestuous impulses with extensive taboos. In addition, it is possible to deduce the original meanings of totemism and taboos from the thoughts of children and the regressive ideas of neurotics, who represent earlier stages of psychological development.

Freud's notions of the universality of the Oedipus complex and its consequences, though framed in a now outmoded theoretical framework of social evolutionism, continue to spark controversy. In *Sex and Repression in Savage Society*, Malinowski contended that sexual conflicts are derived from cultural contexts that vary, not from a universal psychological substrate. Robin Fox presented a renewed version of Freud's ideas in *The Red Lamp of Incest*. Most recently, Melford Spiro, in *Oedipus in the Trobriands* (Chicago: University Press of Chicago, 1982) meticulously reanalyzed Malinowski's data to argue against the idea that the Oedipus complex is culturally variable. (SGF)

PO

954. Gregersen, Edgar. **Sexual Practices: The Story of Human Sexuality.** New York: Franklin Watts, 1983. 320 p. Includes bibliography and index. ISBN 0-531-09899-0.

Gregersen, an anthropologist, explores the richness and diversity of human sexuality in this encyclopedic treatment of varieties of sexual expression; his goal is to "document the culture of sexuality." He begins by explaining why an anthropological approach is particularly appropriate for investigating sexual behavior and then provides informative overviews of Western cultural background as it relates to sexuality, a history of the study of sex, and the evolution of sexuality. Most of the chapters in part 1 concentrate on describing the variety of ways that specific sexual themes are expressed (sexual techniques, physical types, physical attractiveness, clothing and modesty, marriage and incest, prostitution). He concludes this part with a discussion of current developments in twentieth-century Western sexuality. Part 2 maps the geography of sexual practices by describing their occurrence in different parts of the world. Gregersen presents sexual customs as he would any other kind of custom; he uses the cross-cultural orientation of anthropology to discover where customs occur, how they might have spread, and why they are maintained. He relies heavily on data from the Human Relations Area Files to document his descriptions and updates some of the material contained in Ford and Beach's earlier study, *Patterns of Sexual Behavior*. He consciously avoids large-scale theorizing and prefers to confine his discussions to descriptions of "the facts." This journey through the world of sexual customs is enhanced by 320 illustrations and 9 maps. (SGF)

PR,IL
955. Henriques, Fernando. **Love in Action: The Sociology of Sex.** New York: Dutton, 1960. 432 p. Includes bibliographic references and indexes.

Henriques, a lecturer in social anthropology at Leeds University, relies in this scholarly study on a wealth of primary and secondary sources in order to "survey some aspects of the sexual activity of man in society" (p. 422). The aspects selected for emphasis are related to his theme of describing those customs that relate to the ways in which societies arrange for reproduction and for the satisfaction of their participants' sexual needs. They form the subject matter of the chapters: preparation for sexual life, premarital sexual behavior, modesty, love and love magic, lovemaking, courtship, regulation of sexual life, marriage rites and ceremonies, divorce, coitus and taboo, beauty, and extramarital sexual intercourse.

The contents of each chapter are descriptive in nature, consisting of clusters of specific examples of customs of 126 "simple" societies, often related to customs in technologically advanced cultures. The societies described are characterized by a relatively simple technology but with highly complex systems of social relationships. The societies, listed at the back of the book, are widely dispersed around the world, in Asia, Africa, Eurasia, North America, Latin America, Australia, and throughout the islands of the Pacific. Henriques hopes that "a consideration of the sexual behaviour of societies other than our own might help towards a solution of (contemporary) problems" (p. 422). This cross-cultural work serves as a fund of information for specific examples of sexual and reproductive customs. It is well illustrated with many pertinent drawings and photographs. It is also well documented with historical as well as contemporary materials in English, French, German, Dutch, Italian, and Latin. (SGF/TJW)

IL
956. Mantegazza, Paolo. **Sexual Relations of Mankind.** New York: Anthropological Press, 1932. 258 p. Translated from the Italian by James Bruce.

Mantegazza, Professor of Anthropology at the University of Florence and author of *Physiology of Love* and *Hygiene of Love*, draws on documentary evidence to "present a cursive sexual history of man, based on anthropological principles." Although he includes "curiosa" on the sexual life and customs of "ancient and modern, savage and civilized races," he concentrates more on those of the "savage and uncivilized tribes" because they are closer to the origins of divergent practices.

Mantegazza organizes the concise descriptions of customs around aspects of the life cycle. Beginning with "erotic education," the celebration of puberty, the first six chapters describe variations in sexual permissiveness and modesty, eroticism, love and its perversions, forms of sexual stimulation, and modification of the sex organs. The rest of the book deals with the position of women, sexual coercion (rape, abduction, prostitution), mate selection and constraints (e.g., incest), and marriage (by purchase, fidelity, adultery, monogamy, polygyny, polyandry).

In the brief concluding chapter, Mantegazza specifically eschews analysis, but he does comment on the wide variety of customs and values around the world. The civilized world can be divided into East and West. The East is much more sophisticated in its instructions about love than the West, which has "put a taboo on this supremely vital instruction" (p. 257). In part, Western women suffer from sexual ignorance and "a crass inconsiderateness in man." He concludes that "unless we make wide strides to spread this Eastern knowledge, we shall remain centuries retarded in the blackest ignorance of sexual wisdom which could avoid so many untold ills, diseases, unhappiness in marital relationships, and divorces" (p. 258). (SGF)

PR,IL
957. Marshall, Donald S., and Robert C. Suggs, eds. **Human Sexual Behavior: Variations in the Ethnographic Spectrum.** Englewood Cliffs, N.J.: Prentice-Hall, 1971. 302 p. (Studies in Sex and Society). Includes bibliographies and index.

At the outset, Marshall and Suggs claim that this volume is "neither a reader nor a collection of random essays. We shall use information presented herein as a basis upon which to derive comparative similarities and differences and then to develop a number of generalizations about cultural, social, biological, ecological, and psychological forces as these influence human sexual behavior" (p. xv). The book is an outgrowth of a symposium on human sexuality at the 1965 Central States Anthropological Society convention. With the exception of sociologist Lee Rainwater, all of the contributors (Milton Altschuler, Paul H. Gebhard, Donald S. Marshall, Alan P. Merriam, John C. Messenger, Harold K. Schneider, Robert C. Suggs) are anthropologists. Descriptions of the sexual attitudes and behavior of people in seven different societies (Ireland, Cayapa, Turu, Bala, Mangaia, Marquesas, "Cultures of Poverty") are presented as a "spectrum" that illustrates the range of variation in patterns of sexual behavior.

In the foreword, Gebhard notes that anthropologists have only recently begun to mine the valuable reservoir of information provided by sex studies. He characterizes the majority of the profession as "conservatives" who express a basic prudery in the paucity of data they present on sexuality. However, some "progressives," such as Whiting, Malinowski, Devereaux, Davenport, DuBois, and others, recognize and record the role of sex in society, while "synthesizers" such as Ford and Beach, Murdock, and Mead use a comparative approach to analyze sexual data.

In addition to the case studies presented, several other sections suggest the value and role of anthropology in studying sexual behavior. Summary chapters by Gebhard, Marshall, and Suggs conclude that the findings in the volume reaffirm the "ability of culture to inexorably mold, shape, and channel most areas of human behavior and thought" (p. 242). In a lengthy appendix, Gebhard offers basic definitions of sexual behavior; Marshall presents an outline to "serve as a point of departure for ethnographical analyses of sexual behavior in other parts of the world" as well as a description of informal anthropological tactics that could be used in the field; and Suggs critiques some anthropological methods and theory. (SGF)

PR,IL
958. Martin, M. Kay, and Barbara Voorhies. **Female of the Species.** New York: Columbia University Press, 1975. 432 p. Includes bibliography and index. ISBN 0-231-03876-3.

This book proposes to use a traditional anthropological approach to examine the position of women at the species level. Operating on the belief that culture rather than biology is a more crucial determinant of sexual differentiation of behavior, Martin and Voorhies aim to "gain a clear understanding of the myriad definitions and functions of male and female behavior, and of the way societies manipulate sex to achieve efficient adaptations to the physical and social environments" (p. 1). Nevertheless, they acknowledge that sexual differences have multiple determinants that are appropriately viewed as points on a continuum rather than as polar opposites.

The first few chapters consider biosocial aspects of sex differences. In "Sex as a Biological Process," Voorhies discusses attributes of sexual reproduction in mammals and proceeds to investigate the ways in which sexual identity develops in the individual. "Origins of Some Sex-Linked Traits" analyzes sex-typed personality characteristics (aggression, ambition, intelligence, dependency, nurturance) from developmental and cross-cultural perspectives. Findings indicate that learning plays a major role in the development of these differences and that there are "no absolutely fixed correlations" of personality differences and biological sex. A discussion of "supernumerary" sexes emphasizes the influence of social factors on sex differences. Voorhies describes several societies in which the conception of gender as well as the number of genders categorized within the society varies. Finally, sex differences among humans are compared with those found among nonhuman primates. Voorhies concludes that the range of sex differences among humans is greater than that among any other primate; furthermore, they vary with group ecology.

After an overview of anthropological theories that have been presented to explain variations in sex differences, the rest of the book discusses in detail the ways in which sex differences relate to subsistence type (hunting and gathering, horticulture, pastoralism, agriculture, industrialism). Drawing on ethnographic examples and statistical summaries of data based on Murdock's *Ethnographic Atlas*, Martin examines such issues as the relationship between contribution to subsistence and social power, dominance, and prestige; and the link between ideal sexual behavior and ecological adaptation. Her main theme is that the "nature of human sex roles has an adaptive advantage for societies, and that these adaptations correlate with group ecology" (p. 12). Thus, they vary widely in response to social and ecological factors. The concluding chapter traces the history of change in gender roles in the Soviet Union and the United States in response to increased industrialization. Martin suggests that strict gender roles in the United States will become increasingly unimportant in the future. (SGF)

PR
959. Ortner, Sherry B., and Harriet Whitehead, eds. **Sexual Meanings: The Cultural Construction of Gender and Sexuality.** Cambridge, England: Cambridge University Press, 1981. 435 p. Includes bibliographies and index. ISBN 0-521-28375-2.

The title *Sexual Meanings* reflects the focus of this volume on gender and sexuality as cultural constructs. Using the perspective of symbolic anthropology, each of the contributors, all of whom are anthropologists, explores the meaning of sex and gender as symbols within a specific cultural context and deals with questions about the sources, processes, and consequences of their construction. The ten original essays are divided into two parts. The first part deals with the cultural organization of gender. It includes essays by Salvatore Cucchiari (on the origins of gender hierarchy), Whitehead (on the gender meaning of institutionalized homosexuality in native North America), Fitz John Porter Pool (on female ritual leaders and gender identity among Bimin-Kuskusmin), Marilyn Strathen (on Hagen gender imagery), Bradd Shore (on conceptions of Samoan sexuality and gender), Stanley Brandes (on male sexual ideology in an Andalusian town), and Leslee Nadelson (on an analysis of six Mundurucu myths). The second part of the book is concerned with the political contexts of gender. Jane F. Collier and Michelle Z. Rosaldo provide a model for the study of gender as a cultural system. Melissa Llewelyn-Davies describes how notions of property organize material production and reproduction among the Masai, while Ortner attempts to provide a systematic basis for understanding Polynesian gender culture.

In their introductory essay, Ortner and Whitehead provide an overview of the methodological and theoretical themes that pervade the volume. One group of essays emphasizes a culturalist approach (the analysis of the inner logic and structural relations among symbols) while another concentrates on a sociological approach (an analysis of the relationships among symbols, their meanings, and the social order). Beneath the variety of conceptions of gender presented are some recurring themes about the nature of men and women, sex, and reproduction (e.g., nature/culture, domestic/public, and status and role/relationship). These axes of gender distinctions are shared with other domains of social life, particularly in the organization of kinship and marriage and in the prestige system. Ortner and Whitehead conclude that the organization of prestige is the most important area of social structure that affects notions of gender and sexuality, while the marriage system is the most important cross-sex relational system for male prestige. Ultimately, they think that constructions of sex, gender, and reproduction relate to the ways in which male prestige-oriented action is integrated with the structure of cross-sex relationships. (SGF)

PR

960. Paige, Karen Ericksen, and Jeffery M. Paige, with the assistance of Linda Fuller and Elisabeth Magnus. **The Politics of Reproductive Ritual.** Berkeley, Calif.: University of California Press, 1981. 380 p. Includes bibliography and index. ISBN 0-520-03071-0.

Puberty, pregnancy, childbirth, and menstruation are often the occasions for ritual observance in many preindustrial societies. Genital mutilation, seclusion, and elaborate prescriptive behavior may accompany these events. Three major theoretical traditions have supplied explanations for these behaviors. Psychoanalytic theories view reproductive rituals as the result of psychological processes (castration, conflict, penis envy, womb envy, unconscious sexual hostility, and aggression toward the opposite sex) shared by all human beings. Transition-rite theories, following van Gennep, stress the need for dramatic role transition rites while the structural-functional explanations center on the importance of these rituals as symbolic expressions of structural tensions in society. Paige and Paige propose to view reproductive rituals as "political tactics used to solve social dilemmas that become crucial at certain points in the human reproductive cycle" (p. 43). Based on bargaining-exchange theory, this interpretation rests on three premises: (1) reproductive events marked by rituals are potential crises (dilemmas) for those in power in preindustrial societies; (2) ritual is an indirect political solution to the dilemmas, where direct political or legal solutions are not possible; and (3) the political and economic resources of the society determine the use and form of ritual. In essence, ritual is the end result of a causal chain from economy to polity. It is the purpose of this book "to demonstrate the validity of this general causal scheme, to trace these intervening causal linkages, and to test the specific hypotheses the theory generates" (p. 44). Two chapters analyze the dilemmas of female and male puberty, another looks at birth, and another considers menstruation. The final chapter summarizes the main argument and shows its application to complex societies.

Data are drawn from ethnographic accounts or codings of information on a selection of preindustrial societies in George Murdock and Douglas White's "Standard Cross-Cultural Sample" or Murdock's *Ethnographic Atlas*. Appendixes present the code book and codes, description of sample, and an ethnographic source bibliography. (SGF)

PR,IL

961. Reiss, Ira L. **Journey into Sexuality: An Exploratory Voyage.** Englewood Cliffs, N.J.: Prentice-Hall, 1986. 282 p. Includes bibliography, indexes, and glossary. ISBN 0-13-511478-0.

Emphasizing a macro-level sociological approach, Reiss, Professor of Sociology at the University of Minnesota and a past president of the International Academy of Sex Research, proposes to "develop an overall explanation of human sexuality that will apply cross-culturally and will explain how society organizes and shapes our sexual lives" (p. xiv). Drawing on cross-cultural, sociological, and psychological research, he first defines universal aspects of sexuality and then proceeds to analyze variations in terms of the social framework that he establishes.

Reiss defines sexuality as "those scripts shared by a group that are supposed to lead to erotic arousal and in turn to produce genital response" (p. 20). Physical pleasure and self-disclosure often accompany sexual behavior and are the basis for the universal importance of sexuality, which results in its regulation by cultural scripts. Therefore, the way in which sexuality is expressed reflects the characteristics of a particular social system. These attributes lay the foundation for a societal-level explanation of sexuality.

He posits three major areas where sexuality will be linked to society: in the systems of kinship and marriage, power, and ideology. The connection to kinship and marriage is demonstrated by sexual jealousy, a boundary-setting mechanism that is tied to important sexual relationships, particularly marital ones. Gender roles reflect the power structure and determine some of the sex customs of males and females. Ideologies, which can be characterized as emotive or cognitive and as equalitarian or nonequalitarian, define what a group regards as normal or abnormal behavior or attitudes. Reiss discusses how all three of these areas affect a group's degree of acceptance of homosexuality and erotica, which his evidence shows are normal human activities. In the course of his journey into sexuality, Reiss also discusses such topics as differing beliefs about pornography, the relationship between erotica and aggression, and differences in male and female erotic fantasies.

The final chapter summarizes the theoretical framework of the book by presenting it in narrative form and also by listing twenty-five explanatory propositions. Reiss unifies the logic of his argument in one sentence: "The importance of sexuality in human relationships is the basis for the boundaries placed upon sexuality and for those in power seeking sexual rights that become part of the ideologies and the elements in any social change in sexual customers" (p. 217). He acknowledges that his "only dogma" is a strong commitment to a sociological, societal level explanation. (SGF)

PR,IL
962. Rosaldo, Michelle Zimbalist, and Louise Lamphere. **Women, Culture, and Society.** Stanford, Calif.: Stanford University Press, 1974. 352 p. Includes bibliographic notes and index. ISBN 0-8047-0851-7.

In 1971, Rosaldo participated in teaching a course entitled "Women in Cross-Cultural Perspective" at Stanford University. After she shared copies of the lectures with Lamphere, they agreed that a new anthropological perspective on women was needed. Convinced that the "lack of interest in women in conventional anthropology constitutes a genuine deficiency that has led to distorted theories and impoverished ethnographic accounts" (p. vi), Rosaldo and Lamphere decided to produce this anthology of papers, which they say represents "a first generation's attempt to integrate an interest in women into a general theory of society and culture" (p. vi). Most of the sixteen contributors are feminist anthropologists. With the exception of two chapters, all of the contributions are original essays written for this volume.

In the introduction, Rosaldo and Lamphere present the query, Why does sexual asymmetry seems to be such a universal feature of social life? Although biological factors appear to provide the conditions and rationale for female subordination, they do not determine this position. The first three essays (by Rosaldo, Nancy Chodorow, and Sherry B. Ortner) address the question of why asymmetry between the sexes persists despite variation and change in social organization, and they conclude that the social roles of women, particularly in the areas of reproduction and childrearing, channel them into secondary positions.

With the theoretical orientation of the initial papers as background, the rest of the papers (by Jane Fishburne Collier, Lamphere, Carol B. Stack, Nancy Tanner, Margery Wolf, Carol P. Hoffer, Peggy R. Sanday, Karen Sacks, Nancy B. Leis, Bette S. Denich, Joan Bamberger, Lois Paul, and Bridget O'Laughlin) explore in detail the nature of women's roles by using case studies and comparative data from a variety of cultural contexts; they draw on a broad range of ethnographic material from the United States, Africa, Indonesia, Latin America, and Europe. Consistent themes running through these papers include the types and determinants of women's status and power, strategies that women use to cope with and actively influence their positions, and the ideological bases for the maintenance of the status quo.

Overall, Rosaldo and Lamphere think that the contributions to this volume have considerable value in several respects. First, the essays demonstrate a great deal of interesting cross-cultural variation in the nature and significance of women's roles and statuses. Second, by their critical evaluation of the universal subordination of women, the papers reveal that sexual asymmetry is a "cultural product accessible to change." Third, social and economic factors, particularly women's contribution to subsistence and control over the distribution of economic products, are especially important in accounting for variations in women's status and power. Last, but not least, these papers challenge old assumptions about the nature of human society and women's place in it. (SGF)

PR

963.   Sanday, Peggy Reeves. **Female Power and Male Dominance: On the Origins of Sexual Inequality.** Cambridge, England: Cambridge University Press, 1981. 295 p. Includes bibliography and index. ISBN 0-521-28075-3.

Drawing on data from 150 tribal societies from a standard cross-cultural sample and from ethnographic case studies, anthropologist Sanday addresses the fundamental question of why cultures select different styles of interaction between the sexes. Questions about differential power roles between men and women stem from this basic inquiry. Using a "modified" semiotic approach, Sanday begins with cultural premises and then explores their impact on sexual status. Her main theme is that ancient concepts of sacred power are the roots for secular power roles.

In the first part of the book, Sanday establishes the range of variation in male and female power roles. She suggests that each society has a sex-role plan (a template that guides the organization of male/female behavior) that is expressed symbolically. There is a correlation between the gender of the creator god, conceptions of creative forces in nature, and the secular expression of male and female power. People usually ascribe power to those forces that they think are most responsible for providing them with the necessities of life. Therefore, environment, subsistence activities, and sex differences shape these concepts. An outer orientation (usually expressed by males) prevails when the forces of life focus on life-taking activities (such as hunting animals) and migration while an inner orientation (usually expressed by females) occurs when forces of life focus on life-giving activities (such as gathering plants) and balance with nature. Both orientations can be present in the same society.

The rest of the book considers how power relationships become asymmetrical. In order for domination to occur, the sexes have to be segregated. This can occur in the sexual division of labor or in separation channeled by cultural ideas of pollution, for example, notions that intercourse or menstrual blood is dangerous. Such separation divides the worlds of men and women, who then have different sets of meaning and rules for behavior. An emphasis on an inner orientation provides a basis for female economic and political power, but if social change gives males more access to strategic resources, the orientation may shift so that female power diminishes. Sanday traces the rise of secular male dominance as a response to cultural disruption by such circumstances as European colonialism and explains the behavioral and symbolic process that aids in its establishment. Because a people's orientation to nature and sacred symbols varies, so too will their responses to stress. Male dominance is not the only reaction to cultural disruption, and female subordination is not a universal trait. Sanday concludes that both male and female types of power are valued across cultures. However, a symmetrical or asymmetrical evaluation of each type of power lays the foundation for the elaboration of secular power roles. (SGF)

PR
964. Schlegel, Alice, ed. **Sexual Stratification: A Cross-Cultural View.** New York: Columbia University Press, 1977. 371 p. Includes bibliographies and indexes. ISBN 0-231-04215-9.

Schlegel, notable for her earlier cross-cultural study of male dominance and sexual equality in domestic arrangements (*Male Dominance and Female Autonomy*, 1972), attempts in this book to formulate the basis for a theory of sexual stratification by focusing on the dimensions of equality/inequality between the sexes. In the lengthy introduction, she defines and assesses issues relevant to such a formulation. Rewards, prestige, and power are all aspects of sexual stratification, but Schlegel thinks that power is probably the most important of the three. Of particular significance is the degree of control that one gender has over central institutions that set priorities for the distribution of time, goods, and personnel. Sexual stratification is the product of group responses to both internal and external forces. When it occurs, women are excluded from decision-making positions. An adequate theory of sexual stratification has to assess the relative status of the sexes as well as to elucidate the biological, social, political, economic, and ideological components that shape the definition and role of sex status.

Given the complexity of conditions that give rise to sexual stratification, societies vary in the degree to which they are stratified by gender, if at all. Male dominance is by no means a universal social condition. Fourteen contributors, primarily anthropologists and other social scientists, present thirteen case studies that document the range of variation in sexual stratification. At one extreme are societies in which male dominance prevails: in Sicily, Morocco, and India, and among the Bantu of Africa. However, even in these contexts women develop strategies to ameliorate or circumvent this dominance. At the other extreme are groups in which an ideology of sex stratification is absent: among the Hopi and Bontoc and in Barbados and the Israeli kibbutz. The ways in which women activate their equal status in each of these groups are described. Between these extremes are groups in which male dominance is qualified by tactics that women use to gain some influence: in the Ivory Coast and Sudan, and among the Yoruba. Social change in sex roles in Ghana and Yugoslavia illustrates the detrimental impact that external factors such as colonialism and industrialization can have on women's autonomy.

Schlegel reiterates the importance of the multidimensional nature of sexual stratification. "Sexual stratification . . . is not panhuman but rather poses a problem that must be explained, for each society in terms of the forces to which it is responsive, and cross-culturally in terms of variables that exist across societies. It is an enormously complex problem" (p. 356).

Readers interested in sexual stratification can also refer to sociologist Chafetz's study, *Sex and Advantage: A Comparative, Macro-Structural Theory of Sex Stratification* (Totowa, N.J.: Rowman & Allanheld, 1984), which argues that the organization of production activities and the family are the most important factors in explaining the degree of sexual stratification. Chafetz draws on sociological and anthropological literature to develop a theory that explains "variance in the degree of sex inequality cross-culturally and historically" (p. x). (SGF)

PR
965. Unwin, Joseph Daniel. **Sex and Culture.** London: Oxford University Press, 1934. 676 p. Includes bibliography and index.

Sex and Culture is the complete version of an earlier summary entitled *Sexual Regulations and Human Behavior* (1933). In the preface, Unwin states that he began this classic work "with care-free openmindedness" in order to test "a somewhat startling conjecture that had been made by the analytical psychologists: if the social regulations forbid direct satisfaction of the sexual impulses the emotional conflict is expressed in another way, and that what we call 'civilization' has always been built up by compulsory sacrifices in the gratification of innate desires" (p. vii). While psychologists relied on data associated with mental disturbance, Unwin proceeds to draw on a large body of cultural data about eighty societies, most of which he terms "uncivilized peoples."

The first chapter indicates the precision and scientific perspective that Unwin brings to his materials: he not only defines his terms but also establishes a rationale for using a survey approach. The bulk of the study centers on testing the hypothesis that a limitation in sexual opportunity is accompanied by a rise in cultural condition. Sexual opportunity means "the opportunity which is afforded a man or woman to gratify a sexual desire" (p. 23) while cultural condition refers to the way in which members of a society conceive of powers manifested in the universe and the steps taken to maintain a right relation with them. The findings from societies in Melanesia, Polynesia, Africa, Asia, and America are meticulously presented and form a major part of the book. A lengthy reference section as well as charts in the appendix supplement these findings.

Unwin concludes that among the eighty societies he studied, three great patterns of uncivilized culture (zoistic, manistic, and deistic) "invariably" accompanied three patterns of prenuptial sexual opportunity (permit prenuptial, occasional or irregular continence, and prenuptial chastity) respectively. Compulsory continence does not produce neurosis but, rather, social energy that may then be used to further social aims; all uncivilized groups are characterized by low energy while civilized ones are accompanied by higher energy. The strength of the association is so great that it can be stated as a law applicable to all human societies: "The cultural condition of any society in any geographical environment is conditioned by the past and present methods of regulating the relations between the sexes."

This work is significant not only for its development of an early form of cross-cultural analysis but also because it tests rather than assumes a link between social traits and cultural forms. (SGF)

PR

966. Whitam, Frederick L., and Robin M. Mathy. **Male Homosexuality in Four Societies: Brazil, Guatemala, the Philippines, and the United States.** New York: Praeger, 1986. 208 p. Includes bibliography and index. ISBN 0-03-004298-4.

From 1975 through 1984, sociologist Whitam investigated male homosexuality in four societies: Guatemala, Brazil, the Philippines, and the United States. Deriving his primary data from questionnaires, notes, diaries, recorded conversations, anecdotes, gossip, and observation, he attempts to fill a gap in the sociological study of homosexuality: a cross-cultural perspective. Because homosexuality occurs within a cultural setting, its outward form is influenced by culture; however, many important elements are similar in all societies. "One of the fundamental aims of this book is to delineate those behavioral elements that appear to be related to homosexual orientation, and in so doing to sketch out the unique functions that homosexuals perform in society" (p. 1). Defining homosexuals as people who are exclusively or nearly exclusively sexually attracted to persons of the same sex, Whitam uses historical, cross-cultural, and previous research to assert that homosexuals exist in all societies—past and present—regularly making up about 5 percent of the population. Psychosexual development of homosexuals seems to proceed along similar lines in all societies; it is often marked by cross-gender behavior in childhood, and the timing of emerging sexual expression tends to parallel that of heterosexual development, regardless of family type or socialization pressures. Homosexual subcultures generally emerge whenever sufficient population exists, and they are remarkably similar, characterized by some transvestic homosexuals, common occupational choices in fields stressing embellishment, entertainment, the arts, language, travel, helping professions, and grooming; few have interests in competitive athletics.

Given the universality of homosexuality, all societies respond to them in some way. Although no society unequivocally encourages or fosters homosexuality, groups vary in their tolerance of homosexuals according to different erotic traditions, i.e., a "complex system of norms regulating sexual behavior." Anglo-Saxon traditions tend to be repressive; Latin traditions are tolerant; Southeast Asian traditions are extremely tolerant. Consequently, the hostility of many Americans to homosexuals is not mirrored by people from Latin or Southeast Asian traditions, who may view homosexuals as acceptable secondary sexual outlets.

Whitam acknowledges that his perspective "suggests not only that homosexual orientation has a biological basis but that some aspects of gender behavior may also be biologically derived" (p. 157), in contrast to traditional sociological and psychiatric interpretations of homosexuality as learned behavior. However, attributing the origins of homosexuality to social learning does not necessarily result in more tolerance for homosexuality; the belief that homosexuality is natural and biological may be more conducive to tolerance. Unlike many other places in the world, many people in the United States regard homosexuals as an authentic minority. (SGF)

ASIA & AFRICA

(For related material see also entries 373, 376, 380, 385, 655)

PO
967. Bornoff, Nicholas. **Pink Samurai: Love, Marriage & Sex in Contemporary Japan.** New York: Pocket Books, 1991. 479 p. ISBN 0-671-74265-5.
Pink Samurai records Bornoff's observations and feelings about the sexual customs and behavior of the Japanese. A British journalist who spent eleven years in Tokyo, he covers the historical past as well as the present, showing that Japanese society in the years since World War II has been experiencing profound changes. In particular, intergenerational tensions, male/female relationships, and the entertainment infrastructure, including prostitution, have undergone rapid and radical development ever since a democratic constitution, enfranchising women, was imposed on the country in 1946.

By way of background, Bornoff discusses early creation myths, Shintoism, the influence of Chinese culture (Confucianism and Buddhism), and various periods of Japanese history as they impact on contemporary Japan, especially in the area of sex. He goes on to examine the compulsive Japanese work ethic, the educational system, including sex education, childrearing, marriage customs and family life, and how foreign sexual terminology has penetrated the Japanese language. Japanese is peppered with "japlish" terms like *deeto* for date, *garufurendo* for girlfriend, *sopu-reedi* for soap lady, and even *sekkishyaru harassumento* for sexual harassment.

Interweaving observations about sexual behavior with social, cultural, and religious customs, Bornoff examines at length phallic worship and shrines, fertility and ancestor cults, classical literature with sexual themes (*The Tale of Genji*), sex manuals based on Chinese erotic works, the beginning of the shogunates, the rise and decline of the samurai, the unification of Japan in 1600, the establishment of the Yoshiwara brothel district, and the origin of certain durable institutions, such as the kubuki theater and the geisha tradition.

Although prostitution is illegal in modern Japan, the institution flourishes throughout the country in various kinds of establishments located in well-designated entertainment districts. In contrast to the highly organized brothel districts of an earlier era, modern establishments include the ubiquitous love hotels, hostess bars and cabarets, soapland parlors, telephone and date clubs, call girl networks, pink salons, and the like. Bornoff estimates that there are well over 250,000 prostitutes working in Japan today, many of them foreign workers from Thailand, Taiwan, the Philippines, and elsewhere. Enticed to labor-shortage Japan, these so-called japayuki are brought to slave markets and sold to the highest bidders. Bornoff explores other facets of Japan's sex world as well, including stripteasing, sex tourism, and sadomasochistic activities.

One conclusion reached by Bornoff is that among the many changes in Japanese society one of the most positive is the slow but gradual liberation of women. While men remain entrapped in a harsh work ethic, women have made inroads into the economic and political life of the country. What lasting effect this will have on Japan's male dominated society remains an open question. (TJW)

IL

968. Croutier, Alev Lytle. **Harem: The World Behind the Veil.** New York: Abbeville Press, 1989. 224 p. Includes bibliography and index. ISBN 0-89659-903-5.

In this colorful book by Croutier, one reads about a world that no longer exists, that is hard to imagine, but which thrived from the mid-fifteenth century to the early 1920s. Croutier, born in Ixmir (Smyrna), Turkey, came to the United States when she was eighteen years old and, in 1978, returned to Istanbul to visit relatives and to gather information about harem life under the sultans of the Ottoman Empire in the Topkapi Palace, known in the West as the Grand Seraglio. In 1909 ordinary harems as well as the one in the Topkapi Palace were abolished and declared illegal.

Croutier's sources for this descriptive study are accounts by Western travelers and diplomats; smuggled letters; poems by the harem inmates; and some studies of royal life and palace politics. She defines the word *harem* as being derived from the Arabic word *haram*, meaning "unlawful," "protected," or "forbidden." *Haram*, for example, applies to the sacred area around Mecca and Medina. Here it refers to "a place where women are separated and cloistered, sacrosanct from all but the one man who rules their lives," and also "a place in a noble and rich house, guarded by eunuch slaves, where the lord of the manor keeps his wives and concubines."

In a series of chapters, Croutier describes (1) the origins of the harem, polygamy under Islam, slave markets and the acquisition and training of slaves to be odalisques (servants and potential concubines); (2) daily life in the sultan's harem, including games, poetry, use of opium, shopping excursions, festivals, etc.; (3) costumes and finery; (4) the baths; (5) food; (6) the life of the sultans, including sexual regimes with wives and concubines; (7) the life of eunuchs, especially their duties, the practice of castration, and sexual behavior; (8) life in lower-class harems; and (9) how harems have been treated in the literature and art of Western culture. Last, a chapter on twentieth-century orientalism gives a Western interpretation of the Orient, with depictions of harem life in the movies and comments about vestiges of the harem in the modern world.

The book is lavishly illustrated with reproductions of the paintings of such artists as Gérôme (*The Slave Market*), Ingres (*Odalisque and Slave*), Lecomte de Nouy (*The White Slave*), Leon Bakst (*Yellow Sultana*), Matisse (*Odalisque with Magnolias*), and others. It also contains a chronology of Ottoman sultans from 1299 to 1922. (TJW)

PO

969. Douglas, Nik, and Penny Slinger. **The Pillow Book: The Erotic Sentiment and the Paintings of India, Nepal, China & Japan.** New York: Arlington House, 1981. 142 p. Includes bibliography. ISBN 0-517-36993-1.

Pillow books are illustrated erotic manuals traditionally given to a couple before the consummation of their marriage. They were popular in the cultures of China, Japan, India, and Nepal until about the beginning of the twentieth century, after which they were abandoned due to Western influences. These Oriental love manuals focus on drawings, prints, or paintings that depict particularly a great variety of male/female sexual positions. The illustrations appear on scrolls, fold-out albums, or small bound volumes and are often accompanied by quotations from classical erotic works and brief descriptions of the illustrations. The Chinese, Japanese, Indian, and Nepalese art included in the book dates from the eighteenth century. The Chinese erotic art reproduced in this book represents Taoist teachings about the cosmic function of physical love; as the Taoist aphorism declares: "The union of man and woman is like the mating of Heaven and Earth." The Japanese erotic illustrations often show the influence of the Shinto religion by their depiction of grotesquely enlarged genitalia and a very flamboyant style. The Indian paintings represented here clearly express the influence of the Tantric philosophy, manifesting itself in the "love postures, yogic gestures, symbolic color combinations, and the presence of ritual items." In Nepal, where both the Hindus and Buddhists have coexisted for centuries, the erotic art shows both Tantric and Taoist influences. Interestingly, the Nepalese erotic paintings "depict various historical personages in sexual union" (p. 15). The selection of 130 illustrations of erotic postures in "this collection of paintings . . . speaks to the modern heart, freed from the sexual inhibition of the past and ready for the joyous experience of the ecstatic." (TJW)

IL,PO
970. Douglas, Nik, and Penny Slinger. **Sexual Secrets: The Alchemy of Ecstasy.** New York: Destiny Books, 1979. 383 p. Includes bibliography and index. ISBN 0-89281-011-4.

Text and illustration complement each other in this compilation of sexual secrets found in over 2,000 years of Oriental medical, philosophical, and sexual texts, including information from such sex manuals as *The Kama Sutra of Vatsyayana*, the *Ananga Ranga*, *The Perfumed Garden* of Sheikh Nefzawi, and numerous Tantric and Taoist texts. Douglas, the author, who mastered Sanskrit and Tibetan languages and spent many years in the Himalayas, has studied the sexual practices of the East from original texts and from participation in the culture of Tibet; Slinger, the illustrator, has created hundreds of stimulating drawings based on the regalia of Eastern erotica. Intended for "couples or individuals wanting to become couples," this unique book is divided into three parts corresponding "to the Hindu triad of forces that pervades all activity. This triad is the Creative, the Transcendental, and the Preserver. . . . In the Tantric cosmology these forces are formalized as three aspects of one single Divine Unity. Separately they are known as *Brahma*, the Creative; *Shiva*, the Transcendental; and *Vishnu*, the Preserver. Each of these forces is understood as inseparable from a feminine Energy counterpart of *Shakti*. According to Tantra, every higher principle can only exist through a combination of male and female" (p. 13). In part 1, "Brahma the Creative," the Tantric lifestyle is outlined; the significance of the art of love in creation; an emphasis on the senses (seeing, smelling, hearing, and touching) in a context of sexuality; the fostering of yoga positions and techniques (all illustrated); the importance of food, water, sleep, dreams, mantras and yantras, massage, clothing, and so forth. In part 2, "Shiva the Transcendental," sexual secrets are revealed in the dialogues between (1) Shiva and the goddesses Kali and Parvati, with Shiva providing the answers to provocative sexual questions; and (2) the Yellow Emperor and three young and beautiful Oriental women in a Taoist pleasure garden, with the emperor eliciting sexual secrets by asking the girls questions. In part 3, "Vishnu the Preserver," the role of eroticism and preserving and maintaining all that has been created, especially life and love, is examined. On the basis of the literature of Tantrism and Taoism, a host of sexual questions is explored and depicted: lovemaking positions, secret techniques for maintaining sensuous awareness, oragenitalism, group sex, masturbation, sexual aids, and so forth. This book brings to the attention of readers in the West the vital quality of the mystical sexuality of Tantric and Taoist teachings. It is meant to be read as well as experienced as an avenue toward sexual liberation within a spiritual context, for it is through sexual union that a couple has the mystical experience of ecstasy. (TJW/SGF)

PR,IL
971. Gulik, Robert Hans van. **Sexual Life in Ancient China: A Preliminary Survey of Chinese Sex and Society from ca. 1500 B.C. till 1644 A.D.** Leiden, Netherlands: E. J. Brill, 1961. 392 p. Includes bibliographic footnotes and indexes.

Characterizing himself as "an Orientalist with a general interest in anthropology," van Gulik claims that *Sexual Life in Ancient China* is "the first book on the subject." He attributes the paucity of literature about Chinese sex to the excessive prudery during the Manchu Dynasty from 1644 to 1912. In that period, nothing was written on sex, and older materials were systematically destroyed. Fortunately, such material exists outside China, in Japan and elsewhere, and it is to this abundant material that van Gulik turns for information. He contends that until the thirteenth century "the separation of the sexes was not strictly enforced, and sexual relations freely talked and written about" (p. xii). The handbooks of sex, written for the householder, were widely studied. Sexual behavior, unfortunately, became secretive under Confucian puritanism after the twelfth century.

Van Gulik divides his book into four distinct historical parts and each part into two or three chapters. Chapters I and II of the first part, "The Feudal Kingdom," cover the "Early Period and the Former Chou Dynasty, ca. 1500-771 B.C." and the "Later Chou Dynasty, 770-222 B.C." respectively. Intended as a general introduction to Chinese sexual life, they describe social and cultural matters—housing, dress, and adornment. In the second part, "The Growing Empire," van Gulik stresses sex in society in chapter III, "Ch'in and Former Han Dynasty, 221 B.C.-24 A.D."; sex and Taoism in chapter IV, "Later Han Dynasty, 25-220 A.D."; and sex and family life in chapter V, "The Three Kingdoms and the Six Dynasties, 221-590 A.D." In the third part, "The Heyday of Empire," he concentrates on the handbooks of sex in chapter VI, "Sui Dynasty, 590-618 A.D."; high-class prostitution, and the influence of neo-Confucianism on sexual relations in chapter VIII, "Five Dynasties and Sung Period, 908-1279 A.D." In the fourth part, "Mongol Rule and Ming Restoration," he describes sex relations under Mongol occupation, with special reference to Lamaism in chapter IX, "Mongol or Yüan Dynasty, 1279-1367 A.D."; and sex in art and letters in chapter X, "Ming Dynasty, 1358-1644 A.D."

This pioneering work examines for the first time in English, Chinese sexual behavior over a 3,000-year span of time. Van Gulik hopes that sinologists and others will continue the investigation he has started. (TJW)

PR,IL
972. Hirschfeld, Magnus. **Men and Women: The World Journey of a Sexologist.** New York: Putnam, 1935. 325 p. Includes index.

During 1931-1932, Hirschfeld, founder of the Institut für Sexualwissenschaft in Berlin (1919) and author of monumental works dealing with homosexuality (*Die Homosexualität*, 1920) and transvestism (*Die Transvestiten*, 1910), traveled through Asia and the Middle East, delivering 176 invited lectures on sexual topics to interested parties and examining the sexual behavior and customs of the host societies. His extensive background in sex ethnology enabled him to probe more than superficially into the sexual practices of many peoples and institutions in Japan, China, the Philippines, Indonesia, India, Egypt, and Palestine. He observed, for example, the extent to which matriarchy prevails in Tibet, Sumatra, and among the Tuaregs and the Taiwanese. He visited the brothel districts in some of the great cities of the world (Hong Kong, Macao, Tokyo) and observed firsthand the conditions and circumstances of prostitution in each society. He discussed the pros and cons of male and female circumcision with local experts. In India he inquired into the Lingam cult, the uninhibited worship of the phallus, intended to induce fertility. He comments on the widespread practice of infanticide in Asian countries and examines many other areas of study of intense interest to the sexologist, including marriage customs, sex education, erotic art, and the relationship between religion and sex. Hirschfeld believed that "sex is the basic principle around which all the rest of human life, with all of its institutions, is pivoted" (p. 308). In this book he tries to engender a positive and nonjudgmental view toward the sexual customs of the cultures visited. His lecture tour was enormously successful. It is indeed unfortunate that shortly thereafter, in Berlin, the Nazis destroyed Hirschfeld's institute, publicly burning his unique collection of books and research materials. He died a refugee in France in 1935. (TJW)

PO
973. Humana, Charles, and Wang Wu. **Chinese Sex Secrets: A Look Behind the Screen.** New York: Gallery Books, 1984. 159 p. Includes bibliography. ISBN 0-8317-1245-7.

Written by two experienced China watchers, this vividly illustrated history of sex in China covers an enormous stretch of time from as far back as the twenty-seventh century B.C. to as recent as the post-Mao period. In part 1, "The Bridge to the Bamboo Grove," Humana and Wu focus on the sexual behavior of prominent rulers and their court attendants. Court life in China was elaborate, with courtesans, concubines, prostitutes, and eunuchs providing entertainment and diversion. Counselors, often female, tendered advice on sexual matters, such as potent aphrodisiacs and recommended practices for enlarging the penis. Preoccupied with sex, the emperors cultivated stunning reputations of sexual prowess. An elaborate literature of sex manuals and pillow books (for newlyweds) came into existence, and a special vocabulary of sex emerged, providing a refined means of addressing sexual matters (e.g., Jade Stalk stood for penis, Jewel Terrace for the clitoris, and The Clouds and the Rain for intercourse).

The oldest extant treatise on sex, the *N'ei Ching Su Wen*, written by the Yellow Emperor, Huang-Ti (2697-2598 B.C.) is inscribed on bamboo and tortoiseshell in the form of questions from the emperor and answers provided by his counselor. This work antedates the two great philosophies, Confucianism and Taoism, which became the basis of Chinese sexual attitudes and behavior. While radically different in many respects, these philosophies came together in the acceptance of the two vital forces in life: the female principle of Yin and the male principle of Yang, which, in ideal male/female relationships, balance each other out to produce Harmony. Implied in these systems, however, is the equation of dominance/submission with male/female.

In part 2, "The Art of the Bedchamber," Humana and Wu discuss (1) the male preoccupation with the female body, especially "the one square inch"; (2) positions of sexual intercourse in varying circumstances; (3) the prolongation of sexual pleasure; (4) sex aids and sexual perversions; and (5) the highly regarded institution of prostitution. Poems and excerpts from Chinese novels highlight the topics covered.

Part 3, "From Fragrant Silhouettes to the Great Leap Forward," reviews the Chinese classical literature, focusing on the authors and themes of erotic novels. The last chapter of the book, "The Great Leap Forward," brings the history of sex in China up to the present. With the communist takeover following World War II, the traditional rules governing behavior, including sex, were changed overnight. Concubinage and prostitution were abolished, and by 1950 new marriage regulations emerged, guaranteeing the equality of women in Chinese society. "Modern China," Humana and Wu summarize, "is therefore a society in which the sexual side of marriage, extramarital relations and romantic feelings between Yin and Yang are either ignored, discouraged, or prohibited. If there has been a degree of relaxation in the post-Mao society, it is only apparent among those small groups most likely to come into contact with the foreign influences of Western and Japanese visitors. For the great majority, sex remains a relatively joyless function, socially acceptable only between those legally married" (p. 150). Only the overseas Chinese, especially in the Golden Triangle (Taiwan-Hong Kong-Bangkok), seem to be carrying on many of the old traditions and holding on to the time-honored philosophies. (TJW)

PR,IL

974. Nanda, Serena. **Neither Man nor Woman: The Hijras of India.** Belmont, Calif.: Wadsworth, 1990. 170 p. (Wadsworth Modern Anthropology Library). Includes bibliography, index, and glossary. ISBN 0-534-12204-3.

The hijras of India are neither men nor women but rather an institutionalized third gender role. They are anatomical males who have undergone an operation to remove their penis and testes; who wear women's clothes and behave like women; and who make up a religious community, the culture of which focuses on the worship of Buhuchara Mata, a version of the Mother Goddess. Hijras are tolerated rather than scorned and hold a special place in Indian culture. This book is an ethnography of the hijras, based on lengthy personal narratives and conversations with hijras during Nanda's fieldwork in south central India and Bombay from 1981 to 1986.

The theoretical questions underlying the ethnography relate to gender categorization and human sexual variation. Using the beliefs of their culture, how do hijras define and present themselves to their society? In occupying marginal roles, how do they perceive their culture? How do the options for gender roles in India affect human sexual development? How do different individuals perceive and play their roles as hijras? The ten chapters of the book address these questions in various ways.

Hijras are able to construct a sense of self using mythological themes of a third gender role and transformation of gender; they can legitimize themselves in terms of their social roles as culturally significant ritual performers and as homosexual prostitutes. They demonstrate their commitment to their role by undergoing the emasculation operation, transforming impotence to creativity through asceticism, thus enacting an identification with Shiva, one of the greatest ascetic deities, and giving them the power to confer the blessings of fertility on others. The social organization of hijras around their occupation functions like a caste, allowing them to live in households, perform domestic tasks, and remain economically viable.

The personal narratives of four hijras demonstrate how individuals become part of the hijra subculture and commit themselves to new gender identities and roles. Kamladevi is a prostitute; Meera is a hijra leader and wife; Sushila is a former prostitute who has become a wife, mother, and grandmother; and Salima is a performer and wife who was born intersexed. Personal history and a sense of self channel the ways in which individuals interpret hijra roles and behave in them. Nanda analyzes hijra lives in terms of more general concerns about gender identity and role.

The concluding chapter discusses the hijras in cross-cultural perspective by looking at institutionalized alternative sex and gender roles in other cultures: the xanith in Oman, the Mohave alyha, the mahu of Tahiti, and the place of transsexuals in the West. Nanda hopes that her research prompts people in the West to ponder their own gender categories and realize that the Western view of two permanent genders, based on physical anatomy, is not universal. Gender is constructed within and derives its meaning from the culture in which it occurs. (SGF)

PR,IL

975. Rawson, Philip, David James, and Richard Lane. **Erotic Art of the East: The Sexual Theme in Oriental Painting and Sculpture.** Introduction by Alex Comfort. [London]: Minerva, 1973, 384 p. (World History of Erotic Arts). Includes bibliography and index.

Four separate studies of erotic art in India, China, Japan, and the Islamic world comprise this handsome volume. An introduction by Comfort on the sexual in art sets the tone for all subsequent volumes in the series by discussing why sexual representation in art is what art is all about. Sexual representations are the closest tie that Western culture has to others in providing a "technology of the emotions." Thirty-two color plates of erotic painting and sculpture as well as numerous black-and-white photographic images provide illustrations in support of the scholarly texts.

Rawson's lengthy paper on India, which has an abundance of erotic art reaching back to the earliest times, discusses many aspects of the subject: sexuality as intrinsically divine with its roots in the sacred literature of Hinduism, the worship of sexual images, the reflection in art of erotic secular hedonism, the depiction of the sexual role of women and the cult of pleasure, erotic techniques expressed in literature and art, erotic temple art at Khajuraho and Kondarak, Tantrism as a philosophy of sex, yoga rituals, and the worship of gods and goddesses (Shiva and Shakti, Krishna and Radhu).

As to the Islamic world, James's study of the Arab countries and Persia (now Iran) examines fragments of extant erotic art appearing on walls, in baths, on illuminated manuscripts, and in sex manuals. Unlike the abundant erotic literature, most of this artwork, dating from the eighth century on, was destroyed on occasions of overzealous reform. The evidence, James contends, points to a flourishing eroticism in both art and literature in the Islamic world. There was nothing in the Koran to prohibit it. He goes on to say, moreover, that the segregation of women in harems, the prohibition of fornication and adultery, did not lead to widespread homosexuality, lesbianism, bestiality, and other deviations from heterosexuality; this is expressed in the erotic art and literature of Turkey, Persia, and the Arab world, particularly in the eighteenth and nineteenth centuries.

In the third study, on China, Rawson describes the centuries-old Confucian code with its "hostile attitude towards the open discussion of sex and love." Sex in China is deemed a private matter; there has been no guilt feeling associated with sexual pleasure. All Chinese erotic art dates from the late Ming and Ch'ing dynasties; none has been preserved from ancient times. In contrast to Confucianism, the Taoist philosophy permeates the domain of erotic art. Confucianism and Taoism accept the reality of two forces in life—the male and the female—as explained in the *I Ching* or *Book of Changes*. Called Yin and Yang in Taoism, these two forces are in continuous interaction, and sexual intercourse is one manifestation. Thus, the sexual practices of the Chinese, as well as their erotic art, are in accordance with this basic conception. Throughout these pages, attractive illustrations of jade and porcelain objects, embroidered robes, hardstone carvings, paintings, and so forth display male and female sex symbols and depict Chinese sexual behavior in accordance with the Taoist perspective. Rawson concludes with a discussion of erotically illustrated novels and stories, manuals of sexual practice known as The Art of the Bedchamber, and erotic print albums.

The final study, on Japan, is by Lane, who claims that his paper is "the first detailed, fully illustrated account of shunga to be published" (p. 283). It closely traces the development of Shunga, a branch of pictorial art that glorifies the erotic. Shunga means "Spring Pictures" or "Sex Pictures." It captured the spirit of the sex act that in Japanese eyes was "simply the joyful union of the sexes, a natural function that represented man's greatest pleasure—almost, his *raison d'etre*."

The Shunga pictures, painted in the ukiyo-e style, were a normal part of an artist's work in Japan—no stigma was attached to them. For centuries, until banned along with the nude in art in the latter part of the nineteenth century, they served a useful function in sex education. Shunga painting and print appeared in books, albums, and scrolls, which offered erotic stories. Lane identifies the major ukiyo-e artists who made Shunga a part of their work. He concludes by showing the effects of Western influences on Japanese art. (TJW)

PR,IL
976. Ruan, Fang Fu. **Sex in China: Studies in Sexology in Chinese Culture.** New York: Plenum Press, 1991. 208 p. (Perspectives in Sexuality). Includes bibliography and index. ISBN 0-306-43860-7.

Claiming to be one of the foremost scholars of Chinese sexual behavior and customs, Ruan comments in the preface to this survey of sex in China, that for 4,000 years China adhered to the Yin-Yang philosophy of life, which boasted a positive attitude toward sex, and that only in the past 1,000 years has China resorted to sex repression and censorship. The result has been the wholesale destruction of "materials relating to sex, including ancient medical classics, vibrant fiction, and wonderful paintings." Unfortunately, modern China under the Communists has such a terrible record of sexual suppression that pornographers fear the death penalty for their actions.

Ruan's survey combines a history of sex in China with special attention to specific topics, including sexual philosophy, classical sexological literature, Taoist sexual myths and techniques, erotic fiction, prostitution, homosexuality, transvestism and transsexualism, and changing attitudes toward sex in China today.

Ruan also examines China's oldest sex literature, the studies of Chinese sexology in English, the significance of these studies, and the need for the study of sex in China. The major English language study, R. H. van Gulik's *Sexual Life in Ancient China*, takes one only to the end of the Ming Dynasty in 1644 A.D. Ruan also discusses in some detail Chinese sexual philosophy based on the harmony of Yin and Yang and explores sexual attitudes in the Confucian, Taoist, and Buddhist traditions. He looks at classical Chinese sexology: the earliest Chinese sex books, materials preserved in Japanese collections, and the lack of availability of these materials in modern China. He also describes the sexual elements in Taoism, especially its myths and methods.

Four chapters are devoted to prostitution and its latter-day persecution; classical Chinese erotica, both its former expression and its modern suppression; homosexuality, primarily male homosexuality; and transvestism and transsexualism, about which nothing at all has been written in Chinese but which has the potential to be developed and investigated. A final chapter explores changing attitudes toward sex in China today. Despite negative official attitudes toward anything of a sexual nature that goes beyond heterosexual intercourse in monogamous marriage, the Chinese have expressed their opinions about sex. According to a survey of 23,000 people in fifteen provinces conducted by the Shanghai Sex Sociology Research Center in 1989-1990, "86% of the respondents said they approved of premarital sex" (p. 162).

According to Ruan, in China today there is an official ban on nudity, plays and films must not be "obscene," personal adornment is carefully watched, social contacts between young men and women hardly exist, and a censorious atmosphere prevails throughout the country. In this repressive climate, sex crimes, including rape, have increased.

Encouraged by the late Chou En-lai's call for sex education in schools, which has resulted in courses being taught at different levels, young people, taking advantage of the "Democracy Wall" movement in 1978 and 1979, expressed their hope for greater sexual freedom by writing poems and placing posters on the wall. Similar activities occurred in the Tiananmen Square disturbances in 1989.

Ruan's last sentence provides a hopeful sign of change in China: "As the tide of modernization overtakes China, sexual freedom will certainly have its place among the vital human rights the people will enjoy in the future." (TJW)

PR,IL

977. Shostak, Marjorie. **Nisa: The Life and Words of a !Kung Woman.** New York: Vintage Books, 1983. 402 p. Originally published by Harvard University Press in 1981. Includes bibliographic notes, glossary, and index. ISBN 0-394-71126-2.

In this narrative about !Kung life, anthropologist Shostak, an associate of the Peabody Museum of Archaeology and Ethnology at Harvard University, juxtaposes ethnographic details about the social organization and developmental cycle of the !Kung with an autobiographical account of the life of Nisa, a !Kung woman in her fifties, who is unusually articulate but basically typical of other women of the group. Most of the information presented is based on Shostak's fieldwork from 1969 to 1971 among the !Kung San of the Dobe region in northwestern Botswana. However, she also incorporates information from earlier ethnographic descriptions of the area.

The !Kung are a tribe of hunters and gatherers who dwell in the semiarid environment of the Kalahari Desert of Africa. They cluster in semipermanent camps or villages of from ten to thirty people and maintain a relatively egalitarian, flexible way of life. Women contribute the majority of food consumed (with the products of their gathering) while men provide highly valued meat by hunting. Women have high status and considerable influence in the community.

The book traces life among the !Kung from birth to death and includes discussions of family life, discovering sex, trial marriages, wives and co-wives, birth, the relationship between men and women, taking lovers, and growing old. Each chapter is enriched by Nisa's perspective on the events in her own life.

During the course of her work with the !Kung, Shostak noticed their preoccupation with personal relationships, particularly sexual ones. Sex is an integral, important part of !Kung life. Children openly engage in sex play and are prepared by adults for their future sex lives as adults. They are able to observe sex and engage in premarital sexual relationships. Women first marry when they are sixteen and a half, while boys do so between the ages of twenty and thirty. Men are able to have more than one spouse, but marriage with co-wives is difficult. Whether monogamous or polygynous, marriages often end in divorce. Extramarital affairs are common but may engender jealousy or conflict between marriage partners. Despite the shift in partners, sex is regarded as a wonderful experience; both men and women strive to satisfy their partners, even though they may have to deal with lack of desire, impotence, premature ejaculation, and orgasmic dysfunction. Both men and women discuss sexual topics and are enthusiastic about participation in sexually satisfying relationships. Such interest does not wane with age.

Selected by the *New York Times* as one of the notable books of 1981, *Nisa* proves a personal dimension to ethnographic description of life in another culture. In so doing, it illustrates some universal concerns that all people share. (SGF)

NEAR EAST/MIDDLE EAST

(For related material see also entry 790)

IL
978.   Edwardes, Allen. **Erotica Judaica: A Sexual History of the Jews.** New York: Julian Press, 1967. 238 p. Includes bibliographic footnotes and index.

Edwardes, who has written several books on Oriental erotica, surveys Judaism in terms of sexual rules and practices. Rather than a comprehensive analysis, this is a series of reflections on selected passages from the Bible, the Talmud, and writings of both Jewish and non-Jewish observers. Judaism is interpreted as a phallic religion including ancient elements of ritual masturbation. Mental and physical purity became essential as the religion matured, with reverence for procreative, conjugal sex making masturbation as well as sexual activities that "wasted the seed" abhorrent. Edwardes reinterprets many passages of the Bible as euphemistic treatment of sexual themes. Circumcision is the central distinguishing characteristic and has always set the Jews off from the surrounding culture. The Greeks found the practice repellent, the Romans taxed circumcision, and the right to circumcision was the motive for the Maccabean revolt. Although the Judaic code emphasizes purity, the actual sexual practices have been influenced by the surrounding culture, and the Jews have shared their neighbors' practices of homosexuality, bestiality, prostitution (including sacred and homosexual variants), adultery, etc. (JA)

PR,IL
979.   Edwardes, Allen. **The Jewel in the Lotus: A Historical Survey of the Sexual Culture of the East.** Introduction by Dr. Albert Ellis. New York: Julian Press, 1964. 293 p. Original copyright 1959. Includes bibliography.

In the introduction, Ellis recommends this book as the best summary of knowledge available concerning sex customs in the East, primarily the Middle East before the twentieth century. However, he notes that the contents should be interpreted with a grain of salt since literary materials (stories, myths, tales) rather than scientific studies are often the source of much of the information. He adds another caveat to the intelligent layperson, for whom this book is intended: "Many of the customs described herein are no longer practiced today" (p. xv). Nevertheless, he believes that an appreciation of certain basic attitudes—a fatalistic vision of life, the view that sensuality and continence are matters of taste, a candid and realistic feeling about sex, the belief that women are inferior beings—are essential for an understanding of the peoples of the Middle East. As a consequence of their beliefs, Edwardes claims, these peoples sometimes slipped into open debauchery, made a principle of sensuality, became arrogant, superstitious, intolerant, and cruel. Hence, the sexual practices that have shocked and offended Western society.

The area mapped out by Edwardes for study—called the Sotadic Zone by Sir Richard Burton—embraced chiefly the Sudan, Egypt, Syria, Persia, Afghanistan, and India. Within this zone, Islam and Hinduism (religions that condition and define the sexual beliefs and practices of the faithful) prevailed overwhelmingly. Since Edwardes's goal is to survey the past sexual culture of the East, he devotes eight chapters to a historical treatment of the sexual mores of these countries. Each chapter gives detailed accounts of sexual attitudes and behavior, all justified in the name of religion and a disarming fatalism. Topics include the passive role of women, the genitals in symbol and reality, circumcision, autoerotism, female prostitution, eunuchism, sexual perversion, and hygiene. The rituals and practices, however appalling and cruel they may appear to Western eyes, are a part of the heritage of the peoples of the Middle East.

Relying heavily on Eastern source materials, Edwardes uses Arabic words and expressions parenthetically throughout the text to impart a romantic and Asian flavor to the writing. (TJW)

PR,IL
980. Spiro, Melford E. **Gender and Culture: Kibbutz Women Revisited.** Durham, N.C.: Duke University Press, 1979. 116 p. Includes bibliography and index. ISBN 0-8223-0427-9.

This is the third in a series of books that psychological anthropologist Spiro has written on the Israeli kibbutz. Based on one year (1951-1952) of participant observation in a kibbutz, the first book, *Kibbutz: Venture in Utopia* (1955), described the social and cultural nature of the kibbutz. Predicated on cultural ideals that stress common humanity, equality, and freedom, the social organization of the kibbutz was characterized by group living, communal ownership, and cooperative enterprise. The family was not an economic unit. Though husbands and wives shared a room, their children lived in children's houses where they were collectively educated. Both men and women worked nine hours a day; domestic and economic functions previously performed in the family were provided by the kibbutz. Thus, traditional sex roles were shifted into a more egalitarian cast.

In his second book, *Children of the Kibbutz* (1958), Spiro used a psychoanalytic orientation to investigate the impact of the collective care and training of children ("the educational revolution") on their psychological development. These data became the foundation for a more general exploration of the link between culture and personality.

Gender and Culture is based on Spiro's findings about the kibbutz when he returned to the site of his original fieldwork in 1975. Spiro observed a dramatic shift in one aspect of kibbutz organization, which he characterizes as a counterrevolution in sex roles. Women had withdrawn from heavy agricultural work and chosen to raise their children within the context of a nuclear family. Men gravitated toward traditional male roles. High school students objected to the sexually enlightened settings of mixed dormitories and showers. The book describes and interprets the reasons for this counterrevolution.

In contrast to his earlier view that the social experiment of kibbutz organization showed the dominance of cultural influences in molding human behavior, Spiro now thinks that the current situation demonstrates the "triumph of nature over culture." He rejects a cultural interpretation of current *sabra* (people born and raised in the kibbutz) behavior in favor of a precultural interpretation. He argues that counterrevolutionary changes in marriage, the family, and sex role differentiation were brought about by "precultural motivational predispositions." Precultural needs are panhuman and include biological, psychosocial, and psychobiological needs; they can be genetically or experientially acquired and are part of human, precultural adaptation. The female parenting need that Spiro perceives as the cornerstone of changes that have occurred in the counterrevolution is presented as a compelling example. Although he admits that "the kibbutz case does not prove the existence of precultural sex differences," it "challenges the current intellectual and political pieties which deny the existence of such differences . . . on the grounds that to be different is ipso facto to be unequal" (p. 109). Kibbutz women now seek status equivalence rather than identity with men, within a system of sex-role differentiation.

Related materials on the kibbutz include Rochelle Shain's 1974 dissertation, "The Functional Nature of the Sexual Division of Labor in an Israeli Kibbutz" (University of California, Berkeley) and Lionel Tiger and Joseph Shepher's book, *Women in the Kibbutz* (New York: Harcourt Brace Jovanovich, 1975). (SGF)

EUROPE

(For related material see also entries 85, 764)

PR
981. Cohen, David. **Law, Sexuality, and Society: The Enforcement of Morals in Classical Athens.** Cambridge, Eng.: Cambridge University Press, 1991. 259 p. Includes bibliography and index. ISBN 0-521-37447-2.

The regulation of sexuality and the problems of social control in classical Athens are examined in this work by Cohen, of the Department of Rhetoric, University of California, Berkeley. The study suggests that law cannot enforce morality and that legal statutes alone do not provide the historian with a comprehensive account of a society's moral order.

After extensive analysis of the public-private dichotomy in Athenian society and a generalized discussion of social action that includes definition of key concepts such as the politics of reputation, the politics of gender, and the politics of spatial differentiation, Cohen focuses on adultery, homosexuality, and impiety within the context of Athenian society, identifying specifics of the law and of the social norms related to those practices. He develops an understanding of the interplay among legal, religious, and social norms. He interprets the means of social control used by Athenians to regulate sexual and religious activities. He uses a comparative approach, extending his analyses to anthropological studies in other Mediterranean countries, such as Algeria, Cyprus, Egypt, Italy, Lebanon, Malta, Morocco, Portugal, Spain, and Turkey. Sexuality and sexual practices represent an aspect of life where significant cross-cultural differences exist in patterns of enforcement by law of social norms. Detailed information about gender roles is presented. The text is enriched by full use of related research findings by anthropologists, historians, legal scholars, and sociologists. The complexity of social structure is carefully detailed. Interpretations are based on scholarly findings and theories.

Cohen offers a deep and complex view of the role of law in society. He also instructs his readers that social morality is not comprised of a rational, internally consistent set of ethical principles, but rather reflects conflict, contradiction, and ambivalence. (LF)

PR,IL
982. Copley, Antony. **Sexual Moralities in France, 1780-1980: New Ideas on the Family, Divorce, and Homosexuality.** London: Routledge, 1989. 283 p. Includes bibliography and index. ISBN 0-415-00360-1.

In this study, Copley, Senior Lecturer in History at the University of Kent in England, explores the long-term origins of libertarianism by tracing the development of sexual moralities in France from the 1780s to the 1980s. He focuses his explorations on changing attitudes toward divorce and homosexuality, key aspects involving French morality during several periods of French history, especially the revolutionary and Napoleonic regimes, the Third Republic, and the Fourth Republic.

Copley presents the debates on divorce and homosexuality as reflected in the changing French law and the evolving French attitudes toward sexual morality. He also examines the attitudes of moralists and intellectuals toward sexual morality in general, selecting four prominent individuals: the Marquis de Sade, Charles Fourrier, Andre Gide, and Daniel Guerin. Their writings were "a critical response and a search for a more progressive and libertarian sexual morality" and transcended "the constraints of guilt at the heart of a catholic and conservative morality."

Covering as it does such a long period of French history, this study is fully documented with copious notes and an extensive thematic bibliography. (TJW)

PR,IL
983. Costlow, Jane T., Stephanie Sandler, and Judith Vowles, eds. **Sexuality and the Body in Russian Culture.** Stanford, Calif.: Stanford University Press, 1993. 357 p. Includes bibliographic notes and index. ISBN 0-8047-2113-0.

With the goal of attempting "to document the history of sexuality and the body in Russian culture," the editors have assembled twelve papers on a diverse range of subjects. Most of these papers were presented in 1989 at a symposium funded by the Amherst College Russian Department. The editors' introduction focuses on Russian views, past and present, that attempt to distinguish between sexuality in Russia and the West. The importance of this distinction highlights both the current reform movement and the liberalization of sexual attitudes and behavior in Russia since *glasnost* and *perestroika*.

The first chapter of part 1, "The Cultural History of Sexual Representation," deals with sexual vocabulary in medieval Russia. In it Eve Levin writes etymologically about the highly euphemistic terms and expressions employed in both ecclesiastical and secular texts, and shows how they reflect attitudes toward sexuality. In "Marriage à la russe," Vowles describes the transformation in male/female relationships brought about by Peter the Great's efforts to westernize Russia. But in the early nineteenth century, foreign observers were dismayed by the crudity of Russian female aggressiveness in society. In "A Stick with Two Ends, or, Misogyny in Popular Culture," Catriona Kelly analyzes the text of "Petrushka" to show how women and women's sexuality were represented in the puppet theater in the late nineteenth century and early twentieth century. Jane A. Sharp, in "Redrawing the Margins of Russian Vanguard Art," examines censorship in Russian modern art by discussing the nudes of Natalia Goncharova, who "has the distinction of being the only Russian artist ever tried before for pornography in the 'high' genre of the nude life study." Finally, Elizabeth A. Wood, in "Prostitution Unbounded," addresses the problem of prostitution in postrevolutionary Russia during the periods of "war communism" and the New Economic Policy (NEP), when the prostitute was viewed as a danger to the new order.

Part 2, "Literary Versions of Sex and Body," consists of four papers about Russian literature and criticism. Cathy Popkin in "Kiss and Tell" analyzes a Chekhov story, "The Kiss," as a model for storytelling in which desire is stimulated by a kiss, the ensuing fantasies, and telling the story to an audience. The paper "Loving in Bad Taste" is an analysis of Marina Tsvetaeva's novella *The Tale of Sonechka* (1937), an unconventional love story involving multiple relationships among women. It attempts to "reinvent love and 'women in love' from a feminist perspective." In "Laid Out in Lavender" Diana Lewis Burgin describes lesbian love as purveyed by Russian writers and critics of the Silver Age, from 1893 to 1917. Finally, Helena Goscilo in her paper "Monsters, Monomaniacal, Marital, and Medical" satirizes specific gender stereotypes, examining Tatiana Tolstaya's fiction, which portrays implausible candidates seeking sexual love.

Part 3 contains three papers. Costlow in "The Pastoral Source," concentrates on representations of the maternal breast in nineteenth century Russia. Barbara Heldt assesses the poetry and career of Maria Shkapskaya in "Motherhood in a Cold Climate," applying a feminist perspective rather than the usual Russian patriarchal stance, and Eric Naiman, in his paper "Historectomies," explores the metaphysical views of several Russian philosophers bearing on androgyny, misogyny, and immortality. (TJW)

IL

984. Forberg, Friedrich Karl. **Manual of Classical Erotology (De Figuris Veneris).** New York: Grove Press, 1966. 2 v. in 1. Includes extensive footnotes.

Forberg (1770-1848) was a philologian, professor of philosophy, and court librarian at Coburg in Bavaria. This work is a facsimile, reproducing the original English edition that was privately published for the translator, Julian Smithson, in 1884. The Latin and English texts are printed on facing pages. Lacking illustrations, the work consists primarily of excerpts from ancient Greek and Roman authors describing sexual practices and attitudes. Forberg organized the material into categories of copulation, pederasty, fellatio, cunnilingus, masturbation, lesbianism, intercourse with animals, and sexual acts involving more than two participants. The extensive notes are textual and philological in content. No attempt is made to distinguish between presumed actual occurrences and literary invention. (JA)

PR

985. Halperin, David M., John J. Winkler, and Froma I. Zeitlin, eds. **Before Sexuality: The Construction of Erotic Experience in the Ancient Greek World.** Princeton, N.J.: Princeton University Press, 1990. 526 p. Includes bibliographies and indexes. ISBN 0-691-03538-5.

Various perspectives on sex and sexuality in ancient Greece are the subject of this collection of fifteen conference papers. Rather than a comprehensive examination of Greek antiquity, the editors consider these perspectives as "a series of glimpses . . . through different peepholes placed in the wall around a large construction site" (p. 4-5). The contributors chiefly include historians, classical scholars, and cultural anthropologists. They examine religious, social, political, philosophical, medical, literary, and artistic aspects of the Greek world.

The first essay, "Herakles: The Super-Male and the Feminine," by Nicole Loraux, explores the feminine aspects of the Greek hero's character. François Lissarrague in "The Sexual Life of Satyrs" looks at the sexual aggression of satyrs as depicted in paintings on Attic vases. In "Aspects of Baubo: Ancient Texts and Contexts," Maurice Olender describes an odd group of terra-cotta statuettes, where large heads set directly "on the top of legs, blending into and replacing the hips of the atrophied body." Female genitals fuse with the figures' chins. Dubbed Baubo after the woman who made Demeter laugh, these little monsters represent "a sexuality lying beyond the accepted limits of everyday social interactions."

James Redfield in "From Sex to Politics" studies basic "social patterns informing rites of passage preparatory to marriage" by considering a myth and rites at Patras. In "Putting Her in Her Place: Woman, Dirt, and Desire," Anne Carson explores the importance of boundaries in Greek life, especially the breaching of boundaries by women through marriage. John Winkler studies the sexual norms for proper male citizenship and how they were applied in "Laying Down the Law: The Oversight of Men's Sexual Behavior in Classical Athens." In "From Ambiguity to Ambivalence," Françoise Frontisi-Ducroux and François Lissarrague review a series of Attic vases depicting bearded men in apparently feminine apparel. Editor Halperin in "Why Is Diotima a Woman?" analyzes the various strategies by which Plato and his friends (in the *Symposium*) spoke about women by speaking of women.

Ann Ellis Hanson in "The Medical Writers' Woman" and Giulia Sissa in "Maidenhood Without Maidenhead" investigate medical writings about women, giving their attention to such topics as reproduction, virginity, and the function of the hymen. S. R. F. Price in "The Future of Dreams" compares the dream systems of Freud and Artemidoros for their different assumptions about sex. In "The Semiotics of Gender," Maud W. Gleason "reconstructs the ways that men practised, faked, and impugned masculinity in late antique town life."

Froma I. Zeitlin in "The Poetics of *Eros*" views Longus's *Daphnis and Chloe* as a "kind of encyclopedia of multiple erotic acts" rather than a pastoral romance. Then Jean-Pierre Vernant in "One . . . Two . . . Three: *Eros*" looks at the underlying causes that "produce Hesiodic, Orphic, Platonic, and Plotinian *eros*." Finally, Peter Brown explores sexual renunciation in early Christianity in "Bodies and Minds."

Where required, numerous illustrations support the scholarship of this well-documented compilation. (TJW)

PR

986. Keuls, Eva C. **The Reign of the Phallus: Sexual Politics in Ancient Athens.** New York: Harper & Row, 1985. 452 p. Includes bibliography and index. ISBN 0-06-015300-8.

The question of sexuality in ancient Athens has long been a sensitive subject for scholars. In *The Reign of the Phallus*, Keuls examines Greek sexual history, focusing on fifth century (B.C.) Athens. Mythology and literature are used as sources, and more than 300 photographs of vase paintings are used to illustrate Keuls's points. Although this is a scholarly work, Keuls has attempted "to make the book accessible to the general (educated) reader" (p. 12).

Keuls maintains that, until the end of the Periciean age (430 B.C.), Athens can be described as a "phallocracy" marked by extreme dominance of a male elite and symbolized by the public display of the phallus as a sign of power and sovereignty. Greek mythology, permeated with an obsessive fear of women, teaches that rape, brutal punishment, and execution of women are accepted male actions. Women in Athens were considered and treated much the same as slaves. Wives of Athenian citizens were completely dominated by their husbands, were allowed no education or public contact, and were kept cloistered in the home. Their lives were defined by the labors of spinning, weaving, and childbearing. Men sought affection and sexual gratification with prostitutes and concubines. Male homosexual activity was accepted within strict limits: superficial relationships between older man and youths were encouraged while loving relationships between peers were scandalous. Sexual activity between men most frequently involved the older partner copulating between the thighs of the youth. Anal copulation was considered demeaning or obscene.

Athenian life provided opportunities for emotional release through the theater and various religious rituals, particularly the Dionysiac rituals of Maenadism in which women in ecstatic trances danced, sang, handled snakes, and tore apart living animals. Sexual molestation by men dressed as satyrs was part of the ritual activities.

In 415 B.C. the sexual antagonism in Athens came to a symbolic climax with the "mutilation of the herms," in which the noses and penises of hundreds of statues of Hermes were broken off by unidentified vandals. Keuls hypothesizes that rebellious Athenian women mutilated the herms in protest of the ongoing Peloponnesian War. (SDH)

PR,IL

987. Kiefer, Otto. **Sexual Life in Ancient Rome.** London: Routledge & Kegan Paul, 1951. 379 p. First published in 1934. Translated from the German by Gilbert Highet and Helen Highet. Includes index.

Kiefer divides his comprehensive study of sex in ancient Rome into seven chapters, each devoted to a large segment of Roman life. In the introduction Kiefer describes the "early Romans as a race of simple and homely farmers" who later became "a nation striving to conquer the world." With power and wealth came a multiplication of pleasures that led to the eventual decline and destruction of an empire through avarice and sadism.

Chapter I, "Woman in Roman Life," refers to major theories concerning the early history of Rome, especially speculation about Etruscan matriarchy and the subsequent establishment of patriarchal rule over the Roman family, the *patria potestas*. Following a section on "Marriage," Kiefer provides a section on "Divorce, Adultery, Celibacy, and Concubinage." He closes the chapter with a section on "The Emancipation of Roman Women" and one on "Free Love."

In chapter II, "The Romans and Cruelty," Kiefer refers to Wilhelm Stekel's study *Sadism and Masochism*, which states "cruelty is the expression of hatred and of the will to power" (p. 65). He then shows how cruelty is reflected in various aspects of Roman culture: education, conquest, law, slavery, public executions, and in the arena.

In chapter III, "Roman Religion and Philosophy in Relation to Sexual Life," Kiefer first discusses Roman sexual life as reflected in religion. According to Kiefer, the Romans, and earlier the Greeks, considered the generative faculties as deserving of honor and worship. After discussing such indigenous Roman deities as Jupiter, Saturn, Ceres, and Mutunus Tutunus, a sexual deity, Kiefer introduces the popular cults of Dionysus, Venus, Liber, Phallus, Priapus, Bacchanalia, Cybele, Isis, and Bona Dea.

Kiefer devotes chapter IV, "The Physical Life," to those elements of Roman life that were linked to sexuality: dress and ornament, the toilet, dancing, and the theater. In chapter V, "Love in Roman Poetry," he discusses the poetry of twenty-one of Rome's leading poets, including Plautus, Lucretius, Catullus, Vergil, Horace, Ovid, the Priapeia, and others in terms of erotic content. In chapter VI, "Men and Women of the Imperial Age," Kiefer reviews the sexual lives of select Romans, including Augustus, the Elder

Julia, the Younger Julia, Ovid, Tiberius, Caligula, Claudius, Nero, Domitian, Antinous, and Heliogabalus.

In chapter VII, "The Fall of Rome and Its Causes," Kiefer examines reasons for Rome's decline and fall, including sexual decadence, immorality, sadism, and cruelty. Numerous photographic plates complement each chapter of this scholarly study based primarily on original sources. (TJW)

IL

988.   Kon, Igor, and James Riordan, eds. **Sex and Russian Society.** Bloomington, Ind.: Indiana University Press, 1993. 168 p. Includes bibliographies and index. ISBN 0-253-33200-1.

In this collection of papers, Kon, author of the first Russian language textbook on sexuality (*Introduction to Sexology*, 1988); Riordan, Professor of Russian Studies at the University of Surrey in the United Kingdom; and several contributors (four of them Russian), provide a groundbreaking survey of sex in Russian society. Riordan gives a brief overview of the subject, touching on the deplorable state of ignorance about sex in the former Soviet Union, signs of change, both negative and positive, taking place today, and what the West might do to accelerate the process of change. Kon's first paper is a general review of sex in Russian society, including an historical introduction going back several centuries to "holy Rus," and highlighting the negative impact of Christianity on sexual matters since the ninth century. Kon emphasizes the sexual aspects of Russian popular culture as reflected in folklore, painting, and literature up to Soviet times. He provides an overview of the liberal attitudes toward sex that prevailed after the Revolution up to the time of Stalin, when repressive measures were initiated affecting many aspects of Soviet sex culture that endure to this day. Following Stalin's death and during the "thaw," some positive steps were taken to improve the situation: sexology had its beginning, the systematic study of child and juvenile sexuality got underway, and textbooks and statistical surveys were undertaken and sometimes published on sex topics.

Six contributions from experts in Soviet studies explore specific areas of sexuality in Russian society. Larissa I. Remennick writes about induced abortion as the principal means of birth control in the former Soviet Union, pointing out that the contraceptive revolution in the West in the 1960s "never reached the USSR," where approximately 6,818,000 induced abortions took place in 1987. Lynne Atwood, an expert on Soviet women, describes in her paper the inclusion of sex and pornography in recent films produced in Russia. She focuses on the treatment of women in such films as *Little Vera* (1988), which gave Russians their first taste of explicit sex scenes in the country's history. She also comments on the treatment of prostitution and sexual violence against women in other recent films.

Kon returns with a detailed examination of sexual minorities, mainly homosexuals, and their deplorable status throughout the course of Soviet history. Since homosexuality under Article 121 of the Russian criminal code was deemed a criminal offense, the efforts to decriminalize it have been long and arduous. Only now is a new code being debated on television and in the press. In her paper, "Soviet Beauty Contests," Elizabeth Waters reports that the first contests were held in 1988 in the USSR. The first Miss USSR was selected at the All-Union Beauty Contest in Moscow in May 1989. The Soviets have been ambivalent about the role of beauty queens in society. Is it advertising for the fashion industry? Is it just to have a sex symbol, like Marilyn Monroe? Waters believes that contests "will be performed in the future by a range of social institutions, by a diversifying cultural life, by the fashion and sex industries, and by an expanding civil society" (p. 132).

Sergei Golod in "Sex and Young People" reports on the results of sex surveys he has personally conducted with Soviet youth (essentially students) in regard to premarital sex, motives for sexual intercourse, and satisfaction with sexual relationships. The final paper, by Lev Shcheglov, concerns the history and development of medical sexology and sexual pathology in the USSR. He points out that the lack of sex education in the country, the need for professional training in sexology, and the shortage of trained sexopathologists point to the pressing need for change and development in the medical sexology field. (TJW)

PR,IL
989.   Licht, Hans. **Sexual Life in Ancient Greece.** Translated by J. H. Freese. London: Routledge & Kegan Paul, 1963. 556 p. First published in England in 1932. Includes bibliographic footnotes and indexes.

Writing pseudonymously as Hans Licht, Paul Brandt, of Leipzig University, has produced a comprehensive work on the sexual aspects of life in ancient Greece. Intended for the intelligent and educated layperson as well as the scholar, this well-illustrated study examines and describes the sex customs and morals of the ancient Greeks from mythological times to well into the last centuries of the dying Roman Empire. Licht claims that "Greek culture in all its divergences has its root and its prime cause in sexuality" (p. 523). His study reveals the pervasiveness of sex in religion, art, literature, social and public life, festivals, and theatrical performances; indeed "everywhere sexuality is the predominant component." If the erotic is the prime cause of old Greek culture, it follows that the Greeks necessarily felt that an erotic attitude toward life was natural and not to be hemmed in by any moral qualms.

Drawing heavily on literature (prose and poetry) and art (sculpture, vase painting, inscriptions), Licht, in part I, provides detailed discussion of the institutions of social and cultural life. He covers marriage and the life of women; care of the body (clothing, nakedness, gymnastics, beauty contests, and bathing); festivals (national, popular); the theater (tragedy and comedy); dance, games, meals, hospitality; religions and the erotic; and Greek literature (Classical Period, Hellenistic Period, Post-Classical Age).

Licht points out that the Greeks looked upon the physical part of love as a disease, a more or less violent form of madness. Love "results from a disturbance of the healthy equilibrium of body and mind, so that . . . the mind loses its mastery of the body" (p. 307). Part II treats the love of man and woman; masturbation; tribadism, i.e., lesbianism, prostitution, male homosexuality (as expressed in art, poetry, and prose); sexual perversions, which the evidence shows barely existed (voyeurism, transvestism, exhibitionism, flagellation, bestiality, necrophilia). Sexuality, openly expressed in the major aspects of Greek life, hardly left room for what today are called the paraphilias.

In retrospect, Licht comments that "because the almost unchecked sensuality of the Greeks was always dignified by the desire for beauty, their sexual life developed in overflowing force, but also in enviable healthiness" (p. 525). Indeed, the beautiful both in body and soul expresses the lofty ethics of the Greeks. (TJW)

PR,IL
990.   Linnér, Birgitta. **Sex and Society in Sweden.** In collaboration with Richard J. Litell. With a preface by Lester A. Kirkendall. Photographs by Lennart Nilsson. New York: Harper & Row, 1972. 225 p. Originally published in 1967. Includes bibliography and index.

It was "to convey the true nature of sex in Swedish society" to an outside world that harbored notions about free erotic practices in Sweden, that Linnér undertook to write this book. A lawyer and family life counselor with years of experience in the fields of family planning and sex education, she writes about the role of sex in the Swedish welfare state, examining such questions as abortion, venereal disease, provisions for unwed mothers and their children, and sexual equality before the law. She also expresses the views of the church on such important issues as abortion, family planning, and premarital sex. Finally, she focuses her attention on the compulsory sex education program in schools and among the adult population.

While she surmises that Sweden may be years ahead of other countries in matters of sex education and sexual behavior, she does not think that Sweden should be set up as a model for others. Sweden has discarded the double standard; much of the success should be attributed to social legislation over the years providing for equal roles, and mutual rights and responsibilities for husbands and wives. Although patriarchal ways continue to survive in Sweden, there has been an acceptance of the single standard generally and multiple roles for men and women.

Linnér emphasizes sex education and provides in the appendix samples of sex education material for all school age groups and for young adult groups. The last item in the book is an address by Linnér to a United States Government Operations Subcommittee in August 1965. After describing the state of Swedish family planning programs, she concludes with a declaration of faith in the Swedish approach to sexual and family life: "It is my belief that the rules of a new morality, if it is to be a good one, can and should be formed by men and women in cooperation" (p. 215). (TJW)

PR,IL
991.   Melville, Robert. **Erotic Art of the West.** With a short history of Western erotic art, by Simon Wilson. New York: G. P. Putnam's Sons, 1973. 318 p. Includes bibliography and index. ISBN 0-399-11102-6.

In this attractive volume, Melville, noted British art critic, discusses eroticism and sexuality as illustrated by 2,000 years of Western art. The selection of art and the analyses appear to be personal and subjective. Artists include da Vinci, Titian, Dürer, Cranach, Tintoretto, Bruegel, Bosch, Boucher, Beardsley, Rowlandson, Dali, Picasso, Degas, Botero, Munch, Magritte, and many more. Their treatment ranges from the reverent and romantic to satiric, salacious, and morbid. There are many illustrations of varying quality and definition. The text is topical, featuring various kinds of sexual contact, combinations, and preferences, and such subjects as the bath, violence and violation, prostitutes, genitalia, hair, the mouth, clothing, and erotic symbolism. Of particular interest are his explanations of the sexual symbolism in paintings on Christian and mythological themes. His interpretation of symbol, metaphor, and allegory in painting leads to a better understanding of the classic portrayals of St. Sebastian, St. Anthony, and others depicted in the art of the European masters. (JA)

IL
992.   Mosse, George L. **Nationalism and Sexuality: Respectability and Abnormal Sexuality in Modern Europe.** New York: Howard Fertig, 1985. 232 p. Includes bibliographic notes and index. ISBN 0-86527-350-2.

How such themes as nationalism and respectability affected society's attitude toward the human body and its sexuality, is the subject of this book. Mosse, a historian, traces these themes through the nineteenth and twentieth centuries, emphasizing their development in Germany and England primarily but giving attention also to France and Italy. He describes their impact upon arts and letters and upon the women's rights movement. He also points out that the main stream for these notions were the middle classes and the bourgeoisie, although those living on the fringes of society, e.g., homosexuals, were also affected.

Mosse elucidates the relationship between nationalism, which he calls "the most powerful ideology of modern times," and respectability, the adherence to accepted codes of manners and morals, by "tracing the development of the most important norms that have informed our society," e.g., the ideals of manliness and physical beauty, and by analyzing the history of sexuality in terms of normal and abnormal sexuality. Mosse describes how in Germany the effort to direct and control human sexuality in the interests of nationalism and respectability led to the excesses of National Socialism, including the persecution of homosexuals, Jews, and other so-called undesirables. He illustrates how painting and sculpture, aping the classical Greek ideas of beauty, mirrored the nationalistic and racist policies of the country.

Mosse notes that the family, supported by physicians, educators, and the clergy was the indispensable agent of sexual control and respectability. Thus, the family became the focus of attention in the development of national iconographies in art and literature. Too, the female figures of Marianne, Germania, and Britannia became national symbols of strength and stability. Additional artistic efforts showing devotion to the fatherland, reverence for the national past, and attention to unspoiled nature, personal beauty, and sexual purity became manifest in the support of nationalism and respectability. Mosse provides analyses of these efforts in chapters on "Friendship and Nationalism," "What Kind of Woman?" "War, Youth, and Beauty," "Race and Sexuality: The Role of the Outsider," and "Fascism and Sexuality."

Mosse concludes that "from the early nineteenth century onward, general agreement that respectability must be preserved, so closely had it become associated with the coherence of society, and any departure from its norms with chaos, solitude, even death" (p. 184). Furthermore, "the very strength of respectability and nationalism, their appeal, and the needs they filled, meant that those who stood apart from the norms of society were totally condemned. It was no longer the specific sexual acts alone that were considered abnormal, but the entire physical and mental structure of the person practicing these acts. Such a person was excluded from society and the nation. Solitude was the price exacted for abnormal behavior, and the outsider, as we have seen, was supposed to live a lonely life and die a lonely death" (p. 186). (TJW)

PR

993. Rousselle, Aline. **Porneia: On Desire and the Body in Antiquity.** Oxford: Basil Blackwell, 1988. 213 p. (Family, Sexuality and Social Relations in Past Times). First published in France in 1983. Includes bibliography and index. ISBN 0-631-13837-4.

In the introduction Rousselle gives the meaning of the word *porneia* as "any manifestation of desire for another's body." Concern for the body and sexual relations in the last days of antiquity rest on a social background that is the subject of this study. Rousselle's focus is on everyday behavior in Roman times.

Source materials for this study are the writings of men, including letters written to women as well as medical, legal, and philosophical works providing advice and commentary. Women left no writings whatsoever, although they were instrumental in preserving correspondence.

The first three chapters—"The Bodies of Men," "The Bodies of Women," "The Bodies of Children"—are based primarily on the writings of the doctors of antiquity, including Hippocrates, Galen, Rufus of Ephesus, Oribasius (Emperor Julian's private physician), and the Roman Soranus, whose treatise *Gynaecology* was so influential. Advice and comment from these pagan physicians cover a wide range of topics: the sexual relations of upper-class Roman men and women; the activities of wives, concubines, and slaves; sexual habits; diet, exercise, and massage; the nature of sperm; selecting a mate; women's ills in relation to their genitalia; Greek views on intercourse, conception, and pregnancy; early marriage (e.g., marriage of twelve-year-old girls in Greece and Rome); and child care and the influence of the nurse. Throughout all this commentary, the domination of the male over the female body is apparent.

A series of thematic chapters, based on legal, religious, and philosophical sources, follows: virginity and hysteria; adultery and illicit love; separation, divorce, and prostitution; salvation by child sacrifice and castration; and female virginity and male continence. On these topics the medical texts are silent, except for warnings against sexual excesses, the symptoms of hysteria and their treatment, and the related problems of continence and virginity.

In the final chapters—"The Strength of Desire," "From Abstinence to Impotence," and "From Virginity to Frigidity"—Rousselle traces the growth of the ascetic movement in northern Africa, the Near East, and Roman Europe. Without possessions the church fathers went into the desert to discover solitude and silence and to combat evil thoughts and sexual desire. They deprived themselves of sleep, comfort, and food. They resisted temptations derived from contact with women, young boys, other monks, and the urge to masturbate.

During the fourth century "thousands of men from all over Egypt joined the first hermits and begged them to guide them" (p. 154). In this manner the early monasteries were established with regulations to control, resist, and channel the temptations of the flesh. This Christian movement, aided by the freedom of Roman and Egyptian women and admired by the Roman aristocracy, spread throughout the Mediterranean world. Fostering abstinence and virginity, whole families embraced the ascetic approach to life with encouragement from the Christian Church.

Rousselle sums up her study by stating that "once the monks had recognized desire they quickly repressed it and then denied it, pushing out one temptation to desire after another" (p. 197). This led to a hierarchy of values in the Christian Church that favored virginity and chastity over expressions of sexual desire. (TJW)

PR,IL
994. Shlapentokh, Vladimir. **Love, Marriage, and Friendship in the Soviet Union: Ideals and Practices.** New York: Praeger, 1984. 276 p. (Praeger Special Studies). Includes bibliography and index. ISBN 0-03-071541-5.

Shlapentokh was a prominent Soviet sociologist with the USSR Academy of Sciences in Moscow, who emigrated from the Soviet Union in 1979. He is now a professor of sociology at Michigan State University at East Lansing. For the subject of his first book in English, he has written about "the microworld of the Soviet people: the interpersonal relationships between spouses, lovers, and friends" (p. 1). Underlying and directly affecting human relationships in the post-Stalin era are two factors: a reduction in fear of repression and a decline in the acceptance of communist ideology. Shlapentokh hypothesizes "that as a socialist society leaves the period of mass repression, it moves toward a condition of widespread anomie, as people rapidly lose confidence in the dominant values and norms and, indeed, trespass against them in their everyday behavior" (p. 5). The data in this book have been gleaned from a review of the work of both Soviet and non-Soviet sociologists.

Shlapentokh, using a value-oriented approach, traces the changing official conception of marriage and the family since the Revolution. Initially supportive of an open attitude toward love and sex and opposed to legal marriage and the family, Soviet ideology soon adopted a conservative approach, making divorce difficult and emphasizing marriage and the family. Love remains a respected value in Soviet society today. However, among the people, various romantic, hedonistic, even negative attitudes toward love are observed. Sex is either ignored or avidly pursued. Marriage is important to women and enjoys the support of the majority of the population. Yet it is seen as an institution in confrontation with the state, a belief resulting from the erosion of Soviet ideology.

Four modes of marriage prevail in the USSR. As represented in literature, art, and the writings of sociologists, they are the official romantic model, once fostered by Stalin and based on lifelong love and undying faithfulness; the pragmatic model, stressing fidelity, durability, and stability while recognizing the tenuous nature of romance and passion; the permissive model, grounded in the growing influence of eroticism and hedonism, that attempts to link passion with stability in marriage (it is tolerant of extramarital sex if discretion is used); and the serial marriage model, adhered to by those who follow a course proclaimed at the time of the Revolution (they want marriage based on strong mutual passion but prefer divorce and a new alliance to lifelong marriage with stagnation).

Soviet authorities are increasingly bothered by (1) the hedonistic aspirations and egotistical inclinations of people, mostly men but also women, who shun marital ties altogether, and (2) the prevalence in modern society of premarital and extramarital sex. Shlapentokh rounds out his picture of marriage and love with a discussion of the problems of single women. Male/female conflicts have been exacerbated in recent decades both by the growing alcoholism of men and by the educational and cultural progress of Soviet women. Shlapentokh finally deals with friendship, generally regarded as one of the leading personal values, which, however, like marriage, is perceived as confronting the state both economically and ideologically. Concluding remarks concern the deteriorating moral atmosphere and anomie in Soviet society, unquestionably phenomena of great domestic and international significance. (TJW)

IL

995.   Stern, Mikhail, and August Stern. **Sex in the USSR.** New York: Times Books, 1980. 304 p. Translation of *La vie sexuelle en U.R.S.S.*, published in France in 1979. Includes index. ISBN 0-8129-0942-9.

Stern, endocrinologist, sex therapist, and former Party member, practiced medicine in the Ukrainian city of Vinnitsa, a "typical Soviet City," for thirty years; he left the USSR following a prison term from 1974 to 1977. This book on the sexual behavior of the Soviet people is based primarily on his experience both as a civilian and prison doctor. Most of it is written from memory with the aid of notes, photographs, and letters, since his files were confiscated by the police. In the introduction, "The Land Where Sex Is Forbidden," Stern sets the tone for the rest of the book, claiming that the Soviet government has established prohibitions and taboos and created a social environment in which sexual freedom is discouraged. In the USSR "neither the scientific discipline of sexology nor the clinical practice of sex therapy exists" (p. x). As a civilian doctor, seeing people from all walks of life, he noted that their common sexual problems included sexual immaturity, impotence, premature ejaculation, and frigidity. He learned that in sexual matters the Soviet people are abysmally ignorant; they lack sex education in both the family and the school, and nonmedical books on sex are nonexistent.

Part I is devoted to a history of sexuality and the Soviet regime. After briefly reviewing sexuality in Russia before the turn of the century, Stern examines the turbulent years of revolution, focusing on first the free love movement of the 1920s, when the wholesale dissolution of traditional values and institutions took place and people were giddy with freedom. He then turns to the reaction against this trend under Stalin, when the family was rehabilitated and sex became the enemy of the revolution. In part II, "Husbands, Wives, and Lovers," Stern examines the family, marriage and divorce, sexual disorders, and the breakdown of official morality. In part III, he carefully scrutinizes forbidden practices: masturbation, exhibitionism and voyeurism, eroticism and pornography, prostitution, sex crimes, homosexuality, and transsexualism. In the final part, he exposes the sexual life of the power elite and the shocking sexual practices in the prison camps, which he concludes are a mirror of Soviet society. (TJW)

NORTH AMERICA

PO

996.   Chapple, Steve, and David Talbot. **Burning Desires: Sex in America.** New York: Doubleday, 1989. 378 p. Includes index. ISBN 0-385-24412-6.

In an effort to better understand the forces both "impeding sex" in the 1980s and "keeping sexual pulses strong and true," journalists Chapple and Talbot conducted hundreds of interviews around the United States. The resulting narrative is "a celebration of smart and dirty sex in dangerous times."

Chapple and Talbot chronicle shifts in attitudes toward sex in their reports of interviews with significant public figures, narratives about political and professional responses to sexual issues, and analyses of social movements about gender. Each of the three parts describes an aspect of a 1980s' trend to submerge and possibly blot out the desires so rife in the 1960s and 1970s.

Part I, "Repression," examines some ways in which pleasure has been punished. The pursuit of fantasy and pleasure espoused by the "King of Swing" Bob McGinley contrasts with the dampening effect of Dr. Keith Henry's crusade to educate swingers about AIDS and, to the horror of mainstream sexologists, Patrick Carnes's efforts to turn ardent sexual behavior into sexual addiction. Tipper Gore declares war on "porn rock," which results in record companies putting warning labels on albums and in a toning down of lyrics. Parents attempt to regulate and suppress teenage sexuality. Communities like Key West, Florida; Aspen, Colorado; and Chico, California have changed from erotic zones in the United States to sites of reformation. The nation reacts with indignation at the sexual antics of such well-known political figures as Congressman Wilbur Mills and Senator Gary Hart and the surprising sexual behavior of such televangelists as Jimmy Swaggart and Jim Bakker.

Part II, "Sex Wars," expresses the confusion engendered by gender conflicts and the resulting precariousness of heterosexual relationships. Women seem ambivalent about what they want from men. The men's movement, as exemplified by Robert Bly, encourages more distance from women. Feminists, ranging from the "fun kind" (e.g., Susan Forward, Erica Jong) to the militant types (e.g., Germaine Greer, Andrea Dworkin, Shere Hite), express disenchantment with men's sexual behavior while wanting sex on women's terms.

Part III, "Rebirth," offers some examples of the ways in which sex is being retooled to fit modern specifications: women writing erotica, women producing pornographic films, Surgeon-General C. Everett Koop's agenda for safe sex in the AIDS crisis, and the glamorization of birth and children as part of baby boomers' sex lives.

The overall message is that the pleasure of sex still remains despite attempts to quench it. Repression only serves to foster "burning desires." (SGF/TJW)

PR,IL

997. Roscoe, Will. **The Zuni Man-Woman.** Albuquerque, N.M.: University of New Mexico Press, 1991. 302 p. Includes bibliography and index. ISBN 0-8263-1253-5.

Journalist Roscoe's ethnohistorical narrative reconstructs Zuni culture as it was a century ago and focuses on the life of We'Wha, "Zuni's most famous berdache and perhaps the most renowned 'man-woman' in recorded American Indian history" (p. 28). We'Wha's story not only opens up a discussion of his remarkable life but also embraces stories of Matilda Coxe Stevenson, one of the first female anthropologists, who was We'Wha's good friend; pressures for culture change resulting from contact between the Zuni and missionaries, the military, settlers, and the U.S. government; the meaning of the berdache in Zuni society; and the role and acquisition of gender among the Zuni and their implications for assessing Western concepts of gender.

As explained by Roscoe, a berdache is a "man who combined the work and social roles of men and women, an artist and a priest who dressed, at least in part, in women's clothes" (p. 2). Terms like hermaphrodite, transvestite, homosexual, and transsexual do not appropriately translate the fullness of the berdache role, that combines aspects of male and female genders into one personality and indicates an institutionalized third gender. Roscoe thinks that berdaches were "representatives of a form of solidarity and wholeness that transcended the division of humans into men and women. The third gender role of the berdache was one of native North America's most striking social inventions" (p. 146).

In describing the organization of Zuni life, Roscoe explains Zuni social and gender roles as a background for presenting We'Wha's life. The Zunis, a pueblo group of native Americans who live along the Zuni River near the Arizona/New Mexico border, believe that gender is acquired through a series of ritual initiations and the acquisition of gender symbols; the "raw," ungendered child is transformed into the "cooked" gendered human being. If a child's behavior showed a "different road" from male or female, Zunis adapted their child-rearing practices and accepted the child's formative role as a berdache. He became an "integral, productive, and valued" member of his community, not an anomaly. Myths explain the origin of berdaches and their value. Because of We'Wha's personality as a berdache, he was able to become a cultural specialist, undertaking creative, respected roles in his group. As Stevenson's invited emissary to Washington, he became a social sensation as an Indian "princess" and shook hands with President Cleveland.

The psychological and spiritual dimensions that underlie the Lhamana (berdache) role help one to understand We'Wha's career. Acceptance of the berdache status entailed flexible beliefs about gender, not tied to anatomy and a rigid dualism of man-woman. As Roscoe explains, the berdache is both man and woman and neither—"two-fold, one kind." The psychological dynamics of gender among the Zuni prompt us to consider that the psychology of gender is culturally specific, a product of childrearing and attitudes toward gender and sexuality. Roscoe concludes with how aspects of the traditional role of the berdache became secularized as a result of the sexual politics of missionaries and European/American acquisition of native lands. "As long as perceptions are filtered through a dual gender ideology and arbitrary distinctions based on biological sex, berdache patterns cannot be appreciated for what they really are . . . a third gender" (p. 212). (SGF)

PR,IL,PO

998.   Rubin, Lillian B. **Erotic Wars: What Happened to the Sexual Revolution?** New York: Harper, 1991. 207 p. Includes bibliography. ISBN 0-06-096564-9.

Has the sexual revolution really ended? To find out what has happened to sexual freedom, psychologist/sociologist Rubin interviewed a total of 375 people (75 teens and 300 adults) and distributed 600 thirteen-page questionnaires to students in eight colleges and universities. Her inquiry focused on several issues, among which were: How do men and women feel about their pasts? What changes in attitudes, behavior, and feelings have occurred over the past few decades? What have been the effects of the sexual revolution, the gender revolution, and the therapy revolution on the lives of younger people today? In sum, how has the context and meaning of sex changed over the past few decades?

Before the "big IT," teenage sexuality meant engaging in everything but "IT" because virginity meant an intact reputation, a woman's bargaining tool for a good marriage partner. Men feigned experience while women pretended to be naive. Now behaviors unacceptable in the past have become more common: masturbation, intercourse, and oral sex. Nevertheless, the "first time" does not mean physical and emotional satisfaction; rather, males regard it as passing a threshold of adulthood while females respond to it with sexual ambivalence. Orgasm, sensuality, and pleasure are usually absent. The behavior may have changed, but the old ideology of female submission and male conquest remains.

Today's teenagers focus on the importance of tolerance and entitlement in sexual behavior. Although 60 percent of teens have intercourse by the time they finish high school, they expect their peers to have sex with only one person at a time and to be faithful to the relationship; serial monogamy is the rule, regardless of gender. Teens want their privacy respected, particularly by their parents. Because of differences in their gender development, females focus on relationships while males focus on sex. Sexual experience with bondage, pornography, homosexuality, group sex, prostitution, and anal sex has increased.

Nevertheless, the quest for relationships continues. Both males and females are ambivalent and confused about what they want from sex, love, marriage, and the family. The sexual, gender, and therapeutic revolutions converge to foster a search for perfection in partnerships. The expectations of relationships have escalated as has anxiety about them. While women have had more access to sex without social fetters and men have had sexual access to more women, the structure within which these relationships occur has changed very little. Unfortunately, sex is more an obstacle than a route to gratification and pleasure. Differences in socialization and power maintain the status quo. (SGF)

PR,IL

999.   Schlesinger, Benjamin, ed. **Sexual Behaviour in Canada: Patterns and Problems.** Toronto: University of Toronto Press, 1977. 326 p. Includes bibliography and glossary. ISBN 0-8020-2262-6.

Intended as a companion volume to *Family Planning in Canada: A Source Book* (1974), this book, under the editorship of Professor Schlesinger of the Faculty of Social Work, University of Toronto, is the first Canadian collection of readings on human sexuality. Schlesinger states that he "introduced the first course on human sexuality at a Canadian school of social work," and was "pleased to find that by 1976 quite a few universities had included this topic in their varied professional schools (medicine, nursing, social work, etc.)." Until recently, Canadians had relied primarily on American writing and research on the subject. The twenty-seven papers, written by doctors, psychiatrists, educators, lawyers, social workers, sociologists, and natural scientists, present a variety of views about sex and sexuality and attempt to fill the void of Canadian materials on human sexuality. Part I, "An Overview," examines attitudes, sexual identity, and current sex research in Canada; part II, "Sexuality and the Life Cycle," discusses changes in fertility patterns in Canada, family planning in Quebec and among the poor, taboos and myths about sex and the aged, and the treatment of sexual dysfunctions; part III, "Sexual Behaviour Among Selected Groups," focuses on male and female homosexuality, transsexualism, sex and the handicapped, parenthood and the mentally retarded, and the influence of drugs on sexual behavior; part IV, "Sexuality and the Law," explores rape, pedophilia, incest, prostitution, and obscenity in a Canadian setting; part V, "Education for Sexuality," deals with various aspects of Canadian sex education. A special resources section contains a glossary, a basic library of sexuality, Canadian references on human sexuality, and a list of Canadian and American organizations active in the field. (TJW)

PR,IL

1000. Schur, Edwin M. **The Americanization of Sex.** Philadelphia: Temple University Press, 1988. 229 p. Includes bibliographic notes and index. ISBN 0-87722-521-4.

Schur is committed to the importance of a sociocultural model of human sexuality. He assumes that sexual attitudes and behavior are patterned and systematically linked to more general social and cultural trends. He argues that the specifics of sexual behaviors and attitudes cannot be understood without looking at overall sociocultural themes that pervade them. In this sense, "Sexual issues are necessarily social issues."

The focus of this book is on elucidating the cultural meanings and social structures that have led to a distinctive Americanization of sex in the latter half of the twentieth century. Three major tendencies define the Americanization of sex: depersonalization, commoditization, and coercion. These tendencies stem from and are related to the following general cultural features: (1) superficiality and optimistic pragmatism, (2) individualism and compulsive competitiveness, (3) power seeking and violence, and (4) a fixation with success, entrepreneurial instinct, and runaway consumerism. Sexism and capitalism lie at their core.

Each chapter discusses one major theme of the Americanization of sex. The emphasis is on contemporary issues rather than on historical interpretations. Depersonalization means treating sex as a thing or as a possession to be had rather than as a human relationship. It takes many forms: recreational sex, objectification of women, rationalization of sex as science. Depersonalization opens the door for commoditization of sex: a playboy mentality, mass marketing of consumer goods and services by using sexual images and associations, prostitution, and pornography. Attitudes expressed in the commercial realm set the tone for those in the noncommercial area. They set the stage for coercive forms of sex: rape, incest, sexual harassment. These violent forms of sex are not "deviant" from our sexual system but are part of the way in which American society organizes sex.

Although Schur believes that "the sexual scene in America remains disheartening," recognition of the sociocultural factors that shape sexuality is the first step in changing current trends. Paying greater attention to primary relationships, combating sexism, and reducing socioeconomic inequality are routes to restoring human relationships. Adherence to medical and scientific models that naturalize and demystify sex will only perpetuate an avoidance of the roots of the problems. (SGF)

IL

1001. Seidman, Steven. **Embattled Eros: Sexual Politics and Ethics in Contemporary America.** New York: Routledge, 1992. 220 p. Includes bibliographic notes and index. ISBN 0-415-90356-4.

Seidman focuses on social and cultural definitions of and responses to sexuality in the post-World War II era, particularly the 1970s and 1980s. He notes that the "sexual revolution" of the 1960s and 1970s was a continuation of a movement that began in the early twentieth century as a reaction to the Victorian period and resulted in a greater emphasis on enjoyment of sex within marriage and a relaxation of strict social and legal controls on sex. The post-World War II period saw an increase in premarital sex, sexual experimentation, and pornography in the public realm, and the entrance of women and homosexuals into the social mainstream. During the 1980s, however, a reaction to this liberalization took place with increasing pressure for social control.

Two conflicting sexual ideologies have developed in this century: the liberationist, that approves all consensual sex acts and focuses on individual bodily pleasure, and the romanticist, that views sex as legitimate only in the context of long-term, monogamous, preferably heterosexual, marital relationships. These views cannot be defined by young/old, left/right differences; in fact, most populations are split in their opinions. Many feminists object to liberationist philosophy on the grounds that it objectifies partners, focuses on vaginal intercourse, and exploits women. Cultural feminists reject lesbian S/M as reflecting the male-dominant society. Mainstream homosexual society, with a multiple-partner culture centered around gay bars, bathhouses, and social clubs, often involves casual, short-term relationships; AIDS has forced a new focus on long-term, monogamous relations.

Neither liberationist nor romantic ideologies successfully address the moral questions of sexuality: liberationist philosophy is too open, requiring only consent, while romanticism is too restrictive and fails to consider social and cultural variations. Seidman proposes a sexual ethic that has as its defining factors consent and responsibility, thus addressing both individual desires and the social/cultural environment without making moral judgments on sexuality or sexual acts. (SDH)

PO

1002.   Talese, Gay. **Thy Neighbor's Wife.** Garden City, N.Y.: Doubleday, 1980. 568 p. Includes index. ISBN 0-385-00632-2.

Nine years of investigative reporting enabled Talese to produce this analysis of the changing sexual scene in the United States, from the immediate post-World War II years to 1980. Largely based on interviews with the makers and movers of the sexual revolution, the book is an intimate look at those attitudes, changes, and events "that in recent decades had influenced the redefinition of morality in America" (p. 522). In the interest of balance and perspective, Talese provides historical background of sex laws, censorship, and varieties of attitudes toward sexuality. Expressive of these themes is the fascinating story of the Oneida Community in upstate New York, where John Humphrey Noyes had established in 1848 a theocratic community that promoted sexual freedom among its members, which lasted until 1882. Instrumental in the demise of Noyes's community was Anthony Comstock, special anti-obscenity agent of the Post Office Department and founder of the New York Society for the Suppression of Vice. In 1873 he had persuaded Congress to pass a federal bill banning from the mails "every obscene, lewd, lascivious or filthy book, pamphlet, picture, paper, letter, writing, print or other publication of an indecent character."

In delineating the so-called sexual revolution in the postwar years, Talese delves into various events that reflected the dramatic changes taking place in the sexual attitudes and behavior of Americans: the rise of Hugh Hefner and the hedonistic philosophy portrayed in *Playboy* magazine; the legal battles over what constitutes obscenity and pornography in literature, magazines, the movies, and the theater (in the cases of Samuel Roth, Alvin Goldstein of *Screw* magazine fame, and William Hamling); the establishment in the 1970s of Sandstone Retreat in California, a small community that fostered open sexuality among couples willing to pay a modest annual fee; and the activities of the artist/feminist Betty Dodson, who conducted conscious-raising seminars in her apartment in New York City where women learned about their sexuality. In his attempt to take America's sexual pulse, Talese actively participated in many of the events affecting the moral climate: for a time he managed a massage parlor, he frequently attended X-rated movies, for several months he resided at Sandstone Retreat, and he familiarized himself with swing clubs and orgiasts across the country. What enticed Talese into this investigation were his feelings about "America's new openness about sex, its expanding erotic consumerism, and the quiet rebellion that he sensed within the middle class against the censors and clerics that had been an inhibiting force since the founding of the Puritan republic" (p. 524). This book is the result. (TJW)

PR

1003. Thompson, Roger. **Sex in Middlesex: Popular Mores in a Massachusetts County, 1649-1699.** Amherst, Mass.: University of Massachusetts Press, 1986. 252 p. Includes bibliographic notes and index. ISBN 0-87023-516-8.

In the seventeenth century, Middlesex County, Massachusetts, embraced an area to the north and west of Boston, including such towns as Cambridge, Charlestown, Reading, Concord, Groton, and Framingham. *Sex in Middlesex* examines sexual mores in this Massachusetts county over a fifty-year period from 1649 to 1699. It is a study of sexual misdemeanors and family and community life based on county court records, including depositions made by hundreds of witnesses and those charged with criminal behavior, as well as town, church, and genealogical records. David Hall points out in the foreword that the records "strongly suggest that the puritan social system was not so rigid and the relationships between the sexes not so regulated as some historians have suggested."

This revisionist view is borne out by the text wherein Thompson dissects adolescent mores, married mores, and the family and community. For example, Thompson shows that "from the 1660s the ratio of bastardy and prenuptial fornication were on the rise" and "in the 1680s marital infidelity reached a peak unimagined a generation before" (p. 193).

The major historical issue Thompson addresses is the strength and rigidity attributed by such social historians as Lawrence Stone (*Sex and Marriage in England 1500-1800*) to the restricted patriarchal nuclear family. From the small sample of deviants studied in this work, Thompson concludes that "Middlesex criminals and witnesses are representative of society at large" (p. 195) and that their behavior bears little resemblance to the programmed behavior of the constrained members of the nuclear family that Stone espouses. Thompson states: "Though the laws of Massachusetts invested patriarchs with power to control courtship, the courtiers [motivated by physical attraction and love] chose their own partners, circumventing parental supervision by guile or by gall," and furthermore, "the unmarried, far from being erotically repressed, were fascinated by sexuality. They read and talked about it; they seem to have relieved sexual tensions by various means short of, or including, intercourse" (p. 195).

The picture of Middlesex society that emerges from this study is not one of a society dominated by a patriarchal despotism but rather one of a society pervaded by a religiosity that was benign, forgiving, and tolerant. (TJW)

PR,IL

1004. Williams, Walter L. **The Spirit and the Flesh: Sexual Diversity in American Indian Culture.** Boston: Beacon Press, 1986. 344 p. Includes bibliography and index. ISBN 0-8070-4602-7.

Williams, an ethnohistorian at the University of Southern California, uses his detailed presentation of the berdache tradition in American Indian culture to "examine how a culture can accommodate gender variation and sexual variation beyond man-woman opposites, without being threatened by it" (p. 5). He is particularly concerned with presenting the native view of berdaches and bases his portrayal on historical records, anthropological literature, and direct fieldwork with berdaches in a number of different tribes.

The first part of the book defines the characteristics of the berdache tradition. A spiritual dimension lies at its core. A berdache is a morphological male who has a nonmasculine character and does not perform society's standard male role; he has a spirit that falls between male and female. A berdache has a clearly recognized and accepted social status, which is respected and, at times, revered. Berdaches grow up in families that support rather than stigmatize their character and take positions as mediators between male and female and between the psychic and the physical ("the spirit and the flesh"). They do not become women, nor is it appropriate to characterize them as transvestites, transsexuals, hermaphrodites, or homosexuals. Their position is defined in terms of their gender role and personal characteristics, not by their sexual behavior. They are best described as an alternative gender.

However, as the second part of the book demonstrates, the Western emphasis on sexual behavior and only two genders has had a major impact on the institution of the berdache. The intolerance of the Spanish as well as censure by the government and Christianity have resulted in the concealment of berdache status. More recently, the gay movement has allowed for a renewed recognition of the berdache.

The concluding part of the book surveys a variety of other cultures that have special gender categories and then considers the overall implications of alternative genders to an understanding of gender and sexual variation. Williams thinks that his research shows that categories of homosexuality/heterosexuality, normal/abnormal, and man-woman hinder a full comprehension of sexual diversity. "The next frontier of research on both sexual and gender variance is to understand the many varieties of identities and roles" (p. 275). (SGF)

LATIN AMERICA & THE CARIBBEAN

PR
1005. Brody, Eugene B. **Sex, Contraception, and Motherhood in Jamaica.** Cambridge, Mass.: Harvard University Press, 1981. 278 p. Includes bibliography and index. ISBN 0-674-80277-2.

This study records the results of a forty-month period of investigation (1972-1975) of family planning in Jamaica. In Jamaica, as elsewhere, "early sexual intercourse without contraception, followed by pregnancy, delivery, and single-handed rearing of the new infant by an adolescent mother seems to constitute a definable behavioral pattern" (p. 6). This study searches for the reasons why contraceptive services have not been adequately used in Jamaica.

Brody's method of studying the sexual-reproductive behavioral pattern of his subjects consisted of (1) in-depth interviews with men and women who came to family planning clinics in Kingston, Jamaica, seeking information and assistance, and (2) getting to know Jamaicans of all social levels and learning about their lifestyles. In this manner, Brody came to understand the psychosocial barriers to contraceptive use in Jamaica. He learned how Kingston men and women feel and think and act about sexual intercourse and the use of contraceptives, and about their "living, loving, and relating with each other; about becoming parents or not; and about having few or many children" (p. 14).

Brody summarizes his study results by stating that Jamaicans "may not be able to achieve modern status without a reduction in the rate of population increase." This will "require attention to private aims and conflicts and to shared cultural patterns. All these will influence not only the nature, advertisement, and presentation of family planning services but also the gradual development of an ethos favoring parent-child communication, sex education at puberty, increased autonomy for women, delayed first pregnancy, spaced births, small ultimate family size, and a reduction in passing children on to be reared by others. The promotion of stable conjugal unions with adequate communication between partners is essential in the achievement of these aims" (p. 262). (TJW)

PR,IL

1006. Burg, Barry Richard. **Sodomy and the Perception of Evil: English Sea Rovers in the Seventeenth-Century Caribbean.** New York: New York University Press, 1983. 215 p. Includes bibliographic notes and index. ISBN 0-8147-1040-9.

Sodomy as defined by law in seventeenth-century England included various kinds of homosexuality; in his study, Burg, of Arizona State University, limits it to homosexual acts between adult males. Despite the law condemning sodomy as a felony and calling for the ultimate penalty, the English courts generally imposed a lesser penalty. In fact, homosexual acts were often ignored and rarely condemned in England. Amid this tolerance, according to Burg, "flourished one of the most unusual homosexually oriented groups in history, the Caribbean pirates who spread terror from South America northward to Bermuda and occasionally into the Pacific throughout the latter half of the seventeenth century" (p. xvi). Furthermore, homosexual acts "were the only form of sexual expression engaged in by members of the buccaneer community" (p. xvii). Unhampered by outside constraints from either England or the surrounding predominantly heterosexual communities, the buccaneers for three-quarters of a century evolved their own sexual lifestyle.

Denying that his work is a history of piracy, Burg employs modern methods of psychosociology, making use of demographic data, travelers' accounts, court records, etc., to reconstruct the behavior of this unique homosexual community that flourished 300 years ago. Burg proceeds on "the premise that homosexuality is not an inherently pathological condition but rather a variant form of sexual expression well within the range of normal human behavior" (p. xix).

In chapters 1 and 2, Burg examines the social and cultural milieu of Stuart England, bringing out certain aspects of that society that were conducive to the development of a pirate community providing security and safety for the homosexual. Chapter 3 analyzes the various kinds of source data concerning life in the Barbados, Jamaica, and other West Indian islands in the seventeenth century. As in England, a tolerant attitude toward homosexuality prevailed; actually the patterns of population distribution fostered this attitude. Chapter 4 presents theories and plausible explanations about the homosexual practices of the pirates. Finally, in chapter 5, Burg relates the pirate community to the larger society in which it existed, discussing various aspects of pirate life: the use of special language for communication purposes, the prevalence of torture, alcoholism, and the lack of effeminacy in the pirate homosexual role, and reveals that the pirates had no need to hide their sexual orientation. Burg concludes this work with an extensive bibliographic essay on piracy and homosexuality in England and the English West Indies in the seventeenth century. (TJW)

PR,IL,PO

1007. Gregor, Thomas. **Anxious Pleasures: The Sexual Lives of an Amazonian People.** Chicago: University of Chicago Press, 1985. 223 p. Includes bibliography and index. ISBN 0-226-30742-5.

According to anthropologist Gregor, who conducted fieldwork in a village of eighty-five Mehinaku in central Brazil in 1967, 1968, and 1977, sex is an "organizing metaphor" for the Mehinaku. An account of their sexuality is an account of their culture. And the lessons learned from analyzing Mehinaku sexuality can shed light on American sexuality. "Mehinaku culture, in many ways like our own, is an eroticized culture. Sex, as the villagers say, is the pepper that gives life and verve" (p. 4). However, the pleasure of sex in this apparently sex-positive culture is tempered by fear and anxiety. Males learn to desire and fear females. In addition to understanding Mehinaku sexuality, another purpose of this book is to show that "there are universalities in the male experience, and even a common symbolic vocabulary for its expression. If we look carefully, we will see reflections of our sexual nature in the life ways of an Amazonian people" (p. 11).

Using indirect information (biographies, dreams, drawings), myths, and interviews with men and women, Gregor elucidates the sexual culture of the Mehinaku—beliefs and attitudes that channel sexual behavior and engender anxiety about sex. The oppositional nature of male/female interaction is reflected in the activity of men in a men's house in the center of the plaza while the women and children live and work in dwellings surrounding the plaza. Children grow up in an open setting where sex is not "walled off." Premarital sex is tolerated, but not premarital pregnancy. Most women marry soon after menarche. Males are more overtly sexual; females exchange sex for food and support. Extramarital affairs add to village cohesion by consolidating relationships between people in different kindreds. Though they can create tension, extramarital affairs often occur.

Myths, interpretation of dreams, clothing, ornaments, eating and sleeping arrangements, and the division of labor define differences between the sexes as well as appropriate sexual behavior. Although males learn that they are dominant over women (they have sacred flutes, a men's house, the power to gang rape a woman if she enters the men's house), Gregor says the facade of patriarchy is a "citadel of papier-mâché." Men suffer from an "all too fragile sense of being men," who fear castration, the "toothed vagina" of women, the contamination of menstrual fluids, illness from inappropriate sex, or loss of strength from too much sex. Consequently, men cannot experience unabandoned sex, where they merge with their partners, free from anxiety. There are too many hazards to release their guard. The ambivalence that men feel toward women may be a product of a childhood marked by initial maternal comfort for three years, followed by rejection and separation when new siblings are born and are incorporated into male culture. Consequently, they belittle women in order to deny their desire to be comforted and cared for by women. Gregor notes: "Between us and the Mehinaku there remains the common bond of masculine gender with all of its uncertainty and ambivalence" (p. 210). (SGF)

PR

1008. Kauffmann Doig, Federico. **Sexual Behaviour in Ancient Peru.** Lima, Peru: Kompaktos, 1979. 181 p. Includes bibliography, index, and glossary.

This book is essentially a description and interpretation of erotic pottery identified as belonging to various ancient Peruvian cultures. As an expert archaeologist and a professor of Peruvian Archaeology and History of Ancient Peru at the Federico Villarreal National University in Lima, Peru, Kauffmann Doig has been able to bring about the public display of these erotic artifacts in the National Museum of Anthropology and Archaeology in Lima.

Most of the material described and illustrated in this volume is found today in various Peruvian museums and private collections. It can be traced as far back as Peruvian high culture in the central Andes some 3,000 years ago. In the main, ancient Peruvian artifacts are devoid of representations of sexual themes. Only a few cultures along the Peruvian coast, principally the Moche culture, which flourished from the fourth to the eighth centuries A.D. and the earlier Vicús culture, produced any pottery with sexual themes. Indeed, even in these cultures, such pottery represents but a fraction of the total legacy in artifacts; so it should not be concluded from the emphasis on erotic artifacts in this volume that these ancient cultures overemphasized sex in any way or that they were depraved. Sexuality was simply dealt with in a straightforward, albeit artistic, manner.

The extant material falls within a broad spectrum of sexual themes pertaining to fertility rites, the family, myths, and magic-religious rituals. It depicts explicitly a wide range of sexual activities. In addition to displaying male and female genitalia and outsized erections, it shows kissing, caressing, genital fondling, masturbation, various coital positions, anal intercourse, fellatio (but not cunnilingus), and bestiality. The pottery consists mainly of containers of different kinds, various types of figurines, amulets, dildoes, and so forth. Among the more startling pieces of pottery are anthropomorphic jars endowed with genitals used for drinking.

With the Spanish conquest of Peru in the sixteenth century, the Inca Empire came to an end, and with it a cessation in the production of erotic pottery. According to Kauffmann Doig, the various Spanish chronicles from the sixteenth and seventeenth centuries (the only written records mentioning Peruvian sexual behavior) support his conclusions about sexual behavior on the basis of the archaeological evidence described in this book. An appendix in the form of a glossary discusses ancient Peruvian sexuality based on the Spanish chronicles. Forty-two color plates, as well as hundreds of line drawings throughout the text, highlight the descriptions of extant erotic and nonerotic artifacts. (TJW)

PR,IL
1008a. Leiner, Marvin. **Sexual Politics in Cuba: Machismo, Homosexuality, and AIDS.** Boulder, Colo.: Westview Press, 1994. 184 p. (Series in Political Economy and Economic Development in Latin America). ISBN 0-8133-8654-3.

Despite the very real accomplishments of the Cuban socialist revolution, especially in education and health care, some very serious and interrelated social and cultural problems remain. Leiner, Professor Emeritus of Education at Queens College of the City of New York and author of the highly acclaimed study *Children Are the Revolution: Day Care in Cuba* (1978), explores these seemingly intractable problems, placing the blame on the doorstep of the Cuban revolutionary leadership.

An internationally recognized scholar and expert on the Cuban educational system, Leiner focuses his attention on (1) the deep-rooted concept of Latin machismo that pervades Cuban society and works toward the detriment of women; (2) the homophobic attitudes of Cubans toward gays and lesbians; and (3) the treatment of people testing HIV positive, who are quarantined in sanitariums and hospitals until the time when a cure for AIDS is found. Aside from highly unlikely political solutions to these problems from Fidel Castro himself, Leiner believes that progress in these areas is possible through sex education.

Leiner discusses the early attempts to consider sex education as a part of Cuba's successful educational system, the formation and work of Grupo Nacional de Trabajo de Educacion Sexual (GNTES), the lack of qualified sex education teachers and the problem of training them, the eventual introduction of sex education courses in the elementary and secondary school in the late seventies and early eighties, and the adoption of East German textbooks on sexuality that had to be translated.

In what he labels "The Cuban Revolution in Crisis," Leiner identifies the many shortcomings of the Cuban dictatorship: one-party rule, lack of freedom to criticize, fear of external political forces, absence of democracy, and so forth, all of which have an impact on efforts to solve the pressing social and cultural problems of the country. Leiner hopes that this book "offers not only to Cubans but to all of us, useful insights and a key to examining our own sexual prejudices. AIDS has brought to the fore deeply entrenched attitudes toward men, women, and homosexuals in cultures around the world. This look at Cuba provides clues to attitudes that, if changed, can help effectively address the disease of AIDS that threatens us all" (p. 14). (TJW)

PR
1009. Parker, Richard G. **Bodies, Pleasures, and Passions: Sexual Culture in Contemporary Brazil.** Boston: Beacon Press, 1991. 203 p. Includes bibliography and index. ISBN 0-8070-4102-5.

Based on cultural anthropologist Parker's many years of field research in Brazilian urban centers like Rio de Janeiro and Sao Paulo, this book examines "the sometimes contradictory cultural patterns, the ideological constructs, and the value systems that work to shape and structure the sexual universe in contemporary Brazilian life" and tries to "extrapolate the underlying, and often unconscious, rules that organize sexual life there—a kind of cultural grammar . . . " (p. 177). Unlike many anthropological works that focus on coherence of sexual meanings within small-scale settings, this book focuses on layers of sexual meanings within a diverse, large-scale, contemporary society. Multiple subsystems of meaning, different frames of reference, and conflicting logic define the wider structure of the Brazilian sexual system, which opens up a variety of diverse erotic possibilities for men and women. Sensuality is an intrinsic part of the Brazilian identity, and diversity is a basic part of its history. Therefore, this book "focuses, above all else, on the question of diversity, and on the social and historical construction of sexual diversity in Brazilian culture" (p. 1). Parker hopes that his analysis of sexual meanings in Brazil may provide insights about broader aspects of human sexual experience.

Myths of origin recount themes of beauty and innocence; sexuality and miscegenation of the Indians, Portuguese, and Africans; sadness and guilt; cultural fusion and creativity. The informal ideology of gender is one level of meaning that organizes this complex social and cultural background. Parker analyzes the tradition of patriarchy, the language used to refer to male and female bodies, the system of sexual classifications, and sexual socialization to explain the gender hierarchy of masculinity and femininity, articulated in terms of activity and passivity. Another way that sexual meanings are organized is in the formal context of organized religion, social hygiene, medicine, and science, which provide their definitions of sexual normalcy and perversion, often in terms of reproduction. These social and cultural frameworks link sexuality to systems of power. Erotic ideology reframes the messages of gender hierarchy and formal discourse into a third way of organizing sexual experience—according to erotic meaning and behavior. The symbolism of the body and its anatomy is transformed within the erotic context, expanding their meanings beyond gender and reproductive function. Bodies and pleasures, embracing variety and transgression of proscriptions, mark the erotic world. Carnival encapsulates and expresses much of the Brazilian sexual universe described in the rest of the book. Parker concludes that "the picture that emerges . . . is less singular than plural" (p. 165) and contains much ambivalence and ambiguity, perhaps because it reflects the complex nature of social life in contemporary Brazil. (SGF)

INSULAR PACIFIC. AUSTRALIA

PR
1010. Berndt, Ronald M., and Catherine H. Berndt. **Sexual Behavior in Western Arnhem Land.** New York: Johnson Reprint Corporation, 1963. 247 p. + 24 plates. (Viking Fund Publications in Anthropology, no. 16). Originally published by The Viking Fund in 1951. Includes bibliographic footnotes.

In the foreword, Australian anthropologist A. P. Elkin comments that this is the "first anthropological study yet made of Australian aboriginal sexual behavior and its ramifications" (p. 9). Based on the Berndts' fieldwork conducted in Goulbourn Island, the Oenpelli area, and the Liverpool district in Northwestern Arnhem Land in 1947, 1949, and 1950, this book attempts to describe aboriginal sexual behavior within its cultural context, from the native point of view. The primary emphasis is on the social and psychological implications of sexual behavior rather than on sexual activities per se or their erotic aspects.

Sex is regarded as a normal, natural activity that is expressed throughout the life cycle. Young children who sleep in the camp of their parents or older relatives have an opportunity to listen to and furtively watch the sexual activities of their elders. Girls usually begin to engage in intercourse when they are about nine years old while boys start a bit later, usually when they are twelve to fourteen, after they have been initiated. Both boys and girls are very interested in and do engage in premarital sex. In their single male camps, boys masturbate alone and in groups as well as engage in homosexual encounters. Girls and women accept gifts in return for sexual favors. Although both men and women desire to marry, they also expect to engage in extramarital affairs as an adjunct to this relationship. An active sex life may continue well into a person's sixties and seventies.

Sexual activities are channeled by social rules, particularly kinship regulations, and are supported by cultural beliefs, especially in the contexts of religion and storytelling. The

Berndts detail many of the myths, stories, and rituals that legitimize the current system of sexual behavior. In addition, "gossip songs," that express incidents in the social life of the group, often deal with marital and extramarital relationships. Overall, the Berndts elucidate the social principles that underlie sexual relations and their expression in Western Arnhem Land. (SGF)

PR

1011.   Herdt, Gilbert H., ed. **Rituals of Manhood: Male Initiation in Papua New Guinea.** With an introduction by Roger M. Keesing. Berkeley, Calif.: University of California Press, 1982. 365 p. Includes bibliography and index.

In *Guardians of the Flutes: Idioms of Masculinity* (1981), Herdt, a professor of anthropology at Stanford University, describes in rich detail how Sambian men, who live in the Highlands of New Guinea, experience their sexual development. In particular, he attempts to understand why the culture encourages homosexual practices for all men before they marry. In the process, he articulates the ways in which Sambians conceptualize masculinity and femininity, childhood and adolescence, and sexual behavior and relationships.

In *Rituals of Manhood*, he continues his line of inquiry about the development of masculinity by seeking an understanding of male cults and initiation practices. He claims that this book presents "the first substantial data on the subject to appear in years [and] is the first collection of comparative ethnography to ever appear on tribal initiation in Papua, New Guinea" (p. ix). The book grew out of a symposium at the seventh meeting of the Association for Social Anthropology in Oceania (1979), and all of the contributors are anthropologists who have had one or more major periods of fieldwork in New Guinea. The contributors all address questions about the meaning of male initiation rites in cultures of four major ethnographic subregions of Papua, New Guinea: the Provinces of East Sepik (Deborah B. Gewertz on the Chambri; Donald F. Tuzin on the Ilahita Arapesh), West Sepik (Fitz John Porter Poole on the Bimin-Kuskusmin), Eastern Highlands (Terence E. Hays and Patricia H. Hays on the Ndumba; Philip L. Newman and David J. Boyd on the Awa; and Herdt on the Sambia), and Southern Highlands (Edward L. Schieffelin on the Kaluli).

Rather than looking at male cults and initiation rites in terms of social organization and kinship, as earlier studies have done, these essays stress a multidimensional perspective and demonstrate the importance of interpreting them in terms of the cultural system and native experience. In the introduction, Roger Keesing highlights the themes presented in the essays. He characterizes the male cults and initiation rituals of New Guinea as a distinct genre that share common foci, for example, the assumption that males and females are different in physiology and psychological being; that the fluids, essences, and powers of women are dangerous; that women are inimical to male powers. Initiation ceremonies are viewed as a process by which men are culturally created from boys. Keesing suggests that an adequate explanation of these beliefs and practices has to include a consideration of ecological factors, social structure, the symbolic system, psychological experience, and sexual politics. In essence, these essays investigate values about men and women that channel gender-related behavior and raise fundamental questions about the formation of gender identity. (SGF)

PR

1012.   Herdt, Gilbert, and Robert J. Stoller. **Intimate Communications: Erotics and the Study of Culture.** New York: Columbia University Press, 1990. 467 p. Includes bibliography and index. ISBN 0-231-06900-6.

There is a paucity of material on sexuality across cultures. Furthermore, anthropology accords sexuality only a minor role as a focus for study, particularly subjects like sexual excitement, gender identity, orientation or development. Anthropologist Herdt and psychoanalyst Stoller ask: Why? Herdt and Stoller explain the void as more than avoidance of a socially tabooed topic or a product of the prudery of researchers. They think that the reasons lie at the heart of anthropology's epistemology which is expressed by the importance of fieldwork and the emphasis on participant observation. With some exceptions, ethnographers describe normative behavior, institutions, and an idealized version of culture. Consequently, experiences of the fieldworker, the interpreters (a term that seems more accurate than "informants"), and the people described are left out. True to the canons of science, anthropologists try to be objective about their research; subjectivity and personal experience are omitted from their ethnographies. However, Herdt and Stoller contend that it is "only through dialogue, through interpersonal and intimate communication, that certain cultural points of interest to the study of gender and erotics in culture are revealed" (p. vii). Therefore, anthropologists need to use a method that explores the subjective experience of themselves as researchers and of the individuals in the society they are studying, for it is through individuals that culture is expressed. Such a method is particularly important in investigating the "sensitive, intimate nature of erotic feelings." (Herdt and Stoller prefer to use "erotic" rather than "sexual" because it refers more precisely to sexual excitement.) Therefore, this book is not only a study of erotics among the Sambia, a people in the New Guinea Highlands, but also a proposal for the use of a new approach to fieldwork: clinical ethnography, a sub-type of participant observation where context is of major importance and the focus is on communicating with real people with whom the researcher creates and exchanges meanings.

Part I is an introduction to clinical ethnography. Herdt and Stoller detail the need for the method in the context of traditional anthropological methods of fieldwork and participant observation. A summary of Sambian sexual culture provides a structural basis for evaluating the dialogues that occur in part II, which forms the core of the book. This part demonstrates how Herdt and Stoller used and reported the results of their clinical ethnography. Each chapter reports a dialogue between the researcher and an interpreter, revealing experiences of eroticism, masculinity, hermaphroditism, a woman's role, and deviance. Each is a detailed analysis of sex talk. The study of the developmental context and subjective experience of individual erotic behavior leads to hypotheses about the broader cultural expressions of erotics presented in part I. It leads to a juxtaposition of norms in relation to individual thought, feeling, and behavior. It focuses attention on the link between objective experience and culture. The ethnographer's role becomes that of a translator who transforms the experiences of individuals into descriptions that others can understand.

Part III highlights the conclusions of the study, where Herdt and Stoller claim to have provided an "experience-near" narrative of Sambian sexual culture, which they regard as "pathbreaking in cross-cultural studies of sex and gender" (p. 349). Only when anthropologists regard the study of the individual as a legitimate focus of study will there be an appropriate avenue for anthropologists to study erotics, gender orientation, and gender identity. (SGF)

PR,IL,PO

1013. Malinowski, Bronislaw. **The Sexual Life of Savages in North-Western Melanesia: An Ethnographic Account of Courtship, Marriage, and Family Life Among the Natives of the Trobriand Islands, British New Guinea.** 3rd ed. With a preface by Havelock Ellis. London: Routledge, 1932. 505 p. Includes index.

In the preface to this work, noted sexologist Ellis perceptively comments that "it may be safely said that *The Sexual Life of Savages* will become a classic of which the value must increase with the passage of time" (p. xi). Malinowski is acknowledged as the father of fieldwork in anthropology; the self-proclaimed originator of the functional method, which countered prevailing historical and evolutionary interpretations of culture at the beginning of the twentieth century; and a prolific ethnographer and ethnologist, whose works on the Trobriand Islands include *Argonauts of the Western Pacific* (1922), *Sex and Repression in Savage Society* (1927), and *Coral Gardens and Their Magic* (1935).

The goal of *The Sexual Life of Savages* is to describe sexual, family, and kinship relationships as an integrated part of the social and cultural life of the Trobriand Islanders, who live on a group of coral islands northeast of New Guinea. In the foreword, Malinowski asserts that sex is more than the physical connection of bodies; it is a "sociological and cultural force" that cannot be properly studied apart from its cultural context. Therefore, the book describes a whole range of customs related to this context: matrilineal principles of kinship and their link to male and female statuses and roles in society; specific dimensions of sex related to married life (courting, premarital sex, betrothal, marriage, multiple spouses, procreation, pregnancy, childbirth, extramarital sex, divorce, death); moral standards (modesty, decency, taboos); and more general aspects of erotic life ("customary forms of license") in ritual contexts; bases of attraction and beauty, attachment, love, jealousy, and sexual techniques; love magic; erotic dreams and fantasies; and mythology. Although many of the customs Malinowski describes are often different and more permissive than those in American society, Malinowski stresses the importance of viewing them from the native's point of view, as a part of a functioning social system. Although the book was well received, Malinowski was disappointed that his overall aim seemed to be glossed over in the sensationalism that followed its publication. He said, "I wanted to show that only a synthesis of facts concerning sex can give a correct idea of what sexual life means to a people" (p. xx). He had hoped that the book would enhance the value of fieldwork and demonstrate the main principles of the functional method. It remains one of the most detailed anthropological accounts of sexuality in another culture. Suggs's *Marquesan Sexual Behavior* (London: Constable, 1966) is another notable contribution to a detailed understanding of sexuality in this region of the world.

Readers interested in the life of this major figure in anthropology can refer to the publication of Malinowski's diary that he kept during his fieldwork in the Trobriands, *A Diary in the Strict Sense of the Term* (1967). (SGF)

PO
1014. Mead, Margaret. **Male and Female: A Study of the Sexes in a Changing World.** New York: Dell, 1968. 445 p. Originally copyrighted in 1949. Includes bibliographic notes and indexes.

Originally presented as the Jacob Gimbel lectures in sex psychology at Stanford University in 1946, this book focuses on the acquisition and meaning of sex roles. In part 1, renowned anthropologist Margaret Mead reiterates a theme characteristic of her applied orientation in anthropology: the comparative, fieldwork-based method of anthropology produces findings that can shed light on issues of concern in contemporary America. In her classic work, *Coming of Age in Samoa* (1928), she describes a relatively smooth transition from childhood to adulthood in Samoa, compared with the tumultuous transition experienced by American adolescents. She concludes that conflicts during adolescence are not a biological given but a result of the type of society in which a person grows up. (See Derek Freeman's *Margaret Mead and Samoa* [Cambridge, Mass.: Harvard University Press, 1983] for a scathing critique of Mead's approach.) In *Growing Up in New Guinea* (1930), she compares socialization in Manus, with its values of sexual restraint, competition, and economic achievement, to the values of American society. And, in *Sex and Temperament* she compares very different definitions of male and female roles in three New Guinea groups (Arapesh, Mundugumor, Tchambuli) to demonstrate that sex roles and attitudes are not inborn, but a product of learning; thus, sexual stereotypes in American society are not fixed. In *Male and Female*, Mead describes how the process of becoming a male or female in other societies can aid in understanding changing sex roles in American society. All of the foregoing books share another important theme that runs through much of Mead's work: the impact of childhood learning on the formation of personality and its impact in transmitting cultural patterns from one generation to the next. *Male and Female* synthesizes previous works into a general statement about the acquisition of sex roles and the importance of sex differences.

In part 2, "The Ways of the Body," Mead draws on fourteen years of field experience in seven Pacific cultures (Bali, Manus, Samoa, Iatmal, Mundugumor, Arapesh, Tchambuli) to describe the way in which children learn about sex roles. She attempts to show how children's experiences of differences and similarities in their bodies as well as adults' responses to them shape children's conception of sex and the relationship between males and females. In part 3, Mead discusses the relationship of sex differences to issues of social life: the division of labor; the importance of the family, particularly fatherhood; courtship and marriage; and reproduction (fertility, parenthood). Finally, in part 4, Mead applies the lessons learned from other societies to issues relevant to the relationship between the sexes in contemporary America. However, in the preface to her 1962 edition, she warns that this section is "extraordinarily out of date." She updates some of the information in prefaces to subsequent editions.

In sum, Mead points out that all societies acknowledge a difference between the sexes which is not necessarily biologically based. It is important to recognize that sex involves both limitations and possibilities. Males and females are shaped from the beginning of their lives by the behavior of both sexes, and each is dependent on the other. Mead concludes that "we must think . . . of how to live in a two-sex world so that each sex will benefit at every point from each expression of the presence of two sexes" (p. 346).

Readers interested in the life of this significant figure in anthropology can refer to Mead's own description of her earlier years, *Blackberry Winter* (1972); to daughter Mary Catherine Bateson's moving account of her mother and father's (eminent anthropologist Gregory Bateson) lives, *With a Daughter's Eye* (New York: Morrow, 1984); or to Jane Howard's journalistic account of Mead's life and works, *Margaret Mead: A Life* (New York: Simon & Schuster, 1984). (SGF)

PR,IL

1015. Mead, Margaret. **Sex and Temperament in Three Primitive Societies.** New York: Morrow, 1963. 335 p. Includes index.

Originally published in 1935, this classic work by the noted anthropologist Margaret Mead is "an account of how three primitive societies have grouped their social attitudes towards temperament about the very obvious factor of sex-difference" (p. viii). Sex refers to a biologically given sex difference while temperament is innate individual endowment. Mead chose three societies of New Guinea which were located within 100 miles of each other to explore the patterning of gender roles and attitudes to temperament. She bases her findings on interviews and observations of the people while she lived with them. The bulk of the book is a description of life in each of the three groups.

She describes the Arapesh, a mountain-dwelling people, as gentle, cooperative, and nurturant. In contrast, the Mundugumor, a fierce, cannibalistic people, are competitive and violent. In both societies, there are few differences in the temperaments of males and females. The Arapesh emphasize the traditional Western feminine traits while the Mundugumor portray the more masculine ones. A third society, the Tchambuli, graceful headhunters, reverse the traditional Western expectation of male and female traits: males pursue artistic activities, spend time enhancing their appearance, and are very sensitive; females are the main providers, are domineering, and are practical. Each group dramatizes sex differences in temperament in very different ways.

Mead concludes that there are no universal temperamental differences between males and females; many, if not all, of the personality traits that we have called masculine or feminine are as lightly linked to sex as are the clothing and the manners that a society at a given period assigns to either sex. Differences between individuals are due to cultural conditioning in childhood, not to the physical constitution of the two sexes. Therefore, it may be more productive to view the temperament of the sexes as variations on a human theme. (SGF)

PR,IL,PO

1016. Suggs, Robert C. **Marquesan Sexual Behavior.** New York: Harcourt, Brace & World, 1966. 251 p. Includes bibliography and index.

Supported primarily by horticulture and fishing, a few thousand Marquesans inhabit the rugged terrain of six of the nine islands in the Marquesan archipelago (located on the extreme eastern side of Polynesia in the Pacific). Each tribe inhabits a separate valley and is composed of extended families that reside patrilocally and are organized according to principles of patrilineality. Using the ethnographic techniques of interviews, observation, and conversation monitoring, anthropologist Suggs and his wife, Rae, a nurse, collected information about Marquesan sexuality. During their ten-month stay (1957-1958) in the Marquesas, Robert concentrated on approaching the topic from a male point of view while Rae dealt with it from a female point of view. The book attempts to present not only "an objective report . . . of cultural patterns of modern Marquesan sexual behavior and sexuality in Marquesan culture" but also "a reconstruction of the aboriginal behavior patterns" and a clarification of the "dynamics and processes of culture change which have produced the present culture of the Marquesas" (p. vii).

After a brief description of modern, historic, and prehistoric Marquesan life, Suggs proceeds to portray the life cycle of Marquesans from conception and birth through infancy, childhood, puberty, and adolescence, to marriage and adulthood. Each description of modern customs is followed by a reconstruction of these behaviors in aboriginal culture. Overall, the culture is characterized by a wide variety and number of permissible sexual behaviors, including heterosexuality, homosexuality, autoeroticism, and bestiality. As Suggs puts it, sex in the Marquesans is "something of a national sport" (p. 170). Much of the sexual behavior concentrates on physical, genital aspects of sex and rarely seems repressed. According to Suggs, one of the most unusual features of Marquesan sexual behavior is the "precocious development of infantile sexual behavior," during which female genitals are treated with herbs to prepare girls for their later sexual roles in adolescence and adulthood, and children begin sex play at a very early age. Sex permeates every part of the culture, including religious ritual and mythology.

Despite the lack of other detailed studies of Polynesian sexual behavior, Suggs pieces together scattered information from other sources in order to compare Marquesan sexual behavior with that of other cultures in the area. While Marquesan approval of masturbation, homosexuality, and heterosexuality does not differ much from the behavior and attitudes in other Polynesian societies, the Marquesans are somewhat more sexually unrestricted in the types of behavior they permit. Suggs concludes that a good deal of cultural consistency about sexuality characterizes Polynesia. And, despite the advent of Europeans and subsequent depopulation of the Marquesas, many aspects of their aboriginal sexual practices have persisted. (SGF)

PART

III

BIBLIOGRAPHIES

(For related material see also entries 28, 137, 174a, 259, 372, 471, 640, 809, 815, 818)

14

Bibliographies

A reliable source of current bibliographies on human sexuality topics is The Sex Information & Education Council of the U.S. (SIECUS). Requests for available bibliographies should be addressed to SIECUS, 130 West 42nd St., Suite 350, New York, NY 10036-7802.

ABORTION

PR
1017. Muldoon, Maureen. **Abortion: An Annotated Indexed Bibliography.** New York: Edwin Mellen Press, 1980. [165] p. (Studies in Women and Religion, vol. 3). Includes index. ISBN 0-88946-972-5.

This partially annotated bibliography on abortion contains 3,397 entries arranged in a single alphabetical listing. It covers journal articles, meeting papers, symposia, reports, and books published to 1980. The index, at the front of the book, is organized into seven general groupings: Bibliographies on Abortion, Ethical and Theological Aspects of Abortion, Medical and Social Aspects of Abortion, Legal Aspects of Abortion, Abortion Studies in the States (arranged by state), Abortion Studies in Other Countries (arranged by country), and Collected Articles and Symposia Proceedings (arranged by journal and symposia name). Entry numbers may appear under more than one heading in the index. The bibliography presents different sides of the abortion controversy. (TJW)

PR
1018. Winter, Eugenia B., comp. **Psychological and Medical Aspects of Induced Abortion: A Selective, Annotated Bibliography, 1970-1986.** New York: Greenwood Press, 1988. 162 p. (Bibliographies and Indexes in Women's Studies, No. 7). Includes indexes. ISBN 0-313-26100-8.

One of a series of titles on women's studies, this bibliography by Winter (Acquisitions Librarian and Bibliographer at California State College, Bakersfield), was compiled because of the strong interest in induced abortion, especially its medical and psychological aspects. She has prepared annotated citations for 500 of the most representative articles and books on the subject. Among the articles and books is a selection of films, videos, and audio recordings that Winter has personally examined. All of the entries are for items in the English language, including a number of translations. The time period covered is 1970-1986, an active period starting three years preceding the 1973 *Roe* v. *Wade* decision. In her annotations, Winter avoids making evaluative statements, preferring an impartial approach to the literature.

The bibliography is organized under ten major subject divisions: Abortion (General), Abortion Clinics, Abortion Decisions, Abortion Techniques (General), Abortion Techniques (Specific), Counseling, Morbidity and Mortality, Abortion Effects on Subsequent Pregnancy, Psychological Effects, and Psychosocial Aspects. Author, title, and subject indexes provide quick access to the numbered bibliographic citations.

Winter acknowledges the assistance of Planned Parenthood Centers in Bakersfield and Los Angeles, the National Abortion Federation, Catholics for a Free Choice, and Birthright of Bakersfield, all of which provided research materials and helpful suggestions in the course of this endeavor. (TJW)

AGING

PR
1019. Wharton, George F., III. **Sexuality and Aging: An Annotated Bibliography.** Metuchen, N.J.: Scarecrow Press, 1981. 251 p. Includes index. ISBN 0-8108-1427-7.

This bibliography contains 1,106 citations to books and articles on the general topic of sex and the aging process. Both popular and technical materials are included, and most of the items are accompanied by a paragraph-long annotation. Because Wharton compiled the bibliography through computer searches in standard indexing and abstracting sources, he has included references to published abstracts with the bibliographical citations. The chronological coverage is limited in part by the available bibliographic databases. Most references date from the 1960s and 1970s. Although Wharton asserts that most major works related to sex and aging are included, he clearly does not extend the scope of the bibliography to older works and historical materials.

The book is arranged by topic, with author and title indexes but no subject index. A section titled "Unclassified" contains references to works that Wharton categorizes as foreign, dated, hard to obtain, out-of-print, or "of little professional value." This bibliography will be useful for those in search of general information and research studies on the topic. (**ARBA 82**)

ALCOHOL & DRUGS

PR
1020. Abel, Ernest L. **Drugs and Sex: A Bibliography.** Westport, Conn.: Greenwood Press, 1983. 129 p. Includes index. ISBN 0-313-23941-X.

Abel is a research scientist who has prepared several bibliographies on topics related to drug abuse. This work focuses on substances that may have an effect on sex drive or performance and may be particularly useful for medical specialists such as pharmacologists, psychopharmacologists, urologists, obstetricians, gynecologists, and fertility specialists. The current consensus is that there is no such thing as an aphrodisiac. However, the rise of the drug culture has increased interest in investigating substances that may have a negative impact on sexuality, sexual performance, or the physiology of sex. There is also interest in scrutinizing certain substances that are used to treat nonsexual problems because they may have side effects that cause sexual dysfunction.

Abel's rather comprehensive bibliography begins with an essay that defines some of the technical terms he uses; discusses mechanisms of action of drugs; and individually treats alcohol, amphetamines, antidepressants, barbituates, benzodiazepines, caffeine, cocaine, LSD, marijuana, methaqualone, narcotics, nitrites, phencyclidine, and tobacco. The 1,432 references are then listed alphabetically by author under these headings plus "Antipsychotics" and "General Reviews." (**ARBA 84**)

PR
1021. O'Farrell, Timothy J., Carolyn A. Weyand, with Diane Logan. **Alcohol and Sexuality: An Annotated Bibliography on Alcohol Use, Alcoholism, and Human Sexual Behavior.** Phoenix, Ariz.: Oryx Press, 1983. 131 p. Includes index. ISBN 0-89774-040-8.

This annotated bibliography addresses the important subject of alcohol's effects on sexual attitudes and behaviors. The 542 annotated citations drawn from the monographic and journal literature, 1900 to 1982, serve as a reference guide for psychiatrists, physicians, social workers, counselors, and nurses who work in this emerging health care field.

The bibliography focuses on the following key aspects of the alcohol-sex relationship: the short-term influence of alcohol on sexual behavior, the long-term effects of chronic alcohol abuse on sexual activity, the adjustments made by both male and female alcoholics to deal with their sexual dysfunctions, the sex education and sex therapy available for alcoholics, and the cultural and social issues involved with alcohol's impact on sexual attitudes and behavior. This literature survey does not cover alcohol's impact on sex differences, sex roles, or reproduction. Each chapter includes very short introductory comments, and the citations vary in length from one sentence to an extensive paragraph. The appendixes provide brief lists of additional information resources and journals that cover the separate areas of sexuality and alcohol. (**ARBA 84**)

BIRTH CONTROL & CONTRACEPTION

PR
1022. Kolbe, Helen K., comp. **Oral Contraceptives Abstracts: A Guide to the Literature, 1977-1979.** New York: IFI/Plenum, 1980. 563 p. (Population Information Library, v. 2). Includes index. ISBN 0-306-65192-0.

The 1,058 citations, with abstracts, included in this bibliography were taken from the POPLINE database and reproduced from camera-ready copy. The POPLINE base, which broadly covers population materials, is made available through MEDLARS, the computerized literature retrieval service of the U.S. National Library of Medicine. POPLINE, originally called POPINFORM, was developed by the Population Information Program at Johns Hopkins University in collaboration with the Center for Population and Family Health at Columbia University. Online services were provided by Informatics, Inc., from 1973 until 1980, when the base was transferred to the National Library of Medicine as POPLINE.

The years 1977-1979 are comprehensively covered in this compilation. Included are references to scientific journal articles, books, pamphlets, and technical reports in a number of languages. The lengthy abstracts, all in English, allow the user to competently judge the usefulness of the source item. Author and subject indexes are provided. The material is most suitable for researchers, clinicians, and health professionals. (**ARBA 82**)

CINEMA

PR,IL
1023. Limbacher, James L. **Sexuality in World Cinema.** Metuchen, N.J.: Scarecrow Press, 1983. 2 v. (1,511 p.). Includes bibliography and index. ISBN 0-8108-1609-1.

Written for sociologists, teachers, movie buffs, and programmers, this guide to sexuality in world cinema briefly describes and categorizes the content of over 13,000 films, approximately 40 percent of which Limbacher claims he viewed himself! The initial sections orient the reader by providing (1) notes on the history of censorship, pornography, and obscenity as they apply to film; (2) a glossary of sex and media terms, including slang; and (3) an index of films arranged in twenty-six subject categories ("The World's Oldest Profession," "The Beast in All of Us," "It Hurts So Good"), each introduced by a short history of the class. The bulk of the work is composed of an annotated filmography. A bibliography of over 700 books and articles concludes this work.

This massive two-volume work is useful as a compilation of films containing sexual content. Annotations, though frequently humorous, are narrowly focused on the sexual content of the films, and do not include overviews of the films' contents. The style of the book is a mixture of interest in the subject matter and somewhat flip comments. (SGF)

DISABILITY

PR
1024. Sha'ked, Ami. **Human Sexuality in Physical and Mental Illnesses and Disabilities: An Annotated Bibliography.** Bloomington, Ind.: Indiana University Press, 1978. 303 p. ISBN 0-253-10100-X.

Despite the need for counseling on the sexual adjustment of disabled or chronically ill persons to become an integral part of comprehensive rehabilitation care, a lack of knowledge, training, and experience, as well as various misconceptions on that topic, still prevails. This bibliography makes it possible to locate more easily sources in this area of increasing concern.

Sha'ked provides abstracts of journal articles, books, monographs, and other published materials pertaining to a wide range of interrelationships between sexual behavior and various medical conditions and disabilities. Covered are numerous sources published from 1940 through 1977. Basic resources, such as *Psychological Abstracts, Index Medicus, Excerpta Medica,* and many others, were searched for relevant references. Assembled materials are grouped according to illness or disability type. The main areas relate to internal medical conditions, genitourinary conditions, disorders of the nervous system, muscular and joint pain, sensory disabilities, miscellaneous medical conditions, substance abuse, and psychiatric and mental disorders. Special chapters are devoted to sex and the aged, as well as to sex education for the disabled. Finally, a chapter entitled "Media Review" (compiled and edited by Susanne M. Bruyer) covers audiovisual materials that are useful for instruction and illustration.

This bibliography should be of interest to all practitioners, educators, and researchers concerned with effective sex counseling. It might also prove valuable to disabled persons searching for advice in sexual matters. (**ARBA 80**)

PR,IL
1024a. Sobsey, Dick, Sharmaine Gray, Don Wells, Diane Pyper, and Beth Reimer-Heck. **Disability, Sexuality, and Abuse: An Annotated Bibliography.** Baltimore, Md.: Brookes, 1991. 185 p. Includes indexes. ISBN 1-55766-068-9.

As Sandra S. Cole points out in the foreword, society has regarded people with disabilities as asexual. By this definition, they are not candidates for sexual abuse. Yet current research shows that most people with disabilities will experience abuse as children or assault as adults. Ironically, the services provided for people with disabilities are a major source of risk for sexual abuse.

The authors developed this annotated bibliography of over 1,100 sources related to disability, sexuality, and abuse with two goals in mind: to provide a better means to identify assault and abuse of people with disabilities, and to assure "accessible, appropriate" services for victims. Sources include newspaper articles, books, journal articles, reports, newsletters, legal cases and acts, and "cassettes." Most sources were developed in the 1980s, although many are from the 1970s. Abstracts are informative and full, averaging about seventy-five words, but often longer. Entries are arranged alphabetically by author. Subject and author indexes are provided.

The authors claim that this book is the most comprehensive, single source of information available" (p. x), embracing "all relevant research and related theoretical and practical information" (p. xi). They found that the variety and scarcity of materials relating to the links between disability, sexuality, and abuse indicate cultural biases that hinder attention to and research on this important social issue. Consequently there are relatively few materials from which to draw because research in the area is recent, rare, limited in distribution, and not identified as a scholarly research area for electronic literature searches.

Among the professionals who would benefit from using this bibliography are therapists, who can use it to treat and counsel victims; physicians, to diagnose problems; teachers, to identify sexual abuse; and lawyers, to prepare cases and develop legislation. (SGF)

EROTIC LITERATURE

PR
1025.   Kearney, Patrick J., comp. **The Private Case: An Annotated Bibliography of the Private Case Erotica Collection in the British (Museum) Library.** With an Introduction by G. Legman. London: Landesman, 1981. 354 p. Includes index. ISBN 0-905150-24-4.

In 1926 Havelock Ellis wrote to Montague Summers suggesting that a catalog or bibliography of the Private Case (P.C.), a collection of erotica and pornographic literature in the British Museum Library, be compiled. Nothing came of it. In 1936 Alfred Rose had a listing of the library's contents up to about 1934 privately printed. Then in 1966, Peter Fryer, in *Private Case-Private Scandal*, provided historical information about the development of this collection.

Most of the material in the P.C. derives from private donations and posthumous bequests, including Henry Spencer Ashbee's bequest of 1900 containing mostly French material; Charles Reginald Dawes's bequest of 1964, also including many French works of the period 1880-1930; and finally the donation of the American Beecher Moore in 1964, featuring English language erotica from the 1950s and 1960s. A number of small collections have been added to the P.C. from time to time. Interestingly, nothing in the P.C. is based on purchase or copyright deposit.

Kearney's meticulously compiled and annotated bibliography of 1,920 items represents the current contents of this remarkable collection. He points out that a great deal of material has been shifted from the P.C. to the general collections of the British Library so that today the P.C. contains fewer items than previously. Entry 143 shows the descriptive detail of one of Kearney's entries:

> 143. LYSISTRATA (The) . . . Now wholly translated into English and illustrated with eight full-page drawings by Aubrey Beardsley. London: 1896. (Leonard Smithers.) 4to. pp. vi. 61. Original blue paper boards, printed label on front cover. Edges uncut. No. 15 of 100 copies on *Van Gelder.* P.C. 31.1.6.

In the preface, Kearney states that "All erotica are 'rare' by nature." The British Library has "opted for the realistic policy of accepting everything given, simply because these things are rare and becoming more so daily" (p. 66). The rarities in this collection, in English and a number of foreign languages, cover a span of about 300 years. The *Private Case* lists mainly printed books, pamphlets, albums, copies of typescripts, and periodicals, many in translation. Most of them are illustrated novels, stories, and poetry. Bibliographies of erotica are included.

Gershon Legman, the well-known folklorist, bibliographer, and historian of erotica, enhances this work with a lengthy introduction to the world of the erotica collector and bibliographer, the preservation of their collections in the great libraries of the world, and the strange occupation of writing erotica. (TJW)

FEMALE PSYCHOLOGY

PR
1026.   Schuker, Eleanor, and Nadine A. Levinson, eds. **Female Psychology: An Annotated Psychoanalytic Bibliography.** Hillsdale, N.J.: Analytic Press, 1991. 678 p. Includes indexes. ISBN 0-88163-087-X.

Until recently, few psychoanalytic institutes offered specialized courses in female psychology, a subject that was not Freud's central focus. This book fills a gap in the resources offered for developing such courses. It is more than an annotated bibliography; it is an overview of articles, papers, and books pertinent to psychoanalytic views of female psychology. Spanning the period from Freud through 1990, the book concentrates on materials in English, primarily drawn from contemporary American sources, and includes not only psychoanalytic views but also alternatives, revisions, reactions, and dissent from them. Organized in five sections, the first three make up the bulk of the text. The four chapters in section I, "Historical Views," includes Freud's writings and early psychoanalytic views as well as modern commentaries and theoretical formulations. The thirteen chapters in section II, "Developmental Perspective," concentrate on such developmental issues as influences on gender differences, preoedipal development in girls, adolescence, the menstrual cycle, love, the relationship between the sexes, and adult development. The eight chapters in section III, "Female Sexuality, Character, Psychopathology," deal with topics such as sexuality, gender identity disorders, paraphilias, masochism, narcissism, eating disorders, and sexual abuse. The last two sections are particularly relevant to clinicians and curriculum planners; they address questions of transference and countertransference, the clinical implications of a pregnant analyst, reading lists of feminist writings, and a series of suggested readings for courses presenting a psychoanalytic perspective on female psychology. Frequent use of cross-references links the chapters; subject and author indexes facilitate retrieval of specific materials.

Schuker, M.D., Associate Clinical Professor of Psychiatry at Columbia University College of Physicians and Surgeons, and Levinson, D.D.S., F.A.C.D., compiled over 2,000 annotations for this comprehensive, encyclopedic text designed not only for psychoanalysts in planning their curricula and programs but also for other scholars, teachers, and clinicians in allied fields. Over sixty psychoanalysts, mainly those attending the COPE Workshop on Issues for Women in Psychoanalytic Education of the American Psychoanalytic Association, contributed to this volume, which was five years in the making.

A brief commentary introduces the contents of each chapter, places them in historical and theoretical context, highlights major ideas, and assesses their relevance to contemporary psychoanalytic theory. The annotations in each chapter are arranged in chronological order and are often lengthy descriptions of the main ideas and significance of the works cited. Schuker and Levinson provide an overview of the subject area as well as an annotated bibliography. (SGF)

HOMOSEXUALITY

PR,IL
1027. Bullough, Vern L., W. Dorr Legg, Barrett W. Elcano, and James Kepner. **An Annotated Bibliography of Homosexuality.** New York: Garland, 1976. 2 v. (Garland Reference Library of Social Science, v. 22). Includes indexes. ISBN 0-8240-9959-1.

This comprehensive bibliography of books and articles covering the literature of homosexuality contains over 12,794 entries. Sponsored by The Institute for the Study of Human Resources, it draws on material from various fields of knowledge, which are reflected in the specially devised classification for the homosexual literature. The fields encompassed by this interdisciplinary work are bibliography; general studies, including anthropology, history, psychology, and sociology; education and children; medicine and biology, including psychiatry; law and its enforcement; military; religion and ethics; biography and autobiography; studies: literature and the arts; fiction: novels, short stories, drama; poetry; the homophile movement; periodicals: movement and others; and transvestism and transsexualism. An informative bibliographic essay by Bullough introduces and orients the reader to the field of homosexuality and its literature. Each volume has an author index and an index of pseudonyms. A history of the gay movement in the United States from 1948 to 1960 by Salvatore J. Licata is included in an appendix to the second volume. Finally, contrary to the claim of the title, there are no annotations! (TJW)

PR

1028. Dynes, Wayne R. **Homosexuality: A Research Guide.** New York: Garland, 1987. 853 p. Includes indexes. ISBN 0-8240-8692-9.

In compiling this wide-ranging bibliography on homosexuality, Dynes has provided access not only to specific, well-known, and predictable citations, but also to a previously undocumented wealth of materials. At the same time representing diachronic and synchronic perspectives, Dynes has spent twelve years in creating an interdisciplinary research tool concerning homosexuality.

This descriptive (but nonevaluative) annotated bibliography is intended to be comprehensive but not all-inclusive, demonstrating the breadth and available materials as well as breaking new ground in such areas as music and economics as they relate to homosexuality. Not restricted to English-language works, the entries are international in scope, arranged by topic, and the bibliography includes a personal names index along with a subject index. Used carefully, and with an awareness of embedded citations, the guide provides access to books, periodical articles, brochures, official records, government documents, and the gay press. As a rule fiction, poetry, and dramatic works are excluded.

The major topical divisions comprise such themes as pioneer sex research, reference works, libraries and archives, lesbian studies, history and area studies (including Near and Far Eastern materials), anthropology, travel guides, the humanities, philosophy and religion, language studies, lifestyle studies, economics, education, politics, the military, sociology, psychology, psychiatry, family studies, transvestism and transsexualism, legal issues, violence, medicine, and biology, among other fields of inquiry. (NW)

IL

1029. Horner, Tom. **Homosexuality and the Judeo-Christian Tradition: An Annotated Bibliography.** Metuchen, N.J.: Scarecrow Press, 1981. 131 p. (ATLA Bibliography Series, No. 5). Includes indexes. ISBN 0-8108-1412-9.

All 459 items in this succinctly annotated bibliography are within the framework of Jewish and Christian traditions, including modern works reflecting the gay movement in the United States since 1969. Antihomosexual literature is also represented. Horner states that he refrained from rendering value judgments in the annotations. The material is organized by form into four sections: books, articles and essays, pamphlets, and bibliographies. Biblical references to homosexuality are in appendix A, and a list of periodicals of gay religious organizations is in appendix B. (TJW)

PR,IL

1030. Parker, William. **Homosexuality: A Selective Bibliography of Over 3,000 Items.** Metuchen, N.J.: Scarecrow Press, 1971. 323 p. Includes indexes. ISBN 0-8108-0425-5.

This selective, albeit comprehensive, bibliography presents significant writings on homosexuality through 1969. All items are in English and a few are translations. Parker arranges 3,188 items in numerical order under fourteen headings by type of publication: books, pamphlets and documents, theses and dissertations, articles in books, newspaper articles, magazine and journal articles, court cases, articles in homophile publications, literary works (novels, plays, and short stories), and miscellaneous works (movies, television programs, and phonograph records). As a result of compiling this bibliography, Parker concludes that "homosexuality is now being approached more and more in terms of sexual preference, minority status, and personal rights" rather than "as a sickness, sin, or crime." Furthermore, "where once only the works of medical specialists, criminologists, and moralists found their way into print, we now see sociologists, religious leaders, journalists, and homosexuals themse'ves writing on the subject." While the material in this bibliography is not evaluated, Parker does warn that "the reader must be most careful in evaluating what he reads on the subject of homosexuality." Parker has, however, listed by entry number 135 items that he considers the "most significant or influential writings on the subject." An interesting feature of the book is the appendix, in which the 1970 statutes applicable to consensual adult homosexual acts are listed by state. Offenses are given and the status of each offense is provided. (For example, in Colorado a "crime against nature" is a felony.)

In 1977, Parker followed through with the 337-page *Homosexuality Bibliography: Supplement 1970-1975*, which is a listing of 3,136 additional items, with appendixes listing motion pictures and television shows with a homosexual theme, audiovisual materials, and a further listing of laws on homosexuality as of January 1, 1976. (TJW)

PR
1031.   Weinberg, Martin S., and Alan P. Bell, eds. **Homosexuality: An Annotated Bibliography.** New York: Harper & Row, 1972. 550 p. Includes index. SBN 06-014541-2.

With support from the National Institute of Mental Health, investigators at the Institute for Sex Research (founded by Alfred C. Kinsey) at Indiana University undertook in 1969 an in-depth examination of the research literature on homosexuality. Limiting themselves to books and periodical articles, they identified and annotated 1,265 items written in the English language during the years 1940-1968. The material was drawn primarily from psychology, psychiatry, and sociology. The belles-lettres, including biography and autobiography, were excluded, as were popular magazines (excepting *Sexology*) and newspaper articles. A selection of material was made from religion, social work, counseling, medicine, and law. The homophile literature, with rare exceptions, was eschewed altogether.

Classified under three broad categories, "Psychological Considerations," "Physiological Considerations," and "Sociological Considerations," the literature was abstracted in ways that reflect primary emphases. Within the first two categories the literature is further arranged according to etiology, assessment, and treatment of homosexuality, and literature on female homosexuality is separated from male homosexuality within each section. The sociological literature covers the social and demographic aspects of the homosexual community, homosexuality in history, non-Western societies, and special settings, societal attitudes, and the law. Entries are numbered consecutively throughout the bibliography; at the end of each section are cross-references to literature in other sections. Easy access to the contents of the bibliography is provided by detailed author and subject indexes. (TJW)

HUMAN SEXUALITY

PR
1032.   Brewer, Joan Scherer, and Rod W. Wright, comps. **Sex Research: Bibliographies from the Institute for Sex Research.** Phoenix, Ariz.: Oryx Press, 1979. 212 p. Includes index. ISBN 0-912700-48-3.

This is a collection of the most frequently requested bibliographies from the Institute for Sex Research, established in 1947 by Alfred C. Kinsey. It is a volume on human sex behavior and attitudes, broad in scope, with sources encompassing books and book chapters, journal articles, dissertations, conference papers, and nonprint materials, such as cassette tapes and films.

The more than 4,000 numbered entries are arranged into eleven broad categories, each with several subcategories: "Sex Behavior," with relation to age and some special groups, as well as to drugs; "Sex Variations"; "Sexual Response Physiology"; "Sex Counseling"; "Sex and Gender"; "Marriage"; "Sex Education"; "Sex and Society"; "Legal Aspects of Sex Behavior"; and chapters on "Erotica" and "Research" (involving methodology and ethical issues in sex research). No annotations are provided, nor is there an introduction to the individual categories. There was no attempt to make the bibliographies comprehensive. While some foreign sources are included, on the whole the selection emphasizes English-language materials, as well as current rather than historical works.

Complete with author and subject indexes, this well-organized sourcebook provides a multidisciplinary overview that may be useful for facilitating further research work in diverse disciplines. It is not intended to be used as self-help material. (**ARBA 80**)

PO

1033.   Mair, George. **The Sex-Book Digest: A Peek Between the Covers of 113 of the Most Erotic, Exotic, and Edifying Sex Books.** New York: Quill, 1982. 309 p. ISBN 0-688-01336-8.

Impressed by the number of books being written on sex—more than 800 over a ten-year period according to a computer search he conducted at the Library of Congress—Mair, editor and publisher of the *Alexandria* (Virginia) *Gazette*, made up his mind to review those that in his opinion are the best of the lot. The result is this anthology, wittily and perceptively written, about books on a wide range of subjects in the sexual field. From one to six books are reviewed under forty-nine headings ranging from "Aphrodisiacs, Magic, and the Occult" through "The Biology of Sex," "Celibacy and Sex," "Elderly People and Sex," "Forbidden Sexual Behavior," "The History of Sex," "Incest," "Orgasm," "Prostitution," "Religion and Sex," "Teenage Sex," to "Transvestites and Transsexuals," and "Young Men and Older Women." The selection covers 113 popular books on sex written between 1966 and 1981; it includes such well-known works as Alex Comfort's *The Joy of Sex*, *The Redbook Report on Female Sexuality*, and Nancy Friday's *Men in Love*. One could easily pass a pleasant, even stimulating, evening reading randomly the reviews in this book and join with Mair in hoping that "it will encourage you to read more and learn more about sex as a natural, healthy body function." (TJW)

PR

1034.   Mason, Mervyn L. **Human Sexuality: A Bibliography and Critical Evaluation of Recent Texts.** Westport, Conn.: Greenwood Press, 1983. 207 p. Includes indexes. ISBN 0-313-23932-0.

In this bibliography, intended for various professionals, Mason describes, summarizes, and critically evaluates 180 books on the subject of human sexuality, the majority of which have been published since 1970. The books have been selected on the basis of availability, quality, popularity, reputation, and scientific-sexological approach to the subject. They are arranged alphabetically by author under nine broad categories, including female sexuality, history and sex, male sexuality, philosophy and sex, physiology and sex, sex education, sex research, sex therapy and counseling, and sexual minorities (a category embracing lesbians, male homosexuals, bisexuals, handicapped persons, swingers, transsexuals, etc.). Accompanying each bibliographical entry is a brief summary followed by a critique that itemizes strengths and deficiencies of the particular work. Mason, a former editor of the newsletter of the Association of Sexologists and a Ph.D. from the Institute for Advanced Study of Human Sexuality, states in the introduction that he has assessed each work on the basis of its objectivity, factual coverage of the subject, attention to history and cross-cultural comparisons, and use of illustrations. The bibliography has indexes for author, subject, and title. (TJW)

PR

1035.   **Sex in Contemporary Society: A Catalog of Dissertations.** Ann Arbor, Mich.: Xerox University Microfilms, 1973. 14 p. Includes index.

This catalog lists 436 doctoral dissertations available from University Microfilms International for the years 1938-1973. They are grouped into broad subject categories ("The Emerging Woman," "Sex-Roles and Sexual Identity," "The Unwed Mother,"

"Fertility Patterns," "Sex and the Law," "Religion and Sex," etc.) that show the research concerns of scholars since 1938 in the field of human sexuality. Each category lists titles from the social sciences, the humanities, and the sciences, providing the reader with an overall perspective of available materials. The titles do reflect the changing research interest over the years on such key issues as sex education programs, homosexual behavior, birth control and contraception, and abortion. The entries, arranged alphabetically by author under each subject category, consist of title, degree granted, granting institution, and year. An order number is provided for each dissertation, which may be ordered in hard copy or on microfilm. An update of this listing could be obtained by requesting a database search from UMI. (TJW)

INCEST

PR,IL
1036. Rubin, Rich, and Greg Byerly. **Incest: The Last Taboo: An Annotated Bibliography.** New York: Garland, 1983. 169 p. (Garland Reference Library of Social Science, v. 143). Includes index. ISBN 0-8240-9185-X.

Intended for researchers, social workers, health care professionals, and interested laypersons, this selected bibliography of 419 items brings together English-language books, dissertations, journal articles, and audiovisual materials chosen for their analysis of incest in the United States and for their accessibility and usefulness as research tools. Significant works published in the 1960s and earlier are included, but the major emphasis is on works appearing in the 1970s. Accounts dealing mainly with child abuse or child pornography, predominantly historical works, and studies focusing primarily on nonhuman populations are not included.

The broad scope of this bibliography is reflected in the variety of periodicals covered in separate chapters: psychological, sociological and legal, anthropological, medical and scientific, popular, and literary (covering criticism of literary works employing an incest motif). The general subject access provided by this arrangement is enhanced by a detailed subject index; author and periodical indexes are also included. The descriptive annotations are clearly written and consistent in style. Reviews of books are cited wherever possible. Materials not personally examined by the compilers are summarized from other abstracts or reviews, as cited in the annotations. The sixteen audiovisual items and thirty-four dissertations are all annotated in this manner.

A search of the latest *Subject Guide to Books in Print* and *Bibliographic Index* since 1973 reveals no other book-length bibliography on incest. Rubin and Byerly have thus filled an obvious gap in describing the rapidly expanding literature of a serious social problem that has increasingly engaged the attention of researchers, practitioners, and policy makers. (**ARBA 84**)

MEDIEVAL SEXUALITY

PR,IL
1037. Salisbury, Joyce E. **Medieval Sexuality: A Research Guide.** New York: Garland, 1990. 210 p. (Garland Medieval Bibliographies, v. 5; Garland Reference Library of Social Science, v. 565). Includes indexes. ISBN 0-8240-7642-7.

The 815 entries in this research guide to medieval sexuality span materials from the second through the fifteenth centuries. Because there is no clear agreement on when the medieval period began and ended, Salisbury includes Christian works from the second century that influenced medieval thought and ends with works from northern Europe, which experienced the Renaissance later. Secular sources included begin in the fifth century. Geographically, the works concentrate on western Europe: Spain, Portugal, France, Italy, Germany, and England.

Salisbury restricted her selection of works by their content. Any work that describes or discusses sexual behavior or attitudes is included; those concerned only with spiritual love, marriage, and family to the exclusion of sexual consummation are not included.

The guide is divided alphabetically into primary and secondary sources arranged by author. Primary sources are organized by discipline—law, history, literature, religion, and science. Because historical references to sex are scattered and scarce, they are the least comprehensive of the primary sources. Literature on love is rich in its variety, and sources from the law are quite informative. Religious materials tend to be didactic while scientific literature is informative. Because secondary sources draw from a variety of disciplines, they are divided into books and articles rather than by discipline. Most sources have brief annotations indicating the kind of information available in them. Specific cross-references to another source in the guide are also noted.

Three indexes supplement the numbered entries: a subject index; author, editor, translator index; and an index of primary sources by century. All refer back to the numbered entries in the guide. (SGF)

MEN'S STUDIES

PR,IL
1038. August, Eugene R. **The New Men's Studies: A Selected and Annotated Interdisciplinary Bibliography.** Englewood, Colo.: Libraries Unlimited, 1994. 440 p. Includes indexes. ISBN 1-56308-084-2.

This new version of *Men's Studies* (1985) reflects the dramatic growth in men's studies since 1990. With over 1,000 annotated entries—almost double the size of the original edition—August's compilation covers a wide spectrum of subjects drawn primarily from the fields of anthropology, sociology, psychology, history, politics, literature, and the arts. The table of contents, arranged alphabetically in twenty-seven chapters, brings out specific topics such as divorce and custody, erotica and pornography, feminism, health, humor, masculinity, men's rights, patriarchy, sexuality, spirituality, war and peace, and work and play. Each section is cross-referenced to books on related subjects. In addition to the categorical approach to the material annotated, an author/title and a subject index provide direct access to the entries.

August notes that "the presence of gender-conscious content marks an essential difference between traditional studies and the new men's studies" (p. xv). Writers became more gender-conscious in the 1990s. Such a stance emerged in large part as a reaction to the success of earlier, similar feminist endeavors

In recent decades, mythopoetic men, led by such figures as Joseph Campbell and Robert Bly, sought "a spiritual redefinition of masculinity based on myths, archetypes, and, in some cases, mainstream religious beliefs" (p. xvi). This movement generated a body of new studies. August takes note of the increasing use of mysandric and anti-male sexist comments in the recent literature. These trends have been identified in the books selected and annotated for this new edition. (TJW).

PORNOGRAPHY

IL
1039. Sellen, Betty-Carol, and Patricia A. Young. **Feminists, Pornography, & the Law: An Annotated Bibliography of Conflict, 1970-1986.** Hamden, Conn.: Library Professional Publications, 1987. 204 p. Includes index. ISBN 0-208-02124-8.

In its coverage of the literature on the antipornography debate that raged across the country during the 1970s and 1980s, this bibliography highlights the "conflicts and concern over freedom of speech versus restrictions on sexually explicit materials" (p. 1).

Taking a neutral stand toward the materials included, Sellen and Young have annotated a wide range of publications: books and papers in books, magazine and newspaper articles, nonprint media, and unpublished materials. Each annotation attempts to capture the gist of the ideas presented in an impartial manner. A separate chapter lists feminist and gay/lesbian organizations involved in the pornography controversy. Separate appendixes list various sources (magazines and newspapers) of material relevant to the subject.

An interesting introduction points out the conflict between the liberal perspective on pornography, that believes pornography serves "as a safety valve to keep males from acting out violent fantasies," and a feminist viewpoint that "pornography reinforces the subordination of women and leads to actual violence against them." This bibliography traces and reflects that conflict in a crucial period in the United States. (SGF)

PROSTITUTION

PR,IL
1040. Bullough, Vern, Barrett Elcano, Margaret Deacon, and Bonnie Bullough. **A Bibliography of Prostitution.** New York: Garland, 1977. 419 p. Includes index. ISBN 0-8240-9947-8.

There are 6,494 alphabetically arranged entries in this comprehensive bibliography of books, articles, papers, and government documents related to prostitution. They include older materials as far back as ancient Greece as well as current English- and foreign-language imprints. The materials are organized into nineteen categories, including anthropology; area studies; bibliography; biography and autobiography; business; fiction—primarily in English; guides and descriptive history; history; juveniles; legal and police regulations; literature; males; medicine and public health; organizations, societies, and publications; psychiatry; psychology; religion and morality; sociology; and war. Occasionally the entries are annotated with brief one-liners. An author index is provided. The editors point out that changing attitudes toward prostitution are reflected in the bibliography which, they say, is "the first of its kind." Because the information in this bibliography has been stored on computer at the Center for Sex Research at California State University, Northridge, the editors hope to update it from time to time by means of supplements. (TJW)

PR
1041. Bullough, Vern L., and Lilli Sentz, eds. **Prostitution: A Guide to Sources, 1960-1990.** New York: Garland, 1992. 369 p. (Garland Reference Library of Social Science, v. 670). Includes indexes. ISBN 0-8240-7107-8.

Bullough and Sentz hope that this guide to sources in prostitution from 1960 through 1990 will complement materials in Bullough et al.'s *A Bibliography of Prostitution* (New York: Garland, 1977) to provide the "most complete and comprehensive guide to prostitution available" (preface). Because of increased feminist research on prostitution, the willingness of scholars to investigate homosexuality and homosexual prostitution, and concern with the transmission of AIDS, the literature on prostitution has burgeoned during the last thirty years. This bibliography includes books and articles in English, European languages (usually without abstracts), and non-European languages (where English abstracts are available), spanning a wide range of perspectives on the many facets of prostitution.

The 1,965 entries are arranged according to broad, alphabetical headings, the scope of which includes general sources (bibliographies, feminist studies, studies on sexuality and prostitution, etc.), area studies, biographies, histories, humanities, legal, males and prostitution, medicine, sociology, substance abuse, and pornography, among others. Area studies and histories are segmented according to geographical region, facilitating cross-cultural comparisons. Many sources are merely listed without annotations while others are briefly annotated. Two lengthy indexes of personal names and subjects guide the user to specific entries. (SGF)

PR,IL
1041a.   Nash, Stanley D. **Prostitution in Great Britain, 1485-1901: An Annotated Bibliography.** Metuchen, N.J.: Scarecrow Press, 1994. 226 p. Includes index. ISBN 0-8108-2734-4.

Nash, Humanities Resource Librarian for American and British History at the Alexander Library of Rutgers, The State University of New Jersey, recognized that "the serious study of the history of prostitution has produced a sizable body of literature" (p. vii), but much of it was not easily accessible. Nash's purpose is to "provide access to this material and to guide the historian and the history student through both the secondary and key primary sources in a way that will point them to the type of coverage they require for any study in which prostitution is related" (p. vii). Previous bibliographies are incomplete because they include brief, uncritical annotations of sources, are not comprehensive, or neglect earlier periods of British history. This bibliographic survey is developed to fill those gaps by placing together important primary and secondary sources as they relate to the history of prostitution in Great Britain from 1485 to 1901 and then providing longer, critical annotations to accompany them.

The text begins with a bibliographic essay that traces major themes in the evolution of historical literature on prostitution, thus providing the scholar with an overview of the cultural and social contexts within which the literature was written. Nash explains why social attitudes toward prostitution changed and how scholarship and interest in prostitution as a topic for study have shifted. He concludes the lengthy introduction with an analysis of secondary sources, written primarily since the 1960s by twentieth-century historians of prostitution (e.g., Vern L. Bullough and Bonnie Bullough's *Women and Prostitution: A Social History* [1987] and Judith Walkowitz's *Prostitution and Victorian Society: Women, Class, and the State* [1980]).

The 390 works in the bibliography derive from a variety of published (e.g., pamphlets, newspaper articles, books) and unpublished (e.g., court records, diaries, personal journals, doctoral dissertations) sources. Nash includes and points out the relevance of sources that might otherwise be overlooked in research on prostitution (e.g., documents relating to the transportation of felons, responses to cosmetics, and reactions to poor laws). The critical reviews (i.e., "annotations") of the sources are divided into primary and secondary types and then alphabetically arranged according to three arbitrarily chosen time periods (1485-1700, 1700-1800, 1800-1901) during which attitudes toward prostitution differed. An index of names, concepts, subjects, and titles of works appearing within the entries concludes this systematic, thoughtful contribution to the bibliographic literature on prostitution. (SGF)

RAPE

PR
1042.   Chappell, Duncan, and Faith Fogarty. **Forcible Rape: A Literature Review and Annotated Bibliography.** Washington, D.C.: Government Printing Office, 1978. 84 p. Includes index.

This selective bibliography lists 152 books and articles dealing with various aspects of rape. The well-annotated entries are arranged under six sections: "Sociocultural and Descriptive Features of Rape," "Rape Victimization," "Rape Offenders," "Investigation of Rape: Police Procedures and Criminalistics," "Legal Issues and Legislative Reform," "Rape in Foreign Countries and Cultures." The material is indexed by author. The introduction presents a brief overview of current rape literature and specifies the criteria for inclusion in the bibliography—only recent (1970s) English-language publications available to most readers were included. This inexpensive bibliography could be of use to women's studies courses requiring a limited reading list of rape literature. (**ARBA 80**)

PR

1043. Wilson, Carolyn F. **Violence Against Women: An Annotated Bibliography.** Boston: G. K. Hall, 1981. 111 p. (A Reference Publication in Women's Studies). Includes index. ISBN 0-8161-8497-6.

Written from a feminist perspective and directed to women's studies courses, this bibliography considers four forms of violence: battered women, rape (including four entries on sexual harassment), sexual abuse of children (male adult/female child incest), and pornography. The 213 entries concentrate on materials appearing between 1975 and August 1980. While some "new classics from the early seventies" are included, a conscious attempt has been made to avoid repeating many of the pre-1975 books that achieved enough prominence to appear in other bibliographies. Two earlier bibliographies are Dorothy L. Barnes's *Rape: A Bibliography, 1965-1975* (Troy, N.Y.: Whitston Publishing Company, 1977) and Elizabeth Jane Kemmer's *Rape and Rape-Related Issues* (New York: Garland, 1977). The Barnes work is not annotated. Kemmer's book covers materials through mid-1976 and is annotated.

Each of Wilson's chapters is preceded by a three- to six-page, state-of-the-art essay in which the author presents historical background, current thinking and research efforts, and social policy implications related to the subject that follows. Within the main subject categories, entries are arranged under headings designating format or perspective, such as anthologies; personal accounts; legislative, judicial, and police attitudes; medical aspects; and so on. Materials were selected from a variety of sources, including newsletters, journals likely to be found in most college and university libraries, and popular magazine literature. Wilson provides a list of journals consulted and points out in the preface that most materials included "support to some degree the point of view of the Women's Movement." (**ARBA 82**)

SEX EDUCATION

PR,IL

1044. Campbell, Patricia J. **Sex Guides: Books and Films About Sexuality for Young Adults.** New York: Garland, 1986. 374 p. Includes bibliographies and index. ISBN 0-8240-8693-7.

Campbell, a columnist for the *Wilson Library Bulletin* and a former librarian, attempts to "provide the definitive guide to sex guides, a resource that will give background and understanding and specific title suggestions to librarians, teachers, parents, youth advocates, and young adults themselves" (p. ix). Her sophisticated bibliographic approach to this genre of literature is a narrative style that discusses each title individually as well as comparing and contrasting it with other current titles. Background material on the events of the day (e.g., World Wars I and II), social and cultural attitudes, and scientific research on sexuality (e.g., Masters and Johnson) is presented as a context within which the sex advice books can be interpreted. Her review of almost all 400 books in this genre serves as an indication of American attitudes toward adolescent sexuality and provides a vehicle to comprehend current problems about sexuality. A listing of sex advice books discussed follows each chapter.

The first half of the book, most of which was published by R. R. Bowker as *Sex Education Books for Young Adults, 1892-1979* (1979), traces the history of the teen sex manual from its inception in 1892 to its present form. Arranged chronologically, each chapter in this section covers about a decade of an eighty-seven year span of time. When sex education books for young adults first appeared (1892), educators emphasized the importance of self-restraint for individual development and social progress. Campbell traces the evolution of the sexual advice literature from Victorian sex educators' denunciation of masturbation, prostitution, and venereal disease to the more tolerant material available today in which activities such as masturbation and premarital sex are looked upon with greater understanding.

The second half of the book analyzes contemporary sex guides for adolescents as well as sources of noncurricular sex education, including young adult fiction, religious sex books, specific aspects of teen sexuality (STDs, contraception, rape, abortion, pregnancy, etc.), and film. Modern sex guides for teenagers express a departure from the emphases in the past that have attempted to prevent and/or control teenage sexuality by emphasizing the danger involved in such encounters. The last chapter suggests how professionals can become responsible, effective providers of sex information and develop an adequate reference collection. The appendixes specify core reading lists appropriate for different levels of readers and types of libraries.

Overall, the volume provides a rich social and cultural interpretation of sex guides for adolescents as well as a critical overview of materials that influence sex education. (SGF/TJW)

PR,IL

1045.   Center for Early Adolescence. University of North Carolina at Chapel Hill. **Early Adolescent Sexuality: Resources for Parents, Professionals, and Young People.** Carrboro, N.C.: The Center for Early Adolescence, 1983. 32 p.

This bibliographic guide to resources on early adolescent sexuality was compiled for the use of parents and professionals who recognize that "early adolescence is a time of great physical, emotional, and social growth." It should satisfy the need for a resource guide to help in the selection of materials for ten- to fifteen-year-olds—the early adolescents. The materials intended for parents and professionals are arranged in several sections: general reading, bibliographies, journals and periodicals, and training materials. A section on curriculum guides for use with adults and adolescents follows. These are all simple listings without annotations or abstracts. The next sections cover general reading for young adolescents and include separate listings for nonfiction and fiction. Entries are briefly annotated to help the professional in choosing specific titles. A final section lists, but does not annotate, films for young adolescents. A speech by Joan Lipsitz, "Sexual Development of Young Adolescents," given before the American Association of Sex Educators, Counselors, and Therapists in March 1980 concludes this short resource guide. (TJW)

PR,IL

1046.   Seruya, Flora C., Susan Losher, and Albert Ellis. **Sex and Sex Education: A Bibliography.** New York: Bowker, 1972. 336 p. Includes indexes. ISBN 0-8352-0544-4.

This comprehensive human sexuality bibliography covers an estimated 3,000 monographs (books and pamphlets) available in the English language. Not limited to current imprints, it includes older material as well. The compilers, who had the subject specialist support of Albert Ellis, Executive Director, Institute for Advanced Study in Rational Psychotherapy, state: "Our aim in this work is to reach anyone confronted with the teaching or learning of sex, be he parent, educator, or adult who wishes self-instruction, or a professional who is seeking information or materials for recommended reading" (p. xi).

The entries are arranged alphabetically within fourteen categories representing the major aspects of sexuality: biology, psychology, religion, anthropology, medicine, education, sex in literature, love and courtship, ethics, and various social science problems (abortion, illegitimacy, prostitution, sex offenses and offenders). The work is enhanced by occasional annotations providing edition data and explaining unclear titles. Quick access to the material is also provided by author, title, and subject indexes. (TJW)

PO

1047.   **Sex Education for Adolescents: A Bibliography of Low-Cost Materials.** Chicago: American Academy of Pediatrics, 1980. 32 p. ISBN 0-8389-3248-7.

This briefly annotated listing of eighty-three readily available items—paperbacks, booklets, pamphlets, folders—was compiled for "parents, health professionals, educators, librarians, clergy, and youth workers" who "share a common goal of providing young people with accurate, responsible information on sexuality." Intended to replace previously issued lists needing revision, this pocket-sized booklet is the result of the collaborative effort of the American Academy of Pediatrics, the American Library Association, and the Planned Parenthood Federation of America. Sexuality issues are addressed under the headings "General Information"; "Sexuality, Decisions, and Values"; "Contraception"; "Health Issues and Health Care"; and "Special Interests" (pregnancy, sexuality and the disabled, and homosexuality). All items listed have been evaluated in terms of content and adolescent appeal. All items were published or revised between approximately 1975 and 1979 and are expected to be available for a number of years. The addresses of forty-two sources are given in the back of the booklet. (TJW)

PR,IL
1048. Snyder, Susan Untener, and Sol Gordon, eds. **Parents as Sexuality Educators: An Annotated Print and Audiovisual Bibliography for Professionals and Parents (1970-1984).** Phoenix, Ariz.: Oryx Press, 1984. 212 p. Includes index. ISBN 0-89774-087-4.

This annotated bibliography of human sexuality source materials created or revised between 1970 and 1984 was developed as an aid to professionals in guiding perplexed parents to become primary educators in sexuality. Three main themes influence the organization of the bibliography and the selection of materials for it. First, sexuality is defined as a behavioral domain that extends beyond anatomy and physiology into the psychological realm. Second, sex educators ought to "encourage responsible, nonexploitative behavior." Finally, and most important, "parents are the sexuality educators of their own children, whether they do it well or not"; public institutions and professionals occupy secondary roles. The resources presented reflect these themes and include books, pamphlets, periodical articles, and other print materials as well as audiovisual resources for both parents and professionals.

Part I focuses on materials for parents. The first chapter is devoted to resources to assist parents in their role as sexuality educators, while chapters 2 and 3 are devoted to special audiences (e.g., specific age groups, pregnant teens, teen parents, etc.) and parent/family situations ((e.g., single parents, fathers, parents of lesbians/homosexuals, etc.). The last chapter in this section provides a list of general parenting materials for parents and parents to be. Part II is geared to professionals. Chapter 5 provides general sexuality resources for professionals ranging from sexuality texts and reference books and resources for working with families to materials for training professionals. Chapters 7 and 8 present specialized resources appropriate for selected audiences (religious groups, the disabled, etc.) and special parent/family situations (e.g., adolescent sexuality, adoptive families, divorced families, etc.). Six appendixes supplement the text by providing listings of professional periodicals, distributors of audiovisual and printed materials, training manuals, resource guides, organizational sources of information, and Spanish materials. This bibliography provides an overview of materials available in this important area; the annotations are quite brief. (SGF)

SEX & THE FAMILY

PR,IL
1049. Soliday, Gerald L., ed. **History of the Family and Kinship: A Select International Bibliography.** Millwood, N.Y.: Kraus International Publications, 1980. 410 p. Includes index. ISBN 0-527-84451-9.

A project of the *Journal of Family History*, this 6,205-entry bibliography on the history of family and kinship includes books and periodical articles written up to 1978. Although the work is broad in scope, its editors and contributors have been meticulous in choosing entries for this retrospective work.

Focusing on works about family and kinship, the compilers have accumulated under this broad umbrella many related items on abortion, premarital sex, birth control, prostitution, incest, adultery, sex roles, and sex education. In effect, the work deals extensively with the human sexuality aspect of family and kinship.

The geographic editors, aware of "the rapid development of research in family history over the past ten years," arrange the material by country (France, China, United States, etc.), region (Africa south of the Sahara, Latin America, etc.), and continent (Europe, etc.) with one division for classical antiquity. Within each area the division is generally chronological, although each area has categories for general surveys, bibliographies, collections, and review essays. Each numbered entry follows standard bibliographic practice for the books and articles. A single name index ends the volume.

This bibliography will prove useful to researchers, teachers, students, and scholars in historical studies, as well as demography, sociology, anthropology, and psychology. (TJW)

SEX & THE MASS MEDIA

PR,IL
1050.   Alali, A. Odasuo, ed. **Mass Media Sex and Adolescent Values: An Annotated Bibliography and Directory of Organizations.** Jefferson, N.C.: McFarland, 1991. 138 p. Includes index. ISBN 0-89950-518-X.

Average American viewers see over 14,000 instances of sexual behavior on television in a year. Expressions of sexual behavior in the mass media have increased over the past few decades. What roles do mass media's portrayals of sexuality play in the construction of adolescents' views of sexual reality? This annotated bibliography, developed and edited by Assistant Professor of Communications (University of California at Bakersfield) Alali, is an attempt to address this complex question. The three goals of the book are to document works that have investigated the links between adolescents' involvement with the mass media and their construction of sexual reality; "illuminate some of the dark alleys" that professionals dealing with adolescent sexuality run into; and identify gaps in the literature. To do this, Alali organized this book into sections that relate to one of the book's three major goals. Four chapters (sex-role portrayals; sexual curricula and media use; adolescents' attitudes and values; contraception, pregnancy and health issues) examine the connection between mass media and adolescent attitudes, values, social learning and development, and sexual behavior. Although different forms of the media are considered in some of the studies, the impact of television is the main focus in most of the research included. The 227 entries in the annotated bibliography include journal articles, pamphlets, dissertations, newspaper and magazine articles, and some books, primarily published between 1975 and 1990. Annotations are often lengthy and range from brief comments on content to indicative and informative abstracts. Following the annotations is a directory of twenty-eight organizations that offer workshops, seminars, and technical assistance to those involved in processing and confronting adolescent issues and problems. (SGF)

SEX CUSTOMS

PR
1051.   Goodland, Roger. **A Bibliography of Sex Rites and Customs: An Annotated Record of Books, Articles, and Illustrations in All Languages.** London: Routledge, 1931. 752 p. Includes index.

Intended primarily for anthropologists, Goodland's massive bibliography contains 9,000 references appearing in literature dealing with the sexual rites and customs of different societies. Recognizing that phallic ideas in various religions have been considerable,

Goodland searched the relevant collections of major libraries in England and America to find the books, periodical articles, and illustrations that he carefully arranges, describes, and annotates in this compilation. Goodland has added an eighty-three page index of names, places, and subjects to provide ready access to the entries in the bibliography. Typical entries are Africa, amulets, coitus, India, lingam, phalli, prostitutes, and pudenda. Although dated, this work is an important contribution to cross-cultural studies. (TJW)

SEX DIFFERENCES

PR
1052.   Grambs, Jean Dresden, and John C. Carr. **Sex Differences and Learning: An Annotated Bibliography of Educational Research, 1979-1989.** New York: Garland, 1991. 280 p. (The Garland Bibliographies in Contemporary Education, 11). Includes indexes. ISBN 0-8240-6641-3.

According to Grambs and Carr, this bibliography "testifies to our growing awareness of, and concern about sex differences in the educational process" (p. xi). Schools are examining ways in which their curricula, language use, and organization reinforce gender stereotypes. However, differential messages about social behavior and academic expectations persist. Administrators, teachers, and students continue to channel males into science, mathematics, computer science, and leadership positions; females, into less intellectually challenging courses and authoritative roles. Understanding the ways in which gender relates to differences in learning allows educators to foster the unique potential of each student. Building on the considerable literature that has developed over the past twenty-five years (after the publication of E. E. Maccoby's influential *The Development of Sex Differences* in 1966), this book is designed to contribute to that goal.

Conceived as a convenient, quick, reference tool for professionals (educational researchers, classroom teachers K-12, school administrators, curriculum developers, supervisory personnel, faculties and administrators of schools, colleges, and departments of education, relevant researchers outside of education), the book includes 787 entries chosen from the period 1979-1989. The entries were chosen from research studies and professional journals, and focus on studies using American subjects and research concerned with subjects in grades K-12. The identified material suggested twenty-three topical categories into which the entries are organized, e.g., academic achievement, cultural and cross-cultural studies, help seeking/helping behavior, testing/tests, toys/play/games. A very brief description accompanies each entry, usually an indicative abstract that includes the type of research used to reach conclusions about sex differences, which are sometimes but not always specified. The book suggests areas for future research, as indicated by the paucity of studies in the following areas: specific subject areas (industrial arts and technology, home economics, social studies, foreign languages, theater, dance); specialized school settings; students in rural and inner-city schools; students from dysfunctional, itinerant, and abusive families; students from minority populations (Hispanic and Asian, homosexual and lesbian, with handicaps, drug and alcohol abusers); qualitative research; topics related to religion, popular culture, and creativity. (SGF)

SEX ROLES

PR
1053.   Astin, Helen S., Allison Parelman, and Anne Fisher. **Sex Roles: A Research Bibliography.** Washington, D.C.: Center for Human Services, 1975. 362 p. (DHEW Publication No. (ADM) 75-166). Includes index.

This 456-item bibliography completed under contract to the National Institute of Mental Health, U.S. Public Health Service, and the Department of Health, Education, and Welfare, covers "research investigations into the influence of sex roles on individual behavior and on social institutions." Intended for students and professionals in such diverse fields as psychology, anthropology, sociology, economics, and biology, it encompasses a wealth of literature written during the years 1960-1972, including selected material from foreign sources.

The material falls into five categories: descriptive studies of measured or observed sex differences, studies on the origin of sex differences and development of sex roles, studies covering the manifestation of sex roles in institutional settings, cross-cultural overviews and historical accounts of the relative status of the sexes in the United States and in other cultures and nations, and general reviews and theoretical position papers.

Each entry provides the user with the following information: complete bibliographic data; an informative abstract highlighting such elements as purpose of research, original hypotheses, theoretical orientation, study sample(s), methodology, findings, and conclusions; and the number of references cited.

An author index and a subject index make for easy access to the 346 periodical articles, 54 books, 49 book chapters, 2 conference proceedings, and 5 unpublished papers and speeches making up this research bibliography. (TJW)

PR
1054.   Grady, Kathleen E., Robert Brannon, and Joseph H. Pleck. **The Male Sex Role: A Selected and Annotated Bibliography.** Rockville, Md.: National Institute of Mental Health, 1979. 196 p. Includes index.

The National Institute of Mental Health, having sponsored five conferences between 1971 and 1978 on male and female sex roles and their changes (with emphasis on female aspects), came out with this work as a basis to stimulate further needed research on an "important and rapidly evolving subject." More than 250 entries (mostly articles, but also books and unpublished dissertations) were selected, with an emphasis on the more scientific and data-based research, leaving aside articles from the popular press in spite of the provocative ideas to be garnered from that source. Most of the longer annotations are subdivided into subjects, method, findings, and comments. Fourteen topics are listed, each with several subsections. The range of works is wide and precise, with cross-references after most subsections. An author index completes the volume. (**ARBA 81**)

SEXUAL ABUSE

PR
1055.   de Young, Mary. **Child Molestation: An Annotated Bibliography.** Jefferson, N.C.: McFarland, 1987. 176 p. Includes indexes. ISBN 0-89950-243-1.

In response to a growing need for information on the origin, dynamics, and effects of child molestation, de Young, an associate professor of social thought and public policy at Grand Valley State College in Michigan, developed this book with two purposes in mind: to demonstrate that publications on child molestation form a body of scientific knowledge and to define and illustrate different dimensions of the subject.

The main criterion that guided the selection of references was de Young's definition of child molestation as "the exposure of a prepubescent child to sexual stimulation inappropriate for the child's age, psychological development, and psychosexual maturity, by a person at least ten years older, who may either be unfamiliar to or unacquainted with the child, but who is not related to the child by blood or legal means." This definition distinguishes child molestation from incest, for which de Young has previously published *Incest: An Annotated Bibliography* (1985). The contents range from the general (literature reviews, historical and statistical studies, legal issues) to the particular (child pornography and sex rings, pedophile groups). Most of the contents are grouped according to clinically oriented topics: descriptions of child molesters (including homosexual encounters), the effects of molestation on children, the treatment of child molesters and molested children, and the prevention of child molestation.

Although the bibliography contains a few annotations to books, 527 of the 557 references are to articles drawn from the social, medical, and legal literature; the references are often fully annotated with descriptions that often provide the method and findings of a particular study. Each topic has a brief introductory commentary that provides a context for the references that follow. De Young concludes that child molestation (1) can be examined from a variety of perspectives, (2) is fruitfully explored from an interdisciplinary perspective, and (3) needs more research. (SGF)

PR
1056.   McCaghy, M. Dawn. **Sexual Harassment: A Guide to Resources.** Boston: G. K. Hall, 1985. 181 p. Includes indexes. ISBN 0-8161-8669-3.

Since the term *sexual harassment* was coined in 1975, the literature on the subject has mounted. McCaghy presents nearly 300 references—books, chapters of books, organizational and advocacy publications, government reports, dissertations, periodical articles, and audiovisual materials. General newspaper accounts are omitted. Covering sexual harassment "in employment, in education, on the street, and on the telephone" (p. ix), the bibliography's scope is interdisciplinary, and the long annotations descriptive but uncritical. Chapters are devoted to general works (including writings from a feminist perspective, general overviews, surveys and research reports, studies of specific occupations and settings, and bibliographies), the academic setting, coping strategies (both legal and personal), the legal perspective, and management response. Each chapter opens with a cogent and concise analysis of the major streams of thought and significant findings in the citations that follow. (**Women's Studies**, 1987)

PR
1057.   Schlesinger, Benjamin. **Sexual Abuse of Children: A Resource Guide and Annotated Bibliography.** Buffalo, N.Y.: University of Toronto Press, 1982. 200 p. Includes index. ISBN 0-8020-6481-7.

This resource guide is a first attempt to bring together information on the sexual abuse of children from a wide variety of sources in Canada. It is intended to be used by faculty, students, and social welfare workers as a selective guide so that they can expand their own research and study in any of several areas. Since this type of sexual abuse appears mainly in a family situation, the book stresses sex in the family and devotes most of its findings to this area. It includes bibliographies, basic library lists, film suggestions, interviewing the child victim, legal aspects, recommendations, and services. There is a sixty-page annotated bibliography of books and journal articles arranged by topic and a list of nine U.S. and one Canadian addresses for major sources of information on sexual abuse of children. (**ARBA 84**)

WOMEN'S STUDIES

IL
1058.   Brewer, Joan Scherer. **Sex and the Modern Jewish Woman: An Annotated Bibliography.** Fresh Meadows, N.Y.: Biblio Press, 1986. 37 + 88 p. Includes index. ISBN 0-930395-01-8.

Biblio Press specializes in fostering an appreciation of Jewish women's accomplishments and concerns; this bibliography is in line with that focus. Assembled and annotated by Brewer, a former information officer of the Kinsey Institute, the bibliography includes a multidisciplinary selection of books and articles, published between 1960 and 1985, which relate to the current state of knowledge about the sexual attitudes and behavior of and toward Jewish women. The organizational classification includes such specialized headings as "Stereotypes of the Sexuality of the Jewish Woman,"

"Halakhic Views on Women and Sexuality," "Niddah and Mikveh," "Orthodoxy and Sexuality," and "Judaism and Homosexuality," as well as more general categories such as premarital, marital, extramarital, and nonmarital sexuality; sexual dysfunction; aging and sexuality; and contraception and reproduction. However, the contents relate to broader contemporary issues: (1) the role of religion in modern society, (2) feminism, and (3) changes in traditional roles and practices.

Two lengthy introductory essays make up the first third of the book. Sociologist Lynn Davidman presents an overview of the general topic, sex and the modern Jewish woman. She says that the works cited in the bibliography address issues in three major areas: inquiry about and definition of a distinct Judaic sexual tradition, the interpretation of such a tradition by contemporary professionals and laypersons, and the extent to which the sexual practices and attitudes of modern American Jews are affected by the tradition. She concludes that there is a wide variety of conclusions and interpretations of each of these areas. English professor Evelyn M. Avery complements the social perspective of Davidman with a survey of Jewish fiction from 1920 to 1985, particularly in terms of the ways in which the authors deal with male-female relationships. The survey highlights a change in attitudes over time, for example, from women as victims to feminists, and the dynamics at work in this shift. These two essays provide a context for the bibliographic materials that follow them. (SGF)

PR,IL
1059. Sahli, Nancy Ann. **Women and Sexuality in America: A Bibliography.** Boston: G. K. Hall, 1984. 404 p. Includes index. ISBN 0-8161-8099-7.

Sahli selects published writings from the nineteenth and twentieth centuries to document changing concepts of female sexuality in the United States. She emphasizes the professional literature of such fields as medicine, psychiatry, history, sociology, and women's studies. She excludes literary pieces, biographies, heavily scientific or technical studies, and popular publications. Separate chapters cover historical interpretations, social and political analysis and theory, legal and ethical questions, contributions of psychoanalysis, medical and scientific writings, prescriptive literature, and studies of sexual behavior and attitudes. Sahli also devotes several chapters to more specific populations and concerns: children and adolescents, masturbation, nymphomania, lesbians, older women, disabled women, women prisoners and girl delinquents, transsexuals, and sexual dysfunction. Each chapter opens with a short note on the literature, followed by annotated entries for books and pamphlets, and an unannotated checklist of journal articles. The lengthy annotations frequently suggest a work's usefulness to particular lines of inquiry. Sahli's bibliography provides a historical, cross-disciplinary synthesis. (**Women's Studies**, 1987)

PR
1060. Stineman, Esther F., with the assistance of Catherine Loeb. **Women's Studies: A Recommended Core Bibliography.** Littleton, Colo.: Libraries Unlimited, 1979. 670 p. Includes indexes. ISBN 0-87287-196-7.

This comprehensive, annotated, interdisciplinary, feminist bibliography of 1,763 items in the English language provides a recommended collection of literature on women's issues that is organized around traditional disciplines and is based on the premise that all women are important. It covers such issues as abortion, alcoholism, lesbianism, rape, and sexuality as well as the role of women in different fields of endeavor, including anthropology, business, economics, labor, education, fine arts, law, health and medicine, politics, psychology, sociology, and sports. Each entry is thoroughly described and evaluated. A large section is devoted to the belles-lettres, with separate chapters for anthologies, drama, essays, fiction, history and criticism, and poetry. Another lengthy section consists of separate chapters for a variety of audiovisual, bibliographic, biographical, and general reference materials. One chapter lists periodicals devoted to women's issues. Compiled by the Librarian-at-Large for Women's Studies at the University of Wisconsin, with assistance from her colleagues, this basic work provides thorough bibliographic support for women's studies programs and curricula in colleges and universities, and facilitates the efforts of scholars and bibliographers involved in collection building in this area. Author, title, and subject indexes allow direct access to individual entries.

This core bibliography has been updated by *Women's Studies: A Recommended Core Bibliography, 1980-1985* (1987). Organized along the same lines as the 1979 work, it contains 1,211 annotated entries. According to the compilers (Catherine R. Loeb, Susan E. Searing, Esther F. Stineman, and Meredith J. Ross), women's studies has changed radically in recent years; the entries in this volume reflect the diversity of feminist scholarship in the 1980s, including a debate over "the very nature of the field of women's studies itself." (TJW)

About the Authors

Suzanne G. Frayser is a social science consultant, educator, and author. She received her B.A. in sociology and anthropology from the College of William and Mary, and her M.A. and Ph.D. in anthropology from Cornell University. She has served as Secretary/Treasurer of the Society for Cross-Cultural Research; a member of the Board of Directors and President of the Western Region of the Society for the Scientific Study of Sex; a consulting editor for *The Journal of Sex Research*; and a member of the Executive Council of the Colorado Association for Sex Therapy. She was recently elected to the International Academy of Sex Research, and is the author of *Varieties of Sexual Experience: An Anthropological Perspective on Human Sexuality* (HRAF Press, 1985). Involved in research on and the teaching of human sexuality for over twenty-five years, she is currently a member of the faculty of University College at the University of Denver and is a Visiting Associate Professor of Anthropology at The Colorado College, Colorado Springs.

Thomas J. Whitby, Associate Professor Emeritus, University of Denver, received his Ph.B. (1947) and A.M. (1952) degrees from the University of Chicago. After thirty-five years in the library and information field, including nine years with the Library of Congress, eight years directing libraries for Olin Mathieson Chemical Corporation and Martin-Marietta Corporation, and eighteen years on the faculty of the Graduate School of Librarianship at the University of Denver, Professor Whitby continues to pursue his main academic interests of Soviet libraries and bibliography and the classification of knowledge. His most recent works include *Introduction to Soviet National Bibliography* (Libraries Unlimited, 1979) and "Russian and Soviet Bibliography" in *Books in Russia and the Soviet Union: Past and Present* (Wiesbaden, Germany: Otto Harrassowitz, 1991). Professor Whitby is a member of the Society for the Scientific Study of Sexuality.

Author Index

Prepared by Thomas J. Whitby

Reference is to entry number.

Title Index

Prepared by Thomas J. Whitby

Reference is to entry number.

713

Subject Index

Prepared by Thomas J. Whitby

References are to entry number. Personal names, corporate names, and titles (in italics) appear as subjects in this index.

Love *(continued)*
   in literature, 405, 409, 805, 841
   and marriage, 408, 409
   in the movies, 403a
   philosophical perspectives, 42, 405, 419, 421-426
   psychoanalytic perspectives, 404, 412, 416, 420
   quotations about, 404, 937
   United States, 87, 408, 417
   USSR, 994
   and war, 409
   and will, 46
   See also Courtly love; Erotic love; Friendship; Married love; Romantic love; Sex: and love
Love letters, 417
Lovelace, Linda, 99, 141
Lovemaking, 6, 103, 205-210, 212, 217, 219, 220, 223, 244
   story of Richard Rhodes, 103
Lovemaps, 483, 576
Lovesickness, 350

Machismo, 703, 1008a
Madame Bovary (Flaubert), 405, 547
Madonna, 107, 806, 941
Maimonides, Moses, 770
Male couples, 482
Male/female relationships, 84, 93, 108, 133, 204, 224, 227, 264, 265, 389a, 411, 418, 420, 433, 437, 549, 685, 699, 707, 710-712, 715-717, 720, 721, 723, 724, 783, 786, 800, 945
   in art, 856
   cognitive therapy, 712
   United States, 723
Male nudes, 864
Male orgasm, 528
Male reproductive system, 316
Male sex organs, 291. *See also* Penis; Prostate
Male sexuality, 151, 155, 161, 217, 227, 228, 291, 583, 719, 739
   surveys, 154, 155
Mann Act, 672
Mapplethorpe, Robert, 876
Marital rape. *See* Rape: in marriage
Marital therapy, 551
Marquesans, 1016
Marriage, 36, 439, 454, 748, 769, 792, 796
   alternatives to, 787
   cognitive therapy, 712, 961
   cross-cultural perspectives, 803
   encyclopedias, 788
   England, 799
   and the family, 793
   history, 81, 785, 799, 803
   Iran, 790
   as sexual contract, 744
   surveys, 438, 789
   United States, 403, 445, 786, 789, 798
   USSR, 994

   See also Companionate marriage; Open marriage; Polygamy; Teenage marriage; Temporary marriage
Married love, 158, 409, 435, 440, 441, 752, 796
Married people: surveys, 157
Married women: sexual behavior, 146, 148, 168, 443, 445
Masculine beauty, 824, 873, 992
Masculinity, 552, 561-563, 701, 706-708, 719, 1011
   cross-cultural perspectives, 703
   See also Machismo
Masochism, 108, 420, 566, 568, 734, 901. *See also* Sadomasochism
Massage, 512-514
Masters, William H., 41, 175
Masturbation, 35, 75, 103, 132, 215, 292, 392, 508, 515-517, 528, 533, 541, 575, 711, 757, 936
Mating, 389a
   interspecies comparisons, 57
Matlovich, Leonard, Jr., 487
Matriarchy, 785
Matriliny, 44
Medieval medicine, 350
Mehinaku, 1007
Men, 938
   body image, 718
   and communication, 724
   and power, 65, 702
   psychology, 699, 702
   sexual behavior, 151, 155, 158, 161-163, 390, 455, 507, 707
   success, 717
   surveys, 151
   United States, 699
Menarche, 960
Menopause, 267, 305, 307, 308
Men's studies: bibliography, 1038
Menstruation, 302, 304, 306, 308, 392
   history, 303
   See also Menarche; Menopause
Merry Muses of Caledonia (Robert Burns), 818
Midwifery, 301, 342, 344
   United States, 711
   See also Childbirth
Miscegenation, 542
Misogyny, 411, 713, 722, 847, 938
Modesty, 35
Money, John, 137
Monroe, Marilyn, 120, 890, 911
Mormons, 755
Morris, Jan, 100
Morrow, Prince Albert, 352
Mosher Survey, 75
Motherhood, 301, 334
Mothers: psychoanalytic perspectives, 545
Motion pictures
   filmography, 898, 899, 902, 1023
   masochism in, 901
   sex symbols of the, 890, 894

Sex *(continued)*
  United States, 51, 71, 76, 80, 87, 152, 153,
    159a, 164, 389, 689, 732, 756, 891,
    996, 998, 1000-1002
  USSR, 723, 958, 988, 995, 1001
  and witchcraft, 761
  See also Human sexuality; Love; Sex cus-
    toms; Sexual behavior
Sex addicts: rehabilitation, 582
Sex anatomy, 7, 258, 283, 288, 290. *See also*
  Breasts; Clitoris; Penis; Vagina;
  Vulva
Sex counseling, 172
Sex crimes, 600, 603, 728-730, 1003
  England, 604
  United States, 600
  See also Incest; Rape; Sex murder; Sex
    offenders; Sexual harassment
Sex customs
  Arnhem Land, 1010
  bibliography, 1051
  Botswana, 977
  Brazil, 1007, 1009
  Burkino Faso, 380
  Canada, 999
  cross-cultural perspectives, 813
  China, 385, 971-973
  Egypt, 972
  Europe, 85, 86, 991
  France, 748a
  Gambia, 380
  Greece, 984-986, 989
  India, 972
  Indonesia, 972
  Insular Pacific, 1016
  Japan, 972
  Near East, 972, 978, 979
  Papua New Guinea, 1011
  Rome, 984, 987, 993
  Russia, 983
  Senegal, 380
  Sudan, 373
  Trobriand Islands, 1013
  Turkey, 968
Sex differences, 54, 63, 64, 74, 124, 132, 252-
  255, 258-266, 274, 284, 285, 684,
  697, 917
  bibliography, 259, 1052
  cross-cultural perspectives, 958, 1014,
    1015
  interspecies comparisons, 264
  in nonverbal behavior, 947, 948
  pictorial guide, 251a
  See also Femininity; Gender identify;
    Gender roles; Masculinity
Sex education, 25, 139, 188, 192, 592
  bibliography, 1044-1048
  Canada, 999
  criticism of, 191
  Cuba, 1008a
  and the law, 728
  and religion, 191
  Sweden, 990

  United States, 183-186, 234
  See also Sex instruction
Sex games. *See* Erotic games
Sex hormones, 124, 130, 137, 255, 483. *See*
  also Testosterone
Sex in offices. *See* Office sex
Sex industry, 643, 935
Sex Information and Education Council of the
  United States (SIECUS), 184
Sex instruction, 206, 208, 210, 211, 214, 215,
  225
  for boys, 250
  case studies, 190
  for children, 192, 229, 230, 233, 236
  for girls, 247
  for handicapped persons, 387
  for men, 207, 217, 226, 528
  for women, 214, 292, 526, 529, 530, 534,
    535
  for youth, 230, 237, 240, 242, 244, 248,
    249, 251
Sex literature: reviews, 342
Sex magazines
  treatment in libraries, 895
  See also Girlie magazines
Sex manuals, 41
  criticism, 222
  See also Ananga Ranga; *Kama Sutra*
    (Vatsyayana); *The Perfumed Gar-*
    den (al Nefzāwī); Pillow books
Sex media, 217. *See also* Adult films; Girlie
  magazines; Sex magazines
Sex murder, 636, 637
Sex offenders, 600, 603, 625, 637, 727, 729
  and the law, 728
  treatment, 601, 728
  See also Sex crimes
Sex physiology, 6, 283, 288, 290
Sex psychology, 6, 35
Sex ratio, 65
Sex research, 137, 139, 171, 172, 253·
  bibliography, 174a, 1035
  Canada, 999
  ethics, 130, 181, 296
  history, 172a, 173
  interviewing, 182
  methodology, 72, 147, 155, 156, 171, 177-
    179, 182, 1012
  taking a sex history, 182
  tests and measures, 177, 179
  United States, 170, 174
Sex researchers, 171, 175
Sex roles. *See* Gender roles
Sex surgery, 191, 221, 711. *See also* Castra-
  tion; Circumcision; Clitoridectomy;
  Genital mutilation; Vasectomy
Sex surveys. *See* Sexual behavior: surveys
Sex therapists, 29
  directories, 29, 217
Sex therapy, 58, 127, 130, 132, 139, 215, 279,
  295, 532, 548, 551, 580, 584-587,
  589-592
  criticism of, 191, 391a

For Reference

Not to be taken from this room